The IDG Books Bible Advantage

Access 97 Bible is part of the Bible series brought to you by IDG Books Worldwide. We designed Bibles to meet your growing need for quick access to the most complete and accurate computer information available.

Bibles work the way you do: They focus on accomplishing specific tasks — not learning random functions. These books are not long-winded manuals or dry reference tomes. In Bibles, expert authors tell you exactly what you can do with your software and how to do it. Easy-to-follow, step-by-step sections; comprehensive coverage; and convenient access in language and design — it's all here.

The authors of Bibles are uniquely qualified to give you expert advice as well as to provide insightful tips and techniques not found anywhere else. Our authors maintain close contact with end users through feedback from articles, training sessions, e-mail exchanges, user group participation, and consulting work. Because our authors know the realities of daily computer use and are directly tied to the reader, our Bibles have a strategic advantage.

Bible authors have the experience to approach a topic in the most efficient manner, and we know that you, the reader, will benefit from a "one-on-one" relationship with the author. Our research shows that readers make computer book purchases because they want expert advice. Because readers want to benefit from the author's experience, the author's voice is always present in a Bible series book.

In addition, the author is free to include or recommend useful software in a Bible. The software that accompanies a Bible is not intended to be casual filler but is linked to the content, theme, or procedures of the book. We know that you will benefit from the included software.

You will find what you need in this book whether you read it from cover to cover, section by section, or simply one topic at a time. As a computer user, you deserve a comprehensive resource of answers. We at IDG Books Worldwide are proud to deliver that resource with *Access 97 Bible*.

Brenda McLaughlin
Senior Vice President and Group Publisher
Internet: YouTellUs@idgbooks.com

Access 97
Bible

Access 97 Bible

Cary N. Prague and Michael R. Irwin

IDG Books Worldwide, Inc.
An International Data Group Company

Foster City, CA ✦ Chicago, IL ✦ Indianapolis, IN ✦ New York, NY

Access 97 Bible

Published by
IDG Books Worldwide, Inc.
An International Data Group Company
919 E. Hillsdale Blvd.
Suite 400
Foster City, CA 94404
www.idgbooks.com (IDG Books Worldwide Web site)
www.dummies.com (Dummies Press Web site)

Library of Congress Catalog Card No.: 96-78778

ISBN: 0-7645-3035-6

Printed in the United States of America

10

IB/SQ/RR/ZY/IN

Distributed in the United States by IDG Books Worldwide, Inc.

Distributed by Macmillan Canada for Canada; by Transworld Publishers Limited in the United Kingdom; by IDG Norge Books for Norway; by IDG Sweden Books for Sweden; by Woodslane Pty. Ltd. for Australia; by Woodslane (NZ) Ltd. for New Zealand; by Addison Wesley Longman Singapore Pte Ltd. for Singapore, Malaysia, Thailand, and Indonesia; by Norma Comunicaciones S.A. for Colombia; by Intersoft for South Africa; by International Thomson Publishing for Germany, Austria and Switzerland; by Distribuidora Cuspide for Argentina; by Livraria Cultura for Brazil; by Ediciencia S.A. for Ecuador; by Ediciones ZETA S.C.R. Ltda. for Peru; by WS Computer Publishing Corporation, Inc., for the Philippines; by Contemporanea de Ediciones for Venezuela; by Express Computer Distributors for the Caribbean and West Indies; by Micronesia Media Distributor, Inc. for Micronesia; by Grupo Editorial Norma S.A. for Guatemala; by Chips Computadoras S.A. de C.V. for Mexico; by Editorial Norma de Panama S.A. for Panama; by Wouters Import for Belgium; by American Bookshops for Finland. Authorized Sales Agent: Anthony Rudkin Associates for the Middle East and North Africa.

For general information on IDG Books Worldwideís books in the U.S., please call our Consumer Customer Service department at 800-762-2974. For reseller information, including discounts and premium sales, please call our Reseller Customer Service department at 800-434-3422.

For information on where to purchase IDG Books Worldwideís books outside the U.S., please contact our International Sales department at 317-596-5530 or fax 317-596-5692.

For information on foreign language translations, please contact our Foreign & Subsidiary Rights department at 650-655-3021 or fax 650-655-3281.

For sales inquiries and special prices for bulk quantities, please contact our Sales department at 650-655-3200 or write to the address above.

For information on using IDG Books Worldwideís books in the classroom or for ordering examination copies, please contact our Educational Sales department at 800-434-2086 or fax 317-596-5499.

For press review copies, author interviews, or other publicity information, please contact our Public Relations department at 650-655-3000 or fax 650-655-3299.

For authorization to photocopy items for corporate, personal, or educational use, please contact Copyright Clearance Center, 222 Rosewood Drive, Danvers, MA 01923, or fax 978-750-4470.

 is a trademark under exclusive license to IDG Books Worldwide, Inc., from International Data Group, Inc.

About the Authors

Cary N. Prague

Cary Prague is an internationally best-selling author and lecturer in the database industry. He is the owner of Cary Prague Books and Software, the world's largest Microsoft Access add-on vendor; this direct-mail company creates and markets add-on software, books, and video training for personal computer databases. Formerly, he has held numerous management positions in corporate information systems, including Director of Managed Care Reporting for MetraHealth (MetLife and Travelers Insurance joint venture), Director of Software Productivity at Travelers Insurance where he was responsible for software support and trai ning for 35,000 end users, Director in Corporate Finance where he was responsible for the selection and installation of Fixed Asset and Payroll Systems and Manager of Information Centers for Northeast Utilities.

Cary also runs a consulting company named Database Creations that specializes in Microsoft Access applications and training. His local and national clients include many software companies, manufacturers, public utilities, and broadcast companies. His client list includes Microsoft, Borland International, Pratt and Whitney Aircraft, Otis Elevator, State of Connecticut, United Healthcare, Travelers Insurance, Omar Coffee, Rockwell International, and SNET telephone company.

He is one of the best selling authors in the computer database management market having written over thirty five books which have sold nearly one million copies on software including Microsoft Access, Borland's dBASE IV, Paradox, R:Base and Framework. Cary's books include the *PC World's Microsoft Access Bible*, recently on several top 10 national bestseller lists, *Access 95 Secrets, dBASE for Windows Handbook, dBASE IV Programming,* winner of the 1989 Computer Press Association's Book of the Year award for Best Software Specific Book, and *Everyman's Database Primer Featuring dBASE IV*. He is currently writing several new Access 97 books.

Cary has developed and markets several add-on software products for Microsoft Access including Yes! I Can Run My Business With Access, a business sales and accounting program, The Access Business Forms Library distributed by Microsoft with Access 2.0 upgrades, TabMaster Wizard, User Interface Construction Kit winner of the 1996 Access Advisor Readers Choice award, the Calendar Construction Kit, the Picture Builder Add-On Picture Pack, and the Command Bar Image Editor and Image Pack.

Cary is a Microsoft Solutions Provider and Certified Access Professional and is a frequent speaker at seminars and conferences around the country. He has been voted the best speaker by the attendees of several national conferences. In the last year, he was a speaker for Microsoft sponsored conferences in Phoenix, Chicago, Toronto, Palm Springs, Boston and Orlando. He has also spoken at Borland's Database Conference, Digital Consulting's Database World, Microsoft's

Developer Days, Computerland's Technomics Conference, COMDEX, and COMPAQ Computer's Innovate. He is also a contributing editor to Access Advisor magazine. In 1997 he will be speaking at the Access Advisor confrences in Hawaii and Nashville.

Cary holds a master's degree in computer science from Rensselaer Polytechnic Institute, and an M.B.A and Bachelor of Accounting from the University of Connecticut. He is also a Certified Data Processor.

Michael R. Irwin

Michael Irwin is considered one of the leading authorities on automated database management systems. He is a noted worldwide lecturer, a winner of national and international awards, best-selling author, and developer of client/server and PC-based database management systems.

Mr. Irwin has extensive database knowledge, gained by working with the Metropolitan Police Department in Washington, D.C. as a developer and analyst for the Information Systems Division. He retired in June 1992. Now he runs his own consulting firm, specializing in database integration and emphasizing client/server solutions. His range of expertise includes database processing in and between mainframe, minicomputer, and PC-based database systems; he is a leading authority on PC-based databases.

He has authored numerous database books over the last three years, with several of them consistently on the best sellers lists. His most recent works include *The OOPs Primer* (Borland Press) and *dBASE 5.5 for Windows Programming* (Prentice Hall).

ABOUT IDG BOOKS WORLDWIDE

Welcome to the world of IDG Books Worldwide.

IDG Books Worldwide, Inc., is a subsidiary of International Data Group, the world's largest publisher of computer-related information and the leading global provider of information services on information technology. IDG was founded more than 30 years ago by Patrick J. McGovern and now employs more than 9,000 people worldwide. IDG publishes more than 290 computer publications in over 75 countries. More than 90 million people read one or more IDG publications each month.

Launched in 1990, IDG Books Worldwide is today the #1 publisher of best-selling computer books in the United States. We are proud to have received eight awards from the Computer Press Association in recognition of editorial excellence and three from Computer Currents' First Annual Readers' Choice Awards. Our best-selling ...*For Dummies*® series has more than 50 million copies in print with translations in 31 languages. IDG Books Worldwide, through a joint venture with IDG's Hi-Tech Beijing, became the first U.S. publisher to publish a computer book in the People's Republic of China. In record time, IDG Books Worldwide has become the first choice for millions of readers around the world who want to learn how to better manage their businesses.

Our mission is simple: Every one of our books is designed to bring extra value and skill-building instructions to the reader. Our books are written by experts who understand and care about our readers. The knowledge base of our editorial staff comes from years of experience in publishing, education, and journalism — experience we use to produce books to carry us into the new millennium. In short, we care about books, so we attract the best people. We devote special attention to details such as audience, interior design, use of icons, and illustrations. And because we use an efficient process of authoring, editing, and desktop publishing our books electronically, we can spend more time ensuring superior content and less time on the technicalities of making books.

You can count on our commitment to deliver high-quality books at competitive prices on topics you want to read about. At IDG Books Worldwide, we continue in the IDG tradition of delivering quality for more than 30 years. You'll find no better book on a subject than one from IDG Books Worldwide.

John Kilcullen
John Kilcullen
Chairman and CEO
IDG Books Worldwide, Inc.

Steven Berkowitz
Steven Berkowitz
President and Publisher
IDG Books Worldwide, Inc.

VIII WINNER — Eighth Annual Computer Press Awards 1992

IX WINNER — Ninth Annual Computer Press Awards 1993

1995 COMPUTER CURRENTS 1997 READERS CHOICE

X WINNER — Tenth Annual Computer Press Awards 1994

XI WINNER — Eleventh Annual Computer Press Awards 1995

IDG is the world's leading IT media, research and exposition company. Founded, in 1964, IDG had 1997 revenues of $2.05 billion and has more than 9,000 employees worldwide. IDG offers the widest range of media options that reach IT buyers in 75 countries representing 95% of worldwide IT spending. IDG's diverse product and services portfolio spans six key areas including print publishing, online publishing, expositions and conferences, market research, education and training, and global marketing services. More than 90 million people read one or more of IDG's 290 magazines and newspapers, including IDG's leading global brands — Computerworld, PC World, Network World, Macworld and the Channel World family of publications. IDG Books Worldwide is one of the fastest-growing computer book publishers in the world, with more than 700 titles in 36 languages. The "...For Dummies®" series alone has more than 50 million copies in print. IDG offers online users the largest network of technology-specific Web sites around the world through IDG.net (http://www.idg.net), which comprises more than 225 targeted Web sites in 55 countries worldwide. International Data Corporation (IDC) is the world's largest provider of information technology data, analysis and consulting, with research centers in over 41 countries and more than 400 research analysts worldwide. IDG World Expo is a leading producer of more than 168 globally branded conferences and expositions in 35 countries including E3 (Electronic Entertainment Expo), Macworld Expo, ComNet, Windows World Expo, ICE (Internet Commerce Expo), Agenda, DEMO, and Spotlight. IDG's training subsidiary, ExecuTrain, is the world's largest computer training company, with more than 230 locations worldwide and 785 training courses. IDG Marketing Services helps industry-leading IT companies build international brand recognition by developing global integrated marketing programs via IDG's print, online and exposition products worldwide. Further information about the company can be found at www.idg.com.   10/8/98

Credits

Acknowledgments

When we first saw Access in July of 1992, we were instantly sold on this new-generation database management and access tool. We've both spent the last three years using Access daily. After four short years, Access has nearly 20 million users worldwide.

Now we have rewritten this book again for all the incredible new features in Access 97. We've covered every new feature and added a programming and Internet section. Nearly 250,000 copies of our *Access Bibles* have been sold for Access 1.0, 1.1, 2.0, and 95; we thank all of our loyal readers.

We've also written countless systems, designed and brought to market many add-on products for Access, and created the largest Access add-on software and book distribution company in the world. We've served nearly 20,000 customers, our staff has answered thousands of technical support questions, and we've received critical acclaim from readers and reviewers alike. Our first acknowledgment is to all the users of Access who have profited and benefitted beyond everyone's wildest dreams.

There are many people who assisted us in writing this book. We'd like to recognize each of them.

To Diana Smith, who wrote the original introductory chapters (2, 3, and 5) and also was the technical editor for the previous 4 versions of this book. To her we offer an additional and special thank you. Thanks also to Mary Lynn Maurice for her assistance in writing Chapters 4 and 6, so very long ago.

Additional thanks to Diana Smith for running Cary's business while he disappeared for two months. To Phuc Phan, our technical support specialist and developer in training. Phuc helped take many of the screen dumps you see in this book. Without Phuc, this book would not have been on time. To Jennifer Reardon, one of my top developers, for stepping in as always and who wrote Chapters 34 and 35. To Bill Amo, for always being there when I ask *How do you get this to work?* To Ken Getz and F. Scott Barker for always answering my strange questions. To John S. Dranchak for designing the reports in Chapters 21 and 23, and creating the logo for Mountain Animal Hospital.

To our agents, Matt Wagner and Bill Gladstone at Waterside Productions.

To the pilgrims at IDG Books: To Greg Croy, head pilgrim, for always harassing us even when we are on time. To Andy Cummings (who only calls me when there are real problems) and especially to our editors — Pat O'Brien (making books and making friends), Barry Childs-Helton, Becky Whitney, Faithe Wempen, Kelly Oliver, and Kyle Looper — thanks for the incredible job you did managing the project and editing our book.

(The publisher would like to give special thanks to Patrick J. McGovern, without whom this book would not have been possible.)

Dedications

This book is dedicated to the memory of Max Zaretsky. Uncle Mutt would always have a song and a smile no matter the occasion. A male version of my mom, he always brought joy to me in the best and worst of times and always made me laugh. I will never forget his sharp wit and his incredible personality. We'll all miss him.

CNP

This book is dedicated to Aurelia Irwin, my mother. With her guidance during my youth and her advice today, I am clearly a better person. Thank you, Mom.

MRI

Contents at a Glance

Table of Contents

· ·

Chapter 20: Using OLE Objects, Graphs, and ActiveX Custom Controls 499

Part IV: Advanced Database Features   673

Chapter 24: Working with External Data 675

Part VI: Appendixes — 1027

Introduction

Welcome to the *Access for Windows 97 Bible* — your personal guide to a powerful, easy-to-use database management system.

This book examines Microsoft Access 97. We think that Microsoft Access is an excellent database manager and the best Windows database on the market today. Our goal with this book is to share what we know about Access and, in the process, to help make your work and your life easier.

This book contains everything you need in order to learn Microsoft Access to a fairly advanced level. You'll find that the book starts off with the basics and builds, chapter by chapter, on topics previously covered. In places where it is essential that you understand previously covered topics, we present the concepts again and review how to perform specific tasks before moving on. Although each chapter is an integral part of the book as a whole, each chapter can also stand on its own. You can read the book in any order you want, skipping from chapter to chapter and from topic to topic. (Note that this book's index is particularly thorough; you can refer to the index to find the location of a particular topic you're interested in.)

The examples in this book have been well thought out to simulate the types of tables, queries, forms, and reports most people need to create when performing common business activities. There are many notes, tips, and techniques (and even a few secrets) to help you better understand the product.

This book can easily substitute for the manuals included with Access. In fact, many users do not get manuals today, often relying on just the online help. This book will guide you through each task you might want to do in Access. We even created appendixes to be used as reference manuals for common Access specifications. This book follows a much more structured approach than the Microsoft Access manuals — going into more depth on almost every topic and showing many different types of examples.

Is This Book for You?

We wrote this book for beginning, intermediate, and advanced users of Microsoft Access. With any new product, most users start at the beginning. If, however, you've already read through the Microsoft Access manuals and worked with the North Winds sample files, you may want to start with the later parts of this book. Note, however, that starting at the beginning of a book is usually a good idea so you don't miss out on the secrets and tips in the early chapters.

We think this book covers Microsoft Access in detail better than any other book currently on the market. We hope you will find this book helpful while working with Access, and that you enjoy the innovative style of an IDG book.

Yes — If you have no database experience

If you're new to the world of database management, this book has everything you need to get started with Microsoft Access. It then offers advanced topics for reference and learning.

Yes — If you've used other database managers like dBASE or Paradox

If you're abandoning another database (such as dBASE, Paradox, Approach, R:Base, or Alpha Four) or even upgrading from Access 2.0 or Access for Windows 95, this book is for you. You'll have a head start because you're already familiar with database managers and how to use them. With Microsoft Access, you will be able to do all the tasks you've always performed with character-based databases — *without* programming or getting lost. This book will take you through each subject step by step.

Yes — If you want to learn the basics of Visual Basic Applications Edition (VBA) programming

VBA has replaced the Access Basic language. We know that an entire book is needed to properly cover VBA, but we took the time to put together two introductory chapters that build on what you learn in the macros chapters of this book. The VBA programming chapters use the same examples you will be familiar with by the end of the book. These are included on the CD-ROM in electronic form as a bonus for you to use and learn from.

Conventions Used in This Book

The following conventions are used in this book:

✦ When you are instructed to press a *key combination* (press and hold down one key while pressing another key), the key combination is separated by a plus sign. Ctrl+Esc, for example, indicates that you must hold down the Ctrl key and press the Esc key; then release both keys.

✦ *Point the mouse* refers to moving the mouse so that the mouse pointer is on a specific item. *Click* refers to pressing the left mouse button once and releasing it. *Double-click* refers to pressing the left mouse button twice in rapid succession and then releasing it. *Right-click* refers to pressing the right mouse button once and releasing it. *Drag* refers to pressing and holding down the left mouse button while moving the mouse.

✦ When you are instructed to *select* a menu, you can use the keyboard or the mouse. To use the keyboard, press and hold down the Alt key (to activate the menu bar) and then press the underlined letter of the menu name; press Alt+E to select the Edit menu, for example. Or you can use the mouse to click on the word Edit on-screen. Then, from the menu that drops down, you can press the underlined letter of the command you want (or click on the command name) to select it.

✦ When you are instructed to select a command from a menu, you will often see the menu and command separated by an arrow symbol. Edit⇨Paste, for example, indicates that you need to select the Edit menu and then choose the Paste command from the menu.

✦ *Italic* type is used for new terms and for emphasis.

✦ **Bold** type is used for material you need to type directly into the computer.

✦ A special typeface is used for information you see on-screen — error messages, expressions, and formulas, for example.

Icons and Alerts

You'll notice special graphic symbols, or *icons,* used in the margins throughout this book. These icons are intended to alert you to points that are particularly important or noteworthy. The following icons are used in this book:

Note This icon highlights a special point of interest about the topic under discussion.

Tip This icon points to a useful hint that may save you time or trouble.

Caution This icon alerts you that the operation being described can cause problems if you're not careful.

Cross-Reference This icon points to a more complete discussion in another chapter of the book.

This icon highlights information for readers who are following the examples and using the sample files included on the disk accompanying this book.

CD-ROM

NEW FEATURE This icon calls attention to new features of Access 97.

Sidebars

In addition to noticing the icons used throughout this book, you will also notice material placed in grey boxes. This material offers background information, an expanded discussion, or a deeper insight about the topic under discussion. Some *sidebars* offer nuts-and-bolts technical explanations, and others provide useful anecdotal material.

How This Book Is Organized

This book contains 33 chapters (and two bonus chapters on the CD-ROM), divided into five main parts. In addition, the book contains three appendixes.

Part I: First Things First

Part I consists of the first six chapters of the book. In Chapter 1, you receive background information on Microsoft Access and an overview of its features. Chapter 2 covers installation — what you need in terms of hardware and software, as well as how to get Access running properly. In Chapter 3, you learn how to start and stop Access, plus several techniques for moving between Access and other applications. Chapter 4 provides an explanation of database concepts for new users of a database product. Chapter 5 is a hands-on test drive of Access, provided to give you a quick look at some of its features. And Chapter 6 is a case study of the up-front design that is necessary to properly implement a database system; otherwise, you must go through many false starts and redesigns when creating an application. You will design on paper the tables, forms, queries, reports, and menus necessary for creating the application.

Part II: Basic Database Usage

The next six chapters make up Part II. You learn how to create a database table in Chapter 7, and you also examine how to change a database table, including moving and renaming fields without losing data. You also learn about the new internet data types in Access 97. In Chapter 8, you learn how to enter, display, change, and delete data. Chapter 9 teaches the basics of creating data-entry forms and using Wizards to simplify the creation process; using data-entry forms is also discussed. In Chapter 10, you examine the concept of queries; then you create several queries to examine how data can be rearranged and displayed. Chapter 11 covers the basics of report creation and printing. In Chapter 12, you create the many tables used in the case study, and then learn how to relate multiple tables.

Part III: Using Access in Your Work

Part III contains 11 chapters that go into more depth on creating and using forms, queries, and reports. In Chapter 13, you take a look at how to create the expressions and built-in functions that are so important in forms and reports. In Chapter 14, you learn how to create relations and joins in queries. Chapter 15 discusses basic selection queries, using many examples and pictures. In Chapter 16, you examine the concepts of controls and properties, and then learn how to manipulate controls in a form. Chapter 17 examines in detail how to create and use data-entry forms. Chapter 18 covers how to use visual effects to create great-looking forms and reports that catch the eye and increase productivity. In Chapter 19, you learn how to add complex data validation to tables and data-entry forms. Chapter 20 explains the use of pictures, graphs, sound, video, and other OLE objects. Chapters 21–23 cover reports — from simple controls to complex calculations, summaries, printing, and desktop publishing.

Part IV: Advanced Database Features

This part contains six chapters that present advanced topics on each of the basic tasks of Access. Chapter 24 examines how to import, export, and attach external files, and how to copy Access objects to other Access databases. Chapter 25 discusses advanced select query topics, including total, cross-tabulation, top-value, and union queries. Chapter 26 covers action queries, which change data rather than simply displaying records. Chapter 27 is a compendium of advanced query topics that will leave you amazed at the power of Access. Creating forms and subforms from multiple tables is the subject of Chapter 28; this chapter examines how to create the one-to-many relationship found in many database systems. Part IV ends with Chapter 29, which offers a look at additional types of reports not previously covered, including mail-merge reports and mailing labels.

Part V: Applications in Access

This part looks at Access as an application environment. Chapter 30 covers the concept of event-driven software and how Access uses macros to automate manual processes. This chapter also examines what a macro is, how macros are created, and how to debug them. Chapter 31 explains data manipulation, including posting totals and filling in data-entry fields. In Chapter 32, you learn how to create button menus known as switchboards, as well as traditional pull-down menus, custom toolbars, and dialog boxes using the new Access 97 tab control. In Access 97, you will also learn about the new command bars used to build menus and toolbars. Chapter 33 teaches you all of the new internet features including publishing to the Web as well as using hyperlinks. Chapter 34 on the CD-ROM is an introduction to modules using VBA, which teaches you how to create a basic module and debug a program. Chapter 35 on the CD-ROM builds on the discussion of modules, teaching you logical constructs, error processing, DAO, and recordset processing.

The appendixes and reference material

Three appendixes are included in this book. Appendix A presents a series of tables listing Access specifications, including maximum and minimum sizes of many of the controls in Access. Appendix B displays a database diagram of the many database tables used in this book so you can create your own system. Appendix C describes the CD-ROM.

First Things First

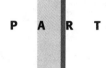

P A R T

◆ ◆ ◆ ◆

In This Part

◆ ◆ ◆ ◆

What Is Access 97?

Before you begin to use a software product, it is important to understand its capabilities and the types of tasks it is designed to perform. Microsoft Access 97 (subsequently referred to simply as Access) is a multifaceted product whose use is bounded only by your imagination.

Access Is . . .

Essentially, Access is a *database management system* (DBMS). Like other products in this category, Access stores and retrieves data, presents information, and automates repetitive tasks (such as maintaining accounts payable, performing inventory control, and scheduling). By using Access, you can develop easy-to-use input forms like the one shown in Figure 1-1. You can process your data and run powerful reports.

Access is also a powerful Windows application; for the first time, the productivity of database management meets the usability of Microsoft Windows. Because both Windows and Access are from Microsoft, the two products work very well together. Access runs on the Windows 95 or Windows NT platform, so all the advantages of Windows are available in Access. You can cut, copy, and paste data from any Windows application to and from Access. You can create a form design in Access and paste it into the report designer.

Using OLE (Object Linking and Embedding) objects in Windows 95 and Microsoft Office 97 products (Excel, Word, PowerPoint, and Outlook), you can extend Access into being a true database operating environment through integration with these products. With the new Internet extensions, you can create forms that interact with data directly from the World Wide Web and translate your forms directly into HTML that works with products like Microsoft Internet Explorer and Netscape Navigator.

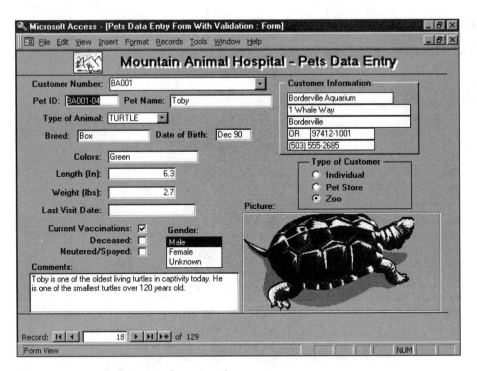

Figure 1-1: A typical Access data-entry form.

Even so, Access is more than just a database manager. As a *relational* database manager, it gives you access to all types of data and gives you the use of more than one database table at a time. It can reduce the complexity of your data and make it easier to get your job done. You can link an Access table with mainframe or server data or use a table created in Paradox or dBASE. You can take the results of the link and combine the data with an Excel worksheet quickly and easily. If you use Microsoft Office 97, you will find complete interoperability between Access and Word, Excel, and PowerPoint.

Figure 1-2 shows the original Microsoft marketing concept for Access. This simple figure conveys the message that Access is usable at all levels. Beginning at the lowest level of the hierarchy and moving upward, you see *Objects* listed first; these give the end user the capability of creating tables, queries, forms, and reports easily. You can perform simple processing by using *expressions,* also known as functions, to validate data, enforce a business rule, or display a number with a currency symbol. *Macros* allow for automation without programming, whereas VBA (Visual Basic for Applications) code lets the user program complex processes. Finally, by using Windows API calls to functions or DLLs written in other languages such as C, Java, or even Visual Basic, a programmer can write interfaces to other programs and data sources.

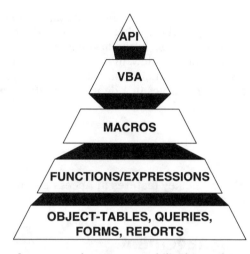

Figure 1-2: The Access usability hierarchy.

Access is a set of tools for end-user database management. Access has a table creator, a form designer, a query manager, and a report writer. Access is also an environment for developing applications. By using macros or modules to automate tasks, you can create user-oriented applications as powerful as those created with programming languages — complete with the buttons, menus, and dialog boxes you see in Figure 1-3. By programming in Visual Basic for Applications (known as VBA), you can create programs as powerful as Access itself. In fact, many of the tools in Access (such as Wizards and Builders) are written in VBA.

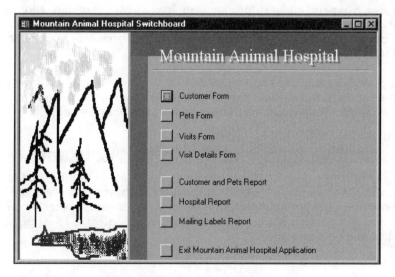

Figure 1-3: A macro switchboard.

The power and usability of Access make it, by far, the best database management software on the market today. Simply telling you about what Access can do, however, doesn't begin to cover the material in this book. In the first 450 pages, you learn how to use Access from an end user's point of view. In the next 450 pages, you will learn Access from the power user's view. Finally, you will learn the basics of VBA and the Internet; you will examine many topics in a depth your reference manuals can only begin to touch.

What Access Offers

The following paragraphs briefly describe some key features in Access and help prepare you for some of the subjects covered in this book.

True relational database management

Access provides true *relational database management*. Access includes definitions for primary and foreign keys and has full referential integrity built in at the level of the database engine itself (which prevents inconsistent updates or deletions). In addition, tables in Access have data-validation rules to prevent inaccurate data regardless of how data is entered, and every field in a table has format and default definitions for more productive data entry. Access supports all the necessary field types, including Text, Number, AutoNumber (counter), Currency, Date/Time, Memo, Yes/No, Hyperlink, and OLE objects. When values are missing in special processing, Access provides full support for null values.

The relational processing in Access fills many needs with its flexible architecture. It can be used as a stand-alone database management system, in a file-server configuration, or as a front-end client to products such as an SQL server. In addition, Access features ODBC (Open Database Connectivity); you'll be able to connect to many more external formats, such as SQL/Server, Oracle, Sybase, or even mainframe IBM DB/2.

The program provides complete support for transaction processing, ensuring the integrity of transactions. In addition, user-level security provides control over assigning user and group permissions to view and modify database objects.

Context-sensitive help and the Office Assistant

The Microsoft Help feature is still the best in the industry, for beginners and experienced users alike. Access provides context-sensitive Help; you can press the F1 key whenever you're stuck. Help information about the item you're working on appears instantly. Access also has an easy-to-use table of contents, a search facility, a history log, and bookmarks.

In Access 97, Microsoft goes a few steps further by introducing the Office Assistant and Screen Tips. As you can see in Figure 1-4, the *Office Assistant* responds in plain English when you ask for help. *Screen Tips* (also known as What's This?) give you short, on-screen explanations of what something is. The assistants are cute at first, and you can choose from a gallery of ten different assistants. You can also turn them off at any time if they become overly annoying.

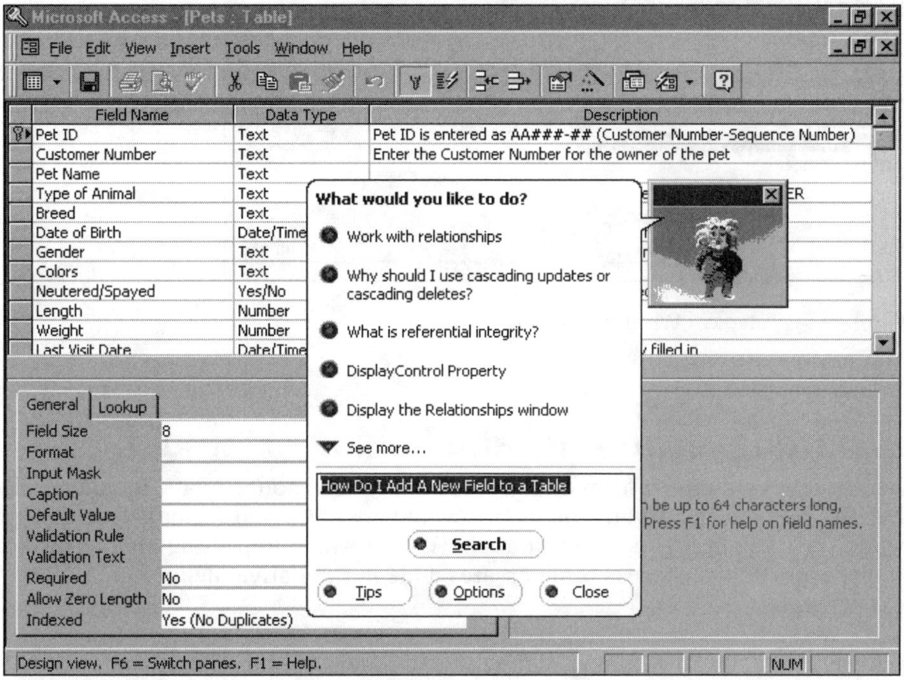

Figure 1-4: The Access 97 Office Assistant.

Ease-of-use Wizards and Builders

A *Wizard* can turn hours of work into minutes. Wizards ask you questions about content, style, and format; then they build the object for you automatically. Access features nearly 100 Wizards to design databases, applications, tables, forms, reports, graphs, mailing labels, controls, and properties. Figure 1-5 shows a Form Wizard screen. You can even customize Wizards for use in a variety of tasks.

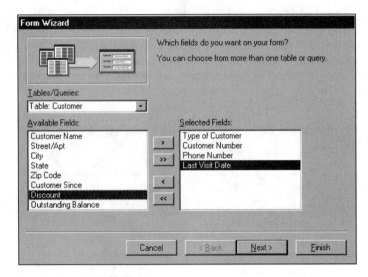

Figure 1-5: A typical Wizard screen.

Importing, exporting, and linking external files

Access lets you import from or export to many common formats, including dBASE, FoxPro, Excel, SQL Server, Oracle, Btrieve, many ASCII text formats (including fixed width and delimited), as well as data in HTML format. Importing creates an Access table; exporting an Access table creates a file in the native file format you are exporting to.

Linking (formally known as *attaching*) means that you can simply use external data without creating an Access table. You can link to dBASE, FoxPro, Excel, ASCII, and SQL data. Linking to external tables and then relating them to other tables is a powerful capability; you can link to Access, FoxPro, dBASE, and SQL server.

WYSIWYG forms and reports

The Form and Report Design windows share a common interface and power. Your form or report is designed in a WYSIWYG environment. As you add each control, you see the form take shape as you build your design.

You can add labels, text data fields, option buttons, tab controls, check boxes, lines, boxes, colors, shading — even pictures, graphs, subforms, or subreports — to your forms and reports. In addition, you have complete control over the style and presentation of data in a form or report, as shown in Figure 1-6. Forms can have multiple pages; reports can have many levels of groupings and totals.

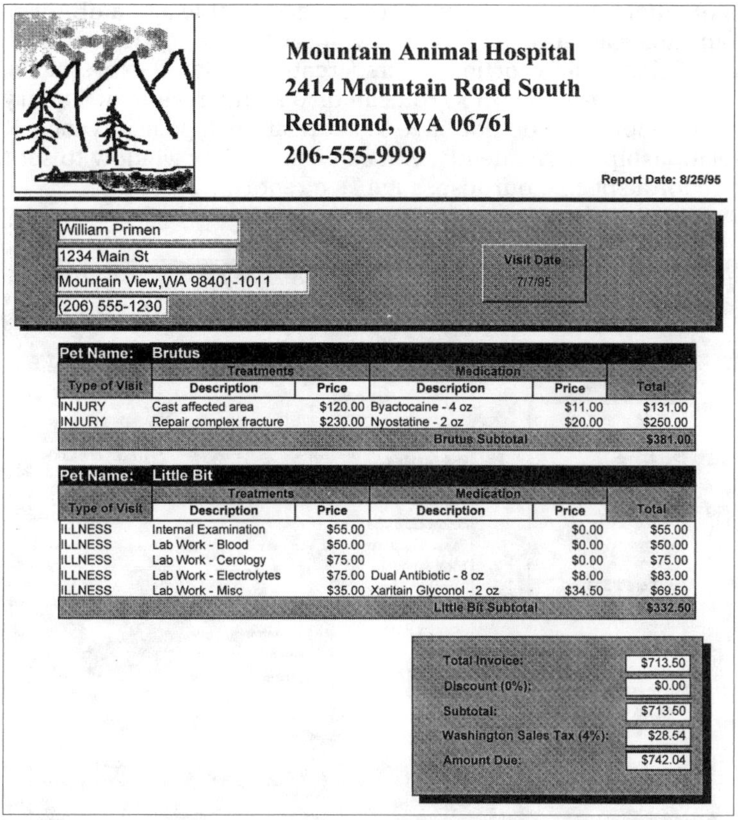

Mountain Animal Hospital
2414 Mountain Road South
Redmond, WA 06761
206-555-9999

Report Date: 8/25/95

William Primen
1234 Main St
Mountain View,WA 98401-1011
(206) 555-1230

Visit Date
7/7/95

Pet Name: Brutus

	Treatments		Medication		
Type of Visit	Description	Price	Description	Price	Total
INJURY	Cast affected area	$120.00	Byactocaine - 4 oz	$11.00	$131.00
INJURY	Repair complex fracture	$230.00	Nyostatine - 2 oz	$20.00	$250.00
			Brutus Subtotal		$381.00

Pet Name: Little Bit

	Treatments		Medication		
Type of Visit	Description	Price	Description	Price	Total
ILLNESS	Internal Examination	$55.00		$0.00	$55.00
ILLNESS	Lab Work - Blood	$50.00		$0.00	$50.00
ILLNESS	Lab Work - Cerology	$75.00		$0.00	$75.00
ILLNESS	Lab Work - Electrolytes	$75.00	Dual Antibiotic - 8 oz	$8.00	$83.00
ILLNESS	Lab Work - Misc	$35.00	Xaritain Glyconol - 2 oz	$34.50	$69.50
			Little Bit Subtotal		$332.50

Total Invoice:	$713.50
Discount (0%):	$0.00
Subtotal:	$713.50
Washington Sales Tax (4%):	$28.54
Amount Due:	$742.04

Figure 1-6: A database-published report.

You can view your form or report in *page preview mode,* zooming out to get a bird's-eye view. You can also view your report with sample data when you're in design mode so that you don't waste valuable time waiting for a large data file to be processed.

Most important, the Report Writer is very powerful, allowing up to ten levels of aggregation and sorting. The Report Writer performs two passes on the data; you can create reports that show the row percentage of a group total, which can be done only by having a calculation based on a calculation that requires two passes through the data. You can create many types of reports that include mailing labels and mail-merge reports.

Multiple-table queries and relationships

One of the most powerful features in Access is also the most important. As you can see in Figure 1-7, the relationship lets you link your tables graphically. You can even link tables of different file types (such as an Access table and a dBASE table); when linked, your tables act as a single entity you can query about your data. You can select specific fields, define sorting orders, create calculated expressions, and enter criteria to select desired records. You can display the results of a query in a datasheet, form, or report. You do not have to set relationships in advance. Rather than set your relationships permanently, you can use a query window to set them when you need to for a specific purpose, such as a report.

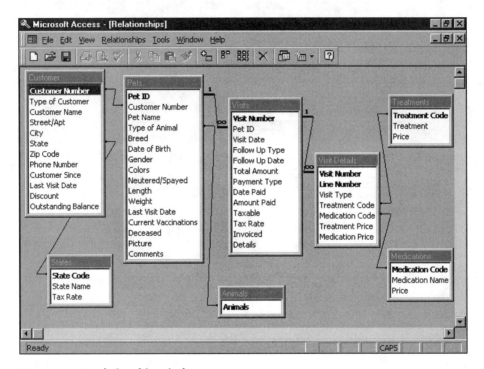

Figure 1-7: A relationship window.

Queries have other uses as well. You can create queries that calculate totals, display cross-tabulations, and then make new tables from the results. You can even use a query to update data in tables, delete records, or append one table to another.

Business graphs and charts

You will find the same graph application found in Microsoft Word, Excel, PowerPoint, and Project built into Access. You can create hundreds of types of business graphs and customize the display to meet your every business need. You can create bar charts, column charts, line charts, pie charts, area charts, and high-low-close charts — in two and three dimensions. You can add free-form text, change the gridlines, adjust the color and pattern in a bar, display data values on a bar or pie slice, and even rotate the viewing angle of a chart from within the Access Graph program.

In addition, you can link your graph with a form to get a powerful graphic data display that changes from record to record in the table. Figure 1-8 shows an example.

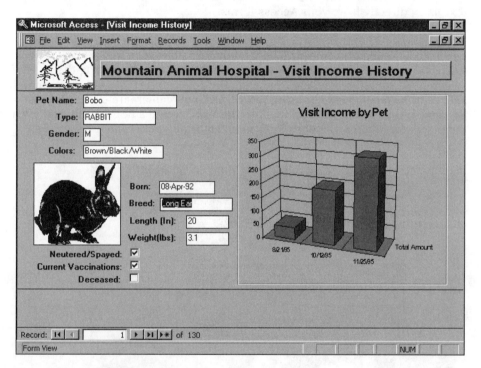

Figure 1-8: A typical form linked to a graph.

DDE and OLE capabilities

Through the capabilities of DDE (Dynamic Data Exchange) and OLE (Object Linking and Embedding), you can add exciting new objects to your Access forms and reports. Such objects may be sound, pictures, graphs, and even video clips. You can embed OLE objects (such as a bitmap picture) or documents from word processors (such as Word or WordPerfect) or link to a range of cells in an Excel spreadsheet. By linking these objects to records in your tables, you can create dynamic database forms and reports and share information between Windows applications.

The Internet is now accessible

Access is now full of features that allow you to easily make your applications Internet/intranet ready. With just a click of the mouse, you can save tables, queries, reports, and form datasheets as HTML. A Publish to the Web Wizard allows even a neophyte to place the HTML code generated from an object out on a Web site, ready for the perusal of all who surf the Internet! Hyperlinks allow you and others to access your published data (and others' published data) as hypertext links, directly from your Access forms.

Many people feel that the process of publishing data to the Web is something to be left to a Webmaster. Access 97 definitely turns this idea into a myth. The Publish to the Web Wizard walks you through the steps of creating the HTML for selected database objects and of placing the generated HTML out on your Web site. As shown in Figure 1-9, using the Wizard, you can create either static or dynamic publications, publish them to the Web, create a home page, and even use templates to obtain a standard look and feel for all your HTML publications!

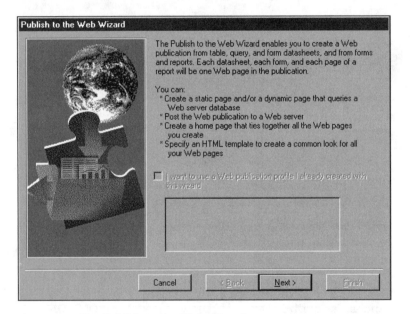

Figure 1-9: The Publish to the Web Wizard.

Built-in functions

Access contains more than 100 *functions* (small built-in programs that return a value); these perform tasks in a wide variety of categories. Access includes database, mathematics, business, financial, date, time, and string functions. You can use them to create calculated expressions in your forms, reports, and queries.

Macros: Programming without programming

For nonprogrammers (or power users who simply don't want to program), there are *macros*. Macros let you perform common tasks without user intervention. Nearly 50 macro actions let you manipulate data, create menus and dialog boxes, open forms and reports, and basically automate any task you can imagine. Macros can probably solve 90 percent of your processing problems.

Modules: Visual Basic for Applications — database programming

Access is a serious development environment with a full-featured programming language. The Visual Basic Application edition (VBA, for short, and formerly known as Access Basic) features an event-driven programming model that lets you do more things than you can do with just forms and reports. VBA Code is a powerful structured programming language; VBA is also fully extensible, featuring API call routines in any dynamic link library for the Windows 95 and Windows NT operating systems.

A full-featured development environment allows multiple windows for color-coded editing and debugging, automatic syntax checking, watchpoints, breakpoints, single-step execution, and even syntax help that displays each possible commands option as you type.

Information for Database Users

If you're already a database user, chances are that you're ready to jump right in and start using Access. A word of warning: *This is not your father's Oldsmobile.* You may be an expert in relational database management software, such as dBASE, FoxPro, or Paradox, but you may never have used a database under Windows.

You should try to become familiar with Windows software before you jump right in to a database package. Play with Windows Paint; experiment with Word or Excel. Learn how to use the mouse to click, double-click, select, drag, and drop. Create a graph in Excel, use a Wizard, and try the Help system. All these tasks will make your learning experience much faster when you use Access.

You also need to get used to some new terminology. Table 1-1 lists the Access terminology and its dBASE and Paradox equivalents.

Table 1-1
Access, dBASE, and Paradox Terminology

Microsoft Access	Borland dBASE	Borland Paradox
Database	Catalog	Directory of related files
Table	Database file	Table
Datasheet	BROWSE command	View command
Table Design	MODIFY STRUCTURE	Modify Restructure
Text data type	Character data type	Alphanumeric data type
Primary key	Unique Index	Key field
Index	Index	Tools QuerySpeed
Validation rule	PICTURE/VALID Clause	ValChecks
Query	Query, QBE, View	Query
Form	Screen	Forms
Subform	Multiple File Screen	Multiple-record selection
Open a form	SET FORMAT TO, EDIT	Image PickForm
Find command	LOCATE AND SEEK	Zoom
Data entry command	APPEND	Modify DataEntry
List box, combo box	Pick list	Lookup
Exclusive/shared access	SET EXCLUSIVE ON/OFF	Edit/Coedit mode
Module	Program file	Script

Information for Spreadsheet Users

If you are an Excel or 1-2-3 expert, you'll find that many things about Access are similar to Excel. First of all, both programs are Windows products, so you should already have experience using the Windows-specific conventions you will use with Access. Access has a spreadsheet view of the data in a table or query, known as a *datasheet.* You'll find that you can resize the rows and columns in much the same way as within Excel worksheets. In fact, Access 97 has a data-entry mode exactly like that of Excel. You simply enter data and define column headings; Access will create a table for you automatically (see Figure 1-10).

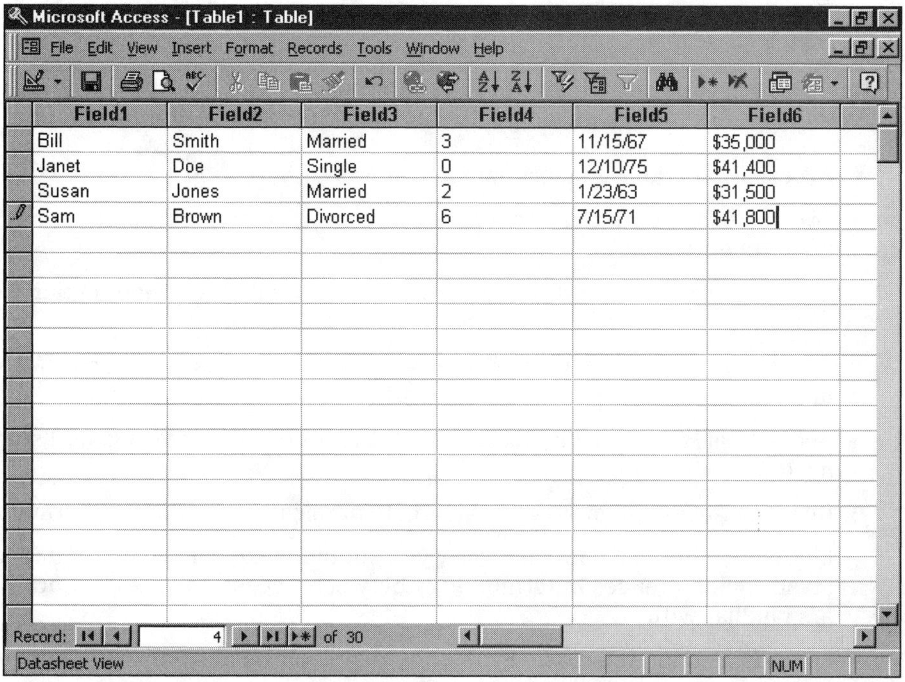

Figure 1-10: Creating a new table using an Access datasheet.

Access has a WYSIWYG drawing capability like that of Excel, and it shares the same graph application. Thus, you can create the same types of graphs in both programs and annotate the graphs in the same way. Also, Access uses graph Wizards that you might have used in Excel.

Access 97 contains a Pivot Table Wizard just like Excel's; in fact, it can create Excel pivot tables. You can also drag and drop information from an Access database to an Excel spreadsheet and link Access databases to Excel spreadsheets. You can query and sort data in both products as well, using a common query interface. (If you've used the Excel menu options for queries and sorting, you already are familiar with these concepts.) You will find Access 97 interoperable with all Microsoft Office 97 products.

Summary

In this chapter, you learned about the capabilities of Access and got an idea of the types of tasks Access can accomplish. The following points were introduced:

✦ Access is a database management system (DBMS).

✦ You can use Access to store and retrieve data, present information, and automate repetitive tasks.

✦ Using Access, you can develop easy-to-use input forms, process your data, and run powerful reports.

✦ Access 97 has powerful new features to publish Access forms as HTML documents and can also exchange data with Internet and intranet sites.

✦ Access features Query By Example (QBE) for selecting, sorting, and searching data.

✦ By using Access macros, you can create applications without programming.

✦ If you already are a database user, you should make sure that you understand the differences in terminology between Access and the product you are familiar with.

✦ Spreadsheet and database users should already be familiar with many of the key concepts used in Access.

In the next chapter, you learn how to install Access.

✦   ✦   ✦

Installing Access 97

◆ ◆ ◆ ◆

In This Chapter

What hardware and software you need to run Access

How to install Access successfully and run it on your computer

How to install the Access 97 upgrade

How to convert Access 1.x, 2.x, and 95 databases

How to handle problems that occur during installation

◆ ◆ ◆ ◆

Access 97 must be installed on your computer before you can use it. Since the majority of copies of Microsoft Access today are purchased through the Microsoft Office suite, it will be used to install the Access 97 programs on your computer. Whether you install Microsoft Office 97 or the stand-alone version of Access 97, after you get to the portion of the setup routine that lets you select the Access 97 options, both installation routines are the same.

Access 97 is installed in a manner similar to Windows 95 or NT software products. If your company has a special person or team designated to install and troubleshoot software, you may want to have this person or department install Access for you so that your system will be installed like the other systems in your company.

If you are installing an upgrade or competitive version of Access or Office 97, the older program must already be installed on your machine. New installations of Access 97 do not require a previous version to be already installed on your machine.

Determining What You Need

Access 97 requires specific hardware and software to run. Before you install Access, check to see that your computer meets the minimum requirements needed to run it.

Hardware requirements

To use Access 97 successfully, you'll need an IBM (or compatible) personal computer with an 80486SX-33 or higher processor and 12MB of RAM. To get reasonable performance from Access 97, we recommend an 80486DX-66 computer with at least 16MB of RAM. With more memory, you'll be able to run more applications simultaneously, and overall performance will be increased. A fast video card is also recommended to display pictures and graphs.

You will also need between 60MB and 191MB of hard disk space for a typical installation of Microsoft Office 97. If you are installing only Access 97, you will still need about 50MB because many of the Office shared files are used by Access and are loaded in the stand-alone version. Keep in mind that you will need additional space to store your database files when you create them.

If space is a problem, you can perform a partial installation, or you can delete unwanted files from your hard disk to free up space needed for the installation. You can also run it directly from the CD-ROM, which installs only 60MB on your hard drive. Unfortunately, this method forces Office to run from the CD-ROM and can be incredibly slow.

Access needs a VGA monitor as a minimum requirement, but we recommend an SVGA (or better) display. This configuration allows you to view more information at one time and to get a sharper resolution.

A mouse or some other compatible pointing device (trackballs and pens will work) is mandatory for you to use Access 97.

If you're planning to print from Access, you need a printer. Any printer that is supported by Windows 95 or Windows NT works.

Software requirements

Access requires that Microsoft Windows 95 or Windows NT be installed on your computer. Windows 95 or NT does *not* come with Access; it must be purchased separately. If Windows 95 or Windows NT is not installed on your computer, install it before you install Access or Office 97. Microsoft Office 97 does not run on OS/2 or Windows 3.1.

Upgrading to Access 97 from Access 2.0 or 95

Before you upgrade to Access 97 from earlier versions of Access, you should consider a few things. Earlier versions of Access databases must be converted to Access 97 format before they are usable. After a database is converted to Access 97 format, it cannot be converted back; it's unusable by Access 2.0 or 95. As an Access 97 user, you can open and work with Access 2.0 or 95 data by attaching to them as external databases, but you cannot modify any of the objects (forms, reports, queries, and so on) you find in them.

If you are sharing data files with people who use older versions of Access, think about leaving the older version of Access on your machine and reinstalling it under Windows 95 or NT. Then you can create files in Access 97 but still use Access 2.0 or 95 to work with files that are shared with others.

Installing Access 97 or Office 97

You can now install Office 97 or Access 97. Insert your CD-ROM into your CD-ROM drive and then select Run from the Windows 95 or NT 4.0 Start menus. If you are using Windows NT 3.51, select run from the Program Manager. Windows 95 or NT will display the Run dialog box. In the Open box, type D:\SETUP (or use whatever letter corresponds to the drive containing your installation CD-ROM, as shown in Figure 2-1. Click on OK to begin the installation. This procedure works for both new installations and upgrades to Access 97.

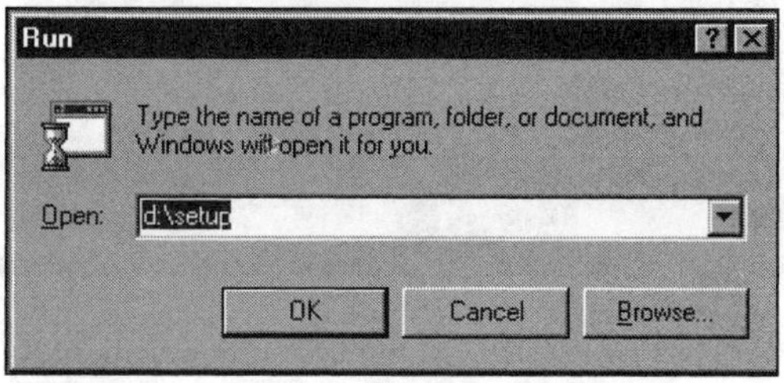

Figure 2-1: The Run dialog box.

Because some Windows 95 and NT programs interfere with the Setup program, Access may warn you to shut down any applications currently running. You can simply click on the Continue button to continue the setup, or you can click on the Exit Setup button to cancel the installation and shut down your applications (you then can run Setup later). The program then welcomes you, as shown in Figure 2-20.

The Setup program now requires some information from you. If you are installing Access for the first time, you are asked to customize your copy of the program by entering your name and (optionally) a company name.

Next, a screen appears with your product ID number. You should write this number down; you'll need it if you call Microsoft Support for help.

Tip You can always find your product ID and the software version number in any Microsoft product by selecting the About option on the Help menu.

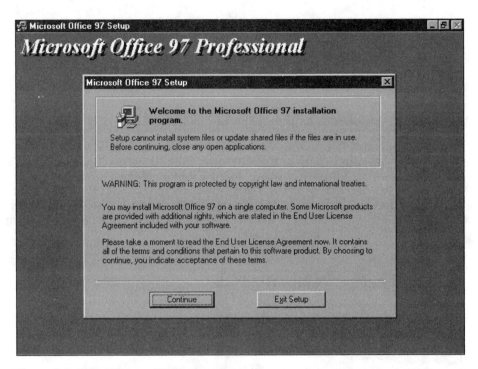

Figure 2-2: The Office 97 Welcome screen.

Next, Setup wants to know where you want to install Access (as shown in Figure 2-3). The default is either C:\Program Files\Access or C:\Program Files\Microsoft Office if you have Microsoft Office Professional. If this location is satisfactory, click on OK to continue with the installation. If you want to change this folder, type the new drive and folder name. For example, to have Access installed in a subfolder located on drive D, you type **D:\ACCESS**. If you type the name of a folder that does not exist, one is created for you.

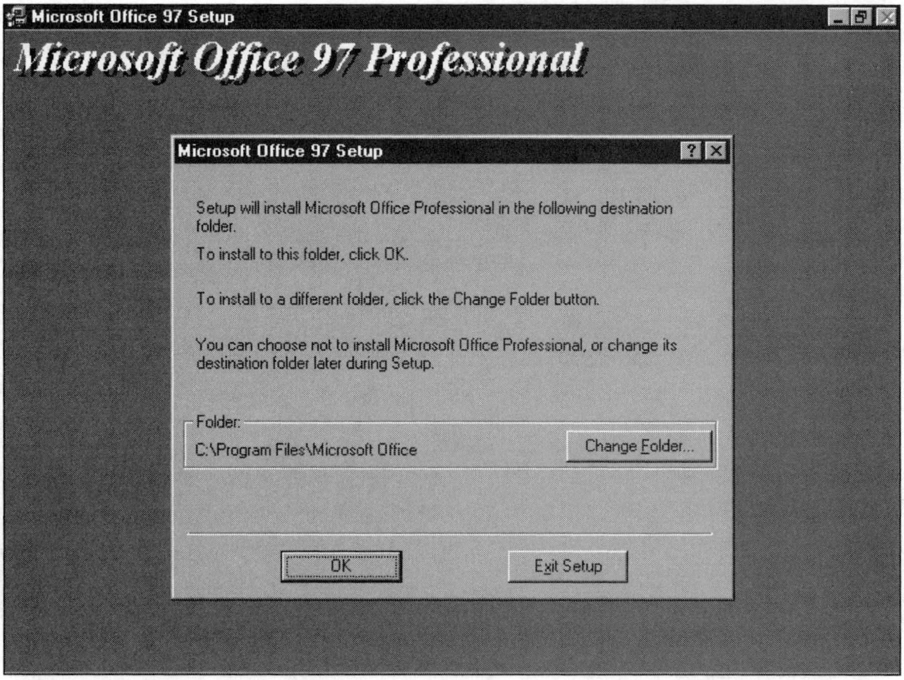

Figure 2-3: Selecting the folder to run Office.

Setup then takes some time to check for available disk space or existing copies of Access files. When this verification step is completed, Setup asks you to choose which type of installation you want, as shown in Figure 2-4. You can choose from the following three options:

Typical	This option installs all the Office files into the folder you specify. This installation uses about 120MB of space.
Custom	This option lets you choose which files you want added. You can install omitted options in the future by rerunning Setup. A full install (choosing every option) can take more than 190MB of hard disk space.
Run from CD-ROM	This option keeps the majority of the program files on the CD-ROM. You will need to have your CD in your drive to use Office 97 or Access 97. Although the software will run very slow, you need only 60MB of hard disk space. This is not a recommended option.

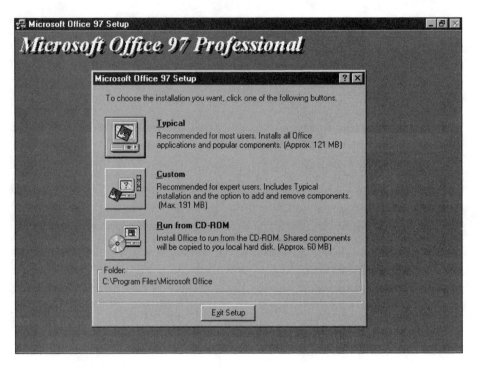

Figure 2-4: Selecting the type of installation.

If you choose Custom installation, you see the screen displayed in Figure 2-5. Setup provides you with a list of options you can install. If you are installing the entire Office suite, you can change the options for each Office product you see in the figure. For example, if you want to change the options for Microsoft Office 97, you choose Microsoft Access and press the Change Option button.

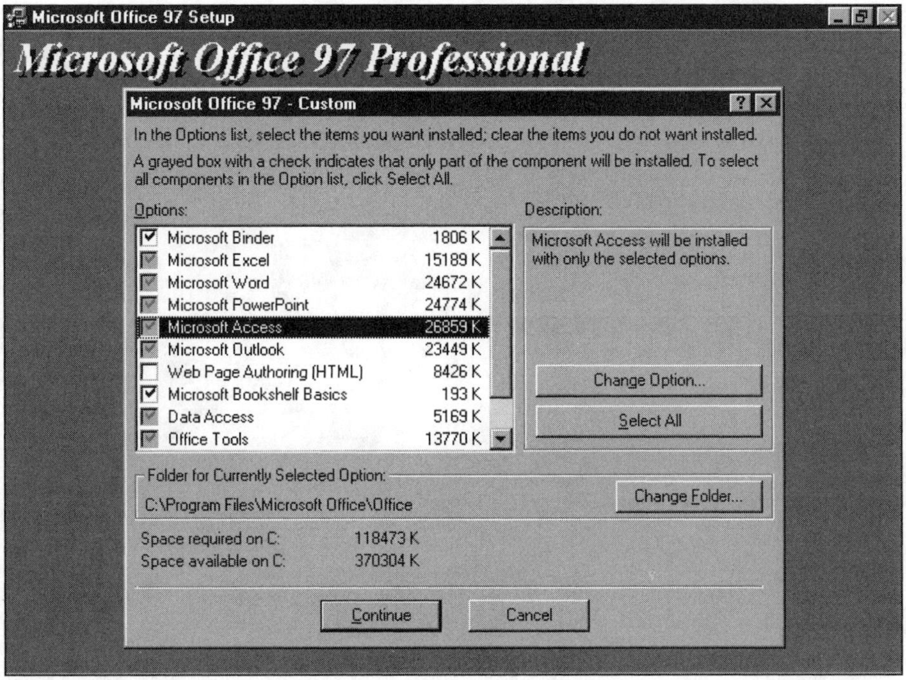

Figure 2-5: Installation options for Microsoft Office 97.

This action displays the Microsoft Access options screen, as shown in Figure 2-6. If you are installing the stand-alone version of Microsoft Access 97, you will see only this screen because the other Office components are not available. However, some of the shared Office components from the previous screen will also be on this screen.

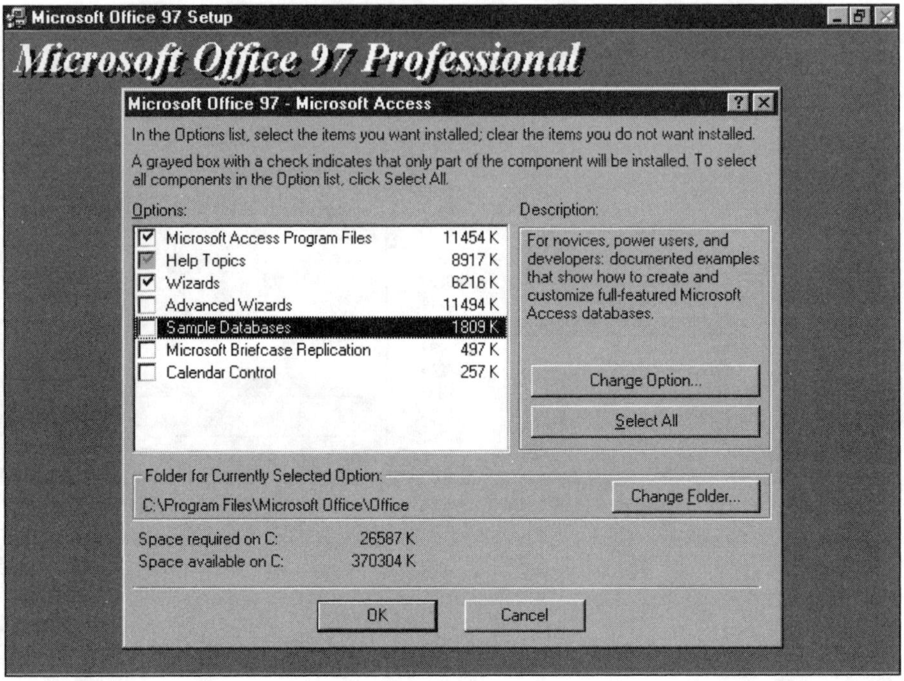

Figure 2-6: Installation options for Microsoft Access 97.

At this point, the default options to be installed are selected as indicated with the check mark in front of the selected options. To select or deselect one, click on the check box next to the option you want to install or that you do not want installed. The check mark will be displayed to indicate that the option will be installed or disappear to indicate that the option will not be installed. Some items are mandatory, and you must install them.

Tip

To select all the options, click the Select All button.

When you have chosen all the items you need, press the Continue button. Setup next determines which disks and files to copy. The installation proceeds. This process will take some time — approximately 10 to 35 minutes for a complete installation, depending on your processor speed, CD-ROM drive speed, and hard disk speed.

If you have an older version of Microsoft Office 4.3 or Microsoft Office 95 products, the Setup routine will ask you if you want to remove them. You may want to keep these versions because Access 97 files can be used only by someone with Access 97. If you are sharing files with Access 2.0, Access for Windows 95 users may need to keep the older versions.

Caution   Although Access 97 can convert older versions of Access .MDB database files, it cannot convert an Access 97 file to either Access 95 or Access 2.0 format.

Tip   You can convert Access 97 data files only to a common format, such as fixed width or delimited, and then import them to an older version of Access.

As the installation continues, a series of pictures appears on-screen. These provide some basic information about various features of Office and Access and how you can use them.

After the installation is complete, you are returned to wherever you were when the installation began. If you installed the stand-alone version of Access, a new program named `Microsoft Access` will be on your Start menu. If you installed the entire Office suite, you will see an entry for each Office product. You can run Access by either choosing Microsoft Access from the Start menu or locating the Microsoft Access folder on the desktop or in Windows 95 Explorer and then finding the Access icon and double-clicking on it. If the Office 97 shortcut bar is present, you can start Access by pressing the Access (key) icon.

Converting Access 1.*x*, 2.0, and 95 Files

Access 97 can convert and read databases created in older versions of Access; you can add, change, and delete data. You can run Access 1.*x*, 2.*x*, and 95 queries, forms, reports, macros, and even Access BASIC modules. Even so, you cannot change any objects (tables, queries, forms, reports, macros, or modules). To redesign an Access 1.*x*, 2.*x*, or 95 object, you must either use Access 1.*x*, 2.*x*, or 95 itself or convert the object to Access 97.

If you attempt to open a database created in a previous version of Microsoft Access, you will be given the option to convert it or open it in read-only mode, as shown in Figure 2-7.

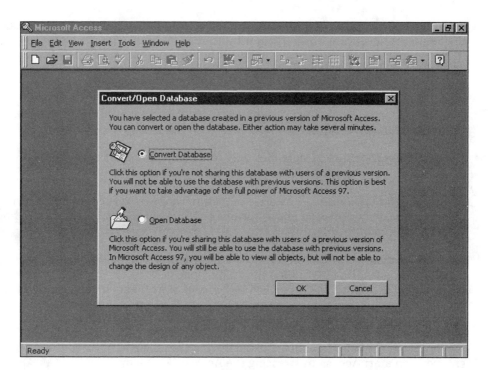

Figure 2-7: Converting an Access database.

Note   You can convert older Access databases by selecting Tools⇨Database Utilities⇨Convert Database in the Access Database window. It is just as easy to open them and let Access ask you, as you can see in Figure 2-7. No database can be open if you want to see the Convert Database menu option.

A standard Windows 95 file-selector dialog box appears. You select the database to be converted and give it a new name. The database is converted.

Note   If the database is already in Access 97 format, Access tells you and the database is not converted.

Caution   If you try to convert the database and save it to the same path and name, you get an error message; the conversion does not take place.

Before you convert a database, check for a few peculiar things that are not converted correctly by the conversion utility:

✦ If you use Microsoft Access security, you must own the database or be a member of the Admins group that was in effect when the database was created.

✦ After you convert a database to Access 97, the attachments of its tables into older-version databases are no longer valid. To use the attached tables, you must convert the attaching database as well.

✦ If Access can't find linked tables while converting the linking database, you should use the Linked Table Manager to relink them.

Troubleshooting

If you run into problems while installing Office or Access, Setup displays a message telling you what the problem may be. Some common problems include lack of disk space and problems reading the CD-ROM.

If you receive a message saying that an error has occurred during Setup, you may have run out of disk space. You need to delete some files before proceeding with the installation. You can delete files from the Windows 95 or NT 4.0 Explorer. Remember to be careful not to delete important files. If you find that you have plenty of available disk space, something else has failed in the installation; you should contact Microsoft Product Support for help.

If your CD-ROM or floppy disk drive has problems reading the installation disks, there may be a problem with your drive. You may want to contact someone in your company's MIS or tech-support department to check the drive for you. Then, if you still receive this message and cannot find the problem, call Microsoft Product Support for help in troubleshooting the problem.

Summary

In this chapter, you learned about the equipment you need to install Access, how to install Access, and how to convert Access 1.x, 2.x, and 95 databases. The chapter covered the following points:

✦ You need to have Microsoft Windows 95 or NT installed on your system before you can install Access.

✦ At least 50MB of free hard disk space is needed to fully install Access 97, and 150MB for installing Office 97.

✦ If available hard disk space is a problem, you can select Custom or Run from CD-ROM installation to limit the options that are installed. (You can install the omitted options at a later time by rerunning Setup.)

✦ You must convert older Access databases to work with Access 97.

Now that you have successfully installed Access, it's time to learn a little about how to use this software. Chapter 3 provides information on how to get started using Access.

✦   ✦   ✦

Getting Started with Access 97

◆   ◆   ◆   ◆

In This Chapter

How you can start
Access 97 in several
different ways

How to add options
to the Access com-
mand line

How to exit Access

How to get help

How to use various
Help options

◆   ◆   ◆   ◆

After you've installed Access successfully, you are ready to learn the various ways to start the Access database program. If you haven't installed Access yet, read Chapter 2 before proceeding.

Starting Access

You can start Access in several ways:

◆ From the Windows Start menu

◆ From an Access shortcut icon

◆ From the Access icon in a folder

◆ From the Windows Explorer

Starting from the Windows Start menu

When you use Windows 95 or Windows NT 4.0 to install Access 97, Windows adds Access to the Start menu's Programs selection automatically. A simple way to start Access 97 is to click on the Start menu, select the Programs submenu, and then select Microsoft Access. This will start Microsoft Access and display the initial Access screen.

Starting from an Access shortcut icon

If you've gotten the hang of Windows 95, you've probably learned how valuable a *shortcut* can be. Figure 3-1 shows the Windows 95 desktop belonging to one of the authors. The top part of the screen shows the Office 97 toolbar along with a separate shortcut to Access 97. In particular, note the copy of the Access 97 icon; dragging it to the Windows 95 desktop from the MSOFFICE\ACCESS folder creates a shortcut. You can start Access 97 quickly by clicking on this icon.

Figure 3-1: The Windows 95 desktop, showing a shortcut to Access.

Starting from an Access icon

If you purchased Access as part of Microsoft Office, then one of your folders in Windows 95 is probably the MSOFFICE folder (or in this example, the Office97 folder), as shown in Figure 3-2. Inside that folder you should find a shortcut icon to launch Access 97 and each Office 97 product. You will also find a file, perhaps in a folder named Office or ACCESS, that contains the file MSACCESS.EXE, which is the actual icon for launching Access 97. You can start Access by clicking on either one of these icons.

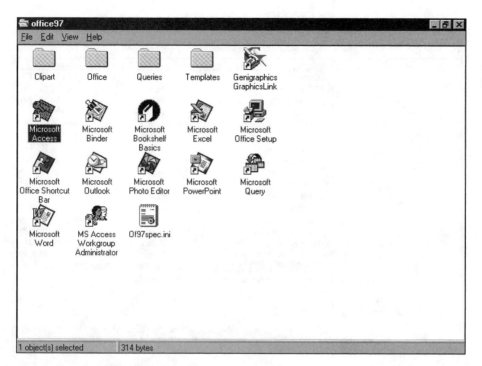

Figure 3-2: The Office97 folder.

Starting from Windows Explorer

You can also start Access from the Windows Explorer (which has kind of replaced Program Manager and File Manager) by selecting the database file you want to load. Figure 3-3 shows the Windows Explorer with the file Mountain Animal Hospital.mdb selected. This is the name of one the sample database files shipped with this book.

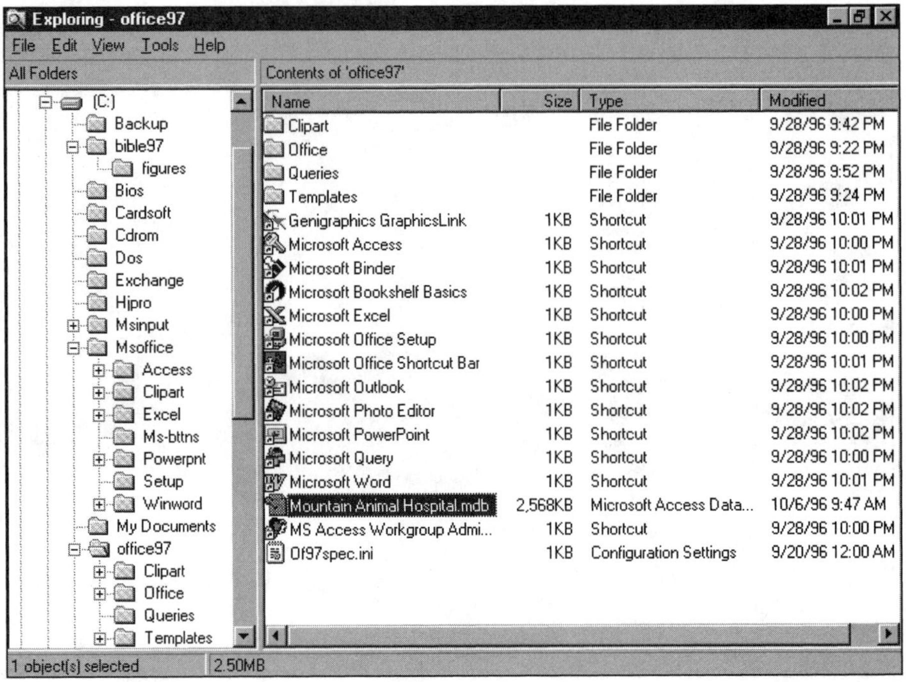

Figure 3-3: Starting a database file in Windows Explorer.

When you find the database file you want to load, double-click on the filename. Windows then starts Access and opens the database you selected. If you are unsure of which file you should choose, check to see that it has a proper file extension. Microsoft Access database files normally have the file extension MDB. Because Microsoft Access is a registered application in Windows 95, you will launch Access whenever you select a file with the .MDB extension. You may also find files with an .MDA or .MDE file extension. These will also launch Access 97. MDA files are library files typically containing add-ins or wizards. MDE files are Access databases that contain preprogrammed applications but in which all the module source code has been removed. You can run the application, but you cannot see any of the modules.

Note If you already have Access running and you double-click on a file in the Windows Explorer, another copy of Access will start, which will load the file you selected. You may want to do this if you want more than one database open at a time. (Access does not let you open more than one database at a time if you are running only one occurrence of Access.)

Options for starting Access

You can customize how Access starts by adding options to the MSACCESS command line from the properties of a shortcut icon. For example, you can have Access open a database, execute a macro, or supply a user name or password — automatically. Table 3-1 identifies the options available for starting Access.

Table 3-1
Command-Line Options for Starting Access

Option	Effect
<database>	Opens the specified database. Include a path if necessary.
/Excl	Opens the specified database for exclusive access. To open the database for shared access in a multiuser environment, omit this option.
/RO	Opens the specified database for read-only access.
/User <user name>	Starts Microsoft Access using the specified user name.
/Pwd <password>	Starts Microsoft Access using the specified password.
/Profile <user profile>	Starts Microsoft Access using the options in the specified user profile instead of the standard Windows Registry settings (created when you installed Microsoft Access). This replaces the /ini option used in previous versions of Microsoft Access to specify an initialization file. However, the /ini option will still work for user-defined .INI files from earlier versions of Microsoft Access.
/Compact <target database>	Compacts the database specified before the /Compact option and then closes Microsoft Access. If you omit a target database name following the /Compact option, Access compacts the database using the original database name. To compact to a different name, specify a target database.
/Repair	Repairs the specified database and then closes Microsoft Access.
/Convert <target database>	Converts a database in an earlier version (1.x, 2.0, or 95) to a Microsoft Access 97 database with a new name and then closes Microsoft Access. Specify the source database before using the /Convert option.

(continued)

Table 3-1 *(continued)*	
Option	**Effect**
/X <macro>	Starts Microsoft Access and runs the specified macro. Another way to run a macro when you open a database is to use an AutoExec macro or the Database Startup properties.
/Cmd	Specifies that what follows on the command line is the value that will be returned by the Command function. This option must be the last option on the command line. You can use a semicolon (;) as an alternative to /Cmd.
/Nostartup	Starts Microsoft Access without displaying the Startup dialog box (the second dialog box you see when you start Microsoft Access).

Tip To run a VBA procedure when you open a database, use the RunCode action in a command-line macro or the AutoExec macro, or use the Access 97 Startup dialog box. You can also run a VBA procedure when you open a database by creating a form with a VBA procedure defined for its OnOpen event. Designate this as the startup form by using the right mouse button to click in the database window, click on Startup, and then enter that form in the Display Form box.

For example, to have Access automatically execute a macro called MYMACRO, you enter the following parameter in the Shortcut Properties section of an Access shortcut. (You may find the command MSACCESS.EXE preceded by its path.)

> **MSACCESS.EXE /X MYMACRO**

You can also use a special option that Access runs automatically when you first open a Microsoft Access database (you will learn more about this in Part V). This is the *Startup form*. You can use it to open certain tables or forms every time you enter a database or to perform complex processing, change the menus, change the title bar, hide the database window, or do just about anything you can think of.

Note In Access 2.0, you created a macro named Autoexec to do this. In Access 97, the startup form is an easier way to run a program automatically when you open a database.

Tip To prevent a startup form from running automatically, hold down the Shift key as you open the database.

Exiting Access

When you are finished using Access (or any application), you should always exit gracefully. It bears repeating: Simply turning off your system is not a good method and can cause problems. Windows and your applications use many files while they are running, some of which you may not be aware of. Turning off your system can cause these files not to be closed properly, which can result in hard disk problems in the future.

Another reason for exiting gracefully is to ensure that all your data is saved before you exit the application. If you have spent quite a bit of time entering data and then you turn off your system, accidentally forgetting to save this work, all this unsaved data will be lost! Save yourself time and grief by exiting your applications the correct way.

You can exit Access in several safe ways:

✦ Double-click on the Control icon on the Access title bar.

✦ From the Access menu, select File➪Exit.

✦ Press Alt+F4.

✦ Display the taskbar and select Microsoft Access. Then right-click and select Close. You can use this method to close Access from within another application.

When you exit Access with one of these methods, you may see a message displayed on-screen that prompts you to save any changes you may have made. You can select Yes to save the changes and exit Access. Selecting No will exit Access without saving the changes you made. Cancel stops Access from closing, and you are returned to Access. You can also choose Help for more information on exiting Access.

Getting Help

Now that you have learned how to start Access, you may need some help in learning how to use the software. After you have started Access, you can choose from any of the Help options that are available. Some of these include:

✦ Office Assistant

✦ Standard Windows 95 Help (Contents, Index, and Find tabs)

✦ Screen Tips (What's This?)

✦ Introduction to Microsoft Access 97

✦ Web-based resources on the Microsoft Web site

✦ Northwinds database

✦ Solutions database

Office Assistant

When you first press F1 to request help, Access displays the friendly new Office Assistant, as shown in Figure 3-4. The default assistant is Clipit, your guide to help. As you can see in the figure, the Office Assistant provides you with a list of options. You can type a request in standard English (or whatever language you use), get helpful tips and hints, or select options to change the Office Assistant character. There are several to choose from, including Clipit, Dot, the Office Logo, Albert Einstein, William Shakespeare, Power Pup, or even Mother Nature or an origami cat named Scribble.

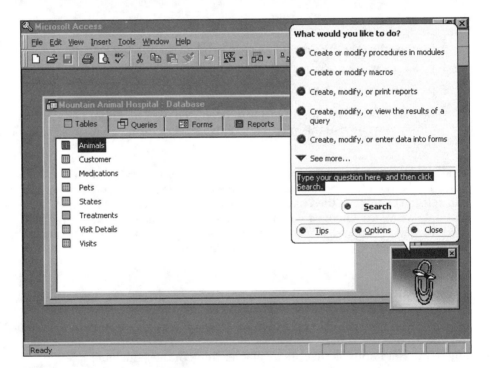

Figure 3-4: The Office Assistant.

Tip   Right-click on the Assistant and select Animate. You will be treated to an amazing show. Each character comes with between 10 and 30 different shows.

Tip   If you have access to the Microsoft Web site, you can use a variety of other characters in the Office pages.

Standard Help

When you choose the <u>H</u>elp menu on the command bar and select Contents and Index, Access presents you with a tabbed dialog box (as shown in Figure 3-5). This dialog box provides several ways to help you get started using Access. You have three options to choose from:

Contents   As shown in Figure 3-5, the Table of Contents lists major topics grouped by task. When you select a topic, a menu of subtopics appears and leads you to various Help screens.

Index   This displays an alphabetical list of Help topics. You can type the first few letters of the Help topic you are searching for or scroll through the list.

Find   This feature conducts a finer search than you can do using the Index. First you enter a single keyword. A list of potential topics appears; you select one of these to see a list of Help topics.

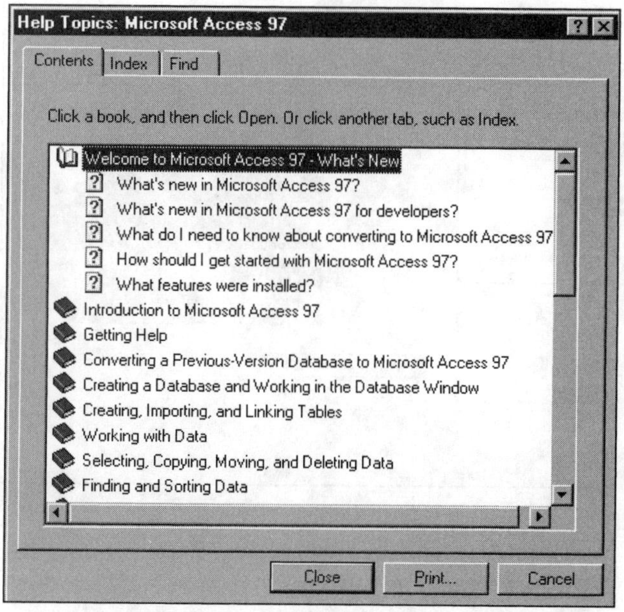

Figure 3-5: The Access 97 Help Topics dialog box.

Note If you have used Access 2.0, the topics under What's New will give you a thorough explanation of the new features in Access 97.

As you can see in Figure 3-5, the list of Help topics is very general. When you select an option, the icon will appear as an open book indicating a list of subtopics. When you see the icon with a question mark, you can click on it and then click on the place you want Help to display the actual help you need or another menu of topics.

From these menus, you can select any topic and receive more help. A good example of this is shown in Figure 3-6. This is some of the more explanatory help used to explain concepts. This is a screen from the Introduction to Help section. As you can see in Figure 3-6, this Help screen also contains buttons you can click on to receive even more detailed help.

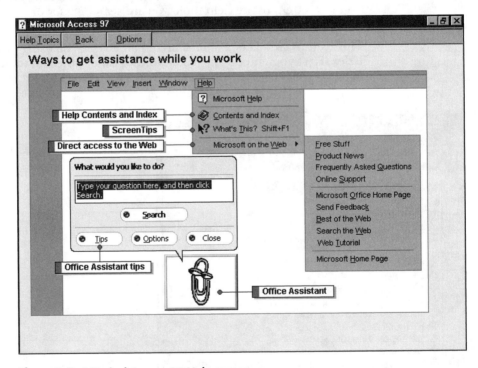

Figure 3-6: A Typical Access 97 Help screen.

Essentials of standard online help

Help in Access is always a keystroke away. There are many easy ways to get help:

✦ Press the F1 key to get the Assistant and then ask a question or select a help suggestion.

✦ Click on the Help button that resembles a cursor arrow and a question mark (on the Access toolbar), and then click on the desired item to get Screen Tip help. You can also press Shift+F1 to display the question-mark cursor or select What's This from the Help menu. More on Screen Tips later.

✦ Select Help from the Access pull-down menu and then choose Contents and Index.

You can get help at any time in Access, no matter what you are doing. Help is available for every aspect of Access — commands, menus, macros, Access terms and concepts, and even programming topics. Figure 3-5 showed the Help Table of Contents window that is displayed when you press F1 (if no activity is in progress).

Help is a separate program from Access and has its own window. Therefore, you can move, size, minimize, or close the Help window.

Help options

When Help is displayed, it shows an Options menu that contains several choices. These appear in Table 3-2.

Table 3-2 Help Menu Options	
Option	**Description**
Annotate	Lets you add text to the current Help topic. Annotations are marked with a paper-clip icon in front of the topic heading. This is a good way to add your own notes to a Help topic for future reference. You can also copy and paste annotations to other Help topics or into other applications or documents.
Copy	Copies the text of the current Help topic to the Clipboard. From the Clipboard, you can paste the text into another application or document. You can generally highlight the specific text you want to copy.
Print Topic	Prints the current topic in the Help window. You can print only entire topics.

(continued)

	Table 3-2 (continued)
Option	**Description**
<u>F</u>ont	Sets the font size to Small, Normal, or Large.
<u>K</u>eep Help on Top	Determines whether a Help window is sent to the background when another function is selected in Access. Choices are Default, On Top, and Not On Top.
<u>U</u>se System Colors	Uses the default system colors rather than Access 97 Help colors.
Bookmarks...	Displays any predefined bookmarks so that you can quickly go to a Help topic you have previously marked.
Define Bookmarks...	Defines a bookmark at the current location that allows you to quickly go back to the specific Help topic using the previous option.

Note   A major change in Office 97 is the conversion of all Help files from RTF (Revisable Text Format) to HTML-based file format. HTML is the language of the Internet.

Screen Tips (What's This?)

Screen Tips are a new type of help found in all Microsoft Office products. They give you short explanations of tasks in the various products. They are text only, generally displayed in a small rectangle. Although standard toolbar ToolTips display only a word or two, Screen Tips display a paragraph. When you select the Help icon on the toolbar, the cursor changes to an arrow with a question mark. You can then click on various parts of an Access 97 screen and receive a short explanation of the task or function you clicked on. You can also press Shift+F1 for the same effect. For example, if you press Shift+F1 and then click on the Tables tab in the Database window, you will see a Screen Tip explaining what you can do with a table, as shown in Figure 3-7.

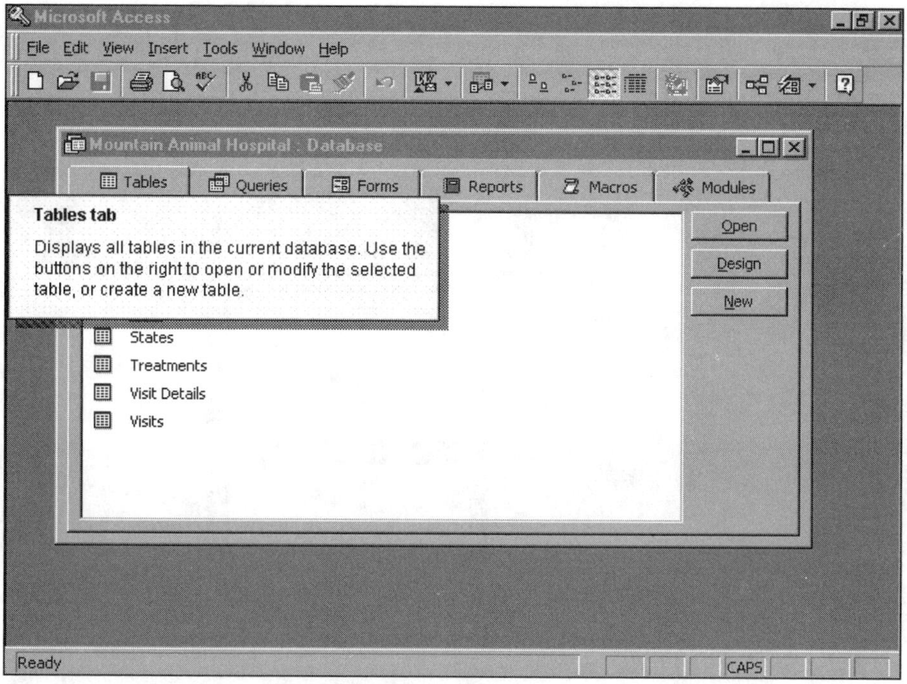

Figure 3-7: An Access 97 Screen Tip.

Tip   You can create your own Screen Tips in your applications, using the same techniques that create standard Access 97 Help.

A visual tour of Access 97

In Figure 3-4, you may have noticed that one of the options in the Access 97 Help contents was Introduction to Microsoft Access 97. This is a very basic conceptual introduction to database concepts using Microsoft Access. Using this type of help, you have more than 50 screens of introductory information. Figure 3-8 shows a typical card from the visual introduction. This is a great place to start if you are new to database terminology and techniques.

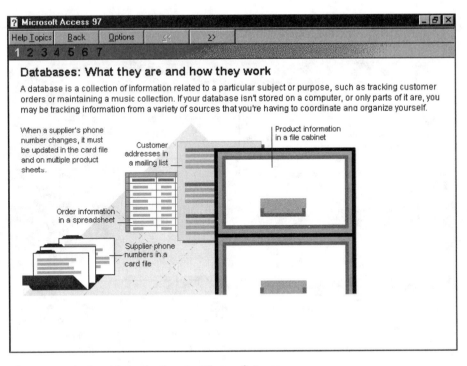

Figure 3-8: A visual introduction to Microsoft Access.

Web-based resources on the Microsoft Web site

On the Access 97 <u>H</u>elp menu is a group of options to give you access to the Microsoft Web site and a plethora of free resources to help you use any Microsoft product. All the options launch the Microsoft Internet Explorer Web browser and take you right to the appropriate page on the Microsoft Web site. This page includes Free Stuff, Product News, the Access Developer Forum, FAQs (Frequently Asked Questions), and Online Support. The bottom most options also let you go directly to the Office Home Page, send Feedback to Microsoft, go to a list of the best Web sites, search the Web, take a tutorial about using the Web, and go to the general Microsoft Home Page.

Sample databases

You should be aware of one more place you can get help. The Office Samples directory contains several special databases: Northwind.MDB (the Northwinds Example file used throughout the Access documentation), ORDERS.MDB (a sample order-entry program also used in the Access programmer's documentation), and SOLUTIONS.MDB (a teaching database).

When you open SOLUTIONS.MDB, a Help-like interfaceappears. You can select a global topic in the top list box and then choose from a set of specific subtopics in the lower list box. When you double-click on a subtopic, a working example from Northwinds is displayed along with instructional Help. This allows you to work with a real example while learning some of the more complex topics. Unlike the visual introduction, which explains concepts, the Solutions database is used to show you how to solve a particular problem using Access.

Summary

In this chapter, you learned various ways to start Access and how to exit the program. You learned about the many ways to use the Access Help system. The following points were covered:

✦ You can start Access in various ways; the easiest and most common method is using the Start menu or double-clicking on an Access shortcut icon.

✦ You can add options to the Access command line that can automatically open a database, execute a macro, or set a user name or password.

✦ You should use one of the suggested ways to exit Access. If you exit by simply turning off your system, the result can be loss of data.

✦ Using the Office Assistant, you can ask questions in plain language and see various Help topics that match your question.

✦ Many types of Help are in Access. Help can provide step-by-step instructions for learning Access; it can walk you through the setups needed to create your own database objects.

✦ You can press F1 to activate the Help feature, which gives information on how to use Access or defines various concepts used in Access.

✦ Microsoft provides direct access to its Web site for free software and many free resources to help you get started and to be productive.

✦ Help appears in a window of its own that can be minimized or resized; you can keep it open as you work on your database.

✦ The Access Introduction will teach you the fundamental concepts of working with databases using Microsoft Access 97.

✦ Three sample databases will help you get started: Northwind, Orders, and Solutions.

In the next chapter, you review basic database concepts as you begin the journey to understanding database management with Access.

✦   ✦   ✦

A Review of Database Concepts

In This Chapter

What is a database?

What are the differences among databases, tables, records, fields, and values?

Why are multiple tables used in a database?

What are database objects?

Before you begin to use a database software package, you must understand several basic concepts. The most important concept is that the data is stored in a "black box" known as a *table* and that by using the tools of the database, you can retrieve, display, and report the data in any format you want.

What Is a Database?

Database is a computer term for a collection of information concerning a certain topic or business application. Databases help you organize this related information in a logical fashion for easy access and retrieval.

Figure 4-1 shows a conceptual view of a typical manual filing system that consists of people, papers, and filing cabinets. This lighthearted view of a manual database makes the point that paper is the key to a manual database system. In a real manual database system, you probably have in/out baskets and some type of formal filing method. You access information manually by opening a file cabinet, taking out a file folder, and finding the correct piece of paper. Paper forms are used for input, perhaps with a typewriter. You find information by sorting the papers manually or by copying desired information from many papers to another piece of paper (or even into a computer spreadsheet). You might use a calculator or a computer spreadsheet to analyze the data further or to report it.

Figure 4-1: A typical manual filing system.

A computer database is nothing more than an automated version of the filing and retrieval functions of a manual paper filing system. Computer databases store information in a structured format that you define. They can store data in a variety of forms, from simple lines of text (such as name and address) to complex data structures that include pictures, sounds, or video images. Storing data in a precise, known format enables a database management system (DBMS) to turn the data into useful information through many types of output, such as queries and reports.

Figure 4-2 shows a conceptual view of an automated database management system such as Access. The person uses a computer to access the data stored in tables — entering data in the tables through data-entry forms and retrieving it by using a query. Queries retrieve only the desired data from the tables. Then a report outputs the data to the screen or a printer. Macros and modules allow the user to automate this process and even create new menus and dialog boxes.

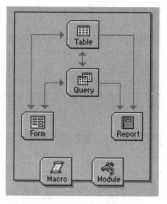

Figure 4-2: A computer database system.

A *relational* database management system (RDBMS) such as Access stores data in many related tables. The user can ask complex questions from one or more of these related tables; answers come back to the user as forms and reports.

Databases, Tables, Records, Fields, and Values

Microsoft Access follows traditional database terminology. The terms *database, table, record, field,* and *value* indicate a hierarchy from largest to smallest.

Databases

In Access, a *database* is the overall container for the data and associated objects. Database *objects* include tables, queries, forms, reports, macros, and modules, as shown in Figure 4-2. In some computer software products, the database is the object that holds the actual data; in Access, this is called a *table*.

Access can work with only one database at a time. Within a single Access database, however, you can have hundreds of tables, forms, queries, reports, macros, and modules — all stored in a single file with the file extension .MDB.

Tables

A table is a container for raw data. When you enter data in Access, a table stores it in logical groupings of similar data (the Pets table, for example, contains data about pets); the table's design organizes the information into rows and columns. Figure 4-3 shows a typical Access table design; its *datasheet* (also known as a *browse table* or *table view*) displays multiple lines of data in neat rows and columns.

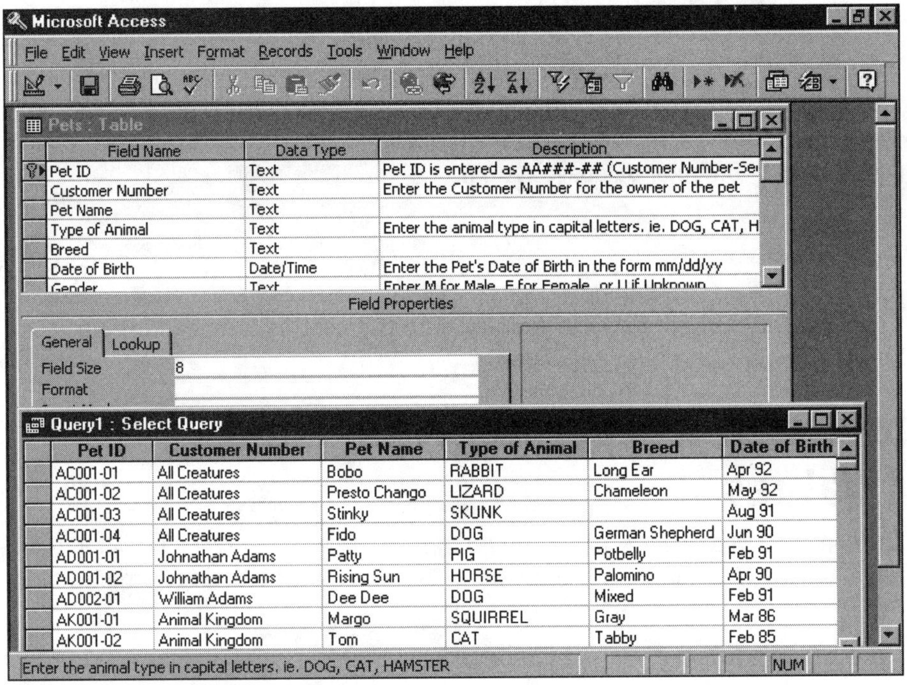

Figure 4-3: A Database table design and datasheet.

Records and fields

As shown in Figure 4-3, the datasheet is divided into rows called *records* and columns called *fields*. The data shown in the table has columns of similar information, such as Pet Name, Customer Number, Breed, or Date of Birth; these columns of data items are fields. Each field is identified as a certain type of data (Text, Number, Date, and so on) and has a specified length. Each field has a name that identifies its category of information.

The rows of data within a table are its records. Each row of information is considered a separate entity that can be accessed or sequenced as desired. All the fields of information concerning a certain pet are contained within a specific record.

Values

At the intersection of a row (record) and a column (field) is a *value* — the actual data element. For example, Bobo, the Pet Name of the first record, is one data value. (How do you identify the first record? It's the record with the rabbit. But what if there is more than one rabbit?) Whereas fields are known by the field name, records are usually known by some unique characteristic of the record. In the Pets table, one field is the Pet ID; Pet Name is not unique because there could be two pets named Fido in the table.

Sometimes it takes more than one field to find a unique value. Customer Number and Pet Name could be used, but it's possible for one customer to have two pets with the same name. You could use the fields Customer Number, Pet Name, and Type of Animal. Again, theoretically you could have a customer come in and say, "Hi, my name's Larry — this is my pet snake Darryl, and this is my other pet snake Darryl." Creating a unique identifier (such as Pet ID) helps you tell one record apart from another without having to look through all the values.

Why Use More Than One Table?

A database contains one or more tables (that is, logical groupings of similar data). Most applications that you develop in Access have several related tables to present the information efficiently. An application that uses multiple tables can manipulate data more efficiently than it could with one large table.

Multiple tables simplify data entry and reporting by decreasing the input of redundant data. By defining two tables for an application that uses customer information, for example, you don't need to store the customer's name and address every time the customer purchases an item.

Figure 4-4 shows a typical table relation: the Customer table related to the Pets table. If there were only one table, the customer name and address would have to be repeated for each pet record. Two tables let the user look up information in the Customer table for each pet by using the common field Customer Number. This way, when a customer changes address (for example), it changes only in one record in the Customer table; when the pet information is on-screen, the correct customer address is always visible.

By separating your data into multiple tables within your database, your system is easier to maintain because all records of a given type are within the same table. You will significantly reduce your design and work time if you invest the extra time to segment your data properly into multiple tables.

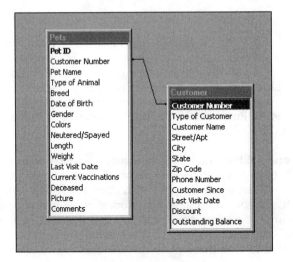

Figure 4-4: Related tables.

 Tip It is also a good idea to create a separate database for just your tables. By separating your design objects (queries, forms, reports, macros, and modules) and the tables into two different databases, you make it easier to maintain your application.

Later in this book, you will have the opportunity to work through a case study for the Mountain Animal Hospital that consists of eight tables. You will also learn how to use the Access 97 Application Splitter to separate the tables from the design objects.

Database Objects and Views

If you are new to databases (or are even an experienced database user), you should understand some key concepts in Access before starting to use the product. The Access database contains six objects; these consist of the data and tools you need to use Access:

Table	Holds the actual data (uses a datasheet to display the raw data)
Query	Lets you search, sort, and retrieve specific data
Form	Lets you enter and display data in a customized format
Report	Lets you display and print formatted data, including calculations and totals

Macro   Gives you easy-to-use commands to automate tasks without programming

Module   Program written in VBA

Datasheets

Datasheets are one of the many ways you can view data. Although not a database object, a datasheet displays a list of records from your table in a format commonly known as a *browse screen,* or *table view.* A datasheet displays data as a series of rows and columns (comparable to a spreadsheet), as shown in Figure 4-5. A datasheet simply displays the information from a table in its raw form. This spreadsheet format is the default mode for displaying all fields for all records.

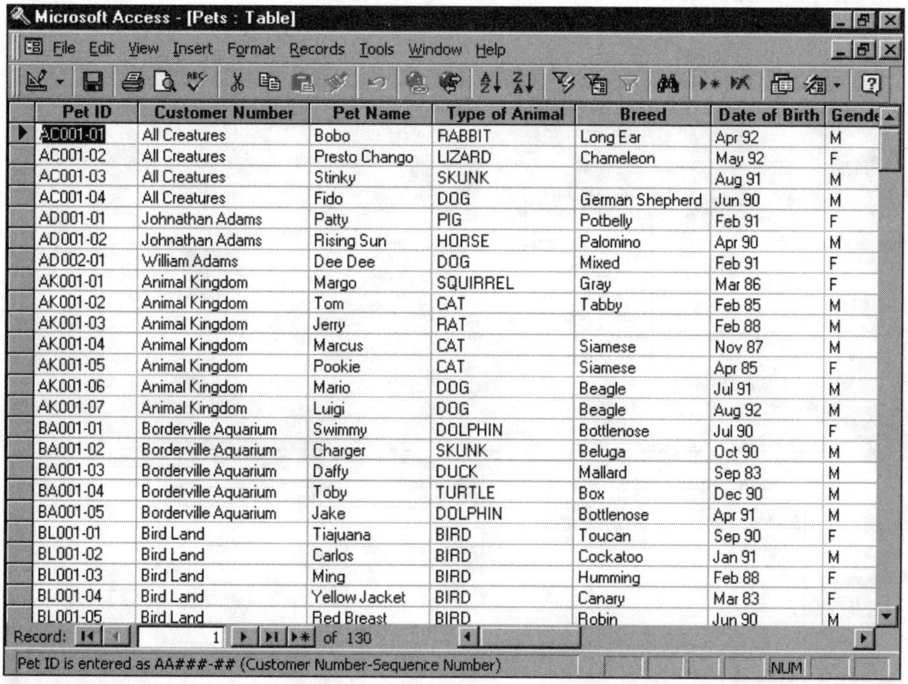

Pet ID	Customer Number	Pet Name	Type of Animal	Breed	Date of Birth	Gender
AC001-01	All Creatures	Bobo	RABBIT	Long Ear	Apr 92	M
AC001-02	All Creatures	Presto Chango	LIZARD	Chameleon	May 92	F
AC001-03	All Creatures	Stinky	SKUNK		Aug 91	M
AC001-04	All Creatures	Fido	DOG	German Shepherd	Jun 90	M
AD001-01	Johnathan Adams	Patty	PIG	Potbelly	Feb 91	F
AD001-02	Johnathan Adams	Rising Sun	HORSE	Palomino	Apr 90	M
AD002-01	William Adams	Dee Dee	DOG	Mixed	Feb 91	F
AK001-01	Animal Kingdom	Margo	SQUIRREL	Gray	Mar 86	F
AK001-02	Animal Kingdom	Tom	CAT	Tabby	Feb 85	M
AK001-03	Animal Kingdom	Jerry	RAT		Feb 88	M
AK001-04	Animal Kingdom	Marcus	CAT	Siamese	Nov 87	M
AK001-05	Animal Kingdom	Pookie	CAT	Siamese	Apr 85	F
AK001-06	Animal Kingdom	Mario	DOG	Beagle	Jul 91	M
AK001-07	Animal Kingdom	Luigi	DOG	Beagle	Aug 92	M
BA001-01	Borderville Aquarium	Swimmy	DOLPHIN	Bottlenose	Jul 90	F
BA001-02	Borderville Aquarium	Charger	SKUNK	Beluga	Oct 90	M
BA001-03	Borderville Aquarium	Daffy	DUCK	Mallard	Sep 83	M
BA001-04	Borderville Aquarium	Toby	TURTLE	Box	Dec 90	M
BA001-05	Borderville Aquarium	Jake	DOLPHIN	Bottlenose	Apr 91	M
BL001-01	Bird Land	Tiajuana	BIRD	Toucan	Sep 90	F
BL001-02	Bird Land	Carlos	BIRD	Cockatoo	Jan 91	M
BL001-03	Bird Land	Ming	BIRD	Humming	Feb 88	F
BL001-04	Bird Land	Yellow Jacket	BIRD	Canary	Mar 83	F
BL001-05	Bird Land	Red Breast	BIRD	Robin	Jun 90	M

Record: ◄ ◄ 1 ► ►► ►* of 130

Pet ID is entered as AA###-## (Customer Number-Sequence Number)

Figure 4-5: A typical datasheet.

You can scroll through the datasheet by using the directional keys on your keyboard. In addition, you can make changes to the displayed data. You should use caution when making any changes or allowing a user to make any modifications in this format. When you change a record in a datasheet, you are actually changing the data in the underlying table.

Queries and dynasets

You use a *query* to extract information from a database. A query can select and define a group of records that fulfill a certain condition. You can use queries before printing a report so that only the desired data is printed. Forms can also use a query so that only certain records (that meet the desired criteria) will appear on-screen. You can use queries within procedures that change, add, or delete database records.

An example of a query is when a doctor at Mountain Animal Hospital says, "Show me which of the pets we treat are dogs or cats and are located in Idaho; show them to me sorted by customer name and then by pet name." Instead of asking the question in actual English, the doctor would use a method known as *QBE,* which stands for Query By Example. Figure 4-6 shows a typical query screen that asks the doctor's question.

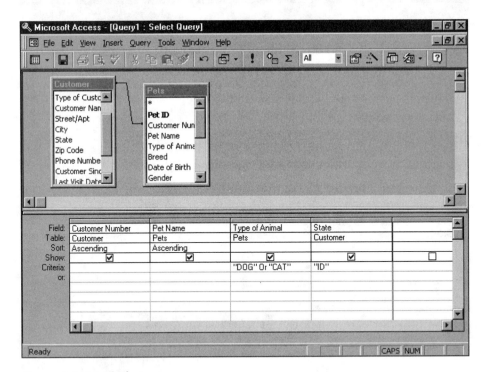

Figure 4-6: A typical query.

When you enter instructions into the QBE window, the query translates them and retrieves the desired data. In this example, first the query combines data from both the Customer and Pets tables, using the related field Customer Number (the common link between the tables). Then it retrieves the fields Customer Name, Pet Name, Type of Animal, and State. Access then filters the records, selecting only those in which the value of State is ID and the value of Type of Animal is dog or cat. It sorts the resulting records, first by customer name and then by pet name within the customer names that are alike. Finally, the records appear on-screen in a datasheet.

These selected records are known as a *dynaset* — a *dyna*mic *set* of data that can change according to the raw data in the original tables.

After you run a query, you can use the resulting dynaset in a form, which you can display on-screen in a specified format or print on a report. In this way, you can limit user access to only the data that meets the criteria in the dynaset.

Data-entry and display forms

Data-entry forms help users get information into a database table in a quick, easy, and accurate manner. Data-entry and display forms provide a more structured view of the data than does a datasheet. From this structured view, you can view, add, change, or delete database records. Entering data through the data-entry forms is the most common way to get the data into the database table. Figure 4-7 shows a typical form.

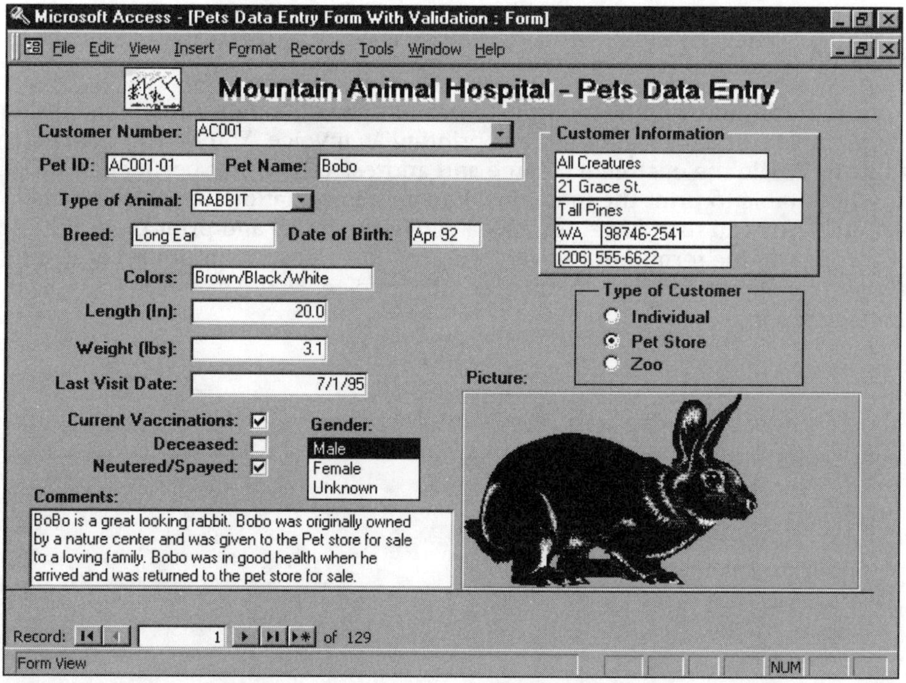

Figure 4-7: A typical data-entry form.

You can use data-entry forms to restrict access to certain fields within the table. You can also use these forms to check the validity of your data before you accept it into the database table.

Most users prefer to enter information into data-entry forms rather than datasheet tables; data-entry forms can be made to resemble familiar paper documents. Forms make data entry self-explanatory by guiding the user through the fields of the table being updated.

Display-only screens and forms are solely for inquiry purposes. These forms allow for the selective display of certain fields within a given table. Displaying some fields and not others means that you can limit a user's access to sensitive data while allowing inquiry into other fields.

Reports

Reports present your data in printed format. You can create several different types of reports within a database management system. For example, your report can list all records in a given table, such as a customer table. You can also create a report that lists only the customers who meet a given criterion, such as all those who live in the state of Washington. You do this by incorporating a query into your report design.

The query creates a dynaset consisting of the records that contain the state code WA.

Your reports can combine multiple tables to present complex relationships among different sets of data. An example is printing an invoice. You access the customer table to obtain the customer's name and address (and other pertinent data) and the sales table to print the individual line-item information for the products ordered. You can then have Access calculate the totals and print them (in a specific format) on the form. Additionally, you can have Access output records into an *invoice report,* a table that summarizes the invoice. Figure 4-8 shows a typical invoice report.

Mountain Animal Hospital
2414 Mountain Road South
Redmond, WA 06761
206-555-9999

Report Date: 8/25/95

William Primen

1234 Main St

Mountain View, WA 98401-1011

(206) 555-1230

Visit Date
7/7/95

Pet Name:	Brutus					
	Treatments		Medication		
Type of Visit	Description	Price	Description	Price	Total
INJURY	Cast affected area	$120.00	Byactocaine - 4 oz	$11.00	$131.00
INJURY	Repair complex fracture	$230.00	Nyostatine - 2 oz	$20.00	$250.00
				Brutus Subtotal	$381.00

Pet Name:	Little Bit					
	Treatments		Medication		
Type of Visit	Description	Price	Description	Price	Total
ILLNESS	Internal Examination	$55.00		$0.00	$55.00
ILLNESS	Lab Work - Blood	$50.00		$0.00	$50.00
ILLNESS	Lab Work - Cerology	$75.00		$0.00	$75.00
ILLNESS	Lab Work - Electrolytes	$75.00	Dual Antibiotic - 8 oz	$8.00	$83.00
ILLNESS	Lab Work - Misc	$35.00	Xaritain Glyconol - 2 oz	$34.50	$69.50
				Little Bit Subtotal	$332.50

Total Invoice:	$713.50
Discount (0%):	$0.00
Subtotal:	$713.50
Washington Sales Tax (4%):	$28.54
Amount Due:	$742.04

Figure 4-8: A typical invoice report.

When you design your database tables, keep in mind all the types of information you want printed. Doing so ensures that the information you require in your various reports is available from within your database tables.

Summary

You can find more new concepts (and thorough discussions of them) throughout this book. Chapter 12, for example, provides an in-depth discussion of database concepts when working with multiple tables as well as primary and foreign keys, referential integrity, and relationships. This chapter covered the following points:

✦ Database is a computer term for a collection of information related to a certain topic or business application.

✦ Databases let you organize this related information in a logical fashion for easy access and retrieval.

✦ An Access database is a single file with an MDB file extension; it holds all the database objects used in Access.

✦ Database objects include tables, queries, forms, reports, macros, and modules.

✦ A table holds the raw data in fields and contains a definition for every field.

✦ A record is a row in the table, identified by some unique value.

✦ A field is a column in the table, identified by a field name.

✦ The value is an element of data found at the intersection of a record and a field.

✦ Relational database management systems use more than one table to simplify database reporting and eliminate redundant data.

✦ A datasheet (also called a browse table or table view) is a spreadsheet-type view of your data. The datasheet lets you view raw data in a table.

✦ A query lets you ask questions of your data; you use the Query By Example (QBE) screen to select fields, sort the data, and select only specific records by specified criteria. The result of a query is a dynaset. This dynamic set of data can be used with a datasheet, form, or report.

✦ Forms let you view your data in a more structured format. You can enter data into a form or make the form read-only.

✦ Reports are used mainly for calculating and summarizing data and are frequently printed.

In the next chapter, you take a guided tour through Access and see how some of these objects are used.

✦   ✦   ✦

A Hands-On Tour of Access 97

◆ ◆ ◆ ◆

In This Chapter

Learning how to navi-
gate the screen by
using the mouse, the
keyboard, or a com-
bination of the two

Seeing a brief
overview of the basic
components on the
Access screen

Take a hands-on tour
through a simple
Access 97 session,
where you learn how
to open a database
and a table, display
a form, create a
query, and display a
report

◆ ◆ ◆ ◆

A Tour of the Screen

In this book, you see many Access windows and shortcut dialog boxes, and you learn many specific terms. It's a good idea
to become familiar with these terms. If you've used another
database software package before learning Access, you'll
need to translate the terms you already know into the words
Microsoft Access uses to refer to the same task or action.

Using the mouse and the keyboard

You can navigate the Access screen by using the mouse, the
keyboard, or a combination of both. The best way to get
around in Access is by using a mouse or some other pointing
device. You'll find the keyboard useful for entering data and
for moving around the various data-entry areas. You'll find it
unproductive, however, to try using only the keyboard when
designing new forms, queries, or reports. In this book, you
learn how to complete tasks by using both the keyboard and
the mouse. In most cases, using the mouse is preferable.

The Access window

The Access window is the center of activity for everything
you do in Access. From here, you can have many windows
open, each of which displays a different view of your data.
Figure 5-1 shows the Access window with a Database window
open inside it.

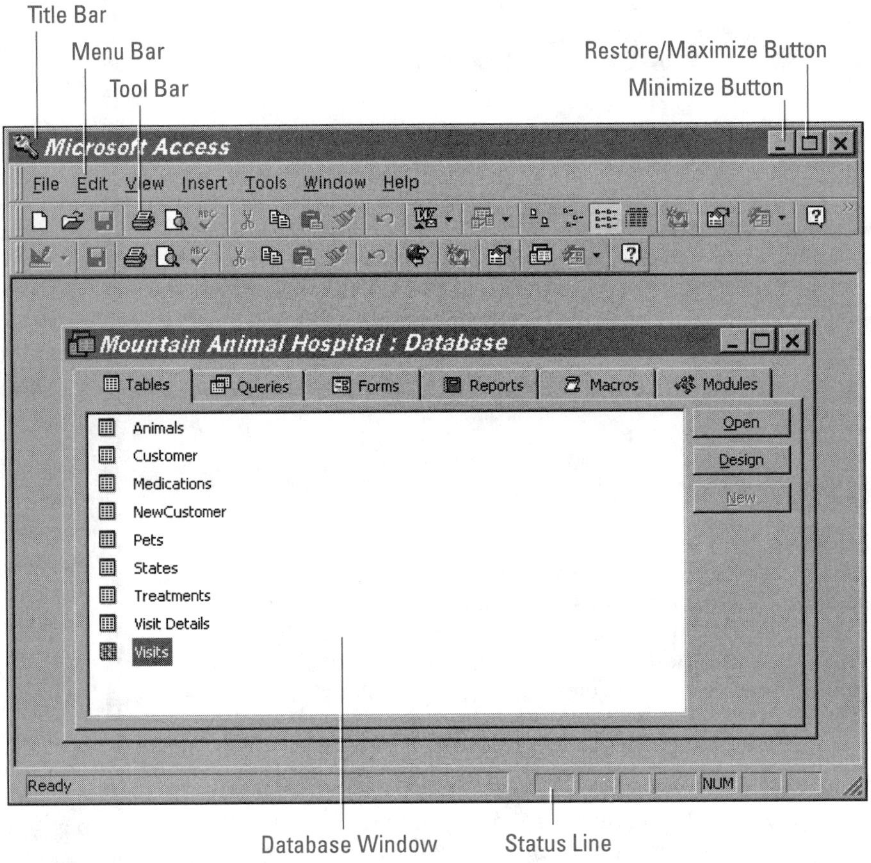

Title Bar

Menu Bar

Tool Bar

Restore/Maximize Button

Minimize Button

Figure 5-1: The Microsoft Access window.

Database Window

Status Line

Following are a number of Access window features you should be familiar with:

Title bar

You know what program is currently active by the name of the program you see displayed on the title bar. The title bar always displays the program name Microsoft Access.

Tip You can change the title bar display by entering a different application title in the Startup dialog box, which you can display by right-clicking in the gray area of the database container and selecting Startup.

Control-menu button

You'll find this button in the upper left corner of nearly every application window. When you click on this button once, a menu appears that lets you do certain tasks, such as move, size, minimize, or close the current application window.

	When you double-click on the Control button, you exit the application automatically.
Minimize button	Clicking on this button reduces Access to an icon on the Windows 95 taskbar. Access will still be running, and you can reactivate it by clicking on the taskbar.
Restore/Maximize button	You can use this middle button (displayed only when the Access window is maximized) to restore the window to its previous size. The Maximize button (a square with a dark top border) resizes the Access window to a full-screen view. The Maximize button does not appear in Figure 5-1 because Access is already maximized.
Close button	This button with an X on it closes Access when pressed.
Command bar	The command bar (previously called the menu bar) contains several menu choices. When you click on one, a menu drops down, offering further choices. The items on the menu bar and the choices you find on each menu will vary in Access, depending on what you are working on. The pictures on the command bars correspond to pictures on the toolbar. In Access 97, you can completely program the command bars and toolbars.
Toolbar	The toolbar is a group of picture buttons just below the command bar; it provides shortcuts for running commands. The buttons on the toolbar vary, depending on what you are working on at the time. The toolbar can be resized and moved by clicking between buttons and moving it around the screen. You can also select View⇨ Toolbars to show, hide, define new, or customize different toolbars; you can use the same command to select large or small buttons, turn off tooltips, and even display monochrome buttons.
Status line	The left side of the status line displays helpful information about what you are doing at the time. In Figure 5-1, the status line simply says Ready. The right side of the status line tells you whether certain keyboard settings are active. For example, if you have the Caps Lock feature turned on, the word CAPS appears on the status line. In Figure 5-1, you can see NUM, indicating that the Num Lock key is down.

Database window   This window appears whenever a database is open; it is the control center of your database. You use the Database window to open the objects contained within a database, including tables, queries, forms, reports, macros, and modules.

Tip   You can change the display on the title bar by changing the Database Startup form. You can display this by selecting Tools⇨Startup⇨Application Title from the Database window.

The Database window

The Database window always displays on the title bar the name of the open database. In Figure 5-1, for example, you see the Mountain Animal Hospital database name on the title bar. The Mountain Animal Hospital database is on the CD-ROM that comes with this book; it contains all the tables, forms, and other objects demonstrated in this book.

The Database window has three basic parts to it. You see a set of six object buttons in a horizontal row on top, a set of three command buttons along the right side of the window, and a list of files.

Object buttons   These buttons are located in a horizontal row along the top of the Database window. With these buttons, you can select the type of object you want to work with. For example, selecting the Form button displays a list of forms created for that database. Selecting this button also lets you create a new form or redesign an existing one.

Command buttons   You can use the command buttons, located along the right side of the Database window, to place a database object in a different window or view. These buttons let you create, open, or design a database object.

Object list   This list displays existing files for the database object you select. You can choose a name from the list to display or redesign the object.

NEW FEATURE   You can change the view of the objects in the object list by selecting View from the Database window menu bar. There are four choices:

Large Icons   Displays a large icon with the type of object and the object name

Small Icons   Displays a small icon with the type of object and the object name

List   The default view, as shown in Figure 5-1

Details   Lists the object name, date created, and date last modified (see Figure 5-2)

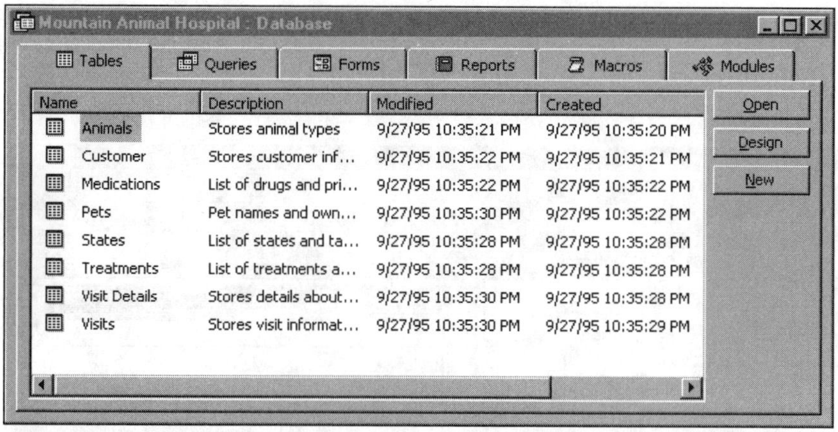

Figure 5-2: The Microsoft Access Database window in Details view.

As you can see in Figure 5-2, Details view shows you more information about each object. Most important is the date last modified. If you are trying to maintain different versions of a database, this gives you a great way to see which database contains your latest version. Of course, you can also use the new Briefcase replication features in Access 97 to keep multiple databases synchronized.

You can click on the column headers in the Database window and re-sort the data by the value in the column. Each time you click on a column, you change the order of the sort. For example, clicking on the Name column sorts the data by Name in ascending order. Click on the Name column again, and you re-sort the window by descending name. You can sort the details of the Database window objects by any of the columns. You can also change a column's width by placing your cursor on the divider between column names and then dragging the column cursor that appears to the right to make a column wider or to the left to make it narrower.

Tip You can enter a description for an object by right-clicking on the object name and then selecting Properties. You can enter a long description for the object and even hide the object if you want.

Design windows

The Database window is just one of several windows you use for your many tasks in Access. Several other windows you commonly see are the *object design windows,* which let you design such objects as tables, queries, forms, reports, macros, and modules. There are also windows that let you view or edit your data in datasheets, forms, and report previews.

Figure 5-3 shows the Database window, along with the Form Design window and several other windows that assist you in designing forms and reports. These are generally known as *design windows*. The Form window is shown with several fields displayed. The form you see in the figure, named Animals, can be used for displaying information about each pet in the Pets table.

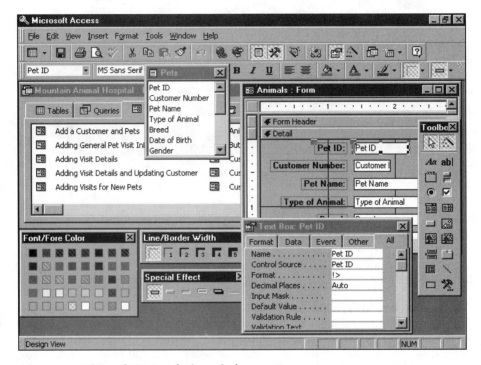

Figure 5-3: Microsoft Access design windows.

In Figure 5-3, you see the most common design windows: the toolbox, foreground color window, field list, special effect window, borders window, and property window. Because the Form window is active, you may also notice that the toolbar is different.

NEW FEATURE Access 97 features tear-off windows on the design toolbar. After a window is displayed from the toolbar, it can be dragged anywhere on the desktop and resized.

The Toolbox

Figure 5-3 displays the Toolbox in the bottom right portion of the screen. You use the Toolbox when you design a form or report. The Toolbox is similar to a toolbar, but the Toolbox is initially arranged vertically and can be moved around. The Toolbox shown in the figure contains toggle buttons you can select to add objects to a form or report, such as labels, text boxes, option group boxes, and so on. You can move the Toolbox or close it when you don't need it. You can also resize it by clicking and dragging the Toolbox border. You can also anchor it as another tool-bar by dragging it to an edge of the screen.

Color, special effect, and border windows

The Font/Fore Color window is shown in the bottom left corner of the screen in Figure 5-3. There is also a background color window and a border color window. In the figure, you can also see the Special Effect and Line/Border Width windows. You can use these windows to change the colors of objects, such as text (foreground), lines, rectangles, and background and borders of a control. You can use the Special Effect window to give their appearance a three-dimensional look (sunken or raised, for example), add a shadow, or add the Windows 95 chiseled look. As with the Toolbox, the size of the palette is resizable. The border width window lets you change the thickness of lines, rectangles, and control borders.

The Field List window

The Field List window displays a list of fields from the currently open table or query dynaset. Field List windows are used in Query Design, Form Design, and Report Design windows. You can select fields from this window by double-clicking on them, and you can drag the fields onto a query, form, or report. If you first select a control type in the Toolbox and then drag a field from the Field List, a control is created (using the selected control type) that is automatically bound to the data field in the Field List.

The Property window

In a form or report, each field (called a *control* in Access) has properties that further define the characteristics of the control. The form or report itself and sections of the form or report also have properties. In Figure 5-3, in the lower right-hand area, you see a Property window displaying the section properties for a form. Usually, a Property window displays only a portion of the properties available for a specific control, so a tabbed dialog box and a vertical scrollbar in the window let you scroll through the complete list. You can also resize a Property window and even move it around the screen.

You'll soon see that having many windows open at once and resizing and rearranging them on-screen helps you use information productively as you create such objects as forms and reports and use the features in Access. Each of the windows is described in detail in the appropriate chapters in this book.

A Simple Access Session

Cross-Reference Now that you are familiar with the Access screen, you can go through a simple Access session even before you know much about Access. Before proceeding, make sure that you are ready to follow along on your own computer. Your computer should be on, and Access should be installed. Chapters 2 and 3 showed you how to install and start Access. You can refer to those chapters for details. If you have not done so already, perform the following steps to get ready for this session:

1. Start your computer. Turn on your computer and start Windows 95 or Windows NT.

2. Start Access 97. Start Access from the Programs menu or find the Access 97 icon or shortcut and double-click on the icon with the left mouse button to start Access. See Chapter 3 if you need more help starting Access.

3. Remove the Microsoft Access dialog box that asks you to Create a New Database or Open an Existing Database by pressing the Cancel button (for now) to display the Access window without opening or creating a database.

4. Maximize the Access window. In the upper right corner of the Access window, you might see a gray box containing a square. If the box shows two rectangles, Access is already maximized; you can go on to the next section. If there is only one square, click on the box to maximize the Access screen. Your screen should now look like the one in Figure 5-4.

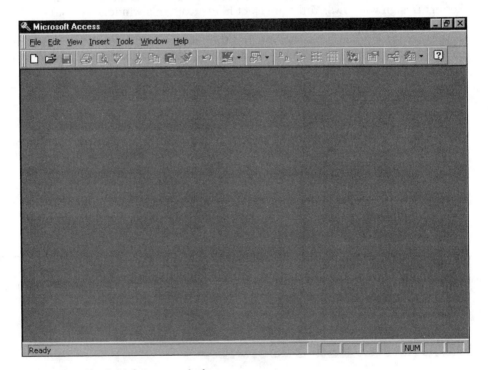

Figure 5-4: The initial Access window.

The CD-ROM in the back of the book

In the back of your book is a CD-ROM that contains several files. It contains several database files that you'll use throughout this book as well as some dBASE and Paradox files used in Chapter 24 and a variety of other goodies. To use this CD-ROM, follow the directions in the back of the book on the pages opposite the CD-ROM envelope. Following is a description of the two main database files used in this book:

Mountain Animal Hospital.MDB: A database containing all the tables, queries, forms, reports, and macros used in this book

Mountain Start.MDB: A file containing only tables

You can use the Mountain Start database file, beginning with Chapter 8, to create your own queries, forms, and reports. You can use the Mountain Animal Hospital database file to see how the final application is created and used.

If you haven't used the CD-ROM in your book yet, now is a good time to take it out and run the Setup routine to copy the files to the Access folder or another folder (perhaps named Bible) on your hard disk.

You are now ready to move on. Your goal for this session is to open a database and then perform such simple steps as opening a table, displaying a form, and creating a query. You'll be using the Mountain Animal Hospital database that came with this book (Mountain Animal Hospital.MDB).

Opening a database

The first thing you'll want to do is open the Mountain Animal Hospital database. When you first start Access, you can open an existing database or create a new database. When you press the Cancel button, you see a blank screen, as shown in Figure 5-4. To open the database, follow these steps:

1. Select File⇨Open Database.

2. Select the folder where you placed the files for the book.

3. Click on the name MOUNTAIN ANIMAL HOSPITAL and click on OK.

A dialog box similar to the one in Figure 5-5 appears, listing all the databases available in the current folder. If you don't see the MOUNTAIN ANIMAL HOSPITAL database listed, you may have to change the folder Access is looking in. To do so, select the drive and folder in which you stored this database. After you tell Access where to find the database, the name should appear in the File List window of the dialog box.

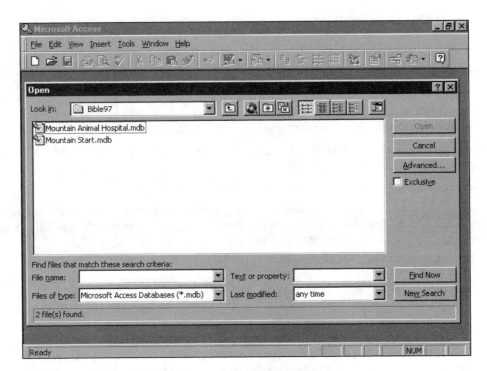

Figure 5-5: The standard Windows 95 Open dialog box.

Access opens the database. You should find the name MOUNTAIN ANIMAL HOSPI-TAL at the top of the Database window.

Opening a table

Now that you've opened the database, you'll open a table so that you can view some of the data stored in the Mountain Animal Hospital database. You should open the table named Pets. This table contains information about the various pets that are treated at the hospital, including the pet and customer identifications, type of animal, pet name, breed, gender, height, weight, and so on. Follow these steps to open the Pets table:

1. Click on the Tables tab in the Database window if it is not already selected.

2. Select the table called Pets.

3. Select the Open command button in the right part of the Database window.

4. Maximize the window by selecting the Maximize button in the top right part of the window.

Access now opens the Pets table, and your screen should look like Figure 5-6.

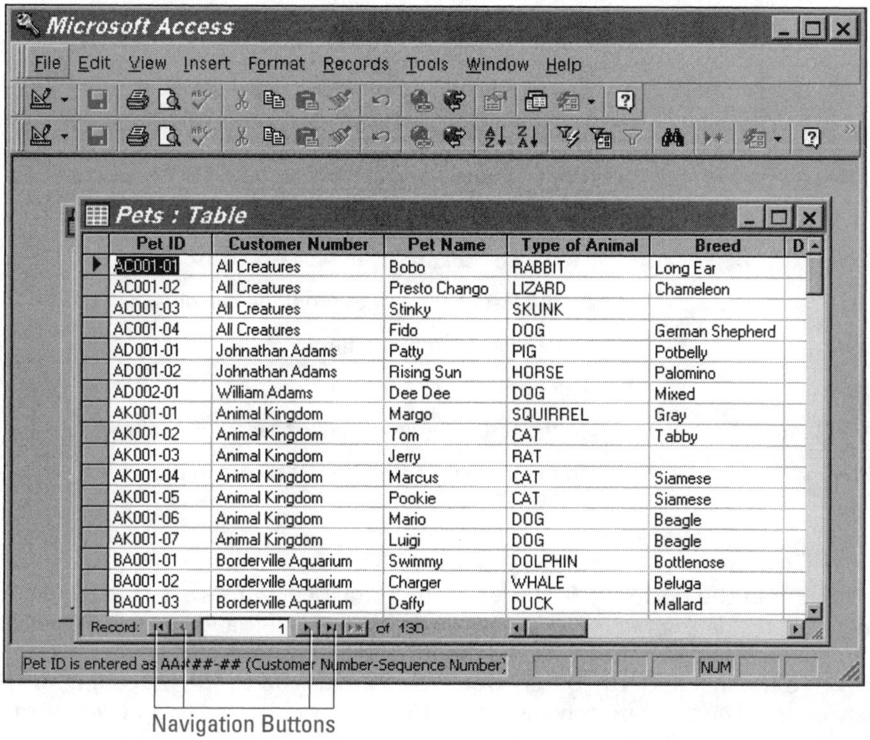

Navigation Buttons

Figure 5-6: The Pets table opened.

Tip   You can also open a table by double-clicking on the table name in the Database window or by clicking the right mouse button while the table name is highlighted. The latter choice displays a shortcut menu, and selecting Open from the shortcut menu opens a table.

Displaying a datasheet

When you open the Pets table, you see a datasheet that contains all the data stored in the Pets table. The data is displayed in a column-and-row format. You can move around the datasheet to view the different types of data stored here. Table 5-1 shows how to move around the Table window using the keyboard. You can also use the mouse to navigate throughout the table. Simply click on any cell with the left mouse button to move the cursor to that cell. You can also use the mouse to move the elevators to navigate around the table.

Table 5-1
Keyboard Techniques for Moving around the Window

Keyboard Keys	Where It Moves
Left- and right-arrow	Left or right one column at a time
Up- and down-arrow	Up or down one row at a time
PgUp and PgDn	Up or down one screen at a time
Ctrl+PgUp and Ctrl+PgDn	Left or right one screen at a time
Home	To the first column of the row the cursor is in
End	To the last column of the row the cursor is in
Tab	Right one column at a time
Shift+Tab	Left one column at a time
Ctrl+Home	To the first column of the first record in the table
Ctrl+End	To the last column of the last record in the table

You can also move through the table with the mouse by using the navigation buttons found in the bottom left corner of the Datasheet window. (These are sometimes called *VCR buttons*.) The arrows located at the left and right ends with a vertical line next to them move you to the first or last record of the table. The two arrows to the inside of the outer two arrows move you to the preceding or the next record. The right-pointing arrow with the asterisk goes to a new record.

Between these arrows is a rectangle that displays the current record number. To the right of the arrows is the number of records. If you know which record you want to move to, you can get there quickly by clicking the mouse on the record number (or by pressing F5), typing the number of the record you want to move to, and pressing Enter.

Tip   You can also use the GoTo command (found on the Edit menu) to go to the First, Last, Next, Previous, or New record.

Viewing a table design

Now that you've seen what kind of information is contained in the Pets table and how to navigate around the datasheet, you can look at the design of the table. You first need to be in Design view to see the design of the Pets table.

To get to Design view, click on the Design button on the toolbar; it is the first button on the Access toolbar and shows a triangle, ruler, and pencil and has an arrow next to it. When you press the arrow, the icon reveals three icons that represent a set of choices (which include the possible views of the data, such as Design and Datasheet). When you click on the Design icon, the Pets datasheet will disappear and be replaced by the Design window for the Pets table. Figure 5-7 displays the Pets Design window.

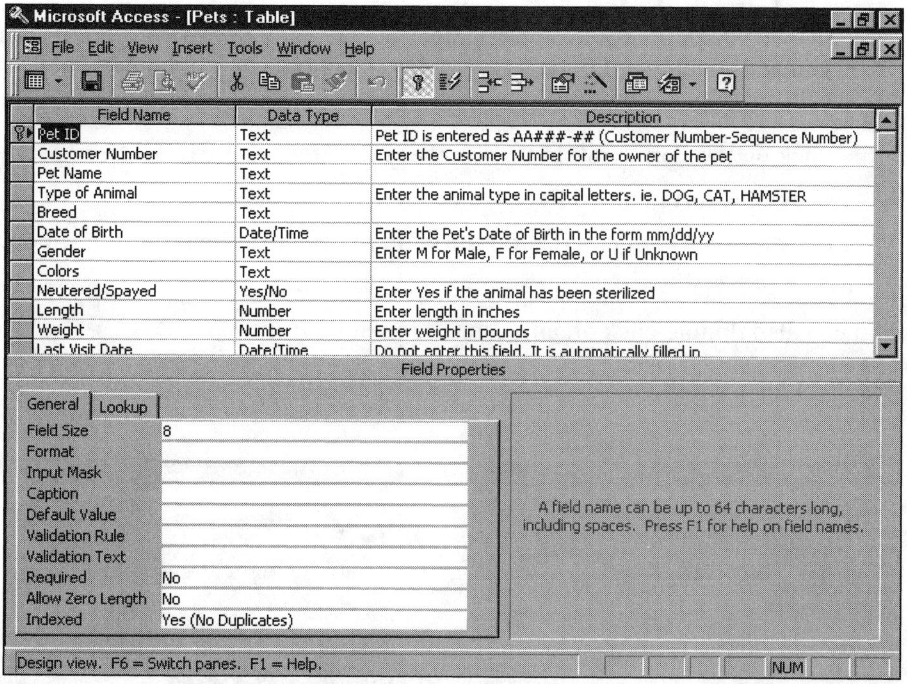

Figure 5-7: The Pets Design window.

Here in Design view is where the fields for the Pets table were set up. When the Pets table was created, fields that were to be included in the table were added here. Depending on the type of information to be entered in each field, a specific data type is given to each field. Some data types you can choose are Text, Currency, Date/Time, and Memo. A field is also provided for a description of the type of data the field will contain.

The Design window has two parts. In Figure 5-7, you see that the top half of the window lists the field names and field types and a description for each field of the Pets table. Moving around this window is similar to moving around the Pets datasheet.

The bottom half of the Pets Design window displays the field properties. Different properties can be set up for each field in the table. You can use the mouse or the F6 key to move between the top and bottom panes of the Design window.

The next object you'll display is a form. At this time, you should close the Design window by selecting File⇨Close. This selection closes the Table Design window and returns you to the Database window.

Displaying a form

The steps for displaying a form are similar to the steps for opening a table. In this case, you are opening a different type of database object. Follow these steps for opening the form called Pets:

1. Click on the Forms tab in the Database window.

2. Select the form named Pets.

3. Click on the Open command button on the right of the Database window to open the form.

Tip

You can also double-click on any name to open the form.

The Pets form should look like the one in Figure 5-8.

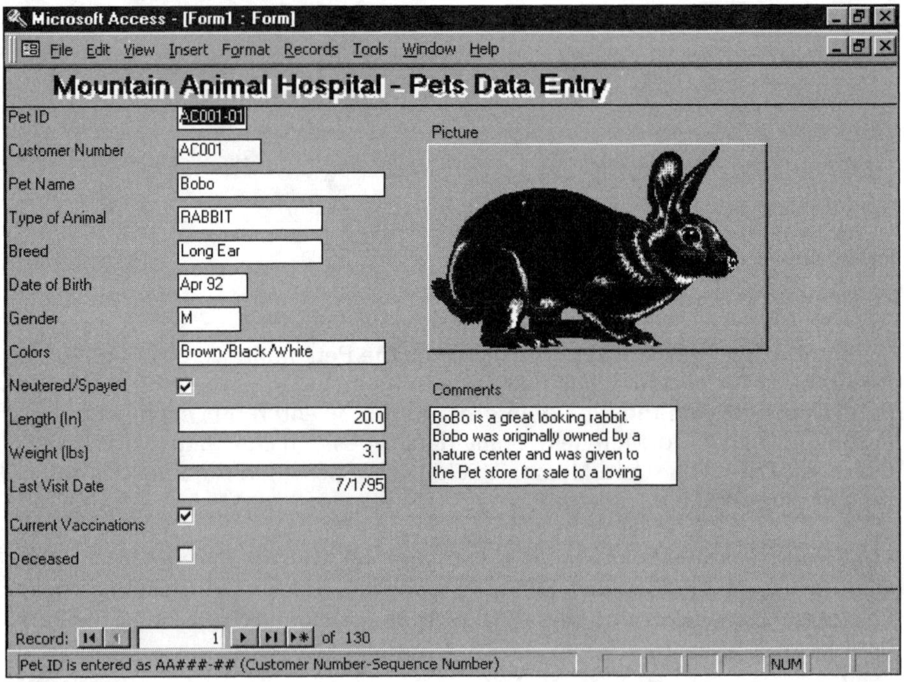

Figure 5-8: The Pets form.

A form provides another way of displaying or changing data. The Pets form is an example of a simple form. You enter information in each text box just as you would enter information in a table. There are some advantages when using a form instead of a datasheet; in a form, you can view more fields on-screen at once, and you can use many data-entry and validation shortcuts. Also note that you can view the picture of each animal on a form and the contents of the Comments Memo field. You cannot do this when you are using a datasheet.

To see how this form was created, click on the Design button located on the Access toolbar (the first button on the left with the triangle, ruler, and pencil). Your form should now look like Figure 5-9.

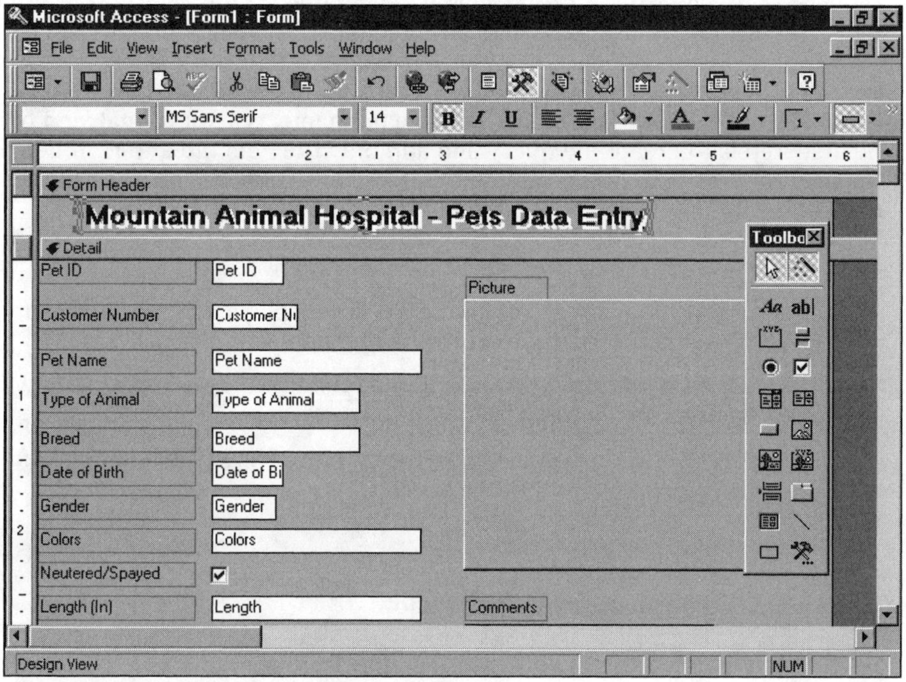

Figure 5-9: The Pets form in Design view.

In Figure 5-9, on the right side of the form, is a long, rectangular box containing several buttons. This is the Form Toolbox. You can move the Toolbox anywhere on-screen. The Toolbox lets you add controls to the form. A *control* is a graphical object, such as a label, text box, check box, or command button that you can place on a form to display data from a field or enhance the look of the form.

Now that you've seen two different methods of entering data — datasheets and forms — you may have some questions about the data stored in the Pets table. You can find the answers to your questions through queries. Before creating a query, you should close the form by selecting File⇨Close. This selection closes both the form and the Form Toolbox and returns you to the Database window. If you made any changes to the form, Access will prompt you to save your changes before closing the form.

Creating a query

A query lets you ask questions about the data stored in your database. The data produced by the query can be saved in its own table for future use or printed as a report. You next learn how to create a simple query by using the Pets table.

Suppose that you want to see only the records in the Pets table in which the type of animal is a dog. You want to see only the pet name, type of animal, and breed. The first step is to create the query and add only the Pets table to it. You can add as many tables as you want to a query, but for this example you add only the Pets table. To create the query and add the Pets table, follow these steps:

1. Select the Queries tab from the Database window.

2. Click on New to create a new query. Access displays a list of all available Query Wizards. Design view should be highlighted.

3. Click on the OK button. The Show Table tabbed window appears showing tables, queries, or both.

4. Select Pets by clicking on the table name in the Show Table dialog box.

5. Click on Add.

6. Click on Close.

You should now see an empty Query window.

The query form consists of two panes. The top pane contains a Field List window of the Pets table fields. You use the Field List window to choose which fields will appear in the query datasheet. The bottom part of the Query screen contains a series of rows and columns. In this pane, you'll ask questions about the fields in your tables. To view the fields Pet Name, Type of Animal, and Breed and to select only the records where the value of Type of Animal is DOG, follow these steps:

1. Double-click on the Pet Name field from the Field List window to add the field to the query.

2. Add the Type of Animal field to the query.

3. Use the scrollbar to display more fields and add the Breed field to the query.

4. Press F6 to move to the lower pane and place the cursor on the Criteria: row of the Type of Animal column of the query.

5. Type **DOG** in the cell.

Your query should now look like Figure 5-10. You added the three fields to the query you want to see in your results. In addition, you want to see only the dogs. Placing the word DOG in the criteria range tells Access to find only records where the value of Type of Animal is DOG.

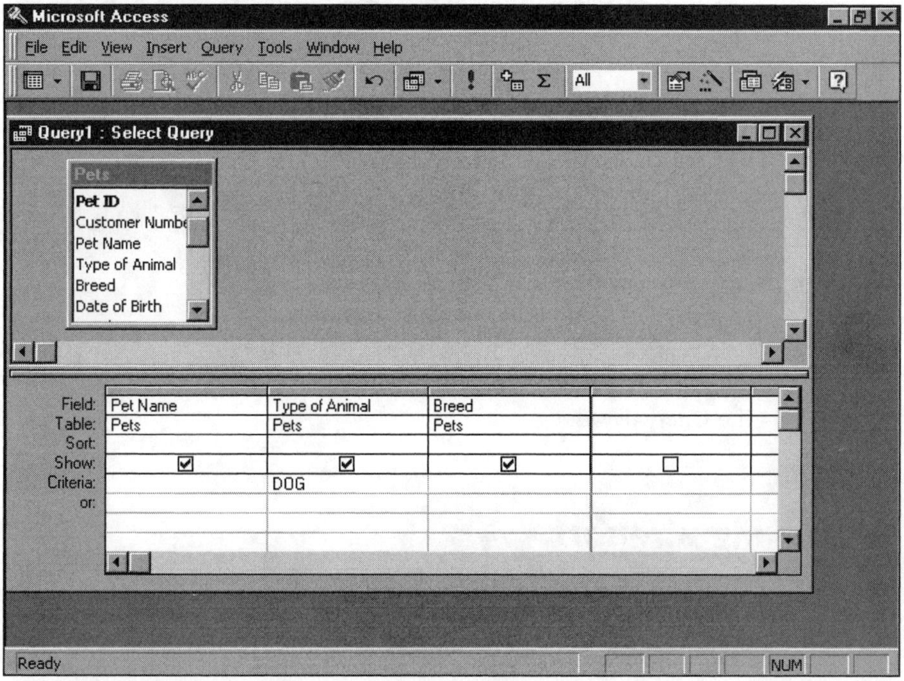

Figure 5-10: The completed Query Design window.

To run the query, you need to select the Run button. This button shows an exclamation point and is on the toolbar. After you select this button, Access goes to work to process your query and produce the results in what is called a dynaset. Your dynaset should look like the one in Figure 5-11. The dynaset displays the pet name, type of animal, and breed for each pet that is a dog.

The results from a query can be saved and used for creating a report you can view or print. The next section explains how to display a report. Select File⇨Close to close the query. Select No because you don't want to save the query.

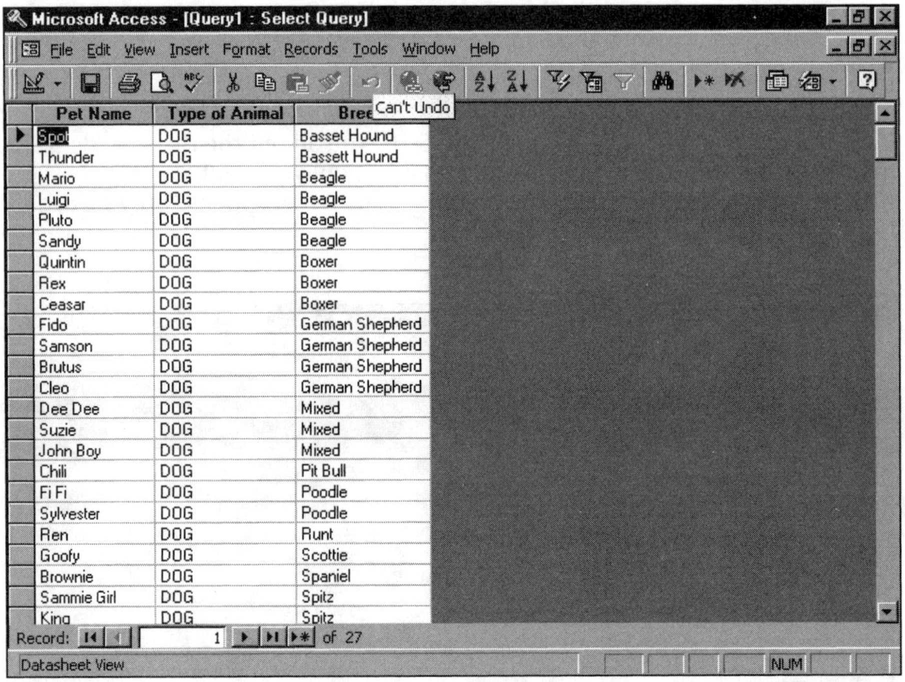

Figure 5-11: The Query dynaset.

Displaying a report

Queries or tables can be formatted and placed in a report for output to a printer. Next, you view and print a report that was already created. You'll be using a report of all the pets in the Pets table. Follow these steps for displaying and printing this report:

1. Click on the Reports tab in the Database window.
2. Select Pet Directory from the File List.
3. Select the Preview button (or double-click on the report name).

   The report is displayed in the zoomed preview mode. You can display the entire page by clicking the cursor anywhere on-screen (the cursor is currently shaped like a magnifying glass).

4. Click anywhere on the screen to display the entire page.
5. Click on the two-page icon on the toolbar to display two pages.

The report should look like Figure 5-12.

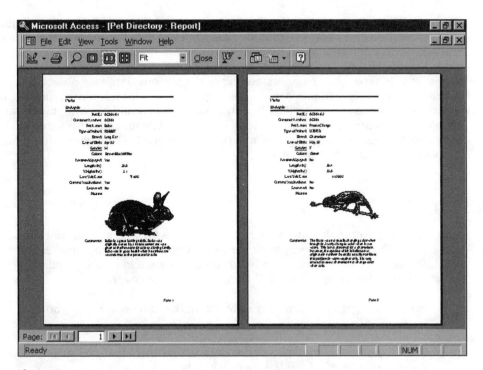

Figure 5-12: The Pets Report in print preview mode.

Tip You can see as many as six pages at a time by clicking on the four-page icon located to the right of the two-page icon. You can then select any combination up to 2 X
3 pages.

The Pets Report shows all the fields from the first two records of the Pets table.
You can use the PgDn key or the navigation buttons in the bottom left corner of
the window to see other pages of the report. The report can also be printed to the
Windows printer, or you can return to the Design window to enhance the report.

Select the Close button to return to the Database window.

Ready for More

You now have experienced many of the different capabilities of Access. If you had
problems with this chapter, you should start again from the beginning. Make sure
that you follow the directions exactly and don't move on to the next steps until
you understand what you were supposed to do. Hopefully, this quick view of

Access will make you eager to learn how to use Access in detail. Don't be afraid to experiment. You can always reload the files from the disk in the back of this book. You can't hurt Access or your computer.

Now that you have a basic understanding of the various database objects in Access, you are ready to move on to creating your own tables, forms, queries, and reports. Before moving on to Part II of this book, you should have an understanding of how to design a database system. In Chapter 6, you learn how some of the tables, forms, queries, reports, and macros are designed. Throughout the book, you will see this design implemented.

Summary

In this chapter, you took a quick tour through Access to learn about the windows you can use. You learned some basic terms that you need as you progress through this book, and you now have some hands-on experience in creating and using forms, reports, and queries. The following points were covered:

✦ You can navigate through Access by using the mouse or the keyboard.

✦ The Access Database window contains several menus and a toolbar.

✦ When you open a database, all the database objects that comprise the database are displayed in the Database window.

✦ When you open a database table, you see the information stored in the table as a datasheet.

✦ You can make your data entry easier by creating a form from an existing table.

✦ You can ask questions about data in a table by assembling a query and creating a view known as a dynaset.

✦ You can save a query to a report for output to a printer.

✦   ✦   ✦

A Case Study in Database Design

The most important lesson to learn as you create a database is good design. Without a good design, you'll be reworking your tables constantly, and you may not be able to extract the information you want from your database. Throughout this book, you learn not only how to use queries, forms, and reports but also how to design each of these objects before you attempt to create one. A case study of the Mountain Animal Hospital provides examples throughout this book and specifically in this chapter; although the examples are fictitious, the concepts are not.

This chapter is not simple to understand; some of its concepts and ideas are fairly complex. If your goal is to get right into Access, you may want to read this chapter later. If you are fairly familiar with Access but new to designing and creating tables, you may want to read it before you begin the actual process of creating your tables.

Throughout this book, specifically, you learn to design forms and reports that range from simple to complex. You begin by learning to create simple forms and reports with just a few fields from a single table. Then you learn how to create multiple-page forms and reports that use multiple tables. Eventually the forms and reports you create use advanced controls (option buttons, list boxes, combo boxes, and check boxes) and use one-to-many relationships displayed as subforms and subreports. Finally, you learn how to design customer mailing labels and mail-merge reports. Most importantly, you use the tables in the Mountain Animal Hospital application to learn how to do data design.

The Seven-Step Method for Design

To create database objects such as tables, forms, and reports, you must first complete a series of tasks known as *design.* The better your design, the better your application. The more you think through your design, the faster you can complete any system. Design is not some necessary evil, nor is its intent to produce voluminous amounts of documentation. The sole intent of design is to produce a clearcut path to follow as you implement it.

Figure 6-1 shows a modified version of this method, designed especially for Access.

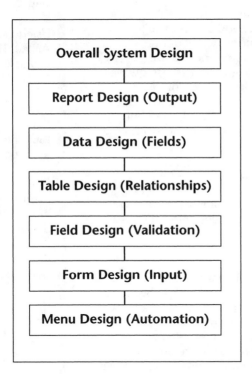

Figure 6-1: The seven-step design flowchart.

These seven design steps, along with the database system illustrated by the examples, will teach you almost all there is to know about Access. You will be able to create and use databases, tables, queries, forms, reports, and macros.

As you read through each step, you'll look at the design in terms of outputs and inputs. Although you see actual components of the system (customers, pets, visits, and visit details), remember that the focus of this chapter is how to design each step. As you watch the Mountain Animal Hospital system being designed, pay attention to the design process, not the actual system.

Step 1: The overall design—from concept to reality

All software developers and end users face similar problems. The first set of problems you encounter is in gathering requirements that will meet the needs of the end user (typically your client, your coworker, or yourself). It is important to understand the overall needs the system must meet before you begin to zero in on the details.

The seven-step design method shown in Figure 6-1 can help you create the system you need, at a price (measured in time or dollars) you can afford. The Mountain Animal Hospital, for example, is a medium-size animal hospital that services individuals, pet stores, and zoos across three states. Basically, Mountain Animal Hospital needs to automate several tasks:

✦ Entering customer information — name, address, and financial history

✦ Entering pet information — pet name, type, breed, length, weight, picture, and comments

✦ Entering visit information — details of treatments performed and medications dispensed

✦ Asking all types of questions about the information in the database

✦ Producing a current Pets and Owners directory

✦ Producing a monthly invoice report

✦ Producing mailing labels and mail-merge reports

The design process is an *iterative* procedure; as you finish each new step, you'll need to look at all the previous steps again to make sure that nothing in the basic design has changed. If (for example) you are creating a data-entry rule and decide that you need another field (not already in the table) to validate a field you've already defined, you have to go back and follow each previous step needed to add the field. You have to be sure to add the new field to each report in which you want to see it. You also have to make sure that the new field is on an input form that uses the table the field is in. Only then can you use this new field in your system.

Now that you've defined Mountain Animal Hospital's overall systems in terms of what must be accomplished, you can begin the next step of report design.

Step 2: Report design — placing your fields

Design work should be broken up to the smallest level of detail you know at the time. You should start each new step by reviewing the overall design objectives. In the case of Mountain Animal Hospital, your objectives are to track customers, track pets, keep a record of visits and treatments, produce invoices, create a directory of pets and owners, and produce mailing labels.

Laying out fields in the report

When you look at the reports you create in this section, you may wonder, "What comes first — the duck or the egg?" Does the report layout come first, or do you first determine the data items and text that make up the report? Actually, these items are conceived together.

It is not important how you lay out the fields in this conception of a report. The more time you take now, however, the easier it will be when you actually create the report. Some people go so far as to place gridlines on the report so that they will know the exact location they want each field to occupy. In this example, you can just do it visually.

The Pets and Owners Directory

Mountain Animal Hospital will begin with the tasks of tracking customers and pets. The first report that must be developed will show important information about pets and their owners and will be sorted by customer number. Each customer's name and address will appear with a listing of the pets the customer has brought into the Mountain Animal Hospital.

The hospital staff has already decided on some of the fields for the customer file. First, of course, is the customer's name (individual or company), followed by address (the customer's street, city, state, and ZIP code) and phone number.

The last visit date is another field the hospital will maintain on file and use on the report. This field will be used to let Mountain Animal Hospital know when it's time to remove a pet from the Pets table; a pet will be removed if it hasn't been in for a visit in the last three years. The plan is to purge the Pets table each year; recording the last visit is the way to find this information. This field will also alert Mountain Animal Hospital when an animal is due for its yearly checkup so that the staff can send out reminder notices.

With that information in mind, the Mountain Animal Hospital people create the report form design shown in Figure 6-2.

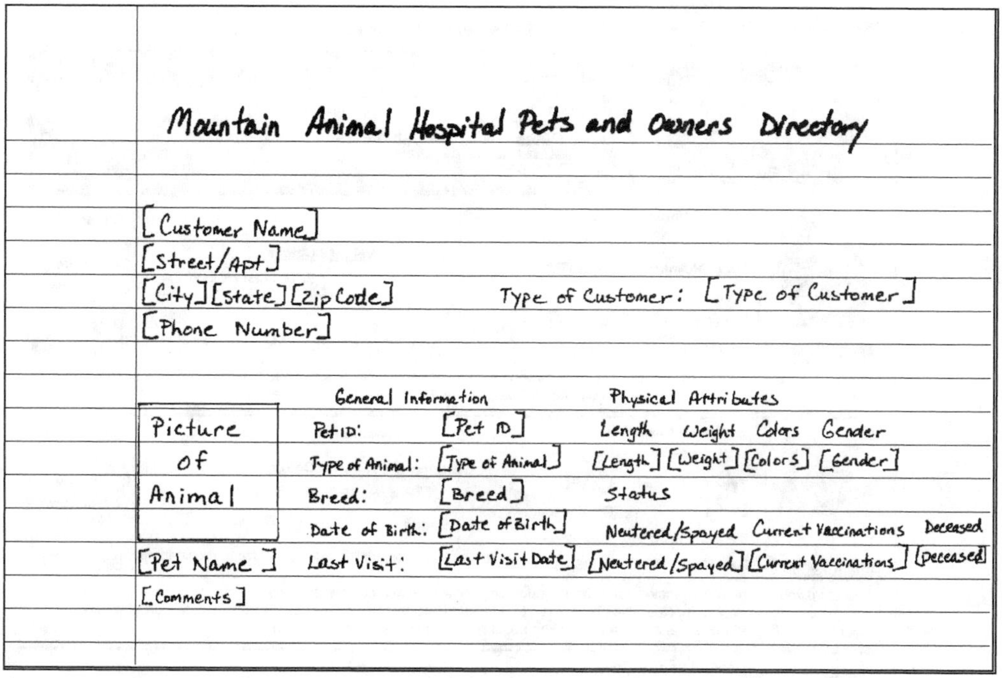

Mountain Animal Hospital Pets and Owners Directory

[Customer Name]
[Street/Apt]
[City] [State] [Zip Code]   Type of Customer: [Type of Customer]
[Phone Number]

	General Information		Physical Attributes			
Picture	Pet ID:	[Pet ID]	Length	Weight	Colors	Gender
of	Type of Animal:	[Type of Animal]	[Length]	[Weight]	[Colors]	[Gender]
Animal	Breed:	[Breed]	Status			
	Date of Birth:	[Date of Birth]	Neutered/Spayed	Current Vaccinations		Deceased
[Pet Name]	Last Visit:	[Last Visit Date]	[Neutered/Spayed]	[Current Vaccinations]		[Deceased]
[Comments]						

Figure 6-2: The Pets and Owners report design.

Cross-Reference   If you want to see how to implement this report, Chapter 21 teaches you how to create it. If you want to see how to complete this report with advanced database-publishing enhancements, see Chapter 22.

Figure 6-3 shows the final hard-copy printout of this report; it shows you the capabilities of Access.

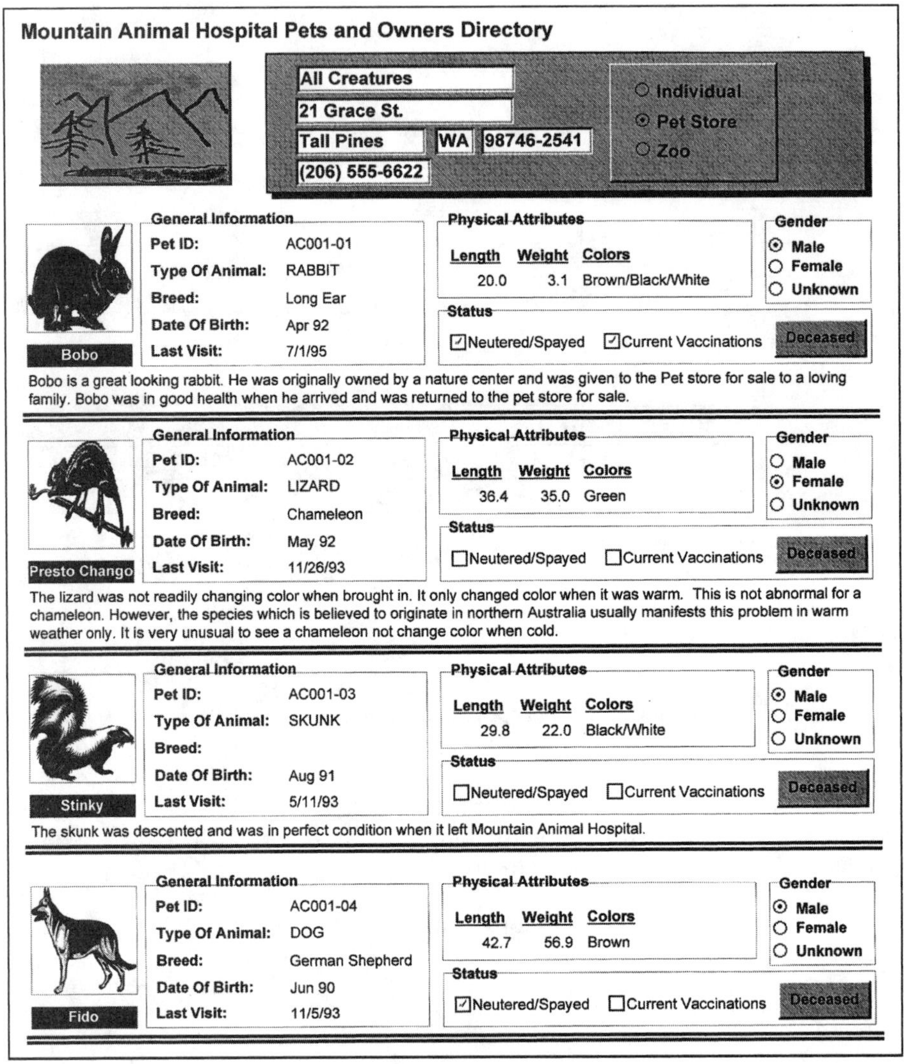

Mountain Animal Hospital Pets and Owners Directory

All Creatures
21 Grace St.
Tall Pines WA 98746-2541
(206) 555-6622

○ Individual
⊙ Pet Store
○ Zoo

Bobo

General Information
Pet ID: AC001-01
Type Of Animal: RABBIT
Breed: Long Ear
Date Of Birth: Apr 92
Last Visit: 7/1/95

Physical Attributes

Length	Weight	Colors
20.0	3.1	Brown/Black/White

Gender: ⊙ Male ○ Female ○ Unknown

Status: ☑ Neutered/Spayed ☑ Current Vaccinations Deceased

Bobo is a great looking rabbit. He was originally owned by a nature center and was given to the Pet store for sale to a loving family. Bobo was in good health when he arrived and was returned to the pet store for sale.

Presto Chango

General Information
Pet ID: AC001-02
Type Of Animal: LIZARD
Breed: Chameleon
Date Of Birth: May 92
Last Visit: 11/26/93

Physical Attributes

Length	Weight	Colors
36.4	35.0	Green

Gender: ○ Male ⊙ Female ○ Unknown

Status: ☐ Neutered/Spayed ☐ Current Vaccinations Deceased

The lizard was not readily changing color when brought in. It only changed color when it was warm. This is not abnormal for a chameleon. However, the species which is believed to originate in northern Australia usually manifests this problem in warm weather only. It is very unusual to see a chameleon not change color when cold.

Stinky

General Information
Pet ID: AC001-03
Type Of Animal: SKUNK
Breed:
Date Of Birth: Aug 91
Last Visit: 5/11/93

Physical Attributes

Length	Weight	Colors
29.8	22.0	Black/White

Gender: ⊙ Male ○ Female ○ Unknown

Status: ☐ Neutered/Spayed ☐ Current Vaccinations Deceased

The skunk was descented and was in perfect condition when it left Mountain Animal Hospital.

Fido

General Information
Pet ID: AC001-04
Type Of Animal: DOG
Breed: German Shepherd
Date Of Birth: Jun 90
Last Visit: 11/5/93

Physical Attributes

Length	Weight	Colors
42.7	56.9	Brown

Gender: ⊙ Male ○ Female ○ Unknown

Status: ☑ Neutered/Spayed ☐ Current Vaccinations Deceased

Figure 6-3: The completed Pets and Owners Directory report.

The Monthly Invoice Report

Whereas the Pets and Owners Directory concentrates on information about customers and pets, the Monthly Invoice Report displays information about the individual visits of specific customers and pets. Mountain Animal Hospital needs to produce a monthly report that lists all the daily visits by each customer and the customer's pets. Figure 6-4 shows the design of this report.

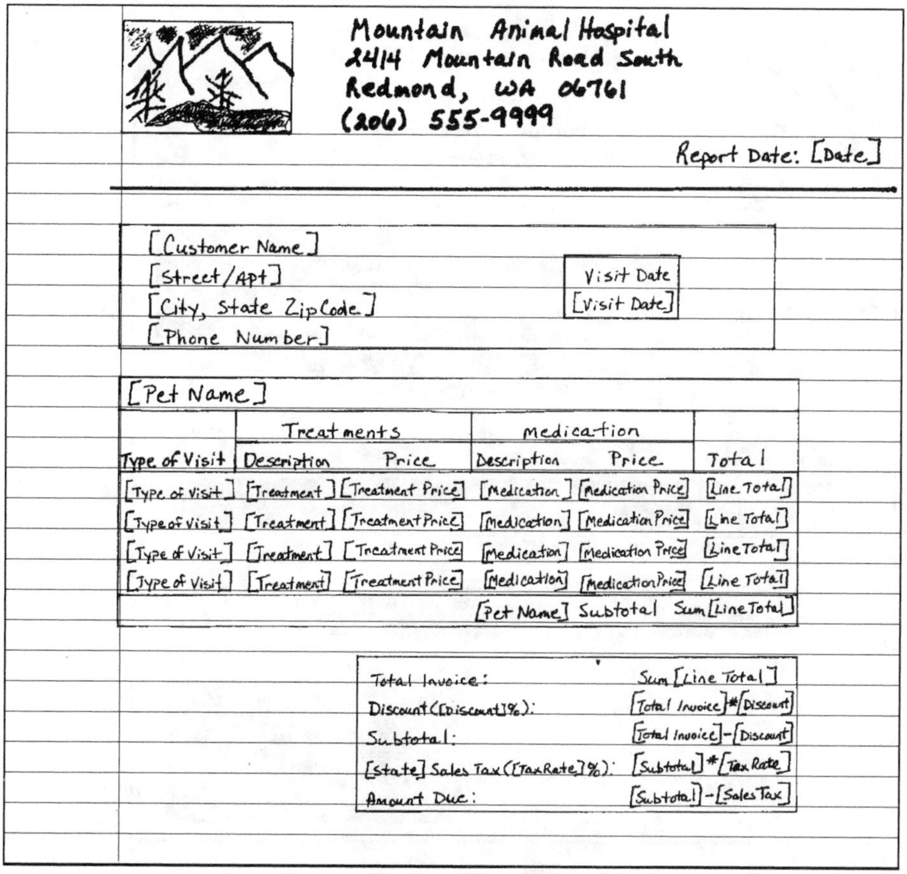

Figure 6-4: The design for the Monthly Invoice Report.

The design of this report shows customer information at the top and data about each visit in the middle. The middle block appears as many times as each customer had visits on the same date. If a customer brings three pets to the hospital on the same day, the report shows the middle block of data three times — once for each pet. The prices are totaled for each line; the sum of these line totals appears at the bottom of the block.

All the data items in the bottom block are summarized and calculated fields. (Because these fields can be calculated whenever necessary, they are not stored in a table.) After subtracting the discount from the subtotal, the report shows a taxable amount. If the customer's visit is subject to tax, the report calculates it at the current tax rate and shows it. Adding the tax to the taxable amount gives the total for the invoice; the customer pays this amount. Figure 6-5 shows the final report (created in Chapter 23).

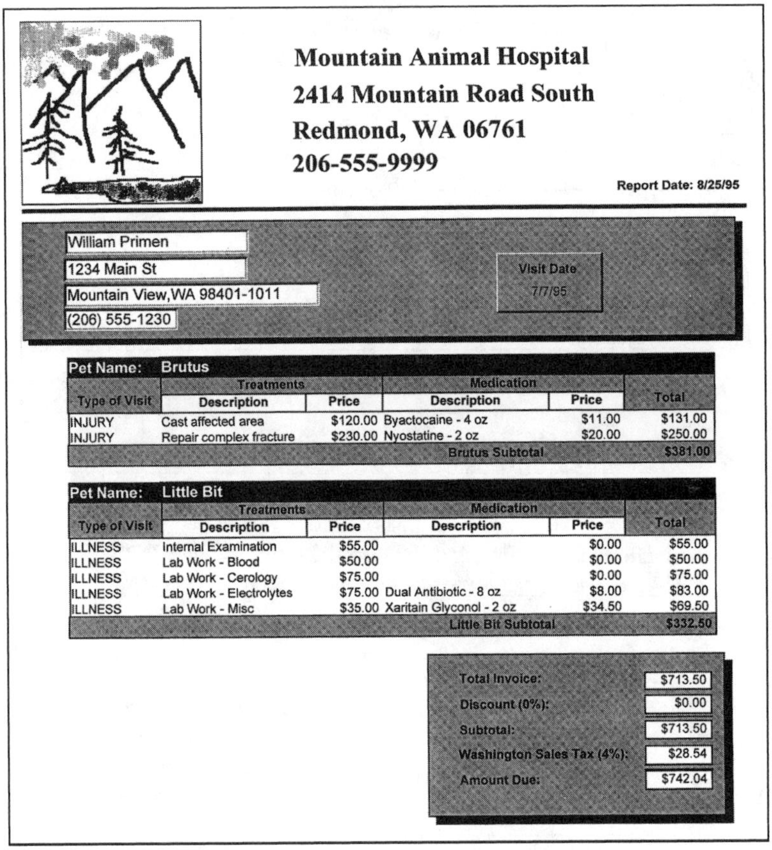

Mountain Animal Hospital
2414 Mountain Road South
Redmond, WA 06761
206-555-9999

Report Date: 8/25/95

William Primen
1234 Main St
Mountain View,WA 98401-1011
(206) 555-1230

Visit Date
7/7/95

Pet Name: Brutus

Type of Visit	Treatments: Description	Treatments: Price	Medication: Description	Medication: Price	Total
INJURY	Cast affected area	$120.00	Byactocaine - 4 oz	$11.00	$131.00
INJURY	Repair complex fracture	$230.00	Nyostatine - 2 oz	$20.00	$250.00
			Brutus Subtotal		$381.00

Pet Name: Little Bit

Type of Visit	Treatments: Description	Treatments: Price	Medication: Description	Medication: Price	Total
ILLNESS	Internal Examination	$55.00		$0.00	$55.00
ILLNESS	Lab Work - Blood	$50.00		$0.00	$50.00
ILLNESS	Lab Work - Cerology	$75.00		$0.00	$75.00
ILLNESS	Lab Work - Electrolytes	$75.00	Dual Antibiotic - 8 oz	$8.00	$83.00
ILLNESS	Lab Work - Misc	$35.00	Xaritain Glyconol - 2 oz	$34.50	$69.50
			Little Bit Subtotal		$332.50

Total Invoice:	$713.50
Discount (0%):	$0.00
Subtotal:	$713.50
Washington Sales Tax (4%):	$28.54
Amount Due:	$742.04

Figure 6-5: The final Mountain Animal Hospital Invoice Report.

In reality, you would design many more reports. In the interest of time and pages, however, the preceding two report designs will suffice.

Step 3: Data design — what fields do you have?

Now that you've decided what you want for output, it's time to think about how you'll organize your data into a system to make it available for the reports you've already defined (as well as for any ad hoc queries). The next step in the design phase is to take an inventory of all the data fields you will need to accomplish the output. One of the best methods is to list the data items in each report. As you do so, take careful note of items that are in more than one report. Make sure that the name for a data item in one report that is the same as a data item in another report is really the same item.

Another step is to see whether you can begin to separate the data items into some logical arrangement. Later, you'll have to group these data items into logical table structures and then map them on data-entry screens that make sense. You should enter customer data, for example, as part of a customer table process — not as part of a visit entry.

Determining customer information

First you must look at each report. For the Mountain Animal Hospital customer reports, you start with the customer data and list the data items, as shown in Table 6-1.

Table 6-1 Customer-Related Data Items Found in the Customer Reports	
Pets and Owners Directory	*Monthly Invoice Report*
Customer Name	Customer Name
Street	Street
City	City
State	State
ZIP Code	ZIP Code
Phone Number	Phone Number
Type of Customer	Discount
Last Visit Date	

As you can see, most of the data fields pertaining to the customer are found in both reports. The table shows only the fields that are used. Fields appearing on both reports appear on the same lines in the table, which allows you to see more easily which items are in which reports. You can look across a row instead of looking for the same names in both reports. Because the related row and the field names are the same, it's easy to make sure that you have all the data items. Although locating items easily is not critical for this small database, it becomes very important when you have to deal with large tables.

Determining pet information

After extracting the customer data, you can move on to the pet data. Again, you need to analyze the two reports for data items specific to the pets. Table 6-2 lists the fields in the two reports that contain information about the animals. Notice that only one field in the Monthly Invoice Report contains pet information.

Table 6-2
Pet Data Items Found in the Reports

Pets and Owners Directory	Monthly Invoice Report
Pet ID	
Pet Name	Pet Name
Type of Animal	
Breed	
Date of Birth	
Last Visit Date	
Length	
Weight	
Colors	
Gender	
Neutered/Spayed	
Current Vaccinations	
Deceased	
Picture	
Comments	

Determining visit information

Finally, you'll need to extract information about the visits from the Monthly Invoice Report, as shown in Table 6-3. You would use only this report because the Pets and Owners Directory report does not deal with visit information.

Table 6-3
Extracting Visit Information

Monthly Invoice Report	
Visit Date	Discount
Type of Visit	Tax Rate
Treatment	Total Amount
Treatment Price	Medication Price
Medication	Line Total

The table does not list some of the calculated fields, but you can re-create them easily in the report. Unless a field needs to be specifically stored in a table, you simply recalculate it when you run the report.

Combining the data

Now for the difficult part. You must determine the fields that are needed to create the tables that make up the reports. When you examine the multitude of fields and calculations that make up the many documents you have, you begin to see which fields actually belong to the different tables. (You already did some preliminary work by arranging the fields into logical groups.) For now, include every field you extracted. You will need to add others later (for various reasons), though certain fields will not appear in any table.

After you have used each report to display all the data, it is time to consolidate the data by function — and then compare the data across functions. To do this step, first you look at the customer information and combine all its different fields to create one set of data items. Then you do the same thing for the pet information and the visit information. Table 6-4 shows the comparison of data items from these three groups of information.

Table 6-4
Comparing the Data Items from the Three Groups

Customer Data Items	Pet Data Items	Visit Data Items
Customer Name	Pet ID	Visit Date
Street	Pet Name	Type of Visit
City	Type of Animal	Treatment
State	Breed	Treatment Price
ZIP Code	Date of Birth	Medication
Phone Number	Last Visit Date	Medication Price
Type of Customer	Length	Discount
Last Visit Date	Weight	Tax Rate
Discount	Colors	Total Amount
	Gender	
	Neutered/Spayed	
	Current Vaccinations	
	Deceased	
	Picture	
	Comments	

This is a good way to start creating the table definitions for Mountain Animal Hospital, but there is much more still to do. First, as you learn more about how to perform a data design, you also learn that the information in the Visits column must be split into two columns. Some of these items are used only once for the visit; other items are used for each detail line in the visit. This is the part of the design process called *normalization.* One customer (for example) has one pet, which has one visit with many visit details. The customer and pet data items each represent one customer or one pet, but a visit may require multiple detail lines.

Table 6-5 shows the Visits column broken into two columns. The visit date is no longer a unique field for the second table, which contains multiple items for each visit. You will have to add another field (which you will see in a minute in Table 6-6).

Table 6-5
Dividing the Visits Information

Visits	Visit Details
Visit Date	Visit Date
Discount	Type of Visit
Tax Rate	Treatment
Total Amount	Treatment Price
	Medication
	Medication Price

When you look at Table 6-5, you may wonder how to link these two files together so that Access knows which visit-detail information goes with which visit. A *unique field* (often an identification number or code) can do this job. By adding the same field to each group of information, you can keep like information together. You can create a field called **Visit Number**, for example, and use a consistent methodology to assign it. If you use a numeric sequence of year, the day number of the year, and a sequence number, then the third pet to visit on January 12, 1997, becomes **1997012-03.** The first four digits record the year, the next three digits tell you the number of days since January 1, and then a hyphen separates the date from a sequence number. After you have added this field to both columns for the Visits and Visit Details tables, you can tie the two files together.

There is one more identification number to assign. The Visit Details table does not have a unique identifier, though it does have a *partially* unique identifier. The Visit Number identifier is unique for an individual visit, but not for a visit that has multiple detail lines. A common practice is simply to assign a sequential number (for example, 001, 002, 003, and so on) for each visit detail.

Cross-Reference Commonly, in a one-to-many type of relationship, you need more than one field to make a record unique. See Chapter 12 for a complete discussion of keys and relationships.

Table 6-6 shows a list of the original data items and the reworked items for the Visits and Visit Details tables. The identification fields are shown in bold italics to set them apart.

Table 6-6
A Final Design of Data Items

Customer	*Pets*	*Visits*	*Visit Details*
Customer Number	*Pet ID*	*Visit Number*	*Visit Number*
Customer Name	Pet Name	Visit Date	*Line Number*
Street	Type of Animal	Discount	Type of Visit
City	Breed	Tax Rate	Treatment
State	Date of Birth	Total Amount	Treatment Price
ZIP Code	Last Visit Date		Medication
Phone Number	Length		Medication Price
Type of Customer	Weight		
Last Visit Date	Colors		
Discount	Gender		
	Neutered/Spayed		
	Current Vaccinations		
	Deceased		
	Picture		
	Comments		

These are not the final fields used in the Mountain Animal Hospital database. Actually, many more changes will be made as the design is examined and enhanced.

Step 4: Table design and relationships

After you complete the data design, the next step is the final organization of the data into tables. Figure 6-6 shows the final design for the four tables; it's an actual database diagram found in Microsoft Access.

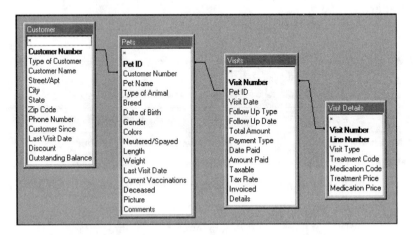

Figure 6-6: The final design, separating the data by function.

Tip   Creating the final set of tables is easy if you have lots of experience. If you don't, that's all right too because Access lets you change a table definition after you've created it — without losing any data. In Chapter 7, you'll actually create a table in Access.

In Figure 6-6, you can see the relationships that join one table to another. Notice the relationship between customers and pets, created by adding the Customer Number field to the Pets table. Each pet has a link to its owner, the customer. You can use the same method to establish a relationship between pets and visits. When you add the Pet ID field to the Visits table, each visit itself involves a pet in the Pets table. The Visit Number field establishes a similar relationship between Visits and Visit Details.

Setting relations

Cross-Reference Later, in Chapter 12, you learn all about using multiple tables and how to set relations in Access. For now, a brief discussion of this topic will show you how to design the relations between the various tables you've identified.

Tables are related to each other so that information in one table is accessible to another. Usually, in systems designed with Access, you have several tables that are all related to one another. You establish these *relations* by having fields in the various tables that share a common value. The field names in these tables need not be the same; only the values have to match. In the Pets table, for example, you have the customer number. By relating the customer number in the Pets table to the customer number in the Customer table, you can retrieve all there is to know about the customer.

This saves you from having to store the data in two places, and it is the first reason to have a relation — for a *table lookup*. A field in one table can look up data in another table. Another example: You can use the Pet ID field to create a table-lookup relation from the Visits table to the Pets table. Then, as you enter each item, Access passes data about the item (such as pet name, type of animal, breed, and date of birth) from the Pets table to the Visits table.

There is a second reason to set a relation, however. As you decide how to relate the tables you have already designed, you must also decide how to handle multiple occurrences of data. In this system design, there can be multiple occurrences of visit details for each visit. For example, each treatment or medication is entered on a separate detail line. When this happens, you should split the table into two tables. In this design, you need to place the visit number of the visit in a separate table from the single-occurrence visit. This new Visit Details table is related by the Visit Number field found in the Visits table.

The Visits and Visit Details tables are the central focus of the system. The Visits table needs to be related not only to the Pets table but also to the Customer table so that you can retrieve information from it for the invoice report. Even so, you don't have to link the Visits table directly to the Customer table; you can go through the Pets table to get there. Figure 6-6 shows these *chain link* relationships graphically in an actual Access screen (the Query window), where you can set relations between tables.

In the course of a visit, the Pet ID field would be entered, linking the pet information to the Visits table. The Pets table uses the Customer Number field to retrieve the customer information (such as name and address) from the Customer table. Although the name and address are not stored in the Visits table itself, this information is needed to confirm that a pet in for a visit belongs to a particular customer.

Step 5: Field design data-entry rules and validation

The next step is to define your fields and tables in much greater detail. You also need to determine data-validation rules for each field and even define some new tables to help with data validation.

Designing field names, types, and sizes

First, you must name each field. The name should be easy to remember but descriptive so that you recognize the function of the field by its name. It should be just long enough to describe the field but not so short that it becomes cryptic. Access allows up to 64 characters (including spaces) for a field name.

You must also decide what type of data each of your fields will hold. In Access, you can choose any of several data types (as shown in Table 6-7).

Table 6-7
Data Types in Access

Data Type	Type of Data Stored
Text	Alphanumeric characters; up to 255 characters
Memo	Alphanumeric characters; long strings up to 64,000 characters
Number	Numeric values of many types and formats
Date/Time	Date and time data
Currency	Monetary data
AutoNumber	Automatically incremented numeric counter
Yes/No	Logical values, Yes/No, True/False
OLE object	Pictures, graphs, sound, video, word processing, and spreadsheet files

NEW FEATURE   The Lookup Wizard is not actually a data type but a way of storing a field one way and displaying a related value in another table instead. Generally, these are text fields, but they can also be numeric. For example, you could store 1, 2, or 3 for the Type of Customer and then look up and display the values Individual, Pet Store, and Zoo instead.

NEW FEATURE   The AutoNumber data type was formerly called Counter in Access 2.0.

One of these data types must be assigned to each of your fields (the next part of the book explains data types in more detail). You also must specify the length of the text fields.

Designing data-entry rules

The last major design decision concerns *data validation,* which becomes important when data is entered. You want to make sure that only *good* data gets into
your system — data that passes certain tests you define. There are several types
of data validation. You can test for *known individual items,* stipulating (for example) that the Gender field can accept only the values Male, Female, or Unknown.
You can test for *ranges* (specifying, for example, that the value of Weight must be
between 0 and 1,500 pounds). Finally, you can test for *compound conditions,* such
as whether the Type of Customer field indicates an individual (in which case the
discount is 0 percent), a pet store (the discount field must show 20 percent), or a
zoo (the discount is 50 percent). In the next chapter, you learn where you can
enter conditions to perform data validation.

Designing lookup tables

Sometimes you need to design entire tables to perform data validation or just to
make it easier to create your system; these are called *lookup tables.* For example,
because Mountain Animal Hospital needs a field to determine the customer's tax
rate, you decide to use a lookup table that contains the state code, state name,
and state tax rate. This also allows you to enter no more than a two-digit state
code in the Customer table and then look up the state name or tax rate when necessary. The state code then becomes the field that relates the tables. Because the
tax rate can change, Access looks up the current tax rate whenever a visit record
is created, storing the tax-rate value in the Visits table to capture the tax rate for
each visit.

Tip This is the perfect time to use a Lookup Wizard in the Customer table — to look
up and display the state instead of the state code.

Although you can create a field on a data-entry form that limits the entry of valid
genders to Male, Female, and Unknown, there are too many allowable animal types
to create a field for animal type in a form. Rather, you can create a table with only
one field — Type of Animal — and then use the Type of Animal field in the Pets
table to link to this field in the Animals lookup table.

Tip You create a lookup table in exactly the same way as you would any other table,
and it behaves in the same way. The only difference is in the way you use the table.

In Figure 6-7, notice that four lookup tables are added to the design. The States
lookup table is necessary for determining an individual's tax rate. The Animals
lookup table is added to ensure that standard animal types are entered into the
Pets table (for the sake of consistency). The Animals lookup table is designed as
an alphabetized listing of valid animal types.

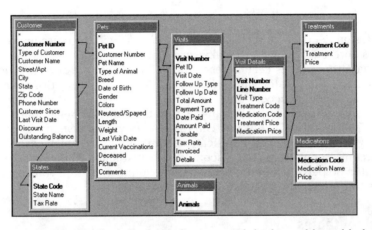

Figure 6-7: The final database diagram, with lookup tables added.

The two tables on the far right, Treatments and Medications, are added for several reasons. The last thing you want is to require that doctors enter a long name to complete the Treatment or Medication fields after an animal's visit. Doctors should be able to choose from a list or enter a simple code. Then the code can be used to look up and retrieve the name of the treatment or medication along with its current price. In fact, the price that the doctor looks up must be stored in the Visit Details table; prices can change between the time of the visit and the time the invoice is sent out. You would add the Treatments lookup table, then, for storing a list of treatments and their associated prices. Similarly, you would add a Medications table for keeping a list of available medications and their associated prices.

Creating test data

After you define your data-entry rules and how the database should look, it's time to create *test data*. You should prepare this data very scientifically (in order to test many possible conditions), and it should have various purposes. It should let you test the process of data entry — do all the conditions you created generate the proper acceptance or error messages? In addition, you may find some conditions you should test for that you hadn't considered. What happens (for example) when someone enters a blank into a field? How about numbers in a character field? Access automatically traps such things as bad dates or characters in Date and Numeric fields, but you must take care of the rest yourself.

You'll be creating two types of test data. The first is simply data that allows you to *populate,* or fill, the databases with meaningful data. This is the initial *good* data that should end up in the database and then be used to test output. Output will consist mainly of your reports. The second type of test data is for testing data entry. This includes designing data with errors that display every one of your error conditions, along with good data that can test some of your acceptable conditions.

Test data should let you test routine items of the type you normally find in your data. You should also test for *limits.* Enter data that is only one character long for some fields, and use every field. Create several records that use every position in the database (and thereby every position in the data-entry screen and in the reports).

Create some "bad" test data. Enter data that tests every condition. Try to enter a customer number that already exists. Try to change a customer number that's not in the file. These are a few examples of what to consider when testing your system. Testing your system begins, of course, with the test data.

Step 6: Form design — input

After you've created the data and established table relationships, it is time to design your forms. *Forms* are made up of the fields that can be entered or viewed in edit mode. If at all possible, your screens should look much like the forms you would use in a manual system. This setup makes for the most user-friendly system.

Designing data-entry screens

When you're designing forms, you will need to place three types of objects on-screen:

- ✦ Labels and text box data-entry fields
- ✦ Special controls (multiple-line text boxes, option buttons, list boxes, check boxes, business graphs, and pictures)
- ✦ Graphic enhancements (color, lines, rectangles, and three-dimensional effects)

You should place your data fields just where you want them on the form. Although the cursor normally moves from top to bottom and from left to right when you enter data, you can specify cursor movement from one field to another. You can also specify any size entry you want. As you place the fields, be sure to leave as much space around them as you'll need. A calculated field, such as a total that would be used only for data display, can also be part of a data-entry form.

You can use *labels* to display messages, titles, or captions. *Text boxes* provide an area where you can type or display text or numbers contained in your database. *Check boxes* indicate a condition and are either unchecked or checked (selected). Other types of controls available with Access include list boxes, combo boxes, option buttons, toggle buttons, and option groups.

Cross-Reference
Chapter 16 covers the various types of controls available in Access. Access also provides a tool called Microsoft Graph that you can use to create a wide variety of graphs. You can also display pictures, using an OLE object stored in a database table, as you will learn in Chapter 20.

In this book, you create several basic data-entry forms:

✦ Customer

✦ Pets

✦ Visits general information

✦ Visit Details

The Customer form

Cross-Reference
The Customer Data Entry Form shown in Figure 6-8 is the simplest of the data-entry forms you create in this book. It is very straightforward, simply listing the field descriptions on the left and the fields themselves on the right. The unique *key field* is Customer Number. At the top of the form is the main header, a title that identifies this data-entry form by type: the Customer Data Entry Form. You can create this simple form by using a Form Wizard (see Chapter 11 for details).

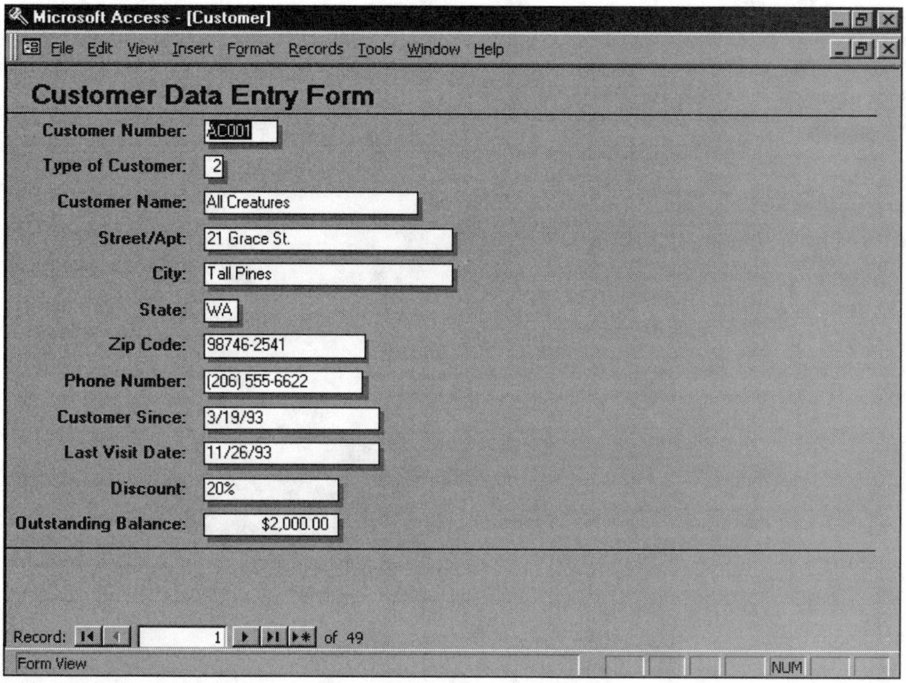

Figure 6-8: The Customer Data Entry Form.

The Pets form

Cross-
Reference

The Pets Data Entry form is more complicated. It contains several types of controls, including option buttons, a list box, several combo boxes, check boxes, a picture, and a memo field. As shown in Figure 6-9, the form contains two sections; one contains pet information, the other contains customer information. You learn how to create this form in Chapter 19.

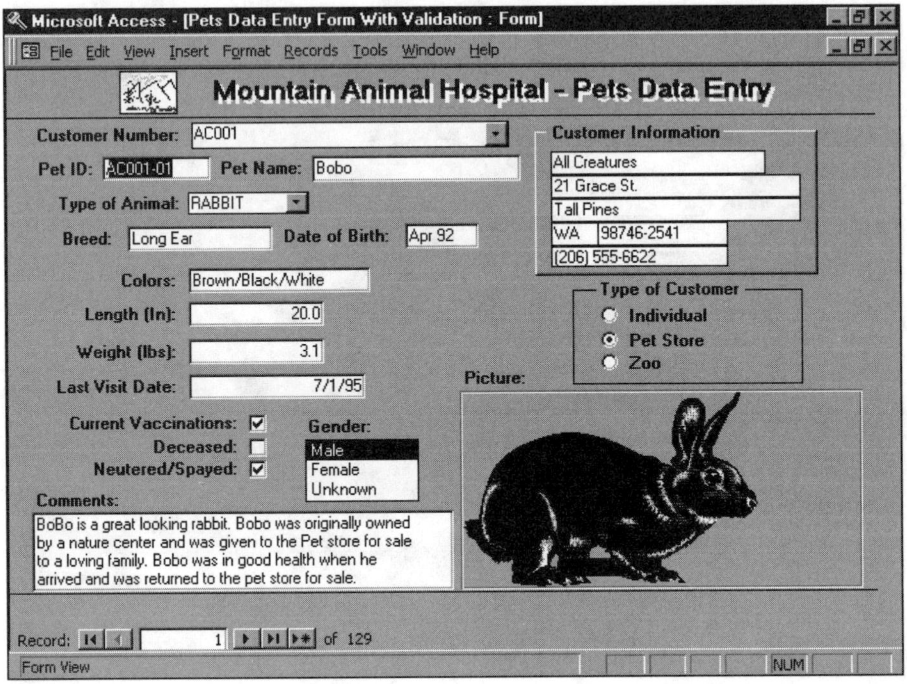

Figure 6-9: The Pets Data Entry form.

The General Visits form

As shown in Figure 6-10, the next data-entry form combines data from several tables to provide general information about visits. This form contains information about customers, pets, and visits; its main purpose is to allow a user to enter such information into the database. Visit Number is the key field for this form.

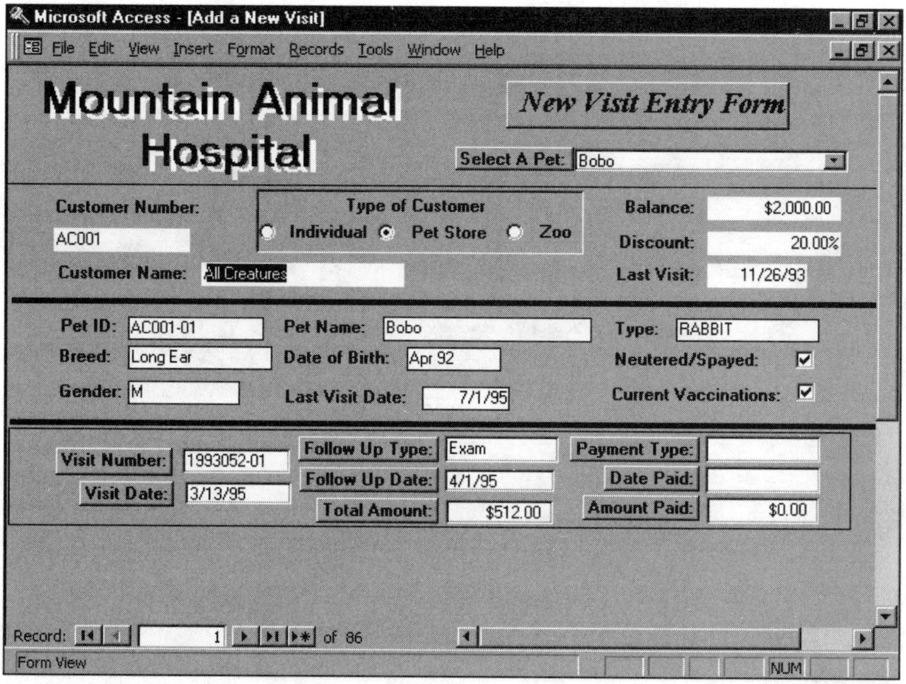

Figure 6-10: The general Visits data-entry form.

The Visit Details form

The final form you'll see in this book (shown in Figure 6-11) is for adding the details of individual visits. (You create this form in Chapter 28.) This form contains a *subform* so that you can see many visit details at once. Many types of subforms can be linked to a form; you can even have a graph as a subform, as you discover in Chapter 20.

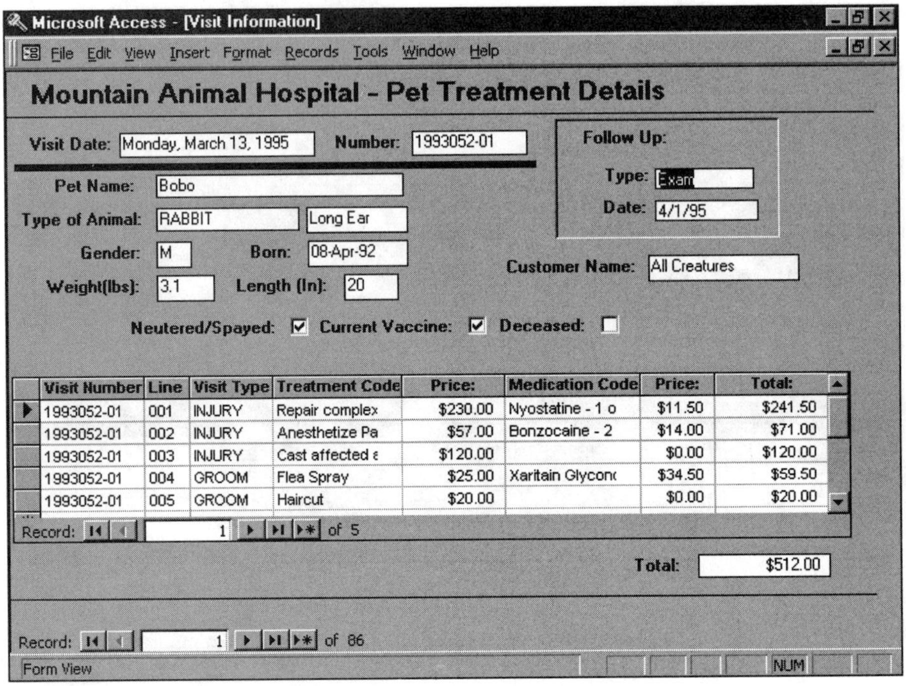

Figure 6-11: The Visit Details data-entry form.

Step 7: Automation design — menus

After you've created your data, designed your reports, and created your forms, it's time to tie them all together using *switchboards* and *menus.* Figure 6-12 shows a switchboard form that also contains a custom menu bar. Switchboards are graphical menus in the center of a form usually built with command buttons with text or pictures on them. Menus refer to the pull-down menus at the top of a screen.

Menus are the key to a good system. A user must be able to follow the system to understand how to move from place to place. Usually each form or report is also a choice on a menu. This means that your design must include decisions on how to group the menus. When you examine the overall design and look at all your systems, you begin to see a distinct set of combinations.

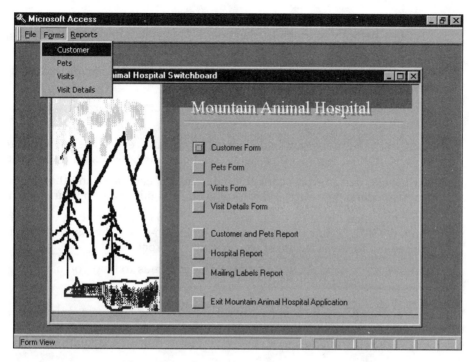

Figure 6-12: A switchboard and menu for Mountain Animal Hospital.

You can use Access macros to create a menu on the top menu bar of the switchboard. This menu gives the user the choice of using pull-down menus or switchboard buttons. You create this switchboard, along with the menus and a complicated dialog box, in Chapter 32.

Summary

In this chapter, you learned how to design reports properly and how to extract data items. You learned how to set relations, and you saw the design process for the forms and menus that serve as examples in this book. You became acquainted with the Mountain Animal Hospital, a fictitious entity used to illustrate database processing. Mountain Animal Hospital is a medium-size veterinary hospital serving individuals, pet stores, and zoos in three states. This chapter explained the following points:

✦ The seven-step method for design includes overall system design, report design, data design, table design, field design, form design, and menu design.

✦ The overall design phase helps you think through your system from concept to reality before you touch the keyboard. This makes implementation much more efficient.

✦ Report design lets you plan for the output necessary to provide information from your system.

✦ In data design, you extract fields from your report in order to group them logically.

✦ After you can group your fields logically, you can create tables in which to store your data. You can then define relationships between related tables.

✦ During field design, you define the data types of each field and their sizes. You also define data-entry rules to allow only valid data into your system.

✦ You can design forms by using the Access Form Design window, which gives you a WYSIWYG view of your data; designing on-screen forms to resemble printed-out forms is the most user-friendly approach.

✦ In Access, you can create switchboards and menus to help you navigate through a system.

This chapter completes the first part of this book. In the next part, you learn how to create a table, enter and display data in datasheets, and create simple data-entry forms, queries, and reports. Finally, you learn how to use multiple files.

✦   ✦   ✦

Basic Database Usage

Creating Database Tables

I n this chapter, you learn how to start the process of database and table creation. You create a database container to hold the tables, queries, forms, reports, and macros that you create as you learn Access. You also create the Pets database table, which stores data about the pets serviced by the Mountain Animal Hospital.

Creating the Pets Table

The Pets table is one of the best examples in the Mountain Animal Hospital database because it illustrates the major field types used by Access. In most tables, you will find that the majority of fields are *text fields*. Most data in the world is either numbers or text. The Pets table contains many text fields to fully describe each animal, but also contains several *numeric fields* to give the animal's length and weight. Another common field type is *date and time*; the Pets table uses a date/time field to record the date of birth. The Pets table also contains several *yes/no fields* used for making a single choice. Examples of this field are Neutered or Current Vaccination. Large amounts of text are stored in a *memo field* to record notes about the animal, such as special customer preferences or known allergies. Another field type is the *OLE field*, used for storing sound, pictures, or video. In the Pets example, this field will store a picture of the animal.

Before you can create a table, however, you must first create the overall database container.

Creating a Database

The Database window displays all the various object files from your database that you may create while using Access. Actually, a database is a single file. As you create new *object files*, they are stored within the database file. They are not DOS files in themselves; instead, they are stored objects. The database file will start off at about 65,000 bytes and grow as you create new objects — tables, queries, forms, reports, macros, and modules. Adding data to an Access database will also increase the size of the file.

You can create a new database by selecting File⊃New Database from the main Access menu (as shown in Figure 7-1), or by clicking on the first icon in the toolbar.

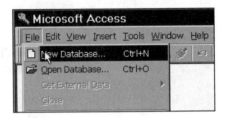

Figure 7-1: Creating a new database by using File⊃New Database.

Tip You can also create a new database by clicking on the New Database icon. This is the first icon in the toolbar. It looks like a sheet of paper with the right top corner bent down.

Create a new database now by clicking on the first toolbar icon.

The New Database window appears, as shown in Figure 7-2. There is one tab, General, which contains one icon, the Blank Database icon. Select the Blank Database icon and click OK.

Tip When you first start Access, a Database selection window appears automatically. You can choose a blank database, choose the Database Wizard, open an existing database, or cancel (not start or open anything).

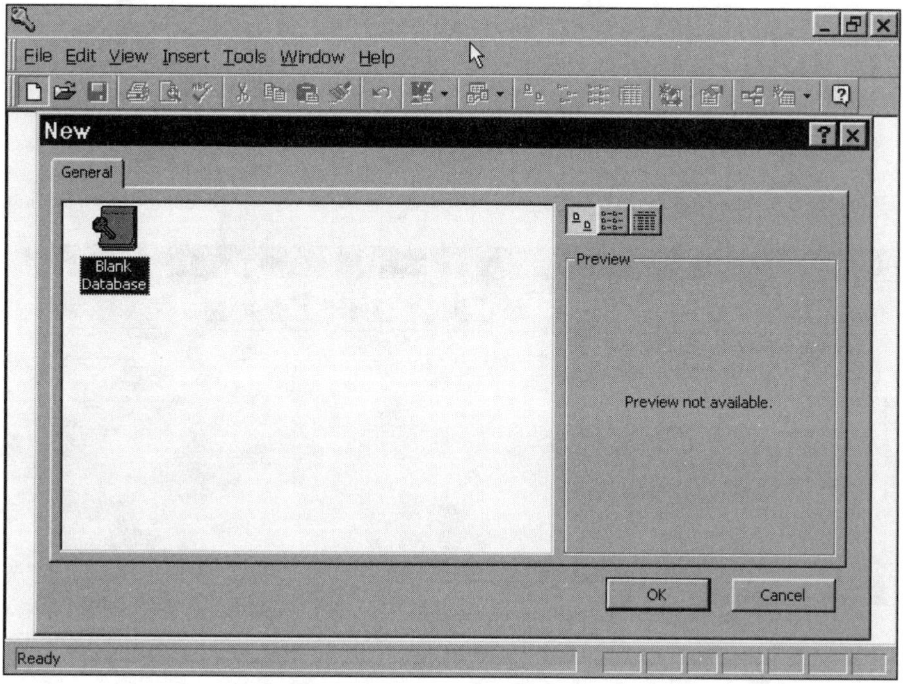

Figure 7-2: The New Database window.

After you start the creation process, you must create a name for the database. Figure 7-3 shows a standard Windows 95/NT file box, which has several areas, including a combo box and a file list. A default name db1.mdb appears in the File name combo box. You can simply type the name you want right over the default name. Adding the .MDB file extension is optional; Access adds it automatically when you create the file container. Because the database is a standard Windows 95/NT file, its filename can be any valid Windows 95/NT long filename. You can also see the existing .MDB files in the file list part of the window. Although the Save in combo box may be set to the My Documents folder initially, you can change this setting to any folder you have. In this example, that folder is C:\ACCESS97.

Caution

An Access 97 database cannot be used by previous versions of Access.

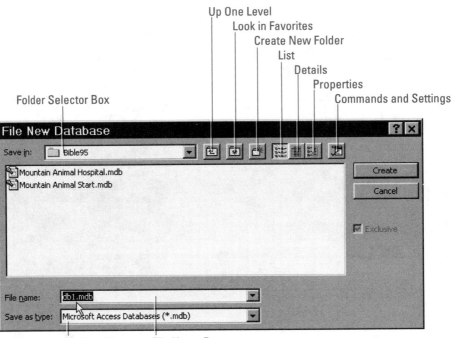

Up One Level
Look in Favorites
Create New Folder
List
Details
Properties
Commands and Settings
Folder Selector Box

File Type Box   File Name Box

Figure 7-3: Entering a filename for the database container.

Caution Type **My Mountain Animal Hospital** in place of db1.mdb as the name for your database. Click on Create to save and open the new database.

If you enter a file extension other than MDB, Access saves the database file but does not display it when you open the database later. By default, Access searches for and displays only those files with an MDB file extension.

The File Selector box displays a list of Access databases in the current subfolder The list is for reference only; you use it to see what databases already exist. All the database filenames appear *grayed out*; they are not selectable. You can switch to a different subfolder or drive to save the new database container by clicking on the arrow to the right of the Save in box and selecting a new folder or drive from the list.

If you are following along with the examples in this book, note that we have chosen the name My Mountain Animal Hospital for the name of the database you create as you complete the chapters. This database is for our hypothetical business, the Mountain Animal Hospital. After you enter the filename, Access creates the empty database. The disk that comes with your book contains two database files named Mountain Animal Hospital Start (only the database tables), and Mountain Animal Hospital (the completed application, including tables, forms, queries, reports, macros, and modules).

The Database Window

The empty Database window is shown in Figure 7-4. After you create or open a database, the look of the screen changes; Access displays additional menus that enable you to perform a variety of tasks. A toolbar appears so that you can quickly create a new query, form, or report, or get help.

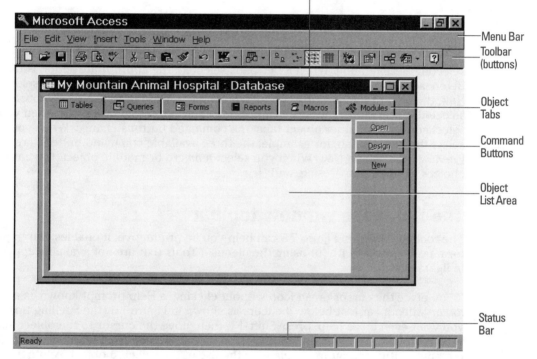

Figure 7-4: The Database window and the empty database.

Object tabs

The Database window contains six tabs; using them, you can quickly select any of these six objects available in Access:

✦ Tables

✦ Queries

✦ Forms

✦ Reports

✦ Macros

✦ Modules

As you create new object files, the names of the files appear in the Database window. You see only the files for the particular type of object selected. You can select an object type by clicking on one of the object buttons.

The Database window command buttons

The command buttons in the Database window enable you to create a New object or Open an existing object. You can also open an existing object for changes by selecting Design mode. When a button is selected, the appropriate action is taken. Before selecting Open or Design, you should select a filename. When you select New, the type of the new object depends on the object tab that you previously selected. If you chose the Tables tab, a new table is created. Note that when you select some of the other object tabs, the command buttons change. When you select the Reports tab, for example, the three available command buttons are Preview, Design, and New. When you select a macro or module object, the button choices become Run, Design, and New.

The Database window toolbar

The toolbar shown in Figure 7-5 can help you be productive; it enables you to perform tasks quickly without using the menus. (Tools that are not available appear in light gray.)

Tip If you place the cursor on an icon without clicking, a Help prompt known as a *tooltip* will appear just below the icon, as shown in Figure 7-5 (the Spelling tip). If you want even more help, press Shift+F1, then move the cursor to the object you want more information about and click on it. You will see *What's This* help: a small rectangle with a paragraph explaining the use of the selected object. Another method is to select the Office Assistant icon at the far right end of the toolbar (it has a question mark inside a bubble), and then type a question in the Office Assistant box.

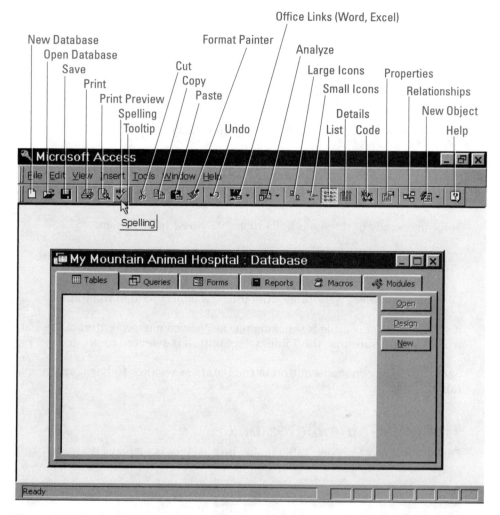

Figure 7-5: The Database window toolbar.

Creating a New Table

After you design your table on paper, you need to create the table design in Access. Although you can create the table interactively without any forethought, carefully planning out any database system is a good idea. You can make any changes later, but doing so wastes time; generally the result is a system that is harder to maintain than one that is well planned from the beginning. Before you get started, you should understand the table design process.

The table design process

Creating a table design is a multi-step process. By following the steps in order, you can create your table design readily and with minimal effort. Follow these steps:

1. Create a new table.

2. Enter each field name, data type, and description.

3. Enter properties for each field you have defined.

4. Set a primary key.

5. Create indexes for necessary fields.

6. Save your design.

You can use any of three methods to create a new table design:

✦ You can click on the <u>N</u>ew command button in the Database window

✦ You can select <u>I</u>nsert⇨<u>T</u>able from the menus.

✦ You can select New Table from the New Object icon in the toolbar.

Tip If you create a new table by clicking on the <u>N</u>ew command button in the Database window, make sure that the Table object button is selected first.

Select the <u>N</u>ew command button in the Database window to begin creating a new table.

The New Table dialog box

Figure 7-6 shows the New Table dialog box as Access displays it.

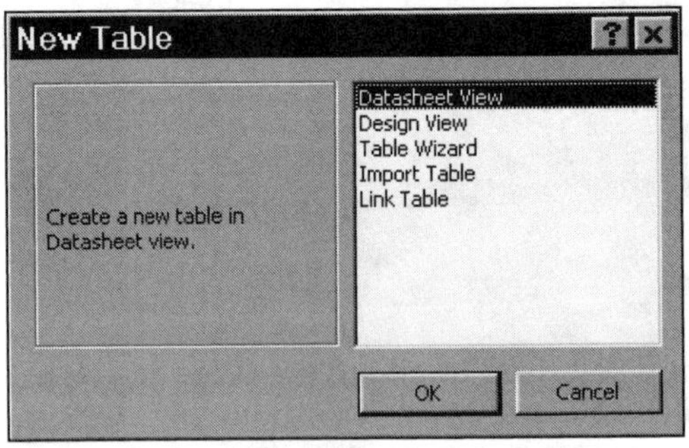

Figure 7-6: The New Table dialog box.

Use this dialog box to select one of five ways to create a new table. These choices are shown in this list:

Datasheet View	Enter data into a spreadsheet
Design View	Create a table design
Table Wizard	Select a pre-built table
Import Table	Import external data formats into a new Access table
Link Table	Link to an existing external data source

Access 97 provides several ways to create a new table. You can design the structure of the table (such as field names, data types, and size) first, and then add data. Another method is to use the Table Wizard (also found in Access 2.0 and 95) to choose from a list of predefined table designs. Access 97 gives you three new ways to create a new table easily. First, you can enter the data into a spreadsheet-like form known as Datasheet view; Access will create the table for you automatically. You can also use the Import Table Wizard to select an external data source and create a new table containing a copy of the data found in that source; the Wizard takes you through the import process. The Link Table Wizard (the third easy method) is similar to the Import Table Wizard, except the data stays in the original location and Access links to it from the new table.

To create your first table, the Datasheet view is a great method for getting started; then you can use the table's Design view to make any final changes and adjustments.

Cross-Reference The Import Table and Link Table are covered in Chapter 24.

Using the Table Wizard

When you create a new table, you can type in every field name, data type, size, and other table property information, or you can use the Table Wizard (as shown in Figure 7-7) to select from a long list of predefined tables and fields. Unlike the Database Wizard (which creates a complete application), the Table Wizard creates only a table and a simple form.

Wizards can save you a lot of work; they are meant to save you time and make complex tasks much easier. Wizards work by taking you through a series of screens that ask you what you want. You answer these questions by clicking on buttons, selecting fields, entering text, and making yes/no decisions.

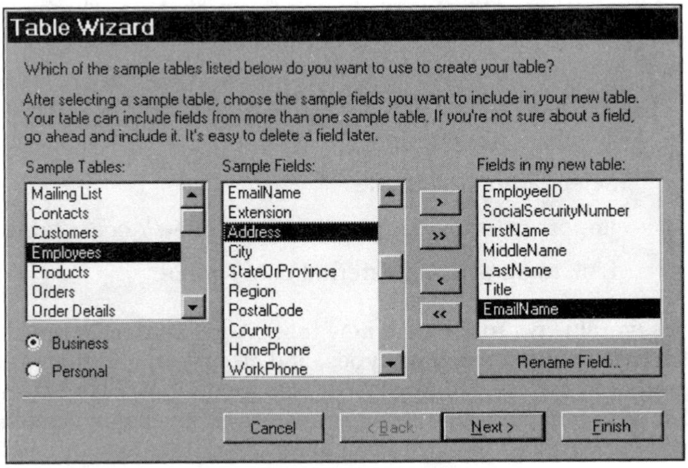

Figure 7-7: A Table Wizard screen.

In the Table Wizard, first you choose between the lists of Business or Personal tables. Some of the Business tables include Mailing List, Contacts, Employees, Products, Orders, Suppliers, Payments, Invoices, Fixed Assets, and Students. The Personal list includes Guests, Recipes, Exercise Log, Plants, Wine List, Photographs, Video Collection, and more.

When you select a table, a list appears and shows you all the fields you might want in the table. Select only the fields you want. Although they are all predefined for data type and size, you can rename a field once it's selected. Once you've chosen your fields, another screen uses input from you to create a primary key automatically. Other screens can then help you link the primary key automatically to another table and establish relationships. Finally, the Wizard can display the table, let you enter records into a datasheet, or even create an automatic form for you. The entire process of creating a simple table and form can take less than one minute! Whenever you need to create a table for an application on the Wizard's list, you can save a lot of time.

Select Datasheet View and click on the OK button to display a blank datasheet with which you can create a new table.

Creating a new table with a Datasheet view

The empty datasheet appears, ready for you to enter data and create a new table. You begin by entering a few records into the datasheet. Each column is a field. Each row will become a record in the table. You will learn more about these terms later in this chapter. For now, all you have to do is add data. The more records you add, the more accurately Access can tell what type of data you want for each field, and the approximate size of each data item.

When you first see the datasheet, it's empty. The column headers that will become field names for the table are labeled Field1, Field2, Field3, and so on. You can change the column header names if you want; they become the field names for the table design. You can always change the field names after you have finished creating the table. The table datasheet is initially named Table followed by a number. If there are no other tables named Table with a number, Access uses the name Table1; the next table would be named Table2, and so forth. You can always change this name when you save the table.

Add the five records as shown in Figure 7-8, and change the column headers to the names shown.

Note You can change a column name by double-clicking on the column name and then editing the value. When you're done, press Enter to save the new column header. If you enter a column header name wider than the default column width, you can adjust the column width by placing the cursor on the line between the column names and then dragging the column line to the right to make it wider or to the left to make it narrower.

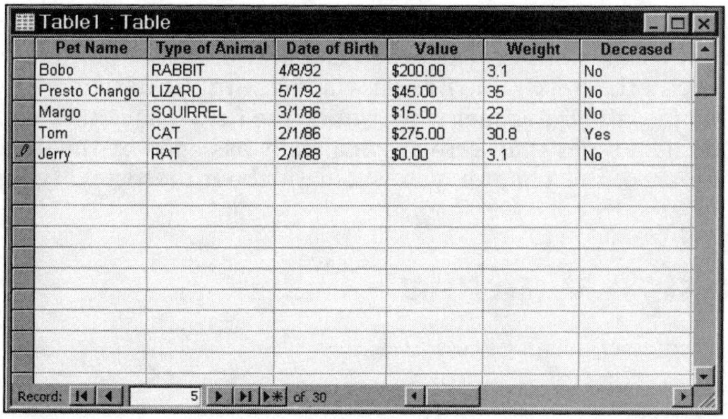

Pet Name	Type of Animal	Date of Birth	Value	Weight	Deceased
Bobo	RABBIT	4/8/92	$200.00	3.1	No
Presto Chango	LIZARD	5/1/92	$45.00	35	No
Margo	SQUIRREL	3/1/86	$15.00	22	No
Tom	CAT	2/1/86	$275.00	30.8	Yes
Jerry	RAT	2/1/88	$0.00	3.1	No

Figure 7-8: A partially completed Datasheet view of the data.

Tip The Datasheet window works very similarly to a Microsoft Excel spreadsheet. Many techniques are the same for both products; even many menus and toolbar icons are exactly the same.

Once you have finished entering the data, you can save the table and give it a name. To close the table and save the data entered, you can either choose Close from the File menu or click on the Close button in the upper right corner of the Table window (the button with the X on it). You can also click on the Save icon on the toolbar, but this only saves the table; you still have to close it.

Click on the Close button in the window to close the table and save the data entry. A dialog box appears, asking whether you want to save changes to the table named Table1. You can select Yes to save the table and give it a name, No to forget everything, or Cancel to simply return to the table for more data entry.

Select Yes to continue the process to save the table. Another dialog box appears because the table is unnamed (it has the default table name).

Enter Pets and click on OK to continue to save the table. Yet another dialog box appears, asking whether you want to create a primary key — a unique identifier for each record, which you will learn about later in the chapter. For now, just select the No button.

Access saves the table and returns you to the Database window. Notice that the table name Pets now appears in the table object list. If you did everything correctly, you have successfully created a table named Pets that has five fields and five records. The next step is to edit the table design and create the final table design you saw in Chapter 6.

To display the Table Design window, select the Pets table and click on the Design button. Figure 7-9 shows the Pets Table Design window with the design created by the data you entered into the Datasheet view. Notice the field names that you created. Also notice the data types that were automatically assigned by the data you entered. In the next part of this chapter, you will learn about these field types.

The Table Design window

The Table Design window consists of two areas:

✦ The field entry area
✦ The field properties area

The *field entry area* is for entering each field's name and data type; you can also enter an optional description. The *property area* is for entering more options for each field, called *properties*. These include field size, format, input mask, alternate caption for forms, default value, validation rules, validation text, required, zero length for null checking, and index specifications. You will learn more about these properties later in the book.

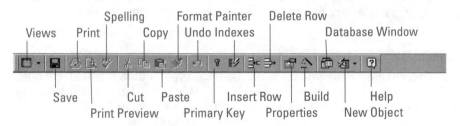

Figure 7-9: The Table Design window.

Tip

You can switch between areas (also referred to as *panes*) by clicking the mouse when the pointer is in the desired pane, or by pressing F6.

Using the Table window toolbar

The Table window toolbar, shown in Figure 7-10, contains many icons to assist you in creating a new table definition.

Figure 7-10: The Table window toolbar.

Working with Fields

You create fields by entering a field name and a field data type in each row of the field entry area of the Table window. The *field description* is an option to identify the field's purpose; it appears in the status bar during data entry. After you enter each field's name and data type, you can further specify how each field is used by entering properties in the property area. Before you enter any properties, however, you should enter all your field names and data types for this example. You have already created some of the fields you will need.

Naming a field

A *field name* identifies the field both to you and to Access. Field names should be long enough to identify the purpose of the field, but not overly long. (Later, as you enter validation rules or use the field name in a calculation, you'll want to save yourself from typing long field names.)

To enter a field name, position the pointer in the first row of the Table window under the Field Name column. Then type a valid field name, observing the following rules:

✦ Field names can be from 1 to 64 characters.

✦ Field names can include letters, numbers, and many special characters.

✦ Field names cannot include a period (.), exclamation point (!), brackets ([ ]), or accent grave (`` ` ``).

✦ You cannot use low-order ASCII characters, for example J or L (ASCII values 0-31).

✦ You cannot start with a blank space.

You can enter field names in upper, lower, or mixed case. If you make a mistake while typing the field name, you can simply position the pointer where you want to make a correction, and then type the change. If you spell a field name incorrectly (or simply want to change it later), you can change it at any time — even if it's in a table and the field contains data.

Caution Once you save your table, if you change a field name that is used in queries, forms, or reports, you will have to change it in those objects as well.

Specifying a data type

After you name a field, you must decide what type of data the field will hold. Before you begin entering data, you should have a good grasp of the data types your system will use. Ten basic types of data are shown in Table 7-1; you'll note that some types (such as numbers) have several options.

NEW
FEATURE

Table 7-1
Data Types Available in Microsoft Access

Data Type	Type of Data Stored	Storage Size
Text	Alphanumeric characters	0 - 255 characters
Memo	Alphanumeric characters	0 - 64,000 characters
Number	Numeric values	1, 2, 4, or 8 bytes
Date/Time	Date and time data	8 bytes
Currency	Monetary data	8 bytes
AutoNumber	Automatic number increments	4 bytes
Yes/No	Logical values: Yes/No, True/False	1 bit (0 or -1)
OLE Object	Pictures, graphs, sound, video	Up to 1GB
HyperLink	Link to an Internet resource	0 - 6,144 characters
Lookup Wizard	Displays data from another table	Generally 4 bytes

Figure 7-11 shows the Data Type menu. When you move the pointer into the Data Type column, a down arrow appears in the text-entry box. To open this menu, move the cursor into the Data Type column and click on the down arrow.

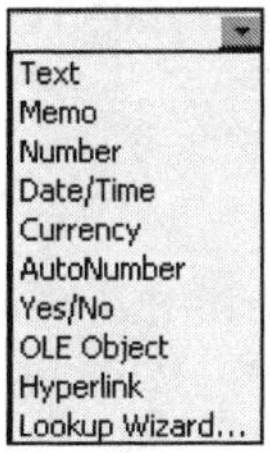

```
Text
Memo
Number
Date/Time
Currency
AutoNumber
Yes/No
OLE Object
Hyperlink
Lookup Wizard...
```

Figure 7-11: The Data Type menu.

Text data is any type of data that is simply characters. Names, addresses, and descriptions are all text data — as are numeric data that are not used in a calculation (such as phone numbers, Social Security numbers, and ZIP codes). Although you specify the size of each text field in the property area, you can enter no more than 255 characters of data into any text field. Access uses variable length fields to store its data. If you designate a field to be 25 characters wide and you only use 5 characters for each record, then that is all the space you will actually use in your database container. You will find that the .MDB database file can get large very quickly but text fields will not cause this. However, rather than allow Access to createeevery text field with the default 50 characters or the maximum 255 characters, it is good practice to limit text field widths to the maximum you believe they will be used for. Names are tricky because some cultures have long names. However, it is a safe bet that a postal code might be less than 12 characters wide while a state abbreviation in the U.S. is always 2. By limiting the size of the text width, you also automatically limit the number of characters the user can type when the field is used in a form.

The *Memo* data type holds a variable amount of data, from 0 to 64,000 characters for each record. Therefore, if one record uses 100 characters, another requires only 10, and yet another needs 3,000, you still use only as much space as each record requires. You would therefore cut down considerably on the amount of space your database requires.

The *Number* data type enables you to enter *numeric* data, that is, numbers that will be used in mathematical calculations. (If you have data that will be used in monetary calculations, you should use the *Currency* data type, which enables you to specify many different currency types.)

The *Date/Time* data type can store dates, times, or both types of data at once. Thus, you can enter a date, a time, or a date/time combination. You can specify many types of formats in the property entry area, and then display date and time data as you prefer.

The *AutoNumber* data type stores an integer that Access increments (adds to) automatically as you add new records. You can use the AutoNumber data type as a unique record identification for tables having no other unique value. If, for example, you have no unique identification for a list of names, you can use an AutoNumber field to identify one John Smith from another.

The *Yes/No* data type holds data that has one of two values, and can therefore be expressed as a binary state. Data is actually stored as –1 for yes and 0 for no. You can, however, adjust the format setting to display Yes/No, True/False, or On/Off. When you use a Yes/No data type, you can use many of the form controls especially designed for it.

The *OLE Object* data type provides access for data that can be linked to an OLE server. This type of data includes bitmaps (such as Windows 95 Paint files), audio files (such as WAV files), business graphics (such as those found in Access and Excel), and even full-motion video files. Of course, you can play the video files only if you have the hardware and necessary OLE server software.

NEW FEATURE

The *Hyperlink* data type field holds combinations of text and numbers stored as text and used as a hyperlink address. It can have up to three parts: (1) the visual text that appears in a field (usually underlined); (2) the Internet address — the path to a file (UNC path) or page (URL); and (3) any subaddress within the file or page. An example of a subaddress would be the name of an Access 97 form or report. Each part is separated by the pound symbol (#).

The *Lookup Wizard* data type creates a field that lets you use a combo box to choose a value from another table or from a list of values. This is especially useful when you are storing key fields from another table in order to link to data from that table. Choosing this option in the Data Type list starts the Lookup Wizard, with which you define the data type and perform the link to another table. You will learn more about this field type later.

Entering a field description

The *field description* is completely optional; you use it only to help you remember a field's uses or to let another user know its purpose. Often you don't use the description column at all, or you use it only for fields whose purpose is not readily recognizable. If you enter a field description, it appears in the status bar whenever you use that field in Access. The field description can help to clarify a field whose purpose is ambiguous, or give the user a fuller explanation of the values valid for the field during data entry.

Completing the Pets Table

Table 7-2 shows the completed field entries for the Pets table. If you are following along with the examples, you should modify the table design now for these additional fields. Enter the field names and data types exactly as shown. You will also have to rearrange some of the fields and delete the Value field you created. You may want to study the next few pages in this chapter to understand how to change existing fields (this includes rearranging the field order, changing a field name, and deleting a field).

	Table 7-2	
	Structure of the Pets Table	
Field Name	*Data Type*	*Description*
Pet ID	Text	Pet ID is entered as AA###-## (Customer # - Sequence).
Customer Number	Text	Enter the Customer Number for the owner of the pet.
Pet Name	Text	
Type of Animal	Text	Enter the animal type in capital letters, for example, DOG, CAT.

(continued)

Table 7-2 *(continued)*

Field Name	Data Type	Description
Breed	Text	
Date of Birth	Date/Time	Enter the Pet's Date of Birth in the form mm/dd/yy.
Gender	Text	Enter M for Male, F for Female, or U if Unknown.
Colors	Text	
Neutered/Spayed	Yes/No	Enter Yes if the animal has been sterilized.
Length	Number	Enter length in inches.
Weight	Number	Enter weight in pounds.
Last Visit Date	Date/Time	Do not enter this field. It is automatically filled in.
Current Vaccinations	Yes/No	Do not enter this field. It is automatically filled in.
Deceased	Yes/No	Enter Yes if pet has died.
Picture	OLE Object	Copy this in from the photograph scanner or picture library.
Comments	Memo	

The general process for adding fields to a table structure is:

1. Place the pointer in the Field Name column in the row where you want the field to appear.

2. Enter the field name and press Enter or Tab.

3. In the Data Type column, click on the down arrow and select the data type.

4. Place the pointer in the Description column and type a description (optional).

Repeat each of these steps to complete the Pets data entry for all fields. You can press the down-arrow key to move between rows, or simply use the mouse and click on any row.

Tip   You can also type in the name of the data type or the first unique letters. The type will be validated automatically to make sure it's on the drop-down list. A warning message appears for an invalid type.

Changing a Table Design

As you create your table, you should be following a well-planned design. Yet sometimes, changes are necessary, even with a plan. Often you may find you want to add another field, remove a field, change a field name or data type, or simply rearrange the order of the field names. You can make these changes to your table at any time. After you enter data into your table, however, things get a little more complicated. You have to make sure that any changes you make don't affect the data entered previously.

In Access 2.0, changes to the table design could be made only in the Table Design window. In Access 97, you can make changes to the table design in a datasheet, including adding fields, deleting fields, and changing field names.

Inserting a new field

To insert a new field, place your cursor on an existing field and select Insert⇨Row or click on the Insert Row icon in the toolbar. A new row is added to the table, and any existing fields are pushed down. You can then enter a new field definition. Inserting a field does not disturb other fields or existing data. If you have queries, forms, or reports that use the table, you may need to add the field to those objects as well.

Deleting a field

You can delete a field in one of three ways:

✦ Select the field by clicking on the row selector, and then press Delete.

✦ Select the field and then choose Edit⇨Delete Row.

✦ Select the field and then click on the Delete Row icon in the toolbar.

When you delete a field containing data, you'll see a warning that you will lose any data in the table for this field. If the table is empty, you won't care. If your table contains data, however, make sure you want to eliminate the data for that field (column). You will also have to delete the same field from queries, forms, and reports that use the field name.

Tip   When you delete a field, you can immediately select the Undo button and return the field to the table. But you must do this step *before* you save the changed table's definition.

If you delete a field, you must also delete all references to that field throughout Access. Because you can use a field name in forms, queries, reports, and even table-data validation, you must examine your system carefully to find any instances where you may have used the specific field name.

Changing a field location

One of the easiest changes to make is to move a field's location. The order of your fields, as entered, determines the initial display sequence in the datasheet that displays your data. If you decide that your fields should be rearranged, you can simply click on a field selector twice and then drag the field to a new location.

Changing a field name

You can change a field name by simply placing your cursor over an existing field name in the Table Design screen and entering a new name; Access updates the table design automatically. As long as you are creating a new table, this process is easy.

Caution
If you used the field name in any forms, queries, or reports, however, you must also change it in them. (Remember that you can also use a field name in validation rules and calculated fields in queries, as well as in macros and module expressions — all of which must be changed.) As you can see, it's a good idea not to change a field name; it creates more work.

Changing a field size

Making a field size larger is simple in a table design. However, only text and number fields can be increased in size. You simply increase the Field Size property for text fields or specify a different field size for number fields. You must pay attention to the decimal-point property in number fields to make sure you don't select a new size that supports fewer decimal places than you currently have.

When you want to make a field size smaller, make sure that none of the data in the table is larger than the new field width. (If it is, the existing data will be truncated.) Text data types should be made as small as possible to take up less storage space.

Tip
Remember that each text field uses the maximum size of the field, regardless of the value of the data in the field. If your largest data value is 20 bytes long, set the Field Size to 20 and no more.

Changing a field data type

You must be very careful when changing a field's data type if you want to preserve your existing data. Such a change is rare; most data types limit (by definition) what kind of data you can input. Normally, for example, you cannot input a letter into a Numeric field or a Date/Time field.

Some data types do, however, convert readily to others. For example, a Numeric field can be converted to a Text data type, but you lose the understanding of mathematics in the value because you can no longer perform mathematical calculations with the values. Sometimes you might accidentally create a phone number or ZIP code as Numeric and want to redefine the data type correctly as Text. Of course, you also have to remember the other places you've used the field name (for example, queries, forms, or reports).

Caution The OLE data type cannot be converted to any other format.

You'll need to understand four basic conversion types as you change from one data type to another. The paragraphs that follow describe each of these types.

To Text from other data types

Converting to Text is easiest; you can convert practically any other data type to Text with no problems. Number or Currency data can be converted with no special formatting (dollar signs or commas) if you use the General Number format; the decimal point remains intact. Yes/No data converts as is; Date/Time data also converts as is, if you use the General Date format (mm/dd/yy hh:mm:ss AM/PM). Hyperlink data will easily convert to Text. The displayed text will lose its underline and the remaining Internet resource link information will be visible.

From Text to Number, Currency, Date/Time, Yes/No, or Hyperlink

Only data stored as numeric characters (0, 1, 2, 3, 4, 5, 6, 7, 8, 9) or as periods, commas, and dollar signs can be converted to Number or Currency data from the Text data type. You must also make sure that the maximum length of the text string is not larger than the field size for the type of number or currency field you use in the conversion.

Text data being converted to Date data types must be in a correct date or time format. You can use any legal date or time format (such as, for example, 10/12/95, 12-Oct-95, or October 95), or any of the other date/time formats.

You can convert text fields to either a Yes or No value, depending on the specification in the field. Access recognizes Yes, True, or On as Yes values, and No, False, or Off as No values.

Tip Access can also convert Number data types to Yes/No values. Access interprets Null values or 0 as No, and any nonzero value as Yes.

NEW FEATURE A text field that contains correctly formatted hyperlink text will convert directly to hyperlink format — display text and address.

From Currency to Number

You can convert data from Currency to Number data types as long as the receiving field can handle the size and number of decimal places. Remember that the Field Size property in numeric fields determines the size (in bytes) of the storage space and the maximum number of decimal places. Anything can be converted to Double, which holds 8 bytes and 15 decimals, whereas Single holds only 4 bytes and 7 decimal places. (For more information, refer to the section "Entering Field Size Properties" earlier in this chapter, and to Table 7-2.)

From Text to Memo

You can always convert from Text to Memo data types because the maximum length of a text field is 255 characters, whereas a memo field can hold 64,000 characters. You can convert from Memo to Text, however, only if every value in the memo fields is less than the text field size — that is, no more than 255 characters. Values longer than the field size are truncated.

Understanding Field Properties

After you enter the field names, data types, and field descriptions, you may want to go back and further define each field. Every field has properties, and these are different for each data type. In the Pets table, you must enter properties for several data types. Figure 7-12 shows the property area for the field named Length; ten options are available.

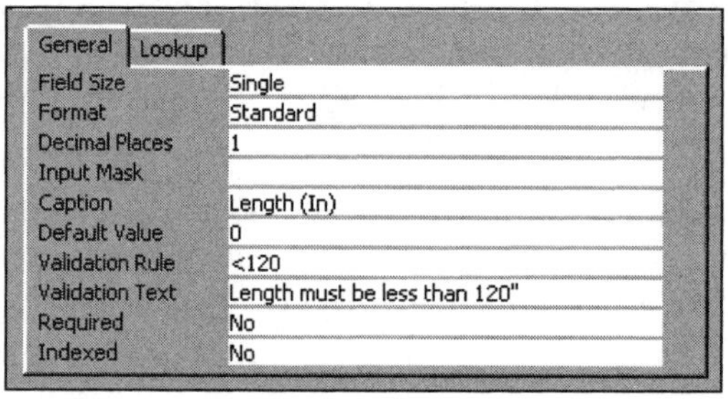

General	Lookup	
Field Size	Single	
Format	Standard	
Decimal Places	1	
Input Mask		
Caption	Length (In)	
Default Value	0	
Validation Rule	<120	
Validation Text	Length must be less than 120"	
Required	No	
Indexed	No	

Figure 7-12: Property area for the Length Numeric field.

You can switch between the field entry area and the property area by pressing F6. You can also move between panes simply by clicking on the desired pane. Some properties will display a list of possible values, along with a downward-pointing arrow, when you move the pointer into the field. When you click on the arrow, the values appear in a drop-down list.

Here is a list of all the general properties (note that they may not all be displayed, depending on which data type you chose):

Field Size	Text: limits size of the field to the specified number of characters (1-255); default is 50
Numeric	Allows specification of numeric type
Format	Changes the way data appears after you enter it (upper-case, dates, and so on)
Input Mask	Used for data entry into a predefined and validated for-mat (Phone Numbers, ZIP Codes, Social Security Numbers, Dates, Custom IDs)
Decimal Places	Specifies number of decimal places (Numeric/Currency only)
Caption	Optional label for form and report fields (replacing the field name)
Default Value	The value filled in automatically for new data entry into the field
Validation Rule	Validates data based on rules created through expres-sions or macros
Validation Text	Displays a message when data fails validation
Required	Specifies whether you must enter a value into a field
Allow Zero Length	Determines whether you may enter the value " " into a text field type to distinguish it from a null value
Indexed	Speeds up data access and (if desired) limits data to unique values

Entering field-size properties

Field Size has two purposes. For text fields, it simply specifies the storage and dis-play size. For example, the field size for the Pet ID field is 8 bytes. You should enter the size for each field with a Text data type. If you don't change the default field size, Access will use a 50-byte size for each text field in every record. You should limit the size to the value equal to the largest number of characters.

For Numeric data types, the field size enables you to further define the type of number, which in turn determines the storage size. Figure 7-12 shows the property area for the Length numeric field. There are five possible settings in the Numeric Field Size property, as described in Table 7-3.

	Table 7-3 Numeric Field Settings		
Field Size Setting	*Range*	*Decimal Places*	*Storage Size*
Byte	0 to 255	None	1 byte
Integer	-32,768 to 32,767	None	2 bytes
Long Integer	-2,147,483,648 to 2,147,483,647	None	4 bytes
Double	-1.797×10^{308} to 1.797×10^{308}	15	8 bytes
Single	-3.4×10^{38} to 3.4×10^{38}	7	4 bytes
Replication ID	N/A	N/A	16 bytes

You should make the field size the smallest one possible; Access runs faster with smaller field sizes. Note that the first three settings don't use decimal points, but allow increasingly larger positive or negative numbers. The last two choices permit even larger numbers: Single gives you 7 decimal places, and Double allows 15. Use the Double setting when you need many decimal places or very large numbers.

Tip Remember: Use the Currency data type to define data that stores monetary amounts.

Using formats

Formats allow you to display your data in a form that differs from the actual keystrokes used to enter the data originally. Formats vary, depending on the data type you use. Some data types have predefined formats, others have only user-defined formats, and some types have both. Formats affect only the way your data appears, not how it is actually stored in the table or how it should be entered.

Text and Memo data-type formats

Access uses four user-defined format symbols in Text and Memo data types:

@   Required text character (character or space)

&   Text character not required

<   Forces all characters to lowercase

>   Forces all characters to uppercase

The symbols @ and & work with individual characters you input, but the < and > characters affect the whole entry. If you want to make sure that a name is always displayed as uppercase, for example, you enter > in the Format property. If you want to enter a phone number and allow entry of only the numbers, yet display the data with parentheses and a dash, you enter the following into the Format property: **(@@@)@@@-@@@@**. You can then enter **2035551234** and have the data displayed as (203)555-1234.

Number and Currency data type formats

You can choose from six predefined formats for Numeric or Currency formats, and many symbols for creating your own custom formats. The predefined formats are as shown in Table 7-4, along with a column showing how to define custom formats.

Table 7-4
Numeric Format Examples

Format Type	Number as Entered	Number as Displayed	Format Defined
General	987654.321	987654.321	######.###
Currency	987654.321	$987,654.32	$###,##0.00
Fixed	987654.321	987654.321	######.###
Standard	987654.321	987,654.321	###,###.###
Percent	.987	98.7%	###.##%
Scientific	987654.321	9.87654321E+05	#.####E+00

Date/Time data-type formats

The Date/Time data formats are the most extensive of all, giving you these seven predefined options:

General Date	(Default) Display depends on the value entered; entering only a date will display only a date; entering only time will result in no date displayed; standard format for date and time is 2/10/93 10:32 PM
Long Date	Taken from Windows Regional Settings Section Long Date setting; example: Wednesday, February 10, 1993
Medium Date	Example: 10-Feb-93
Short Date	Taken from Windows Regional Settings Section Short Date setting; example: 2/10/93

Long Time	Taken from Windows Regional Settings Section Time setting; example: 10:32:15 PM
Medium Time	Example: 10:32 PM
Short Time	Example: 22:32

You can also use a multitude of user-defined date and time settings, including the following:

: (colon)	Time separator; taken from Windows Regional Settings Section Separator setting
/	Date separator
c	Same as General Date format
d, dd	Day of the month — 1 or 2 numerical digits (1 – 31)
ddd	First three letters of the weekday (Sun – Sat)
dddd	Full name of the weekday (Sunday – Saturday)
ddddd	Same as Short Date format
dddddd	Same as Long Date format
w	Day of the week (1 – 7)
ww	Week of the year (1 – 53)
m, mm	Month of the year — 1 or 2 digits (1 – 12)
mmm	First three letters of the month (Jan – Dec)
mmmm	Full name of the month (January – December)
q	Date displayed as quarter of the year (1 – 4)
y	Number of the day of the year (1 – 366)
yy	Last two digits of the year (01 – 99)
yyyy	Full year (0100 – 9999)
h, hh	Hour — 1 or 2 digits (0 – 23)
n, nn	Minute — 1 or 2 digits (0 – 59)
s, ss	Seconds — 1 or 2 digits (0 – 59)
ttttt	Same as Long Time format
AM/PM or A/P	Twelve-hour clock with AM/PM in uppercase as appropriate
am/pm or a/p	Twelve-hour clock with am/pm in lowercase as appropriate
AMPM	Twelve-hour clock with forenoon/afternoon designator, as defined in the Windows Regional Settings Section forenoon/afternoon setting

Yes/No data-type formats

Access stores Yes/No data in a manner different from what you might expect. The Yes data is stored as a –1, whereas No data is stored as a 0. You'd expect it to be stored as a 0 for No, with a 1 for Yes, but this simply isn't the case. Without a format setting, you must enter –1 or 0, and it will be stored and displayed that way. With formats, you can store Yes/No data types in a more recognizable manner. The three predefined format settings for Yes/No data types are as follows:

Yes/No   (Default) Displays –1 as Yes, 0 as No

True/False   Stores –1 as True, 0 as False

On/Off   Stores –1 as On, 0 as Off

You can also enter user-defined formats. User-defined Yes/No formats have two to three sections. The first section is always a semicolon (;). Use the second section for the –1 (Yes) values, and the last section for the 0 (No) values. If (for example) you want to use the values Neutered for Yes and Fertile for No, you enter **";Neutered;Fertile"**. You can also specify a color to display different values. To display the Neutered value in red and the Fertile value in green, you enter **";Neutered[Red];Fertile[Green]"**.

NEW FEATURE

Hyperlink data-type format

Access displays and stores Hyperlink data in a manner different than what you would expect. The format of this type can be comprised of up to three parts:

Display Text   The visual text that is displayed in the field or control

Address   The path to a file (URC) or page (URL) on the Internet

Sub-Address   A specific location within a file or page

The parts are separated by pound signs. The Display Text will be visible in the field or control, while the address and sub-address will be hidden. For example, **Microsoft Net Home Page#http://www.msn.com**.

Entering formats

The Pets table uses several formats. Several of the text fields have a > in the Format property to display the data entry in uppercase. The Date of Birth field has an *mmm yy* display of the date of birth as the short month name, a space, and a two-digit year (Feb 90).

Numeric custom formats can vary, based on the value. You can enter a four-part format into the Format property. The first part is for positive numbers, the second for negatives, the third if the value is 0, and the last if the value is null — for example, **#,##0;(#,##0);"- -";"None"**.

Table 7-5, for example, shows several formats.

Table 7-5
Format Examples

Format Specified	Data as Entered	Formatted Data as Displayed
>	Adam Smith	ADAM SMITH
#,##0;(#,##0);"-0-";"None"	15 -15 0 No Data	15 (15) -0- None
Currency	12345.67	$12,345.67
"Acct No. "0000	3271	Acct No. 3271
mmm yy	9/11/93	Sep 93
Long Date	9/11/93	Friday, September 11, 1993

Entering input masks

Input masks allow you to have more control over data entry by defining data-validation placeholders for each character you enter into a field. For example, if you set the property to **(999)000-0000**, parentheses and hyphens appear as shown, and an underscore (_) appears in place of each 9 or 0 of this phone number template. You would see (_) in your data entry field. Access will automatically add a \ character before each placeholder; an example would be **\(999\)000\-0000**. You can also enter a multipart input mask, for example **(999)000-0000!;0;" "**. The input mask can contain up to three parts separated by semicolons.

The first part of a multipart mask specifies the input mask itself (for example, (999) 000-0000!). The ! is used to fill the input mask from right to left when optional characters are on the left side. The second part specifies whether Microsoft Access stores the literal display characters in the table when you enter data. If you use 0 for this part, all literal display characters (for example, the parentheses and hyphen) are stored with the value; if you enter 1 or leave this part blank, only characters typed into the text box are stored. The third part specifies the character that Microsoft Access displays for spaces in the input mask. You can use any character; the default is an underscore. If you want to display a space, use a space enclosed in quotation marks (" ").

Note   When you have defined an input mask and set the Format property for the same data, the Format property takes precedence when Access displays the data. This means that even if you've saved an input mask with data, it is ignored when data is formatted.

Some of the characters that can be used are shown in Table 7-6.

<table>
<tr><td colspan="2" align="center">Table 7-6
Input Mask Characters</td></tr>
<tr><td>*Character*</td><td>*Description*</td></tr>
<tr><td>0</td><td>Digit (0-9, entry required, plus [+] and minus [–] signs not allowed)</td></tr>
<tr><td>9</td><td>Digit or space (entry not required, [+] and [–] not allowed)</td></tr>
<tr><td>#</td><td>Digit or space (entry not required, blanks converted to spaces, [+] and [-] allowed)</td></tr>
<tr><td>L</td><td>Letter (A–Z, entry required)</td></tr>
<tr><td>?</td><td>Letter (A–Z, entry optional)</td></tr>
<tr><td>A</td><td>Letter or digit (entry required)</td></tr>
<tr><td>a</td><td>Letter or digit (entry optional)</td></tr>
<tr><td>&</td><td>Any character or a space (entry required)</td></tr>
<tr><td>C</td><td>Any character or a space (entry optional)</td></tr>
<tr><td><</td><td>Causes all characters that follow to be converted to lowercase</td></tr>
<tr><td>></td><td>Causes all characters that follow to be converted to uppercase</td></tr>
<tr><td>!</td><td>Causes input mask to fill from right to left, rather than from left to right, when characters on the left side of the input mask are optional. You can include the exclamation point anywhere in the input mask.</td></tr>
<tr><td>\</td><td>Causes the character that follows to be displayed as the literal character (for example, \A appears as just A)</td></tr>
<tr><td>.,:;-/</td><td>Decimal placeholder, thousands, and date time separator determined by Regional Settings section of the Control Panel</td></tr>
</table>

Tip Setting the Input Mask property to the word **Password** creates a password entry text box. Any character typed in the text box is stored as the character, but appears as an asterisk (*).

The Input Mask Wizard

If you are creating a common input mask, you should use the Input Mask Wizard instead of setting the property to create the mask. When you click on the Input Mask property, the builder button (three periods) appears. You can click on the Build button to start the Wizard.

Figure 7-13 shows the first screen of the Input Mask Wizard. The Wizard shows not only the name of each predefined input mask, but also an example for each name. You can choose from the list of predefined masks; click on the Try It text box to see how data entry will look. Once you choose an input mask, the next Wizard screen lets you customize it and determine the placeholder symbol. Another Wizard screen lets you decide whether to store any special characters with the data. When you complete the Wizard, Access places the actual input mask characters in the property sheet.

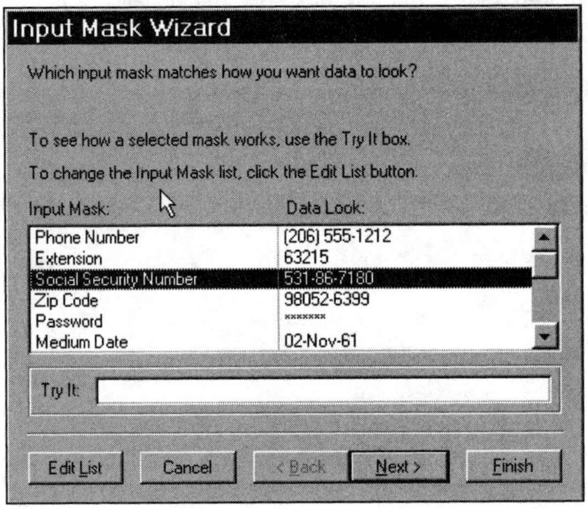

Figure 7-13: The Input Mask Wizard.

You can also enter as many custom masks as you need, and even determine the international settings so you can work with multiple country masks.

Entering decimal places

Decimal places are valid only for Numeric or Currency data. The number of decimal places can be from 0 to 15, depending on the field size of the numeric or currency field. If the field size is Byte, Integer, or Long Integer, you can have 0 decimal places. If the field size is Single, you can enter from 0 to 7 for the Decimal Places property. If the field size is Double, you can enter from 0 to 15 for the Decimal Places property. If you define a field as Currency (or use one of the predefined formats, such as General, Fixed, or Standard), Access sets the number of decimal places to 2 automatically. You can override this setting by entering a different value into the Decimal Places property.

Creating a caption

You use *captions* when you want to display an alternative to the field name on forms and reports. Normally, the label used to describe a field in a form or a report is the field name. Sometimes, however, you want to call the field name one thing while displaying a more (or less) descriptive label. You should keep field names as short as possible, which makes it easier to use them in calculations. You may then want a longer name to be used for a label in forms or reports. For example, you may use the field name Length but want the label Length (in) on all forms.

Setting a default value

A *default value* is the one Access displays automatically for the field when you add a new record to the table. This value can be any value that matches the data type of the field. A default is no more than an initial value; you can change it during data entry. To enter a default value, simply enter the desired value into the Default Value property setting. A default value can be an expression, as well as a number or a text string. See Chapter 13 to learn how to create expressions.

Note Numeric and Currency data types are set automatically to 0 when you add a new record.

Understanding data validation

Data validation enables you to limit the values that will be accepted into a field. Validation may be automatic, such as the checking of a numeric field for text or a valid date. Validation can also be user-defined. User-defined validation can be as simple as a range of values (such as those found in the Length or Weight fields), or it can be an expression like the one found in the Gender field.

Figure 7-12 (shown earlier) displays the property area for the Length field. Notice the validation options for the Length field. The Validation Rule <120 specifies that the number entered must be less than 120. The Validation Text Length must be less than 120" appears in a warning dialog box (see Figure 7-14) if a user tries to enter a length greater than 120.

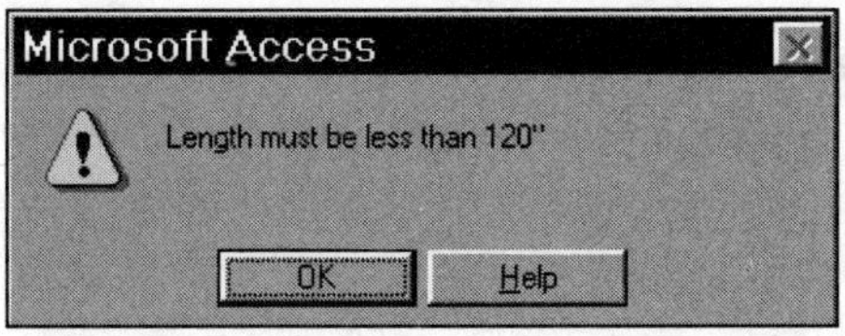

Figure 7-14: A data-validation warning box.

You can also use Date values with Date/Time data types in range validation. Dates are surrounded, or *delimited*, by pound signs when used in data-validation expressions. If you want to limit the Date of Birth data entry to dates between January 1, 1980, and December 31, 1996, you enter **Between #1/1/80# and #12/31/96#**.

If you want to limit the upper end to the current date, you can enter a different set of dates, such as **Between #1/1/80# and Date( )**.

The Gender field contains a validation rule based on an expression. The Gender field validation rule is to limit the data entry to three values: M for Male, F for Female, and U for Unknown. The validation rule for this is `InStr("MFU",[Gender])>0`. The expression `InStr` means Access must validate that the entry is in the string specified.

Following the design displayed in Figure 7-15, you should now be able to complete all the property areas in the Pets database. You can also find this database (and others you see throughout this book) in the Mountain Animal Start and Mountain Animal Hospital files on the disk that accompanies this book.

Pets Table Properties

Field Name	Field Size	Format	Input Mask	Caption	Default Value	Validation Rule	Validation Text	Required	Allow Zero Length	Index
Pet ID	8		LL000-00;0					Yes		Yes
Customer Number	10							Yes		No
Pet Name	35									No
Type of Animal	20									No
Breed	20									No
Date of Birth		mmm yy				#1/1/70 - DATE()	Date of Birth is Invalid	Yes		No
Gender	7	>@				M, F, U	Value must be M, F, or U			No
Colors	50									No
Neutered Spayed					No					No
Length	Single	Standard 1 decimal		Length(In)	0	< 120	Length must be less than 120"			No
Weight	Single	Standard 1 decimal		Weigth(lbs)	0	0 - 1500	Weight must be less than 1500lbs			No
Last Visit Date										No
Current Vaccinations										No
Deceased										No
Picture										No
Comments										No

Figure 7-15: Properties for the Pets table.

Understanding the Lookup Property window

Figure 7-16 shows the Lookup Property window for a yes/no field. There is only one property named Display Control. As you can see in the figure, this property has three choices: Text Box, Check Box, and Combo Box. Choosing one of these determines the default control type when a particular field appears on a form. Previous versions of Access created all controls as text boxes; this is still the default. For Yes/No data types, however, you'll probably want to use the Check Box setting. If you know a certain text field can only be one of a few combinations, you may want to use a combo box. When you select the combo-box control type as a default, the properties change to allow you to define a combo box.

Cross-Reference You will learn about combo boxes in Chapter 19.

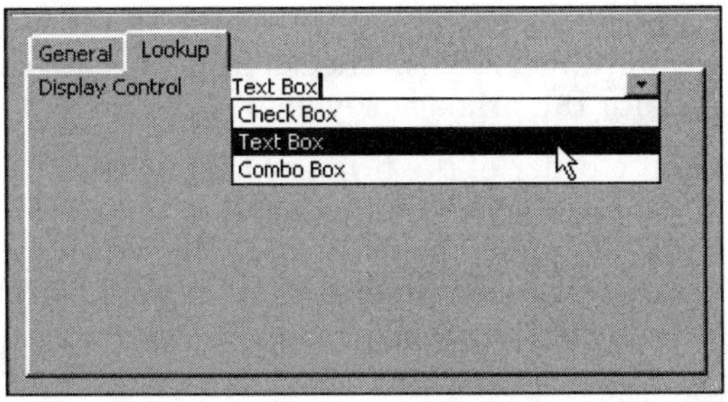

Figure 7-16: The Lookup properties for a field.

Note The properties for a lookup field are different. Because a lookup field is really a combo box (you'll learn more about these later), you will see the standard properties for a combo box when you select a Lookup field data type.

Determining the Primary Key

Every table should have a *primary key* — one or more fields that make a record unique. (This principle is called *entity integrity* in the world of database management.) In the Pets table, the Pet ID field is the primary key. Each pet has a different Pet ID field so you can tell one from another. If you don't specify a unique value, Access creates one for you.

Creating a unique key

Cross-Reference Without the Pet ID field, you'd have to rely on another field for uniqueness. You couldn't use the Pet Name field because two customers could have pets with the same name. You could use the Customer Number and Pet Name fields as a multiple-field key, but theoretically it's possible a customer could have two pets, each with the exact same name and even some of the same characteristics (such as Type of Animal and Breed). You will see a multiple-field primary key in Chapter 12.

If you don't designate a field as a primary key, Access creates an AutoNumber field and adds it to the beginning of the table. This field will contain a unique number for each record in the table, and Access will maintain it automatically. For several reasons, however, you may want to create and maintain your own primary key:

✦ A primary key is an index.

✦ Indexes maintain a presorted order of one or more fields that greatly speeds up queries, searches, and sort requests.

✦ When you add new records to your table, Access checks for duplicate data and doesn't allow any duplicates for the primary key field.

✦ Access will display your data in the order of the primary key.

By designating a field such as Pet ID as the unique primary key, you can see your data in an order you'll understand. In our example, the Pet ID field is made up of the owner's customer number followed by a dash and a two-digit sequence number. If the Adams family (for example) is the first customer on our list of those whose last name begins with AD, their customer number is AD001. If they have three pets, their Pet IDs will be designated AD001-01, AD001-02, and AD001-03. This way, the Pet ID field shows our data in the alphabetical order of customers by using the first two letters of their last name as a customer number.

Creating the primary key

You can create the primary key in any of four ways:

✦ Select the field to be used as the primary key and choose Edit➪Primary Key.

✦ Select the field to be used as the primary key and select the Primary Key button (the key icon) in the toolbar.

✦ Right-click the mouse to display the shortcut menu and select Primary Key.

✦ Save the table without creating a primary key, and Access will create an AutoNumber field for you.

Before you click on the key icon or select the menu choice, you must click on the gray area in the far left side of the field you want as the primary key. A right-pointing triangle appears. After you select the primary key, a key appears in the gray area to indicate that the primary key has been created.

The Indexes window

A primary key is really an *index*. Notice the key icon in the Pet ID column, indicating that this is the primary key for the table. You can also see the primary key by looking at the Indexes window. (Figure 7-17 shows a primary key entered into the Indexes window.) You can display or remove this sheet from sight by toggling the Indexes button on the toolbar.

You can determine whether an index is a primary key, whether or not it is unique, and whether null values should be ignored.

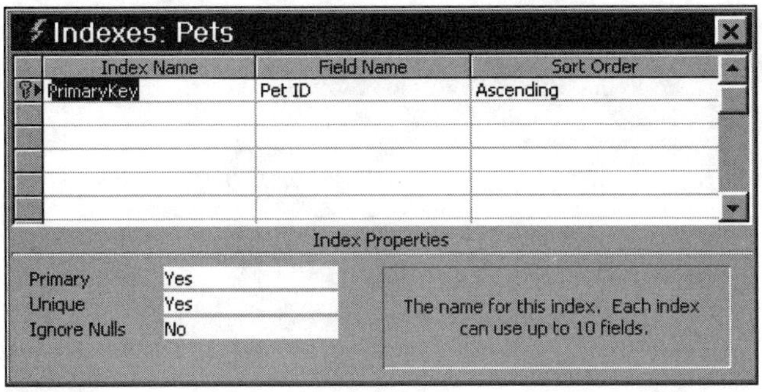

Figure 7-17: Working with indexes and primary keys.

The Table Properties window

Just as each field has a property area, the overall table has one too. Figure 7-18 shows the Table Properties window. Here you can enter a validation rule and message that are applied when you save a record. You can also set up a default sorting order (other than by primary key), and even a default filter to only show a subset of the data.

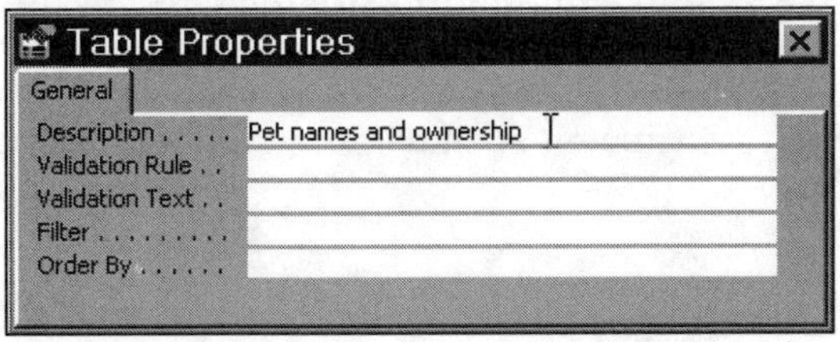

Figure 7-18: Setting general Table properties.

Printing a Table Design

You can print a table design by using Tools⇨Analyze⇨Documenter. The *Database Documenter* is a tool included with Access for Windows 95 to make it easy to explore your database objects. When you select this menu item, Access shows you a form that lets you select objects to analyze. In Figure 7-19, there is only one object, the Pets table.

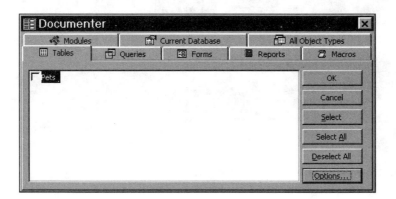

Figure 7-19: The Access Documenter form.

You can also set the various options for printing. When you click on the Options button, a dialog box appears that lets you select what information from the Table Design to print. You can print the various field names, all their properties, the indexes, and even network permissions.

Once you select which data you want to view, Access generates a report; you can view it in a Print Preview window or send the output to a printer.

Tip   The Database Documenter creates a table of all the objects and object properties you specify. You can use this utility to document such database objects as forms, queries, reports, macros, and modules.

Saving the Completed Table

You can save the completed table design by choosing File⇨Save or by clicking on the Save icon in the toolbar. If you are saving the table for the first time, Access will ask you the name of the table; enter it and click on OK. Table names can be up to 64 characters long, and follow standard Access field-naming conventions. If you have saved this table before and want to save it with a different name, choose

File⇨Save As and enter a different table name. You will create a new table design and still leave the original table with its original name untouched. If you want to delete the old table, select it in the Database window and press Delete. You can also save the table when you close it.

Manipulating Tables in a Database Window

As you create many tables in your database, you may want to use them in other databases or copy them for use as a history file. You may want to copy only the table structure. You can perform many operations on tables in the Database window, including the following:

✦ Renaming tables

✦ Deleting tables

✦ Copying tables in a database

✦ Copying a table from another database

You can perform these tasks both by direct manipulation and by using menu items.

Renaming tables

You can rename a table with the following steps:

1. Select the table name in the Database window.

2. Click once on the table name.

3. Type the name of the new table and press Enter.

You can also rename the table by selecting Edit⇨Rename or by right-clicking on a table and selecting Rename from the shortcut menu. After you change the table name, it appears in the Tables list, which re-sorts the tables in alphabetical order.

Caution If you rename a table, you must change the table name in any objects where it was previously referenced, including queries, forms, and reports.

Deleting tables

You can delete a table by simply selecting the table name and then pressing the Delete key. Another method is to select the table name and then select Edit⇨Delete or by right-clicking on a table and selecting Delete from the shortcut menu. Like most delete operations, you have to confirm the delete by selecting Yes in a Delete Table dialog box.

Copying tables in a database

By using the Copy and Paste options from the Edit menu or the toolbar icons, you can copy any table in the database. When you paste the table back into the database, you can choose from three option buttons:

✦ Structure Only

✦ Structure and Data

✦ Append Data to Existing Table

Selecting the Structure Only button creates a new table design with no data. This allows you to create an empty table with all the same field names and properties as the original table. You typically use this option to create a temporary table or a history structure to which you can copy old records.

When you select Structure and Data, you create a complete copy of the table design and all its data.

Selecting the button Append Data to Existing Table adds the data of one table to the bottom of another. This option is useful for combining tables, as when you want to add data from a monthly transaction table to a yearly history table.

The following steps show how to copy a table:

1. Select the table name in the Database window.

2. Select Edit⇨Copy.

3. Select Edit⇨Paste.

4. Type the name of the new table.

5. Choose one of the Paste Options.

6. Click on OK to complete the operation.

Figure 7-20 shows the Paste Table As dialog box, where you make these decisions. To paste the data, you have to select the type of paste operation and type the name of the new table. When you are appending data to an existing table, you must type the name of an existing table.

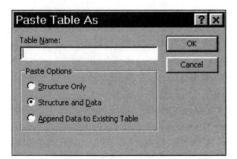

Figure 7-20: Pasting a table.

Copying a table to another database

Just as you can copy a table within a database, you can copy a table to another database. There are many reasons why you may want to do this. Possibly you share a common table among multiple systems, or you may need to create a back-up copy of your important tables within the system.

When you copy tables to another database, the relationships between tables are not copied; Access copies only the table design and the data. The method for copying a table to another database is essentially the same as for copying a table within a database. To copy a table to another database, follow these steps:

1. Select the table name in the Database window.
2. Select Edit⇨Copy.
3. Open another database.
4. Select Edit⇨Paste.
5. Type the name of the new table.
6. Choose one of the Paste Options.
7. Click on OK to complete the operation.

Summary

In this chapter, you learned about creating database tables by creating a database window and then examining the types of fields and properties you will typically use in a table. The following points were covered:

✦ Databases contain objects, such as tables, queries, forms, reports, macros, and modules.

✦ You can create a table by using a Datasheet View, Design View, Table Wizard, Import Table Wizard, or Link Table Wizard.

✦ Table designs consist of field names, data types, and descriptions.

✦ You can choose from ten basic data types: Text, Number, Currency, AutoNumber, Date/Time, Yes/No, Memo, OLE, Hyperlink, and Lookup Wizard.

✦ Each field has properties: Field Size, Format, Caption, Default Value, Validation Rule, Validation Text, and Indexed.

✦ Each table has a primary key field, which is an index and must contain a unique value for each record.

✦ When a table design is complete, you can still rearrange, insert, delete, and rename fields.

✦ You can rename, delete, or copy and paste tables in the Database window.

The next step is to input data into your table, which you can do in a variety of ways. In the next chapter, you learn how to use a datasheet to input your data.

✦   ✦   ✦

Entering, Changing, Deleting, and Displaying Data

In this chapter, you continue to use a datasheet to put data into a Microsoft Access table. This method enables you to see many records at once, as well as many of your fields. Using the Pets table created in the preceding chapter, you learn how to add, change, and delete data, and you learn about features for displaying data in a datasheet.

Understanding Datasheets

Using a datasheet is one of the many ways you can view data in Access. Datasheets display a list of records in a format commonly known as a browse screen in dBASE, a table view in Paradox, and a spreadsheet in Excel or 1-2-3. A datasheet is like a table or spreadsheet in that data is displayed as a series of rows and columns. Figure 8-1 shows a typical datasheet view of data. Like a table or spreadsheet, a datasheet displays data as a series of rows and columns. By scrolling the datasheet up or down, you can see records that don't fit on-screen at that moment, and by scrolling left or right, you can see more columns.

Datasheets are completely customizable, so you can look at your data in many ways. By changing the font size, you can see more or less of your table on-screen. You can rearrange the order of the records or the fields. You can hide columns, change the displayed column width or row height, and even lock several columns in position so they continue to be displayed as you scroll around other parts of your datasheet.

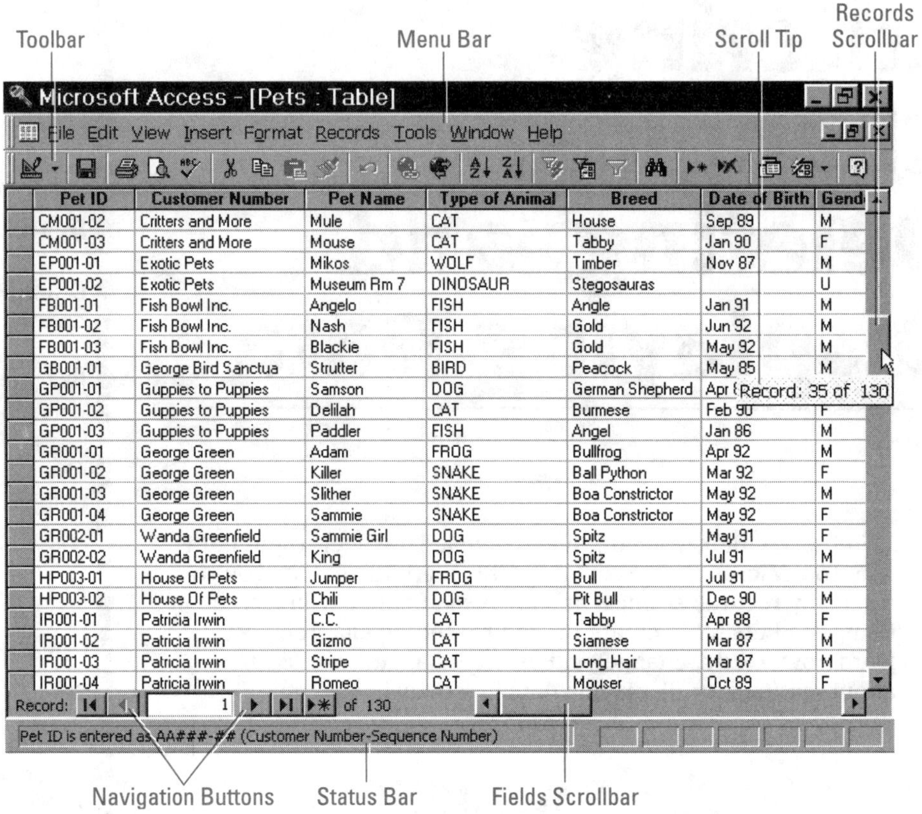

Toolbar   Menu Bar   Scroll Tip   Records Scrollbar

Pet ID	Customer Number	Pet Name	Type of Animal	Breed	Date of Birth	Gend
CM001-02	Critters and More	Mule	CAT	House	Sep 89	M
CM001-03	Critters and More	Mouse	CAT	Tabby	Jan 90	F
EP001-01	Exotic Pets	Mikos	WOLF	Timber	Nov 87	M
EP001-02	Exotic Pets	Museum Rm 7	DINOSAUR	Stegosauras		U
FB001-01	Fish Bowl Inc.	Angelo	FISH	Angle	Jan 91	M
FB001-02	Fish Bowl Inc.	Nash	FISH	Gold	Jun 92	M
FB001-03	Fish Bowl Inc.	Blackie	FISH	Gold	May 92	M
GB001-01	George Bird Sanctua	Strutter	BIRD	Peacock	May 85	M
GP001-01	Guppies to Puppies	Samson	DOG	German Shepherd	Apr 8 Record: 35 of 130	
GP001-02	Guppies to Puppies	Delilah	CAT	Burmese	Feb 90	F
GP001-03	Guppies to Puppies	Paddler	FISH	Angel	Jan 86	M
GR001-01	George Green	Adam	FROG	Bullfrog	Apr 92	M
GR001-02	George Green	Killer	SNAKE	Ball Python	Mar 92	F
GR001-03	George Green	Slither	SNAKE	Boa Constrictor	May 92	F
GR001-04	George Green	Sammie	SNAKE	Boa Constrictor	May 92	F
GR002-01	Wanda Greenfield	Sammie Girl	DOG	Spitz	May 91	F
GR002-02	Wanda Greenfield	King	DOG	Spitz	Jul 91	M
HP003-01	House Of Pets	Jumper	FROG	Bull	Jul 91	F
HP003-02	House Of Pets	Chili	DOG	Pit Bull	Dec 90	M
IR001-01	Patricia Irwin	C.C.	CAT	Tabby	Apr 88	F
IR001-02	Patricia Irwin	Gizmo	CAT	Siamese	Mar 87	M
IR001-03	Patricia Irwin	Stripe	CAT	Long Hair	Mar 87	M
IR001-04	Patricia Irwin	Romeo	CAT	Mouser	Oct 89	F

Record: 1 of 130

Pet ID is entered as AA###-## (Customer Number-Sequence Number)

Navigation Buttons   Status Bar   Fields Scrollbar

Figure 8-1: A typical datasheet.

You can sort the datasheet quickly into any order you desire with one toolbar button. You can filter the datasheet for specific records, making other records invisible. You can also import records directly to the datasheet, or export formatted records from the datasheet directly to Word, Excel, or other applications that support OLE 2.0.

The Datasheet Window

The Datasheet window is similar to other object windows in Access. At the top of the screen, you see the title bar, menu bar, and toolbar. The center of the screen displays your data in rows and columns. Each record occupies one row; each column, headed by a field name, contains that field's values. The display arranges the records initially by primary key, and the fields by the order of their creation in the table design.

The right side of the window contains a *scrollbar* for moving quickly between records. As you scroll between records, a Scroll Tip (shown in Figure 8-1) tells you precisely where the scrollbar will take you. In Access 97, the size of the scrollbar *thumb* gives you a proportional look at how many of the total number of records are being displayed. In Figure 8-1, the scrollbar thumb takes about 15 percent of the scroll area, and 20 of 130 records are shown onscreen. There is also a proportional scrollbar at the bottom of the screen for moving among fields.

The last line at the bottom of the screen contains a *status bar*. The status bar displays the Field Description you entered for each field in the table design. If there is no Field Description for a specific field, Access displays the words `Datasheet View`. Generally, error messages and warnings appear in dialog boxes in the center of the screen rather than in the status bar. If you need help understanding the meaning of a button in the toolbar, move the mouse over the button and a *tooltip* appears with a one- or two-word explanation, while the status bar displays a more comprehensive explanation.

Navigation inside a datasheet

You can move easily around the Datasheet window by using the mouse pointer to indicate where you want to change or add to your data: just click on a field and record location. In addition, the menus, toolbars, scrollbars, and navigation buttons make it easy to move among fields and records. You can think of a datasheet as a spreadsheet without the row numbers and column letters. Instead, your columns have field names, and your rows are unique records that have identifiable values in each cell.

Table 8-1 lists the navigational keys used for moving around within a datasheet.

Table 8-1 Navigating in a Datasheet	
Navigational Direction	*Keystrokes*
Next field	Tab
Previous field	Shift+Tab
First field of current record	Home
Last field of current record	End
Next record	Down arrow

(continued)

	Table 8-1 *(continued)*	
Navigational Direction	*Keystrokes*
Previous record	Up arrow
First field of first record	Ctrl+Home
Last field of last record	Ctrl+End
Scroll up one page	PgUp
Scroll down one page	PgDn
Go to record number box	F5

The navigation buttons

The *navigation buttons* (shown in Figure 8-2) are six controls used to move between records. You can simply click on these buttons to move to the desired record. The two leftmost controls move you to the first record or the previous record in the datasheet (table). The three rightmost controls position you on the next record, last record, or new record in the datasheet (table). If you know the *record number* (the row number of a specific record), you can click on the record number box, enter a record number, and press Enter.

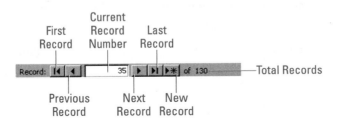

Figure 8-2: Navigation buttons.

Note If you enter a record number greater than the number of records in the table, an error message appears. The message states that you can't go to the specified record.

The Datasheet toolbar

The Datasheet toolbar (shown in Figure 8-3) provides another way for navigating around the datasheet. The toolbar has many familiar objects on it, as well as some new ones.

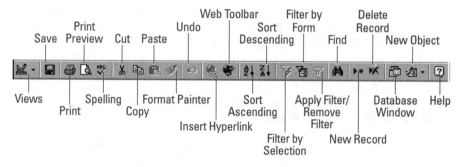

Figure 8-3: The Datasheet toolbar.

The first icon lets you switch between the Table Design and the Datasheet views. By clicking on the Table Design icon, you can make changes to the design of your table. You can then click on the Datasheet icon to return to the datasheet.

Note If you originally displayed a data-entry form, this icon will have three choices: Table Design, Datasheet, and Form.

The next icon, Save, saves any layout changes to the datasheet.

Caution Save does not allow you to roll back changes to the data. As you move from record to record, the data is forever changed.

The next set of three icons includes Print (which looks like a printer and sends your datasheet values to your printer) and Print Preview (which looks like a printed-page-with-magnifying-glass and shows you on-screen how your datasheet would look printed). The third icon lets you spell-check your data using the standard Microsoft Office spell-checking feature.

The objects you can paste include a single value, datasheet row, column, or range of values. You can copy and paste objects to and from other programs (such as Microsoft Word or Excel), but the Format Painter is not available in a datasheet.

The next icon lets you Undo a change to a record or (more globally) undo formatting.

NEW FEATURE The next two icons are the Internet icons. The first lets you insert a hyperlink, and the second displays the Web toolbar.

The next two icons are the QuickSort icons. You can select one or more columns and click on one of these buttons to sort the data instantly, in ascending or descending order, using the selected columns as the sorting criteria.

The next three icons in this toolbar look like funnels. They let you determine and display only selected records. The first icon, Filter by Selection, lets you filter records to match a specific highlighted value. Each time you highlight a value, you add the selection to the filter. This additive process continues until you clear the filter. (See the detailed discussion of this filter later in this chapter.) The second icon, Filter by Form, turns each column of data into a *combo box* where you can select a single value from the datasheet and filter for matching records. The last icon in the group turns any filters on or off.

The Find Specified Text icon is a pair of binoculars; you click on it to display a dialog box that lets you search for a specific value in a specific field. Clicking on the Database Window icon displays the Database window. The New Object icons give you pull-down menus so you can create new objects like tables, queries, forms, reports, macros, and modules. The last icon displays Small Card Help.

Opening a Datasheet

You can view your data in a datasheet in many ways. From the Database window, you should follow these steps:

1. Click on the Table tab.
2. Click on the table name you want to open. (In this example, it will be Pets.)
3. Click on Open.

An alternative method for opening the datasheet is to double-click on the Pets table name.

Tip   If you are in any of the design windows, you can click on the Datasheet button and view your data in a datasheet.

Entering New Data

When you open a datasheet, you see all the records in your table; if you just created your table design, you won't see any data in the new datasheet yet. Figure 8-4 shows an empty datasheet. When the datasheet is empty, the record pointer on the first record is displayed as a right-pointing triangle.

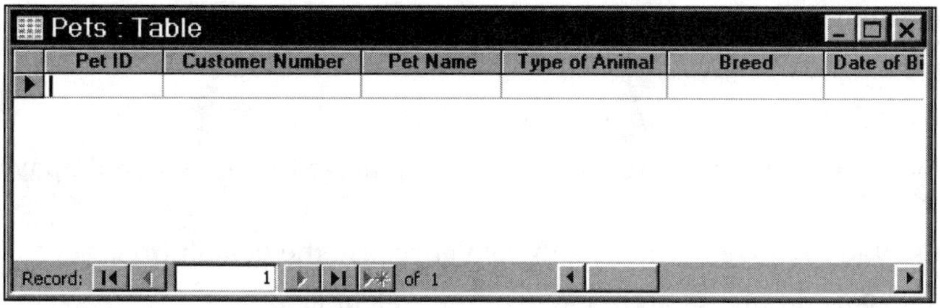

Figure 8-4: An empty datasheet.

You can enter a record into a datasheet field simply by moving the cursor to the field and typing the value. As you begin to edit the record, the record pointer turns into a pencil, indicating that the record is being edited. A second row also appears as you begin to enter the record; this row contains an asterisk in the record-pointer position, indicating a new record. The new-record pointer always appears in the last line of the datasheet; after you enter a record, all new records appear there as well.

The cursor generally starts in the first field of the table for data entry.

If you performed the steps in Chapter 7, you already have five partial records. If not, you have an empty datasheet. To enter or edit the first record in the Pets table, follow these steps. (A portion of the record is shown in Figure 8-5.)

1. Position the cursor in the Pet ID field.

2. Type **AC-001** and press Tab to move to the Customer Number field.

3. Type **AC001-01** and press Tab to move to the Pet Name field.

4. Type **Bobo** and press Tab to move to the Type of Animal field.

5. Type **RABBIT** and press Tab to move to the Breed field.

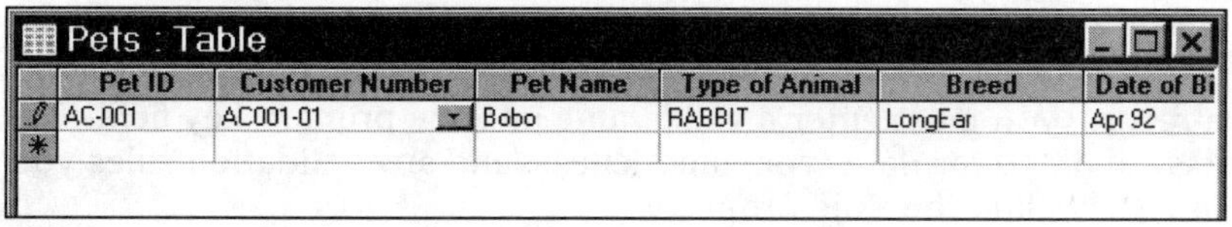

Figure 8-5: A record being entered into the datasheet.

6. Type **Long Ear** and press Tab to move to the Date of Birth field.

7. Type **4/8/92** and press Tab to move to the Gender field.

8. Press **M** and press Tab to move to the Colors field.

9. Type **Brown/Black/White** and press Tab to move to the Neutered/Spayed field.

10. Press Tab to move to the Length field (because the default No is acceptable).

11. Type **20.0** and press Tab to move to the Weight field.

12. Type **3.1** and press Tab twice to move to the Current Vaccination field.

13. Type **Yes** (over the default No) and press Tab three times to move to the Comments field.

14. Once in the Comments field, press Shift+F2 to open the Zoom window.

15. While in the Zoom window, type **Bobo is a great looking rabbit. He was originally owned by a nature center and was given to the pet store for sale to a loving family. Bobo was in good health when he arrived and was returned to the pet store for sale**.

16. Press Enter to move to the Pet ID field of the second record.

While adding or editing records, you may see four different record pointers:

✦ Current record

✦ Record being edited

✦ Record is locked (multi-user systems)

✦ New record

Saving the record

After you enter all the values in the record, normally you move to the next record. This action saves the record. Any time you move to a different record or close the table, the last record you worked with is written to the database. You'll see the record pointer change from a pencil to a right-pointing triangle.

To save a record, you must enter a valid value into the primary key field. The primary key is validated for data type, uniqueness, and any validation rules you entered into the Validation Rule property.

Tip   The Undo Current Field/Record icon in the toolbar will undo changes to only the current record. After you move to the next record, you must use the regular Undo icon. After you change a second record, you cannot undo the first record.

Tip You can save the record to disk without leaving the record by selecting Records⇨Save Record or by pressing Shift+Enter.

Now that you've seen how to enter a record, you should understand what happened as you entered the first record. Next you learn about how Access validates your data as you make entries into the fields.

Understanding automatic data-type validation

Access validates certain types of data automatically, without any intervention. You don't have to enter any data-validation rules for these when you specify table properties. Data types that Access validates automatically include

✦ Number/Currency

✦ Date/Time

✦ Yes/No

Number or Currency fields allow only valid numbers to be entered into the field. Initially, Access will let you enter a letter into a Number field. When you move off the field, however, a dialog box appears with the message `The value you entered isn't appropriate for this data type or field size property for this field`. The same is true of any other inappropriate characters. If you try to enter more than one decimal point, you get the same message. If you enter a number too large for a certain Number data type, you will also get this message.

Date and Time fields are validated for valid date or time values. If you try to enter a date such as 14/45/90, a time such as 37:39:12, or a single letter in a Date/Time field, a dialog box will show you the error message `The value you entered isn't appropriate for this field`.

Yes/No fields require that you enter one of these defined values: Yes, True, 1, or a number other than 0 for Yes; or No, False, Off, or 0 for No. Of course, you can also define your own acceptable values in the Format property for the field, but generally these are the only acceptable values. If you try to enter an invalid value, the dialog box appears with the usual message to indicate an inappropriate value.

Using various data-entry techniques

Because field types vary, you use different data-entry techniques for each type. You have already learned that some data-type validation is automatic. Designing the Pets table, however, meant entering certain user-defined format and data-validation rules. The following sections examine the types of data entry.

Standard text data entry

The first five fields you entered in the Pets table were Text fields. You simply entered each value and moved on. The Pet ID field used an *input mask* for data entry. There wasn't any special formatting for the other fields. Note that if you enter a value in lowercase, it is displayed in uppercase. Text can be validated for specific values, and it can be displayed with format properties.

Tip   Sometimes you want to enter a Text field on multiple lines. You can press Ctrl+Enter to add a new line. This is useful (for example) in large text strings for formatting a multiple-line address field. It is also useful in Memo fields for formatting multiple-line entries.

Date/Time data entry

The Date of Birth field is a Date/Time data type, formatted using the *mmm yy* format. Thus, even though you typed **4/8/96**, Access displays the value Apr 96 when you leave the field. The value 4/8/96 is really stored in the table; you can display it whenever the cursor is in the Date of Birth field. As an alternative choice, you can enter the value in the format specified. You can enter **Apr 96** in the field, and the value Apr 96 will be stored in the table.

Cross-
Reference   Date of Birth also has the validation rule Between #1/1/70# And Date(), which means you can enter Date of Birth values only between January 1, 1970, and the current date.

Tip   Formats affect only the display of the data. They do not change storage of data in the table.

Text data entry with data validation

The Gender field of the Pets table has a data-validation rule entered for it in the Validation Rule property. This rule limits valid entries to M, F, or U. If you try to enter a value other than M, F, or U into the Gender field, a dialog box appears with the message Value must be M, F, or U, as shown in Figure 8-6. The message comes from the Validation Text property that was entered into the Pets table Gender field.

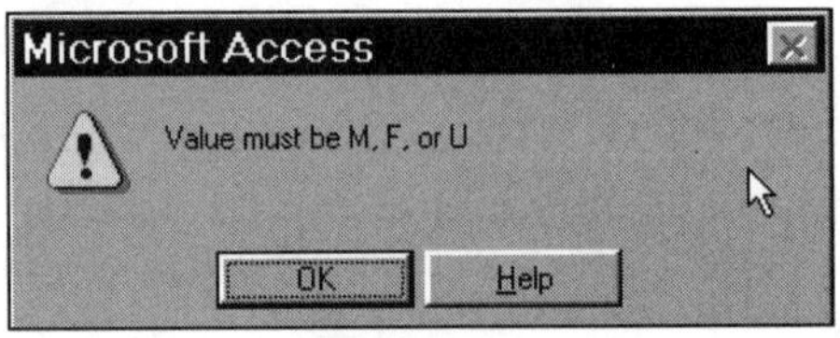

Figure 8-6: Dialog box for a data-validation message.

Numeric data entry with data validation

The Length and Weight fields both have validation rules. The Length field has a Validation Rule property to limit the size of the animal to a realistic length below 10 feet. The Weight field has a Validation Rule property to limit the weight of the animal to below 1,500 pounds. If either of the rules is violated, a dialog box appears with the validation text entered for the field. If an animal arrives that weighs more than 1,500 pounds or is more than 10 feet long, the validation rule can simply be changed in the table design.

OLE object data entry

The OLE data-type field named Picture can be entered into a datasheet, even though you don't see the picture of the animal. An OLE field can be many different items, including the following:

✦ Bitmap pictures

✦ Sound files

✦ Business graphs

✦ Word or Excel files

Any object that an OLE server supports can be stored in an Access OLE field. OLE objects are generally entered into a form so you can see, hear, or use the value. When OLE objects appear in datasheets, you see text that tells what the object is (for example, you might see `Paintbrush Picture` in the OLE field). You can enter OLE objects into a field in two ways:

✦ Pasting in from the Clipboard

✦ Inserting into the field from the Insert⇨Object menu dialog box

Cross-Reference For thorough coverage of using and displaying OLE objects, see Chapter 20.

Memo-field data entry

The last field in the table is Comments; it is a Memo data type. This type of field allows up to 64,000 characters of text for each field. Recall that you entered a long string (about 160 characters) into the Memo field. As you entered the string, however, you saw only a few characters at a time. The rest of the string scrolled out of sight. By pressing Shift+F2, you can display a *Zoom box* with a scrollbar (see Figure 8-7) that lets you see about 1,000 characters at a time.

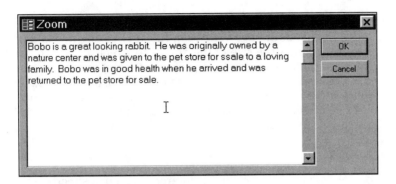

Figure 8-7: The Zoom box for a memo field.

Navigating Records in a Datasheet

If you are following along with the examples, you may want to use the Mountain Start database file now. For the remainder of this section, you'll work with all the data in the Pets table.

CD-ROM

Generally you will want to make changes to records after you enter them. You may want to change records for several reasons:

✦ You receive new information that changes existing values.

✦ You discover errors that change existing values.

✦ You need to add new records.

When you decide to edit data in a table, the first step is to open the table, if it is not open. From the Database window, open the Pets datasheet by double-clicking on Pets in the list of tables.

Note   If you are in any of the Design windows, you can click on the Datasheet button to make changes to the information within the table.

Moving between records

You can move to any record you want by simply scrolling through your records and positioning your cursor on the desired record. When your table is large, however, you probably want to get to a specific record as quickly as possible.

You can use the vertical scrollbar to move between records. The scrollbar arrows move the record pointer only one record at a time. You must use the scrollbar elevator (known as a thumb in Windows 95/NT) to move through many records at a time. You can also click on the area between the scrollbar elevator and the scrollbar arrows to move through many records at once.

The Edit⇨GoTo menu, shown open in Figure 8-8, contains several choices to help you quickly move around the worksheet.

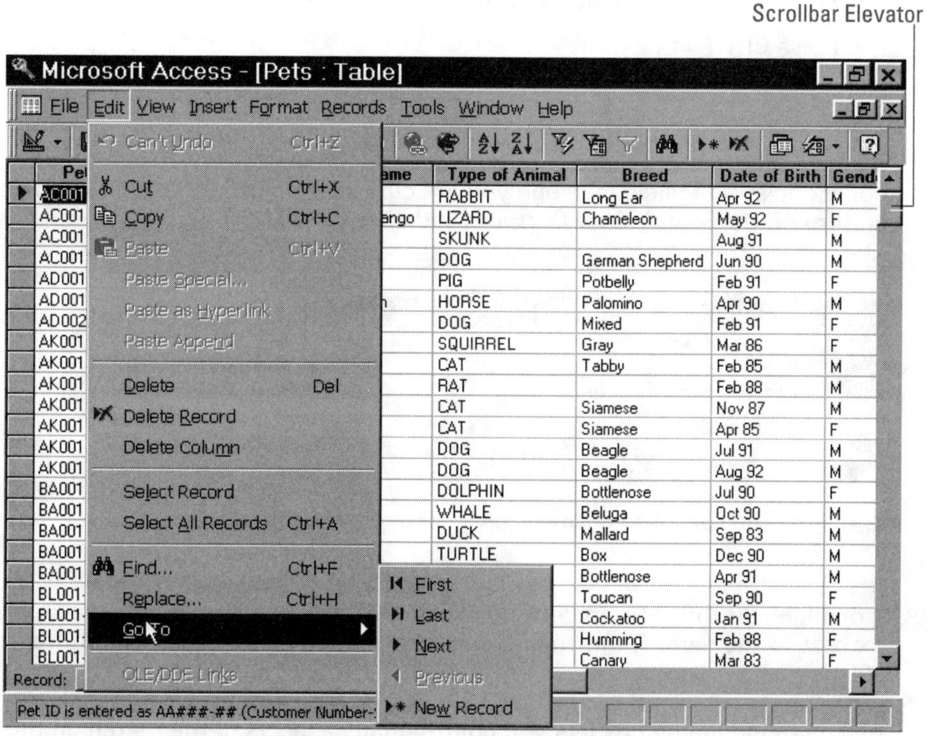

Figure 8-8: Moving between records.

The five navigation buttons, located along the bottom of the Datasheet window (also shown in Figure 8-4), can also be used for moving between records. You simply click on these buttons to move to the desired record. If you know the record number (row number of a specific record), you can click on the record number box, enter a record number, and press Enter. You can also press F5 to move to the record number box.

Tip

Watch the Scroll Tips when you use scrollbars to move to another area of the datasheet. Access does not update the record number box until you click on a field.

Finding a specific value

Although you can move to a specific record (if you know the record number) or to a specific field in the current record, most of the time you really want to find a certain value in a record. You can use three methods to locate a value in a field:

✦ Select Edit⇨Find.

✦ Select the Find Specified Text button in the toolbar (a pair of binoculars).

✦ Press Ctrl+F.

When you choose any of these methods, a dialog box appears (as shown in Figure 8-9). To limit the search to a specific field, make sure your cursor is on the field you want to use in the search before you open the dialog box. Access finds a value in only one specific field (the one you are currently pointing to) at a time unless you turn off the Search Only Current Field check box.

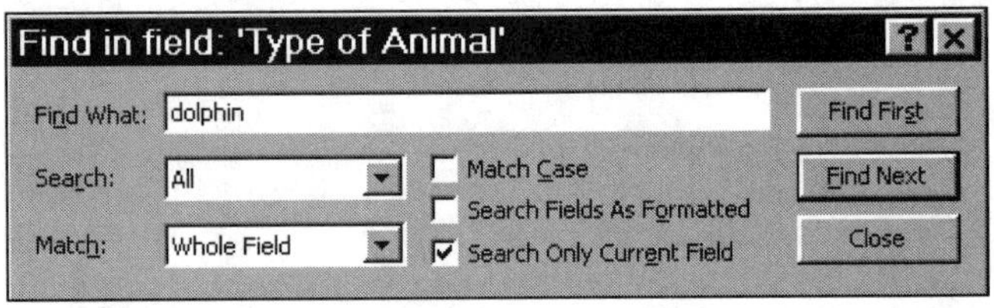

Find in field: 'Type of Animal'		
Find What:	dolphin	Find First
Search:	All ▼ ☐ Match Case ☐ Search Fields As Formatted	Find Next
Match:	Whole Field ▼ ☑ Search Only Current Field	Close

Figure 8-9: The Edit⇨Find dialog box.

Tip   If you highlight the entire record by clicking on the record selector (the small gray box next to the record) the Find dialog box will automatically search through all fields.

The Edit⇨Find dialog box lets you control many aspects of the search. In the Find What text box, you enter the value to be searched for. You can enter the value just as it appears in the field, or you can use three types of wildcards:

      *   Any number of characters

      ?   Any one character

      #   Any one number

To look at how these wildcards work, first suppose that you want to find any value beginning with AB; for this, you can enter **AB***. Then suppose that you want to search for values ending with 001, so you search for ***001**. To search for any value that begins with AB, ends with 001, and contains any two characters in between, you enter **AB??001**. If you want to search for any street number that ends in *th*, you can enter **#th** to find 5th or 8th. To find 5th or 125th, you can use ***th**.

The Match drop-down list contains three choices:

✦ Any Part of Field

✦ Whole Field

✦ Start of Field

The default is Whole Field. This option finds only the whole value you enter. For example, it finds the value SMITH only if the value in the field being searched is exactly SMITH. If you select Any Part of Field, Access searches to see whether the value is contained anywhere in the field; this search finds the value SMITH in the field values SMITHSON, HAVERSMITH, and ASMITHE. A search for SMITH using the Start of Field option searches from the beginning of the field, returning only values like SMITHSON. You can click on one or more of three choices (Up, Down, All) in the Search combo box.

The choice Search Only Current Field searches only a single field for the value. Unchecking this option searches all fields of the datasheet. Match Case determines whether the search is case-sensitive. The default is not case-sensitive. A search for SMITH finds smith, SMITH, or Smith. If you check the Match Case check box, you must then enter the search string in the exact case of the field value. (Obviously, the data types Number, Currency, and Date/Time do not have any case attributes.) If you have checked Match Case, Access does not use the value Search Fields as Formatted, which limits the search to the actual values displayed in the table. (If you format a field for display in the datasheet, you should check the box.) In the Date of Birth field, for example, you can accomplish a search for an animal born in April 1992 by checking the box and entering **Apr 92**. Without this entry, you must search for the exact date of birth, which may be 4/8/92.

Caution Using Search Fields as Formatted may slow the search process.

When you click on the Find First or Find Next button, the search begins. If Access finds the value, the cursor highlights it in the datasheet. To find the next occurrence of the value, you must click on the Find Next command button on the right side of the dialog box. You can also select Find First to find the first occurrence. The dialog box remains open so you can find multiple occurrences. When you find the value you want, select the Close command button to close the dialog box.

Changing Values in a Datasheet

Usually, you change values by simply moving to the value you want to change or edit. You edit a value for several reasons:

◆ Adding a new value

◆ Replacing an existing value

◆ Changing an existing value

If the field you are in has no value, you can simply type a new value into the field. When you enter any new values into a field, follow the same rules as for a new-record entry.

Replacing an existing value

Generally you enter a field with either no characters selected or the entire value selected. If you use the keyboard to enter a field, normally you select the entire value. (You know that the entire value is selected when it is displayed in reverse video.) You can erase a selected entire value by pressing any key, which replaces the value with that of the pressed key. Pressing Delete simply deletes the value without replacing it. Pressing the Spacebar erases the value and replaces it with a space.

To select the entire value with the mouse, you can use any of these methods:

◆ Click just to the left of the value when the cursor is shown as a large plus sign.

◆ Select any part of the value and double-click the mouse button. (This works most of the time unless there is a space in the text).

◆ Click to the left of the value, hold down the left mouse button, and drag the mouse to select the whole value.

◆ Select any part of the value and press F2.

Tip

You may want to replace an existing value with the default from the Default Value table property. To do so, select the value and press Ctrl+Alt+Spacebar.

If you want to replace an existing value with that of the same field from the preceding record, you can press Ctrl+" (quotation mark).

Caution

Be sure not to press Ctrl+– (hyphen) because the current record will be deleted.

Changing an existing value

If you want to change an existing value instead of replacing the entire value, you can use the mouse and click in front of any character in the field. When you position the mouse pointer in front of an individual character, you activate Insert mode; the existing value moves to the right as you type the new value. If you press Insert, your entry changes to Overstrike mode; you replace one character at a time as you type. You can use the arrow keys to move between characters without disturbing them. Erase characters to the left by pressing Backspace, or to the right of the cursor by pressing Delete.

Table 8-2 lists various editing techniques.

Table 8-2 Editing Techniques	
Editing Operation	**Keystrokes**
Move the insertion point within a field	Press the right- and left-arrow keys
Insert a value within a field	Select the insertion point and type new data
Select the entire field	Press F2 or double-click the mouse button
Replace an existing value with a new value	Select the entire field and type a new value
Replace a value with the value of the previous field	Press Ctrl+'
Replace the current value with the default value	Press Ctrl+Alt+Spacebar
Insert a line break in a Text or Memo field	Press Ctrl+Enter
Save the current record	Press Shift+Enter or move to another record
Insert the current date	Ctrl+; (semicolon)
Insert the current time	Ctrl+: (colon)
Add a new record	Ctrl++ (plus sign)
Delete the current record	Ctrl+– (minus sign)
Toggle values in a check box or option button	Spacebar
Undo a change to the current record	Press Esc or click on the Undo button

Fields that you can't edit

Some fields cannot be edited. These are the individual field types you cannot edit:

AutoNumber fields	Access maintains AutoNumber fields automatically, calculating the values as you create each new record. AutoNumber fields can be used as the primary key.
Calculated fields	Access creates calculated fields in forms or queries; these values are not actually stored in your table.
Locked or disabled fields	You can set certain properties in a form to disallow entry for a specific field. You can lock or disable a field when you designate Form properties.
Fields in multiuser locked records	If another user locks the record, you won't be able to edit any fields in that record.

Using the Undo Features

Often the Undo button is dimmed in Access so it can't be used. As soon as you begin editing a record, you can use this button to undo the typing in the current field. You can also undo a change with the Esc key; pressing Esc cancels either a changed value or the previously changed field. Pressing Esc twice will undo changes to the entire current record.

Several Undo menu commands and variations are available to undo your work. The following list shows how you can undo your work at various stages of completion:

Edit⇨Can't Undo	Undo is not available
Edit⇨Undo Typing	Cancels the most recent change to your data
Edit⇨Undo Current Field/Record	Cancels the most recent change to the current field. Cancels all changes to the current record
Edit⇨Undo Saved Record	Cancels all changes to last saved record

As you are typing a value into a field, you can select Edit⇨Undo or use the toolbar undo buttons to undo changes to that value. After you move to another field, you can undo the change to the preceding field's value by selecting Edit⇨Undo Current Field/Record or by using the Undo button. You can also undo all the changes to a current record that has not been saved by selecting Edit⇨Undo Current Field/ Record. After a record is saved, you can still undo the changes by selecting Edit⇨Undo Saved Record. However, after the next record is edited, changes are permanent.

Copying and Pasting Values

Copying or cutting data to the Clipboard is a Microsoft Windows 95/NT task; it is not actually a specific function of Access. After you cut or copy a value, you can paste it into another field or record by using Edit⇨Paste or the Paste button in the toolbar. Data can be cut, copied, or pasted from any Windows application or from one task to another in Access. Using this technique, you can copy entire records between tables or even databases, and you can copy datasheet values to and from Microsoft Word and Excel.

Globally Replacing Values

Just as you can find a specific value, you can replace one existing value with another. The Edit⇨Replace menu choice (or pressing Ctrl+H) gives you a dialog box you can use to replace values, as shown in Figure 8-10.

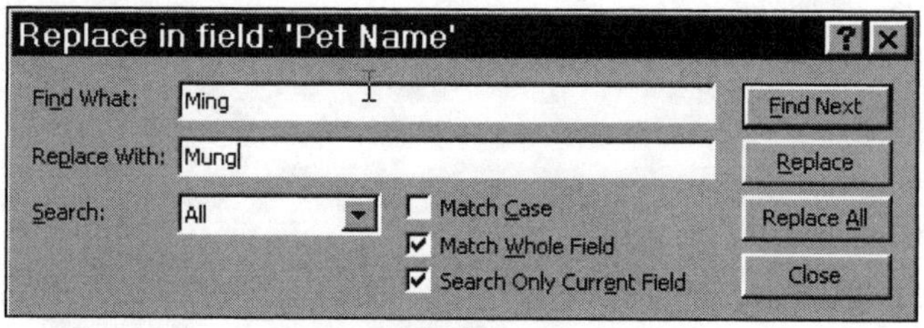

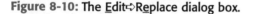

Figure 8-10: The Edit⇨Replace dialog box.

The Replace dialog box is very similar to the Find dialog box. In addition to the Find What text box, you see a Replace With text box that lets you enter not only the search string but also its replacement value. When you press Enter, the search begins. When Access finds the Find What value, the cursor highlights the value. Then you have to select Replace to change the value. If you want to change multiple occurrences, you can select Replace All; Access locates all remaining occurrences and replaces them.

Adding New Records

You add records to the datasheet by positioning the cursor on its last line (where the record pointer is an asterisk) and then entering the new record. There are many ways to go to a new record. You can also select Insert⇨Record or you can go directly to a new record by using the new-record button in the toolbar, the navigation button area, or the menu selection Edit⇨GoTo⇨New. Another way to move quickly to the new record is to go to the last record and press the down-arrow key.

Sometimes you want to add several new records and make all existing records temporarily invisible. The menu item Records⇨Data Entry will clear the screen temporarily of all records while you are editing new records. When you want to restore all records, select Records⇨Remove Filter/Sort.

Deleting Records

You can delete any number of records by selecting the record(s) and pressing the Delete key. You can also select the records and choose Edit⇨Delete or simply place your cursor in a record and select Edit⇨Delete Record. When you press Delete or choose the menu selection, you'll see a dialog box asking you to confirm the deletion (see Figure 8-11). The dialog box forces you to confirm the delete. If you select Yes, the records are deleted. If you select Cancel, no changes are made.

Figure 8-11: The Delete Record dialog box.

Caution   The Default value for this dialog box is Yes. Pressing the Enter key will automatically delete the records. If you accidentally erase records using this method, there is no way to reverse the action.

You can select multiple contiguous records. To do so, click on the record selector of the first record you want to select, and then drag the record-pointer icon (right-pointing arrow) to the last record you want to select.

Adding, Changing, and Deleting Columns

A very dangerous feature in Access 97 is the ability to add, delete, and rename columns in a datasheet. This feature actually changes the data design. When you go to the Table Design screen and make changes, you know you are changing the underlying structure of the data. Within a datasheet, however, you may not realize the consequences of changes you are making. If you are creating applications for others, you should not allow users to use a datasheet to make the changes described in this part of the book.

Deleting a column from a datasheet

You can delete a column from a datasheet by selecting one or more entire columns and then pressing the Delete key or by placing your cursor in one or more columns and selecting Edit⇨Delete Column. When you take this action, a dialog box warns you that you are going to delete all the data in this column, as well as the field itself, from the table design. More importantly, if you have used this field in a data-entry form or a report, you will get an error the next time you use any object that references this field name.

Adding a column to a datasheet

You can add new columns to a datasheet by selecting Insert⇨Column, which creates a new column to the right of the column your cursor was in, labeling it Field1. You can then add data to the records for the column.

Adding a new column also adds the field to the table design. When you save the datasheet, Access writes the field into the table design, using the characteristics of the data for the field properties.

Changing a field name (column header)

When adding a new field, you will want to change the column name before you save the datasheet. You can change a column header by double-clicking on the column header and then editing the text in the column header. When you save the datasheet, this column header text is used as a field name for the table design.

Caution   When you change a column header, you are changing the field name in the table. If you have used this field name in forms, reports, queries, macros, or modules, they will no longer work until you change them in the other objects. This is a dangerous way to change a field name; only experienced users should use it.

Displaying Records

A number of mouse techniques and menu items can greatly increase your productivity when you're adding or changing records. Either by selecting from the Format menu or by using the mouse, you can change the field order, hide and freeze columns, change row height or column width, change display fonts, and even change the display or remove gridlines.

Changing the field order

By default, Access displays the fields in a datasheet in the same order they would follow in a table or query. Sometimes, however, you need to see certain fields next to each other in order to analyze your data better. To rearrange your fields, select a column (as you see in Figure 8-12) and drag the column to its new location.

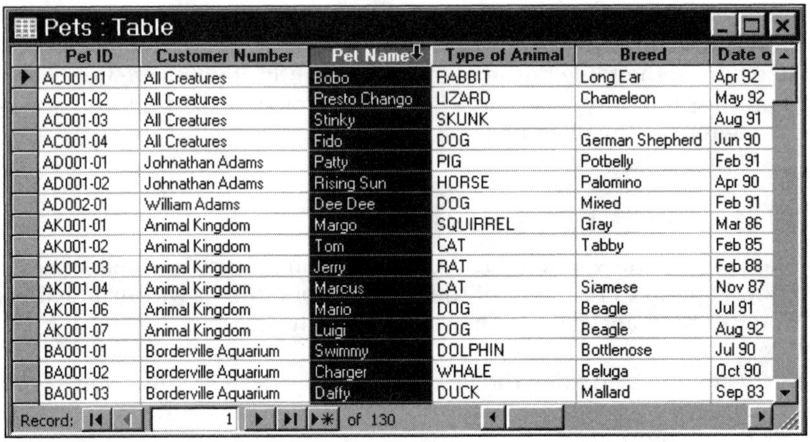

Pet ID	Customer Number	Pet Name	Type of Animal	Breed	Date o
AC001-01	All Creatures	Bobo	RABBIT	Long Ear	Apr 92
AC001-02	All Creatures	Presto Chango	LIZARD	Chameleon	May 92
AC001-03	All Creatures	Stinky	SKUNK		Aug 91
AC001-04	All Creatures	Fido	DOG	German Shepherd	Jun 90
AD001-01	Johnathan Adams	Patty	PIG	Potbelly	Feb 91
AD001-02	Johnathan Adams	Rising Sun	HORSE	Palomino	Apr 90
AD002-01	William Adams	Dee Dee	DOG	Mixed	Feb 91
AK001-01	Animal Kingdom	Margo	SQUIRREL	Gray	Mar 86
AK001-02	Animal Kingdom	Tom	CAT	Tabby	Feb 85
AK001-03	Animal Kingdom	Jerry	RAT		Feb 88
AK001-04	Animal Kingdom	Marcus	CAT	Siamese	Nov 87
AK001-06	Animal Kingdom	Mario	DOG	Beagle	Jul 91
AK001-07	Animal Kingdom	Luigi	DOG	Beagle	Aug 92
BA001-01	Borderville Aquarium	Swimmy	DOLPHIN	Bottlenose	Jul 90
BA001-02	Borderville Aquarium	Charger	WHALE	Beluga	Oct 90
BA001-03	Borderville Aquarium	Daffy	DUCK	Mallard	Sep 83

Record: 1 of 130

Figure 8-12: Selecting a column to change the field order.

You can select and drag columns just one at a time, or you can select multiple columns to drag. Say that you want the fields Pet Name and Type of Animal to appear first in the datasheet. The following steps take you through making this type of change:

1. Position the cursor on the Pet Name field (column) name. The cursor changes to a down arrow.

2. Click to select the column and hold down the mouse button. The entire Pet Name column is now highlighted.

3. Drag the mouse to the right to highlight the Type of Animal column.

4. Release the mouse button; the two columns should now be highlighted.

5. Click the mouse button again; the pointer changes to an arrow with a box under it.

6. Drag the two columns to the left edge of the datasheet.

7. Release the mouse button; the two columns now move to the beginning of the datasheet.

With this method, you can move any individual field or contiguous field selection. You can move the fields left or right or even past the right or left boundary of the window.

Note Moving fields in a datasheet does not affect the field order in the table design.

Changing the field display width

You can change the *field display width* (column width) either by specifying the width in a dialog box (in number of characters) or by dragging the column gridline. When you drag a column gridline, the cursor changes to the double-arrow symbol.

To widen a column or to make it narrower, follow these two simple steps:

1. Place the cursor between two column names on the field separator line.

2. Drag the column border to the left to make the column smaller, or to the right to make it bigger.

Tip You can resize a column instantly to the best fit (based on the longest data value) by double-clicking on the right column border.

Note Resizing the column will not change the number of characters allowable in the table's field size. You are simply changing the amount of viewing space for the data contained in the column.

Alternatively, you can resize a column by choosing Format⇨Column Width or right-clicking the mouse and selecting Column Width from the menu. Figure 8-13 shows the dialog box where you enter column width in number of characters. You can also return the column to its default size by checking the Standard Width check box.

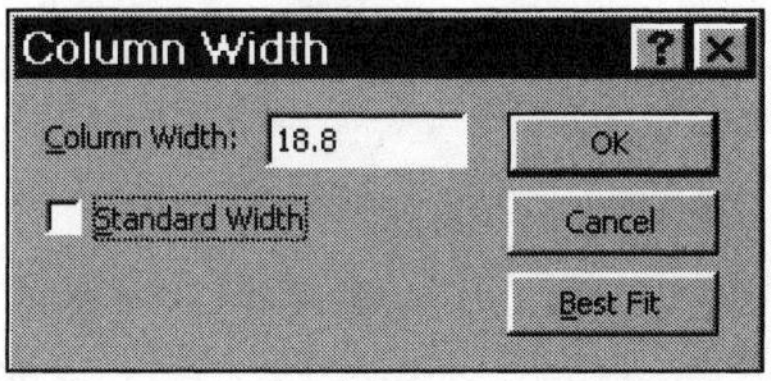

Figure 8-13: The Column Width dialog box.

Caution If you drag a column gridline to the gridline of the next column to the left, you'll hide the column. This also happens if you set the column width to 0 in the Column Width dialog box. If you do this, you must use Format⇨Unhide Columns to redisplay the columns.

Changing the record display height

You can change the record (that is, row) height of all rows. Drag a row's gridline to make the row height larger or smaller, or select Format⇨Row Height. Sometimes you may need to raise the row height to accommodate larger fonts or text data displays of multiple lines.

When you drag a record's gridline, the cursor changes to the vertical two-headed arrow you see at the left edge of Figure 8-14.

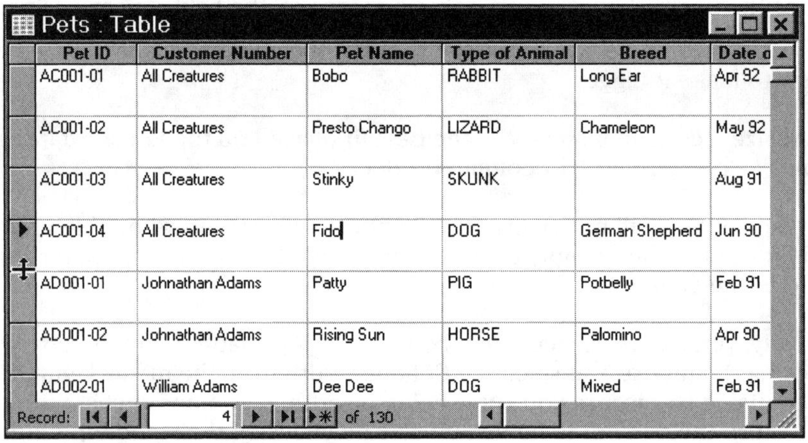

Figure 8-14: Changing a row's height.

To raise or lower a row's height, follow these steps:

1. Place the cursor between two rows on the record separator line.

2. Drag the row border upward to shrink all row heights. Drag the border downward to increase all row heights.

Note The procedure for changing row height changes the row size for all rows in the datasheet.

You can also resize rows by choosing Format⇨Row Height. A dialog box appears so you can enter the row height in point size. You can also return the rows to their default point size by checking the Standard Height check box.

Caution If you drag a record's gridline up to meet the gridline immediately above it in the previous record, you will hide all rows. This also occurs if you set the row height close to 0 (for example, a height of .1) in the Row Height dialog box. In that case, you must select Format⇨Row Height and reset the row height to a larger number to redisplay the rows.

Displaying cell gridlines

Normally gridlines appear between fields (columns) and between records (rows). By selecting Format⇨Cells, you can determine whether to display gridlines and how they will look. Figure 8-15 shows the Cells Effects dialog box you would use.

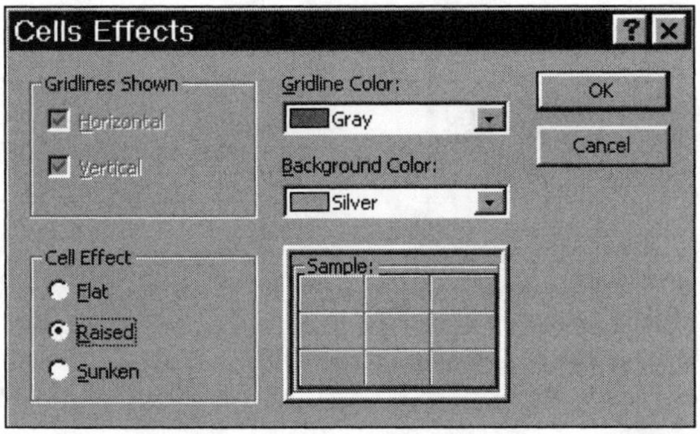

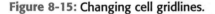

Figure 8-15: Changing cell gridlines.

The Cells Effects dialog box gives you complete control over gridlines. Using the Gridlines Shown check boxes, you can eliminate both Horizontal and Vertical gridlines. If you choose to keep the gridlines, you can change both the Gridline Color and the Background Color. A sample shows you what the effect you have chosen will look like. You can also determine whether the gridlines are Flat (default white background with silver gridlines), Raised (default silver background with gray gridlines), or Sunken (default silver background with white gridlines).

Changing display fonts

You can resize the row height and column width automatically by changing the *display font*. By default, Access displays all data in the datasheet in the MS Sans Serif 8-point Regular font. You may find this font does not print correctly because MS Sans Serif is only a screen font. Arial 8-point Regular is a good match. Select Format⇨Font to change the font type style, size, and style.

Setting the font display affects the entire datasheet. If you want to see more data on the screen, you can use a very small font. You can also switch to a higher-resolution display size if you have the necessary hardware. If you want to see larger characters, you can increase the font size.

To change the font to Arial 10-pt. bold, follow these steps:

1. Select Format⇨Font. A dialog box, appears.

2. Select Arial from the Font combo box, as shown in Figure 8-16.

3. Select Bold from the Font style combo box.

4. Enter 10 into the text box area of the Size combo box.

5. Click on OK.

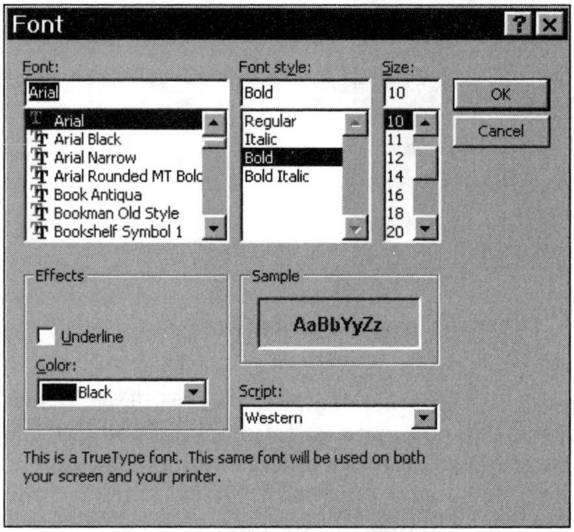

Figure 8-16: Changing to a different font and font size in the datasheet.

As you change font attributes, a sample appears in the Sample area. This way, you can see what changes you are making before you make them. You can also change the font color if you want.

Hiding and unhiding columns

You can hide columns by dragging the column gridline to the preceding field or by setting the column size to 0. You can also use the Hide Columns dialog box to hide one or more columns. Hide a single column by following these steps:

1. Position the cursor anywhere within the column you want to hide.

2. Select Format⇨Hide Columns. The column disappears. Actually, the column width is simply set to 0. You can hide multiple columns by first selecting them and selecting Format⇨Hide Columns.

After a column is hidden, you can redisplay it by selecting Format⇨Unhide Columns. This action displays a dialog box that lets you hide or unhide columns selectively by checking off the desired status of each field. When you are finished, click on Close; the datasheet appears, showing the desired fields.

Freezing columns

When you want to scroll among many fields but want to keep certain fields from scrolling out of view, you can use Format⇨Freeze Columns. With this selection, for example, you can keep the Pet ID and Pet Name fields visible while you scroll through the datasheet to find the animals' lengths and weights. The columns you want to keep remain frozen on the far left side of the datasheet; other fields scroll out of sight horizontally. The fields must be contiguous if you want to select more than one at a time to freeze. (Of course, you can first move your fields to place them next to each other.) When you're ready to unfreeze the datasheet columns, simply select Format⇨Unfreeze All Columns.

Saving the changed layout

When you close the datasheet, you save all your data changes, but you lose all your layout changes. As you make all these display changes to your datasheet, you probably won't want to make them again the next time you open the same datasheet. By default, however, Access does not save the datasheet's layout changes. If you want your datasheet to look the same way the next time you open it, you can select File⇨Save Layout; this command saves your layout changes with the datasheet.

CD-ROM

If you are following along with the example, do not save the changes to the Pets table.

Saving a record

As you move off a record, Access saves it. You can press Shift+Enter to save a record without moving off it. A third way to save a record is to close the table. Yet another way is to select Records⇨Save Record.

Sorting and Filtering Records in a Datasheet

Finding a value lets you display a specific record and work with that record. If you have multiple records that meet a find criteria, however, you may want to display just that specific set of records. Using the Filter and Sort toolbar icons (or the Records menu options Filter and Sort), you can display just the set of records you want to work with. You can also sort selected records instantly into any order you want; use the two QuickSort buttons to sort the entire table, or use the three filter buttons to select only certain records.

Using the QuickSort feature

There may be times when you simply want to sort your records into a desired order. The QuickSort buttons on the toolbar let you sort selected columns into either ascending or descending order. There is a different button on the toolbar for each order. Before you can click on either the Ascending (A-Z) or Descending (Z-A) QuickSort buttons, you must select the fields you want to use for the sort.

You select a field to use in the sort by placing your cursor on the field in any record. Once the cursor is in the column you want to use in the sort, click on the QuickSort button. The data redisplays instantly in the sorted order.

If you want to sort your data on the basis of values in multiple fields, you can highlight more than one column: highlight a column (as previously discussed), hold the Shift key down, and drag the cursor to the right. These steps select multiple contiguous fields. When you select one of the QuickSort buttons, Access sorts the records into major order (by the first highlighted field) and then into orders within orders (based on subsequent fields). If you need to select multiple columns that aren't contiguous (next to each other), you can move them next to each other, as discussed earlier in this chapter.

Tip

If you want to redisplay your records in their original order, use Records⇨Remove Filter/Sort.

Cross-Reference

You can learn more about sorting in Chapter 10.

Using Filter by Selection

Filter by Selection is a technology within Access 97 that lets you select records instantly on the basis of the current value you have selected. For example, suppose you move your cursor to the Type of Animal column and click on the Sort

Ascending button. Access sorts the data by type of animal. Now highlight any of the records that contain DOG. When you press the Filter by Selection button, Access selects only the records where the Type of Animal is DOG. In the Pets table, there are 130 records. Once you have selected DOG and pressed the Filter by Selection button, you will only see 27 records and all have the value DOG in the Type of Animal field.

You may also notice that the navigation button area tells you the database is currently filtered; in addition, the Apply Filter/Remove Filter icon (third filter icon that looks like a large funnel) is depressed, indicating that a filter is in use. When you toggle this button, it removes all filters or sorts. The filter specification does not go away; it is simply turned off.

Filter by Selection is additive. You can continue to select values, each time pressing the Filter by Selection button. If (for example) you place your cursor in the Gender column in a record where the value of Gender is M and press the Filter by Selection button, you will see only 21 records now: the male dogs. If you then place your cursor in the Colors column in a record where the value of Colors is Brown and press the Filter by Selection button, you will see only 6 records now: the brown male dogs.

If you want to specify a selection and then see everything that doesn't match the selection, right-click on the datasheet and select Filter Excluding Selection. For example, when filtering by selection, move the cursor to the Breed column and select one of the German Shepherd fields, and then right mouse click, selecting Filter Excluding Selection. You will be left with four records This selects everything *but* the two selected German Shepherd records (an *inverse* selection).

Imagine using this technique to review sales by salespeople for specific time periods or products. Filter by Selection provides incredible opportunities for drilldown into successive layers of data. As you add to Filter by Selection, it continues to add to its own internal query manager (known as Query by Example). Even when you click on the Remove Filter icon to redisplay all the records, Access still stores the query specification in memory. If you click on the icon again (now called Apply Filter), only the six records return. Figure 8-17 shows this Filter by Selection screen in both a Datasheet view (at the top) and in a query screen (at the bottom). As you can see in Figure 8-17, each of the successive sorts and filters ends up in the QBE grid.

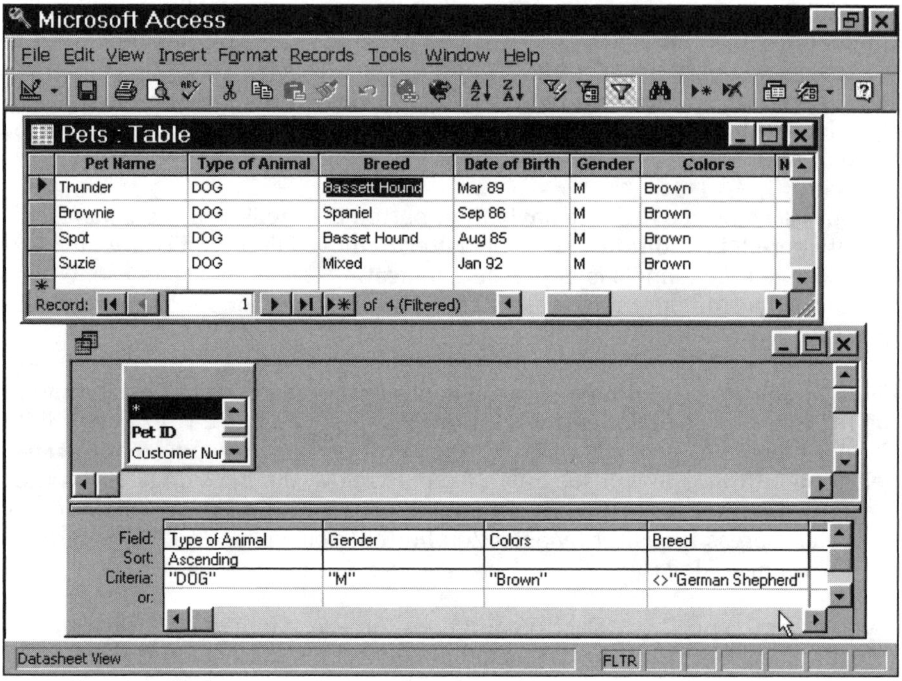

Figure 8-17: Using Filter by Selection.

Filter by Selection has some limitations. Most important, all of the choices are *anded* together. This means that the only operation you can perform is a search for records that meet all of the conditions you specify. Another option, Filter by Form, lets you create more complex analyses.

Using Filter by Form

Filter by Selection is just one way to filter data in Access 97. Another way is known as Filter by Form. Selecting the second filter icon changes the datasheet to a single record; every field becomes a combo box that enables you to select from a list of all values for that field. As you can see in Figure 8-18, the bottom of the form lets you specify the OR conditions for each group of values you specify.

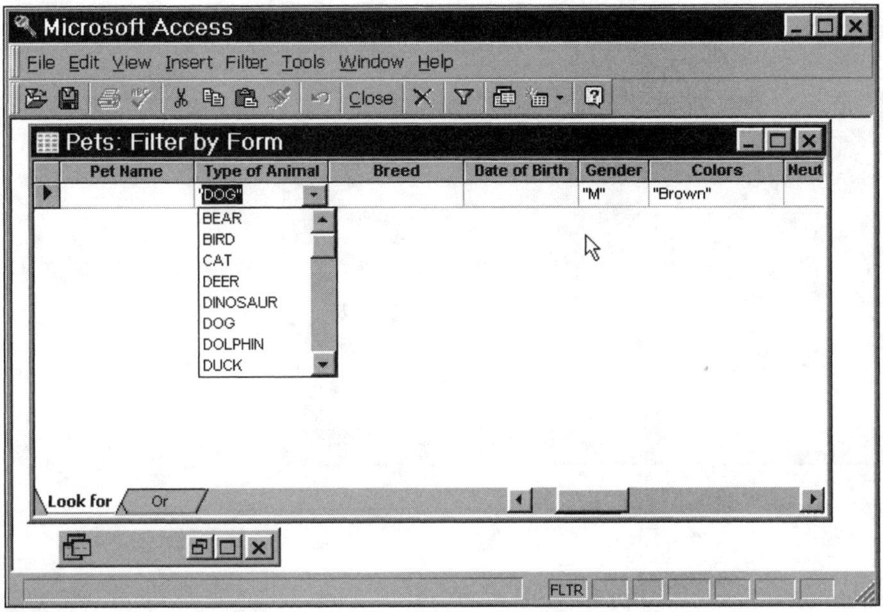

Figure 8-18: Using Filter by Form.

In Figure 8-18, you can see the three conditions created in the Filter by Selection example (described previously in this chapter) in the single line of the Filter by Form screen. If you click on one of the Or tabs, you can enter a second set of conditions. Suppose you want to see brown male dogs or any male ducks. You already have the specification for brown male dogs. You would click on the Or tab and then select DUCK from the now-empty Type of Animal combo box and M from the Gender column. When you click on the Apply Filter button (the large funnel), seven records would be shown.

You can have as many conditions as you need. If you need even more advanced manipulation of your selections, you can choose Records⇨Filter⇨Advanced Filter/Sort and get an actual QBE screen used to enter more complex queries.

Cross-Reference Later chapters explain more advanced concepts of queries.

Printing Records

You can print all the records in your datasheet in a simple row-and-column layout. Later on, you learn how to produce formatted reports. For now, the simplest way to print is to select File⇨Print or use the Print icon in the toolbar. This selection displays the dialog box shown in Figure 8-19.

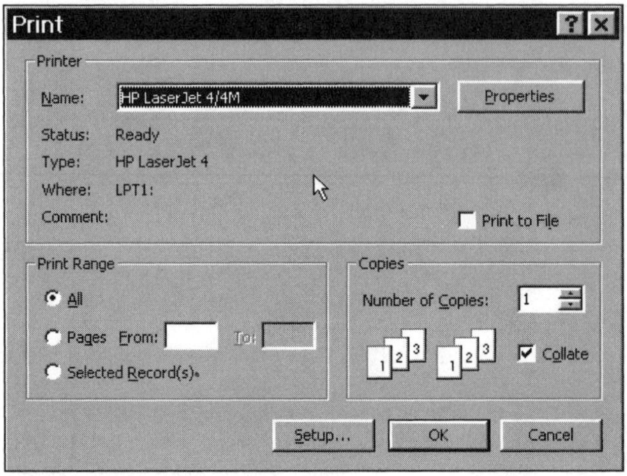

Figure 8-19: The Print dialog box.

Assuming you set up a printer in Microsoft Windows 95/NT, you can select OK to print your datasheet in the font you selected for display (or the nearest printer equivalent). The printout also reflects all layout options that are in effect when the datasheet is printed. Hidden columns do not print. Gridlines print only if the cell gridline properties are on. The printout reflects the specified row height and column width as well.

Only so many columns and rows can fit on a page; the printout will take up as many pages as required to print all the data. Access breaks up the printout as necessary to fit on each page. As an example, the Pets table printout is four pages long. Two pages across are needed to print all the fields; the records take two pages in length.

Printing the datasheet

You can also control printing from the Print dialog box, selecting from several options:

Print Range   Prints the entire datasheet or only selected pages or records.

Copies   Determines the number of copies to be printed.

Collate   Determines whether multiple copies are collated.

You can also click on the Properties button and set options for the selected printer or select the printer itself to change the type of printer. The Setup button allows you to set margins and print headings.

Using the Print Preview window

Often, though you may have all the information in the datasheet ready to print, you may be unsure of whether to change the width or height of the columns or rows or whether to adjust the fonts to improve your printed output. For that matter, you might not want to print out the entire datasheet; you may need printed records from only pages 3 and 4. Before making such adjustments to the datasheet properties, you'll probably want to view the report on-screen.

To preview your print job, you can either click on the Print Preview button on the toolbar (a sheet of paper with a magnifying glass) or select File⇨Print Preview. The Print Preview window appears (see Figure 8-20).

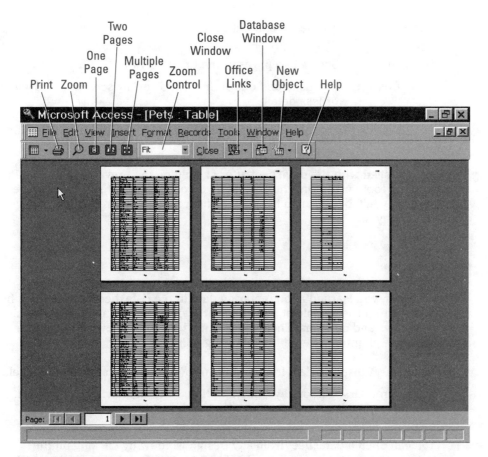

Figure 8-20: Print preview of a datasheet.

After you select the Print Preview button, the screen changes to *print preview mode.* You see a representation of your first printed page; a set of icons appears on the toolbar.

You can use the navigation buttons (located in the lower left section of the Print Preview window) to move between pages, just as you use them to move between records in a datasheet.

The toolbar buttons provide quick access to printing tasks:

Close Window	Returns to Datasheet view
Print	Displays the Print dialog box, accessible when you select File➪Print from the menu bar
One Page	Toggles in and out to make the Print Preview show a single page
Two Pages	Shows two pages in the Print Preview
Zoom Control	Zooms in and out of the Print Preview screen to show more or less detail

Tip   You can view more than two pages by selecting View➪Pages and then selecting 1, 2, 4, 8, or 12.

If you are satisfied with the datasheet after examining the preview, select the Print button on the toolbar to print the datasheet. If you are not satisfied, select the Close button; you'll be returned to the datasheet mode to make further changes to your data or layout.

Summary

In this chapter, you learned about entering data into a datasheet. You learned how to navigate within the datasheet and change the data, as well as how to reposition and resize rows and columns. Then you learned how to preview and print the datasheet. The chapter covered the following points:

✦ A datasheet displays data from a table in rows (records) and columns (fields).

✦ Using scrollbars, cursor keys, menu options, and the navigation buttons, you can move quickly around the datasheet and position the cursor on any record or field.

✦ You can open a datasheet from any Design window by clicking on the Datasheet button (or, from the Database window, by choosing Open with a table selected).

✦ Data is entered into a datasheet at the new-record indicator.

✦ Access performs automatic data validation for various data types. These are Number, Currency, Date/Time, and Yes/No fields. You can add your own custom data validation at the table or form level.

✦ You can paste or insert OLE objects (such as sound, pictures, graphs, Word documents, or video) into OLE fields with Insert⇨Object.

✦ The navigation buttons enable you to move quickly between records.

✦ You can find or replace specific values by using Edit⇨Find or Edit⇨Replace.

✦ You can press Ctrl+Alt+Spacebar to insert the default value into a field or press Ctrl+' to insert the preceding record's value into a field.

✦ Some types of fields can't be edited. These include AutoNumber, calculated, locked, disabled, and record-locked fields, as well as fields from certain types of queries.

✦ The Undo feature can undo typing, a field value, the current record, or a saved record.

✦ You can delete a record by selecting it and pressing Delete or by selecting Edit⇨Delete.

✦ You can change the display of your datasheet by rearranging fields, changing the field display's width or row height, or changing display fonts.

✦ You can hide or reshow columns, freeze or unfreeze columns, and remove or show gridlines.

✦ You can save any layout changes by using File⇨Save Layout.

✦ Using the QuickSort buttons, you can instantly change the order the records are displayed in.

✦ Using Filter by Selection or Filter by Form, you can specify sort orders or filters to limit the record display of a datasheet. This is a limited version of QBE (Query by Example).

✦ File⇨Print prints your datasheet; File⇨Print Preview previews the pages on the screen.

In the next chapter, you learn how to create a form and how to use a form for data entry.

✦   ✦   ✦

Creating and Using Simple Data-Entry Forms

CHAPTER

9

Forms provide the most flexible way for viewing, adding, editing, and deleting your data. In this chapter, you see how to use Form Wizards as the starting point for your form. You learn about how forms work and the types of forms you can create with Access.

Understanding Data-Entry Forms

Although you can view your data in many ways, a form provides the most flexibility for viewing and entering data. A form lets you view one or more records at a time while viewing all of the fields. A datasheet also lets you view several records at once, but you can see only a limited number of fields. When you use a form, you can see all your fields at once, or at least as many as you can fit on a screen. By rearranging your fields in a form, you can easily get 20, 50, or even 100 fields on one screen. You can also use forms to create multipage screens for each record. Forms are useful for simply viewing data in a formatted display, as well as for entering, changing, or deleting data. You can also print them with all the visual effects you have created.

What types of forms can you create?

You can create six basic types of forms:

- ✦ Columnar (also known as full-screen) forms
- ✦ Tabular forms
- ✦ Datasheets
- ✦ Main/subforms
- ✦ Pivot table forms
- ✦ Graphs

Figure 9-1 shows a *columnar form*; you see the fields arranged as columns on-screen. The form can occupy one or more screen pages. Generally you would use this type of form to simulate the hard-copy entry of data; you can arrange the fields any way you want. Most standard Windows controls are available with Access forms and make data entry more productive and understandable. Lines, boxes, colors, and even special effects (such as shadows or three-dimensional looks) enable you to make great-looking, easy-to-use forms.

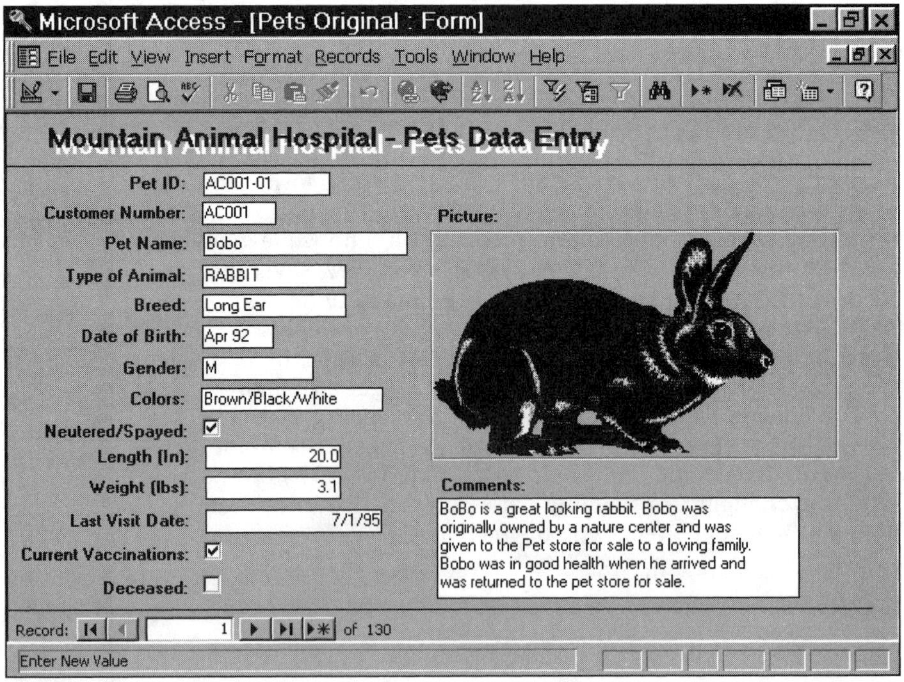

Figure 9-1: A full-screen form.

Figure 9-2 displays a tabular form; note that you can see several records at one time. You can format any part of a tabular form; your column headers can span multiple lines and be formatted separately from the records (unlike datasheets, which do not allow you to customize the column headers). Tabular forms can also have multiple lines per record, and you can add special effects (such as shadows or three-dimensional effects) to the fields. Field controls can also be option buttons or even push buttons.

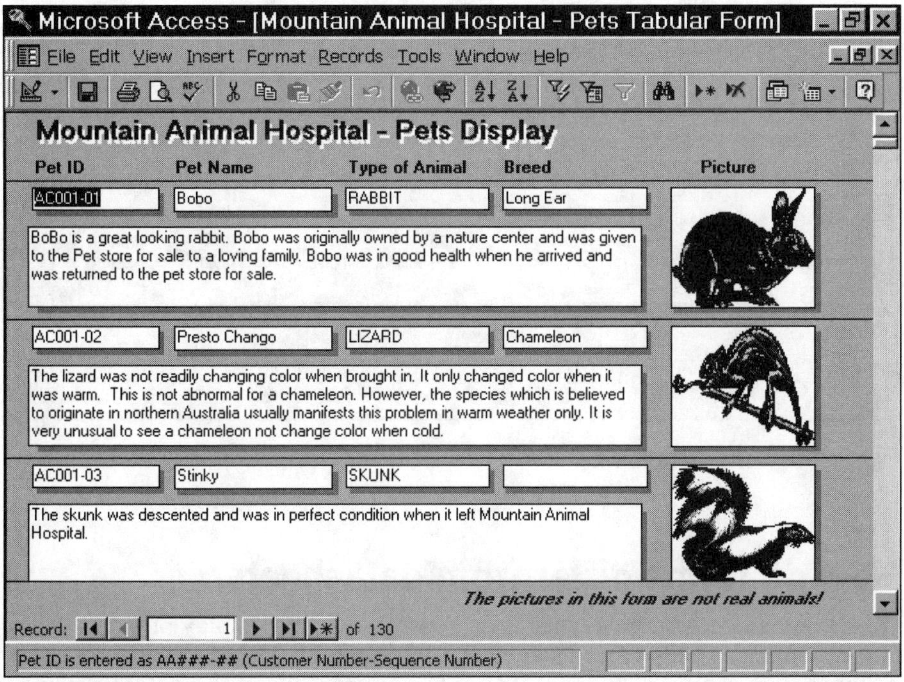

Figure 9-2: A tabular form.

A main/subform, shown in Figure 9-3, is a type of form commonly used to display one-to-many relationships. The main form displays the main table; the subform is frequently a datasheet or tabular form that displays the many portion of the relationship. For example, each pet's visit information shows up once, while the subform shows many visit detail records. This type of form combines all the benefits of a form and a datasheet. A subform can show just one record or several records, each on multiple lines.

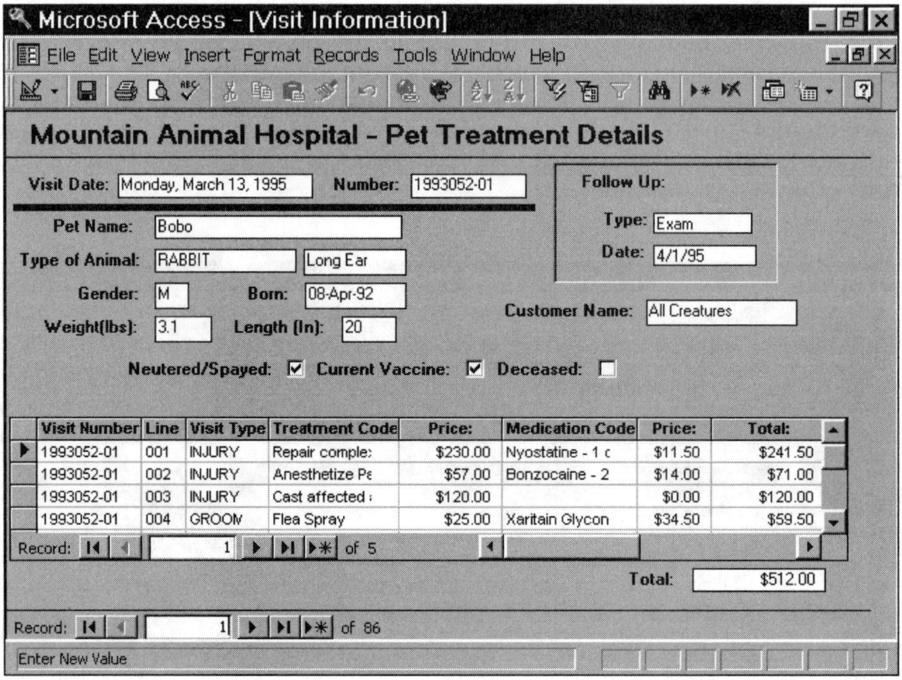

Figure 9-3: A main/subform.

How do forms differ from datasheets?

With a datasheet, you have very little control over the display of data. Although you can change the type and size of the display font, and rearrange, resize, or hide columns, you cannot significantly alter the appearance of the data. By using forms, you can place each field in an exact specified location, add color or shading to each field, and add text controls to make data entry more efficient.

A form gives you more flexibility in data entry than a datasheet. You can not only add calculated fields to your form, but you can also add enhanced data-validation and editing controls (such as option buttons, check boxes, and pop-up list boxes). Adding lines, boxes, colors, and static bitmaps can enhance the look of your data, make your form easier to use, and improve productivity.

In addition, OLE objects (such as pictures or graphs) are visible *only* in a form or report. And although you can increase a datasheet's row size to see more of a Memo field, using a form makes it easier to display large amounts of text in a scrollable text box.

Tip Once you create a form with editing controls or enhanced data validation, you can switch into *datasheet mode*, which lets you use data-validation rules and controls, such as pop-up lists.

Creating a form with AutoForm

From the Table or Query tab in the Database window, a datasheet, or nearly any design screen in Access, you can create a form instantly by clicking on the New Object button in the toolbar (a form with a lightning bolt through it) and then choosing one of the AutoForm icons. Another method is to use Insert⇨Form and select one of the AutoForm choices from the dialog box that appears. When you use the AutoForm button, the form appears instantly with no additional work. You can create columnar, tabular, or datasheets with AutoForm. To create a columnar AutoForm using the Pets table, follow these steps:

1. From the Mountain Animal Hospital Database Window, click on the Table tab.

2. Select Pets.

3. Click on the New Object button in the toolbar.

4. Select AutoForm.

The form instantly appears, as shown in Figure 9-4.

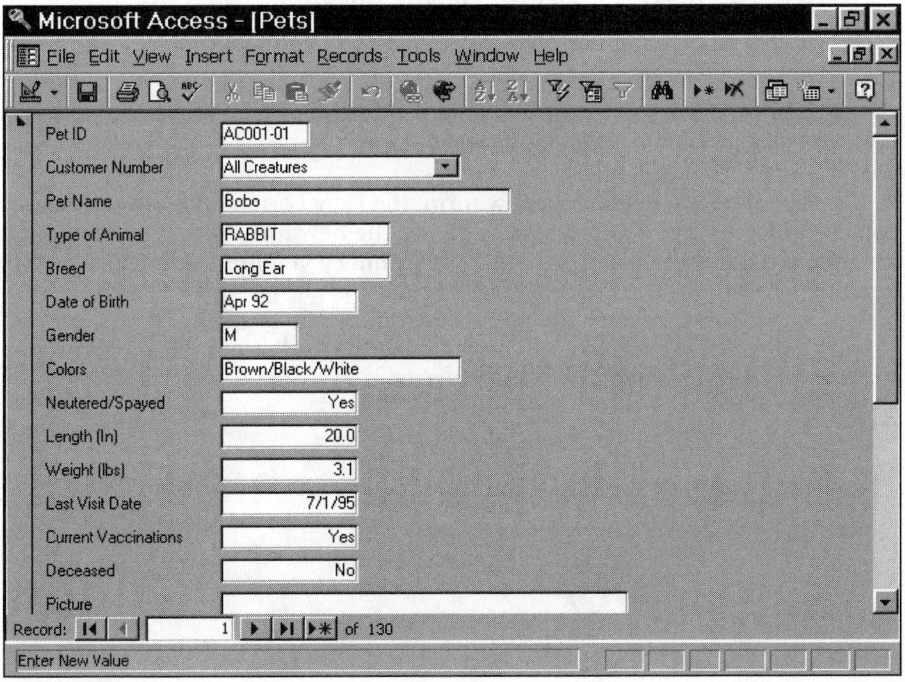

Figure 9-4: The AutoForm form.

If you look at different areas of the form, you can see that some values are not properly displayed. For example, if you scroll down and look at the picture of the rabbit (yes, it's the hindquarter of a rabbit) in the first record, you see only a portion of the rabbit. Later, you learn how to fix this, as well how to customize the form exactly as you want.

AutoForm is the quickest way to create a form. Generally, however, you want more control over your form creation. Other Form Wizards can help you create a more customized form at the outset.

Creating a Form with Form Wizards

Form Wizards simplify the layout process for your fields. The Form Wizard visually steps you through a series of questions about the type of form you want to create and then creates it for you automatically. In this chapter, you learn how to create single-column forms with a Form Wizard, using the columnar form as a starting point for creating a full-screen form.

Creating a new form

You can choose from these three methods to create a new form:

✦ Select Insert⇨Form from the Database window menu.

✦ Select the Form tab and then select the New command button from the Database window.

✦ Select the New Object button from the Database window, the datasheet, or the Query toolbar, and choose New Form.

Regardless of how you create a new form, the New Form dialog box appears, as you see in Figure 9-5. If you began to create the new form with a table highlighted (or from a datasheet or query), the table or query you are using appears in the text box labeled `Choose the table or query where the object's data comes from`. You can enter the name of a valid table or query (if you are not already using one) before continuing; choose from a list of tables and queries by clicking on the combo box's selection arrow.

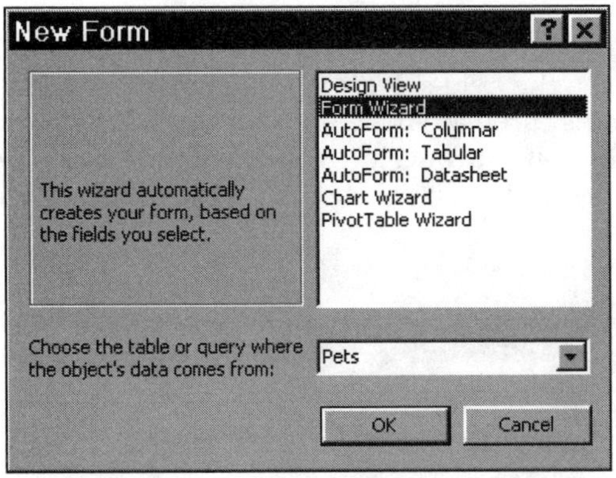

Figure 9-5: The New Form dialog box.

Selecting the New Form type and data source

The New Form dialog box gives you seven choices for creating a form:

Design View — Displays a completely blank form for you to start with in Form design

Form Wizard — Creates a form with one of three default layouts; columnar, tabular, or datasheet, using data fields that you specify in a step-by-step process that lets you customize the form creation process

AutoForm: Columnar — Instantly creates a columnar form

AutoForm: Tabular — Instantly creates a tabular form

AutoForm: Datasheet — Instantly creates a datasheet form

Chart Wizard — Creates a form with a business graph

PivotTable Wizard — Creates an Excel Pivot Table

As you make selections in a Wizard form, notice how the bitmap picture in the left of the Wizard form changes to show you your selection before you make it.

For this example, choose the Form Wizard option.

CD-ROM

Choosing the fields

After you select Form Wizard, you see the field-selection box shown in Figure 9-6. The field-selection dialog box contains three areas where you work. The first area lets you choose fields from multiple tables or queries; you can create many types of forms, including those with subforms. As you select each table or query, the Available Fields list will change.

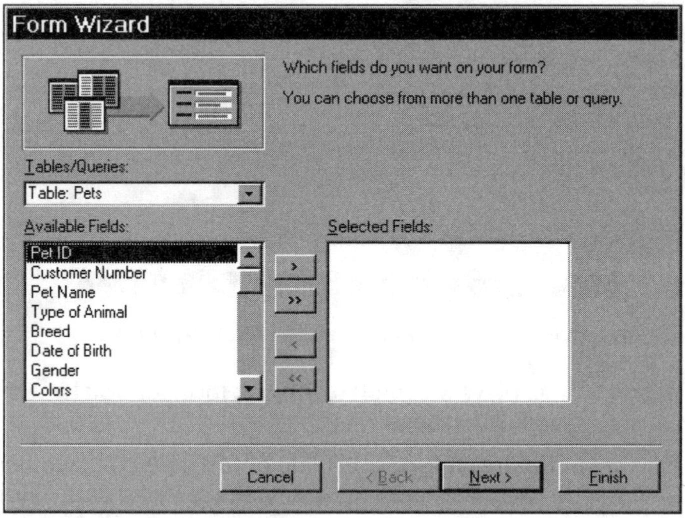

Figure 9-6: Choosing the fields for the form.

Note If you are an experienced Access 2.0 user, you will find this process very different in Access 97. There is no longer a separate subform Wizard. Instead, Access 97 figures out when you have selected data related in a one-to-many relationship and adds extra screens to create a subform.

The field-selection area consists of two list boxes and four buttons. The Available Fields: list box on the left displays all fields from the selected table/query used to create the form. The Selected Fields: list box on the right displays the fields you have selected for this form. You can select one field, all the fields, or any combination of fields. The order in which you add the fields to the list box on the right is the order in which the fields will appear in the form. You can use the buttons to place or remove fields in the Selected Fields: box. Following is a description of these buttons:

>   Add selected field

>>   Add all fields

<   Remove selected field

<<   Remove all fields

When you highlight a field in the Available Fields: list box and click on >, the field name appears in the Selected Fields: list box. You can add each field you want to the list box. If you add a field by mistake, you can select the field in the Selected Fields: list box and click on < to remove it from the selection. If you decide to change the order in which your fields will appear in the form, you must remove any fields that are out of order and reselect them in the proper order.

Note You can double-click on any field in the Available Fields: list box to add it to the Selected Fields: list box.

At the bottom of the form, you find a series of buttons to be used when field selection is completed. The types of buttons available here are common to most Wizard dialog boxes.

Cancel   Cancel form creation and return to the starting point

< Back   Return to the preceding dialog box

Next >   Go to the next dialog box

Finish   Go to the last dialog box (usually the form title)

Tip If you click on Next > or Finish without selecting any fields, Access selects all the fields automatically when creating the form.

CD-ROM Select all of the fields by clicking on the >> button. When you are finished, click on the Next > button to display the dialog box that lets you choose a form layout.

Choosing the form layout

Once you choose the fields, you have to choose the type of layout. As you can see in Figure 9-7, there are four types of layouts:

Columnar

Tabular

Datasheet

Justified

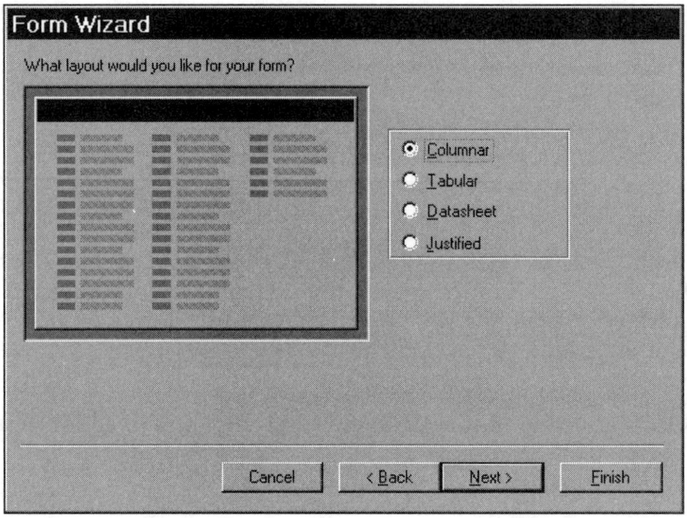

Figure 9-7: Choosing the type of layout for the form.

As you click on the radio button choices, the display changes to show how the form will look.

NEW FEATURE The Justified form layout is new to Access 97. It lets you display your information in fields appended to each other from left to right, top to bottom.

CD-ROM Select the Columnar layout. Once you choose the type of layout, you can click on the Next> button to display the style of the form.

Choosing the style of the form

After you select the form layout, you can choose the style for the look of your form from the dialog box shown in Figure 9-8.

You can choose from many different selections by clicking on the desired name in the list box. As you select one of the styles, the display on the left changes to illustrate the special effect used to create the look.

As you can see in Figure 9-8, the default look uses clouds in the background. The next-to-last selection, Standard, is a more traditional look, with a dark gray background and sunken controls. For the first form you create in this chapter, select Clouds. Once you select the style of your form, you are ready to create a title and view the form.

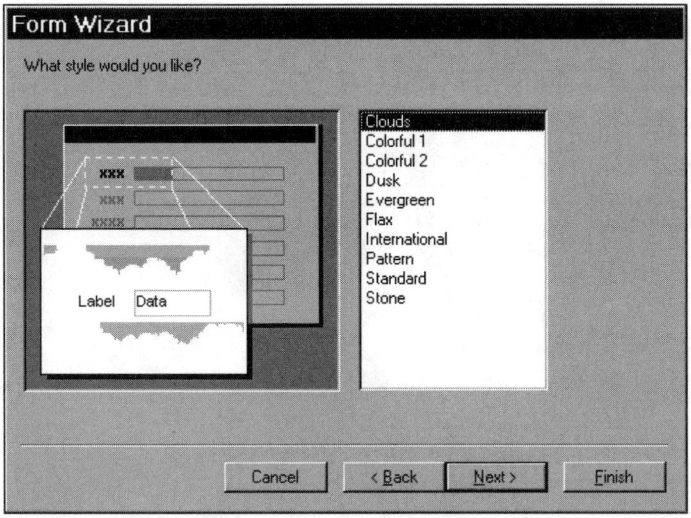

Figure 9-8: Choosing the style of your form.

The style you select will be used as the default the next time you use the Wizard.

Tip You can customize the style by changing a form and then using the AutoFormat function in the Form design screen.

Creating a form title

The form title dialog box is usually the last dialog box in a Form Wizard. It always has a checkered flag to let you know you are at the finish line. By default, the text box for the form title contains the name of the table or query used for the form's data. You can accept the entry for the form title, enter your own, or erase it and have no title. As you can see, the title in Figure 9-9 is Pets, the name of the table.

Figure 9-9: Choosing a form title.

Completing the form

After you complete all the steps to design your form, you can open your new form in one of two ways:

✦ Open the form to view or enter information

✦ Modify the form's design

In this example, you would select the former and then click the Finish button. Once you click the Finish button, the form appears in the Form View window (as shown in Figure 9-10).

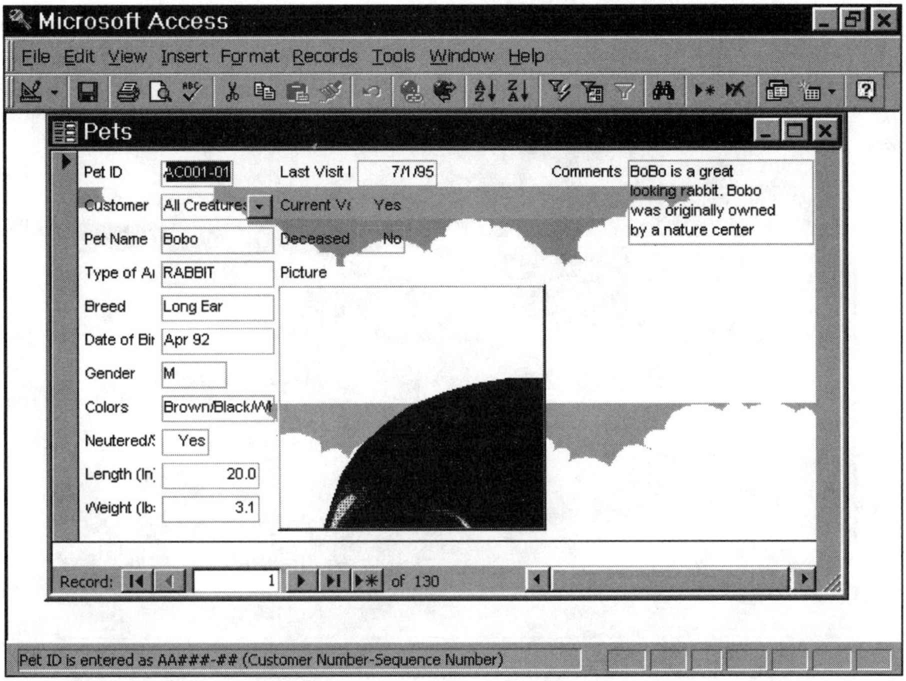

Figure 9-10: A form design created with a Form Wizard.

Changing the Design

As an example of how easy it is to manipulate the field controls, you can change the way the Picture field appears. If you look at Figure 9-10, you see a lovely view of the hind part of the rabbit going over the fence; it would be nice to see the whole rabbit. To fix this, follow these steps:

1. Click on the Design button to open the form the Form Design window.

2. Click on the Picture field (the large, empty rectangle under the Picture label).

3. Click on the Property icon in the toolbar (picture of a hand and a sheet of paper, the fifth icon from the right).

4. Click on the Size Mode property and change it from Clip to Stretch (as shown in Figure 9-11).

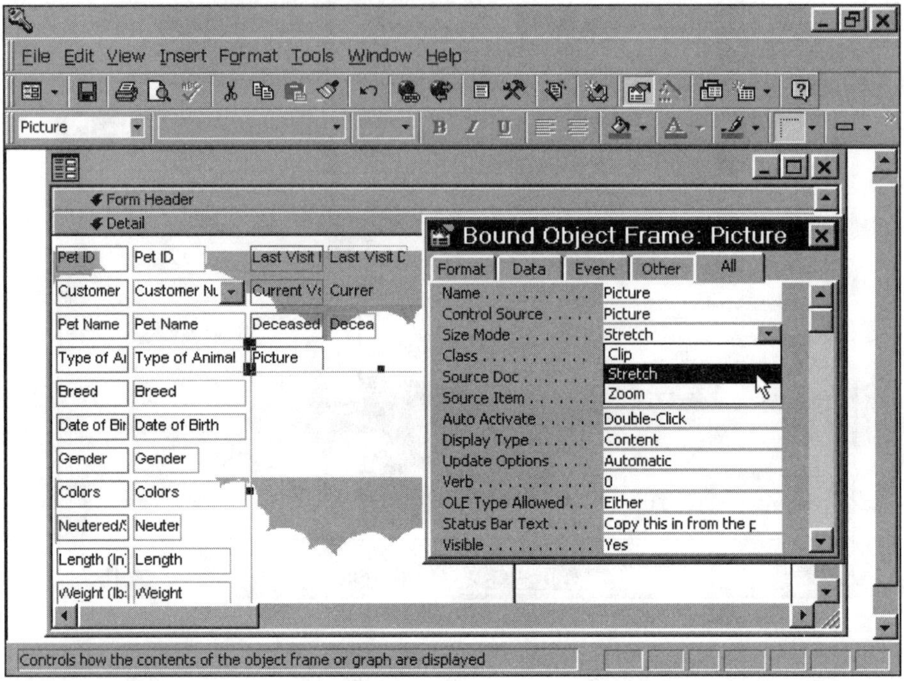

Figure 9-11: Changing a control property.

Tip

If you do not like the Grid or Ruler to be displayed (as in Figure 9-11), you can turn them off by selecting View⇨Ruler and/or View⇨Grid.

After you complete the move, click on the Form button to redisplay the form. Notice the whole rabbit, as shown in Figure 9-12.

Cross-
Reference

In Chapters 16-20, you learn how to completely customize a form. You learn how to use all the controls in the toolbox, add special effects to forms, create forms with graphs and calculated fields, and add complex data validation to your forms.

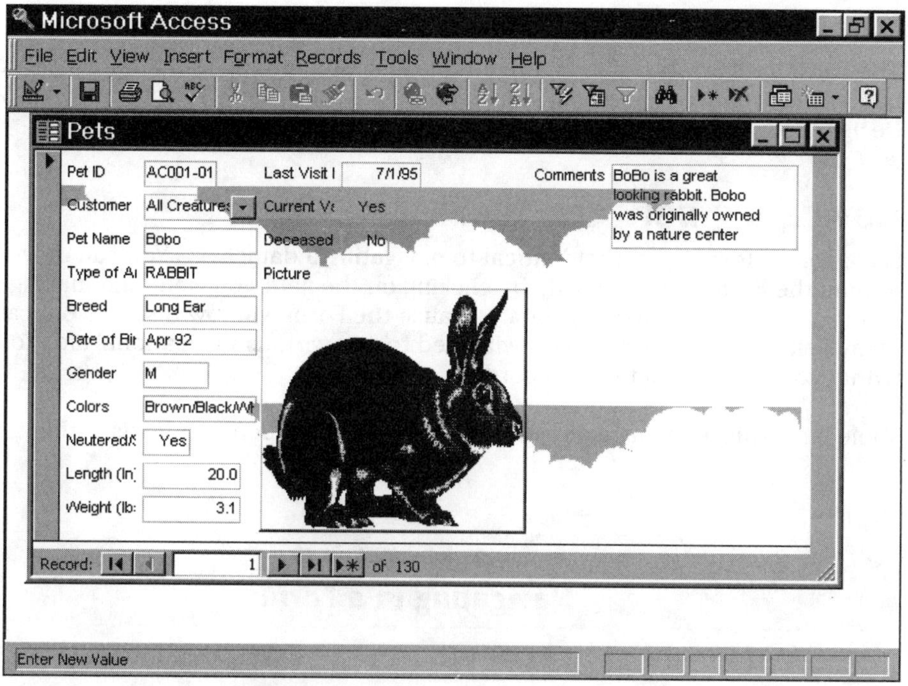

Figure 9-12: The form redisplayed to show the full picture.

Using the Form Window

If you look at the Form window, as shown in Figure 9-12, you see that this window is very similar to the Datasheet window. At the top of the screen you will find the title bar, menu bar, and toolbar. The center of the screen displays your data, one record at a time, in the form window (unless you have the form window maximized). If the form contains more fields than will fit on-screen at one time, Access 97 automatically displays a horizontal and/or vertical scrollbar that can be used to see the remainder of the record. You can also see the rest of the record by pressing the PgDn key. The last line at the bottom of the screen contains a status bar. The status bar displays the Field Description you entered into the table design for each field. If there is no Field Description for a specific field, Access displays the words Form View. Generally, error messages and warnings appear in dialog boxes in the center of the screen (rather than in the status bar). You can also find the navigation buttons at the bottom of the screen. This feature lets you move quickly from record to record.

The Form toolbar

The Form toolbar, shown in Figure 9-12, is almost identical to the Datasheet toolbar. The only difference is that the first icon contains three selections: Form View, Design View, and Datasheet View.

Navigating between fields

Navigating a form is nearly identical to navigating a datasheet. You can move around the Form window easily by clicking on the field you want and making changes or additions to your data. Because the Form window displays only as many fields as fit on-screen, you will need to use various navigational aids to move within your form or between records.

Table 9-1 displays the navigational keys used to move between fields within a form.

Table 9-1 Navigating in a Form	
Navigational Direction	**Keystrokes**
Next field	Tab, right- or down-arrow key, or Enter
Previous field	Shift+Tab, left-arrow, or up-arrow
First field of current record	Home or Ctrl+Home
Last field of current record	End or Ctrl+End
Next page	PgDn or Next Record
Previous page	PgUp or Previous Record

If you have a form with more than one page, you see a vertical scrollbar. You can use the scrollbar to move to different pages on the form. You can also use the PgUp and PgDn keys to move between form pages. You can move up or down one field at a time by clicking on the scrollbar arrows. With the elevator, you can move between many fields at once.

Moving between records in a form

Although you generally use a form to display one record at a time, you will still want to move between records. The easiest way to do this is to use the navigation buttons.

The navigation buttons offer the same five controls at the bottom of the screen that you saw in the datasheet. You can click on these buttons to move to the desired record.

Pressing F5 moves you instantly to the record number box.

You can also press Ctrl+PgDn to move to the current field in the next record, or Ctrl+PgUp to move to the current field in the preceding record.

Displaying Your Data with a Form

In Chapter 8, you learned techniques to add, change, and delete data within a datasheet. The techniques you learned there are the same ones you use within a form. Table 9-2 summarizes these techniques.

Table 9-2 Editing Techniques	
Editing Technique	**Keystrokes**
Move insertion point within a field	Press the right- and left-arrow keys
Insert a value within a field	Select the insertion point and type the new data
Select the entire field	Press F2 or double-click the mouse button
Replace an existing value with a new value	Select the entire field and type a new value
Replace value with value of preceding field	Press Ctrl+' (apostrophe)
Replace current value with default value	Press Ctrl+Alt+Spacebar
Insert current date into a field	Press Ctrl+; (semicolon)
Insert current time into a field	Press Ctrl+: (colon)
Insert a line break in a Text or Memo field	Press Ctrl+Enter
Insert new record	Press Ctrl++ (plus sign)
Delete current record	Press Ctrl+– (minus sign)
Save current record	Press Shift+Enter or move to another record
Undo a change to the current record	Press Esc or click on the Undo button

Working with pictures and OLE objects

In a datasheet, you cannot view a picture or any OLE object without accessing the OLE server. In a form, however, you can size the OLE control area large enough to display a picture, business graph, or visual OLE object. You can also size the Memo controls on forms so you can see the data within the field — you don't have to zoom in on the value, as you do with a datasheet field. Figure 9-12 displays both the picture and the Memo data displayed in the form. Each of these controls can be resized.

Recall from Chapter 8 that any object supported by an OLE server can be stored in an Access OLE field. You generally enter OLE objects into a form so that you can see, hear, or use the value. As with a datasheet, you have two ways to enter OLE fields into a form:

✦ Paste them in from the Clipboard or the Edit menu.

✦ Insert them into the field from the Insert⇨Object menu.

Cross-
Reference   Chapter 20 covers using and displaying OLE objects in forms in more detail.

Memo field data entry

The last field in the form shown in Figure 9-12 (the rightmost column), Comments:, is a Memo data type. This type of field allows up to 64,000 bytes of text for each field. You can see the first two sentences of data in the Memo field. When you move the cursor into the Memo field, a vertical scrollbar appears (see Figure 9-13). Using this scrollbar, you can view the rest of the data in the field. You can resize the Memo control in the Form Design window if you want to make it larger. You can also press Shift+F2 and display a Zoom dialog box in the center of the screen, which lets you view about 12 lines at a time.

Figure 9-13: A vertical scrollbar appears
in a Memo field when the text cursor is in it.

Switching to a datasheet

While in the form, you can display a Datasheet view of your data by one of two methods:

> ✦ Click on the Datasheet button in the toolbar.
>
> ✦ Select View⇨Datasheet.

The datasheet is displayed with the cursor on the same field and record it occupied in the form. If you move to another record and field and then redisplay the form, the form now appears with the cursor on the field and record it last occupied in the datasheet.

To return to the form from a datasheet, you can use either of two methods:

> ✦ Click on the Form button in the toolbar.
>
> ✦ Select View⇨Form.

Sorting and filtering form records

You can use the same techniques to manipulate records in a form as you do in a datasheet (as you learned in the preceding chapter). The only difference is that instead of positioning on a specific record, you display a single record.

Cross-Reference If you need to review the techniques for finding and replacing data or filtering and sorting your records, see the appropriate sections in Chapter 8.

Saving a Record and the Form

As you move off each record, Access automatically saves any changes to the record. You can also press Shift+Enter to save a record without moving off it. The final way to save a record is to save the form. You can save any changes to a form design by selecting Records⇨Save Record. This saves any changes and keeps the form open. When you are ready to close a form and return to the Database window (or to your query or datasheet), you can select File⇨Close. If you made any changes to the form design, you are asked whether you want to save the design.

Printing a Form

You can print one or more records in your form exactly as they look on the screen. (You will learn how to produce formatted reports later in the book.) The simplest way to print is to use the File⇨Print selection or the Print toolbar button. Selecting File⇨Print displays the Print dialog box.

Assuming that you have set up a printer in Windows 95/ NT, you can select OK to print your form. Access then prints your form, using the font you selected for display or using the nearest printer equivalent. The printout contains any formatting you specified in the form (including lines, boxes, and shading) and converts colors to gray shades if you are using a monochrome printer.

The printout prints as many pages as necessary to print all the data. If your form is wider than a single printer page, you will need multiple pages to print your form. Access breaks up the printout as necessary to fit on each page.

Using the Print Preview Window

You may find that you have all the information in your form, but you aren't sure whether that information will print on multiple pages or fit on one printed page. Maybe you want to see whether the fonts need adjustment, or you need only the printed records from pages 3 and 4. In such cases you will probably want to view the report on-screen before printing to make these adjustments to the form design.

To preview your printout, you can either click on the Print Preview button on the toolbar (a sheet of paper with a magnifying glass on top) or select File⇨Print Preview. Figure 9-14 shows the Print Preview window; it works exactly like the datasheet Print Preview window you learned about in Chapter 8.

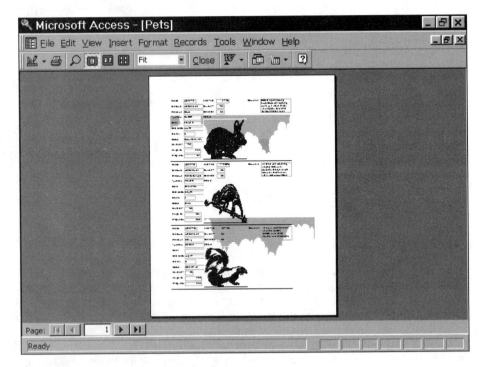

Figure 9-14: The Print Preview window.

If, after examining the preview, you are satisfied with the form, simply select the Print button on the toolbar to print the form. If you are not satisfied, click on the Close button to return to the form to make further changes to your data or design.

Summary

This chapter examined Form Wizards and how you can use them as the starting point for your form. You learned about how forms work and encountered the types of forms you can create with Access. The chapter covered these points:

✦ Data-entry forms provide the most flexible format for viewing your data; you can arrange your fields in any order you want.

✦ Whereas datasheets generally let you view many records at a time, you would use a form to view one record at a time.

✦ AutoForm instantly creates a form for you with just one keystroke.

✦ Form Wizards simplify form creation by giving you a starting point for form design and stepping you through the process.

✦ There are five basic types of forms: full-screen, tabular, main/subforms, pivot tables, and graphs.

✦ A Form Wizard lets you specify the type of form, the fields to be used, the type of look you want, and a title.

✦ You can specify one or more fields in a Form Wizard.

✦ A Form Wizard lets you choose from several types of styles.

✦ A form lets you enter data into Picture and Memo fields and displays the fields as well.

✦ You can switch to a datasheet from a form by selecting the Datasheet button.

✦ You can print a form with all its formatting, or you can preview it on the screen before printing.

In the next chapter, you learn about simple queries.

✦ ✦ ✦

Understanding and Using Simple Queries

In this chapter, you learn what a query is and also about the process of creating queries. Using the Pets table, you create several types of queries for the Mountain Animal Hospital database.

Understanding Queries

The primary purpose of any database, manual or automated, is to store and extract information. Information can be obtained from a database immediately after you enter the data or years later. Of course, even with a manually assembled database, obtaining information requires knowledge of how the database is set up.

For example, reports may be filed manually in a cabinet, arranged first by order of year and then by a *sequence number* that indicates when the report was written. To obtain a specific report, you must know its year and sequence number. In a good manual system, you may have a cross-reference book to help you find a specific report. This book may have all reports categorized by type of report (rather than topic) in alphabetical order. Such a book can be helpful, but if you know only the report's topic and approximate date, you still may have to search through all sections of the book to find out where to obtain the report.

Unlike manual databases, computer-automated databases have a distinct advantage; with their tools, you can easily obtain information to meet virtually any criteria you specify.

This is the real power of a database — the capacity for you to examine the data any way *you* want to look at it. Queries, by definition, ask questions about the data stored in the database. After you create a query, you can use its data for reports, forms, and graphs.

What is a query?

The word *query* comes from the Latin word *quærere,* which simply means to ask or inquire. Over the years, the word "query" has become synonymous with quiz, challenge, inquire, or question. Therefore, you can think of a query as a question or inquiry posed to the database about information found in its tables.

A Microsoft Access query is a question you ask about the information stored in your Access tables. The way you ask questions about this information is by using the query *tools.* Your query can be a simple question about information stored in a single table, or it can be a complex question about information stored in several tables. After you ask the question, Microsoft Access returns only the information you requested.

Using queries this way, you can query the Pets database to show you only the dogs that are named within it. To see the dogs' names, you need to retrieve information from the Pets table. Figure 10-1 shows a typical Query Design window like the one you saw in Chapter 8. This is the same basic format used behind Filter by Selection or Filter by Form.

After you create and run a query, Microsoft Access can return and display the set of records you asked for in a datasheet. This set of records is called a *dynaset,* which is simply the set of records selected by a query. As you've seen, a datasheet looks just like a spreadsheet, with its rows of records and columns of fields. The datasheet can display many records simultaneously.

You can query information from a single table. Many database queries, however, require information from several tables.

Suppose, for example, that you want to send a reminder to anyone living in a certain city that their dog or cat is due for an annual vaccination, based on the town license regulations. This type of query requires getting information from two tables: Customer and Pets.

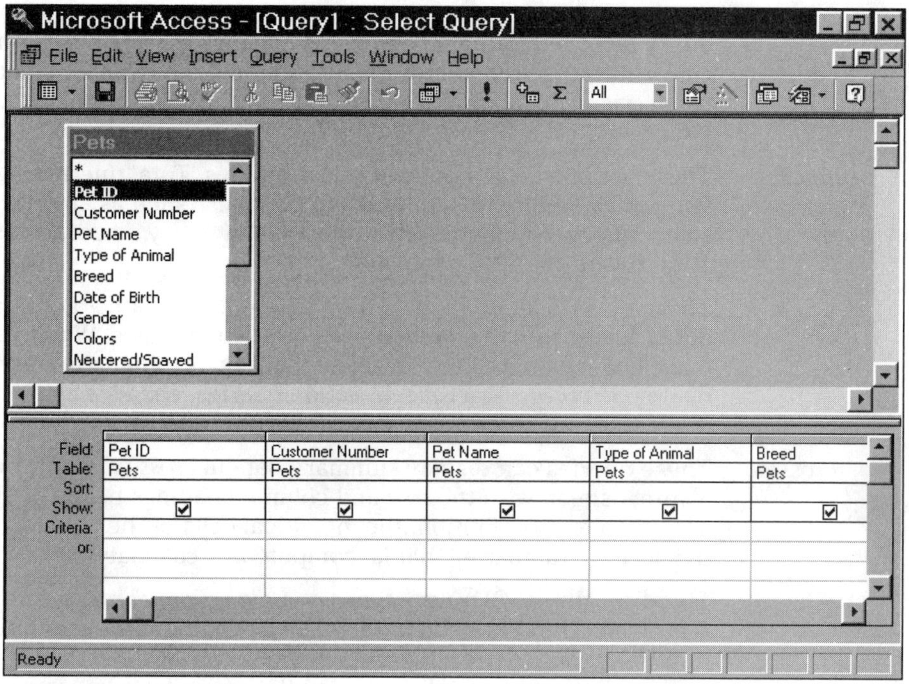

Figure 10-1: A typical select query.

You may want Access to show you a single datasheet of all customers and their pets that meet your specified criteria. Access can retrieve customer names and cities from the Customer table and then pet names, animal type, and current vaccination status from the Pets table. Access then takes the information that's common to your criteria, combines it, and displays all the information in a single datasheet. This datasheet is the result of a query that draws from both the Customer and Pets tables. The database query performed the work of assembling all the information for you. In this chapter, you work with only the Pets table; Part III covers multiple tables.

Types of queries

Access supports many different types of queries. They can be grouped into six basic categories:

Select These are the most common. As its name implies, the select query selects information from one or more tables (based on specific criteria), and displays the information in a dynaset you can use to view and analyze specific data; you can make changes to your data in the underlying tables.

Total These are special versions of select queries. Total queries give you the capability to sum or produce totals (such as count) in a select query. When you select this type of query, Access adds the Total row in the QBE pane.

Action These queries let you create new tables (Make Tables) or change data (delete, update, and append) in existing tables. When you make changes to records in a select query, the changes must be made one record at a time. In action queries, changes can be made to many records during a single operation.

Crosstab These queries can display summary data in *cross-tabular* form like a spreadsheet, with the row and column headings based on fields in the table. By definition, the individual cells of the resultant dynaset are tabular — that is, computed or calculated.

SQL There are three SQL query types — *Union*, *Pass-Through*, and *Data Definition*. They are used for advanced SQL database manipulation (for example, working with client/server SQL databases). You can create these queries only by writing specific SQL commands.

Top(n) You can use this *query limiter* only in conjunction with the other five types of queries. It lets you specify a number or percentage of the top records you want to see in any type of query.

Query capabilities

Queries are flexible. They give you the capability of looking at your data in virtually any way you can think of. Most database systems are continually evolving, developing more powerful and necessary tools. The original purpose they are designed for changes over time. You may decide that you want to look at the information stored in the database in a different way. Because information is stored in a database, you should be able to look at it in this new way. Looking at data in a way that's different from its intended manner is known as performing *ad hoc* queries. You'll find querying tools are among the most powerful features of your database; querying is indeed very powerful and flexible in Microsoft Access. Here is a sampling of what you can do:

Choose tables You can obtain information from a single table or from many tables that are related by some common data. Suppose you're interested in seeing the customer name along with the type of animals each customer owns. This sample task takes information from the Customer and Pets tables. When using several tables, Access returns the data in a combined single datasheet.

Choose fields

You can specify which fields from each table you want to see in the resultant dynaset. For example, you can look at the customer name, customer zip code, animal name, and animal type separated from all the other fields in the Customer or Pets table.

Choose records

You can select the records to display in the dynaset by specifying criteria. For example, you may want to see records for dogs only.

Sort records

Often you may want to see the dynaset information sorted in a specific order. You may need (for example) to see customers in order by last name and first name.

Perform calculations

You can use queries to perform calculations on your data. You may be interested in performing such calculations as averaging, totaling, or simply counting the fields.

Create tables

You may need another database table formed from the combined data resulting from a query. The query can create this new table based on the dynaset.

Create forms and reports based on a query

The dynaset you create from a query may have just the right fields and data you need for a report or form. When you base your form or report on a query, every time you print the report or open the form, your query will retrieve the most current information from your tables.

Create graphs based on queries

You can create graphs from the data in a query, which you can then use in a form or report.

Use a query as a source of data for other queries (subquery)

You can create additional queries based on a set of records you selected in a previous query. This is very useful for performing ad hoc queries, where you may make small changes to the criteria over and over. The secondary query can be used to change the criteria while the primary query and its data remain intact.

Make changes to tables   Access queries can obtain information from a wide range of sources. You can ask questions about data stored in dBASE, Paradox, Btrieve, and Microsoft SQL Server databases.

How dynasets work

Earlier you learned that Access takes the records that result from a query and displays them in a datasheet, in which the actual records are called a dynaset. Physically a dynaset looks like a table; in fact, it is not. The dynaset is a *dynamic* (or virtual) set of records. *This dynamic set of records is not stored in the database.*

Note   When you close a query, the query dynaset is gone; it will no longer exist. Even though the dynaset itself no longer exists, remember that the data that formed the dynaset remains stored in the underlying tables.

When you run a query, Access places the resultant records in the dynaset. When you save the query, the information is *not* saved; only the structure of the query is saved — the tables, fields, sort order, record limitations, query type, and so forth. Consider these benefits of not saving the dynaset to a physical table:

✦ The storage device (usually a hard disk) needs less space.

✦ The query can use updated versions of any records changed since the query was last run.

Every time the query is executed, it goes out to the underlying tables and re-creates the dynaset. Because dynasets themselves are not stored, a query automatically reflects any changes to the underlying tables made since the last time the query was executed — even in a real-time, multiuser environment.

Creating a Query

After you create your tables and place data in them, you are ready to work with queries. To begin a query, follow these steps:

1. From the Database window, click on the Queries tab.

2. Click on the New button.

   The New Query dialog box appears, as shown in Figure 10-2. You can select from the five choices. The first choice displays the Query Design window.

3. Select Design View and click on the OK button.

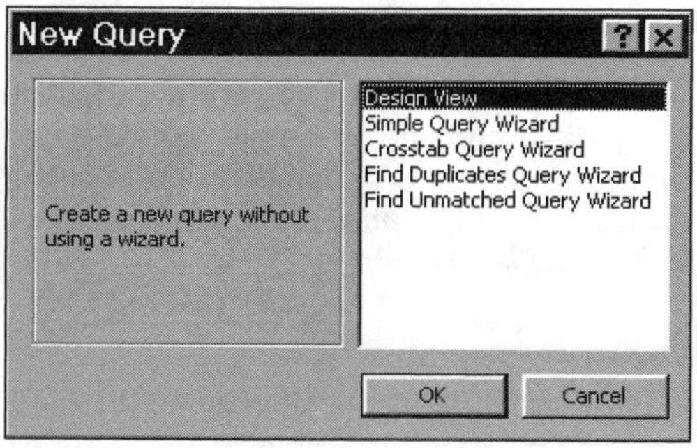

Figure 10-2: The New Query dialog box.

If you select the new query without first selecting a table, Access opens a window and a dialog box. Figure 10-3 shows both windows. The underlying window is the Query Design window. The accompanying Show Table dialog box is *nonmodal,* which means simply that you must do something in the dialog box before continuing with the query. Before you continue, you should add tables for the query to work with.

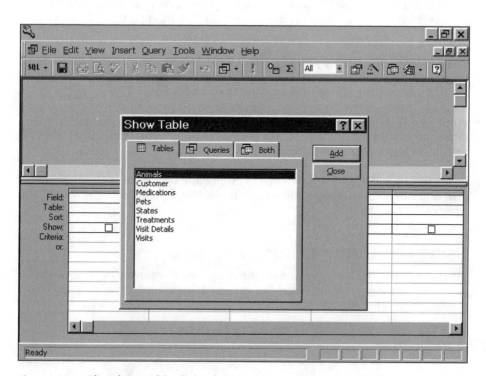

Figure 10-3: The Show Table dialog box in the Query Design window.

Selecting a table

The Show Table dialog box displays all tables and queries in your database. If you are following along with the examples, you should see one table named Pets. If you are using the Mountain Animal Hospital or Mountain Animal Start databases, you should see all the tables in the Mountain Animal Hospital database. You can add the Pets table to the query design with these steps:

1. Select the Pets table.

2. Click on the Add button to add the Pets table to the Query Design window.

3. Click on the Close button.

Tip   Another method of adding the Pets table to the Query Design window is simply double-clicking on the Pets table.

You can also begin a new query by clicking on the New Query button on the toolbar, or you can select Insert⇨Query from the main Access menu. If you select a table or query before you start a new query, Access will load the selected table or query automatically.

You can activate the Show Table dialog box to add more tables at any time; select Query⇨Show Table or click on the Show Table button (picture of table with plus sign).

Tip   You can also add tables by moving the mouse to any empty place in the top half of the window (the Table/Query Pane) and clicking the *right* mouse button. Right-click to activate the shortcut menu and then select Show Table.

When you want to delete a table from the Table/Query pane, you can click on the table name in the query/table entry pane (see Figure 10-4) and either press Delete or select Query⇨Remove Table.

Tip   You also can add a table to the Query/Table Pane by selecting the Database window and dragging and dropping a table name from the Table window into the Query window.

Using the Query window

The Query window has two modes, the *design mode* and the *datasheet mode*. The difference between them is self-explanatory: The design mode is where you create the query, and the datasheet is where you display the query's dynaset.

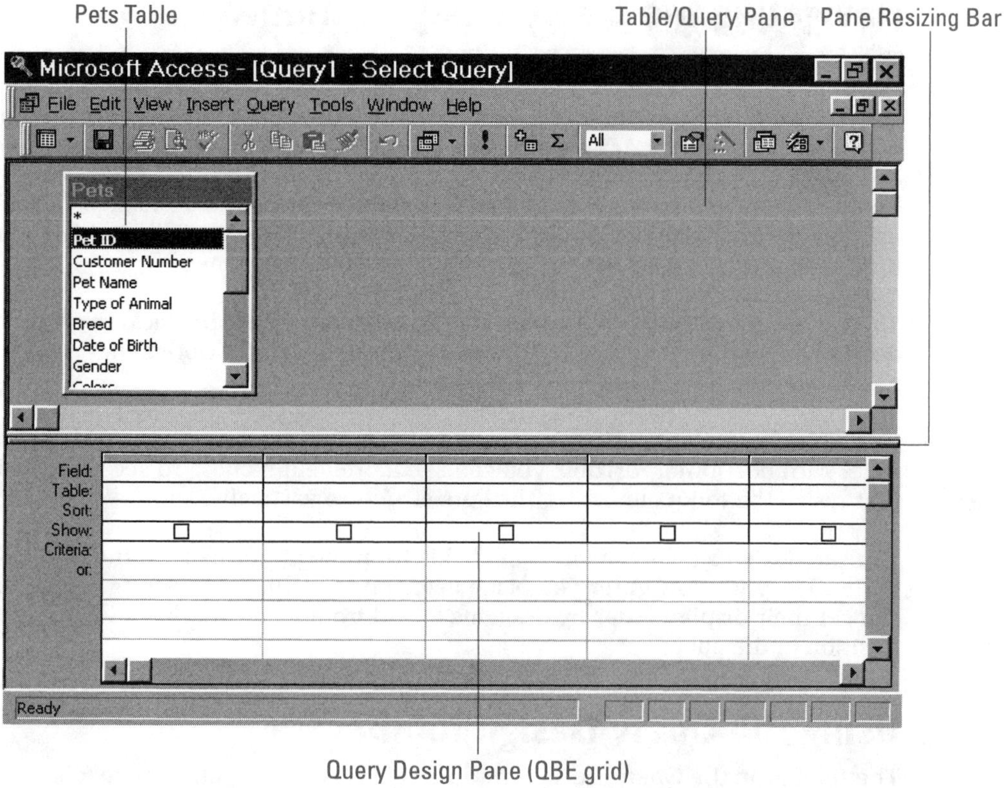

Pets Table   Table/Query Pane   Pane Resizing Bar

Query Design Pane (QBE grid)

Figure 10-4: The Query Design window with the Pets table displayed.

The Query Design window should now look like Figure 10-4, with the Pets table displayed in the top half of the Query Design window.

The Query Design window is currently in the design mode; it consists of two panes:

✦ The table/query entry pane

✦ The query by example (QBE) design pane (also called the *QBE grid*)

The *table/query entry pane* is where tables and/or queries and their design structures are displayed. The visual representation of the table lists each field. The *Query By Example (QBE) pane* is used for the fields and criteria that the query will display in the dynaset. Each column in the QBE design pane contains information about a single field from a table or query in the upper pane.

Navigating the Query Design window

The *title bar* at the top of the Query Design window bears information about a particular window, the type of query, and the query name. Any new query is named Query1. Note that the title bar in Figure 10-4 displays the query type and name as Query1 : Select Query.

The two window panes are separated horizontally by a *pane resizing bar*. You'll use this bar to resize the panes: To enlarge the upper pane, click on the bar and then drag it down; drag the bar up to enlarge the lower pane.

You can switch between the upper and lower panes either by clicking on the desired pane or by pressing F6 to move to the other pane. Notice that each pane has scrollbars to help you move around.

Tip   If you resize the Pets design structure vertically, you can see more fields at one time. With horizontal resizing, you can see more field names. To see more fields, first resize the top pane to size the Pets structure vertically.

You can design a query by dragging fields from the upper pane to the lower pane of the Query window. After you place fields on the QBE pane (lower pane), you can set their display order by dragging a field from its current position to a new position in the pane.

Using the Query Design toolbar

The toolbar in the Query Design window contains several buttons specific to building and working with queries, as shown in Figure 10-5.

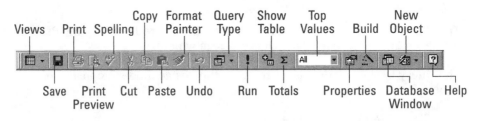

Figure 10-5: The Query Design toolbar.

Using the QBE pane of the Query Design window

Figure 10-4 shows you an empty Query Design pane (QBE grid). You'll see five named rows in this pane:

Field	This is where field names are entered or added.
Sort	This choice lets you enter sort directives for the query.
Show	This check box determines whether to display the field in the resulting dynaset.
Criteria	This is where you enter the first line of criteria to limit the record selection.
Or	This is the first of a number of lines to which you can add multiple values to be used in criteria selection.

You learn more about these rows as you create several sample queries in this chapter.

Selecting Fields

There are several ways to add fields to a query. You can add fields one at a time, select multiple fields, or select all fields. You can use your keyboard or mouse to add the fields.

Adding a single field

You can add a single field in several ways. One method is to double-click on the field name; the field name then appears in the next available column in the Query Design pane. You can also add a field graphically to the Query Design pane by following these steps:

1. Highlight the field name in the table/query entry area.

2. Click on the desired field and drag the Field icon, which appears as you move the mouse.

3. Drop the Field icon in the desired column of the QBE Design pane.

The Field icon looks like a small rectangle when it is inside the Pets table. As the mouse is dragged outside the Pets table, the icon changes to a circle-with-slash (the international symbol meaning "no"). It means you cannot drop the Field icon in that location. When this icon enters any column in the QBE column, the field name appears in the Field: row. If you drop the field between two other fields, it appears between those fields and pushes all existing fields to the right.

Tip If you select a field accidentally, you can deselect it by releasing the mouse button while the icon is the No symbol.

To run the query, click on the Datasheet button on the toolbar (the first icon from the left). When you are finished, click on the Design button on the toolbar (the first one on the left) to return to design mode.

Another way to add fields to the QBE Design pane is to click on the empty Field: cell in the QBE Design pane and then type the field name in the field cell. Another method is to select the field you want from the drop-down list that appears (see Figure 10-6).

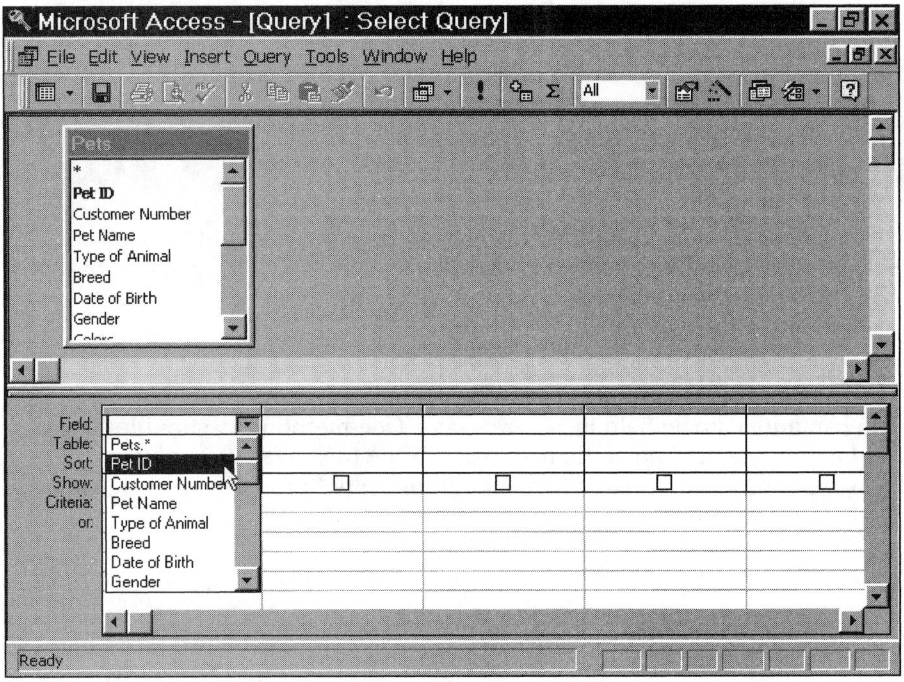

Figure 10-6: Adding a single field in the QBE Design pane (grid).

Adding multiple fields

You can add more than one field at a time by selecting the fields and then dragging the selection to the query pane. For you to add multiple fields from a table simultaneously, the selected fields do not have to be contiguous (one after the other). Figure 10-7 illustrates the process of adding multiple fields.

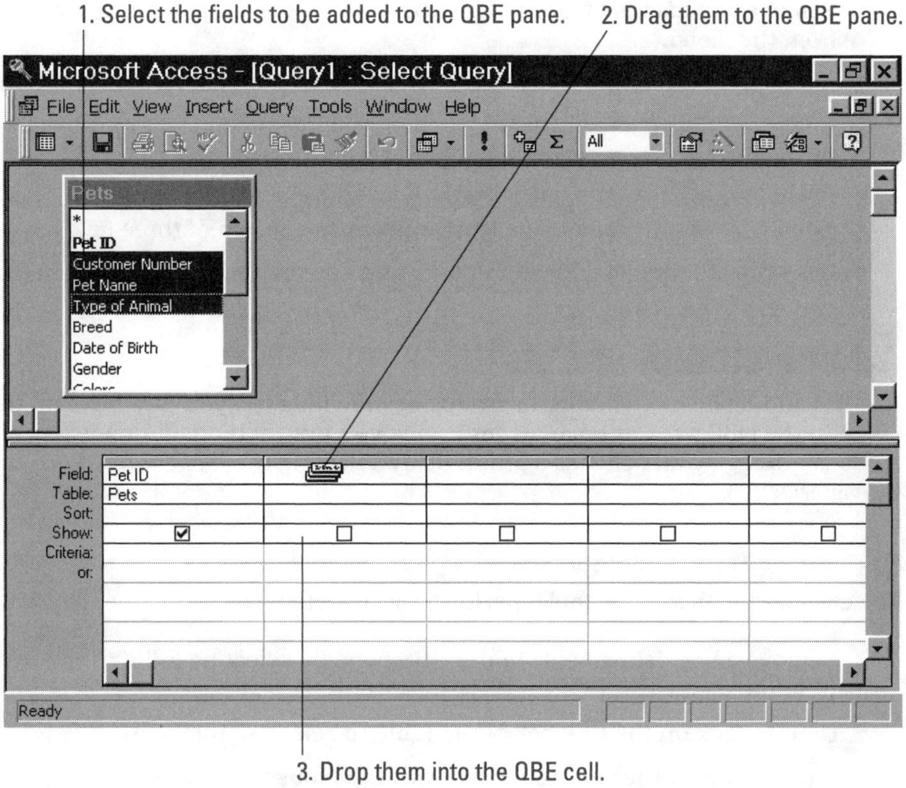

1. Select the fields to be added to the QBE pane.   2. Drag them to the QBE pane.

3. Drop them into the QBE cell.

Figure 10-7: Selecting several fields graphically to move to the QBE Design pane.

To add multiple contiguous fields, follow these steps:

1. Remove any existing fields in the QBE pane by selecting Edit⇨Clear Grid from the menu.

2. Highlight in the table/query entry area the first field name you want to add.

3. Hold the Shift key down and click on the last field you want to select. (All the fields in between will be selected as well.)

4. Click on the selected fields and drag the Multiple Field icon, which appears as you move the mouse. The icon appears as a group of three field icons.

5. Drop the Multiple Field icon in the desired column of the QBE Design pane.

To add multiple noncontiguous fields to the query, follow these steps:

1. Remove any existing fields in the QBE pane by selecting Edit➪Clear Grid from the menu.

2. Highlight in the table/query entry area the first field name you want to add.

3. Hold the Control key down and click on each field you want to select. (Only the fields you select will be highlighted.)

4. Click on the selected fields and drag the Multiple Field icon, which appears as you move the mouse. The icon appears as a group of three field icons.

5. Drop the Multiple Field icon in the desired column of the QBE Design pane.

Adding all table fields

Besides adding fields (whether in groups or individually), you can move all the fields to the QBE pane at once. Access gives you two methods for choosing all fields: by dragging all fields as a group or by selecting the *all-field reference tag* — the asterisk (*).

Dragging all fields as a group

To select all the fields of a table, perform these steps:

1. Remove any existing fields in the QBE pane by selecting Edit➪Clear Grid from the menu.

2. Double-click on the title bar of the table to select all the fields.

3. Point to any of the selected fields with the mouse.

4. Drag the Multiple Field icon down to the QBE pane.

This method fills in each column of the QBE pane automatically. All the fields are added to the QBE pane from left to right, based on their field order in the Pets table. By default, Access displays only the fields that can fit in the window. You can change the column width of each field to display more or fewer columns.

Selecting the all-field reference tag

The first object in the Pets table is an asterisk, which appears at the top of the field list. When you select all fields by using the asterisk, you don't see all the fields moved to the QBE Design pane. You see only that `Pets.*` is displayed in the Field: row, indicating that all fields from the table named Pets are now selected. (This example assumes that the QBE Design pane is empty when you drag the asterisk from the Pets table to the QBE Design pane.)

The asterisk places the fields in a single Field: cell. When you dragged multiple fields with the first technique, you dragged actual table field names to the Query Design window, thus placing each field in a separate Field: cell across the QBE pane. If you change the design of the table later, you must also change the design of the query. The advantage of using the asterisk for selecting all fields is that you won't have to change the query later if you add, delete, or rename fields in the underlying table or query. (Access will automatically add or remove any fields that change in the underlying table or query.)

If you are following along with the examples, you need to delete all fields from the query by selecting Edit⇨Clear Grid from the Query Design menu. When you've cleared all the fields, you can select the first nine fields in the Pets table (Pet ID through Neutered/Spayed, inclusively) and move them to the QBE Design pane.

CD-ROM

To add the all-fields reference tag to the Query Design pane, follow these steps:

1. Click on the asterisk (*) in the Pets table to select this field.
2. Click on the selected field and drag the Field icon to the first cell in the QBE Design pane.

You now have the all-fields reference tag in the QBE pane. When you run this query, all the fields from Pets will be displayed.

Displaying the Dynaset

With multiple fields selected, it is time to display the resultant dynaset. You can switch to the datasheet by selecting either View⇨Datasheet or the Datasheet button on the toolbar. The datasheet should now look like Figure 10-8.

Working with the datasheet

Access displays the dynaset in a datasheet. The techniques for navigating a query datasheet, as well as for changing its field order and working with its columns and rows, are exactly the same as for the other datasheets you worked with in Chapter 8.

Access 97 allows you to sort and filter the results of a datasheet created by a query. All data in Access 97 is editable all the time.

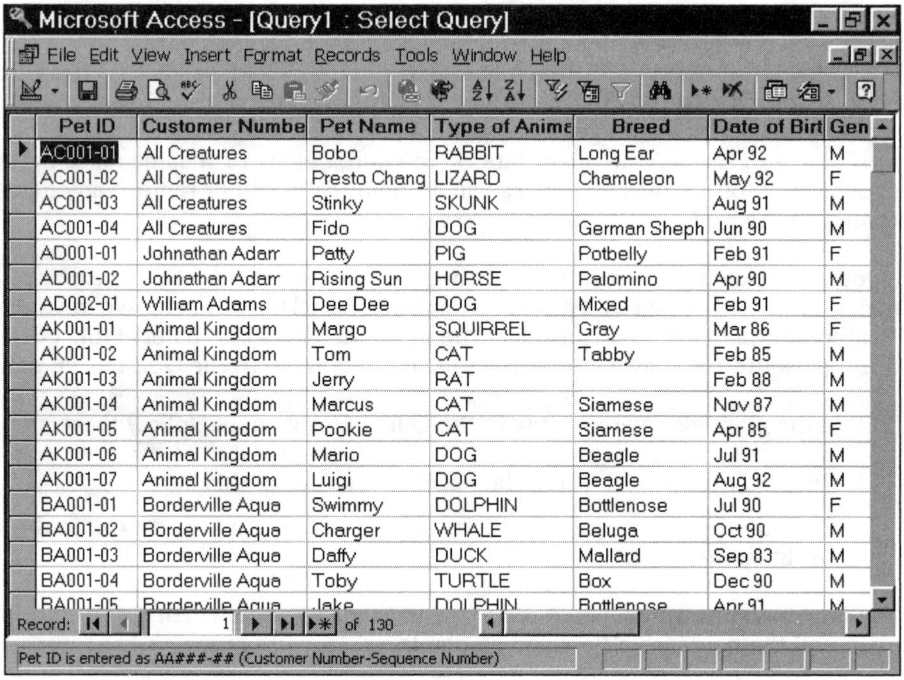

Figure 10-8: The datasheet with several fields.

Changing data in the query datasheet

The query datasheet offers you an easy and convenient way to change data quickly. You can add and change data in the dynaset, and it will be saved to the underlying tables.

When you're adding or changing data in the datasheet, all the table properties defined at the table level are in effect. For example, you cannot enter a length value greater than 120 for any animal.

Returning to the query design

To return to the query design mode, select the Design button on the toolbar (the first one from the left).

Tip   You can also toggle between the design and datasheet mode by selecting View⇨Datasheet or View⇨Query Design from the Query menu.

CD-ROM

Clear the query grid by selecting Edit⇨Clear Grid. Next, add all the fields to the query grid by first double-clicking on the Pets data structure title bar and then dragging all the selected fields to the query grid.

Working with Fields

There are times when you'll want to work with the fields you've already selected — rearranging their order, inserting a new field, or deleting an existing field. You may even want to add a field to the QBE design without showing it in the datasheet.

The *field selector row* is the narrow gray row above the Field: row. This row is approximately half the size of the others; it's important to identify this row because this is where you select columns, whether single or multiple. Recall that each column represents a field. To select the Pet Name field, move the mouse pointer until a small *selection arrow* (in this case, an outlined downward arrow) is visible in the selector row. Then click on the column. Figure 10-9 shows the selection arrow in the next column and the column after it is selected.

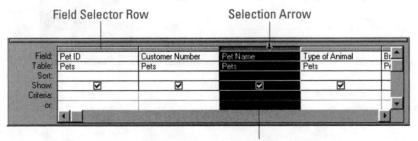

Figure 10-9: Selecting a column in the QBE pane.

If extend mode (F8) is on, the cursor must be in the row whose column you want to select. If the cursor is in an adjacent column and you select a column, you will select the adjacent column (containing the cursor) as well. To deactivate extend mode (EXT), simply press the Escape key.

Changing field order

Several methods are available for changing the order of the fields in the QBE Design pane. One way is to add them in the order you want them to appear in the datasheet, though this method is not always the easiest. You can move fields after they are placed on the QBE design by selecting columns and moving them, just as you learned to move columns in a datasheet. The following steps show you how to move a field:

1. Add several fields to the QBE pane.

2. Select the field you want to move (Breed) by clicking on the field selector above the field name. The column is highlighted.

3. Click on and hold the field selector again; the QBE Field icon, a small graphical box, appears under the arrow.

4. While holding down the left button, drag the column to its new position (to the left of Type of Animal).

5. Release the left mouse button to drop the field in its new position.

Figure 10-10 shows the Breed field highlighted (selected). As you move the selector field to the left, the column separator between the fields Pet Name and Type of Animal changes (gets wider) to show you where Breed will go.

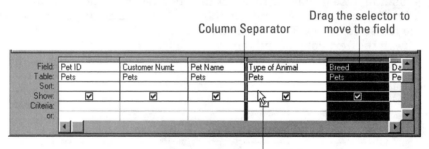

Figure 10-10: Moving the Breed field to between Pet Name and Type of Animal.

Removing a field

You can easily remove a field from the QBE Design pane. Select the field or fields to be deleted in the QBE Design pane, and then press Delete or select Edit⇨Delete. To remove the Customer Number field from the QBE Design pane, follow these steps:

1. Select the Customer Number field (or any other field) by clicking on the field selector above the field name.

2. Press Delete.

Tip If the field is not selected but the cursor is on it, you can select Edit⇨Delete Column. You can delete all the fields in the QBE Design pane in a single operation: Select Edit⇨Clear Grid from the Query Design window's menu bar.

Inserting a field

You insert a field from the table/query entry pane in the QBE Design pane by first selecting the field(s) to be inserted from the table/query entry pane. Next, drag your field selection to the QBE Design pane. The following steps show you how to insert the Customer Number field:

1. Select the Customer Number field from the field list in the table/query entry pane.

2. Drag the field from the field list to the column where you want the field to go.

3. Drop the field by releasing the left mouse button.

When you drag a field to the QBE Design pane, it will be inserted wherever you drop the field. If you drop the field on top of another field, it is inserted before that field. If you double-click on the field name in the table/query entry pane, the field is added to the end of the Field: list in the QBE Design pane.

Changing the field display name

To make the query datasheet easier to read, you may want to rename the fields in your query. The new names you choose will become the tag headings in the datasheet of the query. As an example, to rename the field Breed to Lineage, follow these steps:

1. Click to the left of the *B* in Breed in the Field: row of the QBE Design pane.

2. Type **Lineage** and then type a colon (:) between the new name and the old field name.

The heading now reads Lineage:Breed. When the datasheet is displayed, you'll see Lineage in place of Breed.

Note   Renaming the field by changing the datasheet caption changes *only* the name of the heading for that field in the datasheet. It does *not* change the field name in the underlying table.

Showing a field

While performing queries, you may want to show only some of the fields temporarily. Suppose, for example, that you want to show only the fields Pet ID, Pet Name, and Breed. You can delete all other fields (and restore them when you're done with the temporary dynaset), or you can simply indicate which fields you want to see in the datasheet.

When you select fields, Access makes every field a displayed field automatically. Every Show: property is displayed with a check mark in the box.

To deselect a field's Show: property, simply click on the field's Show: box. The box clears, as you see in Figure 10-11. To reselect the field later, simply click on the Show: box again.

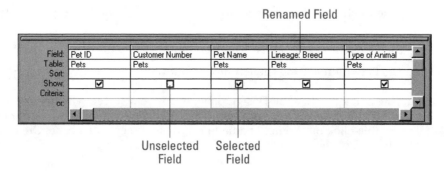

Figure 10-11: The Show: row is checked here only for the fields Pet ID, Pet Name, Breed, and Type of Animal.

Changing the Sort Order

When viewing a dynaset, you may want to display the data in some sorted order. You may want to sort the dynaset to make it easier to analyze the data (for example, to look at all the pets in order by Type of Animal).

Sorting places the records in alphabetical or numeric order. The sort order can be *ascending* (0 to 9 and A to Z) or *descending* (9 to 0 and Z to A).

Just as Access has a Show: property row for fields, there is a Sort: property row for fields in the QBE Design pane. In the following section, you learn how to set this property.

Specifying a sort

To sort the records in the datasheet by Type of Animal in ascending order, perform the following steps:

1. Click on the Sort: cell for the Type of Animal field. An arrow appears in the cell.

2. Click on the down arrow at the right of the cell.

3. Select Ascending from the list.

Figure 10-12 shows the QBE pane with the Type of Animal field selected for sorting by ascending order. Notice that the word *Ascending* appears in the field's Sort: cell.

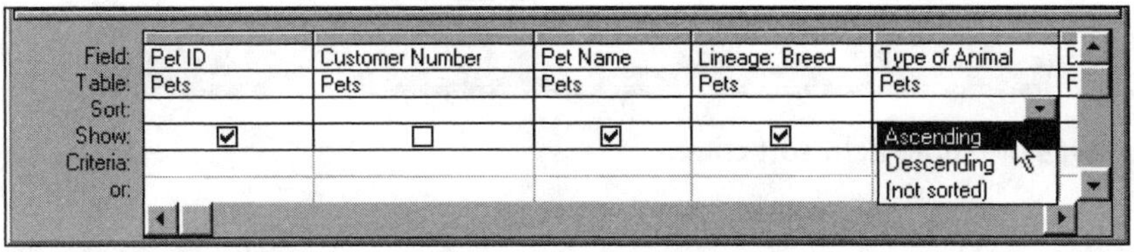

Field:	Pet ID	Customer Number	Pet Name	Lineage: Breed	Type of Animal	C
Table:	Pets	Pets	Pets	Pets	Pets	F
Sort:					▼	
Show:	☑	☐	☑	☑	Ascending	
Criteria:					Descending	
or:					(not sorted)	

Figure 10-12: A field selected for sorting.

Caution If you save a query that has an unused field (its Show: box is unchecked), Access eliminates the field from the query pane.

Note You *cannot* sort on a Memo or an OLE object field.

Sorting on more than one field

Access gives you the capability of sorting on multiple fields. You may, for example, want a primary sort order of Type of Animal and a secondary sort order by Breed. To create this query, start with the query illustrated in Figure 10-12. Then move the Breed field so that it is after the Type of Animal field. Finally, add a sort to the Breed field by selecting Ascending in the Sort: cell.

Access *always* sorts the leftmost sort field first. To make sure that Access understands how you want to sort your data, you must arrange the fields in order from left to right according to sort-order precedence. You can easily change the sort order by simply selecting a sort field and moving it relative to another sort field. Access corrects the sort order automatically.

That's all there is to it. Now the dynaset is arranged in order by two different fields. Figure 10-13 shows the multiple-field sort criteria. The sort order is controlled by the order of the fields in the QBE pane (from left to right); therefore, this dynaset is displayed in order first by Type of Animal and then by Breed, as you see in Figure 10-14. Also notice that Breed has been renamed Lineage in the column header of the datasheet in Figure 10-14.

If you are following along with the examples, start a new query and select all the fields before continuing.

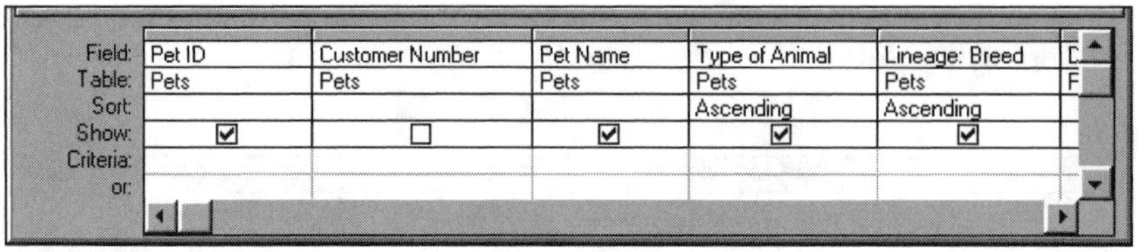

Field:	Pet ID	Customer Number	Pet Name	Type of Animal	Lineage: Breed	
Table:	Pets	Pets	Pets	Pets	Pets	
Sort:				Ascending	Ascending	
Show:	☑	☐	☑	☑	☑	
Criteria:						
or:						

Figure 10-13: Multiple-field sort criteria.

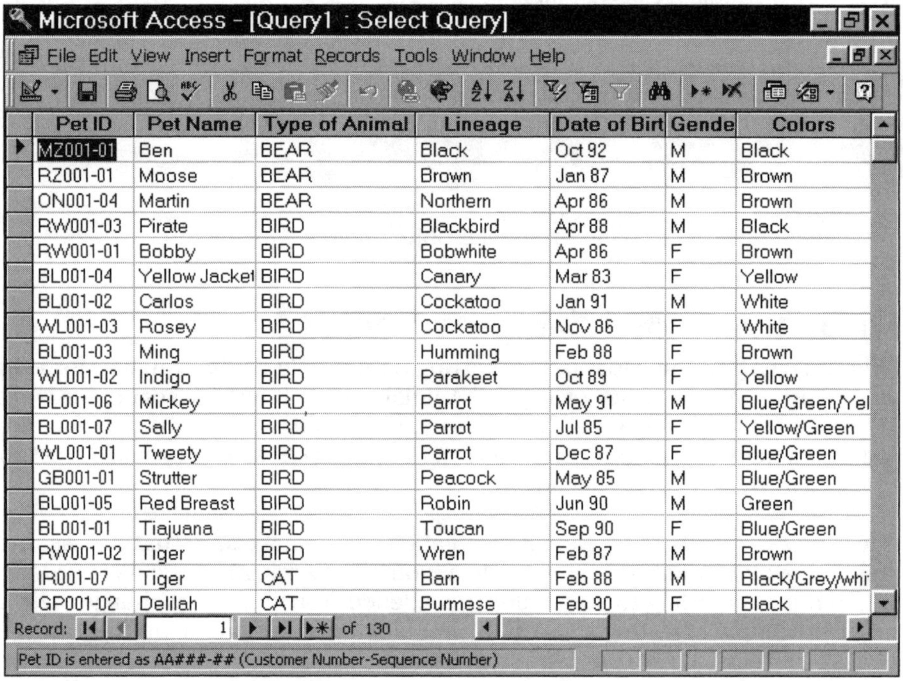

Microsoft Access - [Query1 : Select Query]

File Edit View Insert Format Records Tools Window Help

Pet ID	Pet Name	Type of Animal	Lineage	Date of Birt	Gende	Colors
MZ001-01	Ben	BEAR	Black	Oct 92	M	Black
RZ001-01	Moose	BEAR	Brown	Jan 87	M	Brown
ON001-04	Martin	BEAR	Northern	Apr 86	M	Brown
RW001-03	Pirate	BIRD	Blackbird	Apr 88	M	Black
RW001-01	Bobby	BIRD	Bobwhite	Apr 86	F	Brown
BL001-04	Yellow Jacket	BIRD	Canary	Mar 83	F	Yellow
BL001-02	Carlos	BIRD	Cockatoo	Jan 91	M	White
WL001-03	Rosey	BIRD	Cockatoo	Nov 86	F	White
BL001-03	Ming	BIRD	Humming	Feb 88	F	Brown
WL001-02	Indigo	BIRD	Parakeet	Oct 89	F	Yellow
BL001-06	Mickey	BIRD	Parrot	May 91	M	Blue/Green/Yel
BL001-07	Sally	BIRD	Parrot	Jul 85	F	Yellow/Green
WL001-01	Tweety	BIRD	Parrot	Dec 87	F	Blue/Green
GB001-01	Strutter	BIRD	Peacock	May 85	M	Blue/Green
BL001-05	Red Breast	BIRD	Robin	Jun 90	M	Green
BL001-01	Tiajuana	BIRD	Toucan	Sep 90	F	Blue/Green
RW001-02	Tiger	BIRD	Wren	Feb 87	M	Brown
IR001-07	Tiger	CAT	Barn	Feb 88	M	Black/Grey/whi
GP001-02	Delilah	CAT	Burmese	Feb 90	F	Black

Record: I◄ ◄ 1 ► ►I ►✱ of 130

Pet ID is entered as AA###-## (Customer Number-Sequence Number)

Figure 10-14: A multiple-field sort order displayed.

Displaying Only Selected Records

So far, you've been working with all the records of the Pets table. There are times when you may want to work only with selected records in the Pets table. For example, you may want to look only at records where the value of Type of Animal is DOG. Access makes it easy for you to specify a record's criteria.

Understanding record criteria

Record criteria are simply some rule or rules that you supply for Access. These tell Access which records you want to look at in the dynaset. A typical criterion could be "all male animals" or "only those animals that are not currently vaccinated" or "all animals that were born before January 1990."

In other words, with record criteria, you create *limiting filters* to tell Access which records to find and which to leave out of the dynaset.

You specify criteria starting in the Criteria: property row of the QBE pane. Here you designate criteria with an expression. The expression can be simple example data or can take the form of complicated expressions using predefined functions.

As an example of a simple data criterion, you can type **DOG** in the Criteria: cell of Type of Animal. If you look at the datasheet, you see only records for dogs.

Entering simple character criteria

You would enter character-type criteria into fields that accommodate the Text data type. To use such criteria, you would type in an example of the data contained within the field. To limit the record display to DOG, follow these steps:

1. Click on the Criteria: cell in the Type of Animal column in the QBE Design pane.

2. Type **DOG** in the cell.

3. Click on the Datasheet button.

Only the dogs are displayed. Observe that you did *not* enter an equal sign or place quotes around the sample text, yet Access added double quotes around the value. Access, unlike many other applications, automatically makes assumptions about what you want. This is an illustration of its powerful flexibility. You could enter the expression in any of these other ways:

Dog

= Dog

"Dog"

= "Dog"

In Figure 10-15, you see the expression entered under Type of Animal.

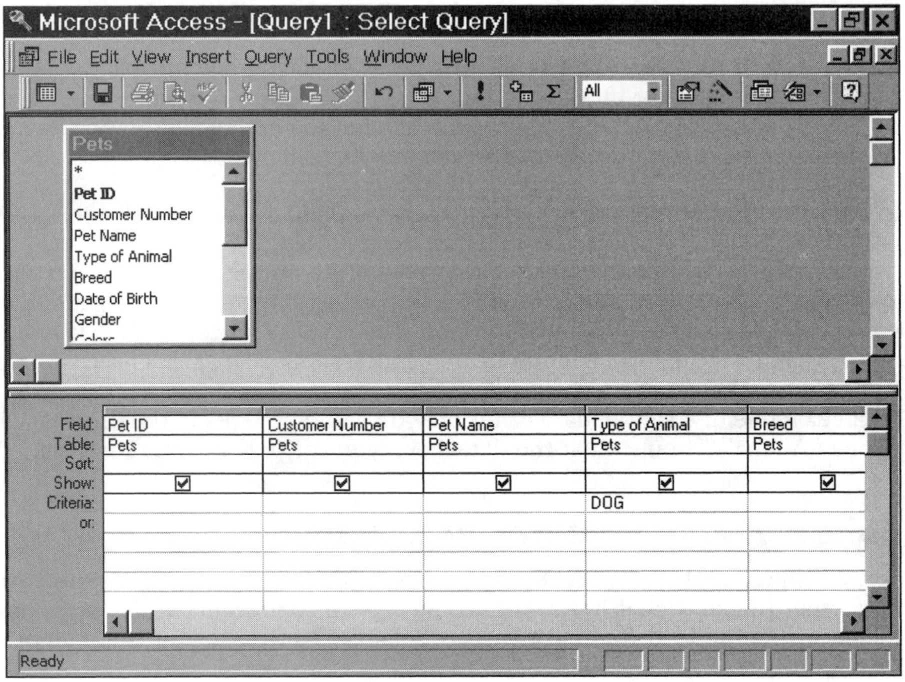

Figure 10-15: Specifying character criteria.

Figure 10-15 is an excellent example to demonstrate options for various types of simple character criteria. You could just as well type **Not Dog** in the criteria column, to say the opposite. In this instance, you would be asking to see all records for animals that are not dogs, adding only **Not** before the example text **Dog**.

Generally, when you deal with character data, you enter equalities, inequalities, or a list of values that are acceptable.

With either of these examples, Dog or Not Dog, you entered a simple expression in a Text-type field. Access took your example and interpreted it to show you all records that equal the example data you placed in the Criteria: cell.

This capability is a powerful tool. Consider that you have only to supply an example and Access not only interprets it but also uses it to create the query dynaset. This is exactly what *Query By Example* means: You enter an example and let the database build a query based on this data.

To erase the criteria in the cell, select the contents and press Delete, or select Edit➪Delete from the Query Design window's menu bar.

If you are following along with the examples, delete the criterion in the Type of Animal field before continuing.

Entering other simple criteria

You can also specify criteria for numeric, date, and yes/no fields. Suppose, for example, that you want to look only at records for animals born after 1/1/95. To limit the display to records where the value of Date of Birth is greater than January 1, 1995, follow these steps:

1. Remove any existing fields in the QBE pane by selecting E̲dit⇨Clea̲r Grid from the menu.

2. Add the following fields: Pet Name, Type of Animal, Breed, and Date of Birth to the QBE grid.

3. Click on the Criteria: cell in the Date of Birth column in the QBE Design pane.

4. Type **> 1/15/93** in the cell.

5. Click on the Datasheet button.

Access also compares Date fields to a value by using *comparison operators,* such as less than (<), greater than (>), equal to (=), or a combination thereof. Notice that Access adds pound-sign (#) *delimiters* around the date value automatically. Access recognizes these delimiters as differentiating a Date field from Text fields. Just as with entering text data examples, however, you don't have to enter the pound signs; Access understands what you want (based on the type of data you enter in the field), and it converts the entry format for you.

Printing a Query Dynaset

After you create your query, you can quickly print all the records in the dynaset. Although you can't specify a type of report, you can print a simple matrix-type report (rows and columns) of the dynaset that your query created.

You do have some flexibility when printing a dynaset. If you know the datasheet is set up just as you want it, you can specify some options as you follow these steps:

1. Specify your record criteria in the query design mode.

2. Switch to the query datasheet mode by clicking on the Datasheet button on the toolbar.

3. Select F̲ile⇨P̲rint from the Query Datasheet window's menu bar, or click on the Print button on the toolbar.

4. Specify the print options you want in the Print dialog box.

5. Click on the OK button in the Print dialog box.

Access now prints the dynaset for you. Assuming that you have set up a printer in Microsoft Windows, you can click on OK to print your dataset. Your dataset prints out in the font selected for display or in the nearest equivalent your printer offers. The printout also reflects all layout options in effect when you print the dataset. Hidden columns do not print; gridlines print only if the Gridlines option is on. The printout reflects the specified row height and column width as well.

Cross-Reference Refer to Chapter 8 to review printing fundamentals; that chapter covers printing the datasheet and using the Print Preview functions.

Saving a Query

To save a query while working in design mode, you can follow this procedure:

Select File⇨Save from the Query Design window, or click on the Save button on the toolbar. If this is the first time you're saving the query, enter a new query name in the Save As dialog box.

To save a query while working in datasheet mode, follow this procedure:

Select File⇨Save from the Datasheet File menu. If this is the first time you're saving the query, enter a new query name in the Save As dialog box.

Tip The F12 key is the Save As key in Access. You can press F12 to save your work and continue working on your query.

Both of these methods will save the query and return you to the mode you were working in. Occasionally, you'll simply want to save and exit the query in a single operation. To do this, select File⇨Close from the query or the datasheet and answer Yes to the question `Save changes to Query 'query name'?`. If this is your first time to save the query, you are prompted to supply a query name and whether you want to save the query to the current database or an external file or database.

You can leave the Query window at any time by one of several ways:

✦ Select File⇨Close from the Query menu.

✦ Select Close from the Query window control box.

✦ Press Ctrl+F4 while inside the Query window.

All three of these methods activate an Access dialog box that asks, Save changes to Query 'Query1'?.

Summary

In this chapter, you learned about the types of queries and the basics of how to use them. You had some practice in creating simple queries and found out about some of the query options Access provides. The chapter covered the following points:

✦ Queries ask questions about your data and return the answers in the form of information.

✦ Types of queries include select, total, crosstab, action, SQL, definition, and Top Values.

✦ Queries let you select tables, fields, sort order, and record criteria.

✦ Queries create a virtual view of the data, known as a dynaset. The data is displayed in a datasheet.

✦ A dynaset is the temporary answer set. Queries save only the instructions and not the data.

✦ The Query window has two panes. The top pane displays the Design view of your tables; the bottom pane is used for entering QBE instructions.

✦ When you add fields with the asterisk button, the query automatically changes if the underlying table changes.

✦ You can display field names differently in the datasheet by adding a new caption with a colon in front of the existing field name.

✦ You can limit records being displayed with record criteria, specifying character, numeric, date/time, and yes/no.

✦ You can use a query's dynaset datasheet just as you would any table — in forms, reports, and other queries.

In the next chapter, you examine how to create and print simple reports.

✦　　　✦　　　✦

Creating and Printing Simple Reports

Reports provide the most flexible way for viewing and printing summarized information. They enable you to display information with the desired level of detail while letting you view or print your information in almost any format. You can add multilevel totals, statistical comparisons, and even pictures and graphics to a report. In this chapter, you see how to use Report Wizards as a starting point for your report. You see how to create reports and what types you can create with Access.

Understanding Reports

Reports are used for presenting a customized view of your data. Your report output can be viewed on-screen or printed to a hard-copy device. With reports, you have the ability to control summarization of the information. You can group your data and sort it in any order you want and then present the data in the order of the groupings. You can create totals that add numbers, calculate averages or other statistics, and even display your data graphically. You can print pictures and other graphics as well as Memo fields in a report. If you can think of a report you want, Access can probably create it.

What types of reports can you create?

Four basic types of reports are used in business today:

Tabular reports   These print data in rows and columns with groupings and totals. Variations include summary and group/total reports.

Columnar reports	These print data as a form; they can include totals and graphs.
Mail-merge reports	These create form letters.
Mailing labels	These create multicolumn labels or snaked-column reports.

Tabular reports

Figure 11-1 shows a typical tabular type report in the Print Preview window. *Tabular reports* (also known as *groups/totals reports*) are generally similar to a table that displays data in neat rows and columns. Tabular reports, unlike forms or datasheets, usually group their data by one or more field values; they calculate and display subtotals or statistical information for numeric fields in each group. Some groups/totals reports also have page totals and grand totals. You can even have *snaked columns* so that you can create directories (such as telephone books). These types of reports can use page numbers, report dates, or lines and boxes to separate information. They can have color and shading and can display pictures, business graphs, and Memo fields, just as forms can. A special type of tabular report, *summary reports* can have all the features of a tabular report; however, they are lacking detail records.

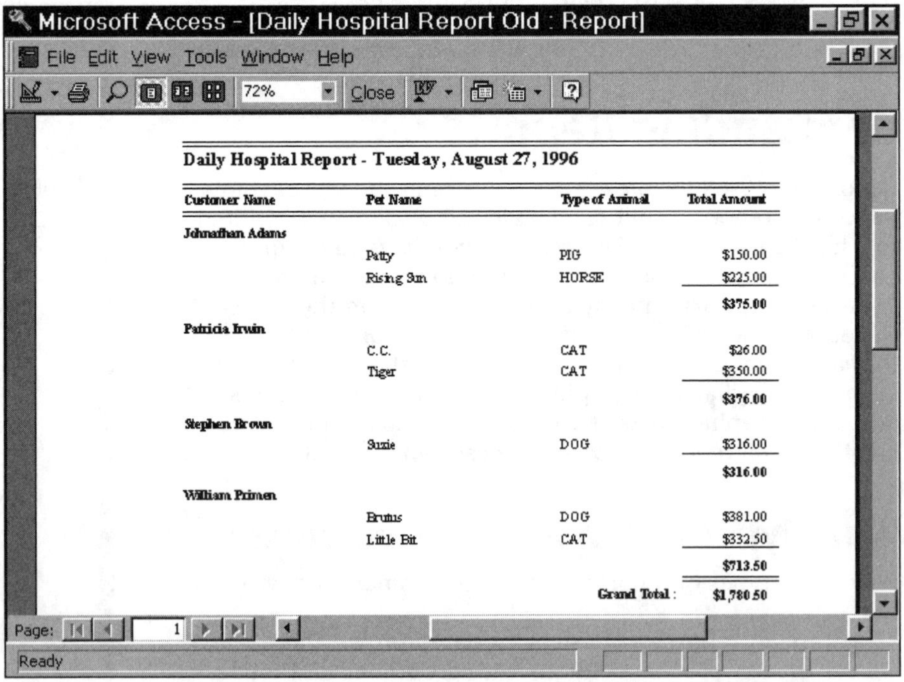

Figure 11-1: A tabular report in the Print Preview window of Access 97.

Columnar reports

Columnar reports (also known as *form reports*) generally display one or more records per page, but do so vertically. Column reports display data very much as a data-entry form does, but the report is used strictly for viewing data and not for entering it. An invoice is a typical example. This type of report can have sections that display only one record and at the same time have sections that display multiple records from the *many* side of a one-to-many relationship — and even include totals. Figure 11-2 shows part of a typical column report from the Mountain Animal Hospital database system in the Print Preview window.

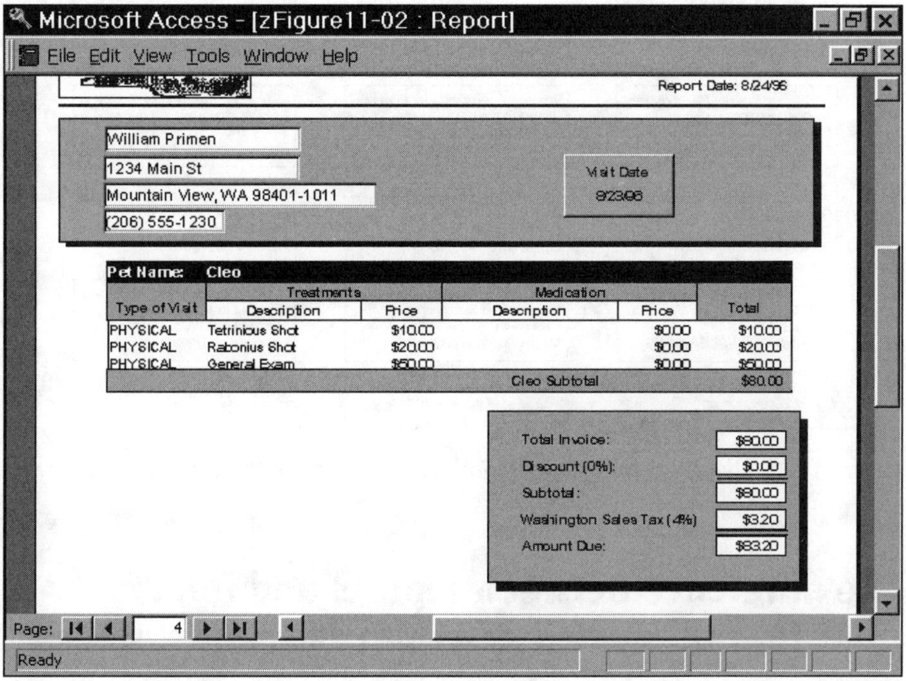

Figure 11-2: The primary part of a form report (columnar) showing multiple records.

Mailing labels

Mailing labels are also a type of report. You can easily create mailing labels, shown in Figure 11-3, by using a report in Access. In fact, you'll want to use the Label Wizard to get you started. The Label Wizard lets you select from a long list of Avery label paper styles, after which Access correctly creates a report design, based on the data you specify to create your label. After the label is created, you can open the report in design mode and customize it as needed.

Cross-Reference Mailing labels are covered in detail in Chapter 29.

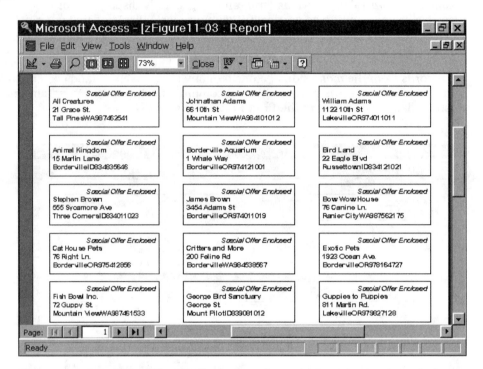

Figure 11-3: A typical mailing label report as shown in the Print Preview window.

The difference between reports and forms

The main difference between reports and forms is the purpose of the output. Whereas forms are primarily for data entry, reports are for viewing data (either on-screen or in hard-copy form). You can use calculated fields with forms and generally have these calculate an amount based on the fields in the record. With reports, you calculate on the basis of a common group of records, a page of records, or all the records processed during the report. Anything you can do with a form — except data input — you can duplicate on a report. In fact, you can save a form *as* a report and then customize the form controls in the Report Design window.

The process of creating a report

Planning a report begins long before you actually create the report design. The report process begins with your desire to view your data in a table, but in a way that differs from datasheet display. You begin with a design for this view; Access begins with raw data. The purpose of the report is to transform the raw data into a meaningful set of information. The process of creating a report involves several steps:

✦ Defining the report layout

✦ Assembling the data

✦ Creating the report design using the Access Report Design window

✦ Printing or viewing the report

Defining the report layout

You should begin by having a general idea of the layout of your report. You can define the layout in your mind, on paper, or interactively, using the Access Report Design window. Figure 11-4 shows a report layout created in this chapter by using the Access Report Designer. This report is first laid out on paper, showing the fields needed and the placement of the fields.

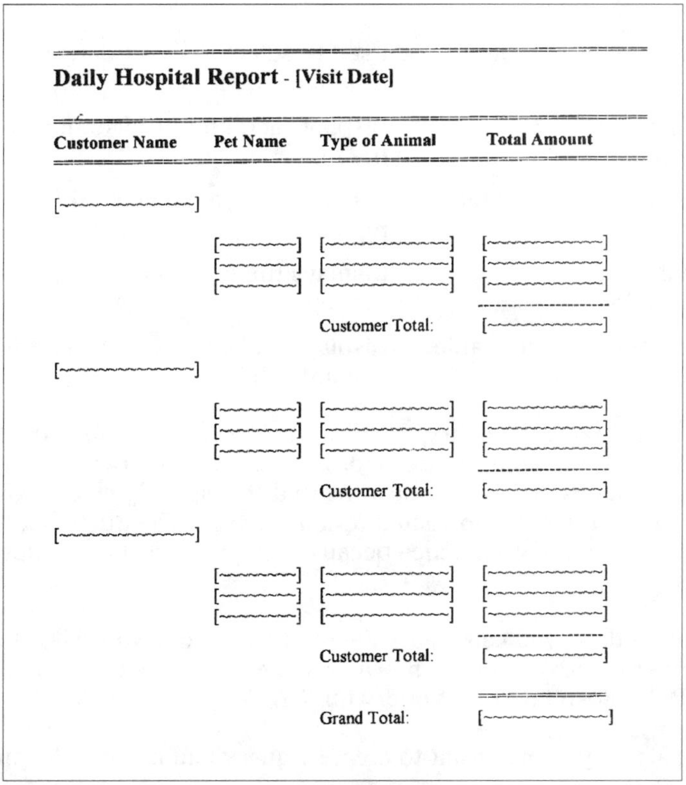

Figure 11-4: A sample report layout.

Assembling the data

After you have a general idea of your report layout, you should assemble the data needed for the report. A report can use data from a single database table or from the results of a query dynaset. You can link many tables together with a query and then use the result of the query (its dynaset) as the record source for your report. A dynaset appears in Access as if it were a single table. As you've learned, you can select the fields, records, and sort order of the records in a query. Access treats this dynaset data as a single table (for processing purposes) in datasheets, forms, and reports. The dynaset becomes the source of data for the report; Access processes each record to create the report. The data for the report and the report *design* are entirely separate. In the report design, you specify the field names that will be used in the report. Then, when you run the report, Access matches data from the dynaset or table against the fields used in the report, and then it uses the data available at that moment to produce the report.

Consider the layout shown in Figure 11-4. Here you want to create a report that shows a daily total of all the pets the hospital treated during a specific day. You call this the Daily Hospital Report. Looking at the layout, you can see that you'll need to assemble the following fields:

Visit Date from the Visits table	Used to select the visit date as a criterion in a query
Customer Name from the Customer table	Displays and groups customers on the report
Pet Name from the Customer table	Displays the pet name on the report table
Type of Animal from the Customer table	Displays the type of animal on the report
Total Amount from the Visits table	Displays and calculates totals for amounts charged

You begin the report by creating a query, as shown in Figure 11-5; notice the three tables linked together and the appropriate fields chosen for the report. The Visit Date field is limited to values of 7/7/95, indicating that this specific view of your data will be limited to customers who visited on July 7, 1995. The Customer Name field is being sorted in ascending sequence because the report will be grouped by customer name.

After you assemble the data, you can create the report design. Figure 11-6 shows the results of this query. The datasheet shown in this figure is the dynaset created when you run the Daily Hospital Report query for 7/7/95.

CD-ROM
If you are following along, you may want to create a query and name it Hospital Report 7/7/95.

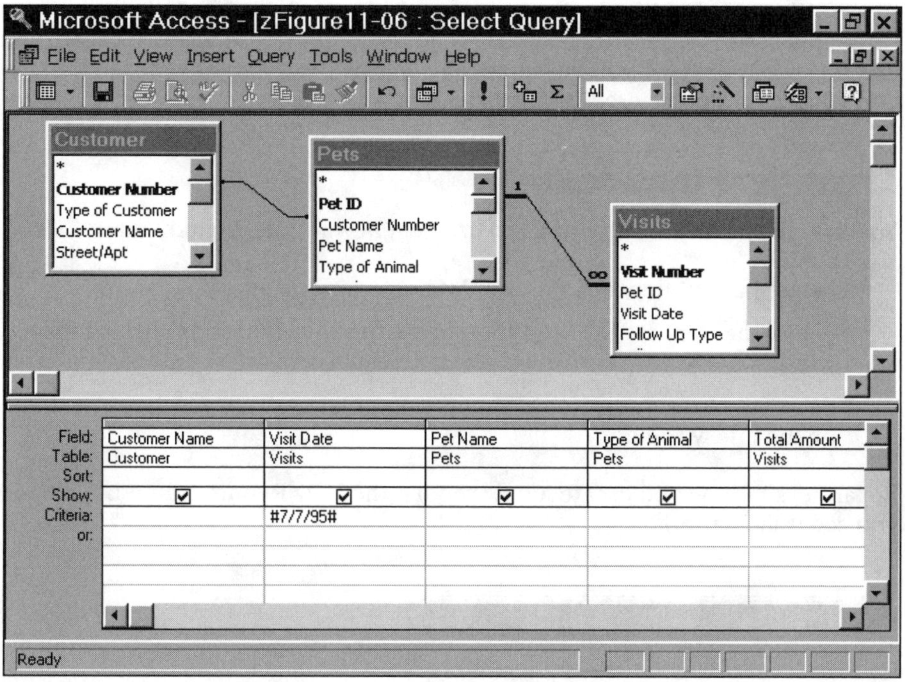

Figure 11-5: Creating a query for a report.

Customer Name	Visit Date	Pet Name	Type of Animal	Total Amount
William Primen	7/7/95	Brutus	DOG	$381.00
William Primen	7/7/95	Little Bit	CAT	$332.50
Stephen Brown	7/7/95	Suzie	DOG	$316.00
Johnathan Adams	7/7/95	Patty	PIG	$150.00
Johnathan Adams	7/7/95	Rising Sun	HORSE	$225.00
Patricia Irwin	7/7/95	C.C.	CAT	$26.00
Patricia Irwin	7/7/95	Tiger	CAT	$350.00

Figure 11-6: The Daily Hospital Report dynaset datasheet.

Creating a Report with Report Wizards

With Access, you can create virtually any type of report. Some reports, however, are more easily created than others; for these, you use a Report Wizard as a starting point. Like Form Wizards, Report Wizards give you a basic layout for your report, which you can then customize.

Report Wizards simplify the layout process of your fields by visually stepping you through a series of questions about the type of report you want to create and then creating the report for you automatically. In this chapter, you will see both tabular and columnar reports created by using Report Wizards.

Creating a new report

You can choose from many ways to create a new report, including the following:

✦ Select Insert⇨Report from the Database window menu.

✦ Select the Reports tab, and then press the New button in the Database window.

✦ Select the New Report object icon from the Database window, the datasheet, or the query toolbar.

Regardless of how you create a new report, the New Report dialog box appears; you see it in Figure 11-7.

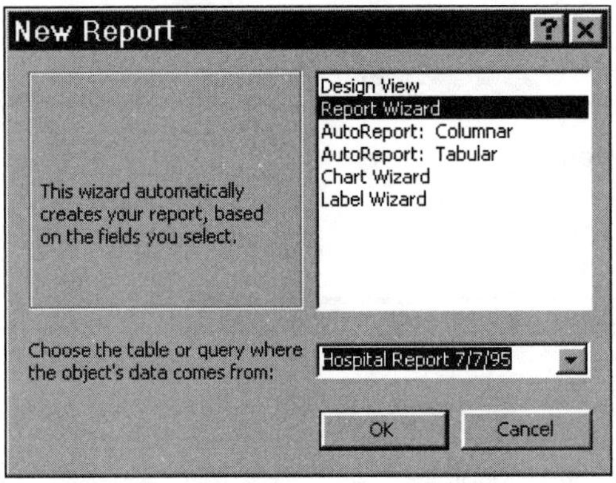

Figure 11-7: The New Report dialog box.

The New Report dialog box lets you choose one of six ways to create a report:

Design View	Displays a completely blank Report Design window for you to start with
Report Wizard	Helps you create a tabular report by asking you many questions
AutoReport: Columnar	Creates an instant columnar report

AutoReport: Tabular	Creates an instant tabular report
Chart Wizard	Helps you create a business graph
Label Wizard	Helps you create a set of mailing labels

To create a new report using a Report Wizard, follow these steps:

1. Create a new report by using any of the methods listed on the previous page.

2. Select Report Wizard.

3. Select the query Hospital Report 7/7/95 in the New Report dialog box.

Choosing the data source

If you begin creating the report with a highlighted table or from a datasheet or query, you will see the table or query you are using displayed in the Choose the table or query text box. Otherwise, you can enter the name of a valid table or query before continuing. You can also choose from a list of tables and queries by clicking on the combo-box selection arrow. In this example, you'll use the Daily Hospital Report query you saw in Figure 11-5, which creates data for customer visits on the date 7/7/95.

Tip   If you begin with a blank report, you don't need to specify a table or query before you start.

Cross-Reference Chapter 21 covers creating a new report without using a wizard.

Choosing the fields

After you select the Report Wizard and click on the OK button, a *field selection box* appears. This box is virtually identical to the field selection box used in Form Wizards (see Chapter 9 for detailed information). In this example, you select all the fields except Visit Date, as shown in Figure 11-8.

1. Click on the All Fields button (>) to place all the fields in the Selected Fields: area.

2. Select the Visit Date field, and then click on the Remove Field button (<) to remove the field.

Tip   You can double-click on any field in the Available Fields list box to add it to the Selected Fields: list box. You can also double-click on any field in the Selected Fields: list box to remove it from the box. Access then redisplays the field in the Available Fields: box.

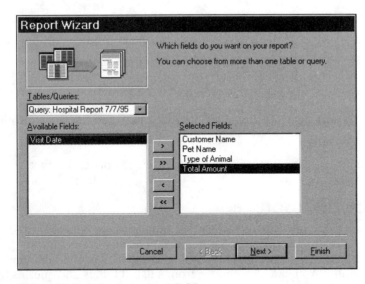

Figure 11-8: Selecting report fields.

In Access 2.0, once you selected the table or query to use with the Report Wizard, you were limited to those fields. In Access 97 and Access for Windows 95, however, you can continue to select other tables or queries by using the Tables/ Queries: combo box in this Wizard screen; you can also display fields from additional tables or queries. As long as you have specified valid relationships so that Access can link the data, these fields are added to your original selection and you can use them on the report. If you choose fields from tables that don't have a relationship, you will see a dialog box asking you to edit the relationship and join the tables. Or you can return to the Report Wizard and remove the fields.

Once you have selected your data, click on the Next> button to go to the next Wizard dialog box.

Selecting the view of your data

The next Wizard dialog box lets you set the view of your data, which can include a grouping. (This is a very confusing screen and will probably be ignored by most people.) The *view* of your data means how you look at the overall data picture. In this example, you have three tables: Customer, Pets, and Visits. The purpose of this report is to look at visits for pets belonging to a specific customer. The visit, however, is the focus of the data.

If you select to view your report by Visits, notice that all the data appears in the sample page on the right. If you choose to view it by Pets or by Customer, only the Total Amount field is shown on the page; the rest of the fields are shown grouped together. Later, you will group the data by Customer; for now, select to view the report by Visits, as shown in Figure 11-9.

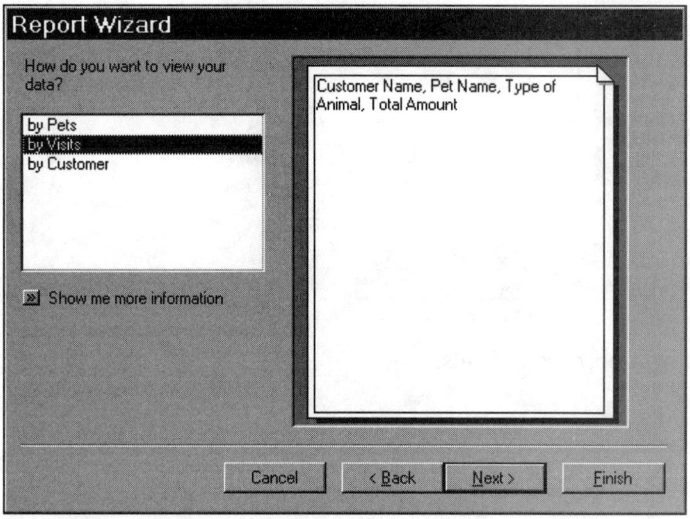

Figure 11-9: Selecting the view of your data.

Selecting the grouping levels

The next dialog box lets you choose which field(s) you want to use for a grouping. In this example, Figure 11-10 shows Customer Name as the only group field. This step designates the field(s) to be used to create group headers and footers. Using the Report Wizard, you can select up to four different group fields for your report; you can change their order by using the Priority buttons. The order you select for the group fields is the order of the grouping hierarchy.

Select the Customer Name field as the grouping field. Notice that the picture changes to graphically show Customer Name as a grouping field.

After you select the group field(s), you can click on the Grouping Options button to display the next dialog box, which lets you further define how your report will use the group field.

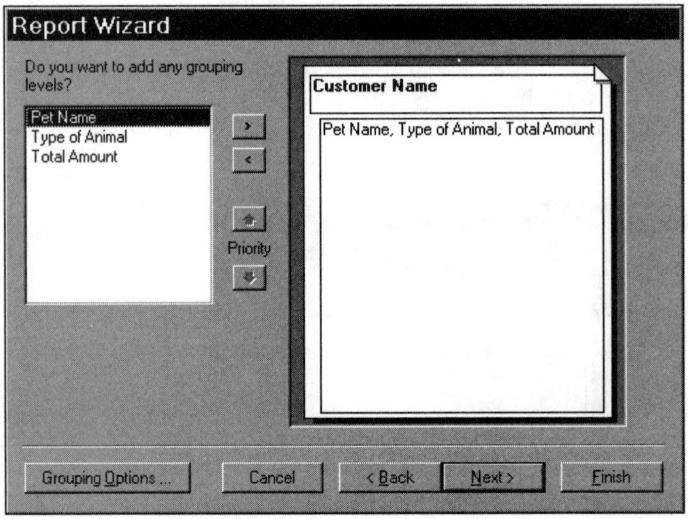

Figure 11-10: Selecting report group fields.

Defining the group data

The Grouping Options dialog box lets you further define the grouping. This selection can vary in importance, depending on the data type.

You will see different values in the list box for the various data types:

Text	Normal, 1st Letter, 2 Initial Letters, 3 Initial Letters, 4 Initial Letters, and so on.
Numeric	Normal, 10s, 50s, 100s, 500s, 1000s, 5000s, 10000s, 50000s, 100000s, 500000s
Date	Normal, Year, Quarter, Month, Week, Day, Hour, Minute

Normal means the grouping will be on the entire field. In this example, you'll want to use the entire Customer Name field. By selecting different values of the grouping, you can limit the group values. For example, suppose you are grouping on the Pet ID field. A typical Pet ID value is AP001-01. The first five characters represent the owner; the two after the hyphen represent the pet number for that owner. By choosing the Pet ID field for the grouping and then selecting 5 Initial Letters as the grouping data, you can group the pets by customer instead of by pet.

In this example, the default text-field grouping option of Normal is acceptable.

Click on the OK button to return to the Grouping levels dialog box, and then click on the Next> button to move to the Sort order dialog box.

Selecting the sort order

Access sorts the Group record fields automatically in an order that helps the grouping make sense. The additional sorting fields specify fields to be sorted in the detail section. In this example, Access is already sorting the data by Customer Name in the group section. As you can see in Figure 11-11, the data is also going to be sorted by Pet Name so that the pets appear in alphabetical order in the detail section.

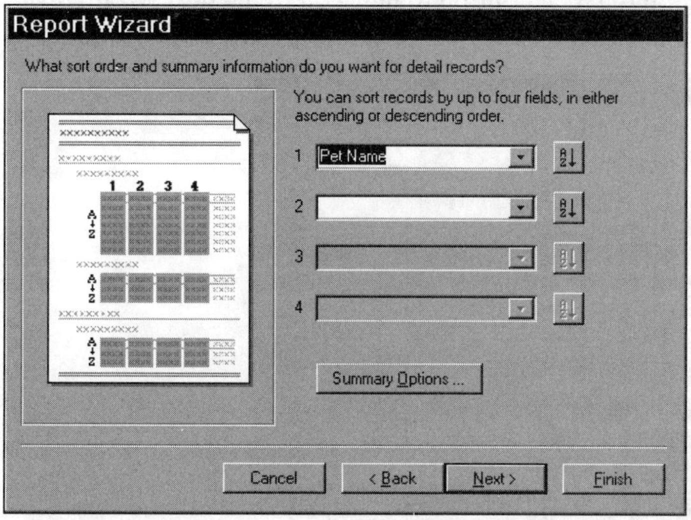

Figure 11-11: Selecting the field sorting order.

You select the sort fields by the same method used for grouping fields in the report. You can select fields you have not already chosen to group and use these as sorting fields. The fields you choose in this dialog box do not affect grouping; they affect only the sorting order in the detail section fields. You can determine whether the order is ascending or descending by clicking on the toggle button to the right of each sort field.

Selecting summary options

At the bottom of the sorting dialog box is a button named Summary Options. Clicking on this button displays the dialog box shown in Figure 11-12. This allows you to determine additional options for numeric fields. As you can see, the field Total Amount will be summed. Additionally, you can display averages, minimums, and maximums.

You can also decide whether to show or hide the data in the detail section. If you select Detail and Summary, the report will show the detail data; selecting Summary Only will hide the detail section showing only totals in the report.

Finally, by checking the box labeled Calculate percent of total for sums, you can add another number below the total in the group footer. Doing so adds the percentage of the entire report that the total represents. If (for example) you had three customers and their total was 15, 25, and 10, they would show (respectively) 30%, 50%, and 20% below their total (that is, 50) — indicating the percentage of the total sum (100%) represented by their sum.

Clicking on the OK button in this dialog box returns you to the sorting dialog box. There you can click on the Next> button to move on to the next Wizard dialog box.

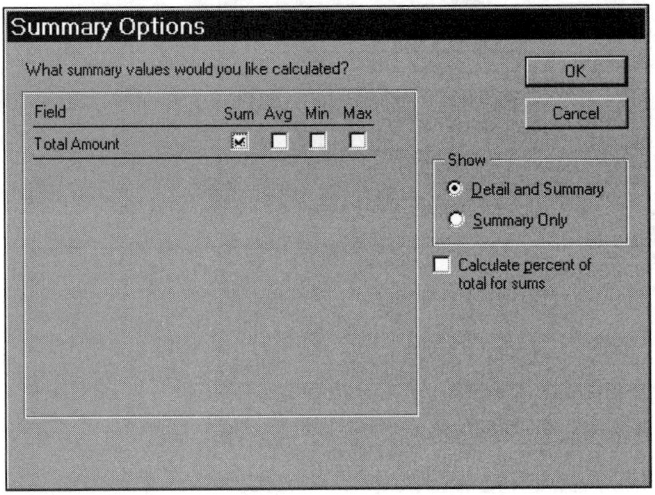

Figure 11-12: Selecting the summary options.

Selecting the layout

Two more dialog boxes affect the look of your report. The first (shown in Figure 11-13) lets you determine the layout of the data. The Layout area lets you choose one of six different layouts; these tell Access whether to repeat the column headers, whether to indent each grouping, and whether to add lines or boxes between the detail lines. As you select each option, the picture on the left changes to show the effect.

The Orientation area lets you decide whether your report will have a Portrait (up-and-down) or a Landscape (across-the-page) layout. This choice affects how it prints on the paper. Finally, put a check mark next to Adjust field width so all fields fit on a page. You can cram a lot of data into a little area. (Magnifying glasses may be necessary!)

For this example, choose Stepped and Portrait, the default values, as shown in Figure 11-13. Then click on the Next> button to move to the next dialog box.

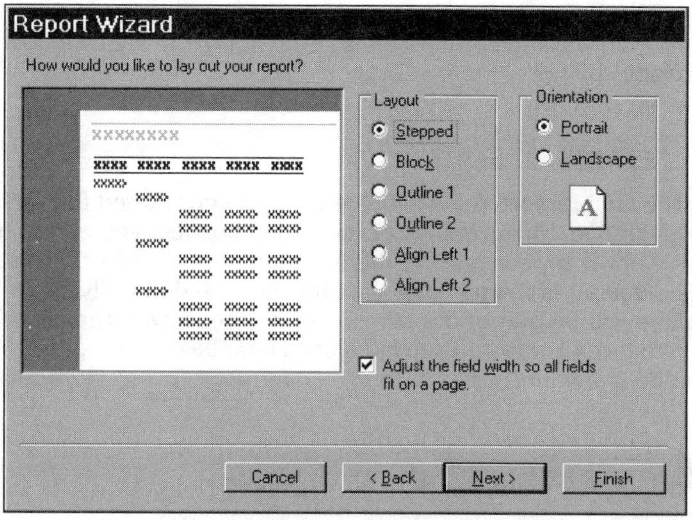

Figure 11-13: Selecting the summary orientation.

Choosing the style

After you choose the layout, you can choose the style of your report from the dialog box shown in Figure 11-14. Each style has different background shadings, font size, typeface, and other formatting. As you select each of these, the picture on the left changes to show a preview. For this example, choose Compact (as shown in Figure 11-14). Finally, click on the Next> button to move to the last dialog box.

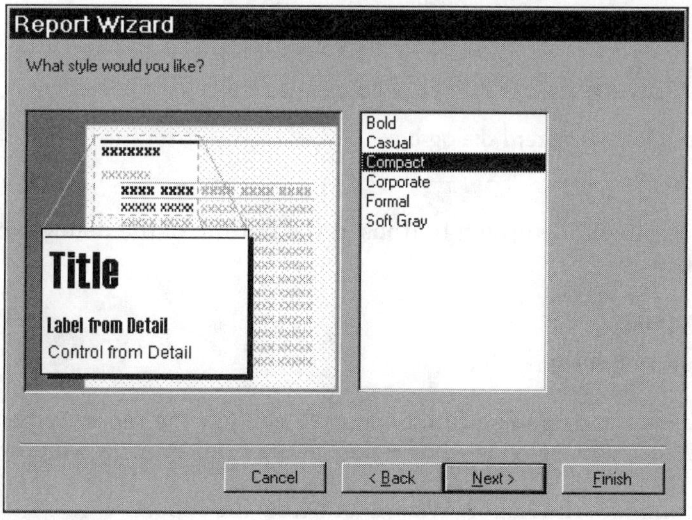

Figure 11-14: Choosing the style of your report.

Tip   You can customize any of the styles, and even add your own, by using the AutoFormat menu option from the Format menu of the Report Design window and choosing Customize.

Opening the report design

Figure 11-15 shows the final Report Wizard dialog box. The checkered flag lets you know you're at the finish line. The first part of the dialog box lets you enter a title for the report. This title will appear once at the beginning of the report, not at the top of each page. The default is the name of the table you used initially. If you used a query, the name will be that of the table used for the view of the data (in this example, it was Visits). As you can see in Figure 11-15, Daily Hospital Report has been typed instead of Visits.

Figure 11-15: The final Report Wizard dialog box.

Next you can choose one of the option buttons at the bottom of the dialog box. You have two choices:

✦ Preview the report

✦ Modify the report's design

For this example, leave the default selection intact to preview the report. When you select the Finish button, you will view your report in the Print Preview window.

Click on Finish to complete the Report Wizard and view the report.

Using the Print Preview window

Figure 11-16 displays the Print Preview window in a zoomed view. This view lets you see your report with the actual fonts, shading, lines, boxes, and data that will be on the printed report. When the Print Preview mode is in a zoomed view, pressing the mouse button changes the view to a *page preview*, where you can see the entire page.

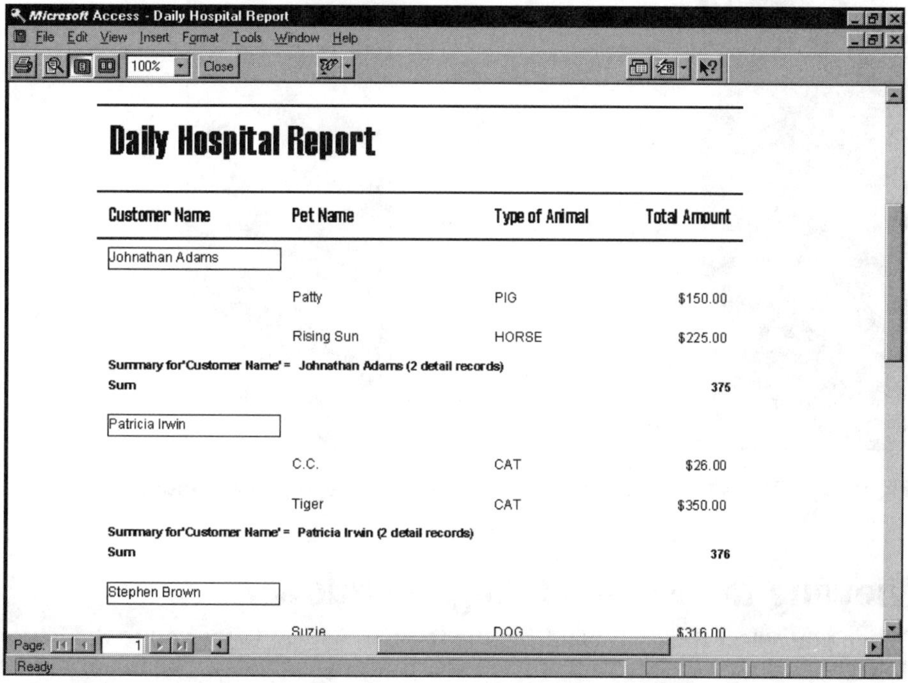

Figure 11-16: Displaying a report in the zoomed preview mode.

You can move around the page by using the horizontal and vertical elevators. Use the Page controls (at the bottom left corner of the window) to move from page to page.

Figure 11-17 shows an entire page of the report as you would see it in the page preview mode of Print Preview. By using the magnifying-glass cursor here, you can select a portion of the page and then zoom in to that portion for a zoomed view.

In Figure 11-17, you can see a representation of the printed page. Use the navigation buttons (in the lower left section of the Print Preview window) to move between pages, just as you would to move between records in a datasheet. A set of icons appears on the toolbar.

If, after examining the preview, you are satisfied with the report, simply select the Printer icon on the toolbar to print the report. If you are dissatisfied, select the Close button to return to the design window; Access takes you to the Report Design window to make further changes.

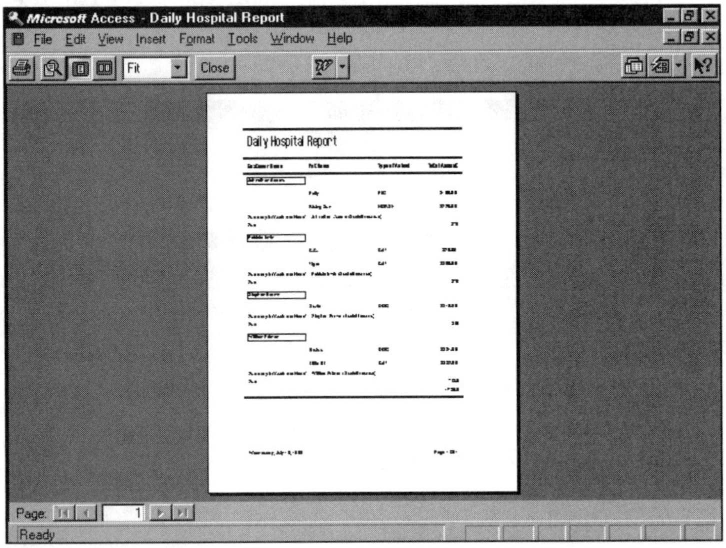

Figure 11-17: Displaying a report in Print Preview's page preview mode.

Viewing the Report Design window

When you select the first icon from the toolbar, Access takes you to the Report Design window, which is similar to the Form Design window. The major difference is in the sections that make up the report design. As you can see in Figure 11-18, the report design reflects the choices you made using the Report Wizard.

Cross-
Reference

You may also see the Toolbox, Sorting and Grouping dialog box, property sheet, and Field List window, depending on whether you have pressed the toolbar buttons to see these tools. You learn how to change the design of a report in Chapters 21 and 22.

You can switch back to the Print Preview mode by selecting the Print Preview icon button on the Report Design toolbar, or by selecting the Print Preview option on the File menu. You can also select Print or Page Setup from the File menu. This menu also provides options for saving your report.

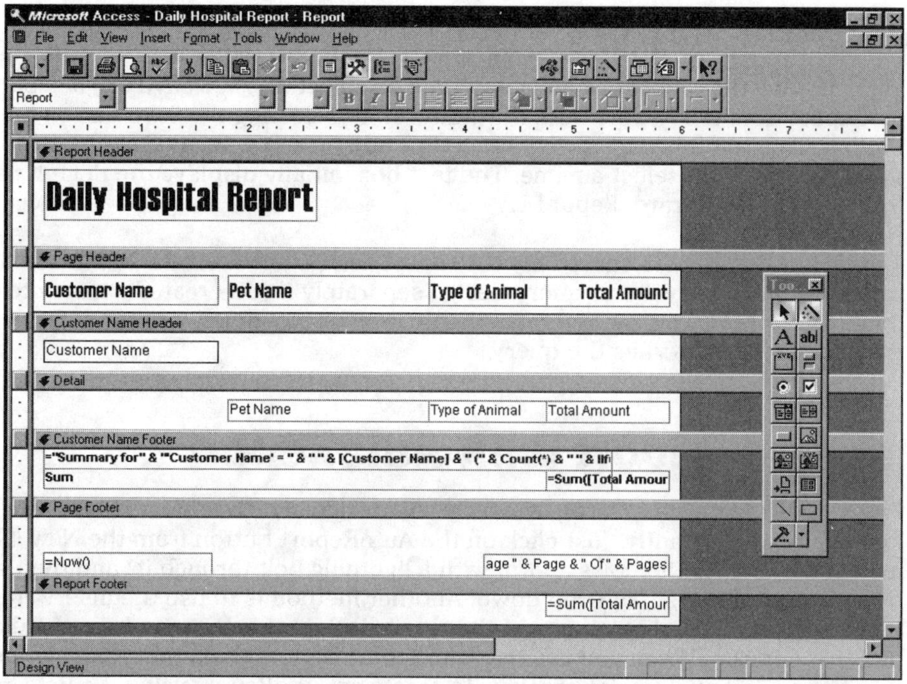

Figure 11-18: The Report Design window.

Printing a Report

You can print one or more records in your report, exactly as they look on-screen, by selecting from any of several places:

✦ File➪Print in the Report Design window

✦ Print button in the Preview window

✦ File➪Print in the Database window (with a report highlighted)

If you select File➪Print, a standard Windows 95/NT Print dialog box appears. You can select the print range, number of copies, and print properties. If you click on the Print icon, the report goes immediately to the currently selected printer, without displaying a Print dialog box.

Cross-Reference For a complete discussion of printing, see Chapter 22.

Saving the Report

You can save the report design at any time by selecting File⇨Save or File⇨Save As/Export from the Report Design window or by selecting the Save button on the toolbar. The first time you save a report (or any time you select Save As/Export), a dialog box lets you select a name. The text box initially displays the default name from the Report Wizard, Report1.

Caution Remember that Access saves only the report *design,* not the data or the actual report. You must save your query design separately if you created a query to produce your report. You can re-create the dynaset at any time by running the report that automatically reruns the query.

Creating a Report with AutoReport

From a table, datasheet, form, or nearly any design screen in Access, you can create a report instantly. Just click on the AutoReport button from the New Object icon in the toolbar (it shows a form with a lightning bolt through it) and then select from the list of icons that drop down. Another method is to use the Insert⇨Report command and then click on one of the two AutoReport selections from the dialog box that appears. When you use the AutoReport button, the report appears instantly with no additional work from you. To create an AutoReport using the Pets table, follow these steps:

1. From the Mountain Animal Hospital or Mountain Animal Start Database Containers, click on the Table tab.

2. Select Pets.

3. Click on the New Object button in the toolbar, and then select AutoReport.

The report instantly appears, as shown in Figure 11-19. Actually, the Picture property of the OLE control has been changed to Stretch to show the whole rabbit. (This was done in the Report Design screen, using the techniques you learned in Chapter 9.)

Using AutoReport is the quickest way to create a report. Generally, however, you will want more control over the process. Other Report Wizards are available to help you create more customized reports, as you have seen.

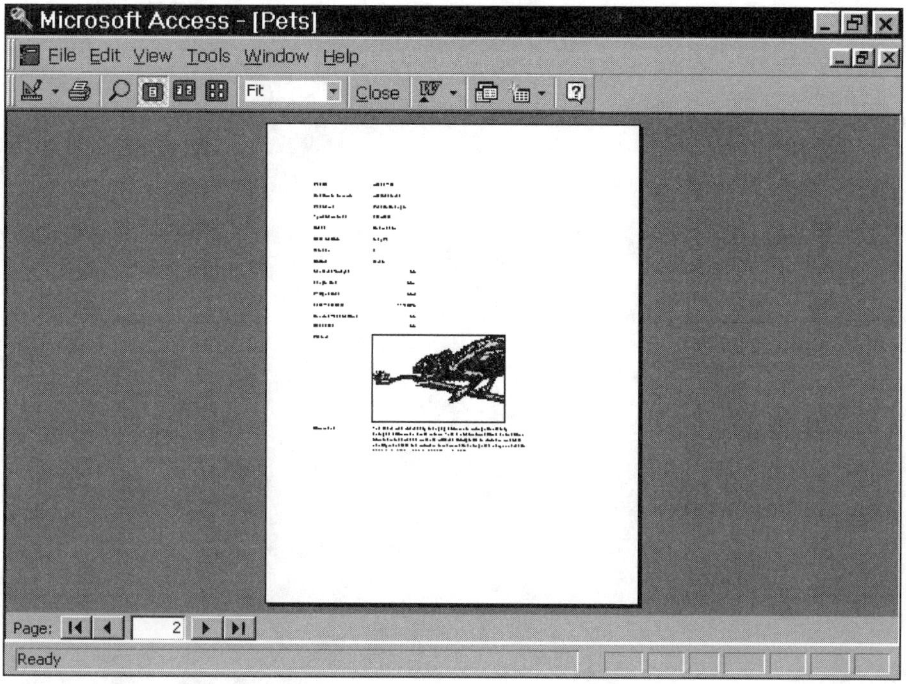

Figure 11-19: The AutoReport report.

Summary

In this chapter, you learned how easily you can create reports in Access. You saw the basic types of reports and how the Report Wizards simplify the process. The chapter covered the following points:

✦ The Access report writer lets you create tabular reports, columnar reports, business graphs, and mailing labels.

✦ The process of creating a report consists of defining the layout, assembling the data, creating the report design, and printing or viewing the report.

✦ Report Wizards let you create reports by filling in a series of dialog boxes.

✦ Reports can be printed or viewed on-screen.

✦ You can view reports on-screen in Print Preview mode.

In the next chapter, you learn how to manipulate multiple tables with Access objects. You'll see how to relate tables to take full advantage of a relational database's capabilities.

✦   ✦   ✦

Setting Relationships Between Tables

◆　◆　◆　◆

In This Chapter

The tables that make up the Mountain Animal Hospital database

What a key is

The benefits of using primary keys

How to create a multiple-field primary key

What a foreign key is

The types of relationships

How referential integrity works

How to create relationships

How to delete relationships

How to use the Table Analyzer Wizard

How to use lookup fields in a table

◆　◆　◆　◆

So far, you have learned how to create a simple table and to enter its data and display it in either a datasheet or a form. Then you learned how to use simple queries and reports. All these techniques were demonstrated, however, with only a single table. The Pets table has been an excellent sample of a single table; it contains many different data types that lend themselves to productive examples.

It's time now to move into the real world of relational database management.

Tables Used in the Mountain Animal Hospital Database

Figure 12-1 diagrams the database of the Mountain Animal Hospital system. You see eight tables in the figure, each of which requires its own table design, complete with field names, data types, descriptions, and properties.

CD-ROM If you're following along with the examples, either use the Mountain Animal Start files on the disk that accompanies this book, or create these tables yourself. If you want to create each of these tables, you can use Appendix B as a reference for each table's description; then use the steps you learned in Chapter 7 to create each one.

Cross-Reference In the diagram in Figure 12-1, you can see lines joining the tables. These are the *relationship lines* between the tables. Each line indicates a separate relationship between two tables; you establish these either at the table level (using the

Relationship Builder feature of Access) or by using a query (Chapter 14 shows you how to establish relationships in a query). In this chapter, you see how to use the Relationship Builder to establish a relationship at the table level.

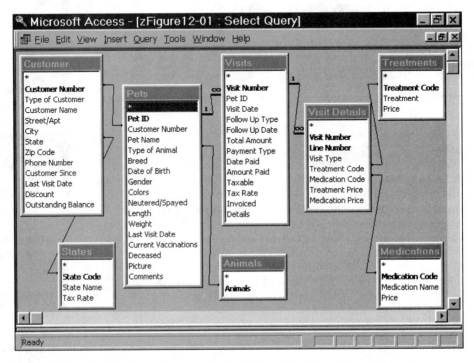

Figure 12-1: The database diagram for the Mountain Animal Hospital system.

Of the eight tables in the database diagram, four actually hold data about Mountain Animal Hospital, and four are used for *lookups*. You can eliminate the lookup tables and still use the system if you want to. These are the four main tables:

Customer	Contains information about each customer
Pets	Contains information about each animal
Visits	Contains information about each visit
Visit Details	Contains multiple records about the details of each visit

Following are the four lookup tables:

States	Used by the Customer table to retrieve state name and tax rate
Animals	Used by the Pets table to retrieve a list of valid animal types

      Treatments   Used by the Visit Details table to retrieve treatment name and price

     Medications   Used by the Visit Details table to retrieve medication name and price

In order to set relations between tables, you must establish a link between fields that contain common information. The fields themselves do not need to have the same name. The field's data type and length must be the same, however, and (even more importantly) the information contained within both fields for a specific record must be the same in both tables for the link to work. Generally you establish a relationship by linking these *key fields* between tables — the *primary* key in one table to a *foreign* key in another table.

Note In Figure 12-1, each table has one or more fields in bold. These are the fields that define the primary key for each table.

Understanding Keys

Every table should have a *primary key* — one or more fields whose contents are unique to each record. For example, the Customer Number field is the primary key in the Customer table — each record in the table has a different Customer Number. (No two records have the same number.) This is called *entity integrity* in the world of database management. By having a different primary key in each record (such as the Customer Number in the Customer table), you can tell two records (in this case, customers) apart. This is important because you can easily have two individual customers named Fred Smith (or pet stores named Animal Kingdom) in your table.

Theoretically, you could use the customer name and the customer's address, but two people named Fred Smith could live in the same town and state, or a father and son (Fred David Smith and Fred Daniel Smith) could live at the same address. The goal of setting primary keys is to create individual records in a table that will guarantee uniqueness.

Remember that when creating Access tables, if you don't specify a primary key, Access asks whether you want one. If you say yes, Access will create a primary key for you as an AutoNumber data type. It will place a new sequential number in the primary key field for each record automatically. Table 12-1 shows a list of tables and their primary keys.

Note In Access, however, you cannot use an AutoNumber data field to enforce referential integrity between tables. Therefore, it is important to specify another data type — like Text or Numeric — for the primary key. (More about this topic later in this chapter.)

	Table 12-1 Tables and Primary Keys	
Table	**Primary Key**	
Customer	Customer Number	
Pets	Pet ID	
Visits	Visit Number	
Visit Details	Visit Number; Line Number	
States	State Code	
Animals	Animals	
Treatments	Treatment Code	
Medications	Medication Code	

Deciding on a primary key

Normally a table has a unique field (or combination of fields) — the primary key for that table — that makes each record unique; often it's some sort of ID field that uses the Text data type. To determine the contents of this ID field, usually you specify some simple method for creating the value in the field. Your method can be as simple as using the first letter of the real value you are tracking along with a sequence number (such as A001, A002, B001, B002, and so on). Sometimes your method may rely on a random set of letters and numbers for the field content (as long as each field has a unique value), or you can use a complicated calculation based on information from several fields in the table.

Table 12-2 shows a list of tables and explains how to define the primary key in each one.

As you can see in Table 12-2, it doesn't take a great deal of work (or even much imagination) to create a key. Any rudimentary scheme and a good sequence number, used together, always seem to work. Because Access tells you automatically when you try to enter a duplicate key value, you can simply add the value of 1 to the sequence number. You may think that all these sequence numbers make it hard to look up information in your tables. Just remember that *normally* you never look up information by an ID field. Generally (instead) you look up information according to the *purpose* of the table. In the Customer table, for example, you can look up information by Customer Name. In some cases, the Customer Name is the same, so you can look at other fields in the table (ZIP code, phone number) to find the correct customer. Unless you just happen to know the Customer Number, you'll probably never use it in a search for information.

	Table 12-2 **Deriving the Primary Key**
Table	**Derivation of Primary Key**
Customer	Individuals: first two letters of last name, three-digit sequence number
	Pet Stores: first letter of first two major words, three-digit sequence number
	Zoos: first letter of first two major words, three-digit sequence number
Pets	Customer Number, a hyphen (–), and then a sequential number
Visits	Four-digit year and then the Julian day (sequential number)
Visit Details	Visit Number and then another field that holds a three-digit sequence number (Line Number field)
Animals	Type of animal
Treatments	Four-digit unique number (arbitrarily selected)
Medications	Four-digit unique number (arbitrarily selected)

Benefits of a primary key

Have you ever placed an order with a company for the first time and then decided the next day to increase your order? You call the people at the order desk. Sometimes they ask you for your customer number. You tell them you don't know your customer number. This type of thing happens all the time. So they ask you for some other information — generally, your ZIP code or telephone area code. Then, as they narrow down the list of customers, they ask your name. Then they tell you your customer number (as if you'd care). Some businesses use phone numbers as a unique starting point. When I call for pizza delivery, I give them my phone number, and they proceed to tell me my wife's name, address, and the last ten types of pizza she ordered! Last week, they didn't even ask for my phone number. Now they have Caller ID hooked into their computer screen. Imagine my surprise when they answered the phone with "Good evening, Mrs. Prague." (And I don't even look like my wife!) Their system didn't quite establish the uniqueness of these two customers.

Database systems usually have more than one table, and these tend to be related in some manner. For example, the Customer table and Pets table are related to each other via a Customer Number. The Customer table will always have one record for each customer, and the Pets table will have a record for each pet the customer owns. Because each customer is *one* physical person, you only have one record about the customer in the Customer table. Each customer can own several pets, however, which means you set up another table to hold information about each pet. Again, each pet is *one* physical animal (a dog, a cat, a bird, and so on). Each animal has one record in the Pets table. Of course, you relate the customers' pets in the Pets table to the right customer in the Customer table by using a common field between both tables. In this case, the field is the Customer Number (which is in both tables).

When linking tables, you should link the primary key field from one table (the Customer Number in the Customer table) to a field in the second table that has the same structure and type of data in it (the Customer Number in the Pets table). If the link field in the second table is *not* the primary key field (and usually it isn't), it's known as a *foreign key* field (this topic is discussed later in the chapter).

Besides being a common link field between tables, a primary key field in Access has other advantages:

✦ A primary key field is an index that greatly speeds up queries, searches, and sort requests.

✦ When you add new records, you must enter a value in primary key field(s). Access will not allow you to enter Null values, which guarantees that you'll have only valid records in your table.

✦ When you add new records to a table that has a primary key, Access checks for duplicate data and doesn't let you enter duplicates for the primary key field.

✦ By default, Access displays your data in the order of the primary key.

If you define a primary key based on part of the data in the record, you can have Access automatically place your data in an understandable order. In the example, the Pet ID field is made up of the owner's Customer Number, followed by a hyphen and a two-digit sequence number. If the All Creatures Pet Store is the first customer on the list whose last name begins with AC, the store's customer number is AC001. If someone from this store brings in three pets, the Pet IDs are designated AC001-01, AC001-02, and AC001-03. This way, the Pet ID field provides you with data in the order of customers displayed alphabetically.

Tip   Primary key fields should be made as short as possible because they can affect the speed of operations in a database.

Creating a primary key

As discussed in Chapter 7, you create a primary key by selecting the field you want to specify as a primary key and clicking on the Primary Key button on the toolbar (the button with the key on it). If you are specifying more than one field, you specify the fields you want for the primary key and again click on the Primary Key button. You specify the fields by selecting each field while holding down the Ctrl key.

When you're specifying multi-field primary keys, the order of the selection is important. Therefore, you should check your selection by clicking on the Indexes button on the toolbar and looking at the field order. Figure 12-2 shows the two-field index for the Visit Details table. Notice that the Visit Number field is before the Line Number field in the index box.

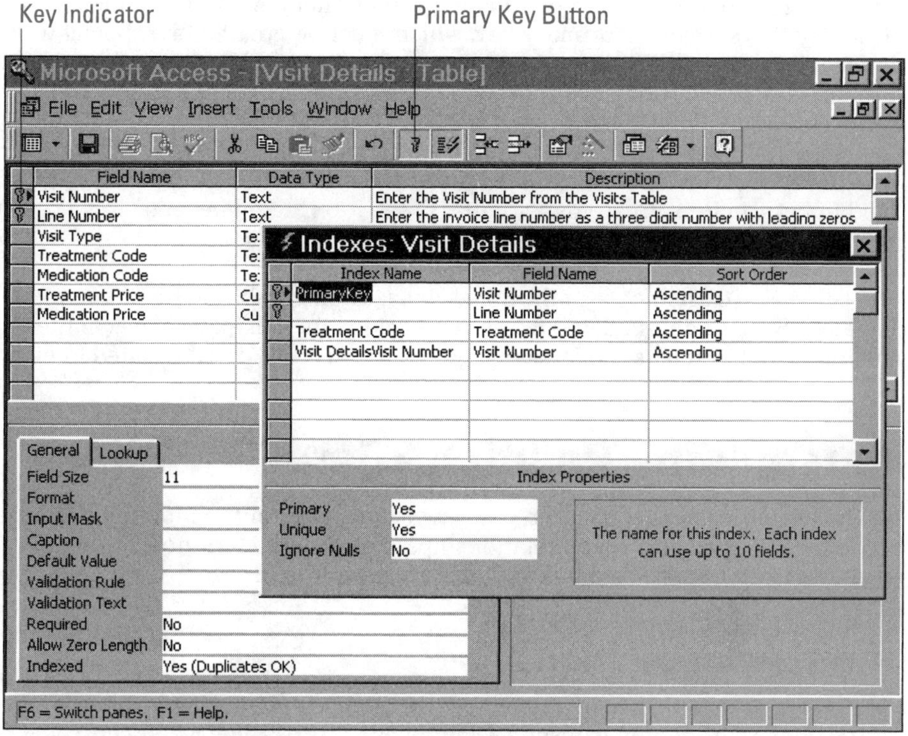

Key Indicator   Primary Key Button

Figure 12-2: The index dialog box showing a two-field primary key.

Note   Also notice that there are two additional index names in the index window. These are not keys but indexes used to speed up sorts used in these tables. If you regularly sort data in tables by the same field or fields, you should create an index for that field. An *index* is an internal table of values that maintains the order of the records. This way, when you need to sort data or find a piece of data instantly, Access can search through the index keys in a known order rather than sequentially through the data.

Caution   Creating indexes will slow down data entry; each new record, deleted record, or change to the indexed field will require a change to the index. Use only the index fields you need, which will speed up sorting your application and balance that need with data-entry speed.

Understanding foreign keys

Primary keys guarantee uniqueness in a table, and you use the primary key field in one table to link to another. The common link field in the other table may not be (and usually isn't) the primary key in the other table. The *common link field* is a field or fields that hold the same type of data as in the primary key of the link table.

The field (or fields) used to link to a primary key field in another table are known as foreign keys. Unlike a primary key, which must be created in a special way, a *foreign key* is any field(s) used in a relationship. By matching the values (from the primary key to the foreign key) in both tables, you can relate two records.

In Figure 12-1, you saw a relationship between the Customer and Pets tables. The primary key of Customer, Customer Number, is related to the Customer Number field in Pets. In Pets, Customer Number is the foreign key because it is the key of a related "foreign" table.

A relation also exists between the States and Customer tables. The primary key of States, State Code, is related to the State field in the Customer table. In the Customer table, State is the foreign key because it is the key of a related foreign table.

Understanding Relations Between Tables

At the beginning of this chapter, you saw eight tables in the Mountain Animal Hospital database and seven relationships. Before you learn how to create these relationships, it is important that you understand them.

A review of relationships

Relationships established at the table level take precedence over those established at the query level. If you can set a relationship at the table level, Access will recognize it automatically when you create a multiple-table query that uses fields from more than one table. Relationships between tables can be grouped into four types:

 ✦ One-to-one

 ✦ One-to-many

 ✦ Many-to-one

 ✦ Many-to-many

Understanding the four types of table relationships

When you physically join two tables (by connecting fields with like information), you create a relationship that Access recognizes. Figure 12-3 shows the relationships between all the tables in the Mountain Animal Hospital system.

The relationship that you specify between tables is important. It tells Access how to find and display information from fields in two or more tables. The program needs to know whether it will look for only one record in a table or look for several records on the basis of the relationship. The Customer table, for example, has a *one-to-many* relationship to the Pets table. There will *always* be one record in the Customer table for *at least* one record in the Pets table; there could be *many* related records in the Pets table. So Access knows to find only one record in the Customer table and to look for any in the Pets table (one or more) that have the same Customer Number.

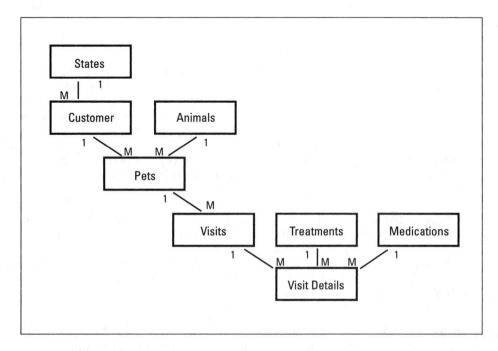

Figure 12-3: The Mountain Animal Hospital relationships.

The one-to-one relationship

The *one-to-one relationship*, though rarely used in database systems, can be a very useful way to link two tables together. A good example of a one-to-one relationship occurs in most billing systems; a billing file is created to allow additional information necessary to invoice customers at a location other than their listed addresses. This file usually contains the customer number and another set of address fields. Only a few customers would have a separate billing address, so you wouldn't want to add this information to the main customer table. A one-to-one relationship between a customer table and billing table may be established to retrieve the billing address for those customers who want to have a separate address. Although all the information on one table could be added to the other, the tables are maintained separately for efficient use of space.

The one-to-many relationship

The *one-to-many relationship* is used to relate one record in a table with many records in another. Examples are one customer to many pets or one pet to many visits. Both of these examples are one-to-many relationships. The Customer-Pets relationship links the customer number (the primary key of the Customer table) to the customer number in the Pets table (which becomes the foreign key of the Customer table).

The many-to-one relationship

The *many-to-one relationship* (often called the lookup table relationship) tells Access that many records in the table will be related to a single record in another table. Normally, many-to-one relationships are not based on a primary key field in either table. Mountain Animal Hospital has four lookup tables, each having a many-to-one relationship with the primary table. The States table has a many-to-one relationship with the Customer table; each state record can be used for many customers. Although (in theory) this relationship is one-to-one, it is known as a many-to-one relationship because it does not use a primary key field for the link, and many records from the primary table link to a single record in the other table.

Some one-to-many relationships can be reversed and made into many-to-one relationships. If you set a relationship from Pets to Customers, for example, the relationship becomes many-to-one; many pets can have the same owner. So relationships depend on how you use and interpret the information in your tables. Thus, one-to-many and many-to-one relationships can be considered the same — just viewed from opposite perspectives.

The many-to-many relationship

The *many-to-many* relationship is the hardest for people to understand. Think of it generally as a *pair of one-to-many relationships* between two tables, as happens in the tables Pets and Visits in the Mountain Animal Hospital database. A pet can be serviced at the hospital on many dates, so you see a one-to-many relationship between Pets and Visits. On the other hand, on each date, many pets can be brought into the hospital; this is also a one-to-many relationship. An individual pet may visit the hospital on many dates, and on a given date, many pets visit the hospital. Thus a pair of separate, two-way, one-to-many relationships creates a many-to-many relationship.

Understanding Referential Integrity

In addition to specifying relationships between tables in an Access database, you can also set up some rules that will help in maintaining a degree of accuracy between the tables. For example, you would not want to delete a customer record in your Customer table if there are related pet records in the Pets table. If you did delete a customer record without first deleting the customer's pets, you would have a system that has pets without an owner. This type of problem could be catastrophic.

Imagine being in charge of a bank that tracks loans in a database system. Now imagine that this system has *no* rules that say, "Before deleting a customer's record, make sure that there is no outstanding loan." It would be disastrous! So a database system needs to have rules that specify certain conditions between tables — rules to enforce the integrity of information between the tables. These rules are known as *referential integrity*; they keep the relationships between tables intact in a relational database management system. Referential integrity prohibits you from changing your data in ways that invalidate the links between tables.

Referential integrity operates strictly on the basis of the tables' key fields; it checks each time a key field, whether primary or foreign, is added, changed, or deleted. If a change to a key creates an invalid relationship, it is said to violate referential integrity. You can set up your tables so that referential integrity is enforced automatically.

When tables are linked together, one table is usually called the *parent*, and the other (the table it is linked to) is usually called the *child*. This is known as a *parent-child relationship* between tables. Referential integrity guarantees that there will never be an *orphan*, a child record without a parent record.

Creating Relationships

Unless you have a reason for not wanting your relationships always to be active, you should create your table relationships at the table level using the *Relationship Builder*. If you need to break the table relationships later, you can. For normal data entry and reporting purposes, however, having your relationships defined at the table level makes it much easier to use a system.

Access 97 has a very powerful Relationship Builder. You can add tables, use drag-and-drop methods to link tables, easily specify the type of link, and set any referential integrity between tables.

Using the Relationship Builder tool

You create relationships in the Database window. From this window, you can select the menu item Tools⇨Relationships or click on the Relationships button on the toolbar. The main Relationships window appears, which lets you add tables and create links between them.

The main Relationships window is shown in Figure 12-4. Notice the new toolbar associated with it. When first opened, the Relationships window is a blank surface. You can add tables to the window by using one of several methods :

✦ Add the tables before entering the Relationship Builder from the dialog box that's first displayed.

✦ Click on the Show Tables button on the toolbar.

✦ Select <u>R</u>elationships⇨Show Table from the menu bar.

✦ While in the Relationships window, click the right mouse button (which calls up the shortcut menu), and select Show Table from the menu.

To start the Relationship Builder and add tables to the Relationships window, follow these steps:

1. Click on the Relationships button on the toolbar. Access opens a Show Table dialog box.

2. Select all the tables by double-clicking on them — Customer, Pets, Visits, Visit Details, States, Animals, Medications, and Treatments.

3. Click on the Close button on the Show Table dialog box. Your screen should look like the one in Figure 12-4. Notice that Access has placed each table in the Relationships window. Each table is in its own box; the title of the box is the name of the table. Inside the table box are the names of the fields for each table. Currently, there are no links between the tables. Now you are ready to set relationships between them.

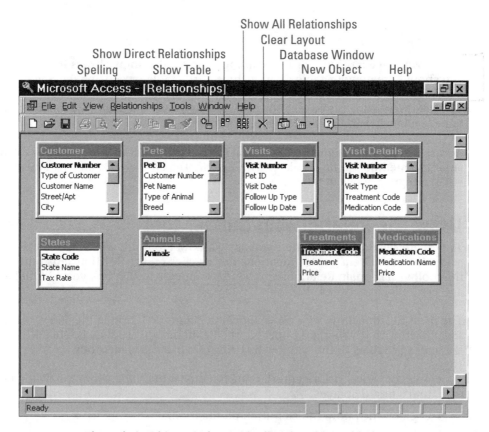

Figure 12-4: The Relationships window with all eight tables added.

Note If you select a table by mistake, you can remove it from the window by clicking in it and pressing the Delete key.

Tip You can resize each table window to see all the fields, as shown in Figure 12-5.

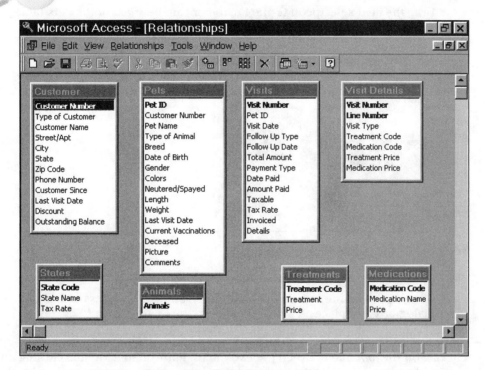

Figure 12-5: Creating relationships (links) between tables.

Creating a link between tables

With the tables in the Relationships window, you are ready to create links between the tables. To create a link between two tables, simply select the common field in one table and drag it over to the field in the table you want to link to, and then drop it on the common field.

Follow these steps to create a link between the tables:

1. Click on the Customer Number field of the Customer table.

Note If you select a field for linking in error, simply move the field icon to the window surface; it turns into the international No symbol. While it is displayed as this symbol, release the mouse button and the field linking will stop.

2. While holding down the mouse button, move the cursor to the Pets table. Notice that Access displays a field select icon.

3. Drag the field select icon to the Customer Number field of the Pets table. Access activates the Relationships dialog box (see Figure 12-6).

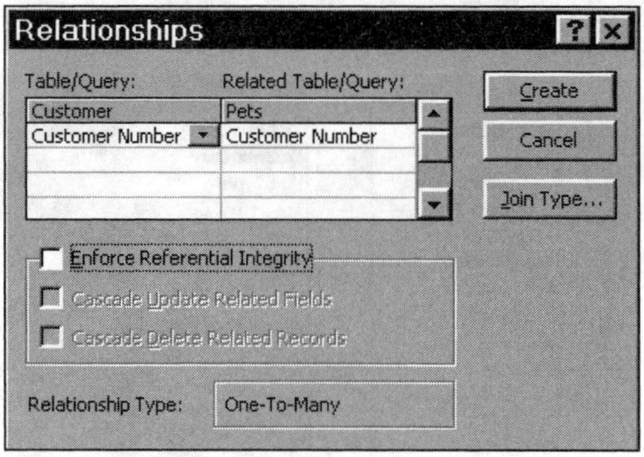

Figure 12-6: The Relationships dialog box.

4. Click on the Create button to create the relationship. Access closes the dialog box and places a join line between the Customer and Pets table.

Note You can reactivate the Relationships dialog box for any *join* (link) by double-clicking on the *join line* between the two tables. For example, double-clicking on the join line between the Customer and Pets table will reactivate the Relationships dialog box for that link.

Specifying relationship options in the Relationships dialog box

The Relationships dialog box has several options you can specify for your relationship between the Customer and Pets tables. Figure 12-6 shows the dialog box and all the options. The dialog box tells you which table is the primary table for the link and whether referential integrity is enforced. The dialog box also tells you the type of relationship (one-to-one or one-to-many) and lets you specify whether you want to allow *cascading* updates and deletes (automatic key changes or deletions in related records) between linked tables when referential integrity is selected.

CD-ROM

For the following sections, you will want to activate the Relationships dialog box for the link between the Customer and Pets tables. To do so, double-click on the join line between the tables.

Specifying the primary table

The top of the dialog box has two table names — Customer on the left and Pets on the right. The Customer table is considered the primary table for this relationship. The dialog box shows the link fields for each table immediately below the table names. Make sure that the correct table name is in both boxes (Customer and Pets) and that the correct link field is specified.

Caution

If you link two tables in the wrong order, simply click on the Cancel button in the dialog box. Access will close the dialog box and erase the join line. Then you can begin again.

Note

If you link two tables by the wrong field, simply select the correct field for each table by using the combo box under each table name.

Enforcing referential integrity

After you specify the link and verify the table and link fields, you can set referential integrity between the tables by clicking on the Enforce Referential Integrity check box below the table information. If you choose not to enforce referential integrity, you can add new records, change key fields, or even delete related records without worrying about referential integrity. You can create tables that are orphans or parents without children. With normal operations (such as data entry or changing information), referential integrity rules should be in force. By setting this option, you can specify several additional options.

Simply click on the check box in front of the option Enforce Referential Integrity. After you do so, Access activates the Cascading choices in the dialog box.

You might find, when you specify Enforce Referential Integrity and click on the Create button (or the OK button if you've reopened the Relationship window to create a relationship between tables), that Access will not allow you to. The reason is that you are asking Access to create a relationship supporting referential integrity between two tables that have records that *violate* referential integrity (the child table has orphans in it). In such a case, Access warns you by displaying a dialog box like the one shown in Figure 12-7. The warning happens in this example because there is a Pet record in the database with no Customer record. (There is also a Customer record with no Pet record. You will learn about these instances later in the book.)

Access returns you to the Relationships window after you click on the OK button, and you will need to re-create the relationship. If you are editing an existing join, Access also returns you to the Relationships window by removing the referential integrity option.

Tip   To solve any conflicts between existing tables, you can create a Find Unmatched query by using the Query Wizard to find the records in the *many*-side table that violate referential integrity. Then you can convert the Unmatched query to a Delete query to delete the offending records. You will learn how to do this in Chapter 14.

With the offending records gone, you can go back in and set up referential integrity between the two tables.

Figure 12-7: A dialog box warning that referential integrity cannot be set between two existing tables.

Choosing the Cascade Update Related Fields option

If you specify Enforce Referential Integrity in the Relationships dialog box, Access lets you select a check box option labeled Cascade Update Related Fields. This option tells Access that a user can change the contents of a link field (the primary key field in the primary table — Customer Number, for example).

When the user changes the contents of the primary key field in the primary table, Access verifies that the change is a new number (because there cannot be duplicate records in the primary table) and then goes through the related records in the other table and changes the link field value from the old value to the new one. Suppose you code your customers by the first two letters of their last names, and one of your customers gets married and changes the name that Access knows to look for. You could change the Customer Number, and all changes would ripple through other related records in the system.

If this option is not checked, you cannot change the primary key field in the primary table that is used in a link with another table.

Note If the primary key field in the primary table is a link field between several tables, this option must be checked for all related tables or it will not work.

Choosing the Cascade Delete Related Records option

If you specify Enforce Referential Integrity in the Relationships dialog box, Access activates the Cascade Delete Related Records check box. If you select this option, you are telling Access that if a user attempts to delete a record in a primary table that has child records, first it should delete all the related child records and then delete the primary record. This can be a very useful option for deleting a series of related records. For example, if you have chosen Cascade Delete Related Records and you try to delete a particular customer (who moved away from the area) by deleting the Customer record, Access goes out to the related tables — Pets, Visits, and Visit Details — and also deletes all related records for the customer. Access deletes all the records in the Visit Details for each visit for each pet owned by the customer, the visit records, the associated pet records, and the customer record, with one step.

If you do not specify this option, Access will not allow you to delete a record that has related records in another table. In cases like this, you must delete all related records in the Visit Details table first, then related records in the Visits table, then related records in the Pets table, and finally the customer record in the Customer table.

Note To use this option, you must specify Cascade Delete Related Records for *all* of the table's relationships in the database. If you do not specify this option for all the tables down the chain of related tables, Access will not allow cascade deleting.

Caution Use this option with caution! Access does not warn you that it is going to do a cascade delete when you press the Delete key. The program simply does it. Later you may wonder where all your records went. It is generally better to delete records programatically, using macros or Visual Basic for Applications (formerly known as Access Basic).

Saving the relationships between tables

The easiest way to save the relationships you created between the tables is to click on the Save button on the toolbar and then close the window. Another method is to close the window and answer Yes to the Save Relationships dialog box that appears.

Adding another relationship

After you specify all the tables, the fields, and their referential integrity status, you can add additional tables to the Relationships window by clicking on the Relationships button on the toolbar and adding new tables.

Again, if data that violates referential integrity exists in the tables being linked, you must fix the offending table by removing the records before you can set referential integrity between the tables.

Deleting an existing relationship

To delete an existing relationship, simply go into the Relationships window, click on the join line you want to delete, press the Delete key, and answer Yes to the question `Are you sure you want to delete the selected relationship?`.

Join lines in the Relationships window

When you create a relationship between two tables, Access automatically creates a thin join line from one table to another. Figure 12-8 shows the join line between States and Customer.

If you specify that you want to enforce referential integrity, however, Access changes the appearance of the join line. It becomes thicker at each end (alongside the table). It also has either a 1 or the infinity symbol (∞) over the thick bar of the line (on each side of the join line).

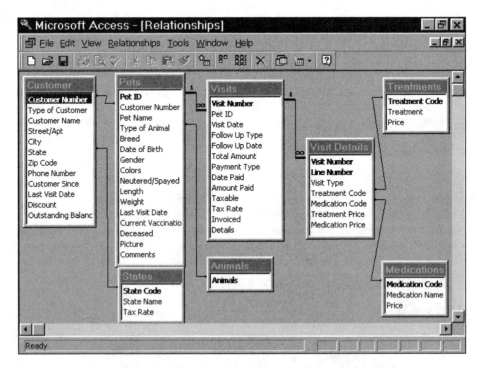

Figure 12-8: The relationships in the Mountain Animal Hospital system.

Tip After referential integrity is specified, Access will add the thick lines to the join in any queries that use the tables. This gives you a visual way to know that referential integrity is active between the tables.

Creating the relationships for the Mountain Animal Hospital system

Table 12-3 shows how the relationships should be set between all the tables in the system. Notice that referential integrity is set between three of the four primary tables. In addition to having referential integrity, each of the four main tables has the Cascade Delete Related Records option checked.

Table 12-3
Relationships in the Mountain Animal Hospital System

Primary Table/ Field	Related Table/ Field	Referential Integrity	Cascade Delete
Customer Customer Number	Pets Customer Number	No*	No*
Pets Pet ID	Visits Pet ID	Yes	Yes
Visits Visit Number	Visit Details Visit Number	Yes	Yes
State State Code	Customer State	No	No
Animals Animals	Pets Type of Animal	No	No
Medications Medication Code	Visit Details Medication Code	No	No
Treatments Treatment Code	Visit Details Treatment Code	No	No

*These will be changed in Chapter 14 after you delete orphan records.

Using the Access Table Analyzer

Everything you have read in this chapter assumes that you have already designed your tables and have normalized relationships in the entire database. With many new systems, however (and especially with new developers), this is not the case. Sometimes you might start by importing an Excel spreadsheet file into Access, or by importing a large mainframe file (commonly known as *flat files* because all the data is contained in a single file). When imported into Access, a flat file becomes one single table.

Access 97 contains a tool called the Table Analyzer that analyzes a single table and attempts to determine whether it is fully normalized. This tool then makes suggestions for splitting up the data into related tables. It creates both primary and foreign keys, search for misspellings of commonly used data, and suggests corrections. If (for example) you have a flat file that contains both sales items and customers in the same table, you might have the customer information (name, address, and so on) repeated over and over. Where the customer name Animals R Us is found many times, it might be listed as `Animals R Us Inc.` or `Animals R Us Company` or `Animals are Us` or even misspelled as `Aminals R Us`. The Table Analyzer will not only split your data into two or more tables, but will also suggest corrections to the data.

CD-ROM

To test this tool, you will need to create a single table consisting of fields from three different tables — Customer, Pets, and Visits. You have a special Make query that exists in both your Mountain Animals Hospital and Mountain Animal Start databases. It is named MAKE: Customer-Pets-Visits. You should run this query to create the Customer-Pet-Visit table. You can use this table to learn how the Table Analyzer tool works.

Starting the Table Analyzer

You can start this tool by selecting Tools➪Analyze➪Table from any design screen. This starts the Table Analyzer Wizard, as shown in Figure 12-9.

Note If you have already used the Analyzer, you may not see the introductory screens shown in Figures 12-9 and 12-10.

This first screen shown in Figure 12-9 is actually one of two introductory screens. They have no function other than to offer Help screens. This first screen introduces you to the concepts performed by the Table Analyzer. You can even click on the arrows in the right center of the screen to get a further explanation of why you should not duplicate information in a table.

Once you finish looking at that screen for the first time, you can click on the Next> button to move to the next screen. This screen tells you how the Table Analyzer will solve the potential problems you have in your table. The first screen's title is Looking At the Problem; the second screen's title is Solving the Problem. Figure 12-10 also shows you some arrows to click on to get even more detailed explanations about data normalization. You will want to click on the Next> button to continue.

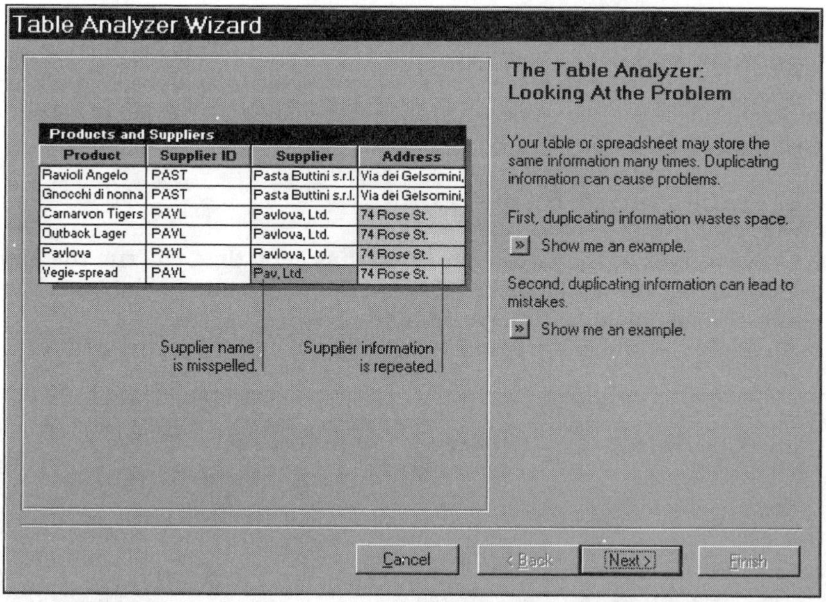

Figure 12-9: Looking At the Problem (the Table Analyzer's first introductory screen).

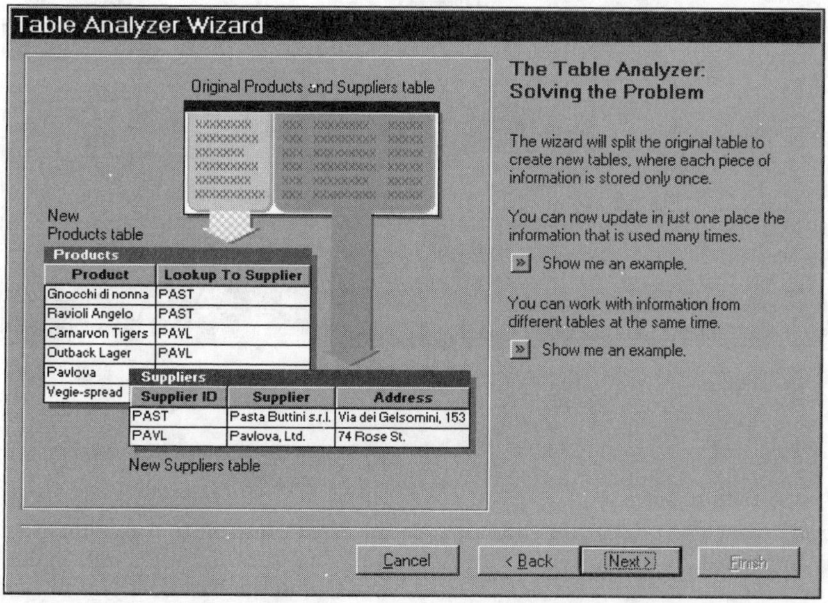

Figure 12-10: Solving the Problem (the Table Analyzer's second introductory screen).

Selecting a table to analyze

After you view the introductory screens, the Table Analyzer displays another screen. This screen is used to select the table you want to analyze. If you are following along in this example, select Customer-Pet-Visit from the list of tables as shown in Figure 12-11.

Only tables can be analyzed, not queries.

Tip You don't have to look at the introductory screens each time you run the Table Analyzer. As you can see in Figure 12-11, there is a check box to eliminate the introductory screens the next time you run the Table Analyzer.

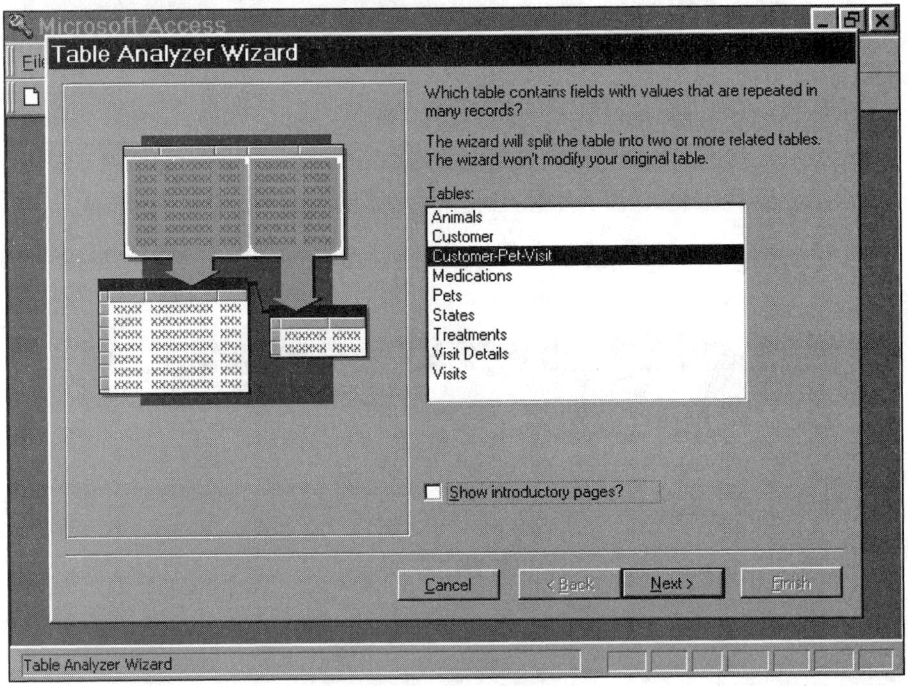

Figure 12-11: Selecting the table to be analyzed.

Analyzing the table

Once you select the table, you can click on the Next> button to move on. The next screen simply asks whether you want Access to analyze the tables and make decisions for you, or whether you want to make your own decisions. If you prefer to make your own choices, Access takes you to the Table Analyzer screen in a special version of the Relationships window. There you can drag and drop fields to create a new table, or drag fields from a related table back into a parent table to undo a relationship. You will learn about this screen later in this section.

At this point, accept the default value of Yes, and press the Next> button. When you select Yes, Let the Wizard Decide, the Table Analyzer performs a multi-step analysis of your data, possibly displaying several progress meters on-screen. When the process is completed, the next Wizard screen appears automatically. It shows the proposed structure of the tables, their relationships, and the primary and foreign keys (as shown in Figure 12-12).

As you can see in Figure 12-12, the Table Analyzer has done a great job in splitting the flat file into several tables. The first table (named Table1) contains data about the Visit. The second table (named Table2) contains Pet information, The third table, named Table3, contains Customer information, and the final table, named Table4, contains City/State information. Each table has a primary key assigned: The Pets and Customer tables have an existing field, the other two assigned a Generated Unique Key. Notice that relationships are already created between suggested tables.

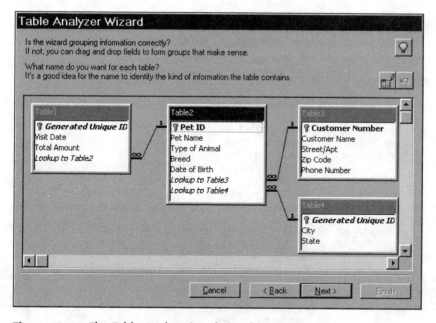

Figure 12-12: The Table Analyzer's Relationships window.

Analyzing a Flat-File Table

The following figure shows part of the data screen of the Customer-Pet-Visit table. As pointed out earlier, the data was created via a Make Table query that combined information from all three tables and eliminated the primary and foreign keys and many of the unimportant fields. The fields used from the Customer table are: Customer Number, Customer Name, Street/Apt, City, State, ZIP Code, and Phone Number. The Pet table fields are: Pet ID, Pet Name, Type of Animal, Breed, and Date of Birth. Finally, the fields from the Visit table: Visit Date and Total Amount.

If you were to sit and study the information in the table, you would see repeating groups. For instance, the Customer information and individual Pet information are repeated across many records. The Table Analyzer should be able to recognize this repetition and create a separate table for customers, pets, and visits. It can do so because all the information is the same for multiple records. The Table Analyzer can recognize information that is or is not part of a repeating group. When the Table Analyzer looks at the Customer Name, Street/Apt, City, ZIP Code, and Phone Number fields, it will find many records with exactly the same data. Therefore, it will move this information into its own table.

Customer Num	Customer Nam	Street/Apt	City	State	Zip Code	Phι
AC001	All Creatures	21 Grace St.	Tall Pines	WA	987462541	206
AC001	All Creatures	21 Grace St.	Tall Pines	WA	987462541	206
AC001	All Creatures	21 Grace St.	Tall Pines	WA	987462541	206
AC001	All Creatures	21 Grace St.	Tall Pines	WA	987462541	206
AC001	All Creatures	21 Grace St.	Tall Pines	WA	987462541	206
AC001	All Creatures	21 Grace St.	Tall Pines	WA	987462541	206
AC001	All Creatures	21 Grace St.	Tall Pines	WA	987462541	206
AC001	All Creatures	21 Grace St.	Tall Pines	WA	987462541	206
AC001	All Creatures	21 Grace St.	Tall Pines	WA	987462541	206
AC001	All Creatures	21 Grace St.	Tall Pines	WA	987462541	206
AD001	Johnathan Adar	66 10th St	Mountain View	WA	984101012	206
AD001	Johnathan Adar	66 10th St	Mountain View	WA	984101012	206
AD001	Johnathan Adar	66 10th St	Mountain View	WA	984101012	206
AD001	Johnathan Adar	66 10th St	Mountain View	WA	984101012	206
AD001	Johnathan Adar	66 10th St	Mountain View	WA	984101012	206
AD001	Johnathan Adar	66 10th St	Mountain View	WA	984101012	206
AD001	Johnathan Adar	66 10th St	Mountain View	WA	984101012	206
AD002	William Adams	1122 10th St	Lakeville	OR	974011011	503
AK001	Animal Kingdom	15 Marlin Lane	Borderville	ID	834835646	208

Record: 1 of 86

Datasheet View

continued

Analyzing a Flat-File Table *(continued)*

In addition to recognizing reoccurring information, the Access 97 Table Analyzer will also attempt to compare data for misspellings. If it finds them, it will report them during the process of analyzing the table.

Before you use the Analyzer, you may want to place your information in a sorted order. This will aid the Analyzer in normalizing your data. For instance, the information stored in the table in the above figure is in order by Customer (Customer Number) first and then pet (Pet ID) second.

Changing the table and field definitions

Examining Figure 12-12, you will notice that the fourth table has City and State information in it. Although the Analyzer linked it to the Pets table, you know that it is really related to the Customer table. At this point, you can interactively work with the Analyzer. You can rename the tables, move fields from table to table, and even delete or create tables from fields in the tables displayed.

All three of the main tables appear to have been split correctly (Visits [Table1], Pets [Table2], and Customer [Table3]) and to have been assigned the correct primary key fields (or to have created one). However, Table4 seems to have some problems. Following normalization rules, you could create a separate table that holds City, State, and ZIP Code information, linking to a table that looks up cities according to the ZIP Code. To guarantee uniqueness of cities, you must use the US Postal Service 9-digit ZIP Code system. If you use 5-digit ZIP codes, it is possible to have multiple cities with the same ZIP Code. So for purposes of this session, you should move the two fields from the fourth table into Table3 (the customer information table).You can move a field from one table to another simply by dragging it from one table to another. Highlight the City and State fields in Table4 and click and drag them to Table3, between Street/Apt and ZIP Code. As you move them, the multi-field icon appears and a horizontal cross bar appears between the Street/Apt and ZIP Code fields. Because all the fields, except the Generated Unique ID field, are moved out of the table, Table4 will be removed from the screen.

Note Likewise, you can drag a field back from one table to another. You can also create a new table by dragging a field from one table to an empty area of the screen. This creates a new table, a primary key for the new table, and a new foreign key in the original table you dragged the field from. You can also change the order of the fields by selecting one and dragging it above or below other fields in the table.

With three tables now left in the Analyzer, you should rename each of the tables. Logically you would rename them Customer, Pets, and Visits. However, these tables already exist, so instead give them the same name with the word "Analyze" before them — from `Table1` to `Analyze Visit`, from `Table2` to `Analyze Pet`, and from `Table3` to `Analyze Customer`.

Note Although you can rename the table in the Analyzer, you can not rename any fields, such as the new primary and foreign key fields. You can rename the new key primary and foreign fields in the tables only by using the standard Table Design screen after the Wizard is complete.

Changing the key fields

Once you complete this Wizard screen, click on the <u>N</u>ext> button to move to the next Wizard screen. This screen lets you change the key fields that the Table Analyzer has created. Figure 12-13 shows this screen with the three tables created and renamed. Since the tables all have a correct primary key assigned, you are done with this screen.

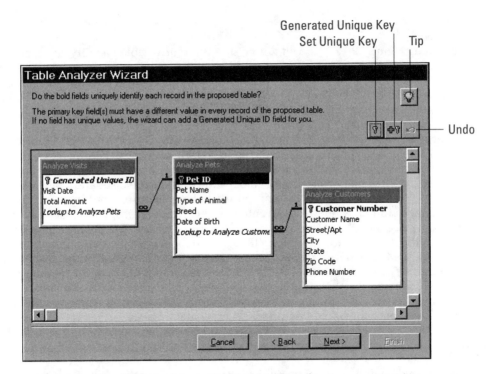

Figure 12-13: The Table Analyzer's Relationships window.

If you need to create a new primary key, or change a primary key to an existing field, this is where to do it. To assign a new unique key, you simply click on the Add Generated Unique Key button. This creates a new field and makes it the primary key. If you need to change the assigned primary key field, simply click on the correct field that should be the primary field and click on the Set Unique Key button. This cancels the previously created primary key assignment. If the previous field was a generated field, it will be removed from the table. Now you should click on the Next> button to continue to the next step of the Analyzer. The next step will begin a search for aberrant data. Misspellings and inconsistencies in like data are the most common types of problem data the Table Analyzer can find.

When performing the analysis, the Table Analyzer will also check your final field choices for fields that belong together. If the Table Analyzer finds data that doesn't appear to fit the rest of the table's data, you will get a warning message like the one in Figure 12-14. If this occurs, you should press the <Back button to go back and make further changes to the tables.

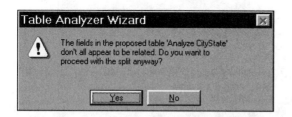

Figure 12-14: Warning message to go back and fix your tables.

Searching for typos and duplicate key data

If during the process of searching for aberrant data in the previous section, the Table Analyzer finds what it believes are inconsistencies or misspellings, it displays a series of screens allowing you to correct what it believes are typographical errors. You may see screens that make no sense, because the Table Analyzer may make a wrong assumption about what to analyze. It might, for example, do some analysis on duplicate key data. These screens will depend totally on the analysis of your data. In this example, the Table Analyzer misses all the misspelled Cities and Companies but it keys in on the similar phone numbers.

Once the typos are corrected, and you click on the Next> button, you will be taken to the final screen of the Analyzer.

If the Analyzer finds no apparent typos, you will immediately be taken to the next, and final, screen.

Completing the Table Analyzer

The final screen (Figure 12-15) lets you complete the analysis process. Notice that the Analyzer offers to create a query using the original name of your table and rename the original table. If you accept this choice, any forms and reports that work with the old flat file table will continue to work. This gives you the best of both worlds — you can start to work with the normalized tables while still being able to work with the old table. If you decide to accept this choice, you should NOT continue to add records into the old table!

Caution One problem the Table Analyzer can cause is to render existing queries, forms, reports, and macros inoperable because all these objects are tied to specific table and field names. When you change the table name or field names within a table, Access will report an error when you try to run the form, report, or macro; they cannot automatically adjust. A solution is to create a new query (with the same name as the original table) that uses the new tables and creates a view identical to the original table.

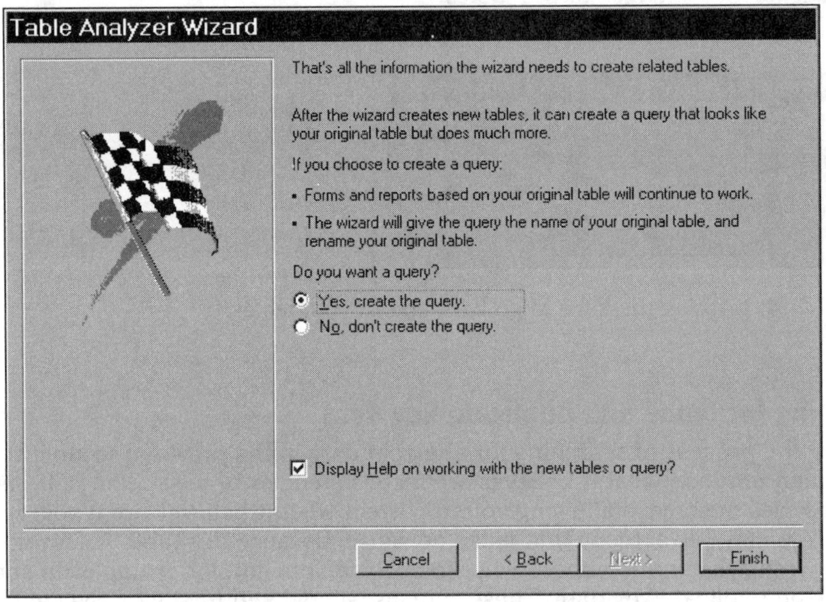

Figure 12-15: Completing the Table Analyzer process.

For the purpose of this exercise, select the choice No, don't create the query and click on the Finish button.

Clicking on the Finish button will make the Table Wizard disappear, and a tiled view of all the new tables appear. When you are finished looking at the new tables, simply close them.

If you want to change the names of any of the fields, you can open each table in Design view and rename any field names. Though the Table Wizard is not perfect, it is an outstanding way to normalize a data table with little effort.

Using the Lookup Wizard in the Table Designer

When you view one table that is related to another, often the table contains a foreign key — generally the primary key of another table. Often the foreign key field is cryptic when you look at it through the related table. Until you relate the two tables and look at the data from a Query view, you cannot tell the real value of the field.

For example, Figure 12-16 shows the Pets table sorted by Type of Animal and Breed. Notice the cryptic value in the Customer Number field. In earlier versions of Access (2.0 and earlier), the only way to see the Customer Name was to create a query and look at the resulting dynaset. In Access 97 you can display the Customer Name in a table that contains only a foreign key lookup to the Customer table. This means that you can display and select and immediately see a Customer Name, like All Creatures, while in the Pets table, instead of using some foreign name like AC001.

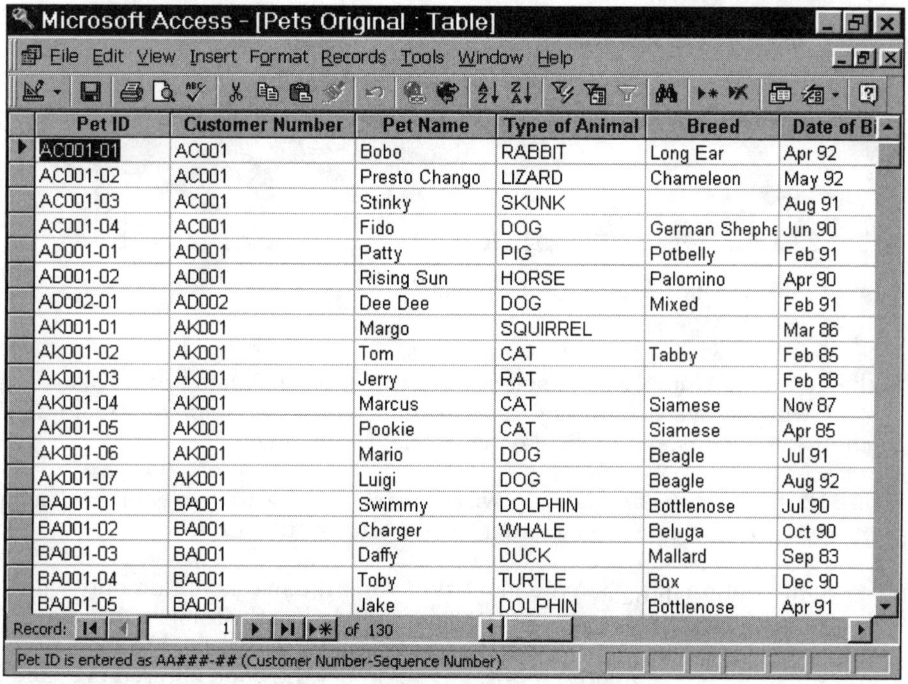

Pet ID	Customer Number	Pet Name	Type of Animal	Breed	Date of Bi
AC001-01	AC001	Bobo	RABBIT	Long Ear	Apr 92
AC001-02	AC001	Presto Chango	LIZARD	Chameleon	May 92
AC001-03	AC001	Stinky	SKUNK		Aug 91
AC001-04	AC001	Fido	DOG	German Shephe	Jun 90
AD001-01	AD001	Patty	PIG	Potbelly	Feb 91
AD001-02	AD001	Rising Sun	HORSE	Palomino	Apr 90
AD002-01	AD002	Dee Dee	DOG	Mixed	Feb 91
AK001-01	AK001	Margo	SQUIRREL		Mar 86
AK001-02	AK001	Tom	CAT	Tabby	Feb 85
AK001-03	AK001	Jerry	RAT		Feb 88
AK001-04	AK001	Marcus	CAT	Siamese	Nov 87
AK001-05	AK001	Pookie	CAT	Siamese	Apr 85
AK001-06	AK001	Mario	DOG	Beagle	Jul 91
AK001-07	AK001	Luigi	DOG	Beagle	Aug 92
BA001-01	BA001	Swimmy	DOLPHIN	Bottlenose	Jul 90
BA001-02	BA001	Charger	WHALE	Beluga	Oct 90
BA001-03	BA001	Daffy	DUCK	Mallard	Sep 83
BA001-04	BA001	Toby	TURTLE	Box	Dec 90
BA001-05	BA001	Jake	DOLPHIN	Bottlenose	Apr 91

Record: 1 of 130

Pet ID is entered as AA###-## (Customer Number-Sequence Number)

Figure 12-16: A confusing foreign-key value.

To do this you need to change the display nature of the field from showing actual content to showing a lookup value from another table or list. This is accomplished by redefining the properties of the field. For instance, to change the display of the Customer Number field in the Pets table so that it displays the actual Customer Name, you would change some properties at the database level of the Pets table.

To start this process, open the Pets table and switch to Design view. Select the data type of the Customer Number field, and click on the down arrow to display the data type list. Notice the last item in the list is Lookup Wizard (as shown in Figure 12-17). This is actually not a data type, of course, but rather a way of changing the Lookup properties.

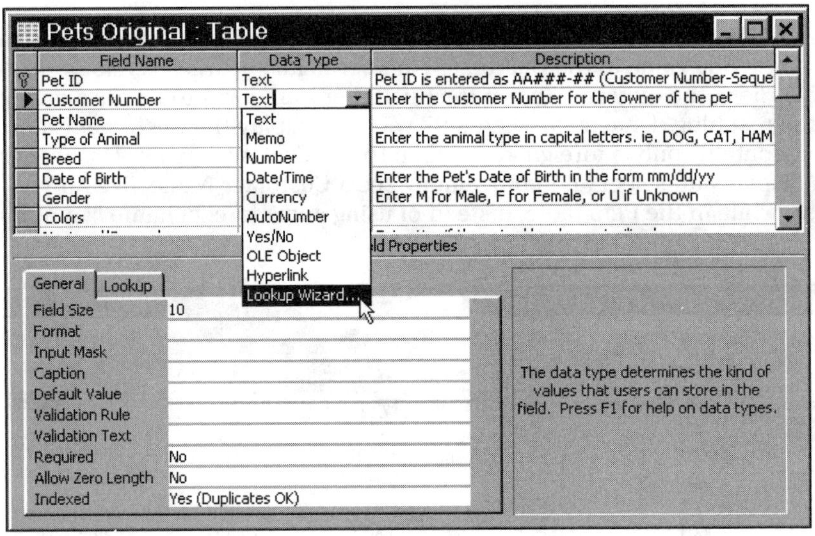

Figure 12-17: Creating a lookup field in a table.

In the Customer Number field, select the Lookup Wizard data type. This starts the Wizard, which takes you through a series of screens that help you create a lookup to another table instead of displaying the field value itself.

Figure 12-18 shows the first Lookup Wizard screen. There are two choices. The first choice lets you use data from another related table as the displayed value in the field.

The second option lets you type in a list of values. Use this option only when you enter a code such as the Type of Customer field in the Customer table. Later you will learn how to change the Lookup properties of that field to display Individual if the code entered is 1, Pet Store if the code entered is 2, and Zoo if the code entered is 3.

In this example, you will display the Customer Name from the Customer table in the Customer Number field in the Pets table. Select the first choice, and then click on the Next> button.

Note   Creating a lookup will not change the stored value in the Pets table for the Customer Number field. Only the display of the value is changed.

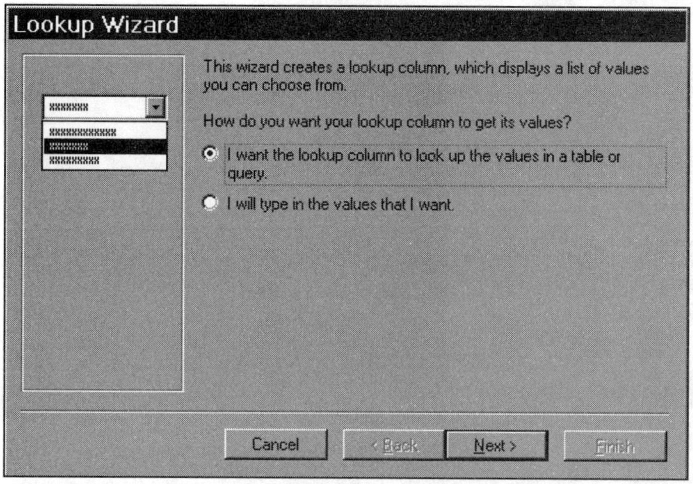

Figure 12-18: Selecting the type of lookup.

The next screen asks `Which table or query contains the fields for the lookup?` and then lets you choose the table or query to use for the lookup. This is the standard table-selection Wizard screen used in most Wizards. Select the Customer table and click on the Next> button.

The next Wizard screen displays a list of all of the fields in the Customer table, and lets you select the fields you want to use in the lookup. This is also a standard field-selection screen. The method here is to select all the fields in the lookup table that will be used in the display, as well as the field that will hold the actual value. Though you can display more than one field in the table, generally you will display only one field. The second field is stored out of sight and used for the actual value that belongs to the table.

You need to select two fields from the Customer table. One field is the link field (used to link to the Pets table), and the other is the field that you want to display in the Pets table. Select the Customer Name and the Customer Number fields. Remember to click on the > button after you select each field (which copies it from the Available Fields list to the Selected Fields list).

Tip   In Access 97, the order you select these fields is NOT important. The Wizard will determine which field is the link field and which is the display field automatically.

After you do this and click on the Next> button, the display and size screen appears (as shown in Figure 12-19).

A list of the data is displayed from the Customer table. As Figure 12-19 shows, the only field visible is the Customer Name. The Customer Number field is hidden from view. If you want to see the hidden field, click the `Hide key column` check box off. (Be sure to turn it back off before continuing.)

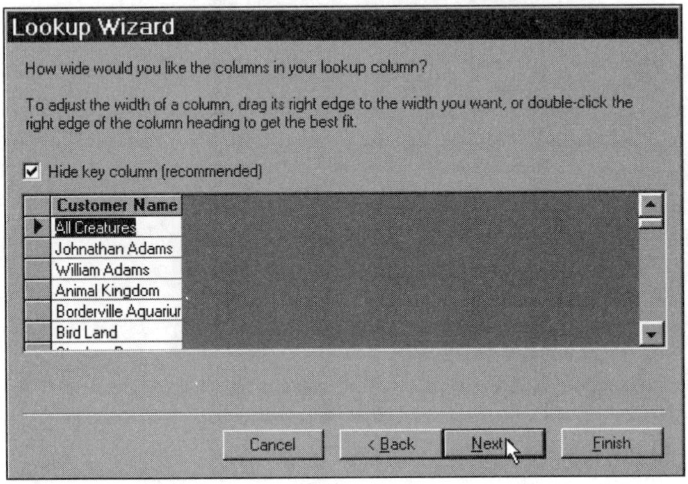

Figure 12-19: Sizing the fields.

Resize the Customer Name field to display all of the contents. Once you have accomplished this, click on the Next> button.

The final screen asks you what name you want to display when the table is viewed. The default name is the original name of the column. Accept the default name of Customer Number, and then click on the Finish button to complete the Wizard. The Wizard displays a dialog box, like in Figure 12-20, telling you that the table must be saved before the relationship between the two tables (Customer and Pets) can be created. Accept the default action of Yes and the lookup table reference is created.

Figure 12-20: Dialog box to save relationship.

Figure 12-21 shows the new settings in the Pets table design window, in the fields set in the Field Properties Lookup tab sheet (bottom half of screen).

The Lookup tab has changed significantly. The first property tells you that the field will now appear as a combo box whenever displayed in a table, or by default when placed on a form. Notice, however, that the data type for the Customer Number field is still Text. Even though you chose the Lookup Wizard from the Data Type list, it still creates a Text data type. The Lookup Wizard merely changes the Lookup properties.

The next two Lookup properties define the type of data for the record. In this case, the source of the data in the record is a table or query. Other choices are Value List (you type them into the Row Source property, separated by semicolons) and Field List (a list of fields in a table).

The Row Source displays a statement in SQL (Standard Query Language), an internal language that Access translates all queries into. You can see only a portion of the SQL statement in Figure 12-21. To see the entire SQL statement, you can open the Zoom window by pressing Shift-F2.

The entire statement is:

```
SELECT DISTINCTROW [Customer].[Customer Number],
      [Customer].[Customer Name] FROM [Customer];
```

This command simply tells Access to use the Customer Name and Customer Number fields from the Customer table. The remaining values tell Access 97 how many columns to use from the Customer table, which field to display (Customer Name, field 0) and which one is used for a link.

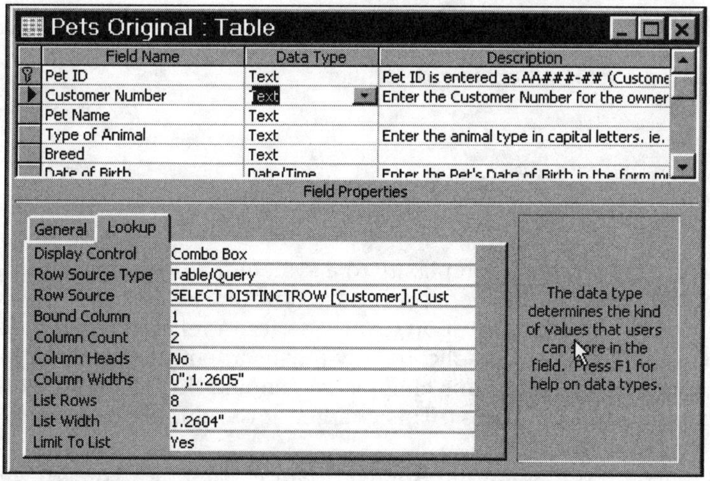

Figure 12-21: Understanding the Lookup properties.

When you display the Pets table in a Datasheet view (as shown in Figure 12-22), you now see Customer Name instead of Customer Number in the Customer Number field. Using this method, you can display and limit the selection of any coded field in a table. You can even use fields found in only one table, like the Gender field in the Pets table. Rather than display an M, F, or U, you can select from Male, Female, or Unknown, and still store the correct code in the field.

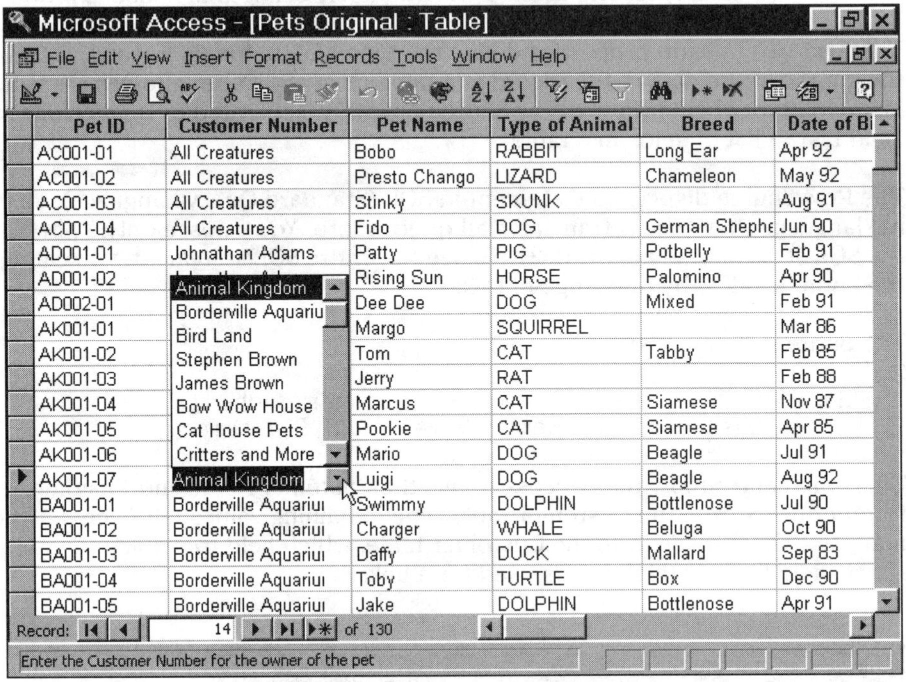

Figure 12-22: Displaying a lookup field in a datasheet.

Summary

Using multiple tables adds far more complexity to a system than working with a single table. Throughout the rest of this book, you learn how to use multiple tables to create more advanced types of forms, reports, and queries. A relational database management system can get quite complicated. By paying attention to details and applying the concepts you learned in this chapter, you should be able to create a system of unlimited complexity with Access. This chapter covered the following points:

✦ Eight tables make up the Mountain Animal Hospital example. The four main tables are Customer, Pets, Visits, and Visit Details; the four lookup tables are States, Animals, Treatments, and Medications.

✦ A primary key designates one or more fields that make a record unique. This uniqueness is called the entity integrity of a record.

✦ A primary key is an index that greatly speeds up searches and query requests.

✦ You create primary keys in the Table Design window by clicking on the Primary Key icon after selecting the primary key field.

✦ A multiple-field primary key is used when one field is not sufficient to guarantee uniqueness.

✦ A foreign key is a field that contains a value matching another table's primary key.

✦ A primary key field and a foreign key field are linked to form a relation.

✦ The four types of relationships are one-to-one, one-to-many, many-to-one, and many-to-many.

✦ Referential integrity is a set of rules that prevents data entry if it will result in an invalid relationship.

✦ When data violates referential integrity, you see an error message.

✦ In a multiple-table system, you cannot simply delete records without regard to referential integrity.

✦ Whenever you make changes to key-field data in a multiple-table system, potentially you violate referential integrity. You must follow special steps to change or delete key-field data.

✦ You create relationships by using the Relationships window from the Database window's Tools menu.

✦ Using the Access 97 Table Analyzer, you can normalize a flat-file table into several related tables automatically.

✦ Using the Access 97 Lookup Wizard, you can place the lookup field properties in a table.

In the next chapter, you learn to use operators, functions, and expressions that are used throughout Access in forms, reports, and queries.

✦　　✦　　✦

Using Access in Your Work

Using Operators, Functions, and Expressions

In This Chapter

What operators, functions, and expressions are and how they are used

Types of operators

Types of functions

How to create an expression

Special identifier operators and expressions

O perators, functions, and expressions are the fundamental building blocks for Access operations. These operations include entering criteria in queries, creating calculated fields in forms, and creating summary controls in reports.

Operators

Operators let you add numbers, compare values, put text strings together, and create complicated relational expressions. You use operators to inform Access that a specific operation is to be performed against one or more items. Access also uses several special operators for identifying an object.

Types of operators

Following are the types of operators you learn about in this chapter:

- ✦ Mathematical (arithmetic) operators
- ✦ Relational operators
- ✦ String operators
- ✦ Boolean (logical) operators
- ✦ Miscellaneous operators

When are operators used?

You use operators all the time. In fact, you use them every time you create an equation. In Access, you use operators to specify data-validation rules for table properties, to create calculated fields in forms, or to specify criteria in queries.

Operators indicate that an operation needs to be performed on one or more items. Following are some common examples of operators:

=

&

And

Like

+

Mathematical operators

There are seven basic mathematical operators. These are also known as arithmetic operators because they are usually used for performing arithmetic calculations:

*	Multiply
+	Add
–	Subtract
/	Divide
\	Integer Divide
^	Exponentiation
Mod	Modulo

By definition, mathematical operators work with numbers. When you work with mathematical operators, numbers can be any numeric data type. The number can be the actual number or one that is represented by a memory variable or a field's contents. Furthermore, the numbers can be used individually or combined to create complex expressions. Some of the examples in this section are quite complex, but don't worry if you don't usually work with sophisticated mathematics.

The * (multiplication) operator

A simple example of when you use the *multiplication operator* is on an invoice entry form. A clerk enters the number of items and the per-item price; a calculated field calculates and displays the total price for that number of items. In this case, the text box contains the formula [Price] * [Quantity]. Notice that the field names are enclosed in brackets, which is standard notation for dealing with field names in an expression.

The + (addition) operator

If you want to create a calculated field in the same form, adding the values in fields such as Gross Amount and Tax, enter the expression [Gross Amount] + [Tax].

This simple formula uses the addition operator to add the contents of both fields and place the result in the object that contains the formula.

Besides adding two numbers, the addition operator can be used for concatenating two character strings. For example, you may want to combine the fields First Name and Last Name to display them as a single field. This expression is as follows:

```
[First Name] + [Last Name]
```

Caution Although you can *concatenate* (put two strings together) text strings by using the addition operator, you should use the ampersand (&). The reason for this appears in the section "String operators," later in this chapter.

The – (subtraction) operator

An example of using the subtraction operator on a form is the calculation of an invoice amount; you might offer a discount to good repeat customers. To determine the Net Amount, you would have a formula that uses the subtraction operator, such as

```
[Gross Amount] - ([Gross Amount]*[Discount]).
```

Note Although parentheses are not mathematical operators, they play an integral part in working with operators, as discussed later, in the section "Operator precedence."

The / (division) operator

You can use the division operator to divide two numbers and (as with the previous operators) place the result wherever you need it. Suppose, for example, that a pool of 212 people wins the $1,000,000 lottery this week. The formula to determine each individual's payoff is 1,000,000 / 212, resulting in $4,716.98 per person.

The \ (integer division) operator

Should you ever need to take two numbers, round them both to integers, divide the two rounded integers, and receive a nonrounded integer, this operator will do it for you in one step. Here is an example:

Normal Division	*Integer Conversion Division*
100 / 6 = 16.667	100 \ 6 = 16
100.9 / 6.6 = 15.288	100.9 \ 6.6 = 14

Tip Access has no specific function for rounding fractional numbers to whole numbers. You can use this operator to round any number. Simply take the number you want to round, and integer-divide (\) it by 1, as in 125.6 \ 1 = 126.

What Are Integer Values?

Integers are whole numbers (numbers that contain no decimal places), which in Access are between -32768 and +32767. Examples are 1, 722, 33, -5460, 0, and 22. To determine the integer part of any number, simply drop any decimal values. For example, the integer of 45.123 is 45; for 2.987, the integer is 3; and so forth.

This can be a confusing operator until you understand just what it does. If you enter the following, it should become clear:

> **? 101 / 6** results in 16.833.

> **? 101.9 / 6.6** results in 15.439.

> **? 102 / 7** results in 14.571.

> **? INT(102 / 7)** results in 14.

> **? 101.9 \ 6.6** results in 14.

The last entry is equivalent to rounding both numbers in the division operation (101.9 = 102 and 6.6 = 7) and then dividing 102 by 7, converting the answer to an integer. In other words, it is equivalent to

INT((101.9 \ 1) / (6.6 \ 1))

Note   Access rounds numbers based on the greater-than-.5 rule: Any number with a decimal value of *x*.5 or less will round down; greater than *x*.5 will round up to the next whole number. This means that 6.5 becomes 6 and 6.6 becomes 7.

The ^ (exponentiation) operator

The exponentiation operator (^) raises a number to the power of an exponent. Raising a number simply means indicating the number of times you want to multiply a number by itself. For example, multiplying the value $4 \times 4 \times 4$ (that is, 4 cubed) is the same as entering the formula 4 ^ 3.

Relational operators

There are six basic relational operators (also known as comparison operators). They compare two values or expressions via an equation. The relational operators include the following:

=	Equal
<>	Not equal
<	Less than

    <=   Less than *or* equal

    >   Greater than

    >=   Greater than *or* equal

The operators always return either a logical value or Null; the value they return says Yes (True), No (not True, that is, False); or it is a Null (unknown/no value).

Note Access actually returns a numeric value for relational operator equations. It returns a –1 (negative 1) for True and a 0 (zero) for False.

If either side of an equation is a Null value, the resultant will always be a Null.

The = (equal) operator

The *equal operator* will return a logical True if the two expressions being compared are the same. Here are two examples of the equal operator in practice:

`[Type of Animal]` = `"Cat"` will be True if the animal is a cat; False is returned for any other animal.

`[Date of Birth]` = `Date()` will be True if the date in the Date of Birth field is today.

The <> (not-equal) operator

The *not-equal operator* is exactly the opposite of the equal operator. Here you see the cat example changed to not-equal:

`[Type of Animal]` <> `"Cat"` will be True if Type of Animal is anything but a cat.

The < (less-than) operator

The *less-than operator* returns a logical True if the left side of the equation is less than the right side, as in this example:

`[Weight]` < 10 will be True if the Weight field contains a value of less than 10.

The <= (less-than-or-equal-to) operator

The less-than-or-equal-to operator will return a True if the left side of the equation is either less than or equal to the right side, as in this example:

`[Weight]` <= 10 will be True if the value of Weight equals 10 or is less than 10.

Note Access is not sensitive to the order of the operators. Access accepts either of these forms as the same:

`(<=)` or `(=<)`

The > (greater-than) operator

The *greater-than operator* is the exact opposite of the less-than operator. This operator returns a True whenever the left side of the equation is greater than the right side. Here is an example:

`[Length (In)] > 22` will return True if the value of Length (In) is greater than 22.

The >= (greater-than-or-equal-to) operator

The *greater-than-or-equal-to operator* returns a True if the left side of the equation is either equal to or greater than the right side. Here is an example:

`[Weight (lbs)] >= 100` will return True if the field Weight (lbs) contains a value equal to or greater than 100.

Note Access is not sensitive to the order of the operator. Access lets you enter either the form (>=) or (=>).

String operators

Access has two *string operators*. Unlike the other operators you've worked with, these work specifically with the Text data type:

    &   Concatenation

    Like   Similar to ...

The & (concatenation) operator

The concatenation operator connects or links (concatenates) two or more objects into a resultant string. This operator works similarly to the addition operator; unlike the addition operator, however, the & operator always forces a string concatenation. For instance, the following example produces a single string:

`[First Name] & [Last Name]`

However, in the resultant string, no spaces are automatically added. If `[First Name]` equals "Fred" and `[Last Name]` equals "Smith," concatenating the field contents yields `FredSmith`. To add a space between the strings, you must concatenate a space string between the two fields. To concatenate a space string between first and last name fields, you enter a formula such as

[First Name] & " " & [Last Name]

This operator can easily concatenate a string object with a number- or date-type object. Using the & eliminates the need for special functions to convert a number or date to a string.

Suppose, for example, that you have a Number field, which is House Number, and a Text field, which is Street Name, and that you want to build an expression for a report of both fields. For this, you can enter the following:

[House Number] & " " & [Street Name]

If House Number has a value of 1600 and Street Name is "Pennsylvania Avenue N.W.," the resultant concatenation of the number and string is

```
"1600 Pennsylvania Avenue N.W."
```

Perhaps you have a calculated field in a report that prints the operator's name and the date and time the report was run. You can accomplish this by using syntax similar to the following:

" This report was printed " & Now( ) & " by " & [operator name]

If the date is March 21, 1996, and the time is 4:45 p.m., this concatenated line will print something like this:

```
This report was printed 3/21/96 4:45:40 PM by Michael R. Irwin
```

Notice the spaces at the end or the beginning of the strings. Knowing how this operator works will make maintenance of your database expressions easier. If you always use the concatenation operator for creating concatenated text strings, you won't have to be concerned with the data types of the concatenated objects. Any formula that uses the & operator converts all the objects being concatenated to a string type for you.

Note Using the & with Nulls: If both objects are Null, the resultant will also be a Null. If only one of the two objects is Null, Access converts the object that is Null to a string type with a length of 0 and builds the concatenation.

The Like (similar to) operator

The Like operator compares two string objects by using wildcards. This operator determines whether one object matches the pattern of another object. The resultant of the comparison will be a True, False, or Null.

The Like operator uses the following basic syntax:

expression object **Like** *pattern object*

Like looks for the *expression object* in the *pattern object*; if it is present, the operation returns a True.

Note

If either object in the Like formula is a Null, the resultant will be a Null.

This operator provides a powerful and flexible tool for string comparisons. The pattern object can use wildcard characters to increase flexibility (see the sidebar "Using Wildcards").

Tip

If you want to match one of the wildcard characters in the Like operation, the wildcard character must be enclosed by brackets in the pattern object. In the example

```
"AB*Co" Like "AB[*]C*
```

the [*] in the third position of the pattern object will look for the asterisk as the third character of the string.

Following are some more examples using the Like operator:

[Last Name] Like "M[Cc]*" will be True for any last name that begins with "Mc" or "MC." "McDonald," "McJamison," "MCWilliams" will all be True; "Irwin" and "Prague" will be False.

[Answer] Like "[!e-zE-Z]" will be True if the Answer is A, B, C, D, a, b, c, or d. Any other letter will be False.

"AB1989" Like "AB####" will result in True. This string looks for the letters *AB* and any four numbers after the letters.

"#10 Circle Drive" Like "[#]*Drive" will result in True. The first character must be the pound sign, and the last part must be the word *Drive*.

Using Wildcards

Access lets you use these five wildcards with the Like operator:

Character	Matches
?	A single character (A to Z, 0 to 9)
F	Any number of characters (0 to *n*)
#	Any single digit (0 to 9)
[*list*]	Any single character in the list
[!*list*]	Any single character *not* in the list

Note that [*list*] and [!*list*] can use the hyphen between two characters to signify a range.

Boolean (logical) operators

Access uses six *Boolean operators*. Also referred to as *logical operators*, these are used for setting conditions in expressions. Many times you'll use Boolean operators to create complex multiple-condition expressions. Like relational operators, these always return either a logical value or a Null. Boolean operators include the following:

And	Logical and
Or	Logical inclusive or
Eqv	Logical equivalence
Imp	Logical implication
Xor	Logical exclusive or
Not	Logical not

The And operator

You use the *And operator* to perform a logical conjunction of two objects; the operator returns the value True if both conditions are true. Following is the general syntax of an And operation:

> *object expression 1* **And** *object expression 2*

Here is an example:

`[State] = "MN" And [Zip Code] = "12345"` will be True only if both conditions are True.

If the conditions on both sides of the And operator are True, the result is a True value. Table 13-1 demonstrates the results.

Table 13-1
And Operator Resultants

Expression 1	Expression 2	Return Resultant
True	True	True
True	False	False
True	Null	Null

(continued)

Table 13-1 *(continued)*

Expression 1	Expression 2	Return Resultant
False	True	False
False	False	False
False	Null	False
Null	True	Null
Null	False	False
Null	Null	Null

The Or operator

You use the *Or operator* to perform a logical disjunction of two objects; the operator returns the value True if either condition is true. This is the general syntax of an Or operation:

object expression 1 Or object expression 2

The following two examples show how the Or operator works:

`[Last Name] = "Williams" Or [Last Name] = "Johnson"` will be True if Last Name is either Williams or Johnson.

`[Animal Type] = "Frog" Or [Animal Color] = "Green"` will be True if the animal is a frog or any animal that is green (a snake, bird, and so forth).

If the condition of either side of the Or operator is True, a True value is returned. Table 13-2 demonstrates the results.

Table 13-2
Or Expression Resultants

Expression 1	Expression 2	Return Resultant
True	True	True
True	False	True
True	Null	True
False	True	True

Expression 1	Expression 2	Return Resultant
False	False	False
False	Null	Null
Null	True	True
Null	False	Null
Null	Null	Null

The Not operator

The *Not operator* is used for negating a numeric object; the operator returns the value True if the condition is not true. This operator reverses the logical result of the expression.

Following is the general syntax of a Not operation:

> **Not** *numeric object expression*

The following example shows how to use the Not operator:

Not [Final Sales Amount] >= 1000 will be true if Final Sales Amount is less than 1000.

If the numeric object is Null, the resulting condition will be Null. Table 13-3 demonstrates the results.

Table 13-3
Not Operator Resultants

Expression	Return Resultant
True	False
False	True
Null	Null

Miscellaneous operators

Access has three miscellaneous operators that can be very useful to you. Their names and what they determine follow:

Between...And	Range
In	List comparison
Is	Reserved word

The Between...And operator

You can use *Between...And* to determine whether an object is within a specific range of values. This is the general syntax:

> *object expression* **Between** *value 1* **And** *value 2*

If the value of the object expression is between value 1 and value 2, the result is True; otherwise, it is False.

Following is an example of the Between...And operator that uses the IIF function for a calculated control:

```
IIF([Amount Owed] Between 0 And 250, "Due 30 Days," "Due NOW")
```

This displays a 30-day-due notice for values of $250 or less, and due-now notices for values over $250.

The In operator

You use the In operator to determine whether an object is equal to any value in a specific list. This is the general syntax:

> *object expression* **In** *(value1, value2, value3, ...)*

If the object expression is found in the list, the result is True; otherwise, the result is False.

The IIF function is used again in this example. Here, the In operator is used for a control value in a form:

```
IIF([Animal Type] In ("Cat," "Dog"), "Common Pet," "Unusual
        Pet")
```

This displays the message `Common Pet` if Animal Type is a cat or dog.

The Is (reserved word) operator

The Is operator is used only with the keyword Null to determine whether an object has nothing in it. This is the general syntax:

object expression **Is Null,** *value 1*

This example is a validation-check message in a data-entry form to force entry of a field:

```
IIF([Customer Name] Is Null, "Name Must be Entered,""")
```

Operator precedence

When you work with complex expressions that have many operators, Access must determine which operator to evaluate first, and then which is next, and so forth. To accomplish this task, Access has a built-in predetermined order, known as *operator precedence*. Access always follows this order unless you use parentheses to specify otherwise.

You use parentheses to group parts of an expression and override the default order of precedence. Operations within parentheses are performed before any operations outside of them. Inside the parentheses, Access follows the predetermined operator precedence.

Precedence is determined first according to category of the operator. The following list ranks operators by order of precedence:

1. Mathematical
2. Comparison
3. Boolean

Each of these categories contains its own order of precedence, which is explained next.

The mathematical precedence

Within the general category of mathematical operators, this order of precedence is in effect:

1. Exponentiation
2. Negation
3. Multiplication and/or division (left to right)
4. Integer division
5. Modulo
6. Addition and/or subtraction (left to right)
7. String concatenation

The comparison precedence

Comparison operators observe the following order of precedence:

1. Equal
2. Not equal
3. Less than
4. Greater than
5. Less than or equal to
6. Greater than or equal to
7. Like

The Boolean precedence

The third general category, Boolean, follows this order of precedence:

1. Not
2. And
3. Or
4. Xor
5. Eqv
6. Imp

What Are Functions?

Functions are small programs that always, by definition, return a value based on some calculation, comparison, or evaluation that the function performs. The value returned can be string, logic, or numeric, depending on the type of function. Access provides hundreds of common functions that are used in tables, queries, forms, and reports. You can also create your own user-defined functions (UDFs) using the Access Visual Basic language.

Using functions in Access

Functions perform specialized operations that enhance the utility of Access. Many times, you find yourself using functions as an integral part of Access. The following gives you a feel for the types of tasks you'll use functions to accomplish:

✦ Determine a default value in a table

✦ Place the current date and time on a report

✦ Convert data from one type to another

✦ Perform financial operations

✦ Display a field in a specific format

✦ Look up and return a value based on another

✦ Perform an action upon the triggering of an event

Access functions can perform financial, mathematical, comparative, and other operations. Therefore, you'll find yourself using functions just about everywhere — in queries, forms, reports, validation rules, and so forth.

Many Access functions evaluate or convert data from one type to another; others perform an action. Some Access functions require use of parameters; others operate without them.

Precedence Order

Simple mathematics provides an example of order of precedence. Bear in mind that Access performs operations within parentheses before operations that are not in parentheses. Also remember that multiplication and division come before addition or subtraction.

For example, what is the answer to this simple equation?

X=10+3*4

If your answer is 52, you need a better understanding of precedence in Access. If your answer is 22, you're right. If your answer is anything else, you need a calculator!

Multiplication is performed before addition by the rules of mathematical precedence. Therefore, the equation 10+3*4 is evaluated in this order:

3*4 is performed first, yielding an answer of 12. Then 12 is added to 10, yielding 22.

Look at what happens when you add parentheses to the equation. What is the answer to this simple equation?

X=(10+3)*4

Now the answer is 52. Within parentheses, the values 10 and 3 are added first; then the result of 13 is multiplied by 4, yielding 52.

Note A parameter is a value you supply to the function when you run it. The value can be an object name, a constant, or a quantity.

Access functions can be quickly identified because they always end with parentheses. If a function uses parameters, the parameters are placed inside the parentheses immediately after the function name.

Following are examples of Access functions:

Now( ) returns the current date and time.

Rnd( ) returns a random number.

Ucase( ) returns the uppercase of an object.

Format( ) returns a user-specified formatted expression.

Types of functions

Access offers several types of functions for you to use. They can be placed in the following general categories:

✦ Conversion

✦ Date/Time

✦ Financial (SQL)

✦ Financial (monetary)

✦ Mathematical

✦ String manipulation

✦ Domain

What Is a Program?

A *program* is a series of defined steps that specify one or more actions the computer should perform. A program can be created by the user or can already exist in Access; all Access functions are programs that are already created for you. For example, a Ucase() function is a small program. If you employ Ucase () on a string, such as "Michael J. Irwin," Access creates a new string from the existing string, converting each letter to uppercase. The program starts at the leftmost letter, first converting *M* to *M* and then *i* to *I*, and so forth, until the entire string is converted. As it converts each letter, the program concatenates it to a new string.

Conversion

Conversion functions change the data type from one type to another. A few common functions are listed here.

Str() returns a numeric as a string:

> **Str(921.234)** returns "921.234".

Val() returns a numeric value from a string:

> **Val("1234.56")** returns 1234.56.
>
> **Val("10 Farmview Ct")** returns 10.

Format() returns an expression according to the user-specified format:

> **Format("Next,"">")** returns NEXT.
>
> **Format("123456789,""@@@-@@-@@@@")** returns 123-45-6789.
>
> **Format(#12/25/93#,"d-mmmm-yyyy")** returns 25-December-1993.

Date/Time

Date/Time functions work with date and time expressions. Following are a couple of common Date/Time functions.

Now() returns the current date and time: 3/4/93 12:22:34 PM.

Time() returns the current time in 12-hour format: 12:22:34 PM.

Financial (SQL)

Financial (SQL) functions perform aggregate financial operations on a set of values. The set of values is contained in a field. The field can be in a form, report, or query. Following are two common SQL functions.

Avg() An example is Avg([Scores]).

Sum() An example is Sum([Gross Amount] + [Tax] + [Shipping]).

Financial (monetary)

Financial (monetary) functions perform financial operations. Following are two monetary functions.

NPV() is the net present value, based on a series of payments and a discount rate. The syntax follows:

> **NPV(*discount rate, cash flow array*())**

DDB() is the double-declining balance method of depreciation return. The syntax follows:

> **DDB(*initial cost, salvage value, life of product, period of asset depreciation*)**

Mathematical

Mathematical functions perform specific calculations. Following are some mathematical functions, with examples of how to use them.

Int() determines the integer of a specific value:

> **Int(1234.55)** results in 1234.
>
> **Int(-55.1)** results in -56.

Fix() determines the correct integer for a negative number:

> **Fix(-1234.55)** results in -1234.

Sqr() determines the square root of a number:

> **Sqr(9)** returns 3.
>
> **Sqr(14)** returns 3.742.

String manipulation

String functions manipulate text-based expressions. Here are several common uses of these functions.

Right() returns the rightmost characters of a string:

> **Right("abcdefg,"4)** returns "defg".

Len() returns the length of a string:

> **Len("abcdefgh")** results in 8.

Lcase() returns the lowercase of the string:

> **Lcase("Michael R. Irwin")** returns michael r. irwin.

Domain

A *domain* is a set of records contained in a table, a query, or an SQL expression. A query dynaset is an example of a domain. Domain aggregate functions determine specific statistics about a specific domain.

Following are two examples of domain functions.

DAvg() returns the arithmetic mean (average) of a set of values:

> **DAvg("[Total Amount],""Visits")** determines the average billing for patients.
>
> **DCount()** returns the number of records specified.

What Are Expressions?

In general, an expression is the means used to explain, or model, something to someone or something. An expression in computer terminology is generally defined as a symbol, sign, figure, or set of symbols that presents or represents an algebraic fact as a quantity or operation. The expression is a representative object that Access can use to interpret something and, based on that interpretation, to obtain specific information. More simply put, an expression is a term or series of terms controlled by operators. Expressions are a fundamental part of Access operations.

You can use expressions in Access to accomplish a variety of tasks. You can use an expression as a property setting in SQL statements, in queries and filters, or even in macros and actions. Expressions can set criteria for a query, filter, or control macros, or perform as arguments in user-defined functions.

Access evaluates an expression each time it is used. If an expression is in a form or report, Access calculates the value every time the form refreshes (as with changing records and so forth). This ensures accuracy of the results. If an expression is used as a criterion in a query, Access evaluates the expression every time the query is executed, thereby ensuring that the criterion reflects any changes, additions, or deletions to records since the last execution of the query. If an expression is used in the table design as a validation rule, Access executes the evaluation every time the field is trespassed to determine whether the value is allowed in the field; this expression may be based on another field's value!

To give you a better understanding of expressions, consider the various examples that follow — all are examples of expressions:

```
=[Customer First Name] & " " & [Customer Last Name]

=[Total Amount] - ([Total Amount] * [Discount])

<25

[Deceased]=Yes

[Animal Type] = "Cat" And [Gender] = "M"

[Date of Birth] Between 1/88 And 12/91
```

All of these are valid expressions. Access can use them in a variety of ways: as validation rules, query criteria, calculated controls, control sources, and control-source properties.

The parts of an expression

As the many examples in the preceding section demonstrated, expressions can be very simple or quite complex. They can include a combination of operators, object names, functions, literal values, and constants.

Keeping in mind that expressions don't need to contain all these parts, you should have an understanding of each of the following uniquely identifiable portions of an expression:

Operators: `>, =, *, And, Or, Not, Like,` and so on.

> Operators indicate what type of action (operation) will be performed on one or more elements of an expression.

Object names: `Forms![Add a Customer & Pets], [Customer Address], [Pet Name]`

> Object names, also known as *identifiers,* are the actual objects: tables, forms, reports, controls, or fields.

Functions: `Date(), DLookUp(), DateDiff()`

> Functions always return a value. The resultant value can be created by a calculation, a conversion of data, or an evaluation. You can use a built-in Access function or a user-defined function (UDF) that you create.

Literal values: `100, Jan. 1, 1988, "Cat," "[A-D]*"`

> These are actual values that you supply to the expression. Literal values can be numbers, strings, or dates. Access uses the values exactly as they are entered.

Constants: `Yes, No, Null, True, False`

> Constants represent values that do not change.

The following illustration demonstrates the parts of an expression:

`[Follow Up Date] = Date() + 30`

> `[Follow Up Date]` is an object name, or identifier.
>
> = is an operator.

Date( ) is a function.

+ is an operator.

30 is a literal.

Creating an expression

Expressions are commonly entered in property windows, action arguments, and criteria grids. As you create expressions, the area is scrolled so that you can continue to enter the expression. Although you can enter an expression in this manner, it is often desirable to see the entire expression as you enter it. This is especially true when you are working with long, complex expressions. Access has a Zoom box you can use to change how much of the expression you see as you enter it. Open this box by clicking where you want to enter your expression and then pressing Shift+F2.

As you enter expressions, Access may insert certain characters for you when you *change focus*. Access will check your syntax and will automatically insert these characters:

✦ Brackets ([]) around control names that have no spaces or punctuation in the name

✦ Pound signs (#) around dates it recognizes

✦ Quotation marks (" ") around text that contains no spaces or punctuation in the body

Note   The term *changing focus* refers to the movement of the cursor out of the location where you are entering the expression. You accomplish this by pressing Tab or by moving the mouse and clicking on another area of the screen.

Caution   Access reports an error when it changes focus under the following conditions: Access doesn't understand the date form you enter, the name of the control contains spaces, or a control is not placed in brackets.

Entering object names

You identify object names by placing brackets ([]) around the element. Access requires the use of brackets when the object contains a space or punctuation in its name. If these conditions are not present, you can ignore the brackets — Access inserts them automatically. Therefore, the following expressions are syntactically identical:

```
Breed + [Type of Animal]
```

```
[Breed] + [Type of Animal]
```

Notice that in both cases the brackets are placed around Type of Animal because this object name contains spaces.

Although it isn't necessary to enter brackets around objects like Breed in the second example, it is good programming practice always to surround object names with brackets for consistency in entry.

Entering text

You identify text by placing quotation marks around the text element of an expression. Access automatically places the quotation marks for you if you forget to add them.

As an example, you can type **Cat, Dog**, and **Frog** into separate criteria cells of a query, and Access automatically adds the quotation marks around each of these three entries. Access recognizes these as objects and helps you.

Entering date/time values

You identify date/time data by placing the pound signs (#) around the date/time element. Access will evaluate any valid date/time format automatically and place the pound signs around the element for you.

Expression Builder

Access has added an *Expression Builder* tool that helps you build complex expressions. You can use it anywhere you can build an expression (such as when specifying criteria for a query or creating a calculated field on a form or report). You can activate the builder in two ways:

✦ Press the Build button on the toolbar (the button with the ellipsis on it).

✦ Click the *right* mouse button and select Build from the shortcut menu.

Special identifier operators and expressions

Access has two special *identifier operators*: the dot (.) and the exclamation point (!). When you work with Access tables, you have a diverse range of ways to display and access objects. You can use fields and their contents; any field object can be used over and over. You can display the field object in numerous forms and reports by using the same reference, the field object name, in every form and report.

For example, the field Pet Name in the Pets table can be used in six or seven different forms. When you want to use the Pet Name field in an expression for a comparison, how do you tell Access which copy of the field Pet Name it should use for the expression? Because Access is a Windows database, it is possible to have several different forms in the same session on the same computer. In fact, it is possible to have multiple copies of Access running the same data and forms.

A Few Words About Controls and Properties

When you create a form or report, you place many different objects on the form — fields in text boxes, text labels, buttons, check boxes, combo boxes, lines, rectangles, and so on.

As you select and place these objects on a form, each object is assigned a *control name*. Access supplies the control name according to predefined rules. For example, control names for fields default to a control-source name of the field name. The field name appears in the text box on the form. The label for the text box is assigned the control name Text, with a sequence number attached to it (for example, Text11 or Text12). The sequence number is added to make each control name unique.

After all objects are placed on the form, you can identify any object on the form (line, button, text box, and so on) by its unique control name. This control name is what you use to reference a specific table field (or field on a form). You can change the name of the control that Access assigned to the object if you want. The only requirement for the new control name is that it must be unique to the form or report that contains it.

Every object on the form (and don't forget that the form itself is an object) has associated *properties.* These are the individual characteristics of each object; as such, they are accessible by a control name. Properties control the appearance of the object (color, size, sunken, alignment, and so forth). They also affect the structure, specifying format, default value, validation rules, and control name. In addition, properties designate the *behavior* of a control — for instance, whether the field can grow or shrink and whether you can edit it. Behaviors also affect actions specified for the event properties, such as On Enter and On Push.

With all this confusion, there must be a way to specify to Access which Pet Name field object you want the expression to use. That is the purpose of the dot and exclamation point as operator identifiers. These symbols identify and maintain clarity in determining which field to use.

The ! (exclamation) identifier operator

The exclamation mark (!) is a key symbol that is used in conjunction with several reserved words. One such reserved word is Forms. When this word is followed by !, you are telling Access that the next object name will be the form object name you want to reference.

As an example, say that you have a Date of Birth field that is in two forms — [Customer & Pets] and [Pet Specifics]. (Note that these two form names are objects; you will need to use brackets to reference them.) You want to refer to the Date of Birth field in the [Pet Specifics] form. The way to specify this form is by use of the ! and the *Forms* reserved word:

```
Forms![Pet Specifics]
```

Now that the form is specified, you need to further refine the scope to add the field Date of Birth.

Note Although Chapter 16 covers controls and properties, by this point you should have a partial understanding of what properties and controls are (for a refresher, see the preceding sidebar).

Actually, what you are specifying is a control on the form. That control will use the field you need, which is Date of Birth. The control has the same name as the field. Therefore, you access this specific object by using the following expression:

```
Forms![Pet Specifics]![Date of Birth]
```

The second exclamation mark specifies a control on a form — one identified by the reserved word *Forms*.

By following the properties of each object, starting with the object Forms, you can trace the control source object back to a field in the original table.

In summary, the exclamation-point identifier is always followed by an object name. You define this object name by using the name of a form, report, field, or other control name you created in the database. If you don't use the existing name for the desired object, you can change the default value name of the source.

The . (dot) identifier operator

The . (dot) is also a key symbol that is used in conjunction with expression identification operators. Normally it is placed immediately after a user-defined object. Unlike the !, the . (dot) usually identifies a property of a specific object. Therefore, if you want to determine the value of the Visible property of the same control you worked with before, you specify it as follows:

```
Forms![Pet Specifics]![Date of Birth].Visible
```

This gives you the value for the Visible property of the specific field on the specific form.

Note Normally the . (dot) identifier is used to obtain a value that corresponds to a property of an object. Sometimes, however, you can use it between a table name and a field name when you are accessing a value associated with a specific field in a specific table, as shown here:

```
[Pets].[Pet Name]
```

A thorough analysis of the two special identifier operators is beyond the scope of this book. Even so, you'll find that these identifiers enable you to find any object and the values associated with its properties.

Summary

In this chapter, you learned about the building blocks of Access operations: operators, functions, and expressions. The chapter covered the following points:

✦ Operators let you add numbers, compare values, put strings together, and create complicated relational expressions.

✦ The many types of operators include mathematical, relational, string, Boolean, and a group of miscellaneous operators.

✦ The relational operators =, <>, >, >=, <, and <= make comparisons.

✦ To concatenate two strings, use the & operator.

✦ You can use five pattern-matching wildcards with the Like operator: *, ?, #, [*list*], and [!*list*].

✦ The Boolean operators are And, Or, Eqv, Imp, Xor, and Not.

✦ Operator precedence determines the order in which Access evaluates the various parts of an expression.

✦ Functions are small programs that return a value. Access has hundreds of built-in functions.

✦ Functions are classified as conversion, date/time, financial, mathematical, string, or domain.

✦ Expressions are used to create a calculation or to model a process.

✦ Expressions use operators, object names, functions, literal values, and constants.

✦ The Expression Builder can be used to create an expression.

✦ Object names are entered in brackets ([ ]) to identify them. Common objects include field names.

✦ The two special identifiers, the exclamation point and the dot, help identify Access objects, such as forms, reports, queries, and tables. These identifiers can also identify properties.

In the next chapter, you examine how to create relationships and joins in queries.

✦   ✦   ✦

Creating Relations and Joins in Queries

In previous chapters, you worked with simple queries by using the single table Pets. Using a query to obtain information from a single table is common; often, however, you need to obtain information from several related tables. For example, you may want to obtain a customer's name and the type of pets the customer owns. In this chapter, you learn how to use more than one table to obtain information.

Adding More Than One Table to the Query Window

In Chapter 12, you learned about the different tables in the Mountain Animal Hospital database system. This system is composed of four primary tables and four lookup tables. You learned about table keys, primary and foreign, and their importance for linking two tables together. You learned how to create relationships between two tables at the table level by using the Tools⇨Relationships menu choice in the Database window. Finally, you learned how referential integrity rules affect data in tables.

After you create the tables for your database and decide how the tables are related to one another, you are ready to begin creating multiple-table queries to obtain information from several tables at the same time.

By adding more than one table to a query and then selecting fields from the tables in the query, you can view information from your database just as though the information from the several tables was in one table. As an example, suppose you need to send a letter to all owners of snakes who brought their pets in for visits in the last two months. For this data, you would need to get the information from three separate tables: Pets, Customer, and Visits. You can do this by using the Pets and Visits tables and creating a query for all animals where the Type of Animal field equals snake and where Visit Date falls between today's date and today's date minus two months. Because of the relationship between the Pets and Customer tables, you then have access to the customer information for each snake. You can then create a report form using the related information from the tables Pets, Visits, and Customer.

The first step in creating a multiple-table query is to open each table in the Query window. The following steps show how to open the Pets, Customer, and Visits tables in a single query:

1. Click on the Query tab in the Database window.

2. Click on the New button to create a new query.

3. Select New Query and click on OK in the New Query dialog box.

4. Select the Pets table by double-clicking on the table name.

5. Select the Customer table by double-clicking on the table name.

6. Select the Visits table by double-clicking on the table name.

7. Click on the Close button in the Show Table dialog box.

Note   You can also add each table by highlighting the table in the list separately and clicking on Add.

The top pane of the Query Design window is shown in Figure 14-1 with three tables: Pets, Customer, and Visits.

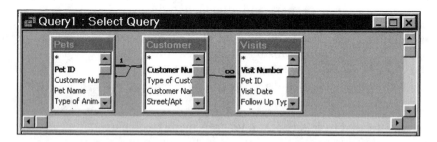

Figure 14-1: The Query Design window with three files added.

Note You can add more tables by selecting Query⇨Show Table from the Query Design window or by clicking on the Show Table icon.

Working with the Table/Query Pane

As you can see in Figure 14-1, each table is connected by a single line from the primary key field to the foreign key field. Actually, on your screen it probably looks as if two lines connect Pets to Customer and a single line runs from Customer to Visits. You'll see how to move the table design so that the lines appear correctly.

The join line

When Access displays each set of related tables, it places a line between the two tables. This line is known as a *join line*. A join line is a graphical line that represents the link between two tables. In this example, the join line goes from the Pets table to the Customer table to connect the two Customer Number fields. A join line also runs from Pets to Visits, connecting the Pet ID fields in these two tables.

This link is created automatically because a relationship was set in the Database window. If Access already knows what the relationship is, it automatically creates the link for you when the tables are added to a query. The relationship is displayed as a join line between two tables.

If Referential Integrity is checked in the relationship between two tables, Access will display a thick portion of the line right at the table window (like the line in Figure 14-2). Notice that the line starts heavy and then becomes thin between Pets and Visits (heavy on both sides). This line variation tells you that Referential Integrity has been set up between the two tables in the Relationship Builder. If a one-to-many relationship exists, the many relationship is denoted by an infinity sign (∞).

Note If you have not specified a relationship between two tables and the following conditions are true, Access 97 will automatically join the tables:

1. The tables have a field in both with the same name.

2. The field with the same name in both tables is the same type (text, numeric, and so on).

3. The field is a *primary key* field in one of the tables.

Tip Access 97 automatically joins the table if a relationship exists. However, you can turn off this property by unchecking the default Enable AutoJoin option from the global options tabbed dialog box. To display this option, select Tools⇨Options⇨ Tables/Queries and then uncheck the Enable AutoJoin option.

Manipulating the Table Design window

Each Table Design window begins at a fixed size, which shows approximately four fields and 12 characters for each field. Each Table Design window is a true window and behaves like one; it can be resized and moved. If you have more fields than will fit in the Table Design window, an elevator is attached to the table design. The elevator lets you scroll through the fields in the Table Design window.

Note After a relationship is created between tables, the join line remains between the two fields. As you move through a table selecting fields, you'll notice that the graphical line will move, relative to the linked fields. For example, if you move the elevator down (toward the bottom of the structure) in the Customer table, you'll notice that the join line moves up with the customer number and eventually stops at the top of the table window.

When you're working with many tables, these join lines can become visually confusing as they cross or overlap. If you move through the table, the line eventually becomes visible, and the field it is linked to will be obvious.

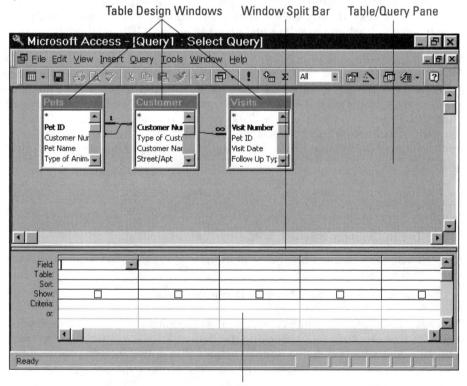

Figure 14-2: Resizing the Query Design panes.

Resizing the table/query pane

When you place table designs on the Table/Query pane, they appear in a fixed size with little spacing between tables. When you add a table to the top pane, it initially shows you five fields. If more fields are in the table, an elevator bar will be added to the box (right side). The table box may show only part of a long field name. (The rest is truncated by the box size.) You can move the tables around the pane and even resize them to show more field names and more of the field name. The first step, however, is to resize the pane itself. The Query Design window is made up of two panes. The top pane displays your table designs, whereas the QBE pane below lets you enter fields, sort orders, and criteria. Often the top pane can be larger than the bottom pane; you may want more space for the design and less space for the QBE pane.

You can resize the Table/Query pane by placing your cursor on the thick line below the elevator. This is the *window split bar*. The cursor changes to a double vertical arrow, as shown in Figure 14-2. You can then drag the split bar up or down. The following steps show how to resize the panes:

1. Place the cursor on the window split bar.

2. Hold down the mouse button and drag the split bar down.

3. Release the bar when it is two lines below the QBE row marked `or:`.

The top pane is now much larger; the bottom pane is smaller but still displays the entire QBE Design area. You now have space to move the table designs around and properly view the Table/Query pane.

Tip   You can build a database diagram so that you view only the table designs by moving the split bar to the bottom of the screen and then positioning the table designs as you want within the full-screen area.

Moving a table

You can move table designs in the Table/Query pane by simply placing the cursor on the top of a table design (where the name of the table is) and then dragging the table to a new location. You may want to move the table designs for a better working view or to clean up a confusing database diagram, (like the one shown in Figure 14-2). To move table designs, follow these steps:

1. Place the cursor on the top of the Customer table on the text `Customer`.

2. Drag the Customer table design straight down until the top of the table design appears where the bottom was when you started.

The screen should now look like Figure 14-3. You can see that each line is now an individual line that goes from one table's primary key to the foreign key in another table.

You can move the table designs anywhere in the top pane. You can spread out the diagram by moving the table designs farther apart. You can also rearrange the table designs. You may want to place the Customer table first, followed by the Pets table and then the Visits table. Remember that, in this example, you are trying to view the snakes that have been in for a visit in the last two months so that you can send a letter to the customer. So the sequence of Pets, Customer, and Visits makes sense. You generally want to view your diagram with a particular business purpose in mind. Pets is the main table in this business example and needs to retrieve information from both the Visits and Customer tables.

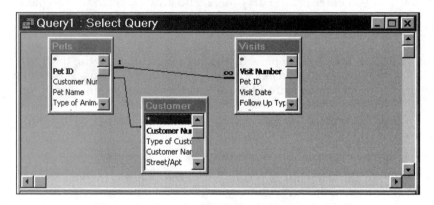

Figure 14-3: A database diagram for the Pets, Customer, and Visits tables.

Removing a table

There are times when you need to remove tables from a query. Any table can be removed from the Query window. Follow these steps to delete the Visits table, bearing in mind that you can restore it later:

1. Select the Visits table in the top pane of the Query window by clicking on either the table or a field in the table.

2. Press the Delete key or select Edit➪Delete.

Note   Only one table at a time can be removed from the Query window. The menu choice Edit➪Clear Grid does *not* remove all tables; this selection is used for removing all fields from the QBE pane. You can also remove a table by right-clicking on a table and selecting Remove Table from the shortcut menu.

When you delete a table, any join lines to that table are deleted as well. When you delete a table, there is no warning or confirmation dialog box. The table is simply removed from the screen.

Adding more tables

You may decide to add more tables to a query or you may accidentally delete a table and need to add it back. You can accomplish this task by either selecting Query⇨Show Table or clicking the *right* mouse button and selecting Show Table from the shortcut menu that appears. When you use one of these methods, the Show Table dialog box that appeared when you created the query is redisplayed. To restore the Visits table to the screen, follow these steps:

1. Move the mouse pointer to the top pane (outside of any existing tables) and press the right mouse button. Select Show Table from the menu.

2. Select the Visits table by double-clicking on the table name.

3. Click on the Close button in the Show Table dialog box.

Access returns you to the Table/Query pane of the Visits table and redisplays the join line.

Resizing a table design

You can also resize each of the table designs by placing the cursor on one of the table design borders. The table design is nothing but a window; thus, you can enlarge or reduce it vertically, horizontally, or diagonally by placing the cursor on the appropriate border. When you enlarge the table design vertically, you can see more fields than the default number (five). By making the table design larger horizontally, you can see the complete list of field names. Then, when you resize the Table/Query pane to take up the entire window, you can create a database diagram.

Creating a database diagram

Figure 14-4 shows a database diagram for these three tables in which you can see all the fields. The more tables and relationships you have, the more important a database diagram becomes in helping you view your data graphically with the proper relationships visible. In upcoming chapters, you'll see many different database diagrams as you use queries to assemble the data for various forms and reports.

In Figure 14-4, the Table/Query pane is expanded to its full size, so you can't see any of the QBE pane below. You can get to the QBE pane by resizing with the split bar. When you're working with fields in the QBE pane, you should keep the screen split so that you can see both panes.

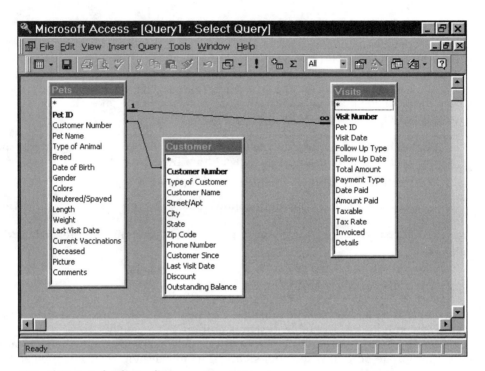

Figure 14-4: A database diagram.

Caution   Although you can switch panes by pressing F6, you can't see where the cursor is in the QBE pane while the Table/Query pane is displayed in full-screen size.

CD-ROM   If you are following along on your computer with the examples in this chapter, resize the panes so that you can see both the Table Design pane and the QBE pane.

Adding Fields from More Than One Table

You can add fields from more than one table to the query in exactly the same way as when you're working with a single table. You can add fields one at a time, many fields grouped together, or all the fields from one or all tables.

Cross-Reference   Adding fields from a single table is covered in detail in Chapter 10; this chapter covers the topic in less detail but focuses on the differences between single- and multiple-table field selection.

Adding a single field

You can select a single field from any table by using any of several methods:

✦ Double-click on a field name in the Table/Query pane.

✦ Click on a field name in the Table/Query pane and drag it to the QBE pane.

✦ Click on an empty Field: cell in the QBE pane and type a field name.

✦ Click on an empty Field: cell and select the field from the drop-down list.

Caution If you type a field name in an empty Field: cell that is in both tables, Access enters the field name from the first table that it finds containing that field. Access will search the tables, starting from the left side in the top pane.

If you select the field from the drop-down list in the Field: cell, you see the name of the table first, followed by a period and the field name. For example, the field Pet ID in the Pets table is displayed as `Pets.Pet ID`. This helps you to select the right field name. Using this method, you can select a common field name from a specific table.

The easiest way to select fields is still to double-click on the query/table designs. To do so, you may have to resize the table designs to see the fields you want to select. To select Customer Name, Pet Name, Type of Animal, and Visit Date, follow these steps:

1. Double-click on Customer Name in the Customer table.

2. Double-click on Pet Name in the Pets table.

3. Double-click on Type of Animal in the Pets table.

4. Double-click on Visit Date in the Visits table.

Viewing the table names

When you're working with two or more tables, the field names in the QBE pane can become confusing. You may find yourself asking, for example, just which table the field Customer Number is from.

Access automatically maintains the table name that is associated with each field displayed in the QBE pane. The default is to display the table name. To choose not to show the table name in the QBE pane, select View⇨Table Names.

This selection controls the display of table names immediately below the corresponding field name in the QBE pane. Figure 14-5 shows the QBE pane with the row Table: below the Field: row. Notice that it contains the name of the table for each field.

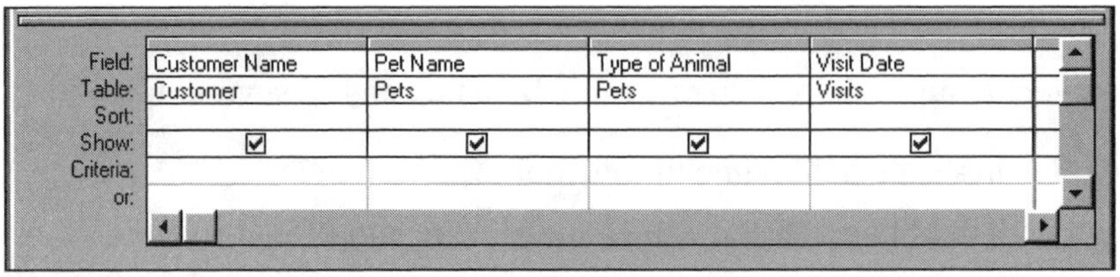

Field:	Customer Name	Pet Name	Type of Animal	Visit Date	
Table:	Customer	Pets	Pets	Visits	
Sort:					
Show:	☑	☑	☑	☑	
Criteria:					
or:					

Figure 14-5: The QBE pane with Table names displayed.

The display of the table name is only for your information. Access always maintains the table name associated with the field names.

After you add fields to a query, you can view your data at any time. Although you'll eventually limit the display of data to snakes that have visited you in the last two months, you can view all the data at any time by selecting the Datasheet icon. Figure 14-6 displays the data as currently selected. The fields have been resized to show all the data values.

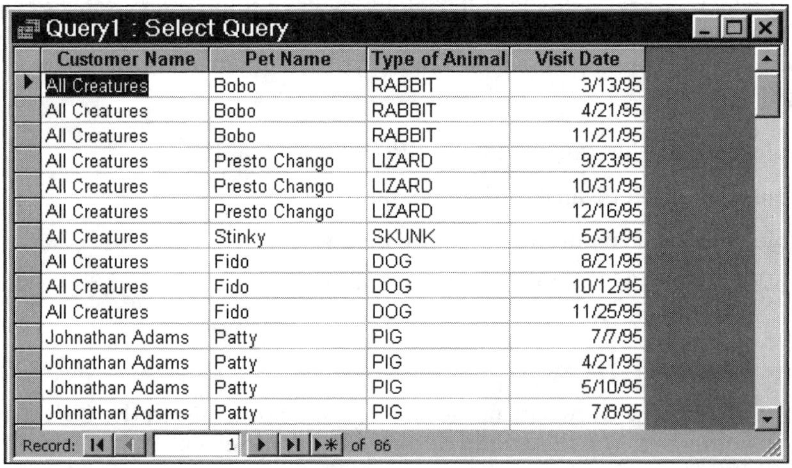

Customer Name	Pet Name	Type of Animal	Visit Date
All Creatures	Bobo	RABBIT	3/13/95
All Creatures	Bobo	RABBIT	4/21/95
All Creatures	Bobo	RABBIT	11/21/95
All Creatures	Presto Chango	LIZARD	9/23/95
All Creatures	Presto Chango	LIZARD	10/31/95
All Creatures	Presto Chango	LIZARD	12/16/95
All Creatures	Stinky	SKUNK	5/31/95
All Creatures	Fido	DOG	8/21/95
All Creatures	Fido	DOG	10/12/95
All Creatures	Fido	DOG	11/25/95
Johnathan Adams	Patty	PIG	7/7/95
Johnathan Adams	Patty	PIG	4/21/95
Johnathan Adams	Patty	PIG	5/10/95
Johnathan Adams	Patty	PIG	7/8/95

Query1 : Select Query — Record: 1 of 86

Figure 14-6: Viewing data from multiple tables.

Adding multiple fields

The process of adding multiple fields is identical to adding multiple fields in a single table query. When you're adding multiple fields from several tables, you must add them from one table at a time. The easiest way to do this task is to select multiple fields and drag them together down to the QBE pane.

You can select multiple fields contiguously by selecting the first field of the list, holding down the Shift key, and using the mouse to go to the last field. You can also select random fields in the list by holding down the Control key (Ctrl) while selecting individual fields with a mouse click.

Adding all table fields

As with adding multiple fields, when you're adding all table fields, you do it by selecting which table you want to add first and then selecting the next table. You can select all the fields by either double-clicking on the title bar of the table name or by selecting the Asterisk (*) field. Remember that these two methods produce very different results.

This method automatically fills in each column of the QBE pane. The fields are added in order of their selection in the table, from left to right (based on their field order in the table). By default, Access displays only the first five fields. You can change the column width of each field to display more or fewer columns.

Selecting all fields with the double-clicking method

One method of selecting all the fields is to double-click on the title bar of the table whose fields you want to select.

Selecting all fields with the Asterisk (*) method

The first object in each table is an asterisk (at the top of the field list), which is known as the *all-field reference tag*. When you select and drag the asterisk to the QBE pane, all fields in the table are added to the QBE pane, but there is a distinct difference between this method and the double-clicking method. When you add the all-field reference tag (*), the QBE pane shows only one cell with the name of the table and an asterisk. For example, if you select the * in the Pets table, you see Pets.* displayed in one field row cell.

Unlike selecting all the fields, the asterisk places reference to all the fields in a single column. When you drag multiple columns, as in the preceding example, you drag actual table field names to the query. If you later change the design of the table, you also have to change the design of the query. The advantage of using the asterisk for selecting all fields is that you won't have to change the query later if you add, delete, or rename fields in the underlying table or query. Changing fields in the underlying table or query will automatically add fields to or remove fields from the query.

Caution   Selecting the * has one drawback: You cannot perform criteria conditions on the asterisk column itself. You have to add an individual field from the table and enter the criteria. If you add a field for a criterion (when using the *), the query displays the field twice — once for the * field and a second time for the criteria field. Therefore, you may want to uncheck the Show: choice of the criteria field.

Understanding the Limitations of Multiple-Table Queries

When you create a query with multiple files, there are limitations to what fields can be edited. Generally, you can change data in a query dynaset, and your changes will be saved to the underlying tables. A primary key field normally cannot be edited if referential integrity is in effect and if the field is part of a relationship (unless Cascade Updates is set to Yes).

In order for you to update a table from a query, a value in a specific record in the query must represent a single record in the underlying table. This means you cannot update fields in a Crosstab or Totals query because they both group records together to display grouped information. Instead of displaying the actual underlying table data, they display records of data that are calculated and stored in a virtual (nonreal) table called a *snapshot*.

Updating limitations

In Access Version 1.*x*, only the records on the *many* side of a one-to-many relationship were updatable. That has changed starting with version 2.0. Table 14-1 shows when a field in a table is updatable. As you can see in Table 14-1, queries based on one-to-many relationships are updatable in both tables (depending on how the query was designed). Any query that creates a *snapshot*, however, is not updatable.

Table 14-1 Updatability Rules for Queries		
Type of Query or Field	*Updatable*	*Comments*
One Table	Yes	
One-to-One relationship	Yes	
One-to-Many relationship	Mostly	Restrictions based on design methodology (see text)
Crosstab	No	Creates a *snapshot* of the data
Totals Query (Sum, Avg, etc.)	No	Works with Grouped data creating a *snapshot*
Unique Value property is Yes	No	Shows unique records only in a *snapshot*
SQL-specific queries	No	Union & Pass-through work with ODBC data

Type of Query or Field	Updatable	Comments
Calculated field	No	Will recalculate automatically
Read-only fields	No	If opened read-only or on read-only drive (CD-ROM)
Permissions denied	No	Insert, Replace, or Delete are not granted
ODBC Tables with no Primary Key	No	A primary key (unique index) must exist
Paradox Table with no Primary Key	No	A primary key file must exist
Locked by another user	No	Cannot be updated while a field is locked by another

Overcoming query limitations

Table 14-1 shows that there are times that queries and fields in tables are not updatable. As a general rule, any query that does aggregate calculations or is an ODBC-based SQL query is not updatable. All others can be updated. When your query has more than one table and some of the tables have a one-to-many relationship, there may be fields that are not updatable (depending on the design of the query).

A unique index (primary key) and updatability

If a query uses two tables that have a one-to-many relationship, the one side of the join must have a unique (primary key) index on the field that is used for the join. If not, the fields from the one side of the query cannot be updated.

Replacing existing data in a query with a one-to-many relationship

Normally, all the fields in the many-side table are updatable in a one-to-many query; the one-side table can update all the fields *except* the primary key (join) field. Normally, this is sufficient for most database application purposes. Also normally, you would never change the primary key field in the one-side table because it is the link to the records in the joined tables.

At times, however, you may need to change the link-field contents in both tables (make a new primary key in the one table and have the database program change the link field in all the related records from the *many* table). Access 97 will let you do this by defining a relationship between the two tables and using referential integrity. If you define a relationship and enforce referential integrity in the Relationship Builder, two check boxes are activated. If you want to allow changes (updates) to the primary key field, check the Cascade Update Related Fields box, as shown in Figure 14-7. By checking this option, you can change the primary key field in a relationship; Access will update the link field to the new value automatically in all the other related tables.

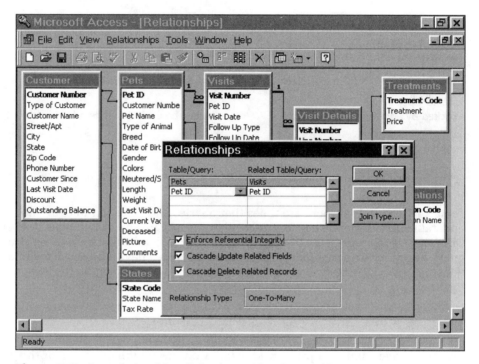

Figure 14-7: The Relationships dialog box with referential integrity in effect.

Design tips for updating fields in queries

✦ If you want to use AutoLookup between forms, be sure to include the join field from the *many* table in your form (instead of the *one* table). Also use a combo or list box to display this field.

✦ If you want to add records to both tables of a one-to-many relationship, be sure to include the join field from the *many*-side table and show the field in the datasheet. After you've done this, you can add records starting with either table. The *one* side's join field will be copied automatically to the *many* side's join field.

✦ If you do not want any fields to be updatable, set the Allow Edits property of the form to No.

✦ If you do not want to update some fields on a form, set the Tab Stop property for the control (field) to No for these fields.

✦ If you want to add records to multiple tables in a form, remember to include all (or most) of the fields from both tables. Otherwise, you will not have a complete record of data in your form.

Temporary non-updatability in a one-to-many relationship

When updating records on the one side of a one-to-many query, you will *not* be able to change the many-side *join* field until you save changes to the one side. You can quickly save changes to the one side by pressing Shift+Enter or selecting File⇨Save Record. Once the one side changes are saved, the join field in the *many*-side record can be changed.

Creating Query Joins

You can create joins between tables in the following three ways:

✦ By creating relationships between the tables when you design the database (Select Tools⇨Relationships from the Database window or click on the Relationship button on the toolbar)

✦ By selecting two tables for the query that have a field that is the same type and name in both, *and* that field is a primary key field in one of the tables

✦ By creating joins in the Query window at the time you create a query

The first two methods are automatic. If you create relationships when designing the tables of your database, Access displays join lines based on those relationships automatically when you add the related tables to a query. It also creates an automatic join between two tables that have a common field, provided that field is a primary key in one of the tables.

There may be times when you add tables to a query that are not already related to a specific file, as in these examples:

✦ The two tables have a common field, but it is not the same name.

✦ A table is not related — and cannot be related to the other table (for example, the Customer table cannot be directly joined to the Treatments table).

If you have two tables that are not automatically joined and you need to relate them, you join them in the Query Design window. Joining tables in the Query Design window does *not* create a permanent join between the tables. Rather, the join (relationship) will apply only to the table for the query you are working on.

Caution All tables in a query must be joined to at least one other table. If, for example, you place two tables into a query and *do not* join them, Access will create a query based on a *Cartesian product* (also known as the *cross product*) of the two tables. This subject will be discussed later in this chapter. For now, note that a Cartesian product means that if you have five records in table 1 and six records in table 2, then the resulting query will have thirty records (5 × 6) that will probably be useless to you.

Joining tables

Figure 14-8 shows the Pets and Customer tables that are being joined. Tables will not be joined automatically in a query if they are not already joined at the table level, do not have a common named field for a primary key, or have the AutoJoin option turned off.

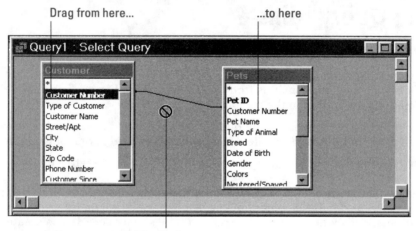

Figure 14-8: Joining tables in the Table/Query pane.

1. Select the Customer Number field in the Customer Table in the Table/Query pane.

2. Drag the highlighted field to the Pets table (as you drag the field, the Field icon appears).

3. Drop the Field icon on the Customer Number field in the Pets table.

Figure 14-8 illustrates the process of joining tables. The Field icon first appears in the Customer Number field of the Customer table; then it moves to the Pets table. As it moves between tables, the Field icon changes to the symbol that indicates the icon cannot be dropped in the area between the tables. When the icon is over the Customer Number field, it changes back to the Field icon, indicating you can drop it in that location. When you release the mouse button, the join line appears.

Of course, you can also create joins that make no sense, but when you view the data, you will get less-than-desirable results. If two joined fields have no values in common, you have a datasheet in which no records are selected or a Cartesian product in which each and every record is joined with each and every record in the second table. If one table has 100 records and the other has 200 records, the Cartesian join will create a table with 20,000 records. Then, your results will make no sense.

Note

You can select either table first when you create a join.

You would never want to create a meaningless join. For example, you would not want to join the City field from the Customer table to the Date of Birth field in the Pets table. Although Access will let you create this join, the resulting dynaset will have no records in it.

Deleting joins

To delete a join line between two tables, you select the join line and press the Delete key. You can select the join line by placing the cursor on any part of the line and clicking once. For example, create a new query by adding the Customer and Pets table to a query, and then, following these steps, you can delete the join line between the Pets and Customer tables:

1. Select the join line between the Customer Number field in the Pets table and the Customer table by placing the cursor on the line and clicking the mouse button.

2. With the join line highlighted, press the Delete key.

After Step 2, the line should disappear. If you delete a join line between two tables that have a relationship set at the database level, the broken join is effective only for the query in which you broke the join. When you exit the query, the relationship between the two tables remains in effect for other operations, including subsequent queries.

You can also delete a join by selecting it and choosing Edit➪Delete.

Caution

Remember that if you delete a join between two tables and the tables remain in the Query window unjoined to any other tables, you will get unexpected results in the datasheet. This is due to the Cartesian product that Access creates from the two tables. The Cartesian product will be effective for only this query. The underlying relationship remains intact.

Note

Access enables you to create multiple-field joins between tables (more than one line can be drawn). Remember that the join must be between two fields that have the same data and data type; if not, the query will not find any records from the datasheet to display.

Understanding Types of Table Joins

In Chapter 12, you learned about table relationships. Access understands all types of table and query relations, which include the following:

✦ One-to-one

✦ One-to-many

✦ Many-to-one

✦ Many-to-many

When you specify a relationship between two tables, you establish rules for the type of relationship, not for viewing the data based on the relationship.

To view data in two tables, you must join them through a link, which you establish via a common field (or group of fields) between the two tables. The method of linking the tables is known as *joining*. In a query, tables with established relationships are shown already joined. Within a query, you can create new joins or change an existing join line; just as there are different types of relationships, there are different types of joins. In the following sections, you'll learn about these types of joins:

✦ Equi-joins (inner joins)

✦ Outer joins

✦ Self-joins

✦ Cross-product joins (Cartesian joins)

Inner joins (equi-joins)

The default join in Access is known as an *equi-join,* or *inner join*. It enables you to tell Access to select all records from both tables that have the same value in the fields that are joined together.

Note   The Access manuals refer to a default join as an equi-join (also commonly referred to as an inner join in database relational theory). The terms are interchangeable and will be used as such throughout this chapter.

For an example of an equi-join, recall the Customer and Pets tables. Bear in mind that you are looking for all records from these two tables with matching fields. The Customer Number fields are common to both, so the equi-join does not show any records for customers that have no pets or any pets that do not relate to a valid customer number. The rules of referential integrity prevent pet records that are not tied to a customer number. Of course, it's possible to delete all pets from a customer or to create a new customer record with no pet records, but a pet should always be related to a valid customer. Referential integrity should keep a customer number from being deleted or changed if a pet is related to it.

Regardless of how it happens, it's possible to have a customer in the Customer table who has no pets. It's less likely, but still theoretically possible, to have a pet with no owner. If you create a query to show customers and their pets, any record of a customer without pets or a pet record without a matching customer record will not be shown in the resulting dynaset.

It can be important for you to find these lost records. One of the features of a query is to perform several types of joins.

Tip
Access can help you find lost records between tables; use the Query Wizards to build a Find Unmatched Query.

Changing join properties

With the Customer and Pets tables joined, certain join behaviors (or *properties*) exist between the tables. The join property is a rule that says to display all records (for the fields you specify) that correspond to the characters found in the Customer Number field of the Customer table and in the corresponding Customer Number field of the Pets table.

To translate this rule into a practical example, this is what happens in the Customer and Pets tables:

✦ If a record in the Customer table has a number for a customer not found in the Pets table, then that Customer record will not be shown.

✦ If a record in the Pets table has a number for a customer number not in the Customer table, then that Pets record will not be shown.

This makes sense, at least most of the time. You don't want to see records for customers without pets — *or do you?*

A join property is a rule that is operated by Access. This rule tells Access how to interpret any exceptions (possibly errors) between two tables. Should the non-corresponding records be shown?

Access has several types of joins, each with its own characteristics or behaviors. Access lets you change the type of join quickly by changing its properties. You can change join properties by selecting the join line between tables and double-clicking on the line. When you do so, a Join Properties dialog box appears. The dialog box in Figure 14-9 is the result of selecting the join line between the Customer and Pets tables.

Figure 14-9: The Join Properties dialog box.

The Join Properties dialog box has three option buttons, which are displayed in this manner for the Pets and Customer tables:

1. Include only rows where the joined fields from both tables are equal. (This is the default.)

2. Include ALL records from the Customer table and only those records from the Pets table where the joined fields are equal.

3. Include ALL records from the Pets table and only those records from the Customer table where the joined fields are equal.

The first choice is commonly known as an *inner join,* and the other two are known as *outer joins.* These joins control the behavior of Access as it builds the dynaset from the query.

Inner and outer joins

Your Query Design window should presently display two tables in the top pane of the Query window — Pets and Customer. The following sections use these tables as examples to explain how inner and outer joins operate.

Displaying an inner join

To display an inner join, follow this procedure: In the QBE pane, select the fields Customer Number and Customer Name from the Customer table and the fields Pet Name and Type of Animal from the Pets table. Then display the dynaset by selecting the Datasheet button on the toolbar. The datasheet should now look like Figure 14-10, displaying each customer, all the customers' pets, and the type of animal for each pet. Scroll through the records until you reach the bottom of the datasheet.

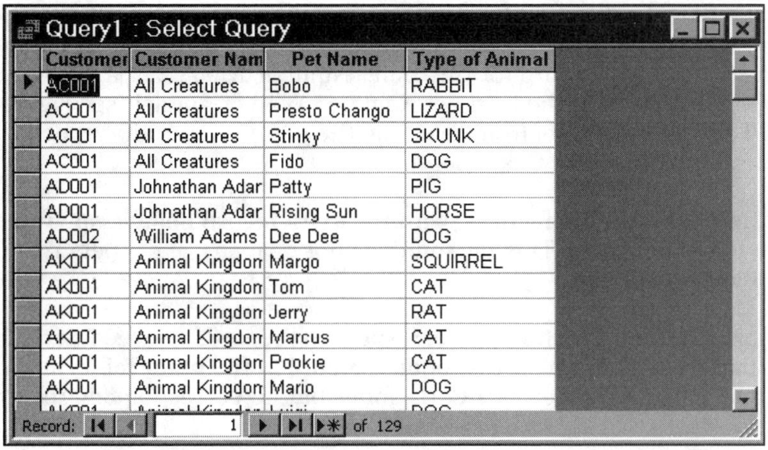

Figure 14-10: The datasheet for an inner join.

Notice that each of the 129 records has entries in all four fields. This means every record displayed from the Customer table has a corresponding record or records in the Pets table.

Return to query design mode by clicking on the Design icon on the toolbar. When you double-click on the join line between the Customer and Pets tables, you see that the join property for these two tables becomes the first selection shown in the Join Properties dialog box (see Figure 14-9). This is an inner join, or *equi-join*, the most common type. These joins show only the records that have a correspondence between tables.

Creating an outer join

Unlike equi-joins (inner joins), outer joins are used for showing all records in one table while showing common records in the other. An outer join will point graphically to one of the tables. When you look at the join line, it says, "Show all records from the main table (the one missing the arrow) while showing only matching records in the table being pointed to." For a further explanation, follow these instructions:

1. Return to the query design and again double-click on the join line between Customer and Pets.

2. Select the second choice from the Join Properties dialog box, which includes all records from the Customer table and only those records from Pets where the joined fields are equal. Then select the OK button. Notice that the join line now has an arrow at one end, pointing rightward to the Pets table. This is known in database terminology as a *right outer join*.

3. Select the Datasheet button to display this dynaset. Everything looks the same as before. Now move down the page until you can see record number 63. You should see a record for Customer Number JO003, Carla Jones but no corresponding entry in the field Pet Name or Type of Animal (see Figure 14-11). This record results from selecting the join property that specifies "include all records from Customer 4."

Notice that there are now 130 records, with the extra record being displayed in a record in the Customer table. This person does not own any of the pets that have been entered into the tables.

Note   Unlike equi-joins, outer joins show all corresponding records between two tables *and* records that do *not* have a corresponding record in the other table. In the preceding example, you see a record for Carla Jones but no corresponding record for any pets she owns.

If you've changed the display order of the tables since adding them to the Query window, Access does not follow the table order you set up; rather, it uses the original order in which you selected the tables. Because the information is normally the same in either table, it won't make a difference which field is selected first.

Select the Design button on the toolbar to return to the Query Design window. When you created the outer join for the Customer table with the Pets table, Access changed the appearance of the graphical join line to show an arrow at one end. As shown in Figure 14-12, the arrow is pointing toward the Pets table. This tells you that Access has created an outer join and will therefore show you *all* records in the Customer table and *only* those that match in the Pets table.

Customer	Customer Nam	Pet Name	Type of Animal
IR001	Patricia Irwin	Gizmo	CAT
IR001	Patricia Irwin	Stripe	CAT
IR001	Patricia Irwin	Romeo	CAT
IR001	Patricia Irwin	Ceasar	CAT
IR001	Patricia Irwin	Juliet	CAT
IR001	Patricia Irwin	Tiger	CAT
JO001	Michael Johnso	Rover	DOG
JO002	Adam Johnson	Fi Fi	DOG
JO003	Carla Jones		
KP001	Kiddie Petting Z	Muncher	GOAT
KP001	Kiddie Petting Z	Whitey	LAMB
KP001	Kiddie Petting Z	Springer	DEER
MC001	Margaret McKin	Rex	DOG

Record: 63 of 130

Figure 14-11: A datasheet with a right outer join.

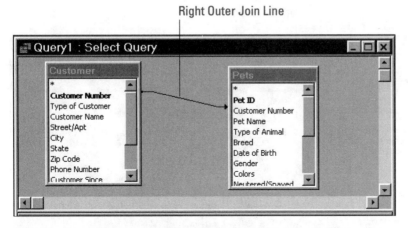

Figure 14-12: The Table/Query pane showing a right outer join.

Creating another outer join

Return to the query design and again double-click on the join line between the Customer and Pets tables.

Select the third choice from the Join Properties dialog box, which asks to "include all records from Pets." Then click on the OK button. Notice that the join line now has an arrow pointing to the Customer table, as shown in Figure 14-13. This is known as a *left outer join*. (If the arrow is pointing to the right in the top pane, the join is known as a right outer join; when the arrow points to the left, it's a left outer join.)

Select the Datasheet button to display this dynaset. Now move down the page until you can see record number 68, as shown in Figure 14-14. You should see a record with nothing in the field Customer Number or Customer Name. All you see is Animal Name (which is Brownie) and the fact that it's a dog. This record results from selecting the join property to include all records from Pets. This is known as a left outer join in database terminology.

Again, there are 130 records in this dynaset. However, unlike before, the extra record is not from the Customer table. Rather, this record (#68 in the dynaset) is in the Pets table. It is known as an orphan record. It is in the Pets table, but there is no Customer that owns it. Because referential integrity is not set up between the Customer and Pets tables, this is possible. If you attempt to set up referential integrity in the Relationships window, you will not be able to because of this record. If you remove the record, you can set up integrity between the two tables. This will be covered more in a later chapter.

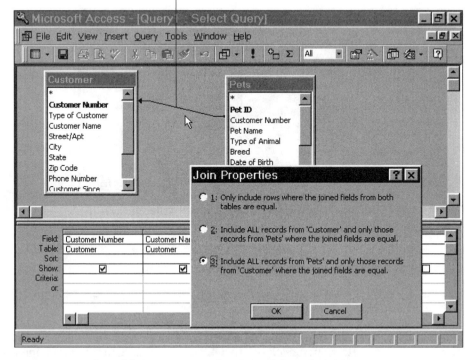

Figure 14-13: The Table/Query pane showing a left outer join.

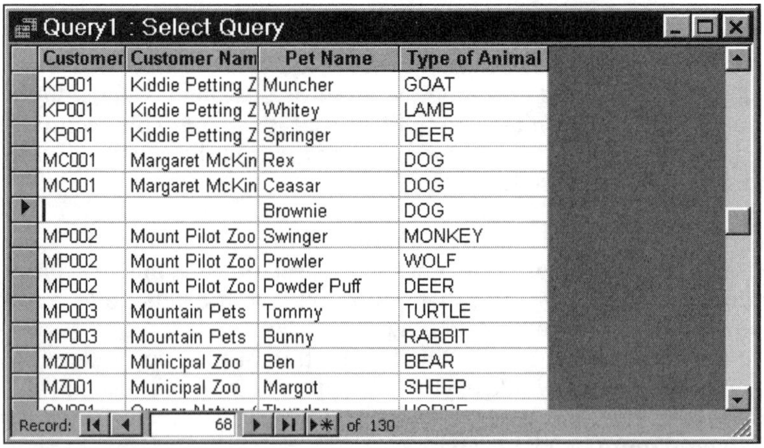

Figure 14-14: A datasheet with a left outer join.

Creating a Cartesian product

If you add both the Customer and Pets tables to a query and don't specify a join between the tables, Access takes the first Customer record and combines it with all the Pets records; then it takes the second record and also combines it with all the Pets records. This combining of records between tables produces a total of 6,321 records in the resultant dynaset. Combining each record in one table with each record in the other results in a Cartesian product (cross product) of both tables.

Summary

In this chapter, you learned about creating relationships between tables and how to use joins in queries. The chapter covered the following points:

- ✦ You can add multiple tables to a query, including multiple copies of the same table.

- ✦ Access creates join lines automatically for any tables that have their relationships set at table level.

- ✦ You can add fields from multiple-table queries in any order. Multiple-table fields are moved and changed in the same way as fields from single tables.

- ✦ To view data from two or more tables, you must join them.

- ✦ You can create joins between two tables by dragging and dropping a field from one table to another. Access draws a graphic join line between the fields.

- ✦ There are two types of joins — inner joins (equi-joins) and outer joins.

- ✦ An inner join (also known as an equi-join) displays records that have a common field in both tables with corresponding data in those fields.

- ✦ An outer join displays all records having corresponding data in both fields and also displays records from one table that do not have corresponding records in the other table.

- ✦ The two types of outer joins are left and right. Access displays a pointer in the Table/Query pane to show the type of outer join you create.

In the next chapter, you examine how to create select queries.

✦   ✦   ✦

Creating Select Queries

Up to this point, you have worked with queries based on criteria against a single field. You also learned how to add multiple tables to a query and how to join tables together. This chapter focuses on extracting information from multiple tables in select queries.

Moving Beyond Simple Queries

Select queries are the most common type of query you will use; they *select* information (based on a specific criterion) from one or more related tables. With these queries, you can ask questions and receive answers about information stored in your database tables. So far, you have worked with queries that pose simple criteria for a single field in a table. You worked with math operators, such as equal (=) and greater-than (>).

Knowing how to specify criteria is critical to designing effective queries. Although queries can be created against a single table for a single criterion, most queries extract information from several tables and more complex criteria. Because of this complexity, your queries retrieve only the data you need, in the order you need it. You may, for example, want to select and display data from the Mountain Animal Hospital database with these limitations:

✦ All owners of horses or cows or pigs

✦ All animals that were given a specific medication during a specific week last year

✦ All owners whose dogs or cats had blood work performed over the past four months

✦ Only the first animal of each type you have treated

✦ Any animal that has the word *color* in the Memo field Comments

As your database system evolves, you will probably ask questions such as these about the information stored in the system. Although the system was not originally developed specifically for these questions, you can find the information needed to answer them stored in the tables. Because the information is there, you find yourself performing *ad-hoc* queries against the database. The ad-hoc queries you perform by using select queries can be very simple or quite complex.

Select queries are the easiest way to obtain information from several tables without resorting to writing programs.

Using query comparison operators

When you're working with select queries, you may need to specify one or more *criteria* to limit the scope of information you want to see. You accomplish this by using *comparison operators* in equations and calculations. The categories of operators include mathematical, relational, logical, and string operators. In select queries, normally you would use operators in either the Field: or Criteria: cell of the QBE pane.

A good rule of thumb to observe is the following:

> *Use mathematical and string operators for creating calculated fields; use relational and logical operators for specifying scope criteria.*

Cross-Reference: Calculated fields will be discussed later in this chapter. You can find an in-depth explanation of operators in Chapter 13.

Table 15-1 shows most of the common operators used with select queries.

Table 15-1
Common Operators Used in Select Queries

Mathematical	Relational	Logical	String	Miscellaneous
* (multiply)	= (equal)	And	& (concatenate)	Between...And
/ (divide)	<> (not equal)	Or	Like	In
+ (add)	> (greater than)	Not		Is Null
– (subtract)	< (less than)			

Using these operators, you can ferret out such types of records as the following:

✦ Pet records that have a picture associated with them

✦ A range of records, such as all patients seen between November and January

✦ Records that meet both And *and* Or criteria, such as all pets that are dogs *and* are not either neutered *or* have a current vaccination

✦ All records that do *not* match a value, such as any animal that is *not* a cat

When you supply a criterion to a query, you use the operator with an *example* that you supply. In Figure 15-1, the example entered is PIG. The operator is equal (=). Notice that the equal sign is *not* shown in the figure. The equal sign is the default operator for criteria selection.

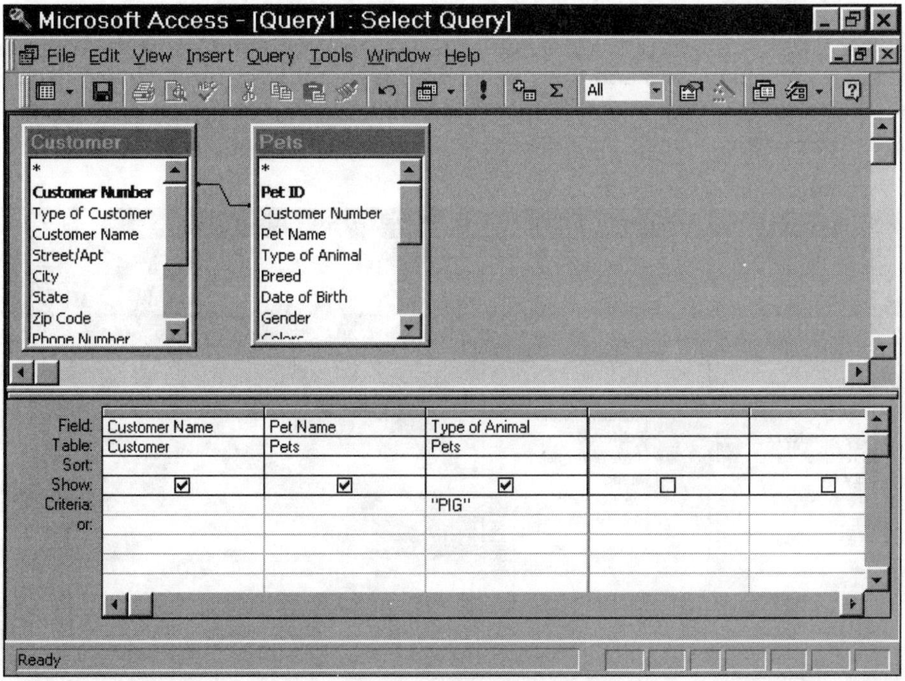

Figure 15-1: The QBE pane with a simple criterion.

Note   When working with criteria for select queries, you supply an example of what type of information Access needs to find in the Criteria: cell of the Query By Example (QBE) pane.

Cross-
Reference   Chapter 10 gives an in-depth explanation of working with queries.

Understanding complex criteria selection

As Table 15-1 shows, you can use several operators to build complex criteria. To most people, complex criteria consist of a series of Ands and Ors, as in these examples:

✦ State must be Idaho *or* Oregon

✦ City must be Borderville *and* state must be Washington

✦ State must be Idaho *or* Washington *and* city must be Borderville

These examples demonstrate use of both the logical operators And/Or. Many times, you can create complex criteria by entering example data in different cells of the QBE pane. Figure 15-2 demonstrates how you can create complex And/Or criteria without having to enter the operator keywords And/Or at all. This example displays all customers and their pets who satisfy these criteria: *Live in the city of Borderville and live in either the state of Washington or the state of Idaho and whose pet is not a dog.*

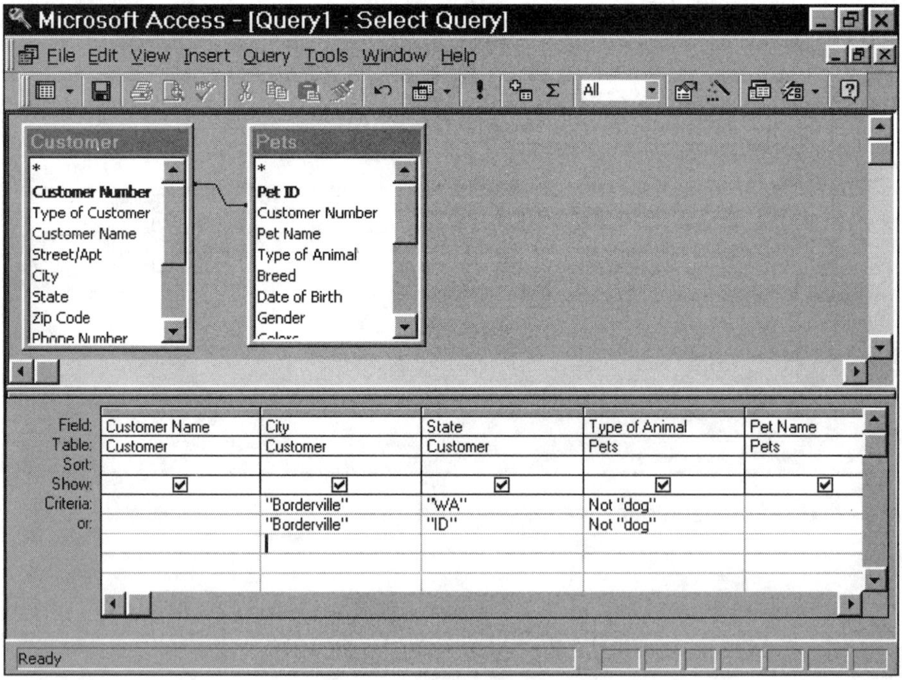

Figure 15-2: Creating complex And/Or criteria by example without using the And/Or operators.

Note Sometimes you see a field name referenced by the table name first and then the field name, with a dot (period) between the two names. This way, you understand which table a field belongs to. This is especially critical when you're describing two fields that have the same name but come from different tables. In a multiple-table query, you see this format in the field list when you add a field to the QBE pane by clicking on an empty column. You can also see this format when you create a multiple table form and use the field list. The general format is *Table Name.Field Name.* Examples are Pets.Type of Animal or Customer.Customer Name.

If you build a mathematical formula for this query, it will look something like this:

```
((Customer.City="Borderville") AND (Customer.State="WA") AND
        (Not Pets.[Type of Animal]="DOG")) OR ((Customer.City=
        "Borderville") AND (Customer.State="ID") AND (Not Pets.
        [Type of Animal]="DOG"))
```

Notice that you must enter the city and pet example for each state line in the QBE pane of Figure 15-2. Later, you use the And/Or operators in a Criteria: cell of the query, eliminating the need for redundant entry of these fields.

Tip To find records that do *not* match a value, use the Not operator with the value. For example, enter the expression *Not Dog* to find all animals except dogs.

The And/Or operators are the most common when you're working with complex criteria. The operators consider two different formulas (one on each side of the And/Or operators) and then determine individually whether they are True or False. Then they compare the resultants of the two formulas against each other for a logical True/False answer. For example, take the first And statement in the formula just given:

```
(Customer.City="Borderville") AND (Customer.State="WA")
```

The first half of the formula, Customer.City = "Borderville", converts to a True if the city is Borderville (False if a different city; Null if no city was entered in the field).

Then the second half of the formula, Customer.State = "WA", is converted to a True if the state is Washington (False if a different state; Null if no state was entered). Then the And compares the logical True/False from each side against the other to give a resulting True/False answer.

Note A field has a *Null value* when it has no value at all; it is the lack of entry of information in a field. Null is neither True nor False; nor is it equivalent to all spaces or zero — it has no value. If you never enter a city name in the City field, simply skipping over it, Access leaves the field empty. This state of emptiness is known as Null.

When the resultant of an And/Or is True, the overall condition is True, and the query displays those records meeting the True condition. Table 15-2 gives a quick review of True conditions for each operator.

Table 15-2 Results of Logical Operators And/Or			
Left Side Is	*Operator Is*	*Right Side Is*	*Resultant Answer Is*
True	AND	True	True
True	OR	True	True
True	OR	False	True
True	OR	Null	True
False	OR	True	True
Null	OR	True	True

Notice that the And operator is True only when *both* sides of the formula are True, whereas the Or operator is True whenever *either* side of the formula is True. In fact, one side can be a Null value, and the Or operator is still True if the other side is True. This is the distinct difference between And/Or operators.

Cross-Reference Refer to Chapter 13 for further details about logical operators.

Using functions in select queries

When you work with queries, you may want to use built-in Access functions to display information. For example, you may want to display such items as the following:

✦ The day of week (Sunday, Monday, and so forth) for visit dates

✦ All customer names in uppercase

✦ The difference between two date fields

You can display all this information by creating calculated fields for the query. This will be discussed in depth later in this chapter.

Referencing fields in select queries

When you work with a field name in queries, as you do with calculated fields or criteria values, you should enclose the field name in brackets ([]). Access requires brackets around any field name that is in a criterion and around any field name that contains a space or punctuation. An example of a field name in brackets is the criterion [Visit Date] + 30. You will find more examples later in this chapter.

Caution If you omit the brackets ([]) around a field name in the criterion, Access automatically places quotes around the field name and treats it as text instead of a field name.

Entering Single-Value Field Criteria

Often you may want to limit query records on the basis of a single field criterion, as in these queries:

✦ Customer information for customers living in the state of Washington

✦ Animals you have treated from the local zoos in the area

✦ Customers and animals you treated during the month of January

All three of these queries require a single-value criterion. Simply put, *single-value criterion* is the entry of only one expression in a field. That expression can be example data or a function: "WA" or DatePart("m",[Visit Date])=1 are both examples of single-value criteria.

You can specify criteria expressions for any type of data, whether Text, Numeric, Date/Time, and so forth. Even OLE Object and Counter field types can have criteria specified.

Cross-Reference For a full explanation of expressions, operators, identifiers, literals, and functions, see Chapter 13.

CD-ROM All the examples in this chapter rely on several tables: Customer, Pets, and Visits. The majority of these examples use only the Customer and Pets tables. You should create a new query and add the Customer and Pets tables.

As you read each series of steps in this chapter, they tell you which tables and fields make up the query. In most examples, you should clear all previous criteria before going to the next example. Each of the examples focuses on the criteria lines of the QBE pane. You can also view each figure to make sure you understand the correct placement of the criteria in each example. Only a few dynasets are shown; you can follow along and view the data. The Mountain Start database contains only the tables used in this chapter.

Entering character (Text or Memo) criteria

Character criteria are used for Text or Memo data-type fields. These are either examples or data about the contents of the field. For example, to create a text criterion to display customers who own birds, follow these steps:

1. Select Customer Name from the Customer table and then Pet Name and Type of Animal from the Pets table.

2. Click on the Criteria: cell of Type of Animal.

3. Type **BIRD** in the cell.

Your query should look similar to Figure 15-3. Notice that only two tables are open and only three fields are selected. You can click on the Datasheet button to see the results of this query.

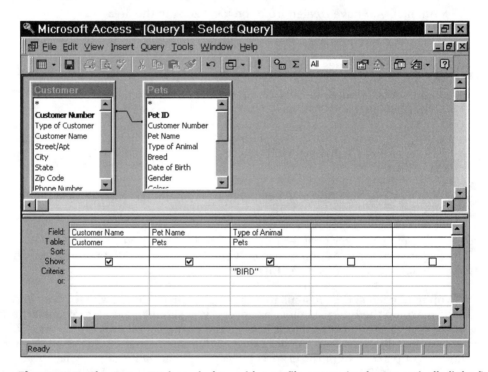

Figure 15-3: The Query Design window with two files open (and automatically linked).

Tip   When you specify example-type criteria, it is not necessary to match capitalization. Access defaults to case-insensitive when working with queries. You can enter *BIRD*, *bird*, or *BiRd* and receive the same results.

Notice that you didn't have to enter an equal sign before the literal word *bird*. This is because Access uses the equal operator as the default. If you want to see all animals except birds, you use either the <> (not equal) or the Not operator before the word *bird*.

You also didn't have to place quotes around the word *bird*. Access understands that you are talking about the example literal *BIRD* and places the quotes for you automatically.

In Version 1.*x*, Access places quotation marks ('') only around example literals that contain no spaces. If the literal has spaces, you must provide the quotes or else Access reports an error on execution. However, in Version 2.0 and for Windows 95, Access automatically places quotation marks around any example data you provide, as long as it is not enclosed in brackets ([]).

Tip   You should use the double quotation mark to surround literals. Access normally uses the single quotation mark as a remark character in its programming language. However, when you use the single quotation mark in the Criteria: cell, Access interprets it as a double quotation mark.

The Like operator and wildcards

To this point, you've been working with *literal* criteria. You specified the exact field contents for Access to find, which in the example was "Bird." Access used the literal to find the specific records. Sometimes, however, you know only a part of the field contents, or you may want to see a wider range of records on the basis of a pattern. For example, you may want to see all pet visits for pets that begin with the letter *G*; you want to check gerbils, goats, and so forth. Perhaps a more practical example is when you have a customer who owns a pig that was born Siamese. You remember making a note of it in the Comments field; you don't, however, remember which pig it was. This requires using a wildcard search against the Memo field to find any records that contain the word *Siamese*.

Access uses the string operator Like in the Criteria: cell of a field to perform wildcard searches against the field's contents. Access searches for a pattern in the field; you use the question mark (?) to represent a single character or the asterisk (*) for several characters. (This is just like working with filenames at the DOS level.) Besides the two characters (?) and (*), Access uses three other characters for performing wildcard searches. Table 15-3 lists the wildcards that the Like operator can use.

The question mark (?) stands for any single character located in the same position as the question mark in the example expression. An asterisk (*) stands for any number of characters in the same position in which the asterisk is placed. Unlike the asterisk at DOS level, Access can use the asterisk any number of times in an example expression. The pound sign (#) stands for any single digit found in the same position as the pound sign. The brackets ([]) and the list they enclose stand for any single character that matches any one character of the list located within the brackets. Finally, the exclamation point (!) inside the brackets represents the *Not word* for the list — that is, any single character that does *not* match any character of the list within the brackets.

	Table 15-3 **Wildcards Used by the Like Operator**
Wildcard	*Purpose*
?	A single character (0-9, Aa-Zz)
*	Any number of characters (0 to *n*)
#	Any single digit (0-9)
[*list*]	Any single character in the list
[*!list*]	Any single character not in the list

These wildcards can be used alone or in conjunction with each other. They can even be used several times within the same expression. The examples in Table 15-4 demonstrate how the wildcards can be used.

To create an example using the Like operator, suppose you want to find that record of the Siamese pig. You know that this fact is referenced in one of the records in the Comments field. To create the query, follow these steps:

1. Remove the criterion field for Type of Animal.

2. Double-click on the Comments field in the Pets table.

3. Click on the Criteria: cell of the Comments field.

4. Type ***Siamese*** in the cell.

	Table 15-4 **Using Wildcards with the Like Operator**	
Expression	*Field Used In*	*Results of Criteria*
Like "Re?"	Pets.Pet Name	Finds all records of pets whose names are three letters long and begin with "Re"; examples: Red, Rex, Ren
Like "*Siamese*"	Pets.Comments	Finds all records with the word "Siamese" somewhere within the Comments field

Expression	Field Used In	Results of Criteria
Like "G*"	Pets.Type of Animal	Finds all records for animals of a type that begins with the letter G
Like "1/*/93"	Visits.Visit Date	Finds all records for the month of January 1993
Like "## Main St."	Customer.Street/Apt	Finds all records for houses with house numbers between 10 and 99 inclusively; examples: 10, 22, 33, 51
Like "[RST]*"	Customer.City	Finds all records for customers who live in any city with a name beginning with R, S, or T
Like "[!EFG]*"	Pets.Type of Animal	Finds all records for animals of types that do not begin with the letters E, F, or G; all other animals are displayed

When you move the cursor, leaving the Criteria: cell, Access automatically adds the operator Like and the quotation marks around the expression. Your query QBE pane should appear similar to Figure 15-4.

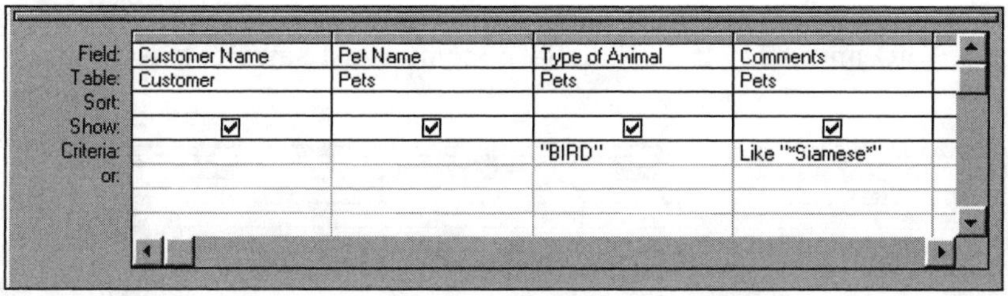

Figure 15-4: Using the Like operator with a selected query.

Access adds the Like operator and quotation marks for you if you meet the following conditions:

✦ There are no spaces in your expression.

✦ You use only the wildcards ?, *, and #.

✦ You use brackets ([ ]) inside quotation marks " " .

If you use the brackets without quotation marks, you must supply the operator Like and the quotation marks.

Using the Like operator with wildcards is the best way to perform pattern searches through Memo fields.

Caution   The Like operator and its wildcards can be used only against three types of fields: Text, Memo, and Date. Using these with any other type can result in an error.

Specifying nonmatching values

To specify a nonmatching value, you simply use either the Not or the <> operator in front of the expression that you don't want to match. For example, you may want to see all customers and their pets for all states, but you want to exclude Washington. You see how to specify this nonmatching value in the following steps:

1. Start with an empty query, using the Customer and Pets tables.

2. Select the Customer Name and State fields from Customer and Pet Name from Pets.

3. Click on the Criteria: cell of State.

4. Type **Not "WA"** in the cell.

The query should now look similar to Figure 15-5. The query will select all records *except* those for customers who live in the state of Washington.

Note   You can use the <> operator instead of Not. In Step 4 of the steps for excluding Washington from the criterion, the resulting dynaset is the same with either operator. These two operators are interchangeable. The exception is with the use of the keyword Is. You cannot say Is <> Null. Rather, you must say Not Is Null.

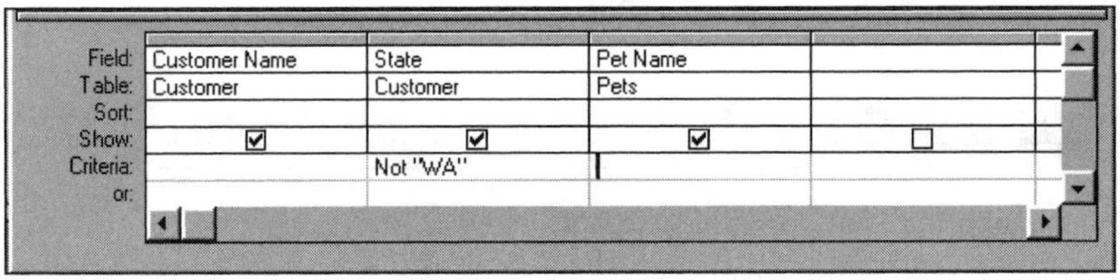

Field:	Customer Name	State	Pet Name		
Table:	Customer	Customer	Pets		
Sort:					
Show:	☑	☑	☑	☐	
Criteria:		Not "WA"			
or:					

Figure 15-5: Using the Not operator in criteria.

Entering numeric (Number, Currency, or Counter) criteria

Numeric criteria are used for Number, Currency, or Counter data-type fields. You simply enter the digits and the decimal symbol, if required. For example, you may want to see all animals that weigh over 100 pounds. To create a query like this, follow these steps:

1. Start with a new query, using the Customer and Pets tables.
2. Select the Customer Name in the Customer table, Pet Name, Type of Animal, and Weight in the Pets table.
3. Click on the Criteria: cell of Weight.
4. Type **>100** in the cell.

When you follow these steps, your query looks similar to Figure 15-6. When working with numeric data, Access does not enclose the expression, as it does with string or date criteria.

Numeric fields are generally compared to a value string that uses comparison operators, such as less than (<), greater than (>), or equal to (=). If you want to specify a comparison other than equal, you must enter the operator as well. Remember that Access defaults to equal for all criteria. That is why you needed to specify greater than (>) 100 in the query for animals over 100 pounds.

Working with Currency and Counter data in a query is exactly the same as working with Numeric data; you specify an operator and a numeric value.

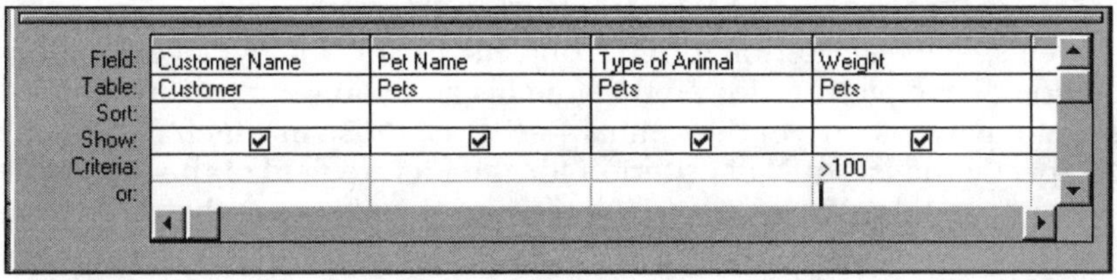

Figure 15-6: Criteria set for weight of animals.

Entering Yes/No (logic) criteria

Yes/No criteria are used for Yes/No type fields. The example data you supply in the criteria can be for only Yes or No states. You can use the Not and the <> operators to signify the opposite, but the Yes/No data also has a Null state you may want to check for.

When entering criteria in a Yes/No field, you are not limited to entering a Yes or No expression. Access recognizes several forms of Yes and No. Table 15-5 lists all the positive and negative values you can use.

Thus, instead of typing Yes, you can enter any of the following in the Criteria: cell: **On**, **True**, **Not No**, **<> No**, **<No**, or **-1**.

Tip

In Access 97, you can enter any number except 0 to represent TRUE or Yes.

Note As stated earlier, a Yes/No field can have only three criteria states: Yes, No, and Null. Checking for Is Null will display only records with no value, and checking for Is Not Null will always display all Yes or No records. After a Yes/No field check box is checked (or checked and then unchecked) it can never be null. It will be Yes or No (-1 or 0).

Table 15-5
Positive and Negative Values Used in Yes/No Fields

| *Yes* | True | On | Not No | <> No | <No | -1 |
| *No* | False | Off | Not Yes | <>Yes | >Yes | 0 |

Entering a criterion for an OLE object

You can even specify a criterion for OLE objects: Is Not Null. As an example, suppose you don't have pictures for all the animals and you want to view only those records that have a picture of the animal -— that is, those in which picture is not Null. You specify the Is Not Null criterion for the Picture field of the Pets table. Once you've done this, Access limits the records to only those that have a picture in them.

Although **Is Not Null** is the correct syntax, you can also type **Not Null** and Access will supply the Is operator for you.

Entering Multiple Criteria in One Field

So far, you've worked with single-condition criteria on a single field at a time. As you learned, single-condition criteria can be specified for any field type. Now you'll work with multiple criteria based on a single field. You may be interested in seeing all records in which the type of animal is either a cat or a squirrel, for example, or perhaps you want to view the records of all the animals you saw between July 1, 1995, and December 31, 1995.

The QBE pane provides the flexibility for solving these types of problems. You can specify several criteria for one field or for several fields in a select query. Using multiple criteria, for example, you can determine which customers and pets are from Idaho or Washington ("ID" or "WA") or which animals you saw for general examinations in the past 30 days (Between Date() and Date()-30).

To specify several criteria for one field, you use the And and the Or operators.

Understanding an Or operation

You use an Or operation in queries when you want a field to meet either of two conditions. For example, you may want to see the customer and pet names of all rabbits and squirrels. In other words, you want to see all records where a customer owns a rabbit *or* a squirrel, *or* both. Following is the general formula for this operation:

```
[Type of Animal] = "Rabbit" Or [Type of Animal] = "Squirrel"
```

If either side of this formula is True, the resulting answer is also True. To clarify this point, consider the following conditions:

✦ Customer One owns a rabbit but does not own a squirrel — the formula is True.

✦ Customer Two owns a squirrel but does not own a rabbit — the formula is True.

✦ Customer Three owns a squirrel and a rabbit — the formula is True.

✦ Customer Four does not own a rabbit and does not own a squirrel — the formula is False.

Specifying multiple values for a field using the Or operator

You use the Or operator to specify multiple values for a field. For example, you use the Or operator if you want to see all records of owners of fish or frogs or ducks. To accomplish this task, follow these steps:

1. Create a new query, using the Customer and Pets tables.

2. Select the Customer Name field in the Customer table and then select Pet Name and Type of Animal in the Pets table.

3. Click on the Criteria: cell of Type of Animal.

4. Type **Fish Or Frog Or Duck** in the cell.

Your QBE pane should resemble Figure 15-7. Notice that Access automatically placed quotation marks around your example data — Fish, Frog, and Duck.

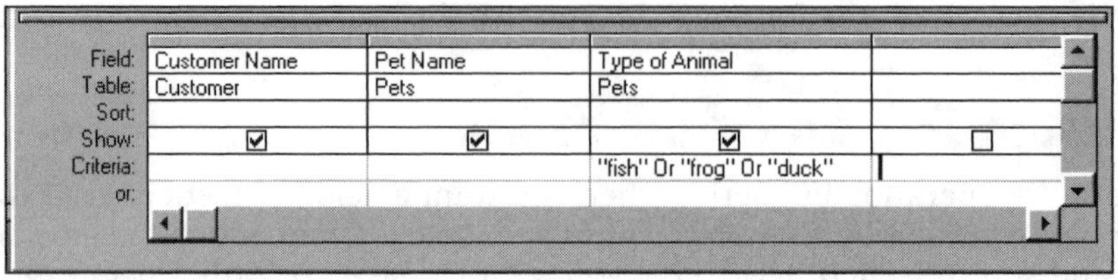

Figure 15-7: Using the Or operator.

This dynaset can be seen in Figure 15-8. Notice that the only records selected contain FISH, FROG, or DUCK in the Type of Animal column.

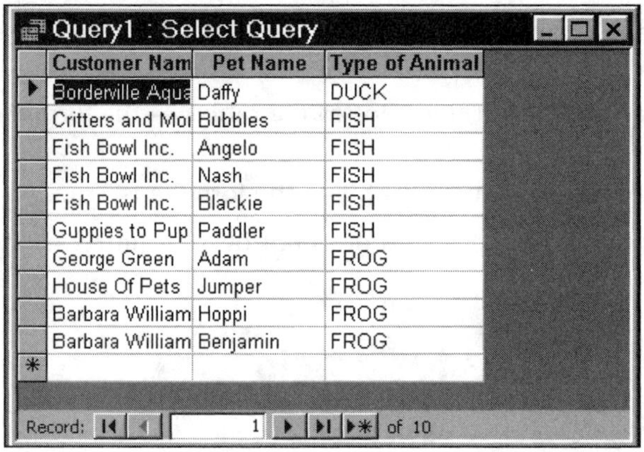

Figure 15-8: Selecting records with the Or operator.

Using the or cell of the QBE pane

Besides using the literal Or operator, you can supply individual criteria for the field on separate lines of the QBE pane. To do this, you enter the first criterion example in the Criteria: cell of the field, just as you have been. Then you enter the criterion example in the or: cell of the field. Enter the next criterion in the cell directly beneath the first example; then continue entering examples vertically down the column. This is exactly equivalent to typing the Or operator between examples. Using the example in which you queried for fish, frogs, or ducks, change your QBE pane to look like the one in Figure 15-9. Notice that each type of animal is on a separate line in the query.

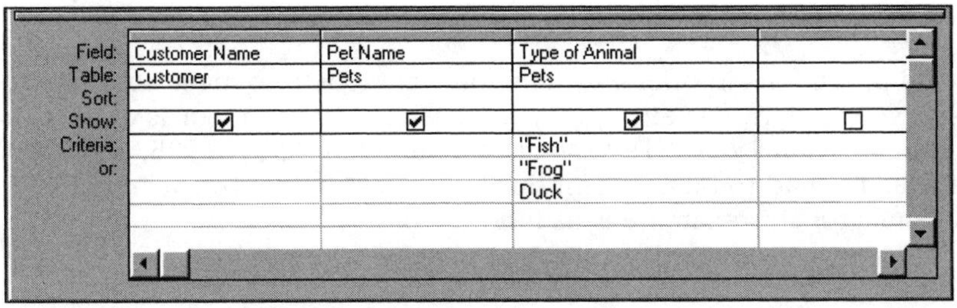

Figure 15-9: Using the or: cell of the QBE pane.

Access gives you five or: cells for each field. If you need to specify more Or conditions, use the Or operator between conditions (for example: `Cat Or Dog Or Pig`).

Using a list of values with the In operator

You can use another method for expressing the multiple values of a single field. This method uses the operator named *In*. The In operator finds a value that is one of a *list of values*. For example, enter the expression **IN(FISH, FROG, DUCK)** under the Type of Animal field. This action creates a list of values, where any item in the list becomes an example criterion. After you create the query, it should resemble Figure 15-10.

In this example, you can see that quotation marks are automatically entered around Fish, Frog, and Duck.

Note When you work with the In operator, each value (example data) must be separated from the others by a comma.

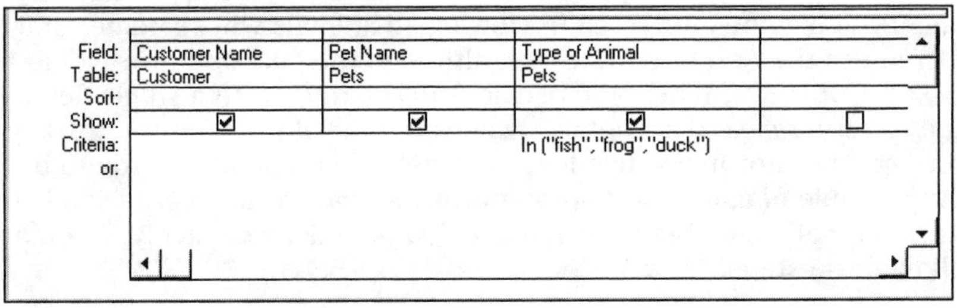

Figure 15-10: Using the In operator.

Understanding an And query

You use And operations in queries when you want a field to meet both of two conditions that you specify. For example, you may want to see records of pets that had a visit date `>= July 1, 1995 And <= December 31, 1995`. In other words, the animal had to be a patient during the last half of the year 1995. The general formula for this example is as follows:

```
[Visit Date] >= 7/1/95 And [Visit Date] <= 12/31/95
```

Unlike the Or operator (which has several conditions under which it is True), the And operator is True only when both sides of the formula are True. When both sides are True, the resulting answer will also be True. To clarify use of the And operator, consider the following conditions:

✦ Visit date (6/22/95) is not greater than 7/1/95, but it is less than 12/31/95 — the formula is False.

✦ Visit date (4/11/96) is greater than 7/1/95, but it is not less than 12/31/95 — the formula is False.

✦ Visit date (11/1/95) is greater than 7/1/95, and it is less than 12/31/95 — the formula is True.

Both sides of the operation must be True for the And operation to be True.

An And operation can be performed in any of several ways against a single field in Access.

Specifying a range using the And operator

You will find And operators used frequently in fields that have Numeric or Date/Time data types. They are seldom used in Text type, although they can be. For instance, you may be interested in viewing all animals whose names start with D, E, or F. You use the And operator here, although the Like operator would be better (`Like" [DEF]*"`). When you use an And operator with a single field, you are using it to set a *range* of acceptable values in the field. Therefore, the key purpose of an And operator in a single field is to define a range of records to be viewed. An example of using the And operator to create a range criterion is to display all animals that weigh between 100 and 300 pounds, inclusively. To create this query, follow these steps:

1. Create a new query, using the Customer and Pets tables.

2. Select the Customer Name field in the Customer table, Pet Name, Type of Animal, and Weight in the Pets table.

3. Click on the Criteria: cell of Weight.

4. Type **>=100 And <=300** in the cell.

The query should resemble Figure 15-11. Note that you can change the formula to **>99 And <301** with identical results.

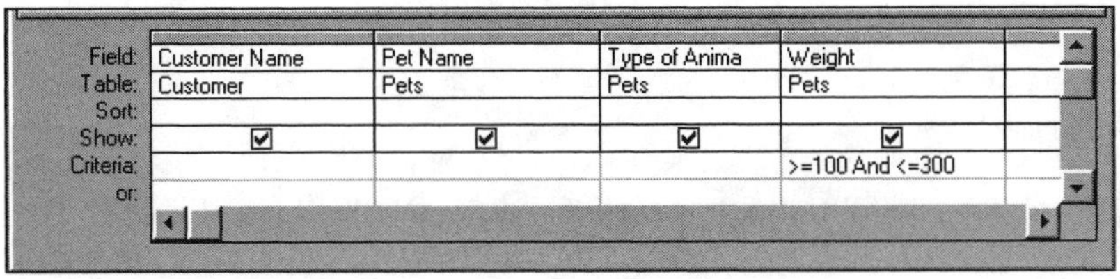

Field:	Customer Name	Pet Name	Type of Anima	Weight	
Table:	Customer	Pets	Pets	Pets	
Sort:					
Show:	☑	☑	☑	☑	
Criteria:				>=100 And <=300	
or:					

Figure 15-11: Using the And operator with numeric fields.

Using the Between...And operator

You can use another method for expressing a range of records from a single field. This method uses the operator called *Between...And*. With the Between...And operator, you can find records meeting a range of values — for example, all pets *Between* Dog *And* Pig. Using the example of animals weighing between 100 and 300 pounds, create the query using the Between...And operator, as shown in Figure 15-12.

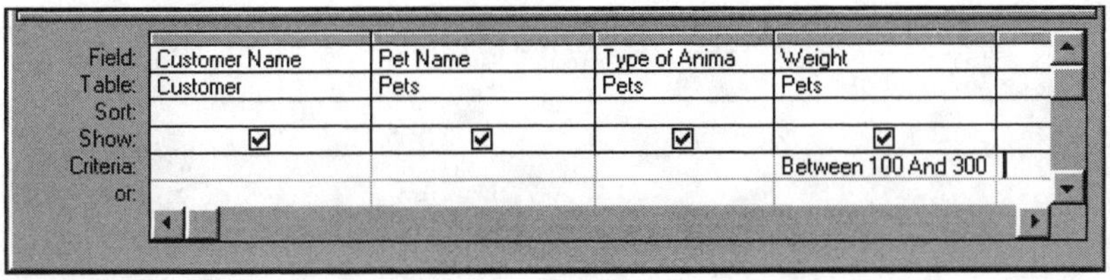

Field:	Customer Name	Pet Name	Type of Anima	Weight	
Table:	Customer	Pets	Pets	Pets	
Sort:					
Show:	☑	☑	☑	☑	
Criteria:				Between 100 And 300	
or:					

Figure 15-12: Using the Between...And Operator.

When you use the Between...And operator, each value (example data) is included in the resulting dynaset.

Searching for Null data

A field may have no contents; possibly the value wasn't known at the time of data entry, or the data-entry person simply forgot to enter the information, or the field's information has been removed. Access does nothing with this field; it simply remains an empty field. (You'll recall that a field is said to be *Null* when it's empty.)

Logically, a Null is neither True nor False. A Null is not equivalent to all spaces or to zero. A Null simply has no value.

Access lets you work with Null value fields by means of two special operators:

> Is Null
>
> Not Is Null

These operators are used to limit criteria based on Null values of a field. You already worked with a Null value when you queried for animals having a picture on file. In the next example, you look for animal records that don't specify gender. To create this query, follow these steps:

1. Create a new query using the Customer and Pets tables.

2. Select the Customer Name field in the Customer table, Pet Name, Type of Animal, and Gender field in the Pets table.

3. Click on the Criteria: cell of Gender.

4. Type **Is Null** in the cell.

Your query should now look like Figure 15-13. If you select the Datasheet button, you'll see that there are no records without a gender.

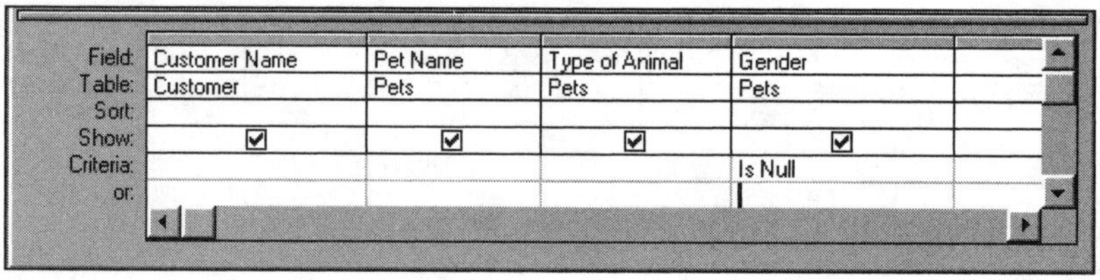

Field:	Customer Name	Pet Name	Type of Animal	Gender	
Table:	Customer	Pets	Pets	Pets	
Sort:					
Show:	☑	☑	☑	☑	
Criteria:				Is Null	
or:					

Figure 15-13: Using the Is Null operator.

Entering Criteria in Multiple Fields

You've worked with criteria specified in single fields up to this point. Now you'll work with criteria across several fields. When you want to limit the records based on several field conditions, you do so by setting criteria in each of the fields that will be used for the scope. Say, for example, that you want to search for all dogs or for all animals in Idaho. Or you may want to search for dogs in Idaho or Washington. Again, you may search for all dogs in Washington or all cats in Oregon. Each of these queries requires placing criteria in multiple fields and on multiple lines.

Using And and Or across fields in a query

To use *And* and *Or* across fields, place your example or pattern data in the Criteria: and the Or: cells of one field relative to the placement in another field. When you want to use And between two fields, you place the example or pattern data across the same line. When you want to use Or between two fields, you place the example or pattern data on different lines in the QBE pane. Figure 15-14 shows the QBE pane and a conceptual representation of this placement.

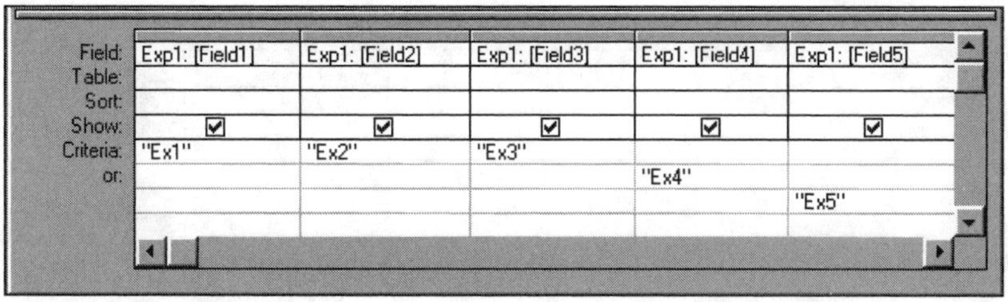

Field:	Exp1: [Field1]	Exp1: [Field2]	Exp1: [Field3]	Exp1: [Field4]	Exp1: [Field5]
Table:					
Sort:					
Show:	☑	☑	☑	☑	☑
Criteria:	"Ex1"	"Ex2"	"Ex3"		
or:				"Ex4"	
					"Ex5"

Figure 15-14: The QBE pane with And/Or criteria between fields.

Looking at Figure 15-14, you see that if the only criteria fields present were Ex1, Ex2, and Ex3 (with Ex4 and Ex5 removed), all three would be Anding between the fields. If only the criteria fields Ex4 and Ex5 were present (with Ex1, Ex2, and Ex3 removed), the two would be Oring between fields. As it is, the selection for this example is (EX1 AND EX2 AND EX3) OR EX4 OR EX5. Therefore, this query is True if a value matches any of these criteria:

EX1 AND EX2 AND EX3   or

EX4   or

EX5

As long as one of these three criteria are True, the record will be selected.

Specifying And criteria across fields of a query

The most common type of condition operator between fields is the And operator. Often you will be interested in limiting records on the basis of several field conditions. For example, you may want to view only the records of customers who live in the state of Washington and own rabbits. To create this query, follow these steps:

1. Create a new query, using the Customer and Pets tables.

2. Select the Customer Name and State fields in the Customer table and then select Pet Name and Type of Animal fields in the Pets table.

3. Click on the Criteria: cell of State.

4. Type **WA** in the cell.

5. Click on the Criteria: cell for Type of Animal.

6. Type **RABBIT** in the cell.

Your query should look like Figure 15-15. Notice that both example data are in the same row.

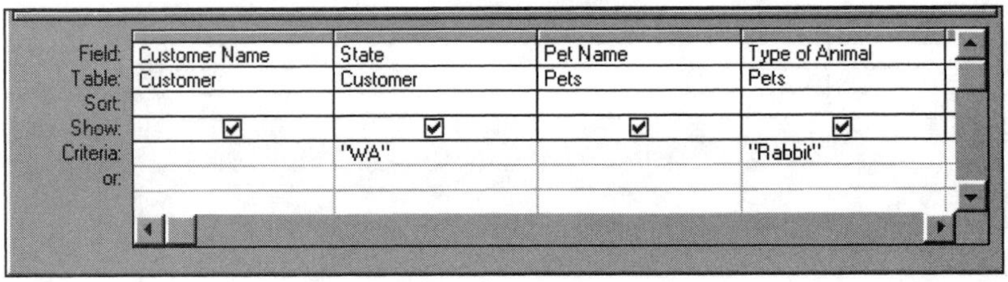

Field:	Customer Name	State	Pet Name	Type of Animal	
Table:	Customer	Customer	Pets	Pets	
Sort:					
Show:	☑	☑	☑	☑	
Criteria:		"WA"		"Rabbit"	
or:					

Figure 15-15: An And operator operation across two fields.

Because you placed data for both criteria on the same row, Access interprets this as an And operation.

Specifying Or criteria across fields of a query

Although the Or operator is not used across fields as commonly as the And, occasionally Or is very useful. For example, you may want to see records of any animals in Washington or you may want all rabbits regardless of the state they live in. To create this query, follow these steps:

1. Use the query from the previous example, emptying the two criteria cells.

2. Click on the Criteria: cell of State.

3. Type **WA** in the cell.

4. Click on the or: cell for Type of Animal.

5. Type **RABBIT** in the cell.

Your query should resemble Figure 15-16. Notice that the criteria entered this time are not in the same row for both fields.

When you place the criterion for one field on a different line from the criterion for another field, Access interprets this as an Or between the fields.

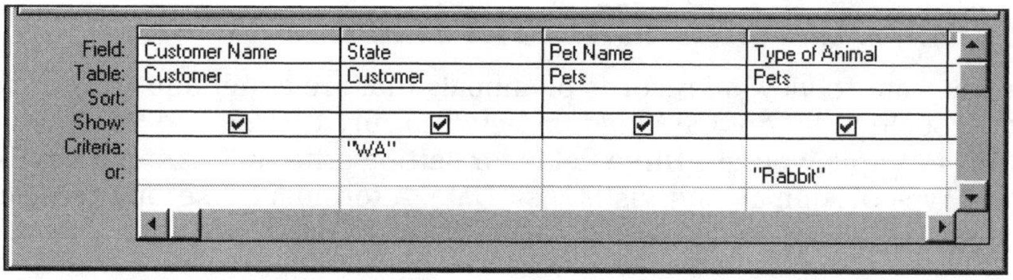

Field:	Customer Name	State	Pet Name	Type of Animal
Table:	Customer	Customer	Pets	Pets
Sort:				
Show:	☑	☑	☑	☑
Criteria:		"WA"		
or:				"Rabbit"

Figure 15-16: Using the Or operator between fields.

Using And and Or together in different fields

Now that you've worked with And and Or separately, you're ready to create a query using And and Or in different fields. In the next example, you want to display information for all skunks in Washington and all rabbits in Idaho. Perform the following steps to create this query:

1. Use the query from the previous example, emptying the two criteria cells.

2. Click on the Criteria: cell of State.

3. Type **WA** in the cell.

4. Click on the or: cell of State.

5. Type **ID** in the cell.

6. Click on the Criteria: cell for Type of Animal.

7. Type **SKUNK** in the cell.

8. Click on the or: cell for Type of Animal.

9. Type **RABBIT** in the cell.

Figure 15-17 shows how the query should look. Notice that WA and Skunk are in the same row; ID and Rabbit are in another row. This query represents two Ands across fields, with an Or in each field.

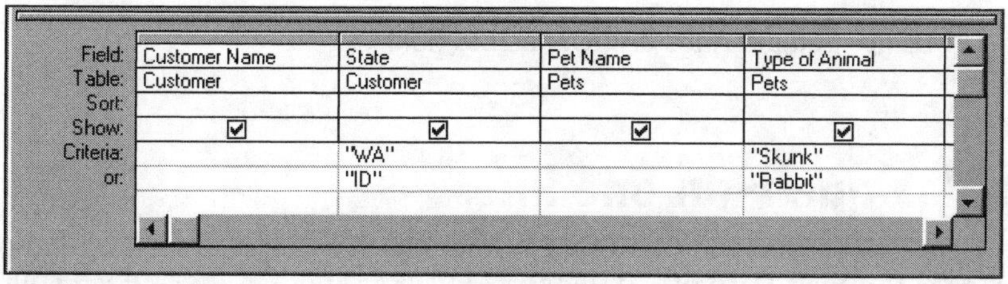

Field:	Customer Name	State	Pet Name	Type of Animal
Table:	Customer	Customer	Pets	Pets
Sort:				
Show:	☑	☑	☑	☑
Criteria:		"WA"		"Skunk"
or:		"ID"		"Rabbit"

Figure 15-17: Using Ands and Ors across fields.

A complex query on different lines

Suppose you want to view all records of animals that are either squirrels or cats that were brought in by Animal Kingdom between July 1, 1995, and December 31, 1995. In this example, you use three fields for setting criteria: Customer.Customer Name, Pets.Type of Animal, and Visits.Visit Date. A formula for setting these criteria follows:

```
(Customer.[Customer Name] = "Animal Kingdom" AND (Pets.[Type of
        Animal] = "SQUIRREL" OR Pets.[Type of Animal]="CAT") AND
        (Visits.[Visit Date] >= #7/1/95# AND <= #12/31/95#)
```

You can display this data by creating the query shown in Figure 15-18.

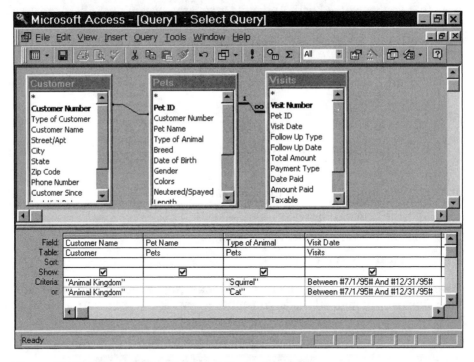

Figure 15-18: Using multiple Ands and Ors across fields.

A complex query on one line

Notice in Figure 15-18 that the Customer Name, Animal Kingdom, is repeated on two lines, as is the Visit Date of Between #7/1/95# And #12/31/95#. This is necessary because the two lines actually form the query:

```
Animal Kingdom AND SQUIRREL AND Between #7/1/95# And #12/31/95#
    OR
Animal Kingdom AND CAT AND Between #7/1/95# And #12/31/95#
```

You don't have to repeat Animal Kingdom in a query such as this. Figure 15-19 shows another approach.

Notice that the criteria in Figure 15-18 have duplicate information in the or: cell of the Customer Name and Visit Date fields. Only the Type of Animal Field has different criteria — "SQUIRREL" or "CAT". By combining the Type of Animal information into a single criterion (using the Or), the Customer Name and Visit Date criteria will have to be entered only once, which creates a more efficient query.

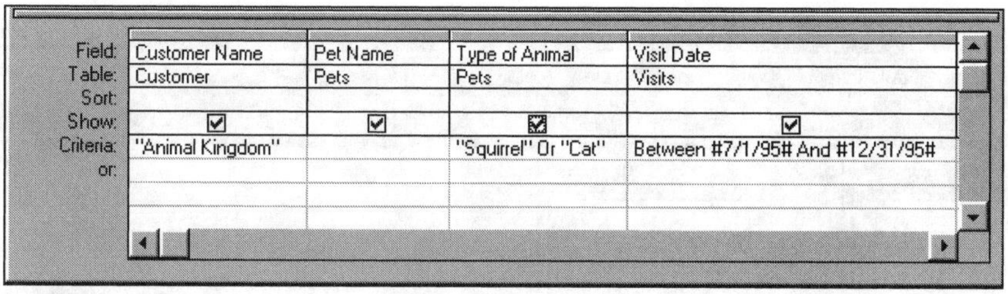

Figure 15-19: Using multiple Ands and Ors across fields on one line.

Creating a New Calculated Field in a Query

When you work with fields in a query, you are not limited to the fields from the tables you use in the query. You can also create *calculated fields* to use in a query — for example, a calculated field named Discount Amount that will display an amount by multiplying the value of Discount times Outstanding Balance in the Customer table.

To create this calculated field, follow these steps:

1. Create a new query, using the Customer table.

2. Select the Customer Name, Discount, and Outstanding Balance fields in the Customer table.

3. Click on the empty Field: cell.

4. Type Discount Amount: **[Discount]*[Outstanding Balance]** and move the cursor off the cell.

If you did this correctly, the cell looks like Figure 15-20. The expression has changed to Discount Amount:[Discount]*[Outstanding Balance]. If you didn't add the field name, Expr1: would precede the calculation.

Note For two reasons, a calculated field has a name (supplied either by the user or by an Access default). First, a name is needed to supply a label for the datasheet column. Second, the name is necessary for referencing the field in a form, a report, or another query.

Notice that the general format for creating a calculated field is as follows:

Calculated Field Name: *Expression to build calculated field*

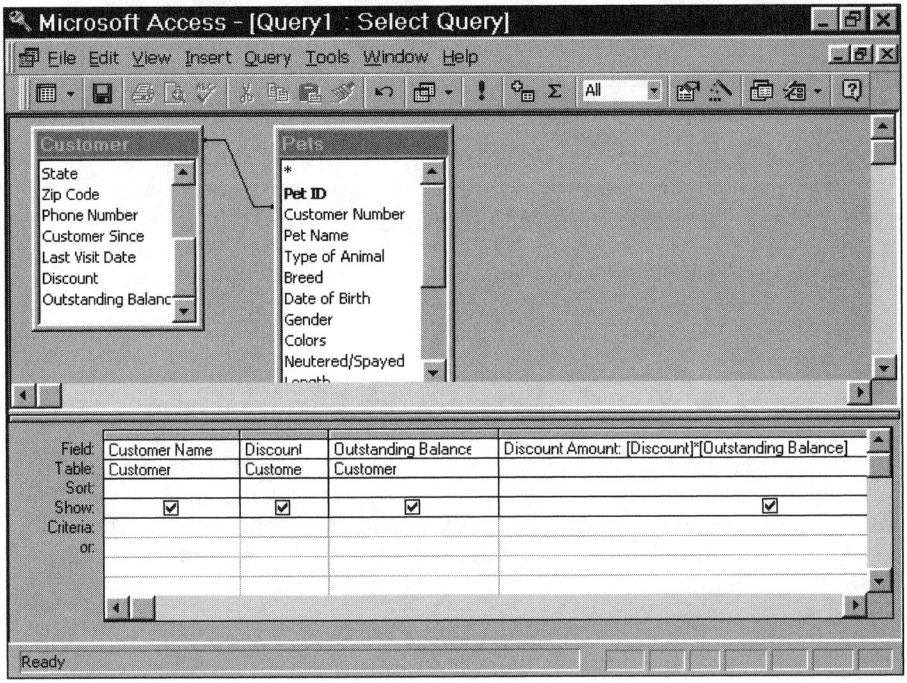

Figure 15-20: A calculated field.

Summary

In this chapter, you learned how to specify criteria to design select queries. You learned about the operators that help you query against fields for the exact information you want. The chapter covered the following points:

✦ With select queries, you select information from tables you can use for datasheets, forms, reports, and other queries.

✦ You can specify record criteria for any type of field.

✦ You can build expressions in the Criteria: cell of a field, based on literal data (examples) or with functions that build the example data.

✦ Access has five distinct wildcards it uses with the Like operator: ?, *, #, [], and !. You can use these operators independently or in conjunction with each other.

✦ The Not operator, similar to the <> operator, specifies nonmatching values as criteria.

✦ The And operator forms a True expression only when both sides of a formula are True. An Or operator is True when either side of the formula is True.

✦ With the Or operator, you can specify a list of values for a field. The And operator lets you specify a range of values in a field.

✦ Often you can use the In operator instead of an Or operator; you can use the Between...And operator in place of the And operator.

✦ You can search fields for empty conditions by using the Is Null operator. A Null is the absence of any value in a field.

✦ Calculated fields are created from an expression. The expression can use one or more fields, functions, or other objects.

In the next chapter, you examine controls and properties.

✦   ✦   ✦

Understanding Controls and Properties

T his is the first of eight chapters in Part III that examine forms and reports in detail. Controls and properties form the basis of forms and reports. It is critical to understand the fundamental concepts of controls and properties before you begin to apply them to forms and reports.

CD-ROM In this chapter, you use the Pets table in the Mountain Animal Hospital database. The chapter explains each control by examining one or more fields in the Pets table. To create the first form you need for this chapter, follow these steps:

1. Open the Mountain Animal Hospital or Mountain Animal Start database.

2. Select Insert⇨Form.

3. Select Design View from the New Form dialog box.

4. Select the Pets table from the combo box in the New Form dialog box.

5. Click on the OK button to display the Form Design window.

6. Maximize the form by clicking on the maximize button in the top right corner of the window.

7. Expand the light gray area of the form to the full-window size by dragging the bottom right corner of the light gray area to the bottom right corner of the window.

What Is a Control?

A *control* has many definitions in Access. Generally, a control is any object on a form or report, such as a label or text box. You enter values into controls and display them by using a control. A control can be bound to a table field, but it can also be an object, such as a line or rectangle. Calculated fields are also controls, as are pictures, graphs, option buttons, check boxes, and objects. There are also controls that aren't part of Access but are developed separately; these are *custom controls* (also known as *OCXs* or *ActiveX controls*). These extend the base feature set of Access 97.

Cross-Reference

Custom controls are covered in Chapter 20.

Whether you're working with forms or reports, you follow essentially the same process to create and use controls. In this chapter, you see controls explained from the perspective of a form.

The different control types

You find many different control types on a form or report. You can create some of these controls by using the Toolbox shown a little later, in Figure 16-1. In this book, you learn how to create and use the most-often-used controls (listed in Table 16-1). In this chapter, you learn when to use each control; you also learn how these controls work.

Table 16-1	
Controls You Can Create in Access Forms and Reports	
Basic Controls	
Label	Literal text is displayed in a label control.
Text box	Data is typed into a text box.
Enhanced Data Entry and Data Validation Controls	
Option group	This group holds multiple option buttons, check boxes, or toggle buttons.
Toggle button	This is a two-state button, up or down, which usually uses pictures or icons.
Option button	Also called a *radio button,* this button is displayed as a circle with a dot when the option is on.
Check box	This is another two-state control, shown as a square that contains a check mark if it's on and an empty square if it's off.

Enhanced Data-Entry and Data-Validation Controls

Combo box	This box is a pop-up list of values that allows entries not on the list.
List box	This is a list of values that is always displayed on the form or report.
Command button	Also called a *push button,* this button is used to call a macro or run a Basic program to initiate an action.
Subform/Subreport	This control displays another form or report within the original form or report.
Tab control	This control can display multiple pages in a file folder type interface.

Graphic and Picture Controls

Image	Displays a bitmap picture with very little overhead.
Unbound object frame	This frame holds an OLE object or embedded picture that is not tied to a table field. Includes graphs, pictures, sound files, and video.
Bound object frame	This frame holds an OLE object or embedded picture that is tied to a table field.
Line	This is a single line of variable thickness and color, which is used for separation.
Rectangle	A rectangle can be any color or size or can be filled in or blank; the rectangle is used for emphasis.
Page break	This is usually used for reports and denotes a physical page break.

Note If the Toolbox is not displayed, display it by selecting View➪Toolbox or clicking on the Toolbox icon.

Tip The Toolbox can be moved, resized, and anchored on the window. You can anchor it to any border, grab it, and resize it in the middle of the window.

Figure 16-1 shows the resulting new form.

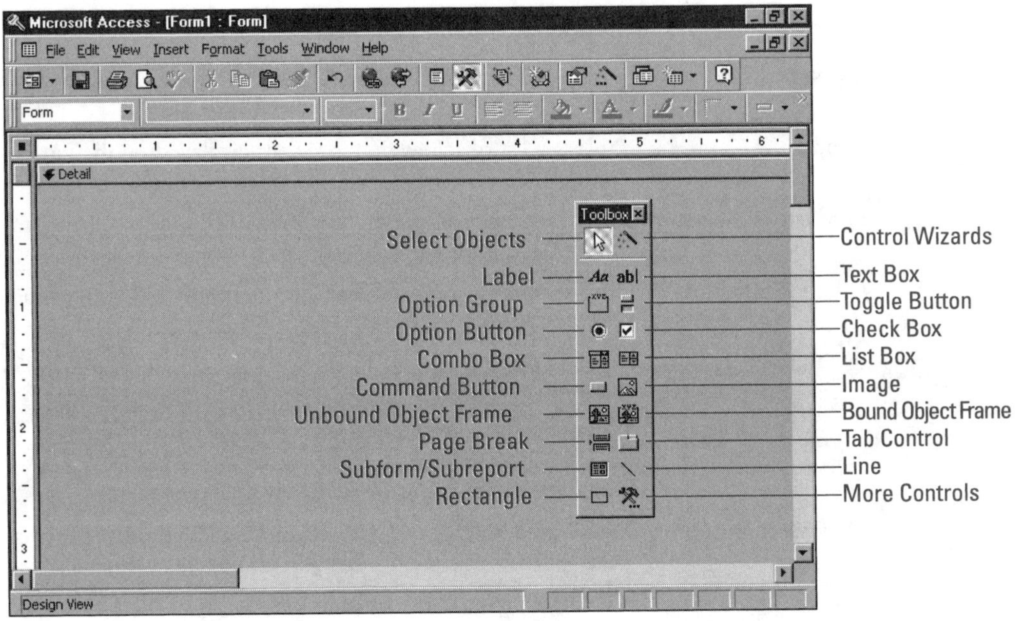

Figure 16-1: A new blank form and the Toolbox.

The Control Wizard icon does not create a control; rather, it determines whether a Wizard is automatically activated when you create certain controls. The option group, combo box, list box, subform/subreport, object frame, and command button controls all have Wizards that Access starts when you create a new control. The More Controls icon is used to display a list of custom controls you can add to Access 97.

Understanding bound, unbound, and calculated controls

There are three basic types of controls:

✦ Bound controls

✦ Unbound controls

✦ Calculated controls

Bound controls are those that are bound to a table field. When you enter a value into a bound control, Access automatically updates the table field in the current record. Most of the controls that let you enter information can be bound; these include OLE fields. Bound controls can be most data types, including text, dates, numbers, Yes/No, pictures, and memo fields.

Unbound controls retain the value entered but do not update any table fields. You can use these controls for text display; for values to be passed to macros, lines, and rectangles; or for holding OLE objects (such as bitmap pictures) that are not stored in a table but on the form itself. Unbound controls are also known as *variables* or *memory variables*.

Calculated controls are based on expressions, such as functions or calculations. Calculated controls are also unbound, as they do not update table fields. An example of a calculated control is =[Medication Price] + [Treatment Price]; this control calculates the total of two table fields for display on a form.

Examples of these three control types are shown in Figure 16-2. The picture of the mountain, which is the company's logo, and the text Mountain Animal Hospital are unbound controls. You can find bound controls that contain field names (including the picture) below the text and logo. You also see one calculated control, which is the animal's age. You can see that the function DateDiff is used to calculate the number of years from the Date of Birth bound control to the function Now(), which returns the current date.

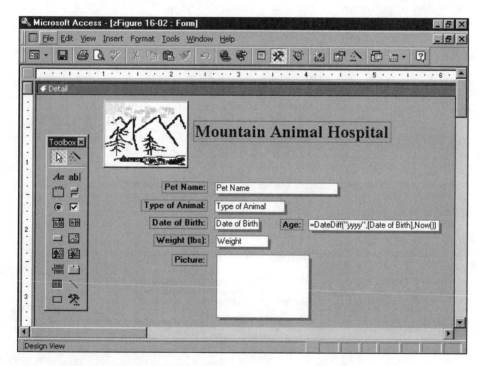

Figure 16-2: The three control types.

Standards for Using Controls

Most of you reading this book have used Microsoft Windows. You have probably used other applications in Windows as well, such as word processing applications (Word for Windows, WordPerfect for Windows, or WordPad) or spreadsheet applications (Excel, 1-2-3 for Windows, or Quattro Pro). There is a difference, however, between using a Windows application and designing one.

The controls in Access 97 have specific purposes. Their uses are not decided by whim or intuition; a scientific method determines which control should be used for each specific situation. Experience will show you that correct screen and report designs lead to more usable applications.

Label controls

A *label control* displays descriptive text (such as a title, a caption, or instructions) on a form or report. Labels can be separate controls, as is common when they are used for titles or data-entry instructions. When labels are used for field captions, often they are attached to the control they describe.

You can display labels on a single line or on multiple lines. Labels are unbound controls that accept no input; you use them strictly for one-way communication (they are read and that's all). You can use them on many types of controls. Figure 16-3 shows many uses of labels, including titles, captions, button text, and captions for buttons and boxes. You can use different font styles and sizes for your labels, and you can boldface, italicize, and underline them.

You should capitalize each word in a label, except for articles and conjunctions, such as *the, an, and, or,* and so on. There are several guidelines to follow for label controls when you use them in other controls, as you can see in Figure 16-3. The following list explains some of these guidelines for placement:

Command buttons	Inside the button
Check boxes	To the right of the check box
Option buttons	To the right of the option button
Text box	Above or to the left of the text box
List or combo box	Above or to the left of the box
Group box	On top of and replacing part of the top frame line

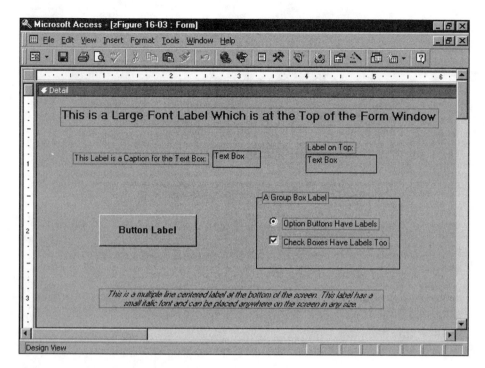

Figure 16-3: Sample label controls.

Text box controls

Text boxes are controls that display data or ask the user to type information at specific locations. In a text box, you can accept the current text, edit it, delete it, or replace it. Text boxes can accept any type of data, including Text, Number, Date/Time, Yes/No, and Memo, and you can create them as bound or unbound controls. You can use text box fields from tables or queries, and the text box can also contain calculated expressions. A text box is the most-used control because editing and displaying data are the main purposes of any database system.

Every text box needs an associated label to identify its purpose. Text boxes can contain multiple lines of data and often do (as when you use one to display Memo field data). Data that is too long for the width of the text field wraps automatically within the field boundaries. Figure 16-4 shows several different text boxes in Form view. Notice how the different data types vary in their alignment within the text boxes. The Comments text box displays multiple lines in the resized text box, which also has a scrollbar added.

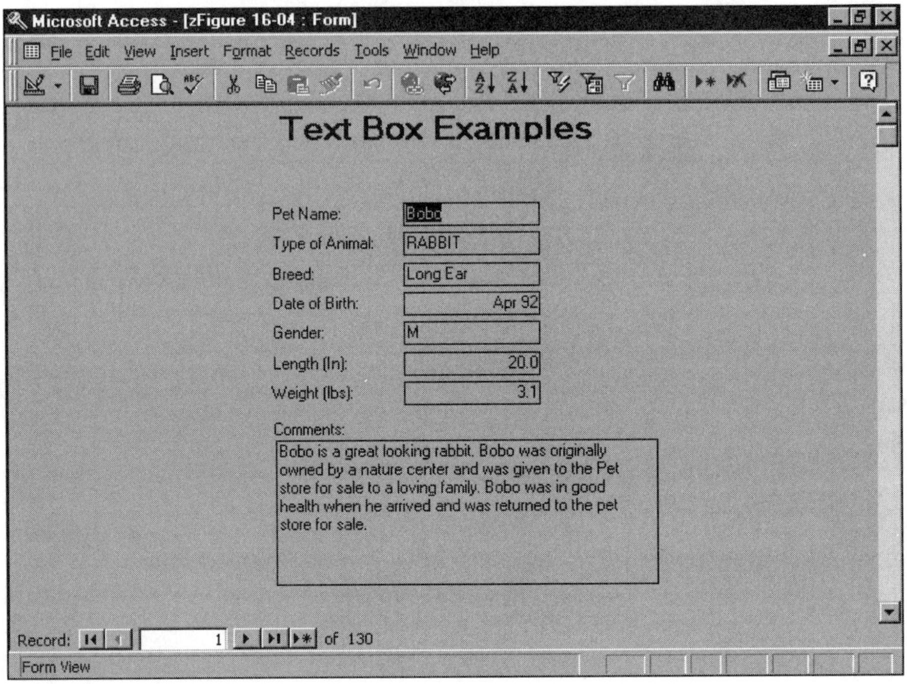

Figure 16-4: Sample text box controls.

Toggle buttons, option buttons, and check boxes

There are three types of buttons that act in the same way, and yet their visual displays are very different:

✦ Toggle buttons

✦ Option buttons (also known as radio buttons)

✦ Check boxes

These controls are used with Yes/No data types. Each can be used individually to represent one of two states, whether Yes or No, On or Off, or True or False. Table 16-2 describes the visual representations of these controls.

	Table 16-2	
	Button Control Visual Displays	
Button Type	*State*	*Visual Description*
Toggle button	True	Button is sunken
Toggle button	False	Button is raised
Option button	True	Circle with a large solid dot inside
Option button	False	Hollow circle
Check box	True	Square with a check in the middle
Check box	False	Empty square

Toggle buttons, option buttons, and check boxes return a value of –1 to the bound table field if the button value is Yes, On, or True; they return a value of 0 if the button is No, Off, or False. You can enter a default value to display a specific state. The control is initially displayed in a Null state if no default is entered and no state is selected. The Null state's visual appearance is the same as that of the No state.

Although you can place Yes/No data types in a text box, it is better to use one of these controls. The values that are returned to a text box (–1 and 0) are very confusing, especially because Yes is represented by –1 and No is 0.

Note As you can see in Figure 16-5, you can change the look of the option button or check box by using the special effects options from the Formatting toolbar. See Chapter 18 for more details.

Tip You can format the display of the Yes/No values in Datasheet or Form view by setting the Format property of the text box control to Yes/No, On/Off, or True/False. If you don't use the Format property, the datasheet will display –1 or 0. Using a default value also speeds up data entry, especially if you set as the default the value selected most often.

Option groups

An *option group* can contain multiple toggle buttons, option buttons, or check boxes. When these controls are inside an option group box, they work together rather than individually. Instead of representing a two-state Yes/No data type, controls within an option group return a number based on the position in the group. Only one control within an option group can be selected at a time; the maximum number of buttons in such a group should be four. If you need to exceed that number, you should switch to a drop-down list box (unless you have plenty of room on your screen).

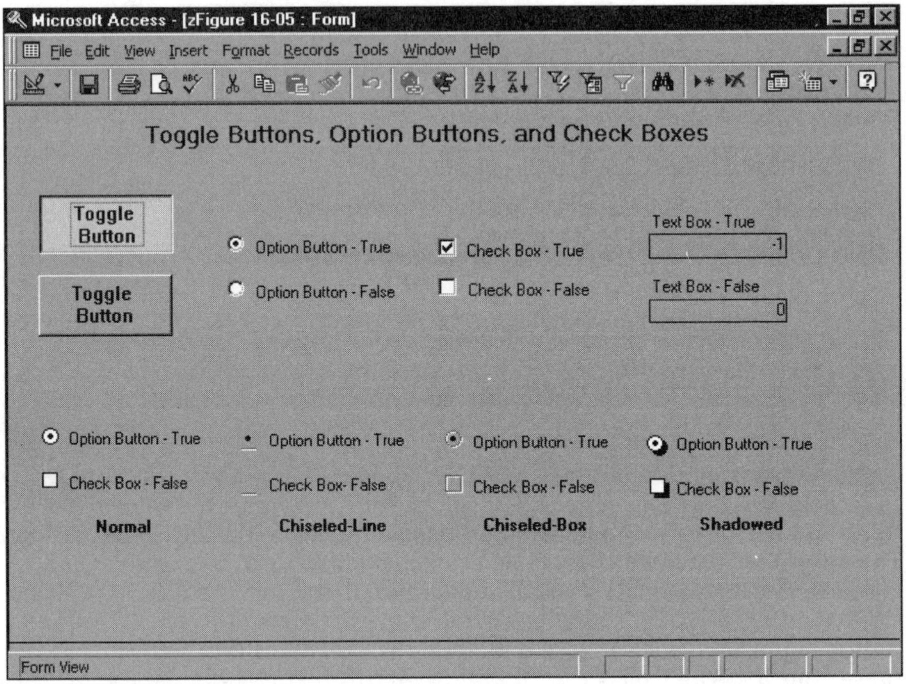

Figure 16-5: Sample toggle buttons, option buttons, and check boxes.

An option group is generally bound to a single field or expression. Each button inside it passes a different value back to the option group, which in turn passes the single choice to the bound field or expression. The buttons themselves are not bound to any field; instead, they are bound to the option group box.

Figure 16-6 shows three types of buttons; two of these types are shown in option group boxes. In the Toggle Buttons option group, the second choice is selected; the same is true of the Option Buttons option group. Notice, however, that the first and third choices are selected in the Check Boxes rectangle; the check boxes are independent and are not part of an option group. When you make a new selection in an option group, the current selection is deselected. If (for example) you click on Option Button 3 in the option group box in the middle of Figure 16-6, the solid dot will appear to move to the third circle, and the second circle will become hollow.

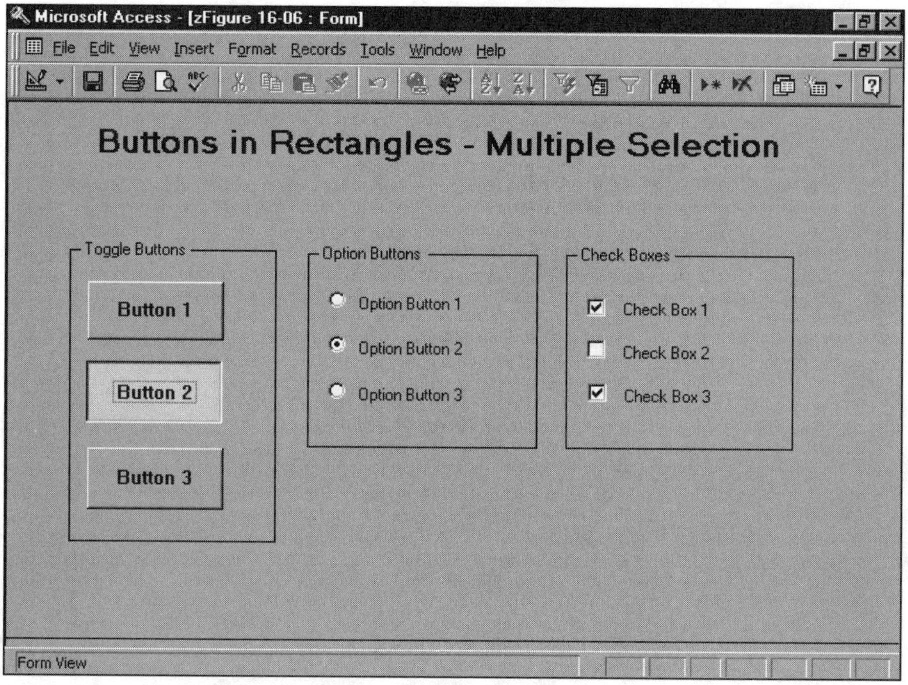

Figure 16-6: Three types of option groups.

Buttons in rectangles

The three types of buttons act very differently, depending on whether they are used individually or in an option group. You can create buttons that look like a group but do not function as a single entity. Figure 16-7 shows a multiple-selection group. Notice that check boxes 2 and 3 are simultaneously selected. This is not an option group; rather, this is a group of controls enclosed in a box. They act totally independently, so they don't have to be in the same box; each control passes either a –1 (True) or a 0 (False) to the field, expression, or control to which it is bound. A common use for this type of grouping is to let a user select from a list of nonexclusive options, such as a list of reports or a list of days on which a process should occur.

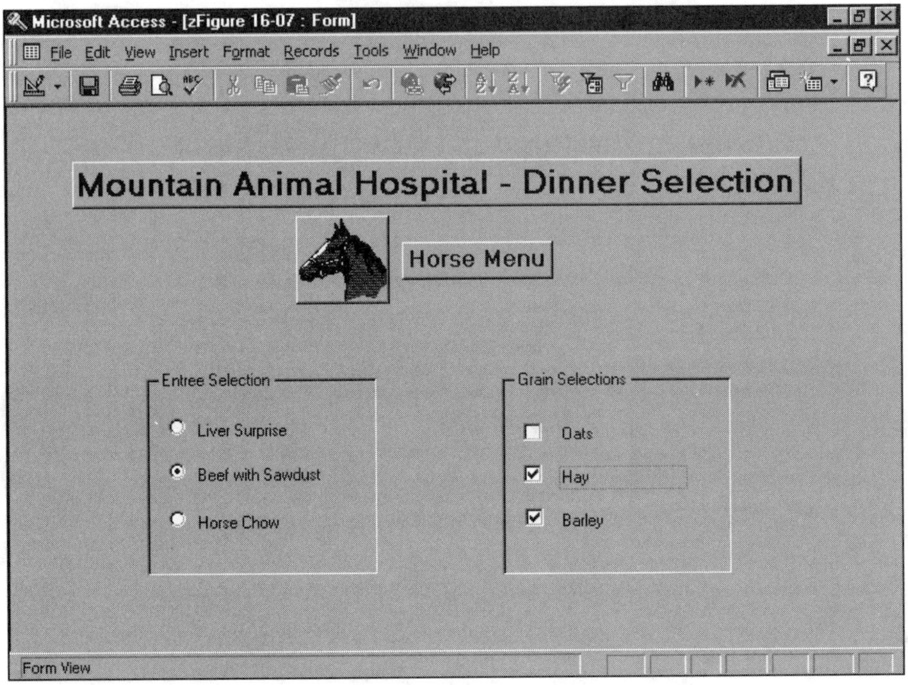

Figure 16-7: Selecting a meal.

Tip   You may want to create groups of buttons that look like option groups but have multiple selections. Rather than use an option button, simply enclose the group of buttons with a rectangle. Each button remains an individual entity instead of becoming part of a group.

List boxes

A *list box* control displays a list of data on-screen just as a pull-down menu does, but the list box is always open. You can highlight an item in the list by moving the cursor to the desired choice and then pressing Enter (or clicking the mouse) to complete the selection. You can also type the first letter of the selection to highlight the desired entry. After you select an item, the item's value is passed back to the bound field.

List boxes can display any number of fields and any number of records. By sizing the list box, you can make it display more or fewer records.

NEW
FEATURE Access 97 list boxes feature a new *Multi-Select* property that allows you to select more than one item at a time. The results are stored in new properties and have to be used with Visual Basic for Applications.

List boxes are generally used when there is plenty of room on-screen and you want the operator to see the choices without having to click on a drop-down arrow. A vertical — and even horizontal — scrollbar is used to display any records and fields not visible when the list box is in its default size. The highlighted entry will be the one currently selected. If no entries are highlighted, either a selection has not been made or the selected item is not currently in view. Only items in the list can be selected.

You also have a choice of whether to display the column headings in list boxes. Figure 16-8 displays list boxes with three layout schemes.

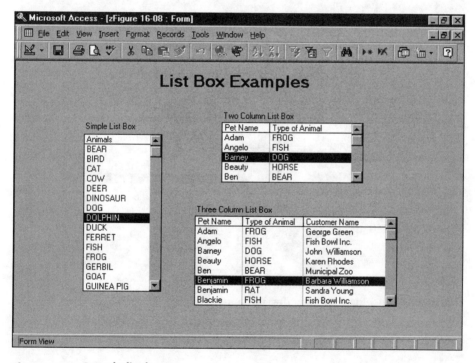

Figure 16-8: Sample list boxes.

Combo boxes

In Access, *combo boxes* differ from list boxes in two ways:

✦ The combo box is initially displayed as a single row with an arrow that lets you open the box to the normal size.

✦ As an option, the combo box lets you enter a value that is not on the list.

You see a list box and a combo box (shown both open and closed) in Figure 16-9.

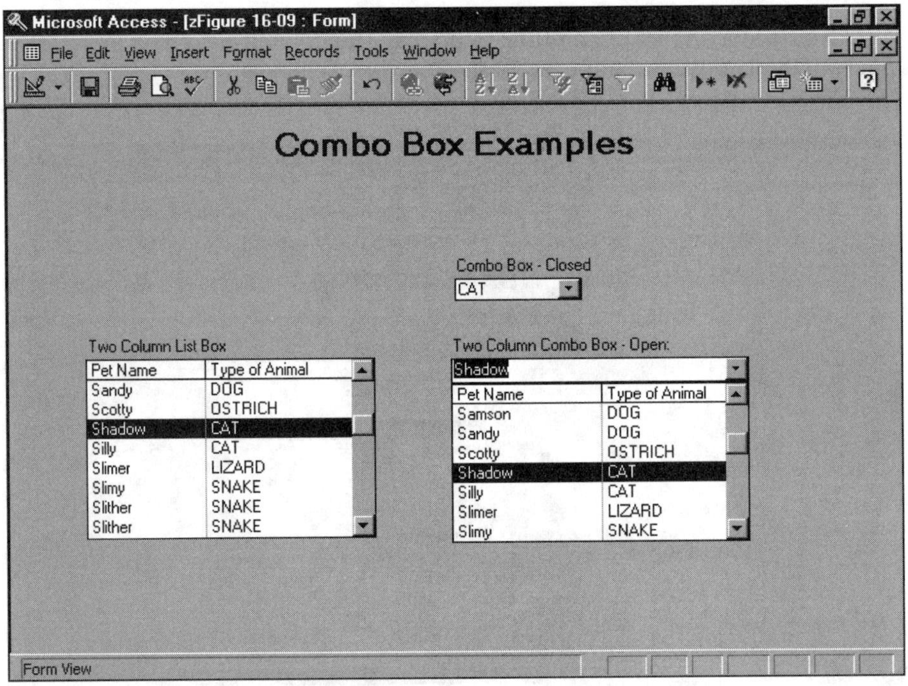

Figure 16-9: Resizing the query design panes.

Tab controls

The tab control is the only control new to Access 97. This may be one of the most important controls because it allows you to create completely new interfaces using the tabbed dialog box look and feel.

Cross-
Reference   Chapter 32 shows you how you use the tabbed dialog box when creating a print dialog box example for Mountain Animal Hospital.

Today, most serious windows applications contain tabbed dialog boxes. Tabbed dialog boxes are very professional looking. They allow you to have many screens of data in a small area by grouping similar types of data and using tabs to navigate between the areas.

The tab control is called a tab control because it looks like the tabs on a file folder when you use it. Figure 16-10 shows the Access 97 Tab Control icon and a tab control already under construction on the design screen. As you can see, the tab control visually looks like the tabs you will see in Form view.

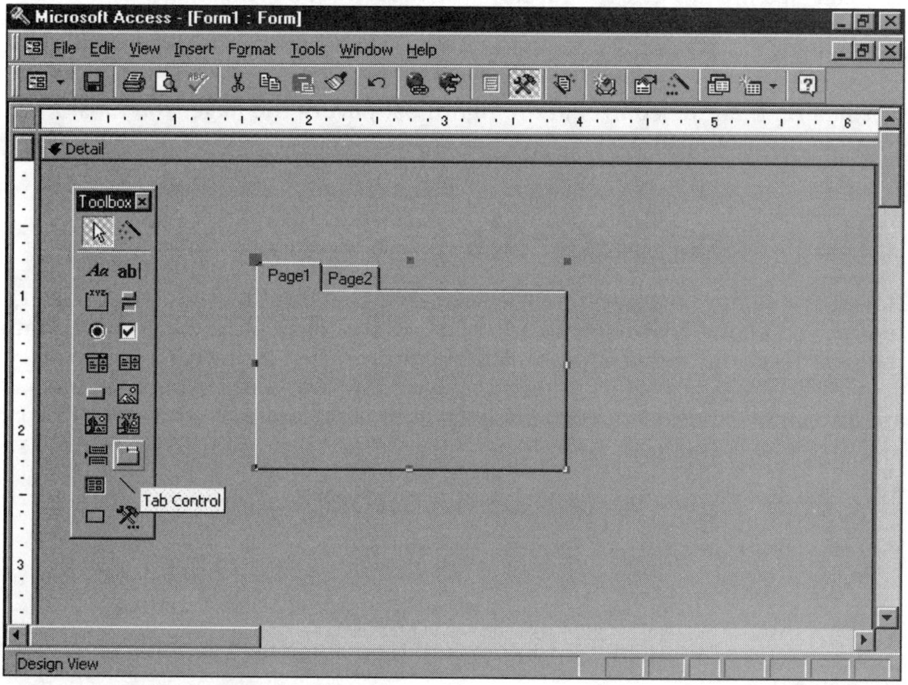

Figure 16-10: Designing a tab control.

You create a new tab control the way you create any Access control. You select the tab control as shown in Figure 16-10 and then draw a rectangle to indicate the size of the control. When the tab control is initially shown, it is displayed with two tab pages. The tab control contains pages. Each tab you define creates a separate page. As you choose each tab in Design view, you see a different page. You can place other controls on each page of the tab control. The control can have many pages. In fact, you can have multiple rows of tabs, each having its own page. You can place new controls on a page or copy and paste them from other forms or other pages. You cannot drag and drop between pages of a tab control. To change the active page for the tab control, just click on the page you want and it will become active (even in design mode).

You insert new pages by right-clicking on a tab and choosing the Insert command. The new page is inserted before the selected page. You delete pages by right-clicking on a tab and choosing the Delete command. This deletes the active page and all the controls on it.

You can size the tab control but not individual pages. Individual pages don't have visual appearance properties — they get these from the tab control itself. You can click on the border of the tab control to select it. You can click directly on a page to select that page. As with an Access detail section, you cannot size the tab control smaller than the control in the rightmost part of the page. You must move controls before resizing.

Creating New Controls

Now that you have learned about the controls that can be used on a form or report, you should learn how to add controls to a form and how to manipulate them in the Form Design window. Although the Form Wizard can quickly place your fields in the Design window, you still may need to add more fields to a form. There are also many times when you simply want to create a report from a blank form.

The two ways to create a control

You can create a control in either of two ways:

✦ Drag a field from the Field List window to add a bound control.

✦ Click on a button in the Toolbox and then add a new unbound control to the screen.

Using the Field List window

The Field List window shown in Figure 16-11 displays all the fields in the open table/query that was used to create a form. This window is movable and resizable and also displays a vertical scrollbar if there are more fields than will fit in the window.

Figure 16-11: The resized Field List window.

You can use one of two methods to display the Field List window:

✦ Click on the Field List button on the toolbar. (This button looks like an Access table).

✦ Select View⇨Field List. . . from the Form menu bar.

Note After you resize or move the Field List window, it remains that size for all forms, even if toggled off or if the form is closed. Only if you exit Access is the window set to its default size.

Generally, dragging a field from the Field List window creates a bound text box in the Form Design window. If you drag an OLE field from the Field List window, you create a bound object frame. Optionally, you can select the type of control by first selecting a control from the Toolbox and then dragging the field to the Form Design window.

Caution When you drag fields from the Field List window, the first control is placed where you release the mouse button. Make sure that there is enough space to the left of the control for the labels. If there is insufficient space, the labels will slide under the controls.

There are several distinct advantages to dragging a field from the Field List window:

✦ The control is bound automatically to the field you dragged.

✦ Field properties inherit table-level formats, status-bar text, and data-validation rules and messages.

✦ The label text is created with the field name as the caption.

Using the Toolbox

By using the *Toolbox buttons* to create a control, you can decide what type of control is to be used for each field. If you don't create the control by dragging it from the Field List window, the field will be unbound and have a default label name such as Field3 or Option11. After you create the control, you can decide what field to bind the control to; you can also enter any text you want for the label and set any properties you want.

The basic deciding factor for using the field list or the Toolbox is simply whether the field exists in the table/query or whether you want to create an unbound or calculated expression. By using the Field List window and the Toolbox together, you can create bound controls of nearly any type. You will find, however, that some data types do not allow all the control types found in the Toolbox. For example, if you attempt to create a graph from a single field, you simply get a text box.

NEW
FEATURE

In Access 97, you can change the type of control after you create it; then you can set all the properties for the control. For example, suppose that you create a field as a text box control and you want to change it to list box. You can use Format⇨Change To and change the control type. Obviously, however, you can change only from some types of controls to others. Anything can be changed to a text box control; option buttons, toggle buttons, and check boxes are interchangeable, as are list and combo boxes.

Dragging a field name from the Field List window

The easiest way to create a text box control is to drag a field from the Field List window. When the Field List window is open, you can click on an individual field and drag it to the Form Design window. This window works in exactly the same way as a Table/Query window in QBE. You can also select multiple fields and then drag them to the screen together. The techniques you would use include the following:

✦ Select multiple contiguous fields by holding down the Shift key and clicking on the first and last field you want.

✦ Select multiple noncontiguous fields by holding down the Ctrl key and clicking on each field you want.

✦ Double-click on the table/query name in the window's top border to select all the fields.

After you select one or more fields, you can drag the selection to the screen.

To drag the Pet Name, Type of Animal, Date of Birth, and Neutered/Spayed fields from the Field List window, follow the next set of steps. If you haven't created a new form, create one first and resize the form as instructed at the beginning of this chapter. When you complete those steps successfully, your screen should look like Figure 16-12.

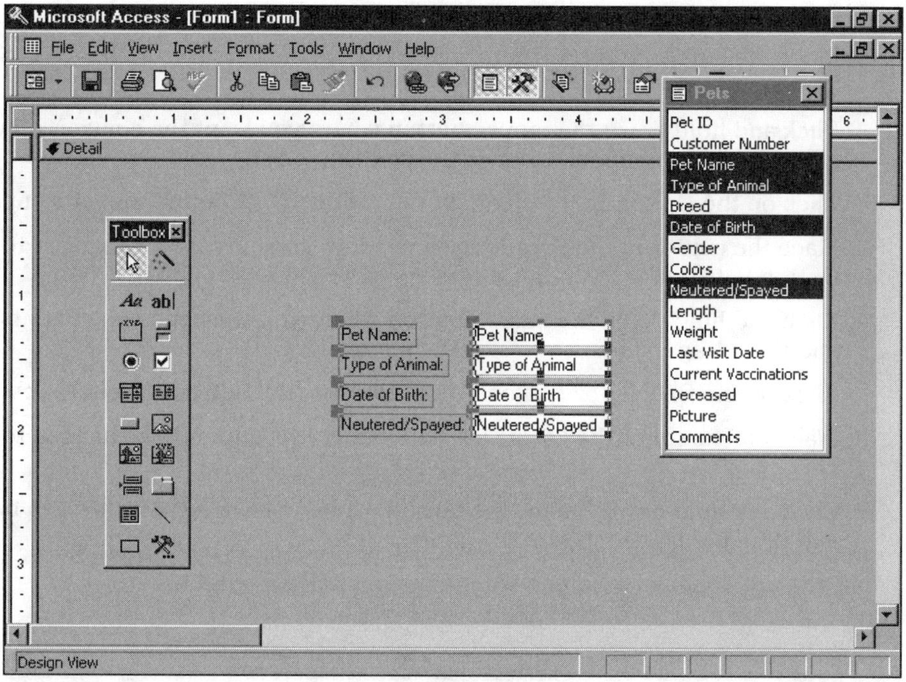

Figure 16-12: Fields dragged from the Field List window.

You can see four controls in the Form Design window, each of them made up of a label control and a text box control (Access attaches the label control to the text box automatically). You can work with these controls as a group or independently, and you can select, move, or delete them. To resize them, you must work with them separately. Notice that each is a text box control, each control has a label with a caption matching the field name, and the text box control displays the bound field name used in the text box.

Note You can close the Field List window by clicking on the Field List button on the toolbar.

Creating unbound controls with the Toolbox

You can create one control at a time by using the Toolbox. You can create any of the controls listed in the Toolbox. Each control becomes an unbound control that has a default label and a name.

To create three different unbound controls, perform the following steps:

1. Click on the Text Box button in the Toolbox (the button appears sunken).
2. Place the cursor in the Form Design window (the cursor has changed to the Text Box button).
3. Click and hold down the mouse button where you want the control to begin, and then drag the mouse to size the control.
4. Click on the Option Button icon on the toolbar (this button appears sunken).
5. Place the cursor in the Form Design window (the cursor has changed to an Option button).
6. Click and hold down the mouse button where you want the control to begin, and then drag the mouse to size the control.
7. Click on the Check Box button on the toolbar (the button appears sunken).
8. Place the cursor in the Form Design window (the cursor has changed to a check box).
9. Click and hold down the mouse button where you want the control to begin, and drag the mouse to size the control.

When you are done, your screen should resemble Figure 16-13.

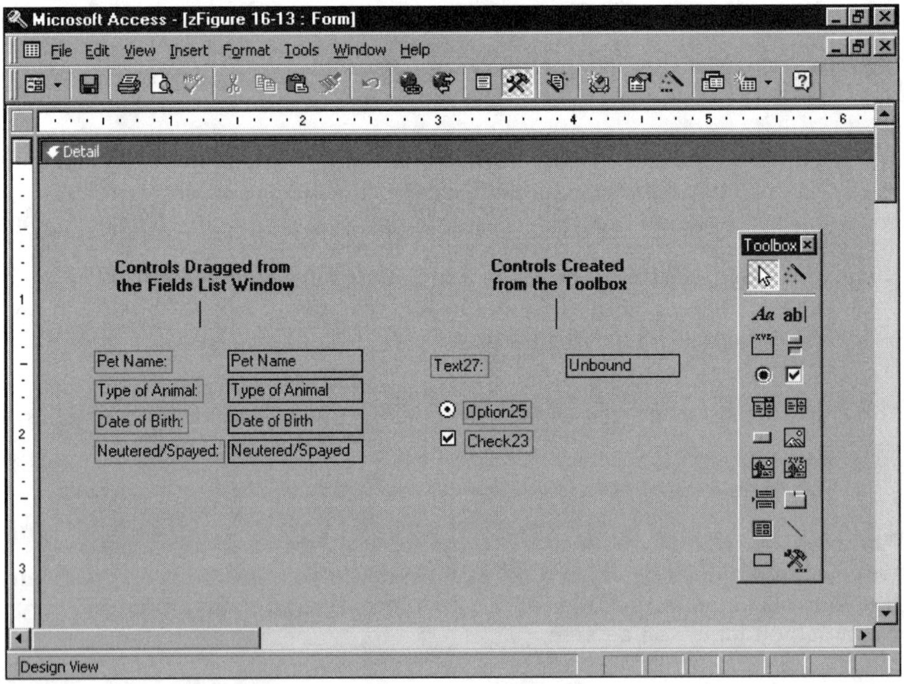

Figure 16-13: Adding three new controls.

Tip

If you just click on the Form Design window, Access will create a default-sized control.

Notice (in Figure 16-13) the difference between the controls that were dragged from the Field List window and the controls that were created from the Toolbox. The Field List window controls are bound to a field in the Pets table and are appropriately labeled and named. The controls created from the Toolbox are unbound and have default names. Notice that control names are assigned automatically according to the type of control and a number.

Later you learn how to change the control names, captions, and properties. Using properties will speed up the process of naming controls and binding them to specific fields.

Selecting Controls

After you have a control on the Form Design window, you can begin to work with it. The first step is to select one or more controls. Depending on its size, a selected control may show from four to eight *handles* (small squares you can drag) around the control box area at the corners and midway along the sides. The handle in the upper left corner is larger than the other handles; use it to move the control. Use the other handles to size the control. Figure 16-14 displays these controls.

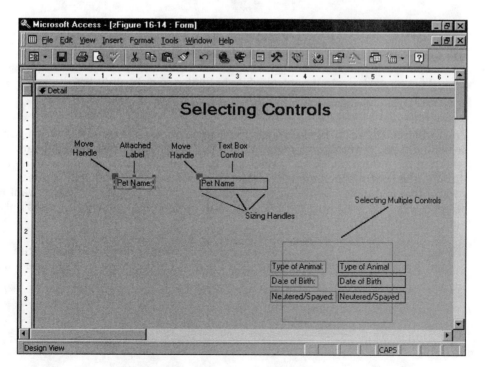

Figure 16-14: A conceptual view of selecting controls.

The pointer tool in the Toolbox must be on for you to select a control. The pointer always appears as an arrow pointing diagonally to the upper left corner. If you selected another button in the Toolbox and then selected the Lock button in the Toolbox, you must click on the pointer again to change the cursor to a selection pointer. If you use the Toolbox to create a single control, Access automatically re-selects the pointer as the default cursor.

Deselecting selected controls

It is good practice to deselect any selected controls before you select another control. You can deselect a control by simply clicking on an unselected area of the screen that does not contain a control. When you do so, the handles disappear from any selected control.

Selecting a single control

You can select any single control by simply clicking anywhere on the control. When you click on a control, all the handles appear. If the control has an attached label, the handle for moving the label appears as well. If you select a single label control that is part of an attached control, all the handles in the label control are displayed, and only the *Move handle* (the largest handle) is displayed in the attached control.

Selecting multiple controls

You can select multiple controls in these ways:

✦ Click on each desired control while holding down the Shift key.

✦ Drag the pointer through the controls you want to select.

The screen in Figure 16-14 shows some of these concepts graphically. When you select multiple controls by dragging the mouse, a light gray rectangle appears as you drag the mouse. When you select multiple controls by dragging the pointer through the controls, be careful to select only the controls you want to select. Any control that is touched by the line or enclosed within it is selected. If you want to select labels only, you must make sure that the selection rectangle encloses only your passes through the labels.

Tip   When you click on a ruler, an arrow appears and a line is displayed across the screen. You can drag the cursor to widen the line. Each control that the line touches is selected.

Tip If you find that controls are not selected when the rectangle passes through the control, you may have the Selection Behavior global property set to Fully Enclosed. This means that a control will be selected only if the selection rectangle completely encloses the entire control. The normal default for this option is Partially Enclosed. You can change this option by first selecting Tools⇨Options... and then selecting Forms/Reports Category in the Options tabbed dialog box. The option Selection Behavior should be set to Partially Enclosed.

By holding down the Shift key, you can select several noncontiguous controls. This lets you select controls on totally different parts of the screen, cut them, and then paste them together somewhere else on-screen.

Manipulating Controls

Creating a form is generally a multistep process. The next step is to make sure that your controls are properly sized and moved into the correct positions.

Resizing a control

You can *resize* controls by using any of the smaller handles on the control. The handles in the control corners let you make the field larger or smaller — in both width and height — and at the same time. You use the handles in the middle of the control sides to size the control larger or smaller in one direction only. The top and bottom handles control the height of the control; the handles in the middle change the control's width.

When a corner handle is touched by the cursor in a selected control, the cursor becomes a diagonal double arrow. You can then hold down the mouse button and drag the control size handles to the desired size. If the cursor touches a side handle in a selected control, the cursor changes to a horizontal or vertical double-headed arrow. Figure 16-15 shows the Pet Name control after resizing. Notice the double-headed arrow in the corner of the Pet Name control.

Tip You can resize a control in very small increments by pressing the Shift and arrow keys. This also works with multiple controls selected. They will change by only one pixel at a time.

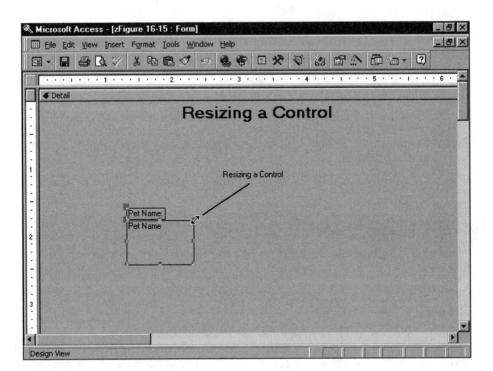

Figure 16-15: Resizing a control.

Moving a control

After you select a control, you can move it. Use either of these methods to move an unselected control:

> ✦ Click on the control and drag it to a new location.
>
> ✦ Select the control and then place your cursor *between* any two Move handles on its border.

If the control has an attached label, you can move both label and control by this method. It doesn't matter whether you click on the control or the label; they are moved together.

You can move a control separately from an attached label by simply grabbing the Move handle of the control and moving it. You can also move the label control separately from the other control by selecting the Move handle of the label control and moving it separately.

Figure 16-16 shows a label control that has been separately moved to the top of the text box control. The Hand button indicates that the controls are ready to be moved together.

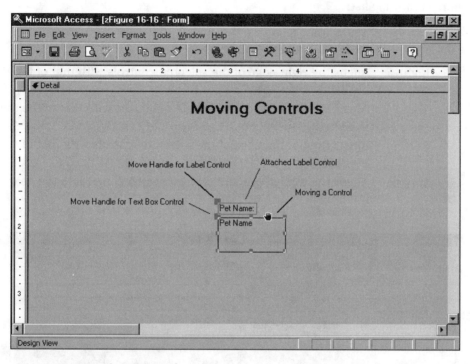

Figure 16-16: Moving a control.

Tip You can move a control in small increments with the keyboard by pressing the Ctrl and arrow keys after you select a control or group of controls.

Tip You can restrict the direction in which a control is moved so that it maintains alignment within a specific row or column. To do so, hold down the Shift key as you press the mouse button to select and move the control. The control will move only in the direction you first move it, either horizontally or vertically.

You can cancel a move or a resizing operation by pressing Esc before you release the mouse button. After a move or resizing operation is complete, you can click on the Undo button or select Edit⇨Undo Move or Edit⇨Undo Sizing to undo the changes.

Aligning controls

You may want to move several controls so that they are all *aligned* (lined up). The Format⇨Align menu has several options, as shown in Figure 16-17 and described in the following list:

Left	Aligns the left edge of the selected controls with that of the leftmost selected control
Right	Aligns the right edge of the selected controls with that of the rightmost selected control
Top	Aligns the top edge of the selected controls with that of the topmost selected control
Bottom	Aligns the bottom edge of the selected controls with that of the bottommost selected control
To Grid	Aligns the top left corners of the selected controls to the nearest grid point

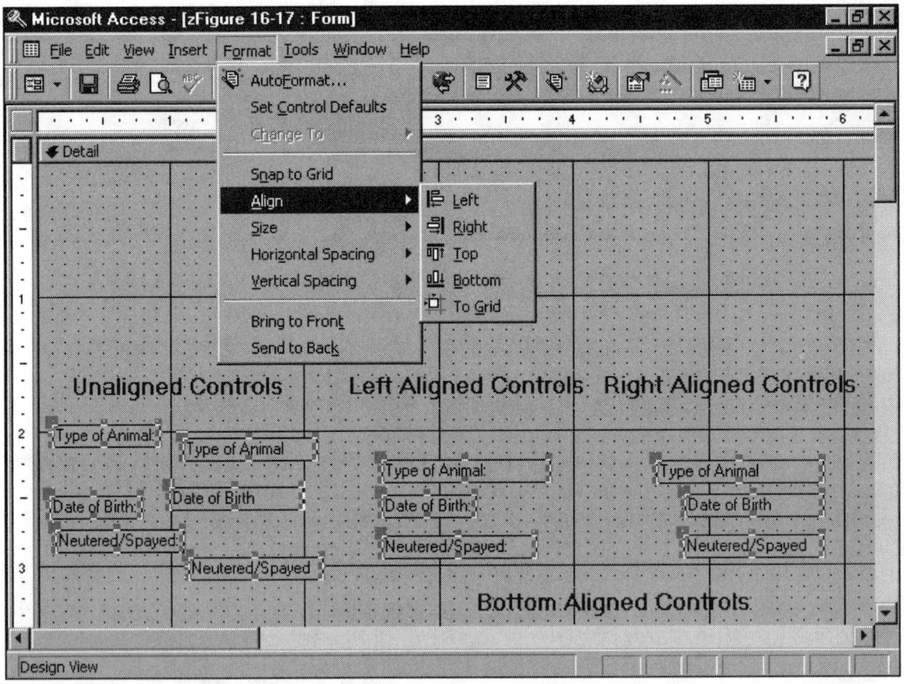

Figure 16-17: Aligning controls and the grid.

By selecting from this menu, you can align any number of controls. When you choose one of the options, Access uses the control that is the closest to the desired selection as the model for the alignment. For example, suppose that you have three controls and you want to left-align them. They will be aligned on the basis of the control farthest to the left in the group of the three controls.

Figure 16-17 shows several groups of controls. The first group is not aligned. The label controls in the second group of controls has been left-aligned. The text box controls in the second group have been right-aligned. Each label, along with its attached text box, has been bottom-aligned.

Each type of alignment must be done separately. In this example, you can left-align all the labels or right-align all the text boxes at once. However, you would have to align each label and text control bottom separately (three separate alignments).

You may notice a series of dots in the background of Figure 16-17. This is the *grid*. The grid is used to assist you in aligning controls. The grid is displayed by selecting View➪Grid.

You can use the Format➪Snap to Grid option to align new controls to the grid as you draw or place them on a form. It also aligns existing controls when you move or resize them.

When Snap to Grid is on and you draw a new control by clicking on and dragging the form, Access aligns all four corners of the control to points on the grid. When you place a new control just by clicking on the form or report, only the upper left corner is aligned.

As you move or resize existing controls, Access 97 lets you move only from grid point to grid point. When Snap to Grid is off, Access 97 ignores the grid and lets you place a control anywhere on the form or report.

Tip You can turn off Snap to Grid temporarily by holding down the Ctrl key before you create a control (or while you're creating or moving it).

The Size option on the Format menu has several options that assist you in sizing controls based on the value of the data, the grid, or other controls. The options of the Size menu are the following:

To Fit	Adjusts the height and width of controls to fit the font of the text they contain
To Grid	Moves all sides of selected controls in or out to meet the nearest points on the grid
To Tallest	Sizes selected controls so that they have the same height as the tallest selected control

To Shortest	Sizes selected controls so that they have the same height as the shortest selected control
To Widest	Sizes selected controls so that they have the same width as the widest selected control
To Narrowest	Sizes selected controls so that they have the same width as the narrowest selected control

Tip The grid's *fineness* (number of dots) can be changed from form to form by using the GridX and GridY Form properties. The grid is invisible if its fineness is greater than 16 units per inch horizontally or vertically. (Higher numbers indicate greater fineness.)

Tip Another pair of alignment options can make a big difference when you have to align the space between multiple controls. The options Horizontal Spacing and Vertical Spacing change the space between controls on the basis of the space between the first two selected controls. If the controls are across the screen, use horizontal spacing. If they are down the screen, use vertical spacing.

Deleting a control

If you find that you no longer want a specific control on the Form Design window, you can delete it by selecting the control and pressing Delete. You can also select Edit⇨Delete to delete a selected control or Edit⇨Cut to cut the control to the Clipboard.

You can delete more than one control at a time by selecting multiple controls and pressing one of the Delete key sequences. If you have a control with an attached label, you can delete the label only by clicking on the label itself and then selecting a delete method. If you select the control, both the control and the label will be deleted. To delete only the label of the Pet Name control, follow the next set of steps (this example assumes that you have the Pet Name text box control in your Form Design window):

1. Select the Pet Name label control only.
2. Press Delete.

The label control should be removed from the window.

Attaching a label to a control

If you accidentally delete a label from a control, you can reattach it. To create and then reattach a label to a control, follow these steps:

1. Click on the Label button in the Toolbox.

2. Place the cursor in the Form Design window (the cursor has become the Text Box button).

3. Click and hold down the mouse button where you want the control to begin; drag the mouse to size the control.

4. Type **Pet Name:** and click outside the control.

5. Select the Pet Name label control.

6. Select Edit⇨Cut to cut the label control to the Clipboard.

7. Select the Pet Name text box control.

8. Select Edit⇨Paste to attach the label control to the text box control.

Copying a control

You can create copies of any control by duplicating it or by copying it to the Clipboard and then pasting the copies where you want them. If you have a control for which you entered many properties or specified a certain format, you can copy it and revise only the properties (such as the control name and bound field name) to make it a different control. This capability is also useful when you have a multiple-page form and you want to display the same values on different pages and in different locations.

What Are Properties?

Properties are named attributes of controls, fields, or database objects; you use them to modify the characteristics of the control, field, or object. These attributes can be the size, color, appearance, or name. A property can also modify the behavior of a control, determining (for example) whether the control is editable or visible.

Properties are used extensively in forms and reports for changing the characteristics of controls. Each control has properties; the form itself also has properties, as does each of its sections. The same is true for reports; the report itself has properties, as does each report section and each individual control. The label control also has its own properties, even if it is attached to another control.

Properties are displayed in a *property sheet* (also commonly called a *Property window* because it is an actual window). The first column contains the property names; you enter properties in the second column. Figure 16-18 shows a property sheet for the Date of Birth text box.

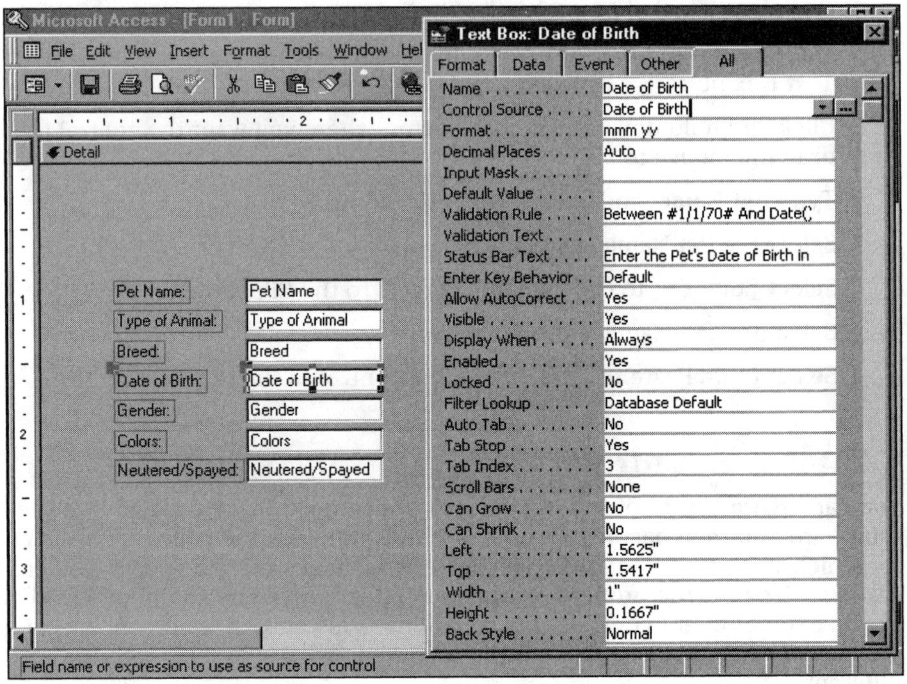

Figure 16-18: The property sheet for the Date of Birth text box.

Viewing a control's properties

There are several ways to view a control's properties:

✦ Select View⇨Properties from the menu bar.

✦ Click on the control and then click on the Properties button on the toolbar.

✦ Double-click on any control.

To display the property sheet for the Date of Birth text box control, follow these steps:

1. Create a new blank form, using the Pets table.

2. Drag the fields Pet Name through Neutered/Spayed from the Field List window to the Form Design window.

3. Click on the Date of Birth text box control to select it.

4. Click on the Properties button on the toolbar.

As you can see in Figure 16-18, a partial property sheet is displayed. It has also been resized larger. By widening the property sheet, you can see more of the its values; by increasing the vertical size, you can see more controls at one time. The vertical scrollbar lets you move between various properties. Only the text box control has more properties than can fit on-screen at one time. Because the property sheet is a true window, it can be moved anywhere on-screen and resized to any size. It does not, however, have Maximize or Minimize buttons.

As a tabbed dialog box, the property window lets you see all the properties for a control; you can also limit the view to specific properties. The specific groups of properties include:

Format   These determine how a label or value looks: font, size, color, special effects, borders, and scrollbars.

Data   These properties affect how a value is displayed and the control it is bound to: control source, formats, input masks, validation, default value, and other table-level properties.

Event   Event properties are named events, such as clicking a mouse button, adding a record, pressing a key for which you can define a response (in the form of a call to a macro or an Access Basic procedure), and so on.

Other   Other Properties shows additional characteristics of the control, such as the name of the control or the description that appears on the status bar.

Cross-
Reference   The number of properties available in Access has increased greatly since Access 2.0. The most important new properties are described in various chapters of this book. For a discussion of new event properties and event procedures, see Chapters 30–34.

The properties displayed in Figure 16-18 are the specific properties for Date of Birth. The first two properties, Name and Control Source, reflect the field name Date of Birth.

The Name is simply the name of the control itself. You can give the control any name you want. Unbound controls have names such as Field11 or Button13. When a control is bound to a field, Access names it automatically to match the bound field name.

The Control Source is the name of the table field to which the control is bound. In this example, the Date of Birth field is the name of the field in the Pets table. An unbound control has no control source, whereas the control source of a calculated control is the calculated expression, as in the example =[Weight] * .65.

The following properties are always inherited from the table definition of a field for a text box or other type of control. Figure 16-17 shows some of these properties inherited from the Pets table:

✦ Format

✦ Decimal Places

✦ Status Bar Text (from the field Description)

✦ Input Mask

✦ Caption

✦ Default Value

✦ Validation Rule

✦ Validation Text

Note Changes made to a control's properties don't affect the field properties in the source table.

Each type of control has a different set of properties, as do objects such as forms, reports, and sections within forms or reports. In the next few chapters, you learn about many of these properties as you use each of the control types to create complex forms and reports.

Changing a control property

You can display properties in a property sheet, and you can use many different methods to change the properties. A list of these follows:

✦ Entering the desired property in a property sheet

✦ Changing a property directly by changing the control itself

✦ Using inherited properties from the bound field

✦ Using inherited properties from the control's default selections

✦ Entering color selections for the control by using the palette

✦ Changing text style, size, color, and alignment by using the toolbar buttons

You can change a control's properties by simply clicking on a property and typing the desired value.

Figure 16-18 displays an arrow and a button with three dots to the right of the Control Source property-entry area. Some properties display the arrow in the property-entry area when you click in the area. This tells you that Access provides a pop-up list of values you can choose. If you click on the down arrow in the Control Source property, you find that the choices are a list of all fields in the open table.

Three dots on a button constitute the *Builder button,* used to open one of the many Builders in Access. This includes the Macro Builder, the Expression Builder, and the Module Builder.

Some properties have a list of standard values such as Yes or No; others display varying lists of fields, forms, reports, or macros. The properties of each object are determined by the object itself and what the object is used for.

NEW FEATURE A new feature in Access 97 is the capability of cycling through property choices by repeatedly double-clicking on the choice. For example, double-clicking on the Display When property will alternately select Always, Print Only, and Screen Only.

Default properties

The properties you see in a specific control's property sheet are for that specific control. You can click on a control to see its properties. You can also create a set of default properties for a specific type of control by clicking on the toolbar button for that control type. For example, to view or change the default properties for a text box in the current form, follow these steps:

1. Make sure that the property sheet is displayed.
2. Click on the Text Box button in the Toolbox.

As you can see in Figure 16-19, these are some of the default properties for a text box. You can set these properties; from then on, each new text box you create will have these properties as a starting point. This set of default properties can determine the color and size for new controls, the font used, the distance between the attached label and the control, and most other characteristics.

By changing the default property settings, you can create customized forms much more quickly than by changing every control.

Access provides many tools for customizing not only your data-entry and display forms but also reports. In addition, you can apply the default properties to existing controls and even save a set of default controls as a template. You can then use the template as the basis for a new form. Learning these techniques can save you even more time when you create new forms and reports.

Cross-Reference Chapter 18 covers saving control settings and using a tool known as AutoFormat to change settings globally.

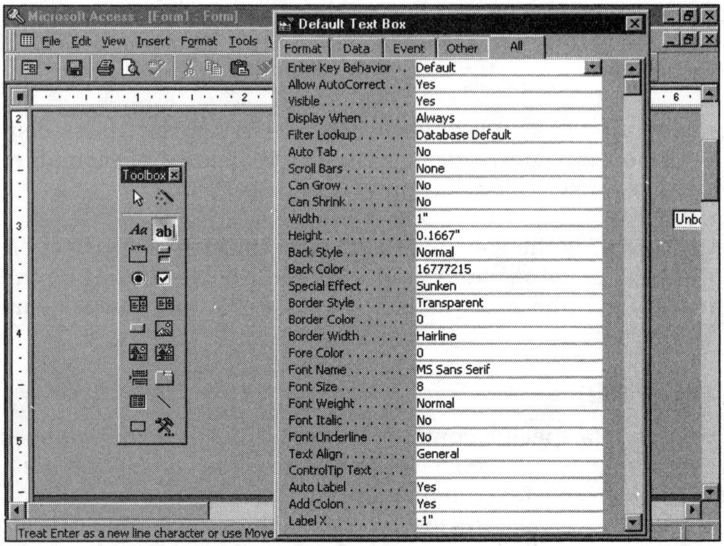

Figure 16-19: Displaying default properties.

Summary

In this chapter, you learned the basic usage of controls and properties for forms and reports. The following points were examined:

✦ You can create a new blank form by selecting Insert⇨Form⇨Design View.

✦ A control is an object on a form or report, such as a label or a text box.

✦ There are three types of controls: bound, unbound, and calculated.

✦ Text boxes, the most common type of control, let you enter and display data.

✦ The tab control is new to Access 97 and helps you create tabbed user interfaces.

✦ Controls often have attached label controls to identify the purpose of the control.

✦ You can create a new control by dragging a field from the Field List window or by using the Toolbox.

✦ The Field List window displays a list of all fields from the current table or query.

✦ You can drag a field from the Field List window to create a bound control.

✦ You can select a control by clicking on it. You can select multiple controls by clicking on them while holding down the Shift key, by dragging a rectangle to enclose the controls, or by dragging the pointer through the controls.

✦ You can resize controls by using the small resizing handles found in a selected control.

✦ You can move controls by dragging them. An attached control can be moved separately from its attached label by use of the larger Move handles in the upper left corner of a selected control.

✦ You can align controls by using the <u>A</u>lign options of the F<u>o</u>rmat menu. Controls can also be copied, duplicated, and deleted.

✦ Using the <u>S</u>ize options of the F<u>o</u>rmat menu, you can change the size of controls consistently.

✦ You can space controls evenly by using the Hori<u>z</u>ontal and <u>V</u>ertical Spacing options in the F<u>o</u>rmat menu.

✦ Properties are named attributes of controls, fields, or database objects. You can set properties that modify the characteristics of the control, such as size, color, or appearance.

✦ Properties are displayed in a property sheet. Each type of control has different properties.

✦ Although an individual control has its own properties, each form maintains a set of default properties for each type of control on the form.

In the next chapter, you learn how to use controls to create a new form.

Creating and Customizing Data-Entry Forms

In Chapter 16, you learned about all the tools necessary to create and display a form. In this chapter, you use all the skills you learned to create several types of data-entry and display forms.

In this chapter, you use the Customer and Pets tables in the Mountain Animal Start database to create several types of simple forms. Each control will be explained by the use of one or more fields in these tables.

Creating a Standard Data-Entry Form

The first form you create in this chapter is a simple data-entry form that uses two tables. In Chapter 9, you created a simple Pets data-entry form by using a Form Wizard. In this section of the chapter, you create the more complicated form you see in Figure 17-1. This form demonstrates the use of label and text box controls from multiple tables as well as embedded pictures. You'll continue to modify this form in the next several chapters, adding more complicated controls and emphasis.

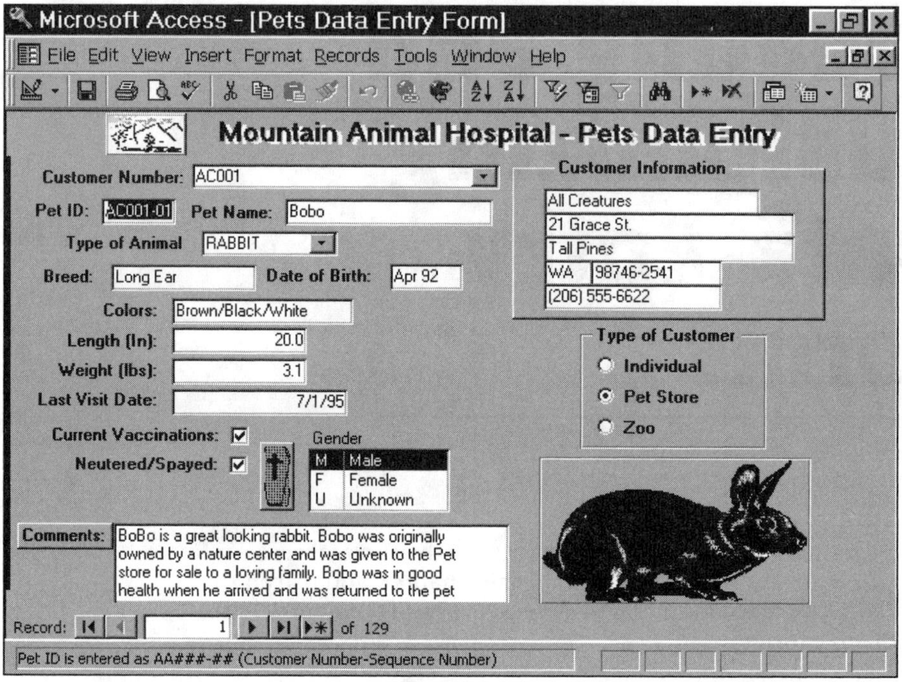

Figure 17-1: A complicated data-entry form.

Assembling the data

With this design in mind, you need to assemble the data. To create this form, you need fields from two tables, Customer and Pets. Table 17-1 lists the necessary fields and their table locations.

To assemble this data, you first need to create a query called Pets and Owners, which includes all fields from both tables, even though you aren't going to use all the fields. These extra fields give you the flexibility to add a field later without redoing the query. This can happen, for example, when you see that you'll need another field from which to derive a calculated control.

Table 17-1
Fields Needed for the Pets Data-Entry Form

Fields from Pets Table	Fields from Customer Table
Pet ID	Customer Name
Customer ID	Street/Apt
Pet Name	City
Type of Animal	State
Breed	ZIP Code
Date of Birth	Phone Number
Colors	Type of Customer
Length	
Weight	
Last Visit Date	
Current Vaccinations	
Deceased	
Neutered/Spayed	
Gender	
Comments	
Picture	

In this example, you also sort the data by the Pet ID. It's always a good idea to arrange your data into some known order. When you display a form, you see the data in its physical order unless you sort the data.

To create the Pets and Owners query, follow these steps:

1. Click on the Query tab in the Database window, and then click on the <u>N</u>ew button to create a new query.

2. Select New Query in the New Query dialog box and click on OK. The Show Table dialog box appears.

3. Add the Customer table.

4. Add the Pets table.

5. Close the Show Table dialog box.

6. Drag the asterisk (*) from the Customer field list to the first column in the QBE design pane.

7. Drag the asterisk (*) from the Pets field list to the second column in the QBE design pane.

8. Drag the Pet ID field from the Pets field list to the third column in the QBE pane.

9. Click on the Pet ID Show: box to turn it off.

10. Change the Sort to Ascending in the Pet ID field, as shown in Figure 17-2.

11. Select File⇨Close, click on Yes, and then name the query **Pets and Owners**.

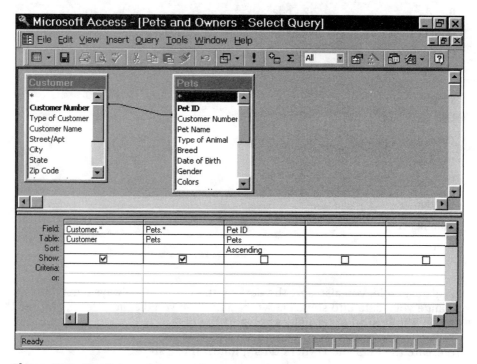

Figure 17-2: The Pets and Owners query.

You use the asterisk (*) to select all fields from each table.

Creating a new form and binding it to a query

Now that you've created the Pets and Owners query, you can create a new form and bind it to the query. Follow these steps to complete this process:

1. Click on the Database icon to display the Database window if it is not already displayed.

2. Click on the Forms tab in the Database window and click on the New button.

3. Select Design View in the Wizard list, and then select the Pets and Owners query from the combo box at the bottom of the dialog box.

4. Click on the OK button to create the new form.

5. Maximize the Form window.

Note If the Toolbox and Property dialog boxes are not open, as in Figure 17-3, you can open them by selecting them from the View menu.

You now see a blank Form Design window, as shown in Figure 17-3. The form is bound to the query Pets and Owners, as you can see in the Property window on the screen. This means that the data from that query will be used when the form is viewed or printed. The fields from the query are available for use in the form design; they will appear in the Field List window.

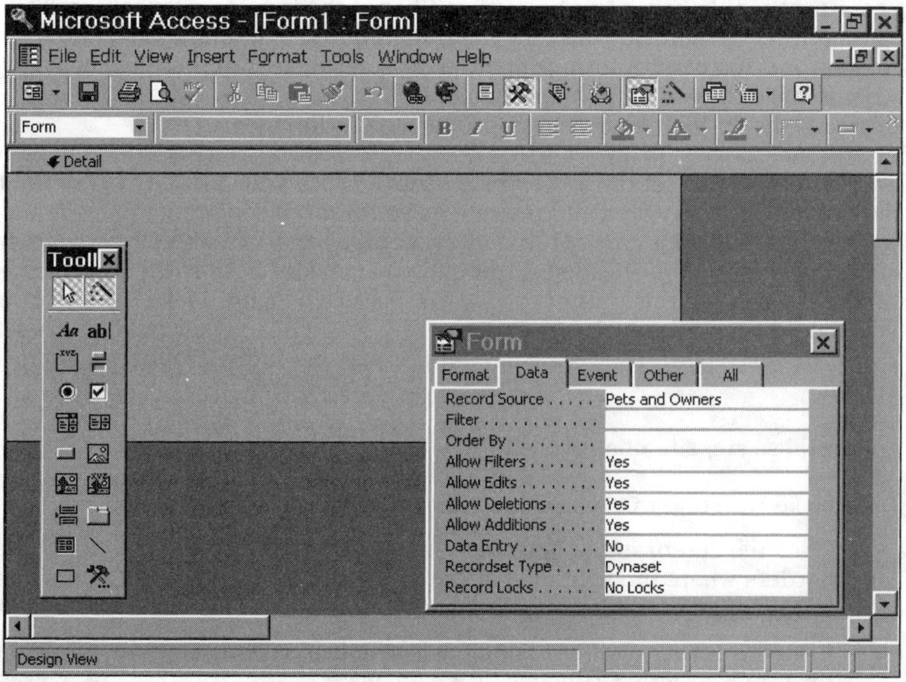

Figure 17-3: The blank Form Design window.

If you need to create a form that contains no field controls, you may want to create a blank form that is not bound to a query. You can do this by simply not selecting a table/query when you select Design view in the New Form dialog box.

Defining the form display size

When you are creating your form, you must resize the workspace of the form. In Figure 17-3, the light gray area in the form is your workspace. If you place controls in the dark gray area outside it, however, the workspace expands automatically until it is larger than the area in which you placed the control. The size of the workspace depends on the size of your form. If you want the form to fill the screen, size it to the size of your screen, which depends on your screen resolution. You can fit more data on-screen if you are using a SuperVGA screen size of 800 X 600 or 1024 X 1024 than you can if you are using the standard VGA size of 640 X 480. You never know who may use a form you create; you should stay with the smallest size any anticipated user may have.

A maximized standard VGA screen set to 640 X 480 in Windows 95/NT can display a full-screen size of approximately $6\frac{1}{4}$ inches by $3\frac{3}{4}$ inches. This includes the space for the title bar, menu bar, and toolbar at the top; the vertical scrollbar areas down the right side; and the navigation buttons/scrollbar and status line at the bottom. You can set form properties to control most of these elements. If you want to have the record pointer column down the left side, you will need to decrease the $6\frac{1}{4}$-inch margin by approximately $\frac{1}{8}$ inch.

The easiest way to set the form size is simply to use your mouse to grab the borders of the light gray area and resize it as you want. If you grab either the top or bottom borders, your cursor turns into a double arrow. If you grab the corner, the cursor becomes a four-headed arrow and you can size both sides at the same time. (You can see this four-headed arrow cursor in Figure 17-4.) For this example, you should set the form size to $6\frac{1}{4}$ inches by $3\frac{3}{4}$ inches, following the next set of steps, and use Figure 17-4 as a guide. At this size, no form scrollbars should appear.

Follow these steps to change the form size:

1. Make sure that the ruler is on; otherwise, select it from the <u>V</u>iew menu.

2. Place the cursor in the bottom right corner of the vertical and horizontal borders where the light gray space meets the dark gray area. The cursor should appear as a four-headed arrow.

3. Grab the corner and (pressing the left mouse button) drag the borders until the size is exactly $6\frac{1}{4}$ inches by $3\frac{3}{4}$ inches.

4. Release the mouse button to accept the new size.

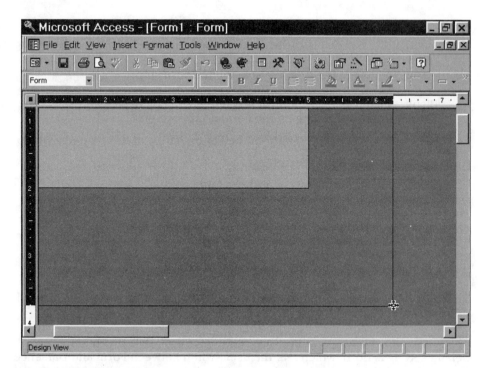

Figure 17-4: Form properties.

If you add controls beyond the right border, you have to scroll the form to see these controls. This is generally not acceptable in a form. If you add controls beyond the bottom border, you have to scroll the form to see these controls as well; this is acceptable because the form becomes a multiple-page form. Later in this chapter, you learn how to control multiple-page forms.

Note   If you try the form and see a horizontal scroll bar along the bottom, either resize the right margin or turn the Record Selector property off for the form. This topic will be covered later.

Working with form properties

You can set many form properties to change the way the entire form is displayed. Table 17-2 (in a later section of this chapter) discusses some of the most important properties. Changing default properties is relatively easy: You select the property in the Property dialog box (also known as the Property window) and set a new value. Following are some of the more important properties for the form.

Changing the title bar text with the Caption property

Normally the title bar displays the name of the form after it is saved. By changing the Caption property, you can display a different title on the title bar when the form is run. To change the title bar text, follow these steps:

1. Display the Property window if it is not already displayed and select the Format sheet by clicking on the Format tab.

2. Click on the Caption property in the Format sheet of the Property window.

3. Type **Pets Data Entry Form**.

4. Click on any other property or press Enter.

You can display the blank form by selecting the Form button on the toolbar to check the result. The caption you enter here overrides the name of the saved form.

Specifying how to view the form

Two properties determine how your form displays records: *Default View* and *Views Allowed.*

The Views Allowed property has three settings: Form, Datasheet, and Both. The default setting is Both, which lets the user switch between Form and Datasheet view. If you set the Views Allowed property to Datasheet, the Form button and the View⇨Form menu selections cannot be selected; you can view the data only as a datasheet. If you set the Views Allowed property to Form, the Datasheet button and the View⇨Datasheet menu selections cannot be selected; you can view the data only as a form.

The Default View property is different; it determines how the data is displayed when the form is first run. Three settings are possible: Single Form, Continuous Forms, and Datasheet. The first setting, Single Form, displays one record per form page, regardless of the form's size. The next setting, Continuous Forms, is the default; it tells Access to display as many detail records as will fit on-screen. Normally you would use this setting to define the height of a very small form and to display many records at one time. Figure 17-5 shows such a form. The records have a small enough height that you can see a number of them at once. The final Default View setting, Datasheet, displays the form as a standard datasheet when run. You should now change this property to Single Form.

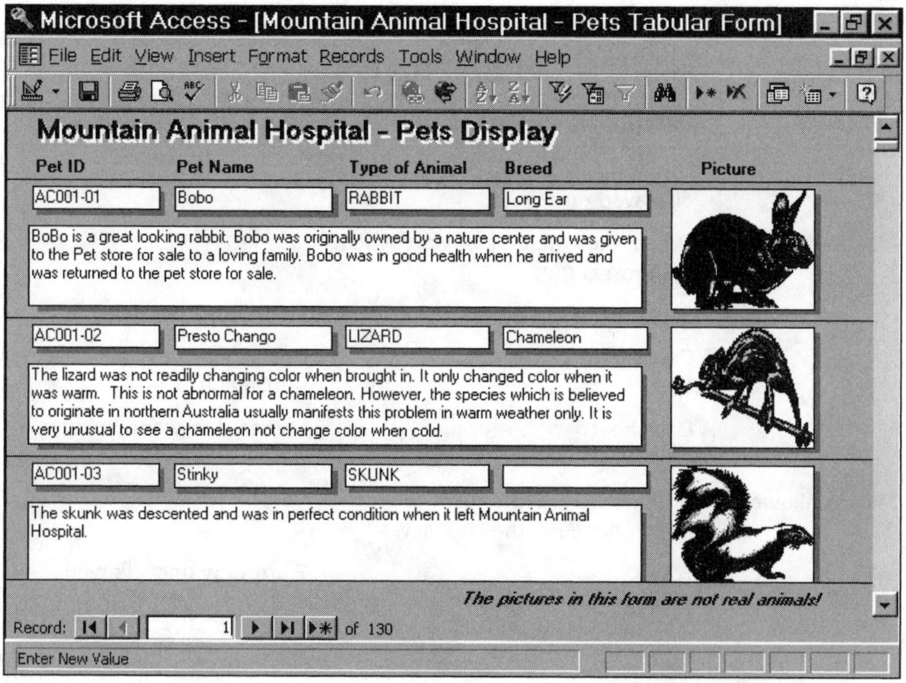

Figure 17-5: Using the Continuous Forms setting of the Default View property.

Eliminating the record selector bar

The Record Selector property determines whether you see the vertical bar on the left side of the form; this bar lets you select the entire record (you see the bar with the editing icon in datasheets). Primarily used in multiple-record forms or datasheets, a right-pointing triangle indicates the current record; a Pencil icon indicates that the record is being changed. Though the record selector bar is important for datasheets, you probably won't want it for a single record form. To eliminate it, simply change the form's Record Selector property to No.

Table 17-2
Form Properties

Property	Description and Options	
Caption	Displayed on the title bar of the displayed form	
Default View	Determines the type of view when the form is run	
	Single Form	One record per page
	Continuous Forms	As many records per page as will fit (Default)
	Datasheet	Standard row and column datasheet view
Views Allowed	Determines whether user can switch between the two views	
	Form	Form view only allowed
	Datasheet	Datasheet view only allowed
	Both	Form or Datasheet view allowed
Allow Edits	Prevents or allows editing of data, making the form read-only for saved records	
	Yes/No	You can/cannot edit saved records
Allow Deletions	Used to prevent records from being deleted	
	Yes/No	You can/cannot delete saved records
Allow Additions	Used to determine whether new records can be added	
	Yes/No	You can/cannot add new records
Data Entry	Used to determine whether form displays saved records	
	Yes/No	Only new records are displayed/ All records are displayed
Recordset Type	Used to determine whether multitable forms can be updated; replaces Access 2.0 Allow Updating property	
	Dynaset	Only default table field controls can be edited

Property	Description and Options	
Recordset Type (continued)	Dynaset	All tables and fields are editable (Inconsistent Update)
	Snapshot	No fields are editable (Read Only in effect)
Record Locks	Used to determine multiuser record locking	
	No Locks	Record is locked only as it is saved
	All Records	Locks entire form records while using the form
	Edited Records	Locks only current record being edited
Scrollbars	Determines whether any scrollbars are displayed	
	Neither	No scrollbars are displayed
	Horizontal Only	Displays only horizontal scrollbar
	Vertical Only	Displays only vertical scrollbar
	Both	Displays both horizontal and vertical scrollbars
Record Selectors	Determines whether vertical record selector bar is displayed (Yes/No)	
Navigation Buttons	Determines whether navigation buttons are visible (Yes/No)	
Dividing Lines	Determines whether lines between form sections are visible (Yes/No)	
Auto Resize	Form is opened to display a complete record (Yes/No)	
Auto Center	Centers form on-screen when it's opened (Yes/No)	
Pop Up	Form is a pop-up that floats above all other objects (Yes/No)	
Modal	For use when you must close the form before doing anything else. Disables other windows; when Pop Up set to Yes, Modal disables menus and toolbar, creating a dialog box (Yes/No)	

(continued)

Table 17-2 *(continued)*

Property	Description and Options	
Border Style	Determines form's border style	
	None	No border or border elements (scrollbars, navigation buttons)
	Thin	Thin border, not resizeable
	Sizeable	Normal form settings
	Dialog	Thick border, title bar only, cannot be sized; use for dialog boxes
Control Box	Determines whether control menu (Restore, Move Size) is available (Yes/No)	
Min Max Buttons		
	None	No buttons displayed in upper right corner of form
	Min Enabled	Minimize button only is displayed
	Max Enabled	Maximize button only is displayed
	Both Enabled	Minimize and Maximize buttons are displayed
Close Button	Determines whether to display Close button in upper right corner and a close menu item on the control menu (Yes/No)	
What's This Button	Determines whether Screen Tips appear when user presses Shift+F1 for Help	
Width	Displays the value of the width of the form; can be entered or Access fills it in as you adjust the width of the work area	
Picture	Enter the name of a bitmap file for the background of the entire form	
Picture Size Mode	Options:	
	Clip	Displays the picture at its actual size
	Stretch	Fits picture to form size (Non-Proportionally)

Property	Description and Options	
Picture Size Mode *(continued)*	Zoom	Fits picture to form size (Proportionally); this may result in the picture not fitting in one dimension (Height or Width)
Picture Alignment	Options:	
	Top Left	The picture is displayed in the top left corner of the form, report window, or image control
	Top Right	The picture is displayed in the top right corner of the form, report window, or image control
	Center	(Default) The picture is centered in the form, report window, or image control
	Bottom Left	The picture is displayed in the bottom left corner of the form, report window, or image control
	Bottom Right	The picture is displayed in the bottom right corner of the form, report window, or image control
	Form Center	The form's picture is centered horizontally in relation to the width of the form and vertically in relation to the topmost and bottommost controls on the form
	Picture Tiling	Used when you want to overlay multiple copies of a small bitmap; for example, a single brick can become a wall
Cycle	Options:	
	All Records	Tabbing from the last field of a record moves to the next record
	Current Record	Tabbing from the last field of a record moves to the first field of that record
	Current Page	Tabbing from the last field of a record moves to the first field of the current page

(continued)

Table 17-2 *(continued)*

Property	Description and Options	
Menu Bar	Used to specify an alternate menu bar; Builder button lets you create a new menu bar if you want	
Shortcut Menu	Determines whether shortcut menus are active	
Shortcut Menu Bar	Used to specify an alternate shortcut menu bar	
Grid X	Determines number of points per inch when X grid is displayed	
Grid Y	Determines number of points per inch when Y grid is displayed	
Layout for Print	Determines whether form uses screen fonts or printer fonts	
	Yes	Printer Fonts
	No	Screen Fonts
Fast Laser Printing	Prints rules instead of lines and rectangles (Yes/No)	
Help File	Name of compiled Help file to assign custom help to the form	
Help Context ID	ID of context-sensitive entry point in the help file to display	

Placing fields on the form

The next step is to place the necessary fields on the form. When you place a field on a form, it is called a *control* and is bound to another field (its *control source*). Therefore, you'll see the terms *control* and *field* used interchangeably in this chapter.

As you've learned, the process of placing controls on your form consists of three basic tasks:

✦ Display the Field List window by clicking on the Field List button on the toolbar.

✦ Click on the desired Toolbox control to determine the type of control that is created.

✦ Select each of the fields you want on your form and then drag them to the Form Design window.

Displaying the field list

To display the Field List window, click on the Field List button on the toolbar (the icon that looks like a list sheet). You can resize the Field List window and move it around. The enlarged window (illustrated in Figure 17-6) shows all the fields in the Pets and Owners query dynaset.

Notice, in Figure 17-6, that the fields Customer.Customer Number and Pets.Customer Number, as well as Customer.Last Visit Date and Pets.Last Visit Date, have the table name as a prefix. This prefix distinguishes fields of the same name that come from different tables within a query.

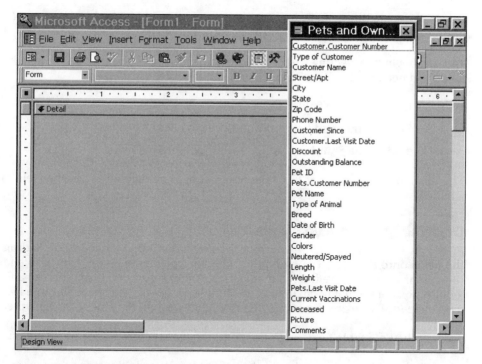

Figure 17-6: The Field List window.

You can move the Field List window simply by clicking on the title bar and dragging it to a new location. You can also select the <u>M</u>ove command from the window's control menu.

Selecting the fields for your form

Selecting a field in the Field List window is the same as selecting that field from a query field list. The easiest way to select a field is simply to click on it, which highlights it; then you can drag it to the Form window.

To highlight *contiguous* (adjacent) fields in the list, click on the first field you want in the field list, and then move the cursor to the last field you want; hold down the Shift key as you click on the last field. The block of fields between the first and last fields are displayed in reverse video as you select them. Drag the block to the Form window.

Tip   You can highlight noncontiguous fields in the list by clicking on each field while holding down the Ctrl key. Each field is then displayed in reverse video and can be dragged (as part of the group) to the Form Design window.

One way this method differs from using the query Field List is that you *cannot* double-click on a field to add it to the Form window.

You can begin by selecting the Pets table fields for the detail section. To select the fields you need for the Pets Data Entry form, follow these steps:

1. Click on the Pet ID field.

2. Scroll down the field list until the Deceased field is visible.

3. Hold down the Shift key and click on the Deceased field.

The block of fields from Pet ID to Deceased should be highlighted in the Field List window.

Dragging fields onto your form

After you select the proper fields from the Pets table, all you need to do is drag the fields onto the form. Depending on whether you choose one or several fields, the cursor changes to reflect your selection. If you select one field, you see a Field icon (a box containing text). If you select multiple fields, you see a Multiple Field icon instead. These are the cursor icons you've seen on the Query Design screens.

To drag the Pets table fields onto the Form Design window, follow these steps:

1. Click within the highlighted block of fields in the Field List window.

2. Without releasing the mouse button, drag the cursor onto the form, placing it under the 1½-inch mark on the horizontal ruler at the top of the screen and the ½-inch mark of the vertical ruler along the left edge.

3. Release the mouse button. The fields now appear in the form, as shown in Figure 17-7.

4. Close the Field List window by clicking on the Field List button on the toolbar.

Notice that there are two controls for each field you dragged onto the form. When you use the drag-and-drop method for placing fields, Access automatically creates a label control that uses the name of the field; it's attached to the text control that the field is bound to. If you followed along with Chapter 14 in this book, you changed the Customer Number field in the Pets table to a lookup field. Figure 17-7 shows this field displayed as a combo box (automatically because it is one of the properties changed in Chapter 14).

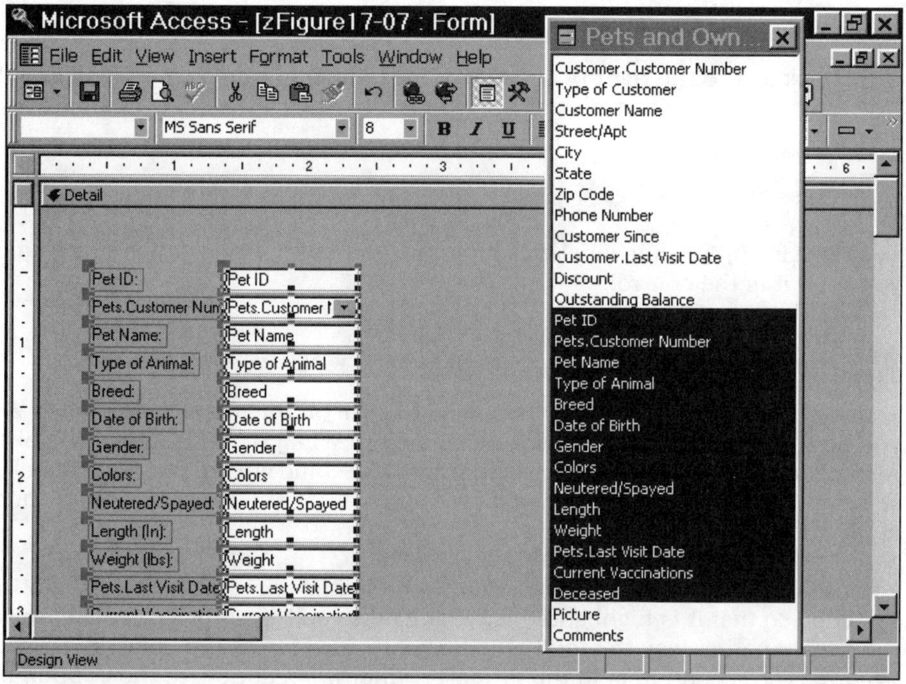

Figure 17-7: Dragging fields to the form.

Working with Label Controls and Text Box Controls

You've already seen how attached label controls are created automatically. With the Text Box button selected in the Toolbox, you drag a field from the Field List window to a form; this creates a text box control with an attached label control. Sometimes, however, you want to add text label controls by themselves to create headings or titles for the form.

Creating unattached labels

To create a new, unattached label control, you must use the Toolbox unless you copy an existing label. The next task in the example is to add the text header *Mountain Animal Hospital Pets Data Entry* to your form. This task is divided into segments to demonstrate adding and editing text. To create an unattached label control, follow these steps:

1. Display the Toolbox.

2. Click on the Label button in the Toolbox.

3. Click just to the right of and above the label that says Pet ID and drag the cursor to make a small rectangle about 3 inches long and ¼-inch high.

4. Type **Pets Data**.

5. Press Enter.

To create a multiple-line label entry, press Ctrl+Enter to force a line break where you want it in the control.

Modifying the text in a label or text control

To modify the text in a control, you need to click on the inside of the label. When you do this, the cursor changes to the standard Windows text cursor, an I-beam. Also notice that the Formatting toolbar icons become grayed out and cannot be selected. This is because within a label control — or any control — you cannot apply specific formatting to individual characters.

You can now make any edits you want to the text. If you drag across the entire selection so that it is highlighted, anything new you type replaces whatever is in this area. Another way to modify the text is to edit it from the control's Property window. The second item in the Property window is Caption. In the Caption property, you can also edit the contents of a text or label control (for a text control, this property is called *Control Source*) by clicking on the Edit box and typing new text. To edit the label so that it contains the proper text, follow these steps:

1. Click in front of the P in Pets Data in the label control.

2. Type **Mountain Animal Hospital -** before Pets Data.

3. Type **Entry** after Pets Data.

4. Press Enter.

If you want to edit or enter a caption that is longer than the space in the Property window, the contents will scroll as you type. Or you can press Shift+F2 to open a zoom box that gives you more space to type.

The Formatting toolbar

Access 97 for Windows 95 features a second toolbar known as the Formatting toolbar (described more fully in Chapter 18). Toolbars are really windows. You can move any toolbar by dragging it from its normal location to the middle of a form, and you can change its size and shape. Some toolbars can be docked to any edge of the screen (such as the left, right, or bottom). The Formatting toolbar can be docked only at the top or bottom of the screen.

The Formatting toolbar integrates objects from the Access 2.0 Form Design toolbar and the Palette. The first area of the Formatting toolbar (on the left side) selects a control or Form section, such as the Form or Page headers or footers, Detail, or the form itself. When you have multiple pages of controls and you want (for example) to select a control that's on page 3 or behind another control, this combo box makes it easy. The next few objects on the Formatting toolbar change text properties. Two more combo boxes let you change the font style and size. (Remember, you may have fonts others do not have. Do not use an exotic font if the user of your form does not have the font.) After the Font Style and Size combo boxes are icons for making a text control Bold, Italic, and Underlined. Beyond those are alignment icons for Left, Center, and Right text alignment. The last five pull-down icons change color properties, line types and styles, and special effects. See Chapter 18 for more complete descriptions.

Modifying the appearance of text in a control

To modify the appearance of text within a control, select the control by clicking on its border (not in it). You can then select a formatting style you want to apply to the label. Just click on the appropriate button on the toolbar. To add visual emphasis to the title, follow these steps:

1. Click on the newly created form heading label.
2. Click on the Bold button on the Formatting toolbar.
3. Click on the drop-down arrow of the Font-Size list box.
4. Select 14 from the Font-Size drop-down list.

The label control still needs to be resized to display all the text.

Sizing a text box control or label control

You can select a control by simply clicking on it. Depending on the size of the control, from three to seven sizing handles appear. One appears on each corner except the upper left, and one appears on each side. When you move the cursor over one of the sizing handles, the cursor changes into a double-headed arrow. When this happens, click on the control and drag it to the size you want. Notice that as you drag, an outline of the new size appears, indicating how large the label will be when you release the mouse button.

When you double-click on any of the sizing handles, Access usually resizes a control to a *best fit* for the text in the control. This is especially handy if you increase the font size and then notice that the text is cut off, either at the bottom or to the right. For label controls, note that this *best-fit sizing* adjusts the size vertically and horizontally, though text controls are resized only vertically. This is because when Access is in form design mode, it can't predict how much of a field you want to display — the field name and field contents can be radically different. Sometimes, however, label controls are not resized correctly and must be manually adjusted.

You see that the text no longer fits within the label control, but you can resize the text control to fit the enhanced font size. To do this, follow these steps:

1. Click on the `Mountain Animal Hospital - Pets Data Entry` label control.

2. Move the cursor over the control. Notice that the cursor changes as it moves over the sizing handles.

3. Double-click on one of the sizing handles.

The label control size may still need readjustment. If so, you can place the cursor in the bottom right corner of the control so that the diagonal arrow appears; then drag the control until it is the correct size. You will also need to move some of the controls down to make room for the label; you'll want to center it over the form. You can select all the controls and move them down using techniques you learned in the previous chapter.

You can also select Format⇨Size⇨to Fit to change the size of the label control text automatically.

As you create your form, you should test it constantly by selecting the Form button on the toolbar. Figure 17-8 shows the form in its current state of completion.

Now that you've dragged the Pets fields to the form design and added a form title, you can move the text box controls into the correct position. You then want to size each control to display the information properly within each field.

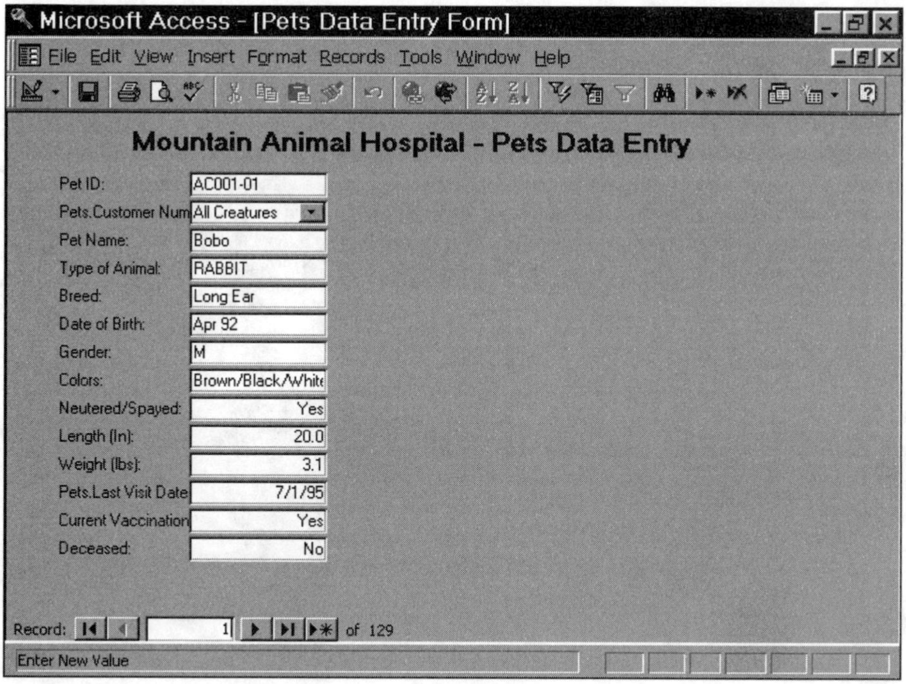

Figure 17-8: A form in progress.

Moving label and text controls

Before you move the label and text controls, it is important to remind you of a few differences between attached and unattached controls. When an attached label is created automatically with a text control, it is called a *compound control* — that is, whenever one control in the set is moved, the other control in the set is also moved.

To move both controls in a compound control, select one of the pair by clicking anywhere on it. Move the cursor over either of the objects. When the cursor turns into a hand, you can click on the controls and drag them to their new location.

Place the controls in their proper position to complete the form design and layout, as shown in Figure 17-9. Notice that the Gender control has its label moved to a position above the text box control and that some of the text labels are updated. Remember that you can do this by selecting the attached label control and then using the Move handle to move only the label. Also notice that some formatting is added, as you'll do in the next section.

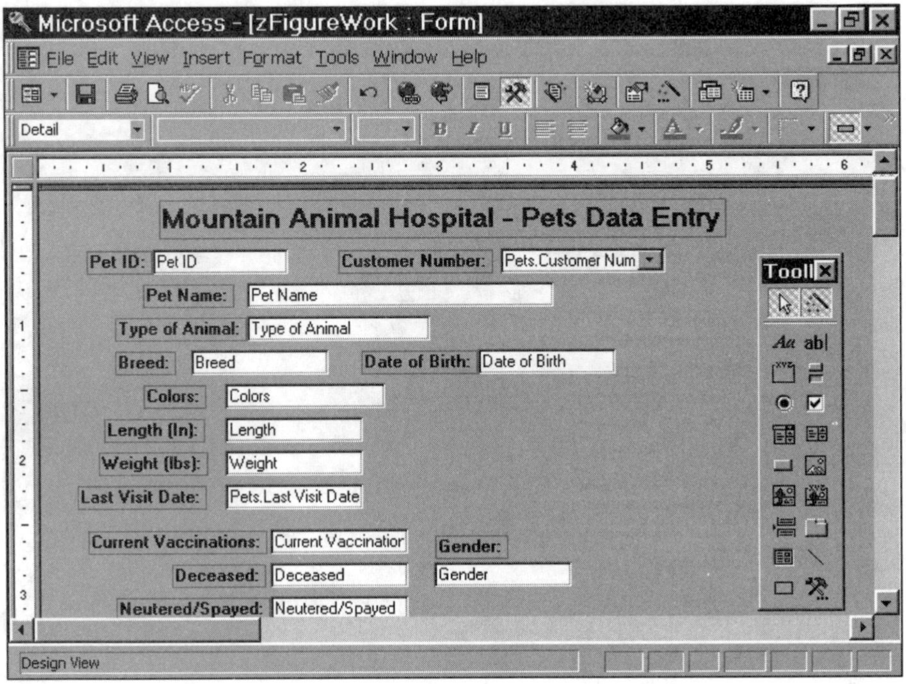

Figure 17-9: Selected and resized label controls in the Detail section.

Modifying the appearance of multiple controls

The next step is to make all the label controls in the form bold. This helps you differentiate between label controls and text controls; some of them currently have the same text. The following steps guide you in this process:

1. Select all the attached label controls in the form by clicking on them individually while holding down the Shift key. There are 14 label controls to select, as shown in Figure 17-9.

2. Click on the Bold button on the toolbar.

3. Select Format⇨Size⇨to Fit to resize all the labels.

You cannot select the label controls in the steps given here if you use the drag-and-surround method and drag the rectangle through the text boxes. That method also selects all the text boxes; you want only to bold and resize the labels.

If you run the form now, you notice that the Length, Width, and Last Visit Date data items are all right-aligned within the text controls. You want to left-align these controls so that values appear left-aligned next to the label. To make this change, follow these steps:

1. Select the Length, Weight, and Pets. Last Visit Date text box controls only; use the cursor to draw a box around the three text box controls.

2. Click on the Left Align button on the toolbar.

Changing the control type

You may notice, in Figure 17-9, that the Customer Number field is a combo box (the default control type you defined in the table using the Lookup Wizard). Though there are times you may want to use a lookup field to display related data, this is not one of those times. In this example, you will need to see the Customer Number for each Pet, not the Customer Name (you'll deal with displaying the Customer information later in this chapter). For now, use these steps to turn the combo box back into an edit box control:

1. Select the Customer Number field.

2. Select Format⇨Change To⇨Edit Box to change the control type.

Setting the tab order

Now that you've completed moving all your controls into position, you should test the form again. If you run the form and press Tab to move from field to field, you notice that the cursor does not move from field to field in the order you expect. It starts out in the first field, Pet ID, and then continues vertically from field to field until it reaches the Date of Birth field. Then the cursor jumps down to Gender, back up to Colors, and then down again to Neutered/Spayed. This route may seem strange, but that is the original order in which the fields were added to the form.

This is called the *tab order* of the form. The form's *default tab order* is always the order in which the fields were added to the form. If you don't plan to move the fields around, this is all right. If you do move the fields around, however, you may want to change the order. After all, though you may make heavy use of the mouse when designing your forms, the average data-entry person still uses the keyboard to move from field to field.

When you need to change the tab order of a form, select the View⇨Tab Order. . . menu option in the Design window to change the order to match your layout. To change the tab order of the form, follow the next set of steps (make sure that you are in the Design window before continuing):

1. Select View⇨Tab Order. . . .

2. Click on the Gender row in the Tab Order dialog box.

3. Click on the gray area in front of the Gender row again; drag the row to the bottom of the dialog box to a point below the Deceased row, as shown in Figure 17-10.

4. Click on the Neutered/Spayed row in the dialog box.

5. Click on the Neutered/Spayed row again; drag the row to the bottom of the dialog box between the Deceased and Gender rows.

6. Click on the OK button to complete the task.

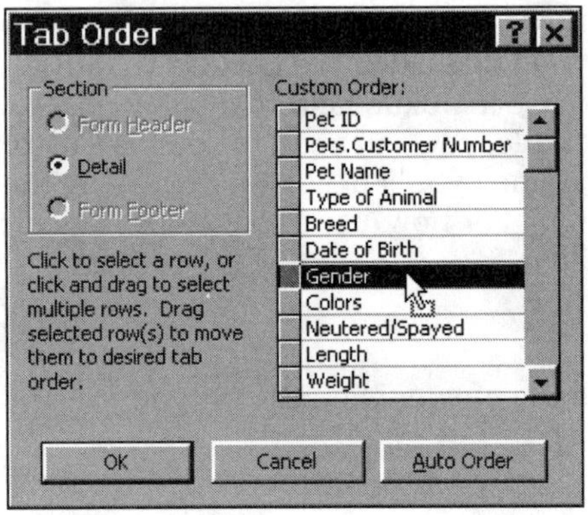

Figure 17-10: The Tab Order dialog box.

The Tab Order dialog box lets you select either one row or multiple rows at a time. You can select multiple contiguous rows by clicking on the first row and then dragging down to select multiple rows. After the rows are highlighted, you can drag the selected rows to their new positions.

The Tab Order dialog box has several buttons at the bottom of the box. The Auto Order button places the fields in order from left to right and from top to bottom, according to their position in the form. This button is a good place to start when you have significantly rearranged the fields.

Each control has two properties that interact with this screen. The Tab Stop property determines whether pressing the Tab key will land you on the field. The default is Yes; changing the Tab Stop property to No removes the field from the tab order. When you set the tab order, you set the Tab Index property controls. In this example, the first field (Pet ID) is set to 1, Customer Number is set to 2, and so on. Moving the fields around in the Tab Order dialog box will change the Tab Index properties of those (and other) fields.

Adding multiple-line text box controls for Memo fields

Multiple-line text box controls are used for Memo data types such as the Comments field in the Pets table. When you add a Memo field to a form, make sure that there is plenty of room in the text box control to enter a large amount of text. You have several ways to make certain that you've allowed enough space.

The first method is to resize the text box control until it's large enough to accommodate any text you may enter into the Memo field, but this is rarely possible. Usually the reason you create a Memo field is to hold a large amount of text; that text can easily take up more space than the entire form.

One of the options in a text box control is a vertical scrollbar. By adding scrollbars to the your Memo field's text box control, you can allow for any size of data entry. To create a Memo field text box control, follow these steps:

1. Display the Field List window.

2. Drag the Comments field to the bottom left corner of the form below the Neutered/Spayed field.

3. Select the Comments label control and click on the Bold button on the toolbar.

4. Resize the Comments text box control so that the bottom of the control is about ½-inch high, and put the right side of the control just past the right side of the Gender text box control (as shown in Figure 17-11).

5. Close the Field List window.

The Comments text box will, by default, display a vertical scrollbar if the text in the box is larger than the display area. If you do not want to display a scrollbar, you can select the Scrollbar property in the Data sheet of the Property window and turn it off.

Figure 17-11 shows the added control.

When you run the form, the scrollbar appears only once when you move into the Comments Memo field.

Adding a bound object frame to the form

When you drag a field that uses the OLE data type to a form, Access creates a bound object frame automatically. You can resize and move this control, just as you can move any control. To add the Picture OLE field to the form, follow these steps:

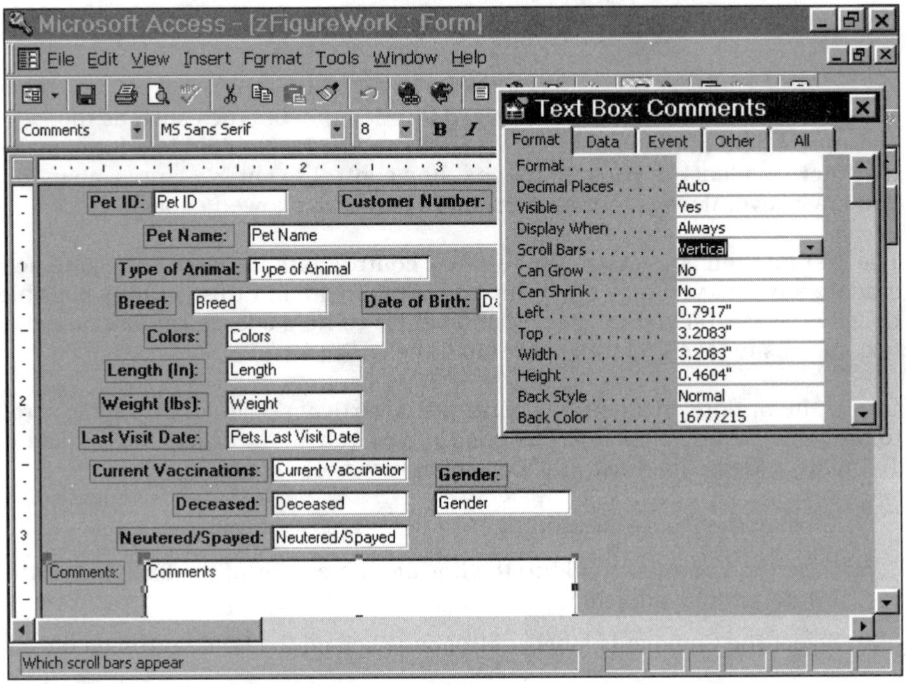

Figure 17-11: Adding a multiple-line text box control.

1. Display the Field List window.

2. Drag the Picture field to the center right area of the form.

3. Select the Picture attached label control by clicking on the small solid box in the top left corner of the text area.

4. Press Delete to delete the attached label control.

5. Move the left edge of the bound object frame just to the right of the Comments text box.

Note One problem you may sometimes have when adding controls is that their default size exceeds the form's borders. When this happens, you must resize the control and also resize the border. If you don't resize the border, you'll find that the form becomes scrollable outside the normal screen boundaries. This may work, but it doesn't create a well-displayed form. To resize the bound object frame control and the form's border, follow these steps:

1. Select the Picture bound object frame.

2. Resize the control so that the right edge is just inside the original form border at 6⅛ inches on the top border. As you resize the control, you can follow the illustration in Figure 17-12.

3. Resize the form borders to make sure that they are at 6¹/₄ inches and 3³/₄ inches.

When you're done, the design should look like Figure 17-12. Before you complete the OLE field, there is one more task to perform. The default value for the Size Mode property of a bound object frame is Clip. This means that a picture displayed within the frame is shown in its original size and truncated to fit within the frame. In this example, you need to display the picture so that it fits completely within the frame. Two property settings let you do this:

Zoom   Keeps picture in its original proportion; may result in extra white space

Stretch Sizes picture to fit exactly into the frame borders

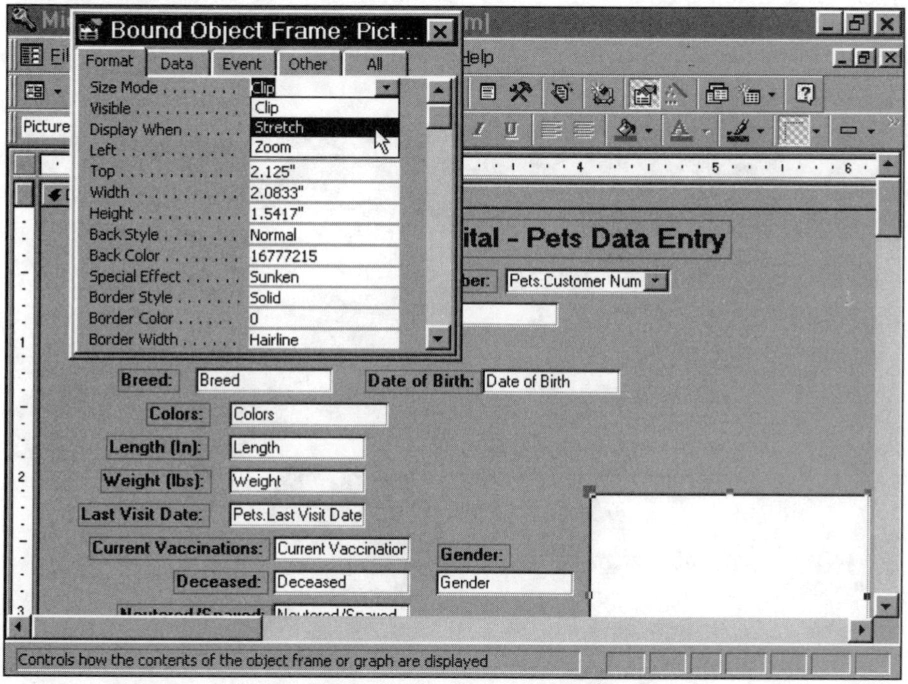

Figure 17-12: Adding an OLE field in a bound object frame control.

Although the Zoom setting displays the picture more correctly, the Stretch setting looks better, unless the picture's proportions are important to viewing the data. To set the Size Mode property of a bound object frame, follow these steps:

1. Select the Picture bound object frame.

2. Display the Property window.

3. Select the Size Mode property.

4. Select Stretch.

Figure 17-12 shows the form design as it currently is completed. Notice the Property window for the bound object frame control. The Size Mode property is set to Stretch.

When you complete this part of the design, you should save the form and then display it. You can now name this form **Pets Data Entry** if you want. Figure 17-13 shows the form.

So far, you've created a blank form and added several types of controls to the form, but only fields from the Pets table are on the form; originally, you created a query that linked the Pets and Customer tables. The Customer table can serve as a lookup table for each Pet record. This allows you to display customer information for each pet.

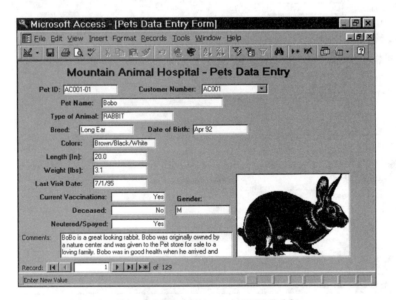

Figure 17-13: The form with a Memo and OLE field.

Creating a Form Using Multiple Tables

When you create a form from a single table, you simply use fields from the one table. When you create a form from multiple tables, normally you use fields from a second table as lookup fields; they let you display additional information. In this section, you learn how to display the customer information.

Adding fields from a second table

You now add the fields from a second table. You want to add the fields to be displayed in the Pets form from the Customer table. These fields will display the customer name and address along with the Type of Customer field. You place these fields in the upper right portion of the form. Follow these steps to add the customer fields to the form:

1. Display the Field List window.

2. Click on the Type of Customer field.

3. Hold down the Shift key and click on the Phone Number field.

4. Click within the highlighted block of fields in the Field List window.

5. Without releasing the mouse button, drag the cursor to the form under the 5-inch mark on the ruler at the top of the screen and the 0.5-inch mark of the ruler along the left edge.

At this point, your form should look like Figure 17-14. You've now placed all the fields needed for the Pets Data Entry form. You may have to adjust some of the other fields to make it look correct.

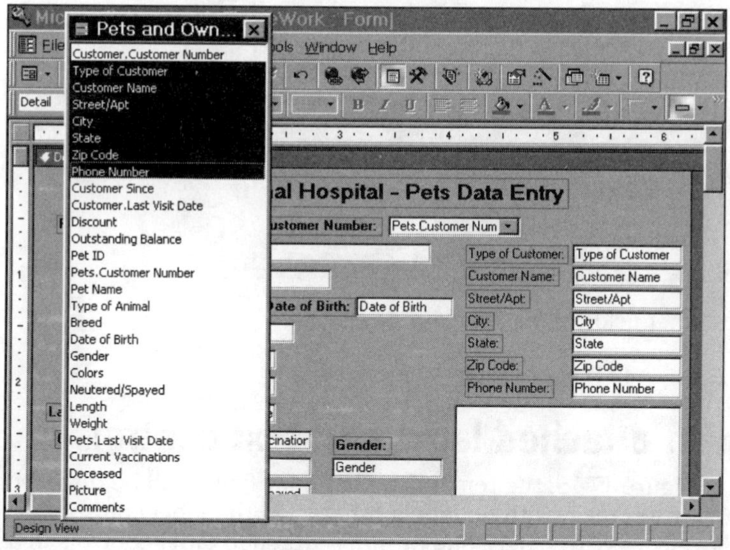

Figure 17-14: Adding the Customer fields.

As you can see in Figure 17-14, the form begins with the Type of Customer field. Actually, you want that field separated from the others (you'll change it to a calculated field later). Use Figure 17-15 as a guide for the final placement of the field.

To move the Type of Customer control below the other customer controls, follow these steps:

1. Deselect all the selected controls by clicking on any empty area of the form.

2. Select just the Type of Customer text box control and its attached label.

3. Move the control just below the Phone Number control so that it's just above the Picture bound object frame control.

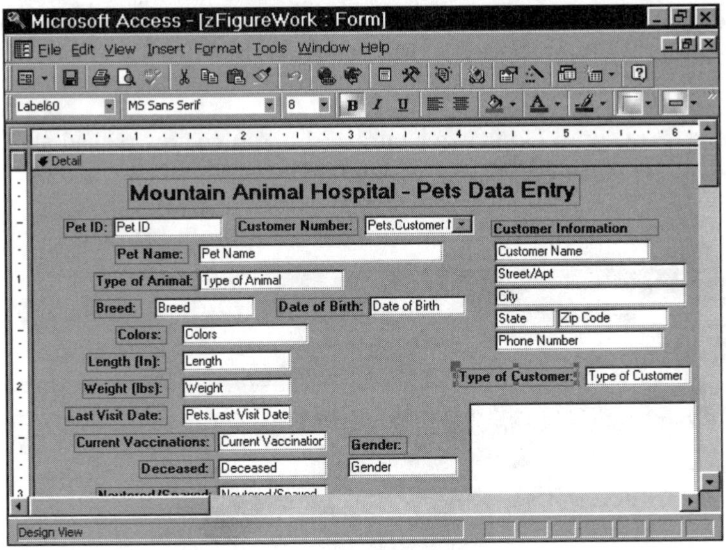

Figure 17-15: Customer fields in the Pets form.

Working with attached label and text controls

As you can see in Figure 17-15, the remaining customer fields will be displayed in a very small area of the screen, with no labels other than the label control Customer Information. It is very easy to delete one or more attached label controls in a form. You simply select the desired label control (or controls) and press Delete. When you delete attached controls, you have two choices:

✦ Delete only the label control.

✦ Delete both the label control and the field control.

If you select the label control and press Delete, only the label control is deleted. If you select the field control and press Delete, both the label control and the field control are deleted. To delete only the Customer label controls (that is, the attached label controls), follow these steps:

1. Draw a box that surrounds only the six label controls from Customer Name through Phone Number.

2. Verify that only the label controls are selected (sizing handles are displayed in all the label controls; only the Move handle is displayed in the text box controls).

3. Press Delete.

If you want to delete the field control yet keep the attached label control, you can do this by first selecting the label control and selecting Edit⇨Copy. Then select the field control and press Delete to delete both the field control and the label control. Finally, choose Edit⇨Paste to paste the copied label control to the form.

As you learned in Chapter 16, you can attach a label to an unlabeled control by cutting the unattached label control and then pasting it onto another control.

The final task is to move the customer controls to their final positions and add a label control, as shown in Figure 17-15. Follow these steps to complete this part of the form:

1. Rearrange the controls in the page header to resemble a typical mailing label's address format with State and Zip Code on the same line.

2. Move the Phone Number text box control under the State and Zip Code text box controls.

3. Move the block of name, address, and phone number controls into position so that it resembles Figure 17-15. Notice that all the control lines need to touch one another.

   You can use the new Format⇨Vertical Spacing⇨Make Equal option to line up all the controls above each other. If there is still space between them, use the Decrease option.

4. Create a label control with the text **Customer Information**, as shown in Figure 17-15.

Creating a calculated field

The field Type of Customer is a numeric field that displays a 1 if the customer is an individual, 2 if the customer is a pet store, and 3 if the customer is a bird sanctuary, aquarium, or municipal zoo. Rather than have the number displayed, you can transform the value into a more recognizable text expression.

The easiest way to do this is to replace the original Type of Customer control with a calculated expression. In Chapter 13, you used the function called the Immediate IF function (IIf) that lets you transform one value to another. In this example, the expression uses two IIf functions together.

The expression must transform the value of 1 to "Individual," the value of 2 to "Pet Store," and the value of 3 to "Zoo." This is the complete expression:

```
=IIf([Type of Customer]=1,"Individual",IIf([Type of
        Customer]=2,"Pet Store","Zoo"))
```

The first IIf function checks the value of the Type of Customer field; if the value is 1, the value of the calculated control is set to Individual. If the value is not 1, another IIf checks to see whether the value of Type of Customer is 2. If the value is 2, the value of the calculated control is set to Pet Store. If not 2, the value of the calculated control is set to the only other possibility, which is Zoo. To create this new calculated control, follow these steps:

1. Select the Type of Customer text box control.

2. Display the Property window and select the Other sheet by clicking on the Other tab.

3. Change the Name property to Calculated Type of Customer.

4. Click on the Control Source property and press Shift+F2 to display the zoom box.

5. In the Control Source property, type the following:

   =IIf([Type of Customer]=1,"Individual",IIf([Type of Customer]=2,"Pet Store","Zoo"))

6. Click on OK.

7. Close the Property window.

Note   The Lookup Wizard for Access 97 helps you create a control to display a different value from the value used in the control. You could use the Lookup Wizard in the Customer table and build a combo box to display Individual, Pet Store, or Zoo but store the values 1, 2, or 3. You will create an option group in Chapter 19, but this method is better for now.

Now that the form is complete, you can test it. Run the form and observe that the customer information is now displayed as you see the third record in Figure 17-16.

Changing the updatability of a multiple-table form

If you run the form you just created, you may notice that you can edit the existing pet data or even add new pet records. As you enter a new pet's valid customer number, the customer information is filled in automatically. You can, however, change the customer information. This information is being looked up in the customer table. Since it can affect all records for this customer, you don't want to allow changes to the information fields.

To prevent changes to the customer information fields, use the Locked property. Select all the fields under Customer information. Change the Locked property, found on the Data sheet of the Property window, to Yes.

You must remember that by updating a field such as Customer Name (which is on the *one* side of a one-to-many relationship), you change the one data field in the Customer table that changes a value for all records of pets owned by that customer.

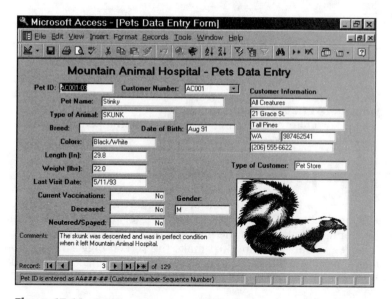

Figure 17-16: The Pets Data Entry form with customer information.

Figure 17-17 shows the Locked property being changed to Yes for the Customer information in the Pets Data Entry form.

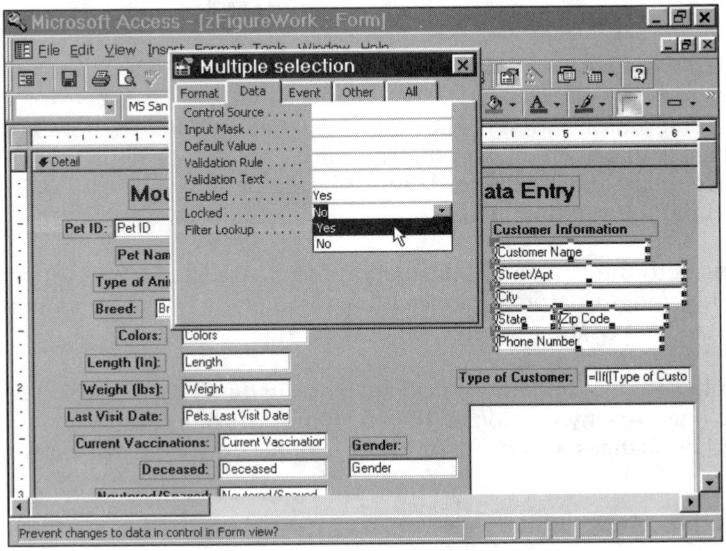

Figure 17-17: Locking the customer data from changes.

You should save this form with all the changes currently made. Name the form **Pets Data Entry Form - Without Formatting**. You use this form later in the chapter and again in the next few chapters, starting with the form in its current state.

Creating a Multiple-Page Form

Suppose that you want to add more information to the form. There is little room to add more fields or labels, but you may want to see a larger picture of the animal and to see all the comments at once in the multiple-line text box. Without getting a larger form, you can't do that. You can't just make the screen bigger unless you change to a higher screen resolution, which means getting the necessary hardware. One solution is to create a *multiple-page form*.

Why use multiple-page forms?

You use multiple-page forms when all your information won't fit on one page or when you want to segregate specific information on separate pages. Multiple-page forms allow you to display less information on a page so that a complicated form looks less cluttered. You can also place data items that are not always necessary on the second (or even the third) page, which makes data entry on the first page easier for the user.

Changing defaults for attached label positioning

Attached label controls are called compound controls because the two controls are attached. Sometimes you want to disable this feature, which you can do by changing a default property named AutoLabel. When AutoLabel is set to Yes, a label control is automatically created that bears the name of the field the text control is bound to. With AutoLabel in effect, a label is created automatically every time you drag a field onto a form. Follow these steps to change the AutoLabel default:

1. Display the Toolbox if it is not already displayed.

2. Display the Property window if it is not already displayed.

3. Click on the Text Box button on the toolbar. The title of the Property window should be Default Text Box.

4. Scroll down until you see the AutoLabel property.

5. Click on the AutoLabel text box.

6. Change the contents in the text box to No.

The next property, AutoColon, automatically follows any text in a new label with a colon if the value of the property is set to Yes.

Two properties control where the label appears relative to the control itself. These are the Label X and Label Y properties. Label X controls the horizontal position of the label control relative to the text box control. The default is −1 (to the left of the text box control). As you make the value a smaller negative number, as with .5, you decrease the space from the attached label to the control. If you want the label after the control (as you may for an option button), you use a positive number, such as 1.5, to move the label to the right of the control.

Label Y controls the vertical position of the label control relative to the text box control. The default is 0, which places the label on the same line as the text box control. If you want to place the label above the control, change Label Y to −1 or a larger negative number. The last option, Label Align, lets you control the alignment of the text within the label.

If you changed the AutoLabel default to No and you now drag fields from the Field List window to the form, you see no label controls attached. The AutoLabel property is in effect for only this form. Because you don't need to add further labeled fields to this form, you can leave the setting of AutoLabel as No.

You can have as many pages as you need on a form, but the general rule is that more than five pages make the form very tedious. There is also a 22-inch size limitation in the form. You can use a macro to attach other forms to buttons on the form; then you can call up the other pages as you need them by selecting a button.

After you add pages to a form, you can move between them by using the PgUp and PgDn keys or you can use macros or Visual Basic for Applications to program navigation keys.

You can create a multiple-page form only when the Default View property of the form is set to Single Form.

Adding a page break

You can add *page breaks* to a form by adding a Page Break control (which you can find third from the bottom left of the Toolbox). Use Figure 17-18 as a guide as you change the Pets Data Entry form to add a separate page for resized Picture and Comments controls.

Follow these steps to add a new page and a page break:

1. Increase the bottom margin of the form to 7½ inches.
2. Move and resize the Comments text box control, as shown in Figure 17-18.
3. Move and resize the Picture text box control.
4. Select the Pet Name text box control in the upper area of the control, and then select Edit⇨Copy.
5. Select Edit⇨Paste and move the copy to the second page of the form.
6. Display the Toolbox.
7. Click on the Page Break button in the Toolbox.
8. Move the cursor to the left corner of the intersection of the two pages (3¼ inches).
9. Click on the mouse to add the page break.

Figure 17-18 shows the completed design.

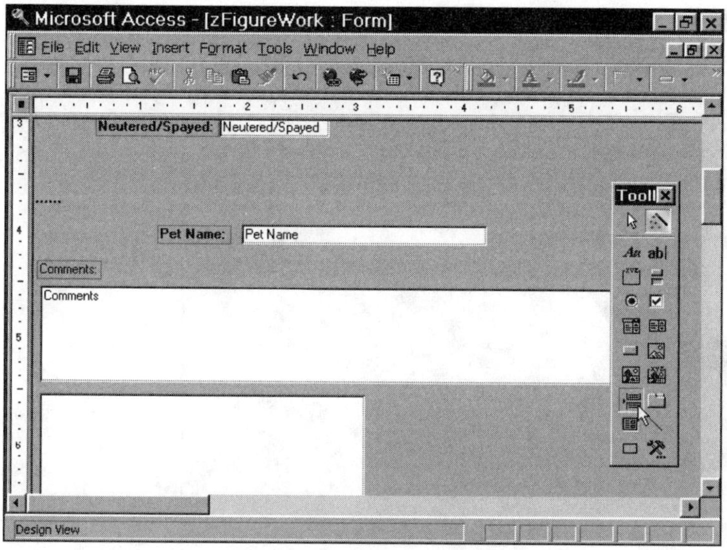

Figure 17-18: Adding a new page and a page break.

Notice that you copied `Pet Name` into the second page. This was for display-only purposes. Unless you change the properties of the second Pet Name control, you can also edit its value. When working with forms that require multiple pages, you may want to place controls that are used as headers in a form header section. If you are working with numeric data, you may also want to add a form footer section to display totals.

Figure 17-19 shows the second page of the form for the first record in the table.

You should not save this last set of changes to create a multiple-page form. Reopen the form you saved as Pets Data Entry Form - Without Formatting.

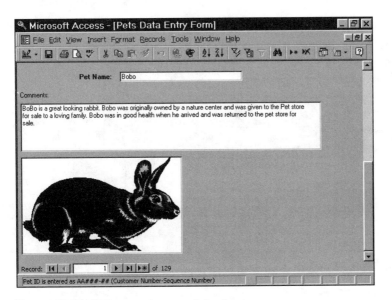

Figure 17-19: The second page of the form.

Using Form and Page Headers and Footers

The most common use of a page or form header is to repeat identification information. In the Pets Data Entry form, for example, the text header is part of the form itself. When you have a second page, you don't see the text header. In Access forms, you can add both form and page sections. Sections include *headers* (which come before the detail controls) and *footers* (which come after the detail controls).

The different types of headers and footers

Several types of headers and footers can appear in a form:

Form header	Displayed at the top of each page when viewed and at the top when the form is printed
Page header	Displayed only when the form is printed; prints after the form header
Page footer	Appears only when the form is printed; prints before the form footer
Form footer	Displayed at the bottom of each page when viewed and at the bottom of the form when the form is printed

Form headers and footers are displayed in the form; you can use them optionally in a printed form. *Page headers and footers* are displayed only when a form is printed. Generally, unless you are printing the form as a report, you won't use the page headers or footers. Because you can create reports easily in Access (and even save a form as a report), you won't find much use for page headers and footers.

Creating a form header and footer

You create form headers and footers by selecting View⇨Form Header/Footer. When you select this menu option, both the form header and form footer sections are added to the form.

You can add page headers and footers by selecting View⇨Page Header/Footer.

To create a form header and move the text header label control into it, follow the next steps:

1. Open the original Pets Data Entry Form - Without Formatting form in Design view.

2. Select View⇨Form Header/Footer to display the form header and footer.

3. Select the label control `Mountain Animal Hospital - Pets Data Entry`.

4. Move the label control straight up from the detail section to the form header section.

5. Resize the form header to fit the label control properly, as shown in Figure 17-20.

6. Close the form footer area by dragging the form footer bottom border to meet the top border.

Sometimes, when you display a form with an added header or footer, you lose that much space from the detail section. You must adjust the size of your detail section to compensate for this space.

In this example, you might need to make the height of the detail section smaller because you moved the text label control to the form header section and moved the other controls up in the detail section. You are not using the form footer section; you'll need to close it.

You change the size of a section by placing the cursor on the bottom border of the section, where it turns into a two-headed arrow. Then drag the section border up or down. You can only drag a section up to the bottom of the lowest control in the section.

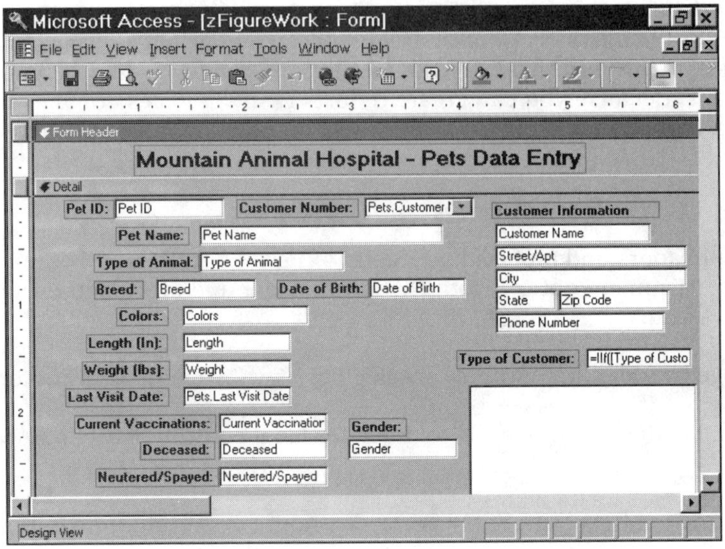

Figure 17-20: Adding a form header.

When you display a form with a header or footer section, you see the sections separated from the detail section by a line. The form headers and footers are literally anchored in place. If you create a scrollable or a multiple-page form, the headers and footers remain where they are while the data in the detail section moves.

After you have completed the form, you should save it.

Printing a Form

You can print a form by selecting the File⇨Print option and entering the desired information in the Print dialog box. Printing a form is like printing anything; you are in a WYSIWYG environment, so what you see on the form is essentially what you get in the printed hard copy. If you added page headers or page footers, you see them at the top or bottom of the printout.

You can also preview the printout by selecting the File⇨Print Preview menu option. This displays a preview of the printed page, as shown in Figure 17-21.

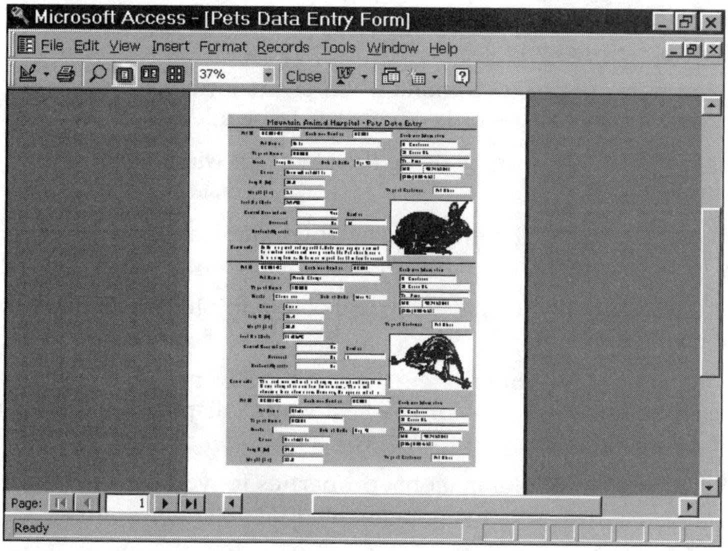

Figure 17-21: A preview of a form.

Converting a Form to a Report

By right-clicking on a form name in the Database window and selecting Save As Report, you can save the form design as a report. The entire form is placed in the report form. If the form has form headers or footers, these are placed in the report header and report footer sections. If the form has page headers or page footers, these are placed in the page header and footer sections in the report. After the design is in the Report Design window, you can enhance it by using the report design features. This allows you to add group sections and additional totaling in a report without having to re-create a great layout!

Summary

In this chapter, you learned how to create several types of forms without Form Wizards.

✦ When you create a form, you can adjust the form size by grabbing the borders and moving them.

✦ The Caption form property changes the text on the title bar.

✦ The Views Allowed form property lets you determine whether the user can switch to the Datasheet view.

✦ The Default View form property determines whether the form can display more than one record at a time.

✦ The Editing form properties determine whether the form is read-only and whether it allows only new records or records to be added, edited, or deleted.

✦ You can place fields on a form by using the Field List window and the Toolbox.

✦ The tab order determines the direction in which the cursor moves within a data-entry form. You can change this order by selecting View⇨Tab Order. . . .

✦ Memo fields are generally displayed by use of a multiple-line text box control with a scrollbar.

✦ Generally, picture fields (which can be OLE objects or non-OLE bitmaps) are displayed in a bound object frame. The best way to display a picture is to set the Scaling control property to either Stretch or Zoom.

✦ The AutoLabel and AutoColumn global properties let you determine where the labels, if any, appear when you create an attached label control.

✦ You can create a multiple-page form with the Page Break control.

✦ Page headers and footers appear only on the printed form.

✦ Form headers and footers appear at the top and bottom of each page in the form.

✦ You can print (or preview) a form by using the options on the File menu.

✦ You can save a form as a report design and later modify it by right-clicking on a form name in the Database window and selecting Save As Report.

In the next chapter, you learn how to add special effects to your forms. These include colors, background shading, and other enhancements such as lines, rectangles, and three-dimensional appearance.

✦   ✦   ✦

Creating Great-Looking Forms

In Chapter 17, you built a form that started with a blank Form Design screen. That form had no special formatting other than some label and text box controls. The most exciting object on the form was the picture of the rabbit. By using the various formatting windows and the Formatting toolbar, the line and rectangle controls, background pictures, and your own imagination, you can create great-looking forms with a small amount of work.

In this chapter, you learn how to format the data-entry form. You enhance the form you created in the preceding chapter, making it more readable and more presentable.

Making a Good Form Look Great

The Access form designer has the capability to do with a form what any good desktop publishing package can do with words. Just as a desktop publishing package can enhance a word-processing document to make it more readable, the form designer can enhance a database form to make it more usable.

To make your database form more usable, you can draw attention to areas of the form you want the reader to notice. Just as a headline in a newspaper calls your attention to the news, an enhanced section of a form makes the information it contains stand out.

The Access form designer gives you a number of tools to make the form controls and sections visually striking:

+ Lines and rectangles
+ Color and background shading
+ Three-dimensional effects (raised, sunken, etched, chiseled, shadowed)

✦ Background pictures

✦ Form headers and footers

In this chapter, you enhance the form you created earlier; you add special text features to create shading, shadows, lines, rectangles, and three-dimensional effects. Figure 18-1 shows the form as it appears after some special effects have been added.

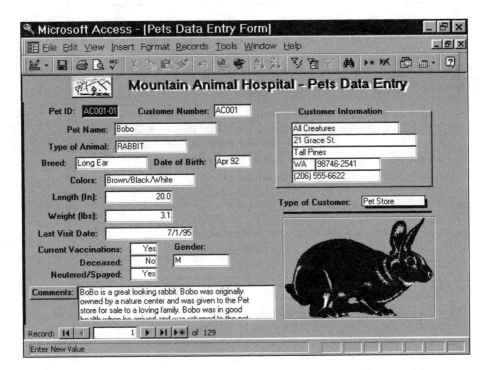

Figure 18-1: An enhanced form.

Understanding WYSIWYG

Access has a WYSIWYG (what-you-see-is-what-you-get) form designer. As you create your controls on-screen, you see instantly what they look like in your form. If you want to see what the data will look like during the form-design process, the on-screen preview mode lets you see the actual data in your form design without using a hard-copy device.

The Access form designer lets you add color and shading to your form text and controls. You can also display them in reverse video, which shows white letters on a black background. You can even color or shade the background of form sections. As you specify these effects, you see each change instantly on the Design screen.

Using the formatting windows and toolbar

Some of the most important controls for enhancing a form are the formatting windows and the Formatting toolbar. There are five formatting windows, including:

✦ Fill/Background color for shading

✦ Font/Foreground color for text

✦ Line/Border Color for lines, rectangles, and control borders

✦ Line/Border Width for lines, rectangles, and control borders

✦ Special Effect, such as raised, sunken, etched, chiseled, or shadowed

Note The Formatting toolbar can be displayed or removed from the screen by selecting View⇨Toolbars and (respectively) either selecting Formatting or right-clicking on the toolbar area and selecting Formatting. Figure 18-2 shows the Formatting toolbar (the third one from the top) and the five formatting windows pulled off the bar and opened. These windows can be used to format the different controls in a form.

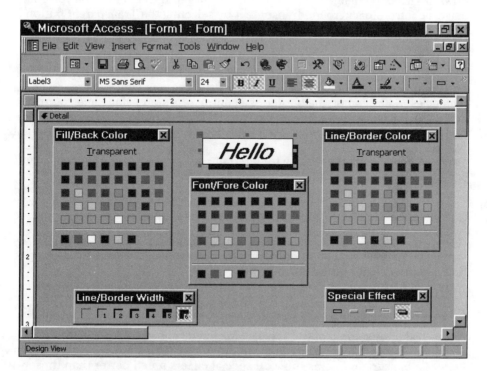

Figure 18-2: The various formatting windows.

Tip You can tell the selected color in the three color icons (background, foreground, and border) by looking at the small rectangle in each picture icon.

You modify the appearance of a control by using a formatting window. To modify the appearance of a control, select it by clicking on it, and then click on one of the formatting windows you need in order to change the control's options. (Refer back to Figure 18-2 to see all five formatting windows.)

Tip A *formatting window* is a window like the Toolbox or the Field List. You can move a formatting window around the screen, but you cannot anchor it the way you can dock a toolbar to a window border. To open the window and place it on the surface, you click on one of the formatting tool icons and then click on the title bar and drag it to where you want it. A formatting window can remain on-screen all the time; you can use it to change the options for one or more controls. To close a formatting window, you click on the Close button or reselect its icon on the Formatting toolbar.

The Font/Fore Color (foreground text) and Fill/Back Color (background color) windows are used to change the color of the text or background of a control. You can make a control's background transparent by selecting the <u>T</u>ransparent button in the Fill/Back Color window. The Line/Border Color window changes the color of control borders, lines, and rectangles. When you click on the <u>T</u>ransparent button in the Line/Border Color window, the border on any selected control becomes invisible.

The Line/Border Width window controls the thickness of control borders, lines, and rectangles. A line can be the border of a control or a stand-alone line control. You define the thickness of the line by using the thickness buttons. Available thicknesses (in points) are hairline, 1 point, 2 points, 3 points, 4 points, 5 points, and 6 points.

There is also a control property to determine the line type; the choices include solid line, dashed line, and dotted line.

Note A *point* (approximately $1/72$ inch) is a unit of measurement for character height.

When you're finished with a formatting window, you can close it by clicking on the X in its upper right corner.

Creating special effects

Figure 18-3 shows some of the special effects you can create easily for controls by using the Special Effect formatting window. In the figure, you see that controls with gray as a background color show off special effects much better than those with white. In fact, a form background in gray or a dark color is almost mandatory to make certain special effects easy to see. The following sections describe each of these effects; you'll apply some of them later to modify the Pets Data Entry form.

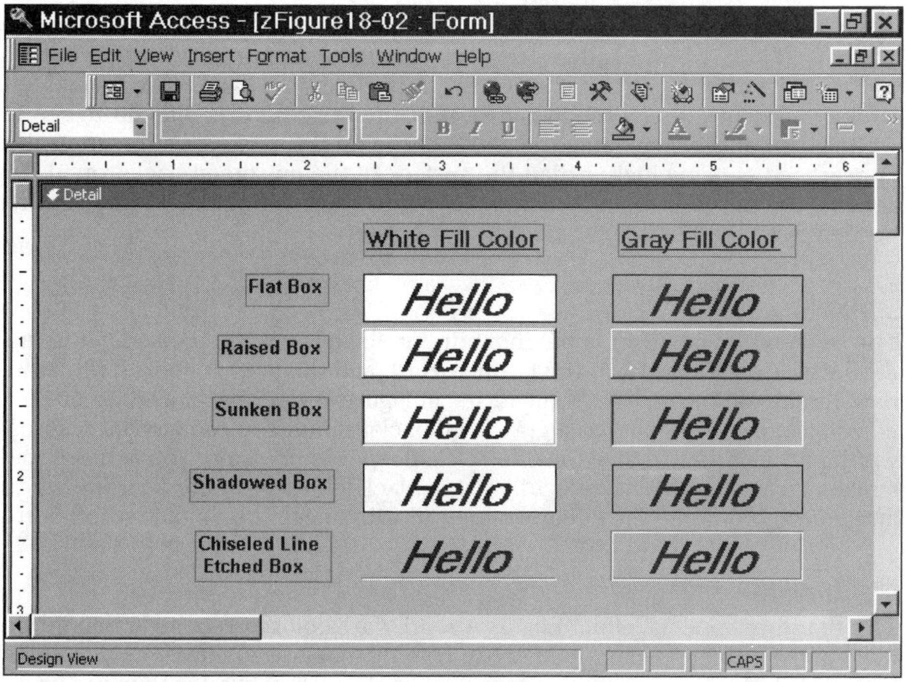

Figure 18-3: Special effects.

Special effects can be applied to rectangles, label controls, text box controls, check boxes, option buttons, and option group boxes. Anything that has a box or circle around it can be raised, sunken, etched, chiseled, or shadowed. Figure 16-5 showed special effects applied to check boxes and option buttons.

By simply selecting the control and adding the special effect, you can make your forms look much better and draw attention to their most important areas.

Flat

In Figure 18-3, you see a pair of label boxes created without any special effect. As you can see in the figure, the flat box stands out better when set against the gray background.

Tip You can also use the Border Width window to increase the width of the border lines, which makes the box more prominent. The Border Color window lets you change the color of the box. A thick white box also stands out.

Raised

The raised box is best used to set off a rectangle that surrounds other controls, or for label controls. This box gives the best effect in a dark color against a dark background. As you can see in Figure 18-3, the raised box is difficult to see with a white fill color. By increasing the width of the box, you can give the control an appearance of being higher than the surface of the on-screen background. You achieve the raised three-dimensional effect by contrasting the white left and top borders with the black right and bottom borders.

Sunken

The sunken special effect is the most dramatic and most often used. (It is the standard Windows 95 format in the Form Wizard, and the default control format in the new version of Access.) As you can see in Figure 18-3, either the white or the gray fill color looks very good on a gray form background. You can also increase the width of the border to give the effect of a deeper impression. You achieve the sunken three-dimensional effect by using black left and top borders and white right and bottom borders. The effect works well with check boxes and option buttons.

Shadowed

The shadowed special effect places a solid, dark-colored rectangle behind the original control, which is slightly offset to give the shadowed effect. As you can see in Figure 18-3, the black shadow works well behind a box filled with white or gray. You can change the border color to change the shadow color.

Etched

The etched effect is perhaps the most interesting of all the special looks. It is, in effect, a sunken rectangle with no sunken inside area. Windows 95 makes heavy use of etched rectangles.

Chiseled

The chiseled effect adds a chiseled line underneath a selected control.

In this chapter, you modify the form you created in Chapter 17 so it looks like Figure 18-1. If you are using Microsoft Access as you follow along in this book, you should have the form named `Pets Data Entry Form - Without Formatting` open in the Form Design window.

Changing the forms background color

If you are usually going to view your form on-screen instead of printing it, it may be beneficial to color the background. A light gray background (the Windows 95 default) seems to be the best neutral color in all types of lighting and visual conditions. To change the background for the form header and detail sections, you select the desired section and then select the appropriate background color.

Tip   When you change the background color of form sections, you also will want to change the background of individual label controls for a more natural look. A label control generally doesn't look good if its background doesn't match the background of the form itself.

Enhancing Text-Based Controls

Generally, it's important to get the label text and data right before you start enhancing display items with shading or special effects. When your enhancements include label and text box control changes, you should begin with them.

Enhancing label and text box controls

You can enhance label and text box controls in several ways:

✦ Change the text font type style (Arial, Times New Roman, Wingdings).

✦ Change the text font size (4–200).

✦ Change the text font style (bold, italic, underline).

✦ Change the text color (using a formatting window).

✦ Add a shadow.

Cross-Reference   In Chapter 17, you changed the title in the form header. You then changed the text font size and font style. Now you will learn how to add a text shadow to the label control.

Creating a text shadow

Text shadows give text a three-dimensional look, by making the text seem to float above the page while its shadow stays on the page. This effect uses the same basic principle as a shadowed box. Use this process to create text shadows:

1. Duplicate the text.

2. Offset the duplicate text from the original text.

3. Change the duplicate text to a different color (usually a lighter shade).

4. Place the duplicate text behind the original text.

5. Change the original text's background color to Clear.

To create a shadow for the title's text, follow these steps:

1. Select the label control that reads Mountain Animal Hospital - Pets Data Entry.

2. Select Edit⇨Duplicate.

3. Select the white Fore color (second from the left) to change the duplicate text's color.

4. Drag the duplicate text up and to the right to create the offset from the text below it.

5. Select Format⇨Send to Back.

After you complete the shadow, you may have to move the text and its shadow to accommodate the changes you made when you moved the controls. You also may have to move the section border. The text now appears to have a shadow, as shown in Figure 18-4.

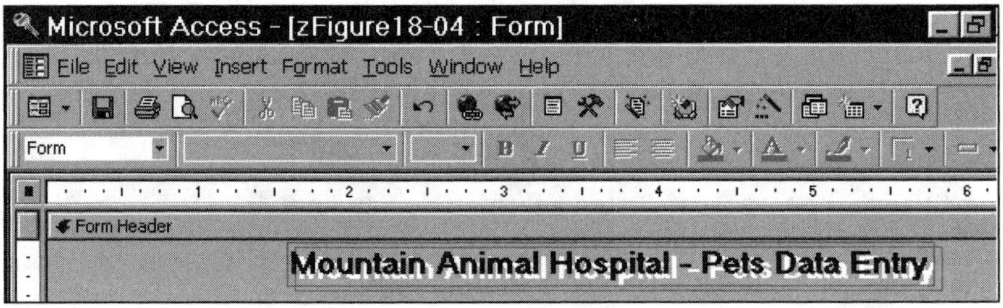

Figure 18-4: Creating text with a shadow and reverse video.

Note

If you do not see the shadow, select the original text and then select the Transparent option on the Fill/Back Color Formatting toolbar.

Tip

The box around the label control is not visible when the form is printed, because the Transparent button in the Border Color window is depressed.

When you duplicated the original text, the duplicate automatically was offset below the original text. When you place the duplicate text behind the original, it's hidden. You redisplay it by placing the original text in front. If the offset (the distance from the other copy), is too large, the effect will not look like a shadow. You can perfect the shadowed appearance by moving one of the label controls slightly.

Caution Although the shadow appears correctly on-screen and looks great, it won't print correctly on most monochrome printers. What you see normally is two lines of black text; they look horrible. If you plan to print your forms and don't have a printer that prints text in color (or prints many shades of gray by using graphics rather than text fonts), you should avoid using shadowed text on a form.

Changing text to a reverse video display

Text really stands out when you create white text on a black background. This setup is called *reverse video*; it's the opposite of the usual black letters on white. You can convert text in a label control or text box to reverse video by changing the Back Color to black and the Fore Color to white. To change the Pet Name text control to reverse video, follow these steps:

1. Select the Pet ID text box control (not the label control).

2. Select Black from the Back Color formatting window.

3. Select White from the Fore Color formatting window.

Tip To make it more dramatic, you may want to set the font to Bold and resize the frame.

Caution If you are using one of the less expensive laser printers, you may not see reverse video if you print your form. The printer drivers may not be able to print it.

Displaying label or text box control properties

As you change values in a label control or text box control by using a formatting window, you are actually changing their properties. Figure 18-5 displays the Property window for the text box control in the form header you just modified. As you see in Figure 18-5, many properties can be affected by a formatting window. Table 18-1 shows the various properties (and their possible values) for both label and text box controls.

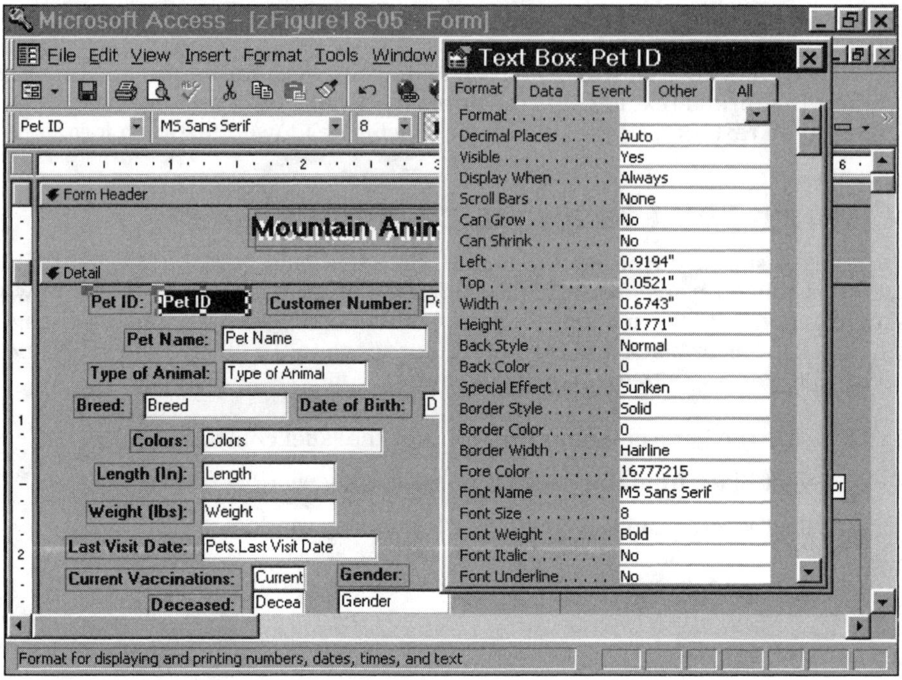

Figure 18-5: Text Box control properties.

Table 18-1
Label or Text Box Format Properties

Property	Options	Description
Format	Various Numeric and Date Formats	Determines how the data is displayed
Visible	Yes/No	Yes: Control is displayed normally No: Control is invisible when displayed
Display When	Always, Print Only, Screen Only	Determines when the control is displayed
Scrollbars	None, Vertical, Horizontal, Both	Specifies when scrollbars are displayed
Can Grow	Yes/No	If multiple lines of text are in the control, does the text box get larger?

Property	Options	Description
Can Shrink	Yes/No	If fewer lines of text are in the control than in its initial size, does the text box height get smaller?
Left	Position of the left corner of the control in the current measure (include an indicator, such as **cm** or **in**, if you use a different unit of measurement)	Specifies the position of an object on the horizontal axis
Top	Position of the top corner of the control in the current measure	Specifies the position of an object on the vertical axis
Width	The width of the control in the current unit of measure	Specifies the width of an object
Height	The height of the control in the current unit of measure	Specifies the height of an object
Back Style	Transparent, Normal	Determines whether a control's background is opaque or transparent
Back Color	Any available background color	Specifies the color for the interior of the control or section
Special Effect	Flat, Raised, Sunken, Shadowed, Etched, Chiseled	Determines whether a section or control appears flat, raised, sunken, shadowed, etched, or chiseled
Border Style	Transparent or Solid, Dashes, Dots, (Lines/Boxes Only)	Determines whether a control's border is opaque or transparent
Border Color	Any available border color	Specifies the color of a control's border
Border Width	Hairline, 1pt, 2pt, 3pt, 4pt, 5pt, 6pt	Specifies the width of a control's border
Fore Color	Any selection from a formatting window	Specifies the color for text in a control or the printing and drawing color
Font Name	Any system font name that appears on the toolbar; depends on fonts installed	Specifies the name of the font used for text or a control

(continued)

Table 18-1 *(continued)*		
Property	**Options**	**Description**
Font Size	Any size available for a given font	Specifies the size of the font used for text or a control
Font Weight	Extra Light, Light, Normal, Medium, Semi-Bold, Bold, Extra Bold, Heavy	Specifies the width of the line Windows uses to display and print characters
Font Italic	Yes/No	Italicizes text in a control
Font Underline	Yes/No	Underlines text in a control
Text Align	General (default), Left, Center, Right	Sets the alignment for text in a control

Although you can set many of these controls from the property sheet, it's much easier initially to drag the control to set the Top, Left, Width, and Height properties or to use a formatting window to set the other properties of the control.

Tip To move the selected control a very small amount, you can press Ctrl+arrow key; the control will move slightly in the direction of the arrow key used.

Displaying Images in Forms

You can display a picture on a form by using *image frames*. This method is different from the way a bound OLE control is used. Normally, you would store an OLE object (sound, video, Word, or Excel document) with a data record or with an unbound OLE object used specifically for storing OLE objects (those same sound, video, Word, or Excel documents) on a form.

Image controls in Access 97 are used only for non-OLE objects, such as Paintbrush (.BMP) pictures. Image controls offer a distinct advantage. Unlike OLE objects (which can be edited but use huge amounts of resources), the image control adds only the size of the bitmap picture to your computer's overhead. Using too many OLE objects in Access causes resource and performance problems. New and existing applications should use image controls only when displaying pictures that don't change or don't need to be edited within Access.

Tip In Access 2.0, many people learned to select an unbound OLE object picture and then select Edit⇨Save As Picture. This technique broke the OLE connection but did not fix the resource problem.

You can add an image control to your form by either pasting a bitmap from the Clipboard or embedding a bitmap file that contains a picture. Suppose that you have a logo for Mountain Animal Hospital. On the disk that accompanies this book is a bitmap file called MTN.BMP. In this section, you add this bitmap to the page header section of the form.

CD-ROM

An image object can be displayed in one of three ways:

Clip   Displays picture in its original size

Stretch   Fits the picture into the control regardless of size; often displayed out of proportion

Zoom   Fits the picture into the control (either vertically or horizontally) and maintains proportions; often results in white space on top or right side

To add the logo to the form, follow these steps:

1. Display the Toolbox by selecting View⇨Toolbox.

2. Click on the Image button in the Standard Toolbox.

3. Click on the left corner below the title; drag the box so that it is sized as shown in Figure 18-1. The Insert Picture dialog box appears, as shown in Figure 18-6.

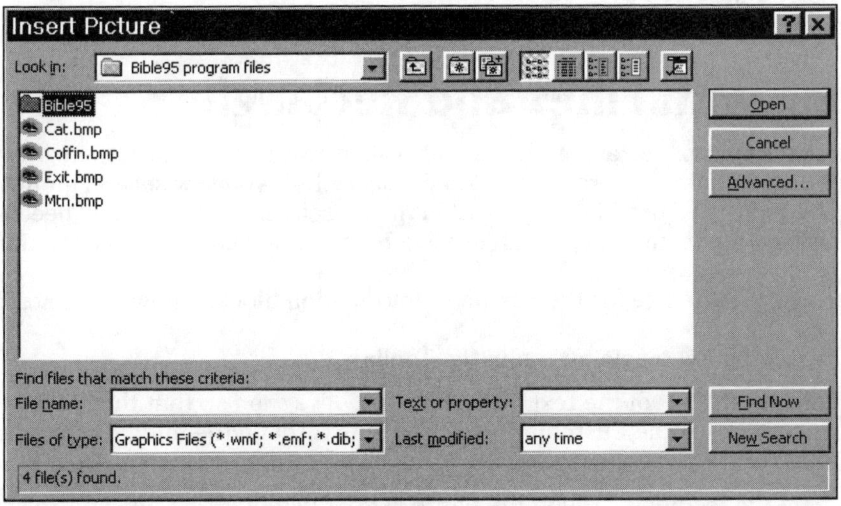

Figure 18-6: Creating an unbound object frame.

From this dialog box, you can select the type of picture object you want to insert into your form. The dialog box supports many picture formats, including .BMP, .TIF, .WMF, .PCX, .ICO, .WPG, .JPG, .PCT, or any picture format your copy of Windows 95 supports.

4. Select Mtn.bmp and click on OK.

If the file does not already exist and you want to create a new object (such as a Paintbrush picture), you must create an unbound OLE frame rather than an image.

After you complete step 5, Access returns you to the Form Design window, where the picture is displayed. You must still change the Size Mode property to Stretch.

5. Display the property sheet.

6. Change the Size Mode property to Stretch.

Finally, you have to change the Border property so that the picture does not simply blend in with the background because there is so much white in it. You can make this modification by changing the border color to black, or you can make the border three-dimensional by selecting the Raised toggle button in the Special Effect formatting window.

7. Display the Special Effect formatting window and click on the Raised toggle button.

The image object frame is complete.

Working with Lines and Rectangles

You can use lines or rectangles (commonly called *boxes*), to make certain areas of the form stand out and attract attention. In Figure 18-1, you saw several groups of lines and rectangles used for emphasis. In the present example, you still need to add the lines and the rectangle. You can use Figure 18-7 as a guide for this procedure.

To create the rectangle for the customer information block, follow these steps:

1. Select the Rectangle button in the Toolbox.

2. Click to the left of the text Customer Information so that the rectangle encompasses the Customer fields and cuts through the middle of the text that reads Customer Information.

3. Drag the rectangle around the entire set of Customer text box controls, and then release the mouse button.

4. Select Format⇨Send to Back to redisplay the text boxes.

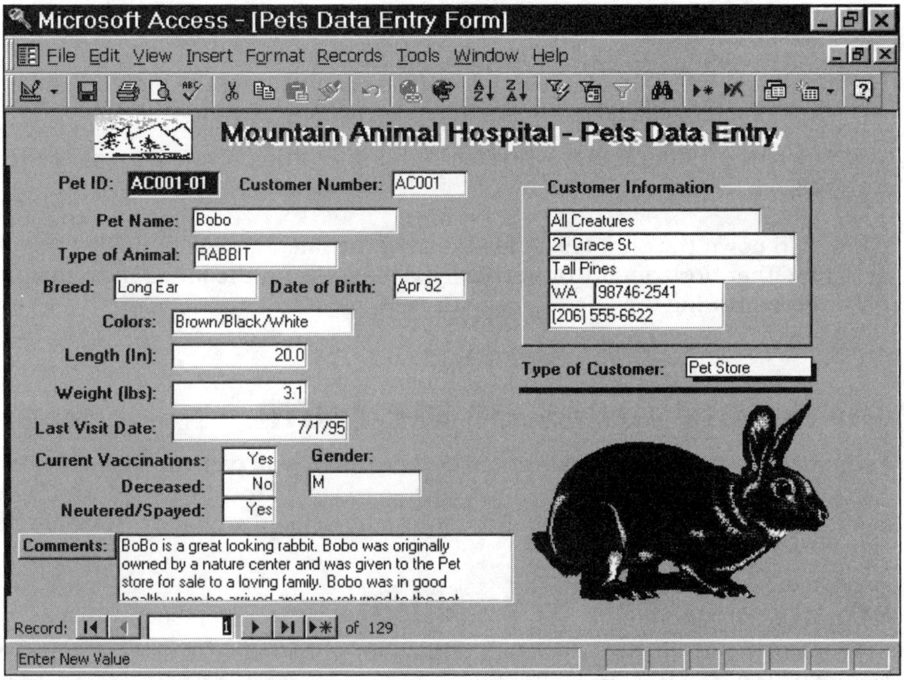

Figure 18-7: Completing the rectangles and lines.

Tip You may notice that when you create the rectangle, it blocks out the controls beneath it. By sending the rectangle to the background, you make the controls reappear.

5. Select the raised effect in the Special Effect formatting window.

Tip You can also redisplay the controls behind the rectangle by checking the Transparent button of the Background Color option in a formatting window. This method, however, does not allow you to add other shading effects. For a rectangle, you should always select Format⇨Send to Back.

You still need to create several lines for the form. You still need to add a single horizontal line just below the Type of Customer control and a thick vertical line down the left side of the form (beginning with Pet ID and ending to the left of the Comments field). To add these lines, complete the following steps (use Figure 18-7 as a guide):

1. Click on the Line button in the Toolbox.

2. Create a new horizontal line just above the image picture control.

3. Select the 2 button in the Line Thickness window to make the line thicker.

4. Create a new vertical line, starting just to the left of the Pet ID field. To keep the line vertical, hold down the Shift key as you drag the line to just left of the Comments field (as shown in Figure 18-7).

5. Select the 3 button in the Border Width formatting window to make the line thicker.

Tip   If you hold down the Shift key while creating the line, the line remains perfectly straight, either horizontally or vertically, depending on the initial movement you make when drawing the line.

Emphasizing Areas of the Form

If you really want to emphasize an area of the form, you can add a shadow to any control. The most common types of controls to which to add a shadow are rectangles and text boxes. You can create shadows by using the Shadow special effect.

Adding a shadow to a control

If the background is light or white, a dark-colored rectangle is needed. If the background is dark or black, use a light-colored or white rectangle. To create a shadow for the Type of Customer text box, follow these steps:

1. Select the Type of Customer control to receive the shadow.

2. Select the Shadow special-effects button.

To give the form a Windows 95/NT look and feel, you may want to change some other objects. The first is the rectangle around the bound OLE object (displaying the rabbit in the first record). A Windows 95/NT look and feel would have an etched gray rectangle rather than a sunken white one. Figure 18-7 shows this change.

Changing the header dividing line

Form headers are footers automatically separated from the Detail section by a solid black line. In Access for Windows 95, you can remove this line by changing the Dividing Lines form property to No. This action removes the line and makes the form appear seamless. This is especially important if you have a background bitmap on the entire form, you're using form headers or footers, and you want a single look.

Figure 18-7 shows the form after it has run. Notice both the raised rectangle around the Customer information and the two new lines. Also notice that the Mountain Animal Hospital logo appears in the form header.

Figure 18-8 shows the final form in the Form Design window.

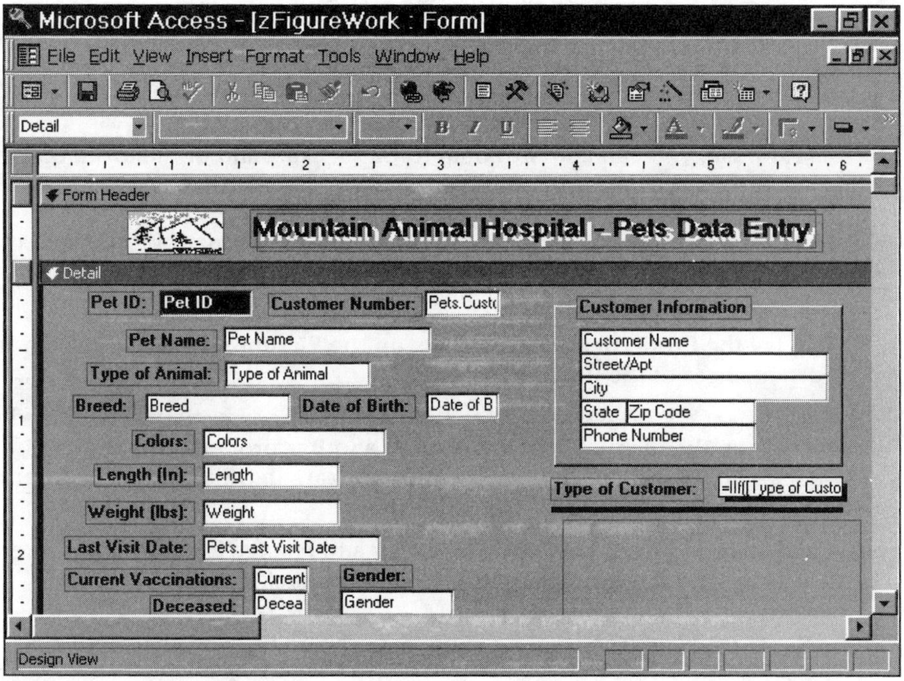

Figure 18-8: The final form.

You'll use this final form in the next chapter, so you should save it now. Select File⇨Save As/Export and name the form **Pets Data Entry - With Formatting.**

Adding a Background Bitmap

To emphasize a form even more (or add a really fun effect), you can add a background bitmap to any form, just as you added one control behind another. In Access 97, you do this by using the form's Picture properties. There are three properties you can work with:

Picture	The name of the bitmap picture; it can be any image-type file.
Picture Size Mode	Clip, Stretch, or Zoom. Clip displays the picture only at its actual size starting at the Picture Alignment property. Stretch and Zoom fill the entire form from the upper left corner of any header to the lower right corner of any footer.

Picture Alignment	Top-Left, Top-Right, Center, Bottom-Left, Bottom-Right, and so on. Use this property only when you use the Clip option in Picture Size mode.
Picture Tiling	Yes/No. When a small bitmap is used with Clip mode, this repeats the bitmap across the entire form. For example, a brick becomes a brick wall.

For this example, you can add Mtn.bmp to the background of the form. Use the following steps to add a background bitmap:

1. Select the form itself by clicking in the upper left corner of the intersection of the two design rulers, or select Form from the combo box at the left margin of the Formatting toolbar.

2. Display the Properties window; click on the Picture property that's on the Format sheet of the property window.

3. Enter **C:\ACCESS\MTN.BMP** (or the path to wherever you have placed your bitmap on the disk). When you click to another property, the Mountain Animal Hospital logo (or your bitmap) appears in the upper left corner of the form background.

4. Click on the Picture Size Mode property and change it from Clip to Stretch. The picture will now occupy the entire form background.

If you are following along with the example, notice that the gray box for the Customer Information is still gray, the fields themselves still have white backgrounds, and the bitmap does not show through. If you want the bitmap to show through, check the Transparent background color of any control; the background will show through the form.

You can do this by choosing Edit⇨Select All to select all the controls and then selecting Transparent from the Fill Back Color formatting window. This action produces the effect shown in Figure 18-9. As you can see, the white background of the picture (along with the thick, black lines) makes it difficult to see the fields.

Tip   The use of background bitmaps can give you some interesting capabilities. For example, you can take this process a step further by incorporating the bitmap into your application. A bitmap can have buttons tied to macros (or Visual Basic for Applications code placed in the right locations). To help the office staff look up a patient, for example, you can create a form that has a map with three states behind it. By adding invisible buttons over each state, you can give the operator the choice of clicking on a state to select the patient records from that state.

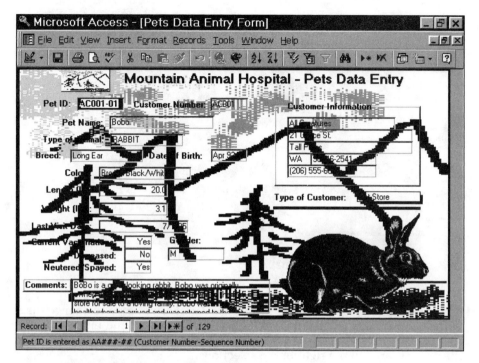

Figure 18-9: A bitmap picture behind a form.

You can also scan a paper form into your computer and use that image as the form background, by placing fields on top of the scanned form itself, without having to spend a great deal of time re-creating the form (which gives the phrase *filling out a form* a whole new meaning).

Using AutoFormat

You can change the format of an entire form by using a new feature in Access 97 known as AutoFormat. This is the first menu option on the Format menu. Auto-Format lets you make global changes to all fonts, colors, borders, background bitmaps, and virtually every property, on a control-by-control type basis. This feature works instantly and completely and is totally customizable.

When you select Format⇨AutoFormat, a window appears, as shown in Figure 18-10. This window lets you select from the standard AutoFormats or any you have created. The figure is shown after you click on the Options >> button. This lets you apply only fonts, colors, or border style properties separately.

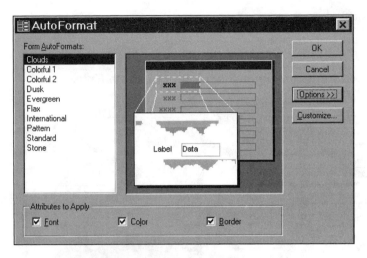

Figure 18-10: Selecting AutoFormat.

In this example, you can choose the Clouds AutoFormat type to change the style of the control fonts and colors and to change the background bitmap. As you move between the different AutoFormats, you can see an example of the look in the preview area to the right of the selections.

For this example, click on the Options >> button and then deselect the check box for color (turn it off). Then press the OK button.

When you're done, the controls appear as shown in Figure 18-11. Notice that the title text size has changed and the shadow box around the Type of Customer has been removed. The reason is that the defaults for these controls are different from what you have selected.

Customizing and adding new AutoFormats

You can modify existing AutoFormats — or define new ones — by simply creating a form, setting various form properties, and starting AutoFormat. Though Auto-Format will change the look of your form totally, it does its job on one control type at a time. This means that it can format a label differently from a text box and differently from a line or rectangle. This capability also lets you define your own formats for every control type, including the background bitmap.

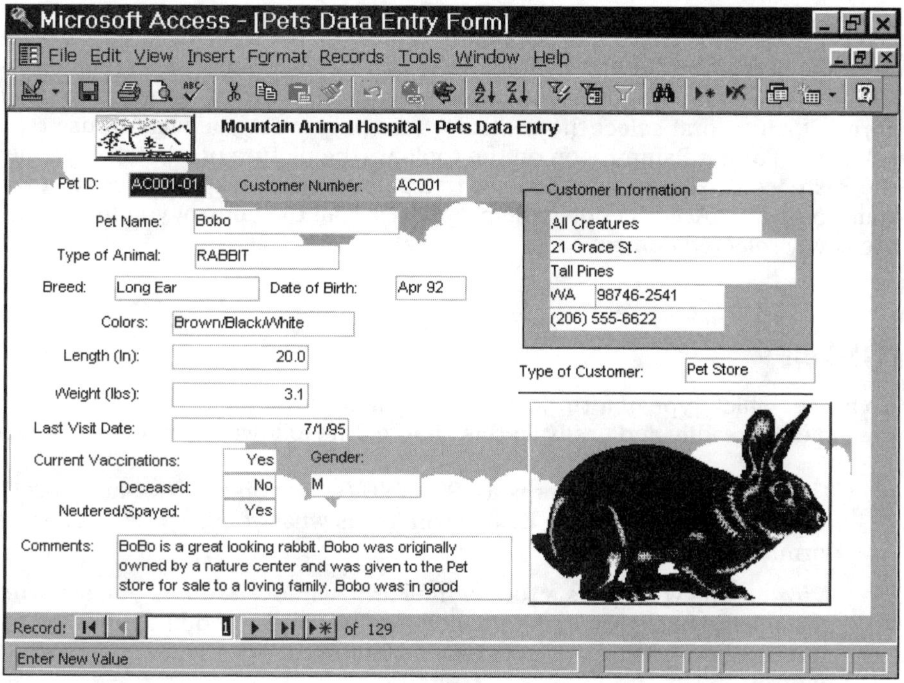

Figure 18-11: Mountain Animal Hospital in the Clouds.

After you have created a form you want to use as a basis for an AutoFormat, you can select AutoFormat and then click on the Customize button, shown in Figure 18-10. Another window appears, as shown in Figure 18-12. This window allows you to update the selected format, add a new format, or delete the selected format.

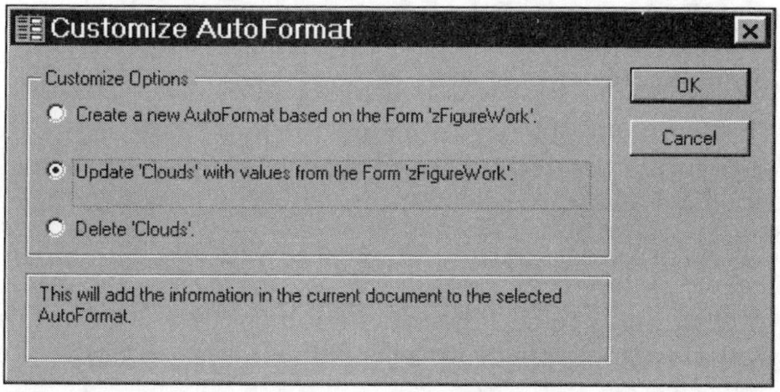

Figure 18-12: Creating your own AutoFormat.

Copying individual formats between controls

A subset of the AutoFormat technology is the Format Painter. This tool allows you to copy formatting properties from one individual control to another. To use the Format Painter, first select the control whose properties you want to use. Then select the Format Painter icon on the toolbar (the picture of a paintbrush, next to the Paste icon). Your cursor changes to a paintbrush. Click on the control you want to update; Access copies the properties from the control you first selected to the newly selected control.

Summary

No matter which type of form you are creating with the tools in Access, you can get the job done readily and easily. In this chapter, the following points were covered:

✦ The Access form designer is a WYSIWYG (what-you-see-is-what-you-get) form tool. What you see in the Design window is what you get when you run the form.

✦ A formatting window is a tool in the Form window that lets you set foreground and background colors, control line widths and line types, as well as add three-dimensional effects (such as a raised or sunken appearance) to controls.

✦ You can enhance label and text box control text by changing the font type style and size and by changing the font style to bold or italic. You can specify font color and even add a shadow by duplicating the text.

✦ To display pictures in forms, you can use bound object frames (attached to a data field in the record) or image controls or unbound object frames (which are embedded in the form).

✦ Lines and rectangles let you separate areas of the form to add emphasis.

✦ You can further emphasize areas of the form by adding color, background shading, and three-dimensional effects. You can also use shadows and reverse video for emphasis.

✦ The Access 97 AutoFormat tool lets you change the look of the entire form by applying a set of formatting properties to every control on the form, including the form itself and form selections.

✦ You can copy formats between controls by using the Format Painter icon.

In the next chapter, you learn how to add data-validation controls to your form, including list boxes, option buttons, check boxes, combo boxes, and other items.

✦   ✦   ✦

Adding Data-Validation Controls to Forms

In the preceding three chapters, you learned how to create a basic form and how to enhance it by using visual effects to make data entry and display easier. In this chapter, you learn techniques for creating several *data-validation* controls; these controls will help you make sure that the data being entered (and edited) in your forms is as correct as possible.

In this chapter, you modify your form from Chapter 18 to look like the one in Figure 19-1. If you are following along with the examples in this book, open either the form you created in Chapter 18 (Pets Data Entry - With Formatting) or the form on the disk that comes with this book (Pets Data Entry Form - Without Validation).

Creating Data-Validation Expressions

You can enter expressions into table design properties (or a form control's property sheet) that will limit input to specific values or ranges of values; the limit will go into effect when a specific control or form is used. In addition, you can display a status line message that advises users how to enter the data properly into the table or form when they move the cursor into a particular field. You can also have Access show an error message if a user makes an invalid entry; you can enter these expressions in a table design or in a form.

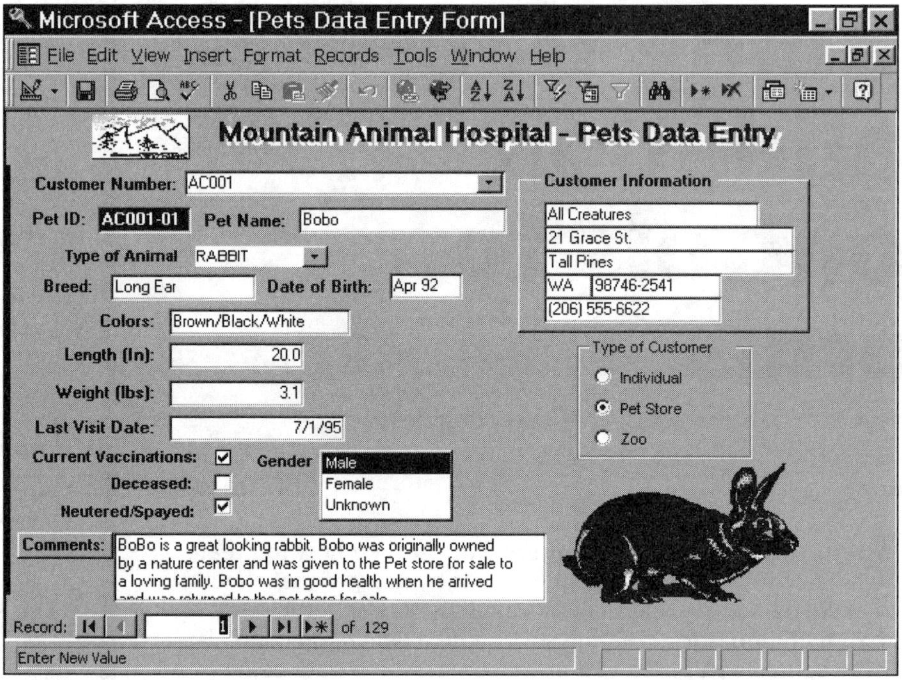

Figure 19-1: The Pets Data Entry form after adding validation controls.

Table-level validation

You can enter several types of validation text into a table design, as shown in Table 19-1. When the user of a form or datasheet moves the cursor into the field, messages appear in the status line at the lower left corner of the screen. In your table design, you would enter these messages into the Description column, as shown in Figure 19-2. In this example, the status line message displays `Enter M for Male, F for Female, or U if Unknown` when the cursor is in the Gender field.

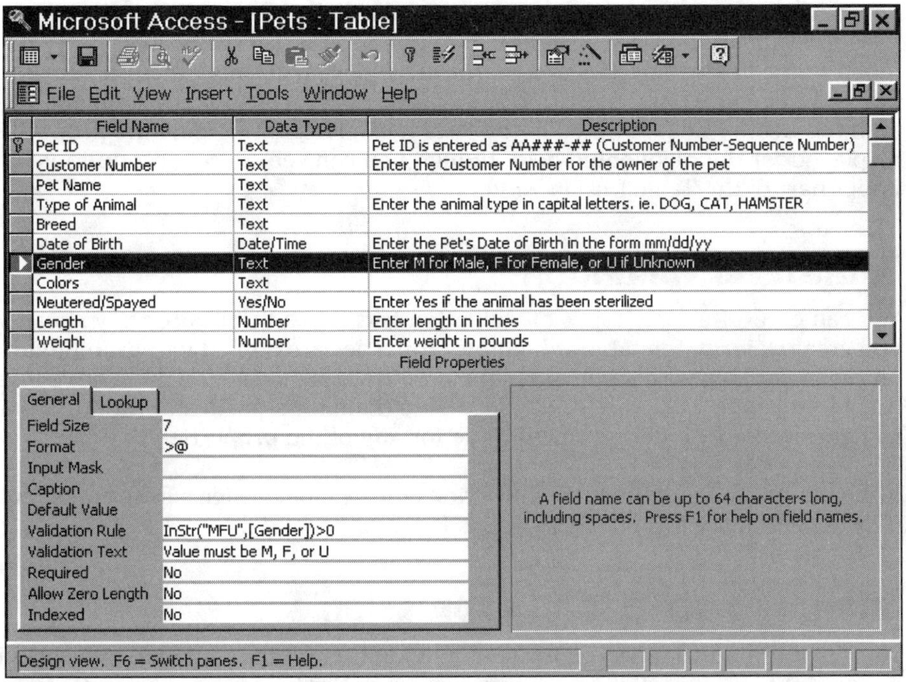

Figure 19-2: The validation properties for the Gender field in the table design.

Table 19-1
Types of Validation Entered into a Table Design

Type of Validation	Stored in	Displayed in Form
Status line message	Description/Status Bar Text	Status bar
Validation expression	Validation rule	Not displayed
Error message	Validation text	Dialog box
Input mask	Input mask	Control text box

Validation expressions are the rules the data must follow. Any type of expression can be entered into the Validation Rule property (found in the field properties area of the table design). In Figure 19-2, the expression `InStr("MFU",[Gender])>0` limits the valid entry to the three letters M, F, or U.

You can also display an error message in a dialog box when data entry does not pass the validation rule. This text is entered into the Validation Text property found in the field properties area of the table design. In this example, the dialog box will tell you `Value must be M, F, or U`. Figure 19-2 shows a table design with the Gender field selected in the Pets table. Notice that only the properties are displayed for the highlighted field, though you can see all the descriptions in the upper part of the Table Design window.

Form-level validation

You can enter the same types of validation text into a form's property sheet. When you create a form, the table validation properties are copied into each bound field on the form. This way, if you enter them at the table level, you don't have to enter them for each form. If you want to override them for a particular form, you can do so here by simply entering a new value for any of the properties.

Note Although you enter status bar instructions into a table design's Description column, they appear in the form design's Status Bar Text property.

Entering a validation expression

You can enter a validation expression in a number of different ways for each field in your table or control in your form. For a number field, you can use standard mathematical expressions such as *less than, greater than,* or *equal to,* using the appropriate symbols (<, >, =). For example, if you want to limit a numerical field to numbers greater than 100, you enter the following validation expression in the appropriate property box:

> **> 100**

To limit a date field to dates before January 1995, you enter

> **< #1/1/95#**

If you want to limit a numeric or date value to a range, you can enter

> **Between 0 And 1500**

or

> **Between #1/1/70# And Date( )**

Cross-Reference You can use a series of the functions included within Access to validate your data. In Figure 19-2, Access interprets the validation expression used to limit the input in the Gender field as "allow only the letters M, F, or U." The Access function `InStr` means *in string.* Access will search the Gender input field and allow only those entries. Chapter 13 details the various functions available to you for validation purposes.

Creating Choices with Option Buttons

Sometimes you won't want to allow a user to enter anything at all — only to pick a valid entry from a list. You can limit input on your form in this way by using an *option button* (also known as a *radio button*), a control that indicates whether a situation is True or False. The control consists of a string of text and a button that can be turned on or off by clicking the mouse. When you click on the button, a black dot appears in its center, indicating that the situation is True; otherwise, the situation is False.

Generally, you would use an option button when you want to limit data entry but more than two choices are available. You should limit the number of choices to four, however, when using option buttons. If you have more than four choices, use a list or combo box (described later in this chapter).

By using option buttons, you can increase flexibility in validating data input. For example, the current control for Type of Customer displays a number: 1 means individual, 2 means pet store, and 3 means zoo. It is much more meaningful to users if all these choices are displayed on-screen. Figure 19-1 shows the numerical field input changed to an option group box that shows the three choices available to users.

Only one of the option buttons can be made True for any given record. This approach also ensures that no other possible choices can be entered on the form. In an option group, the option group box itself is bound to a field or expression. Each button inside passes a different value back to the option group box, which in turn passes a single value to the field or expression. Each option button is bound to the option group box rather than to a field or expression.

Caution Only fields with a Numeric data type can be used for an option group in a form. In a report, you can transform nonnumeric data into numeric data types for display-only option buttons (see Chapter 22). You can also display an alternative value by using the Lookup Wizard on the Table design window and displaying a combo box.

To create an option group with option buttons, you must do two things:

✦ Create the option group box and bind it to a field.

✦ Create each option button and bind each one to the option group box.

Creating option groups

In Access 97, the easiest and most efficient way to create option groups is with the Option Group Wizard. You can use it to create *option groups* with multiple option buttons, toggle buttons, or check boxes. When you're through, all your control's property settings are correctly filled out. This Wizard greatly simplifies the process and allows you to create an option group quickly, but you should still understand a little of the process.

Creating an option group box

When you create a new option group, the Option Group Wizard is triggered automatically. You start this process by clicking on the Option Group icon on the toolbox and then drawing the control box rectangle. Another method is to click on the Option Group button and then drag the appropriate field from the field list window.

Caution   To start any of the Wizards that create controls, you must first depress the Control Wizard button on the toolbox.

Before creating an option group for the Type of Customer field, first you must delete the current display of the field: Highlight it with your mouse and press the Delete key. You may also want to delete the shadow (the thick line below the control) and narrow the height of the picture so that the option group box will fit. Use the completed option group in Figure 19-1 as a guide. If the toolbox and Field List are not open, open them now.

After you have deleted the existing Type of Customer text box control, you can create the Type of Customer option group box by following these steps:

1. Click on the Option Group button from the toolbox. When you release the mouse button, the Option Group button will remain in.

2. Select and drag the Type of Customer field from the Field List window to the space under the Customer Information box.

   The first screen of the Option Group Wizard should be displayed (as shown completed in Figure 19-3). On this screen, you can enter the text label for each option button, check box, or toggle button that will be in your option group. Enter each entry as you would in a datasheet. You can press the down-arrow key to move to the next choice.

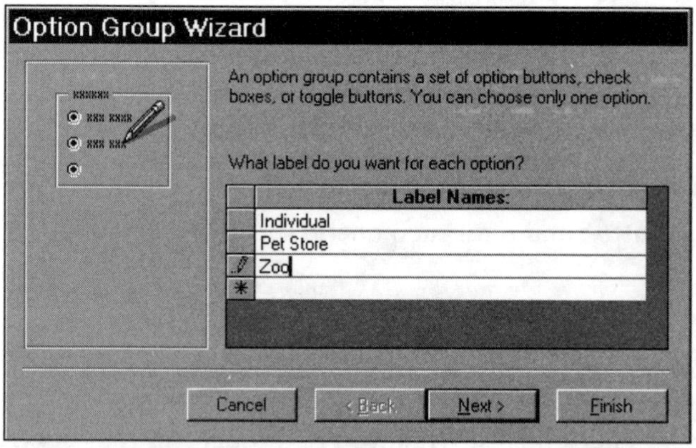

Figure 19-3: Entering the option group choices.

3. Enter **Individual**, **Pet Store**, and **Zoo**, pressing the down-arrow key between choices.

4. Click on the <u>N</u>ext > button to move to the default option Wizard screen.

   The next screen lets you select the default control for when the option group is selected. Normally, the first option is the default. If you want to make a different button the default, you would first select the Yes, the default choice is option button and then select the default value from the combo box that contains your choices. In this example, the first value will be the default automatically.

5. Click on the <u>N</u>ext > button to move to the Wizard screen used for assigning values.

   This screen (shown in Figure 19-4) displays the actual values you entered, along with a default set of numbers that will be used to store the selected value in the bound option group field (in this example, the Type of Customer field). The screen looks like a datasheet with two columns. Your first choice, Individual, is automatically assigned a 1, Pet Store a 2, and Zoo a 3. When Pet Store is selected, a 2 will be stored in the Type of Customer field.

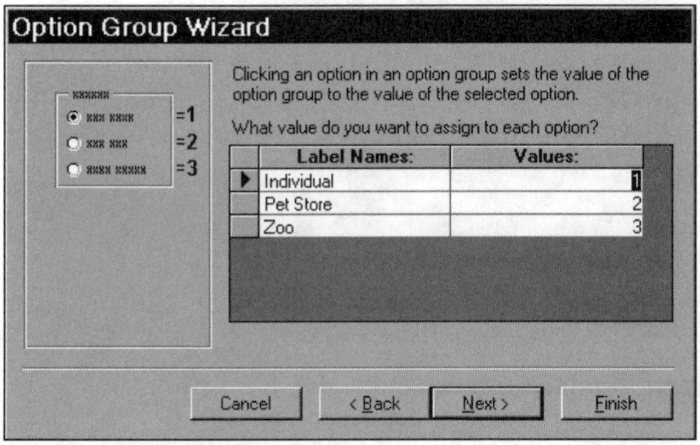

Figure 19-4: Assigning the value of each option button.

   In this example, the default values are acceptable. Sometimes, however, you may want to assign values other than 1, 2, 3. . . . You may want to use 100, 200, and 500 for some reason. As long as you use unique numbers, you can assign any values you want.

6. Click on the <u>N</u>ext > button to move to the next Wizard screen.

   In this screen, you have to decide whether the option group itself is bound to a form field or unbound. The first choice in the Wizard — Save the value for later use — creates an unbound field. If you're going to put the option group in a dialog box that uses the selected value to make a decision, you don't want to store the value in a table field. Thus (in this example) the second value — `Store the value in this field` — is automatically selected because you started with the Type of Customer field. If you want to bind the option group value to a different table field, you can select from a list of all form fields. Again, in this example, the default is acceptable.

7. Click on the <u>N</u>ext > button to move to the option group style Wizard screen.

For this example (as shown in Figure 19-5), select Option buttons and the Etched style. Notice that your actual values are used as a sample. The upper half of this Wizard screen lets you choose which type of buttons you want; the lower half lets you choose the style for the option group box and the type of group control. The style affects the option group rectangle. If you choose one of the special effects (such as Etched, Shadowed, Raised, or Sunken), that value is applied to the Special Effect property of the option group.

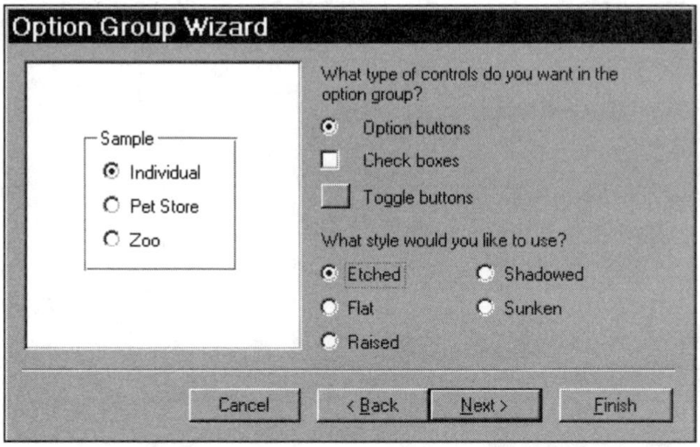

Figure 19-5: Selecting the type and look of your buttons.

Note

As you change your selections, the Sample changes as well.

8. Click on the <u>N</u>ext > button to move to the final Option Group Wizard screen.

This screen lets you give the option group control a label that will appear in the option group border. Then you can add the control to your design and (optionally) display help to additionally customize the control.

9. Enter **Type of Customer** as your caption for the Option Group.

10. Click on the <u>F</u>inish button to complete the Wizard.

Your Wizard work is now complete. Eight new controls appear on the design screen: the option group, its label, three option buttons, and their labels. Even so, you may still have some work to do. If you refer back to Figure 19-1, you may want to boldface the text labels of the option group control and each individual option button. You may want to move the option buttons closer together or change the shape of the option group box, as shown in Figure 19-6. You may want to change the Special Effect property of some controls. As you have learned, you can do this by using the property sheet for the controls.

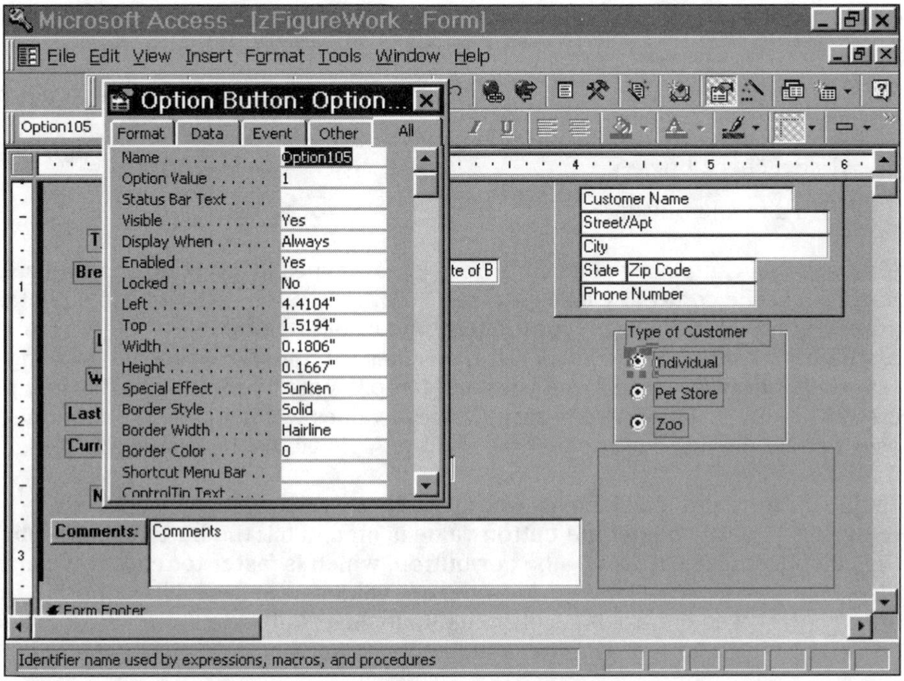

Figure 19-6: The option group controls and property sheet.

Figure 19-6 shows the option group controls and the property sheet for the first option button (as automatically created). Notice the Option Value property; it's found only in controls that are part of an option group. You should make all the suggested modifications to make the control look like Figure 19-1.

If you want to create an option group manually, the best advice is *not* to. If you must, however, the steps are the same as for creating any control. First create the option group box, and then create each button inside it manually. You'll have to set manually all data properties, palette properties, and specific option group or button controls.

Caution If you create the option buttons outside the option group box and then drag or copy them into the option group box, they will not work. The reason is that the automatic setting of the Option Value for buttons is left undone, and the option button control has not been bound to the option group box control.

After this process is complete, you can turn your attention to Yes/No controls.

Creating Yes/No Options

There are three ways to show data properly from Yes/No data types:

✦ Display the values `Yes` or `No` in a text box control, using the Yes/No Format property.

✦ Use a check box.

✦ Use a toggle button.

Although you can place values from Yes/No data types in a text box control and then format the control by using the Yes/No property, it's better to use one of the other controls. Yes/No data types require the values −1 or 0 to be entered into them. An unformatted text box control returns values (−1 and 0) that seem confusing, especially because −1 represents Yes and 0 represents No. Setting the Format property to Yes/No or True/False to display those values will help, but it still requires a user to read the text `Yes/No` or `True/False`. A visual display is much better.

Toggle buttons and check boxes work with these values *behind the scenes* — returning −1 to the field if the button value is on and 0 if the button is off — but they display these values as a box or button, which is faster to read. You can even display a specific state by entering a default value in the Default property of the form control. The control is displayed initially in a Null state if no default is entered and no state is selected. The Null state appears visually the same as the No state.

The check box is the commonly accepted control for two-state selection. Toggle buttons are nice (they can use pictures rather than a text caption to represent the two states) but not always appropriate. Although you could also use option buttons, they would never be proper as a single Yes/No control.

Creating check boxes

A *check box* is a Yes/No control that acts the same as an option button but is displayed differently. A check box consists of a string of text (to describe the option) and a small square that indicates the answer. If the answer is True, a check mark is displayed in the box. If the answer is False, the box is empty. The user can toggle between the two allowable answers by clicking on the mouse with the pointer in the box.

The Pets Data Entry form contains three fields that have Yes/No data types. These are Current Vaccinations, Deceased, and Neutered/Spayed. The choices are easier to understand if they are shown as a check box (rather than as a simple text box control). To change these fields to a check box, you first must delete the original text box controls. The following steps detail how to create a check box for each of the Yes/No fields after you have deleted the original controls:

1. Click on the Check Box icon in the toolbox.

2. While holding down the Ctrl key, select Current Vaccinations, Deceased, and Neutered/Spayed from the Field List window.

3. Using Figure 19-7 as a guide, drag these fields just below the Last Visit Date control. (This process creates each of the check boxes and automatically fills in the Control Source property.)

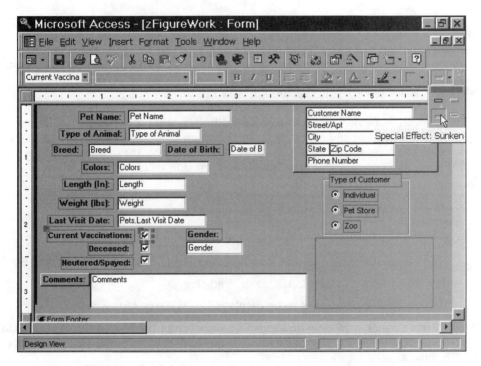

Figure 19-7: Creating check boxes.

4. Rearrange the fields so that they look like Figure 19-7. (Notice that this example calls for the check boxes to be on the right of the labels.)

5. Select each label control and modify it: Change it to the appropriate text, bold it, add a colon to the end of the labels, and then size the controls to fit and align them as necessary.

Tip You can set the Display Control option of the Lookup tab in the Table Design to Check Box for any field with a Yes/No data type. After you have entered this setting, a check box will be created automatically whenever you add this field to a form.

Note Before creating the check box controls, you could change the Default Check Box Label X property to a negative value; this would automatically place the check boxes to the right of the labels when they are created. The value you would enter depends on the length of the labels. You can change the Add Colon property to Yes to add a colon automatically and also change the Special Effect property to Sunken. This would save you several steps when creating a group of similar-looking controls.

The completed check boxes appear in Figure 19-7.

Creating visual selections with toggle buttons

A toggle button is another type of True/False control. Toggle buttons act like option buttons and check boxes but are displayed differently. When a toggle button is set to True (in *pushed* mode), the button appears on-screen as sunken. When it is set to False, the button appears raised.

Toggle buttons provide a capability in addition to what other button controls offer. You can set the size and shape of a toggle button, and you can display text or pictures on the face of the button to illustrate the choice a user can make. This additional capability provides great flexibility in making your form user-friendly.

As an example of how to create a toggle button, you can follow these steps, using the Deceased Yes/No field (this example is not part of the final form):

1. Select the Deceased check box label control and delete the label.

2. Select the Deceased check box and select Format⇨Change To⇨Toggle Button.

3. Resize the toggle button to the desired size.

4. Type the text **Deceased** to be displayed on the face of the button; press Enter.

5. Using the arrows keys on the keyboard, correct the size of the button to fit the text (or select Format⇨Size⇨To Fit) and move it below the other check boxes.

Adding a bitmapped image to the toggle button

As mentioned, you can display a picture on a toggle button rather than display text. You can modify the button you just created in the preceding steps, changing it to display a picture (included in the sample files). Using the following steps to add a bitmap to a toggle button, modify the button for the entry field called

Deceased (this example assumes that you completed the steps to create the toggle button):

1. Select the toggle button.

2. Open the property sheet and select the Picture property.

3. Click on the Builder button.

   The Picture Builder dialog box appears; in it, you can select from more than 100 predefined pictures. In this example, you want to select the bitmap named COFFIN.BMP that came with your *Access 97 Bible* disc; it should be in the same directory your Access book files were copied to (the example assumes that it's C:\ ACCESS97).

4. Click on the Browse button in the Picture Builder dialog box.

5. Select COFFIN.BMP from the C:\ACCESS97 directory; click on the OK button. A sample of the picture appears in the Picture Builder dialog box, as shown in Figure 19-8.

6. Click on the OK button to add the picture to the toggle button. The coffin appears on the toggle button on the design screen. You may need to move it on the screen to make it fit between other controls.

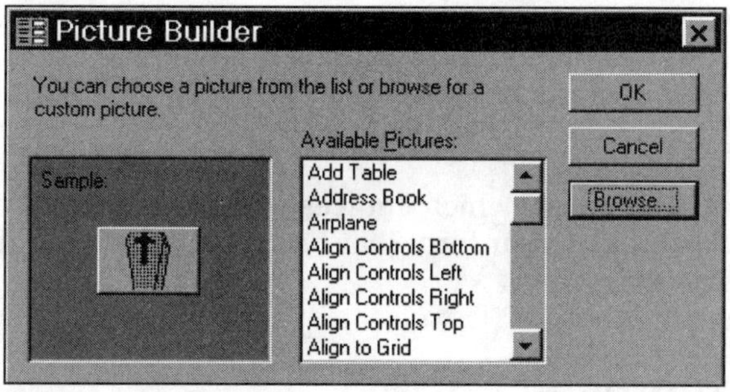

Figure 19-8: The Picture Builder dialog box.

Although option buttons, check boxes, and toggle buttons are great for handling a few choices, they are not a good idea when many choices are possible. Access has other controls that make it easy to pick from a list of values.

Working with List Boxes and Combo Boxes

Access has two types of controls that let you show lists of data a user can select from. These controls are *list boxes* and *combo boxes*.

Understanding the differences between list boxes and combo boxes

The basic difference between a list box and a combo box is that the list box is always open, whereas you have to click on the combo box to open the list for selection. In addition, the combo box lets you enter a value that is not on the list.

Cross-Reference

Chapter 16 contains details on this subject. Review Figures 16-8 and 16-9 if you are not familiar with list boxes and combo boxes.

A closed combo box appears as a single text box field with a downward-pointing arrow on its far right side. A list box, which is always open, can have one or more columns, from one to as many rows as will fit on-screen, and more than one item to be selected. When a combo box is open, it displays a single-column text box above the first row, followed by one or more columns and as many rows as you specify on the property sheet. Optionally, a list box or combo box can display column headers in the first row.

Settling real-estate issues

Note

You have to consider the amount of space on the form needed to display either a list box or combo box. If only a few choices are allowed in a given field, a list box is sufficient. If there is not enough room on the form for the choices, use a combo box (a list box is always open, but a combo box is initially closed). When you use a list box, a user cannot type any new values but instead must choose from the selection list.

When you design a list box, decide exactly which choices will be allowed for the given field. You should select an area of your form that has sufficient room for the open list box to display all selections.

Creating a single-column list box

List boxes and combo boxes can be even more difficult to create than option groups, especially when a combo box uses a query as its source and contains multiple columns. The new List Box Wizard and Combo Box Wizard in Access make the process much easier. This first example uses the List Box Wizard to create a simple list box for the Gender field.

To create the single-column list box, follow these steps:

1. Delete the existing Gender text box field control and its label.
2. Click on the List Box icon in the toolbox.

3. Display the field list and drag the Gender field to the right of the recently created check boxes.

The List Box Wizard starts automatically, as shown in Figure 19-9. The first
screen lets you decide whether to type a list of values, have the values come
from a table/query, or create a query-by-form list box that will display all the
unique values in the current table. Depending on your answer, you either
select the number of columns (and type in the values) or select the fields
you want to use from the selected table/query.

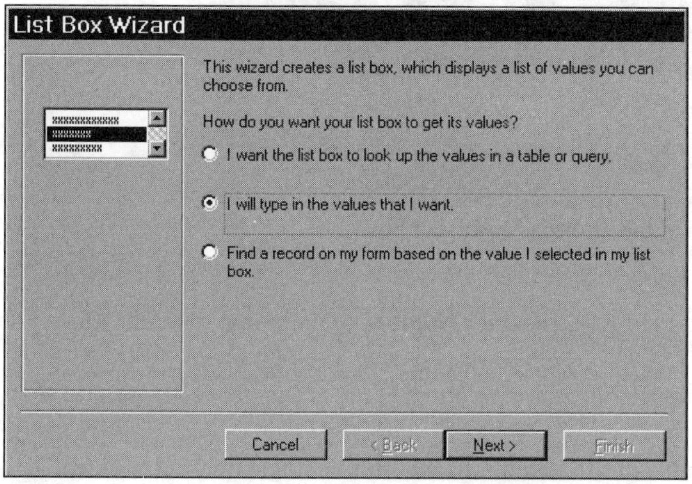

Figure 19-9: Selecting the data source for the list box.

4. Select the second option, `I will type in the values that I want`,
and click on the Next > button.

In the next screen, you can choose the number of columns and enter the values you want to use in the list box. You can also resize the column widths,
just as in any datasheet. In this example, just enter three values in a single
column: **M**, **F**, and **U** (shown completed in Figure 19-10).

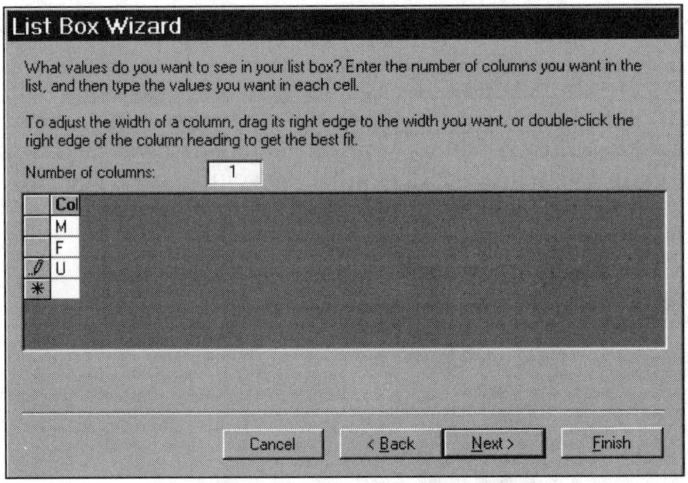

Figure 19-10: Entering the choices for the list box.

5. Enter **1** in the field that specifies Number of columns; then click in the first row under the Col1: header.

6. Enter **M**, press the down arrow, enter **F**, press the down arrow, and then enter **U**.

7. Resize the width of the column to match the single-character entry.

Tip You can double-click on the right side of the column list to size the column automatically.

8. Click on the Next > button to move to the next screen.

Use this screen to specify the field that you will link to. It should currently say Gender. Accept this value.

9. Click on the Next > button to move to the final Wizard screen.

Use this screen to give the list box control a label that will appear with your list box. When you click on the Finish button, your control is added to your design; you can optionally display Help if you want to continue customizing the control.

10. Click on the Finish button to complete the Wizard.

Your work with the Wizard is now complete, and the control appears on the design screen. You will have to move the label control and resize the list box rectangle. The Wizard does not do a good job of sizing the box to the number of entries.

Figure 19-11 shows the list box control and the property sheet for the list box.

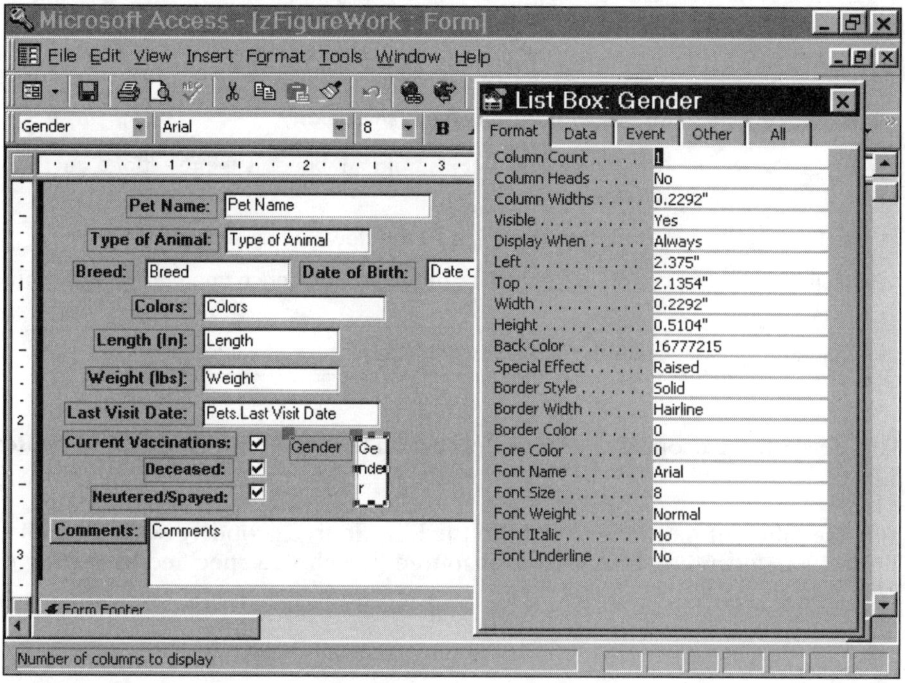

Figure 19-11: The list box control and property sheet.

Understanding list box properties

As you can see in Figure 19-11, several properties define a list box. The Wizard takes care of these (except for the Column Heads property, which adds the name of the column at the top of the list box). Begin by setting the Row Source properties; the first of these is Row Source Type (shown later in this chapter), which specifies the source of the data type.

The Row Source properties are the first two properties you have to set. One of these, Row Source Type, determines the data type. Valid Row Source Type property options are listed in Table 19-2.

Table 19-2
Row Source Type Settings

Row Source Type	Source of the Data Type (see below)
Table/Query	(Default setting) Data is from a table or is the result of a query or SQL statement.
Value List	List of items specified by the Row Source setting.
Field List	List of field names from the Table/Query named by the Row Source setting.
Row Source	Either the Table/Query name or a list of values.

The Row Source property settings depend on the source type specified by Row Source Type.

You use different methods to specify the Row Source property settings, as listed in Table 19-3, depending on the type of source (which you specified by setting the Row Source Type).

Table 19-3
Row Source Property Settings

Row Source Type	Method of Setting the Row Source Property
Table/Query	Enter the name of a table, a query, or an SQL statement.
Value List	Enter a list of items separated by semicolons.
Field List	Enter the name of a table or query.

In this example, you entered the values on the Wizard screen. Therefore, the Row Source Type is set to Value List, and the Row Source is set to **"M";"F";"U"**. As you can see, the values are entered separated by semicolons.

When you specify Table/Query or Field List as the Row Source Type, you can then pick from a list of tables and queries for the Row Source. The table or query must already exist. The list box will display fields from the table or query according to the order they follow in their source. Settings in the property sheet determine the number of columns, their size, whether there are column headers, and which column is bound to the field's control source.

Tip If you want to use noncontiguous table/query fields in the list box, you should use an SQL statement rather than a list of field names. The Wizard can do this for you automatically. The following is an example of an SQL statement for a two-column list, drawn from the Pets table in the Mountain Animal Hospital database:

```
SELECT [Pet Name], [Type of Animal] FROM [Pets] ORDER BY [Pet
    ID];
```

These settings include:

Column Count	The number of columns to be displayed.
Column Heads	Yes or No. Yes displays the first set of values or the field names.
Column Widths	The width of each column. Each value is separated by a semicolon.
Bound Column	The column that passes the value back to the control source field.

Suppose that you want to list Pet Name, Type of Animal, and Breed, returning Pet Name to the field control. You could enter **Table/Query** in the Row Source Type and **Pets** in the Row Source. You would then enter **3** for the Column Count, **1.5;1;1** in the Column Width, and **1** for the Bound Column.

These are valid entries for the Row Source property for a list box from the Value List:

For a one-column list with three rows (Column Count = 1):

```
M;F;U
```

For a two-column list with three rows (Column Count = 2):

```
M;Male;F;Female;U;Unknown
```

For a two-column list with five rows of data and a column header (Column Count = 2, Column Heads = Yes):

```
Pet Name;Type of Animal;Bobo;Rabbit;Fido;Dog;Daffy;Duck;Patty;
    Pig;Adam;Frog
```

Creating a multiple-column list box

List boxes are not limited to a single column of data. It's easy to create a list box with multiple columns of data. You could easily go back and run the Wizard again to create a two-column list box, but it's just as easy to modify the list box you already have on the design screen. Follow these next steps to modify the list box control to change it to a two-column list:

1. Change the Row Source property to **M;Male;F;Female;U;Unknown**.

2. Set the Column Count property to **2**.

3. Enter the Column Widths property as **.25;.75**.

4. Set the Bound Column property to **1**.

5. Resize the list box control to fit the new column widths.

By changing the Number of Columns property to 2 and setting the Column Widths to the size of the data, you can display multiple columns. As you can see in Figure 19-12, there are now multiple columns. The first column's value (specified by the Bound Column property) is passed back to the Gender field.

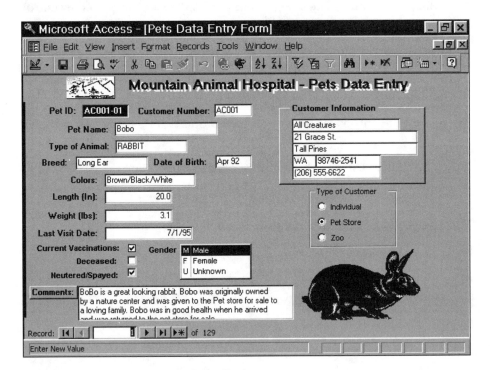

Figure 19-12: Creating a two-column list box.

Cross-Reference You enter the column widths as decimal numbers; Access adds the abbreviation for inches (in) automatically. You can also change it to *cm* or any other unit of measurement.

Caution If you don't size the list box wide enough to match the sum of the column widths, a horizontal scrollbar will appear at the bottom of the control. If you don't size the list box deep enough to display all the items in the list (including the horizontal scrollbar), a vertical scrollbar will appear.

When you look at this list box, you may wonder, "Why display the single-letter code at all?" You may think that you need it to pass the single-letter code back to the Gender field. That *is* the reason, in fact, for the first column, but there is no need to display it. Data in hidden *or* displayed columns can be used as a bound column.

Hiding a column in a list box

When you create a multiple-column list box, Access lets you *hide* any column you don't want displayed. This capability is especially useful when a list box is bound to a field you don't want displayed. You can hide the first column in the list box you just created by following these steps:

1. Display the Properties sheet for the list box.

2. Change the Column Widths property to **0;.75**.

3. Resize the list box control to the new width.

When you display the list box, you see only the one column; the hidden column is used as the bound column. You can bind a list box to a field that isn't even displayed on-screen.

Creating multi-selection list boxes

An option in Access 97 creates list boxes that allow more than one selection. You can build such a *multi-selection* (or *multi-select*) list box by changing the Multi-Select property of a standard list box. To use the multiple selections, however, you have to define a program by using Visual Basic for Applications to capture the selections.

The Multi-Select property has three settings:

None	(Default) Multiple selection isn't allowed.
Extended	Pressing Shift+click or Shift+arrow key extends the selection from the previously selected item to the current item. Pressing Ctrl+click selects or deselects an item.
Simple	Multiple items are selected or deselected by choosing them with the mouse or pressing the spacebar.

Creating and Using Combo Boxes

As mentioned in this chapter, a *combo box* is very similar to a list; it's a combination of a normal entry field and a list box. The operator can enter a value directly into the text area of the combo box or else click on the directional arrow (in the right portion of the combo box) to display the list. In addition, the list remains hidden from view unless the arrow is activated, conserving valuable space on the form. A combo box is useful when there are many rows to display; a vertical scrollbar will give users access to the records that are out of sight.

In this next example, you are going to change the Type of Animal control from a text box to a combo box, using the Combo Box Wizard.

To create a single-column combo box using the Wizard, follow these steps:

1. Delete the existing Type of Animal text box field control and its label.

2. Click on the Combo Box icon in the toolbox.

3. Display the field list and drag the Type of Animal field to the area below Pet Name.

   The Combo Box Wizard starts automatically; its first screen is exactly the same as the first list box screen. You decide whether you want to type in a list of values, or whether the values will come from a table or query. In this example, you will get the values from a table.

4. Select the first option, which displays the text I want the combo box to look up the values in a table or query; then click on the Next > button.

   As shown in Figure 19-13, this Wizard screen lets you choose the table you want to select the values from. By using the row of option buttons under the list of tables, you can view all the Tables, Queries, or Both tables and queries.

5. Select the Animals table and click on the Next > button.

   The next screen lets you pick the fields you want to use to populate the combo box. You can pick any field in the table or query and select the fields in any order; Access creates the necessary SQL statement for you. On this screen, only one field is shown. The Animals table has only one field (Animals), a list of valid animals.

6. Select the Animals field; click on the > button to add it to the Columns list.

7. Click on the Next > button to move to the next Wizard screen.

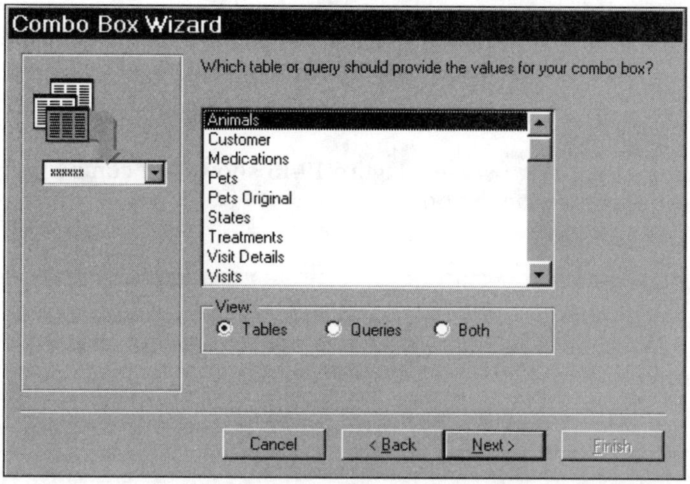

Figure 19-13: Selecting the table for the row source of the combo box.

In this screen, a list of the actual values in your selected field appears (as shown in Figure 19-14). Here, you can adjust the width of any columns for their actual display.

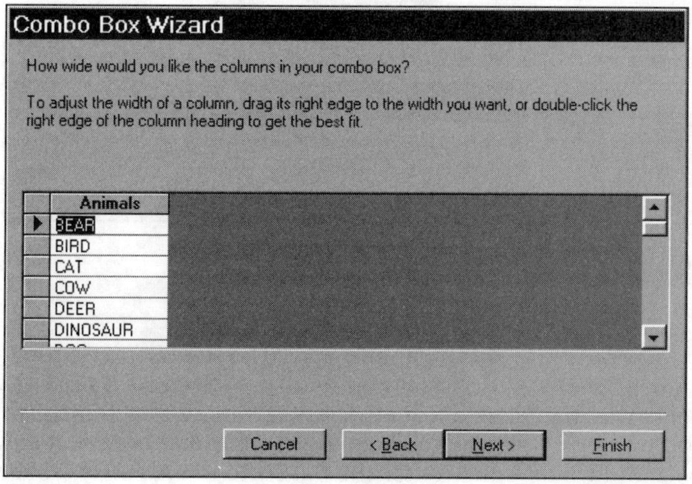

Figure 19-14: Adjusting the column width of the selection.

The rest of the Wizard screens are like the list box. First, you accept or change the name of the bound field; the last screen lets you enter a label name, and the Wizard creates the combo box.

8. Click on <u>F</u>inish to complete the entries with the default choices.

The control appears on the design screen. Figure 19-15 shows the combo box control and the property sheet for the list box.

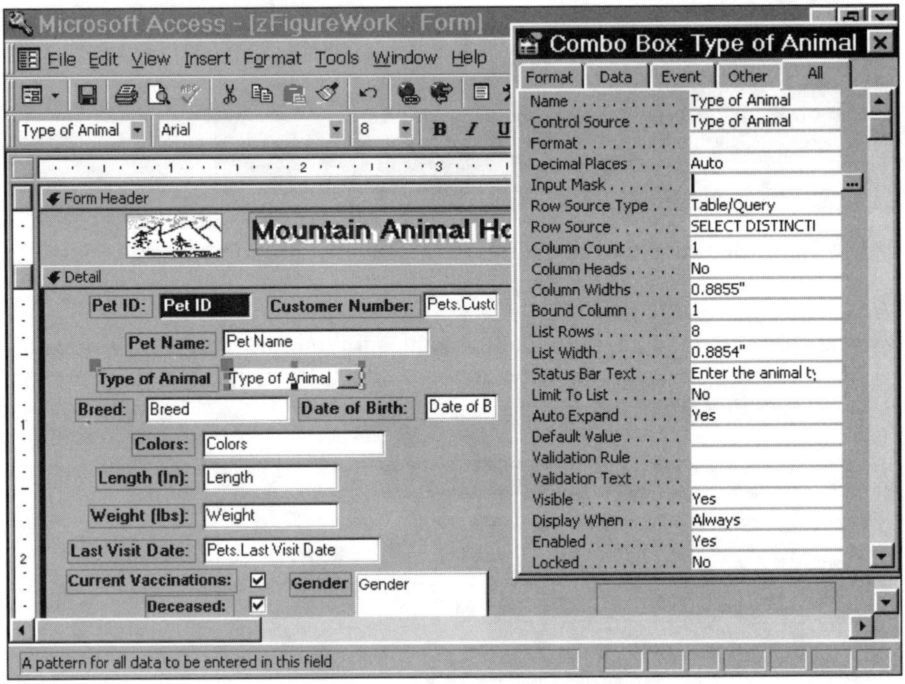

Figure 19-15: The combo box control and property sheet.

The Row Source Type property is set to Table/Query. The Row Source property is set to the SQL statement `Select Distinctrow [Animals] From [Animals]`. This statement selects the Animal field from the Animals table and limits it to unique values. If you wanted to display the animals in a sorted order, you could do it in one of two ways. You would either enter the data into the Animals table in a sorted order or create a simple query to sort the data into the order you want and then use the query as the basis for the combo box. You can also add sorting directives to the SQL statement by adding **Order By [Animals]**.

The List Rows property sets the number of rows to 8 when the combo box is opened, but the Wizard does not allow you to select this. The last property, Limit

To List, determines whether you can enter a value into the Pets table that is not in the list; this property is another one the Wizard does not let you select. You must set it directly from the property sheet. The default No value for Limit To List says that you can enter new values because you are not limiting the entry to the list.

Tip Setting the AutoExpand property to Yes enables the user to select the combo box value by entering text into the combo box that matches a value in the list. As soon as Access finds a unique match, it displays the value without having to display the list.

Creating a multiple-column combo box from a query

Just as with list boxes, combo boxes may have multiple columns of information. These boxes are displayed when the operator activates the field list. Unless you are extracting fields from a single table — in the order in which they appear there — you'll probably want to use a query.

Figure 19-16 displays the combo box you will create next. Notice that this combo box displays the Customer Number and Customer Name in the order of the Customer Name. This task is accomplished by creating a query. Also notice (in Figure 19-16) that the Customer Number and Customer Name heads are displayed.

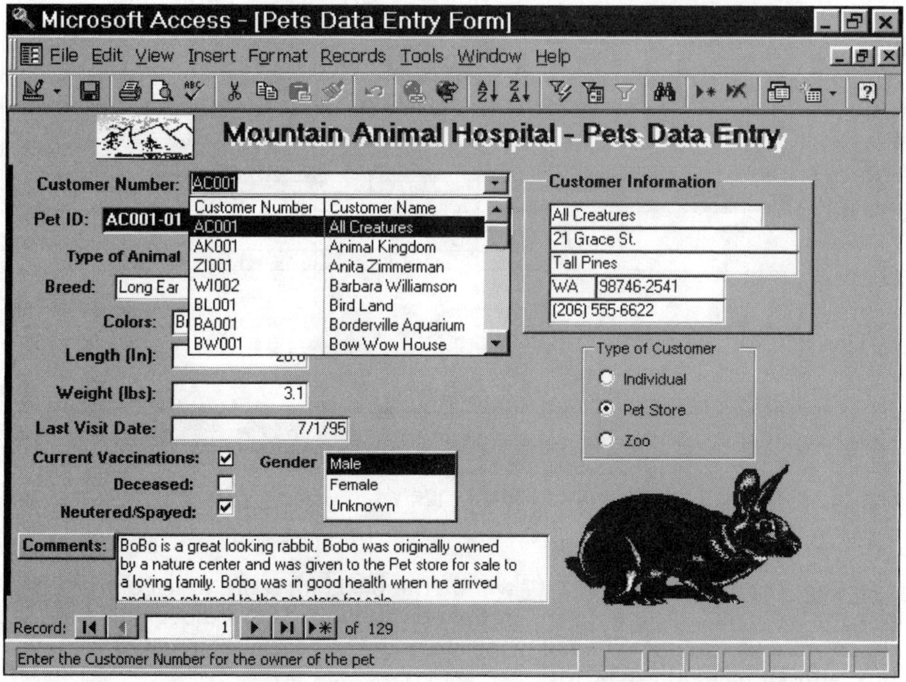

Figure 19-16: Displaying the multi-column combo box.

To understand the selection criteria of a multiple-column combo box, you should first create the query that will select the proper fields.

Before continuing, minimize the form you are working on and create a new query after selecting the Query tab in the Database container. The query you want to create is shown in Figure 19-17. After the query is created, save it to a query named Customer Number Lookup. Note that the Customer table is related to the Pets table; the Customer Name field is selected to be used as the query's sorting field. When used for the combo box, this query will select the Customer Name from the Customer table, match it with the Customer Number in the Customer table, and pass it to the Customer Number in the Pets table. When a Customer is selected, the Customer Number in the Pets table is updated; the correct name is displayed in the Customer area of the form. Thus, you can reassign the ownership of a pet or (more usefully) add a new pet to the system and correctly choose the pet's owner.

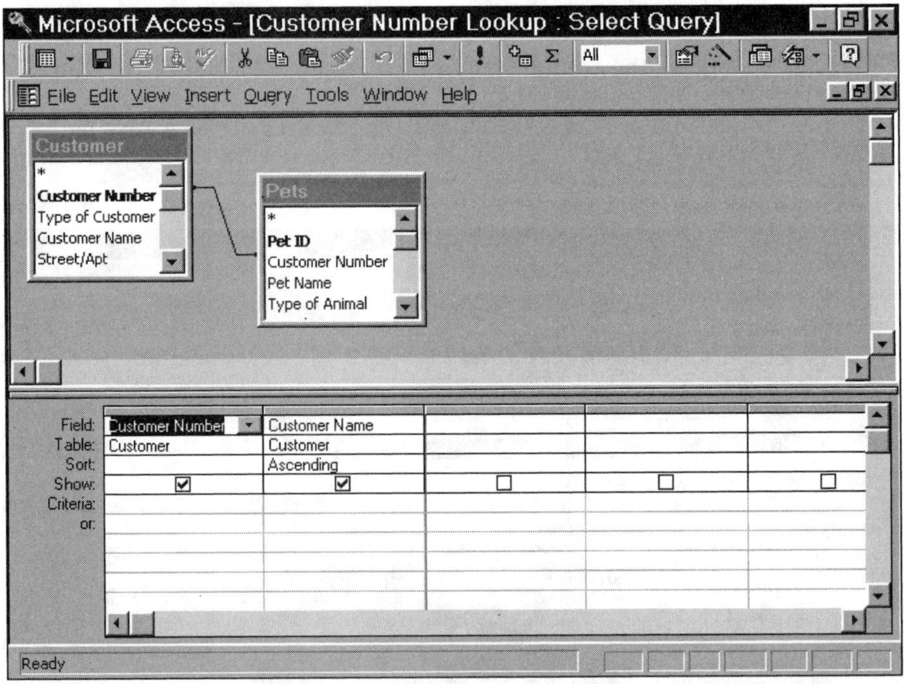

Figure 19-17: Customer Number Lookup query.

The query shown in Figure 19-17 will be the basis for a multiple-column combo box for the Pets.Customer Number field on the form. Before beginning, remaximize the form to work on it. The following steps describe how to create this new combo box without using the Wizard:

1. Select the Pets.Customer Number text box, and then select Format⇨Change To⇨Combo Box from the menu.

2. Move the original Pet ID and Pet Name controls, as shown in Figure 19-18. Also resize the new Customer Number combo box control.

3. Select the Data sheet (Data tab) in the Property window. If the Property window is not open, open it.

4. Enter **Pets.Customer Number** in the Control Source property.

5. Select Table/Query in the Row Source Type property.

6. Set the Row Source property to the query Customer Number Lookup.

7. Set the Bound Column property to 1.

8. Select the Format tab to activate the Format sheet.

9. Enter **2** in the Column Count property.

10. Set the Column Heads property to Yes.

11. Set the Column Widths property to **1;1.25**.

If you have followed the preceding steps properly, your screen form design should resemble the form shown in Figure 19-18, and the Form view should look like Figure 19-16.

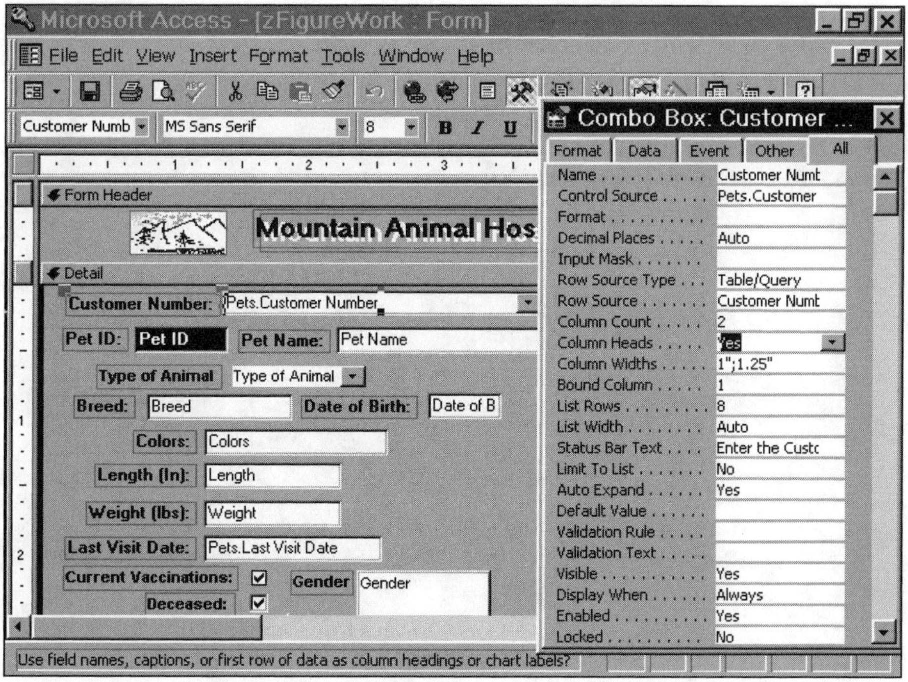

Figure 19-18: A multiple-column combo box.

Summary

In this chapter, you learned many ways to create forms that accept only good data. Validation rules, option buttons, check boxes, list boxes, and combo boxes make it easy. The Control Wizards in Access make it simple. This chapter covered the following points:

✦ Data-validation expressions are entered in either tables or forms.

✦ The Description column in a table becomes the status-bar text on a form.

✦ The Validation Rule and Validation Text properties let you trap for errors and display error messages.

✦ You can use option buttons, check boxes, and toggle buttons individually to display a two-state choice or as part of an option group to display one of several possible choices.

✦ An option button (also called a radio button) is the preferred choice for showing three to four choices.

✦ Yes/No data is best shown with check boxes.

✦ You can also use toggle buttons to display Yes/No data, and you can attach pictures to the face of the button.

✦ List boxes display choices in an open box.

✦ Combo boxes display choices in a closed box that a user must select in order to view the choices.

✦ List boxes and combo boxes can have one column or many.

In the next chapter, you learn how to link and embed pictures and graphs in your forms and reports.

✦   ✦   ✦

Using OLE Objects, Graphs, and ActiveX Custom Controls

Access provides many powerful tools for enhancing your forms and reports. These tools let you add pictures, graphs, sound — even video — to your database application. Chart Wizards make it easy to build business graphs and add them to your forms and reports. OLE custom controls (OCXs or ActiveX controls) extend the power of Access 97; new features borrowed from Microsoft Office 97 make using Access forms more productive than ever. In this chapter, you learn about the different types of graphical and OLE objects you can add to your system. You also learn how to manipulate them to create professional, productive screen displays and reports. You will also learn how to use some of the new Office 97 tools that work with Access 97 forms.

Understanding Objects

Access 97 gives you the capability of embedding pictures, video clips, sound files, business graphs, Excel spreadsheets, and Word documents; you can also link to any OLE (Object Linking and Embedding) object within forms and reports. Access lets you not only use objects in your forms but also edit them directly from within your form.

Types of objects

As a general rule, Access can add any type of picture or graphic object to a form or report. Access can also interact with any application through DDE (Dynamic Data Exchange) or OLE. You can interact with OLE objects with great flexibility. For example, you can link to entire spreadsheets, ranges of cells, or even an individual cell.

Access can embed and store any binary file within an object frame control, including even sound and full-motion video. As long as you have the software driver for the embedded object, you can play or view the contents of the frame.

These objects can be bound to a field in each record (*bound*) or to the form or report itself (*unbound*). Depending on how you want to process the OLE object, you may either place (*embed*) the copy directly in the Access database or tell Access where to find the object (*link*) and place it in the bound or unbound object frame in your form or report. The following sections describe the different ways to process and store both bound and unbound objects by using embedding and linking.

Using bound and unbound objects

A *bound object* is an object displayed (and potentially stored) within a field of a record in a table. Access can display the object in a form or print it on a report. A bound object is bound to an OLE object data type field in the table. If you use a bound object in a form, you can add and edit pictures or documents record by record, the same way you can with values. To display a bound OLE object, you use a *bound object frame*. In Figure 20-1, the picture of the pig is a bound object. Each record stores a photograph of the animal in the field named `Picture` in the Pets table. You can enter a different picture for each record.

An *unbound object* is not stored in a table; it is placed on the form or report. An unbound object control is the graphic equivalent of a label control. These are generally used for OLE objects in the form or report itself; they don't belong to any of the record's fields. Unbound objects don't change from record to record.

An *image control* that displays a picture is another example of an unbound object. Although an unbound OLE object frame allows you to edit an object by double-clicking on it and launching the source application (PC Paintbrush, Word, Excel, a sound or video editor or recorder, and so on), an image control only displays a bitmap picture (usually in .BMP, .PCX, or .WMF format) that cannot be edited.

Tip   Always use an image control for unbound pictures; it uses far fewer computer resources than an OLE control and significantly increases performance.

In Figure 20-1, the picture of the mountain is an image control. The pig is a bound OLE object; the graph is an unbound object. Though the graph is unbound, there is a data link from the graph template to the data on the form. This means the graph is updated each time data in the record changes.

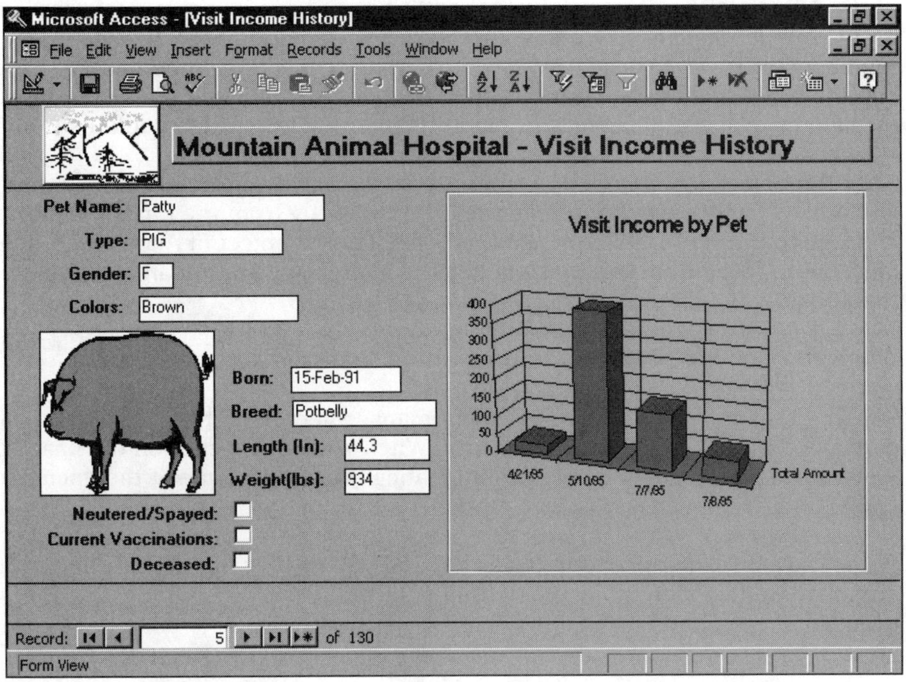

Figure 20-1: Bound and unbound objects.

Linking and embedding

The basic difference between linking and embedding objects within a form or report is that *embedding* the object stores a copy of it within your database. *Linking* an object from another application does not store the object in your database; instead, the external location of the object is stored.

Linking an object gives you two benefits:

✦ You can make changes using the external application, even without opening Access.

✦ The external file does not use any space in the Access MDB database file.

Caution If the external file is moved to another directory (or if the file is renamed), the link to Access is broken; opening the Access form may result in an error message.

One benefit of embedding is that you don't have to worry about someone changing the location or name of the linked file. Because it is embedded, the file is part of the Access MDB database file. Embedding does have its costs, however. The first is that it takes up space in your database — sometimes a great deal of it (some pictures can take several megabytes). In fact, if you embed an .AVI video clip of just 30 seconds in your database for one record, it can use ten or more megabytes of space. Imagine the space 100 records with video could use.

After the object is embedded or linked, you can use the source application (such as Excel or Paintbrush) to modify the object directly from the form. To make changes to these objects, you need only display the object in Access and double-click on it. This automatically launches the source application and lets you modify the object.

When you save the object, it is saved within Access.

Suppose that you've written a document management system in Access and have embedded a Word file in an Access form. When you double-click on the image of the Word document, Word is launched automatically and you can edit the document

Note   When the external application is started and you modify the object, the changes are made to the external file, not within your database.

Note   To edit an OLE object, you must have the associated OLE application installed in Windows. If you have embedded an Excel .XLS file but don't own Excel, you can view the spreadsheet (or use its values), but you won't be able to edit or change it.

CD-ROM   In the next section of this chapter, you use the form shown in Figure 20-2. You can find the form in the Mountain Animal Hospital database file, named Pet Picture Creation - Empty.

Embedding Objects

You can embed objects in both unbound and bound object frames as well as in image frames. Embedding places the object in the Access database, where it is stored in the form, the report design, or a record of a table.

Embedding an unbound object

You can use two methods to embed an unbound object in a form or report:

> ✦ You can simply paste an object on the form or report; an image or unbound object frame is created that contains the object.

✦ You can create an unbound object frame or image frame and then insert the object or picture into the frame.

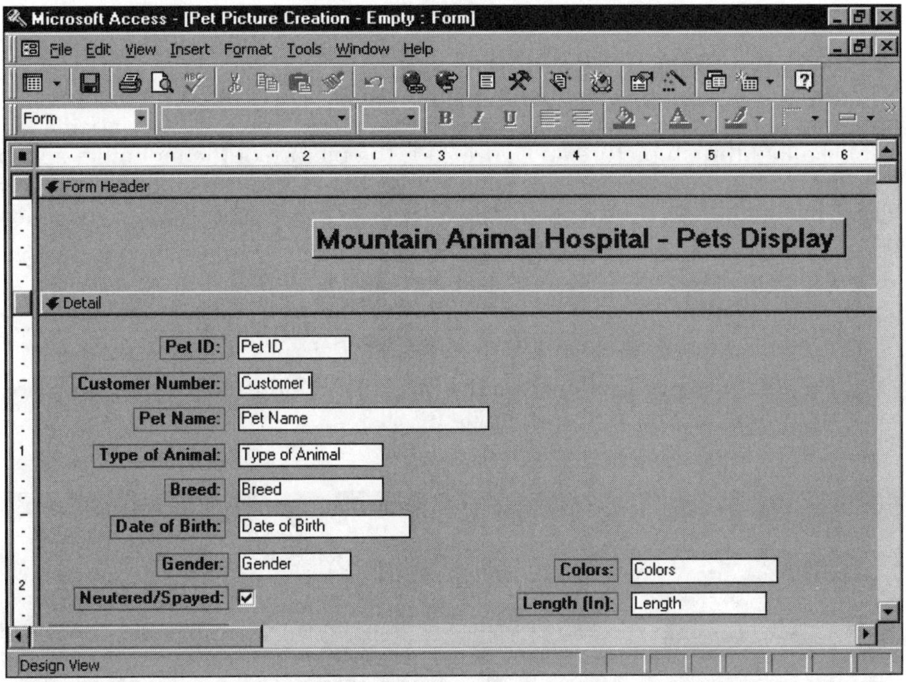

Figure 20-2: The Pet Picture Creation - Empty form.

Pasting an unbound object

If the object you want to insert is not an OLE object, you *must* paste the object on the form. As an example, to cut or copy an object and then paste it into an image or unbound object frame, follow these steps:

1. Create or display the object by using the external application.

2. Select the object and choose Edit⇨Cut or Edit⇨Copy.

3. Display the Access form or report and select Edit⇨Paste.

This process automatically creates an unbound object frame for an OLE object or an image frame for a picture and then embeds the pasted object in it.

If the object you paste into a form is an OLE object and you have the OLE application loaded, you can still double-click on the object to edit it. For example, you can highlight a range of cells in an Excel worksheet and paste the highlighted selection into an Access form or report. You can use the same highlight-and-paste approach with a paragraph of text in Word and paste it on the Access form or report. You can paste both OLE and non-OLE objects on a form or report with this method, but you'll see that there are other ways to add an OLE object.

Inserting an image-type object

You can also use another method to embed OLE objects or pictures into an unbound object frame or image frame. Suppose that you want to embed a file containing a Paintbrush picture. In Figure 20-1, the picture of the mountain appears on the form in the form header; this is an *image frame*. You can embed the picture by either pasting it into the image frame or by inserting the object into the image frame. Follow these steps to create an image frame:

1. Open the form Pet Picture Creation — Empty in Design view.

2. Select the Image Frame button on the toolbar.

3. Create the image frame, using the Image Frame button from the Toolbox to draw a rectangle, as shown in Figure 20-3.

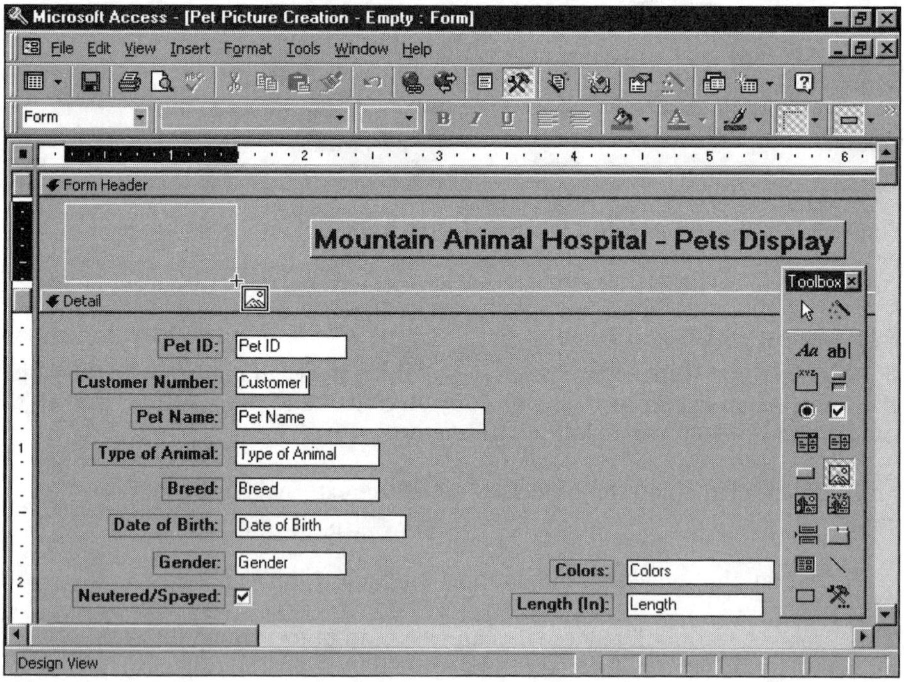

Figure 20-3: Creating an image frame.

When you create an image frame, the Insert Picture dialog box appears. This dialog box, shown in Figure 20-4, displays the image objects you have on your system.

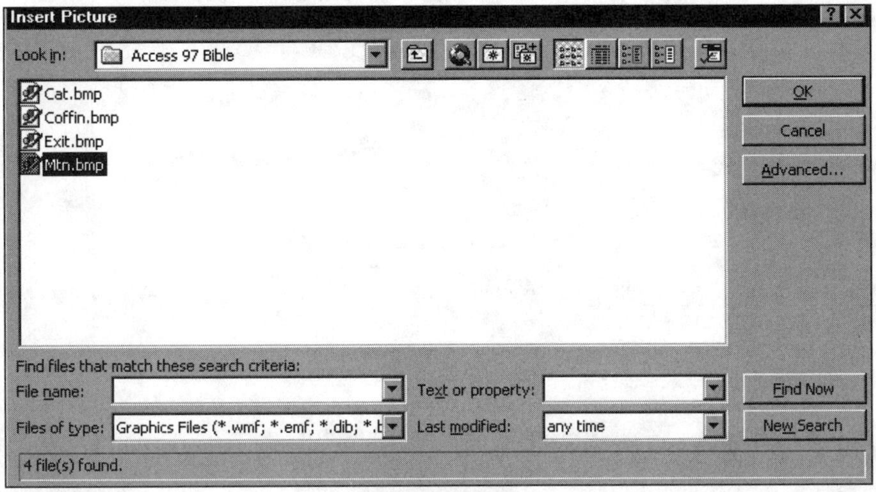

Figure 20-4: The Insert Picture dialog box.

To embed the existing Paintbrush file MTN.BMP in the image frame, follow these steps:

1. Using the standard file explorer dialog box, select MTN.BMP from the folder in which your other database files reside. (This file was installed when you installed files from the *Access 97 Bible* CD-ROM).

2. Click on OK after the filename appears in the Insert Picture dialog box.

Access embeds and displays the picture in the unbound object frame, as you can see in Figure 20-5. Notice that in this figure the picture of the mountain does not seem to be displayed correctly. You can correct this by using the Size Mode property.

Notice some of the other properties of the Image control. The Picture property contains the path and filename of the image you selected. The Picture Type property below has two choices. The default is Embedded and saves a copy of the bitmap picture in the database container in a compressed form. When you save the form and have chosen Embedded, the Picture property will change to (bitmap) rather than the name of the path and file for the original location of the picture. The other Picture Type option is Linked. This would maintain a link to the original picture. However, if you move the bitmap, the picture will no longer be displayed and the link would be broken.

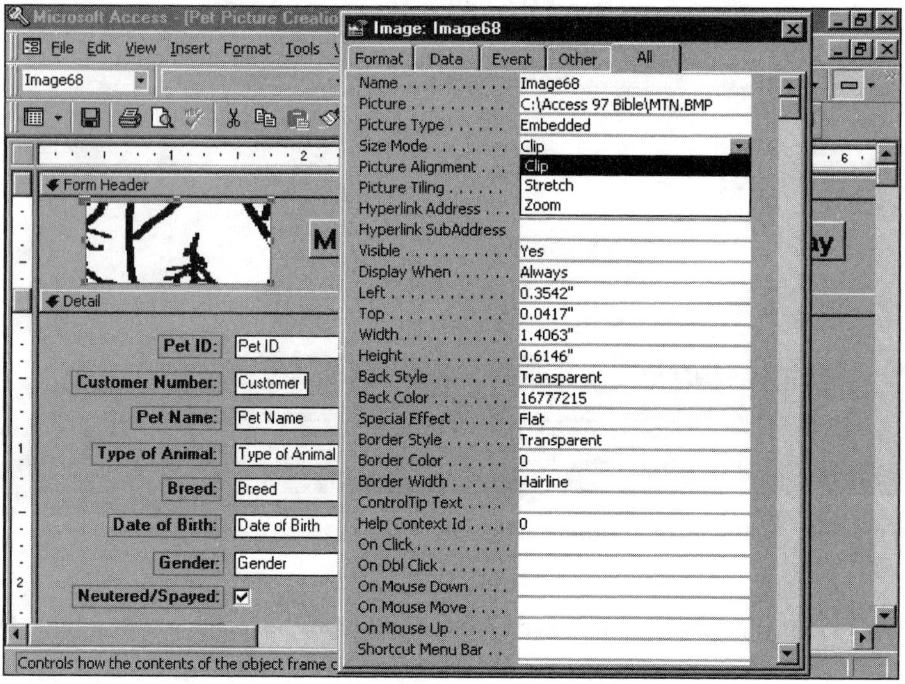

Figure 20-5: The image frame property sheet.

Changing the display of an image

After you add an image to a form or a report, you may want to change the size of the object or the object frame. If you embed a small picture, you may want to adjust the size of the object frame to fit the picture. Similarly, you might want to reduce the size of the picture to fit a specific area on your form or report.

To change the appearance and proportions of the object you embedded, you change the size of the image frame and set the Size Mode property. In Figure 20-6, you see three choices for the Size Mode property:

Clip	Shows the picture using the actual size, truncating both right and bottom
Stretch	Fits the picture within the frame, distorting the picture's proportions
Zoom	Fits the picture proportionally within the frame, possibly resulting in extra white space

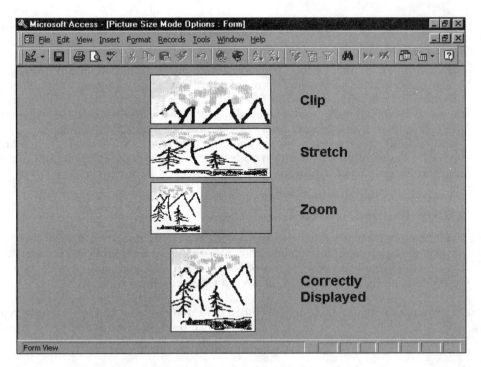

Figure 20-6: Results of using the various scaling options.

Use Clip only when the frame is the exact size of the picture or when you want to crop the picture. Stretch is useful when you have pictures where you can accept a slight amount of distortion. Although using Zoom fits the picture to the frame and maintains the original proportions, it may leave empty space in the frame. Figure 20-6 shows the MTN.BMP file using each of the property selections as well as the correct view of the picture.

To change the Size Mode options for the MTN.BMP file on the Pets form, follow these steps:

1. Select the image frame in Design view.

2. Display the property sheet.

3. Change the Size Mode setting to Stretch.

Tip If you want to return the selected object to its original size, select it and choose Format⇨Size⇨To Fit.

When you have added a picture whose frame (border) is much larger than the picture itself and you have selected a Size Mode of Clip, the picture normally is centered within the frame. You can control this by using one of the Picture Alignment options, which include Center, Top Left, Top Right, Bottom Left, and Bottom Right. These options are also the same ones used when placing a picture in the background of a form using the form's Picture property. Using the Picture Tiling property, you can control how many copies of a picture will fit within a frame. For example, a brick wall is made up of many bricks. You can specify one brick (BRICKS.BMP) in your Windows system directory and then set the Picture Tiling option to Yes to build a wall within your frame. Access copies the bitmap as many times as it needs to fit within the frame.

Embedding bound objects

You can store pictures, spreadsheets, word-processing documents, or other objects as data in a table. You can store (for example) a Paintbrush picture, an Excel worksheet, or an object created in any other OLE application, such as a sound clip, an HTML document, or even a video clip from a movie.

You store objects in a table by creating a field that uses the OLE object data type. After you create a bound object frame, you can bind its Control Source to the OLE object field in the table.

You can then use the bound object frame to embed an object into each record of the table.

Note
You can also insert objects into a table from the Datasheet view of a form, table, or query, but the objects cannot be displayed in a view other than Form. When you switch to Datasheet view, you'll see text describing the OLE class of the embedded object. For example, if you insert a .BMP picture into an OLE object field in a table, the text `Picture` or `Paintbrush Picture` appears in Datasheet view.

Creating a bound OLE object

To create an embedded OLE object in a new bound object frame, follow these steps:

1. Select the Bound Object Frame button from the Toolbox.

2. Drag and size the frame, as shown in Figure 20-7.

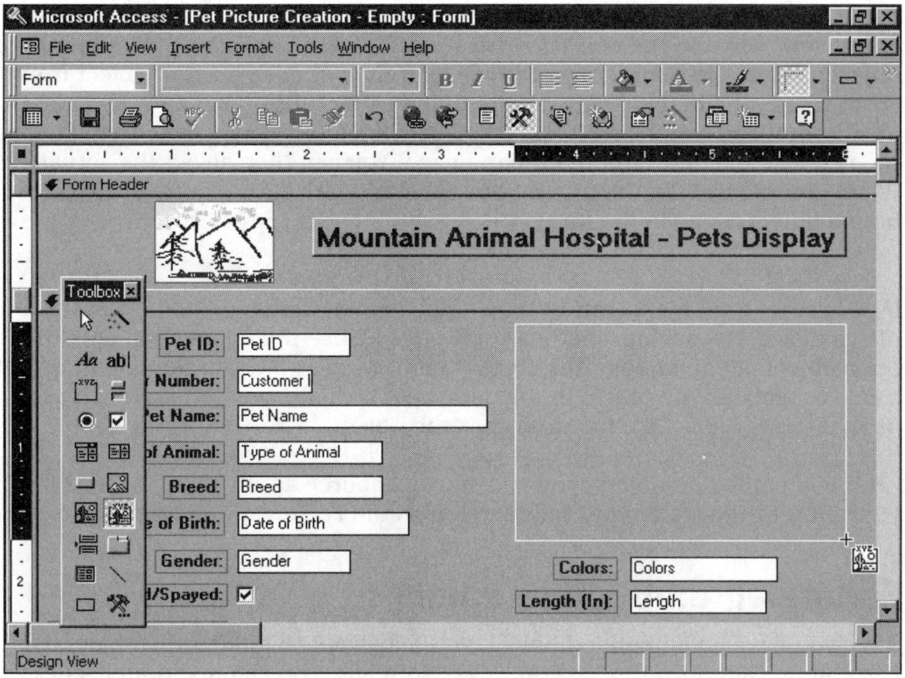

Figure 20-7: Creating a bound object frame.

3. Display the properties sheet.

4. Type **Picture** in the Control Source property. This is the name of the OLE field in the Pets table that contains pictures of the animals.

5. Set the Size Mode property to Zoom so that the picture will be zoomed proportionally within the area you define.

6. Select and delete only the bound object frame label (OLEBoundxx:).

7. Close and save the changes to this form.

Adding a picture to a bound object frame

After you define the bound object frame control and place it on a form, you can add pictures to it in several ways. You can paste a picture into a record or insert a file object into the frame. You insert the file object for a bound frame in nearly the same way you would insert an unbound object or image frame. The only difference is that where an image frame has a picture inserted in the design screen, a bound object frame has a picture inserted in Form view.

To insert a picture or other object into a bound object frame, display the form in Form view, move to the correct record (each record can have a different picture or object), select the bound object frame, and then choose Insert⇨Object from the Form menu. The dialog box is a little different. Because you can insert any OLE object (in this example, a picture), you first have to select Create from File and then choose the first option, Bitmap Image. You can then select the actual picture. When you're through, the picture or object appears in the space used for the bound object frame in the form.

Note   If you create the object (rather than embed an existing file), some applications display a dialog box asking whether you want to close the connection and update the open object. If you choose Yes, Access embeds the object in the bound object frame or embeds the object in the datasheet field along with text (such as Paintbrush Picture) that describes the object.

After you embed an object, you can start its source application and edit it from your form or report. Simply select the object in Form view and double-click on it.

Editing an embedded object

After you have an embedded object, you may want to modify the object itself. You can edit an OLE object in several ways. Normally, you can just double-click on it and launch the source application; then you can edit the embedded OLE object. As an example, follow these steps to edit the picture of the cat in Windows 95 Paintbrush:

1. Display the form Pets Picture Creation — Empty in Form view.

2. Move to record 12 and select the Picture bound object frame of the cat.

3. Double-click on the picture. The screen changes to an image-editing environment with Windows 95 Paint menus and functions available.

Note   As you can see in Figure 20-8, Windows 95 supports full in-place editing of OLE objects. Rather than launch a different program, it changes the look of the menus and screen to match Windows 95 Paint, temporarily adding that functionality to Access. Notice the different menus in Figure 20-8.

4. Make any changes you want to the picture.

5. Click on any other control in the form to close Paint.

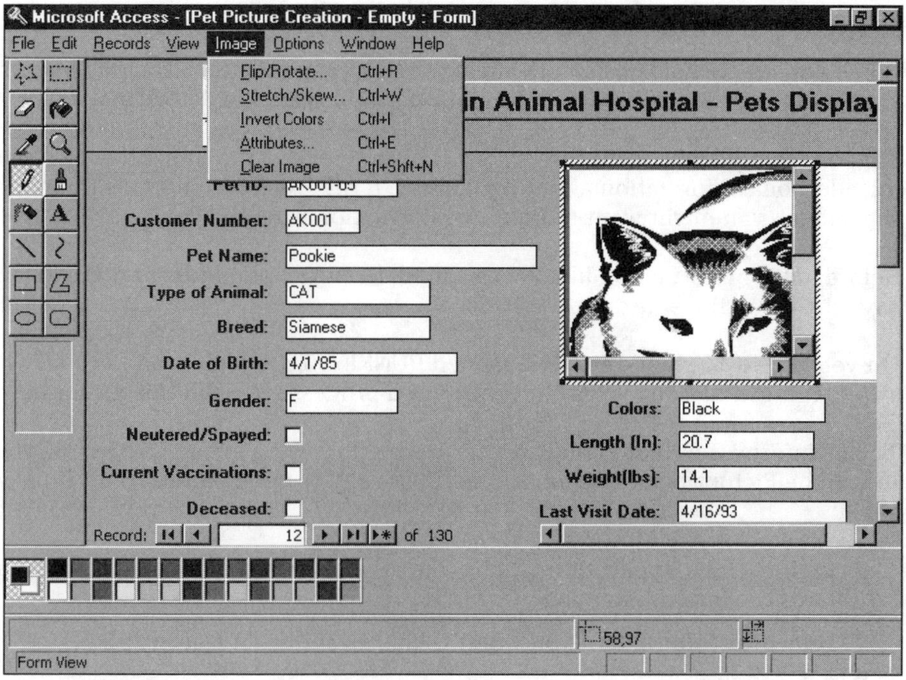

Figure 20-8: Editing the embedded object.

If you make any changes, you will be prompted to update the embedded object before continuing.

Caution In most cases you can modify an OLE object by double-clicking on it. When you attempt to modify either a sound or video object, however, double-clicking on the object causes it to use the player instead of letting you modify it. For these objects, you must use the Edit menu; select the last option, which changes (according to the OLE object type) to let you edit or play the object. You can also convert some embedded OLE objects to static images, which breaks all OLE links and simply displays a picture of the object.

Linking Objects

Besides embedding objects, you can link them to external application files in much the same way as you would embed them. The difference is that the object itself is not stored in the form, the report, or the database table. Instead, Access stores information about the link in those places, saving valuable space in the MDB file. This feature also allows you to edit the object in its source application without having to go through Access.

Linking a bound object

When you create a link from a file in another application (for example, Microsoft Excel) to a field in a table, the information is still stored in its original file.

Suppose that you decide to use the OLE object field to store an Excel file containing additional information about the animal. If the Excel file contains history about the animal, you might want to link the information from the Pet record to this file.

Before linking information in a file to a field, however, you must first create and save the file in the source application.

CD-ROM

On your CD-ROM should be a file named PUNKIN.XLS, which is an Excel 97 worksheet. You can use any spreadsheet or word-processing file in this example.

To link information to a bound object, use the following steps. They show you how to use the Picture bound object frame to link a Pets table record to an Excel worksheet:

1. In the source application (Microsoft Excel), open the document that contains the information you want to link to.

2. Select the information you want to link, as shown in Figure 20-9.

3. Select Edit⇨Copy.

   After you copy the range to the Clipboard, you can paste it into the bound object frame in the Access form by using the Paste Special option of the Edit menu.

4. Switch to Access and open the Pet Picture Creation - Empty form in Form view.

5. Go to record number 32 in the Access form.

6. Select the bound object frame containing the picture of the cat.

7. Select Edit⇨Paste Special.

   The Paste Special dialog box appears as shown in Figure 20-10. When you link a data range to a bound object frame, the link is always manual.

8. Select Paste Link and choose Microsoft Excel worksheet.

9. Click on OK.

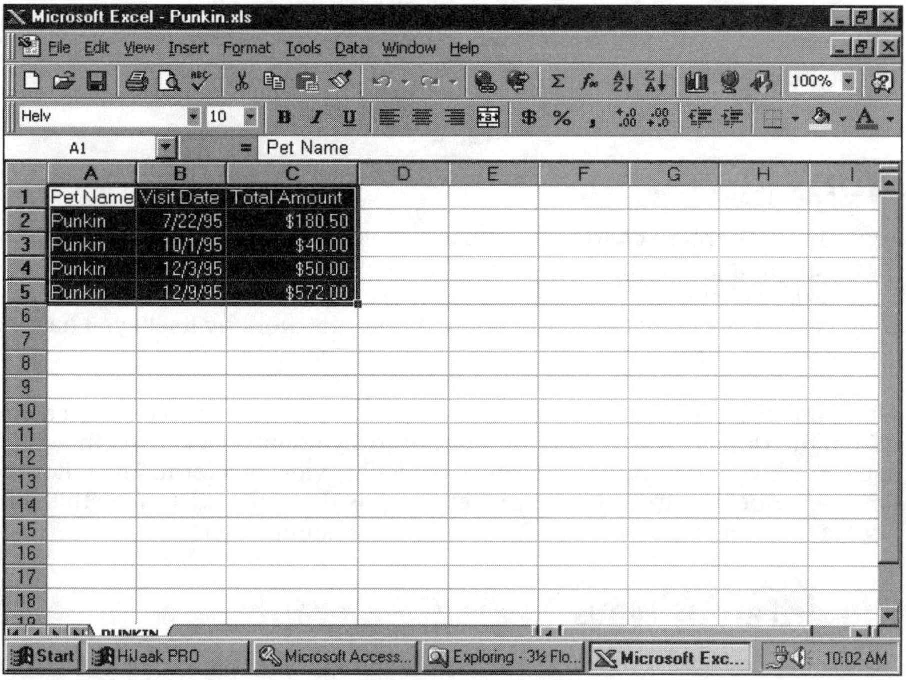

Figure 20-9: Copying a range from Microsoft Excel.

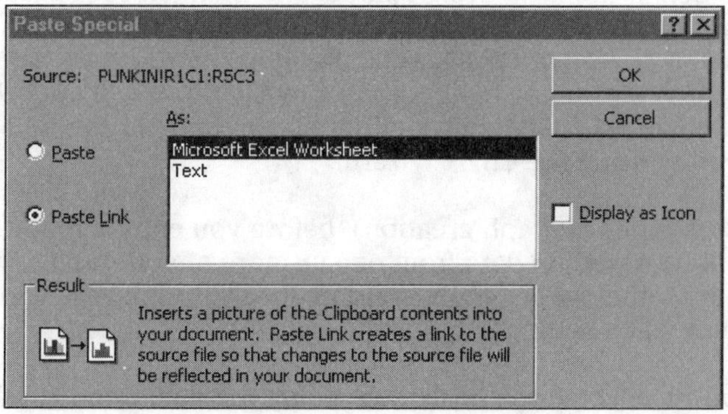

Figure 20-10: Pasting a linked worksheet.

The linked Excel worksheet appears in the bound object frame. Access creates the link and displays the object in the bound object frame or it links the object to the datasheet field, displaying text (such as `Microsoft Excel`) that describes the object. When you double-click on the picture of the worksheet, Excel is launched and you can edit the data.

Creating a Graph

You can use Graph to chart data from any of your database tables or data stored within other applications (such as Microsoft Excel). You can create graphs in a wide variety of styles — bar graphs, pie charts, line charts, and others. Because Graph is an embedded OLE application, it does not work by itself; you have to run it from within Access.

After you embed a graph, you can treat it as any other OLE object. You can modify it from the Design view of your form or report by double-clicking on the graph itself. You can edit it from the Form or Datasheet view of a form. The following sections describe how to build and process graphs that use data from within an Access table as well as from tables of other OLE applications.

The different ways to create a graph

Access provides two ways to create a graph and place it on a form or a report. Using the Graph form or Report Wizard, you can create a graph as a new form or report, add it to an existing form or report, or add it to an existing form and link it to a table data source. (To use this third method, click on the Unbound Object frame button in the Toolbox in the form design mode, and then choose Microsoft Graph 5.0 Chart.) Unless you are already an experienced Graph user, familiar with it from previous versions of Access or Excel, you'll find it easier to create a new graph from the Toolbox. If you examine the Toolbox, however, you will not see a Chart Wizard icon. You must first customize the Toolbox so that you can add a graph to an existing form by using the Chart Wizard.

As a general rule (for both types of graph creation), before you enter a graph into a form or report that will be based on data from one or more of your tables, you must specify which table or query will supply the data for the graph. You should keep in mind several rules when setting up your query:

✦ Make sure that you've selected the fields containing the data to be graphed.

✦ Be sure to include the fields containing the labels that identify the data.

✦ Include any linking fields if you want the data to change from record to record.

Customizing the toolbox

If you are an experienced Access 2.0 user, you may notice that, for the first time, the Chart Wizard button is missing from the Access Toolbox. This is now an optional item, left for you to add. Fortunately, as with toolbars, the Toolbox can be customized.

The easiest way to customize the Toolbox is to right-click on it, display the shortcut menu, and choose Customize. The Customize Toolbars dialog box appears. Click on the Commands tab. You can then select Toolbox from the list of toolbars and then (as shown in Figure 20-11) click on the Chart... command and drag it to the Toolbox. This adds the missing icon permanently. You can rearrange Toolbox icons now by clicking on an icon and dragging it to the desired location in the Toolbox.

Embedding a Graph in a Form

As you learned earlier in this chapter, you can both link and embed objects in your Access tables, and you can create and display objects on your Access forms. Next you create and display a graph based on the Mountain Animal Hospital data and then display it on a form.

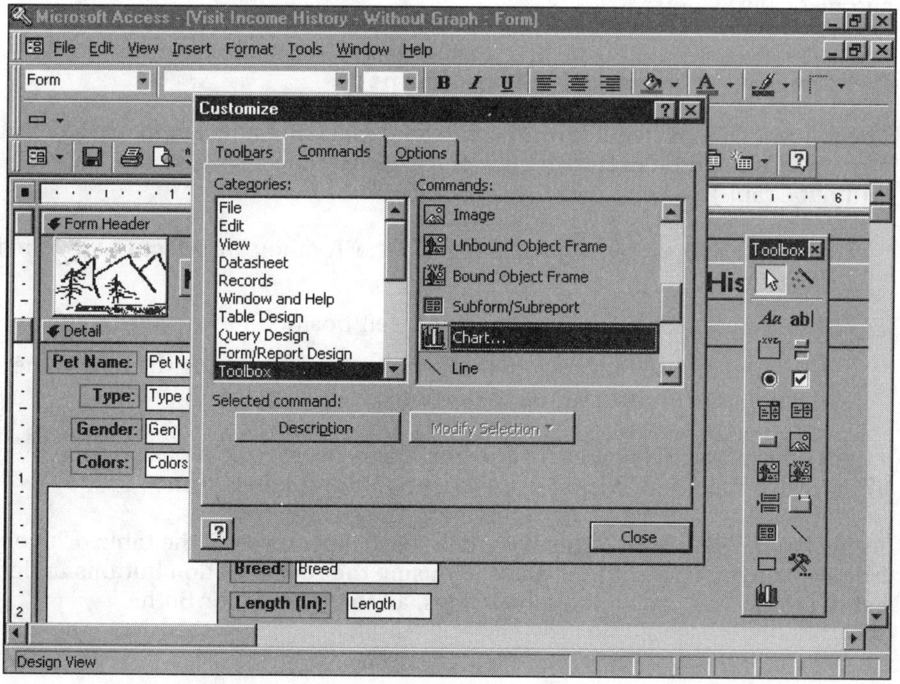

Figure 20-11: Customizing the Toolbox toolbar.

This graph will represent the visits of a pet, showing the visit dates and the dollars received for each visit. When you move through the Pets table, the form recalculates each pet's visits and displays the graph in a graph format. The graph is in the form that Figure 20-1 displayed, which was completed and displayed in Form view. You'll use a form that already exists but doesn't contain the graph: Visit Income History - Without Graph.

The form Visit Income History - Without Graph is in the Mountain Animal Hospital.MDB database, along with the final version (called Visit Income History) that contains the completed graph.

Assembling the data

As a first step in embedding a graph, make sure that the query associated with the form provides the information you need for the graph. In this example, you need both the Visit Date and the Total Amount fields from the Visits table as the basis of the graph. You also need the Pet ID field from the Visits table to use as a link to the data on the form. This link allows the data in the graph to change from record to record.

Sometimes you'll need to create a query when you need data items from more than one table. In this example, you can select all the data you need right from the Wizard; Access will build the query (actually an SQL statement) for you automatically.

Adding the graph to the form

The following steps detail how to create and place the new graph on the existing form (you should be in Design view of the form named Visit Income History - Without Graph):

1. Select the Chart button you added to the Toolbox, or select Chart from the Insert menu.

2. Position the new cursor at the upper left position for the new graph.

3. Click the mouse button and hold it down while dragging the box to the desired size on the righthand portion of the form.

After you size the blank area for the graph and release the mouse button, Access 97 activates the Chart Wizard used to embed a graph in a form.

As shown in Figure 20-12, this Wizard screen lets you select the table or query from which you'll select the values. By using the row of option buttons under the list of tables, you can view all the Tables, all the Queries, or Both.

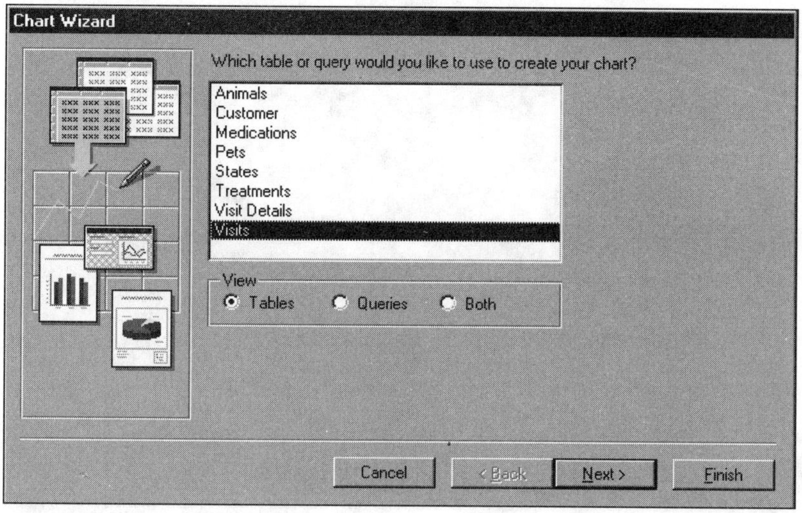

Figure 20-12: Selecting the table for the source of data for the graph.

The following steps take you through the Wizard to create the desired graph and link it to your form:

1. Choose the Visits table as the source for the graph.

2. Click on Next> to go to the next Wizard screen.

   The Chart Wizard lets you select fields to include in your graph.

3. Select the Visit Date and Total Amount fields by double-clicking on them to move them to the Fields for graph box.

4. Click on Next> to go to the next Wizard screen.

   This screen (Figure 20-13) lets you choose the type of graph you want to create and determine whether the data series are in rows or columns. In this example, select a column chart; you'll customize it later using the graph options. As you click on each of the graph types, an explanation appears in the box in the lower right corner of the screen.

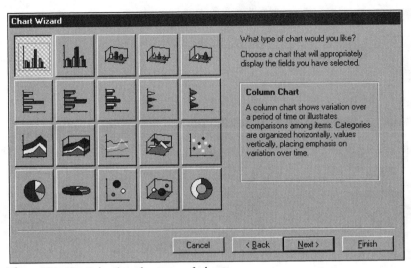

Figure 20-13: Selecting the type of chart.

> **NEW FEATURE** Many new chart types are in Access 97, including 3-D cylinder, cone, pyramid, and bubble charts.

5. Select the Column Chart (as shown in Figure 20-13), and then click on Next> to go to the next Wizard screen. (The Column Chart is easiest to work with.)

The next screen (Figure 20-14) makes choices for you automatically and lets you change the assumptions. Figure 20-14 shows that the Visit Date field has been used for the x-axis and that the Total Amount field is used in the y-axis to determine the height of the bars.

> **NEW FEATURE** This screen is very different from the Access 2.0 Chart Wizard; it replaces three or four Access 2.0 Wizard screens with a single screen.

This screen gives you a graphical way to choose the fields you want for your graph; then you can drag them to the simulated graph window. Figure 20-14 shows the Wizard screen divided into two areas. The right side shows the fields you have selected to work with. The left side displays a simulated graph; you can drag fields from the list of fields on the right to the axis area on the left. If you want to change the Visit Date field chosen for you for the x-axis, drag it back from the left side to the right side. Likewise, to make a selection, drag a field name from the right side of the screen to its proper axis on the left side.

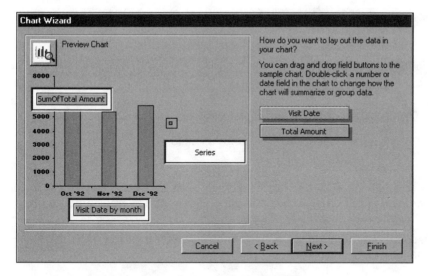

Figure 20-14: Laying out the chart's data elements.

Tip If you had several numeric fields, you could drag them (or any multiple fields) to the left side for a multiple series; these would appear in a legend. You can also drag the same field to both the x-axis and the Series indicator, as long as you're grouping differently. For example, you could group the Visit Date by month and use it again in the Series grouped by year. Without using the Visit Date field a second time as the series variable, you would have one bar for each month in sequential order — for example, Jan95, Feb95, Mar95,... Dec95, Jan96, Feb96.... By adding the Visit Date as a series variable and grouping it by year, you could get pairs of bars. Multiple bars can be created for each month, each a different color and representing a different year and a legend for each year.

For this example, the assumptions made by Access are fine. You may notice (in Figure 20-14) that each of the fields on the left side of the screen is actually a button. When you double-click on one, you can further define how the data is used in the graph.

Generally, the x-axis variable is either a date or a text field. The y-axis field is almost always a number (though it can be a count of values). Only numeric and date fields (such as the y-axis variable Total Amount) can be further defined. If you double-click on the Total Amount field on the left side of the screen, the dialog box shown in Figure 20-15 appears; it lets you define options for summarizing the field. Remember that there may be many records for a given summary; in this example, many pets may have visits in a specific month.

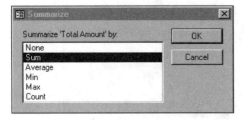

Figure 20-15: Selecting options to summarize the field.

As you can see in Figure 20-15, Sum has been chosen as the summarization type. You could change it to Average to graph the average amount of a visit instead of summing all the visit amounts.

Caution You must supply a numeric variable for all the selections except Count, which can be any data type.

The dialog box shown in Figure 20-16 lets you choose the date hierarchy from larger to smaller roll-ups. The choices include Year, Quarter, Month, Week, Day, Hour, and Minute. If you have data for many dates within a month and want to roll it up by month, you would choose Month. In this example, you want to see all the detail data. Since the data is in Visits by date (mm/dd/yy), you would select Day to view all the detail records. For this example, change the default selection from Month to Day.

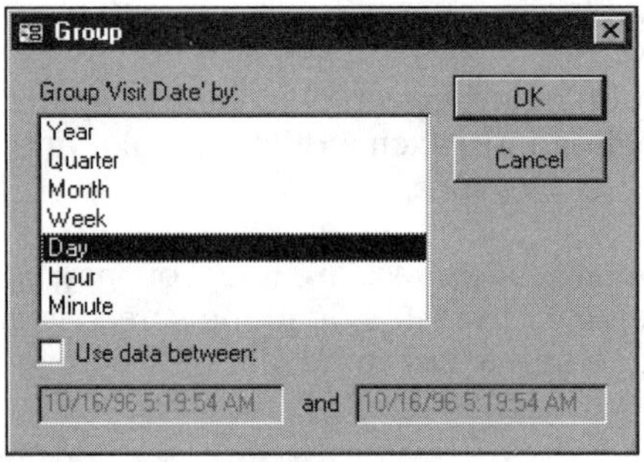

Figure 20-16: Choosing group options for a date field.

You can click on the Preview Chart button at any time to see the results of your choices.

6. Make sure that you changed the group options from Month to Day; click on Next> to go to the next Wizard screen.

Figure 20-17 shows the Field Linking box. If you run the Chart Wizard from inside an existing form, you have the option to link a field in the form to a field in the chart. Even if you don't specify the field when you select the chart fields, you can make the link as long as the field exists in the selected table.

In this example, Access has correctly selected the Pet ID field from both the Visit Income History form and the Visits table. This way, as you move from record to record (keyed by Pet ID) in the Visit Income History form, the graph changes to display only the data for that pet.

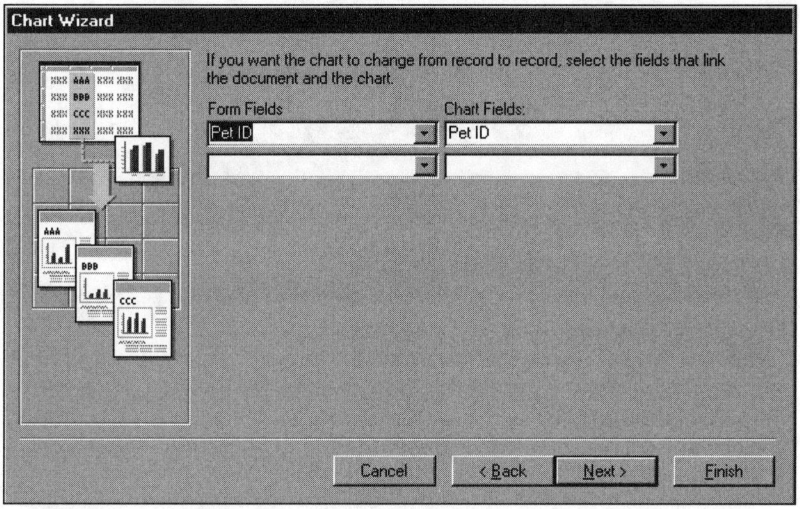

Figure 20-17: Linking fields between the form and the graph.

7. Select Next> to move to the last Wizard screen.

The last Chart Wizard screen, shown in Figure 20-18, lets you enter a title and determine whether a legend is needed. You won't need one for this example because you have only one data series.

Figure 20-18: Specifying a chart title and legend.

8. Enter **Visit Income History** for the graph title.

9. Select the button next to the text `No, don't display a legend.`

10. Click on <u>F</u>inish to complete the Wizard.

   After you complete all these entries, the sample chart appears in the graph object frame on the design screen (as shown in Figure 20-19). Until you display the form in Form view, the link to the individual pet is not established and the graph is not recalculated to show only the visits for the specific pet's record.

   In fact, the graph shown is a sample preview; it doesn't use any of your data. If you were worried about where that strange-looking graph came from, don't be.

11. Click on the Form View button on the toolbar to display the Visit Income History form and recalculate the graph. Figure 20-20 shows the final graph in Form view.

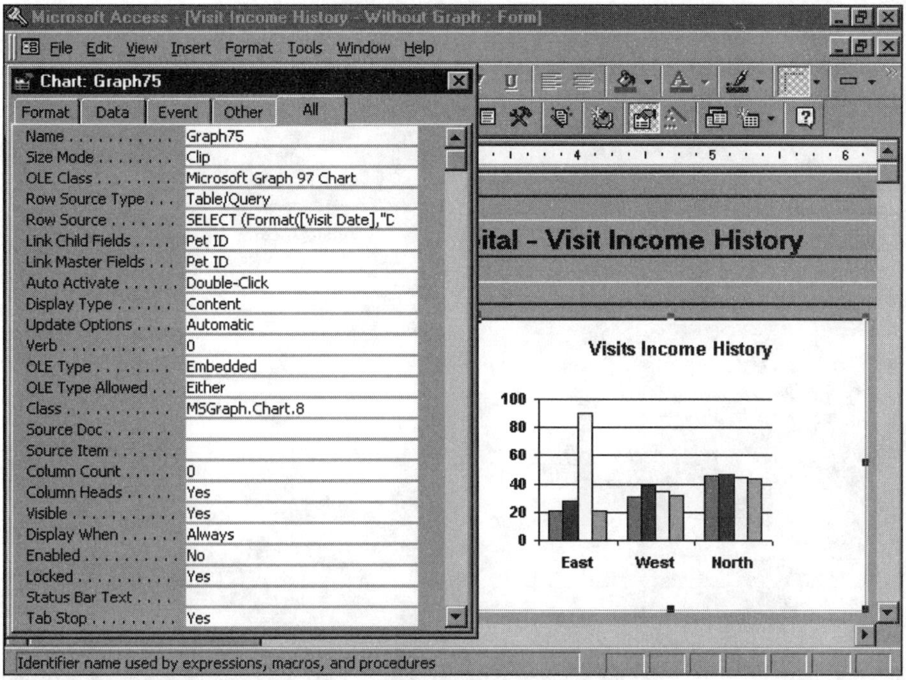

Figure 20-19: The graph in the Form Design window.

In Figure 20-19, you saw the graph and the property sheet. You display a graph by using a *graph frame*, which shows its data in either Form view or Design view. Take note of some properties in the property sheet. The Size Mode property is set initially to Clip. You can change this to Zoom or Stretch, although the graph should always be displayed proportionally. You can size and move the graph to fit on your form. When you work with the graph in the Graph window, the size of the graph you create is the same size it will be in the Design window.

The OLE Class property is Microsoft Graph 97 Chart. This is linked automatically by the Chart Wizard. The Row Source comes from the table of query you used with the graph, but it appears as an SQL statement that is passed to the Graph. The SQL statement (more on this later) created for this graph is:

```
SELECT Format([Visit Date], "DDDDD"), SUM([Total Amount]) AS
      [SumOfTotalAmount]
FROM [Visits] GROUP BY Int([Visit Date]), Format([Visit Date],
      "DDDDD");
```

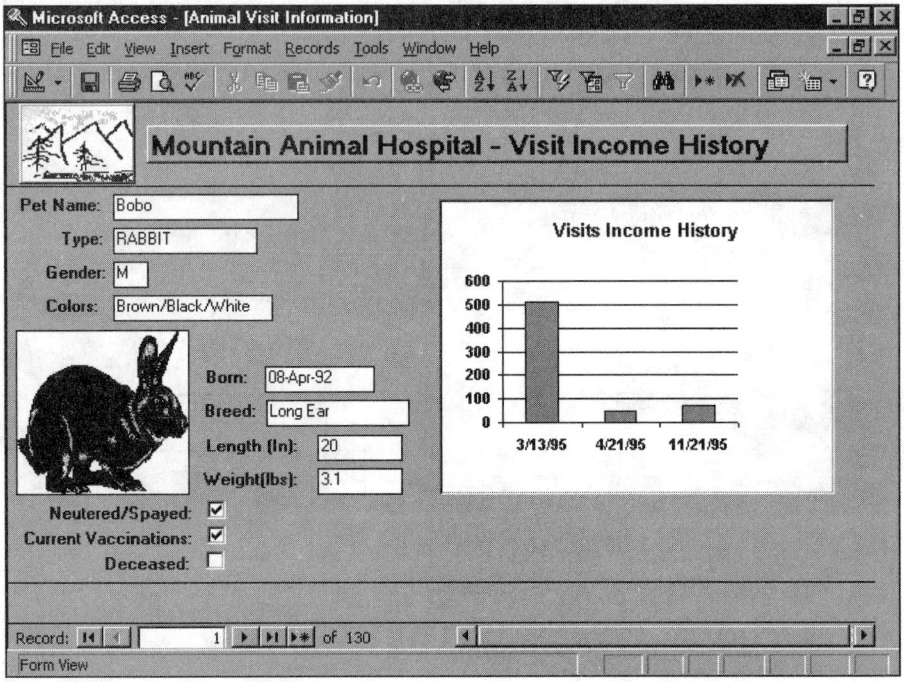

Figure 20-20: Recalculating the graph in Form view.

The next two properties, Link Child Fields and Link Master Fields, control linking of the data to the form data itself. Using the link properties, you can link the graph's data to each record in the form. In this example, the Pet ID from the current Pets record is linked to Visit Details records with the same Pet ID.

To change the appearance of the graph, you can double-click on the graph in Design view to open Microsoft Graph. After you make the changes you want, you can select File⇨Exit, return to Microsoft Access, and go back to Design view.

Customizing a Graph

After you create a graph within Access, you can enhance it by using the tools within Microsoft Graph. As demonstrated in the preceding section, just a few mouse clicks will create a basic graph. The following section describes a number of ways to make your graph a powerful presentation and reporting tool.

In many cases, the basic chart you create presents the idea you want to get across. In other cases, however, it may be necessary to create a more illustrative presentation. You can accomplish this by adding any of these enhancements:

✦ Entering free-form text to the graph to highlight specific areas of the graph

✦ Changing attached text for a better display of the data being presented

✦ Annotating the graph with lines and arrows

✦ Changing certain graphic objects with colors and patterns

✦ Moving and modifying the legend

✦ Adding gridlines to reflect the data better

✦ Manipulating the 3-D view to show your presentation more accurately

✦ Adding a bitmap to the graph for a more professional presentation

✦ Changing the graph type to show the data in a different graphic format, such as Bar, Line, or Pie

✦ Adding or modifying the data in the graph

After the graph appears in the Graph application, you can begin to modify it.

Understanding the Graph window

The Graph window, shown in Figure 20-21, lets you work with and customize the graph. As you can see, there are actually two windows within the Graph window:

Datasheet   A spreadsheet of the data used in the graph

Chart   The displayed chart of the selected data

You can change the look of the graph by resizing the Chart window. Figure 20-21 shows a wider Chart window, which enables you to see labels better. Notice the sample data in the Graph window.

In the datasheet, you can add, change, or delete data. Any data you modify this way is reflected immediately in the graph. After you change the datasheet in the Graph window, you can even tell Access whether to include each row or column when the graph is drawn.

Changing data in a linked record will change data in the graph for only as long as you are on that record. After you move off it, the changes are discarded.

Most important, you can use the Chart portion of the Graph window to change the way the graph appears. By clicking on objects such as attached text (or on areas of the graph such as the columns), you can modify these objects. You can customize by double-clicking on an object to display a dialog box or by making selections from the menus at the top of the window.

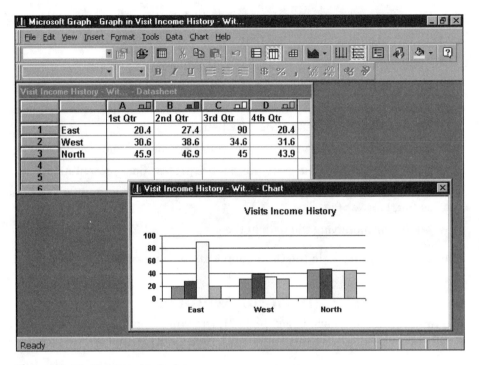

Figure 20-21: The Graph window.

Working with attached text

Text generated by the program is called *attached* text. These graph items are attached text:

✦ Graph title

✦ Value of y-axis

✦ Category of x-axis

✦ Data series and points

✦ Overlay value of y-axis

✦ Overlay value of x-axis

After the initial graph appears, you can change this text. Click on a text object to change the text itself, or double-click on any text item in the preceding list and then modify its properties.

You can choose from three categories of settings to modify an attached text object:

Patterns	Background and foreground colors, borders, and shading
Font	Text font, size, style, and color
Alignment	Alignment and orientation

Note

You can change attributes from the Format menu too.

The Font options let you change the font assignment for the text within the text object, as shown in Figure 20-22.

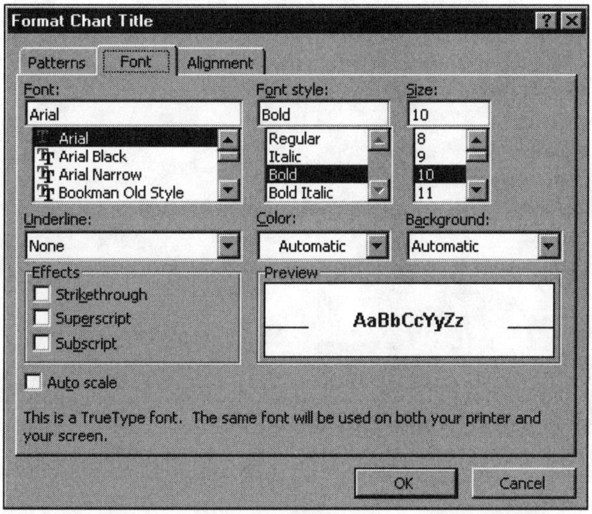

Figure 20-22: The chart fonts dialog box.

The chart fonts dialog box is a standard Windows font-selector box. Here you can select Font, Size, Font Style, Color, and Background effects. To change the text, follow these steps:

1. Double-click on the chart title Visit Income History.

2. Select the Font tab from the Format Chart Title dialog box.

3. Select Times New Roman in the Font list box.

4. Select Italic in the Font Style list box.

5. Select 12 in the <u>S</u>ize list box.

6. Click on OK to complete the changes.

As you make the font changes, a sample of each change appears in the Preview box.

The Alignment tab in the dialog box lets you set the horizontal alignment (left, center, right, or justify), the vertical alignment (top, center, bottom, or justify), and the orientation (a control that lets you rotate your text on a compass). Figure 20-23 shows the Alignment dialog box and the options available.

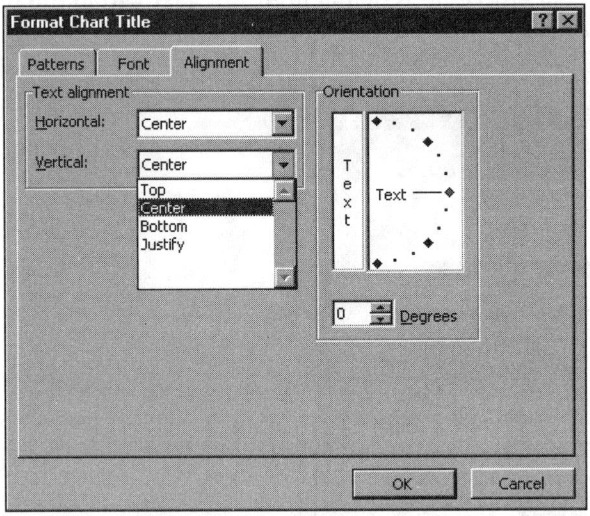

Figure 20-23: The Alignment dialog box.

The most important part of this dialog box is the Orientation setting. Although for some titles it is not important to change any of these settings, it becomes necessary to change them for titles that normally run vertically (such as axis titles).

Sometimes you may need to add text to your graph to present your data better. This text is called *free-form* (or *unattached*) text. You can place it anywhere on your graph and combine it with other objects to illustrate your data as you want. Figure 20-24 shows free-form text being entered on the graph, as well as the changes you previously made to the graph title.

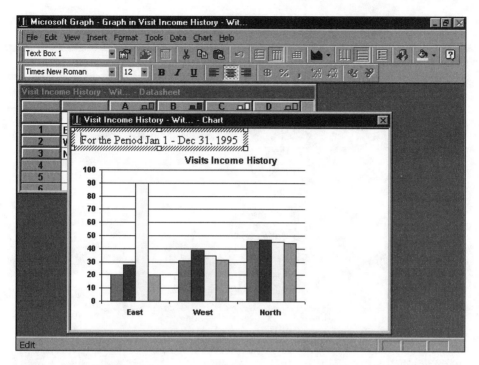

Figure 20-24: Free-form text on a graph.

In the next steps, you see how to add free-form text to the graph:

1. Type **For the Period Jan 1-Dec 31, 1995** anywhere on the graph, as shown in Figure 20-24.

   Microsoft Graph positions the text near the middle of the graph. The text is surrounded by handles so that you can size and position the text.

2. Drag the text to the upper left corner of the graph.

3. Right-click on the text, select Format⇨Text Box, and change the font to Times New Roman, 12 point, regular.

Changing the graph type

After you create your initial graph, you can experiment with changing the graph type to make sure that you selected the type that best reflects your data. Microsoft Graph provides a wide range of graphs to select from; a few mouse clicks can change the type of graph.

The following are the different types of graphs you can select:

Two-Dimensional Charts	*Three-Dimensional Charts*
Column	3-D Column
Bar	3-D Bar
Line	3-D Line
Pie	3-D Pie
XY (Scatter)	3-D Area
Area	3-D Surface
Doughnut	3-D Cylinder
Radar	3-D Cone
Surface	3-D Pyramid
Bubble	
Stock	
Cylinder	
Cone	
Pyramid	

To select a different type of graph, select Chart⇨Chart Type from the menu bar of the Chart window to display the various chart types. When you select any of the graph options, a window opens (as shown in Figure 20-25) to display all the different graphing options available within the selected graph type. Click on one of them to select your new graph type.

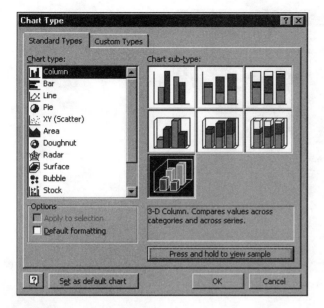

Figure 20-25: The chart types.

To display some different graph types, follow these steps:

1. Select Chart⇨Chart Type, as shown in Figure 20-25.
2. Select Column from the Standard Types tab and select the 3-D Column type.
3. Click on OK to return to the Graph window.

Changing axis labels

You may want to change the text font of the x-axis so that you can see all the labels. Follow these steps to change axis labels:

1. Double-click on the x-axis (the bottom axis with East, West, and North from the Sample data on it). You can see the Format Axis tabbed dialog box in Figure 20-26.
2. Select the Font tab from the Format Axis dialog box.
3. Change the Size setting to 8 points by entering **8** in the Font Size box.
4. Click on OK to return to the chart.

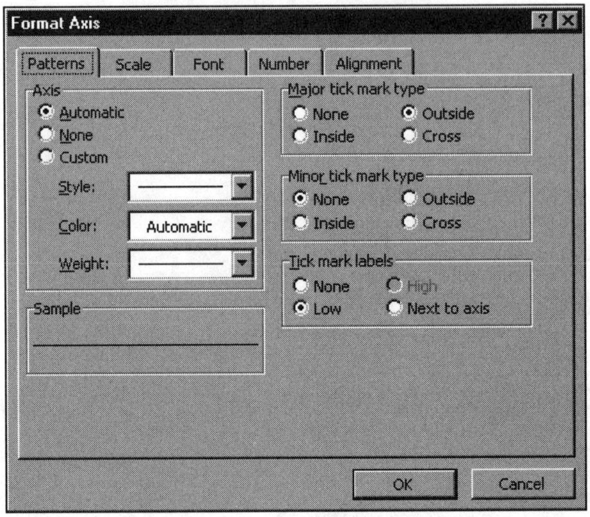

Figure 20-26: The Format Axis dialog box.

Changing a bar color, pattern, and shape

If you are going to print the graph in monochrome, you should always adjust the patterns so that they are not all solid colors. You can change the color or pattern of each bar by double-clicking on any bar in the category you want to select.

The Format Data Series dialog box is displayed. You can change the patterns and color of the bars from the first tab. If you press the Shape tab, as shown in Figure 20-27, you can select from cubes, pyramids, cylinders, or cones.

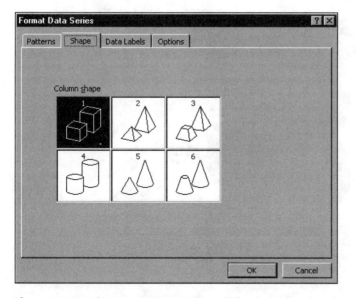

Figure 20-27: The Format Data Series dialog box showing the Shape tab.

Modifying gridlines

Gridlines are lines that extend from the axis across the plotting area of the graph to help you read the graph properly. You can add them for the x-axis and y-axis of your graph; if it's three-dimensional, an additional gridline is available for the z-axis. You can add gridlines for any axis on the graph. The *z-axis gridlines* appear along the back and side walls of the plotting area. The *x-* and *y-axis gridlines* appear across the base and up the walls of the graph.

Select Chart⇨Chart Options... to begin working with gridlines. Select the Gridlines tab, as shown in Figure 20-28. Here, you can define which gridlines are shown. On the left wall are shown the y-axis gridlines; the z-axis gridlines are shown on the back wall; and the x-axis gridlines are shown on the floor. You can change the line type by double-clicking on the gridlines when you're in the normal Design view of the graph and working with the Format Gridlines dialog box to change the Patterns and Scale.

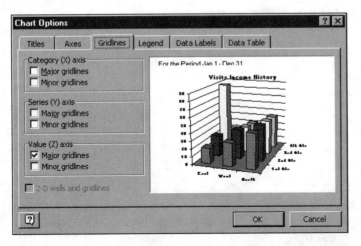

Figure 20-28: The Chart Options dialog box showing the Gridlines tab.

Manipulating three-dimensional graphs

In any of the three-dimensional chart options, you can modify the following graph-display characteristics:

✦ Elevation

✦ Perspective (if the Right angle axes option is turned off)

✦ Rotation

✦ Scaling

✦ Angle and height of the axes

You can change the 3-D view by selecting Chart⇨3-D View. The dialog box shown in Figure 20-29 appears. Then you can enter the values for the various settings or use the six buttons to rotate the icon of the graph in real time. When you like the view you see, click on OK and your chart will change to that perspective.

Note   The Elevation buttons control the height at which you view the data. The elevation is measured in degrees; it can range from –90 to 90 degrees.

An elevation of zero displays the graph as if you were level with the center of the graph. An elevation of 90 degrees shows the graph as you would view it from above center. A –90 degree elevation shows the graph as you would view it from below its center.

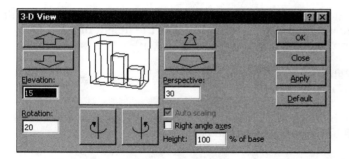

Figure 20-29: The 3-D View dialog box.

The Perspective buttons control the amount of perspective in your graph. Adding more perspective makes the data markers at the back of the graph smaller than those at the front of the graph. This option provides a sense of distance; the smaller data markers seem farther away. If your graph contains a large amount of data, you may want to use a larger perspective value (the ratio of the front of the graph to the back of the graph). This value can range from 0 to 100.

A perspective of 0 makes the back edge of the graph equal in width to the front edge. You can experiment with these settings until you get the effect you need.

The Rotation buttons control the rotation of the entire plotting area. The rotation is measured in degrees, from 0 to 360. A rotation of 0 displays your graph as you view it from directly in front. A rotation of 180 degrees displays the graph as if you were viewing it from the back. (This setting visually reverses the plotting order of your data series.) A rotation of 90 degrees displays your graph as if you were viewing it from the center of the side wall.

The Auto scaling check box lets you scale a three-dimensional graph so that its size is closer to that of the two-dimensional graph using the same data. To activate this option, click on the Auto scaling check box so that the X appears in the box. When this option is kept activated, Access will scale the graph automatically whenever you switch from a two-dimensional to a three-dimensional graph.

Two options within the 3-D View dialog box pertain specifically to display of the axes. The Right angle axes check box lets you control the orientation of the axes. If the check box is on, all axes are displayed at right angles to each other.

Caution If the Right angle axes check box is selected, you cannot specify the perspective for the three-dimensional view.

The Height entry box contains the height of the z-axis and walls relative to the width of the graph's base. The height is measured as a percentage of the x-axis length. A height of 100 percent makes the height equal to the x-axis. A height of 50 percent makes the height half the x-axis length. You can set this height percentage at more than 100 percent; by doing so, you can make the height of the z-axis greater than the length of the x-axis.

Caution If you change the Height setting, your change will not be displayed in the sample graph shown in the 3-D View dialog box.

After you have made the desired changes, you can select File➪Exit and then select Return to (which will bring you back to the Form Design screen).

You might want to make one more change: A graph frame is really an unbound object frame, and you can change its border type and background (as you can for any unbound object frame). Figure 20-30 shows the final graph after the border has been changed to an etched special effect, and the background colored light gray to match the background of the form. This allows the graph to stand out more than it would if you used a sunken white background.

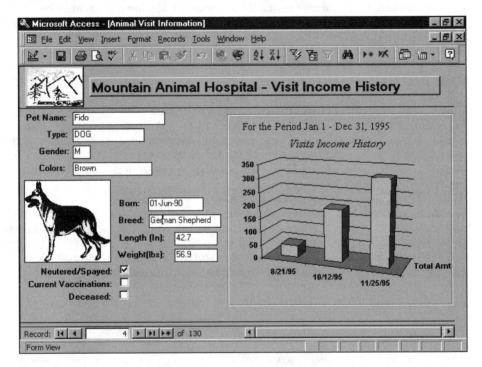

Figure 20-30: The final graph.

Integration with Microsoft Office

Access 97 is not only integrated with Windows 95 or Windows NT, it now shares many major components with Microsoft Office 97. (If you are an Excel 97 or Word 97 user, you will be especially thrilled.) Access 97 has an integrated Spell Checker that is used to make sure that the data stored in Access 97 tables and database objects is spelled correctly. The dictionary is shared across all Office 97 applications, including custom words. Access 97 also shares the Office 97 AutoCorrect features to fix errors while you type.

Checking the spelling of one or more fields and records

You can check the spelling of your data in either Form or Datasheet view. In Form view, you can spell-check only a single record — and field within the record — at a time. To check the spelling of data in Form view, you would select the field or text containing spelling you want to check, and then click on the Spell Check icon on the toolbar (the icon with the check mark and the small letters ABC above it).

When you click on the icon, Access checks the field (or selected text within the field) for spelling, as shown in Figure 20-31.

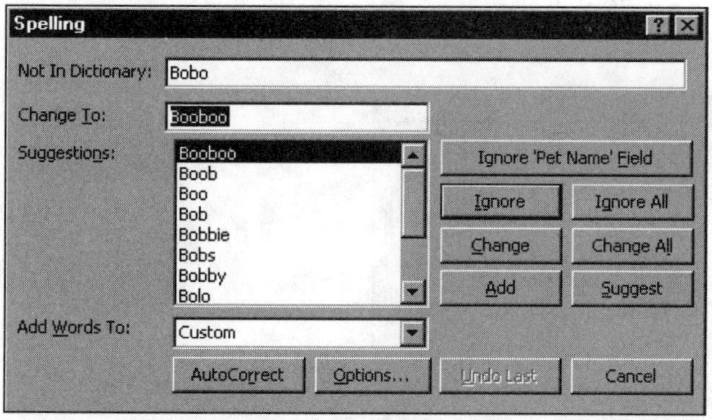

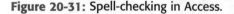

Figure 20-31: Spell-checking in Access.

In the Spelling dialog box that appears, you can click on <u>A</u>dd if you want to add the word in the Not In Dictionary: box to the custom dictionary listed in the Add <u>W</u>ords To: box.

You can select only one field at a time in Form view. You'll probably want to use only Form view to spell-check selected memo data; to select multiple fields or records, you must switch to Datasheet view. To check the spelling of data in

Datasheet view, you would select the records, columns, fields, or text within a field containing spelling you want to check and then click on the Spell Check icon.

You can also check the spelling in a table, query, or form in the Database window by clicking on the table, query, or form object containing spelling you want to check.

You only spell-check the data inside the objects. Access 97 cannot spell-check control names.

Correcting your typing automatically when entering data

You can use the AutoCorrect feature to provide automatic corrections to text you frequently mistype and to replace abbreviations with the long names they stand for (also automatically). For example, you can create an entry "mah" for Mountain Animal Hospital. Whenever you type **mah** followed by a space or punctuation mark, Microsoft Access replaces mah with the text Mountain Animal Hospital.

You can activate AutoCorrect by selecting Tools➪AutoCorrect. The dialog box shown in Figure 20-32 appears. You can select the Replace text as you type check box. In the Replace box, type the text you want corrected. In the With box, type the corrected text. When you click on Add, the word replacement combination will be added to the AutoCorrect dictionary.

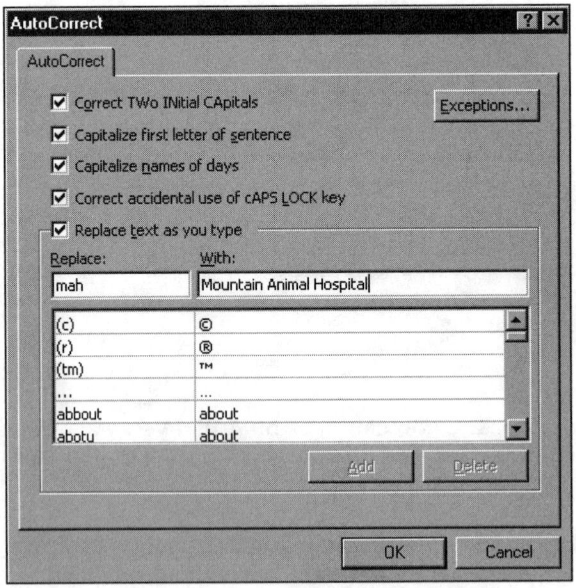

Figure 20-32: Using AutoCorrect in Access 97.

AutoCorrect won't correct text that was typed before you selected the Replace text as you type check box.

Using OLE automation with Office 97

Access 97 takes advantage of drag and drop; you can do it from Datasheet view across Excel and Word. You can instantly create a table in a Word document (or add a table to an Excel spreadsheet) by simply copying and pasting (or dragging and dropping) data from an Access datasheet to a Word document or an Excel spreadsheet. (Obviously, you must have Word or Excel to take advantage of these features.)

Access 97 contains a new PivotTable Wizard to create Excel PivotTables based on Access tables or queries. A *PivotTable* is like a cross-tabulation of your data; you can define the data values for rows, columns, pages and summarization. Figure 20-33 (from the Microsoft Excel 97 Help system) shows a conceptual figure of a PivotTable.

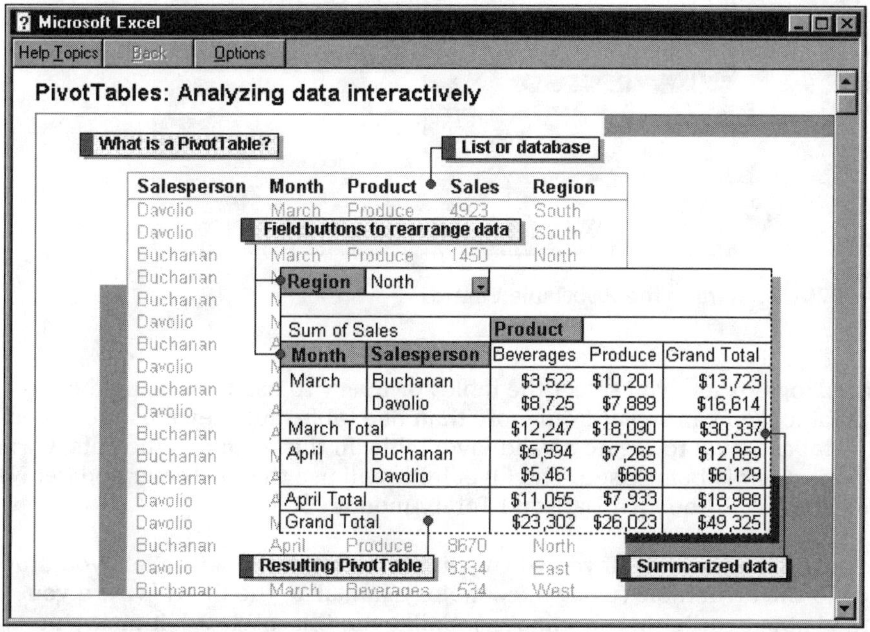

Figure 20-33: A conceptual view of a PivotTable.

A PivotTable can have multiple levels of rows, columns, and even pages. As you can see in the conceptual figure, the center of the table contains numeric data; the rows and columns form a hierarchy of unique data. In this figure, dates and salespeople are the row hierarchies, along with multiple levels of subtotals. The column headers are types of products, and each page of the PivotTable is a different region.

Cross-Reference A PivotTable is like a crosstab query (see Chapter 25), but much more powerful.

You start creating a PivotTable from the New Form dialog box using one of the standard Wizards you can select. After you begin the PivotTable Wizard process, you will first see an introductory screen explaining how a PivotTable works. After you view this screen, press the Next> button to begin selecting the fields for the PivotTable (shown in Figure 20-34).

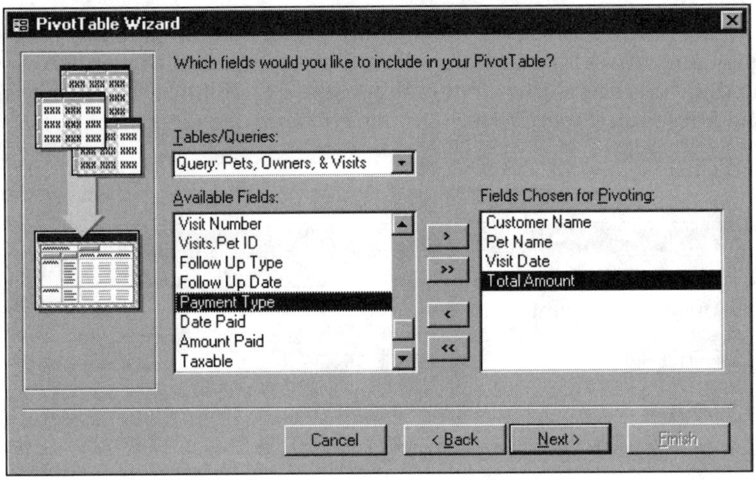

Figure 20-34: Starting the PivotTable Wizard.

This dialog box lets you select the tables or query to use in creating the PivotTable. You can select from more than one table, but they must be joined at the database level to create a valid PivotTable. In this example, the Pets, Owners, & Visits query is being used. The PivotTable will use the Customer and Pet Name fields along with the Visit Date and Total Amount spent.

The next dialog box displayed when you press the Next> button lets you drag the fields to the PivotTable (using a technology similar to the Chart Wizard you learned about earlier in this chapter). Unlike the Chart Wizard, it makes no assumptions for you. You must drag each field from the list on the right to the area on the left. As you can see, Customer Name for the page, Pet Name will be used for the column headers, Visit Date for the row names, and Total Amount will be summed in the center of the PivotTable. You may also notice that Microsoft Excel 97 is started as the PivotTable will be created for this program.

You can double-click on any of the items in the field placement area. You can determine where a field is placed and how subtotals are created for each field (as shown in Figure 20-35). You can see in Figure 20-36 that you can also change the placement of the field by clicking on the Orientation option buttons. You can also determine how subtotals are created for the field.

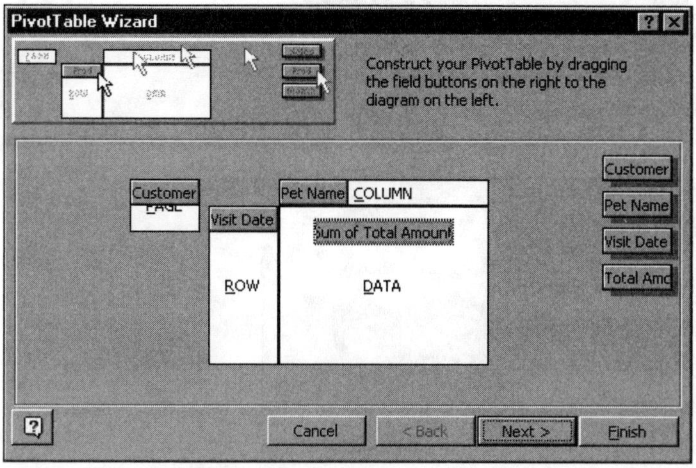

Figure 20-35: Selecting the field locations.

Finally, you can choose to hide any of the data items. Although this doesn't make sense for this example, if you were using date data, you could exclude a range of dates; in the case of a few product lines, you could exclude selected products.

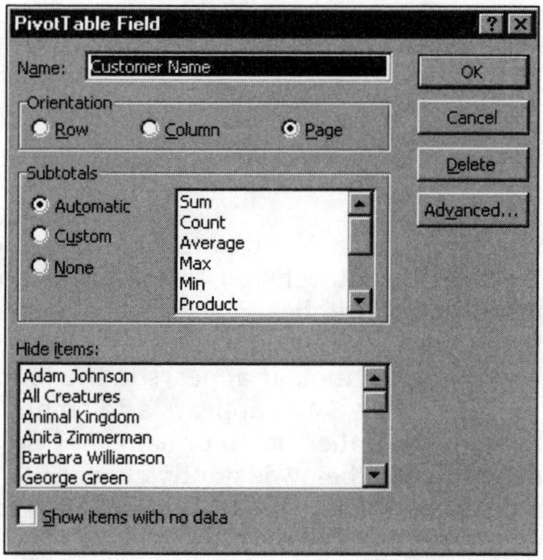

Figure 20-36: Selecting the field locations.

After you complete this screen, you can complete the last Wizard screen. When you press the Options button, the Options screen appears, as shown in Figure 20-37.

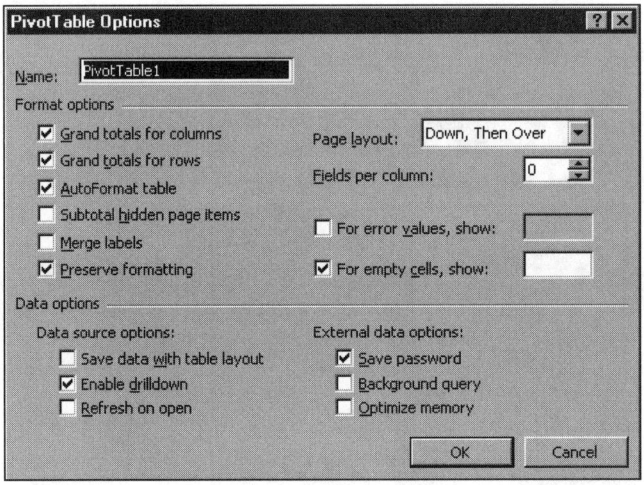

Figure 20-37: Using the final PivotTable Wizard Options screen.

This screen lets you determine whether totals for columns and rows are displayed. You can also determine if the default AutoFormat is used when the PivotTable is created. After you return to the last screen and select the Finish button, a new form is created; you can see your results as shown in Figure 20-38.

The PivotTable in the figure shows the PivotTable in Excel 97. The OLE link is then made to Access 97 and the PivotTable is displayed in an Access form.

Note You must have Excel to use this Wizard.

Using the new OLE capabilities, the Excel PivotTable Wizard appears to be integrated with Access; it's really an embedded Excel object. You can edit this table by pressing the large Edit PivotTable button, which switches to an Excel 97 view (as shown in Figure 20-38) and displays the various options, including one that changes the PivotTable selections. The PivotTable toolbar appears in the lower portion of the screen. The page variable Customer Name appears as a combo box, initially set to All. This has been changed to show the customer name All Creatures. When this selection is made, the data below instantly changes to show only data for pets owned by All Creatures. Notice the row and column totals in the figure.

PivotTables are easy to create and provide a much better analysis than cross-tabulation queries. When you save the form, the link to Excel remains.

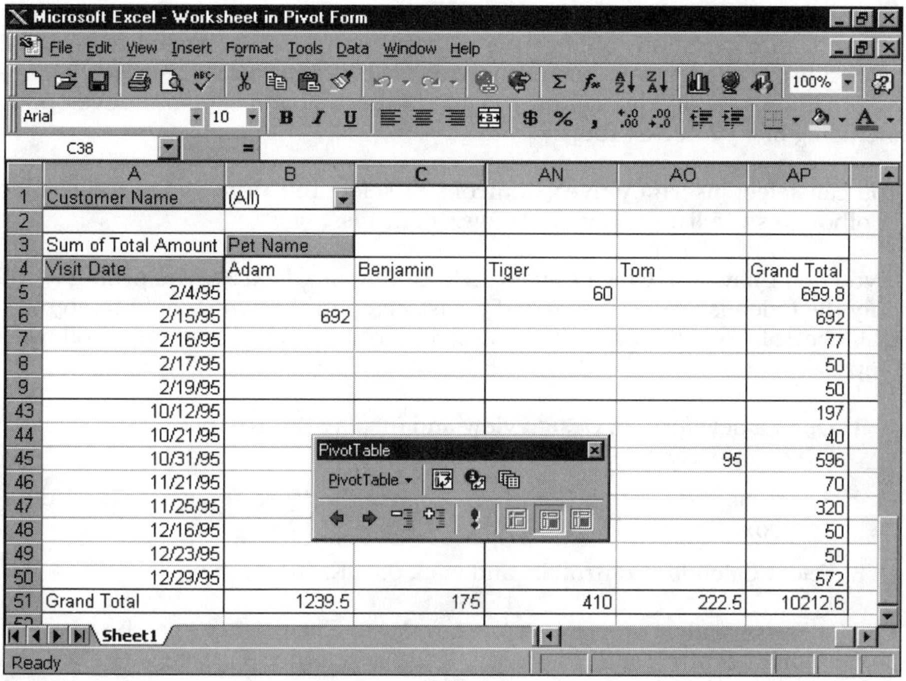

Figure 20-38: The completed PivotTable.

NEW FEATURE Another feature in Excel 97 lets you create a new Access table directly from an Excel 97 spreadsheet — automatically — and link them so that data changes are made with either product. This is not an Access feature, but an Excel feature you should know; it allows Excel users to update and manipulate Access data without knowing Access.

Using the Calendar ActiveX Control

ActiveX controls (also known as OCX and custom controls) are not new to Access. Custom controls extend the number of controls already found in Access. Some of the more popular controls have included Calendars, Tab Dialog box controls, Progress Meters, Spin Box, Sliders, and many others. Though they existed in Access 2.0 (as 16-bit controls), they were seldom used; they required separate sets of properties and were not totally stable. Access for Windows 95 introduced support for the new 32-bit controls, and Access 97 makes them even better. Access 97 comes with one ActiveX control called the Calendar control. If you have Office 97, you have many ActiveX controls from the new Microsoft Forms collection used to create Office forms without Access. There is expected to be a wealth of new ActiveX controls from third parties for Access 97.

Note   The Office Developers Edition is a separate product from Microsoft that allows you to create a run-time application without Access. It also includes the Help compiler, a printed-language reference manual, the Windows Setup Wizard, many other ActiveX controls, and many new tools for Access 97 and Office 97 developers, including many Internet tools.

You can select Insert⇨ActiveX Control... or select the More Tools icon from the Toolbox to see a list of all your ActiveX controls.

If you don't have the Office Developer's Edition or Office 97, you probably will see only the Calendar control. You add a custom control as you would to any unbound OLE control. To add a Calendar custom control to a new blank form, follow these steps:

1. Open a new form in Design view and display the Toolbox. Don't select any table in the New Form dialog box.

2. Select Insert⇨Custom Control or choose the More Tools icon from the Toolbox.

3. Select Calendar Control 8.0 and click on OK.

The Calendar control appears on the new form. The calendar can be resized like any unbound control, and (of course) it has properties. Figure 20-39 shows the Calendar control and its basic properties.

Notice the Property window. This window appears showing the properties specific to a Calendar control. These are the properties displayed by the Other tab. With these properties, you can change some of the display characteristics of the calendar, including the following:

DayLength	Short(SMTWTFS), Medium (Sun, Mon, Tue, . . .), Long (Sunday, Monday, . . .)
FirstDay	First day of week displayed (default is Sunday)
GridCellEffect	Raised, Sunken, Flat
MonthLength	Long (January, February, . . .), Short (Jan, Feb, . . .)
ShowDateSelectors	Display a combo box for month and year in Form view

Many other properties control the various colors and fonts of calendar components. A number of value properties affect the display of the calendar and the selected date. Four properties change the display of the calendar data:

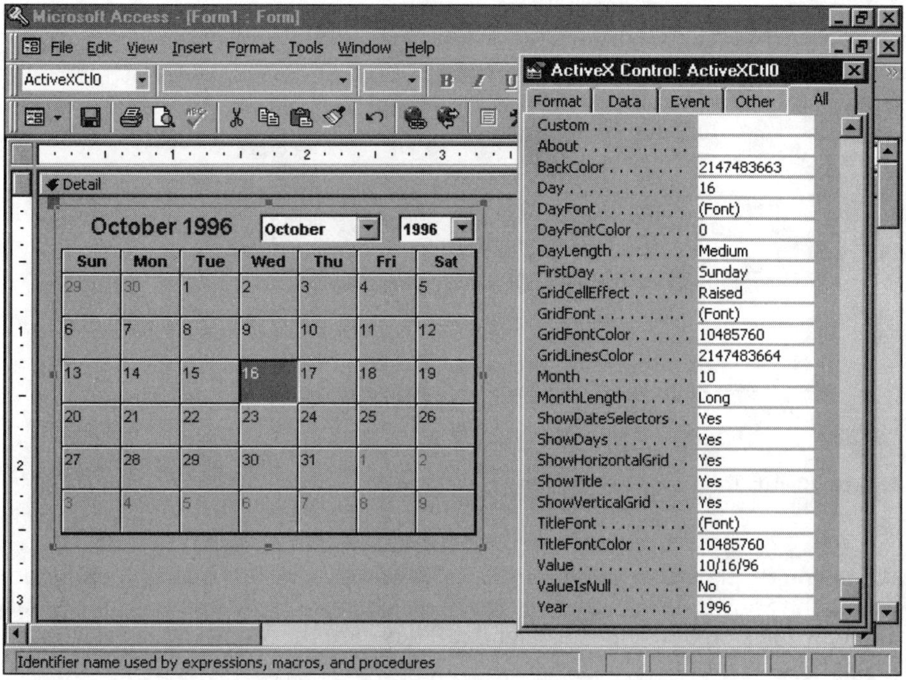

Figure 20-39: The Calendar control and the standard and additional Access properties.

Day	The day of the current month (16 in this example)
Month	The month of the current date (10 in this example)
Year	The year being displayed (1996 in this example)
Value	The date displayed (10/16/96 in this example)

Cross-Reference The values can be changed in several ways. You can click on a date in the calendar in Form view, which changes the Value property. When the Value property changes, so do the Day, Month, and Year properties. You can also change these properties in the Property window or programmatically from a macro or Visual Basic for Applications. You'll learn how to do this in Chapters 32 and 34.

Another way to change properties in a custom control is to display the Calendar Properties dialog box, as shown in Figure 20-40. This provides combo-box access to certain control properties. You can display this dialog box by selecting Edit⇨ Calendar Control Object⇨Properties or by right-clicking on the Calendar control and selecting Calendar Control Object⇨Properties from the shortcut menu.

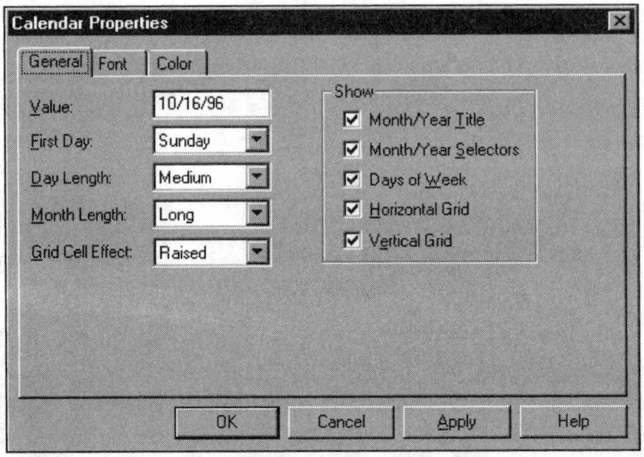

Figure 20-40: The Calendar Properties dialog box.

When you display the calendar in Form view, you can also display combo boxes (using the ShowDateSelectors property) to change the month or year because you can only click on a day in the calendar. These are the Month/Year Selectors in the Property dialog box.

The calendar's real power is that you can link it to a field. When the calendar is changed, the field value changes. Likewise, if the field value changes, the calendar display changes. You can easily do this by linking the calendar to a field by using its Control Source property.

Summary

In this chapter, you learned the differences between linking and embedding graphs and other OLE objects to your forms. You created a graph by using the Chart Wizard, and you used Microsoft Graph to customize the graph to fit your needs. Microsoft Access, because of its Windows compatibility, has the power to share data, pictures, and other objects with other OLE-compatible products. You also learned that you can embed or link a full range of graphs to your forms with just a few keystrokes. In this chapter, the following points were explained:

✦ Access adds any type of picture or graphic object to an Access table, including sound and video, a worksheet, or a document.

✦ A bound object is attached to a specific record, whereas an unbound object is attached only to a form or report.

✦ Embedded objects are stored in a table, form, or report, but linked objects merely link to an external file.

✦ You can embed an object by either pasting it into an object frame or inserting the object.

✦ If the embedded object supports OLE, you can double-click on the object to launch the source application and edit the object.

✦ The easiest way to create graphs is to use the Chart Wizard in a form.

✦ After you create a graph, you can customize the graph by using Microsoft Graph.

✦ To customize a graph, double-click on it; then you can change the graph type, text, axis labels, legend, gridlines, colors, patterns, and view of the graph.

✦ You can embed a graph in a form and link it to the data in the form by using the Chart button in the Toolbox of the Form or Report Design window; then you follow the steps in the Wizard.

✦ You can use various Office 97 features, including spell-checking and AutoCorrect when you're working with Access data.

✦ You can create an Excel PivotTable to analyze your data by using the PivotTable Wizard.

✦ ActiveX controls extend the functionality of Access forms and reports. The Calendar control that comes with Access lets you add calendar functions to Access.

In the next chapter, you learn how to create reports.

✦   ✦   ✦

Creating and Customizing Reports

In previous chapters, you learned how to create a report from a single table by using a Wizard. You also learned how to create multiple-table queries and work with controls. In this chapter, you combine and build on these concepts. You learn how to create — from scratch — a report that lets you view data from multiple tables, group the data, and sort it in meaningful ways.

Starting with a Blank Form

Cross-
Reference

In Chapter 11, you learned how to create a report by using an Access Report Wizard with a single table as the data source. Wizards are great for creating quick and simple reports, but they are fairly limited and give you little control over field type or placement. Although there are advantages to creating a report with a Wizard and then modifying the report, this chapter focuses on creating a report from a blank form without the help of the Wizards. If you haven't read Chapter 11, now is a good time to read or review it. In the chapter you're reading now, you have to understand the basic report concepts covered in Chapter 11. This chapter assumes that you have also read Chapter 16 and are familiar with the basic controls and properties used in forms and reports.

Previous chapters about forms introduced you to all the tools available in the Report Design window. When you create reports, you use some of these tools in a slightly different manner from that used to create forms. It is important to review some of the unique menus and toolbar buttons.

Note Because the Report Design window is set to a width of eight inches, most of the screen printouts in this chapter were taken with a Super VGA Windows screen driver (800 x 600 resolution) rather than with the standard VGA Windows driver (640 x 480). This higher resolution lets you see almost the entire screen in the screen figures.

You can view a report in three different views: Design, Layout Preview, and Print Preview. You can also print a report to the hard-copy device defined for Windows 95. You have already seen the preview windows in previous chapters. This chapter will focus on the Report Design window.

The Report Design window is where you create and modify reports. The empty Report Design window, shown in Figure 21-1, contains various tools, including the Toolbox.

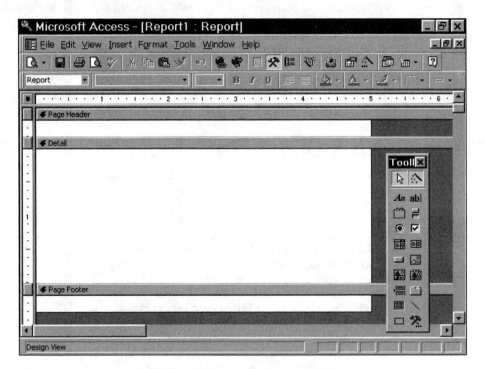

Figure 21-1: The Report Design window showing the Toolbox.

The Design Window Toolbar

The Report Design View toolbar is shown in Figure 21-2. You can click on the button you want for quick access to such design tasks as displaying different windows and activating Wizards and utilities. Table 21-1 summarizes what each item on the toolbar does. (The table defines each tool from left to right on the toolbar.)

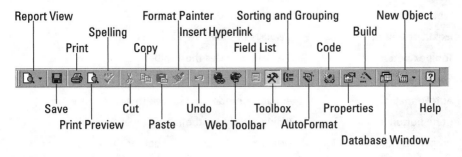

Figure 21-2: The Report Design toolbar.

Note The Report Design toolbar is distinct from the Format toolbar. To make such changes as font selection and justification, you must first make sure that the Format Form/Report Design toolbar is selected.

Table 21-1 The Design View Toolbar	
Toolbar Item	**Description**
Report View button	Drop-down box displays the three types of previews available
Save button	Saves the current report design
Print button	Prints a form, table, query, or report
Print Preview button	Toggles to print preview mode
Spelling button	Spell-checks current selection or document
Cut button	Removes selection from the document and adds it to the Clipboard
Copy button	Copies the selection to the Clipboard
Paste button	Copies the Clipboard contents to the document

(continued)

Table 21-1 *(continued)*

Toolbar Item	Description
Format Painter button	Copies the style of one control to another
Undo button	Undoes the previous command
Insert Hyperlink button	Inserts hyperlink
Web Toolbar	Displays or hides Web toolbar
Field List button	Displays or hides the Field List window
Toolbox button	Displays or hides the Toolbox
Sorting and Grouping button	Displays or hides the Sorting and Grouping box
AutoFormat button	Applies a predefined format to a form or report
Code button	Displays or hides the module window
Properties button	Displays the properties sheet for the selected item
Build button	Displays the Builder or Wizard for selected control or item
Database window	Displays the Database window
New Object button	Creates a new object
Help button	Displays Access Help

Note   The tools on the Report Design screen are virtually identical to the Form Design tools.

Banded Report Writer Concepts

In a report, your data is processed one record at a time. Depending on how you create your report design, each data item is processed differently. Reports are divided into sections, known as *bands* in most report-writing software packages. (In Access, these are simply called *sections.*) Access processes each data record from a table or dynaset, processing each section in order and deciding (for each record) whether to process fields or text in each section. For example, the report footer section is processed only after the last record is processed in the dynaset.

A report is made up of groups of *details* — for example, all animals Johnathan Adams brought in on a certain day and how much he paid. Each group must have an identifying *group header,* which in this case is customer Johnathan Adams. Each group has a footer that calculates the total amount for each customer. For Johnathan Adams, this amount is $375. The *page header* contains column descriptions; the *report header* contains the report title. Finally, the *report footer* contains grand totals for the report, and the *page footer* prints the page number.

The Access sections are as follows:

Report header	Prints only at the beginning of the report; used for title page
Page header	Prints at the top of each page
Group header	Prints before the first record of a group is processed
Detail	Prints each record in the table or dynaset
Group footer	Prints after the last record of a group is processed
Page footer	Prints at the bottom of each page
Report footer	Prints only at the end of a report after all records are processed

Figure 21-3 shows these sections superimposed on a report.

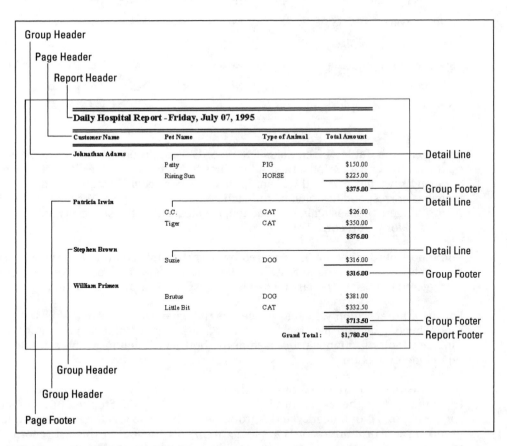

Figure 21-3: Typical Report Writer sections.

How sections process data

Most sections are triggered by the values of the data. Table 21-2 shows the five records that make up the dynaset for the Daily Hospital Report (Yes indicates that a section is triggered by the data).

Table 21-2 Processing Report Sections								
Customer	Pet Name	Report Header	Page Header	Group Header	Detail	Group Footer	Page Footer	Report Footer
Johnathan Adams	Rising Sun	Yes	Yes	Yes	Yes	No	No	No
Johnathan Adams	Patty	No	No	No	Yes	Yes	No	No
Patricia Irwin	C. C.	No	No	Yes	Yes	No	No	No
Patricia Irwin	Tiger	No	No	No	Yes	Yes	No	No
Stephen Brown	Suzie	No	No	Yes	Yes	Yes	No	No
William Primen	Brutus	No	No	No	Yes	No	No	No
William Primen	Little Bit	No	No	Yes	Yes	Yes	Yes	

As you can see, Table 21-2 contains five records. Four groups of records are grouped by the customer name. Johnathan Adams has two records, as does Patricia Irwin; Stephen Brown has one, and William Primen has two records. Each record in the table has corresponding columns for each section in the report. Yes means that the record triggers processing in that section; No means that the section is not processed for that record. This report has only one page, so it is very simple.

The report header section is triggered by only the first record in the dynaset. This section is always processed first, regardless of the data. The report footer section is triggered only after the last record is processed, regardless of the data.

For the first record only, Access processes the page header section after the report header section and then every time a new page of information is started. The page footer section is processed at the bottom of each page and after the report footer section.

Group headers are triggered only by the first record in a group. Group footers are triggered only by the last record in a group. Notice that the Stephen Brown record triggers both a group header and a group footer because it is the only record in a group. If three or more records are in a group, only the first or the last record can trigger a group header or footer; the middle records trigger only the detail section.

Access always processes each record in the detail section (which is always triggered, regardless of the value of the data). Most reports with a large amount of data have many detail records and significantly fewer group header or footer records. This small report has as many group header and footer records as it has detail records.

The Report Writer sections

To get an idea of what a report design looks like in Access, look at Figure 21-4, the Report Design window that produced the Daily Hospital Report. As you can see, the report is divided into sections. One group section displays data grouped by Customer Name, so you see the sections Customer Name Header and Customer Name Footer. Each of the other sections is also named for the type of processing it performs.

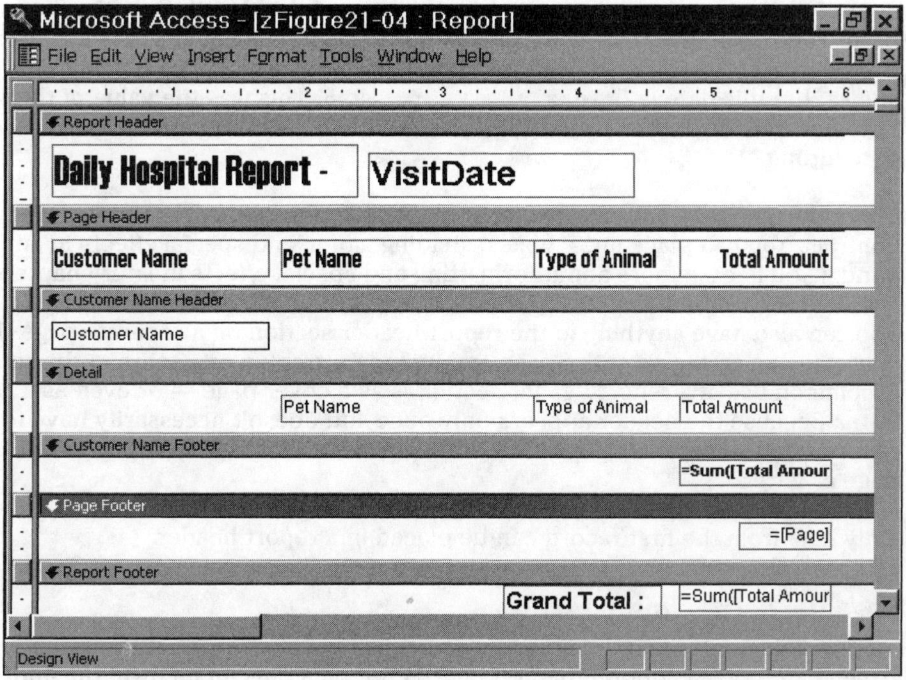

Figure 21-4: The Report Design window.

You can place any type of text or field controls in any section, but Access processes the data one record at a time. It also takes certain actions (based on the values of the group fields, the location of the page, or placement in the report) to make the bands or sections active. The example in Figure 21-4 is typical of a report with multiple sections. As you have learned, each section in the report has a different purpose and different triggers.

Note Page and report headers and footers must be added as pairs. To establish one without the other, simply resize to a height of zero the section you don't want; then set its Visible property to No.

Caution If you remove a header or footer section, you will lose the controls in those sections as well.

Report header section

Anything in the report header is printed once only at the beginning of the report. In the report header section is a text control that places the words Daily Hospital Report in a large font size at the top of the report. Only the first page of the report has this text. You can also see the field control Visit Date; it places the value of the visit date from the first record in the report header. Figure 21-3 shows that this date is Friday, July 07, 1995. This was the value of the Visit Date field for the first record in the dynaset. It has been formatted using the long date format.

The report header section also has a double line placed before the text and field controls. You can place lines, boxes, shading, color, and special effects in any band. (You'll learn more about formatting and special effects in later chapters.)

You can also have anything in the report header section on a separate page. This way, you can create an entire page and include a graphic or picture in the section. A common use of a report header section is as a cover page — or even as a cover letter. Because the header appears only once and doesn't necessarily have to contain any data, a separate page with the report header is a perfect place for a cover page or letter.

Note Only data from the first record can be placed in a report header.

Page header section

Text or field controls in the *page header section* normally print at the top of every page. If a report header on the first page is not on a page of its own, the information in the page header section prints just below the report header information. Typically, page headers serve as column headers in group/total reports; they can also contain a title for the report. In this example, placing the Daily Hospital Report title in the report header section means that the title appears on only the first page. You can move it into the page header section if you want it to appear on every page.

The page header section you see in Figure 21-4 also has double lines above and below the text controls. Each of the text controls is separate; each can be moved or sized individually. You can also control special effects (such as color, shading, borders, line thickness, font type, and font size) for each text control.

Note Both the page header and page footer can be set for one of four settings (this setting can be found in the report's properties):

All Pages	Both the page header and page footer print on every page.
Not with Report Header	Neither the page header nor footer prints on a page with the report header.
Not with Report Footer	The page header does not print with the report footer. The report footer prints on a new page.
Not with Report Header/Footer	Neither the page header nor the footer prints on a page with the report header or footer.

Group header

Because *group headers* normally identify a specific value, you know that all the records displayed in a detail section belong to that group. In this example, the detail records are about animals and the cost of their treatments. The group header field control Customer Name tells you that these animals are owned by the customer who appears in the group header band. Group header sections immediately precede detail sections.

You may have multiple levels of group headers and footers. In this report, for example, the data is only for July 7, 1995. The detail data is grouped by the field, Customer Name. If you want to see one report for the entire month of July 1995, you can change the query and add a second group section. In this second group section, you can group the data by date — and then, within each date, by customer. You can have many levels of groupings, but you should limit the number to between three and six; reports with too many levels become impossible to read. You don't want to defeat the purpose of the report, which is to show information clearly in a summarized format.

Note To set group-level properties such as Group On, Group Interval, Keep Together, or something other than the default, you must first set the Group Header and Group Footer property (or both) to Yes for the selected field or expression.

Detail section

The *detail section* processes *every* record; this section is where each value is printed. The detail section frequently contains a calculated field, such as a price extension that multiplies a quantity times a price. In this example, the detail section simply displays the Pet Name, Type of Animal, and Total Amount (which is the cost of the treatments). Each record in the detail section *belongs* to the value in the group header Customer Name.

Tip   You can tell Access whether you want to display a section in the report by changing the section's Visible property in the Report Design window. By turning off the display of the detail section (or by excluding selected group sections), you can display a summary report with no detail or with only certain groups displayed.

Group footer

Use the *group footer* to summarize the detail records for that group. In the Daily Hospital Report, the expression =Sum(Total Amount) adds the Total Amount fields for a specific customer. In the group for customer Johnathan Adams, this value sums the two Total Amount records ($225.00 and $150.00) and produces the value $375.00. This type of field is reset automatically to 0 every time the group changes. (You learn more about expressions and summary fields in later chapters.)

Tip   You can change the way summaries are calculated by changing the Running Sum property of the field box in the Report Design window.

Page footer

The *page footer section* usually contains page numbers or control totals. In very large reports, you may want page totals as well as group totals (such as when you have multiple pages of detail records with no summaries). For the Daily Hospital Report, you print the page number by combining the text control Page: with the expression Page: (which keeps track of the page number in the report).

Report footer

The *report footer section* is printed once at the end of the report after all the detail records and group footer sections are printed. Report footers typically display grand totals or other statistics (such as averages or percentages) for the entire report. The report footer for the Daily Hospital Report uses the expression =Sum(Total Amount) to add the Total Amount fields for all treatments. This expression, when used in the report footer, is not reset to 0, as it is in the group footer. The expression is used only for a grand total.

When there is a report footer, the page footer band is printed after the report footer.

The Report Writer in Access is a *two-pass report writer*, capable of preprocessing all records to calculate the totals (such as percentages) needed for statistical reporting. This capability lets you create expressions that calculate percentages as Access processes those records that require foreknowledge of the grand total.

Cross-Reference Chapter 23 covers calculating percentages.

Creating a New Report

Fundamental to all reports is the concept that a report is another way to view the records in one or more tables. It is important to understand that a report is bound to either a single table or a query that accesses one or more tables. When you create a report, you must select which fields from a query or table to place in your report. Unless you want to view all the records from a single table in it, you will probably want to bind your report to a query. If you are accessing data from a single table, using a query lets you create your report on the basis of a particular search criterion and sorting order. If you want to access data from multiple tables, you have no choice but to bind your report to a query. In the examples in this chapter, you'll see all the reports bound to a query (even though it is possible to bind a report to a table).

Note Access lets you create a report without first binding it to a table or object, but you will have no fields on the report. This capability can be used to work out *page templates,* which can serve as models for other reports. You can add fields later by changing the underlying control source of the report.

Throughout this chapter and the next chapter, you learn the tasks necessary to create the Mountain Animal Hospital Pets and Owners Directory (the first hard-copy page is shown in Figure 21-5). In this chapter, you will design the basic report, assemble the data, and place the data in the proper positions. In Chapter 22, you will enhance the report by adding lines, boxes, and shading so that certain areas stand out. You will also add enhanced controls (such as option buttons and check boxes) to make the data more readable.

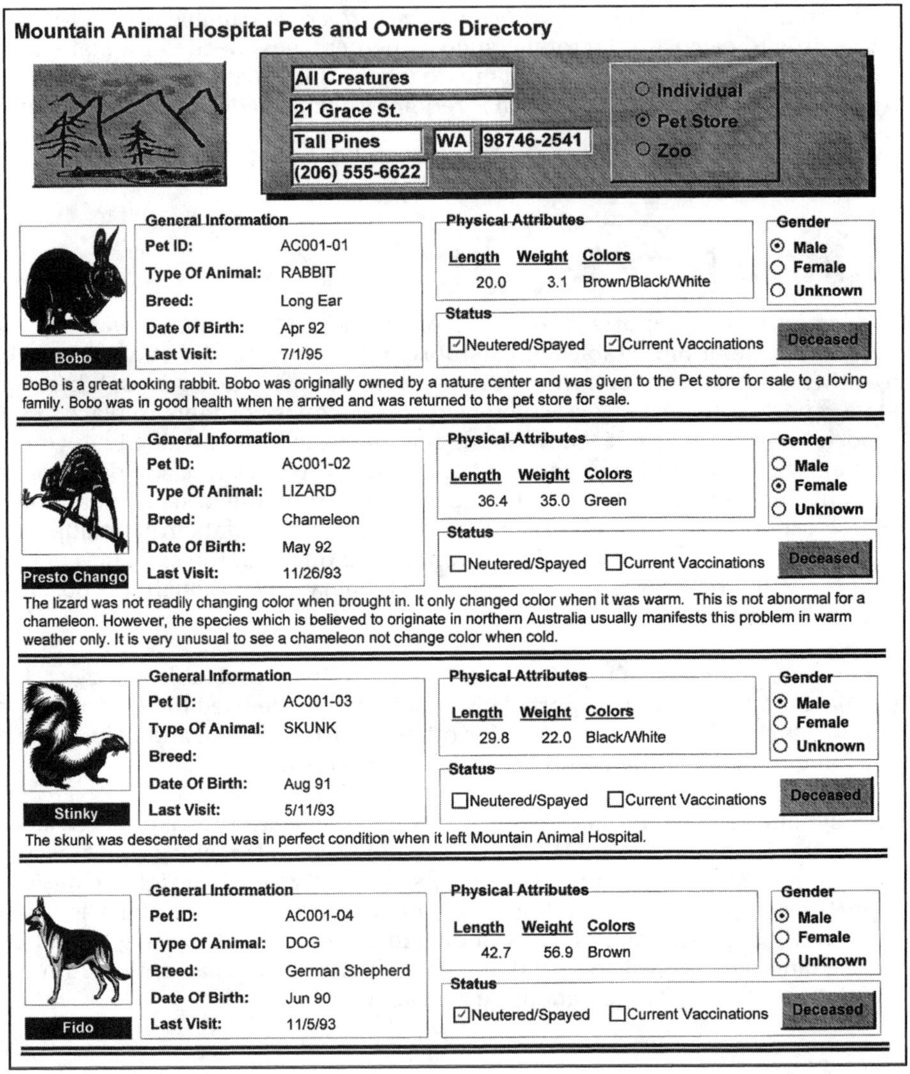
Mountain Animal Hospital Pets and Owners Directory

All Creatures
21 Grace St.
Tall Pines WA 98746-2541
(206) 555-6622

○ Individual
⦿ Pet Store
○ Zoo

Bobo

General Information
Pet ID: AC001-01
Type Of Animal: RABBIT
Breed: Long Ear
Date Of Birth: Apr 92
Last Visit: 7/1/95

Physical Attributes
Length 20.0 Weight 3.1 Colors Brown/Black/White

Gender: ⦿ Male ○ Female ○ Unknown

Status: ☑ Neutered/Spayed ☑ Current Vaccinations Deceased

BoBo is a great looking rabbit. Bobo was originally owned by a nature center and was given to the Pet store for sale to a loving family. Bobo was in good health when he arrived and was returned to the pet store for sale.

Presto Chango

General Information
Pet ID: AC001-02
Type Of Animal: LIZARD
Breed: Chameleon
Date Of Birth: May 92
Last Visit: 11/26/93

Physical Attributes
Length 36.4 Weight 35.0 Colors Green

Gender: ○ Male ⦿ Female ○ Unknown

Status: ☐ Neutered/Spayed ☐ Current Vaccinations Deceased

The lizard was not readily changing color when brought in. It only changed color when it was warm. This is not abnormal for a chameleon. However, the species which is believed to originate in northern Australia usually manifests this problem in warm weather only. It is very unusual to see a chameleon not change color when cold.

Stinky

General Information
Pet ID: AC001-03
Type Of Animal: SKUNK
Breed:
Date Of Birth: Aug 91
Last Visit: 5/11/93

Physical Attributes
Length 29.8 Weight 22.0 Colors Black/White

Gender: ⦿ Male ○ Female ○ Unknown

Status: ☐ Neutered/Spayed ☐ Current Vaccinations Deceased

The skunk was descented and was in perfect condition when it left Mountain Animal Hospital.

Fido

General Information
Pet ID: AC001-04
Type Of Animal: DOG
Breed: German Shepherd
Date Of Birth: Jun 90
Last Visit: 11/5/93

Physical Attributes
Length 42.7 Weight 56.9 Colors Brown

Gender: ⦿ Male ○ Female ○ Unknown

Status: ☑ Neutered/Spayed ☐ Current Vaccinations Deceased

Figure 21-5: The Mountain Animal Hospital Pets and Owners Directory — first page.

As with almost every task in Access, there are many ways to create a report without Wizards. It is important, however, to follow some type of methodology; creating a good report involves a fairly scientific approach. You can follow a set of tasks that will result in a good report every time and then arrange these tasks to create a checklist. As you complete each of the tasks, you can check it off your list. When you are done, you will have a great-looking report. The following section outlines this approach.

Eleven tasks to creating a great report

To create a good report, perform these eleven steps:

1. Design your report.

2. Assemble the data.

3. Create a new report and bind it to a query.

4. Define your page layout properties.

5. Place the fields on the report, using text controls.

6. Add other label and text controls as necessary.

7. Modify the appearance, size, and location of text, text controls, and label controls.

8. Define your sorting and grouping options.

9. Save your report.

10. Enhance your report by using graphics and other control types.

11. Print your report.

This chapter covers tasks 1 through 9. Chapter 22 discusses using other controls, such as group boxes, option buttons, and memo fields, as well as methods to enhance your report visually.

Designing the report

Cross-
Reference

The first step in this process is to design the report. By the nature of the report name, Mountain Animal Hospital Pets and Owners Directory, you know that you want to create a report which contains detailed information about both the customer and the customer's pets. You want to create a report that lists important customer information at the top of a page and then lists detailed information about each pet a customer owns, including a picture. You want no more than one customer on a page. If a customer has more than one pet, you want to see as many as possible on the same page. If a customer has more pets than will fit on one page, you want to duplicate the customer details at the top of each page. (The grouping section of this chapter discusses this task.)

Figure 21-6 shows a design of this data. This is not the complete design for the report shown in Figure 21-5; rather, it is a plan for only the major data items, placed roughly where they will appear in this report. You can sketch this design by hand on a piece of paper or use any good word processor or drawing tool (such as Micrografx Draw or Word for Windows Draw) to lay out the basic design. Because Access has a WYSIWYG report writer, you can also use that to lay out your report. (Personally, I like the pencil-and-paper approach to good design.)

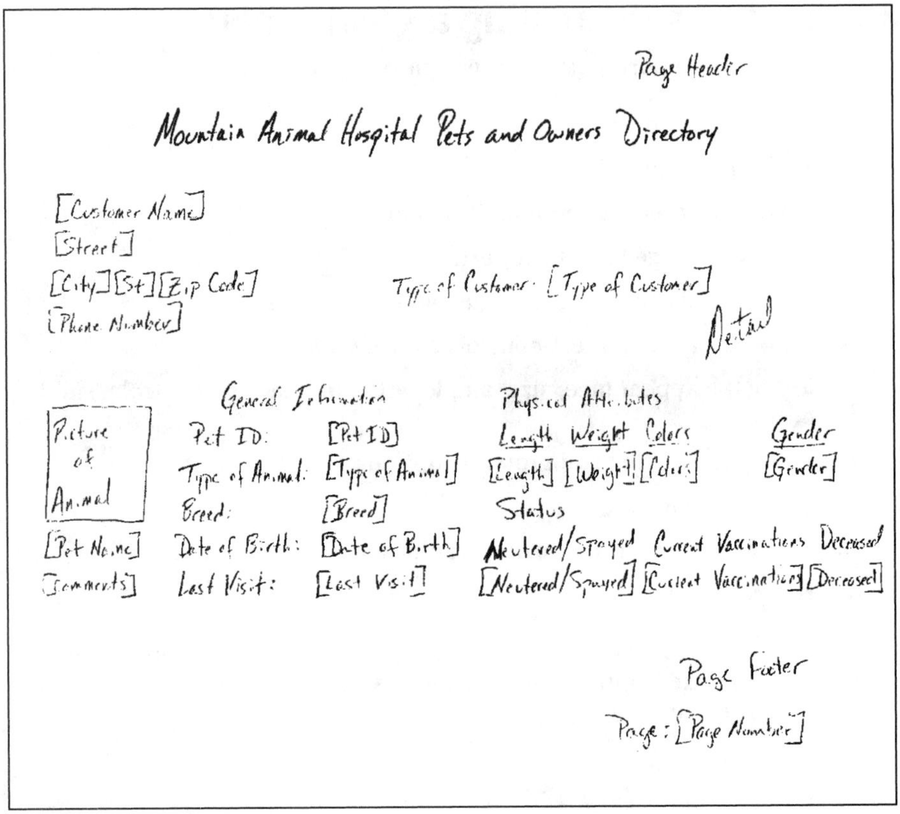

Figure 21-6: The data design for the Mountain Animal Hospital Pets and Owners Directory.

The data design is created only to lay out the basic data elements with no special formatting. Although this design may seem rudimentary, it is nevertheless a good starting point. This layout represents the report you will create in this chapter.

Assembling the data

With this design in mind, you now need to assemble the data. To create this report, you will need fields from two tables: Customer and Pets. Table 21-3 lists the necessary fields and identifies the tables that contain them.

Table 21-3
Tables and Fields Needed for the Pets and Owners Directory

Fields from Pets Table	Fields from Customer Table
Pet ID	Customer Number
Picture	Customer Name
Pet Name	Type of Customer
Type of Animal	Street/Apt
Breed	City
Date of Birth	State
Last Visit Date	ZIP Code
Length	Phone Number
Weight	
Colors	
Gender	
Neutered/Spayed	
Current Vaccinations	
Deceased	
Comments	

To assemble this data, first you need to create a query, which you can call Pets and Owners. This query includes *all* fields from both tables, but you won't use all of them. Some of the fields that don't appear on the report itself are used to derive other fields. Some fields are used merely to sort the data, although the fields themselves are not displayed on the report. In this example, you also create a sort by Pet ID. It is always a good idea to arrange your data in some known order. When reports are run, the data is used in its *physical* order unless you sort the data.

To create the Pets and Owners query, follow Figure 21-7.

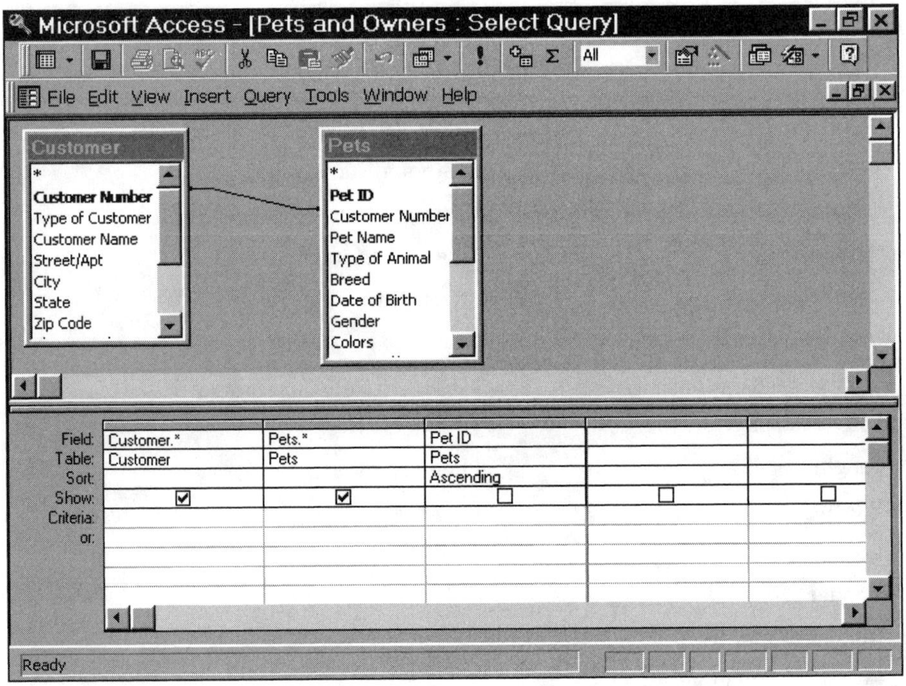

Figure 21-7: The Pets and Owners query.

> **Note**
>
> You use the asterisk (*) to select all fields from each table.

Creating a new report and binding it to a query

Now that you have created the Pets and Owners query, you need to create a new report and bind it to the query. Follow these steps to complete this process:

1. Press F11 to display the Database window if it is not already displayed.

2. Click on the Reports tab.

3. Click on the New command button. The New Report dialog box appears.

4. Select Design View.

5. Click on the combo box labeled Choose a table or query. A drop-down list of all tables and queries in the current database appears.

6. Select the Pets and Owners query.

7. Click on OK.

8. Maximize the Report window.

A blank Report Design window appears (see Figure 21-8). Notice the three sections in the screen display: Page Header, Detail, and Page Footer. The report is bound to the query Pets and Owners. This means that the data from that query will be used when the report is viewed or printed. The fields from the query are available for use in the report design and will appear in the Field List window.

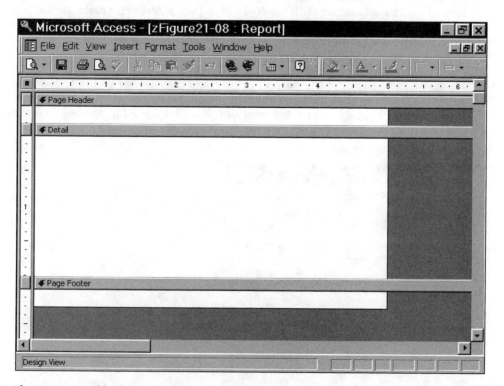

Figure 21-8: A blank Report Design window.

Note

You can also create a new report by using any of these methods:

✦ Click on the New Object toolbar button and then select New Report.

✦ Copy, paste, and rename an existing report.

✦ Start a New Report and then select one of the AutoReport options.

Note

Note that there are two options for the AutoReport: Columnar and Tabular.

Defining the report page size and layout

As you are planning your report, consider the page-layout characteristics as well as the kind of paper and printer you want to use for the output. If you use an Epson dot-matrix printer with a wide-carriage feed, you'll want to design your report with an approach that differs from the one you would use for printing on a Hewlett-Packard LaserJet with 8½-by-11-inch paper. After you make these decisions, you can use several dialog boxes and properties to make adjustments; these items work together to create the output you want. You learn how to use these tools in the next several chapters.

Cross-Reference   First, you need to select the correct printer and page-layout characteristics by selecting File⇨Page Setup. The Page Setup dialog box, shown in Figure 21-9, lets you select your printer and set printer options. Chapter 22 discusses Page Setup options in detail.

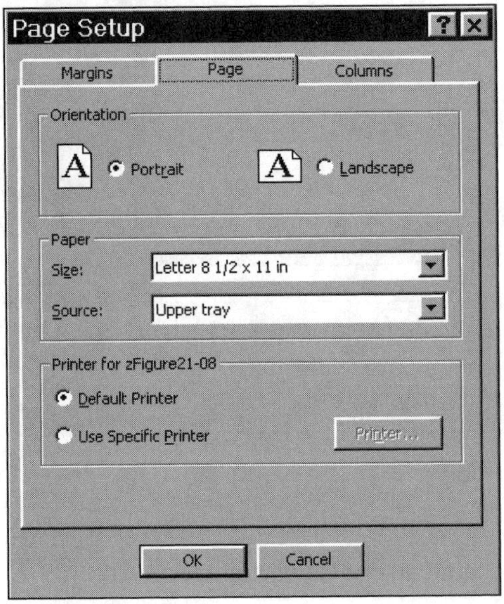

Figure 21-9: The Page Setup dialog box showing the Page tab.

This dialog box is a tab in the Page Setup dialog box. Layout tabs and page margins are also available under the Page Setup dialog box.

The Page dialog box is divided into three sections:

Orientation	Selects the page orientation you want
Paper	Selects the paper size and paper source you want
Printer	Selects the printer you want

Note Select the Printer button; the Page Setup dialog box for the selected printer appears. Pressing Properties will then bring up a more extensive dialog box with all the applicable options.

For the Pets and Owners report, you'll create a *portrait* report, which is taller than it is wide. The paper you'll use is 8½ x 11 inches; the left, right, top, and bottom margins are all set to 0.250.

Follow these steps to create the proper report setup for the Pets and Owners report:

1. Open the Page Setup dialog box and select the Page tab.

2. Click on the Portrait option button.

   Next to the Orientation buttons are two sheet-of-paper icons with the letter A pictured on them. The picture of the sheet is an indication of its setting.

3. Click on the tab named Margins.

4. Click on the Top margin setting and change the setting to **.250**.

5. Click on the Bottom margin setting and change the setting to **.250**.

6. Click on the Left margin setting and change the setting to **.250**.

7. Click on the Right margin setting and change the setting to **.250**.

8. Click on OK to close the Page Setup dialog box.

Tip Access displays your reports in Print Preview view by using the driver of the active printer. If you don't have a good-quality laser available for printing, install the driver for a PostScript printer so that you'll be able to view any graphics you create (and see the report in a high-resolution display). Later, you can print to your dot-matrix or other available printer and get the actual hard copy in the best resolution your printer offers.

Caution In Figure 21-9, you can see the option button (Printer. . .) in the bottom right corner of the Page tab. If you are going to give your database or report to others, you should always select the first option, Default Printer. This way, if you have selected a printer the recipients don't have, the report will use their default printer. If you have selected the second option (Use Specific Printer) and those who run the report don't have that printer, they will get an error message and will not be able to use the report.

After you define your page layout in the Page Setup dialog box, you need to define the size of your report (which is not necessarily the same as the page definition, as you might expect).

To define the report size, place the cursor on the rightmost edge of the report (where the white page meets the gray background). The cursor changes to a two-headed arrow. Drag the cursor to change the width of the report. As you drag the edge, a vertical line appears in the ruler to let you know the exact width if you release the mouse at that point. Be careful not to exceed the width of the page you defined in the Page Setup dialog box.

When you position the cursor at the bottom of the report, it looks similar to the one for determining width. This cursor determines the height not of the page length, but of the page footer section or other specified bottom section. (Predefining a page length directly in the report section doesn't really make sense because the detail section will vary in length, based on your groupings.) Keep in mind that the Report Design view shows not the actual report but only a representation of the various report sections.

To set the right border for the Pets and Owners report to eight inches, follow these steps:

1. Click on the rightmost edge of the report body (where the white page representation meets the gray background). The cursor changes to a two-headed arrow.

2. Drag the edge to the 8-inch mark.

3. Release the mouse button.

Note
You can also select the Width property in the report's property sheet.

Because the Report Design screen is set to a width of eight inches, you see most of the screen printouts in this chapter taken with a Super VGA Windows screen driver (resolution: 800 x 600) rather than with the standard VGA Windows driver (640 x 480). This higher resolution lets you see almost the entire screen in the screen figures.

Placing fields on the report

As you've seen, Access takes full advantage of the drag-and-drop capabilities of the Windows environment. The method for placing fields on a report is no exception. When you place a field on a report, it is no longer called a field; it is called a *control*. A control has a *control source* (a specific field) that it is bound to, so the terms *control* and *field* are used interchangeably in this chapter.

The process of placing controls on your report consists of three basic tasks:

✦ Display the Field List window by clicking on the Field List toolbar button.

✦ Click on the desired Toolbox control to determine the type of control that will be created.

✦ Select each of the fields you want on your report and then drag them to the Report Design window.

Displaying the field list

To display the Field List window, click on the Field List button on the toolbar. A small window with a list of all the fields from the underlying query appears. This window is called a *modeless* dialog box because it remains on-screen even while you continue with other work in Access. The Field List window can be resized and moved around the screen. This enlarged window is illustrated in Figure 21-10, showing all the fields in the Pets and Owners query dynaset.

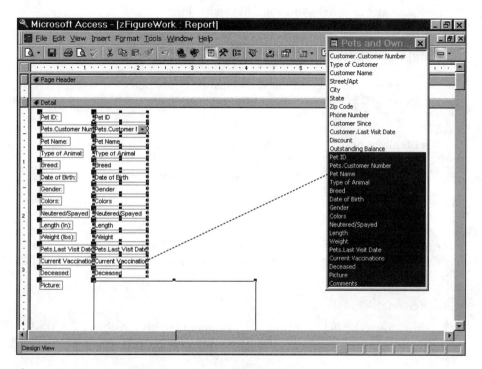

Figure 21-10: Dragging fields to the Design window.

Notice that in Figure 21-10 the fields Customer.Customer Number and Pets.Customer Number as well as Customer.Last Visit Date and Pets.Last Visit Date use the table name as a prefix. This setup is necessary to distinguish fields of the same name that come from different tables used in the query.

Tip   You can move the Field List window by simply clicking on the title bar and dragging it to a new location.

Selecting the fields for your report

Selecting a field in the Report field list is the same as selecting a field in the Query field list. The easiest way to select a field is simply to click on it. As you click on a field, it becomes highlighted. After a field is highlighted, you can drag it to the Report window.

You can highlight *contiguous* (adjacent) fields in the list by following these steps:

1. Click on the first field you want in the field list.

2. Move the cursor to the last field you want from the list.

3. Hold down the Shift key and click on the last field you want.

The block of fields between the first and last field you selected is displayed in reverse video as it is selected. You can then drag the block of fields to the Report window.

You can highlight noncontiguous fields in the list by clicking on each field while holding down the Ctrl key. Each field will be displayed in reverse video; then you can drag the fields as a group to the Report Design window.

Note   Unlike the Query field list, you *cannot* also double-click on a field to add it to the Report window.

You can begin by selecting the Pets table fields for the detail section. To select the fields needed for the detail section of the Pets and Owners report, follow these steps:

1. Click on the Pet ID field.

2. Scroll down the field list until the Comments field is visible.

3. Hold down the Shift key and click on the Comments field.

The block of fields from Pet ID to Comments should be highlighted in the Field List window, as shown in Figure 21-10.

Dragging fields onto your report

After you select the proper fields from the Pets table, all you need to do is drag them to the detail section of your report. Depending on whether you choose one or several fields, the cursor changes to represent your selection. If you select one field, you see a Field icon, which shows a single box with some unreadable text inside. If you select multiple fields, you see a set of three boxes. These are the same icons you saw on the Query Design screens.

To drag the selected Pet table fields into the detail section of the Report Design window, follow these steps:

1. Click within the highlighted block of fields in the Field List window. You may need to move the horizontal elevator bar back to the left before starting this process.

2. Without releasing the mouse button, drag the cursor into the detail section; place the icon under the 1½-inch mark on the horizontal ruler at the top of the screen and next to the 0-inch mark of the vertical ruler along the left edge of the screen.

3. Release the mouse button.

The fields appear in the detail section of the report, as shown in Figure 21-10. Notice that for each field you dragged onto the report, there are two controls. When you use the drag-and-drop method for placing fields, Access automatically creates a label control (attached to the text control the field is bound to) that uses the name of the field.

Note   Notice the OLE (Object Linking and Embedding) control for the field named Picture. Access always creates an OLE control for a picture or an OLE-type object. Also notice that the detail section automatically resizes itself to fit all the controls. Below the OLE control is the control for the memo field Comments.

You also need to place the desired field controls on the report for the customer information you need in the page header section. Before you do this, however, you need to resize the page header frame to leave room for a title you will add later.

Resizing a section

To make room on the report for both the title and the Customer table fields in the page header, you must resize it. You can resize a section by placing the cursor at the bottom of the section you want to resize. The cursor turns into a vertical double-headed arrow; drag the section border up or down to make the section smaller or larger.

To make the page header section larger, resize it by following these steps:

1. Move the cursor between the bottom of the page header section and the top of the detail section.

2. When the cursor is displayed as a double-sided arrow, hold down the left mouse button.

3. Drag the page header section border down until it intersects the detail section's ruler at the ½-inch mark.

4. Release the button to enlarge the page header section.

You can now place the Customer table fields in the page header section by following these steps:

1. Click on the Customer.Customer Number field.

2. Scroll down the field list until the Phone Number field is visible.

3. Hold down the Shift key and click on the Phone Number field.

4. Click within the highlighted block of fields in the Field List window.

5. Without releasing the mouse button, drag the cursor into the page header section; place the icon under the 1½-inch mark on the horizontal ruler at the top of the screen and next to the ⅝-inch mark of the vertical ruler along the left edge of the screen.

6. Release the mouse button; the fields now appear in the page header section of the report, as shown in Figure 21-11.

7. Close the Field List window by clicking on the Field List toolbar button.

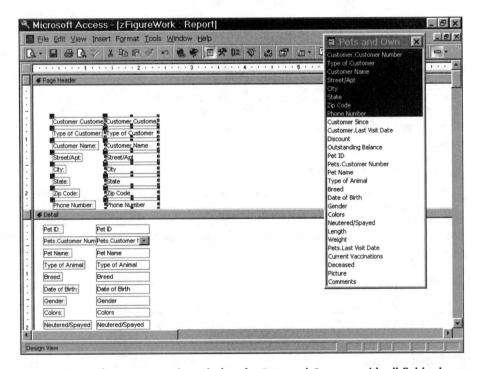

Figure 21-11: The Report Design window for Pets and Owners, with all fields shown.

Notice that the page header section also expanded to fit the fields that were dragged into the section. At this point, your report should look like Figure 21-11. You have now placed all the fields you need for the Pets and Owners report.

Working with label controls and text

As you've learned, when you drag a field from the Field List window to a report while the Text Box button is selected in the Toolbox, Access creates not only a text box control but also a label control that is attached to the text box control. At times, you will want to add text label controls by themselves to create headings or titles for the report.

Creating unattached labels

To create a new, unattached label control, you must use the Toolbox (unless you copy an existing label). The next task in the current example is to add the text header *Mountain Animal Hospital Pets and Owners Directory* to your report. You will do this task in segments to demonstrate adding and editing text.

To begin by creating an unattached label control, follow these steps:

1. Display the Toolbox.
2. Click on the Label tool in the Toolbox.
3. Click near the top left edge of the page header at about the 1-inch mark on the ruler; then drag the cursor to make a small rectangle about 2³/₄-inches wide and ¹/₄-inch high.
4. Type **Mountain Animal Hospital Pets and Owners Directory**.
5. Press Enter.

Tip   To create a multiple-line label entry, press Ctrl+Enter to force a line break where you want it in the control.

Tip   If you want to edit or enter a caption that is longer than the space in the property sheet, the contents will scroll as you type. Otherwise, you can press Shift+F2 to open a Zoom box that gives you more space to type.

Modifying the appearance of text in a control

To modify the appearance of the text in a control, select the control by clicking on its border (not in the control itself). You can then select a formatting style to apply to the label by clicking on the appropriate button on the toolbar.

To make the title stand out, follow these steps for modifying the appearance of label text:

1. Click on the newly created report heading label.

2. Click on the Bold button on the Formatting toolbar.

3. Click on the arrow beside the Font-Size drop-down box.

4. Select 18 from the Font-Size drop-down list box.

The label control appears. You will need to resize it (which you will do later in this chapter) in order to display all the text.

Working with text boxes and their attached label controls

After you enter label controls to display text on the report, you will want to place text box controls (fields) on the report. These text boxes can be bound to fields in tables, or they can be unbound, holding expressions such as the page number, date, or some calculation.

Adding text box controls

Text box controls serve two purposes in reports. First, they let you display stored data from a particular field in a query or table. Their second purpose is displaying the result of an expression. Expressions can be calculations that use other controls as their operands, calculations that use Access functions (either built-in or user-defined), or a combination of the two. You have learned how to use a text box control to display data from a field and how to create that control. Next, you learn about text controls that use expressions.

Entering an expression in a text control

Cross-Reference

Expressions let you create a value that is not already in a table or query. They can range from simple functions (such as a page number) to complex mathematical computations. Chapters 13 and 23 cover expressions in greater detail; for this example, in this chapter, you'll use an expression that is necessary for the report.

A *function* is a small program that is run and returns a single value; it can be one of many built-in Access functions, or it can be user-defined. To facilitate page numbering in reports, Access has a function called Page that returns the value of the current report page. The following steps show you how to use an unbound text box to add a page number to your report:

1. Select the Text Box tool from the Toolbox.

2. Scroll down to the page footer section by using the vertical elevator.

3. Click in the middle of the page footer section, and then create a text box about three-quarters of the height of the section and about ³⁄₄-inch wide.

4. Click on the label control to select it. (It should say something like Text42.)

5. Click on the beginning of the label control text, drag over the default text in the label control, and type **Page:** or double-click on the text to highlight it and then replace it.

6. Click twice on the text box control (it says "unbound"); type **=Page** and press Enter. (Notice that the Control Source property changes on the data sheet of the Property window to =Page, as shown in Figure 21-12. If the Property window is not open, you may want to open it to see the change.)

7. Click on the Page label control's Move handle (upper left corner); move the label closer to the =Page text box control until the right edge of the label control touches the left edge of the text box control. (Later, you will move the entire control to the right side of the page.)

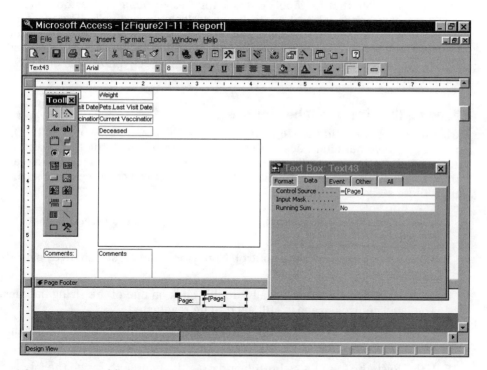

Figure 21-12: Adding a page-number expression in a text box control.

Tip You can always check your result by clicking on the Print Preview button on the toolbar. You may want to zoom in on the page footer section to check the page number.

Sizing a text box control or label control

You can select a control by simply clicking on it. Depending on the size of the control, from three to seven sizing handles will appear — one on each corner except the upper left and one on each side. When you move the cursor over one of the sizing handles, the cursor changes into a double-headed arrow. When the cursor changes, click on the control and drag it to the size you want. Notice that, as you drag, an outline appears; it indicates the new size the label control will be when you release the mouse button.

If you double-click on any of the sizing handles, usually Access will resize a control to the best fit for the text in the control. This feature is especially handy if you increase the font size and then notice that the text is cut off, either on the bottom or to the right. Note that for label controls, this *best-fit sizing* resizes both vertically and horizontally, though text controls can resize only vertically. The reason for this difference is that in the report design mode, Access doesn't know how much of a field you want to display; the field name and field contents might be radically different. Sometimes label controls are not resized correctly, however, and have to be adjusted manually.

Changing the size of a label control

Earlier in this chapter (in the steps that modified the appearance of label text), you changed the characteristics of the Pets and Owners label; the text changed, but the label itself did not adjust. Note that the text no longer fits within the label control. You can resize the text control, however, to fit the enhanced font size. Follow these steps:

1. Click on the Mountain Animal Hospital Pets and Owners Directory label control.

2. Move your cursor over the control. Notice how the cursor changes over the sizing handles.

3. To size the control automatically, double-click on one of the sizing handles. The label control size may still need to be readjusted.

4. Place the cursor in the bottom right corner of the label control so that the diagonal arrow appears.

5. Hold down the left mouse button and drag the handle to resize the label control's box until it correctly displays all of the text (if it doesn't already).

Tip   You can also select Format⇨Size⇨to Fit to change the size of the label control text automatically.

Before continuing, you should see how the report is progressing; you should do this frequently as you design a report. You can send a single page to the printer or view the report in a print preview. Figure 21-13 shows a zoomed print preview of how the report currently looks. The customer information is at the top of the page; the pet information is below that and offset to the left. Notice the title at the top of the page. You can see the page number at the bottom if you click on the magnifying-glass button to zoom out and see the entire page. Only one record per page appears on the report because of the vertical layout. In the next section of this chapter, you move the fields around and create a more horizontal layout.

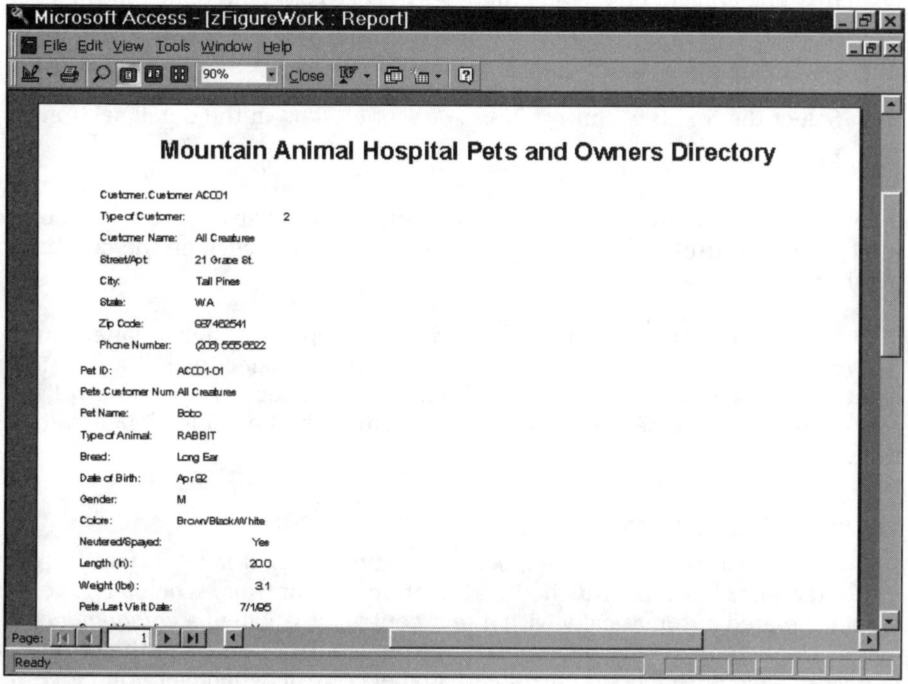

Figure 21-13: A print preview of the report.

Deleting attached label and text controls

As you can see in Figure 21-13, the report begins with the Customer Number field. The original design in Figure 21-6 did not have the Customer Number field on the report. After talking to the report design's architect (who is usually yourself), you find that the Customer Number field is not wanted on the report, either in the page header section or the detail section. It's very easy to delete one or more attached controls in a report. You simply select the desired controls and press Delete. When deleting attached controls, you have two choices:

✦ Delete only the label control.

✦ Delete both the label control and the field control.

If you select the label control and press Delete, only the label control is deleted. If you select the field control and press Delete, both the label control and the field control are deleted. To delete an attached control (in this case, the Customer Number controls and their attached label), follow these steps:

1. Select the Close icon on the toolbar to exit print preview mode. Select the text box control `Customer.Customer (Customer Number)` in the page header.

2. Press Delete.

3. Select the text box control `Pets.Customer Num` in the detail section.

4. Press Delete.

If you accidentally selected the label control that precedes the text box control, the text box control is still visible. You can then simply click on the control and press Delete.

Tip   If you want to delete only the field control and keep the attached label control, you can do so by first selecting the label control and selecting Edit⇨Copy. Next, to delete both the field control and the label control, select the field control and press Delete. Finally, select Edit⇨Paste to paste only the copied label control to the report.

Moving label and text controls

Before discussing how to move label and text controls, it is important to review a few differences between attached and unattached controls. When an attached label is created automatically with a text control, it is called a *compound control*. In a compound control, whenever you move one control in the set, the other control moves as well. With a text control and a label control, whenever you move the text control, the attached label is also moved. Likewise, whenever you move the label control, the text control is also moved.

To move both controls in a compound control, select one of the pair by clicking anywhere on the control. Move the cursor over either of the objects. When the cursor turns into a hand, you can click on the controls and drag them to their new location. Notice that, as you drag, an outline for the compound control moves with your cursor.

Cross-Reference   The concepts of moving controls are covered visually and in more detail in Chapter 16.

To move only one of the controls in a compound control, you must drag the desired control by its *Move handle* (the large square in the upper left corner of the control). When you click on a compound control, it looks like both controls are selected. If you look closely, you'll see that only one of the two controls is selected (as indicated by the presence of both moving and sizing handles). The deselected control displays only a moving handle. A pointing finger indicates that you have selected the Move handles and can now move only one control. To move either control individually, select the control's Move handle and drag it to its new location.

Cross-Reference To move a label that is not attached, simply click on any border (except where there is a handle) and drag it. You can also move groups of controls with the selection techniques you learned about in Chapter 16.

To make a group selection, click on the cursor anywhere outside a starting point and drag the cursor through (or around) the controls you want to select. A gray, outlined rectangle is displayed to show the extent of the selection. When you release the mouse button, all the controls the rectangle surrounds are selected. You can then drag the group of controls to a new location.

Tip The global option Tools⇨Options – Form/Reports – Selection Behavior is a property that controls the enclosure of selections. You can enclose them fully (the rectangle must completely surround the selection) or partially (the rectangle must only touch the control), which is the default.

In the next steps, you begin to place the controls in their proper position to complete the report design and layout as created (see Figure 21-6). You want this first pass at rearranging the controls to look like Figure 21-14. The steps to move all the controls will be broken up into logical groups. This is the way most reports are created. By making a series of block moves (where many controls are selected) and then refining the positioning, you can complete a report design. Follow these steps to begin placing the controls where they should be:

Roughly positioning the page header controls:

1. Move the Type of Customer control to the right and down so that the top of the control intersects 1 inch on the vertical ruler and the left edge is under the P in Pets in the title.

2. In the page header, delete (only) the attached labels from all the text controls except Type of Customer.

3. Rearrange the controls in the page header to resemble a typical mailing-label address format; City, State, and Zip Code should be on the same line.

4. Move the Phone Number text box control under the Zip Code text box control.

5. Move the block of name, address, and phone number controls into position so that the top of the block intersects the ½-inch mark on both the vertical and horizontal rulers.

6. Resize the page header section so that it intersects the 1¾-inch mark on the left vertical ruler.

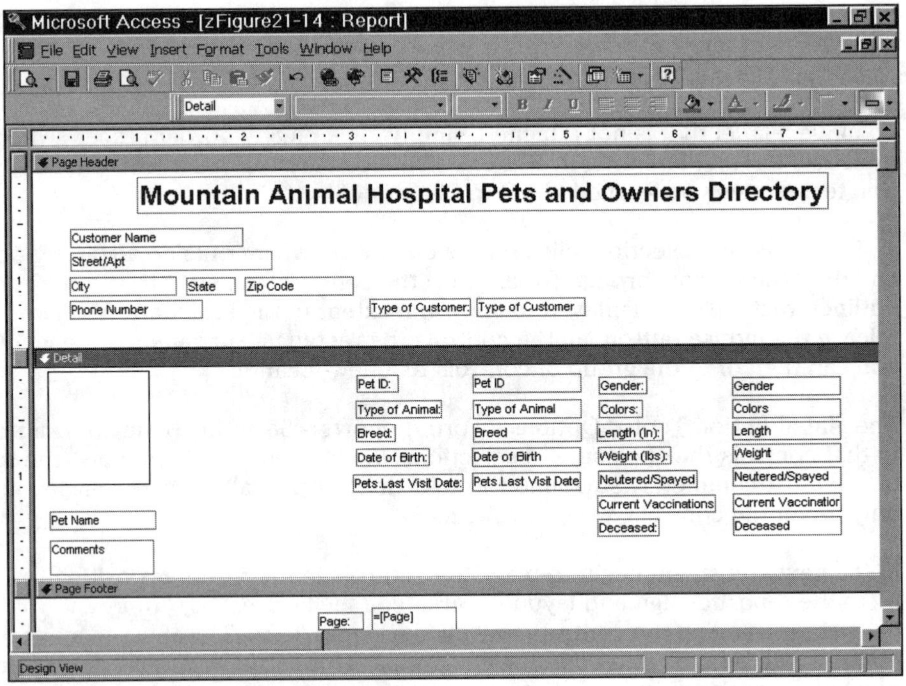

Figure 21-14: Rearranging the controls on the report.

Note Some fields, such as Customer Name, Street/Apt, and Phone Number, may need to be adjusted. You can adjust them now or later in this chapter.

Roughly positioning the detail controls:

1. Select the Pet ID, Type of Animal, Breed, Date of Birth, and Last Visit Date controls (and their attached labels) by clicking on each text control while holding down the Shift key.

2. Drag the block of controls to the right so that the left edge intersects 3 inches on the top ruler.

3. Select (only) the Last Visit Date control and its attached label.

4. Drag the Last Visit Date control up so that it is just under the Date of Birth control.

5. Select the Gender control and its attached label.

6. Drag the control to the right so that the left edge intersects the 5¼-inch mark on the top ruler and the ¼-inch mark on the left-side ruler.

7. Select the Colors, Length, and Weight controls and their attached labels by clicking on each text control while holding down the Shift key.

8. Drag the block of controls to the right so that the left edge intersects the 5¼-inch mark on the top ruler and the ¾-inch mark on the left-side ruler.

9. Select the Neutered/Spayed, Current Vaccinations, and Deceased controls and their attached labels by clicking on each text control while holding down the Shift key.

10. Drag the block of controls to the right so that they are just under the most recently moved block.

11. Select the Current Vaccinations and Deceased controls and their attached labels by clicking on each text control while holding down the Shift key.

12. Drag the block of controls upward so that they are just under the Neutered/Spayed control.

13. Delete (only) the Pet Name label control.

14. Delete (only) the Picture label control.

15. Delete (only) the Comments label control.

16. Select the bottom right handle to resize the Picture control to 1 inch x 1 inch.

17. Move the Picture control to ⅛ inch x ⅛ inch on the rulers (top left corner) of the detail section.

18. Move the Pet Name text box control under the picture so that it intersects the left ruler at the 1½-inch mark.

19. Move the Comments text box control under the picture so that it intersects the left ruler at the 1¾-inch mark.

20. Resize the detail section so that it intersects the 2-inch mark on the left ruler.

At this point, you are about halfway done. The screen should look like Figure 21-14. (If it doesn't, adjust your controls until the screen matches the figure.) Remember that these screen pictures are taken with the Windows screen driver set at 800 x 600. If you are using normal VGA, you'll have to scroll the screen to see the entire report.

The next step is refining the design to get as close as possible to the design created in Figure 21-6. The page header band is complete for now. Later in this chapter, you'll reformat the controls to change the font size and style. In the next set of steps, you complete the layout of the detail section:

1. Group select all the fields starting with Pet ID through Last Visit date (in a column).

2. Select and drag that block to the right of the Picture OLE control, as shown in Figure 21-15.

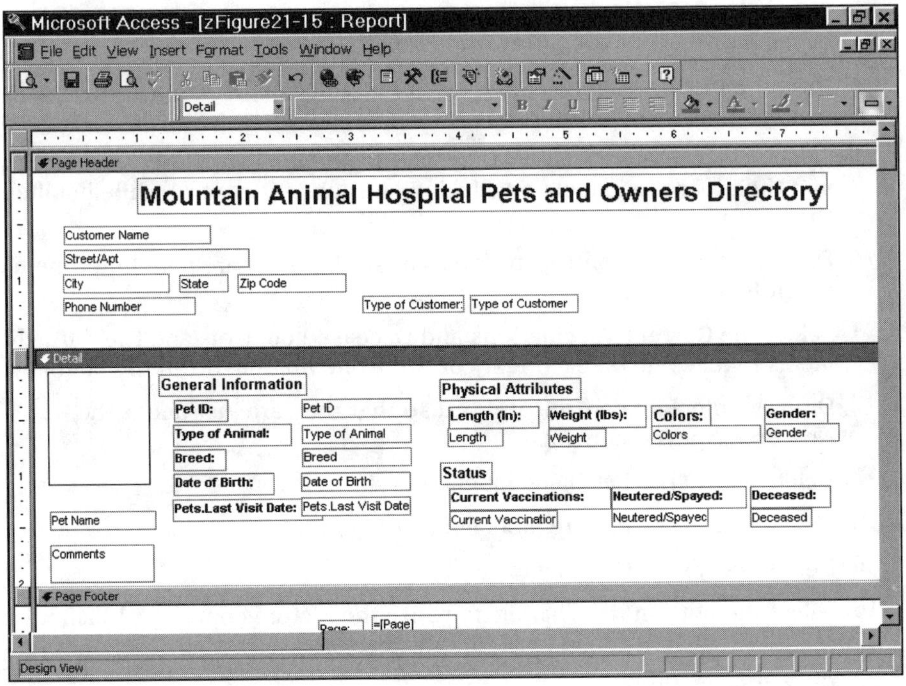

Figure 21-15: The selected and resized label control in the detail section.

3. Drag the controls Neutered/Spayed, Current Vaccinations, and Deceased away from other controls to allow space to move the label controls above the text box controls, as shown in Figure 21-15.

4. Drag each of the label controls to locations above the text box controls by grabbing each Move handle individually and then moving the controls above the text box controls.

5. Select all three label controls and align them by selecting Format⇨Align⇨ Bottom.

6. Repeat Steps 3 and 4 for the Length, Weight, Colors, and Gender controls, moving them into position as shown in Figure 21-15.

7. Move the Comments text box control so that it appears below all other controls.

Again, you may have to resize some of the controls to match the ones shown in Figure 21-15. There is still some text to add as label controls. If you compare the design shown in Figure 21-6 to your screen, you can see that you still need to add some label controls to define the groups. To add the label controls, follow these steps:

1. Double-click the Label Control button in the Toolbox so that you can add more than one label control.

2. Create a new label control above the Pet ID field and enter **General Information**. Make sure that you press Enter after entering the text of each label control so that the control is sized automatically to fit the text. You still may have to resize the label if it is bigger than the text.

3. Create a new label control above the Length field and enter **Physical Attributes**.

4. Create a new label control above the Neutered/Spayed field and enter **Status**.

5. Click on the Pointer button in the Toolbox to unlock the Toolbox.

These steps complete the rough design for this report. There are still properties, fonts, and sizes to change. When you make these changes, you'll have to move fields around again. Use the design in Figure 21-6 only as a guideline. How it looks to *you,* as you refine the look of the report in the Report window, determines the real design.

Modifying the appearance of multiple controls

The next step is to change all the label controls in the detail section to bold and 10-point size. This will help to differentiate between label controls and text controls, which currently have the same text formatting. The following steps guide you through modifying the appearance of text in multiple label controls:

1. Select all label controls in the detail section by individually clicking on them while holding down the Shift key. There are 15 label controls to select, as shown in Figure 21-15.

2. Click on the Bold button on the toolbar.

3. Click on the arrow in the Font-Size drop-down box.

4. Select 10 from the Font-Size drop-down list.

5. Select Format➪Size➪to Fit to resize all the labels.

Note   You cannot select all the label controls in the preceding steps by using the drag-and-surround method. This method would also select all the text boxes; you want only to bold and resize the labels.

You will also need to make all the text box controls bold and increase their font size to 12 points in the page header section. To modify the appearance of text box controls, follow these steps:

1. Select all the controls except the title in the page header section by clicking on the cursor in the top left corner of the section and then dragging the cursor to surround all the controls. Include the Type of Customer label control as well.

2. Click on the Bold button on the toolbar.

3. Click on the Font-Size box drop-down arrow.

4. Select 12 from the Font-Size drop-down list.

5. Select Format⇨Size⇨to Fit to resize all the text box controls.

Caution Notice that the text box controls do not display the entire field name. Remember that sizing to fit works only on the vertical height of a control. It is impossible to know how wide a field's value will be — you'll have to adjust these values manually. You can use the Print Preview window (shown in Figure 21-16) to check on your progress.

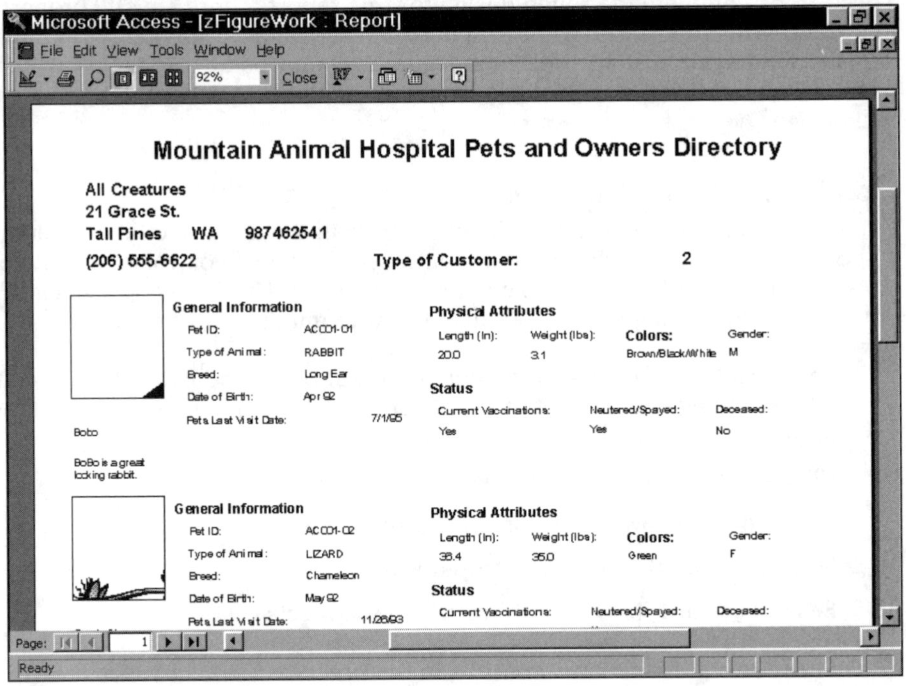

Figure 21-16: Previewing the report.

Looking at the print preview may show some minor problems. If you haven't already made any cosmetic changes, you should notice that the following changes have to be made (some or all of these may need to be fixed on your form):

Page header section:

✦ The Customer Name text box is not wide enough.

✦ There is too much space after the State text box before the ZIP Code.

✦ The Phone Number text box is not wide enough.

✦ The Type of Customer label needs to be longer.

✦ The Type of Customer text box value needs to be left-aligned.

Detail section:

✦ None of the text boxes in the detail section is 10 point; all are 8 point.

✦ The Pet Name needs to be bolded, centered, and moved closer to the picture.

✦ The data under General Information is not lined up properly.

✦ The Pets.Last Visit Date label needs to have the prefix Pets deleted.

✦ Pet ID, Type of Animal, and Breed are left-aligned, whereas the other two values are right-aligned.

✦ The Length and Weight values under Physical Attributes are right-aligned and don't line up with the labels above them.

✦ The Gender control doesn't quite fit.

✦ The Picture OLE control is not correctly displayed.

✦ The Comments memo field displays only the first few words.

Page footer section:

✦ The Page Number control needs to be moved to the right edge of the page.

✦ The page number needs to be left-aligned; both controls should be italicized.

Tip Remember that you may have looked at the data for only one record. Make sure that you look at data for many records before completing the report design, and watch the maximum sizes of your data fields. Another suggestion is to create a dummy record to use only for testing; it should contain values that use each position of the field. For example, a great name to test a 24-character field is Fred Rumpelstiltskin III. (Of course, with proportional fonts, you really can't count characters because an *i* uses less space than an *m*.)

The problems just noted will have to be fixed before this report is considered complete. You can fix many of them easily with the techniques you've already performed. Complete the changes as outlined in the list on the preceding pages. When you're through, your screen should look like Figure 21-17.

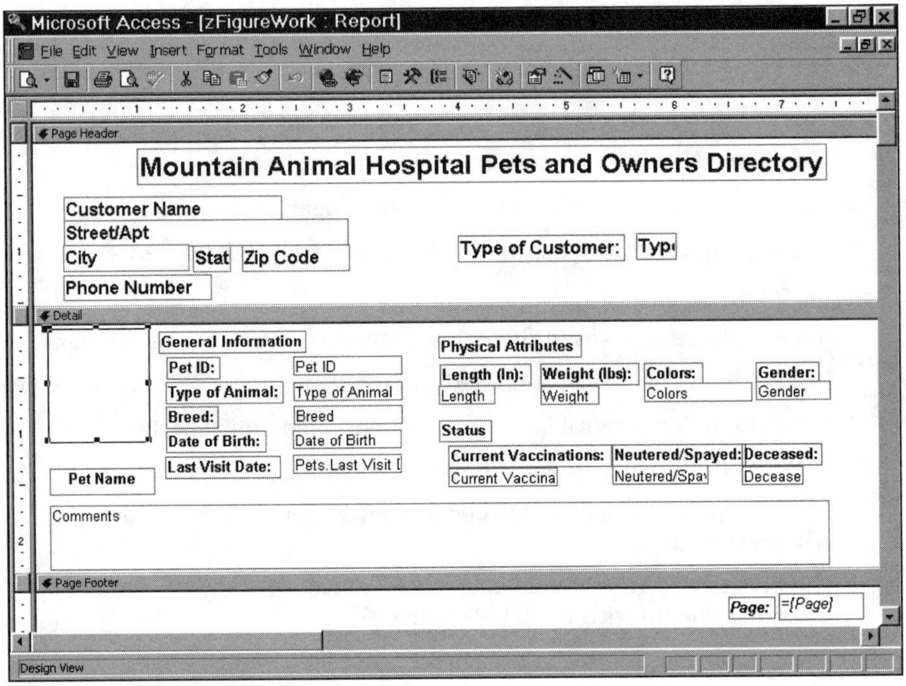

Figure 21-17: The final design layout.

After you make the final modifications, you are finished, except for fixing the picture. To do this, you'll need to change properties, which you do in the next section. This may seem to be an enormous number of steps because the procedures were designed to show you how laying out a report design can be a slow process. Remember, however, that when you are clicking away with the mouse, you don't realize how many steps you are doing as you design the report layout visually. With a WYSIWYG layout like that of the Access report designer, you may need to perform many tasks, but it's still easier and faster than programming. Figure 21-17 shows the final version of the design layout as you'll see it in this chapter. In the next chapter, you will continue to improve this report layout.

Changing label and text box control properties

To change the properties of a text or label control, you need to display the control's property sheet. If it is not already displayed, perform one of these actions:

✦ Double-click on the border of the control (anywhere except a sizing handle or Move handle).

✦ Click on the Properties button on the toolbar.

✦ Select View⇨Properties.

✦ Right-click the mouse and select Properties.

The *property sheet* lets you look at a control's property settings and gives you an easy way to edit the settings. When you use tools such as the formatting windows and text-formatting buttons on the Formatting toolbar, you are changing the property settings of a control. When you click on the Bold button, for example, you are really setting the Font Weight property to Bold. It is usually much more intuitive to use the toolbar (or even the menus), but some properties are not accessible this way. Sometimes, in fact, objects have more options available through the property sheet.

The Size Mode property of an OLE object (bound object frame), with its options of Clip, Stretch, and Zoom, is a good example of a property available only through the property sheet.

The Image control, which is a bound object frame, presently has its Size Mode property set to Clip, which is the default. With Clip, the picture is displayed in its original size. For this example, change the setting to Stretch so that the picture is sized automatically to fit the picture frame.

Cross-Reference Chapter 20 covers the use of pictures, OLE objects, and graphs.

To change the property for the bound object frame control that contains the picture, follow these steps:

1. Click on the frame control of the picture bound object.

2. Click on the Size Mode property.

3. Click on the arrow to display the drop-down list box.

4. Select Stretch.

These steps complete the changes to your form. A print preview of a single record appears in Figure 21-18. Notice how the picture is now properly displayed; the Comments field now appears across the bottom of the detail section.

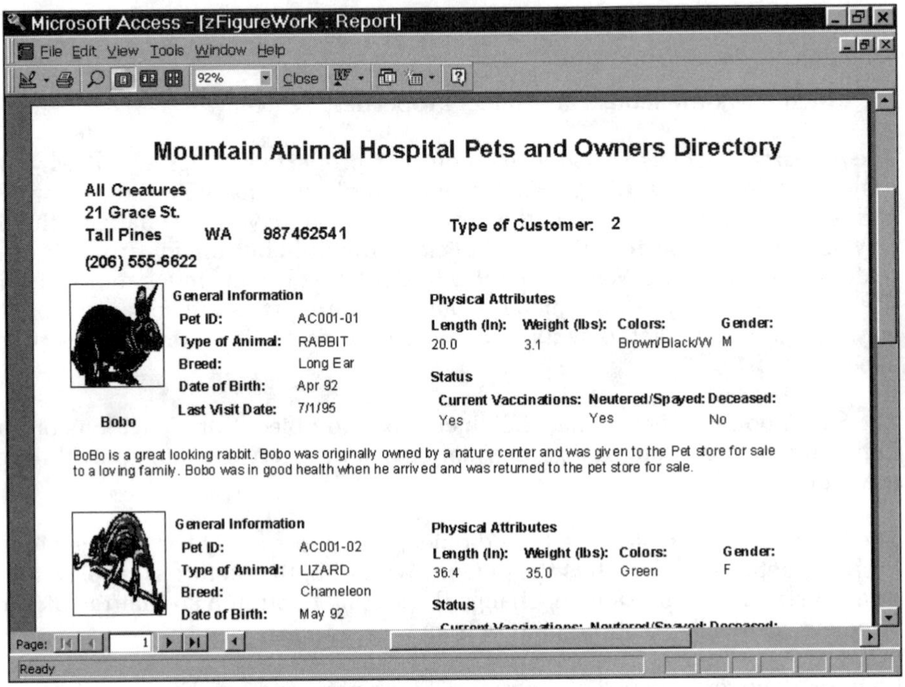

Figure 21-18: The final report print preview.

Formatting the display of text controls

With the Formatting toolbar, you can change the appearance of a control and its text. For example, you can make a control's value bold or change its font size. You can make additional changes by using the property sheet. Depending on the type of field a text box is bound to — or on whether it contains an expression — you can use various types of format masks. You can type the > character to capitalize all letters, or you can create an input mask to add parentheses and hyphens to a phone number. For numeric and date-formatting properties, you can select from a drop-down list box, which lets you add dollar signs to a number or format a date in a more readable way.

Growing and shrinking text box controls

When you print or print-preview fields that can have variable text lengths, Access provides options for enabling a control to grow or shrink vertically, depending on the exact contents of a record. The option Can Grow determines whether a text control will add lines to fit additional text if the record contains more lines of text than the control can display. The option Can Shrink determines whether a control will delete blank lines if the record's contents use fewer lines than the control can display. Although you can use this property for any text field, it is especially helpful for memo field controls.

Table 21-4 explains the acceptable values for these two properties.

Table 21-4
Text Control Values for Can Grow and Can Shrink

Property	Value	Description
Can Grow	Yes	If the data in a record uses more lines than the control is defined to display, the control resizes to accommodate additional lines.
Can Grow	No	If the data in a record uses more lines than the control is defined to display, the control does not resize; it truncates the data display.
Can Shrink	Yes	If the data in a record uses fewer lines than the control is defined to display, the control resizes to eliminate blank lines.
Can Shrink	No	If the data in a record uses fewer lines than the control is defined to display, the control does not resize to eliminate blank lines.

To change the Can Grow settings for a text control, follow these steps:

1. Select the Comments text control.

2. Display the property sheet.

3. Click on the Can Grow property; then click on the arrow and select Yes.

Note The Can Grow and Can Shrink properties are also available for report sections. Use a section's property sheet to modify these values.

As you near completion of testing of your report design, you should also test the printing of your report. Figure 21-19 shows a hard copy of the first page of the Customer and Pets report. You can see three pet records displayed for the Customer named All Creatures.

Mountain Animal Hospital Pets and Owners Directory

All Creatures
21 Grace St.
Tall Pines WA 98746-2541
(206) 555-6622

Type of Customer: 2

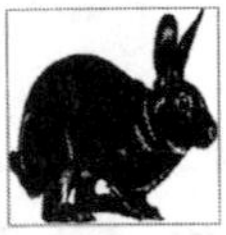

Bobo

General Information

Pet ID:	AC001-01
Type of Animal:	RABBIT
Breed:	Long Ear
Date of Birth:	Apr 92
Last Visit Date:	7/1/95

Physical Attributes

Length (In):	Weight (lbs):	Colors:	Gender:
20.0	3.1	Brown/Black/White	M

Status

Neutered/Spayed:	Current Vaccinations:	Deceased:
Yes	Yes	No

BoBo is a great looking rabbit. Bobo was originally owned by a nature center and was given to the Pet store for sale to a loving family. Bobo was in good health when he arrived and was returned to the pet store for sale.

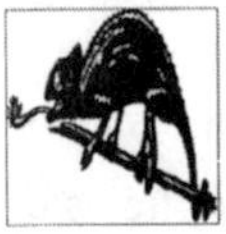

Presto Chango

General Information

Pet ID:	AC001-02
Type of Animal:	LIZARD
Breed:	Chameleon
Date of Birth:	May 92
Last Visit Date:	11/26/93

Physical Attributes

Length (In):	Weight (lbs):	Colors:	Gender:
36.4	35.0	Green	F

Status

Neutered/Spayed:	Current Vaccinations:	Deceased:
No	No	No

The lizard was not readily changing color when brought in. It only changed color when it was warm. This is not abnormal for a chameleon. However, the species which is believed to originate in northern Australia usually manifests this problem in warm weather only. It is very unusual to see a chameleon not change color when cold.

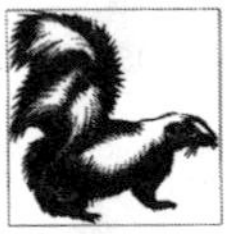

Stinky

General Information

Pet ID:	AC001-03
Type of Animal:	SKUNK
Breed:	
Date of Birth:	Aug 91
Last Visit Date:	5/11/93

Physical Attributes

Length (In):	Weight (lbs):	Colors:	Gender:
29.8	22.0	Black/White	M

Status

Neutered/Spayed:	Current Vaccinations:	Deceased:
No	No	No

The skunk was descented and was in perfect condition when it left Mountain Animal Hospital.

Figure 21-19: The final report's hard-copy printout.

You should, however, print several pages of the report. When you get to page 2, you may see a problem: The animals owned by Johnathan Adams are listed on the page for All Creatures, a pet store. What's wrong? The problem is that you haven't told Access how to group your data. Figure 21-19 displays three records on a page, but All Creatures brought in four pets. The next page begins again with All Creatures in the page header. Then the first record is Fido, the dog belonging to All Creatures. But the next record is Patty the Pig, belonging to Johnathan Adams. This record needs to trigger a page break because the Customer record has changed (later in this chapter, you learn how to do this). You may also notice on page 2 that the Breed field is not fully displayed. You should expand the text box to display the entire text German Shepherd.

Caution If every even-numbered page is blank, you accidentally widened the report past the 8-inch mark. If you move a control to brush up against the right page-margin border or exceed it, the right page margin increases automatically. When it is past the 8-inch mark, it can't display the entire page on one physical piece of paper. The blank page you get is actually the right side of the preceding page. To correct this, make sure that all your controls are within the 8-inch right margin; then drag the right page margin back to 8 inches.

Sorting and grouping data

So far, you have completely designed the layout of your report. You may think that you're done, but some tasks still remain; one of these is sorting.

Sorting lets you determine the order in which you view the records in a datasheet, form, or report, based on the values in one or more fields. This order is important when you want to view the data in your tables in a sequence other than that of your input. For example, new customers are added to the Customer table as they become clients of the hospital; the physical order of the database reflects the date and time a customer is added. Yet when you think of the customer list, you probably expect it to be in *alphabetical* order, and you want to sort it by Customer Number or Customer Name. By sorting in the report itself, you don't have to worry about the order of the data. Although you can sort the data in the query, it is more advantageous to do it in the report. This way, if you change the query, the report is still in the correct order.

You can take this report concept even further by *grouping* — breaking related records into groups. Suppose that you want to list your customers first by Customer Name and then by Pet Name within each Customer Name group. To do this, you must use the Customer Number field to sort the data. Groupings that can create group headers and footers are sometimes called *control breaks* because changes in data trigger the report groups.

Before you can add a grouping, however, you must first define a *sort order* for at least one field in the report. You do this by using the Sorting and Grouping box, which is shown completed in Figure 21-20. In this example, you will use the Customer.Customer Number field to sort on first and then the Pet ID field, which you will use as the secondary sort.

The Customer Name and Customer Number fields

You may have noticed that the Customer Name field is not in last name/first name order and that the Customer Number is generally in a sorted order by the customer's last name. The Customer Number field begins with the first two characters of a customer's last name if the customer is an individual (Type of Customer = 1). If the customer is a pet store (Type of Customer = 2) or zoo (Type of Customer = 3), the Customer Number field begins with the first two logical characters of the pet store or zoo name.

For an illustration, examine the following list, which shows Type of Customer, Customer Name, and Customer Number for the first five records in the Customer table:

Type of Customer	Customer Name	Customer Number
2 - Pet Store	**All C**reatures	AC001
1 - Individual	Johnathan **Ad**ams	AD001
1 - Individual	William **Ad**ams	AD002
2 - Pet Store	**A**nimal **K**ingdom	AK001
3 - Zoo	**B**orderville **A**quarium	BA001

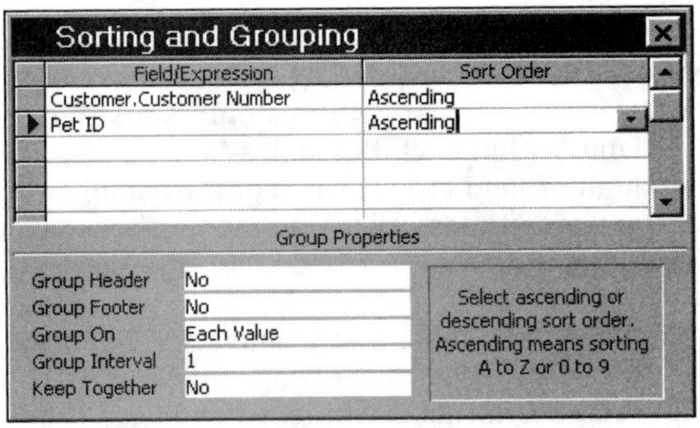

Figure 21-20: The Sorting and Grouping box.

To define a sort order based on Customer Number and Pet ID, follow these steps:

1. Click on the Sorting and Grouping button on the toolbar to display the Sorting and Grouping box.

2. Click on the cursor in the first row of the Field/Expression column of the Sorting and Grouping box. A downward-pointing arrow appears.

3. Click on the arrow to display a list of fields in the Pets and Owners query.

4. Click on the Customer.Customer Number field in the field list. Notice that Sort Order defaults to Ascending.

5. Click on the cursor in the second row of the Field/Expression column.

6. Click on the arrow to display a list of fields in the Pets and Owners query.

7. Scroll down to find the Pet ID field in the field list and select Pet ID. The Sort Order defaults to Ascending.

Tip To see more of the Field/Expression column, you can drag the border between the Field/Expression and Sort Order columns to the right (as shown in Figure 21-20).

Note You can drag a field from the Field List window into the Sorting and Grouping box Field/Expression column rather than enter a field or choose one from the field list in the Sorting and Grouping box Field/Expression column.

Although in this example you used a field, you can alternatively sort (and group) by using an expression. To enter an expression, click in the desired row of the Field/Expression column and enter any valid Access expression, making sure that it begins with an equal sign, as in =[Length]*[Weight].

Note To change the sort order for fields you placed in the Field/Expression column, simply click on the Sort Order column and click on the down arrow to display the Sort Order list; then select Descending.

Creating a group header or footer

In this example, you'll need to sort by the Customer Number and Pet ID. You will also need to create a group header for Customer Number in order to force a new page break before each new customer page. This way, a customer page will display pet records for only that customer; customers who have more pets than will fit on one page will continue to generate new pages, with only the customer information and pets for that customer. You don't need a group footer in this example because there are no totals by customer number or other reasons to use a group footer.

To create a group header that lets you sort and group by Customer Number, follow these steps:

1. Click on the Sorting and Grouping button on the toolbar if the Sorting and Grouping box is not displayed. The field Customer.Customer Number should be displayed in the first row of the Sorting and Grouping box; it should indicate that it is being used as a sort in Ascending order.

2. Click on Customer.Customer Number in the Field/Expression column.

3. Click on the Group Header property in the bottom pane; an arrow appears.

4. Click on the arrow on the right side of the edit box; a drop-down list appears.

5. Select Yes from the list.

6. Press Enter. (A header separator bar appears on the report.)

After you define a header or footer, the row pointer changes to the grouping symbol shown in Figure 21-21. This is the same symbol you see in the Sorting and Grouping button on the toolbar. In Figure 21-21, you can see not only the grouping row pointer but also a newly created section. The Customer.Customer Number header section appears between the page header and detail sections. If you define a group footer, it appears below the detail section. If a report has multiple groupings, each subsequent group becomes the one closest to the detail section. The groups defined first will be farthest from the detail section.

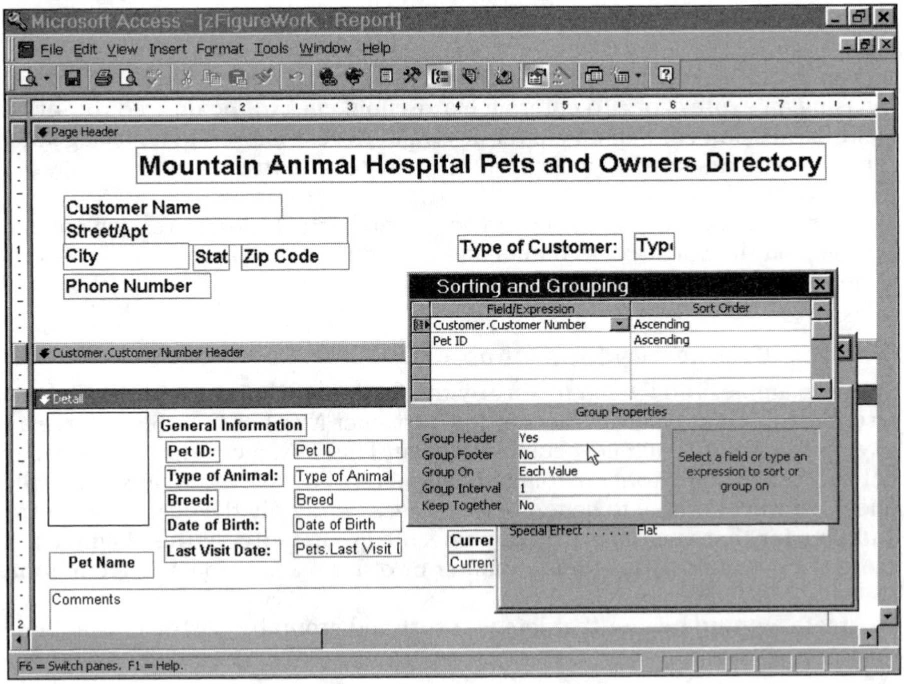

Figure 21-21: The group header definition.

The Group Properties pane (displayed at the bottom of the Sorting and Grouping box) contains the following properties:

Group Header	Yes creates a group header. No removes the group header.
Group Footer	Yes creates a group footer. No removes the group footer.
Group On	Specifies how you want the values grouped. The options you see in the drop-down list box depend on the data type of the field on which you're grouping. If you group on an expression, you see all the options. Group On has more choices to make:

For Text data types, you have two choices:

Each Value	The same value in the field or expression
Prefix Characters	The same first *n* number of characters in the field

For Date/Time data types, you have additional options:

Each Value	The same value in the field or expression
Year	Dates in the same calendar year
Qtr	Dates in the same calendar quarter
Month	Dates in the same month
Week	Dates in the same week
Day	Dates on the same date
Hour	Times in the same hour
Minute	Times in the same minute

With AutoNumber, Currency, or Number data types, you have two options:

Each Value	The same value in the field or expression	
Interval	Values falling within the interval you specify	
Group Interval	Specifies any interval that is valid for the values in the field or expression you're grouping on	
Keep Together	Whole Group	Prints header detail and group footer on one page
	With First Detail	Prevents the contents of the group header from printing without any following data or records on a page
	No	Doesn't keep together

After you create the Customer Number group header, you are done with the Sorting and Grouping box for this report. You may need to make additional changes to groupings as you change the way a report looks; the following three sections detail how to make these changes. You should not make any of these changes, however, if you are following along with the examples. If you want to practice these skills, you can save the report before practicing and then retrieve the original copy of the report you saved. After the next three sections, you will have to size the group header section and change its properties.

CD-ROM

Changing the group order

Access lets you easily change the Sorting and Grouping order without moving all the individual controls in the associated headers and footers. Here are the general steps to change the sorting and grouping order:

1. Click on the selector of the field or expression you want to move in the Sorting and Grouping window.
2. Click on the selector again and hold down the left mouse button.
3. Drag the row to a new location.
4. Release the mouse button.

Removing a group header or footer

To remove a page or report header/footer section, use the <u>V</u>iew⇨<u>P</u>age Header/Footer and <u>V</u>iew⇨Report <u>H</u>eader/Footer toggles as detailed earlier in this chapter. To remove a group header or footer but leave the sorting intact, follow these steps:

1. In the Sorting and Grouping window, click on the selector of the field or expression you want to remove from the grouping.
2. Click on the Group Header edit box.
3. Change the value to **No**.
4. Press Enter.

To remove a group footer, follow the same steps but click on Group Footer in Step 2.

To permanently remove both the sorting and grouping for a particular field (and thereby remove the group header and footer sections), follow these steps:

1. Click on the selector of the field or expression you want to delete.
2. Press Delete. A dialog box will appear, asking you to confirm the deletion.
3. Click on OK.

Hiding a section

Access also lets you hide headers and footers so that you can break data into groups without having to view information about the group itself. You can also hide the detail section so that you see only a summary report. To hide a section, follow these steps:

1. Click on the section you want to hide.

2. Display the section property sheet.

3. Click on the Visible property's edit box.

4. Click on the drop-down list arrow on the right side of the edit box.

5. Select No from the drop-down list box.

Note Sections are not the only objects in a report that can be hidden; controls also have a Visible property. This property can be useful for expressions that trigger other expressions.

CD-ROM If you are following along in the examples, you should complete the steps in the following section.

Sizing a section

Now that you have created the group header, you must decide what to do with it. Its only purpose in this example is to trigger a page break before a new customer record is displayed. (You learn how to do this later in this chapter.) For this example, you don't need to place any controls within the section. Unless you want to see the empty space on the report from the height of the group header section, close the section. You can do this by resizing the section height to 0.

To modify the height of a section, drag the border of the section below it. If (for example) you have a report with a page header, detail section, and page footer, change the height of the detail section by dragging the top of the page footer section's border. You can make a section larger or smaller by dragging the bottom border of the section. For this example, change the height of the group header section to zero with these steps:

1. Move your cursor over the section borders. Notice that the cursor changes to a horizontal line split by two vertical arrows.

2. Select the top of the detail section border.

3. Drag the selected border until it meets the bottom of the header Customer.Customer Number. Notice the gray line that indicates where the top of the border will be when you release the mouse button.

4. Release the mouse button.

Adding page breaks

Access lets you add page breaks based on group breaks; you can also insert forced breaks within sections, except in page header and footer sections.

In some report designs, it's best to have each new group begin on a different page. In the Pets and Owners report you created in this chapter, one of the design criteria is that no more than one customer will appear on a page (though a customer can appear on more than one page). You can achieve this effect easily by using the Force New Page property of a group section, which lets you force a page break every time the group value changes.

The four Force New Page settings are as follows:

None	No forced page break (the default)
Before Section	Starts printing the current section at the top of a new page every time there is a new group
After Section	Starts printing the next section at the top of a new page every time there is a new group
Before & After	Combines the effects of Before Section and After Section

To create the report you want, you must force a page break before the Customer Number group by using the Force New Page property in the Customer Number header. To change the Force New Page property on the basis of groupings, follow these steps:

1. Click anywhere in the Customer.Customer Number header.

2. Display the Property window format sheet.

3. Select the Force New Page property.

4. Click on the drop-down list arrow on the right side of the edit box.

5. Select Before Section from the drop-down list box.

Figure 21-22 shows this property sheet.

If you run the report now, you'll see that page 2 has correctly printed only the last record from All Creatures. Page 3 now contains the two pets owned by Johnathan Adams.

Tip
Alternatively, you can create a Customer Number footer and set its Force New Page property to After Section.

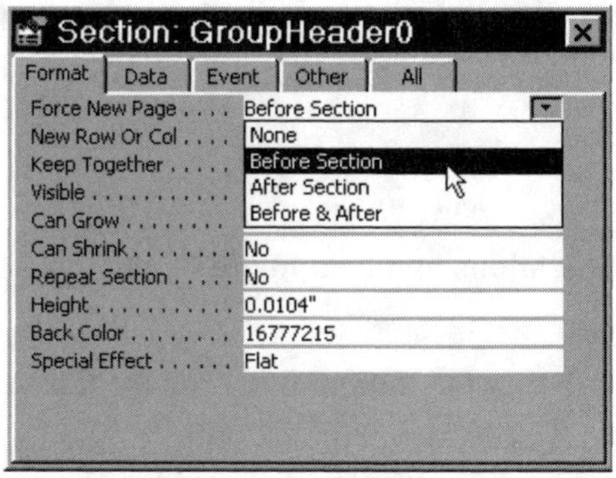

Figure 21-22: Forcing a page break in a group header.

Sometimes you don't want to force a page break on the basis of a grouping but still want to force a page break. For example, you may want to split a report title across several pages. The solution is to use the Page Break tool from the Toolbox; the general steps follow:

1. Display the Toolbox.

2. Click on the Page Break tool.

3. Click in the section where you want the page break to occur.

4. Test the results by using Print Preview.

Note   Be careful not to split the data in a control. Place page breaks above or below controls; do not overlap them.

Saving your report

After all the time you spent creating your report, you'll want to save it. As a matter of fact, even though it is covered at the end of this chapter, it is good practice to save your reports frequently, starting as soon as you create them. This prevents the frustration of losing your work because of a power failure or human error. Save the report as follows:

1. Select File⇨Save. If this is the first time you have saved the report, the Save As dialog box appears.

2. Type a valid Access name. For this example, type **Pets and Owners - Unformatted**.

3. Click on OK.

If you already saved your report, Access silently (or not so silently, depending on your disk drive) saves your file, with no message about what it is up to.

Summary

In this chapter, you learned the basic operations involved in creating a report. Concepts covered include the following:

✦ A report gives you a different way of viewing data in one or more tables.

✦ Because of the advanced capabilities of Access, you are limited only by your imagination and your printer in the types of reports you can create.

✦ In the Report Design window, Access provides you with powerful but easy-to-use tools. These tools are the toolbars, the Properties window, the Sorting and Grouping box, and the Field List.

✦ The Report Design View toolbar gives you quick access to such design tasks as displaying various windows and applying formatting styles.

✦ With the Toolbox, you can create, place, or select the controls on a report.

✦ The Field List window displays all fields available to a report from the query or table the report is bound to.

✦ Properties for a control can be viewed and edited from the control's property sheet.

✦ The Sorting and Grouping box lets you create group or summary sections on the report and define sort orders.

✦ You can place fields on a report by displaying the field list, selecting your fields, and then dragging the fields to your report.

✦ You can edit control properties by direct manipulation (by using the various tools in the Report Design window), or you can edit these properties from the property sheet.

✦ You can create a summary report by hiding the detail section.

✦ Sorting lets you organize your data in a different order from the order you used during input.

✦ Grouping lets you organize your data in related groups that make the data easier to understand.

In the next chapter, you learn how to publish your reports using the Access database publishing features.

✦   ✦   ✦

Database Publishing and Printing

In Chapter 21, you built a report from a blank form. That report was fairly simple. You worked with only label and text box controls, and the report had no special formatting. There were no lines or boxes and no shading to emphasize any areas of the report. Although the report displays all the necessary data, you can make the data more readable by using check boxes, option buttons, and toggle buttons to display certain fields.

In this chapter, you see how to complete the formatting of the report you created in the preceding chapter, enhancing it to make it more readable and presentable.

Note Because the Report Design window is set to a width of eight inches, most of the screen printouts in this chapter appear as though an 800 x 600-resolution Super VGA Windows screen driver is used rather than the standard 640 x 480 VGA Windows driver. This setup lets you see almost the entire screen in the figures.

Database Publishing with Access

The term *database publishing* generally refers to the process of enhancing a report from a database by using special effects that desktop publishing packages provide. The Access Report Writer can accomplish with data, reports, and forms what any good desktop publishing package can do with words. Just as a desktop publishing application can enhance a word-processing document to make it more readable, a database publisher can enhance a database report to make it more usable.

You can, for example, draw attention to areas of the report you want the reader to notice. Just as a headline in a newspaper screams out the news, an enhanced section of the report screams out the information.

Cross-Reference You accomplish database publishing in reports with a variety of controls and by enhancing the controls with color, shading, or other means of emphasis. In Chapters 18, 19, and 20, you learned how to add to a form many of the controls you work with in this chapter. You use a somewhat different process to add and enhance these controls in a report. One major difference is the ultimate viewing medium. Because the output of these controls is usually viewed on paper, you have design concerns that differ from those of creating a design to be viewed on-screen. Another difference is the use of each data control. In a form, you input or edit the data; in a report, you just view it.

Figure 22-1 shows the hard copy of the final report you create in this chapter. Notice that it has been significantly enhanced by adding special effects and more control types than mere labels or text boxes. Important information, such as the type of customer, gender, and current vaccinations, is easily understood at a glance; readers need only look at an option button(◉/◯) or check box (☐/☑) rather than a numeric code or text.

The Access Report Writer offers a number of tools to make the report controls and sections stand out visually. These tools enable you to create such special effects as

> ◆ Lines and rectangles
>
> ◆ Color and background shading
>
> ◆ Three-dimensional effects (raised, sunken, shadowed, flattened, etched, and chiseled)

In this chapter, you use all these features as you change many of the text box controls into option buttons, toggle buttons, and check boxes. You also enhance the report with special text options: shading, shadows, lines, rectangles, and three-dimensional effects.

Caution When you add shading to a report, you can increase printing time dramatically. Also, avoid adding colors unless you plan to print on a color printer.

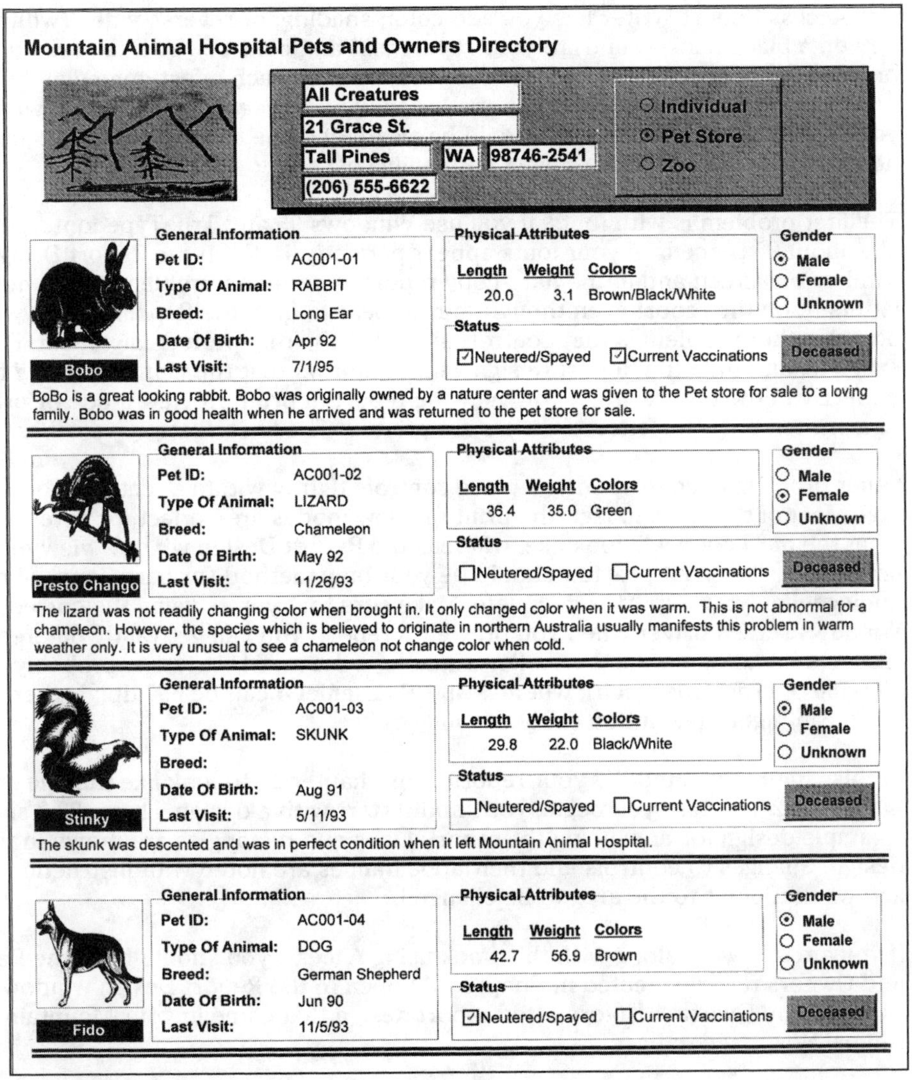

Mountain Animal Hospital Pets and Owners Directory

All Creatures
21 Grace St.
Tall Pines   WA 98746-2541
(206) 555-6622

○ Individual
◉ Pet Store
○ Zoo

General Information

Pet ID:	AC001-01
Type Of Animal:	RABBIT
Breed:	Long Ear
Date Of Birth:	Apr 92
Last Visit:	7/1/95

Bobo

Physical Attributes

Length   Weight   Colors
20.0   3.1   Brown/Black/White

Status

☑Neutered/Spayed ☑Current Vaccinations   Deceased

Gender
◉ Male
○ Female
○ Unknown

BoBo is a great looking rabbit. Bobo was originally owned by a nature center and was given to the Pet store for sale to a loving family. Bobo was in good health when he arrived and was returned to the pet store for sale.

General Information

Pet ID:	AC001-02
Type Of Animal:	LIZARD
Breed:	Chameleon
Date Of Birth:	May 92
Last Visit:	11/26/93

Presto Chango

Physical Attributes

Length   Weight   Colors
36.4   35.0   Green

Status

☐Neutered/Spayed ☐Current Vaccinations   Deceased

Gender
○ Male
◉ Female
○ Unknown

The lizard was not readily changing color when brought in. It only changed color when it was warm. This is not abnormal for a chameleon. However, the species which is believed to originate in northern Australia usually manifests this problem in warm weather only. It is very unusual to see a chameleon not change color when cold.

General Information

Pet ID:	AC001-03
Type Of Animal:	SKUNK
Breed:	
Date Of Birth:	Aug 91
Last Visit:	5/11/93

Stinky

Physical Attributes

Length   Weight   Colors
29.8   22.0   Black/White

Status

☐Neutered/Spayed ☐Current Vaccinations   Deceased

Gender
◉ Male
○ Female
○ Unknown

The skunk was descented and was in perfect condition when it left Mountain Animal Hospital.

General Information

Pet ID:	AC001-04
Type Of Animal:	DOG
Breed:	German Shepherd
Date Of Birth:	Jun 90
Last Visit:	11/5/93

Fido

Physical Attributes

Length   Weight   Colors
42.7   56.9   Brown

Status

☑Neutered/Spayed ☐Current Vaccinations   Deceased

Gender
◉ Male
○ Female
○ Unknown

Figure 22-1: An enhanced report.

Understanding WYSIWYG Printing

Access has a *WYSIWYG* (*what you see is what you get*) report writer. As you create controls on-screen, you see instantly how they will look in your report. If you want to see how the data will look, you can take advantage of several types of on-screen preview modes. These modes enable you to see the actual data without involving a hard-copy device.

The Access Report Writer lets you add color, shading, or reverse video (white letters on a black background) to your report text and controls. You can even color or shade the background of report sections; you see each effect immediately. Although what you see on the Report Design window *seems* to be exactly what you'll see when you print, you should be aware of some factors that affect just how close what you see is to what you really get.

The first problem is with fonts. If you use Windows 95 and TrueType fonts, generally about 95 percent of your fonts appear perfectly, both on the Report Design window on-screen and in the hard-copy report. A common problem is that not all letters fit on the report even though they appear to fit in the Report Design window. Another problem is that controls shift slightly from perfect alignment. For example, although the Report Design window shows that the word *Deceased* fits perfectly in the report, when you view the report in print preview mode or print it to a printer, only the letters *Decease* are printed. The final *d* simply vanishes.

Other problems occur when you place controls tightly within a rectangle or group box. Most of the time, in fact, the print preview modes are perfect for determining what the hard copy will look like, whereas the Report Design window view may differ slightly. The print preview should be your only method (or hard copy) of determining when your report is complete. Make sure that you're using the correct Windows screen driver when you preview a report; you can get vastly different results depending on the driver. For example, a dot-matrix driver is probably only 100–150 dpi (dots per inch), whereas an HP LaserJet 4 can be 600 dpi; higher values mean higher resolution (a clearer image).

In this chapter, you modify your report from Chapter 21 to look like the one shown in Figure 22-1. Before you begin, you should start with a design. Figure 22-2 shows a sample design for enhancing the report. Lines and rectangles are drawn in the design. Changes to controls and their appearances are noted with instructions and arrows that point to the area to be changed.

CD-ROM

If you are following along with this book using Access, you should have the Pets and Owners report (created in Chapter 21) open in the Report Design window or the Pets and Owners - Unformatted report design that came in your Mountain Animal Hospital database.

Enhancing Text-Based Controls

Before you begin using such display items as shading or three-dimensional effects, it's important to get the data right. If your enhancements include control changes, start with these changes.

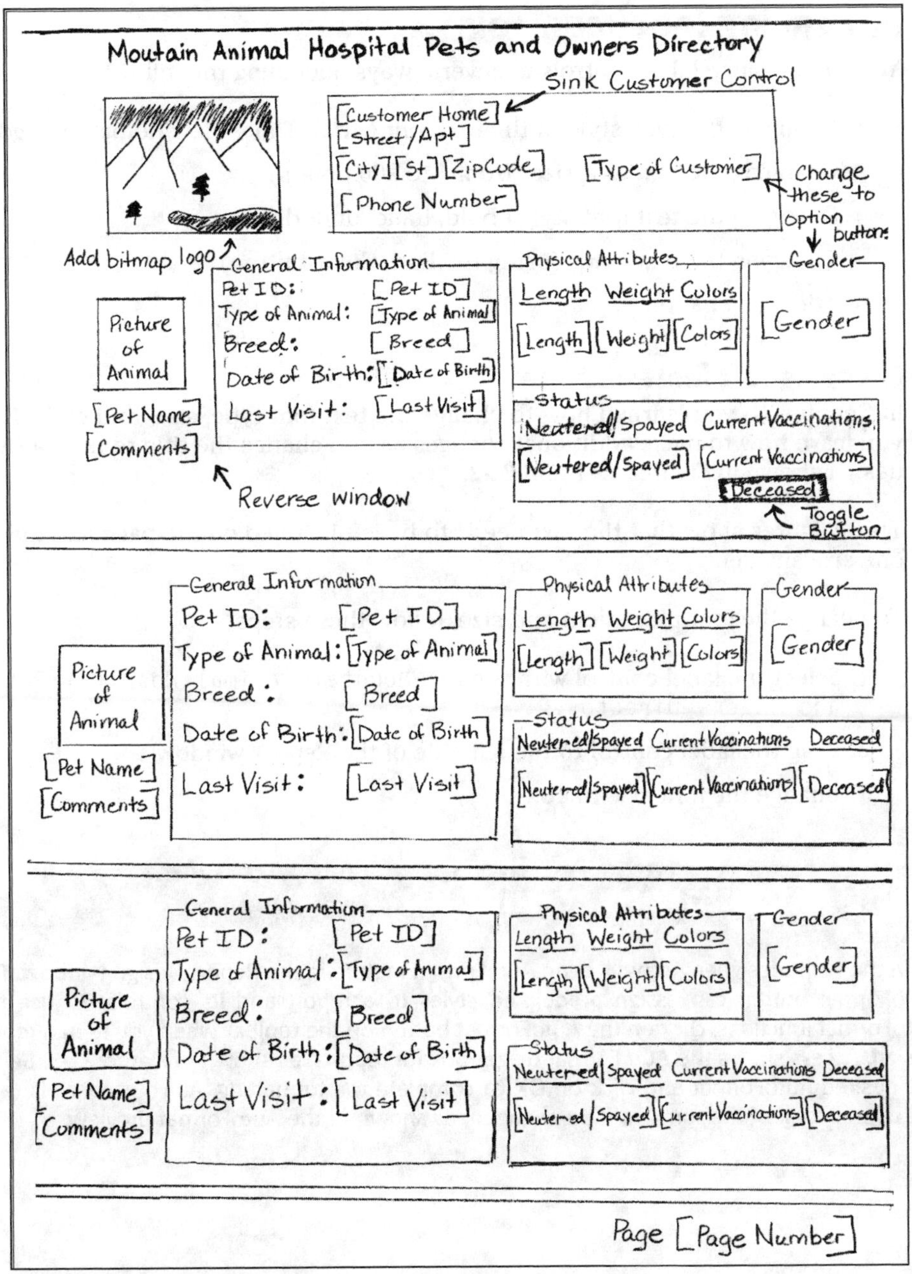

Figure 22-2: A design for report enhancements.

Enhancing label controls

You can enhance label controls in several ways, including the following:

✦ Changing the type style of the text font (Arial, Times New Roman, Wingdings)

✦ Changing the text font size (from 4 to 200 points)

✦ Changing the text font style (bold, italic, underline)

✦ Changing the text color (using the Fore Color button)

✦ Adding a shadow

Changing text fonts and size

In Chapter 21, you learned how to change the text font type, size, and style. Now you learn how to make additional changes as you change the title to match the design shown in Figures 22-1 and 22-2.

These figures show that the text needs to be left-justified on the page and made one size smaller.

To change the font placement and size, follow these steps:

1. Select the label control with the text Mountain Animal Hospital Pets and Owners Directory.

2. Drag the label control to the left side of the Report window.

3. Change the font size to **16**.

Using the AutoFormat button

As in the Form designer, Access has an AutoFormat feature in the Report Design window. The AutoFormat button can assign predefined styles to a report and its controls. To use the AutoFormat functions, click on the AutoFormat button on the toolbar when you're in a report design. Access shows the AutoFormat dialog box for reports, as shown in Figure 22-3. Select the desired AutoFormat and click on OK to complete the formatting. All your controls (and the overall look of the form) will be changed, as shown in the AutoFormat preview.

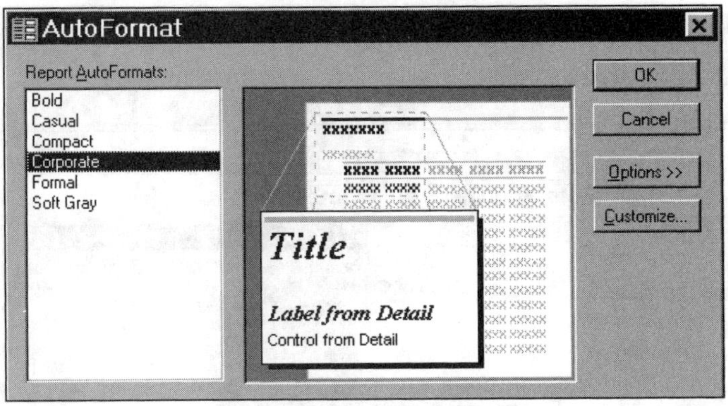

Figure 22-3: The AutoFormat dialog box.

Creating a text shadow

Text shadows create a three-dimensional look. They make text seem to float above the page while text shadows stay on the page. You can create text shadows for a report by using these techniques:

- ✦ Duplicate the text.
- ✦ Offset the duplicate text from the original text.
- ✦ Change the duplicate text to a different color (usually a lighter shade).
- ✦ Place the duplicate text behind the original text.
- ✦ Change the original text Back Color Transparent button.

Note   Access has a shadow effect on the Special Effects button under the Formatting toolbar. This effect creates a shadow only on boxes or on the text box, not on the text itself. Compare the Mountain Animal Hospital Pets and Owners Directory in Figure 22-4 and Figure 22-5.

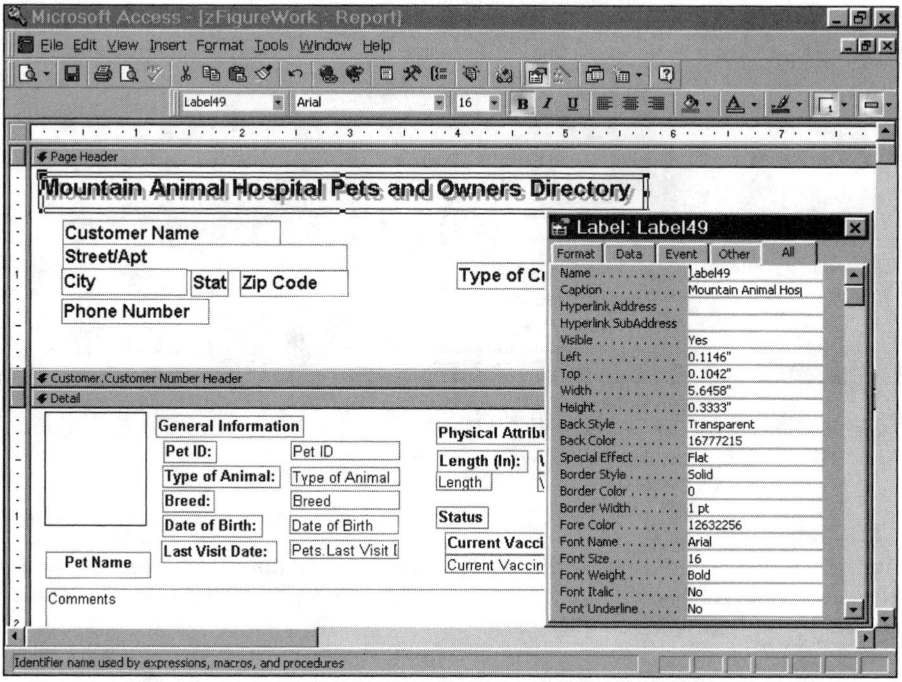

Figure 22-4: Label control properties.

To create a shadow for the title's text, follow these steps:

1. Select the label control with the text Mountain Animal Hospital Pets and Owners Directory.

2. Select Edit⇨Duplicate.

3. Select light gray from the Foreground Color window to change the duplicate text color.

4. Drag the duplicate text slightly to the right and upward to lessen the offset from the original text below.

5. Select Format⇨Send to Back.

6. Select the original copy of the text (the one now in front).

7. Click on the Transparent button in the Back Color window.

The text now appears to have a shadow, as you see in Figure 22-4. The box around the label control will not be visible when the report is printed.

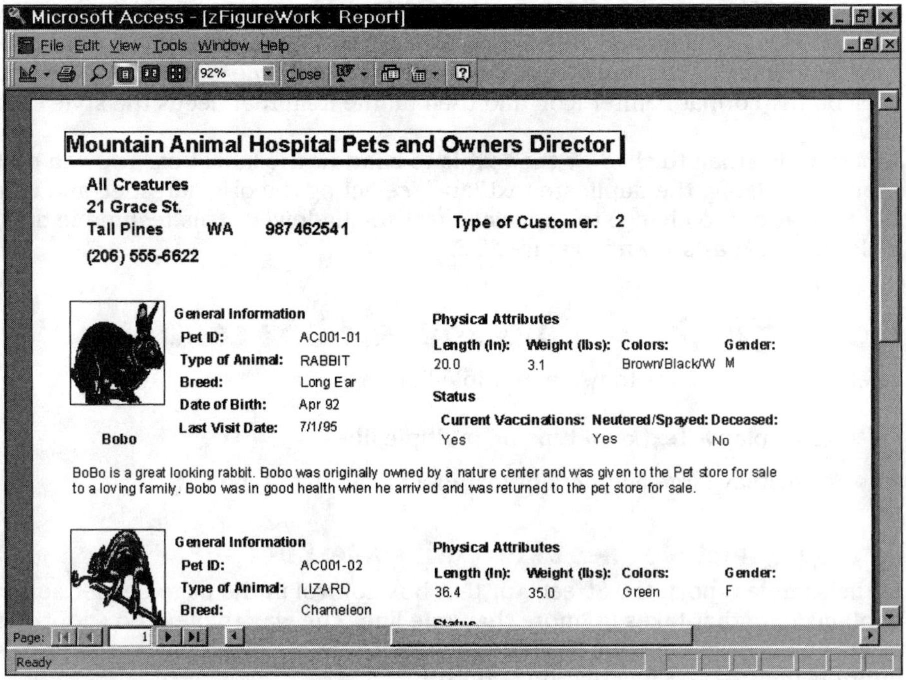

Figure 22-5: Displaying the Print Preview window.

Caution

Although the on-screen shadow looks great, it does not print correctly on most monochrome printers. Normally, you get just two lines of black text that look horrible. Unless you have a printer that prints text in shades of gray (using graphics rather than text fonts) or a color printer that prints in gray, avoid using shadowed text on a report.

CD-ROM

For the purpose of this book, select the shadow box you just created and remove it to continue with the tutorials.

Displaying label or text box control properties

As you use formatting to change values in a label or text box control, you change their properties. Figure 22-4 displays the property sheet for the label control you just created. As you can see in the figure, many properties (described in Chapter 18) can be affected by the formatting windows.

Although you can set many of these controls from the property sheet, it's much easier to drag the control to set the Top, Left, Width, and Height and to use the Formatting toolbar to set the other properties of the control.

Tip   Access (like other Microsoft Office products) has a Format Painter on the standard toolbar. This excellent and convenient tool allows you to copy styles from one selection to the next. Simply click on the item whose style you want to copy; then click on the Format Painter icon and then on the item that needs the style change.

Tip   A better idea than to shadow the text is to shadow the label box. You can do this easily by deleting the duplicate text label, selecting the original label, and using the Format bar to change the special effect to Shadowed. This technique displays a cleaner look, as shown in Figure 22-5.

Working with multiple-line text box controls

There are two reasons to use a multiple-line text box:

- ✦ To display a Text data type on multiple lines
- ✦ To display large amounts of text in a Memo data type

Displaying multiple lines of text using a text box

In the sample report, the Street/Apt text box control in the page header sometimes contains data that takes up more than one line. The way the text box control is sized, you can see only the first line of data. There are generally two ways to see multiple lines of text in a text box control:

- ✦ Resize the control vertically to allow more lines to be displayed.
- ✦ Change the Can Grow or Can Shrink properties.

When you resize a control by making it larger vertically, it uses as much space as you created for the field of the record. This leaves excess space for the field if the content's length changes from record to record. For example, most of the values of the Street/Apt text box control use one line; some use two. If you resize the Street/Apt text box control to display two lines, the control displays two lines for *every* customer. This leaves a blank line between the Street/Apt control and the City control whenever the Street/Apt value uses only one line.

One solution to this problem is to use the Can Grow or Can Shrink properties of the text box control instead of resizing the control. If you change the value of the Can Grow property to Yes, the control grows vertically if there are more lines than can be displayed in the default control. Another solution is to resize the control so that it's larger and then use the Can Shrink property to remove any blank lines if the value of the data does not use the full size of the control.

When you set the Can Grow property in a text box control to Yes, the property is also set for the detail, group header, and group footer or report header or footer sections.

Displaying memo fields in multiple-line text box controls

The Memo data type fields generally use large amounts of text. You can display these fields on a report by simply placing the text box in the desired section (usually the detail section) and resizing it to the desired width and height.

In a form, you can add *scrollbars* to display any text that doesn't fit the space allotted. In a report, you don't have that option; to display text properly, use the Can Grow and Can Shrink properties. In Chapter 21, you created a large text box control to accommodate several lines of memo text, and you set the Can Grow and Can Shrink properties to Yes. You should check the Can Grow and Can Shrink properties to verify that they are set to Yes for the Comments text box control and resize the field. To do so, follow these steps:

1. Select the Properties button on the toolbar to display the property sheet.
2. Select the Comments text box control.
3. Change the height of the control to one line to fit the Comments caption.
4. Verify that the Can Grow property is Yes.
5. Verify that the Can Shrink property is Yes.
6. Shrink the detail section height by dragging the page footer border upward until it's just below the Comments control.

To see the effect of the Can Grow and Can Shrink properties, display the report in the Print Preview window. Notice the Comment line and the shadowed line in Figure 22-5, which shows the Print Preview window. If you look at the print preview in zoom mode, you'll see that the spaces between the records are the same, regardless of the size of the Comments field. If no comment text is present, the next record begins immediately below the preceding record's information.

Adding New Controls

You can change many data types to control types other than text boxes. These data types include Text, Number, and Yes/No. The other control types you can use are

◆ Option buttons

◆ Check boxes

◆ Toggle buttons

Note Access lets you change some control types from one to another. Generally, text box controls can become combo box or list box controls; check boxes, option buttons, and toggle buttons are interchangeable.

Displaying values with option groups and option buttons

In your design, as shown in Figure 22-2, you see two text box controls that should be changed to option buttons within an option group. These text box controls are the Type of Customer field in the page header section and the Gender field in the detail section.

An option group is generally bound to a single field or expression. Each button in the group passes a different value to the option group, which in turn passes the single choice to the bound field or expression. The buttons themselves are not bound to a field — only to the option group box.

Cross-Reference   If you haven't used an option button or option group yet, read Chapter 16 before continuing.

You can use only numeric data values to create an option button within an option group. The Type of Customer field is relatively easy to change to an option group; its values are already numeric, expressed as customer types 1, 2, or 3.

Creating the option group

To create the option group for the Type of Customer control, you must first delete the existing Type of Customer control. Then you can create a new option group and use the Option Group Wizard to create the option buttons.

Cross-Reference   Chapter 19 offers a more complete example of creating an option group and option buttons with the Option Group Wizard.

Follow these steps to create an option group using the Option Group Wizard:

1. Delete the existing Type of Customer control.

2. Select the Option Group button from the Toolbox.

3. Drag the Type of Customer field from the field list to the space in the page header section.

   The first screen of the Option Group Wizard should be visible (as shown completed in Figure 22-6). Enter the text label for each option button that will be in your option group, just as you would do in a datasheet. You can press the down-arrow key to move to the next choice.

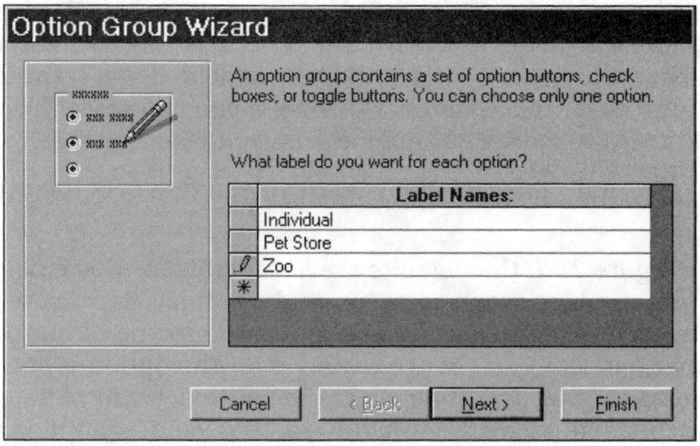

Figure 22-6: Entering the option group choices.

4. Enter **Individual**, **Pet Store**, and **Zoo**, pressing the down-arrow key between choices.

5. Click on the <u>N</u>ext> button to move to the default option Wizard screen.

   The next screen lets you select the default control for when the option group is selected. Normally, the first option is the default. To make a different button the default, you first select the Yes option button and then select the new default value from the combo box that shows your choices. In this example, the first value will be the default automatically.

6. Click on the <u>N</u>ext> button to move to the Assigning Values screen of the Wizard.

   The next Wizard screen displays the actual values you entered, along with a default set of numbers that will be used to store the selected value in the bound option group field. The screen looks like a datasheet with two columns. In this example, this is the Type of Customer field. Your first choice, Individual, is automatically assigned a 1, Pet Store a 2, and Zoo a 3. When Pet Store is selected, a 2 will be stored in the Type of Customer field.

   In this example, the default values are acceptable. Sometimes you may want to assign values other than 1, 2, 3, and so on. For example, you might want to use 100, 200, and 500 for some reason. As long as you use unique numbers, you can assign any values you want.

7. Click on the <u>N</u>ext> button to move to the next Wizard screen.

   In this Wizard screen, you have to decide whether to bind the option group itself to a form field or to leave it unbound. The first choice in the Wizard, Save the value for later use, creates an unbound field. When you are using the option group in a dialog box that uses the selected value to make a decision, you don't want to store the value in a table field. In this example, the second value, Store the value in this field, is selected automatically because you started with the Type of Customer field. If you want to bind the option group value to a different table field, you can select from a list of all form fields. Again, in this example, the default is acceptable.

8. Click on the Next> button to move to the Wizard screen that sets the option group style.

Again, as shown in Figure 22-7, the defaults are acceptable for this example. Notice that your actual values are used as a sample. In this Wizard screen, the lower half of the Wizard screen lets you choose which type of buttons you want. The upper half lets you choose the style for the option group box and the type of group control. The style affects the option group rectangle. If you choose Raised, Sunken, Etched, or Shadowed, that value is applied to the Special Effect property of the option group. Additionally, for Option buttons and Check boxes, if you choose any of the special effects, the property for each option button or check box is set to the special effect.

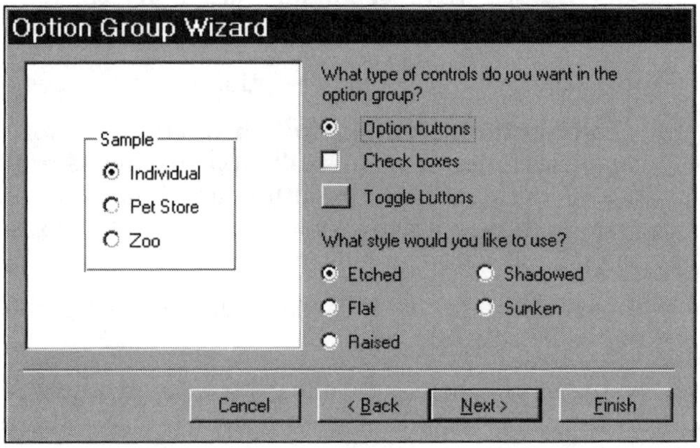

Figure 22-7: Selecting the type and look of your buttons.

Note

As you change your selections, the Sample changes as well.

9. Click on the Next> button to move to the final option group Wizard screen.

The final screen lets you give the option group control a label that will appear in the option group border. You can then add the control to your design and optionally display help.

10. Accept Type of Customer as your label for the Option Group.

11. Click on the Finish button to complete the Wizard.

Your Wizard work is now complete, and the controls appear on the design screen. Eight controls have been created: the option group, its label, three option buttons, and their labels. In this example, you don't want the option group label.

12. Select the option group label `Type of Customer`, and click on the Delete key to remove it.

Creating an option group with a calculated control

You also want to display the Gender field as a set of option buttons. There is one problem, however. The Gender field is a text field with the values of M, F, and U. You can create option buttons only with a numeric field. You can do this easily with the Type of Customer field, which is numeric. How can you solve this problem with the Gender field? The solution is to create a new calculated control that contains an expression. The expression must transform the values M to 1, F to 2, and U to 3. You create this calculation by using the Immediate IF function (IIf), with this expression:

=IIf([Gender]="M","1",IIf([Gender]="F","2","3"))

The first IIf function checks the value of Gender; if the value is "M," the value of the calculated control is set to 1. If the value is not "M," another IIf checks for a Gender value of "F." If the value is "F," the calculated control value is set to 2. If the value is not "F," the value of the calculated control is set to 3. To create this new calculated control, follow these steps:

1. Create a new text box control alongside the Status text control, as shown in Figure 22-8.

2. Delete the attached label control.

3. Display the All sheet of the Properties window for the text box control.

4. Change the Control Name property to **Gender Number**.

5. Type **=IIf([Gender]="M","1",IIf([Gender]="F","2","3"))** in the Control Source property. (Remember that you can press Shift+F2 to zoom.)

6. Change the Visible property to **No**.

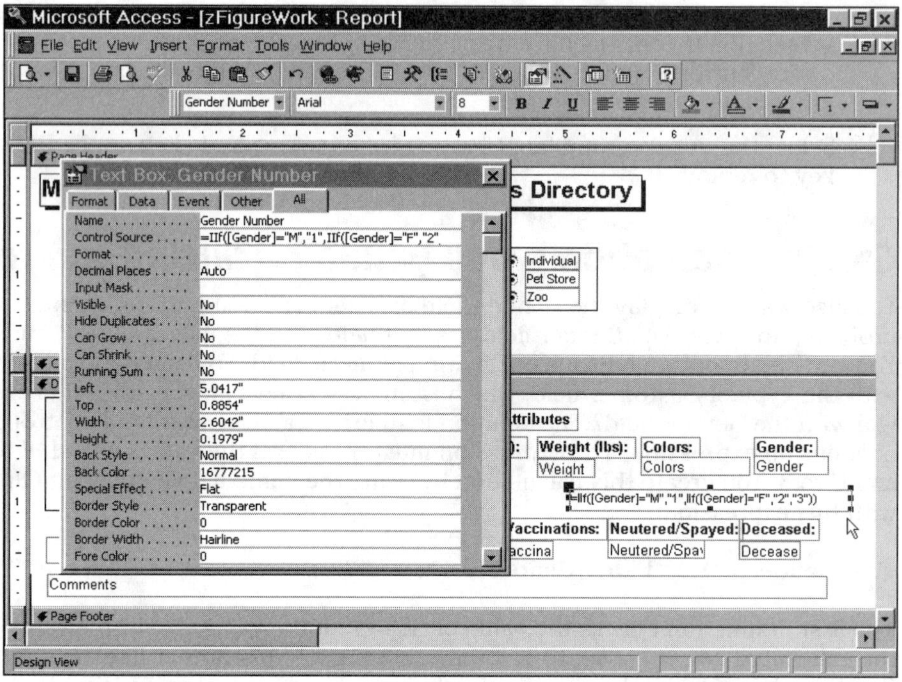

Figure 22-8: Creating a calculated control.

Because you change the Visible property of the calculated control to No, the control is not displayed when you produce the report. After you create the calculated control, you can use it as the control source for an option group. Figure 22-8 shows this new calculated control on the bottom right side of the screen. If you look at the report in print preview, you will see that the control is not visible.

To create the option group for Gender (based on this calculated control), follow these steps:

1. Delete the existing Gender text box and label control in the detail section.

2. Select the Option Group button from the Toolbox.

3. Drag the Option Group rectangle to the space in the detail section. The first screen of the Option Group Wizard should be displayed.

4. Enter **Male**, **Female**, and **Unknown**, pressing the down-arrow key between choices.

5. Click on the Next> button three times to move to the Control Source screen.

In this Wizard screen, you have to decide whether the option group itself will be bound to a form field or unbound. In this example, you will use the first choice in the Wizard, `Save the value for later use`, which creates an unbound field. You cannot select a calculated field in the Wizard; after completing it, you will change the control source of the option group.

6. Click on the <u>N</u>ext> button to move to the Option Group Style Wizard screen.

   Again, for this example, the defaults are acceptable. Notice that your actual values are used as a sample.

7. Click on the <u>N</u>ext> button to move to the final Option Group Wizard screen.

8. Accept **Gender**.

9. Click on the <u>F</u>inish button to complete the Wizard.

   Your Wizard work is now complete, and the controls appear on the design screen. Currently, as an unbound control, the Control Source property is blank. You must set this to the calculated control Gender Number.

10. Select the option group control and change the Control Source property to =**[Gender Number]**, as shown in Figure 22-9.

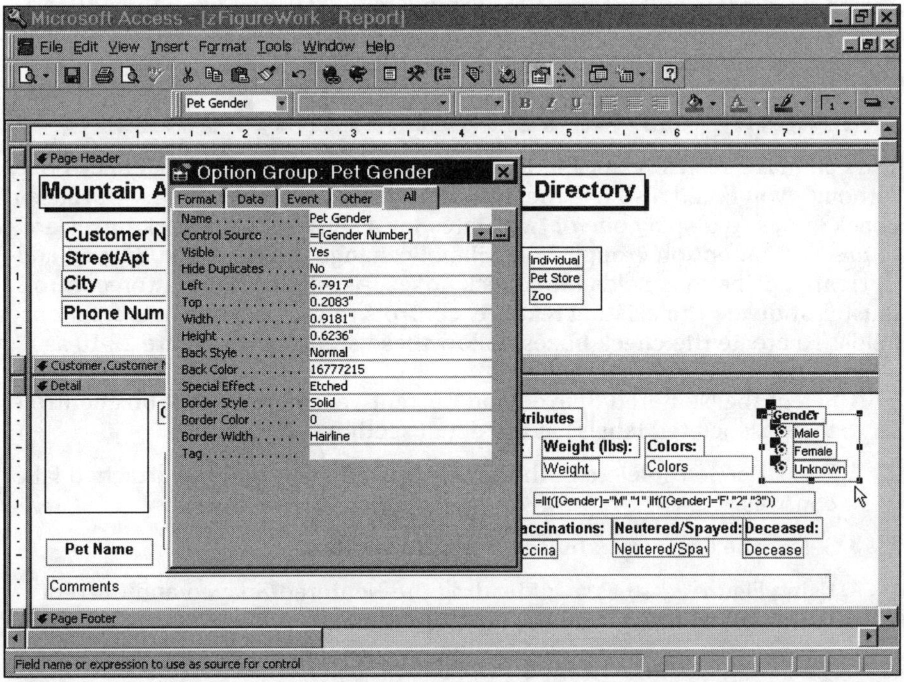

Figure 22-9: Completing an option group for a calculated control.

11. Name the control Pet Gender by changing the Name property to **Pet Gender**.

Caution

You must not name this control **Gender**. The pets table already has a field named Gender; if you duplicate the name as a control, you will receive an error.

You may need to change the size of the rectangle to fit within the 8-inch margin. If you have to make it smaller, remember to change the margin (which may be larger than 8 inches now).

12. Resize the option group rectangle and reset the right margin to **8** inches.

The last task is to enhance all the text on the control buttons to 12-point bold. To accomplish this, follow these steps:

1. Select the entire Gender option group box, all the buttons, and their attached labels.

2. Click on the Bold button on the toolbar.

3. Select Format⇨Size⇨to Fit to resize the label control boxes.

You may still need to align the labels before your task is complete. The final design for the option buttons is shown in Figure 22-9, including the option button properties.

Displaying Yes/No values with check boxes

You can make Yes/No values more readable on a report by using check boxes. Although you could also use them in an option group, the primary purpose of a check box is to display one of two states for a single value; check boxes are easier to create than option groups. You will now change the Neutered/Spayed and Current Vaccinations fields into check boxes. As with option button controls, you must first delete the existing text box controls to create a check box that uses the fields. To create the check boxes, follow these steps, using Figure 22-10 as a guide:

1. Select the Neutered/Spayed and Current Vaccinations text box controls (and their associated labels) in the detail section.

2. Press Delete to delete both the text box controls and the attached label controls.

3. Select the Check Box button from the Toolbox.

4. Using Figure 22-10 as a guide, drag the Neutered/Spayed and Current Vaccinations fields from the field list to create two new check boxes.

5. Select both check box controls; change the font size to **10**.

6. Size the controls to fit; move them as necessary.

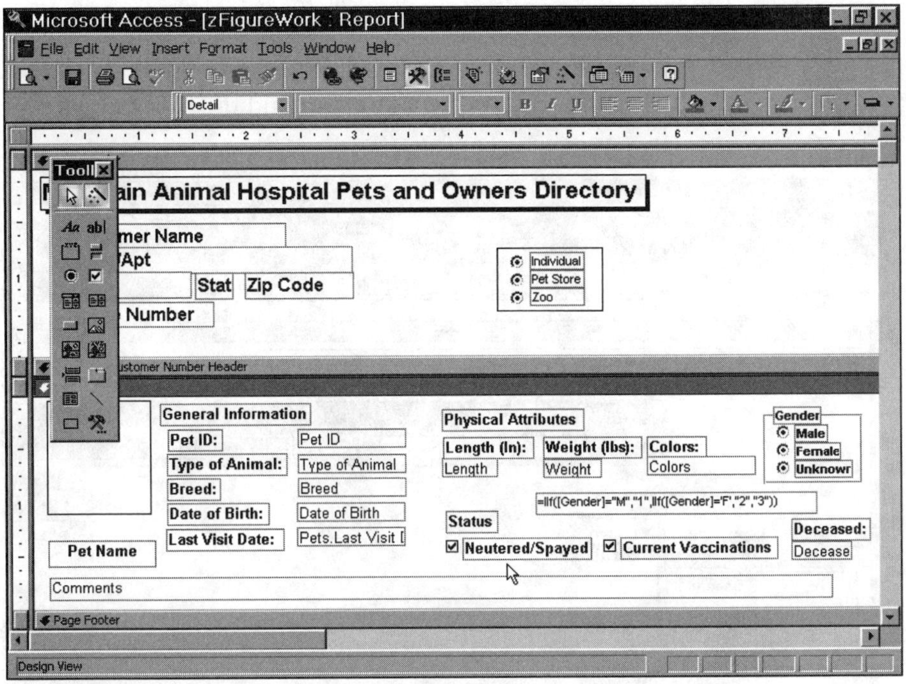

Figure 22-10: The completed check boxes.

The completed check boxes are shown in Figure 22-10.

Displaying values as toggle buttons

You can use toggle buttons as another way to make Yes/No data types easier to read. A toggle button appears to sit above the screen if the value of the Yes/No data type is No. If the value is Yes, the button appears to be pressed into the screen. To create a toggle button for the Deceased field, follow these steps:

1. Select the Deceased text box control (and its associated label) in the detail section.

2. Press Delete to delete both the text box control and the attached label control.

3. Select the Toggle Button icon from the Toolbox and the field Deceased from the field list.

4. Using Figure 22-11 as a guide, create a new toggle button by dragging the Deceased field from the field list.

5. Double-click on the toggle button and type **Deceased**.

6. Select Bold and the 10 point Font size from the Formatting toolbar.

7. Select Format⇨Size⇨to Fit to fit the button around the caption text.

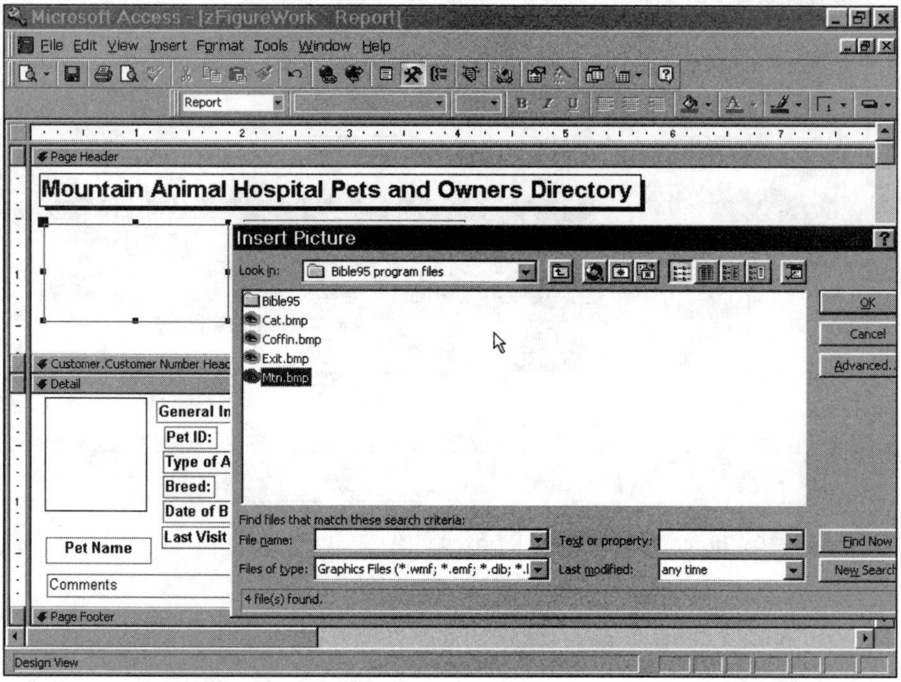

Figure 22-11: Creating toggle buttons.

The toggle button is displayed with the caption centered within the control.

Note You can also display a picture rather than text on the face of the toggle button by entering the filename of a bitmap image in the Picture property of the toggle button.

Tip Remember that Access allows you to change some controls from one type to another; first you select the control (right-click to display the shortcut menu), and then select the new control style from the Change To option.

Displaying bound OLE objects in reports

In the report you are creating in this chapter, a picture of each animal is shown in the detail section. Some animals are displayed as they look, but others appear stretched out of proportion. Presto Chango (who is not really a hunchbacked lizard) illustrates this distortion.

Pictures are stored in OLE controls. The two types of OLE controls are as follows:

Bound object frames	Pictures are stored in a record.
Image frames	Pictures are embedded or linked to a report section itself.

In this report, there is already a bound object frame. The Picture field is an OLE data type that has bitmaps embedded in each record. The Picture bound object control gets its values from the Picture field in the Pets table.

Displaying an image in a report

CD-ROM

You can also add an image object to your report. Do this by pasting a bitmap from the Clipboard or by either embedding or linking a bitmap file that contains a picture. Suppose that you have a logo for the Mountain Animal Hospital. On the disk that accompanies this book is a bitmap called MTN.BMP. In this section, you can add this bitmap to the page header section (if you copied it to your Access directory).

Using Figure 22-11 as a guide, you will move the customer information to the right side of the page header section and then add the bitmap to the left side after creating the image frame. To add an unbound object frame, follow these steps:

1. Select the customer information in the page header section and move it to the right, as shown in Figure 22-11.

2. Click on the Image Frame button in the Toolbox.

3. Click on the left corner below the title; drag the box so that it's sized as shown in Figure 22-11. The Insert Picture dialog box appears.

   From this dialog box, you can select the picture filename you want to insert into your report.

4. Select MTN.BMP from your Access directory (or wherever you copied the files for the book) and click on OK.

5. Display the property sheet.

6. Change the Size Mode property to Stretch.

   Finally, change the Border property so that the picture does not simply blend into the background (there is too much white in the picture); change the border color to black or make the border three-dimensional (as shown in the next step).

7. Click on the Raised button in the Special Effect formatting window.

The image frame is now complete. This is a good time to view the report in the Print Preview window. Figure 22-12 shows the report in print preview mode.

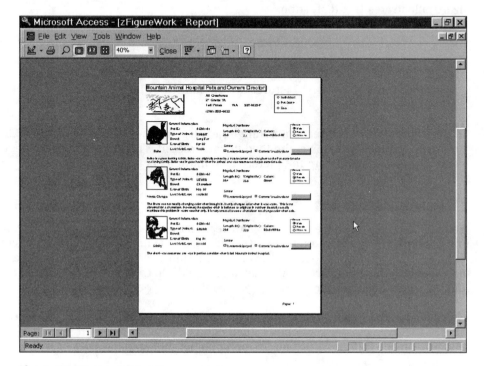

Figure 22-12: Previewing the report.

Note You can see that the toggle button does not display the text correctly in the button. At this size, no text font can display text correctly (in the previewed size) on a button. When the report is printed, however, the text will appear correctly.

Working with Lines and Rectangles

You can use lines and rectangles (commonly called boxes) to make certain areas of the report stand out or to bring attention to desired areas of the report. In Figure 22-1, you saw several groups of lines and rectangles that were used to emphasize data in the report. You need four rectangles and two different lines to complete the lines and boxes in this report. Figure 22-13 will be used as a guide for creating emphasis, boxes, and lines.

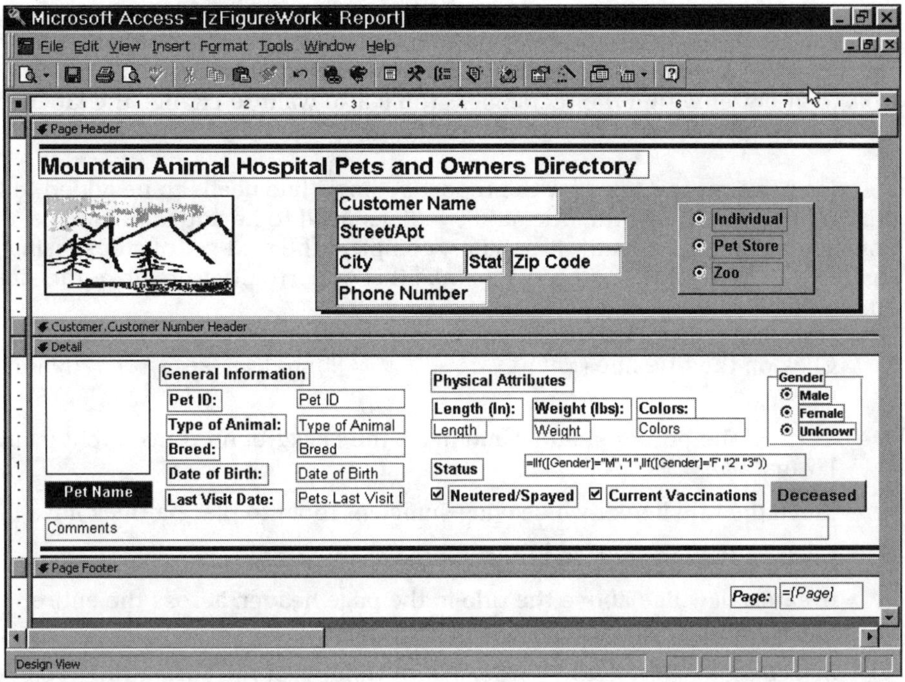

Figure 22-13: The final report.

To create the rectangle for the page header, follow these steps, using Figure 22-13 as a guide:

1. Select the Rectangle button in the Toolbox.

2. Click on the upper left part of the page header section to the right of the picture and just below the title.

3. Drag the rectangle around the entire set of customer text boxes and option buttons.

4. Select Format⇨Send to Back to redisplay the text boxes and option buttons.

Tip You may notice that when you create the rectangle, it blocks out the controls beneath it. By sending the rectangle to the background, you make the controls reappear.

You can also redisplay the controls by changing the Transparent button of the Back Color. This option, however, does not let you add other shading effects. For a rectangle, you should always select Send to Back.

The next three rectangles are in the detail section. You can create the rectangles by following the same steps you used to create the rectangle in the page header section. As you create them, you may find yourself rearranging some of the controls to fit better within the rectangles. You'll also want to change the label controls for Length, Weight, and Colors, as shown in Figure 22-13.

You also need several lines for the report. A single line needs to be added to the top of the report above the title, and two lines need to be added below the Comments text box. To add these lines, complete the next set of steps, using Figure 22-13 as a guide (you can also take this opportunity to remove the shadow on the title if you added it earlier):

1. Click on the title line (Mountain Animal Hospital Pets and Owners Directory).

2. Turn off the border shadow and make the background transparent using the Format bar.

3. Move the title line down, leaving sufficient room to place a thick line.

4. Click on the Line button in the Toolbox.

5. Create a new line above the title in the page header, across the entire width of the report.

6. Select choice 3 from the Border Width window of the Formatting toolbar to make the line thicker.

7. Create a new line below the Comments text box in the detail section.

8. Again, make the line thickness 3 from the Border Width window to make the line thicker.

9. Duplicate the line below the comments and align it with the line above.

Tip   If you hold down the Shift key while creating a line, the line remains perfectly straight, either horizontally or vertically, depending on the initial movement of drawing the line.

Emphasizing Areas of the Report

The report is now almost complete, but several tasks remain. According to the original printout and design shown in Figures 22-1 and 22-2, you still need to shade the rectangle in the page header, add a shadow to the rectangle, sink the Customer text box controls, raise the Type of Customer option group box, and change Pet Name to reverse video.

Adding background shading

You can add a background shade to any control. Adding background shading to a rectangle shades any controls contained within the rectangle. You can, however, add background shading to all controls that are selected at one time. To add background shading to the rectangle in the page header section, follow these steps:

1. Select the Rectangle control in the page header section.

2. Select the light gray Back Color.

Sinking controls

Generally, in a report, you cannot sink controls; they don't look sunken on a white background. You can, however, use a gray background to enhance the depth of a control; both sunken and raised controls stand out on a gray background. Because you just added a gray background to the rectangle in the page header, you can sink or raise controls within the rectangle. To give the Customer text box controls a sunken appearance, follow these steps:

1. Select each of the Customer text box controls in the page header section.

2. Click on the Sunken selection from the Special Effects button.

Raising controls

Just as you can sink a control, you can raise one. Raised controls, like sunken controls, look much better on a gray or dark background. To raise the Type of Customer option group control, follow these steps:

1. Select the Type of Customer option group control.

2. Click on the Raised selection from the Special Effects button.

Tip
If you sink or raise a check box, Access uses a different, smaller check box that has the appearance of depth.

Creating a shadow on a rectangle

If you want to emphasize an area of the report, you can add a shadow to any control. Most commonly, rectangles and text boxes are the types of controls given this effect. You create the shadows by adding a solid-color rectangle that is slightly offset and behind the original control. If the background is light or white, you need a dark-colored rectangle. If the background is dark or black, you need a light-colored or white rectangle. To create a shadow for the page header rectangle, follow these steps:

1. Select the rectangle in the page header.
2. Click on the Special Effects button in the Formatting toolbar.
3. Select Shadow from the window.

Changing text to a reverse video display

Text really stands out when you create white text on a black background. This is called *reverse video;* it's the opposite of the usual black on white. You can convert text in a label control or text box to reverse video by changing the fill color to black and the text color to white. To change the Pet Name text control to reverse video, follow these steps:

1. Select the Pet Name text control (not the label control).
2. Click on the black Back Color button.
3. Click on the white Fore Color button.

Figure 22-13 shows the final report in the Report Design window.

Seeing Your Output in Different Ways

You can see your output from a report in several ways:

✦ Print previewing (to multiple pages)
✦ Printing to hard copy
✦ Printing to a file
✦ Printing the report definition

Using the Print Preview window

Throughout this chapter, you used the Print Preview window to view your report. Figure 22-5 displayed your report in the Print Preview window in a zoomed view. This lets you see your report with the actual fonts, shading, lines, boxes, and data that will be on the printed report. When the print preview mode is in a zoomed view, you can press the mouse button to change the view to a page preview (where you can see the entire page).

You can use the horizontal and vertical elevators to move around the page or move from page to page by using the page controls in the bottom left corner of the window.

The *page preview mode* of the Print Preview window displays an entire page of the report, as shown in Figure 22-14. The cursor is shaped like a magnifying glass in Print Preview windows; using this cursor during page preview lets you select a portion of the page and then zoom in to that portion for a detailed view.

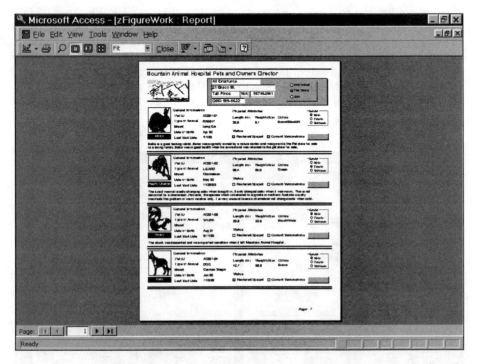

Figure 22-14: Displaying a report in page preview mode in the Print Preview window.

In Figure 22-14, you see a representation of the printed page. You can use the navigation buttons (located in the lower left section of the Print Preview window) to move between pages, just as you would use them to move between records in a datasheet.

The first six buttons displayed on the toolbar provide quick access to printing tasks:

Print	Displays the Print dialog box
Zoom	Toggles in and out of Page Preview and Zoomed view
One Page	Displays a single page in the Print Preview window
Two Pages	Displays two pages in the Print Preview window

Zoom Control   Select Percent of Size to Zoom: 200%, 150%, 100%, 75%, 50%, 25%, 10%, Fit (you can also type a specific percentage in this control)

Close Window   Returns to Design view

You are not limited to a one- or two-page preview; Access for Windows 95 lets you view as many as 12 pages on a single screen. As you can see in Figure 22-15, the View⇨Pages menu lets you select 1, 2, 4, 8, or 12 pages to preview. In Figure 22-15, eight pages have been selected and are visible. You can also right-click on the Print Preview page and select pages or the Zoom percentage. When you use the shortcut menus, you can select as many as 20 pages to preview at a time; you can also determine their arrangement in rows and columns (2 x 4, 5 x 4, 3 x 4, and so on).

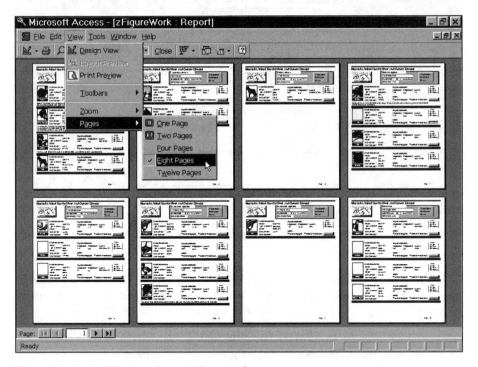

Figure 22-15: Multipage print preview mode.

If you are satisfied with the report after examining the preview, simply select the Print button on the toolbar and print it. If you are not satisfied with your report, select the Close button to return to the Report Design window and make additional changes.

Using layout previews

Layout preview is different from a print preview. A print preview uses a query's dynaset; layout preview displays sample data (ignoring criteria) or joins in an underlying query.

The purpose of a layout preview is strictly to show you the field placement and formatting. Thus you can create a report design without having to assemble your data properly; in a large query, this can save considerable time. You can see a sample preview by one of two methods: Select View⇨Layout Preview, or click on the Report View button and then select the Layout Preview icon (the bottom one) on the Report Design toolbar. You can switch back to the Report Design window by selecting the Close Window button if you entered the Print Preview from the Report Design window. If you entered from the Database window, you are returned there.

> **Note** You can also zoom in to a layout page preview on the sample data or print the sample report from the Layout Preview window.

Printing a report

You can print one or more records in your form (exactly as they look on-screen) from several places:

✦ Select File⇨Print in the Report Design window.

✦ Select File⇨Print in the Preview window.

✦ Select File⇨Print in the Database window with a report highlighted.

> **Note** If you are in the Print Preview window, your actual data prints. If you are in the Layout Preview window, only sample data prints.

> **Caution** If you select the Print button in the Preview window, *all* your data will start printing immediately and you will not be able to control which data is to be printed.

The Print dialog box

After you decide to print your report, the Print dialog box is displayed, as shown in Figure 22-16. The Print dialog box lets you control several items by giving you the following choices:

Name	Lets you select the printer
Print Range	Prints the entire report or selected pages
Copies	Selects the number of copies

Collate	Selects whether to collate copies
Print to File	Prints to a file rather than to the printer

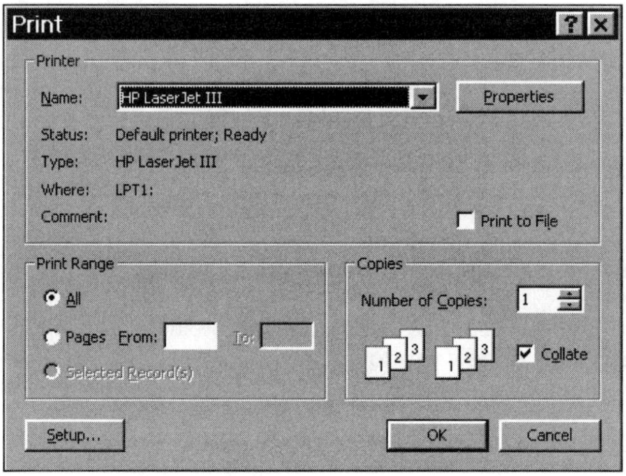

Figure 22-16: The Print dialog box.

The Print dialog box that is displayed is specific to your printer and based on your setup in Microsoft Windows. Although each printer is different, the dialog box is essentially the same. Generally, dot-matrix or impact printers have a few more options for controlling quality than do laser printers.

Assuming that you set up a printer in Windows 95, you can click on OK to print your form. Your form is printed using the font you selected for display (or the nearest printer equivalent). The printout contains any formatting in the form, including lines, boxes, and shading. Colors are converted to shades on a monochrome printer.

If you need to additionally set up your Windows printer options, you can choose the Properties button in the Print dialog box. This dialog box sets up your printer, not your report. If you want to fine-tune the setup of your report, use the Setup button (which provides more options).

You can display print setup options in other ways as well, including the following:

✦ Select File➪Page Setup from the Report Design window.

✦ Select File➪Page Setup from the Database window.

The Page Setup dialog box

The Page Setup dialog box, shown in Figure 22-17, is divided into three tabbed dialog boxes: Margins, Page, and Layout. (You will use the Layout tab in Chapter 29 when you work with labels and multicolumn reports.)

Margins   Sets the page margins; also has option for Print Data Only

Page   Selects page orientation, paper size and source, and printer device

Layout   Selects grid settings, item size, and layout items

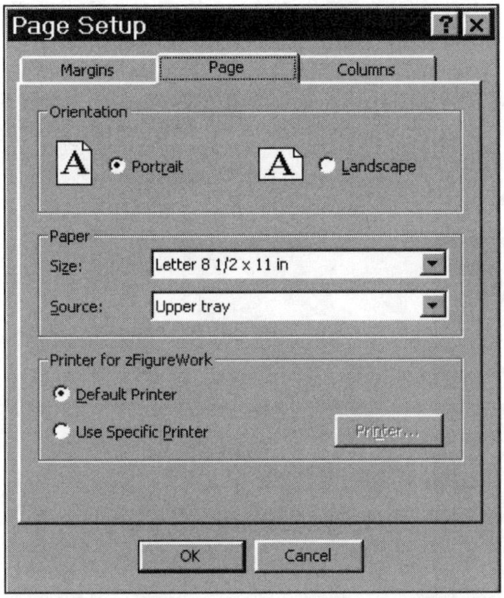

Figure 22-17: The Page tab in the Page Setup dialog box.

On the Page tab, you can control the orientation of the report. You have two choices: Portrait and Landscape. Clicking on the Portrait button changes the report so that the page is taller than it is wide. Clicking on the Landscape button changes the report orientation so that the page is wider than it is tall.

Tip   A good way to remember the difference between landscape and portrait is to think of paintings. Portraits of people are usually taller than they are wide; landscapes of the outdoors are usually wider than tall. When you click on either button, the Page icon (the letter A) changes to show your choice graphically.

The Paper section indicates the size of the paper you want to use, as well as the paper source (for printers that have more than one source available). Clicking on <u>S</u>ource displays a drop-down list of paper sources available for the printer you selected. Depending on the printer selected, you may have one or more paper trays or manual feed available. Click on the source you want to use.

Clicking on Si<u>z</u>e displays a drop-down list box showing all the paper sizes available for the printer (and paper source) you selected. Click on the size you want to use.

If you click on the Print Data Only check box on the Margins tab, Access prints only the data from your report and does not print any graphics. (This feature is handy if you use preprinted forms.) Also, printing complex graphics slows down all but the most capable printers; not printing them saves time.

The Margins section shown in Figure 22-18 displays (and allows you to edit) the left, right, top, and bottom margins. To edit one or more of these settings, click on the appropriate text box and type a new number.

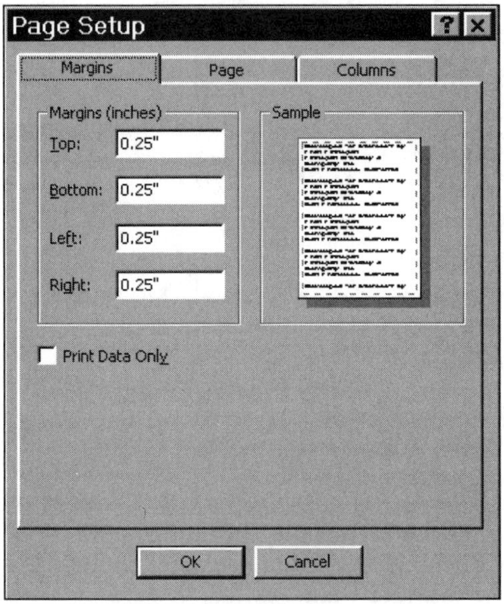

Figure 22-18: The Margins tab in the Page Setup dialog box.

Tip   Page Setup settings are stored with each report. It's therefore possible to use several different printers for various reports, as long as you don't use the default Windows printer. This can also be a problem, though, because if you exchange files with another user who doesn't have the same printer installed, the other user must modify the Page Setup settings.

Note   Someone may send you a report you can't view or print because a Windows printer driver you don't have was used. If the report was created with a driver not installed on your system, Access will display a dialog box and let you print with your default printer.

Summary

In this chapter, you learned how to enhance your reports and how to print them. The chapter covered the following points:

✦ Database publishing is a term that generally describes report formatting from a database application that offers lines, boxes, shading, and other types of desktop publishing enhancements.

✦ The Access Report Writer is a WYSIWYG (what-you-see-is-what-you-get) report writer. What you see in the Design window is generally what you get on the hard-copy report.

✦ The form- and report-formatting buttons in the Report window let you set text, fill colors, and control line widths; and add three-dimensional effects to controls, such as a raised or sunken appearance.

✦ You can enhance the text of label and text box controls by changing the font type style, font size, and such font style attributes as bold, italic, or font color. You can even add a shadow by duplicating the text or selecting the special effects.

✦ Multiple-line text box controls can display large amounts of text. To avoid leaving blank lines, you can set the Can Grow and Can Shrink properties to control the precise amount of space needed.

✦ Controls such as option buttons, check boxes, and toggle buttons make it easier to view your data. You must delete an existing control before you can create one of these controls using the same data field.

✦ When any of these controls is placed inside an option group, they act together rather than separately, and only one is active at a time.

✦ Option buttons are generally used to let a user select only one of a group, whereas check boxes and toggle buttons represent a two-state selection from Yes/No data types.

✦ You can display pictures in reports by using object frames. The two types of object frames are bound (the objects are attached to a data field in each record) and unbound (the objects are embedded in the report itself).

✦ Lines and rectangles let you separate areas of the report to add emphasis.

✦ You can further emphasize areas of the report by adding color, background shading, three-dimensional effects, shadows, and reverse video.

✦ You can view your report by previewing it or by printing it to a hard-copy device.

✦ You can view as many as 20 pages at a time on one screen in the Print Preview window.

✦ Two types of print previews are available: print preview and layout preview. With print preview, you see your actual data; a layout preview uses only portions of your table data, but it is very fast.

✦ You can set printing selections from the Page Setup dialog box.

In the next chapter, you learn how to create reports with totals and summaries.

✦   ✦   ✦

Creating Calculations and Summaries in Reports

In the preceding two chapters, you learned how to design and build reports from a blank form as well as how to create striking and effective output by using many of the advanced features in Access. In this chapter, you learn how to use expressions to calculate results.

CD-ROM

If you don't want to build the reports created in this chapter, they are included on your sample disk in the Reports tab. The reports are named Monthly Invoice Report – No Cover, Monthly Invoice Report, Monthly Invoice Report – Percentages, and Monthly Invoice Report – Running Sum.

Note Because the Report Design window is set to a width of eight inches, you see most of the screen printouts in this chapter taken with an 800 × 600 resolution Super VGA Windows screen driver (rather than the standard 640 × 480 VGA Windows driver), which lets you see almost the entire screen in the figures.

Creating a Multilevel Grouping Report with Totals

You now create a report that displays information about visits to the hospital for each customer's pets on specific days. This report displays data in an invoice format that lists the type of visit, treatments given, medication dispensed, and the cost of each of these items. The data is totaled for each line item and summarized for each visit. The report can display multiple pets for the same customer on the same day. Finally, totals are shown for each visit by a customer, including the total amount spent, any discounts, and tax. A sample hard-copy page of the report is shown in Figure 23-1. Later in this chapter, you see how to enhance this report to display individual line-item percentages and cumulative running totals.

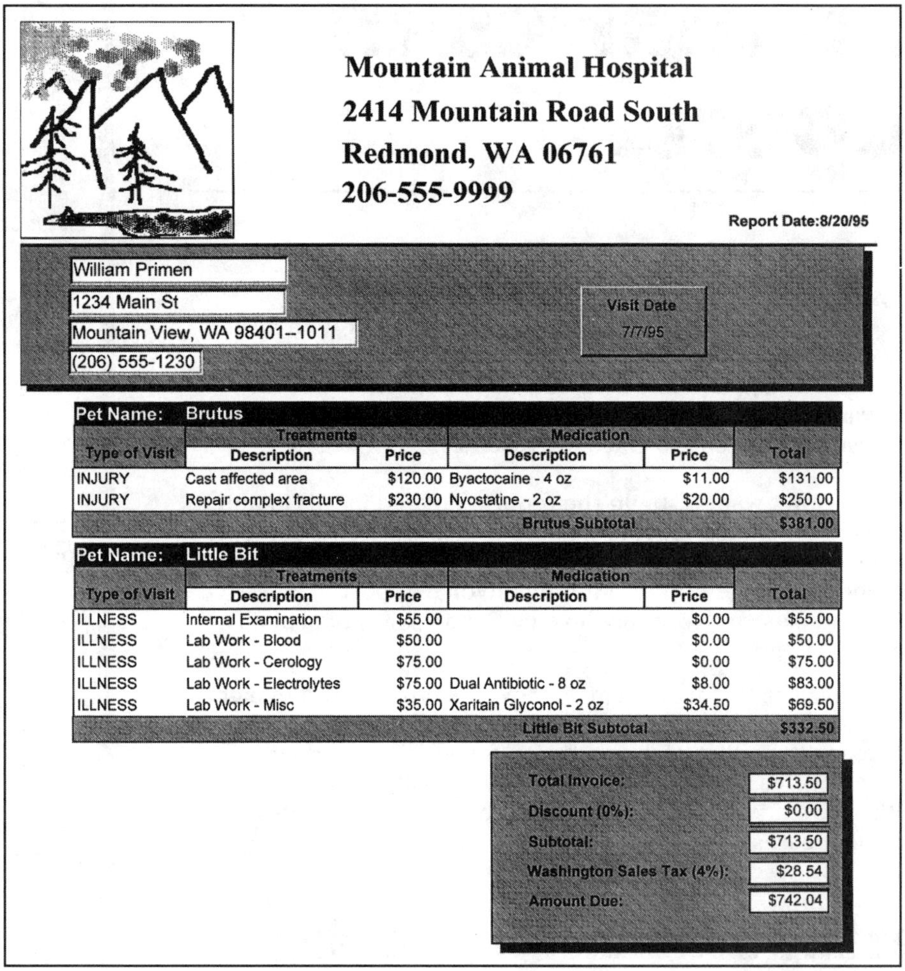

Mountain Animal Hospital
2414 Mountain Road South
Redmond, WA 06761
206-555-9999

Report Date:8/20/95

William Primen
1234 Main St
Mountain View, WA 98401--1011
(206) 555-1230

Visit Date
7/7/95

Pet Name: Brutus

| Type of Visit | Treatments | | Medication | | Total |
	Description	Price	Description	Price	
INJURY	Cast affected area	$120.00	Byactocaine - 4 oz	$11.00	$131.00
INJURY	Repair complex fracture	$230.00	Nyostatine - 2 oz	$20.00	$250.00
				Brutus Subtotal	$381.00

Pet Name: Little Bit

| Type of Visit | Treatments | | Medication | | Total |
	Description	Price	Description	Price	
ILLNESS	Internal Examination	$55.00		$0.00	$55.00
ILLNESS	Lab Work - Blood	$50.00		$0.00	$50.00
ILLNESS	Lab Work - Cerology	$75.00		$0.00	$75.00
ILLNESS	Lab Work - Electrolytes	$75.00	Dual Antibiotic - 8 oz	$8.00	$83.00
ILLNESS	Lab Work - Misc	$35.00	Xaritain Glyconol - 2 oz	$34.50	$69.50
				Little Bit Subtotal	$332.50

Total Invoice:	$713.50
Discount (0%):	$0.00
Subtotal:	$713.50
Washington Sales Tax (4%):	$28.54
Amount Due:	$742.04

Figure 23-1: The sample Invoice Report page.

Designing the Invoice Report

The Invoice Report is an excellent example for showing the types of tasks necessary to create common types of reports. It uses many of the advanced report-writing features in Access — sorting and grouping, group summaries, text expressions, and graphical objects. Following is a summary of what the Invoice Report's design includes:

✦ The Mountain Animal Hospital name, address, phone number, and logo on the top of every page

✦ Owner detail information (customer name, street/apt., city, state, ZIP code, and telephone)

✦ Visit date

✦ Pet name

✦ Visit detail information for each pet (including type of visit, treatment, treatment price, medication, medication price, and total cost)

✦ A subtotal that summarizes each pet's visit details (total cost subtotal for the pet)

✦ A subtotal that summarizes the total cost for each pet on a visit date for a particular owner and then calculates a total that lists and incorporates the owner's discount and proper state sales tax

The report design also must be shaped according to the following considerations:

✦ The report must be sorted by the field's Visit Date, then Customer Number, and then Pet ID.

✦ No more than one visit date per printed page should appear.

✦ No more than one customer per printed page should appear.

✦ One or more pets belonging to the same owner can appear on each printed page.

✦ If there is more than one pet per invoice, the pets should be listed in Pet ID order.

The design for this report is shown in Figure 23-2. As you can see, each section is labeled, and each control displays either the field name control or the calculated control contents. With the exception of the Mountain Animal Hospital logo (an unbound object frame) and several lines and rectangles, the report consists primarily of text box controls.

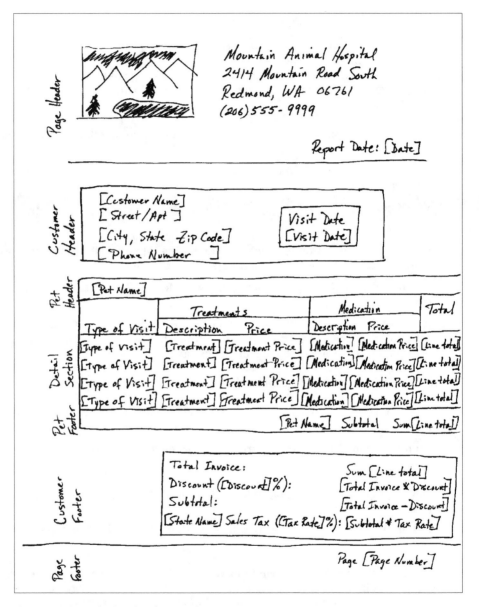

Figure 23-2: A design for the Invoice Report.

Designing and creating the query for the report

The Invoice Report uses fields in practically every table you've seen in the Mountain Animal Hospital database. Although the design in Figure 23-2 shows the approximate position and use of each control, it is equally important to perform a data design that lists each table field or calculated control. This data design should include the purpose of the field or control and the table in which the field originates. Using such a design plan, you can be sure to build a query that contains all the fields you may need. Table 23-1 lists these controls, the section in the report where they are used, and the originating table. Important: Do this type of data design *before* creating the query from which to build your report.

Table 23-1
The Data Design for the Invoice Report

Report Section	Control Purpose	Type of Control	Table Field/ Calculation	Table
Page header	Logo	Unbound object frame		
Page header	Name and address	Label controls (4)		
Page header	Report date	Calculated text box	Date Function	
Customer header	Customer name	Bound text box	Customer Name	Customer
Customer header	Street and apt.	Bound text box	Street/Apt	Customer
Customer header	City	Bound text box	City	Customer
Customer header	State	Bound text box	State	Customer
Customer header	ZIP code	Bound text box	Zip Code	Customer
Customer header	Phone number	Bound text box	Phone Number	Customer
Customer header	Visit date	Bound text box	Visit Date	Visits
Pet header	Pet name	Bound text box	Pet Name	Pets
Pet header	Text labels	Label controls (8)		
Detail	Type of visit	Bound text box	Visit Type	Visit Details
Detail	Treatment	Bound text box	Treatment	Treatments
Detail	Treatment price	Bound text box	Treatment Price	Visit Details
Detail	Medication	Bound text box	Medication Name	Medications
Detail	Medication price	Bound text box	Medication Price	Visit Details

(continued)

Table 23-1 *(continued)*

Report Section	Control Purpose	Type of Control	Table Field/ Calculation	Table
Detail	Line total	Calculated text box Price	Treatment Price + Medication	
Pet footer	Pet name	Calculated text box	Pet Name + Text	Pets
Pet footer	Line total sum	Calculated text box	Sum(Line Total)	
Customer footer	Text labels	Label controls (3)	Lines 1, 3, 5	
Customer footer	Discount label	Calculated text box	Text + Discount	Customer
Customer footer	State sales tax	Calculated text box	State Name + Tax Rate	States/Visits
Customer footer	Total invoice	Calculated text box	Sum(Line Total)	
Customer footer	Discount amount	Calculated text box	Total Invoice * Discount	
Customer footer	Subtotal	Calculated text box	Total Invoice − Discount	
Customer footer	Sales tax	Calculated text box	Subtotal * Tax Rate	Visits
Customer footer	Amount due	Calculated text box	Subtotal + Sales Tax	
Page footer	Page number	Calculated text box	Text + Page Number	

After you complete the data design for a report, you can skim the Table column to determine the tables necessary for the report. When you create the query, you may not want to select each field individually; if not, use the asterisk (*) field to select all the fields in each table. This way, if a field changes in the table, the query can still work with your report.

Caution   Remember that if a table field name changes in your query, you'll need to change your report design. If you see a dialog box asking for the value of a specific field when you run your report — or the text #Error appears in place of one of your values after you run it — chances are that a table field has changed.

After examining Table 23-1, you may notice that every table in the Mountain Animal Hospital database is needed for the report — with the exception of the Animals lookup table. You may wonder why you need *any* of the four lookup tables. The States, Animals, Treatments, and Medications tables are to be used primarily as lookup tables for data validation when you're adding data to forms, but you can also use them to look up data when printing in reports.

In the Invoice Report, the State Name field from the States table is used for looking up the full state name for the sales tax label in the Customer footer. The Tax Rate field can also be found in the States table, but at the time of the visit, the current tax rate is copied to the Visits table for that record. Only the codes are stored in the Visit Details table, so Access looks up the Treatment and Medication Name fields from their respective tables.

These seven tables are all joined together using the Monthly Invoice Report query, as illustrated in Figure 23-3.

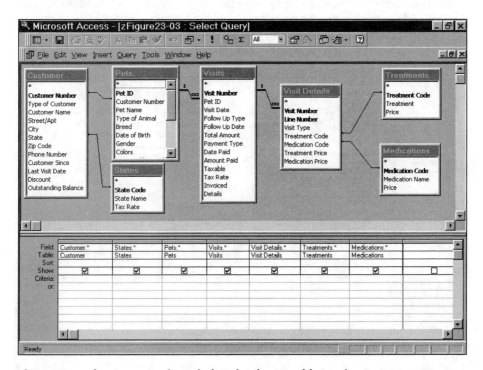

Figure 23-3: The Query Design window for the Monthly Invoice Report query.

After your query is completed, you can create your report.

Cross-Reference — Chapter 21 contains a detailed explanation of how to create a new report from a blank form; it also shows you how to set page size and layout properly. If you are unfamiliar with these topics, read Chapter 21 before continuing. The present chapter focuses mainly on multiple-level groupings, calculated and summarized fields, and expressions.

Designing test data

One of the biggest mistakes you can make when designing and creating complex reports is not checking the results your report displays. Before you create your complete report, you should have a good understanding of your data. One way is to create a query using the same sorting order the report will use and then create any detail line calculations. You can then check the query's datasheet results, using them to check the report's results. When you are sure that the report is using the correct data, you can be sure that it will always produce great results. Figure 23-4 shows a simple query (the Monthly Invoice Report – Test Data) to use for checking the report you create in this chapter.

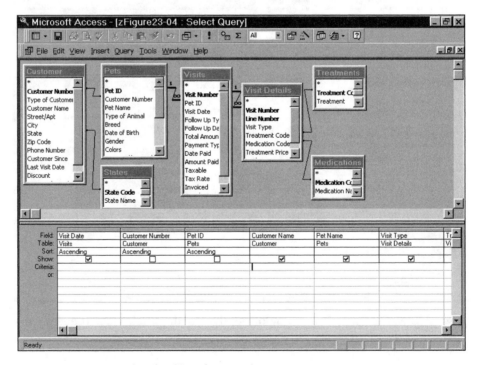

Figure 23-4: A query for checking data results.

Notice that the query in Figure 23-4 has three fields for sorting: Visit Date, Customer Number, and Pet ID. Only the first one is being viewed in the dynaset; the other two have the Show check box turned off. When you save this query and reopen it, the Customer Number and Pet ID fields will be moved to the end of the query skeleton.

Normally, you can make a copy of the report query, adding the sorting orders and using only the detail fields you need to check totals. You can then add the numbers manually or convert the query to a Total query to check group totals. Figure 23-5 shows the datasheet produced by this query; you can compare the results of each task in the report design to this datasheet.

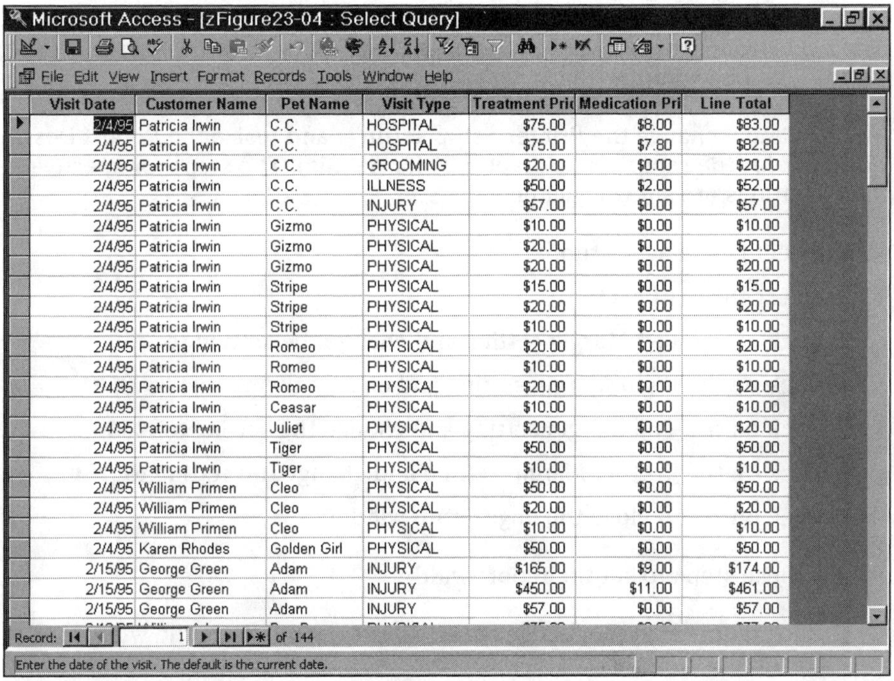

Visit Date	Customer Name	Pet Name	Visit Type	Treatment Price	Medication Price	Line Total
2/4/95	Patricia Irwin	C.C.	HOSPITAL	$75.00	$8.00	$83.00
2/4/95	Patricia Irwin	C.C.	HOSPITAL	$75.00	$7.80	$82.80
2/4/95	Patricia Irwin	C.C.	GROOMING	$20.00	$0.00	$20.00
2/4/95	Patricia Irwin	C.C.	ILLNESS	$50.00	$2.00	$52.00
2/4/95	Patricia Irwin	C.C.	INJURY	$57.00	$0.00	$57.00
2/4/95	Patricia Irwin	Gizmo	PHYSICAL	$10.00	$0.00	$10.00
2/4/95	Patricia Irwin	Gizmo	PHYSICAL	$20.00	$0.00	$20.00
2/4/95	Patricia Irwin	Gizmo	PHYSICAL	$20.00	$0.00	$20.00
2/4/95	Patricia Irwin	Stripe	PHYSICAL	$15.00	$0.00	$15.00
2/4/95	Patricia Irwin	Stripe	PHYSICAL	$20.00	$0.00	$20.00
2/4/95	Patricia Irwin	Stripe	PHYSICAL	$10.00	$0.00	$10.00
2/4/95	Patricia Irwin	Romeo	PHYSICAL	$20.00	$0.00	$20.00
2/4/95	Patricia Irwin	Romeo	PHYSICAL	$10.00	$0.00	$10.00
2/4/95	Patricia Irwin	Romeo	PHYSICAL	$20.00	$0.00	$20.00
2/4/95	Patricia Irwin	Ceasar	PHYSICAL	$10.00	$0.00	$10.00
2/4/95	Patricia Irwin	Juliet	PHYSICAL	$20.00	$0.00	$20.00
2/4/95	Patricia Irwin	Tiger	PHYSICAL	$50.00	$0.00	$50.00
2/4/95	Patricia Irwin	Tiger	PHYSICAL	$10.00	$0.00	$10.00
2/4/95	William Primen	Cleo	PHYSICAL	$50.00	$0.00	$50.00
2/4/95	William Primen	Cleo	PHYSICAL	$20.00	$0.00	$20.00
2/4/95	William Primen	Cleo	PHYSICAL	$10.00	$0.00	$10.00
2/4/95	Karen Rhodes	Golden Girl	PHYSICAL	$50.00	$0.00	$50.00
2/15/95	George Green	Adam	INJURY	$165.00	$9.00	$174.00
2/15/95	George Green	Adam	INJURY	$450.00	$11.00	$461.00
2/15/95	George Green	Adam	INJURY	$57.00	$0.00	$57.00

Figure 23-5: The datasheet for checking data results.

Creating a new report

With the report planning and data testing completed, it's time to create the new report. In Chapter 21, you learned how to create a report from a blank form. The steps to create a new report (and bind it to a query) are repeated for you here:

1. Press F11 to display the Database window if it is not already displayed.

2. Click on the Report tab.

3. Click on the New command button. The New Report dialog box appears.

4. Select the Monthly Invoice Report query.

5. Select Design View.

6. Click on OK.

7. Maximize the Report window.

A blank Report Design window appears, showing three sections (Page Header, Detail, and Page Footer). The report is bound to the query Monthly Invoice Report; data from that query will be used when the report is viewed or printed. The fields from the query are available for use in the report design and will appear in the Field List window.

You must also change the Printer Setup settings and resize the Report Design window area for the report (see Chapter 21 for details). The steps for specifying Page Setup settings are shown again here:

1. Select File⇨Page Setup.

2. Select the Margins tab.

3. Click on the Left Margin setting and change the setting to .250.

4. Click on the Right Margin setting and change the setting to .250.

5. Click on the Top Margin setting and change the setting to .250.

6. Click on the Bottom Margin setting and change the setting to .250.

7. Click on OK to close the Page Setup window.

Follow these steps to set the report width:

1. Click on the rightmost edge of the report body (where the white area meets the gray).

2. Drag the edge to the 8-inch mark on the ruler.

3. Release the mouse button.

These steps should complete the initial setup for the report. Next, you create the report's sorting order.

Creating the sorting orders

In a query, you can specify sorting fields as you did in the test query you created earlier. In a report, however, you must also specify the sorting order when you create groups; Access ignores the underlying query sorting. In the underlying query for this report, no sorting is specified because it must be entered here as well.

This report design has three sorting levels: Visit Date, Customer Number, and Pet ID. You'll need to use all these levels to define group headers, and you need the latter two for group footers. If you look back at the original design in Figure 23-2, you see that Visit Date is not shown as a group. Later, as you create your report, you'll see why a grouping to use the Visit Date header section is necessary.

Before you can add a grouping, you must first define the sort order for the report. You've learned to do this task with the Sorting and Grouping box (shown completed on the blank Report Design window in Figure 23-6).

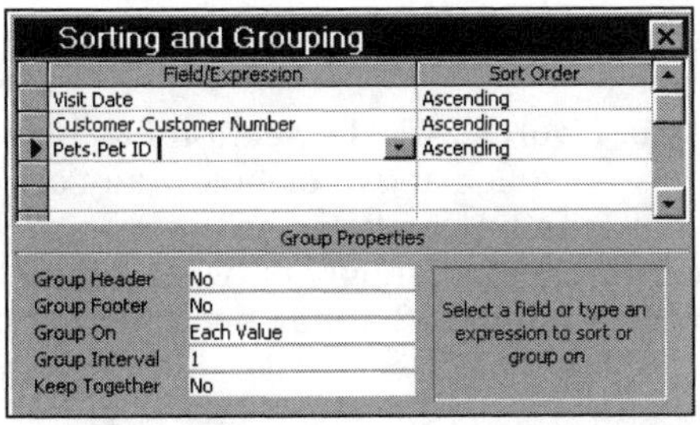

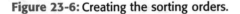

Figure 23-6: Creating the sorting orders.

To complete the sorting orders as shown in Figure 23-6, follow these steps:

1. Click on the Sorting and Grouping button on the toolbar to display the Sorting and Grouping box.

2. Click on the cursor in the first row of the Field/Expression column of the Sorting and Grouping box. A downward-pointing arrow appears.

3. Click on the arrow to display a list of fields in the Monthly Invoice Report query.

4. Click on the Visit Date field in the field list. Notice that Sort Order defaults to Ascending.

5. Click on the cursor in the second row of the Field/Expression column.

6. Click on the arrow to display a list of fields in the Mountain Invoice Report query.

7. Click on the Customer.Customer Number field in the field list. Notice that Sort Order defaults to Ascending.

8. Click on the cursor in the third row of the Field/Expression column.

9. Click on the arrow to display a list of fields in the Mountain Invoice Report query.

10. Click on the Pets.Pet ID field in the field list. Notice that Sort Order defaults to Ascending.

Tip To see more of the Field/Expression column, you can drag the border between the Field/Expression and Sort Order columns to the right (as shown in Figure 23-6).

You next see how the detail section is created for this report. Because this chapter's intent is to focus on expressions and summaries, be sure that you have read Chapters 21 and 22 and that you understand how to create and enhance the labels and text boxes in a report.

Creating the detail section

The detail section is shown in its entirety in Figure 23-7. The section has been completed and resized. Notice that there is no space above or below any of the controls, which allows multiple detail records to be displayed as one comprehensive section on a report. Because this section must fit snugly between the Pet header and Pet footer, as shown in Figures 23-1 and 23-2, it has been resized to the exact size of the controls.

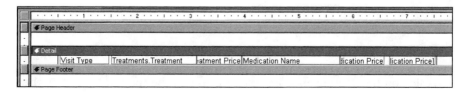

Figure 23-7: The detail section.

Creating the detail section controls

The detail section has five unlabeled bound text box controls, two line controls, and one calculated control:

✦ A Vertical line control

✦ Visit Details.Visit Type, bound text box control

✦ Treatments.Treatment, bound text box control

✦ Visit Details.Treatment Price, bound text box control

✦ Medications.Medication Name, bound text box control

✦ Visit Details.Medication Price, bound text box control

✦ Calculated unbound text control (formula is =[Treatment Price]+
  [Medication Price]

✦ A Vertical line control

You need to drag each of these bound text box controls from the Report window
field list onto the detail section and then properly size the controls. The default
text box property Auto Label should be set to No.

The two line controls are vertical lines. One is on the left side of the detail section
under the left edge of the Type of Visit text box control. The other is on the right
side of the detail section under the right edge of the calculated control.

The last control is a calculated text box control. This control calculates the total
of the Treatment Price and the Medication Price for each detail line. You need to
enter the formula into a new unlabeled text box: **=[Treatment Price]+[Medication
Price]**. A calculated control always starts with an equal sign (=), and each field
name must be placed in brackets. Figure 23-7 also shows the property sheet for
this calculated text box control, which is named Pet Line Visit Total. The Pet Line
Visit Total control is also formatted with the Currency format property so that the
dollar signs appear. If any of the totals is over $1,000.00, the comma also appears.
The Decimal Place property is set to Auto, which is automatically set to 2 for the
Currency format.

Creating calculated controls

You can use any valid Access expression in any text control. Expressions can contain operators, constants, functions, field names, and literal values. Some examples of expressions are shown next:

=Date()	Date function
=[Customer Subtotal]*[Tax Rate]	A control name multiplied by a field name
=Now()+30	A literal value added to the result of a function

The control (Control Source property) shown in Figure 23-7 calculates the total for
each individual line in the detail section. To create this calculated control, follow
these steps:

1. Create a new text control in the detail section, as shown in Figure 23-7.

2. Display the property sheet for the new text box control.

3. Enter **=[Treatment Price]+[Medication Price]** in the Control Source property cell.

4. Set the Format property to Currency.

Naming controls used in calculations

Every time you create a control, Access automatically inserts a name for it into the Control Name property of the control's property sheet. The name is really a description that defines which kind of control it is; for example, text controls show the name Field, and label controls show the name Text. Each name is followed by a sequential number. An example of a complete name is Field13. If the next control you create is a label, it is named Text15. These names can be replaced with user-defined names, such as Report Date, Sales Tax, or any other valid Access name, which lets you reference other controls easily (especially those containing expressions).

For example, if you have the fields Tax Rate and Subtotal and want to calculate Amount of Tax Due, you enter the expression **=[Tax Rate]*[Subtotal]** and call it Amount of Tax Due. You can then calculate Total Amount Due by entering the expression **=[Subtotal]+[Amount of Tax Due]**. This expression lets you change an expression in a calculated field without having to change all other references to that expression. To change the name of the control for Treatment Price + Medication Price Total, follow these steps:

1. Select the calculated control (=[Treatment Price]+[Medication Price]).

2. Display the property sheet.

3. Select the Name property.

4. Replace the default with **Pet Visit Line Total.**

Caution Later, you learn that you cannot use a calculated control name in a *summary* calculation. You'll learn that you must summarize the original calculation. For example, rather than create an expression such as =Sum(Pet Visit Line Total), you must enter the summary expression **=Sum([Treatment Price]+[Medication Price])**.

Testing the detail section

As you complete each section, you should compare the results against the test datasheet you created, as shown in Figure 23-5. The easiest way to view your results is either to select the Print Preview button on the toolbar (and view the report on-screen) or print the first few pages of the report. Figure 23-8 displays the Print Preview screen. If you compare the results to the test data in Figure 23-5, you'll see that all the records are correctly displayed. You may notice, however, that the records are not exactly in the right order. This is acceptable as long as groups of the same visit date for the same customer and pet are together. In Figure

23-5, the first five total amounts are $83.00, $82.80, $20.00, $52.00, and $57.00. In Figure 23-8, the first five totals are $83.00, $20.00, $52.00, $57.00, and $82.80. Because the data is not also sorted by the line number in the Visit Details table, the final sort is not precise.

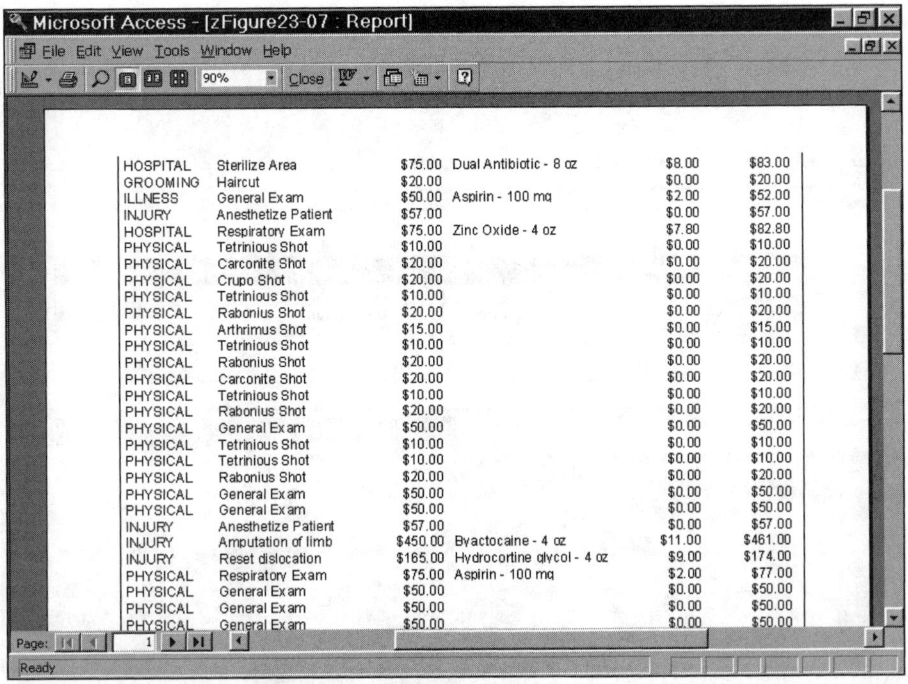

HOSPITAL	Sterilize Area	$75.00	Dual Antibiotic - 8 oz	$8.00	$83.00
GROOMING	Haircut	$20.00		$0.00	$20.00
ILLNESS	General Exam	$50.00	Aspirin - 100 mg	$2.00	$52.00
INJURY	Anesthetize Patient	$57.00		$0.00	$57.00
HOSPITAL	Respiratory Exam	$75.00	Zinc Oxide - 4 oz	$7.80	$82.80
PHYSICAL	Tetrinious Shot	$10.00		$0.00	$10.00
PHYSICAL	Carconite Shot	$20.00		$0.00	$20.00
PHYSICAL	Crupo Shot	$20.00		$0.00	$20.00
PHYSICAL	Tetrinious Shot	$10.00		$0.00	$10.00
PHYSICAL	Rabonius Shot	$20.00		$0.00	$20.00
PHYSICAL	Arthrimus Shot	$15.00		$0.00	$15.00
PHYSICAL	Tetrinious Shot	$10.00		$0.00	$10.00
PHYSICAL	Rabonius Shot	$20.00		$0.00	$20.00
PHYSICAL	Carconite Shot	$20.00		$0.00	$20.00
PHYSICAL	Tetrinious Shot	$10.00		$0.00	$10.00
PHYSICAL	Rabonius Shot	$20.00		$0.00	$20.00
PHYSICAL	General Exam	$50.00		$0.00	$50.00
PHYSICAL	Tetrinious Shot	$10.00		$0.00	$10.00
PHYSICAL	Tetrinious Shot	$10.00		$0.00	$10.00
PHYSICAL	Rabonius Shot	$20.00		$0.00	$20.00
PHYSICAL	General Exam	$50.00		$0.00	$50.00
PHYSICAL	General Exam	$50.00		$0.00	$50.00
INJURY	Anesthetize Patient	$57.00		$0.00	$57.00
INJURY	Amputation of limb	$450.00	Byactocaine - 4 oz	$11.00	$461.00
INJURY	Reset dislocation	$165.00	Hydrocortine glycol - 4 oz	$9.00	$174.00
PHYSICAL	Respiratory Exam	$75.00	Aspirin - 100 mg	$2.00	$77.00
PHYSICAL	General Exam	$50.00		$0.00	$50.00
PHYSICAL	General Exam	$50.00		$0.00	$50.00
PHYSICAL	General Exam	$50.00		$0.00	$50.00

Figure 23-8: A print preview of the detail section.

Notice that the calculated control correctly calculates the sum of the two numeric price text box controls and displays them in the Currency format.

Creating the Pet ID header and footer sections

When the detail section is complete, you can move *outward* to create the inner group headers and footers. The innermost group is the Pet ID group. You need to create both a header and a footer for this section.

As you've learned, to create group headers and footers for the Pet ID sort you already created, you only have to change the Group Header and Group Footer properties of the Pets.Pet ID Field/Expression to Yes (as shown in Figure 23-9). To display the group headers and footers to make this change, follow these steps:

1. Display the Sorting and Grouping box if it is not displayed.

2. Click on the Pets.Pet ID row in the window.

3. Click on the Group Header property and change it to **Yes**.

4. Click on the Group Footer property and change it to **Yes**.

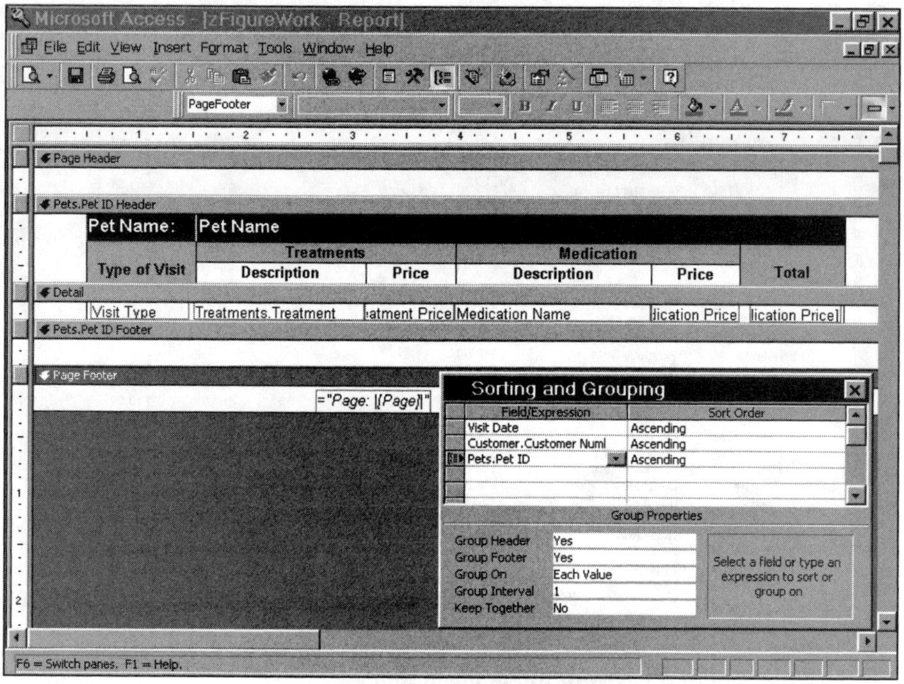

Figure 23-9: The Report Design window for the Pets.Pet ID group header.

Note After a group header or footer is defined, the first column of the Sorting and Grouping box for the field you created in the header or footer displays a grouping icon (the same icon you see when you select the Sorting and Grouping button on the toolbar).

The Pet ID header and footer sections should now be displayed.

Creating the Pet ID header controls

The Pets.Pet ID group header, shown in Figure 23-9 along with the Sorting and Grouping box, creates a group break on Pet ID, which causes each pet's individual visit details to be grouped together. This is the section where the pet's name is displayed, as well as labels that describe the controls that appear in the detail section.

No calculated controls are in this header. There are no lines or rectangles. With the exception of the pet name itself, in fact, all controls are label controls. Each label control is stretched so that the borders make perfect rectangles on the desired areas and the text is centered where appropriate. The Fore Color and Back Color buttons are then used for coloring the background and the text.

Notice the use of reverse video in the Pet Name label and text control. Also notice that the Type of Visit, Treatments, Medication, and Total label controls display black text on a light gray background. This setup, along with the borders, creates a visually appealing section. Notice that there is no room between the bottom of the controls and the bottom of the section. This (along with the lack of space in the detail section) creates the illusion that several sections are really one. You create the label controls Type of Visit and Total by pressing Ctrl+Enter before you enter the text, which makes it use two lines.

Creating the Pet ID footer controls

The Pets.Pet ID group footer, shown in Figure 23-10, is where you subtotal all the visit detail information for each pet. Thus, if a pet has more than one treatment or medication per visit, the report summarizes the visit detail line items in this section. In fact, even if there is only one detail record for a pet, a summary is displayed.

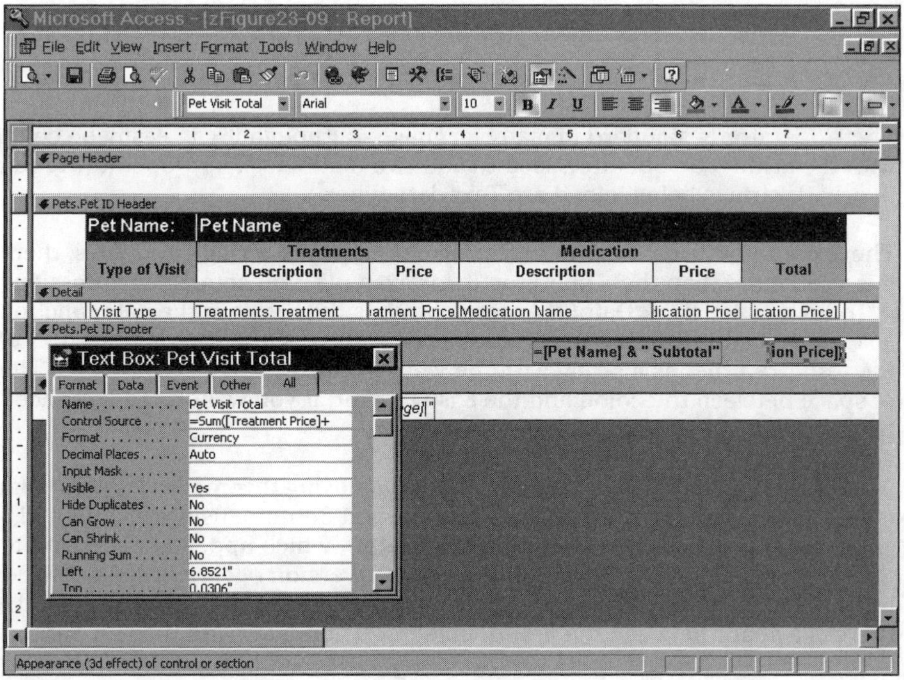

Figure 23-10: Creating a group summary control.

The Pets.Pet ID footer section contains three controls:

Rectangle	Displays the boundaries of the section and is shaded in light gray
Label control	Displays Pet Name and the text Subtotal
Summary text box control	Displays the total of all Pet Visit line totals for each pet

The rectangle completes the area displayed under the detail section; it serves as a *bottom cap* on the preceding two sections. Notice that there is no space between the top of the controls and the top of the section. Notice also how the edges line up, setting the entire section (Pet ID header, detail section, Pet ID footer) apart from other areas of the report.

The first control combines the Pet Name field with the text Subtotal. You use a process known as *concatenation*.

Using concatenation to join text and fields

You can use the concatenation operators to combine two strings. (A *string* is either a field or an expression.) Several different operators can be used for concatenation, including the following:

+   Joins two Text data type strings

&   Joins two strings; also converts non-Text data types to Text data

The + operator is standard in many languages, although it can easily be confused with the arithmetic operator used to add two numbers. The + operator requires that both strings being joined are Text data types.

The & operator also converts nonstring data types to string data types; therefore, it is used more than the + operator. If, for example, you enter the expression ="Today's Date Is:" & Date(), Access converts the result of the date function into a string and adds it to the text Today's Date Is:. If the date is August 2, 1995, the result returned is a string with the value Today's Date Is:8/2/95. The lack of space between the colon and the 8 is no error; if you want to add a space between two joined strings, you must add one.

Access can join any data type to any data type using this method. If you want to create the control for the Pet Name and the text Subtotal using this method, you enter the expression =**[Pet Name] & "Subtotal"**, which appends the contents of the Pet Name field to the text Subtotal. No conversion occurs because the contents of Pet Name and the literal value Subtotal are both already text. Notice that there is a space between the first double quotation mark and the text Subtotal.

Note   If you use the + operator for concatenation, you must convert any nonstring data types; an example would be by using the CStr( ) function to return a date with the Date( ) function to a string data type. If you want to display the system date with some text, you have to create a text control with the following contents:

=**"Today's Date Is:" +cstr(Date())**

You can insert the contents of a field directly into a text expression by using the ampersand (&) character. The syntax is

```
="Text String "&[Field or Control Name]&" additional text string"
```

or

```
[Field or Control Name]&" Text String"
```

You can use this method to create the control for the Pet Name text box control; follow these steps:

1. Create a new text control in the Pets.Pet ID footer section.

2. Enter the expression = **[Pet Name]&" Subtotal"** (as shown in Figure 23-10).

Calculating group summaries

Creating a sum of numeric data within a group is very simple. Following is the general procedure for summarizing group totals for bound text controls:

✦ Create a new text control in the group footer (or header).

✦ Enter the expression =**Sum([Control Name])** where *Control Name* is a valid field name in the underlying query or the name of a control in the report.

If, however, the control name is for a calculated control, you will have to repeat the control expression. Suppose that in the Pets.Pet ID footer you want to enter the following expression into the text box control to display the total of the detail line:

```
=Sum([Pets Line Visit Total])
```

If you try this, it won't work; that is simply a limitation of Access. To create a sum for the totals in the detail section, you have to enter

=**Sum([Treatment Price]+[Medication Price])**

This is how the summary shown in Figure 23-10 was created.

Access 97 knows to sum the detail lines for the Pet ID summary because you put the summary control in the Pets.Pet ID section. Each time the value of the Pet ID changes, Access resets the summary control automatically. Later, when you create this same summary control in the Customer ID footer section, Access will reset the total only when the value of Customer ID changes.

You can use expressions in a report in two ways. The first is to enter the expression directly in a text control. For example, enter

[Treatment Price]+[Medication Price]

The second way is to create the expression in the underlying query, as you saw in Figure 23-4, where you created a field named Line Total in the query itself. You can then use the calculated field of the query in a text control on the report. The advantage of the former method is that you have the flexibility to create your expressions *on the fly* as well as the ability to reference other report objects, such as text controls with expressions. The disadvantage is that you cannot use summary expressions on calculated controls.

If you add a calculated field to your underlying query, you can then refer to this field in the detail section or in any group section. The syntax you use is

```
=Sum([Calculated Field Name])
```

If you want to create the detail section Line Total and Pet ID Subtotal by using the calculation from the query, first you create the query's calculated field as

Line Total: [Treatment Price]+[Medication Price]

Then you create the summary control in the report as

=Sum([Line Total])

Either method works; either is acceptable.

You can use the Print Preview window to check the progress of your report. Figure 23-11 displays the report created so far; notice how the three sections come together to form one area.

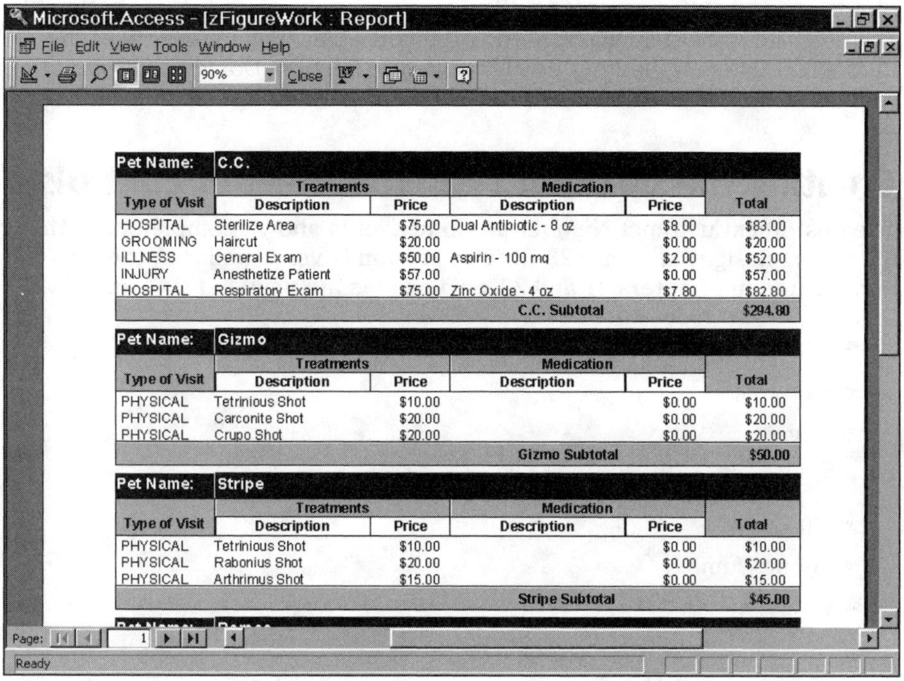

Figure 23-11: The Print Preview window of a report's Pet ID group header, the detail, and the group Pet ID footer sections.

Creating the Customer Number header and footer sections

Cross-Reference

When the Pet ID sections are complete, you can move *outward* again to create the next outer group header and footer. The next group as you move outward is Customer Number; you can create a header and footer for this section by following these steps:

1. Display the Sorting and Grouping box if it is not already displayed.

2. Click on the Customer.Customer Number row in the window.

3. Click on the Group Header property and change it to Yes.

4. Click on the Group Footer property and change it to Yes.

One task remains: Each new customer for a specific date should be displayed on a separate page. If you view the report as it currently exists, you will notice that there are no specific page breaks. You can create a page break every time the customer number changes by setting the Force New Page property of the Customer.Customer Number header to Before Section. Doing so will ensure that each customer's information is printed on a separate page.

Creating the Customer Number header controls

Cross-Reference

The Customer.Customer Number group header is shown completed (at the top of the report design) in Figure 23-12. This section is very similar to the Customer section created in Chapters 21 and 22. Seven fields are used in this section:

✦ Customer Name

✦ Street/Apt

✦ City

✦ State

✦ Zip Code

✦ Phone Number

✦ Visit Date

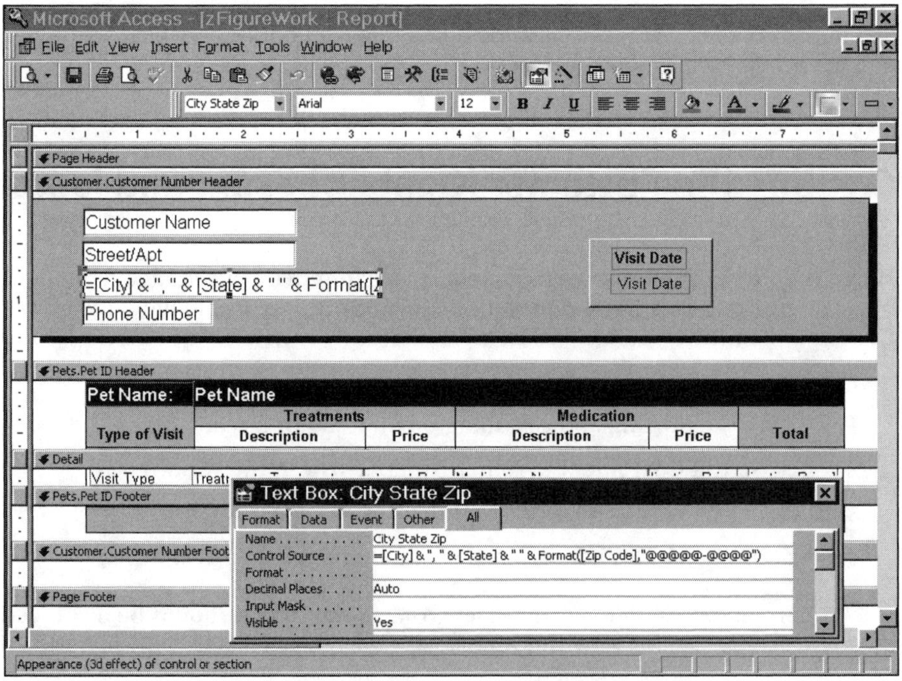

Figure 23-12: The Report Design window for the Customer.Customer Number group header.

Cross-Reference The first six controls are from the Customer table; the Visit Date control is from the Visits table. The entire section is surrounded by a gray shaded rectangle and a shadow box. (Chapter 22 explains how to create this effect.) The Visit Date control has an attached label and is surrounded by a transparent rectangle (which you create by setting the Back Color window's <u>T</u>ransparent button). The control uses the <u>R</u>aised appearance option; the Customer controls are sunken (a three-dimensional effect created by selecting the <u>S</u>unken button in the Special Effect window).

One change you can make is to rearrange the display of the City, State, and Zip Code fields. Rather than display these fields as three separate controls, you can concatenate them to appear together. You can save space by compressing any trailing spaces in the city name, adding a comma after city, and also by compressing the space between State and Zip Code. You can make the changes by creating a concatenated text box control. Follow these steps:

1. Delete the City, State, and Zip Code controls in the Customer Number header.

2. Create a new unlabeled text box control.

3. Enter =[City]&", "&[State]&" "&[Zip Code] in the Control Source property of the text box control.

The only problem with this expression is that the ZIP code is formatted in the Zip Code table field, using the @@@@@-@@@@ format to add a hyphen between the first five and last four characters. As currently entered, the control may display the following value when run: Lakeville, OR 974011021.

You still need to format the Zip Code field. Normally, the function Format( ) is used for formatting an expression. In this example, the function should be written as

Format([Zip Code],"@@@@@-@@@@")

You can add this function to the concatenation expression, substituting the Format expression in place of the Zip Code field. To complete this example, change the control to

=[City]&", "&[State]&" "&Format([Zip Code],"@@@@@-@@@@")

To check the Customer Number group heading, you can view the report in the Print Preview window, as shown in Figure 23-13.

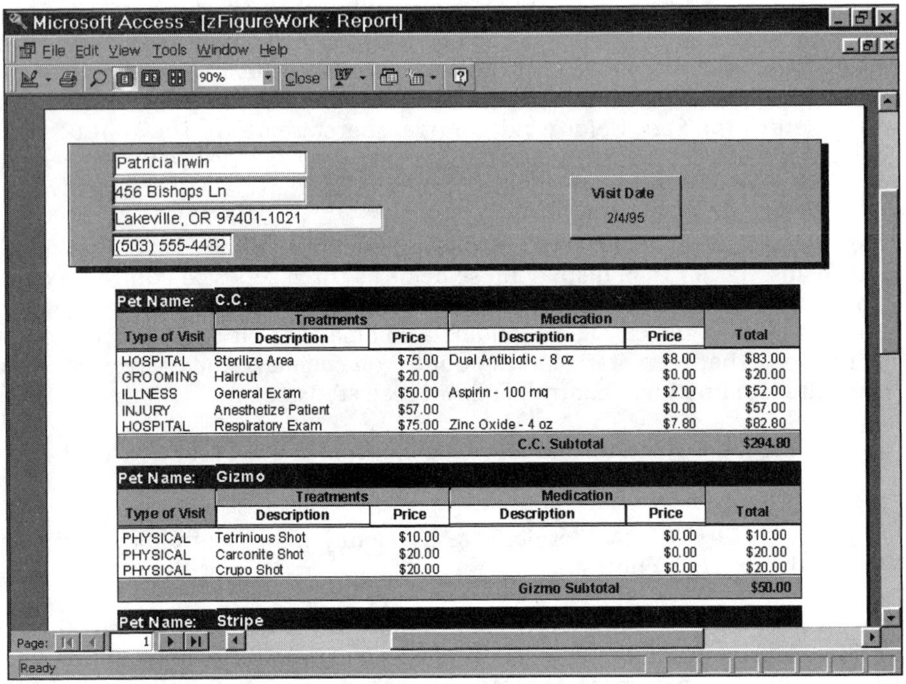

Figure 23-13: Viewing the report in the Print Preview window.

Creating the Customer Number footer controls

The Customer.Customer Number footer section contains ten controls: five label controls and five text box controls. The text box control expressions (and their associated labels) appear in Table 23-2.

Each of the concatenated label controls uses the same standard notation you learned about in this chapter; each of the text box controls is a simple expression. Notice that Customer Total uses exactly the same expression as the Pet ID total, except that now it resets the total by Customer Number.

Table 23-2
Expressions in the Customer Number Footer

Expression Name	Label Control	Text Box Control
Customer Total	Total Invoice:	=Sum([Treatment Price]+[Medication Price])

Expression Name	Label Control	Text Box Control
Discount Amount	="Discount	=[Customer Total] *[Discount] ("&[Discount]*100&"%):"
Customer Subtotal	Subtotal:	=[Customer Total]-[Discount Amount]
State Sales Tax	=[State Name]&"	=[Customer Subtotal] *[Visits.Tax Rate]Sales Tax ("&[Visits.Tax Rate]*100&"%):"
Amount Due	Amount Due:	=[Customer Subtotal]+[State Sales Tax]

The Customer.Customer Number footer (shown in Figure 23-14) is where you create and summarize the line-item totals for each pet for a particular owner for a particular visit. You also want to display a customer's discount rate, the amount of the discount in dollars, the customer's state, the state sales tax as a percentage, the state sales tax in dollars, and (finally) a total for the amount due. All this information will appear in separate boxes with shadows; you create these boxes by using the shadow special effect on the rectangle. If you are following along with this example, the steps for each of the controls follow.

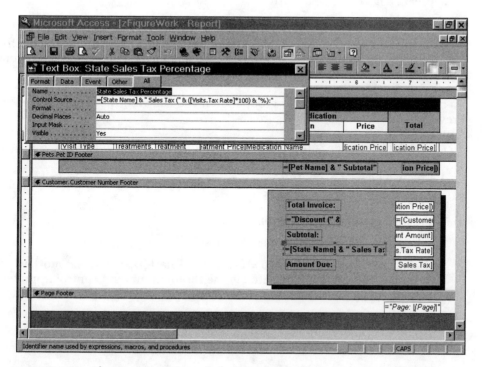

Figure 23-14: The Report Design window for the Customer.Customer Number group footer.

Because the first group has many pets and visit detail lines, you'll have to look at page 3 to see the first customer number footer. To create the label for Total Invoice (and for the text box controls), follow these steps:

1. Create a new label control.

2. Change the Caption property to **Total Invoice:**.

3. Create a new text box control.

4. Change the Name property to **Customer Total**.

5. Change the Control Source property to **=Sum([Treatment Price]+ [Medication Price]).**

Follow these steps to create the Discount Amount label and text box controls:

1. Create a new label control.

2. Change the Control Source property to **="Discount ("&[Discount]*100&"%):"**, which concatenates the word *Discount* with the customer's discount rate and then multiplies by 100 to give a percentage.

3. Create a new text box control.

4. Change the Name to **Discount Amount**.

5. Change the Control Source to **=[Customer Total]*[Discount]**, which multiplies the customer's discount rate by the amount calculated in the Customer Total control.

To check the Customer Number group footer, you can view the report in the Print Preview window, as shown in Figure 23-15.

To create the Customer Subtotal label and text box controls, follow these steps:

1. Create a new label control.

2. Change the caption to **Subtotal:**.

3. Create a new text box control.

4. Change the Name to **Customer Subtotal**.

5. Change the Control Source to **=[Customer Total]-[Discount Amount]**, which subtracts the amount calculated in the Discount Amount control from the sum calculated in the Customer Total control.

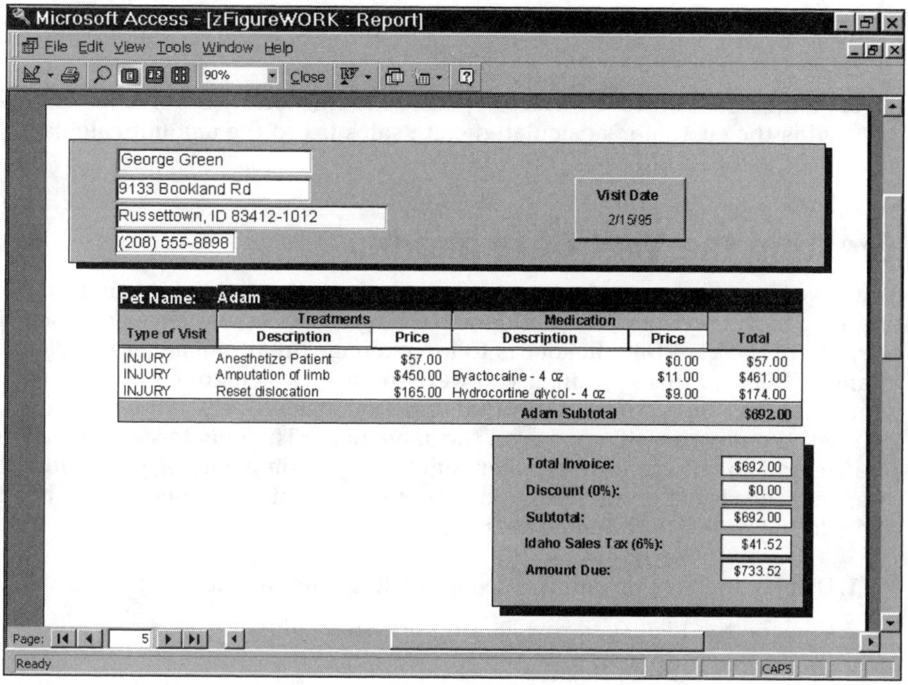

Figure 23-15: Viewing the report in the Print Preview window.

Create the State Sales Tax label and text box controls with these steps:

1. Create a new label control.

2. Change the Control Source to **=[State Name]&" Sales Tax ("&[Visits.Tax Rate]*100&"%):",** which concatenates the customer's state name (full spelling) and the words *Tax Rate* with the customer's tax rate, and then multiplies by 100 to give a percentage.

3. Create a new text box control.

4. Change the Name to **State Sales Tax.**

5. Change the Control Source to **=[Customer Subtotal]*[Tax Rate],** which multiplies the customer's state tax rate by the amount calculated in the Customer Subtotal control.

Next, create the Amount Due label and text box controls:

1. Create a new label control.

2. Change the Caption to **Amount Due:.**

3. Create a new text box control.

4. Change the Name to **Amount Due**.

5. Change the Control Source to **=[Customer Subtotal]+[State Sales Tax],** which adds the customer's calculated state sales tax to the amount calculated in the Customer Subtotal control.

Creating the Visit Date header

You have one more group header to create — Visit Date — but it won't display anything in the section. The section has a height of 0; essentially, it's *closed.* The purpose of the Visit Date header is to force a page break whenever the Visit Date changes. Without this section, if you were to have two customer records for the same customer on different dates that appear consecutively in the report's dynaset, the records will appear on the same page. The only forced page break you created so far was for Customer Number; by adding one for Visit Date, you complete the report groupings. To create the Visit Date grouping for the header and add the page break, follow these steps:

1. Display the Sorting and Grouping box if it is not already displayed.

2. Click on the Visit Date row Field/Expression column.

3. Click on the Group Header property.

4. Click on the arrow and select Yes from the drop-down list.

5. Double-click on the section to display its property sheet.

6. Change the Height property to **0**.

7. Change the Visible property to No.

8. Change the Force New Page property to Before Section.

Creating the page header controls

The page header appears at the top of every page in the Invoice Report. The page header and footer controls are not controlled by the Sorting and Grouping box; you have to select View⇨Page Header/Footer. In this report, the page header has been open all the time. This section contains a small version of the Mountain Animal Hospital logo in the upper left corner, as well as the name, address, and phone number for the hospital. The section also contains the report date and a horizontal line at the bottom to separate it visually from the rest of the page. By default, the page header and footer are created and displayed automatically when a new report is created. All you have to do is change the height and add the proper controls.

Cross-Reference In Chapter 22, you learned how to add the unbound bitmap MTN.BMP to the report. The label controls that display the Mountain Animal Hospital page header are four separate controls. The only control that needs explanation is the Report Date control.

Access offers several built-in functions that let you display and manipulate date and time information. The easiest to start with is the Date( ) function, which returns the current system date when the report is printed or previewed. To add a text control to the report header that displays the date when the report is printed, follow these steps:

1. Create a new text control in the page header, as shown in Figure 23-16.

2. Display the control's property sheet.

3. In the Control Source property cell, type =**"Report Date: "&Date( )**.

This process concatenates the text Report Date with the current system date.

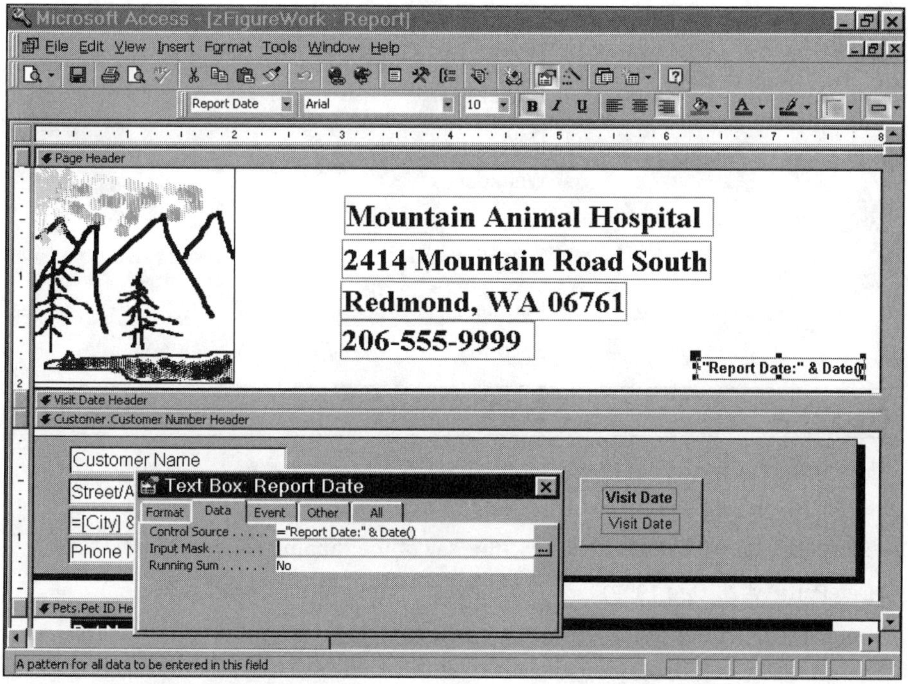

Figure 23-16: The page header.

Another date function Access offers is DatePart( ), which returns a numeric value for the specified portion of a date. The syntax for the function is

```
DatePart(interval,date,firstweekday,firstweek)
```

where *interval* is a string expression for the interval of time you want returned and *date* is the date to which you want to apply the function.

Table 23-3 lists some valid intervals and the time periods they represent.

The date can be a literal date (such as 1-Jan-1993) or a field name that references a field containing a valid date.

	Table 23-3 DatePart( ) Intervals
Interval	*Time Period*
yyyy	Year
q	Quarter
m	Month
y	Day of year
d	Day
w	Weekday
ww	Week
h	Hour
n	Minute
s	Second
Expression	*Result*
=DatePart("yyyy",25-Dec-1992)	1992 (the year)
=DatePart("m",25-Dec-1992)	12 (the month)
=DatePart("d",25-Dec-1992)	25 (the day of the month)
=DatePart("w",25-Dec-1992)	6 (the weekday; Sunday=1, Monday=2 . . .)
=DatePart("q",25-Dec-1992)	4 (the quarter)

Creating the page footer controls

Normally, you would use the page footer to place page numbers or to hold page totals. For this report, the footer's only purpose is to display a thick, horizontal line at the bottom of every page, followed by the page number in the bottom right corner.

To number the pages in your report, Access provides the Page function. You access it by using it in an expression in a text control that returns the current page of the report. As with all expressions, one that has the Page property in it must be preceded by an equal sign (=). To create a footer with a page number, follow these steps:

1. Create a new text control in the lower right section of the page footer.

2. Display the control's property sheet.

3. In the Control Source property cell, type =**"Page: "&Page**.

4. Select the Italics button on the toolbar.

Although it makes the most sense to put the page number in the page header or page footer, you can place a control with the Page property in any section of your report. You can also use the Page property as part of an expression. For example, the expression =Page*10 will display the result of multiplying the actual page number by ten.

You have now completed the Monthly Invoice Report. Compare your report design with the one shown originally in Figure 23-2 and then with the final output in Figure 23-17. Figure 23-17 shows page 14 of the report, a good example of displaying all the sections on one page. (Look back at Figure 23-1 to see a hard copy of the report page.)

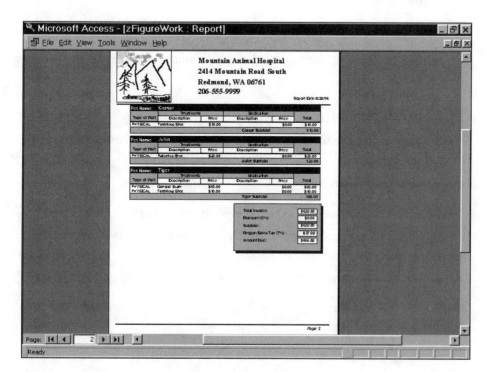

Figure 23-17: The report design output on-screen.

Before moving on, you need to create a few more controls. You can create controls based on knowledge of the final report because Access features a *two-pass report writer* that makes it possible. For example, you can create a control that displays the percentage of one total to a grand total or create a cumulative total to display cumulative totals.

Calculating percentages using totals

You can calculate a line percentage to determine what percent of the total cost for a pet's visit each line is. By comparing the line item to the total, you can calculate the percentage of a particular item to a whole. To do so, you'll need to move all the controls for the Pet ID header and footer and the detail section to the far left side of the report. To create a new control that displays what percentage of the whole (Mountain Animal Hospital Charges) is for each pet, follow these steps:

1. Duplicate the Pet Visit Line Total control.

2. Position the duplicate to the right of the original.

3. Change the Control Source to **=[Pet Visit Line Total]/[Pet Visit Total]**.

4. Change the Format property to **Percent**.

5. Create a new label control with the caption Percent above it, as shown in Figure 23-18.

The calculation takes the individual line total control [Pet Visit Line Total] in the detail section and divides it by the summary control [Pet Visit Total] in the page header section. The Percent format automatically handles the conversion and displays a percentage.

Calculating running sums

Access also lets you calculate *running sums* (also known as *cumulative totals*) easily; simply change the Running Sum property for a control. If you want to create a running total of how much is spent as each pet's charges are totaled, for example, follow these steps:

1. Duplicate the rectangle and its controls in the Pets.Pet ID footer section.

2. Display the new rectangle just below the existing one, as shown in Figure 23-19.

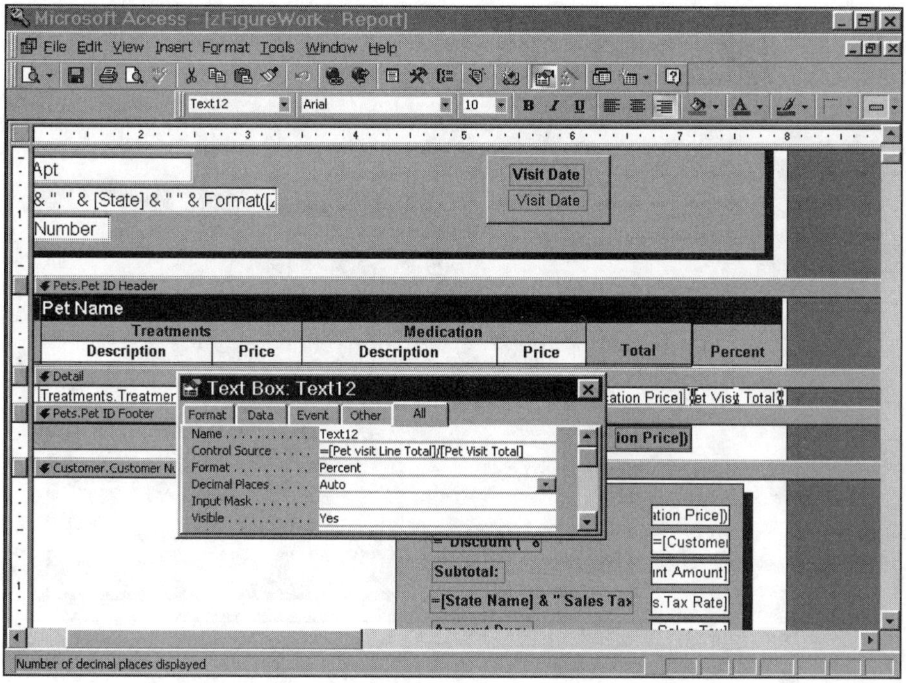

Figure 23-18: Creating a percentage control.

3. Select the label control and change the caption to
   =[**Customer Name]&"'s Running Total"**.
4. Select the new control with this expression:
   =**Sum([Treatment Price]+[Medication Price])**.
5. Display the control's property sheet.
6. Change the Name to **Running Total**.
7. Click on the Running Sum property.
8. Select Over Group from the drop-down list shown in Figure 23-19.

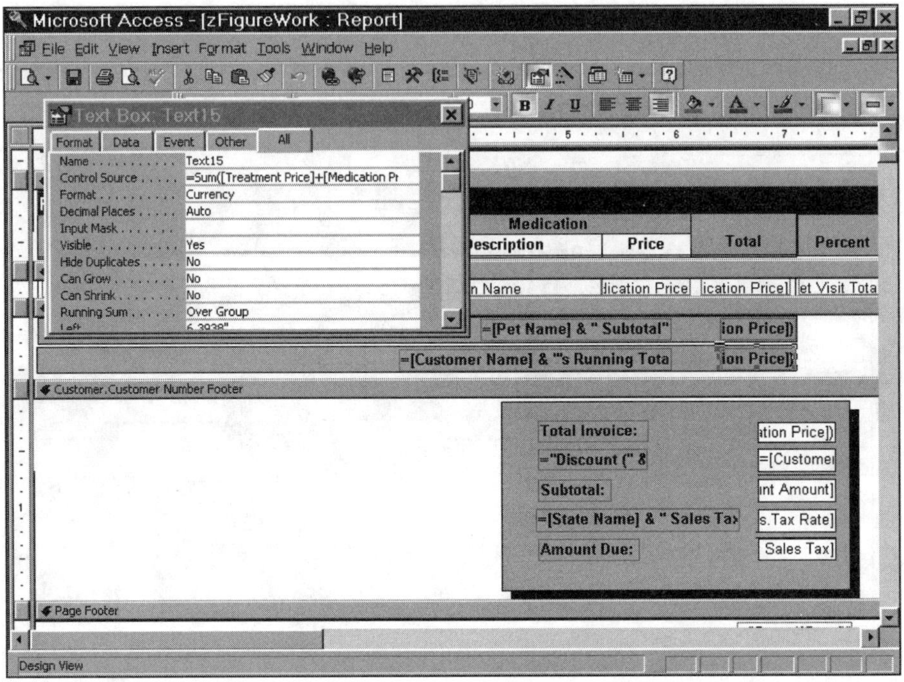

Figure 23-19: Creating a running sum control.

Access will now add the current subtotal to all previous subtotals for each owner. Alternatively, you can create a running sum across all values in a report. This is useful if you want to present an overall summary in the report's footer section.

You can display the percentages and the running total by performing a print preview, as shown in Figure 23-20.

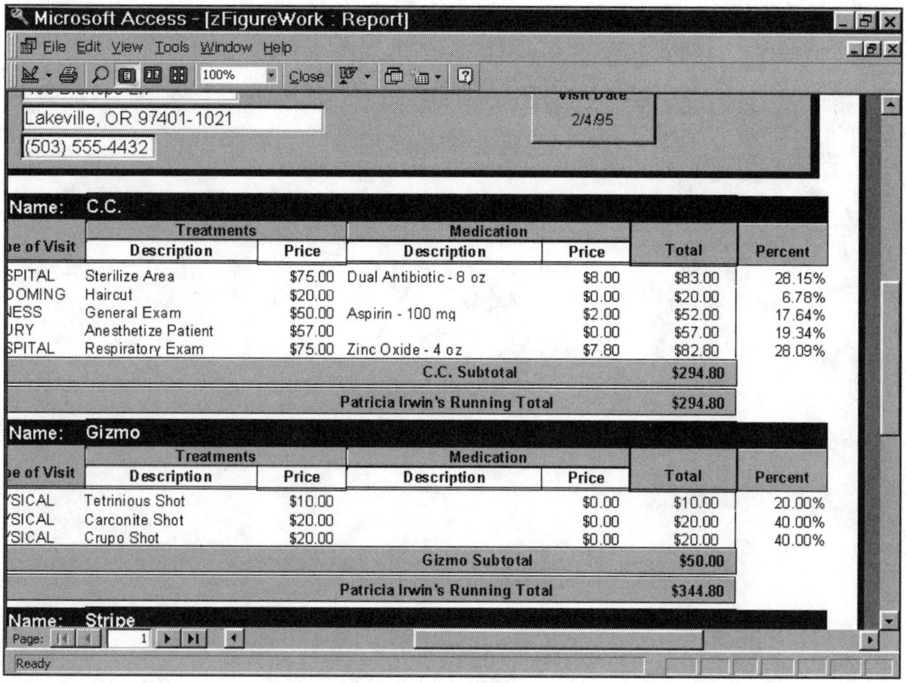

Figure 23-20: A print preview displaying percentages and running totals.

Creating a title page in a report header

The main purpose of the report header (illustrated in Figure 23-21) is to provide a separate title page. From the report description given earlier, you know that the report header must contain Mountain Animal Hospital's logo, name, address, and phone, as well as a report title. In the sample Monthly Invoice Report file, all these controls are created for you.

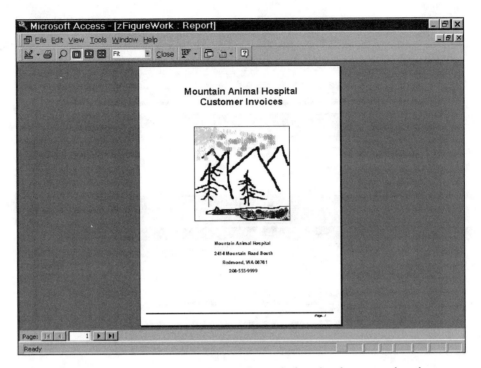

Figure 23-21: The Report Design Print Preview window for the report header.

If you created the report from scratch, you can follow these steps to create a report header:

1. Select View➪Report Header.

2. Click on the report header section and then open its Properties sheet.

3. Resize the height of the report header section to about 9½ inches.

4. Set the Force New Page property of the report header section to After Section so that a page break occurs after the report header.

5. Create label controls for the report title, name, address, and phone.

6. Create an image picture control (using MTN.BMP) and change the Size Mode property to Stretch.

Using the report footer

The report footer is not actually used in this report; it's displayed because the report header cannot be displayed in Design view without it. The normal use of the report footer is for grand totals that occur once in the report. You can also use it in an accounting type of report or in a letter concerning the totals for an audit trail.

Summary

In this chapter, you learned how to create multilevel reports as well as subreports. The following points were covered:

✦ Access lets you easily create multilevel grouping reports.

✦ A calculated control contains mathematical expressions.

✦ Text box controls can contain field names or expressions.

✦ Text expressions use the concatenation operators + or & to combine text strings and/or text strings and other data types.

✦ The Date( ) function returns the current system date.

✦ The DatePart( ) function returns a numeric value for the specified portion of a date.

✦ Controls can, and should be, named. You can then reference them in other controls.

✦ When you use the =Sum( ) function in a group header or footer (or page or report header or footer), it summarizes all the values of a field within that group.

✦ Access can use summary totals to calculate line-item or group-total percentages.

✦ Access can perform running sums within a group as well as across groups.

In the next chapter, you learn how to link to external data by attaching, importing, and exporting.

✦　　✦　　✦

Advanced Database Features

Working with External Data

So far, you have worked only with data in Access tables. In this chapter, you explore the use of data from other types of files. You learn to work with data from database, spreadsheet, and text-based files.

Access and External Data

Exchanging information between Access and another program is an essential capability in today's database world. Information is usually stored in a wide variety of application programs and data formats. Access (like many other products) has its own native file format, designed to support referential integrity and provide support for rich data types such as OLE objects. Most of the time, this format is sufficient; occasionally, however, you need to move data from one Access database file to another or even to a different software program's format.

Types of external data

Access has the capability to use and exchange data among a wide range of applications. For example, you may need to get data from other database files (such as FoxPro, dBASE, or Paradox files) or obtain information from an SQL Server, Oracle, or a text file. Access can move data among several categories of applications:

- ✦ Other Windows applications
- ✦ Spreadsheets
- ✦ PC database management systems
- ✦ Server-based database systems (ODBC)
- ✦ Text or mainframe files

Methods of working with external data

Often you will need to move data from one application or file into your Access database. You may need to obtain information you already have in an external spreadsheet file. You can reenter all the information by hand — or have it *imported* into your database. Perhaps you need to put information from your Access tables into Paradox files. Again, you can reenter all the information into Paradox by hand or have the information *exported* to the Paradox table. Access has tools that allow you to move data from a database table to another table or file. It could be a table in Access, dBASE, or Paradox; it could be a Lotus 1-2-3 spreadsheet file. In fact, Access can exchange data with more than 14 different file types, including the following:

✦ Access database objects (all types, all versions)

✦ dBASE III+, IV, and 5

✦ FoxPro 2.*x* and 3.0

✦ Paradox 3.*x*, 4.*x*, and 5.0

✦ Text files (ANSI and ASCII; DOS or OS/2; delimited and fixed-length)

✦ Lotus 1-2-3 2.*x* and 3.*x*

✦ Excel 3.0 and greater

✦ ODBC (Microsoft SQL Server, Sybase Server, Oracle Server, and other ODBC 1.1-compliant databases)

✦ HTML tables and lists

✦ IDC/HTX (Internet Information Services) resources

Access can work with these external data sources in several ways; Table 24-1 shows how and to what purpose.

Table 24-1
Methods of Working with External Data

Method	Purpose
Link	Creates a link to a table in another Access database or uses the data from a different database format
Import	Copies data *from* a text file, another Access database, or another application's format into an Access table
Export	Copies data from an Access table *to* a text file, another Access database, or another application's format

Should you import or link data?

As Table 24-1 shows, you can work with data from other sources in two ways: linking or importing. Both methods allow you to work with the external data.

There is a distinct difference between the two methods:

✦ Importing makes a copy of the external data and brings the copy into the Access table.

✦ Linking uses the data in its current file format (such as a dBASE or Paradox file).

Each method has clear advantages and disadvantages.

Linking in Access 97 was called *attaching* in Access 2.0 and 1.*x*.

When to import external data

Access cannot link to certain file formats; these include 1-2-3 spreadsheet files. If you need to work with data from formats that cannot be linked to, you must import it. You can, however, link to Excel files in Access 97.

NEW
FEATURE Because Access 97 has added the ability to link to HTML and text tables for read-only access, you can use and look at tables in HTML or text format. However, the tables cannot be updated nor records added to them using Access 97.

Of course, importing data means that you have doubled the storage space required for that particular data because it now resides in two different files on the storage device.

Caution Because importing makes another copy of the data, you may want to erase the old file after you import the copy into Access. Sometimes, however, you won't want to erase it. For example, the data may be sales figures from a spreadsheet still in use. In cases such as this, simply maintain the duplicate data and accept that storing it will require more space.

Working with other Access databases

Access can open only one database at a time; therefore, you can't work directly with a table in a different database. Even so, if you need to work with tables or other Access objects (such as forms and queries) from another Access database, you don't have to close the current one. Instead, simply import or link the object in the other database to your current database. You'll be able to view or edit data directly in more than one database table.

One of the principal reasons to import data is to customize it to meet your needs. You can specify a primary key, change field names (up to 64 characters), and set other field properties. With linked tables, on the other hand, you are restricted to setting very limited field properties. For example, you cannot specify a primary key, which means that you can't enforce integrity against the linked table.

Note When you link to another Access database, you can do everything you can do with tables in the primary database, including defining primary keys and enforcing referential integrity.

When to link to external data

If you leave data in another database format, Access can actually make changes to the table while the original application is still using it. This capability is useful when you want to work with data in Access that other programs also need to work with. For example, you might need to obtain updated personnel data from a dBASE file (maintained in an existing networked dBASE application) so that you can print a monthly report in Access. Another example is when you use Access as a front end for your SQL database; you can link to an SQL table and update the data directly to the server, without having to "batch upload" it later.

The biggest disadvantage of working with linked tables is that you lose the internal capability of Access to enforce referential integrity between tables (*unless* you are linked to an Access database).

Linking External Data

Access can directly link to several database management system (DBMS) tables individually or simultaneously. After an external file is linked, Access builds and stores a link to the table.

Database connectivity

As the database market continues to grow, the need to obtain information from many different sources will escalate. If you have information captured in an SQL Server table or a Paradox table, you don't want to reenter the information from these tables into Access. Ideally, you want to open the table and use the information in its native format, without having to copy it or write a translation program to access it. For many companies today, this capability of accessing information from one database format while working in another is a primary goal.

Copying or translating data from one application format to another is both time-consuming and costly. The time it takes can mean the difference between success and failure. Therefore, you want a *heterogeneous* environment between your DBMSs and the data. Access provides this environment through linking tables.

Types of database management systems

Access lets you connect, or *link,* to several different DBMSs, directly accessing information stored in them. Following are the database systems Access supports:

✦ Other Access database tables

✦ dBASE (versions III, IV, and 5)

✦ FoxPro (versions 2.*x* and 3.0)

✦ Paradox (versions 3.0, 4.*x*, and 5.0)

✦ Microsoft SQL Server, Sybase Server, Oracle, or any ODBC-aware database

You can link to any of these table types, individually or mixed together. If you link to an external file, Access displays the filename in the Database Table window (just as it does for other Access tables), but the icon linked with the table will be different. It starts with an arrow pointing from left to right and points to an icon. A table icon tells you that it's an Access table, a dB icon tells you that it's a dBASE table, and so on. Figure 24-1 shows several linked tables at the top of the list, which are all external tables. These tables are linked to the current database. Notice that all the linked tables have an icon with an arrow. (The icon clues you in to the type of file that is linked).

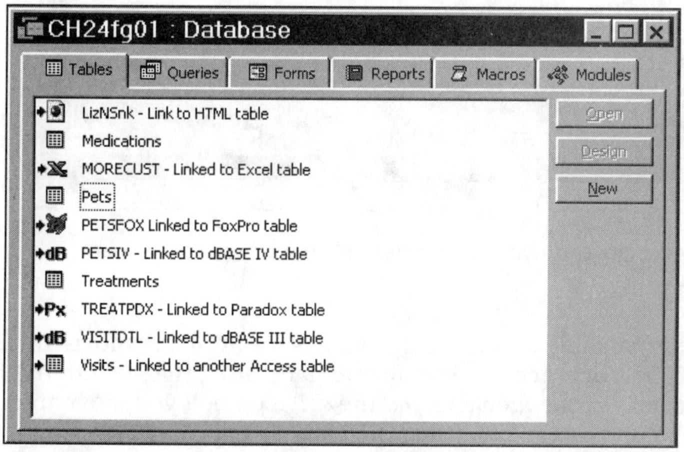

Figure 24-1: Linked tables in the database.

In Figure 24-1, the tables that have a left-pointing arrow next to them are linked. In addition to the link arrow reference, you can tell by their icon which type of file they are linked to. For instance, FoxPro has a picture of a fox, Excel has the X symbol, Paradox has the Px symbol, and dBASE tables have the dB symbol.

After you link a table to your Access database, you can use it as you would any other table. You can query against it, link another table to it, and so on. For example, Figure 24-2 shows a query design and dynaset using several linked tables Customer (from Excel), PETSIV (from dBASE), and Visits (from another Access database). You don't have to use an Access table; you can just as easily link to the Paradox and FoxPro tables.

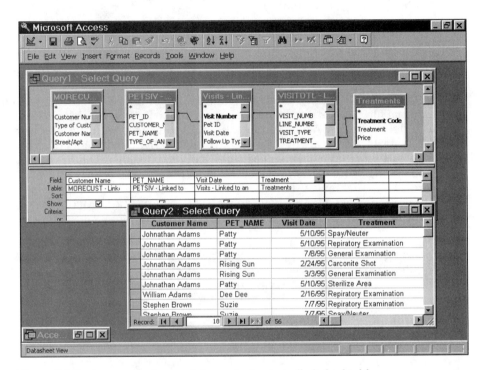

Figure 24-2: A query design and dynaset of externally linked tables.

Caution After you link an external table to an Access database, you *cannot* move the table to another drive or directory. Access does not actually bring the file into the MDB file; it maintains the link via the filename *and* the drive:path. If you move the external table, you have to update the link using the Linked Table Manager.

CD-ROM The examples in this chapter use the database Access Import-Export.mdb. This database is included on your CD-ROM along with several different types of DBMS files: Paradox, dBASE IV, dBASE III+, and FoxPro 2.x with indexes.

Linking to other Access database tables

When you work with an Access database, normally you create every table you want to use in it. If the table exists in another Access database, however, you can link to this other Access database and use the table (rather than re-creating it and duplicating its data).

You may, for example, want to link to another Access table that is on a network. After you link to another Access table, you use it just as you use another table in the open database. To link to the Visits table in the Mountain Animal Hospital Access database from the Access Import-Export.mdb database file, follow these steps:

1. Open the Access Import-Export.mdb (IMEXPORT.MDB) database.

2. Select File⇔Get External Data⇔Link Tables... (as shown in Figure 24-3). Access opens the Link dialog box.

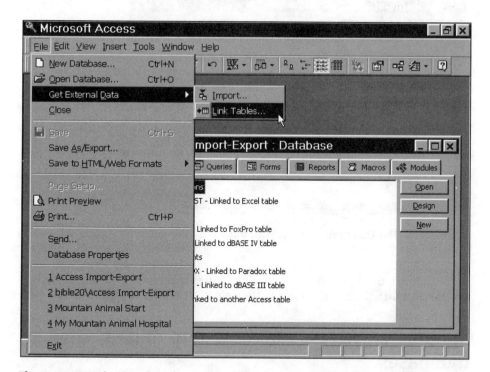

Figure 24-3: Selecting the File⇔Get External Data⇔Link Tables... menu commands.

You can select the .MDB file you want to link to. You can also change the type of files displayed in the Link dialog box; it can link to any type of external data. Though the default is to show only Access files (.MDB), you can link to any of the supported file types.

3. Find and select the Mountain Animal Hospital.MDB file in the dialog box. You may have to search for a different drive or directory.

4. Double-click on the Mountain Animal Hospital.MDB file (or select it and click on the Link button). Access will close the dialog box and display the Link Tables dialog box.

5. Select Visits and click on OK.

After you link the Visits table from the Mountain Animal Hospital database, Access returns to the Database window and shows you that the Visits table is now linked to your database. Figure 24-4 shows the Visits table linked to the current database. Notice the arrow on the Visits table's icon; it shows that the table has been linked from another source.

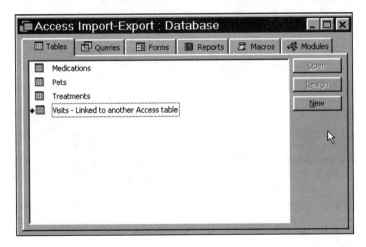

Figure 24-4: The Database window with the Visits table added.

Tip   You can link more than one table at a time by selecting each table before you click on the OK button. You can also use the Select All button to select all the tables.

Splitting an Access database into multiple linked databases

Generally, you split an Access application into two databases. One contains only your tables; the other contains all your queries, forms, reports, macros, and modules. This is extremely important when moving an application to a multiuser environment. The database with the queries, forms, reports, macros, and modules go on each client machine, and the database with the tables goes on the server. This arrangement has several major benefits:

✦ Everyone on the network shares one common set of data.

✦ Many people can update data at the same time.

✦ When you want to update the forms, reports, macros, or modules, you don't have to interrupt processing or worry about data corruption.

If you start with your database split when you create a new application, it's easier to complete your application later. Some things you just can't do with a linked table without doing a little extra work; these tasks include finding records and importing data. By using different techniques with linked tables, however, you can do anything you can do with a single database.

If you're starting from scratch, you first create a database with just the tables for your application. You then create another new database and link the tables from the first database to the second (as you learned in the preceding section).

After you have built a system with all your objects (including the tables) in one database file, however, it's a little more difficult to split your tables. One method is to duplicate your database file in Windows by copying and pasting it. In one version, you delete everything except the tables from the duplicate database file. In the other version, you delete only the tables. Then you use the database file without the tables as a starting point and then link to all the tables in the database.

Access 97 features a Wizard that can do this for you automatically. Using the Mountain Animal Hospital database, for example, you can split all the tables into a separate database file. Later, you can import all those tables into the original database if you want or continue to use the split database file.

You start the Database Splitter Wizard by selecting Tools➪Add-ins➪Database Splitter. This displays a set of Wizard screens to help you split a single database into two. The first Wizard screen simply confirms that you want to split the database, as shown in Figure 24-5.

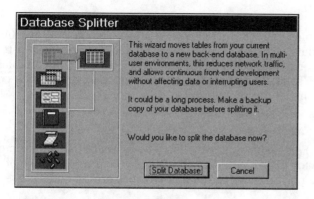

Figure 24-5: The Database Splitter Wizard.

When you click on the Split Database button, you see the standard Windows 95 File Save dialog box (named the Database Splitter window). Here, you can enter the name of the new database you want Access to create with just the tables. When you're ready for Access to split the tables, click on the Split button.

Access creates the new database, copies all the tables from the original database to the new database, and then links to them. When the process is done, a message tells you that the database was successfully split. Figure 24-6 shows the original database file with linked tables.

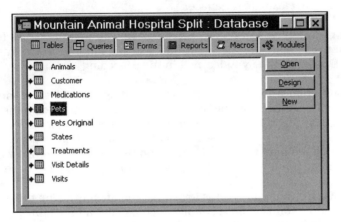

Figure 24-6: Linked tables in the Mountain Animal Hospital database.

Linking to dBASE and FoxPro databases (tables)

You can link to DBF files in either dBASE or FoxPro format. As with other Access database tables, after an *x*BASE (dBASE or FoxPro) file is linked, you can view and edit data in the DBF format.

dBASE and FoxPro save tables in individual files with the extension DBF. In *x*BASE, these DBF files are called databases. In Access, however, a *table* is equivalent to an *x*BASE *database*. (Access considers a *database* a complete collection of all tables and other related objects.) To maintain consistency in terminology, this book considers *x*BASE databases to mean the same thing as dBASE or FoxPro tables.

Access and dBASE/FoxPro indexes

When you link a dBASE or FoxPro file, you can also tell Access to use one or more index files (NDX and MDX for dBASE, and IDX and CDX for FoxPro). The use of these indexes will improve performance of the link between *x*BASE and Access.

If you inform Access of the associated index files, Access will update the indexes every time it changes the DBF file. By linking a DBF file and its associated indexes, Access can link to DBFs in real time in a network environment. Access recognizes and enforces the automatic record-locking feature of dBASE and FoxPro as well as the file and record locks placed with *x*BASE commands and functions.

Tip You should always tell Access about any indexes associated with the database. If you don't, it will not update them; dBASE or FoxPro will have unexpected problems if their associated index files are not updated.

When you tell Access to use one or more associated indexes (NDX, MDX, IDX, or CDX) of a dBASE or FoxPro file, Access maintains information about the fields used in the index tags in a special information file. This file has the same name as the dBASE or FoxPro file with an INF extension.

Caution If you link a dBASE or FoxPro file and associated indexes, Access must have access to the index files in order to link the table. If you delete or move the index files or the Access INF file, you will not be able to open the linked DBF file.

Linking to dBASE IV tables

Linking to FoxPro tables and dBASE tables works the same. For example, to link the dBASE IV table PETSIV.DBF and its associated memo file (DBT), follow these steps:

1. Open the ATCIMPEX database and select File➪Get External Data➪Link Tables....

2. In the Link dialog box, select Files of type: dBASE IV. Access displays just the dBASE IV DBF files.

3. Double-click on PETSIV.DBF in the Select Index Files list box. (The memo file PETSIV.DBT is linked automatically and given the DBF extension.) Access activates the Select Index Files box and displays all NDX and MDX files.

4. Click on the Cancel button (there are no related indexes for this table). Access closes the Select Index Files box and displays a dialog box to indicate that the link was successful.

   Note: If there are any indexes to associate with this table, you select them here.

5. Click on the OK button. Access redisplays the Select File dialog box.

6. Click on the Close button to finish linking dBASE files. Access displays the Database window with the file PETSIV linked.

Note You can cancel linking at any time by clicking on the Cancel button in the Select File dialog box before you select a table.

Caution   When you add index files, Access automatically creates and updates an Access information file. This file contains information about the index and associated dBASE or FoxPro file, has the same name, and ends in the extension INF.

Linking to Paradox tables

You can link DB files in either Paradox 3.*x* or Paradox 4.*x* format. As with other Access database tables, after a Paradox file is linked, you can view and edit data in the DB format.

Access and Paradox index files

If a Paradox table has a primary key defined, it maintains the index information in a file that ends in the extension PX. When you link a Paradox table that has a primary key defined, Access links the associated PX file automatically.

Caution   If you link a Paradox table that has a primary key, Access needs the PX file in order to open the table. If you move or delete the PX file, you will not be able to open the linked table.

Tip   If you link a Paradox table to Access that does not have a primary key defined, you will not be able to use Access to update data in the table; you can only view it.

Access can link to DBs in real time in a network environment. Access recognizes and enforces the file- and record-locking features of Paradox.

Linking to nondatabase tables

You can also link to Excel, HTML tables, and text tables. When you select one of these types of data sources, Access will run a Link Wizard that will prompt you through the process.

If you link to an Excel table, you can update its records from within Access 97 or any other application that can update Excel spreadsheets.

NEW FEATURE   Linking to HTML and text tables will let you view and use tables in queries, forms, and reports. However, you cannot change the current record contents or add new records. Linking to both HTML tables (local or on the Internet) and text tables is a new feature of Access 97. Earlier versions could not work with HTML tables, and they could import or export only text files.

The Access 97 Link Wizard

When you link to an Excel spreadsheet, HTML table, or text file, Access 97 will automatically run a Link Wizard to help you. In each case, you will be asked whether the first line (record) contains the field names for the fields. If it does, click on the check box to turn it on. If the first record does not hold the field names, you will be given the option of specifying a name for each field or accepting the default names (field1, field2, field3, and so on).

Working with Linked Tables

After you link to an external table from another database, you can use it just as you would use another Access table.

After external tables are linked, you can use them with forms, reports, and queries. When working with external tables, you can modify many of their features; for example, you can rename the table, set view properties, and set links between tables in queries.

Setting view properties

Although an external table can be used like another Access table, you cannot change the structure (delete, add, or rearrange fields) of an external table. You can, however, set several table properties for the fields in a linked table:

- ◆ Format
- ◆ Decimal Places
- ◆ Caption
- ◆ Input Mask

Setting relationships

Access does not let you set permanent relations at the table level between non-Access external tables and Access tables. If you need to set a relationship between an external table and another Access table, you must do it in a query. Then you can use the query in a form, another query, or a report.

Setting links between external tables

To set a link between an external table and another Access table, simply create a query and use the drag-and-drop method of setting links. After a link is set, you can change the join properties from equi-join (inner join) to external join by double-clicking on the link.

Using external tables in queries

When using a query, you can join the external table with another table, internal or external. This gives you powerful flexibility when working with queries. Figure 24-7 shows a query using several different database sources:

✦ An Excel spreadsheet

✦ An HTML document (table)

✦ Access tables (both internal and linked)

✦ A Paradox table

✦ A dBASE IV table

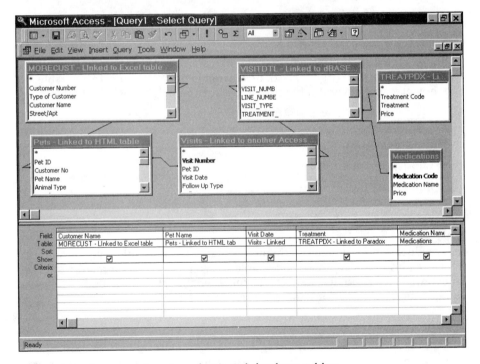

Figure 24-7: A query using several external database tables.

Notice that the query in Figure 24-7 has joins between all tables. This query will obtain information from all the tables and display a datasheet similar to the one in Figure 24-8.

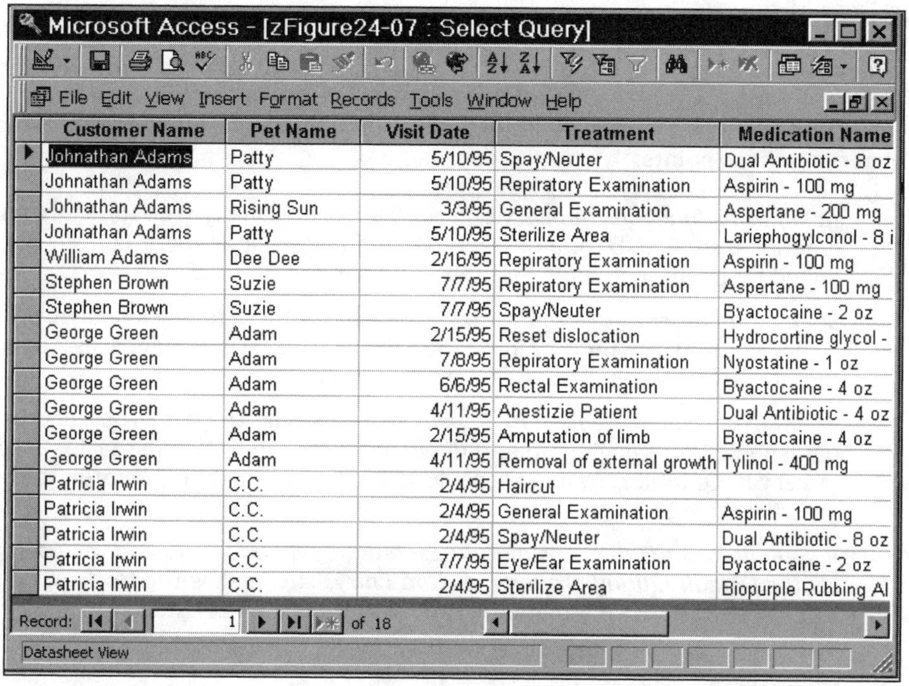

Customer Name	Pet Name	Visit Date	Treatment	Medication Name
Johnathan Adams	Patty	5/10/95	Spay/Neuter	Dual Antibiotic - 8 oz
Johnathan Adams	Patty	5/10/95	Repiratory Examination	Aspirin - 100 mg
Johnathan Adams	Rising Sun	3/3/95	General Examination	Aspertane - 200 mg
Johnathan Adams	Patty	5/10/95	Sterilize Area	Lariephogylconol - 8 i
William Adams	Dee Dee	2/16/95	Repiratory Examination	Aspirin - 100 mg
Stephen Brown	Suzie	7/7/95	Repiratory Examination	Aspertane - 100 mg
Stephen Brown	Suzie	7/7/95	Spay/Neuter	Byactocaine - 2 oz
George Green	Adam	2/15/95	Reset dislocation	Hydrocortine glycol -
George Green	Adam	7/8/95	Repiratory Examination	Nyostatine - 1 oz
George Green	Adam	6/6/95	Rectal Examination	Byactocaine - 4 oz
George Green	Adam	4/11/95	Anestizie Patient	Dual Antibiotic - 4 oz
George Green	Adam	2/15/95	Amputation of limb	Byactocaine - 4 oz
George Green	Adam	4/11/95	Removal of external growth	Tylinol - 400 mg
Patricia Irwin	C.C.	2/4/95	Haircut	
Patricia Irwin	C.C.	2/4/95	General Examination	Aspirin - 100 mg
Patricia Irwin	C.C.	2/4/95	Spay/Neuter	Dual Antibiotic - 8 oz
Patricia Irwin	C.C.	7/7/95	Eye/Ear Examination	Byactocaine - 2 oz
Patricia Irwin	C.C.	2/4/95	Sterilize Area	Biopurple Rubbing Al

Figure 24-8: A datasheet display of the dynaset created by the query in Figure 24-7.

Renaming tables

You can rename a linked external table. Because Access lets you name a table with as many as 64 characters (including spaces), you may want to rename a linked table to be more descriptive. For example, you may want to rename the dBASE table called PETSIV to Pets Table from dBASE.

To rename a file, you can select Edit⇨Rename... from the Database menu. Another (quicker) method is to click on the filename, click on it again, and enter a new name.

Note When you rename an external file, Access does not rename the actual DOS filename or SQL Server table name. It uses the new name only in the Table object list of the Access database.

Optimizing linked tables

When working with linked tables, Access has to retrieve records from another file. This process takes time, especially when the table resides on a network or in an SQL database. When working with external data, you can optimize performance by observing these points:

✦ *Avoid using functions in query criteria.* This is especially true for aggregate functions, such as DTotal or Dcount, which retrieve all records from the linked table automatically and then perform the query.

✦ *Limit the number of external records to view.* Create a query specifying a criterion that limits the number of records from an external table. This query can then be used by other queries, forms, or reports.

✦ *Avoid excessive movement in datasheets.* View only the data you need to in a datasheet. Avoid paging up and down and jumping to the last or first record in very large tables. (The exception is when you're adding records to the external table.)

✦ *If you add records to external linked tables, create a form to add records and set the Default Editing property to Data Entry.* This makes the form an entry form that starts with a blank record every time it's executed.

✦ When working with tables in a multiuser environment, minimize locking records. This will free up records for other users.

Deleting a linked table reference

To delete a linked table from the Database window, follow these steps:

1. In the Database window, select the linked table you want to delete.

2. Either press the Delete key or select Edit⇨Delete from the Database menu.

3. Click on OK in the Access dialog box to delete the file.

Note   Deleting an external table will delete only its name from the database object list. The actual file will not be deleted at the DOS level.

Viewing or changing information for linked tables

After a table is linked, it or its associated indexes shouldn't be moved. If they are, Access will not be able to find them. You can use the Linked Table Manager to reestablish linked files.

If you move, rename, or modify tables or indexes associated with a linked table, you can use the Linked Table Manager to update the links. To use this tool, select Tools⇨Add-ins⇨Linked Table Manager. Access will display a dialog box similar to the one shown in Figure 24-9. Select the linked table that needs the information changed; Access will verify that the file cannot be found and will prompt you for the new information.

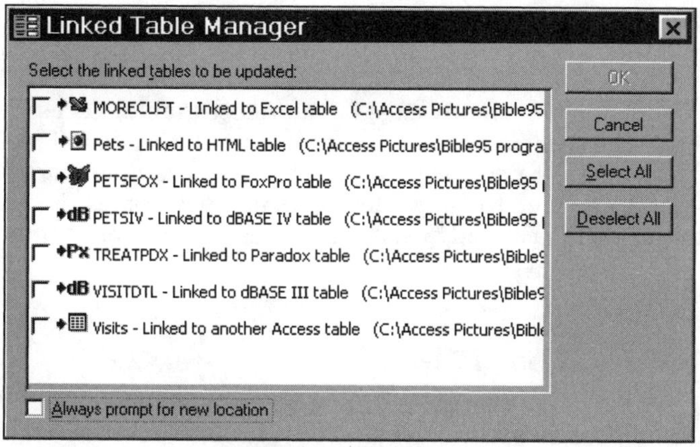

Figure 24-9: The Linked Table Manager.

Importing External Data

When you import a file (unlike when you link tables), you copy the contents from an external file into an Access table. You can import external file information from several different sources:

✦ Microsoft Access (other unopened database objects: forms, tables, and so on)

✦ Paradox 3.x, 4.x, and 5.0

✦ FoxPro 2.x and 3.0

✦ dBASE III, IV, and 5

✦ SQL databases (Microsoft SQL Server, Sybase Server, and Oracle Server)

✦ Delimited text files (fields separated by a delimiter)

✦ Fixed-width text files (specific widths for each field)

✦ Microsoft Excel (all versions)

✦ Lotus 1-2-3 and 1-2-3 for Windows (versions WKS, WK1, and WK3)

✦ An HTML document

✦ IDC/HTX (Microsoft Internet Information Server)

You can import information to either new tables or existing tables, depending on the type of data being imported. All data types can be imported to new tables, but only spreadsheet and text files can be imported to existing tables.

When Access imports data from an external file, it does not erase or destroy the external file. Therefore, you will have two copies of the data: the original file (in the original format) and the new Access table.

Note If the filename of the importing file already exists in an Access table, Access adds a chronological number (1, 2, 3, and so on) to the filename until it has a unique table name. If an importing spreadsheet name is Customer.XLS (for example) and there is an Access table named Customer, the imported table name becomes Customer1. If Customer and Customer1 tables already exist, Access creates a table named Customer2.

Importing other Access objects

You can import other Access database tables or any other object in another database. You can therefore import an existing table, query, form, report, macro, or module from another Access database.

NEW FEATURE In addition to the standard Access objects, Access 97 allows you to import custom toolbars and menus into the current database.

As an example, use these steps to import the States table from the Mountain Animal Hospital Access database:

1. Open the Access Import-Export database and select File⇨Get External Data⇨Import. (An Import dialog box appears.)

2. In the Import dialog box, select Files of type: Microsoft Access.

3. Double-click on Mountain Animal Hospital.MDB. Access closes the Import select database dialog box and opens the Import Objects dialog box, as shown in Figure 24-10. At the bottom of this selection box, you can click on the Options>> button to specify import options.

4. In the box, select the States table by clicking on States and then clicking on the OK button.

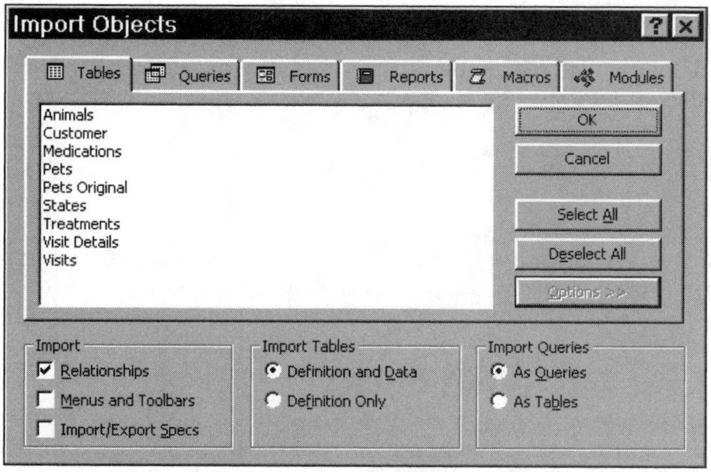

Figure 24-10: The Import Objects dialog box.

Access imports the States table into the Access Import-Export database and closes the Import Objects dialog box. You can select more than one item at a time, using the Select All and Deselect All buttons to select or deselect all the objects in a specific category. The Options>> button lets you further define how to import Access data.

You can choose to import relationships, custom toolbars, and import/export specifications from an Access database. You can determine whether the tables you import come in with just the table design or with the data as well. Finally, the last set of options lets you decide whether queries you import come in as queries or run as make-table action queries to import a new table. (See Chapter 26 for details about make-table queries.)

The States table appears in the Database window display without a link symbol in the icon. Unlike linking the table, you have copied the States table and added it to the current database. Therefore, because it's not linked but instead an actual part of the database, it occupies space like the original Access table does.

Besides adding tables from other Access databases, you can also add other objects (including queries, forms, reports, macros, or modules) by clicking on each of the tabs in the Import Objects dialog box. You can select objects from each and then import them all at one time.

Importing PC-based database tables

When importing data from personal-computer-based databases, you can import two basic categories of database file types:

✦ xBASE (dBASE, FoxPro)

✦ Paradox

Each type of database can be imported directly into an Access table. The native data types are converted to Access data types during the conversion.

Importing a PC-based database

You can import any Paradox, dBASE III, dBASE IV, dBASE V, FoxPro, or Visual FoxPro database table into Access. To import one of these, simply select the correct database type in the Files of type: box during the import process.

After selecting the type of PC-based database, you select which file you want to import; Access imports the file for you automatically.

If you try to import a Paradox table that is encrypted, Access prompts you for the password after you select the table in the Select File dialog box. Enter the password and click on the OK button to import an encrypted Paradox table.

When Access imports xBASE fields, it converts them from their current data type into an Access data type. Table 24-2 lists how the data types are converted.

Table 24-2 Conversion of Data Types from *xBASE* to Access	
xBASE Data Type	*Access Data Type*
Character	Text
Numeric	Number (property of Double)
Float	Number (property of Double)
Logical	Yes/No
Date	Date/Time
Memo	Memo

When importing any *x*BASE database file in a multiuser environment, you must have exclusive use of the file. If other people are using it, you will not be able to import it.

As with *x*BASE tables, when Access imports Paradox fields, the Paradox fields are converted from their current data type into an Access data type. Table 24-3 lists how the data types are converted.

Table 24-3
Conversion of Data Types from Paradox to Access

Paradox Data Type	Access Data Type
Alphanumeric	Text
Number	Number (property of Double)
Short Number	Number (property of Integer)
Currency	Number (property of Double)
Date	Date/Time
Memo	Memo
Blob (Binary)	OLE

Importing spreadsheet data

You can import data from Excel or Lotus 1-2-3 spreadsheets to a new or existing table. The key to importing spreadsheet data is that it must be arranged in tabular (columnar) format. Each cell of data in a spreadsheet column must contain the same type of data. Table 24-4 demonstrates correct and incorrect columnar-format data.

Table 24-4
Spreadsheet Cells with Contents

A	B	C	D	E	F
1	TYPE	WEIGHT	BDATE	JUNK	GARBAGE
2	DOG	122	12/02/92	123	YES
3	CAT	56	02/04/89	22	134.2
4	BIRD	55	05/30/90	01/01/91	DR SMITH
5	FROG	12	02/22/88	TEST	$345.35
6	FISH	21	01/04/93	=====	==
7	RAT	3	02/28/93	$555.00	<== TOTAL

Table 24-4 represents cells in a spreadsheet, in the range A1 through F7. Notice that the data in columns A, B, and C and rows 2 through 7 is the same type. Row 1 contains field names. These columns can be imported into an Access table. Column D is empty and cannot be used. Columns E and F do *not* have the same type of data in each of their cells; they may cause problems when you try to import them into an Access table.

Figure 24-11 shows an Excel spreadsheet named MORECUST.XLS (actually a spreadsheet with some of the same fields and data as other Mountain Animal Hospital tables).

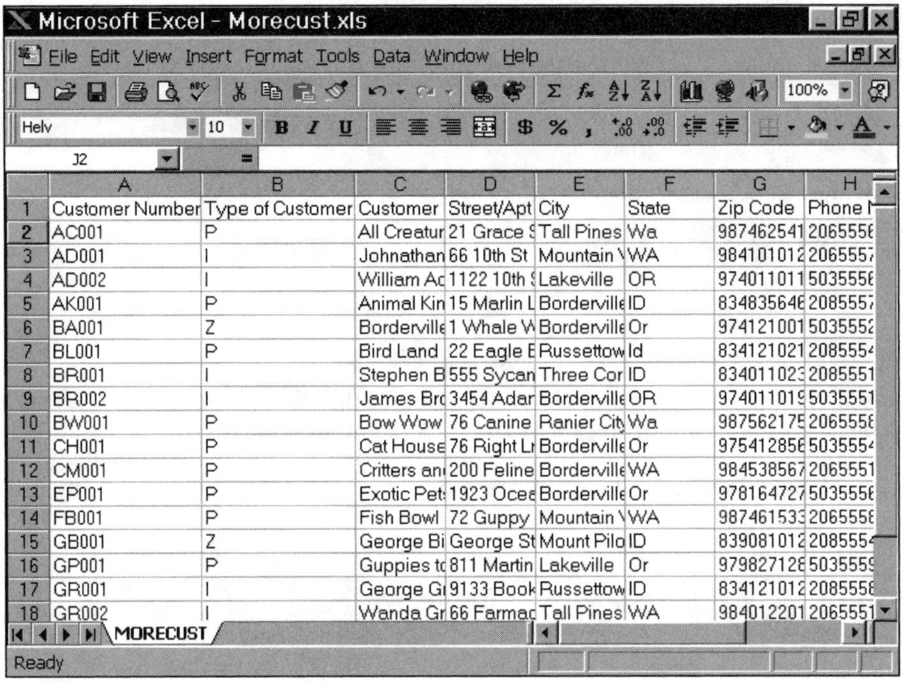

Figure 24-11: An Excel spreadsheet.

To import the Excel spreadsheet named MORECUST.XLS, follow these steps:

1. Open the Access Import-Export database and select File⇨Get External Data⇨Import.

2. In the Import dialog box, select Files of type: Microsoft Excel (*.xls). Then double-click on MORECUST.XLS in the select box. Access closes the Import box and displays the first Spreadsheet Import Wizard screen.

3. Access opens the first Import Spreadsheet Wizard screen for the table MORE-CUST.XLS; the screen resembles the one shown in Figure 24-12.

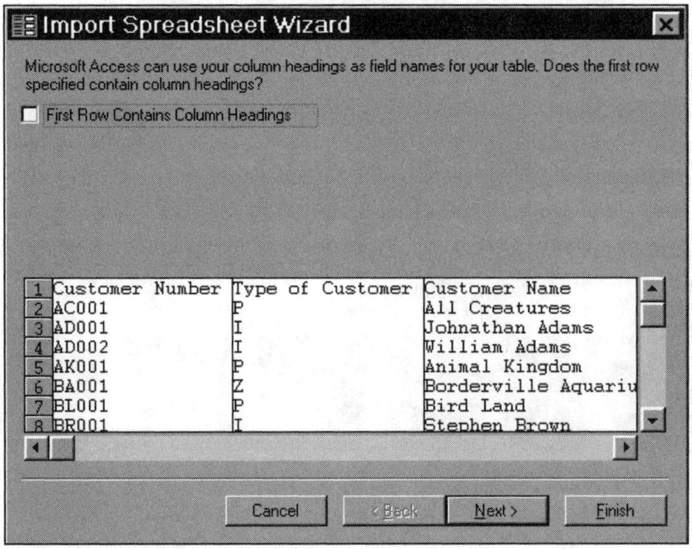

Figure 24-12: The first Import Spreadsheet Wizard screen.

This screen displays a sample of the first few rows and columns of the spreadsheet. You can scroll the display to see all the rows and columns if you want. Enter the starting row number to import the data. To use the first row of the spreadsheet to name fields in the table, use the check box.

4. Click on the First Row Contains Column Headings check box. The display changes to show the first row and column headings.

5. Click on Next> to display the second screen.

This screen lets you determine where the data will go. You can create a new table or add to an existing table.

6. Click on Next> to display the third screen.

This screen (shown in Figure 24-13) lets you click on each column of the spreadsheet to accept the field name, change it, and decide whether it will be indexed; the Wizard determines the data type automatically. You can also choose to skip each column if you want.

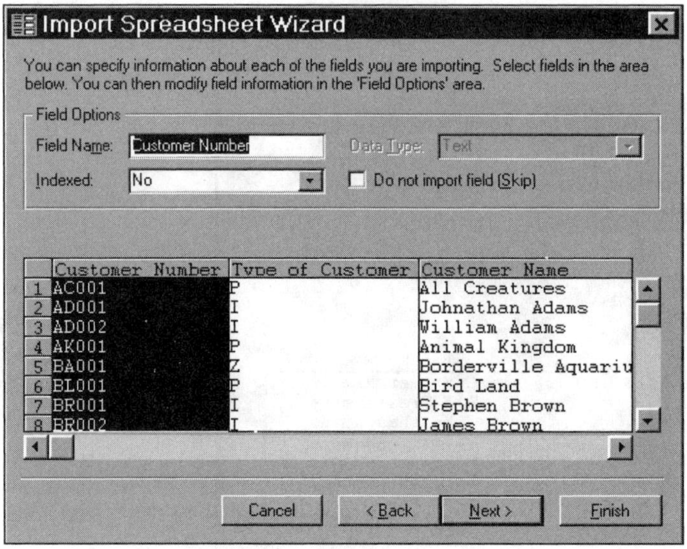

Figure 24-13: Determining the field names and data types.

7. Click on Next> to display the next Import Spreadsheet Wizard screen.

This screen lets you choose a field for the primary key. You can let Access create a new AutoNumber field (by choosing Let Access add Primary Key), enter your own (by selecting Choose my own Primary Key and selecting one of the columns), or have no primary key. Figure 24-14 shows these options.

8. Select Choose my own Primary Key and select the Customer Number field.

9. Click on Next to display the last Import Spreadsheet Wizard screen.

The last screen lets you enter the name for the imported table and (optionally) run the Table Analyzer Wizard.

10. Click on Finish to import the spreadsheet file. Access 97 informs you that it imported the file successfully.

The filename now appears in the Access database window. A standard Access table has been created from the original spreadsheet file.

Importing from word-processing files

Access does not offer a specific way to import data from word-processing files. If you need to import data from a word-processing file into Access, convert the word-processing file to a simple text file first and then import it as a text file. Most word processors have the capability to convert their formatted text to text files or ASCII files.

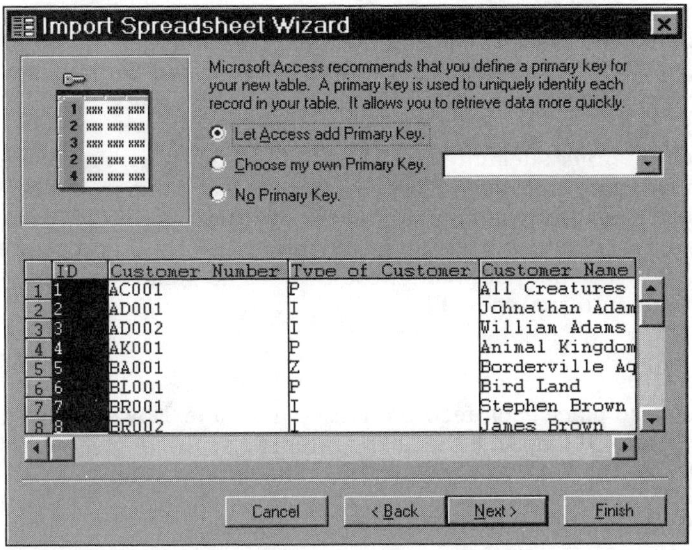

Figure 24-14: Determining the primary key.

Importing text file data

You can import from two different types of text files: *delimited* and *fixed-width*. These types of files use, in turn, an *import/export specification* file. Unformatted mainframe data is generally transferred from the mainframe to a personal computer as a text file.

NEW
FEATURE
Access 97 uses one Wizard for both types of text files. It will graphically assist you in identifying the fields for the import/export specification.

Delimited text files

Delimited text files are sometimes known as *CSV* (for *comma-separated values*) files; each record is on a separate line in the text file. The fields on the line contain no trailing spaces, normally use commas as field separators, and require certain fields to be enclosed in a *delimiter* (such as single or double quotation marks). Usually the text fields are also enclosed in quotation marks or some other delimiter, as in these examples:

```
"Irwin","Michael","Michael Irwin Consulting",05/12/72
"Prague","Cary","Cary Prague Books and Software",02/22/86
"Zimmerman-Schneider","Audrie","IBM",01/01/59
```

Notice that the file has three records (rows of text) and four fields. Each field is separated by a comma, and the text fields are delimited with double quotation marks. The starting position of each field, after the first one, is different. Each record has a different length because the field lengths are different.

Tip   You can import records from a delimited text file that has fields with no values. To specify a field with no value, place delimiters where the field value would be, and put no value between them (for example, `"Irwin","Michael",,05/12/72`). Notice that there are two commas after the field content "Michael" and before the field content `05/12/72`. The field between these two has no value; it will be imported with no value into an Access file.

Fixed-width text files

Fixed-width text files also place each record on a separate line. However, the fields in each record are of a fixed length. If the field contents are not long enough, trailing spaces are added to the field, as shown in the following example:

```
Irwin       Michael  Michael Irwin Consulting       05/12/82
Prague      Cary     Cary Prague Books and Software 02/22/86
Zimmerman   Audrie   IBM                            01/01/59
-Schneider
```

Notice that the fields are not separated by delimiters. Rather, they start at exactly the same position in each record. Each record has exactly the same length. If a field is not long enough, trailing spaces are added to fill the field.

You can import either a delimited or a fixed-width text file to a new table or existing Access table. If you decide to append the imported file to an existing table, the file's structure must match that of the Access table you're importing to.

Note   If the Access table being imported has a key field, the text file cannot have any duplicate key values or else the import will report an error.

Importing delimited text files

To import a delimited text file named MEDLIMIT.TXT, follow these steps:

1. Open the Access Import-Export database and select File⇨Get External Data⇨Import.

2. In the Import dialog box, select Files of type: Text files (*.txt,*.csv,*.tab,*.asc).

3. Double-click on MEDLIMIT.TXT in the File Name list box. Access displays the first screen of the Import Text Wizard dialog box for the table MEDLIMIT.TXT. The dialog box resembles the one shown in Figure 24-15.

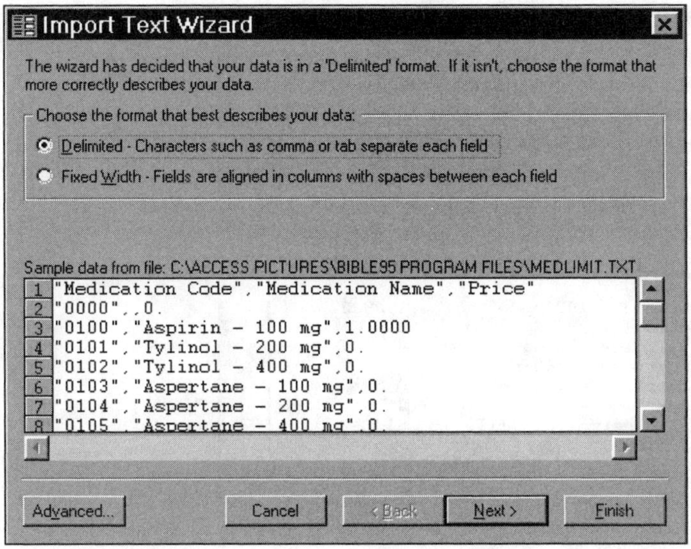

Figure 24-15: The first Import Text Wizard screen.

This screen displays the data in the text file and guesses whether the text file is delimited or fixed width. As you can see, the Wizard has determined correctly that the file is delimited.

Note Notice at the bottom of the screen the button marked Advanced. Click on it to further define the import specifications. You will learn more about this option in the upcoming section about fixed-width text files. Generally, it's not needed for delimited files.

4. Click on the Next> button to display the next Import Text Wizard screen.

As you can see in Figure 24-16, this screen lets you determine which type of separator to use in the delimited text file. Generally this separator is a comma, but you could use a tab, semicolon, space, or other character (such as an asterisk), which you enter in the box next to the Other option button. You can also decide whether to use text from the first row as field names for the imported table.

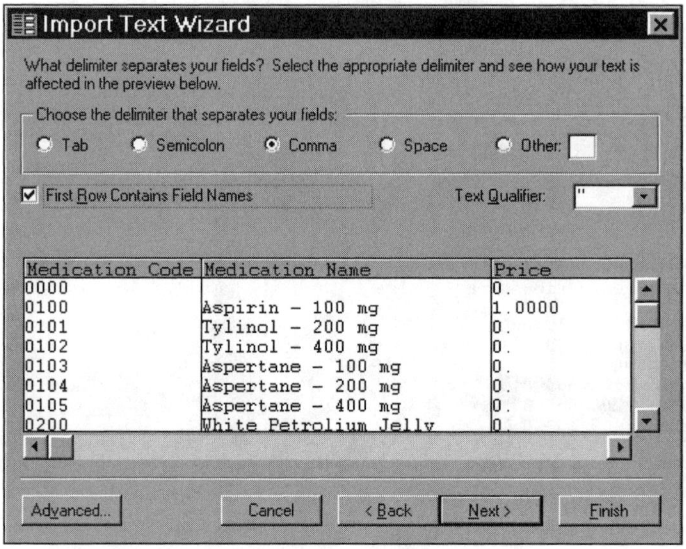

Figure 24-16: The second Import Text Wizard screen.

5. Click on the First Row Contains Field Names check box to use the first row for field names. Access will redisplay the text file with the first row as the column headers.

6. Click on the Next> button to display the next Import Text Wizard screen.

   This screen lets you determine whether you're storing the imported data in a new table or an existing table. If you decide to use an existing table, you have to choose it from a list.

   The next few screens are exactly the same as the Spreadsheet Import Wizard screens you saw earlier in this chapter.

7. Click on the Next> button to display the next Import Text Wizard screen, which lets you select each column of the Text Import grid, accept or change the field name, decide whether it will be indexed, and set the data type (which is also automatically determined by the Wizard). You can choose to skip a column if you want.

8. Click on Next> to display the next Import Text Wizard screen.

   This screen lets you choose a field for the primary key. You can let Access create a new AutoNumber field (by choosing Let Access add Primary Key), enter your own (by selecting Choose my own Primary Key and selecting one of the columns), or have no primary key.

9. Click on the radio button that says Choose my own Primary Key and select the field Medication Code.

10. Click on Next> to display the last Import Text Wizard screen.

   The last screen lets you enter the name for the imported table and (optionally) run the Table Analyzer Wizard.

11. Click on Finish to import the delimited text file.

Access creates a new table, using the same name as the text file's name. The filename appears in the Access Database window, where Access has added the table MEDLIMIT.

Importing fixed-width text files

In *fixed-width* text files, each field in the file has a specific width and position. Files downloaded from mainframes are the most common fixed-width text files. As you import or export this type of file, you must specify an import/export setup specification. You create this setup file by using the Advanced options of the Import Table Wizard.

To import a fixed-width text file, follow these steps:

1. Open the Access Import-Export database and select File⇨Get External Data⇨Import.

2. In the Import dialog box, select Files of type: Text files (*.txt,*.csv,*.tab,*.asc).

3. Double-click on PETFIXED.TXT in the File Name list box. Access opens the first screen of the Import Text Options Wizard dialog box for the table PETFIXED.TXT. (The dialog box resembles the one shown in Figure 24-15.)

   This screen displays the data in the text file and guesses whether the type of text file is delimited or fixed width. As you can see, the Wizard has correctly determined that it's a fixed-width file.

4. Click on Next> to display the next Import Text Wizard screen.

   This screen makes a guess about where columns begin and end in the file, basing the guess on the spaces in the file.

   Figure 24-17 shows that Access has not done a good job in this file. It has recognized the first field correctly, but the second three fields have been lumped together. You'll need to add field break lines at positions 32, 33, and 34. You can do this on this screen by pointing between the columns of data and pressing the mouse button. The idea is to show the end of the Date field, the beginning and end of the Type of Animal field (1, 2, 3), the Gender field (M, F), and the beginning of the Weight field.

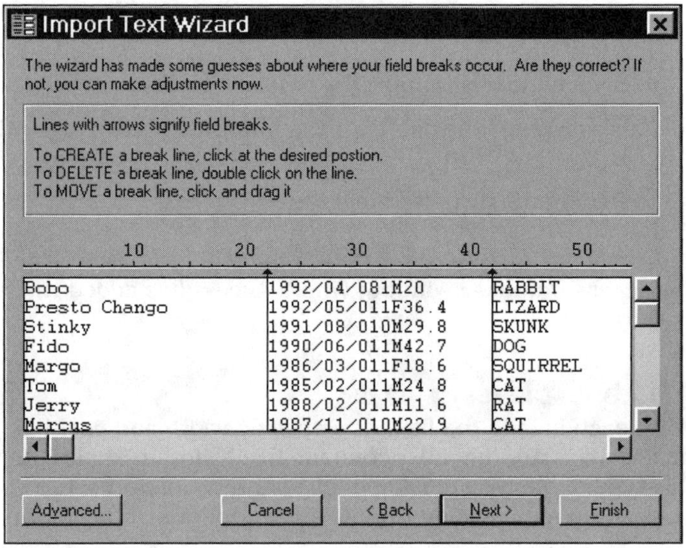

Figure 24-17: Selecting the export function.

As you can see in Figure 24-17, you can drag a field break line, add one, or delete one to tell Access where the fields really are. You continue to graphically move through the data and specify the field lengths graphically.

As you do so, you're completing an internal data table known as Import/Export Specifications.

Figure 24-18 shows the Import Specification screen. If you click on the Advanced button in the Import Text Wizard, the Import Specification screen appears. If you know the specifics about your file, you can type them rather than use the graphical tools. After you complete the information, you simply click on the OK button to leave the window. Any changes made there will be reflected in the Import Text Wizard window when you return.

Although you can manually type the specifications for the file, in this example click on the OK button to return to the Wizard.

5. After you return to the Wizard, press the Next> button to move to the next screen.

This screen lets you determine whether the records should be added to a new table or an existing one.

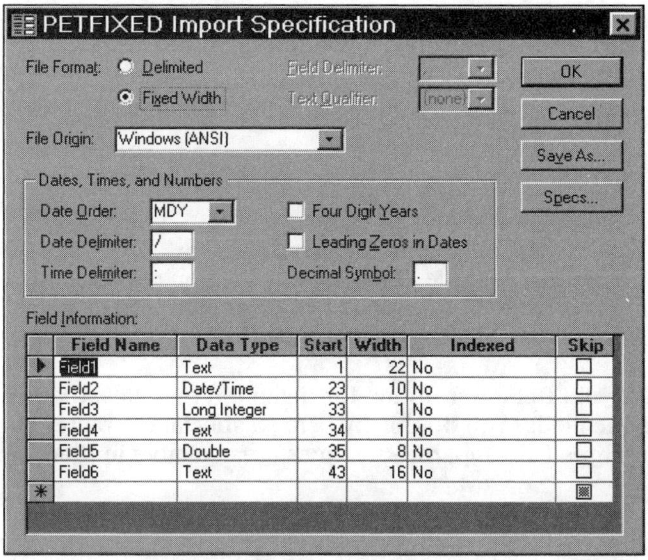

Figure 24-18: The Import Specification screen for fixed-width text files.

6. Click on the Next> button again to move to the next screen.

This screen lets you specify the field names and any indexes for the fields. You can type in fields for each one: Pet Name, Date of Birth, Neutered/Spayed, Gender, Length, and Pet Type. To move from field to field, click on the field heading or the field contents.

7. Click on the Next> button to move to the next screen.

This screen lets you specify a primary key. Click on No Primary Key.

8. Click on the Next> button.

This step takes you to the last screen. Again, you can name your file and then click on the Finish button to save the file to your database.

Using the Import Specification window

Before Access 97, you had to specify the import/export specifications manually, specifying field lengths, delimited or fixed text, type of delimiter, how to export date fields, and so on. Although you can still specify this information by using the Import Specification window, it is easier to use the graphical tools in Access 97.

If you use the specification's window (shown in Figure 24-18), you can change or set all the options on one screen, which can be helpful.

One advantage of using this screen is the ability to specify the type of file to be imported from or exported to — specifically, a Windows text file or a DOS or OS/2 text file. Access offers three pull-down choices:

✦ Windows (ANSI)

✦ DOS or OS/2 (PC-8)

✦ Macintosh

The default value is the Windows text file. If the type of file you're importing is a DOS or OS/2 text file, you select the DOS or OS/2 (PC-8) choice. You can also import a file from a Macintosh by selecting this option.

You can also specify the F̲ield Delimiter option for delimited text files; the delimiter is used to separate the fields. You do this by using a special character such as a comma or semicolon. Three field-separator choices are available in this combo box:

;	Semicolon
{tab}	Tabulation mark
{space}	Single space
,	Comma

When working with delimited files, you can also specify your own field separator directly in this combo box.

Also, when working with delimited files, you can specify the Text Qualifier. It specifies the type of delimiter to be used when you're working with Text-type fields. Normally, the text fields in a delimited file are enclosed by specified delimiters (such as quotation marks). This is useful for specifying Number-type data (such as Social Security numbers) as Text type rather than Number type (it won't be used in a calculation). You have three list box choices:

{none}	No delimiter
"	Double quotation mark
'	Single quotation mark

The default value is a double quotation mark. This list box is actually a combo box; you can enter your own delimiter. If the one you want is not among these three choices, you can specify a different text delimiter by entering a new one directly in the combo box — for example, the caret symbol (^).

Tip   If you use CSV files, you should set the text qualifier to the double quotation mark (") and the field delimiter to a comma (,).

Caution If you specify your own delimiter, it must be the same on both sides of the text. For example, you can't use both of the curly braces ({ }) as user-specified delimiters; you can specify only one character. If you specify the left curly brace, Access looks for only the left curly brace as a delimiter — on both sides of the text:

{This is Text data enclosed in braces{

Notice that only the left brace is used.

When Access 97 imports or exports data, it converts dates to a specific format (such as MMDDYY). In the example MMDDYY, Access converts all dates to two digits for each portion of the date (month, day, and year), separating each by a specified delimiter. Thus, January 19, 1995 would be converted to 1/19/95. You can specify how date fields are to be converted, using one of six choices in the Date Order combo box:

✦ DMY

✦ DYM

✦ MDY

✦ MYD

✦ YDM

✦ YMD

These choices specify the order for each portion of a date. The *D* is the day of the month (1-31), *M* is the calendar month (1-12), and *Y* is the year. The default date order is set to the American format of month, day, and year. When you work with European dates, the order must be changed to day, month, and year.

You use the Date Delimiter option to specify the date delimiter. This option tells Access which type of delimiter to use between the parts of date fields. The default is a forward slash (/), but this can be changed to any user-specified delimiter. In Europe, for example, date parts are separated by periods, as in 22.10.95.

Caution When you import text files with Date-type data, you must have a separator between the month, day, and year or else Access reports an error if the field is specified as a Date/Time type. When you're exporting date fields, the separator is not needed.

With the Time Delimiter option, you can specify a separator between the segments of time values in a text file. The default value is the colon (:). In the example 12:55, the colon separates the hours from the minutes. To change the separator, simply enter another in the Time Delimiter box.

You use the Four Digit <u>Y</u>ears check box when you want to specify that the year value in date fields will be formatted with four digits. By checking this box, you can export dates that include the century (such as in 1881 or 1993). The default is to exclude the century (such as when a year is expressed as 93).

The Leading <u>Z</u>eros in Dates option is a check box where you specify that date values include leading zeros. You can specify, for example, that date formats include leading zeros (as in 02/04/93). To specify leading zeros, check this box. The default is without leading zeros (as in 2/4/93).

Importing HTML tables

NEW
FEATURE
Access 97 lets you import HTML tables as easily as any other database, Excel spreadsheet, or text file. You simply select the HTML file you want to import and use the HTML Import Wizard.

Modifying imported table elements

After you import a file, you can refine the table in Design view. The following list itemizes and discusses some of the primary changes you may want to make to improve your table:

✦ *Add field names or descriptions.* You may want to change the names of the fields you specified when you imported the file. For example, *x*BASE databases allow no more than ten characters in names.

✦ *Change data types.* Access may have guessed the wrong data type when it imported several of the fields. You can change these fields to reflect a more descriptive data type (such as Currency rather than Number, or Text rather than Number).

✦ *Set field properties.* You can set field properties to enhance the way your tables work. For example, you may want to specify a format or default value for the table.

✦ *Set the field size to something more realistic than the 255 bytes Access allocates for each imported text field.*

✦ *Define a primary key.* Access works best with tables that have a primary key. You may want to set a primary key for the imported table.

Troubleshooting import errors

When you import an external file, Access may not be able to import one or more records, in which case it reports an error when it tries to import them. When Access encounters errors, it creates an Access table named Import Errors (with the user's name linked to the table name). The Import Errors table contains one record for each record that causes an error.

After errors have occurred and Access has created the Import Errors table, you can open the table to view the error descriptions.

Import errors for new tables

Access may not be able to import records into a new table for the following reasons:

✦ A row in a text file or spreadsheet may contain more fields than are present in the first row.

✦ Data in the field cannot be stored in the data type Access chose for the field.

✦ On the basis of the first row's contents, Access automatically chose the incorrect data type for a field. The first row is OK, but the remaining rows are blank.

Import errors for existing tables

Access may not be able to append records into an existing table for the following reasons:

✦ The data is not consistent between the text file and the existing Access table.

✦ Numeric data being entered is too large for the field size of the Access table.

✦ A row in a text file or spreadsheet may contain more fields than the Access table.

✦ The records being imported have duplicate primary key values.

The Import Errors table

When errors occur, Access creates an Import Errors table you can use to determine which data caused the errors.

Open the Import Errors table and try to determine why Access couldn't import all the records. If the problem is with the external data, edit it. If you're appending records to an existing table, the problem may be with the existing table; it may need modifications (such as changing the data types and rearranging the field locations). After you solve the problem, erase the Import Errors file and import the data again.

Note Access attempts to import all records that do not cause an error. If you reimport the data, you may need to clean up the external table or the Access table before reimporting. If you don't, you may have duplicate data in your table.

Tip If importing a text file seems to take an unexpectedly long time, it may be because of too many errors. You can cancel importing by pressing Ctrl+Break.

Exporting to External Formats

You can copy data from an Access table or query into a new external file. This process of copying Access tables to an external file is called *exporting*. You can export tables to several different sources:

- ♦ Microsoft Access (other unopened databases)
- ♦ Delimited text files (fields separated by a delimiter)
- ♦ Fixed-width text files (specific widths for each field)
- ♦ Microsoft Excel (all versions)
- ♦ Lotus 1-2-3 and 1-2-3 for Windows (versions WKS, WK1, and WK3)
- ♦ Paradox 3.x, 4.x, and 5.0.
- ♦ FoxPro 2.*x* and Visual FoxPro 3.0
- ♦ dBASE III, dBASE IV, and dBASE 5
- ♦ Rich text formats (RTF)
- ♦ Word Mail Merge (.txt)
- ♦ ODBC Data Sources SQL databases (Microsoft SQL Server, Sybase Server, and Oracle Server)
- ♦ HTML document (as text HTML 1.1 or as tables HTML 2.0 or 3.0)

When Access exports data from an Access table to an external file, the Access table isn't erased or destroyed. This means that you will have two copies of the data: the original Access file and the external data file.

Exporting objects to other Access databases

You can export objects from the current database to another, unopened Access database. The objects you export can be tables, queries, forms, reports, macros, or modules. To export an object to another Access database, follow these steps:

1. Open the database that has the object you want to export and select File⇨Save As/Export from the Database menu.

2. In the Export dialog box, select To an external file or database and click on OK.

   Access opens the standard Save As dialog box — the same one that appears whenever you save an object to another name. The difference is that you can specify a different format (Save as type). When you open the combo box, a list of formats appears. Select the one you want; Access will save the data to that format.

When this process is complete, Access copies to the other database the object you specified and immediately returns you to the Database window in Access.

Caution   If you attempt to export an object to another Access database that has an object of the same type and name, Access warns you before copying. You then have the option to cancel or overwrite.

Exporting objects to other databases or to Excel, HTML, or text files

You can also export objects to databases (such as ODBC, dBASE, Paradox, and FoxPro) and text files (delimited and fixed width). To export any of these objects, simply follow these general steps:

1. Select File⇨Save As/Export... from the Database menu.

2. Select to an External file or database from the selection box and click on the OK button.

3. Select the type of file you want the object to be saved to and specify a name.

4. Click on the Export button.

To export any objects to Internet resources (HTML documents, IDC/HTX Internet Information Server files, or ActiveX Server), you follow these general steps:

1. Select File⇨Save to HTML/Web Formats from the Database menu.

2. Select the type of format you want to save to (Publish, HTML, IDX/HTX, or ActiveX Server).

3. Access will save the file in the format you specify.

Note   If you save a table to an HTML table, Access 97 will create the HTML document and then start your browser to show you the form it created.

Summary

This chapter explored the use of data from other types of files. You worked with data from database, spreadsheet, and text-based files. This chapter covered the following points:

✦ Access can work with various types of external data, including spreadsheets, PC-based databases, SQL Server tables, HTML and IDC/HTX documents, and text files.

✦ Access can link to other Access tables, *x*BASE (dBASE and FoxPro) databases, Paradox tables, and SQL Server tables. When you link to these tables through Access, you can view and edit the files in their native formats. You can also link to Excel spreadsheets, HTML documents, and text files. If you link to an HTML or text file, you can only view the records.

✦ You should always split your Access application into two databases: one with tables and one with all the other objects. You then link the tables from the second database to the first (the one that has only the tables). This approach makes multiuser systems more efficient.

✦ You can use linked tables for queries, forms, and reports. You can set relations between linked tables and Access tables. You can even rename a linked table for better clarity.

✦ When you're working with text files (delimited and fixed width), you have extensive flexibility for importing and exporting them by using the import/-export specifications setup file.

✦ When you create an import/export setup file, you can set several options, such as a specific delimiter, the format of date fields, and so on.

✦ You can import data from other Access objects, dBASE databases, FoxPro databases, Paradox tables, SQL Server tables, Excel spreadsheets, Lotus 1-2-3 spreadsheets, HTML documents, and text files. All these file types can be imported to new tables.

✦ Spreadsheets and text files can also be appended to existing Access tables.

✦ You can export Access table data to several different external files: dBASE databases, FoxPro databases, Paradox tables, SQL Server tables, Excel spreadsheets, Lotus 1-2-3 spreadsheets, HTML documents, ActiveX Server, IDC/HTX resources, and text files.

In the next chapter, you examine advanced select queries.

✦   ✦   ✦

Advanced Select Queries

In this chapter, you work with advanced select queries. So
far, you have worked with relatively simple select queries,
in which you selected specific records from one or more tables
based on some criteria. This chapter shows you queries that
display totals, create cross tabulations, and obtain criteria
from the user at run time.

Your queries have specified criteria for single or multiple
fields (including calculated fields) using multiple tables. You
also have worked with wildcard characters and fields not
having a value (Is Null). You are already accustomed to using
functions in queries to specify record criteria or to create calculated fields. Finally, you've realized that Access queries are
a great tool for performing ad hoc "what-ifs."

This chapter focuses on three specialized types of advanced
select queries:

✦ Total

✦ Crosstab

✦ Parameter

Using these queries, you can calculate totals for records,
summarize data in row-and-column format, and run a query
that obtains criteria by prompting the operator of the query.

Creating Queries That Calculate Totals

Many times, you want to find information in your tables
based on total-type data. For example, you may want to find
the total number of animals you've treated or the total

amount of money each customer spent on animals last year. Access supplies the tools to accomplish these queries without the need for programming.

Access performs calculation totals by using nine aggregate functions that let you determine a specific value based on the contents of a field. For example, you can determine the average weight of all cats, the maximum and minimum length of all animals you have treated, or the total count of all records in which the type of animal is either a duck or a fish. Performing each of these examples as a query results in a dynaset of answer fields based on the mathematical calculations you requested.

To create a total query, you use a new row in the QBE pane — the Total: row.

Displaying the Total: row in the QBE pane

To create a query that performs a total calculation, you create a select query and then activate the Total: row of the QBE pane. You can activate the Total: row by using either of the following two selection methods (first, open a new query using the Pets table):

✦ Select View⇨Totals from the Design menu.

✦ Select the Totals button (the Greek sigma symbol button, Σ, which is to the right of the midway mark) on the toolbar.

Figure 25-1 shows the Total: row after it is added in the QBE pane. Notice that the Totals button is selected on the toolbar and the Total: row is placed in the QBE pane between the Table: and Sort: rows.

Note   If the toolbar is not visible, select View⇨Toolbars... from the Query menu. Then select Query Design and close the dialog box.

If the Table: row is not present on your screen, the Total: row will be between the Field: and Sort: rows. You can activate the Table: row by selecting View⇨Table Names from the Design menu.

Removing the Total: row from the QBE pane

To deactivate the Total: row in the QBE pane, simply reselect either activation method (with the Totals button or the menu choice). The Totals button is a toggle that alternately turns the Total: row on and off.

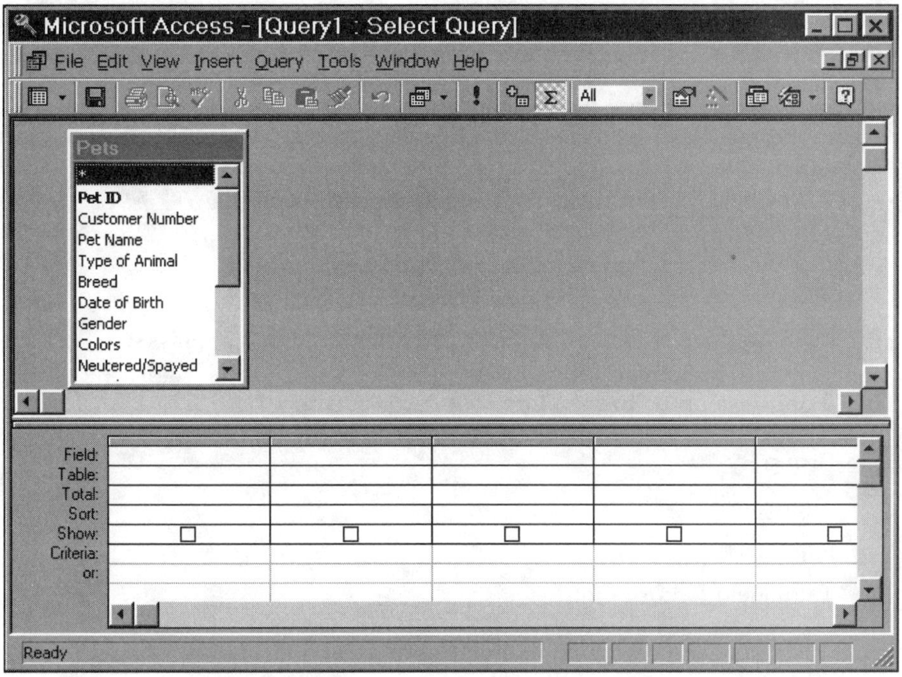

Figure 25-1: Activating the Total: row of the QBE pane.

The Total: row options

You can perform total calculations against all records or groups of records in one or more tables. To perform a calculation, you must select one of the options from the drop-down list box in the Total: row for every field you include in the query, including any hidden fields (with the Show: option turned off). Figure 25-2 shows the drop-down list box active in the Total: row of the field Pet ID.

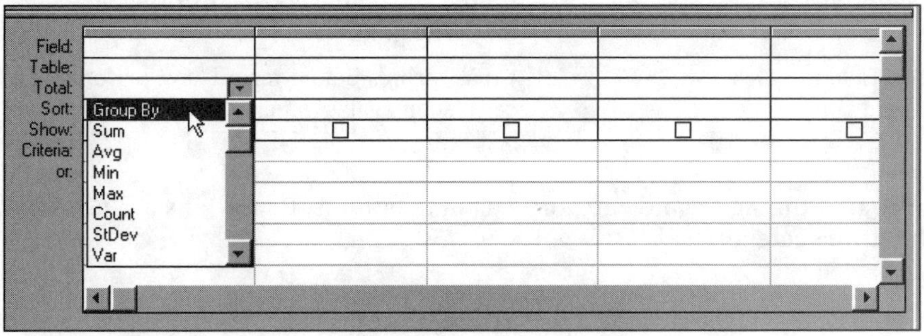

Figure 25-2: The drop-down list box of the Total: row.

What is an aggregate function?

The word *aggregate* implies gathering together a mass (a group or series) of things and working on this mass as a whole — a total. Therefore, an *aggregate function* is a function that takes a group of records and performs some mathematical function against the entire group. The function can be a simple *count* or a complex *expression* you specify, based on a series of mathematical functions.

Although you see only eight options in Figure 25-2, you can choose from 12. You can view the remaining options by using the elevator on the right side of the box. The 12 options can be broken into four distinct categories:

✦ Group By

✦ Aggregate

✦ Expression

✦ Total Field Record Limit

Table 25-1 lists each category, its number of Total options, and its purpose.

Table 25-1
Four Categories of Total Options

Category	Number of Options	Purpose of Operator
Group By	1	Groups common records together against which Access performs aggregate calculations
Aggregate	9	Specifies a mathematical or selection operation to perform against a field
Expression	1	Groups several total operators together and performs the group totals
Total Field Record Limit	1	Limits records before record limit performing a total calculation against a field

Notice that the Aggregate category has nine options. Its options are used by the other three categories.

Group By category

This category has one option, the Group By option. You use this option to specify that a certain field in the QBE pane will be used as a grouping field. For example, if you select the field Type of Animal, the Group By option tells Access to group all cat records together, all dog records together, and so on. This option is the default for all Total: cells; when you drag a field to the QBE pane, Access automatically selects this option. Figure 25-2 shows that this is also the first choice in the drop-down list box. These groups of records will be used for performing some aggregate calculation against another field in the query. This subject will be discussed in more detail later in this chapter.

Expression category

Like the Group By category, the Expression category has only one option: Expression. This is the second-from-last choice in the drop-down list box. You use this option to tell Access that you will create a calculated field by using one or more aggregate calculations in the Field: cell of the QBE pane. For example, you may want to create a query that shows each customer and how much money the customer saved, based on the individual's discount rate. This query requires creating a calculated field that uses a sum aggregate against the Total Amount field in the Visits table, which is then multiplied by the Discount field in the Customer table. This type of calculation is discussed in detail later.

Total Field Record Limit category

The Total Field Record Limit category is the third category that has a single option: the Where option. This option is the last choice in the drop-down list box. When you select this option, you tell Access that you want to specify limiting criteria against an aggregate type field, as opposed to a Group By or an Expression field. The limiting criteria will be performed *before* the aggregate options are executed. For example, you may want to create a query that will count all pets by types of animals that weigh less than 100 pounds. Because the Weight field is not to be used for a grouping (as is Type of Animal) and won't be used to perform an aggregate calculation, you specify the Where option. By specifying the Where option, you are telling Access to use this field only as a limiting criteria field — before it performs the aggregate calculation (counting types of animals). This type of operation is also discussed in detail later in this chapter.

Aggregate category

The Aggregate category, unlike the others, has nine options: Sum, Avg, Min, Max, Count, StDev, Var, First, and Last. These options appear as the second through tenth options in the drop-down list box. Each of these options performs some operation. Seven of the options perform mathematical operations, whereas two perform simple selection operations. When each option is executed, it finds (calculates or determines) some answer or value and supplies it to a cell in the resulting dynaset. For example, you may want to determine the maximum (Max) and minimum (Min) weight of each animal in the Type of Animal field in the Pets table.

On the other hand, you may want the total number (Count) of animals in the Pets table. You use these aggregate options to solve these types of queries.

Options such as these are what most people think about when they hear the words *total query*. Each of the options performs a calculation against a field in the QBE pane of the query and returns a single answer in the dynaset. As an example, there can only be one maximum weight for all the animals. Several animals may have the same maximum weight, but only one weight is the heaviest.

The other three categories of options can be used against any type of Access field (Text, Memo, or Yes/No, for example). However, some of the aggregate options can be performed against only specific field types. For example, you cannot perform a Sum option against Text type data, and you cannot use a Max option against an OLE object.

Table 25-2 lists each option, what it does, and which field types you can use with the option.

Table 25-2
Aggregate Options of the Total: Row

Option	Finds	Field Type Support
Count	Number of non-Null values in a field	AutoNumber, Number, Currency, Date/Time, Yes/No, Text, Memo, OLE object
Sum	Total of values in a field	AutoNumber, Number, Currency, Date/Time, Yes/No
Avg	Average of values in a field	AutoNumber, Number, Currency, Date/Time, Yes/No
Max	Highest value in a field	AutoNumber, Number, Currency, Date/Time, Yes/No, Text
Min	Lowest value in a field	AutoNumber, Number, Currency, Date/Time, Yes/No, Text
StDev	Standard deviation of values in a field	AutoNumber, Number, Currency, Date/Time, Yes/No
Var	Population variance of values in a field	AutoNumber, Number, Currency, Date/Time, Yes/No
First	Field value from the *first* record in a number, table, or query	AutoNumber, Currency, Date/Time, Yes/No, Text, Memo, OLE object
Last	Field value from the *last* record in a number, table, or query	AutoNumber, Currency, Date/Time, Yes/No, Text, Memo, OLE object

Performing totals on all records

You can use total queries to perform calculations against all records in a table or query. For example, you can find the total number of animals in the Pets table, the average weight, and the maximum weight of the animals. To create this query, follow these steps:

1. Select the Pets table.

2. Click on the Totals button on the toolbar to turn it on.

3. Double-click on the Pet ID field in the Pets table.

4. Double-click on the Weight field in the Pets table.

5. Double-click on the Weight field in the Pets table again.

6. In the Total: cell of Pet ID, select Count.

7. In the Total: cell of Weight, select Avg.

8. In the second Total: cell of Weight, select Max.

Your query should look similar to Figure 25-3.

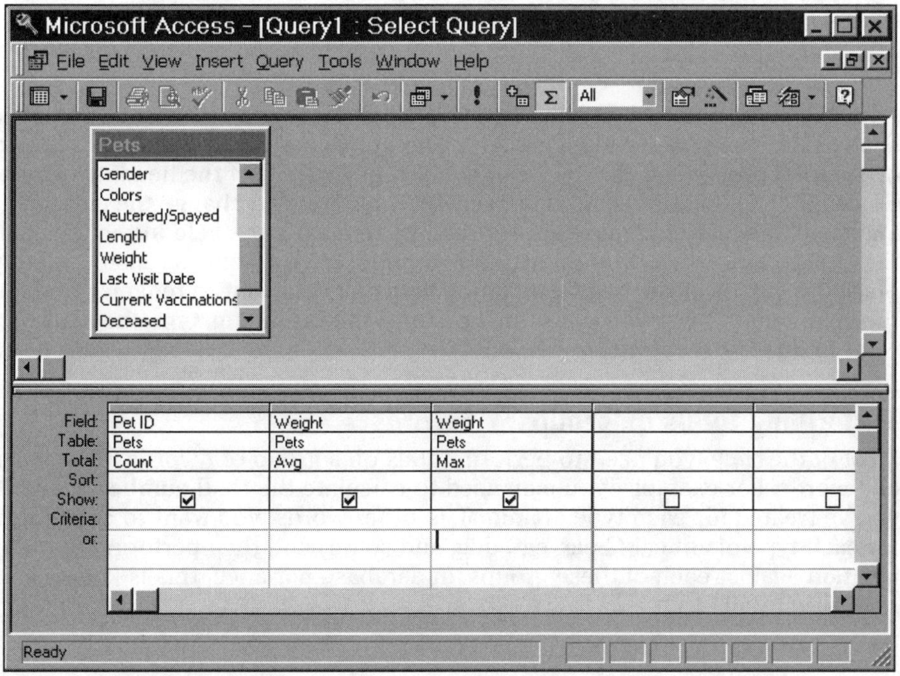

Figure 25-3: A query against all records in the Pets table.

This query calculates the total number of pet records in the Pets table as well as the average weight of all animals and the heaviest weight of all the animals.

Caution The Count option of the Total: cell can be performed against any field in the table (or query). However, Count will eliminate any records that have a Null value in the field you select. Therefore, you may want to select the primary key field on which to perform the Count total because this field cannot have any Null values, thus ensuring an accurate record count.

If you select the Datasheet button on the toolbar, you should see a query similar to Figure 25-4. Notice that the dynaset has only one record. When performing calculations against *all records* in a table or query, the resulting dynaset will have only *one* record.

Figure 25-4: This datasheet of a dynaset was created from a total query against all records in a table.

Note Access creates a default column heading for all total fields in a totals datasheet, such as the one you see in Figure 25-4. The heading name is a product of the name of the total option and the field name. Thus, in Figure 25-4 the heading names are CountOfPet ID, AvgOfWeight, and MaxOfWeight. You can change the column heading name to something more appropriate by renaming the field in the QBE pane of the Design window. As you do with any other field you want to rename, simply place the cursor at the beginning of the field cell you want to rename (to the left of the field name). After you place the cursor at the beginning, type the name you want to display, followed by a colon.

Performing totals on groups of records

Most of the time, you need to perform totals on a group of records rather than on all records. For example, you may need to calculate the total number of animals you've treated for each type of animal. In other words, you want to create a group for each type of animal (bear, cat, dog, and so on) and then perform the total calculation against each of these groups. In database parlance, this is known as *control break* totaling.

Calculating totals for a single group

When you create your query, you specify which field or fields to use for grouping the totals and which fields to perform the totals against. Using the preceding example, to group the Type of Animal field, you select the Group By option of the Total: cell. Follow these steps to create the query:

1. Open a new query and select the Pets table.

2. Click on the Totals button (the Σ) on the toolbar to turn it on.

3. Double-click on the Type of Animal field in the Pets table.

4. Double-click on the Pet ID field in the Pets table.

5. In the Total: cell of Type of Animal, select Group By.

6. In the Total: cell of Pet ID, select Count.

The query in Figure 25-5 groups all like animals together and then performs the count total for each type of animal. Unlike performing totals against all records, this query produces a dynaset of many records — one record for each type of animal. Figure 25-6 demonstrates how the datasheet looks if you select the Datasheet button on the toolbar.

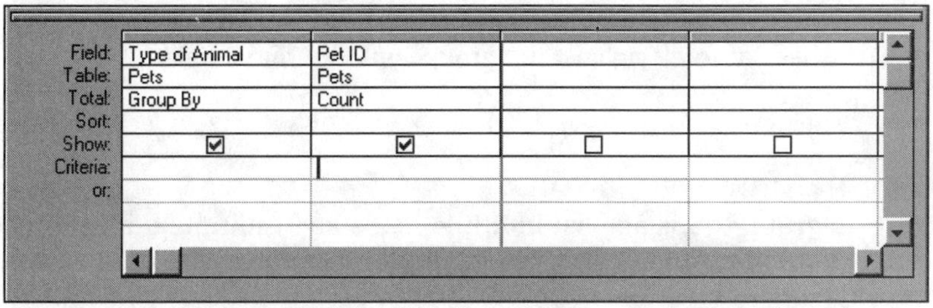

Figure 25-5: Totals against a group of records.

The dynaset in Figure 25-6 has a single record for each type of animal. Notice that the count was performed against each type of animal; there are 3 bears, 14 birds, and so on. Also notice that the Group By field displays one record for each unique value in that field. The Type of Animal field is specified as the Group By field and displays a single record for each type of animal, showing Bear, Bird, Cat, Dog, and so on. Each of these records is shown as a row heading for the datasheet, indicating a unique record for each type of animal specified that begins with the Group By field content (bear, bird, and so on). In this case, each unique record is easy to identify by the single-field row heading under Type of Animal.

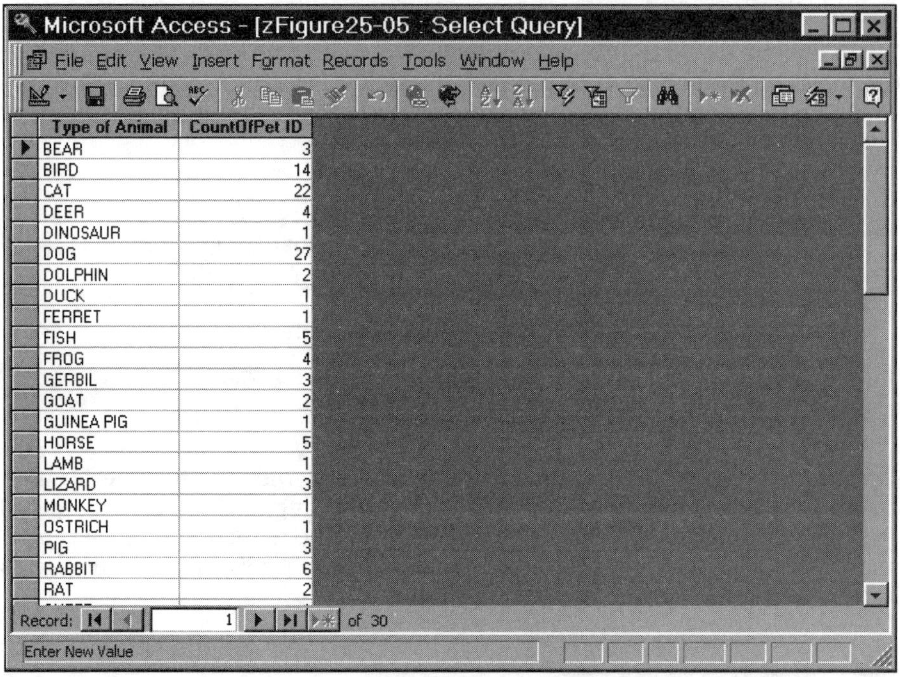

Figure 25-6: Datasheet of totals against the group Type of Animal field.

Calculating totals for several groups

You can perform group totals against multiple fields and multiple tables as easily as with a single field in a single table. For example, you may want to group by both customer and type of animal to determine the number of animals each customer owns by animal type. To create a total query for this example, you specify **Group By** in both Total: fields (Customer Name and Type of Animal).

This query, shown in Figure 25-7, uses two tables and also groups by two fields to perform the count total. First, the query groups by Customer Name and then by Type of Animal. When you select the Datasheet button on the toolbar, you see a datasheet similar to the one shown in Figure 25-8.

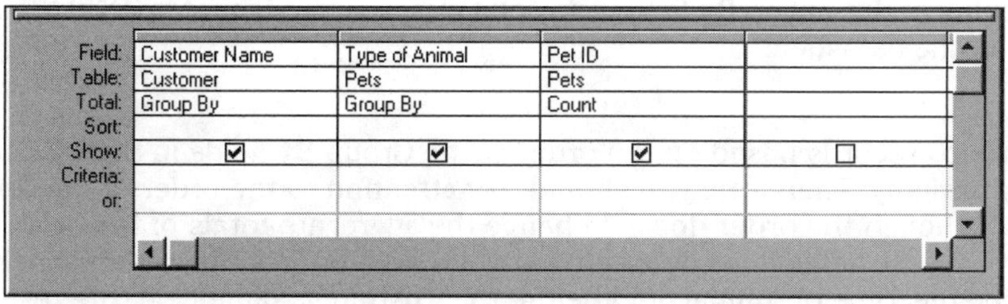

Figure 25-7: A multiple-table, multiple-field Group By total query.

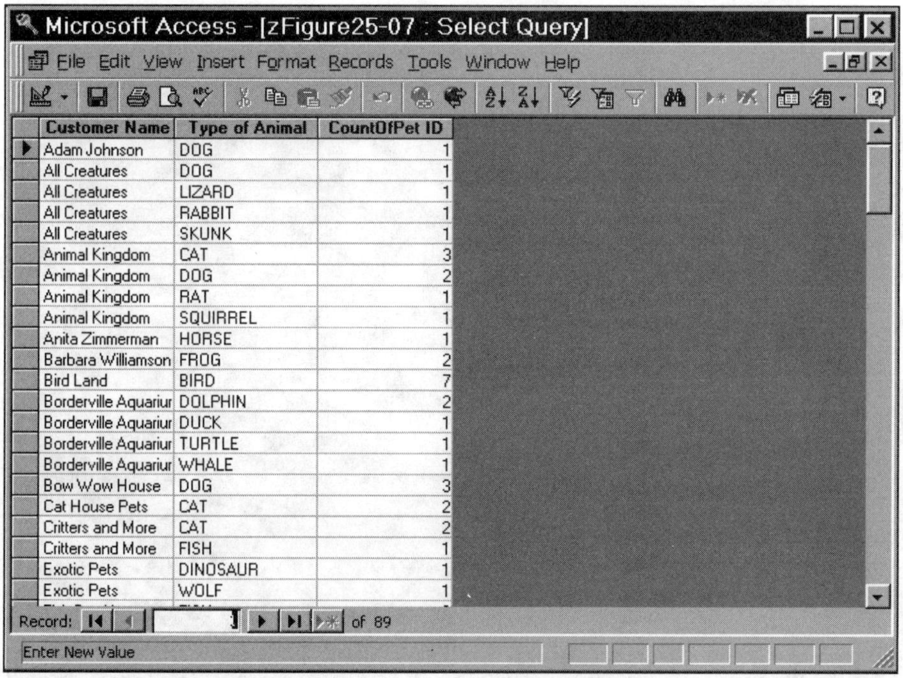

Figure 25-8: Datasheet of a multiple-field Group By query.

The datasheet in Figure 25-8 shows several records for the customer Animal Kingdom. This customer has three cats, two dogs, one rat, and one squirrel. This datasheet has a unique record based on two Group By fields: Customer Name and Type of Animal. Therefore, the unique row headings for this datasheet are created by combining both fields — first the Customer Name and then the Type of Animal.

Note You can think of the Group By fields in a total query as fields that specify the row headings of the datasheet.

Tip Access groups records based on the order of the Group By fields in the QBE pane (from left to right). Therefore, you should pay attention to the order of the Group By fields. Although the order doesn't change the aggregate totals of the fields, the order of Group By fields does determine how you see the results in the datasheet. If you place the Type of Animal field before the Customer Name field, the resulting datasheet shows the records in order by animal first and then customer. Figure 25-9 demonstrates this setup, showing the bear records and their owners (with the total number) and then the bird records and their owners, and so on.

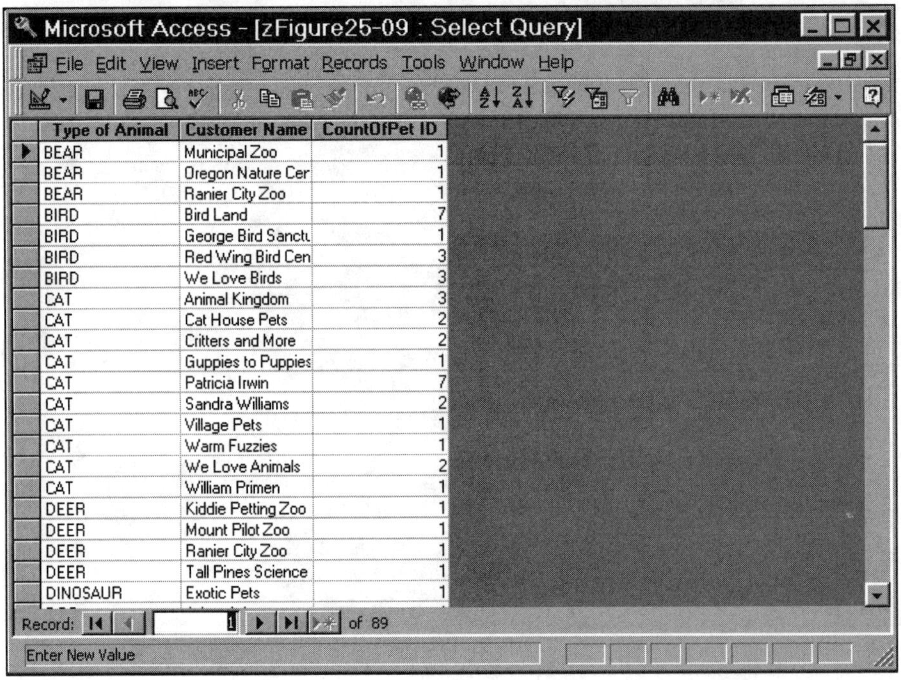

Figure 25-9: Changing the order of Group By fields.

By changing the order of the Group By fields in a totals query, you can look at your data in new and creative ways.

Specifying criteria for a total query

Besides grouping records for total queries, you can also specify criteria to limit the records that will be processed or displayed in a total calculation. When you're specifying record criteria in total queries, several options are available to you. You can create a criterion against any of these three fields:

✦ Group By

✦ Aggregate Total

✦ Non-Aggregate Total

Using any one or all three of these criteria types, you can easily limit the scope of your total query to finite criteria.

Specifying criteria for a Group By field

To limit the scope of records that will be used in a grouping, you specify criteria in the Group By fields. For example, you may want to calculate the average length and weight of only three animals — bears, deer, and wolves. Doing so requires specifying criteria on the Group By field Type of Animal. This type of query looks like Figure 25-10.

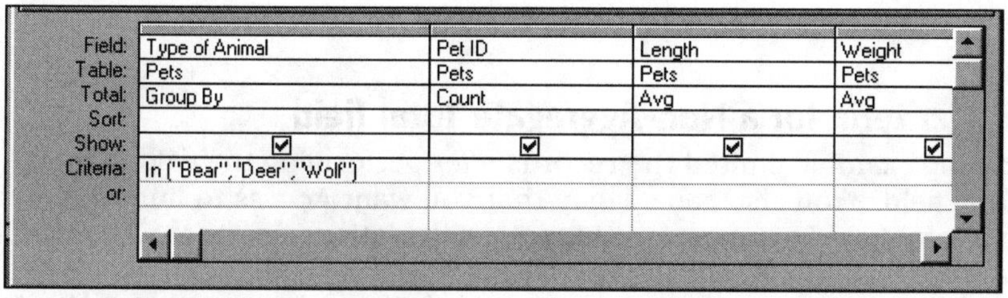

Field:	Type of Animal	Pet ID	Length	Weight
Table:	Pets	Pets	Pets	Pets
Total:	Group By	Count	Avg	Avg
Sort:				
Show:	☑	☑	☑	☑
Criteria:	In ("Bear","Deer","Wolf")			
or:				

Figure 25-10: Specifying criteria in a Group By field.

By specifying criteria in the Group By field, only those records that meet the Group By criteria will have the aggregate calculations performed. In this example, the count, average length, and average weight will be performed only for animals that are bears, deer, and wolves. This results in a three-record dynaset, with one for each animal.

Specifying criteria for an Aggregate Total field

At times you will want a query to calculate aggregate totals first and then display only those totals from the aggregate calculations that meet a specified criterion. In other words, you want Access to determine all totals for each Group By field and then take the totals field and perform the criteria against the totals before creating the resulting dynaset.

For example, you may want a query to find the average length of all animals, grouped by type of animal, where the average length of any animal is greater than 20 inches. This query should look like Figure 25-11. Notice that the criterion >20 is placed in the Aggregate Total field, Length. This query calculates the average length of all animals grouped by type of animal. Then the query determines whether the calculated totals for each record are greater than 20. Records greater than 20 are added to the resulting dynaset, and records less than or equal to 20 are discarded. Note that the criterion is performed *after* the aggregate calculations are performed.

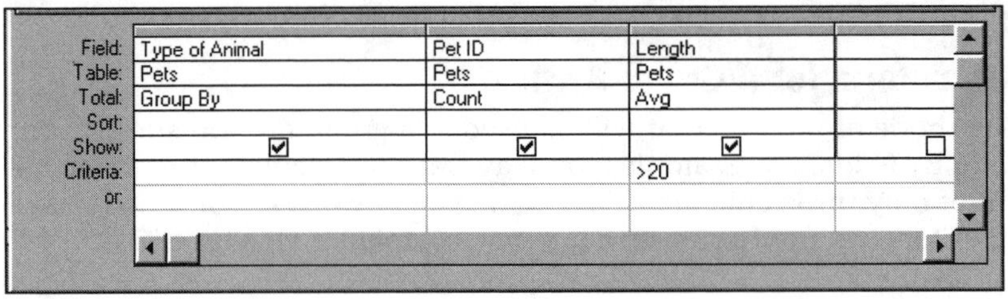

Field:	Type of Animal	Pet ID	Length	
Table:	Pets	Pets	Pets	
Total:	Group By	Count	Avg	
Sort:				
Show:	☑	☑	☑	☐
Criteria:			>20	
or:				

Figure 25-11: A query with a criterion set against an Aggregate Total field.

Specifying criteria for a Non-Aggregate Total field

The preceding example limited the records *after* performing the calculations against total fields. You also can specify that you want Access to limit the records based on a total field *before* performing total calculations. In other words, limit the range of records against which the calculation is performed. Doing so creates a criterion similar to the first type of criteria; the field you want to set a criterion against is not a Group By field.

For example, you may want to display the total amount of money charged for each animal during the first half of 1995 after February 9. You want to use the Visit Date field to specify criteria, but you don't want to perform any calculations against this field or to use it to group by. In fact, you don't even want to show the field in the resulting datasheet.

Figure 25-12 shows how the query should look. Notice that Access automatically turned off the Show: cell in the Visit Date field.

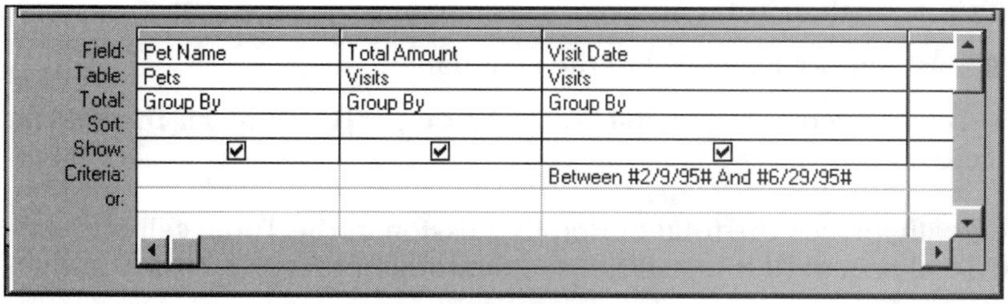

Field:	Pet Name	Total Amount	Visit Date	
Table:	Pets	Visits	Visits	
Total:	Group By	Group By	Group By	
Sort:				
Show:	☑	☑	☑	
Criteria:			Between #2/9/95# And #6/29/95#	
or:				

Figure 25-12: Specifying criteria for a Non-Aggregate field.

Note   Access automatically turns off the Show: cell whenever it encounters a Where option in the Total: cell of a field. Access understands that you are using the field only to specify criteria so you don't want to see the actual field value displayed for the criteria field.

In the query you just completed, Access displays only those records for pets that have visited the hospital from February 9 to June 29, 1995. All other records are discarded.

Caution   When you specify a Where option in a Total: cell, you cannot show the field. The reason is that Access uses the field to evaluate the Where criteria before performing the calculation. Therefore, the contents are useful only for the limiting criteria. If you try to turn on the Show: cell, Access will display an error message.

Creating expressions for totals

Besides choosing one of the Access totals from the drop-down list box, you can also create your own total expression. You can base your total expression on several types of totals in an expression, such as when you use Avg and Sum or multiple Sums together. Or you can base your expression on a calculated field composed of several functions — or a calculated field based on several fields from different tables. Suppose that you want a query that shows the total amount of money each customer owed before discount. Then you want to see the amount of money these customers saved based on their discount. You want the information to be grouped by customer. Follow these steps to create this query:

1. Start a new query and select the Customer, Pets, and Visits tables.

2. Click on the Totals button (the Σ) on the toolbar to turn it on.

3. Double-click on the Customer Name field in the Customer table.

4. Double-click on the Total Amount field in the Visits table.

5. In the Total: cell of Customer Name, select Group By.

6. In the Total: cell of Total Amount, select Sum.

7. Click on an empty Field: cell in the QBE pane.

8. Type **Total Saved:Sum([Visits].[Total Amount]*[Customer].[Discount])** in the cell.

Access generally places the total option Expression in the Total: cell of the calculated field Total Saved: (if it doesn't, place the total option Expression in the Total: cell).

Note Your query should be similar to Figure 25-13. Notice that the query uses two fields from different tables to create the Total Saved: calculated field. You had to specify both the table and the field name for each field the Sum function used.

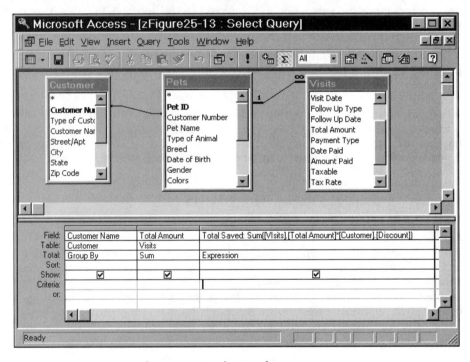

Figure 25-13: A query using an Expression total.

If you click on the Datasheet button on the toolbar, your dynaset should be similar to Figure 25-14.

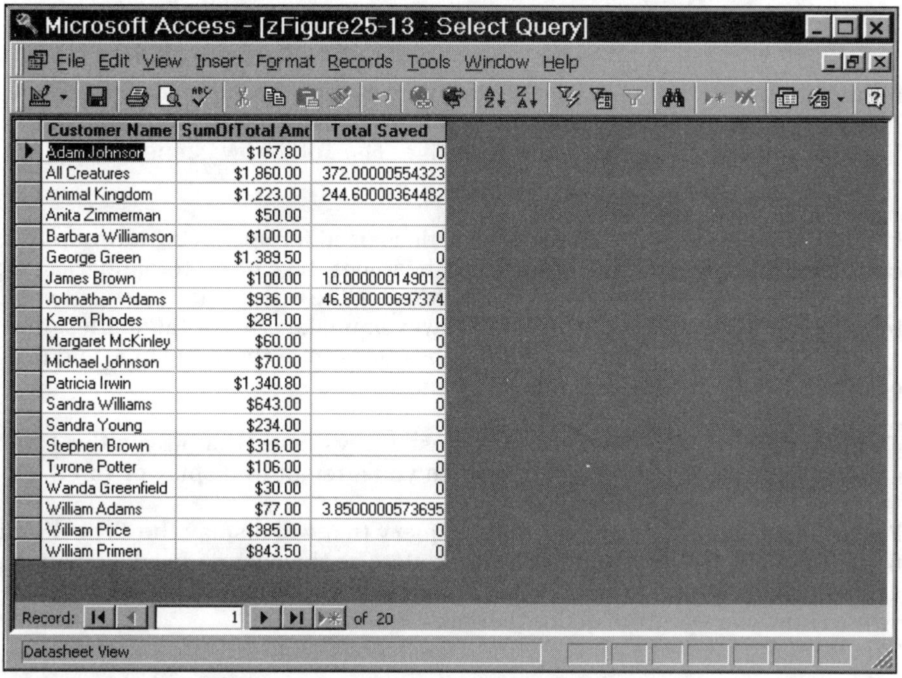

Customer Name	SumOfTotal Amo	Total Saved
Adam Johnson	$167.80	0
All Creatures	$1,860.00	372.00000554323
Animal Kingdom	$1,223.00	244.60000364482
Anita Zimmerman	$50.00	
Barbara Williamson	$100.00	0
George Green	$1,389.50	0
James Brown	$100.00	10.000000149012
Johnathan Adams	$936.00	46.800000697374
Karen Rhodes	$281.00	0
Margaret McKinley	$60.00	0
Michael Johnson	$70.00	0
Patricia Irwin	$1,340.80	0
Sandra Williams	$643.00	0
Sandra Young	$234.00	0
Stephen Brown	$316.00	0
Tyrone Potter	$106.00	0
Wanda Greenfield	$30.00	0
William Adams	$77.00	3.8500000573695
William Price	$385.00	0
William Primen	$843.50	0

Figure 25-14: A datasheet created by an Expression total.

Tip

Notice in the datasheet in Figure 25-14 that the calculated field Total Saved shows as many as 12 decimal places. You can limit the decimal places by using the Format( ) function around the Sum( ) function. To do so, add the following line to the existing criteria formula in the calculated Field: cell:

Total Saved:Format(Sum([Visits].[Total Amount]*[Customer].[Discount]), "Standard")

Creating Crosstab Queries

With Access, you can use a specialized type of total query — the crosstab — to display summarized data in a compact and readable format. A crosstab query summarizes the data in the fields from your tables and presents the resulting dynaset in a row-and-column format.

Understanding the crosstab query

Simply put, a crosstab query is a two-dimensional summary matrix that is created from your tables. This query presents summary data in a spreadsheet-like format that you create from fields you specify. In this specialized type of total query, the Total: row in the QBE pane is always active. The Total: row cannot be toggled off in a crosstab query!

In addition, the Total: row of the QBE pane is used for specifying a Group By total option for both the row and the column headings. Like other total queries, the Group By option specifies the row headings for the query datasheet and comes from the actual contents of the field. However, unlike other total queries, the crosstab query also obtains its column headings from the value in a field (table or calculated) rather than from the field names themselves.

Caution   The fields used as rows and columns must always have Group By in the Total: row. Otherwise, Access reports an error when you attempt to display or run the query.

For example, you may want to create a query that will display the Type of Animal field as the row heading and the owner's state as the column heading, with each cell containing a total for each type of animal in each state. Table 25-3 demonstrates how you want the query to look.

Table 25-3			
A Typical Crosstab Query Format			
Type of Animal	*ID*	*OR*	*WA*
Bear	0	2	1
Bird	11	0	3
Cat	4	12	6
Dog	6	7	13
Pig	0	0	3

In Table 25-3, the row headings are specified by Type of Animal: Bear, Bird, and so on. The column headings are specified by the state: ID, OR, and WA. The cell content in the intersection of any row and column is a summary of records that meets both conditions. For example, the Bear row that intersects the OR column shows that the clinic treats two bears in the state of Oregon. The Dog row that intersects with the WA column shows that the clinic treats 13 dogs in the state of Washington.

This table shows a simple crosstab query created from the fields Type of Animal and State, with the intersecting cell contents determined by a Count total on any field in the Pets table.

Creating the crosstab query

Now that you have a conceptual understanding of a crosstab query, it is time to create one. To create a crosstab query like the one described in Table 25-3, follow these steps:

1. Start a new query and select the Customer and Pets tables.
2. Double-click in the Type of Animal field in the Pets table.
3. Double-click in the State field in the Customer table.
4. Double-click in the Pet ID field in the Pets table.
5. Select Query⇨Crosstab in the Query menu or press the Query Type button on the toolbar (this step will display a drop-down list box listing the types of queries).
6. In the Crosstab: cell of Type of Animal, select Row Heading.
7. In the Crosstab: cell of State, select Column Heading.
8. In the Crosstab: cell of Pet ID, select Value.
9. In the Total: cell of Pet ID, select Count.

Your query should look similar to Figure 25-15. Notice that Access inserted a new row named Crosstab: between the Total: and Sort: rows in the QBE pane.

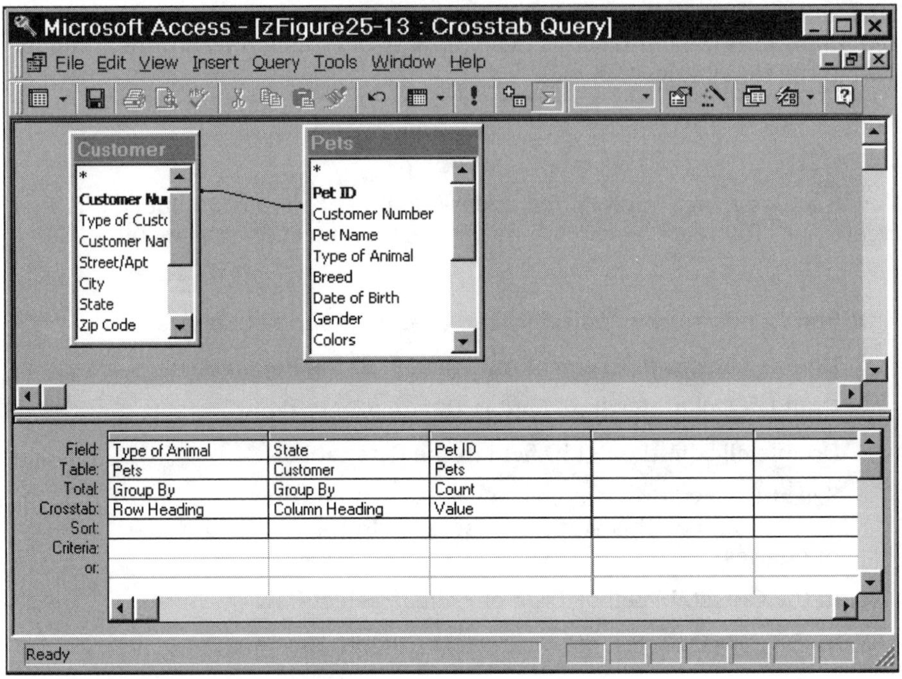

Figure 25-15: Creating a crosstab query.

As Figure 25-15 demonstrates, you *must* specify a minimum of three items for crosstab queries:

- ✦ The Row Heading field
- ✦ The Column Heading field
- ✦ The summary Value field

These three items are specified in the appropriate Crosstab: cells of the fields. After you specify the contents for the three Crosstab: cells, you specify Group By in the Total: cell of both the Row Heading and the Column Heading fields and an aggregate Total: cell operator (such as Count) for the Value field.

If you have done this procedure correctly, selecting the Datasheet button on the toolbar reveals a datasheet similar to the one shown in Figure 25-16.

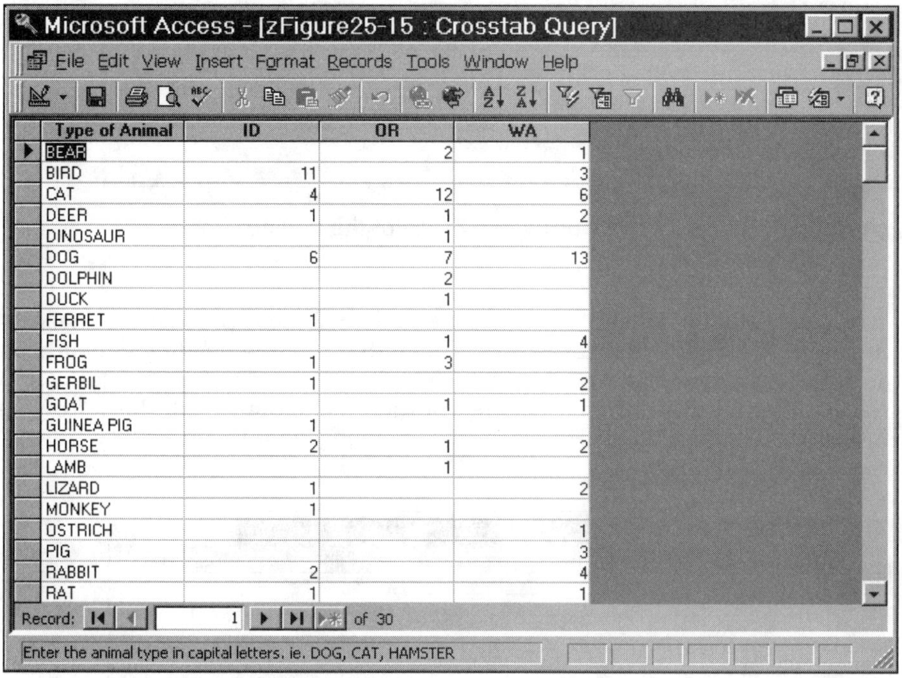

Type of Animal	ID	OR	WA
BEAR		2	1
BIRD	11		3
CAT	4	12	6
DEER	1	1	2
DINOSAUR		1	
DOG	6	7	13
DOLPHIN		2	
DUCK		1	
FERRET	1		
FISH		1	4
FROG	1	3	
GERBIL	1		2
GOAT		1	1
GUINEA PIG	1		
HORSE	2	1	2
LAMB		1	
LIZARD	1		2
MONKEY	1		
OSTRICH			1
PIG			3
RABBIT	2		4
RAT	1		1

Figure 25-16: Datasheet of a crosstab query.

Notice that the dynaset is composed of distinct (nonrepeating) rows of animals, three columns (one for each state), and summary cell contents for each animal against each state; that is, the clinic treats no bears in the state of Idaho, but it does treat two in Oregon and one in Washington.

Entering multiple-field row headings

When you're working with crosstab queries, you can specify only one summary Value field and one Column Heading field. You can add more than one Row Heading field, however. By adding multiple Row Heading fields, you can further refine the type of data you want presented in the crosstab query.

Suppose that you're interested in seeing the types of animals from the last crosstab query further refined to the level of city. In other words, you want to see how many of each type of animal you have from each city within each state. Such a query is shown in Figure 25-17. Notice that it has two Crosstab: cells that show Row Heading for the fields State and City. Access groups the Crosstab: rows first by the State and then by the City. Access specifies the group order from left to right.

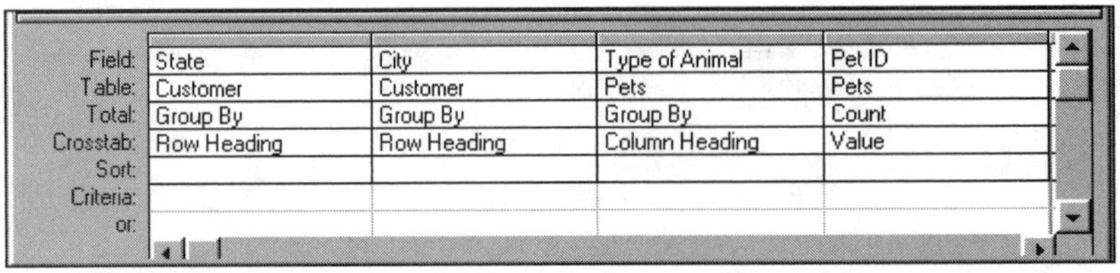

Figure 25-17: Crosstab query using two fields for the row heading.

If you select the Datasheet button on the toolbar, Access presents a datasheet similar to the one shown in Figure 25-18. Notice that the row heading depends on both the State and City fields. The dynaset is displayed in order, first by state (ID, OR, WA) and then by city within the state (Borderville, Mount Pilot, Russettown, and so forth).

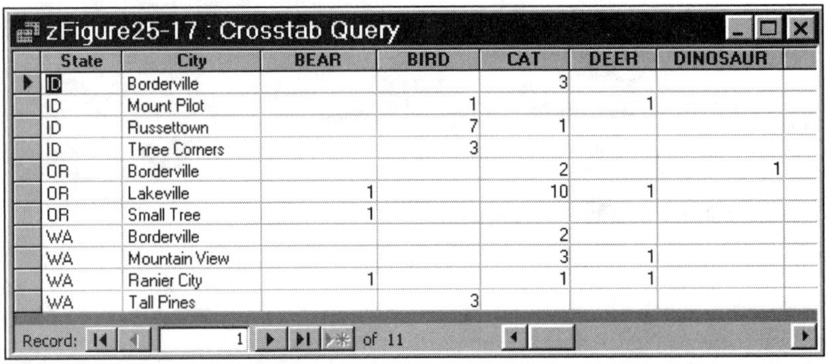

Figure 25-18: Datasheet with multiple-field row headings of a crosstab query.

Tip A crosstab query can have several row headings but only one column heading. If you want to display a several-field column heading and a single-field row heading, simply reverse your heading types. Change the multiple-field column headings to multiple-field row headings and change the single-row heading to a single-column heading.

Specifying criteria for a crosstab query

When you work with crosstab queries, you may want to specify record criteria for the crosstab. Criteria can be specified in a crosstab query against any of these fields:

✦ A new field

✦ A Row Heading field

✦ A Column Heading field

Specifying criteria in a new field

You can add criteria based on a new field that will not be displayed in the crosstab query itself. For example, you may want to create the crosstab query you see in Figure 25-17, in which the two fields, State and City, are used as the row heading. However, you want to see only records in which the type of customer is an individual (or the contents equal the number 1). To specify criteria, simply follow these additional steps:

1. Start with the crosstab query shown in Figure 25-17.

2. Double-click in the Type of Customer field in the Customer table.

3. Select the Criteria: cell of Type of Customer.

4. Type **1** in the cell.

Note   The Crosstab: cell of the Type of Customer field should be blank. If it is not, select (not shown) to blank the cell.

Your query should now resemble the one shown in Figure 25-19. Notice that you added a criterion in a field that will not be displayed in the crosstab query.

Field:	State	City	Type of Animal	Pet ID	Type of Customer	
Table:	Customer	Customer	Pets	Pets	Customer	
Total:	Group By	Group By	Group By	Count	Group By	
Crosstab:	Row Heading	Row Heading	Column Heading	Value		
Sort:						
Criteria:					1	
or:						

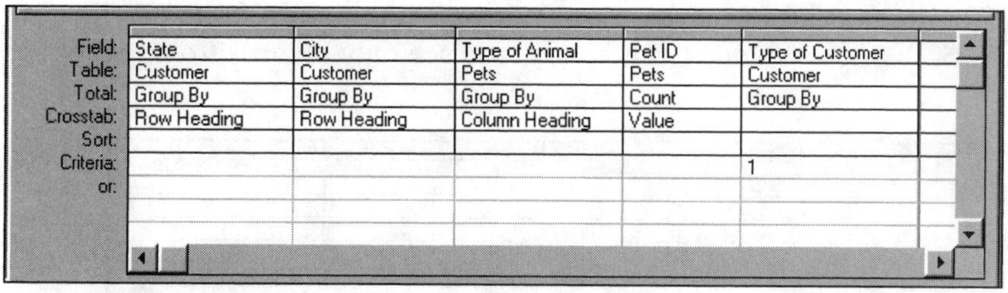

Figure 25-19: Specifying a criterion in a crosstab query on a new field.

Now that the new criterion is specified, you can click on the Datasheet button of the toolbar to see a datasheet similar to the one portrayed in Figure 25-20.

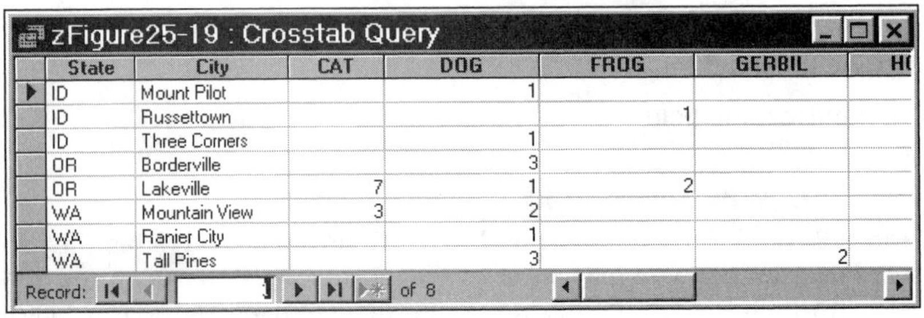

Figure 25-20: The datasheet after specifying a criterion on a new field.

Notice that the datasheet in Figure 25-20 shows only columns in which at least one of the intersecting row cells has a value. For example, only two gerbils appear in the Gerbil column. Several types of animal columns are gone. Bears, birds, deer, and others are missing because none of these types is owned by an individual.

Specifying criteria in a Row Heading field

You can specify criteria for not only a new field but also a field being used for a row heading. When you specify a criteria for a row heading, Access excludes any rows that do not meet the specified criteria.

For example, you may want to view a crosstab query for all animals where the state is Idaho (ID). To create this query, start with the crosstab query shown in Figure 25-17. If you created the last query, simply remove the Type of Customer column from the QBE pane. To create this query, make the QBE pane look like Figure 25-21. When you view this query, you see only records from Idaho.

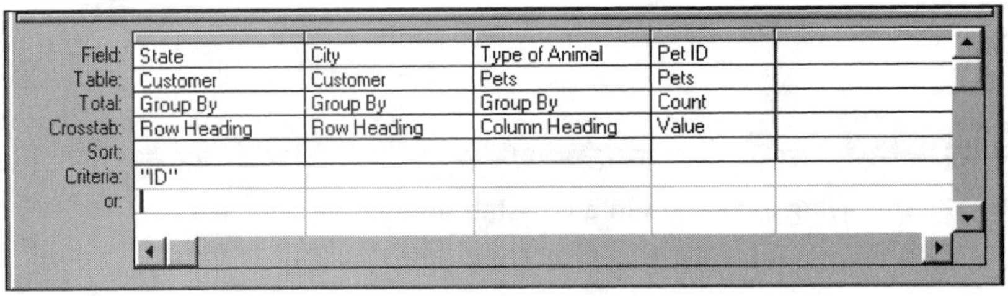

Figure 25-21: Criteria set against a Row Heading field.

You can specify criteria against any field used as a Row Heading field. You can even specify criteria for multiple Row Heading fields to create a finely focused crosstab query.

Specifying criteria in a Column Heading field

You also can specify criteria for the field being used as the column heading. When you specify the criteria for a column heading, Access excludes any columns that don't meet the specified criteria. In the next example, you want a crosstab query for any animal that is either a cat or a dog. To create this query, again start with the crosstab query shown in Figure 25-17. If you created the last query, simply remove the criteria for the State field from the QBE pane. The QBE pane should look similar to the one shown in Figure 25-22.

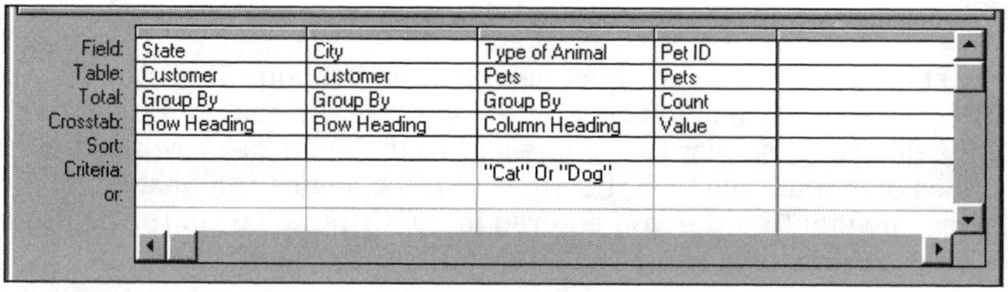

Field:	State	City	Type of Animal	Pet ID		
Table:	Customer	Customer	Pets	Pets		
Total:	Group By	Group By	Group By	Count		
Crosstab:	Row Heading	Row Heading	Column Heading	Value		
Sort:						
Criteria:			"Cat" Or "Dog"			
or:						

Figure 25-22: A criterion specified against the Column Heading field.

Notice that the specified criterion is placed in the Criteria: cell of the Column Heading field Type of Animal. If you now select the Datasheet button on the toolbar, you should see a datasheet that has only two column headings: Cat and Dog. The other headings have been eliminated.

Tip You cannot specify criteria in a field used as the summary Value field for the crosstab query. However, if you need to specify criteria based on this field, simply drag the field again to the QBE pane and set a criterion against this second copy of the field while keeping the Crosstab: cell empty.

Specifying criteria in multiple fields of a crosstab query

Now that you've worked with each type of criterion separately, you may want to specify criteria based on several fields. In the next example, you see how to create a crosstab query with complex criteria. You want a row heading based on the Type of Animal field and a column heading based on the Month value of the Visit Date field. The Value cells are based on the Sum of Total Amount.

Finally, you want to limit the months to part of 1995. To create this complex crosstab query, make the QBE pane look like Figure 25-23. This is clearly the most complex crosstab query you have created. Notice that you specified a column heading based on a calculated field.

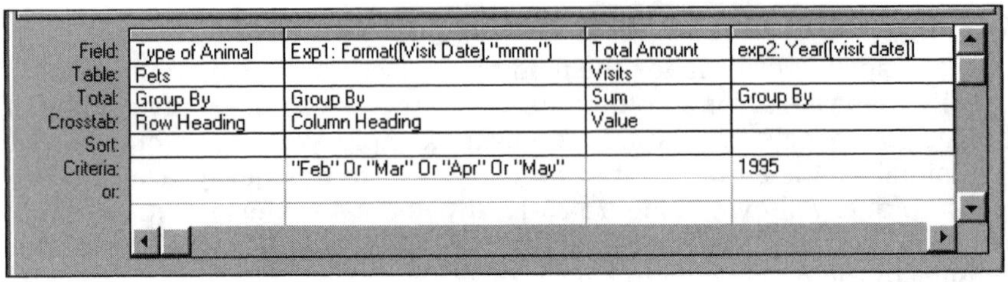

Field:	Type of Animal	Exp1: Format([Visit Date],"mmm")	Total Amount	exp2: Year([visit date])
Table:	Pets		Visits	
Total:	Group By	Group By	Sum	Group By
Crosstab:	Row Heading	Column Heading	Value	
Sort:				
Criteria:		"Feb" Or "Mar" Or "Apr" Or "May"		1995
or:				

Figure 25-23: A complex crosstab query.

This query should display a datasheet in which the columns are Feb, Mar, Apr, or May for the year 1995. When you select the Datasheet button on the toolbar, you should see a datasheet similar to the one shown in Figure 25-24. Notice that the datasheet has only four columns; the order of the columns is alphabetical, not the chronological, by-month order you entered in the Criteria: cell of the field. The next section of this chapter shows you how to fix the column order.

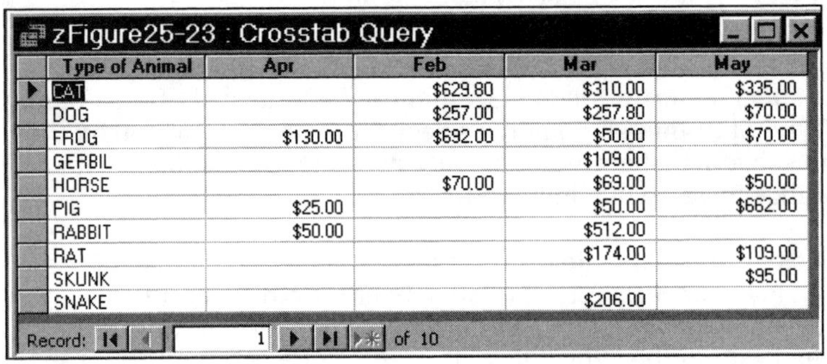

zFigure25-23 : Crosstab Query

Type of Animal	Apr	Feb	Mar	May
CAT		$629.80	$310.00	$335.00
DOG		$257.00	$257.80	$70.00
FROG	$130.00	$692.00	$50.00	$70.00
GERBIL			$109.00	
HORSE		$70.00	$69.00	$50.00
PIG	$25.00		$50.00	$662.00
RABBIT	$50.00		$512.00	
RAT			$174.00	$109.00
SKUNK				$95.00
SNAKE			$206.00	

Record: |◄| |◄| 1 |►| |►I| |►*| of 10

Figure 25-24: A datasheet of very complex crosstab criteria.

Note As the preceding crosstab query shows, you can set criteria in the QBE pane for a number of fields, including calculated fields. Because you have the ability to set either complex or focused criteria, you can create very specific crosstab queries.

Specifying fixed column headings

At times, you will want more control over the appearance of the column headings. By default, Access sorts column headings in alphabetical or numeric order. This sort order can be a problem, as you saw in the preceding example and as illustrated in Figure 25-24. Your columns will be more readable if the columns are in chronological rather than alphabetical order. You can use the option Column Headings in the Query Properties box to solve this problem. This option lets you make these choices:

✦ Specify an exact order for the appearance of the column headings

✦ Specify fixed column headings for reports and forms that use crosstab queries

To specify fixed column headings, follow these steps:

1. Begin with the crosstab query shown in Figure 25-23. Move the pointer to the top half of the query screen and click on it once.

2. Click on the Properties button (a hand holding a piece of paper) on the toolbar or select View➪Properties... from the Query Design menu.

3. Select the Column Headings text box entry area.

4. Type **Feb, Mar, Apr, May** in the box.

Tip

If you double-click in step 1, the Properties window will automatically appear.

The Query Properties dialog box should look like the one shown in Figure 25-25. When you move to another entry area, Access converts your text into "Feb", "Mar", "Apr", "May" in the Query Properties dialog box.

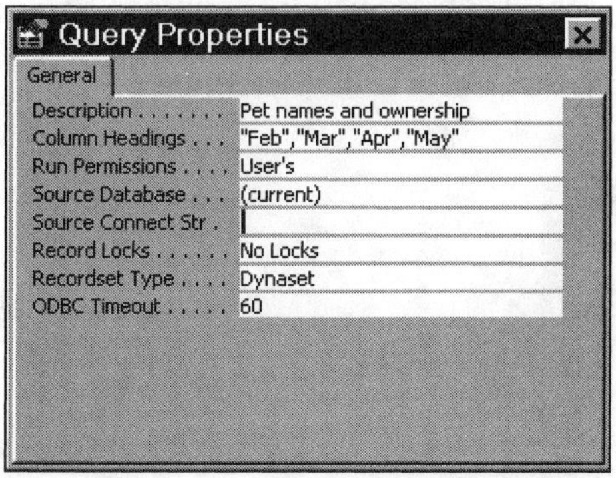

Figure 25-25: The Query Properties dialog box.

If you look at the datasheet, you see that it now looks like Figure 25-26. The order for the column headings is now chronological.

Type of Animal	Feb	Mar	Apr	May
CAT	$629.80	$310.00		$335.00
DOG	$257.00	$257.80		$70.00
FROG	$692.00	$50.00	$130.00	$70.00
GERBIL		$109.00		
HORSE	$70.00	$69.00		$50.00
PIG		$50.00	$25.00	$662.00
RABBIT		$512.00	$50.00	
RAT		$174.00		$109.00
SKUNK				$95.00
SNAKE		$206.00		

zFigure25-25 : Crosstab Query

Record: 14 ◄ [　　　　] ► ►I ►※ of 10

Figure 25-26: The datasheet with the column order specified.

Note The column names you enter *must* match the query headings exactly. If you enter February rather than Feb, Access will accept the heading without reporting an error. When you display the query, however, no records for that column will appear.

You can enter column names without separating them by semicolons. To do so, enter each name on a new line (press Ctrl+Enter to move to a new line).

The Crosstab Query Wizard

Access 97 employs several Query Wizards, which are helpful additions to the query design surface. One such Wizard, the Crosstab Query Wizard (see Figure 25-27), is an excellent tool to help you create a crosstab query quickly.

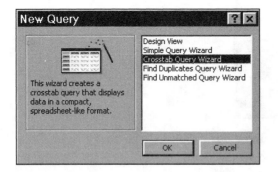

New Query

This wizard creates a crosstab query that displays data in a compact, spreadsheet-like format.

Design View
Simple Query Wizard
Crosstab Query Wizard
Find Duplicates Query Wizard
Find Unmatched Query Wizard

OK   Cancel

Figure 25-27: The Access Query Wizard.

It has some limitations, however:

✦ If you need to use more than one table for the crosstab query, you need to create a separate query that has the tables you need for the crosstab query. For example, you may have a Group By row heading from the Pets table (Type of Animal) and a Group By column heading from the Customer table (State). The Crosstab Query Wizard allows you to select only one table or query for the row and column heading.

   The workaround: Create a query of the Customer and Pets tables, selecting the All Fields reference for each, and then save this intermediate query. Then use this intermediate query as the record source for the Wizard.

✦ You cannot specify the limiting criteria for the Wizard's query.

   The workaround: Make the Wizard do the query and then go in and set the limiting criteria.

✦ You cannot specify column headings or column orders.

   The workaround: Again, have the Wizard create the query and then modify it.

To use the crosstab query, simply click on the New button and then select the Crosstab Wizard (third from the top) in the dialog box. Click on OK and then follow the prompts that Access asks for:

✦ The table or query name for the source

✦ The fields for the row headings

✦ The fields for the column headings

✦ The field for the body

✦ The title

After you specify these things, Access creates your crosstab query and then runs it for you.

Creating a Parameter Query

You can automate the process of changing criteria for queries you run on a regular basis by creating *parameter queries*.

Understanding the parameter query

As the name *parameter* suggests, a parameter query is one you create that prompts the user for a quantity or a constant value every time the query is executed. Specifically, a parameter query prompts the user for criteria every time it is run, thereby eliminating the need to open the query in design mode to change the criteria manually.

Parameter queries are also very useful with forms or reports because you can have Access prompt the user for the criteria when the form or report is opened.

Creating a single-parameter query

You may have queries that require minor modifications to the criteria of a field every time they are run. Suppose that you have a query which displays all pets for a specific customer. If you run the query often, you can design a parameter query to prompt the user for a customer number whenever the query runs. To create the query, follow these steps:

1. Starting with a select query, select the Customer and Pets tables.

2. Double-click in the Customer Number field in the Customer table.

3. Double-click on the Customer Name in the Customer table.

4. Double-click in the Pet Name field in the Pets table.

5. Click on the Criteria: cell for Customer Number.

6. Type **[Enter a Customer Number]** in the cell.

7. Deselect the Show: cell of Customer Number if you don't want this field to show in the datasheet. It has been left in the upcoming example figure.

That's all there is to creating a single-parameter query. Your query should resemble Figure 25-28.

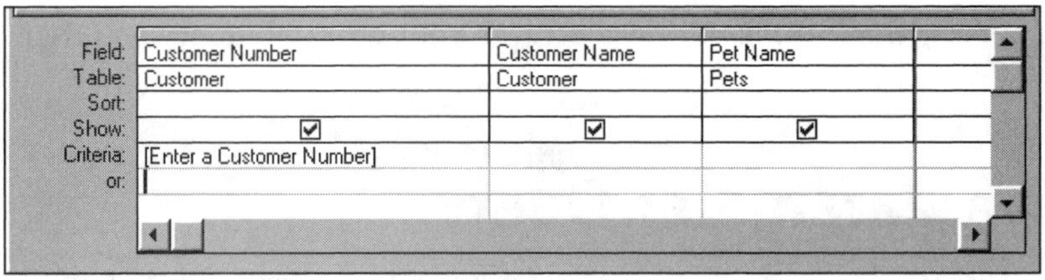

Field:	Customer Number	Customer Name	Pet Name	
Table:	Customer	Customer	Pets	
Sort:				
Show:	☑	☑	☑	
Criteria:	[Enter a Customer Number]			
or:				

Figure 25-28: A single-parameter query.

In the preceding example, you created a parameter query that prompts the user for a customer number by displaying the message Enter a Customer Number every time the query is run. Access will convert the user's entry to an equals criteria for the field Customer Number. If a valid number is entered, Access will find the correct records.

Caution When you specify a prompt message for the parameter, you should make the message meaningful yet brief. When the parameter query is run, Access will display as many as approximately 50 characters of any prompt message. If the message is longer than 50 characters, it will be truncated to approximately the first 50 characters.

Running a parameter query

To run a parameter query, select either the Run button or the Datasheet button on the toolbar. A parameter dialog box appears on-screen, such as the one shown in Figure 25-29, prompting the user for a value.

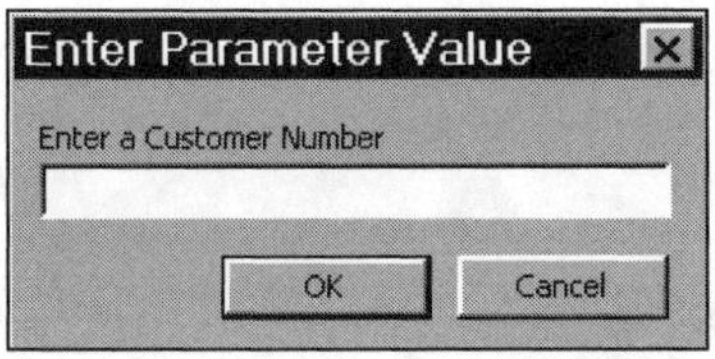

Figure 25-29: The Enter Parameter Value dialog box.

After the user enters a value or presses Enter, Access runs the query, based on the criteria entered. If the criteria is valid, the datasheet will show records matching the criteria; otherwise, the datasheet displays no records.

If the user types **GR001** in the parameter dialog box, Access will display a datasheet similar to the one shown in Figure 25-30.

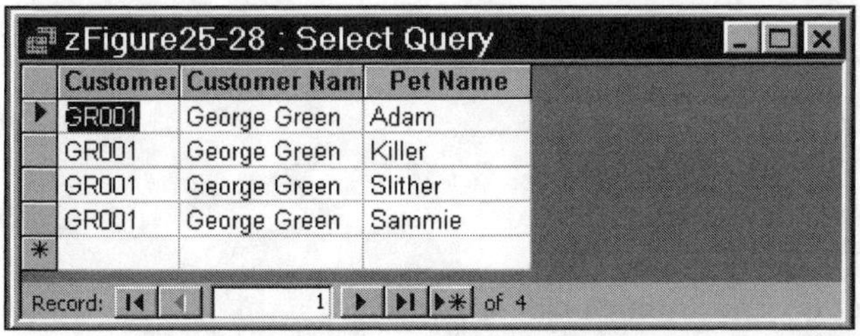

Figure 25-30: Datasheet of records specified by a parameter query.

Notice that the records displayed in Figure 25-30 are only those for George Green, whose customer number is GR001.

Creating a multiple-parameter query

You are not limited to creating a query with a single parameter. You can create a query that asks for multiple criteria. For example, you may want a query that displays all pet and visit information based on a type of animal and a range of visit dates. You can design this multiple-parameter query as simply as you designed the single-parameter query. To create this query, follow these steps:

1. Select the Pets and Visits tables.

2. Double-click in the Pet Name field in the Pets table.

3. Double-click in the Type of Animal field in the Pets table.

4. Double-click in the Visit Date field in the Visits table.

5. Click on the Criteria: cell for Type of Animal.

6. Type **[Enter an Animal Type]** in the cell.

7. Click on the Criteria: cell for Visit Date.

8. Type **Between [Start Date] And [End Date]** in the cell.

Steps 6 and 8 contain the prompt messages you specify for the prompt criteria. This query will display three parameter query prompts. Your query should resemble the one shown in Figure 25-31.

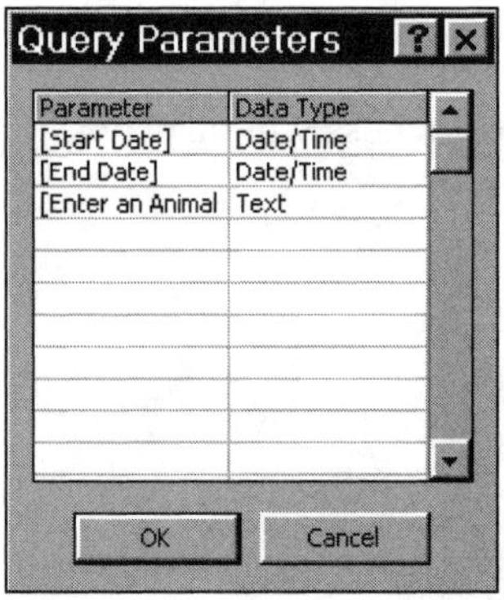

Figure 25-31: A parameter query with three criteria specified.

When you run this query, Access prompts the user for the three criteria in this order:

✦ Enter an Animal Type

✦ Start Date

✦ End Date

Like the single-parameter example, the user must enter valid criteria. If the user enters valid criteria in all three dialog boxes, Access displays all records meeting the specified criteria. Otherwise, it will display no records.

Tip   You can create parameter queries using any valid operator, including the Like operator with wildcards. An example is the query with the parameter Like [Enter a State Abbr or Enter for all States] & *. This parameter lets the user run the query for a single state or for all states.

Viewing the parameter dialog box

Access defaults the prompt order to left to right, based on the position of the fields and their parameters. However, you can override the prompt order by selecting the Query⇨Parameters... Query menu choice and specifying an order.

To specify a prompt order, enter the criteria on the QBE pane just as you have until now. For example, to specify a prompt order of Start Date, End Date, and Animal Type, follow these steps:

1. Start with the query in Figure 25-31.

2. Select Query⇨Parameters... from the Query menu.

3. Type **[Start Date]** in the first cell under the Parameter column.

4. Press Tab to move to the Data Type column.

5. Type **Date/Time** or select the Date/Time type from the drop-down list box.

6. Press Tab to move to the Parameter column.

7. Type **[End Date]** in the first cell under the Parameter column.

8. Press Tab to move to the Data Type column.

9. Type **Date/Time** or select the Date/Time type from the drop-down list box.

10. Press Tab to move to the Parameter column.

11. Type **[Enter an Animal Type]** in the first cell under the Parameter column.

12. Press Tab to move to the Data Type column.

13. Enter **Text** or select the Text type from the drop-down list box.

14. Press Enter or click on the OK button to leave the dialog box.

Your Query Parameters dialog box should look like the one shown in Figure 25-32.

Figure 25-32: The Query Parameters dialog box.

Notice that the message prompt in the Parameter column must match exactly the message prompt in each of the Criteria: cells of the QBE pane. If the prompt message does not match, the query will not work correctly.

Caution   When you specify a parameter order, you must specify the correct data type for each parameter in the Query Parameters dialog box, or else Access will report a data type mismatch error.

Summary

In this chapter, you learned how to work with complex select queries. You learned how to use total, crosstab, and parameter queries. The following points were discussed:

✦ The three specialized select query types are total, crosstab, and parameter.

✦ The Total: row of the QBE pane can be broken into four distinct total categories: Group By, Expression, Total Field Record Limit, and Aggregate.

✦ Access has nine Aggregate Total options. These operators perform mathematical or selection operations.

✦ Total queries can perform calculations against all records of a table or against groups of records in a table.

✦ Total queries can be used to specify criteria which limit the records that can be processed. These criteria can be against a Group By field, an Aggregate Total field after totaling is performed, or a Non-Aggregate Total field before totaling is performed.

✦ You can create a total query based on an expression that uses one or more of the Aggregate Total options and/or a series of Access functions.

✦ A crosstab query is a two-dimensional summary matrix that has field contents specified for both the row and column headings. Each intersecting cell between the row and column heading has a Value content (usually an Aggregate Total option).

✦ Crosstab queries can have multiple fields for specifying row headings but can have only one field for specifying column headings and one for specifying the total operation against the Value cell.

✦ You can specify the order of the column headings in a crosstab query in the Query Properties dialog box by specifying the order in the Column Headings box.

✦ The new Crosstab Query Wizard simplifies the process of creating a crosstab query.

✦ A parameter query is used for obtaining user-specified criteria when the query is run. This eliminates the need to redesign the query every time a user runs it.

✦ A parameter query can prompt the user for more than one parameter. If the user wants the order of prompting to be different from the default, it must be specified in the Query Parameter dialog box.

In the next chapter, you work with action queries. You make tables, perform global updates, and delete records by using queries.

✦   ✦   ✦

Creating Action Queries

As you have seen, queries are tools that let you question or request information from your database. In this chapter, you learn about a special type, called the *action query,* that lets you *change* the field values in your records. For example, you can change a medications field to increase all prices by 10 percent or delete all information from the records of a deceased animal.

What Is an Action Query?

The term *action query,* as you can guess, defines a query that does something more than simply select a specific group of records and present them to you in a dynaset. The word *action* suggests performing some operation — doing, influencing, or affecting something. The word is synonymous with operation, performance, and work. This is exactly what an action query does — some specific operation or work.

An action query can be considered a select query that is given a *duty* to perform against a specified group of records in the dynaset.

When you create any query, Access creates it as a select query automatically. You can specify a different type (such as action) from the Query Design menu. From this menu, you can choose from several types of action queries. (The menu's selections are Make Table, Update, Append, and Delete.)

Like select queries, action queries create a dynaset you can view in a datasheet. To see the dynaset, you simply click on the Datasheet button on the toolbar. Unlike select queries, action queries perform an action — specified in the QBE pane of the query design — when you click on the Run button (the button with the exclamation point) on the toolbar.

You can quickly identify action queries in the Database window by the special exclamation-point icons that sit beside their names. There are four different types of action queries (see Figure 26-1); each has a different icon.

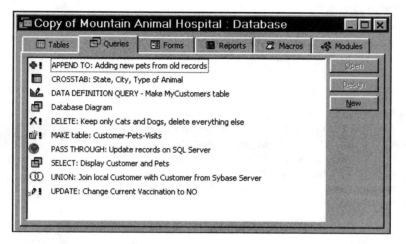

Figure 26-1: The query container of the Database window, showing select and action queries.

Uses of Action Queries

You can use action queries to accomplish the following tasks:

✦ Delete specified records from a table or group of tables

✦ Append records from one table to another

✦ Update information in a group of records

✦ Create a new table from specified records in a query

The following examples describe some practical uses for action queries:

✦ You want to create history tables and then copy all inactive records to them. (You consider a record inactive if a customer hasn't brought a pet to the office in more than three years.) You decide to remove the inactive records from your active database tables.

What to do? Use a make-table query to create the history tables and a delete query to remove the unwanted records.

✦ One of your old clients, whom you haven't seen in more than four years, comes in with a new puppy; you need to bring the old information back into the active file from the backup files.

What to do? Use an append query to add records from your backup tables to your active tables.

Caution Action queries change, add, or delete data. As a result, it's a good idea to observe the following rules:

✦ Always back up your table *before* performing the query.

✦ Always create and view the action query (use the Datasheet button on the toolbar) *before performing it.*

The Process of Action Queries

Because action queries are irreversible, you should consider following this four-step process when you're working with them:

1. Create the action query specifying the fields and the criteria.

2. View the records selected in the action query by clicking on the Datasheet button on the toolbar.

3. Run the action query by clicking on the Run button on the toolbar.

4. Check the changes in the tables by clicking on the Datasheet button on the toolbar.

If you follow the preceding steps, you should be able to use action queries relatively safely.

Viewing the Results of an Action Query

Action queries perform a specific task — many times a destructive task. Be very careful when you're using them. It's important to view the changes they will make before you run the action query and to verify afterward that they made the changes you anticipated. Before you learn how to create and run an action query, it's also important to review the process for seeing what your changes will look like *before* you change a table permanently.

Viewing a query before using update and delete queries

You can click on the Datasheet View button to see with which set of data the action query will work. Meanwhile, when you're updating or deleting records with an action query, the actions take place on the underlying tables of the query currently in use. Therefore, to view the results of an update or a delete query, you can click on the Datasheet button to see whether the records were updated or deleted.

Note If your update query made changes to the fields you used for selecting the records, you may have to look at the underlying table or change the selection query to see the changes. For example, if you deleted a set of records with an action button, the resulting select dynaset of the same record criteria will show that no records exist. By removing the delete criteria, you can view the table and verify that all the records specified have been deleted.

Switching to the result table of a make-table or append query

Unlike the update or delete queries, make-table and append queries copy resultant records to another table. After specifying the fields and the criteria in the QBE pane of the Query Design window, the make-table and the append queries copy the specified fields and records to *another* table. When you run the queries, the results take place in another table, not in the current table.

Pressing the Datasheet button shows you a dynaset of only the criteria and fields that were specified, not the actual table that contains the new or added records. To view the results of a make-table or append query, you need to open the new table and view the contents to verify that the make-table or append query worked correctly. If you won't be using the action query again, do *not* save it. Delete it.

Reversing action queries

Action queries copy or change data in underlying tables. After an action query is executed, it cannot be reversed. Therefore, when you're working with action queries, you should consider creating a select query first to make sure that the record criteria and selection are correct for the action query.

Caution Action queries are destructive; before you perform one, you should always make a backup of the underlying tables.

Scoping criteria

Action queries can use any expression composed of fields, functions, and operators to specify any limiting condition you need to place on the query. Scoping criteria are one form of record criteria. Normally, the record criteria serve as a filter to tell Access which records to find and/or leave out of the dynaset. Because action queries do not create a dynaset, you use *scoping criteria* to specify a set of records for Access to operate on.

Creating an Action Query

Creating an action query is very similar to creating a select query. You specify the fields for the query and any *scoping criteria*.

Besides specifying the fields and criteria, you specify an action-specific property — Append to, Make new table, Update to, or Delete where.

Creating an Update Action Query to Change Values

In this section, you see how to handle an event that requires you to change many records.

Suppose that the city of Mountain View has passed an ordinance that requires horses within its borders to receive a new type of vaccination, starting this year. To create this query, you work with the Customer and Pets tables. First, change the existing status of the Current Vaccinations field in the Pets table from Yes to No wherever the field shows a current vaccination status. Then enter **horse** in the Criteria: row for Type of Animal and **Mountain View** in the Criteria: row for the City field.

It's possible to update each record in the table individually by using a form or a datasheet. Using a select query dynaset to make these changes, however, takes a very long time. The method is not only time-consuming but also inefficient — especially if you have many records to change. In addition, this method lends itself to typing errors as you enter new text into fields.

The best way to handle this type of event is to use an *update* action query to make many changes in just one operation. You save time and eliminate many of those typos that crop up in manually edited records.

To create an update query that performs these tasks, follow a two-phase process:

1. Create a select query. View the data you want to update by pressing the Datasheet button.

2. Convert the select query to an update query. Then run the update query after you're satisfied that it will affect only the records you want to affect.

Creating a select query before an update action

The first step in making an update query is to create a select query. In this particular case, the query is for all customers who live in Mountain View and own horses. Perform the following steps to create this query:

1. Create a new query using the Customer and Pets tables.

2. Select the City field from the Customer table and Type of Animal and Current Vaccinations from the Pets table.

3. Specify a criterion of **"Mountain View"** in the City field and **"Horse"** in the Type of Animal field.

   The Select Query Design window should now resemble the one in Figure 26-2. Notice that the QBE pane shows all three fields but shows criteria in only the fields City and Type of Animal.

4. Examine the datasheet to make sure that it has only the records you want to change. Return to the design surface when you're finished.

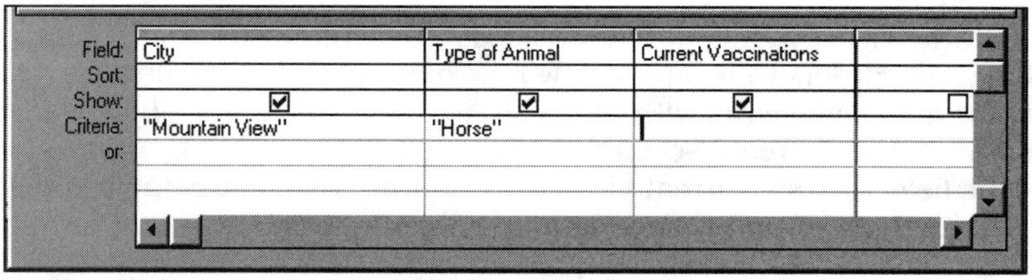

Field:	City		Type of Animal		Current Vaccinations		
Sort:							
Show:		☑		☑		☑	☐
Criteria:	"Mountain View"		"Horse"				
or:							

Figure 26-2: Entering a select query.

The select query datasheet should resemble the one shown in Figure 26-3. Notice that only the records for horses whose owners reside in Mountain View appear in the dynaset.

Figure 26-3: Dynaset showing only the records for horses whose owners live in Mountain View.

You are now ready to convert the select query to an update query.

Converting a select query to an update query

After you create a select query and verify the selection of records, it's time to create the update query. To convert the select query to an update query, follow these steps:

1. Select Update Query from the Query Type button on the toolbar or select Query⇨Update from the menu.

   Access changes the title of the Query window from `Query1: Select Query` to `Query1: Update Query`. Access also adds the `Update To:` property row to the QBE pane, as shown in Figure 26-4.

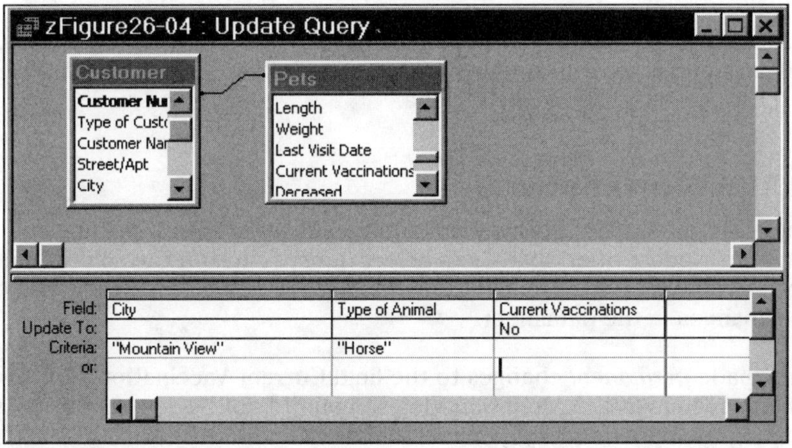

Figure 26-4: The design pane for the update query.

2. In the Update To: cell of Current Vaccinations, enter **No**.

3. Click on the Run button on the toolbar (or select Query⇨Run from the menu).

   Access displays the dialog box shown in Figure 26-5. This dialog box displays a message: You are about to update x row[s]. Once you click Yes, you can't use the Undo command to reverse the changes. Are you sure you want to update these records? Two buttons are presented: Yes and No.

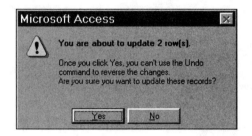

Figure 26-5: The dialog box for updating records.

4. Click on the Yes button to complete the query and update the records. Selecting No stops the procedure (no records are updated).

Note If you're changing tables that are attached to another database, you *cannot* cancel the query.

Tip You can change more than one field at a time by filling in the Update To: cell of any field you want to change. You can even change the field contents of fields you used for limiting the records, that is, the criteria.

Checking your results

After completing the update query, you should check your results. You can do so by changing the update query back to a select query (click on the Select Query button on the toolbar). After changing the query back to a select query, you can review the changes in the datasheet.

The update made *permanent* changes to the field Current Vaccinations for all horses whose owners live in Mountain View. If you did not back up the Pets table before running the update query, you cannot easily restore the contents to their original Yes or No settings. (Hope that you have a good memory.)

Note If you update a field that was used for a limiting criterion, you must change the criterion in the select query to the new value in order to verify the changes.

Creating a New Table Using a Make-Table Query

You can use an action query to create new tables based on scoping criteria. To make a new table, you create a *make-table* query. Consider the following situation that might give rise to this particular task and for which you would create a make-table query.

A local pet-food company has approached you for a mailing list of customers who own dogs or cats. This company wants to send these customers a coupon for a free four-pound bag of food for each animal they own. The pet-food company plans to create the mailing labels and send the form letters if you supply a table of customer information, pet names, and type of animal. The company also stipulates that, because this is a trial mailing, only those customers you've seen in the past six months should receive letters.

You have decided to send the company the requested table of information, so now you need to create a new table from the Customer and Pets tables. To accomplish this task, you create a make-table query that will perform these actions.

Creating the make-table query

You decide to create a make-table query for all customers who own dogs or cats and who have visited you in the past six months. (For this example, assume that six months ago was February 1, 1995.) Perform the following steps to create this query:

1. Create a new query using the Customer and Pets tables.

2. Select Make Table from the Query Type button on the toolbar.

   Access displays the Make Table dialog box, as shown in Figure 26-6.

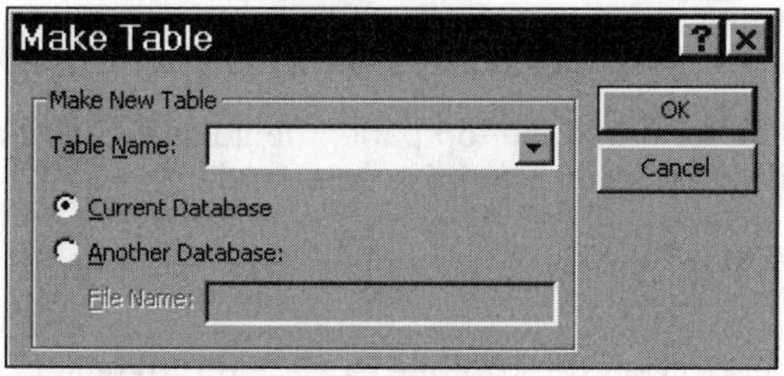

Figure 26-6: The Make Table dialog box.

3. Type **Mailing List for Coupons** in the Table Name: field; press Enter or click on OK. Notice that the name of the window changes from `Query1: Select`

Query to Query1: Make Table Query.

4. Select the mailing information fields (Customer Name through Zip Code) from the Customer table and the fields Pet Name, Type of Animal, and Last Visit Date from the Pets table.

5. Specify the criteria **In("CAT","DOG")** in the Type of Animal field and **>#2/1/95#** in the Last Visit Date field.

The Query Design window should resemble the one shown in Figure 26-7. Notice that the fields are resized so that they all appear in the QBE pane. Two fields (Type of Animal and Last Visit Date) contain criteria.

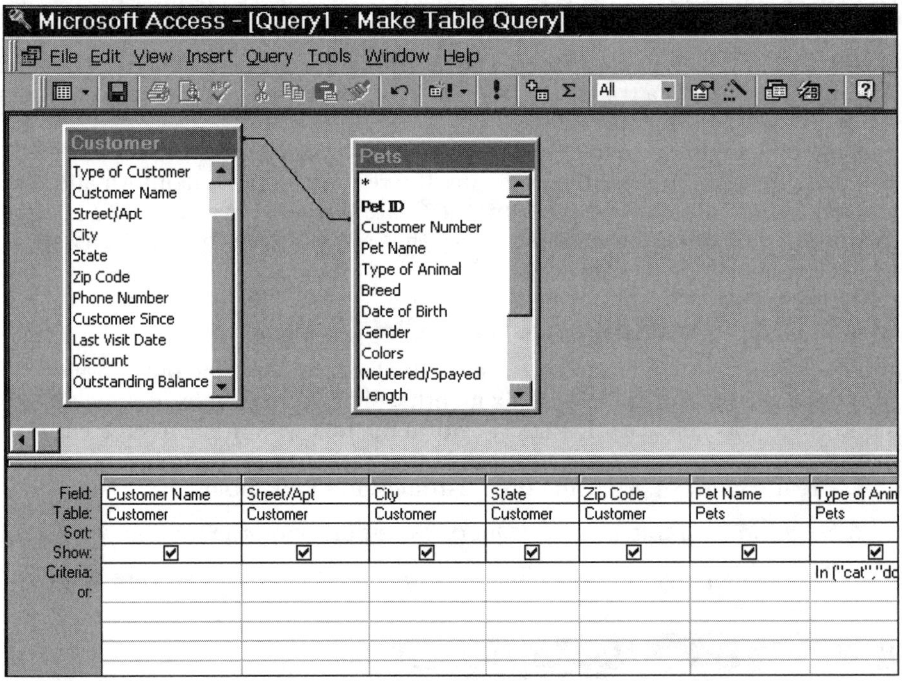

Figure 26-7: The Customer and Pets tables are in the top pane; the fields Customer Name, Street/Apt, City, State, Zip Code, Pet Name, Type of Animal, and Last Visit Date are in the bottom pane.

6. Click on the Datasheet View button on the toolbar to view the dynaset (see Figure 26-8).

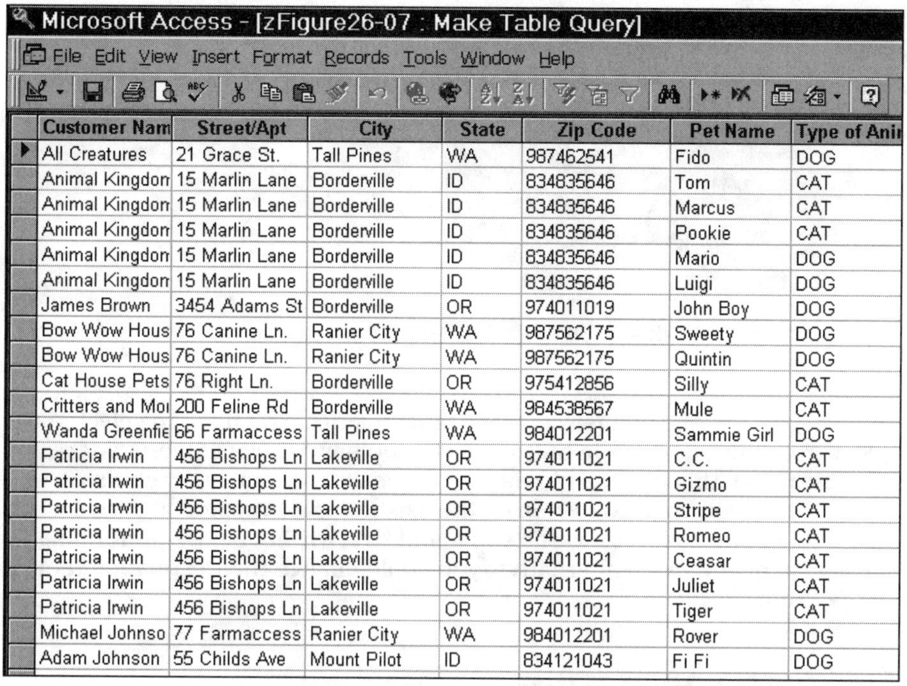

Customer Nam	Street/Apt	City	State	Zip Code	Pet Name	Type of Ani
All Creatures	21 Grace St.	Tall Pines	WA	987462541	Fido	DOG
Animal Kingdon	15 Marlin Lane	Borderville	ID	834835646	Tom	CAT
Animal Kingdon	15 Marlin Lane	Borderville	ID	834835646	Marcus	CAT
Animal Kingdon	15 Marlin Lane	Borderville	ID	834835646	Pookie	CAT
Animal Kingdon	15 Marlin Lane	Borderville	ID	834835646	Mario	DOG
Animal Kingdon	15 Marlin Lane	Borderville	ID	834835646	Luigi	DOG
James Brown	3454 Adams St	Borderville	OR	974011019	John Boy	DOG
Bow Wow Hous	76 Canine Ln.	Ranier City	WA	987562175	Sweety	DOG
Bow Wow Hous	76 Canine Ln.	Ranier City	WA	987562175	Quintin	DOG
Cat House Pets	76 Right Ln.	Borderville	OR	975412856	Silly	CAT
Critters and Moi	200 Feline Rd	Borderville	WA	984538567	Mule	CAT
Wanda Greenfie	66 Farmaccess	Tall Pines	WA	984012201	Sammie Girl	DOG
Patricia Irwin	456 Bishops Ln	Lakeville	OR	974011021	C.C.	CAT
Patricia Irwin	456 Bishops Ln	Lakeville	OR	974011021	Gizmo	CAT
Patricia Irwin	456 Bishops Ln	Lakeville	OR	974011021	Stripe	CAT
Patricia Irwin	456 Bishops Ln	Lakeville	OR	974011021	Romeo	CAT
Patricia Irwin	456 Bishops Ln	Lakeville	OR	974011021	Ceasar	CAT
Patricia Irwin	456 Bishops Ln	Lakeville	OR	974011021	Juliet	CAT
Patricia Irwin	456 Bishops Ln	Lakeville	OR	974011021	Tiger	CAT
Michael Johnso	77 Farmaccess	Ranier City	WA	984012201	Rover	DOG
Adam Johnson	55 Childs Ave	Mount Pilot	ID	834121043	Fi Fi	DOG

Figure 26-8: The dynaset of cats and dogs seen since February 1, 1995.

7. Make sure that the dynaset has only the records you specified.
8. Click on the Design button to switch back to the Query Design view.
9. Deselect the Show: property of the field `Last Visit Date`.

   You do not want to copy this field to the new table Mailing List for Coupons. Only those fields selected with an X in the check box of the Show: row are copied to the new table. By deselecting a field with a criteria set, you can base the scoping criteria on fields that will *not* be copied to the new table.
10. Click on the Run button on the toolbar or select Query➪Run from the menu.

    Access indicates how many records it will copy to the new table (see Figure 26-9).
11. Click on the Yes button to complete the query and make the new table. Selecting No stops the procedure (no records are copied).

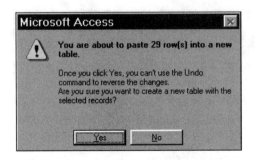

Figure 26-9: The dialog box for copying records.

When you're creating numerous make-table queries, you need to select Make Table Query from the Query Type button on the toolbar or select Query⇨Make Table... from the menu; this command renames the make-table query each time. Access assumes that you want to overwrite the existing table if you don't reselect the make-table option. Access warns you about overwriting before performing the new make-table query; as an alternative, you could change the Destination table name on the Property sheet.

Checking your results

After you complete the make-table query, you should check your results. You can do so by opening the new table Mailing List for Coupons, which has been added to the database container (see Figure 26-10).

Note When you create a table from a make-table query, the fields in the new table inherit the data type and field size from the fields in the query's underlying tables; however, no other field or table properties are transferred. If you want to define a primary key or other properties, you need to edit the design of the new table.

Tip You can also use a make-table action query to create a backup of your tables before you create action queries that change the contents of the tables. Backing up with this method *does not* copy the table's properties or primary key to the new table.

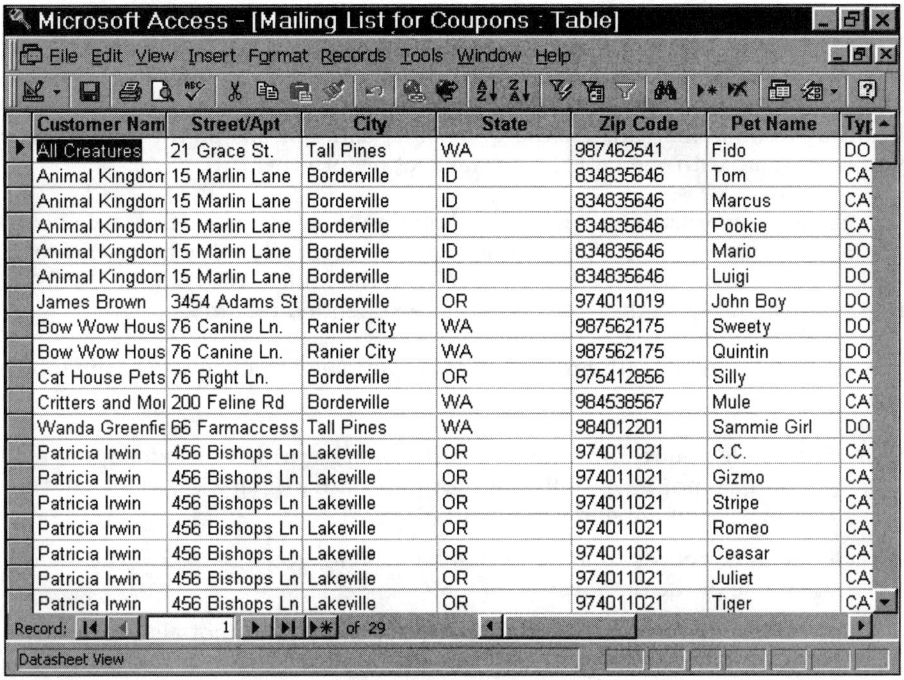

Customer Nam	Street/Apt	City	State	Zip Code	Pet Name	Typ
All Creatures	21 Grace St.	Tall Pines	WA	987462541	Fido	DO
Animal Kingdon	15 Marlin Lane	Borderville	ID	834835646	Tom	CA
Animal Kingdon	15 Marlin Lane	Borderville	ID	834835646	Marcus	CA
Animal Kingdon	15 Marlin Lane	Borderville	ID	834835646	Pookie	CA
Animal Kingdon	15 Marlin Lane	Borderville	ID	834835646	Mario	DO
Animal Kingdon	15 Marlin Lane	Borderville	ID	834835646	Luigi	DO
James Brown	3454 Adams St	Borderville	OR	974011019	John Boy	DO
Bow Wow Hous	76 Canine Ln.	Ranier City	WA	987562175	Sweety	DO
Bow Wow Hous	76 Canine Ln.	Ranier City	WA	987562175	Quintin	DO
Cat House Pets	76 Right Ln.	Borderville	OR	975412856	Silly	CA
Critters and Moi	200 Feline Rd	Borderville	WA	984538567	Mule	CA
Wanda Greenfie	66 Farmaccess	Tall Pines	WA	984012201	Sammie Girl	DO
Patricia Irwin	456 Bishops Ln	Lakeville	OR	974011021	C.C.	CA
Patricia Irwin	456 Bishops Ln	Lakeville	OR	974011021	Gizmo	CA
Patricia Irwin	456 Bishops Ln	Lakeville	OR	974011021	Stripe	CA
Patricia Irwin	456 Bishops Ln	Lakeville	OR	974011021	Romeo	CA
Patricia Irwin	456 Bishops Ln	Lakeville	OR	974011021	Ceasar	CA
Patricia Irwin	456 Bishops Ln	Lakeville	OR	974011021	Juliet	CA
Patricia Irwin	456 Bishops Ln	Lakeville	OR	974011021	Tiger	CA

Figure 26-10: The new table Mailing List for Coupons.

To copy any database object (table, query, form, or other object) while you're in the Database window, follow these steps:

1. Highlight the object you need to copy.
2. Press Ctrl+C (or select Edit⇨Copy) to copy the object to the Clipboard.
3. Press Ctrl+V (or select Edit⇨Paste) to paste the object from the Clipboard.
4. Enter the new object name (table, form, and so forth) and click on the OK button in the dialog box. If the object is a table, you also can specify Structure with or without the data and append it to an existing table.

Creating a Query to Append Records

As the word *append* suggests, an append query attaches or adds records to a specified table. An append query adds records from the table you're using to another table. The table you want to add records to must already exist. You can append records to a table in the same database or in another Access database.

Append queries are very useful for adding information to another table on the basis of some scoping criteria. Even so, append queries are not always the fastest way of adding records to another database. If you need (for example) to append all fields and all records from one table to a new table, the append query is *not* the best way to do it. Instead, use the Copy and Paste options on the Edit menu when you're working with the table in a datasheet or form.

Tip You can add records to an open table. You don't have to close the table before adding records. However, Access does not automatically refresh the view of the table that has records added to it. To refresh the table, press Shift+F9. This action requeries the table so that you can see the appended records.

When you're working with append queries, you need to be aware of the following rules:

1. If the table you're appending records to has a primary key field, the records you add cannot have Null values or duplicate primary key values. If they do, Access will not append the records.

2. If you add records to another database table, you must know the location and name of the database.

3. If you use the asterisk (*) field in a QBE row, you cannot also use individual fields from the same table. Access assumes that you're trying to add field contents twice to the same record and will not append the records.

4. If you append records with an AutoNumber field (an Access-specified primary key), do not include the AutoNumber field if the table you're appending to also has the field and record contents (this causes the problem specified in rule 1). Also, if you're adding to an empty table and you want the new table to have a new AutoNumber number (that is, order number) based on the criteria, do not use the AutoNumber field.

If you follow these simple rules, your append query will perform as expected and become a very useful tool.

Here's an example that will help illustrate the use of append queries: Every February, you archive all records of animals that died in the preceding year. To archive the records, you perform two steps. First, you append them to existing backup files. Second, you delete the records from the active database.

In this case, you want to add records to the backup tables for deceased animals in your active tables. In other words, you will copy records to three tables: Pets, Visits, and Visit Details. You need three backup files to perform this exercise. To create the backup files, perform the following steps:

1. Press F11 or Alt+F1 to display the Database window.

2. Click on the Tables tab to display the list of tables.

3. Click on the Pets table to highlight it.

4. Press Ctrl+C (or select Edit⇨Copy) to copy the object Pets table to the Clipboard.

5. Press Ctrl+V (or select Edit⇨Paste) to display the Paste Table As dialog box.

6. Click on Structure Only in the Paste Options section of the dialog box (or tab to the Paste Options section and click on S).

7. Click on the Table Name: box and type **Pets Backup**.

8. Click on the OK button (or press Enter after typing the filename).

9. Open the Pets Backup table (it should be empty); then close the table.

Repeat this process for both the Visits and Visit Details tables, naming them **Visits Backup** and **Visit Details Backup**, respectively.

To create an append query that copies the deceased animals' records, follow a two-step process:

1. Create a select query to verify that only the records you want to append are copied.

2. Convert the select query to an append query and run it.

Note When you're using the append query, only fields with names that match in the two tables are copied. For example, you may have a small table with six fields and another with nine. The table with nine fields has only five of the six field names that match fields in the smaller table. If you append records from the smaller table to the larger table, only the five matching fields are appended. The other four fields remain blank.

Creating the select query for an append query

To create a select query for all pets that died last year, along with their visit histories, follow these steps:

1. Create a new query using the Pets, Visits, and Visit Details tables.

2. Select the Deceased field from the Pets table.

3. Specify a criterion of Yes in the Deceased field.

   You may want to select some additional fields from each table, such as Pet Name, Visit Date, Visit Type, Treatment Code, and so forth. The Select Query Design window should resemble the one shown in Figure 26-11. Notice that all the fields are resized to appear in the QBE pane. The only field and criterion that must be in this select query is the first field: Deceased. If you add any other fields, make sure that you remove them before converting this query to an append query.

4. Go to the datasheet and make sure that all the Deceased field contents say Yes (see Figure 26-12).

5. Return to design mode. With the select query created correctly, you are ready to convert the select query to an append query.

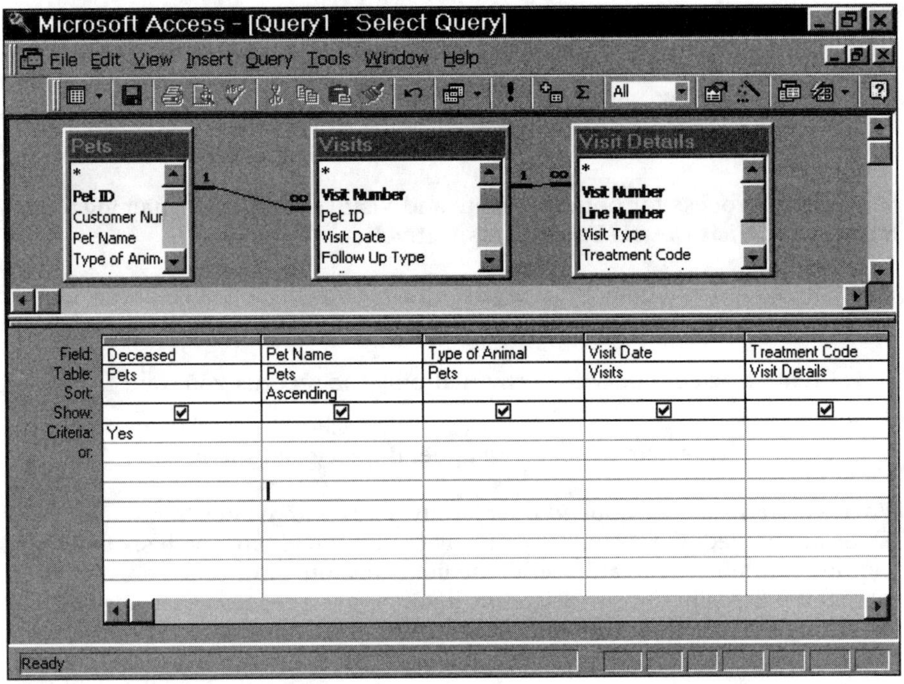

Figure 26-11: The tables Pets, Visits, and Visit Details are in the top pane, and selected fields are in the QBE pane.

Converting to an append query

After you create the select query and verify that it is correct, you'll need to create the append query (actually, three different append queries — one each for the tables Visit Details, Visits, and Pets — because append queries work with only one table at a time). For this example, first copy all fields from the Visit Details table. Then copy all the fields from the Visits table. Finally, copy all the fields from the Pets table.

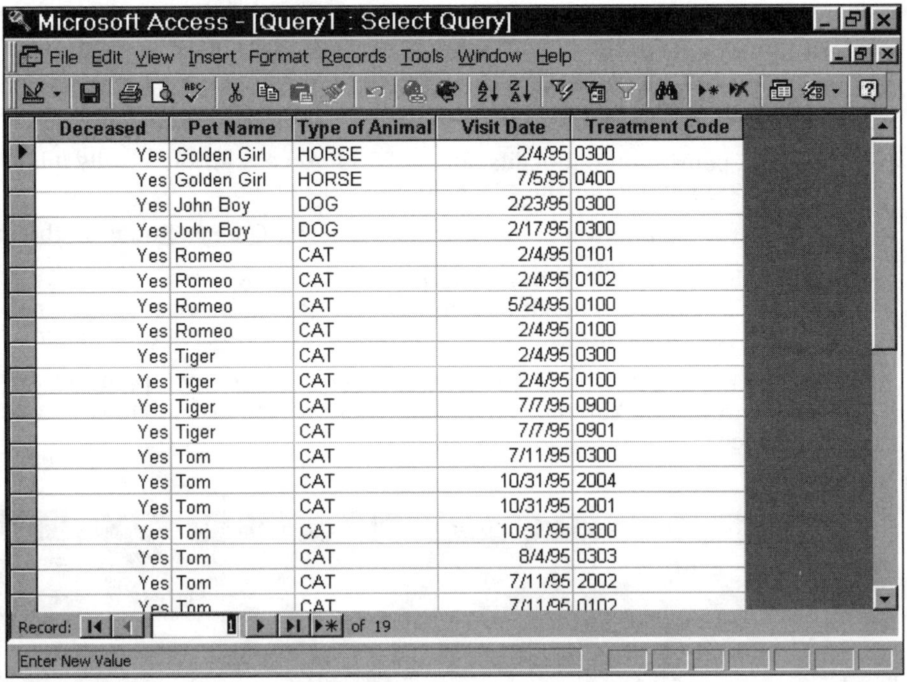

Figure 26-12: A dynaset of records for all deceased animals.

To convert the select query to an append query and run it, perform the following steps:

1. Deselect the Show: property of the Deceased field.

2. Select Append from the Query Type button on the toolbar, or select Query⇨Append... from the Design menu.

   Access displays the Append dialog box, as shown in Figure 26-13.

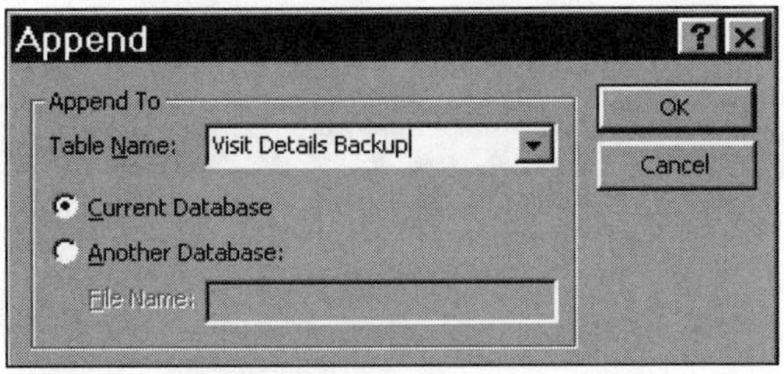

Figure 26-13: The Append dialog box.

   3. Type **Visit Details Backup** in the Table Name: field and either press Enter
      with the cursor in the field or click on OK with the cursor in the dialog box.

   4. Drag the asterisk (*) field from the Visit Details table to the QBE pane to
      select all fields.

      The QBE pane should look like Figure 26-14. Access automatically fills in the
      Append To: field under the A11 field-selector column.

   5. Click on the Run button on the toolbar (or select Query⇨Run from the menu).

      Access displays a dialog box that displays a message: You are about to
      append x row[s]. Then it presents two buttons (Yes and No). After you
      click on Yes, you can't use the Undo command to reverse the changes.

   6. Click on the Yes button to complete the query and copy (append) the
      records to the backup table. Selecting No stops the procedure (no records
      are copied).

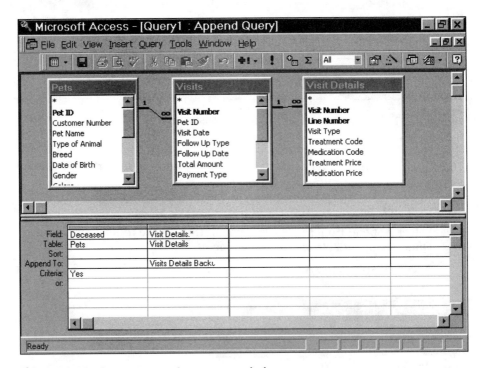

Figure 26-14: The QBE pane for an appended query.

Note After the Visit Details records for deceased animals are backed up, repeat Steps 2 through 5 for the Visits and Pets tables. Before you append fields from these other tables, however, you must remove the previous All selector field [Visit Details.*] from the QBE pane. For example, to move the Visits records, delete the asterisk (*) field for the Visits Details table and select the asterisk (*) field for the Visits table. Reselect Query⇨Append... and type **Visits Backup** for the name of the table to append to. Finally, click on Run.

Caution If you create an append query by using the asterisk (*) field and you also use a field from the same table as the asterisk to specify a criterion, you must take the criteria field out of the Append To: row. If you don't, Access reports an error. Remember that the field for the criterion is already included in the asterisk field. If you leave the Show on, it tries to append the field twice, repeating an error. Then Access halts the append query, appending no records to the table.

Checking your results

After you complete the three append table queries, check your results. To do so, go to the Database window and select each of the three tables to be appended to (Pets Backup, Visits Backup, and Visit Details Backup); view the new records.

Creating a Query to Delete Records

Of all the action queries, the *delete query* is the most dangerous. Unlike the other types of queries you've worked with, delete queries wipe out records from tables permanently and *irreversibly*.

Like other action queries, delete queries act on a group of records on the basis of scoping criteria.

A delete action query can work with multiple tables to delete records. If you intend to delete related records from multiple tables, however, you must do the following:

✦ Define relationships between the tables in the Relationships Builder.

✦ Check the Enforce Referential Integrity option for the join between tables.

✦ Check the Cascade Delete Related Records option for the join between tables.

Figure 26-15 shows the Relationships dialog box for the join line between tables. Notice that the options Enforce Referential Integrity and Cascade Delete Related Records are selected.

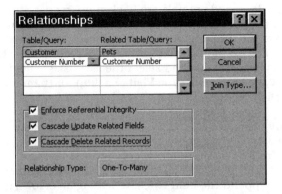

Figure 26-15: The Relationships dialog box.

When working with one-to-many relationships without defining relationships and putting Cascade Delete on, Access deletes records from only one table at a time. Specifically, Access deletes the *many* side of the relationship first. Then you must remove the *many* table from the query and delete the records from the *one* side of the query.

This method is time-consuming and awkward. Therefore, when you're deleting related records from one-to-many relationship tables, make sure that you define relationships between the tables and check the Cascade Delete box in the Relationships dialog box.

Caution Because of the permanently destructive action of a delete query, you should always make backup copies of your tables before working with them.

The following example will help illustrate the use of Access action queries. In this case, you have a large number of records to delete.

In this situation, you are going to delete all records of deceased animals. Recall that you already copied all deceased pet records to backup tables in the append query section. The tables you're dealing with have these relationships:

> ✦ One pet has many visits.
>
> ✦ One visit has many visit details.

Both of these are one-to-many relationships. As a result, if you don't define permanent relationships between the tables and have turned on Cascade Delete, you'll need to create three separate delete queries. (You would need to delete from the Visit Details, Visits, and Pets tables — in that order.)

With relations set and Cascade Delete on, however, you have to delete only the records from the Pets table; Access automatically deletes all related records. Assume for this example that you have already appended the records to another table — or that you have made a new table of the records you're about to delete, set up permanent relationships among the three tables, and turned on Cascade Delete for both relationships (that is, between Pets and Visits and between Visits and Visit Details).

Creating a cascading delete query

To create a *cascading delete query* for all pets that died last year, along with their visit histories, perform the following steps:

1. Create a new query using the Pets, Visits, and Visit Details tables.

2. Select Query⇨Delete from the Design menu.

   Notice that the name of the window changes from `Select Query:Query1` to `Delete Query:Query1`.

3. Select the Deceased field from the Pets table.

4. Specify the criterion **Yes** in the Deceased field.

   The Delete Query Design window is shown in Figure 26-16. The only field and criteria that must appear in this delete query is the first field, Deceased.

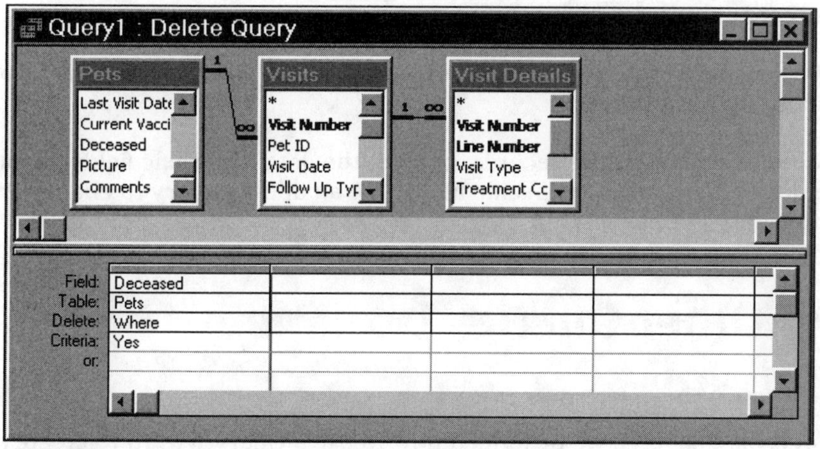

Figure 26-16: The delete query's QBE pane.

5. Go to the datasheet and verify that only records which say `Yes` are there.

6. Return to the Design window.

7. Click on the Run button on the toolbar (or select Query⇨Run from the menu).

   Access displays a dialog box with a message: You are about to delete *x* row[s] from the specified table (Pets).After you click Yes, you can't use the Undo command to reverse the changes. Are you sure that you want to delete the selected records? **Access does not specify how many rows will be deleted from the other tables that may be linked to the table you selected.**

8. Click on the Yes button to complete the query. The records are removed from all three tables. When you click on the Yes button, Access deletes the records in the Pets table and then automatically deletes the related records in the Visits and Visit Details tables. Selecting No stops the procedure (no records are copied).

Remember that a delete query permanently and irreversibly removes the records from the table(s). Therefore, it is important to back up the records you want to delete *before* you delete them.

Checking your results

After completing the delete query, you can check your results by simply pressing the Datasheet button on the toolbar. If the delete query worked correctly, you will see no records in the datasheet.

You have now deleted all records of deceased animals from the database tables Pets, Visits, and Visit Details.

Note   Delete queries remove entire records, not just the data in specific fields. If you need to delete only values in specific fields, use an update query to change the values to empty values.

Creating Other Queries Using the Query Wizards

In the preceding chapter, we described how to use a Query Wizard to create a crosstab query. Access has three other Wizards that can help you maintain your databases:

✦ Find Duplicate Records Wizard: Shows any duplicate records in a single table, on the basis of a field in the table.

✦ Find Unmatched Records Wizard: Shows all records that do not have a corresponding record in another table (for example, a customer with no pets or a pet with no owner).

✦ Archive Wizard: Lets you back up records in a single table and then optionally delete the records you just backed up.

Both the Find Duplicate Records Wizard and Archive Wizard work on a single table. The Find Unmatched Records Wizard compares records from one table with another.

These Wizards (along with all the others, such as the Crosstab Wizard) are listed when you first start a new query.

Find Duplicate Records Wizard

This Wizard helps you create a query that reports which records in a table are duplicated using some field or fields in the table as a basis. Access asks which fields you want to use for checking duplication and then prompts you to enter some other fields you may want to see in the query. Finally, Access asks for a title; then it creates and displays the query.

This type of Wizard query can help you find duplicate key violations, a valuable trick when you want to take an existing table and make a unique key field with existing data. If you try to create a unique key field and Access reports an error, you know that you have either Nulls in the field or duplicate records. Then the query helps you find the duplicates.

Find Unmatched Records Wizard

This Wizard helps you create a query that reports any orphan or widow records between two tables.

An *orphan* is a record in a *many*-side table that has no corresponding record in the *one*-side table. For example, you may have a pet in the Pets table that does not have an owner in the Customer table (the pet is an orphan).

A *widow* is a record in the *one* side of a one-to-many or one-to-one that does not have a corresponding record in the other table. For example, you may have a customer who has no animals in the Pets table.

Access asks for the names of the two tables you want to compare; it also asks for the link field name between the tables. Access prompts you for the fields you want to see in the first table and for a title. Then it creates the query.

This type of query can help you find records that have no corresponding records in other tables. If you create a relationship between tables and try to set referential integrity but Access reports that it cannot activate the feature, some records are violating integrity. This query helps you find them quickly.

Archive Records Wizard

The Archive Records Wizard helps you create a query that will back up records for a specific criterion and then delete the records from the current table (if the user so requests). The query, created by the Wizard, will actually perform two queries, one after the other — a make-table query and a delete query. Even so, this query works with only one table at a time and is based on a single-field criterion (that is, based on one field in the table).

Access prompts you for the table you want to archive and then for a single-field criterion you want to archive for. Then Access reports the number of records to be archived and shows them to you for verification, asking whether you want to delete them after archiving. Finally Access prompts you for a title and runs the query. As it runs, Access again prompts you to verify that you want to archive the records. If you answer Yes, Access copies the records to a table by the same name, adding Arc (for archive) to the name.

The archive records type of query is an excellent way to back up any table in your application. However, the delete archived records option should be used with caution because it removes the records permanently from the tables. When you're working with related tables, this query should back up all child tables first and then parent tables. For example, the Pet table should be backed up before the Customer table. This should be done because the archive records query works with only one table at a time. Working from the bottom of the hierarchy up will ensure that you have archived all tables. When you're working with lookup tables and nonrelated tables, this query offers an excellent way to create a working backup.

Saving an Action Query

Saving an action query is just like saving any other query. From design mode, you can save the query and continue working by clicking on the Save button on the toolbar (or by selecting File⇨Save from the Query menu). If this is the first time you're saving the query, Access prompts you for a name in the Save As dialog box.

You can also save the query and exit, by either selecting File⇨Close from the menu or double-clicking on the Control menu button (in the top left corner of the Query window) and answering Yes to this dialog box question: Save changes to the design of '<query name>'? You also can save the query by pressing F12.

Running an Action Query

After you save an action query, you can run it by simply double-clicking on its name. Access will warn you that an action query is about to be executed and ask you to confirm before it continues with the query.

Troubleshooting Action Queries

When you're working with action queries, you need to be aware of several potential problems. While you're running the query, any of several messages may appear, including messages that several records were lost because of *key violations* or that records were *locked* during the execution of the query. This section discusses some of these problems and how to avoid them.

Data-type errors in appending and updating

If you attempt to enter a value that is not appropriate for the specified field, Access doesn't enter the value; it simply ignores the incorrect values and converts the fields to Null values. When you're working with append queries, Access will append the records, but the fields may be blank!

Key violations in action queries

When you attempt to append records to another database that has a primary key, Access will not append records that contain the same primary key value.

Access does not let you update a record and change a primary key value to an existing value. You can change a primary key value to another value under these conditions:

✦ The new primary key value does not already exist.

✦ The field value you're attempting to change is not related to fields in other tables.

Access does not let you delete a field on the *one* side of a one-to-many relationship without first deleting the records from the *many* side.

Access does not let you append or update a field value that will duplicate a value in a *unique index field* — one that has the Index property set to Yes (No Duplicates).

Record-locked fields in multiuser environments

Access will not perform an action query on records locked by another user. When you're performing an update or append query, you can choose to continue and change all other values. But remember that if you allow Access to continue with an action query, you won't be able to determine which records were left unchanged!

Text fields

When appending or updating to a Text field that is smaller than the current field, Access will truncate any text data that doesn't fit in the new field. Access will *not* warn you that it truncated the information.

Summary

In this chapter, you learned how to create and use a special type of query called the action query. This type of query goes beyond performing searches; it can make changes to the data. This chapter covered the following points:

✦ Action queries perform some operation on the tables you're using. The operation can be deleting records, changing the contents of records, adding records to another table, or making new tables.

✦ The various types of action queries include make-table, append, update, and delete.

✦ Action queries do not create a dynaset. To view the results of an action query, you must convert it to a select query (if it's a delete or update query) or view the affected table.

✦ Always back up your tables before you work with action queries.

✦ When you create an action query, it's best to create a select query first to make sure that the action will affect the correct records.

✦ Append action queries can work with only one table at a time.

✦ Append action queries must already have an existing table to append to. The query does not create a table for you if one doesn't already exist.

✦ The append query is not the best method for appending all records from one table to another. It's better to copy the table to the Clipboard and paste it to the other table.

✦ Make-table action queries can take fields from one or many tables and combine them into a single table.

✦ Delete action queries can delete records from multiple tables that have one-to-one relationships.

✦ Delete action queries for tables with one-to-many relationships require deleting the *many*-side records first; then the *one*-side record can be deleted.

✦ Unless an action query will be executed over and over, do not save it.

✦ Access enforces all referential rules when performing action queries. If an action query attempts to perform an operation that violates referential integrity, Access halts the operation.

In the next chapter, you examine advanced query topics.

✦   ✦   ✦

Advanced Query Topics

In this chapter, you work with queries in more detail and complexity than in earlier chapters. So far, you have worked with all types of queries: select, action, crosstab, and parameter. You have not, however, worked with all the options you can use with these types of queries.

This chapter focuses on a wide range of advanced query topics. You will read about several topics explained in other chapters; this chapter will address them in more detail. A firm understanding of advanced queries can solve unexpected problems for you later.

Using Lookup Tables and Joins

You can use a lookup table to validate the entry of data or find additional information based on a key value. Such a table uses, by definition, a many-to-one relationship; many records in the primary table can reference information from one record in the lookup table. A lookup table can be permanent or transient:

Permanent   Created solely for lookup purposes

Transient   Used as either a lookup table or a primary table

The Mountain Animal Hospital database has four permanent lookup tables: States, Pets, Treatments, and Medications.

The Customer table is an example of a *transient lookup table*. When you're working with a form to add pet personal information (name, type, and so on), the Customer table becomes a lookup table based on the customer number. Although the Customer table is a primary table of the database, in this case it may become a lookup table for the Pets table.

Working with lookup tables in queries does require an understanding of joins and how they work. For example, you may be interested in displaying visit details along with the specific treatment and medication given for each visit. Treatment and medication information will come from the lookup tables — in this case, Treatments and Medications. To create this query, follow these steps:

1. Select the Visit Details, Treatments, and Medications tables and join them if they are not already joined.

2. Double-click on the Visit Number field in the Visit Details table.

3. Double-click on the Visit Type field in the Visit Details table.

4. Double-click on the Treatment field of the Treatments table.

5. Double-click on the Medication Name field of the Medications table.

Your query should look like Figure 27-1. Notice that Visit Details uses both Treatments and Medications as lookup tables.

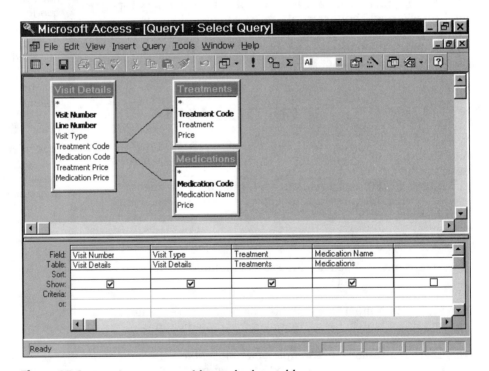

Figure 27-1: Creating a query with two lookup tables.

After you create the query, you can select the Datasheet option from the Query View button on the toolbar to display a dynaset similar to the one in Figure 27-2. (Clicking once will toggle you back and forth between the Design view and the Datasheet. Clicking on the drop-down box will show all three options: Query View, Datasheet, and SQL.)

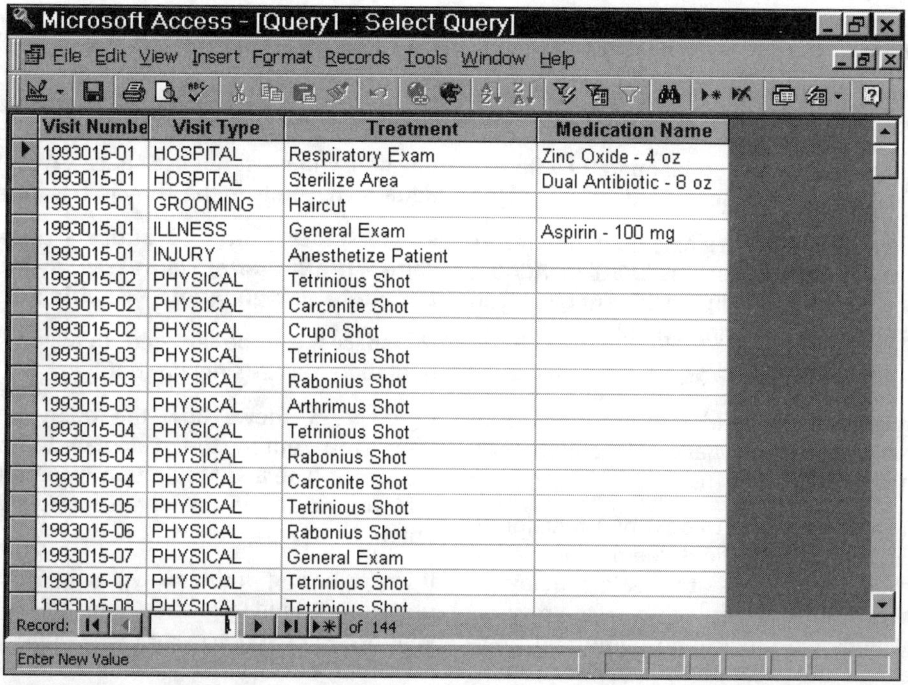

Visit Number	Visit Type	Treatment	Medication Name
1993015-01	HOSPITAL	Respiratory Exam	Zinc Oxide - 4 oz
1993015-01	HOSPITAL	Sterilize Area	Dual Antibiotic - 8 oz
1993015-01	GROOMING	Haircut	
1993015-01	ILLNESS	General Exam	Aspirin - 100 mg
1993015-01	INJURY	Anesthetize Patient	
1993015-02	PHYSICAL	Tetrinious Shot	
1993015-02	PHYSICAL	Carconite Shot	
1993015-02	PHYSICAL	Crupo Shot	
1993015-03	PHYSICAL	Tetrinious Shot	
1993015-03	PHYSICAL	Rabonius Shot	
1993015-03	PHYSICAL	Arthrimus Shot	
1993015-04	PHYSICAL	Tetrinious Shot	
1993015-04	PHYSICAL	Rabonius Shot	
1993015-04	PHYSICAL	Carconite Shot	
1993015-05	PHYSICAL	Tetrinious Shot	
1993015-06	PHYSICAL	Rabonius Shot	
1993015-07	PHYSICAL	General Exam	
1993015-07	PHYSICAL	Tetrinious Shot	
1993015-08	PHYSICAL	Tetrinious Shot	

Figure 27-2: Datasheet of a query with two lookup tables.

Using the DLookUp( ) function for lookup tables

Another way to find specific lookup information based on a field is to create a calculated field using the DLookUp( ) function. You use DLookUp( ) to find information in a table that is not currently open. The general syntax for this function is as follows:

DLookUp("[Field to display]", "[Lookup Table]", "<Criteria for Search>")

"[Field to display]" in quotation marks is the field in the lookup table you want to find.

"[Lookup Table]" in quotation marks is the table containing the field you want to display.

"<Criteria for Search>" in quotation marks signifies criteria used by the lookup function.

(continued)

(continued)

Access suggests that *Criteria for Search* is not necessary, but if you want to use a different criterion for each record, it is essential. When you use DLookUp( ), the format of your criteria is critical. The syntax of *Criteria for Search* is as follows:

"[*Field in Lookup Table*] = '<*Example Data*>' "

You can replace the equal operator with any valid Access operator.

'<*Example Data*>' in single quotation marks is usually a literal, such as 'DOG' or 'AC001'. If the data is a field in the current table, you must use the following syntax:

" & [*Field in This Table*] & "

Notice that the field is surrounded with double quotation marks (") and ampersands (&).

Although using the DLookUp( ) function to build a calculated field seems complex, it can be a simple way to create a query for use by a form or report. To create a query that finds the medication name and treatment in the Treatments and Medications tables, follow these steps:

1. Select the Visit Details table.

2. Double-click on the Visit Type field in the Visit Details table.

3. In an empty field in the QBE pane, type
TreatmentType:DLookUp ("[Treatment]", "[Treatments]","[Treatment Code]=""&[VisitDetails]. [TreatmentCode]&"").

4. In another empty field in the QBE pane, type **MedicationType: DLookUp ("[MedicationName]", "[Medications]","[Medication Code] = ""&[Visit Details]. [Medication Code]&"").**

When you enter the field name of the current table in the criteria for the DLookUp( ) function, you must not use spaces. After the equal sign, you type the entry in this format:

single quote - double quote - ampersand - [*field name*] - ampersand - double quote - single quote - double quote

No spaces can be entered between the quotation marks (single or double).

Figure 27-3 shows how the query looks after you enter the calculated fields Treatment Type and Medication Type. Notice that you don't see the entire formula you entered.

If you're having problems typing in Steps 3 or 4, press Shift+F2 to activate the Zoom window. After you activate the window, the entire contents will be highlighted; press F2 again to deselect the contents and move to the end of them.

If you now select the Datasheet option in the Query View button on the toolbar, you see a datasheet similar to Figure 27-4. Notice that several records have no medication name.

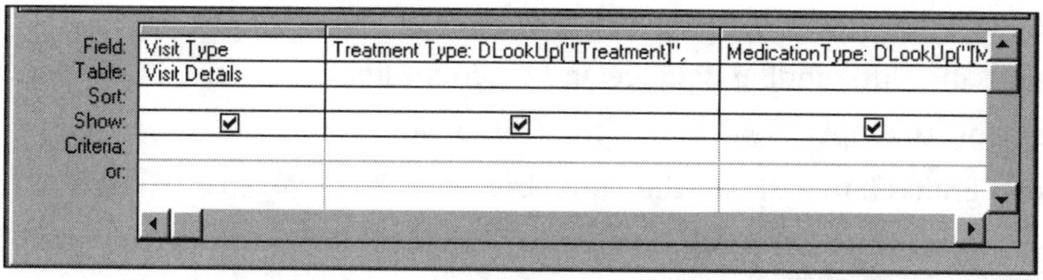

Figure 27-3: The QBE pane showing two calculated fields using the DLookUp( ) function.

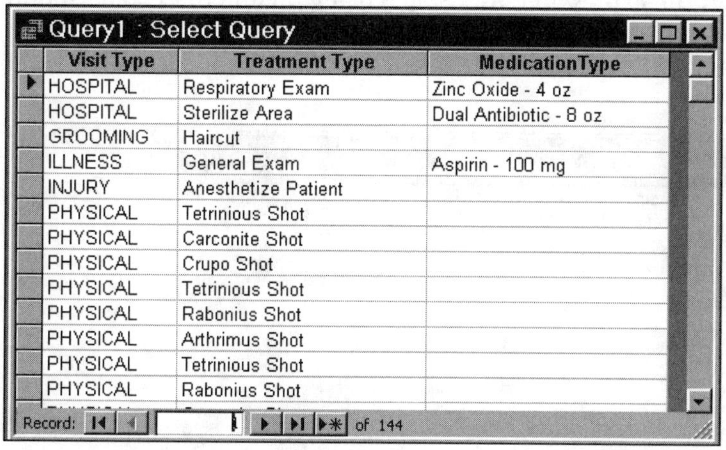

Visit Type	Treatment Type	MedicationType
HOSPITAL	Respiratory Exam	Zinc Oxide - 4 oz
HOSPITAL	Sterilize Area	Dual Antibiotic - 8 oz
GROOMING	Haircut	
ILLNESS	General Exam	Aspirin - 100 mg
INJURY	Anesthetize Patient	
PHYSICAL	Tetrinious Shot	
PHYSICAL	Carconite Shot	
PHYSICAL	Crupo Shot	
PHYSICAL	Tetrinious Shot	
PHYSICAL	Rabonius Shot	
PHYSICAL	Arthrimus Shot	
PHYSICAL	Tetrinious Shot	
PHYSICAL	Rabonius Shot	

Figure 27-4: A datasheet with some of the records for the Medication Name field left blank.

Using Calculated Fields

Queries are not limited to actual fields from tables; you can also use *calculated fields* (created by performing some calculation). A calculated field can be created in many different ways, for example:

✦ Concatenating two Text type fields using the ampersand (&)

✦ Performing a mathematical calculation on two Number type fields

✦ Using an Access function to create a field based on the function

In the next example, you create a simple calculated field, Total Due, from the Outstanding Balance and Discount fields in the Customer table. Follow these steps:

1. Create a new query by using the Customer table.

2. Select the Outstanding Balance and Discount fields from the Customer table.

3. Click on an empty Field: cell of the QBE pane.

4. Press Shift+F2 to activate the Zoom box.

5. Type **Total Due: Format([Outstanding Balance]-[Outstanding Balance]*[Discount],"currency")**.

6. Click on the OK button in the Zoom box (or press Enter).

Figure 27-5 shows the expression from Step 5 being built in the Zoom window. Total Due is the calculated field name for the expression. The field name and expression are separated by a colon.

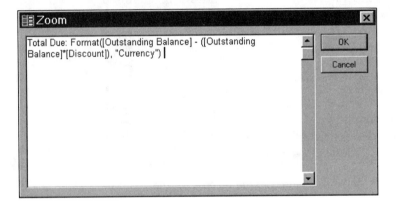

Figure 27-5: Creating a simple calculated field.

Access 97 has an Expression Builder you can use to help you create any expression — for example, a complex calculated field for a query. In the following example, you create a calculated field named Next Visit Date that displays a date six months later. You can use this date for a letter report you plan to send to all customers; the date is based on the Last Visit Date field of the Pets table. To create this calculated field, follow these steps:

1. Create a new query by using the Pets table.

2. Select the Type of Animal and Last Visit Date fields from the Pets table.

3. Click on an empty Field: cell in the QBE pane.

4. Activate the Expression Builder by clicking on the Build button on the toolbar (the wand). Another method: *right*-click to display the shortcut menu and select Build.

Access displays the Expression Builder dialog box, as shown in Figure 27-6.

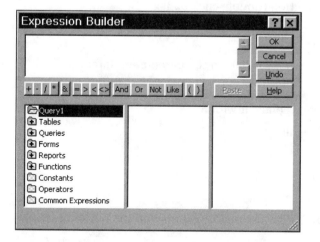

Figure 27-6: The Expression Builder dialog box.

Now build the expression **DateAdd("m",6,[Pets]![Last Visit Date])** for the calculated field.

5. Go to the bottom left window of the Expression Builder dialog box and expand the Functions tree (double-click on it).

6. Select the Built-in Functions choice (double-click on it).

Access places information in the two windows to the right of the one you're in (see Figure 27-7).

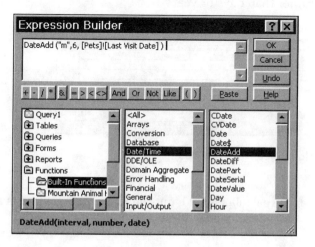

Figure 27-7: Creating a calculated field.

7. Go to the third window (which lists all the functions).

8. Select the DateAdd function (double-click on it).

   Access places the function in the top left window, with information about the necessary parameters.

9. Go to the top left window and click on the parameter <interval>.

10. Type **"m"**.

11. Click on <number> and replace it with **6**.

12. Click on <date> and highlight it.

    The function should look like the one in Figure 27-7.

13. Go back to the bottom left window; double-click on Tables.

14. Select the Pets table (click on it).

15. Select [Last Visit Date] from the middle window on the bottom (double-click on it).

    Access places the table and field name in the last part of the DateAdd function.

16. Click on the OK button in the Expression Builder.

    Access returns you to the QBE pane and places the expression in the cell for you.

17. Access assigns a name for the expression automatically, labeling it Expr1. Should your field now show this name, change it from Expr1 to **Next Visit Date** by simply overwriting it.

If you perform these steps correctly, the cell looks like Figure 27-8. The DateAdd( ) function lets you add six months to Pets.Last Visit Date. The *m* signifies that you are working with months rather than days or years.

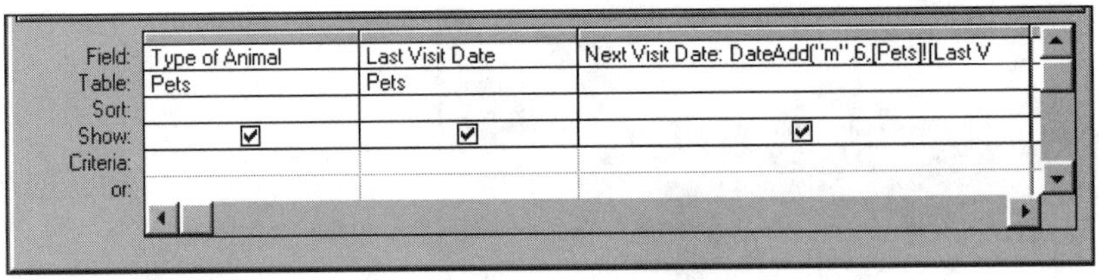

Field:	Type of Animal	Last Visit Date	Next Visit Date: DateAdd("m",6,[Pets]![Last V
Table:	Pets	Pets	
Sort:			
Show:	☑	☑	☑
Criteria:			
or:			

Figure 27-8: A calculated field named Next Visit Date.

Of course, you could type in the calculated field, but the Expression Builder is a valuable tool when you're creating complex, hard-to-remember expressions.

Finding the Number of Records in a Table or Query

To determine quickly the total number of records in an existing table or query, use the Count(*) function. This is a special use of the Count( ) function. For example, to determine the total number of records in the Pets table, follow these steps:

1. Start a new query using the Pets table.

2. Click on the first empty Field: cell in the QBE pane.

3. Type **Count(*)** in the cell.

Access adds the calculated field name Expr1 to the cell in front of the Count( ) function. Your query should now look like Figure 27-9.

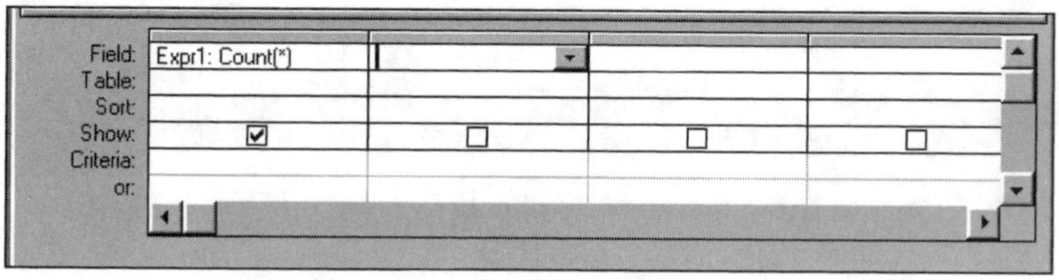

Figure 27-9: Using the Count(*) function.

When you look at the datasheet, you'll see a single cell that shows the number of records for the Pets table. The datasheet should look like the one in Figure 27-10.

Figure 27-10: The datasheet of a Count(*) function.

If you use this function with the asterisk wildcard (*), this is the only field that can be shown in the datasheet. That is why you entered the expression Count(*) in an empty QBE pane.

You can also use the Count(*) function to determine the total number of records that match a specific criterion. For example, you may want to know how many cats you have in the Pets table. Follow these steps to ascertain the number of cats in the table:

1. Start a new query and select the Pets table.

2. Click on the first empty Field: cell in the QBE pane.

3. Type **Count(*)** in the cell.

4. Double-click on the Type of Animal field of the Pets table.

5. Deselect the Show: cell for Type of Animal.

6. Type **"CAT"** in the Criteria: cell for Type of Animal.

Figure 27-11 shows how the query should look. If you select the Datasheet option from the Query View button on the toolbar, Access will again display only one cell in the datasheet; it contains the number of cats in the Pets table.

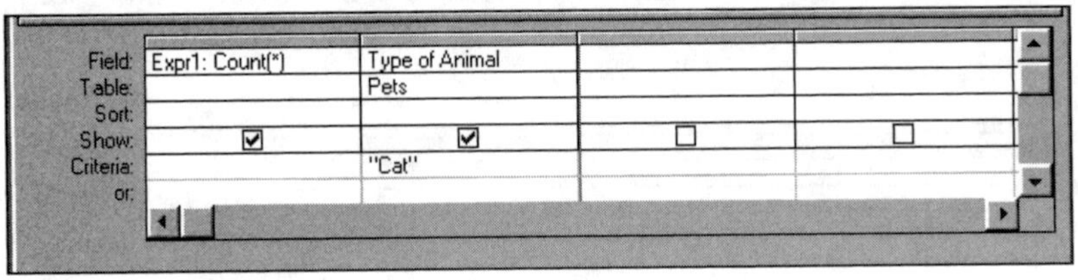

Figure 27-11: The query to show the number of cats.

Remember that only the field that contains the Count(*) function can be shown in the datasheet. If you try to display any additional fields, Access reports an error.

Finding the Top (*n*) Records in a Query

Access 97 not only enables you to find the number of records in an existing table or query but also provides you with the capability of finding the query's first (*n*) records (that is, a set number or percentage of its records).

Suppose that you want to identify the top ten animals you have treated — in other words, for which animal has which owner paid the most to your business? To determine the top ten animals and their owners, follow these steps:

1. Create a new query using the Customer, Pets, and Visits tables.

2. Select Customer Name from the Customer Table, Type of Animal and Pet Name from the Pets table, and Total Amount from the Visits table.

3. Click on the Totals button, Σ, on the toolbar.

4. Change Group By (under the Total Amount field) to **Sum**.

5. Sort the Total Amount field in Descending order.

The resulting query should look like the one in Figure 27-12.

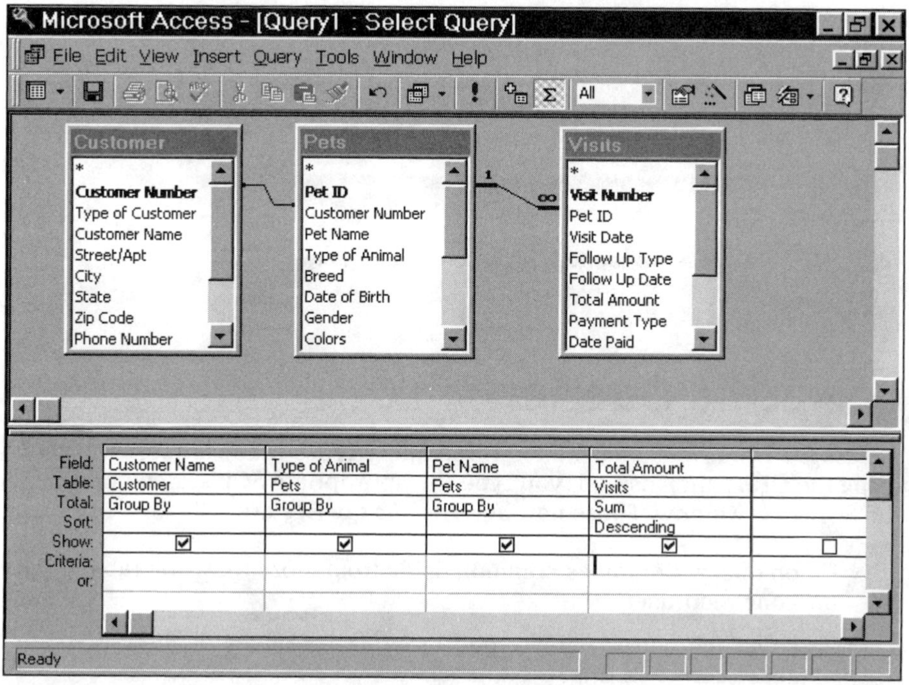

Figure 27-12: A total query with three Group By fields.

6. Click on the combo box next to the Σ button on the toolbar.

7. Select from the combo box or enter **10** in the Top Values property cell.

You are ready to run your query. When you click on the Query View button on the toolbar, you should see the top ten money-producing records in the dynaset, which should look like Figure 27-13.

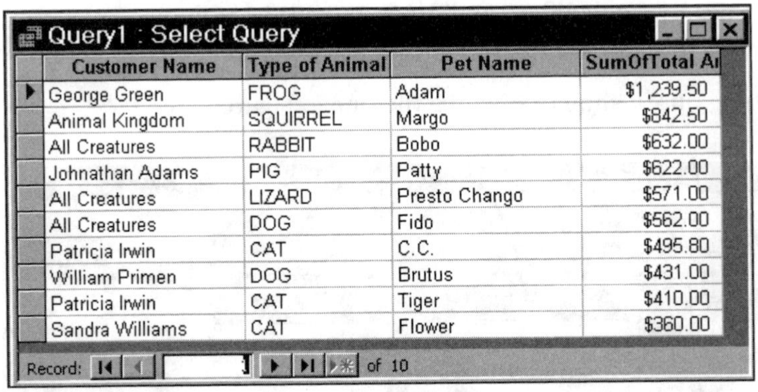

Query1 : Select Query

Customer Name	Type of Animal	Pet Name	SumOfTotal A
George Green	FROG	Adam	$1,239.50
Animal Kingdom	SQUIRREL	Margo	$842.50
All Creatures	RABBIT	Bobo	$632.00
Johnathan Adams	PIG	Patty	$622.00
All Creatures	LIZARD	Presto Chango	$571.00
All Creatures	DOG	Fido	$562.00
Patricia Irwin	CAT	C.C.	$495.80
William Primen	DOG	Brutus	$431.00
Patricia Irwin	CAT	Tiger	$410.00
Sandra Williams	CAT	Flower	$360.00

Record: 1 of 10

Figure 27-13: Dynaset of the top ten records in a query.

SQL-Specific Queries

Access for Windows 95 has added three query types that cannot be created by using the QBE pane; instead, you type the appropriate SQL statement directly in the SQL view window. These new *SQL-specific* queries are

- ✦ Union query: Combines common fields from more than one table or query into one recordset.
- ✦ Pass-through query: Allows you to send SQL commands directly to any SQL database server in the SQL database server's SQL syntax.
- ✦ Data definition query: Lets you create or alter database objects in Access databases directly.

To create any of these queries, select from the Query➪SQL Specific menu the type you want to create. (No applicable button is available on the toolbar.)

Creating union queries

Union queries let you quickly combine several tables that have common fields. The resultant *snapshot* (like a dynaset) is not updatable.

For example, a competing veterinarian retires and gives you all the client records from her practice. You decide to create a union query to combine the data from both practices. Figure 27-14 shows a union query that returns the customer name and city in order (by city).

Query1 : Union Query
SELECT [Customer Name], [City]
FROM Customer
UNION SELECT [Customer Name], [City]
FROM NewCustomer
ORDER BY [City];

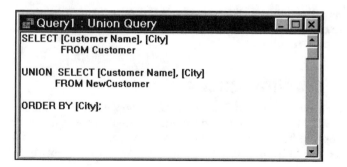

Figure 27-14: An SQL union query.

Notice that a union query has two or more SQL SELECT statements. Each SELECT statement requires the same number of fields, in the same order.

Creating pass-through queries

A *pass-through query* sends SQL commands directly to an SQL database server (such as Microsoft SQL Server, Oracle, and so on). You send the command by using the syntax required by the particular server. Be sure to consult the documentation for the appropriate SQL database server.

Figure 27-15 shows a pass-through query for a Microsoft SQL Server that creates a new table named Payroll and defines the fields in the table.

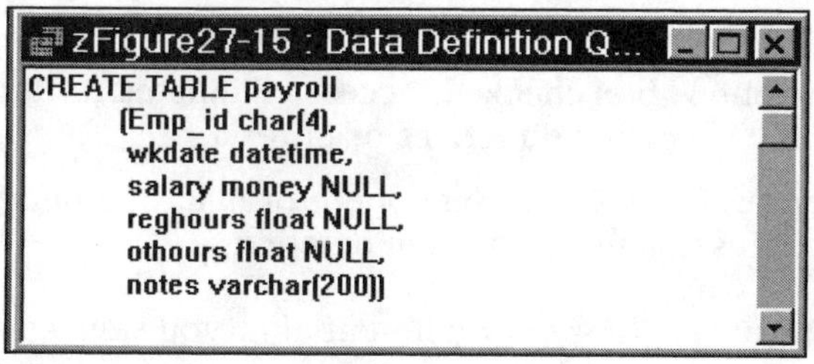

zFigure27-15 : Data Definition Q...
CREATE TABLE payroll
(Emp_id char(4),
wkdate datetime,
salary money NULL,
reghours float NULL,
othours float NULL,
notes varchar(200))

Figure 27-15: A pass-through query for SQL Server.

Caution Never attempt to convert a pass-through query to another type of query. If you do, Access erases the entire SQL statement you typed in.

Caution When working with pass-through queries, you should not perform operations that change the state of the connection. Halting a transaction in the middle (for example) may cause unexpected results.

Creating data definition queries

Of these three SQL-specific queries, the *data definition query* is least useful. Everything you can do with it, you can also do using the design tools in Access. The data definition query is, however, an efficient way to create or change database objects. With a data definition query, you can use any of the following SQL statements:

✦ CREATE TABLE

✦ ALTER TABLE

✦ DROP TABLE

✦ CREATE INDEX

✦ DROP INDEX

How Queries Save Field Selections

When you open a query design, you may notice that the design has changed since you last saved the query. When you save a query, Access rearranges (even eliminates) fields on the basis of several rules. The following list summarizes these rules:

✦ If a field does not have the Show: box checked but has criteria specified, Access moves it to the rightmost columns in the QBE pane.

✦ If a field does not have the Show: box checked, Access eliminates it from the QBE pane column unless it has sorting directives or criteria.

✦ If you create a totaling expression with the Sum operator in a total query, Access changes it to an expression using the Sum function.

Because of these rules, your query may look very different after you save and reopen it. In this section of the chapter, you learn how this happens (and some ways to prevent it).

Hiding (Not Showing) Fields

Sometimes you won't want certain fields in the QBE pane to show in the actual dynaset of the datasheet. For example, you may want to use a field such as Customer Number to specify a criterion or a sort without showing the actual field.

To *hide*, or exclude, a field from the dynaset, you simply click off the Show: box under the field you want to hide. Figure 27-16 demonstrates this procedure. Notice that the field Type of Customer is used to specify a criterion of displaying only individuals ("1"). You don't want the Type of Customer field in the actual datasheet, so you click off the Show: cell for the Type of Customer field.

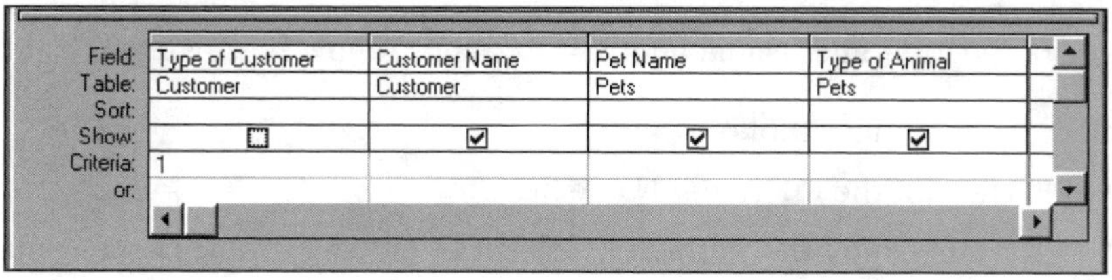

Figure 27-16: Hiding a field.

Any fields that have the Show: cell turned off (and for which you entered criteria) are placed at the end of the QBE pane when you save the query. Figure 27-17 shows the same query as Figure 27-16 after it is saved and brought back into the design screen. Notice that the field `Type of Customer` has been moved to the end (extreme right) of the QBE pane. The location of a hidden field will not change the dynaset. Because the field is not displayed, its location in the QBE pane is unimportant. You always get the same results, even if you've placed a hidden field in the QBE pane.

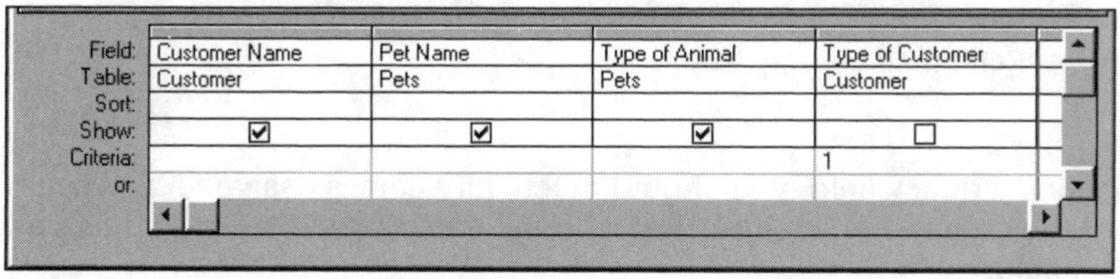

Figure 27-17: A query that has been saved with a hidden field.

Note   If you hide any fields in the QBE pane that are not used for sorts or criteria, Access eliminates them from the query automatically when you save it. If you want to use these fields and need to show them later, you'll have to add them back to the QBE pane.

Caution   If you're creating a query to be used by a form or report, *you must show any fields it will use,* including any field to which you want to bind a control.

Renaming Fields in Queries

When working with queries, you can rename a field to describe the field's contents more clearly or accurately. For example, you may want to rename the Customer Name field to Owner Name. This is useful for working with calculated fields or calculating totals; Access automatically assigns nondescript names such as Expr1 or AvgOfWeight, but it's easy to rename fields in Access queries. To change the display name of the Customer Name field, for example, follow these steps:

1. Select the Customer table.

2. Double-click on the Customer Name field.

3. Place the cursor in front of the first letter of Customer Name in the Field: cell.

4. Type **Owner Name:** (be sure to include a colon).

Figure 27-18 shows the query field renamed. Notice that the field has both the display name, which is Owner Name, and the actual field name, which is Customer Name.

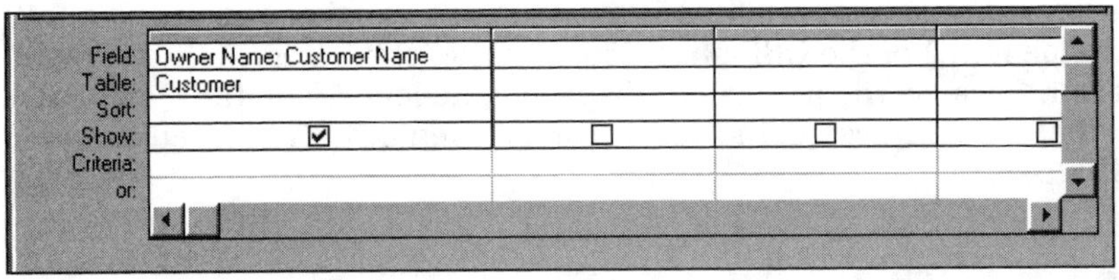

Figure 27-18: Renaming a query field.

Note   When naming a query field, you should delete any names assigned by Access (on the left of the colon). For example, remove the name Expr1 when you name the calculated field.

If you rename a field, Access uses only the new name for the heading of the query datasheet; it does the same with the control source in any form or report that uses the query. Any new forms or reports you create on the basis of the query will use the new field name. (Access does not change the actual field name in the underlying table.)

Note   If you want to change *only* the name that appears on the datasheet, change the Captions property of the Field: cell, typing the new name in this cell. This new name will then appear only when you view the datasheet; it will not show up in the query's Design view.

When working with renamed fields, you can use an *expression name* (the new name you specified) in another expression within the same query. For example, you may have a calculated field called First Name that uses several Access functions to separate an individual's first name from the last name. For this calculated field, you can use the field called Owner Name you created earlier.

Caution   When you work with referenced expression names, you cannot have any criteria specified against the field you're referencing. For example, you cannot have a criterion specified for Owner Name if you reference Owner Name in the First Name calculation. If you do, Access will not display the contents for the expression field Owner Name in the datasheet.

Hiding and Unhiding Columns in the QBE Pane

Sometimes you may want to hide specific fields in the QBE pane. This is not the same as hiding a field by clicking on the Show: box. Hiding a column in the QBE pane is similar to hiding a datasheet column, which is easy: You simply resize a column (from right to left) until it has no visible width. Figure 27-19 shows several fields in the QBE pane; in the next example, you hide one of its columns.

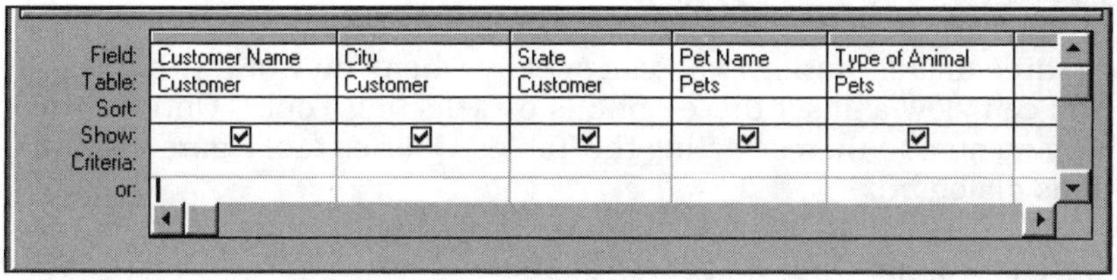

Figure 27-19: A typical QBE pane.

Follow these steps to hide the City column:

1. Move the mouse pointer to the right side of the City field on the *field selector* (a small, thick bar icon with arrows on both sides).

2. Click on the right side of the City field, and drag it toward the Customer Name field until it totally disappears.

Figure 27-20 shows the QBE pane with the City field hidden.

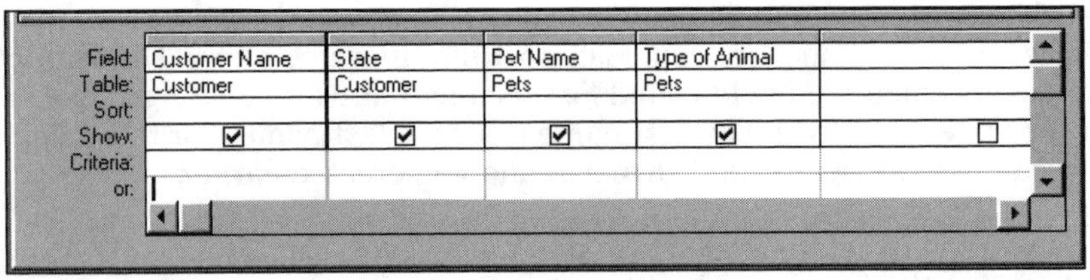

Field:	Customer Name	State	Pet Name	Type of Animal		
Table:	Customer	Customer	Pets	Pets		
Sort:						
Show:	☑	☑	☑	☑		☐
Criteria:						
or:						

Figure 27-20: The QBE pane with a column hidden.

After you hide a field, you can *unhide* it by reversing the process. If you want to unhide the City column, follow these steps:

1. Move the mouse pointer to the left side of the field State on the selector bar (the bar with arrows appears). Make sure that you are to the right of the divider between Customer Name and State.

2. Click on the left side of State and drag it toward the Pet Name field until you size the column to the correct length.

3. Release the button; the field name City will appear in the column you unhide.

Query Design Options

There are three default options you can specify when you work with a query design. You can view and set these options by selecting Tools⇨Options from the main Query menu and then selecting the Tables/Queries tab. Figure 27-21 shows this Options dialog box.

Notice these four items you can set for queries:

+ Output All Fields
+ Run Permissions
+ Show Table Names
+ Enable AutoJoin

Generally the default for Show Table Names and Output All fields is No. Run Permissions offers you a choice of either the Owner's permission or the User's (the default). Finally, Enable AutoJoin controls whether Access will use common field names to perform an automatic join between tables that have no relationships set. Table 27-1 describes each option and its purpose.

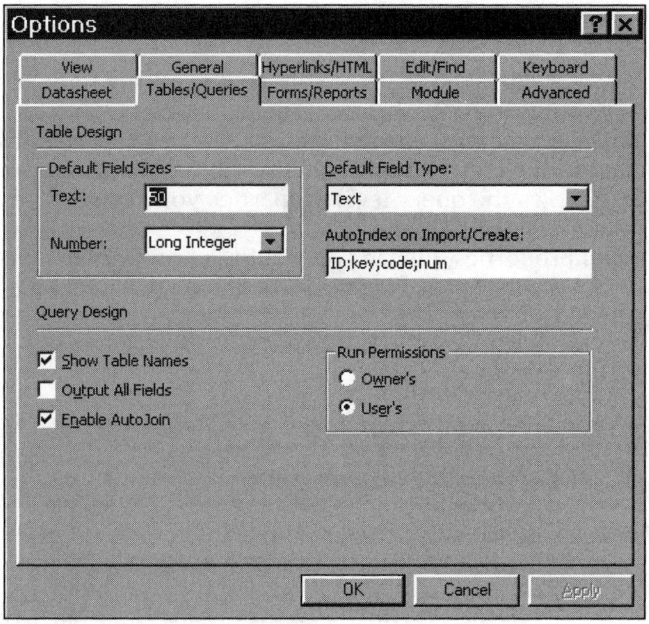

Figure 27-21: The Options dialog box.

Note   When you set query design options, they specify actions for new queries only; they do not affect the current query. To show table names in the current query, select View⇨Table Names from the main Query menu. To specify the other two options for the current query, select View⇨Properties....

Table 27-1
Query Design Options

Option	Purpose
Output All Fields	Shows all fields in the underlying tables or only the fields displayed in the QBE pane
Run Permissions	Restricts use in a multiuser environment; a user restricted from viewing the underlying tables can still view the data from the query
Enable AutoJoin	Uses common field names to perform an automatic join between tables that have no relationships set
Show Table Names	Shows the Table: row in the QBE pane when set to Yes; hides the Table: row if set to No.

Setting Query Properties

To set query properties, either click on the Properties button on the toolbar, *right-click* on Properties and choose it from the shortcut menu, or select View⇨ Properties from the main Query menu. Access displays a Query Properties dialog box. Your options depend on the query type and on the table or field with which you're working. Table 27-2 shows the query-level properties you can set.

You can use the query-level properties, just as you would the properties in forms, reports, and tables. *query-level properties* displayed when you click depend on the type of query being created.

<table>
<tr><td colspan="8" align="center">Table 27-2
Query-Level Properties</td></tr>
<tr><td>***Property***</td><td>***Description***</td><td colspan="6">***Query***</td></tr>
<tr><td></td><td></td><td>*Select*</td><td>*Crosstab*</td><td>*Update*</td><td>*Delete*</td><td>*Make-Table*</td><td>*Append*</td></tr>
<tr><td>Description</td><td>Text describing table or query</td><td>X</td><td>X</td><td>X</td><td>X</td><td>X</td><td>X</td></tr>
<tr><td>Output All Fields</td><td>Show all fields from the under-lying tables in the query</td><td>X</td><td></td><td></td><td></td><td>X</td><td>X</td></tr>
<tr><td>Top Values</td><td>Number of highest or low-est values to be returned</td><td>X</td><td></td><td></td><td></td><td>X</td><td>X</td></tr>
<tr><td>Unique Values</td><td>Return only unique field values in the dynaset</td><td>X</td><td></td><td></td><td></td><td>X</td><td>X</td></tr>
<tr><td>Unique Records</td><td>Return only unique records for the dynaset</td><td>X</td><td>X</td><td>X</td><td>X</td><td></td><td>X</td></tr>
<tr><td>Run Permissions</td><td>Establish permissions for specified user</td><td>X</td><td>X</td><td>X</td><td>X</td><td>X</td><td>X</td></tr>
</table>

Property	Description	Query					
		Select	Crosstab	Update	Delete	Make-Table	Append
Source Database	External database name for all tables/queries in the query	X	X	X	X	X	X
Source Connect Str	Name of application used to connect to external database	X	X	X	X	X	X
Record Locks	Records locked while query runs (usually action queries)	X	X	X	X	X	X
ODBC Time-out	Number of seconds before reporting error for opening DB	X	X	X	X	X	X
Filter	Filter name loaded automatically with query	X	X	X	X	X	X
Order By	Sort loaded automatically with query	X	X	X	X	X	X

An SQL Primer

When you use graphical Query By Example, Access converts what you create into a *Structured Query Language (SQL)* statement. This SQL statement is what Access actually executes when the query runs.

Many relational databases use SQL as a standardized language to query and update tables. SQL is relatively simple to learn and use. Even so, Access does not require you know it or use it — though Access uses it, you won't ever have to know that it's there.

Viewing SQL statements in queries

If you're familiar with SQL, you can view and/or edit an SQL statement. If you make changes to an SQL statement, Access reflects them automatically in the QBE pane.

To view an SQL statement that Access creates, select View⇨SQL... from the Query menu. Figure 27-22 shows a typical SQL statement that will display the fields Customer Name and State for dogs in Idaho or Oregon.

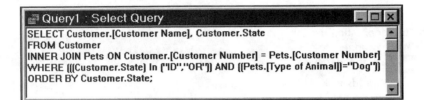

Figure 27-22: An SQL statement in Access.

Note   If you want to modify an existing SQL statement or create your own, enter changes directly into the SQL dialog box. To add new lines in the dialog box, press Ctrl+Enter.

You can use SQL statements directly in expressions, macros, forms, and reports. You might use one, for example, in the RowSource or RecordSource properties of a form or report. Even so, you don't have to "know the language" to use SQL statements directly. You can simply create the needed statement (for such purposes as selecting specific records) in the Query window. Then you activate the SQL dialog box and copy (Ctrl+C) the entire SQL statement you created. Switch to where you want to use the statement, and then paste it (Ctrl+V) where you need it (for example, the RowSource property of the property sheet).

Tip   You can create SQL statements in the SQL dialog box. Whether you write your own statement or edit one, Access updates the Query window when you leave the dialog box. Tables are added to the top portion; fields and criteria are added to the QBE pane.

An SQL primer

Until now, you have created queries using the query designer of Access. You have even been told that you can examine the SQL statement Access builds by selecting View⇨SQL from the menu.

As you already know, one way to learn SQL statements is to build a query graphically and then view the corresponding SQL statement. Earlier, for example, Figure 27-22 showed the following SQL statement:

```
SELECT DISTINCTROW Customer.[Customer Name], Customer.State
FROM Customer
INNER JOIN Pets ON Customer.[Customer Number] = Pets.[Customer
        Number]
WHERE (((Customer.State) In ("ID","OR"))
AND ((Pets.[Type of Animal])="DOG"))
ORDER BY Customer.State;
```

Four common SQL commands

This statement uses the four most common SQL commands. Table 27-3 shows each command and explains its purpose.

Table 27-3
Four Common SQL Keywords

Command	Purpose in SQL Statement
SELECT	This command/keyword starts an SQL statement. It is followed by the names of the fields that will be *selected* from the table or tables (if more than one is specified in the FROM clause/command). This is a *required* keyword.
FROM	This clause/keyword specifies the name(s) of the table(s) containing the fields specified in the SELECT command. This is a *required* keyword.
WHERE	This command specifies any condition used to filter (limit) the records that will be viewed. This keyword is used only when you want to limit the records to a specific group on the basis of the condition.
ORDER BY	This command specifies the order in which you want the resulting dataset (the selected records that were found and returned) to appear.

Using these four basic commands, you can build very powerful SQL statements to use in your Access forms and reports.

The DISTINCTROW keyword

Note   The DISTINCTROW keyword in the preceding SQL statement is an *optional* predicate keyword. Access uses it as a *restricter keyword* to specify which records should be returned. This predicate keyword is not used by other SQL database languages. In Access, it limits the display of duplicate records, basing its restrictions on the values of the entire duplicate record. It works like the DISTINCT predicate of other SQL languages, except that DISTINCT works against duplicate fields within the SELECT statement. DISTINCTROW works against their records (even fields that are not in the SELECT statement). This is covered in more detail later.

The SELECT command

The SELECT command (or *clause*) is the first word found in two query types; in a select query or make-table query, the SELECT clause specifies the field(s) you want displayed in the Results table.

After specifying the keyword SELECT, you need to specify the fields you want to display (for more than one, use a comma between the fields). The general syntax is

SELECT *Field_one, Field_two, Field_three* ...

where *Field_one, Field_two,* and so on are replaced with the names of the table fields.

Notice that commas separate each field in the list from the others. For instance, if you want to specify customer name and city using fields from the Customer table, you would specify the following:

```
SELECT [Customer Name], City
```

If you need to view fields from more than one table, you should specify the name of the tables in which to find the fields. If you want to select fields from both the Customer and Pets table, for example, the SELECT clause would look like this:

```
SELECT Customer.[Customer Name], Customer.City, Pets.[Type of
       Animal], Pets.[Pet Name]
```

When you build a query in Access, it places the table name before the field name automatically. In reality, you need only specify the table name if more than one table in the SQL statement have fields with the same name. For instance, a field named Customer Number appears in both the Customer table and the Pets table. If you want to SELECT a [Customer Number] field in your SQL statement, you *must* specify which of these to use — the one in Customer or the one in Pets.

The following SQL SELECT clause demonstrates the syntax:

```
SELECT Customer.[Customer Number], [Customer Name], City, [Type
       of Animal], [Pet Name]
```

Tip   Although table names are *not* required for nonduplicate fields in an SQL statement, it's a good idea to use them anyway for clarity.

Tip   You can use the asterisk wildcard (*) to specify that all fields should be selected. If you're going to select all fields from more than one table, specify the table, a period (.), and then the name of the field — in this case, the asterisk.

Using the brackets around field names

Notice that the SELECT clause just described uses brackets around the field name Customer Name. Any field name that has spaces within it requires the use of brackets.

Specifying SELECT Predicates

When you create a SQL SELECT statement, several predicates can be associated with the SELECT clause:

✦ ALL

✦ DISTINCT

✦ DISTINCTROW

✦ TOP

Use them to restrict the number of records returned. They can work in conjunction with the WHERE clause of an SQL statement.

The ALL predicate is the default. It selects all records that meet the WHERE condition specified in the SQL statement. Selecting it is optional (it's the default value).

Use the DISTINCT predicate when you want to omit records that contain duplicate data in the fields specified in the SELECT clause. For instance, if you create a query and want to look at both the Customer Name and the Type of Animal the customer owns, *without* considering the number of animals of a given type, the SELECT statement would be:

```
SELECT DISTINCT [Customer name], [Type of Animal]
```

If a customer owns two dogs — that is, has two Dog records (one named Bubba and one named Killer) in the Pets table — only one record will appear in the resulting datasheet. The DISTINCT predicate tells Access to show only one record if the values in the selected fields are duplicates (that is, same customer number and same type of animal). Even though two different records are in the Pets table, only one is shown. DISTINCT eliminates duplicates on the basis of the fields selected to view.

The DISTINCTROW predicate is unique to Access. It works much like DISTINCT, with one big difference: It looks for duplicates on the basis of *all* fields in the table(s), not just the selected fields. For instance, if a customer has two different Dog records in the Pets table and uses the predicate DISTINCTROW (replacing DISTINCT) in the SQL statement just described, *both* records will be displayed. DISTINCTROW looks for duplicates in all the fields of the Customer and Pets tables. If any field is different (in this case, the name of the pet), then both records are displayed in the datasheet.

The TOP predicate is also unique to Access. It lets you restrict the number of dis-played records, basing the restriction on the WHERE condition to the TOP <num-ber> of values. For instance, TOP 10 will display only the first ten records that match the WHERE condition. You can use TOP to display the top five customers who have spent money on your services. For instance, the following SELECT clause will display the top five records:

```
SELECT TOP 5 [Customer Name]
```

The TOP predicate has an optional keyword, PERCENT, that displays the top num-ber of records on the basis of a percentage rather than a number. To see the top 2 percent of your customers, you would use a SELECT clause like this one:

```
SELECT TOP 2 PERCENT [Customer Name]
```

The FROM clause of an SQL statement

As the name suggests, the FROM clause (command) specifies the tables (or queries) that hold the fields named in the SELECT clause. This clause is required; it tells SQL where to find the records.

When you're working with one table (as in the original example), the FROM clause simply specifies the table name:

```
SELECT [Customer Name], City,

FROM Customer
```

When you are working with more than one table, you can supply a TableExpression to the FROM clause to specify which data will be retrieved. The FROM clause is where you set the relationship between two or more tables for the SELECT state-ment. This link will be used to display the data in the resulting data sheet.

The TableExpression can be one of three types:

✦ INNER JOIN ... ON

✦ RIGHT JOIN ... ON

✦ LEFT JOIN ... ON

Use INNER JOIN ... ON to specify the traditional equi-join of Access. For instance, to join Customers to Pets via the Customer Number field in the FROM clause, the command would be

```
SELECT  Customer.[Type of Customer], pets.[Type of Animal]
FROM Customer INNER JOIN pets ON Customer.[Customer Number] =
        pets.[Customer Number]
```

Notice that the FROM clause specifies the main table to use (Customer). Then the INNER JOIN portion of the FROM clause specifies the second table to use (Pets). Finally, the ON portion of the FROM clause specifies which fields will be used to join the table together.

The LEFT JOIN and RIGHT JOIN work exactly the same, except that they specify an outer join instead of an inner join (equi-join).

The WHERE clause of an SQL statement

Use the WHERE clause (command) of the SQL statement only when you want to specify a condition. (This clause is optional, unlike SELECT/DELETE . . . and FROM.)

The original SQL statement you started with (for example) specified the following WHERE clause:

```
WHERE (Customer.[Type of Customer]=2)
```

The WHERE condition can be any valid expression. It can be a simple, one-condition expression (such as the one just given) or a complex expression based on several criteria.

Note If you use the WHERE clause, it *must* follow the FROM clause of the SQL statement.

The ORDER BY clause

Use the ORDER BY clause to specify a sort order. It will sort the displayed data by the field(s) you specify after the clause, in ascending or descending order. In the original example, you specified a sort order by Customer Number:

```
ORDER BY Customer.[Customer Name];
```

Specifying the end of an SQL statement

Since an SQL statement can be as long as 64,000 characters, you need a way to tell the database language that you've finished creating the statement. End an SQL statement with a semicolon (;).

Tip Access is very forgiving about the ending semicolon. If you forget to place one at the end of an SQL statement, Access will assume that it should be there and run the SQL statement as if it were there.

Caution If you place a semicolon *inside* an SQL statement accidentally, Access will report an error and attempt to tell you where it occurred.

Using SELECT, FROM, WHERE, and SORT BY, you can create some very powerful SQL statements to display and view data from your tables.

For instance, build an SQL statement that will do the following:

1. Select the Customer Name and City, Pet Name, and Type of Animal fields.

2. Join FROM the Customer and Pets tables, where the Customer and Pets tables are linked ON the Customer Number.

3. Display only records where the Type of Customer is a pet store (type = 2).

4. Sort the data in order by the Customer Number.

The SQL statement could be:

```
SELECT [Customer Name], City, [Pet Name], [Type of Animal]
FROM Customer INNER JOIN Pets ON Customer.[Customer Number] =
        Pets.[Customer Number]
WHERE [Type of Customer] = 2
ORDER BY Customer.[Customer number];
```

This is simply a quick overview of SQL statements and how to create them in Access for Windows 95; various other clauses (commands) can be used with SQL statements. SQL is relatively easy to understand and work with. It offers several benefits and power over creating graphical queries and using queries.

Summary

In this chapter, you worked with queries in great detail. The chapter covered the following points:

✦ When you're working with lookup tables, always set an outer join that points to the lookup table. An alternative is to use the DLookUp( ) function.

✦ When using tables in queries, open (use) only the tables whose fields you will use. Because Access creates equi-joins automatically, you may not see all the records unless you set outer joins.

✦ You can create calculated fields for display, set criteria against them, and even sort on them in a query.

✦ If you hide a field and save the query, Access moves the hidden field to the end of the display. If you don't use a hidden field for a criterion or sort and you save the query, Access deletes the hidden field from the QBE pane.

✦ Columns in the QBE pane can be hidden and unhidden by clicking on the side of the field on the selector bar and dragging it until the field disappears.

✦ Query properties are optional for all queries except the make-table and append queries.

✦ SQL statements can be viewed and modified. If you modify an SQL statement, Access updates the QBE pane automatically to reflect the changes.

✦ You can use SQL statements in expressions, macros, forms, and reports by copying and pasting them where you need them.

In the next chapter, you learn how to create multiple-table forms.

✦　　✦　　✦

Creating and Using Subforms

Subforms give you great flexibility in displaying and entering data with multiple tables. You can still edit all the fields without worrying about integrity problems. With a subform, you can even enter data into a one-to-many form relationship.

What Is a Subform?

A *subform* is simply a form within a form. It lets you use data from more than one table in a form; you can display data from one table in one format while using a different format for data from the other table. You can, for example, display one customer record on a form while displaying several pet records on a datasheet subform.

Although you can edit multiple tables in a typical form, using a subform gives you the flexibility to display data from several tables or queries at one time.

As you may recall, you can display data on a form in several ways:

Form	Display one record on a form
Continuous	Display multiple records on a form
Datasheet	Display multiple records using one line per record

Including a subform on your form enables you to display your data in multiple formats, as shown in Figure 28-1. This figure shows a form for entering visit details. It shows data from a query that lists information from the Customer, Pets, and Visits tables at the top, in a Form view. At the bottom is a subform that displays information from the Visit Details table. Notice that both the form and the subform have record selectors; each acts independently.

The subform contains data from three tables. In addition to its data from Visit Details, the subform shows descriptions of each treatment from the Treatments table, and medication listings from the Medications table. As you'll learn when you create this form later in this chapter, a drop-down list box appears when you select either of these latter fields in the datasheet. Each one is a combo box that lets you select a description from the Treatments or Medications table; then it will store the appropriate code in the Visit Details table for you.

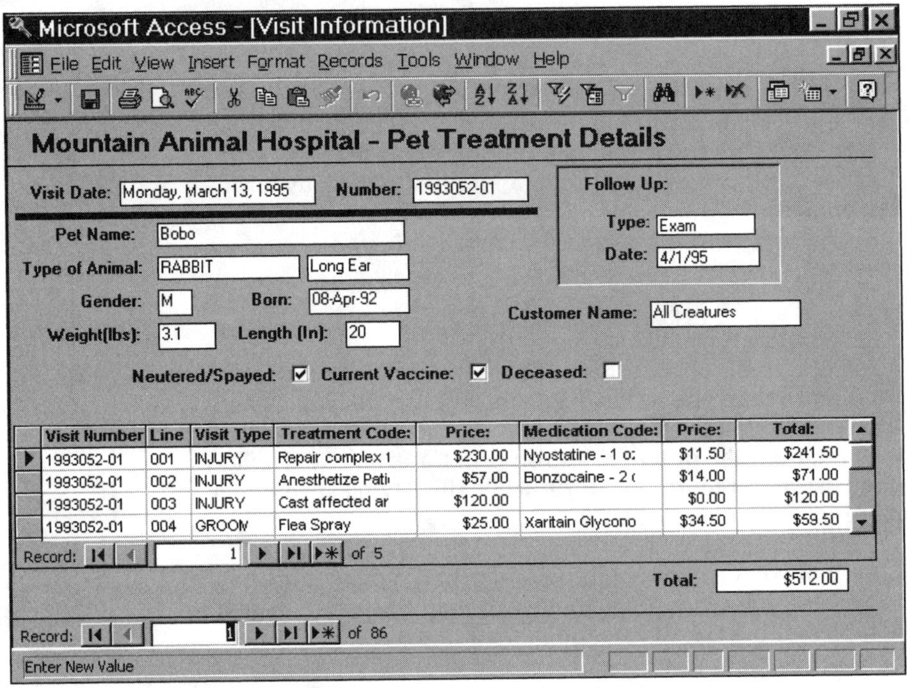

Figure 28-1: The form for adding visit details.

When you create a subform, you link the main form to it by a common field of expression. The subform will then display only records that are related to the main form. The greatest advantage of subforms is their ability to show the one-to-many relationship. The main form represents the *one* part of the relationship; the subform represents the *many* side.

You can create a subform in several ways:

✦ Use the Form Wizard as you create a new form.

✦ Use the Subform Wizard in an existing form.

✦ Use the Subform button in the toolbox and modify control properties.

✦ Drag a form from the Database window to another form.

Creating Subforms with the Form Wizard

The Access Form Wizard can create a form with an embedded subform if you choose more than one table (or use a query with more than one table). If you don't use the Wizard, you have to create both the form and subform separately; then you embed the subform and link it to the main form.

Creating the form and selecting the Form Wizard

Both the form and the subform are created automatically by the Form Wizard when you specify more than one table in a one-to-many relationship. In this example, you create a form that displays information from the Customer table on the main form; the subform shows information from the Pets table. To create the form, follow these steps:

1. Create a new form by selecting the Forms tab in the Database window and clicking on the <u>N</u>ew button.

2. Select Form Wizard in the New Form dialog box; select the Customer table from the tables/queries combo box, as shown in Figure 28-2.

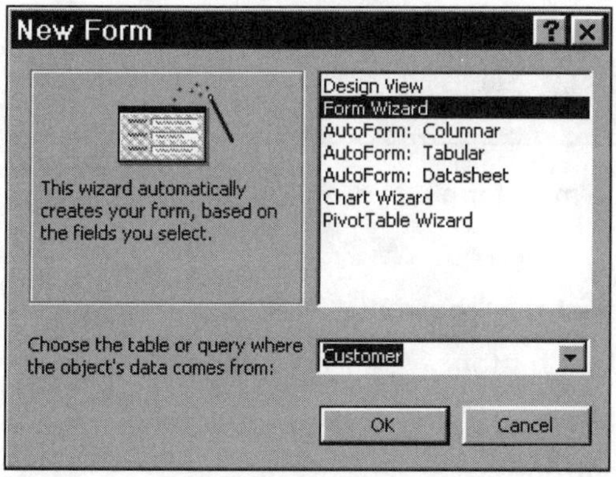

Figure 28-2: Selecting the Form Wizard.

Access 2.0 users should note that there is no Main/Subform Wizard in Access 97. The standard Form Wizard automatically handles the process of creating a new form with a subform.

> **Note** Selecting the Customer table when you begin the Wizard is a mere convenience. You can select a different table in the next dialog box.

After you select the Form Wizard, you need to select the fields for the main part of the form.

Choosing the fields for the main form

You then select each of the fields you want on the main form. The Customer table will be used for these fields. Figure 28-3 shows the completed field selection. To select the fields for this example, follow these steps:

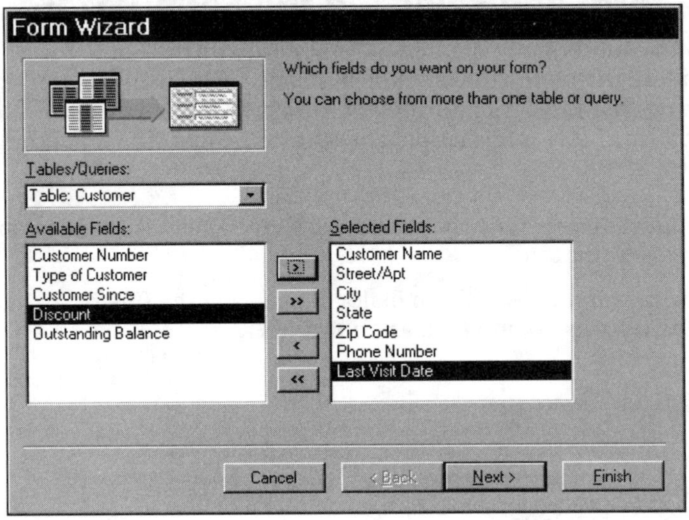

Figure 28-3: Selecting the fields for the main form.

1. Select Customer Name and select the > button.
2. Select Street/Apt and select the > button.
3. Select City and select the > button.
4. Select State and select the > button.
5. Select Zip Code and select the > button.
6. Select Phone Number and select the > button.
7. Select Last Visit Date and select the > button.

Selecting the table or query that will be the subform

Because a subform uses a data source separate from the form, you have to select the table or query to be used on the subform. To select another table/query, select the Pets table from the combo box, as shown in Figure 28-4. This table will be the subform of the primary form.

You will notice after a few seconds that the field list below in the Available Fields list box changes to display fields in the Pets table. The fields already selected from the Customer table in the Selected Fields list box remain.

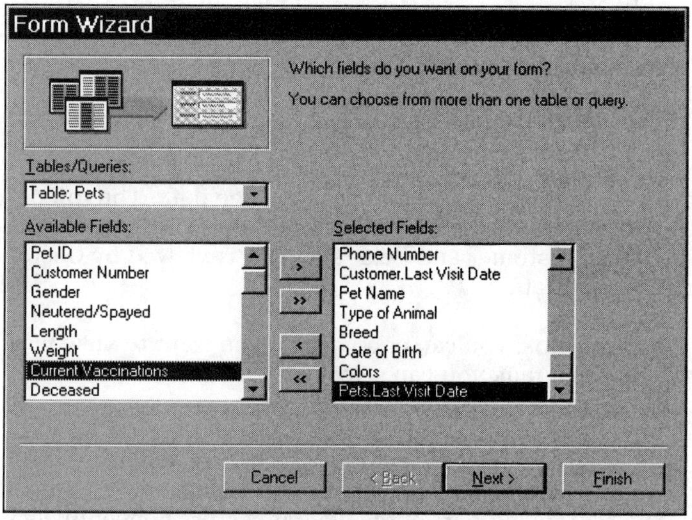

Figure 28-4: Selecting the fields for the subform.

Choosing the fields for the subform

Fields for the subform are selected in exactly the same way as fields for the main form. Those you select from the Pets table will be added to the list of fields already selected from the Customer table.

To select the fields for the subform, follow these steps:

1. Select Pet Name and select the > button.

2. Select Type of Animal and select the > button.

3. Select Breed and select the > button.

4. Select Date of Birth and select the > button.

5. Select Colors and select the > button.

6. Select Pets Last Visit Date and select the > button.

7. Select the Next > button to move to the next dialog box.

Note   Notice the Pets Last Visit Date field in the Selected Fields list box. Because both tables have a field named Last Visit Date, a prefix is added from the table that uniquely identifies the field.

After you select the fields for the Pets table, you can move to the next Wizard screen to decide how the linkage between forms will be built and how the data on the form will look.

Selecting the Form Data Layout

The next dialog box is shown as part of a conceptual diagram in Figure 28-5. A multi-table relationship gives you many ways to lay out the data. The top part of the figure shows an automatic decision Access makes on the basis of the one-to-many relationship between Customer and Pets. The data is viewed by Customer, with a subform with the Pets data.

On the left side of the dialog box, you can choose how you want to view your form. Below the field view diagram, you can select whether you want to see your data as a Form with subform(s) or as Linked forms.

In the top part of the figure that shows the entire Form Wizard dialog box, you can see the form with a subform: Customer fields are on the main form, and Pets fields are on the subform. The bottom left part of the diagram shows conceptually what the data would look like if you viewed the data by Pets instead. The data from both tables would be placed on a single form. The bottom right part of the figure shows how it would look if you chose to view the data by Customer but chose Linked forms instead. Rather than creating a Customer form with an embedded Pets sub-form, Access would create a Customer form with a button to display the Pets form.

After you select the type of form you want (the data is viewed by Customer, with a Form with subform(s) with the Pets data), you can click on the Next> button to move to the subform layout screen.

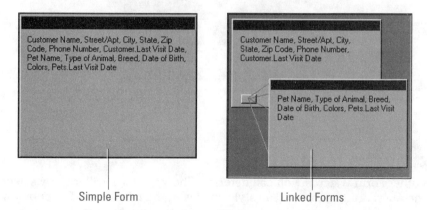

Figure 28-5: Selecting the data layout.

Selecting the Subform Layout

When you create a form with an embedded subform, you must decide which type of layout to use for the subform. The two possibilities are *tabular* and *datasheet*. The datasheet is the default, but it may not be the choice you want to accept. Datasheets are rigid by nature; you cannot change certain characteristics (such as adding multiline column headers or precisely controlling the location of the fields below). You can choose a tabular layout for added flexibility. Whereas a datasheet combines the headers and data into a single control type (the datasheet itself), a tabular form places the column headers in a form header section, placing the field controls in the form's detail section.

Select the Datasheet layout, as shown in Figure 28-6.

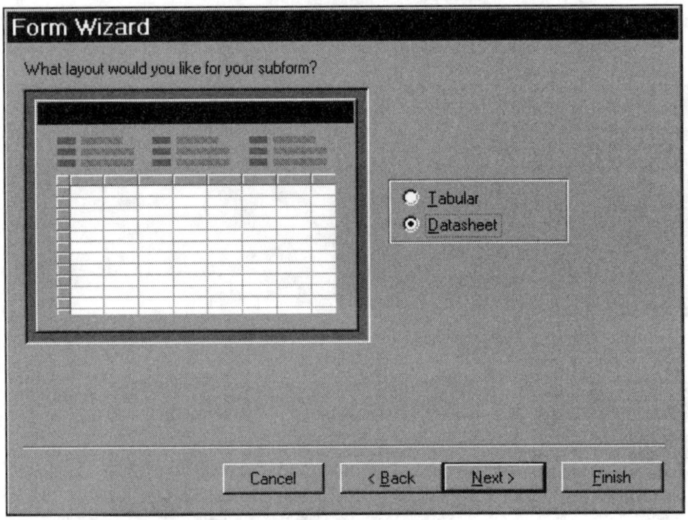

Figure 28-6: Selecting the subform layout.

Selecting the form style

As with other Form Wizards, you can determine how the form will look by selecting one of the AutoFormat choices. The style applies to the main form. The subform, displayed as either a separate tabular form or a datasheet, has the same look.

Cross-Reference: Chapter 9 explains in more detail the process of determining a form's look, and Form Wizards in general.

Click on the Next > button to move to the final dialog box. This box lets you select the title for the form and the subform.

Selecting the form title

You can accept the default titles (the table names Access gives the main form and subform), or you can enter a custom title. The text you enter appears in the form header section of the main form. (See Figure 28-7.)

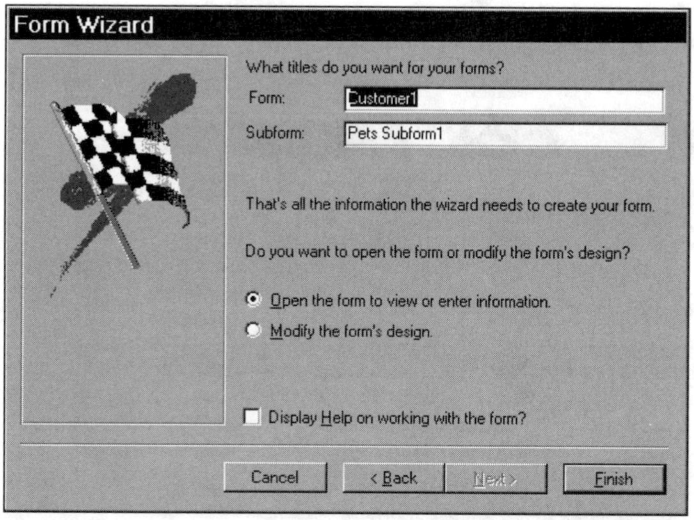

Figure 28-7: Selecting titles for the form and subform.

Note   When you accept the names (or enter a name of your choice), the subform is saved as a form; it will appear in the Database window when you select Forms. You should try to name your forms and subforms something similar so that you can tell that they go together. After you complete this step, you can view your form or its design.

Displaying the form

After the subform is named, the screen displays either the form or its design, depending on the option button you choose. In this example, you see the form, as shown in Figure 28-8.

The tabular form layout was chosen for the subform. Whether you create your subform through a Wizard, by dragging one to the form, or by using the toolbox, Access creates either a datasheet or a tabular (continuous) form. You can change it by changing the Default View property to either Single Form, Continuous Form (Tabular), or Datasheet.

You can change the look of the subform by moving to Design view and double-clicking on the subform control. This action displays the subform's main form; there, you can change the subform all you like. You can move fields around, adjust column widths, change the formatting, modify the distance between rows, and rearrange columns. When you make these changes, you'll see them in effect the next time you view the subform. If you scroll down to the bottom of the subform, you'll notice that the asterisk (*) appears in the record selector column. As with any continuous form or datasheet, you can add new records by using this row.

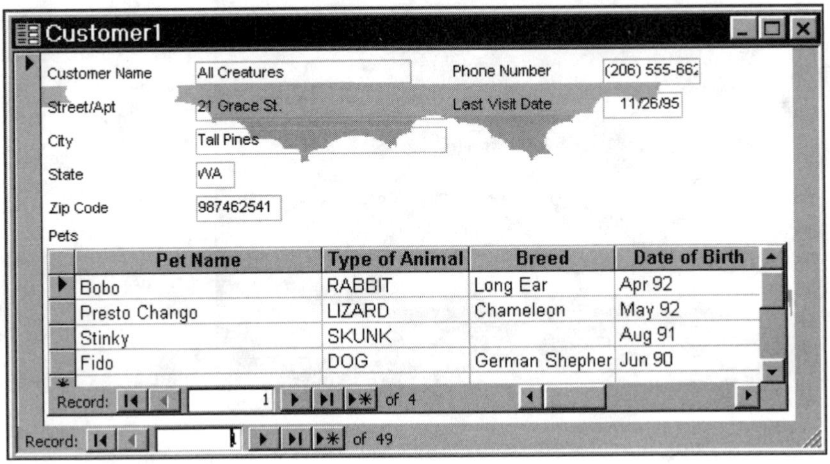

Figure 28-8: The Customer and Pets form.

Both the main form and the subform have record selectors because they are separate forms. As you use the outer record selector on the main form, you move from one customer record to another, and the link automatically changes which pets are displayed. This way, when you look at the record for All Creatures, you see pets for All Creatures. When you switch to Animal Kingdom, its pets are displayed.

When you use the inner record selector of the subform, you can scroll the records within the tabular form or datasheet. This capability is especially important if more records are on the subform than can be displayed in the subform area. You can use the scrollbar too.

Displaying the main form design

To understand how the forms are linked from main form to subform, view the main form in Design view, as shown in Figure 28-9.

The design for the main form shows the fields from the Customer table at the top and the subform control at the bottom. The subform control is similar to other controls (such as the unbound object control). It stores the name of the subform, however, rather than store the names of the fields on the form. When you run the form, Access retrieves the subform, displaying the fields on the subform.

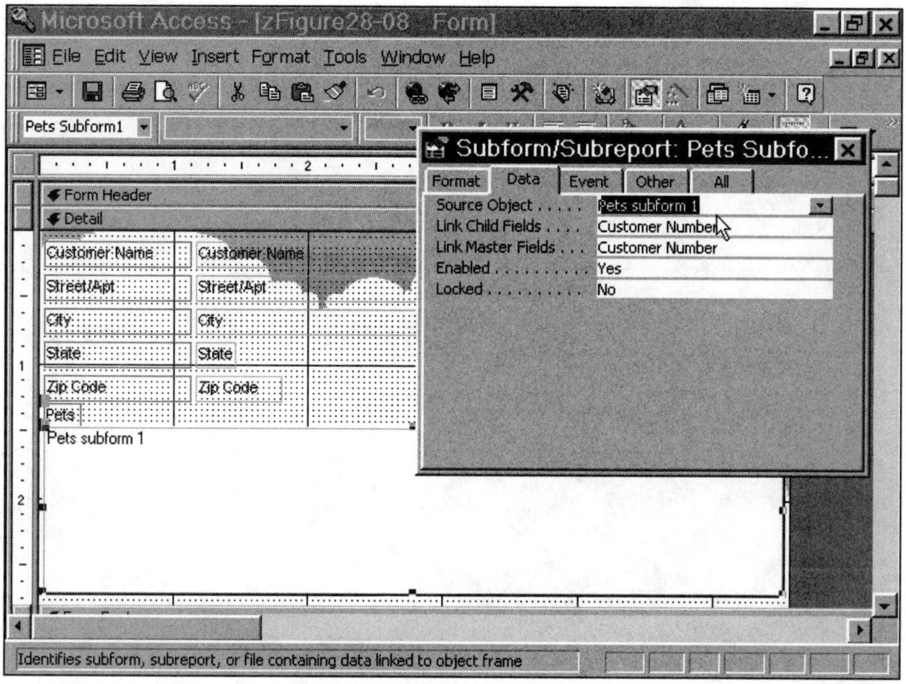

Figure 28-9: The Customer and Pets main form design.

Caution   You must always create first the form you intend to use as a subform; the main form will not be usable until the subform form is created.

The Subform control property sheet is also shown. Notice the two properties Link Child Fields and Link Master Fields; these properties determine the link between the main form and the subform. The field name from the main table/query is entered in the Link Master Fields property. The field name from the subform table/query is entered in the Link Child Fields property. When the form is run, the link determines which records from the child form are displayed on the subform.

Note   This control is used for both subforms and subreports.

Displaying the subform design

To understand how the subform is built, view the subform in Design view (as shown in Figure 28-10). A subform is simply another form; it can be run by itself without a main form. You should always test your subform by itself, in fact, before running it as part of another form.

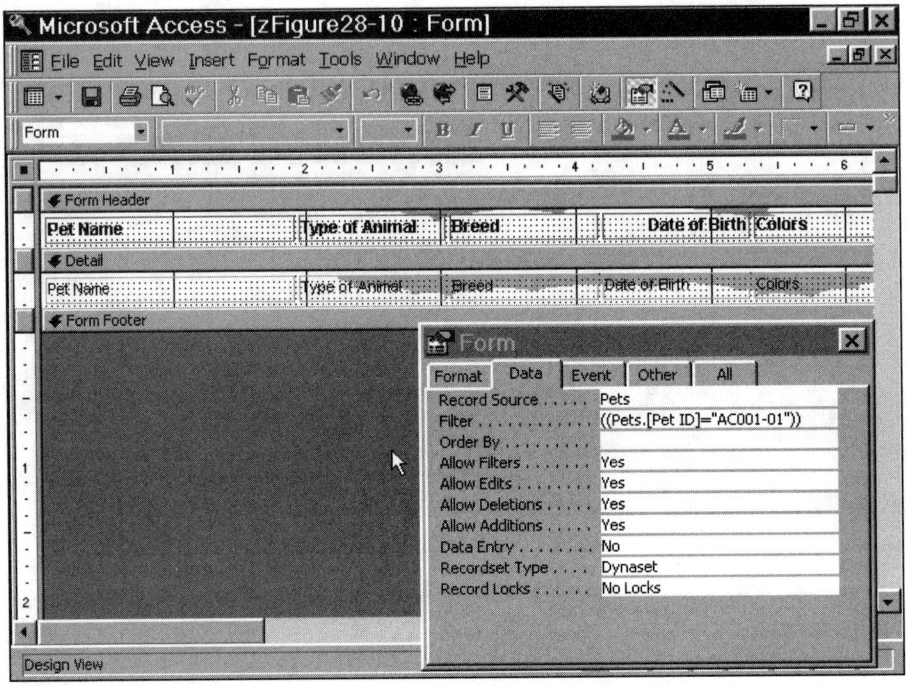

Figure 28-10: The Pets subform design.

Tip   A subform that will be viewed as a datasheet needs only to have its fields added in the order you want them to appear in the datasheet. Remember that you can rearrange the fields in the datasheet.

In Figure 28-10, you can see that all the fields are from the Pets table. You can also create a subform design with fields from multiple tables by using a query as the data source.

Notice that in the Form property sheet for the Pets subform, the Default View property is set to Continuous Forms. This means that the subform is displayed as a continuous form, whether it is run by itself or used in a form. You can change it to a datasheet if you want or create a multiple-line form (which would then display its multiple lines on a subform).

Tip   You can use the form footer of a subform to calculate totals or averages and then use the results on the main form. You learn how to do this later in this chapter.

The Form Wizard is a great place to start when creating a form with a subform. In the next section, however, you learn to create a subform without using a Form Wizard. Then you customize the subform to add combo box selections for some of the fields as well as calculate both row and column totals.

Creating a Simple Subform Without Wizards

As mentioned, there are several ways to create a subform without Wizards. You can drag a form from the Database window to a form, or you can use the Subform tool in the toolbox. The most desirable way is to drag the form from the Database window, because Access will try to create the links for you.

In this section, you create the form shown in Figure 28-11. The entire form is on the CD-ROM that accompanies this book, in the Mountain Animal Hospital database, and is called Adding Visit Details. The completed subform is called Data for CD-ROM Subform Example.

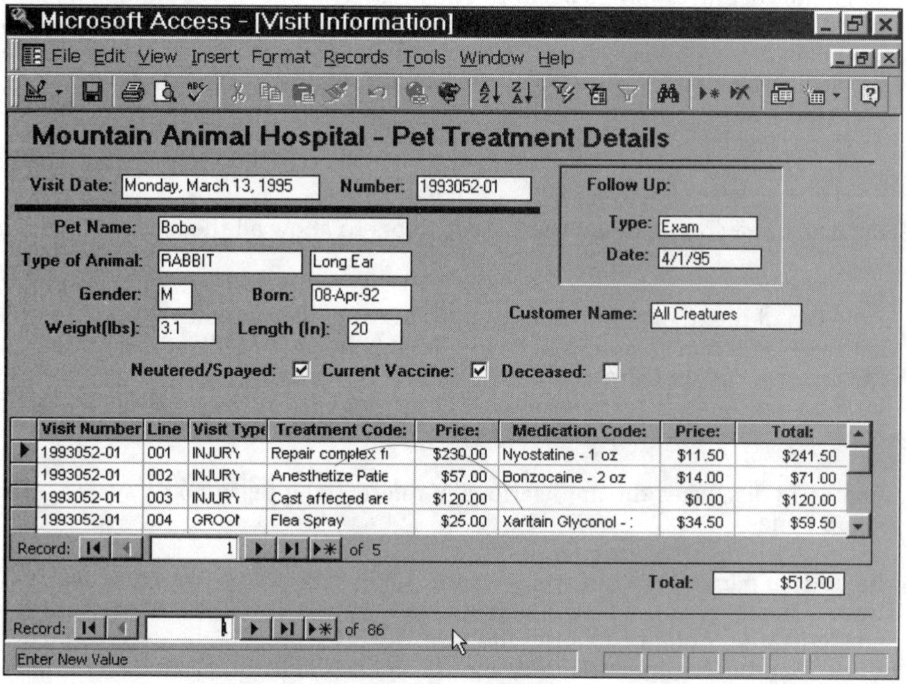

Figure 28-11: The Adding Visit Details form.

In this chapter, you'll work with only the Adding Visit Details form as a main form; you create and embed the Data for Subform Example form as a subform. (You may want to copy the Adding Visit Details form from the example disk and then delete the subform and subform totals box. You can use that copy to create the main form for this section of the chapter and save yourself a great deal of work.)

The Adding Visit Details form is divided into several sections. The top half uses the query Pets, Owners, and Visits to display data from the Pets, Customer, and

Visits tables. The Adding Visit Details form's only purpose is to let you add or review details about an existing visit. The middle of the form contains the subform that displays information about the visit details in a datasheet. Data in this subform comes from the query Data for Subform Example. Finally, there is a total for the data in the subform displayed in a text box control in the main form.

Creating a form for a subform

The first step in creating an embedded subform is to create the form to be used as the subform. Of course, this process begins with a plan and a query. The *plan* is what you see in Figure 28-11. This datasheet, however, is not just a few fields displayed as a datasheet. The field Visit Type is a combo box that uses a value list; you create that layer in this section. The fields Treatment Code and Medication Code do not display codes at all; instead, they display the treatment description and the medication description. The Price fields come from the Treatments table and Medications table by way of links. Finally, Total is a calculated field.

To create this datasheet, you start at the beginning. Figure 28-12 shows the query used for the subform.

Note This figure is a composite of two screen shots to show all the fields selected in the query.

At the top of the query, you can see the three necessary tables. Notice that the Visit Details table is joined to both the Treatments and Medications tables using a right outer join. You learned about this subject in Chapter 14. This is necessary so that if a Visit Detail record has either no treatment or no medication, it will not appear because of referential integrity.

Cross-Reference Chapter 12 discusses the implications of referential integrity on a system using lookup tables.

The bottom pane of the query shows the fields that can be used for the datasheet. These fields include the Visit Number, Line Number, Visit Type, Treatment Code, and Medication Code fields from the Visit Details table. The fields Treatment and Price (from the Treatments table) and the fields Medication Name and Price (from the Medications table) can be used to display the actual data they name rather than the codes. This datasheet can be further enhanced by using the combo boxes, as you'll soon see.

The final field in the query, Total: [Treatments].[Price]+[Medications].[Price], names the field Total and sets the calculation to the total of both Price fields — the one in the Treatments table and the one in the Medications table. This field displays the line totals for each record in the datasheet.

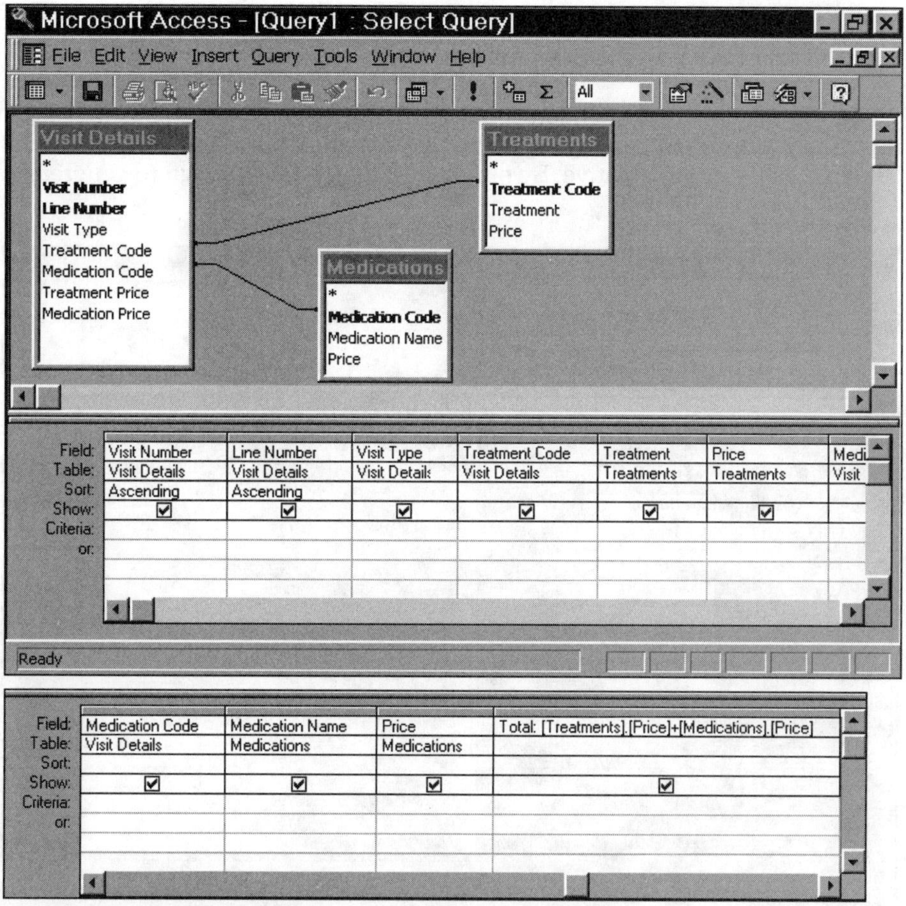

Figure 28-12: A composite figure showing the subform query.

Creating a *subform datasheet* is an iterative process; you have to see how many fields can fit across the screen at one time. If your goal is not to use a horizontal scrollbar, you'll have to use only as many fields as you can fit across the screen.

You can create the basic subform either by using a Form Wizard or by creating a new form and placing all the needed fields in it.

To create the initial subform, follow these steps:

1. Create a new blank form, using the query Data for Subform Example as the Record Source.

2. Open the Field List window and drag all the fields to the form.

3. Change the Default View property to Datasheet, as shown in Figure 28-13.

4. Display the form as a datasheet to check the results.

When you display the datasheet, you see that the fields don't even come close to fitting. There simply isn't enough room to display all of them. There are two solutions: Use a scrollbar or get creative. By now, you have learned enough to get creative!

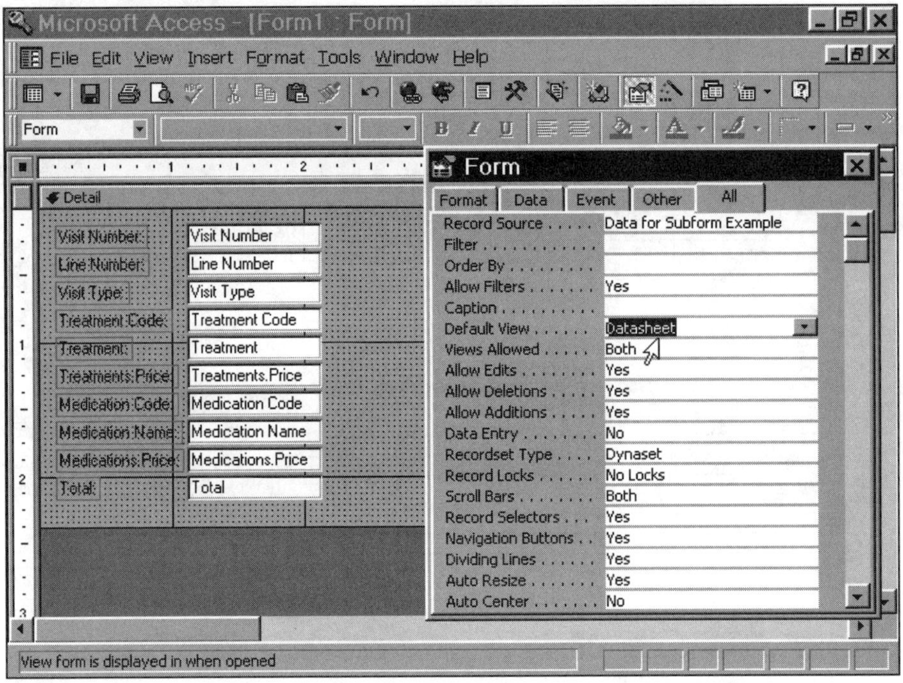

Figure 28-13: Creating the subform.

First, which fields are absolutely necessary to the entry of data, and which are strictly lookup fields? The first necessary field is Visit Number; it's used to link to the main form and must be included. Next is Line Number, the second field that makes up the multiple-field key in Visit Details. You must enter a Visit Type for each record, so that field needs to stay. Next come the details themselves. To enter a treatment, you must enter a treatment code and a medication code (if any). The codes themselves are used to look up the description and price. Therefore, you need only Treatment Code and Medication Code. Even so, you also want to display the prices and the line total. So the only fields you can eliminate are Treatment and Medication Name — and even then the datasheet doesn't fit across the page. To make it all fit, follow these steps:

1. Switch to Form Design view.

2. Delete the fields Treatment and Medication Name.

3. Change the labels for Treatments.Price and Medications.Price to simply **Price**.

4. Switch back to Datasheet view.

5. The fields still don't fit. By changing the column widths, however, you can fix that. Adjust the column widths, as shown in Figure 28-14.

6. Save the form as **Data for Subform Example**.

This is usually a good starting point. Notice that in Figure 28-14 some extra space shows on the right side. Because this datasheet will be placed in the center of another form, you must take into consideration the space the record selector column and scrollbar of the main form will use. After you view the datasheet in the main form, you can make final adjustments. You may also wonder why so much space was left for the Treatment Code and Medication Code columns. Later, when you change these columns into combo boxes, you'll need this amount of space. (Normally, you might not have realized this yet.)

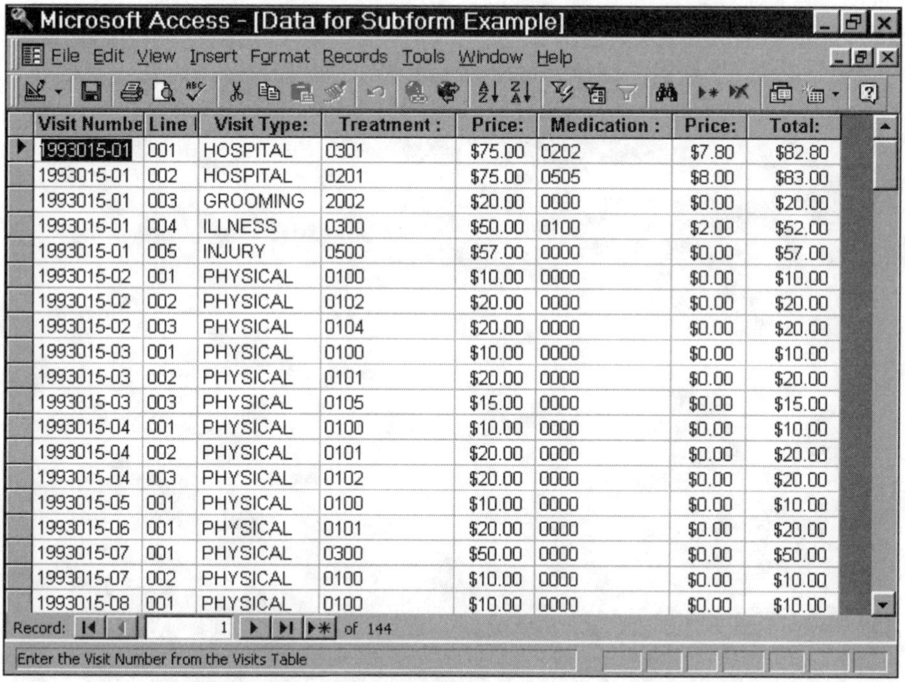

Figure 28-14: Adjusting the subform datasheet.

Adding the subform to the main form

After the subform is complete, you can add it to the main form. The easiest way is to display the main form in a window and then drag the subform to the main form. This action automatically creates the subform object control and potentially links the two forms.

To add the Data for Subform Example to the Adding Visit Details form you're using as the main form, follow these steps:

1. Display the Adding Visit Details form in a window in Design view so that you can also see the Database window.

2. Display the form objects in the Database window.

3. Click on the form name Data for Subform Example and drag it to the Adding Visit Details form, as shown in Figure 28-15.

4. Maximize the Form window.

5. Resize the subform so that it fits on-screen below the three check boxes. It should begin around the 2-inch mark and go down to the 3-inch mark. The width should be approximately 6¼ inches.

6. Delete the subform label control.

7. Display the property sheet for the subform control to verify the link.

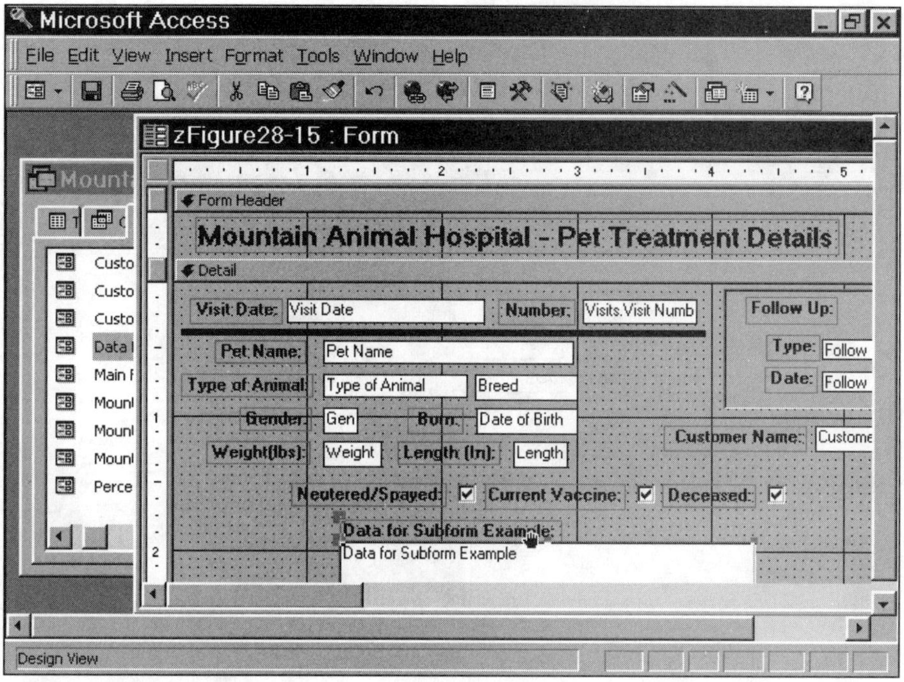

Figure 28-15: The form for Adding Visit Details.

The form should look like Figure 28-16. Notice that the Link Child Fields and Link Master Fields sections are not filled in. This means that the main form (Master) and the subform (Child) are not linked because the primary key for the Visit Details table is a multiple-field key. Access cannot automatically link this type of primary key.

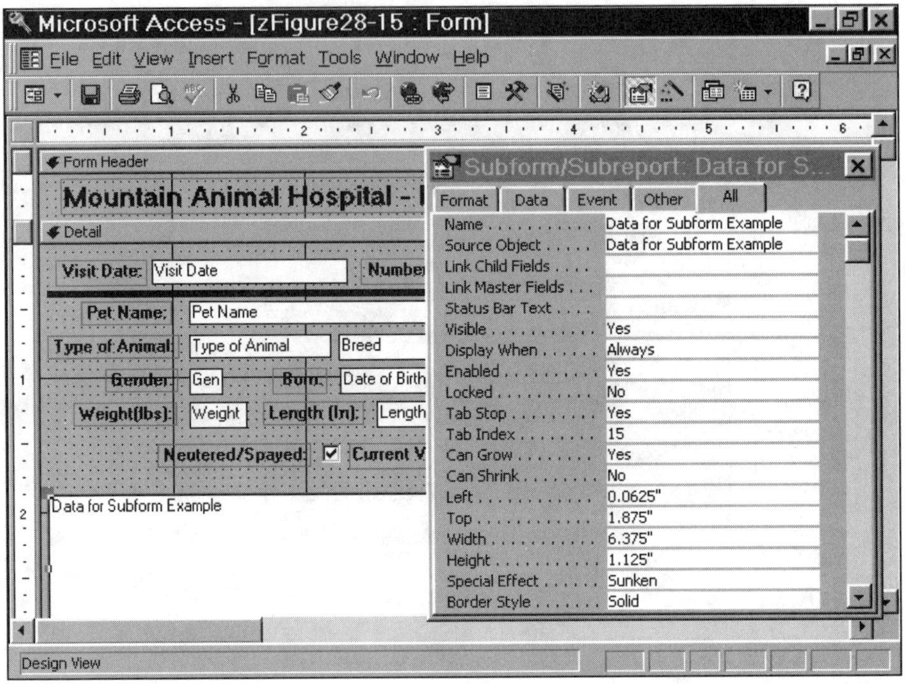

Figure 28-16: The subform in the main form.

Linking the form and subform

When you drag a form from the Database window onto another form to create a subform, Access tries automatically to establish a link between the forms. This is also true when you drag a form or report onto a report.

Access establishes a link under these conditions:

✦ Both the main form and subform are based on tables, and a relationship has been defined with the Relationships command.

✦ The main form and the subform contain fields with the same name and data type, and the field on the main form is the primary key of the underlying table.

If Access finds a relationship or a match, these properties show the field names that define the link. You should verify the validity of an automatic link. If the main form is based on a query, or if neither of the conditions just listed is true, Access cannot match the fields automatically to create a link.

The Link Child Fields and Link Master Fields property settings must have the same number of fields and must represent data of the same type. For example, if the Customer table and the Pets table both have Customer ID fields (one each) that contain the same type of data, you enter **Customer ID** for both properties. The subform automatically displays all the pets found for the customer identified in the main form's Customer ID field.

Although the data must match, the names of the fields can differ. For example, the Customer ID field from the Customer table can be linked to the Customer Number field from the Pets table.

To create the link, follow these steps:

1. Enter **Visit Number** in the Link Child Fields property.
2. Enter **Visit Number** in the Link Master Fields property.

Without the link, if you display the form, you see all the records in the Visit Details table in the subform. By linking the forms, you see only the visit details for the specific visit being displayed on the main form.

Display the form, as shown in Figure 28-17. Notice that the only visit numbers displayed in the datasheet are the same as the visit numbers in the main form. In Figure 28-17, you may notice that the user will have to enter the Treatment Code and Medication Code. In the type of systems that Access lets you create, you should never have to enter a code that can be looked up automatically. You can change some of the fields in the datasheet to use lookup tables by creating combo boxes in the subform.

Adding lookup tables to the subform fields

You can change the way the data is displayed on a subform of a main form by changing the design of the subform itself. You now make three changes:

✦ Display the Visit Type field as a value list combo box.

✦ Display the Treatment Code as a combo box showing the Treatment Name, letting Access enter the Treatment Code automatically.

✦ Display the Medication Code as a combo box showing the Medication Name, letting Access enter the Medication Code automatically.

Cross-Reference Combo boxes are discussed in detail in Chapter 19.

By changing a field in a subform to a combo box, when you click on the field in the datasheet of the subform, the list will drop down and you can select from the list.

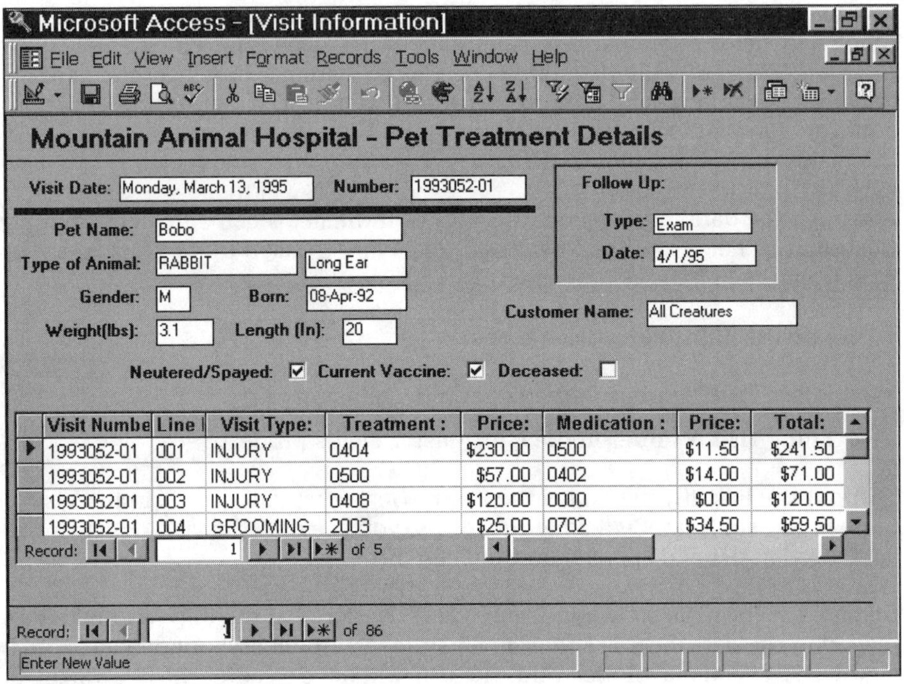

Figure 28-17: Displaying the main form and the subform.

The first control to change is the Visit Type field. To create a value list combo box without using the Wizard, follow these steps:

1. Display the subform in the Design view.

2. Select the existing Visit Type text box control.

3. From the menu bar, select Format⇨Change To⇨Combo Box.

4. With the Visit Type combo box selected, display the property sheet.

5. Select Value List for the Row Source Type property.

6. Enter **INJURY;PHYSICAL;GROOMING;HOSPITAL** in the Row Source property.

7. Set the Column Count property to **1** and the Column Widths to **1"**.

8. Set the Bound Column property to **1** and the List Rows property to **8**.

9. Set the Limit To List property to **No** to allow an alternative treatment type to be added.

This combo box and property sheet are shown in Figure 28-18.

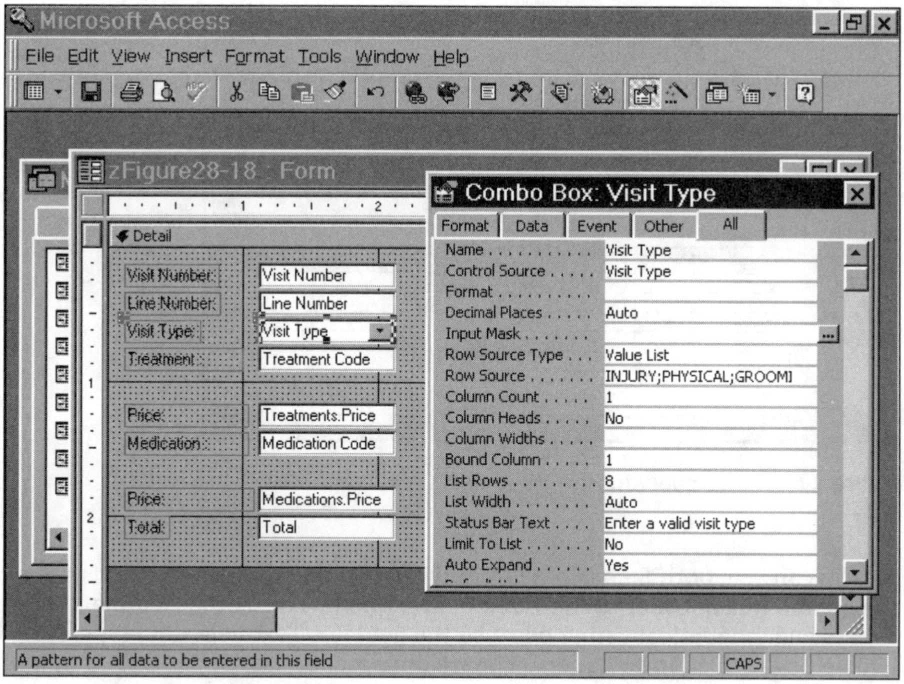

Figure 28-18: Creating a value list combo box for the Visit Type field.

Note   You can also display fields in a datasheet as check boxes or as individual option buttons. You cannot display an option button group, a list box, or a toggle button in a datasheet.

When a user clicks on the Visit Type field in the datasheet, the combo box appears. When a user selects the arrow, the list box is displayed with the values INJURY; PHYSICAL; GROOMING; or HOSPITAL. Because the Limit To List property is set to No, a user can also add new values to the Visit Details table.

The next two combo boxes are very similar. You want to create two combo boxes. The first one allows you to see the treatment descriptions rather than the treatment codes. When you select a treatment description, the code is entered automatically. The second combo box is the same, except that it uses the Medications table rather than the Treatments table.

To create these combo boxes, you need to create several queries. Figure 28-19 shows the query for the Treatment Code combo box. You have to create this query and name it Treatment Lookup.

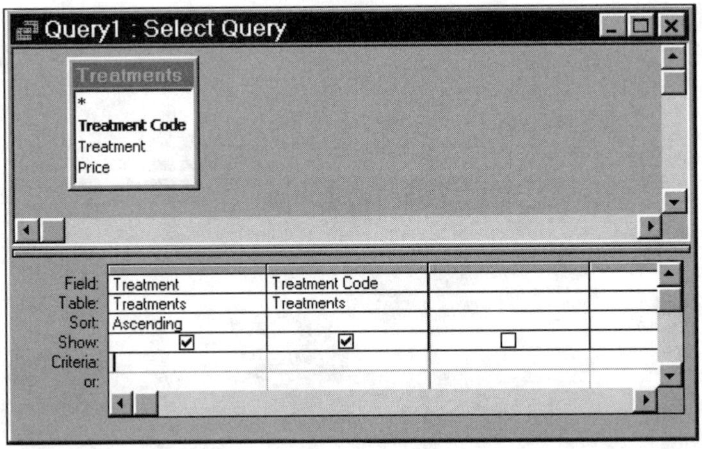

Figure 28-19: The query for the Treatment Code combo box.

As you can see, both fields come from the Treatments table. The fields appear in the combo box in order of the value of Treatment. This is the treatment name. This is an alphabetical listing because the field is a Text field data type. Notice that two fields are used in the query. The treatment code will be hidden so that only the treatment name is displayed.

After you create the query, you can create the combo box. To create the combo box for the treatment code, follow these steps:

1. Display the subform in the Design view.

2. Select the existing Treatment Code text box control.

3. From the menu bar, select Format⇨Change To⇨Combo Box.

4. With the Treatment Code combo box selected, display the property sheet.

5. Select Table/Query for the Row Source Type property.

6. Enter **Treatment Lookup** in the Row Source property.

7. Set the Column Count property to **2** and the Column Heads property to **Yes**.

8. Set the Column Widths property to **2";0"**.

9. Set the Bound Column property to **2** and the List Rows property to **4**.

10. Set the List Width property to **2"**.

11. Set the Limit To List property to **Yes** so that the user must select from the list.

Figure 28-20 shows this combo box completed. When the form is run and the user selects the Treatment Code field, the list of valid treatment codes is shown.

Because the Bound Column is 2 (the hidden Treatment Code column), Access places the value of the Treatment Code in the Treatment Code field in the Visit Details table.

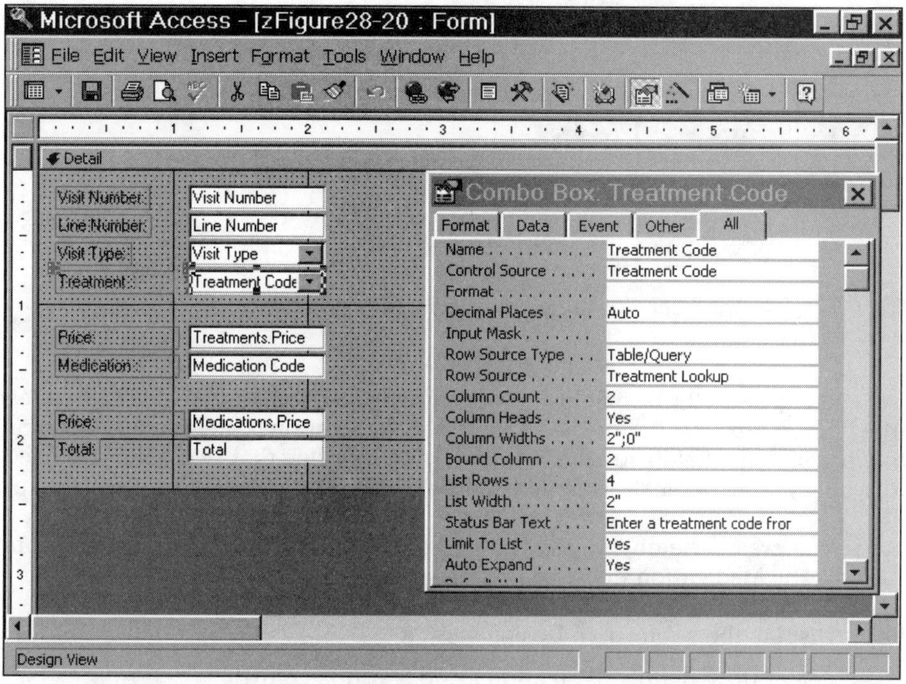

Figure 28-20: Creating a combo box for the Treatment Code.

The Medication Code lookup table is virtually identical to the Treatment Code lookup table; only the field name is different. To create this combo box, you also need to create a query. Figure 28-21 shows the query for the Medication Code combo box.

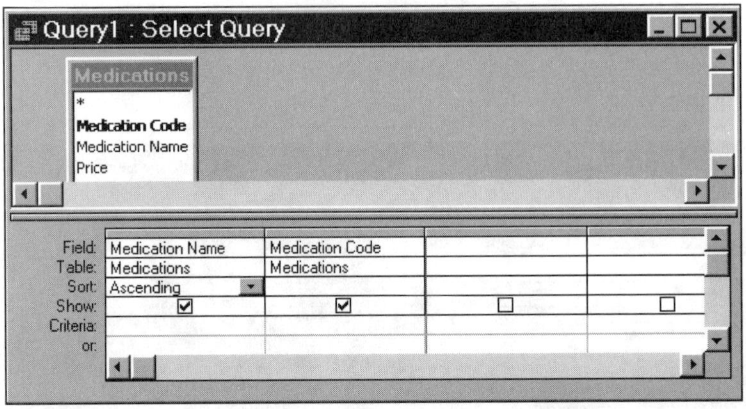

Figure 28-21: The query for the Medication Code combo box.

As you can see, all these fields come from the Medications table. They appear in the combo box in order of the value of the Medication Name (an alphabetical listing because the field uses the Text data type). Notice that two fields are used in the query. The Medication Code is hidden; only the Medication name is displayed.

After you create the query, you can create the combo box. To create the combo box for the Medication Code, follow these steps:

1. Display the subform in Design view.

2. Select the existing Medication Code text box control.

3. From the menu bar, select Format⇨Change To⇨Combo Box.

4. With the Medication Code combo box selected, display the property sheet.

5. Select Table/Query for the Row Source Type property.

6. Enter **Medications Lookup** in the Row Source property.

7. Set the Column Count property to **2** and the Column Heads property to **Yes**.

8. Set the Column Widths property to **2";0"**.

9. Set the Bound Column property to **2** and the List Rows property to **4**.

10. Set the List Width property to **2"**.

11. Set the Limit To List property to **Yes** so that the user must select from the list.

Figure 28-22 shows this combo box completed. When the form is run and the user selects the Medication Code field, the list of valid medication codes is shown. Because the Bound Column is 2 (the hidden Medication Code column), Access places the value of the Medication Code in the Medication Code field in the Visit Details table.

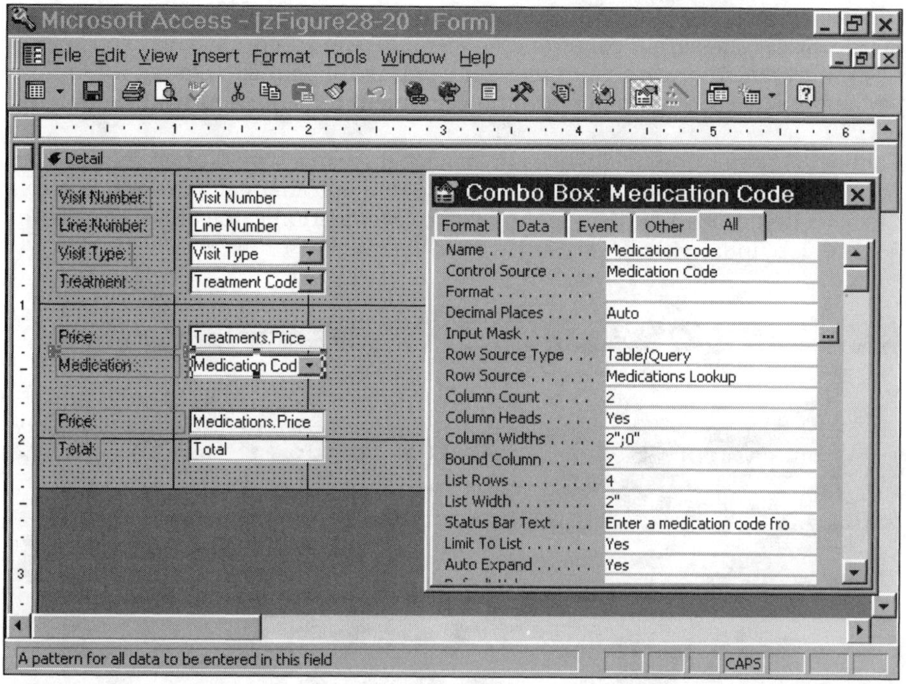

Figure 28-22: Creating a combo box for the Medication Code.

After you make these changes, you can test your changes. You may want first to display the form as a datasheet in the Form view of the subform. You can also close the form and display the subform in the main form. Close the subform and run the main form named Adding Visit Details.

First, you can test the combo boxes. Click on the Visit Type field. An arrow should appear. When you click on the arrow, the list of valid visit types is displayed. You can then select the desired visit type or enter a new one in the combo box. When the combo box is closed, Access enters this data into the Visit Type field of the Visit Details table.

When you select the Treatment Code field and select the arrow, a combo box is also displayed, as shown in Figure 28-23. The combo box displays only three columns because the List Rows property is set to 4 and the Column Heads property is set to Yes.

The treatment description is shown in its entirety, even though the Treatment Code field entry area is smaller. This is controlled by setting the List Width property to 2. If you leave this property set to the default (Auto), your data may be truncated (displayed with too much white space after the values) because the list width will be the size of the actual combo box control on the subform. When you select the desired treatment, Access automatically enters the hidden value of the treatment code in the Treatments table into the Treatment Code field in Visit Details.

The Medication Code field works in exactly the same way. Notice that as you select various treatments, the price is updated automatically in each line to reflect the selection. As either Treatment Price or Medication Price changes, the Total field is also updated.

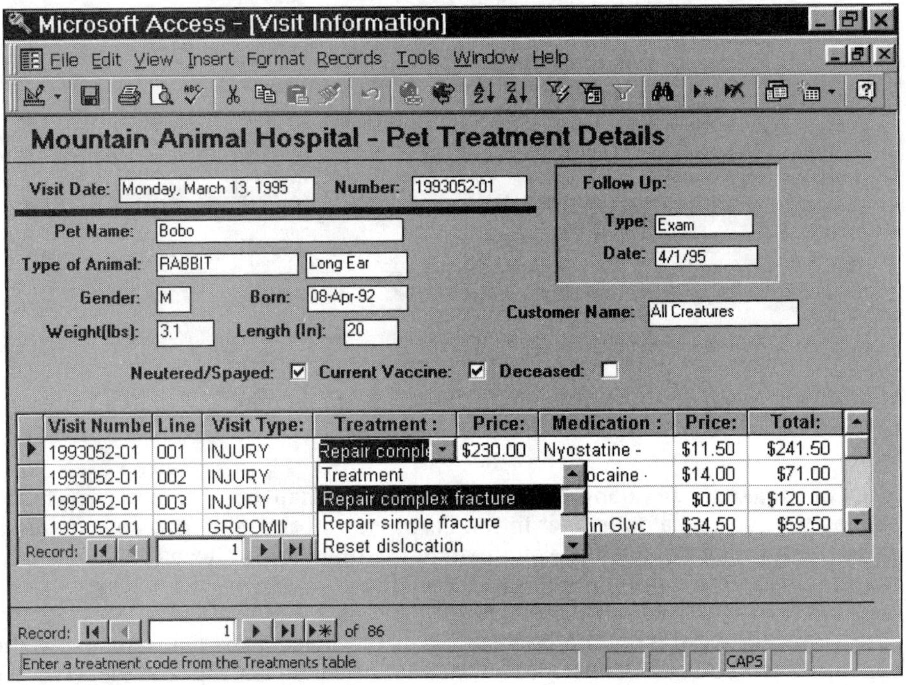

Figure 28-23: Displaying the subform.

The last change to make to the form is to create a field to display totals of all the line items in the datasheet.

Creating totals in subforms

To create a total of the line items in the subform, you have to create an additional calculated field on the form you're using as a subform. Figure 28-24 shows a new field being created in the form footer on this form.

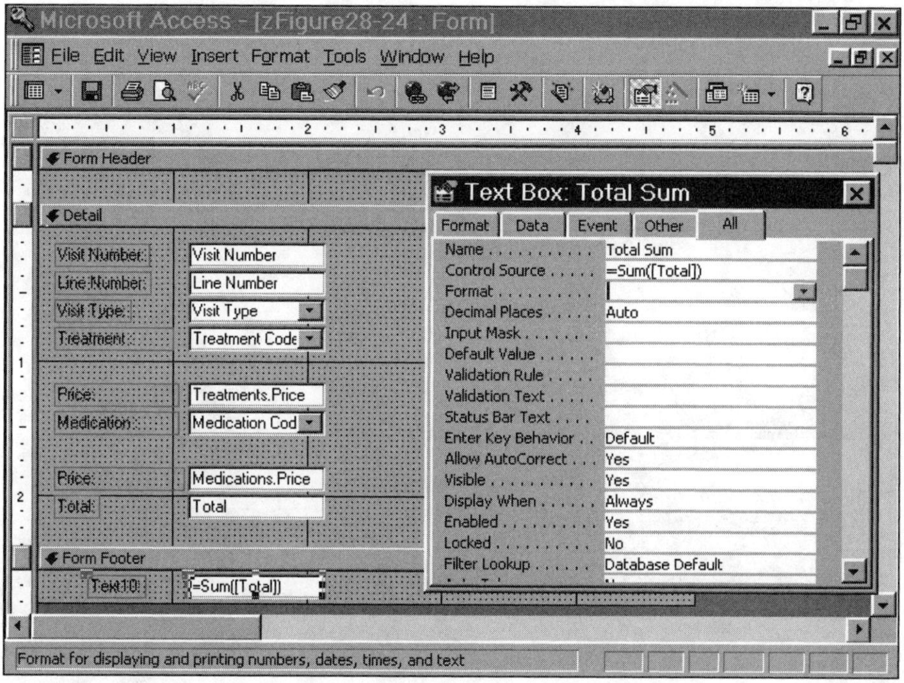

Figure 28-24: Creating a summary calculation.

Just as you can create summaries in reports, you can create them in forms. Use the form footer; that way, the calculation occurs after all the detail records are processed. When the form is displayed in Single-form view, this total is always equal to the detail record. In Continuous-form or Datasheet view, however, this calculation is the sum of the processed record.

As shown in Figure 28-24, the text box Control Source property is the expression =Sum([Total]). This is the sum of all the values in the Total field. To display the data as a dollar amount, the field's Format property should be set to Currency and the number of decimal places set to 2.

Although the text box control was created in the subform, it's displayed by a text box control (which references the subform control) placed in the main form. This control is shown in Figure 28-25.

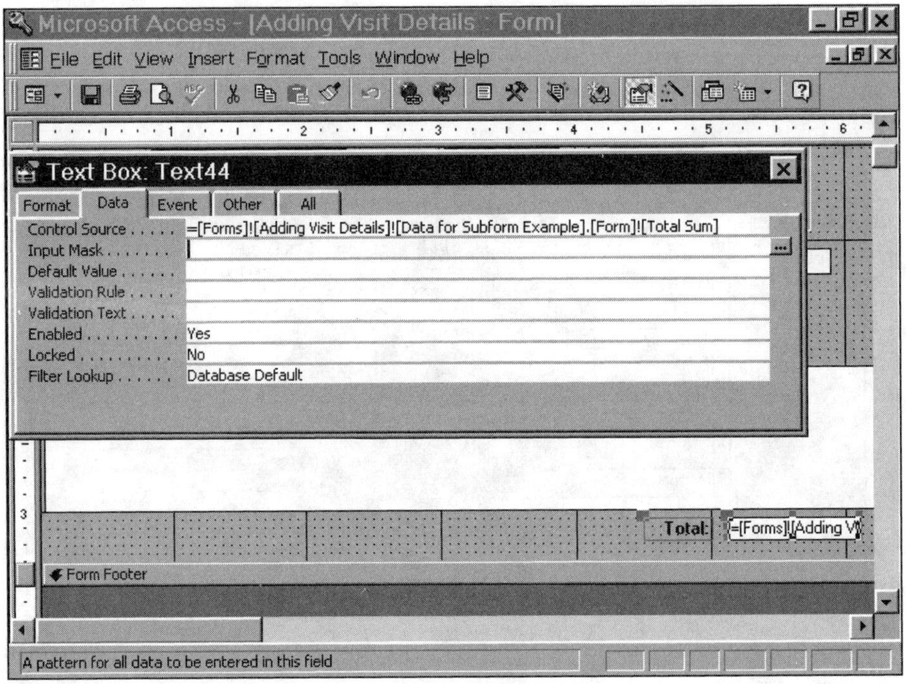

Figure 28-25: Referencing a control in another form.

Because the field is in another form, it must be referenced with the fully qualified terminology (Object type![Form name]![Subform name].Form![Subform field name]).

As you can see in the property sheet, the Control Source property is as follows:

```
=[Forms]![Adding Visit Details]![Data for Subform
        Example].[Form]! [Total Sum]
```

The first part of the reference specifies the name of the form; Form tells Access that it's the name of a form. By using the ! character, you tell Access that the next part is a lower hierarchy. The control name [Total Sum] contains the value to be displayed.

Caution If you are an experienced Access 2.0 user, you may find that many of the field reference calculations you enter no longer work; they just display the #Name? Symbol message in your calculated or referenced text boxes. A major change was made in Access for Windows 95 that makes it mandatory to fully qualify all references. In Access 2.0, you could leave off the first part of the reference (Forms![formname]). In the example just given, you could have used just the subform name first, leaving out the Forms![Adding Visit Details] part.

The final form, including the total for the subform, is shown in Figure 28-26.

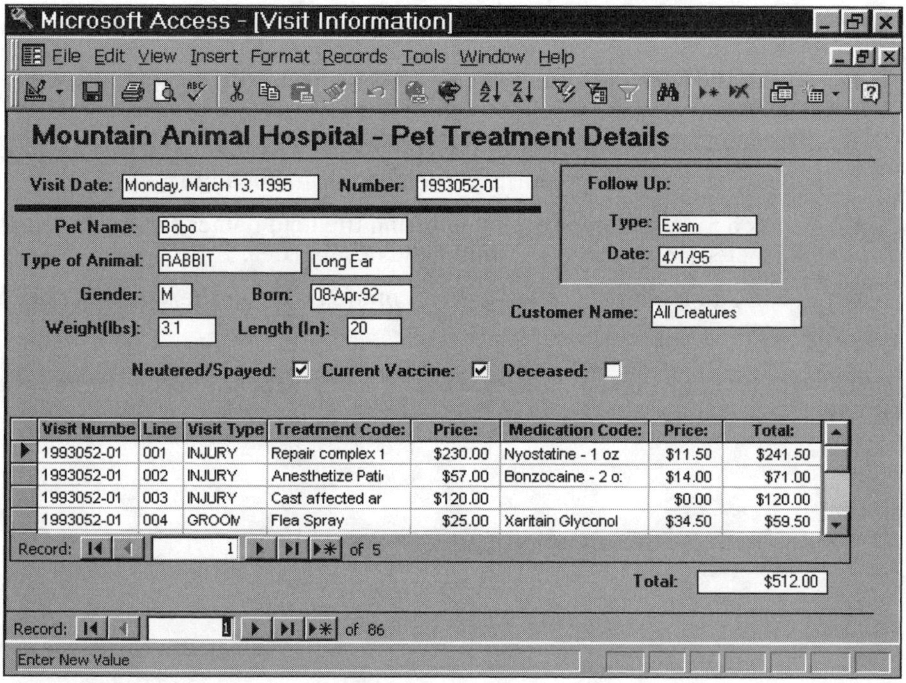

Figure 28-26: Displaying the totals.

Summary

In this chapter, you learned how to use subforms to make displaying data from multiple tables easier. You learned how to create a subform with a Wizard as well as how to create subforms by dragging the form from the Database window to another form. You also learned how to change the display of the subform. This chapter covered the following points:

✦ A subform is simply a form within a form.

✦ There are several ways to create a subform:

- Use the Form Wizard.

- Drag a form from the Database window to another form.

- Use the toolbox and the Form Wizard.

✦ A subform can be displayed as a single form, a continuous form, or a datasheet.

✦ Before adding a subform to an existing form, you must create the subform.

✦ By using the Form Wizard, you can create a form with an embedded subform datasheet.

✦ When you create a subform by dragging a form from the Database window, you may have to link the form to the subform manually.

✦ You link a form and subform by entering the field names for the link in the Link Master Fields and Link Child Fields properties.

✦ You can add lookup tables and even combo boxes to the datasheet used in a subform.

In the next chapter, you learn how to create mailing labels, snaked column reports, and mail-merge reports.

✦   ✦   ✦

Creating Mailing Labels and Mail Merge Reports

For correspondence, you often need to create mailing labels and form letters, commonly known as *mail merges*. The Access Report Writer helps you create these types of reports as well as reports with the multiple columns known as *snaked column reports*.

Note   Because the Report Design window is set to a width of eight inches, some screens in this chapter appear as though an 800×600 resolution Super VGA Windows screen driver is used rather than the standard 640×480.

Creating Mailing Labels

You create mailing labels in Access by using a report. You can create the basic label by starting from a blank form, or you can use the Label Wizard. This Wizard is much easier to use and saves you a great deal of time and effort.

Access 97 has no special report for creating mailing labels. Like any other report, the report for a mailing label is made up of controls; the secret to the mailing label is using the margin settings and the Page Setup screen. In previous chapters, you learned how to use the Page Setup dialog box to change your margins. One of the tabs in the dialog box is Columns. When you select this tab, the Columns dialog box expands to reveal additional choices you use to control the number of labels across the report as well as how the data is placed on the report. You learn how to use this dialog box later in this chapter.

The best way to create mailing labels is to use the Label Wizard.

Creating the new report with the Label Wizard

You create a new report to be used for a mailing label just as you create any other report (see Figure 29-1). To create a new report for a mailing label, follow these steps:

1. From the Database window, click on the Reports tab.

2. Click on New to create a new report.

3. Select Label Wizard.

4. Select Customer from the table/query combo box.

5. Click on OK.

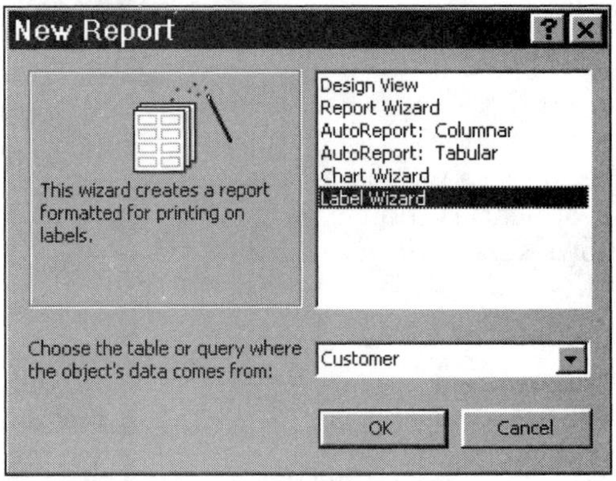

Figure 29-1: Choosing the Label Wizard.

The Label Size dialog box should now be displayed.

Selecting the label size

The first Wizard dialog box you see will ask you to select a label size. You can select the type of label stock you want to print to. Nearly a hundred Avery label stock forms are listed. (Avery is the world's largest producer of label paper.)

You can find in these lists nearly every type of paper Avery makes. You can select from lists of English or metric labels. You can also select sheet feed for laser printers or continuous feed for tractor-fed printers. Select between the two from the option buttons below the label sizes.

Note If you do not see the Avery labels in the Label Wizard, click in the customized sizes check box to turn it off.

The list box shown in Figure 29-2 contains three columns:

Avery number	The model number on the Avery label box
Dimensions	The height and width of the label in either inches or millimeters
Number across	The number of labels that are physically across the page

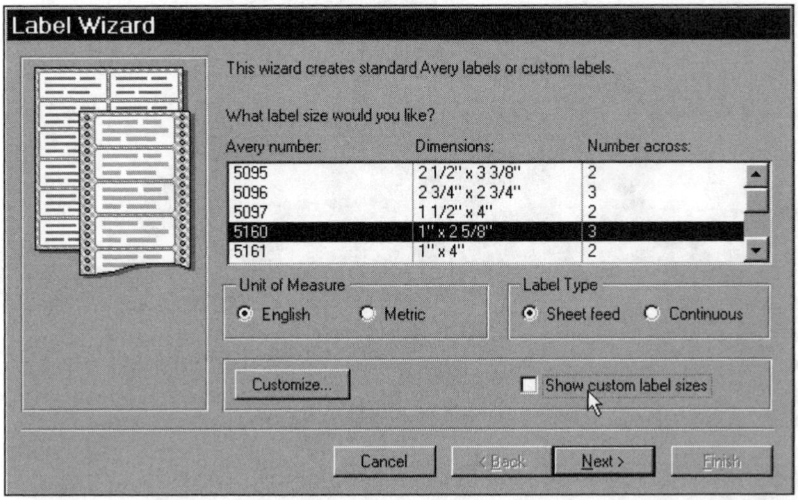

Figure 29-2: Selecting the label size.

When you select a label size, you're actually setting the Page Setup parameters, as you learn later in this chapter.

Select Avery number 5160, as shown in Figure 29-2. Notice that there are three labels across and that the size is shown as 1" x 2 5/8." You'll see these values again when you examine the Page Setup dialog box. After you select the label size, you can again click on the Next> button to go to the next dialog box.

Note You can also select the Customize button to create your own label specifications if the labels you're using are not standard Avery labels.

Selecting the font and color

The next dialog box (shown in Figure 29-3) displays a set of combo boxes to let you select various attributes about the font and color of the text used in the mailing label. For this example, click on the Italic check box to turn on the italic effect. Notice that the sample text changes to reflect the difference. Accept the remaining default choices of Arial, 8, Bold, and black text. Click on the <u>N</u>ext> button to move to the next dialog box.

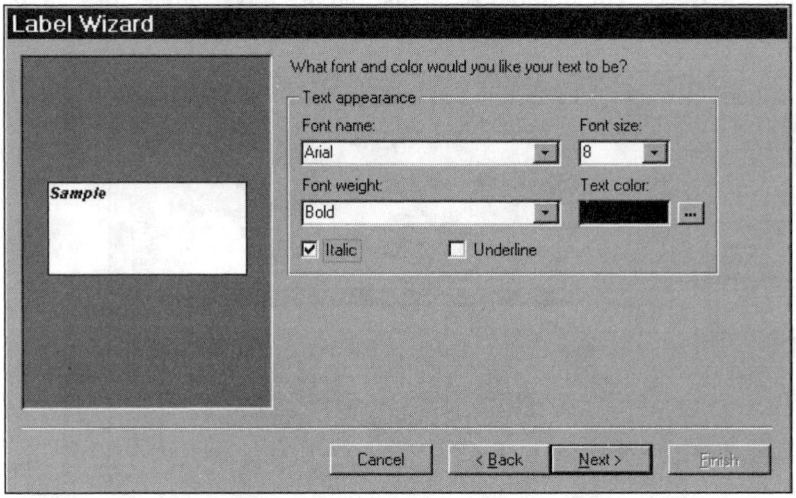

Figure 29-3: Selecting the font type, size, and color.

Creating the mailing-label text and fields

This dialog box lets you choose the fields from the table or query to appear in the label. You can also add spaces, unbound text, blank lines, and even punctuation.

The dialog box is divided into two areas. The left area, titled `Available fields:`, lists all the fields in the query or table. Figure 29-4, shown completed, displays the fields from the Customer table. The right area, titled `Prototype label:`, shows the fields used for the label and displays a rough idea of how the mailing label will look when it's completed.

> **Note** The fields or text you use in this dialog box serve only as a starting point for the label. You can make additional changes later in the Report Design window.

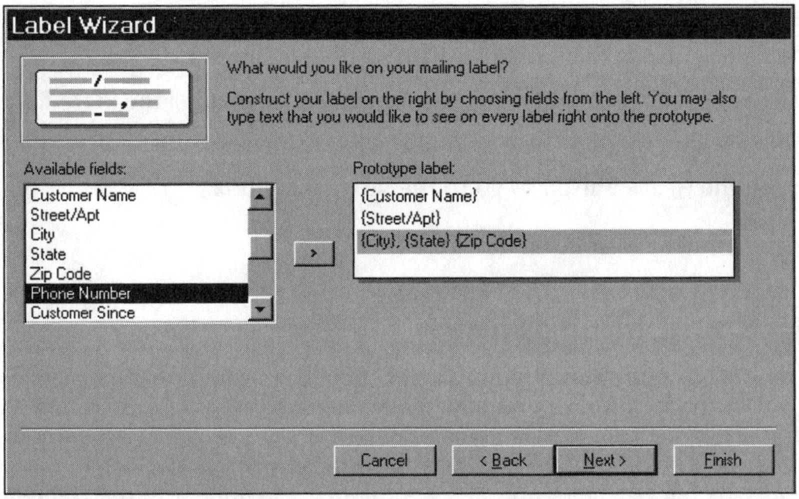

Figure 29-4: The completed label in the Label Wizard.

You can select a field either by double-clicking on the field name in the Available fields: area or by selecting the field name and then clicking on the > command button between the two areas. You can remove a field by highlighting it and then pressing Delete on your keyboard. You move to the next line by pressing the Tab key.

Note You may enter text at any point by simply placing your cursor where you want to insert the text and then typing the text, including spaces and punctuation marks.

Caution If you add a new line to the label and leave it blank, it will appear only as a blank line on the label (provided you have also manually changed the Can Shrink property to No for the unbound text box control you created to display that blank line). The default property for this control is Yes; the blank line is not displayed, and the lines above and below the blank line appear together.

To create the label as shown completed in Figure 29-4, follow these steps:

1. Double-click on the Customer Name field in the Available fields: list.

2. Press the Tab key to go to the next line.

3. Double-click on the Street/Apt field in the Available fields: list.

4. Press the Tab key to go to the next line.

5. Double-click on the City field in the Available fields: list.

6. Position your cursor after the City field and type a comma (,) to add a comma to the label.

7. Press the spacebar to add a blank space to the label after the comma.

8. Double-click on the State field in the Available fields: list.

9. Press the spacebar to add a blank space to the label after the State field.

10. Double-click on the Zip Code field in the Available fields: list.

11. Click on the Next> button to go to the next dialog box.

The completed label is displayed in Figure 29-4.

Sorting the mailing labels

The next dialog box will prompt you to select a field on which to sort, as shown in Figure 29-5. Depending on how you have your database set up (and on how you want to organize your information), you may sort it by one or more fields. The dialog box consists of two sections; one lists the available fields, the other, the selected sort fields. To select a field, double-click on it (it will appear in the right-side column labeled Sort by:) or use the arrow buttons (> and >>). The single > means that only the highlighted field will be selected; the double >> means that every field showing in the column will be selected. In this example, you will select Customer Name as the field to sort by. When you're done, click on Next> to bring up the final dialog box.

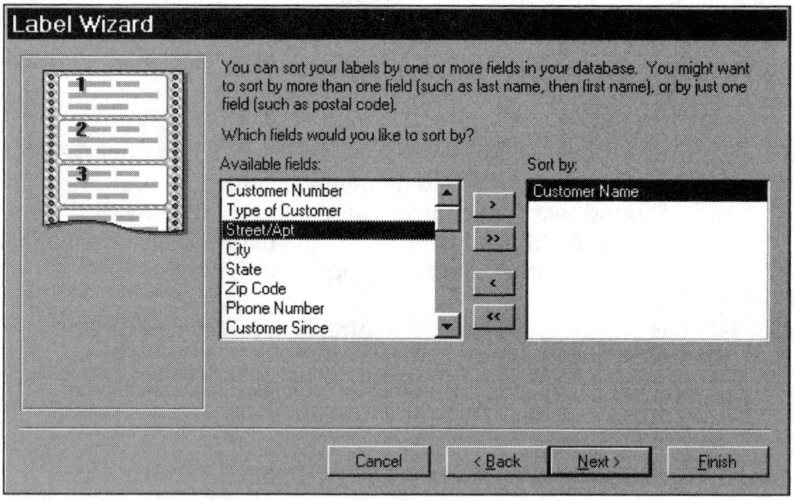

Figure 29-5: The Label Wizard's Sort By dialog box.

Note The order in which the fields are listed in the Sort by: column represents the order in which they will be sorted, from the top down. If you have a database set up in which you have first and last name, you can select the last name and then the first name as the sort order.

The last dialog box in the Label Wizard sequence lets you decide whether to view the labels in the Print Preview window or to modify the report design in the Report Design window. The default name is the word Label followed by the table name. In this example, that's Labels Customer. Change it to a more meaningful name, such as Customer Mailing Labels. This final dialog box is shown in Figure 29-6.

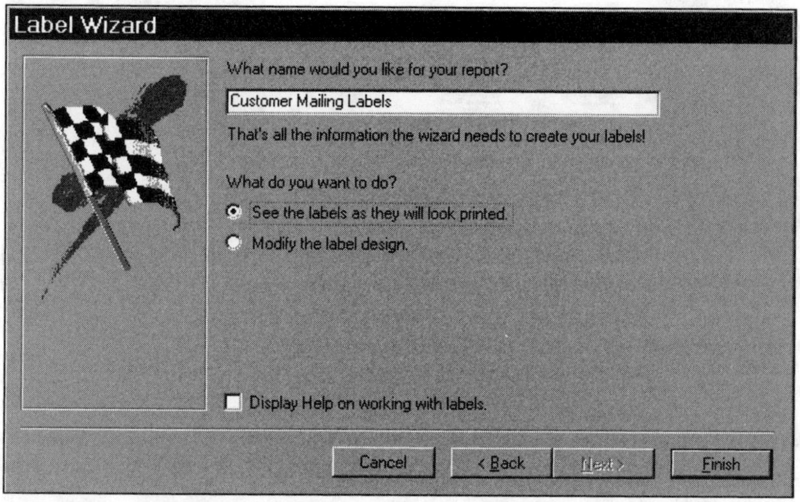

Label Wizard

What name would you like for your report?

Customer Mailing Labels

That's all the information the wizard needs to create your labels!

What do you want to do?

⦿ See the labels as they will look printed.

○ Modify the label design.

☐ Display Help on working with labels.

Cancel   < Back   Next >   Finish

Figure 29-6: The final mailing Label Wizard dialog box.

Displaying the labels in the Print Preview window

When you click on the Finish button, you are taken directly to the Print Preview window (as shown in Figure 29-7). This is the normal Print Preview window for a report. By using the magnifying-glass cursor, you can switch to a page view to see an entire page of labels at one time, or you can zoom in to any quadrant of the report. By using the navigation buttons in the bottom left corner of the window, you can display other pages of your mailing label report.

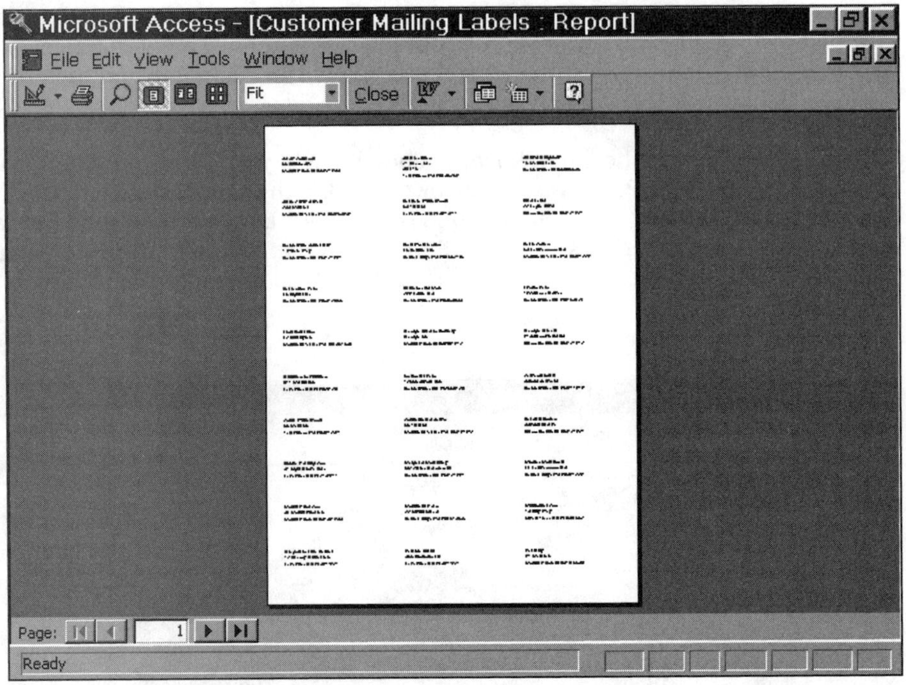

Figure 29-7: Viewing labels in the Print Preview window.

Note Remember that a mailing label is simply a report; it behaves as a report normally behaves.

You can print the labels directly from the Print Preview window, or you can click on the first icon on the toolbar to display the Report Design window.

Modifying the label design in the Report Design window

When you click on the Close Window icon, the label design is displayed in the Report Design window, as shown in Figure 29-8. Notice that the height of the detail band is set at 1 inch and that the right margin of the report is set at 2⅜ inches. This gives you the measurement you defined when you chose the label size of 1" × 2⅝". The difference between 2⅜ and 2⅝ is the settings in the page setup box (discussed later in this chapter).

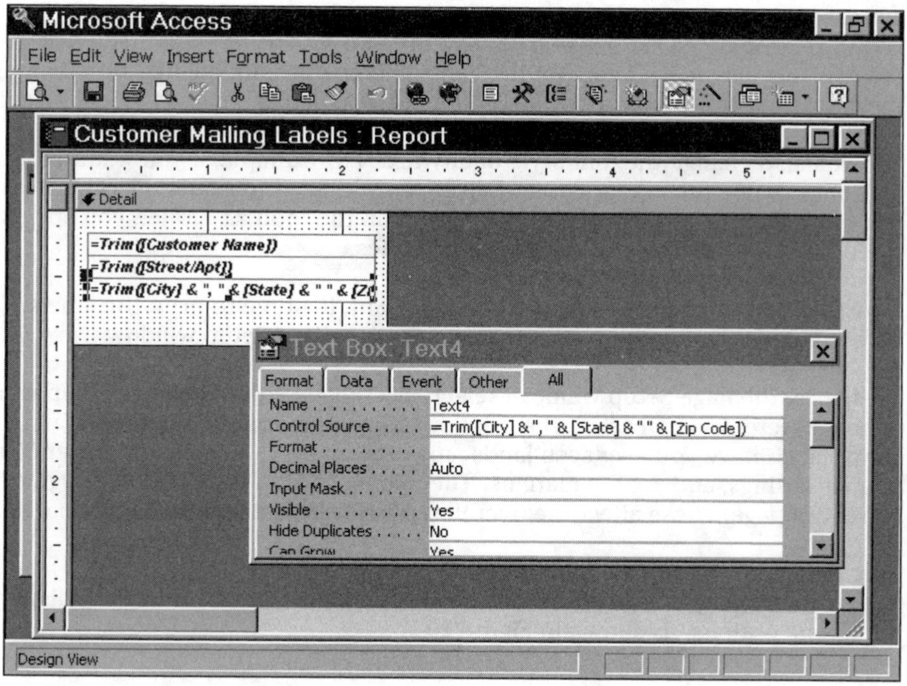

Figure 29-8: The Report Design window.

If you look at the report print preview, you notice that the first record's ZIP code value is 834121043. The Zip Code field is normally formatted using the @@@@@-@@@@ format. This format displays the stored sequence of nine numbers with a hyphen placed where it properly goes.

The Label Wizard uses the ampersand (&) type of concatenation when working with text strings; any formatting is missing. In the property sheet for the third line text box, you must change the control by adding the format function inside the Trim( ) function. Change the source to this:

```
=Trim([City] & ", " & [State] & " " & Format([Zip
     Code],"@@@@@-@@@@")).
```

This control source correctly displays the ZIP code as 83412-1043 when it's printed or displayed. You can make this change by simply selecting the control and adding the Format( ) function.

Another change you could make is to the font size. In this example, Arial (the Helvetica TrueType font) with a point size of 8 is used. Suppose that you want to increase the text size to 10 points. You select all the controls and then click on the Font Size drop-down list box and change the font size to 10 points. The text inside the controls becomes larger, but the control itself does not change size. As long as the text is not truncated or cut off on the bottom, you can make the font size larger.

You can also change the font style of any text. For example, if you want only the Customer Name text to appear in italics, you will need to select the other two text box controls and deselect the Italics button on the toolbar. Earlier, you specified in the Wizard that all three fields should be italics.

Now that you've changed your text as you want, it's time to print the labels. Before you do, however, you should examine the Page Setup window.

To display the Page Setup window, select File➪Page Setup. The Page Setup window appears. Here, you can select the printer, change the orientation to Portrait or Landscape (have you *ever* seen landscape label paper?), change the Paper Size or Source settings, and set the margins. The margin setting controls the margins for the entire page. These affect the overall report itself, not just the individual labels.

To view the settings of each label and determine the size and number of labels across the page, you need to select the Columns tab. The window then displays additional options, as shown in Figure 29-9.

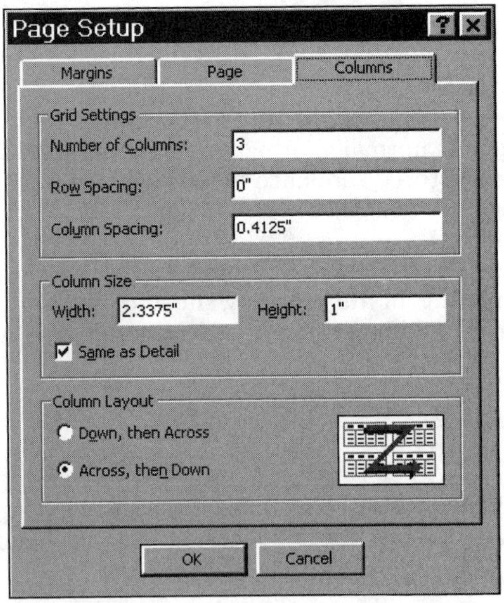

Figure 29-9: The Columns tabbed dialog page from the Page Setup window.

Note Although Figure 29-9 shows the Columns tab as active, you need to click on the Margins tab and set the top and bottom margins to 0.5" and the left and right margins to 0.3".

Several items appear in the Columns dialog box. The first three items (under the Grid Settings) determine the spacing of the labels on the page:

Number of <u>C</u>olumns	Number of columns in the output
Ro<u>w</u> Spacing	Space between the rows of output
Col<u>u</u>mn Spacing	Amount of space between each column (this property is not available unless you enter a value greater than 1 for the Items Across property)

The Column Size settings determine the size of the label:

W<u>i</u>dth	Sets the width of each label
H<u>e</u>ight	Sets the height of each label
S<u>a</u>me as Detail	Sets the Width and Height properties to the same width and height as the detail section of your report

The Column Layout section determines in which direction the records are printed:

D<u>o</u>wn, then Across	Prints consecutive labels in the first column and then starts in the second column when the first column is full
Across, the<u>n</u> Down	Prints consecutive labels across the page and then moves down a row when there is no more room

After the settings are completed, you can print the labels.

Printing labels

After you create the labels, change any controls as you want, and check the Page Setup settings, you can print the labels. It's always a good idea to preview the labels one last time. Figure 29-10 shows the final labels in the Print Preview window. The ZIP code is correctly displayed.

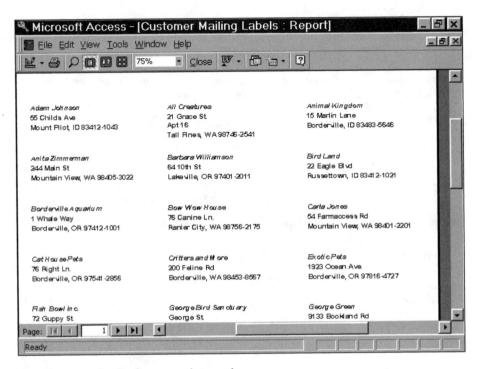

Figure 29-10: The final report print preview.

You can print the labels by simply selecting the Print button on the toolbar and then clicking on OK in the Print dialog box. You can also print the labels directly from the Report Design window by selecting File⇨Print.

Of course, you must insert your label paper first. If you don't have any #5160 label paper, you can use regular paper. The labels will simply be printed in consecutive format, like a telephone directory. In fact, that's another feature of Access reports — the capability to create what is known as a snaked column report.

Creating Snaked Column Reports

All the reports discussed in this book so far are either form-based (that is, free-form) or single-column lists. (*Single column* means that each column for each field appears only once on each page.) Often this is not the best way to present your data. Access gives you another option: *snaking columns.* This option lets you define the sections of a report so that they fit in an area that is less than half the width of the printed page. When the data reaches the bottom of the page, another column starts at the top of the page; when there is no more room on the page for another column, a new page starts.

This technique is commonly used for text in telephone directories or newspapers and other periodicals. An example of a database use is a report that prints several addresses, side by side, for a page of adhesive mailing labels you feed through your laser printer. You just learned how to create labels for mailing. Now you will learn how to apply these same techniques in a report. Snaked column reports have a major difference from mailing labels: They often have group sections, page headers, and footers; mailing labels have only data in the detail section.

The general process for creating a snaked column report is as follows:

✦ Decide how you want your data to be displayed: How many columns do you want? How wide should each column be?

✦ Create a report that has detail and group section controls no wider than the width of one column.

✦ Set the appropriate options in the Page Setup dialog box.

✦ Verify your results by using print preview.

Creating the report

You create a snaked column report in the same way you create any report. You start out with a blank Report Design window. Then you drag field controls to the report design and add label controls, lines, and rectangles. Next, you add any shading or special effects you want. Then you're ready to print your report. The major difference is the placement of controls and the use of the Page Setup window.

Figure 29-11 shows a completed design for the Customers by State (three snaking columns) report. The report displays a label control and the date in the page header, along with some solid black lines to set the title apart from the directory details. The detail section contains information that lists the customer number, customer name, address, and phone number. Then, within this section, you see three information fields about the customer's history with Mountain Animal Hospital. The page footer section contains another solid black line and a page number control.

What's important here is to make sure that the controls in the detail section use no more space for their height or width than you want for each occurrence of the information. Because you're going to be printing or displaying multiple detail records per page in a snaked-column fashion, you must note the size. In this example, you can see that the detail section data is about $1\frac{3}{4}$ inches high and about 2 inches wide. This is the size of the item you will define in the Columns dialog box.

Before continuing, you have to specify a sort order for the report. The report should be placed in order by State and then by Customer Number. You can do this by clicking on the Sort and Group button on the toolbar and typing the names of the fields in the dialog box.

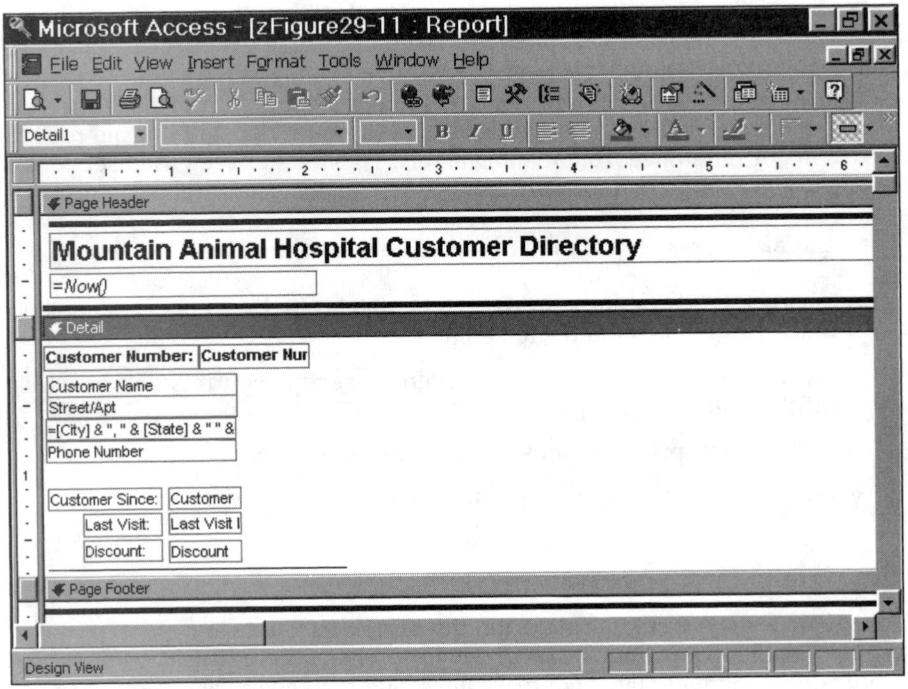

Figure 29-11: Defining a snaked column report design.

Defining the page setup

Earlier in this chapter, in the "Creating Mailing Labels" section, you learned how to use Page Setup settings. Since you created the labels by using the Label Wizard, the values for the Page Setup were automatically adjusted for you. Next, you learn how to enter these values manually. Figure 29-12 shows the Page Setup dialog box and the settings used to produce the Customer Directory report. Again, it doesn't show you the settings for the margins. Before continuing, click on the Margins tab and set the left and right margins to 0.5" (the top and bottom should be 1"). Then click on the Columns tab to continue.

The first group of settings (Grid Settings) to change are the Number of Columns, Row Spacing, and Column Spacing. Notice that the Number of Columns setting is set to 3. This means that you want three customer listings across the page. This and the other two settings actually work together. As you learned in the section about mailing labels, these controls set the spacing between groups of data and how the data is to be shown (the number of columns). The Row Spacing should be set to 0.2" and the Column Spacing set to 0.4". This is one way to set up the multiple columns and allow enough space between both the rows and the columns.

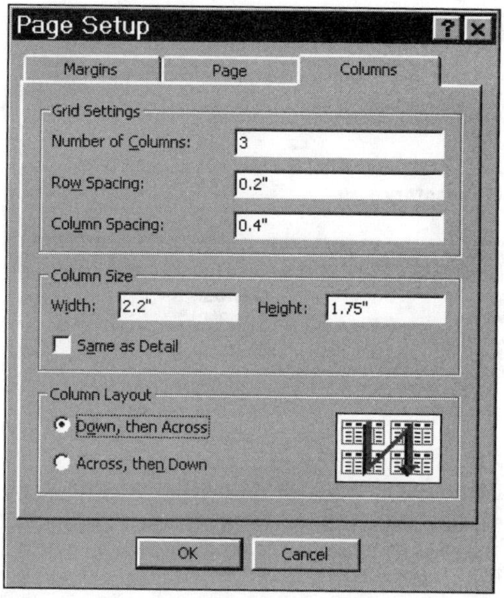

Figure 29-12: Defining the layout setup for a snaked column report.

The next grouping is the Column Size settings. In this example, the data is 1³/₄ inches high and about 2 inches wide in the detail section. You can define Width as **2.2 in** and Height as **1.75 in**. By adjusting the Grid Settings and Column Sizes, you control how your columned report will look.

Notice that the final grouping, Column Layout section, offers two settings: Down, then Across or Across, then down. The icon under Column Layout shows the columns going up and down. You saw in Figure 29-9 that when the setting is Across, then Down, the icon shows rows of labels going across. In this customer directory, you want to fill an entire column of names first before moving to the right to fill another column. Therefore, you select the Down, then Across setting.

Printing the snaked column report

After the expanded Page Setup dialog box settings are completed, you can print your report. Figure 29-13 shows the top half of the first page of the final snaked column report in the Print Preview window. The data is sorted by state and customer number. Notice that the data snakes down the page. The first record is for Customer Number AK001, in Idaho. Below that is customer BL001. There are four customers in the first column. After the fourth customer, the next customer (Customer Number GR001) is found at the top of the middle column.

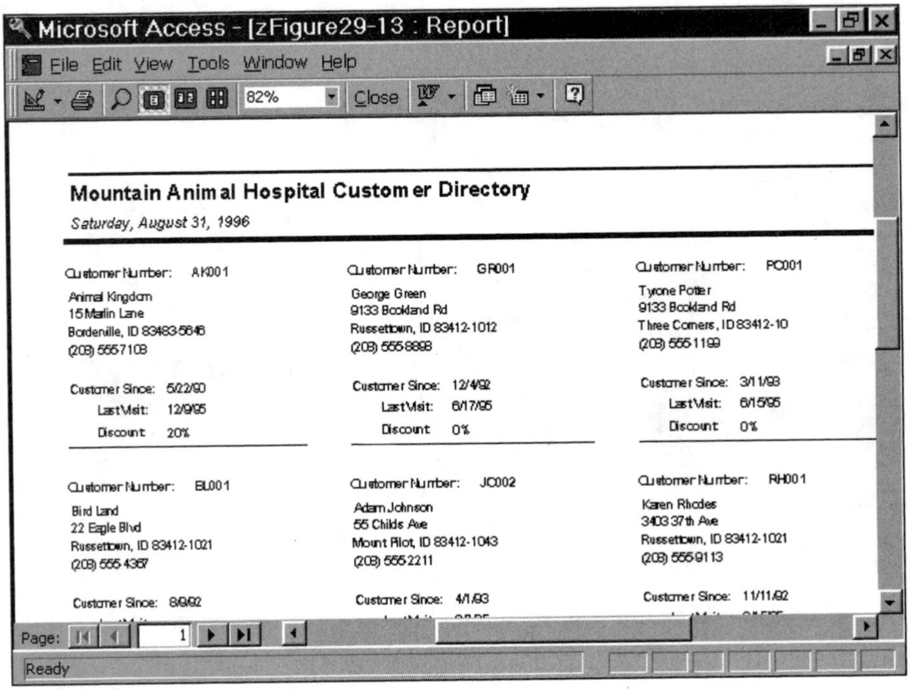

Figure 29-13: A snaked column report.

Creating Mail Merge Reports

Now that you have learned how to create snaked column reports and mailing labels (actually, they are the same thing), there is one more type of report to create — the *mail merge report* (also known as a *form letter*). A mail merge report is simply a report containing large amounts of text that have embedded database fields. For example, a letter may contain within the body of the text the amount a customer owes and the name of a pet.

The problem is how to control the *word wrap*. This means that the text may occupy more than one line, depending on the length of the text and the embedded field values. Different records may have different length values in their embedded fields. One record may use two lines in the report, another may use three, and another may require only one.

Access 97 contains a Report Wizard that exports your data to Microsoft Word and launches the Word Print Merge feature. Why would you want to use a word processor, however, when you're working in a database? What happens if you don't use

Word? Most word processors can perform mail merges using database data. Access itself does not have a specific capability to perform mail merging. Even so, as you see in this section, Access can indeed perform mail merge tasks with nearly the same precision as any Windows word processor!

In the first section of this chapter, you created mailing labels that indicated a special offer. You can use these labels to address the envelopes for the mail merge letter you now create. Suppose that you need to send a letter to all your customers who have an outstanding balance. You want to let them know that you expect payment now.

Figure 29-14 shows a letter created with Access. Many of the data fields embedded in this letter come from an Access query. The letter was created entirely with the Access Report Writer, as were its embedded fields.

Mountain Animal Hospital
2414 Mountain Road South
Redmond, WA 06761
(206) 555-9999

August 06, 1995

All Creatures
21 Grace St.
Tall Pines, WA 98746-2541

Dear All Creatures:

It has come to our attention that you have an outstanding balance of $2,000.00. We must have payment within 10 days or we will have to turn this account over to our lawyers. We give great service to your pets. In fact, according to our records, we have helped care for your animals since March 1993.

The entire staff is very fond of your animals. They especially like Bobo, and they would be very upset if your pet was no longer cared for by us. Since your last visit date on November 26, 1993, we have tried to contact you several times without success. Therefore, we are giving you 10 days to pay at least half of the outstanding balance, which comes to $1,000.00.

In advance, thank you, and we look forward to hearing from you and receiving your payment by August 16, 1995.

Sincerely,

Fred G. Rizzley

President
Mountain Animal Hospital

Figure 29-14: A letter created with the Access Report Writer.

Assembling data for a mail merge report

You can use data from either a table or a query for a report. A mail merge report is no different from any other report. As long as you specify a table or query as the control source for the report, the report can be created. Figure 29-15 shows a typical query used for the letter.

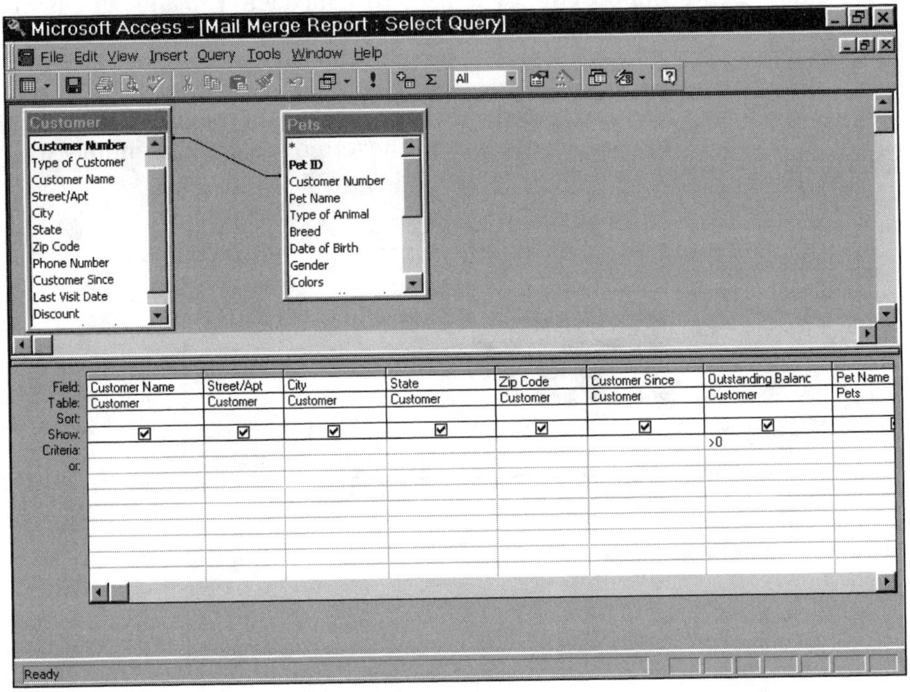

Figure 29-15: A typical query for a mail merge report.

Table 29-1 shows the fields or functions embedded in the text blocks used to create the letter. Compare the values in each line of the letter (shown in Figure 29-14) to the fields shown in the table. Later in this chapter, you'll see how each field or function is embedded in the text.

Table 29-1
Fields Used in the Mail Merge Report

Field Name	Table	Usage in Report
Date( )	Function	Page header; displays current date; formatted as mmmm dd, yyyy
Customer Name	Customer	Page header; displays customer name
Street/Apt	Customer	Page header; displays street in the address block
City	Customer	Page header; part of city, state, ZIP code block
State	Customer	Page header; part of city, state, ZIP code block
Zip Code	Customer	Page header; part of city, state, ZIP code block; formatted as @@@@@-@@@@
Customer Name	Customer	Detail; part of salutation
Outstanding Balance	Customer	Detail; first line of first paragraph; formatted as $#,##0.00
Customer Since	Customer	Detail; fourth line in first paragraph; formatted as mmmm yyyy
Pet Name	Pets	Detail; first line in second paragraph
Last Visit Date	Customer	Detail; second and third lines in second paragraph; formatted as mmm dd, yyyy
Outstanding	Customer	Detail; fifth line in second paragraph; formatted as $#,##0.00 Balance *.5 Calculation
Date Add( );	Function	Detail; second line in third paragraph; Date Add adds ten days Now( ) Function to system date Now( ); formatted as mmmm dd, yyyy

Creating a mail merge report

After you assemble the data, you can create your report. Creating a mail merge report is much like creating other reports. Frequently a mail merge has only a page header and a detail section. You can use sorting and grouping sections, however, to enhance the mail merge report (although form letters normally are fairly consistent in their content).

Usually the best way to begin is with a blank report. Report Wizards don't really help you create a mail merge report. After you create a blank report, you can begin to add your controls to it.

Creating the page header area

A form letter generally has a top part that includes your company's name, address, and possibly a logo. You can print on preprinted forms that contain this information, or you can scan in the header and embed it in an unbound object frame. Usually, the top part of a form letter also contains the current date along with the name and address of the person or company to whom you're sending the letter.

Figure 29-16 shows the page header section of the mail merge report. In this example, an unbound bitmap picture is inserted that contains the Mountain Animal Hospital logo. The text for the company information is created with individual label controls. As you can see in the top half of the page header section, the current date is also displayed along with a line to separate the top of the header from the body of the letter. You can see the calculated text box control's properties at the bottom of Figure 29-16. The Format( ) and Date( ) functions are used to display the date with the full text for month, followed by the day, a comma, a space, and the four-digit year.

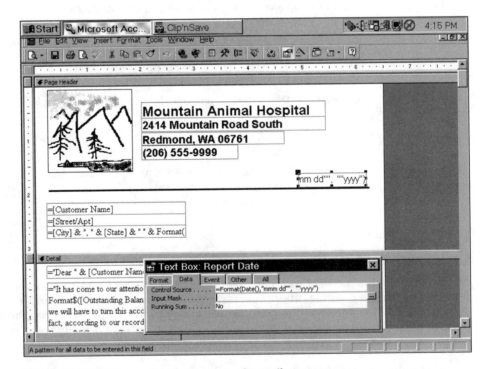

Figure 29-16: The page header section of a mail merge report.

The date expression is entered as

=Format(Date( ),"mmmm dd, yyyy")

and then automatically changed to

```
=Format(Date(),"mmmm dd""","""yyyy")
```

This expression takes the system date of 09/05/96 and formats the date as September 5, 1996.

The customer name and address fields are also displayed in the page header. The standard concatenated expression is used to display the city, state, and ZIP code fields:

```
=[City] & ", " & [State] & " " & Format([Zip Code],"@@@@@-
        @@@@")
```

Working with embedded fields in text

The body of the letter is shown in Figure 29-17. Each paragraph is one large block of text. A standard text box control is used to display each paragraph. The text box control's Can Grow and Can Shrink properties are set to Yes, which allows the text to take up only as much space as needed.

Embedded in each text block are fields from the query or expressions that use the fields from the query. In the page header section, the & method is used to concatenate the city, state, and ZIP code. Although this method works for single concatenated lines, it does not allow word wrapping, which is critical to creating a mail merge report. If you use this method in large blocks of text, you get only a single, truncated line of text.

**Cross-
Reference**
As you learned in Chapter 23, the & method of concatenation handles word wrap within the defined width of the text box. When the text reaches the right margin of a text box, it shifts down to the next line. Because the Can Grow property is turned on, the text box can have any number of lines. It's best to convert nontext data to text when you concatenate with the & method. Although this conversion isn't mandatory, the embedded fields are displayed more correctly when they are correctly converted and formatted.

The first text block is a single-line text box control that concatenates the text "Dear" with the field Customer Name. Notice the special symbols within the first text box control. Remember that each text box is made up of smaller groups of text and expressions. By using the & character, you can concatenate them.

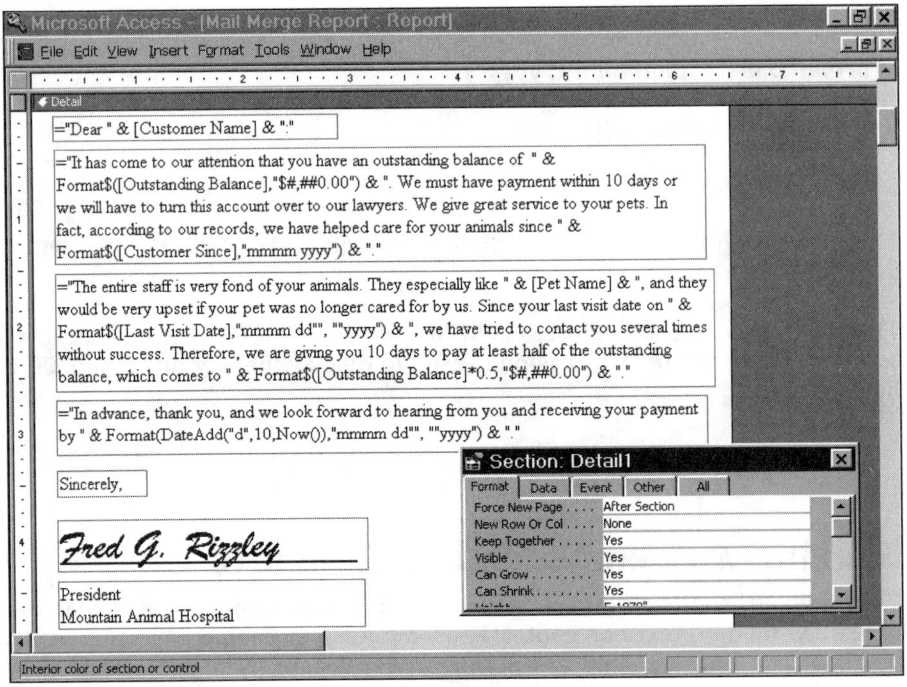

Figure 29-17: The body of the letter in the Report Design window.

The expression **="Dear" & [Customer Name] & ":"** begins with an equal sign and a double quote. Because the first item is text, it's surrounded by " characters. [Customer Name] needs to be enclosed in brackets because it's a field name; it should also be surrounded by & characters for concatenation. The colon at the end of the expression appears in the letter; it too is text and must be surrounded by double quotes.

The next control produces the first paragraph of the letter. Notice that there are five lines in the text box control but only four lines in the first paragraph of the letter (as shown in Figure 29-14). If you compare the two figures carefully, however, you'll see that the text box for the date is on the fifth line of the paragraph in the text control, whereas it's in the fourth line of the paragraph in the printed letter. This is a good example of word wrap. The lines shrank to fit the data.

The first line of the text control simply displays a text string. Notice that the text string is both enclosed in double quotes *and* concatenated to the next expression by the & character. The second line begins with an expression:

```
Format$([Outstanding Balance],"$#,##0.00") & "."
```

The expression converts the numeric expression to text and formats the field Outstanding Balance so that it shows a dollar sign, a comma (if the value is 1,000 or more), and two displayed decimal places. Without the format, the field would have simply displayed 381 rather than $381.00 for the first record.

The rest of the second line of the paragraph through the end of the fourth is one long text string. It's simply enclosed in double quotes and concatenated by the & character. The last line of the first paragraph contains an expression that formats and converts a date field. The expression `Format$([Customer Since],"mmmm yyyy")` formats the date value to display only the full month name and the year. (The date format in the page header demonstrated how to display the full month name, day, and year.)

Caution The maximum length of a single concatenated expression in Access is 254 characters between a single set of quotes. To get around this limitation, just end one expression, add an & character, and start another. The limit on the length of an expression in a single text box is 2,048 characters (almost 40 lines)!

The last line of the second paragraph formats a numeric expression, but it also calculates a value within the format function. This is a good example of an expression within a function. The calculation `[Outstanding Balance] * .5` is then formatted to display dollar signs, and a comma if the number is 1,000 or more.

The last paragraph contains one text string and one expression. The expression advances the current date Now( ) by 10 days by using the expression `DateAdd("d",10,Now())`.

The bottom of the letter is produced using the label controls, as shown in Figure 29-17. These label controls display the closing, the signature, and the owner's title. The signature of Fred G. Rizzley is created here by using the Script font. Normally, you would scan in the signature and then use an unbound frame object control to display the bitmap picture that contains the signature.

One thing you must do is set the Force New Page property of the detail section to After Section so that a page break is always inserted after each letter.

Printing the mail merge report

You print a mail merge report in exactly the same way you would print any report. From the Print Preview window, you can simply click on the Print button. From the Report Design window, you can select File⇨Print. The report is printed out like any other report.

Using the Access Mail Merge Wizard for Word for Windows 6.0, 7.0/95, or 8.0/95

Another feature in Access 97 is a Wizard to open Word automatically and start the Print Merge feature. The table or query you specify when you create the new report is used as the data source for the Word for Windows 6.0, Word for Windows 7.0/95, or Word for Windows 8.0/95 print merge.

Caution   To use the Mail Merge Wizard in Access 97, you must have either Word 6.0 for Windows 3.1, Word for Windows 95 Version 7.0 or 8.0, or the Word in Office 95 or Office 97.

1. From the Database container window, click on either the Tables or Queries tab.

2. Select the table or query you want to merge with Word for Windows.

3. Click on the OfficeLinks drop-down button on the toolbar.

4. Click on <u>M</u>erge It to start the MS Word Mail Merge Wizard, as shown in Figure 29-18.

   After you select the MS Word Mail Merge Wizard, Access displays the Microsoft Word Mail Merge Wizard screen, as shown in Figure 29-19.

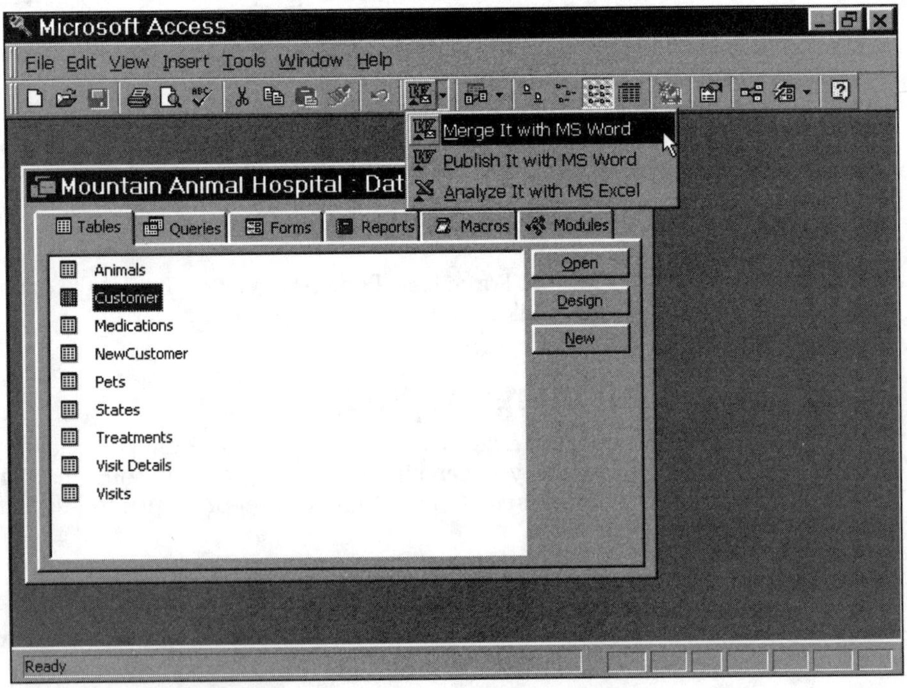

Figure 29-18: Selecting the MS Word Mail Merge Wizard.

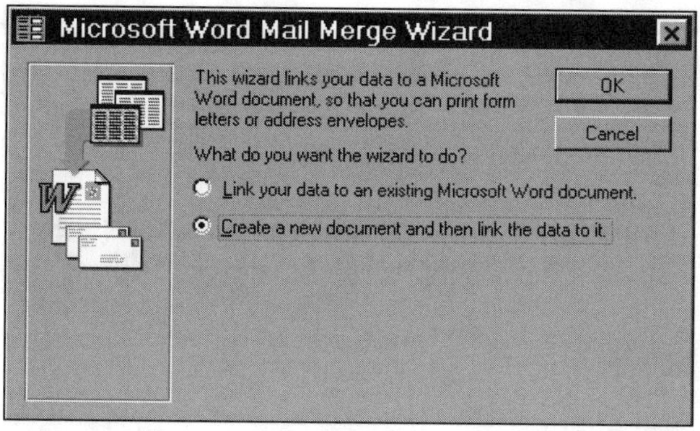

Figure 29-19: The Microsoft Word Mail Merge Wizard screen.

This screen lets you decide whether to link your data to an existing Word for Windows document or to create a new document. If you select the option that says to Link your data to an existing Microsoft Word document, Access displays a standard Windows file-selection box that lets you select an existing document. The document is retrieved, Word is displayed, and the Print Merge feature is active. You can then modify your existing document.

In this example, you start with a new document.

5. Select the option Create a new document and then link the data to it.

6. Click on OK to launch Word and display the Print Merge toolbar.

You may also see a dialog box asking for the field and record delimiter, usually a quote (") and a comma (,), with some type of merged data. You can now create your document, adding merge fields where you want them. As you can see in Figure 29-20, you simply click on the Insert Merge Field button whenever you want to display a field list from your Access table or query. The fields appear with a pair of carets around them.

When you're through, you can use the Mailmerge command button to merge the data and print your mail merge letters. There are some advantages to using the Microsoft Word print merge facility to create your letters. You have the availability of a spell checker, you can properly justify your paragraphs, and you can individually change the font type, size, or weight of individual words or characters. The negatives are that you have to use a word processor, you can't format numeric or date data, and you can't embed other Access objects, such as datasheets or graphs.

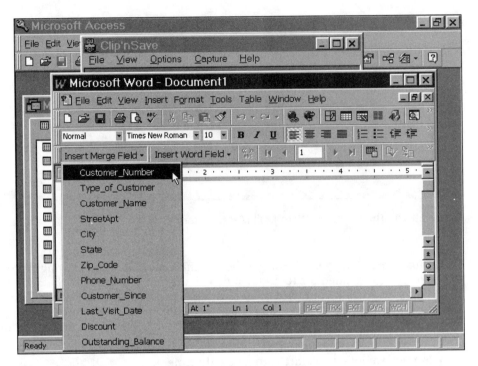

Figure 29-20: The Word for Windows Print Merge screen.

An example of a document created using the Mailmerge feature is shown in Figure 29-21. The merged fields have been highlighted in bold to make them stand out. An example of the hard-copy printout of the form letter is shown in Figure 29-22.

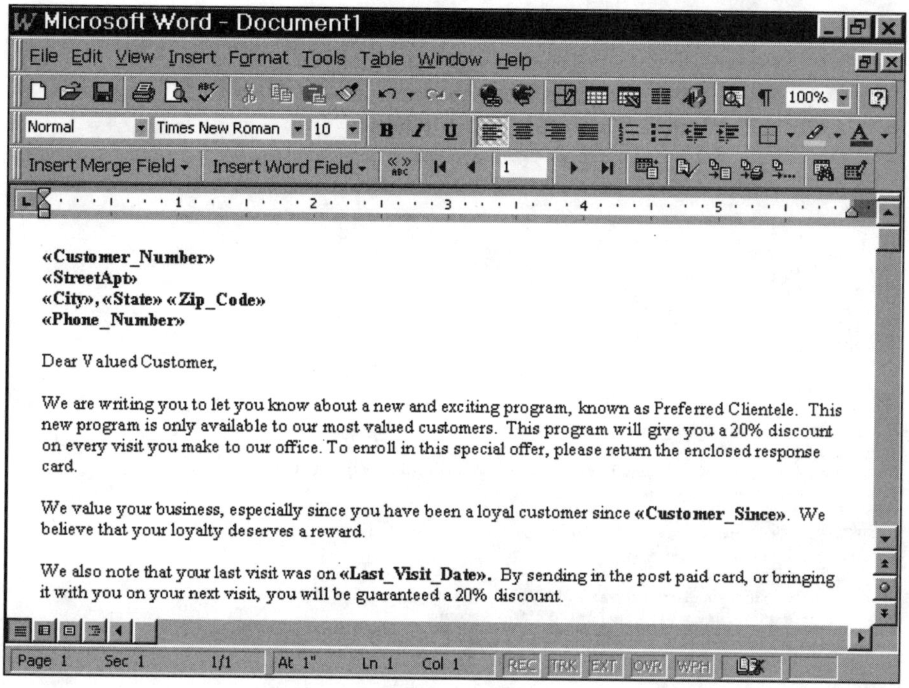

Figure 29-21: An example of a document created with the Mailmerge feature.

To see the merged fields in your document while in Word for Windows, you can click on the Merged Data button on the Word format bar.

When you're through editing and printing your letter, you can return to Access by selecting File⇨Close or File⇨Exit.

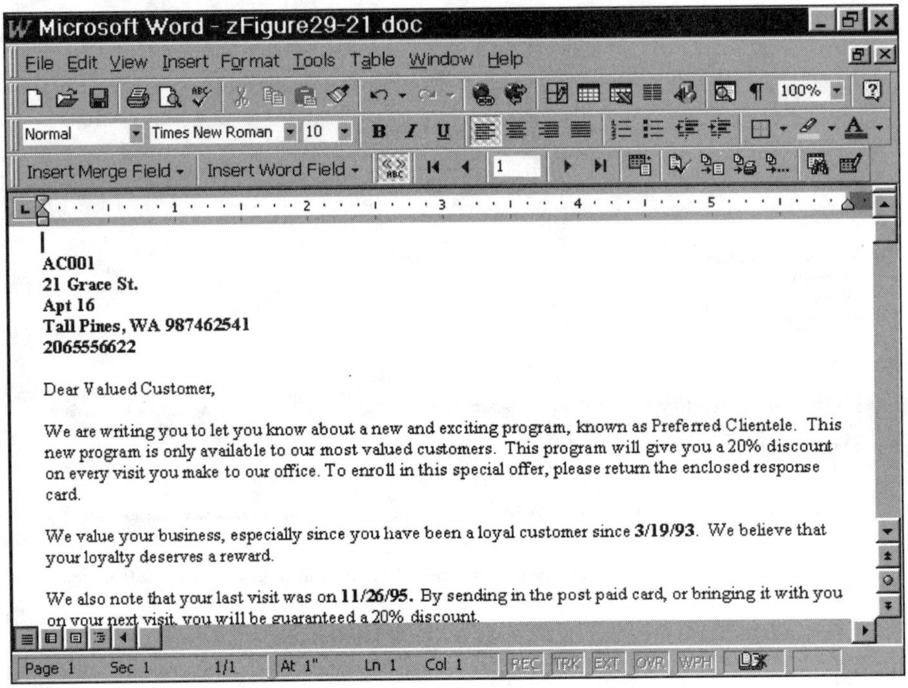

Figure 29-22: A printout of the form letter using the Mailmerge function.

Summary

In this chapter, you learned how to create mailing labels, snaked column reports, and mail merge reports. The following concepts were discussed:

✦ Mailing labels are most easily created using the Access Label Wizard.

✦ The Label Wizard lets you select the fields for the mailing label and also select from more than 100 Avery mailing label forms.

✦ Using the Report Design window, you can further customize the mailing label.

✦ The secret to mailing labels is changing the settings in the expanded Page Setup dialog box.

✦ Snaked column reports can be snaked vertically or horizontally.

✦ Snaked column reports are essentially large labels on paper; they are used for such things as customer directories.

✦ You can create mail merge reports with the Access Report Writer.

✦ By using concatenated text boxes, you can create paragraphs of text with embedded fields that word-wrap to create form letters.

✦ You can use the Format( ) function to reformat numeric and date fields in a mail merge report.

✦ The Word for Windows 6.0, 7.0/95 or 8.0/95 Mail Merge Wizard makes exported Access data easy to use with the Print Merge feature in Word for Windows (all versions after 6.0).

This chapter completes Part IV, which deals with advanced Access query, form, and report topics. Part V covers the use of Access macros you can use to automate tasks without programming.

✦　　✦　　✦

Applications in Access

An Introduction to Macros and Events

When you work with your database system, you may perform the same tasks over and over. Rather than do the same steps every time, you can automate the process by using macros.

Database management systems continually grow as you add records in a form, perform ad hoc queries, and print new reports. As the system grows, you save many of the objects for later use — for a weekly report or monthly update query, for example. You tend to create and perform many tasks repetitively. Every time you add customer records, for example, you open the same form. Likewise, you print the same form letter for customers whose pets are overdue for their annual shots.

You can create Access *macros* to perform these tasks. After you have created these small programs, you may want certain macros to take effect whenever a user performs some action (such as pressing a button or opening a form). Access uses *events* to trigger macros automatically.

Understanding Macros

Access macros automate many repetitive tasks without your having to write complex programs or subroutines. In the example of the form letter for customers whose pets are overdue for annual shots, a macro can perform a query and print the results for all such customers.

What is a macro?

A *macro* is an object like other Access objects (tables, queries, forms, and reports), except that you create it to automate a particular task or series of tasks. Think of each task as the result of one or more steps; each step is an action not found on the Access menu but in the Visual Basic or VBA language. You can also use Access macros to simulate menu choices or mouse movements.

Unlike macros in spreadsheets, Access macros normally are not used to duplicate individual keystrokes or mouse movements. They perform specific, user-specified tasks, such as opening a form or running a report.

Every task you want Access to perform is called an *action*. Access provides 49 actions you can select and perform in your macros. For example, you may have a macro that performs the four actions shown in Figure 30-1:

✦ Place the hourglass on the screen

✦ Automatically open a form

✦ Maximize the form after opening it

✦ Display a message box that says that the macro is complete

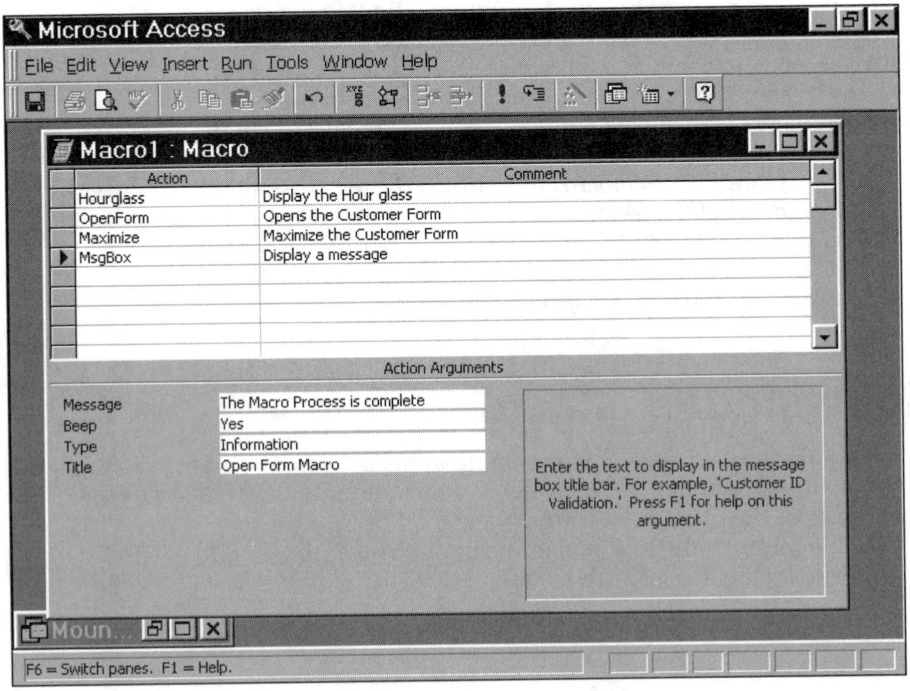

Figure 30-1: A macro designed with four actions (tasks).

Macro actions are created in a Macro Design window. The macros are run by entering the macro name in the Event properties of a form or report.

When to use a macro

You can use macros for any repetitive task you do in Access, so you save time and energy. In addition, because the macro performs the actions in the same way every time, macros add accuracy and efficiency to your database. You can use macros to perform such tasks as

✦ Running queries and reports together

✦ Opening multiple forms and/or reports together

✦ Checking for data accuracy on validation forms

✦ Moving data between tables

✦ Performing actions when a command button is clicked on

As an example, a macro can find and filter records for a report. You can add a button to a form that makes a macro perform a user-specified search. Macros can be used throughout the Access database system.

The Macro Window

As with other Access objects, you create a macro in a graphical design window. To open a new Macro window, follow these steps:

1. In an open database, press F11 (or Alt+F1) to select the Database window.

2. Click on the Macros tab.

3. Click on the New command button in the Database window.

After you complete these steps, Access displays an empty Design window, similar to the one in Figure 30-2. Notice the different parts of the window in this figure.

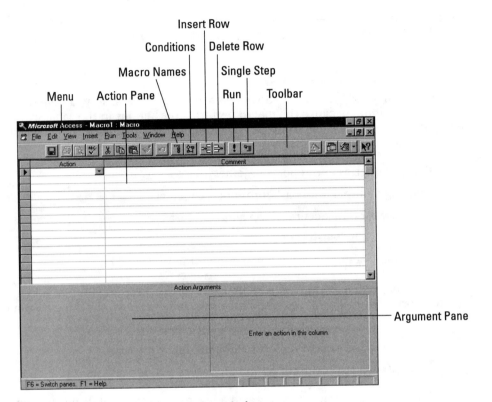

Figure 30-2: An empty Macro Design window.

As Figure 30-2 shows, the Macro Design window has four parts: a menu and a toolbar above the Design window, and these two window panes:

✦ Action pane (top portion of the window)

✦ Argument pane (bottom portion of the window)

The Action pane

By default, when you open a new Macro Design window, as in Figure 30-2, Access displays two columns in the Action pane (top pane): Action and Comment. Two more columns, Macro Name and Condition, can be displayed in the Action pane by selecting View⇨Macro Names and View⇨Conditions or by clicking on the equivalent icons on the toolbar.

Note If you want to change the default so that all four columns are open, select Tools⇨Options and then click on the View tab and place a check mark in both the Show in Macro Design items.

Each macro can have one or many actions (individual tasks you want Access to perform). You add individual actions in the Action column, and you can add a description of each action in the Comment column. Access ignores the comments when the macro is run.

The Argument pane

The lower portion of the window is the *Argument pane*. This pane is where you supply the specific *arguments* (properties) needed for the selected action. Most actions need additional information to carry out the action, such as which object should be used. For example, Figure 30-3 shows the action arguments for a typical action named OpenForm, which opens a specific form and has six different arguments that can be specified:

Form Name	Specifies the Access form to open
View	Specifies the view mode to activate: Form, Design, Print Preview, Datasheet
Filter Name	Applies the specified filter or query
Where Condition	Limits the number of records displayed
Data Mode	Specifies a data-entry mode: Add, Edit, or Read Only
Window Mode	Specifies a window mode: Normal, Hidden, Icon, or Dialog

Note Some actions, such as Beep and Maximize, have no arguments but most require at least one argument.

Creating a macro

To create a macro, you use both panes of the Macro window: Action and Argument. After you supply actions and associated arguments, you can save the macro for later use.

Entering actions and arguments

You can add actions to a macro in any of several ways:

✦ Enter the action name in the Action column of the Macro window.

✦ Select actions from the pull-down list box of actions (in the Action column).

✦ Drag and drop an object from the Database window into an action cell.

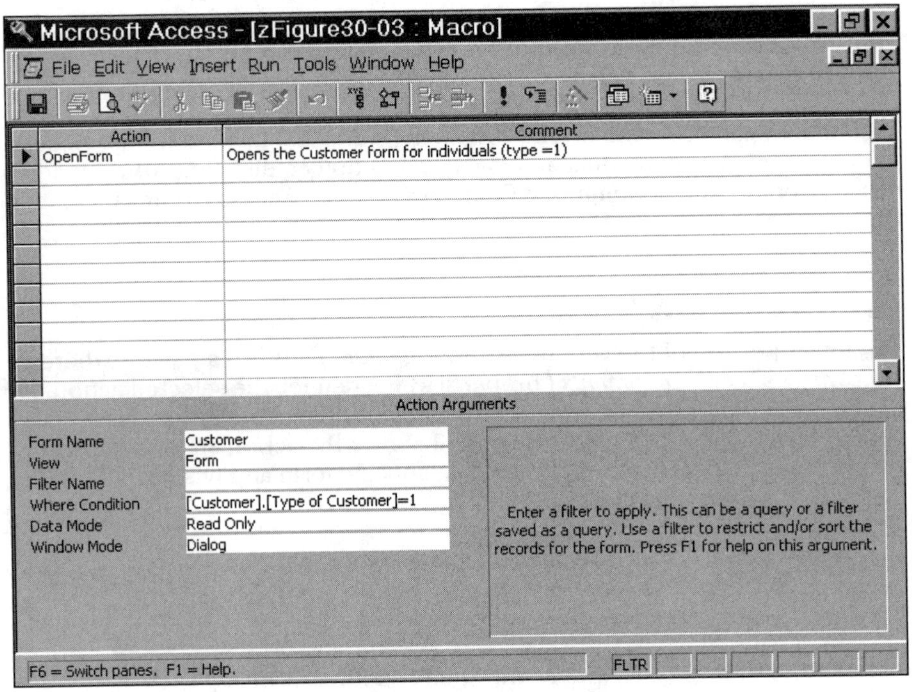

Figure 30-3: Arguments displayed for the OpenForm action.

The last method, drag and drop, is useful for common actions associated with the database. For example, you can drag a specific form to an action cell in the macro Action column; Access will automatically add the action OpenForm and its known arguments (such as the form name).

Selecting actions from the combo box list

The easiest way to add an action is by using the combo box, which you can access in any action cell. For example, if you want to open a form, you specify the action OpenForm. To create the OpenForm action, follow these steps:

1. Open a new Macro Design window.

2. Click on the first empty cell in the Action column.

3. Click on the arrow that appears in the action cell.

4. Select the OpenForm action from the combo box.

Note   You don't have to add comments to the macro, but it's a good idea to document the reason for each macro action (as well as a description of the entire macro).

Specifying arguments for actions

After entering the OpenForm action, you can enter the arguments into the bottom pane. Recall that Figure 30-3, which displays the completed arguments, shows that the bottom pane has six action arguments associated with this specific action. The arguments View, Data Mode, and Window Mode have default values. Because Access does not know which form you want to open, you must enter at least a form name. To open the form named Customer as a dialog box in read-only mode, you enter the three arguments Form Name, Data Mode, and Window Mode, as shown earlier, in Figure 30-3.

To add the arguments, follow these steps:

1. Click on the Form Name cell (or press F6 to switch to the Argument pane).

2. Select the Customer form from the pull-down list box (or type the name).

3. Click on the Data Mode cell.

4. Select the Read Only choice from the pull-down list (or type the choice).

5. Click on the Window Mode cell.

6. Select the Dialog choice from the pull-down list (or type the choice).

Your macro should now resemble the one in Figure 30-3. Notice that the Form Name is specified and the default values of the Data Mode and Window Mode cells are changed.

Selecting actions by dragging and dropping objects

You can also specify actions by dragging and dropping objects from the Database window. When you add actions in this manner, Access adds the appropriate arguments automatically. To add the same form (Customer) to an empty Macro window, follow these steps:

1. Start with an empty Macro Design window.

2. Select Window⇨Tile Vertically from the Design menu. Access places the Macro and Database windows side by side.

3. Click on the Forms tab in the Database window. Access displays all the forms, as shown in Figure 30-4.

4. Click on and drag the Customer form from the Database window. Access displays a Form icon as it moves into the Macro window.

5. Continue to drag and drop the Form icon in any empty action cell of the Macro window.

Access displays the correct action and arguments automatically.

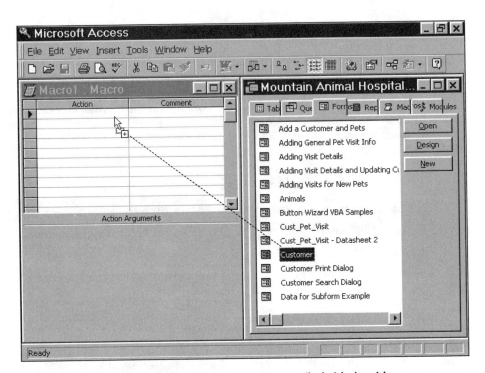

Figure 30-4: The Macro and Database windows are tiled side by side.

Note After using the drag-and-drop method to select actions, you may need to modify the action arguments to further refine them from their default values. Recall that in the last example you changed Data Mode and Window Mode for the form.

Adding multiple actions to a macro

You are not limited to adding a single action in a macro. You can have multiple actions assigned to a macro. For example, you may want to display an hourglass and then, while it's displayed, open two forms. Then you can have the computer beep for the user after completing the macro. To accomplish these multiple actions, follow these steps:

1. Open a new Macro Design window.
2. Click on the first empty cell in the Action column.
3. Select the Hourglass action from the pull-down list box or type it.
4. Click in the Comment cell alongside the Hourglass action.
5. Type **Display the hourglass while the macro is running**.

6. Click on the next empty cell in the Action column.

7. Select the OpenForm action from the pull-down list box, or type the name of the action.

8. Click on the argument cell Form Name.

9. Select the Add a Customer and Pets form.

10. Click on the Comment cell alongside the OpenForm action.

11. Type **Open the Add a Customer and Pets form**.

12. Click on the next empty cell in the Action column.

13. Select the OpenForm action from the pull-down list box or type the action.

14. Click on the argument cell Form Name.

15. Select the Adding Visit Details form.

16. Click on the Comment cell alongside the OpenForm action.

17. Type **Open the Adding Visit Details form**.

18. Click on the next empty cell in the Action column.

19. Select the Beep action from the pull-down list box, or type the action.

Your macro design should now look similar to Figure 30-5. Notice that this macro will open both forms as it displays the hourglass. After both forms are open, the macro beeps to signal that it is finished.

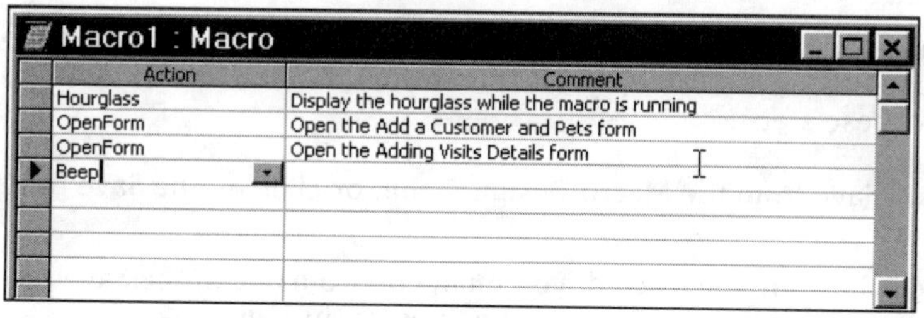

Action	Comment
Hourglass	Display the hourglass while the macro is running
OpenForm	Open the Add a Customer and Pets form
OpenForm	Open the Adding Visits Details form
Beep	

Figure 30-5: Adding multiple actions to a single macro.

Tip When you're adding more than one action, you can specify each action, one after the other, with several rows of spaces between them. These blank rows can contain additional lines of comments for each macro action.

Rearranging macro actions

When you work with multiple actions in a macro, you may change your mind about the order of the actions. For example, you may decide that the macro created in Figure 30-5 should have the Beep action come first in the macro. To move the action, follow these steps:

1. Select the action by clicking on the row selector to the left of the action name.

2. Click on the highlighted row again and drag it to the top row.

Deleting macro actions

If you placed an action in a macro you no longer need, you can delete the action. In the example of the macro shown in Figure 30-5, you may decide that you don't want to open the form Adding Visit Details. To delete the action, follow these steps:

1. Select the action by clicking on the row selector to the left of the action's name.

2. Press Delete or select Edit⇨Delete Row from the menu.

Tip   You can also delete a row by using the right-click shortcut menu: Select the row to delete, press the *right* mouse button, and select Delete Row.

Saving macros

Before you can run a macro, it must be saved. After you save a macro, it becomes another database object you can open and run from the Database window. To save a macro, follow these steps:

1. Select File⇨Save from the Macro Design menu, or click on the Save button on the toolbar.

2. If the macro has not been saved, you must enter a name in the Save As dialog box. Press Enter or click on OK when you're through.

Tip   The fastest way to save a macro is to press F12 or Alt+F2 and give the macro a name. Another way is to double-click on the Macro window's Control menu (top left corner) and answer the appropriate dialog box questions.

Editing existing macros

After you create a macro, you can edit it by following these steps:

1. In the Database window, select the Macros tab.

2. Highlight the macro you want to edit.

3. Click on the Design button in the Database window.

Copying entire macros

To copy a macro, follow these steps:

1. Click on the Macros tab in the Database window.

2. Select the macro you want to copy.

3. Press Ctrl+C or select Edit⇨Copy to copy the macro to the Clipboard.

4. Press Ctrl+V or select Edit⇨Paste to paste the macro from the Clipboard.

5. In the Paste As dialog box, type the new name.

Renaming macros

Sometimes you need to rename a macro because you changed the event property in the form or report property. To rename a macro, follow these steps:

1. Select the Database window by pressing F11 or Alt+F1.

2. Click on the Macros tab to display all the macro names.

3. Highlight the macro name you want to change.

4. Choose Edit⇨Rename from the Database menu or right-click and choose Rename from the shortcut menu.

5. Enter the new name.

Running Macros

After a macro is created, you can run it yourself from several locations within Access:

✦ A Macro window

✦ A Database window

✦ Other object windows

✦ Another macro

Running a macro from the Macro window

You can run a macro directly from the Macro Design window by clicking on the toolbar's Run button (the exclamation mark) or by choosing Run from the Design menu.

Running a macro from the Database window

You can run a macro from the Database window by following these steps:

1. Click on the Macros tab in the Database window.

2. Select the macro you want to run.

3. Either double-click on the macro or choose the Run button.

Running a macro from any window in the database

To run a macro from any window in the database, follow these steps:

1. Select Tools⇨Macro from the menu.

2. In the Macro dialog box, enter the name or select it from the pull-down list box.

3. Click on the OK button or press Enter.

Running a macro from another macro

To run a macro from another macro, follow these steps:

1. Add the action **RunMacro** to your macro.

2. Enter the name of the macro you want to run in the Macro Name argument.

Running a macro automatically when you open a database

You can instruct Access to run a macro automatically every time a database is opened; there are two ways to do this. Access recognizes a special macro name: *AutoExec*. If Access finds it in a database, it executes this macro automatically every time the database is opened. For example, you may want to open some forms and queries automatically and immediately after opening the database.

To run a macro automatically when a database is opened, follow these steps:

1. Create a macro with the actions you want to run when the database is opened.

2. Save the macro and name it **AutoExec.**

If you close that database and reopen it, Access runs the AutoExec macro automatically.

Tip   If you have a macro named AutoExec but you *don't* want to run it when you open a database, hold down the Shift key as you select the database in the Open Database dialog box.

In Access 97, databases have an option for setting Startup properties. Here, as shown in Figure 30-6, you can enter the name of a form you want to start when Access is opened. This form can contain the name of a macro to run when the form is loaded (more about form events later). You display the Startup properties window by selecting Tools⇨Startup from any window. Options you set in the Startup properties window are in effect as long as the Access database is open. You can set many options from the Startup properties window; for instance, you can change the title bar of all windows, specify the name of an icon file to use when Access is minimized, and affect many Access custom menus and toolbars.

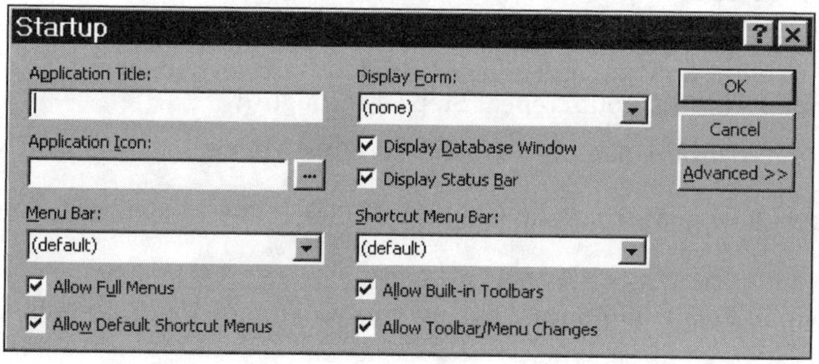

Figure 30-6: Using the Startup properties.

Macro Groups

As you create macros, you may want to group a series of related macros into one large macro. To do this, you need some way of uniquely identifying the individual macros within the group. Access lets you create a *macro group* (a macro file that contains one or more macros).

Creating macro groups

Like individual macros, macro groups are database objects. When you look in the macro object list of the Database window, you see only the macro group's name. Inside the group, each macro has a unique name you assign (along with the actions for each macro).

You may, for example, want to create a macro group of all macros that will open forms. To create this type of macro, follow these steps:

1. In the Database window, select the Macros tab.

2. Click on the New command button in the Database window. Access opens the Macro Design window.

3. Select View⇨Macro Names or select the Macro Names button on the toolbar. Access adds the Macro Name column to the Action pane.

4. In the Macro Name column, enter a name for the macro.

5. In the Action column, next to the macro name you just entered, enter an action for the macro.

6. Select the Action column under the action you just entered so that you can enter the next action.

7. Enter the next action (if the macro has more than one) in the Action column. Continue to enter actions until all are specified for a certain macro. To add another macro to the group, repeat Steps 4 through 7.

8. Save the macro group, naming it **Open and Close Forms**.

Figure 30-7 shows how a macro group will look. Notice that five separate macros are within it.

The macro group in Figure 30-7 shows five macros: Customer, Visits, Details, Close All Forms, and Exit.

The Arguments pane shows only the arguments for the highlighted macro name.

Tip   Although not necessary, it's a good idea to leave a blank line between macros to improve readability and clarity.

Running a macro in a macro group

After you create a macro group, you'll want to run each macro inside the group. To run one, you must specify both the group name and the macro name.

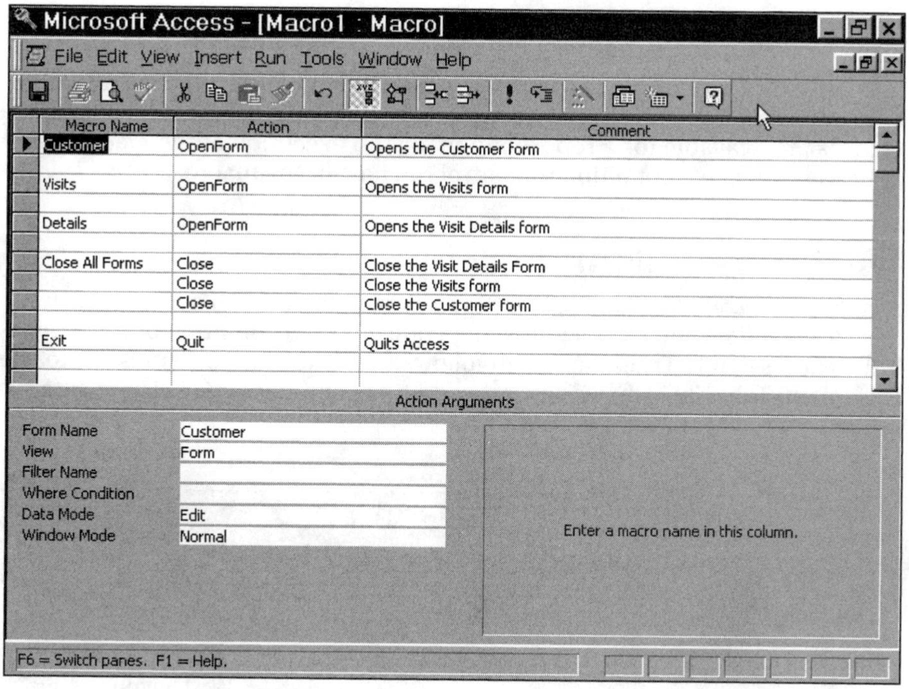

Figure 30-7: A macro group.

Cross-Reference Later in this chapter, you will learn how to use the events that run macros.

To specify both group and macro names, you will have to enter the group name, a period, and then the macro name. If you type **Open and Close Forms.Visits**, for example, you specify the macro Visits in the group macro named Open and Close Forms.

Caution If you run a group macro from the Macro Design window or from the Database window, you cannot specify a macro name inside the macro group. Access will run only the first macro or set of actions specified in the group macro. Access stops executing actions when it reaches a new macro name in the Macro Name column.

To run a macro inside a group macro, using the other windows in the database or another macro, you simply enter both the macro group name and macro name, placing a period between the two names.

Tip You also can run a macro by selecting Macro from the Tools menu and typing the group and macro name.

Supplying Conditions for Actions

In some cases, you may want to run some action or actions in a macro only when a certain condition is true. For example, you may want to display a message if no records are available for a report and then stop execution of the macro. In such a case, you can use a condition to control the flow of the macro.

What is a condition?

Simply put, a *condition* is a logical expression; it can be either True or False. The macro will follow one of two paths, depending on the condition of the expression. If the expression is True, the macro follows the True path; otherwise, it follows the False path. Table 30-1 shows several conditions and the True/False results.

Table 30-1 Conditions and Their Results		
Condition	*True Result*	*False Result*
Forms!Customer!State="WA"	If the state is Washington	Any state except Washington
IsNull(Gender)	If no gender is specified	Gender is male or female (not Null)
Length <= 10 to 10 inches	If length is less than or equal inches	If length is greater than 10
Reports![Pet Directory]! [Type animal] = "CAT" OR Reports! [Pet Directory]! [Type of Animal] = "DOG"	If type of animal is cat or dog	Any animal other than cat or dog

Activating the Condition column in a macro

As Table 30-1 demonstrates, a condition is an expression that results in a logical answer of Yes or No. The answer must be either True or False. You can specify a condition in a macro by following these steps:

1. Enter the Macro Design window by creating a new macro or editing an existing one.

2. Select View⇨Conditions or click on the Conditions button on the toolbar. The Condition column is inserted to the left of the Action column. If the

Macro Name column is visible, the Condition column is between the Macro Name and the Action columns (see Figure 30-8).

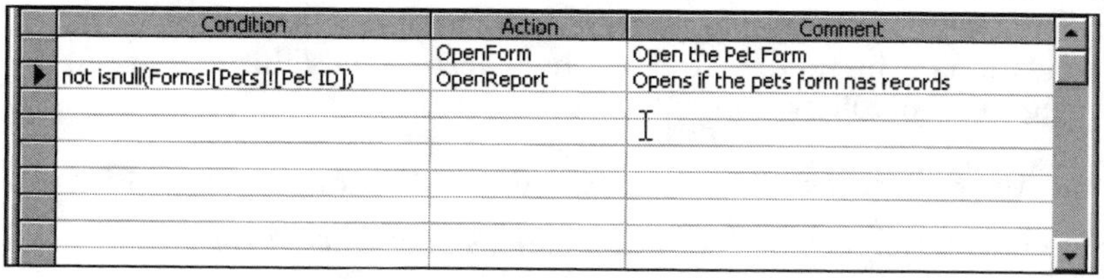

Condition	Action	Comment
	OpenForm	Open the Pet Form
not isnull(Forms![Pets]![Pet ID])	OpenReport	Opens if the pets form has records

Figure 30-8: The Condition column added to the Macro Design window.

With the Condition column visible, you can specify conditions for one or many actions within a macro.

Tip In Figure 30-8, you can see that the Condition and Comment columns are wider than the Action column. You can widen or shrink columns by positioning the cursor on the column border and dragging the column line.

Referring to control names in expressions

When working with macros, you may need to refer to the value of a control in a form or report. To refer to a control in a form or report, use the following syntax:

```
Forms!form-name!control-name
Reports!report-name!control-name
```

If a space occurs within the name of a form, report, or control, you must enclose the name in brackets. For example, Forms![Add a Customer and Pets]!State refers to the State control (field on a form) on the currently open form called Add a Customer and Pets.

If you run a macro from the same form or report that contains the control, you can shorten this syntax to the control name.

Note: To reference a control name on a form or report, first make sure that the form or report is open.

Specifying a condition for a single action

You may want to specify a condition for a single action. An example is activating the report Pet Directory only when there are records in the form Pets, based on a query named Only Cats and Dogs. If no records are present, you want the macro to skip activation of the report. To have the macro specify this condition, as shown in Figure 30-8, follow these steps:

1. In the Macro window, click on the Conditions button on the toolbar.
2. In the first action cell of the Action pane, select OpenForm.
3. In the Form Name cell of the Argument pane, select Pets.
4. In the next Action cell of the Action pane, select OpenReport.
5. In the Report Name cell of the Argument pane, select Pet Directory.
6. Click on the Condition cell next to the action OpenReport.
7. Type **Not IsNull(Forms![Pets]![Pet ID])**.

At the completion of these steps, your macro should resemble the one shown in Figure 30-8.

In this example, the condition specified is True if there are no records (the first Pet ID is Null) in the open form Pets. If the condition is True, when the macro is run, the action OpenReport is not performed; otherwise, the report is opened in print preview mode.

Caution When you specify conditions in a macro and reference a control name (field name), the source (form or report) of the control name must already be open.

Specifying a condition for multiple actions

Besides specifying a condition for a single action, you can specify a condition that will be effective for multiple actions. That is, a single condition will cause several actions to occur. In this way, you can also create an If-Then-Else condition.

If you want Access to perform more than one action, add the other actions below the first one. In the Condition column, place an ellipsis (...) beside each action. Figure 30-9 shows a macro in which two actions are performed based on a single condition. Notice that the condition has been changed from Not IsNull to IsNull.

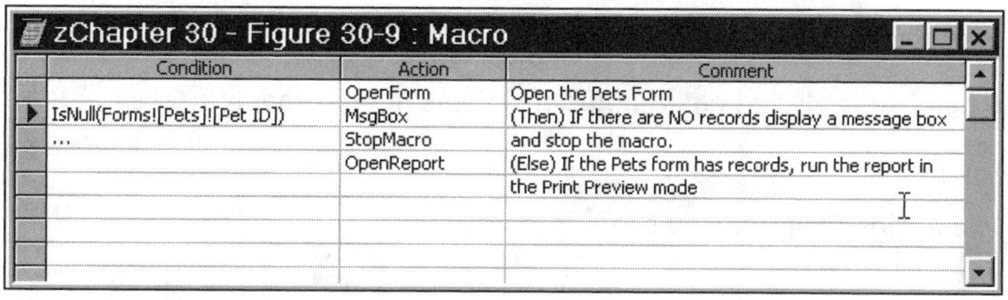

Condition	Action	Comment
	OpenForm	Open the Pets Form
IsNull(Forms![Pets]![Pet ID])	MsgBox	(Then) If there are NO records display a message box
...	StopMacro	and stop the macro.
	OpenReport	(Else) If the Pets form has records, run the report in the Print Preview mode

Figure 30-9: This macro shows two actions based on a single condition.

In Figure 30-9, the condition IsNull(Forms![Pets]![Pet ID]) performs the two actions MsgBox and StopMacro if the condition is True. Notice the ellipsis (...) in the cell immediately under the specified condition, which is the Condition cell for the action StopMacro.

When you run the macro, Access evaluates the expression in the Condition cell. If the expression is True, Access performs the action beside the expression and then all the following actions that have an ellipsis in the Condition column. Access continues the True actions until it comes to another condition (using the new condition from that point on).

If the expression is False, Access ignores the action (or actions) and moves to the next action row that does not have an ellipsis.

Caution If Access reaches a blank cell in the Condition column, it performs the action in that row regardless of the conditional expression. The only way to avoid this is to control the flow of actions by use of a *redirection action,* such as RunMacro or StopMacro. For example, if the second conditional action (StopMacro) is not after the MsgBox action, the OpenReport action is executed regardless of whether the conditional expression is True or False. On the other hand, the MsgBox action takes effect only if the field Pet ID is Null (True).

Controlling the flow of actions

By using conditional expressions, you can control the flow of action in the macro. The macro in Figure 30-9 uses the action StopMacro to stop execution of the macro if the field is Null; it therefore avoids opening the report Pet Directory if the table is empty.

Several macro actions can be used to change or control the flow of actions based on a condition. The two most common are the actions StopMacro and RunMacro; they also control the flow of actions within a macro.

Troubleshooting Macros

Access has two tools to help you find problems in your macros:

✦ Single-step mode

✦ The Action Failed dialog box

Single-step mode

If, while running a macro, you receive unexpected results, you can use *single-step mode* to move through the macro one action at a time, pausing between actions. By single-stepping, you can observe the result of each action and isolate the action or actions that caused the incorrect results.

To use single-stepping, click on the Single-Step button on the toolbar. To use this feature on the macro in Figure 30-9, follow these steps:

1. Edit the macro, bringing it into the Macro Design window.

2. Click on the Single-Step button on the toolbar or select Run⇨Single Step.

3. Run the macro as you normally do or by clicking on the Run button on the toolbar.

Access displays the Macro Single Step dialog box, showing the macro name, the action name, and the arguments for the action (see Table 30-2). Figure 30-10 shows a typical Macro Single Step dialog box.

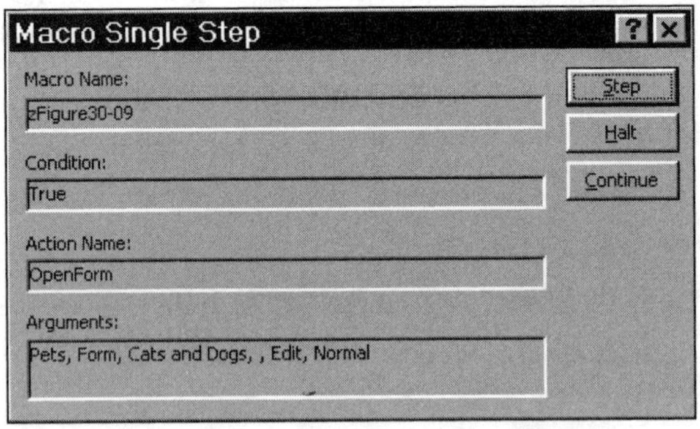

Figure 30-10: The Macro Single Step dialog box.

Table 30-2
Macro Single-Step Button Options

Button	Purpose
<u>S</u>tep	Runs the action in the dialog box. If no error is reported, the next action appears in the dialog box.
<u>H</u>alt	Stops the execution of the macro and closes the dialog box.
<u>C</u>ontinue	Turns off single-step mode and runs the remainder of the macro.

The Action Failed dialog box

If a macro action causes an error (either during single-step mode or when running normally), Access opens a dialog box that looks exactly like the Macro Single Step dialog box, except that the only available button is the <u>H</u>alt button.

To correct the problem, choose <u>H</u>alt and return to the Macro Design window.

Understanding Events

With the actions stored in macros, you can run the macro either via a menu choice or by naming the macro **AutoExec**. The AutoExec macro runs automatically every time you open the database. Access also offers another method to activate a macro: Base it on a user action.

For example, a user can click on a command button to activate a macro or by the action of opening a form. To accomplish this, Access takes advantage of something known as an *event*.

What is an event?

An Access event is the result or consequence of some user action. An Access event can occur when a user moves from one record to another in a form, closes a report, or clicks on a command button on a form.

Your Access applications are *event driven*. Objects in Access respond to many types of events. Access responds to events with behaviors that are built in for each object. Access events can be recognized by specific object properties. For example, if a user clicks the mouse button with the pointer in a check box, the property OnMouseDown recognizes that the mouse button was clicked. You can have this property run a macro when the user clicks the mouse button.

Events in Access 97 can be categorized into seven groups:

✦ **Windows (Form, Report) events:** Opening, closing, and resizing, for example

✦ **Data events:** Making current, deleting, updating, for example

✦ **Focus events:** Activating, entering, and exiting, for example

✦ **Keyboard events:** Pressing or releasing a key, for example

✦ **Mouse events:** Clicking or pressing a mouse button down, for example

✦ **Print events:** Formatting and printing, for example

✦ **Error and timing events:** Happening after an error has occurred or some time has passed

In all, nearly 50 events can be checked in forms and reports to specify some action after they take place.

How do events trigger actions?

You can have Access run a macro when a user performs any one of the 50 events that Access recognizes. Access can recognize an event through the use of special properties for forms, controls (fields), and reports.

For example, Figure 30-11 shows the property sheet for a form. This form has many properties, which may be used to respond to corresponding events. Forms themselves aren't the only objects to have events; so do form sections (page header, form header, detail, page footer, form footer) and every control on the form (labels, text boxes, check boxes, and option buttons, for example).

Where to trigger macros

In Access, you can run event-driven macros by using properties in forms and reports. There are no event properties for tables or queries.

Even so, when you work with forms, you can run macros based on Access switchboards (full-screen button-type menus), command buttons, and pull-down menus. These features make event-driven macros powerful and easy to use. In the next few chapters, you will learn about many events and the macro actions that events can use.

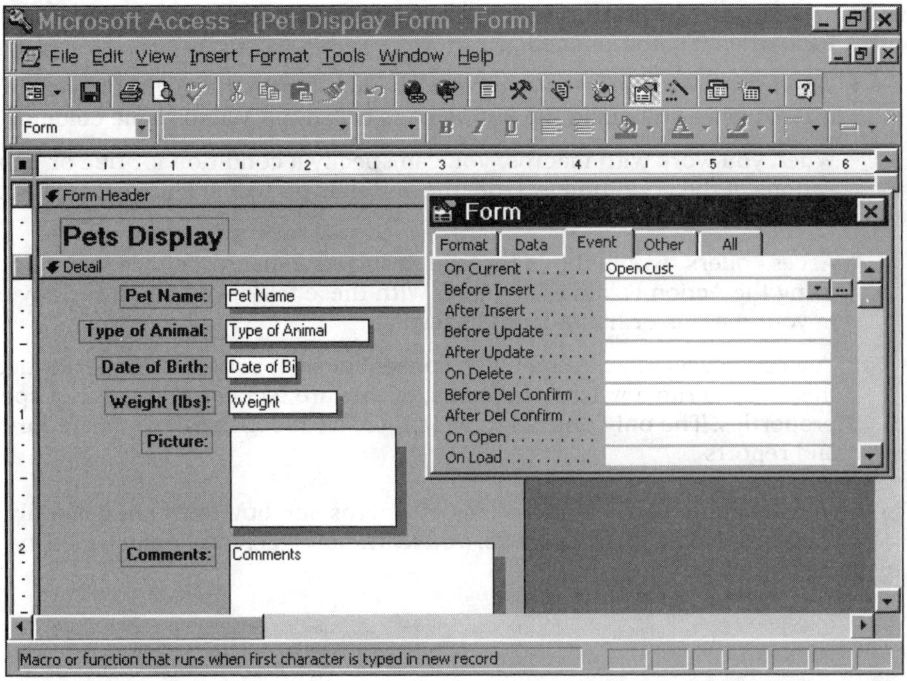

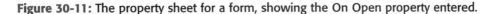

Figure 30-11: The property sheet for a form, showing the On Open property entered.

Summary

In this chapter, you learned the basics of macros and events:

✦ An Access macro is a database object that lets you automate tasks without writing complex programs. Macros should be used to automate repetitive tasks. In Access, the tasks you perform are known as *actions*.

✦ Two panes comprise the Macro Design window: Action and Argument. In the Action pane, you specify Access actions. You can add them from a pull-down list box or by dragging and dropping common objects.

✦ Access requires arguments (variables) in order to perform actions.

✦ Macros can be saved, renamed, edited, and copied just like any other Access object.

✦ Access has a special macro called AutoExec that runs automatically when the database is opened. You can deactivate the AutoExec macro by holding down the Shift key when you open the database.

✦ You can use the Startup window to control many options in an Access database when it's first opened.

✦ When you create macros, you can consolidate them into a group macro. Group macros use a column in the Action pane called the Macro Name column.

✦ When you work with macros, you can specify a condition for one or more actions. If the condition is True, the action is performed; if False, the action is skipped.

✦ Access offers two methods for troubleshooting macros: single-stepping and using the Action Failed dialog box. With these tools, you can trace any errors in your macros or halt a faulty macro.

✦ You can use an *event* (a result or consequence of some action performed by the user) to run a macro. In Access, events are recognized by use of special properties. The only objects in which Access recognizes events are forms and reports.

In the next chapter, you see many uses of macros and how they are generally run from triggered events. In Chapter 32, you learn how to create menu-based systems by using events and macros.

✦   ✦   ✦

Using Macros in Forms and Reports

At this point, you should know how to create and run macros, and you should know how to start a macro automatically when you open a database. In addition, you should be able to create and specify conditions for macros.

Now you're going to learn how to use macros in real examples by using tables, forms, queries, and reports you created in previous chapters.

Types of Macros

Cross-Reference In Chapter 30, you learned how to create macros, and you learned how to associate a macro with a form or report property. *Macros* are Access objects consisting of one or more actions. Macros can open a dialog box, run a report, or even find a record.

Usually, you create macros to perform redundant tasks or a series of required actions after some initial action. For example, macros can synchronize two forms while a user moves from record to record. They can also validate new data after it is entered by a user.

Before activating a macro, you need to decide where and how you will use it. For example, you may have a macro that opens the Customer form, and you want Access to run the macro every time a user opens the Pets form. In this case, you place the name of the macro in the On Open property of the Pets form. Then, every time a user opens the Pets form, the On Open property will trigger the macro that opens the Customer form.

Or you may want to trigger another macro every time a user presses an accelerator key (also known as a hot key). For example, if you want an Import dialog box to be activated when a user presses Ctrl+I, you should attach the macro to the key combination Ctrl+I in a hot-key macro file.

Although the second macro performs some tasks or actions, it is different from the first one. The second macro is activated by a user action (pressing a hot key); the first one is activated when a user performs some specific action recognized by a form property.

Macros can be grouped together based on their usage. The four basic groups follow:

✦ Form

✦ Report

✦ Import/Export

✦ Accelerator keys

The most common macros are those used in forms and reports. Using macros in these objects lets you build intelligence into each form and report. Macros are also used for importing or exporting data to and from other data sources. Finally, macros can be activated by the use of hot keys.

A review of events and properties

Simply put, an *event* is some user action. The event can be an action such as opening a form or report, changing data in a record, selecting a button, or closing a form or report. Access recognizes nearly 50 events in forms and reports.

To recognize one of these events, Access uses form or report *properties*. Each event has an associated form or report property. For example, the On Open property is associated with the event of opening a form or report.

You trigger a macro by specifying the macro name. The name is specified as a parameter for the event property you want to have the macro run against. For example, if you want to run a macro named OpenPets every time a user opens the Customer form, you place the macro name in the parameter field alongside the property On Open in the form named Customer.

Macros for forms

You can create macros that respond to *form events*. These events are triggered by some user action, which may be opening a form or clicking on a control button on a form. Access knows when a user triggers an event through its recognition of event-specific form properties. Forms let you set properties for field controls. These properties can be quite useful during the design phase of a form, such as when you use a property to set a format or validation rule.

However, macros give you added power by letting you specify actions to be performed automatically based on a user-initiated event. The event is recognized by Access by use of event properties such as Before Update, On Delete, or On Enter. Unlike a simple format or field-level validation rule, a macro can perform multiple-step actions based on the user event. For example, after a user presses the Delete key to delete a record but before the deleted record is removed from the table, you can have a macro that automatically runs and asks the user to verify that the record should be deleted. In this case, you use the On Delete property to trigger execution of the macro.

Macros for forms can respond both to *form events* and *control events*. Form events take effect at the form level; control events take effect at the individual control level. Form events include deleting a record, opening a form, or updating a record. These events work at the form and record levels. Control events, on the other hand, work at the level of the individual control. These controls are the ones you specify when you create your form and include such items as a field (text box), a toggle button, an option button — even a command button. Each control has its own event properties that can trigger a macro. These events include selecting a command button, double-clicking on a control, and selecting a control.

By specifying a macro at the control level, you can activate a customer form when the user double-clicks on a field object or its label object. For example, you may have a form that identifies the customer by name but gives no additional customer information. When the user double-clicks on the customer's name, your macro can activate a customer form that shows all the customer information. To accomplish this, you use the field object property On Dbl Click to specify a macro that opens the customer form. Then the macro will run and open the Customer form every time the user double-clicks on the Customer field.

Figure 31-1 shows a form, named Cust_Pet_visit, with a label named Customer Name; note the field containing the name Animal Kingdom. When the user double-clicks on either the label (Customer Name) or the name (Animal Kingdom), the Customer form opens.

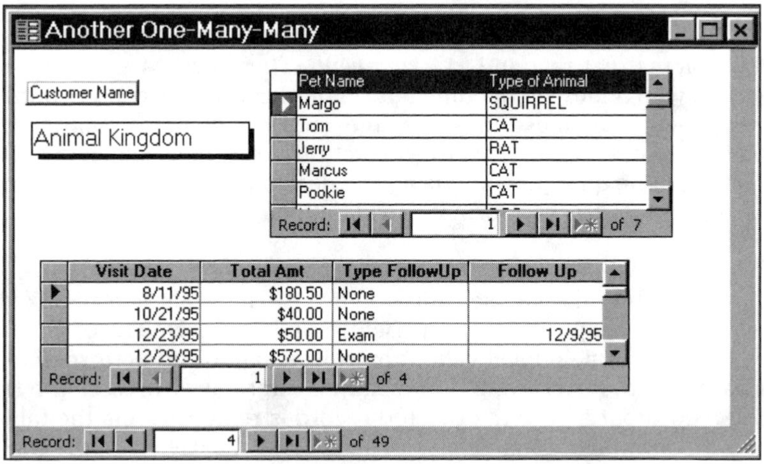

Figure 31-1: A typical form with labels and controls (fields).

Notice that the form in Figure 31-1 does not display any outward sign that a user can initiate a macro by double-clicking the label or field. However, the On Dbl Click property is set for the field to automatically execute the macro that opens the Customer form. In Figure 31-2, you can see that the macro is being specified in the On Dbl Click property. The macro group name is Update Form, and the specific macro name in the group is ShowCustomer.

Tip   By using the properties of text boxes, the event will be triggered when it occurs on the text box (field) or its associated label.

Macros for reports

Just as with forms, macros can also enhance the use of the reports. You may, for example, want to prompt a user for a range of records to be printed before printing the report. You may want to display a message on the report whenever a certain condition is met. You may even want to underline or highlight a field on the basis of its value, such as when the value is too small or too large. Macros give you this type of refined control in reports.

Macros for reports can respond both to *report events* and *report section events.* Report events take effect at the report level; report section events take effect at the section level of the report.

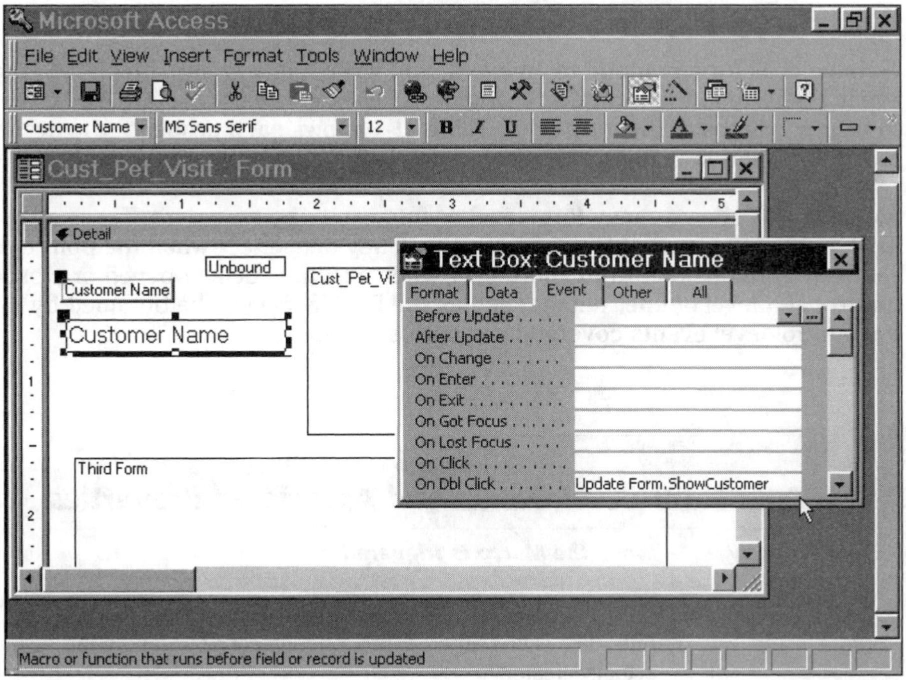

Figure 31-2: Using a form event to call a macro.

Macros for accelerator keys

You can also associate a macro with a specific key or combination of keys. When a macro is assigned to a key combination, it can be activated by a user pressing that key or key combination. For example, you may assign the key combination Ctrl+P to print the current record displayed on-screen. Another example is assigning the key combination Ctrl+N to skip to the next record in the report or form. Creating hot keys gives you additional capabilities in your forms and reports without requiring you to write complicated programs.

You use most hot-key macros when you work with forms and reports, although hot-key macros can be used in queries or other Access objects.

Form-Level Event Macros

When you work with forms, you can specify macros based on events at the form level, the section level, or the control level. If you attach a macro to a form-level event, whenever the event occurs, the action takes effect against the form as a whole (such as when you change the record pointer or leave the form).

Attaching macros to forms

To have your form respond to an event, you write a macro and attach it to the event property in the form that recognizes the event. Many properties can be used to trigger macros at the form level. Table 31-1 shows each property, the event it recognizes, and how the property works.

As Table 31-1 shows, many form-level events can trigger a macro. These events work only at the level of forms or records. They take effect when the pointer is changed from one record to another or when a form is being opened or closed. Control at a level of finer detail (such as the field level) can be obtained by using the control-level events covered later in this chapter.

Table 31-1
The Form-Level Events and Associated Properties

Event Property	When the Macro Is Triggered
On Current	When you move to a different record and make it the current record
Before Insert	After data is first entered into a new record but before the record is actually created
After Insert	After the new record is added to the table
Before Update	Before changed data is updated in a record
After Update	After changed data is updated in a record
On Delete	When a record is deleted but *before* the deletion takes place
Before Del Confirm	Just before Access displays the Confirm Delete dialog box
After Del Confirm	After the Delete Confirm dialog box closes and confirmation has happened
On Open	When a form is opened, but the first record is not displayed yet
On Load	When a form is loaded into memory but not yet opened
On Resize	When the size of a form changes
On Unload	When a form is closed and the records unload and before the form is removed from the screen
On Close	When a form is closed and removed from the screen
On Activate	When an open form receives the focus, becoming the active window
On Deactivate	When a different window becomes the active window but before it loses focus

Event Property	When the Macro Is Triggered
On Got Focus	When a form with no active or enabled controls receives the focus
On Lost Focus	When a form loses the focus
On Click	When you press and release (click) the left mouse button on a control in a form
On Dbl Click	When you press and release (click) the left mouse button twice on a control/label in a form
On Mouse Down	When you press the mouse button while the pointer is on a form
On Mouse Move	When you move the mouse pointer over an area of a form
On Mouse Up	When you release a pressed mouse button while the pointer is on a form
On Key Down	When you press any key on the keyboard when a form has focus; when you use a SendKeys macro
On Key Up	When you release a pressed key or immediately after the SendKeys macro
On Key Press	When you press and release a key on a form that has the focus; when you use the SendKeys macro
On Error	When a run-time error is produced
On Filter	When a filter has been specified but before it is applied
On Apply Filter	After a filter is applied to a form
On Timer	When a specified time interval passes

Opening a form with a macro

Sometimes you may want to open a form with a macro. For example, every time you open the Pets Display form, you may also want to open the Customer form. This will enable a user to click on either form to see information from both at one time.

To accomplish this, you create a macro named OpenCust and attach it to the On Open property of the Pets Display form.

To create the macro, follow these steps:

1. Click on the Macros tab in the Database window to select the Macro Object list.

2. Click on the New button to display the Macro Design window.

3. Click on the first empty Action cell.

4. Select the OpenForm action from the pull-down menu of the Action cell.

5. Click in the Form Name cell of the Action Arguments (bottom part of window).

6. Select or type **Customer**.

7. Save the macro by clicking on the Save button on the toolbar and naming the macro **OpenCust**.

Notice that in Figure 31-3 the OpenCust macro has only one action — OpenForm, with the action argument Form Name of Customer.

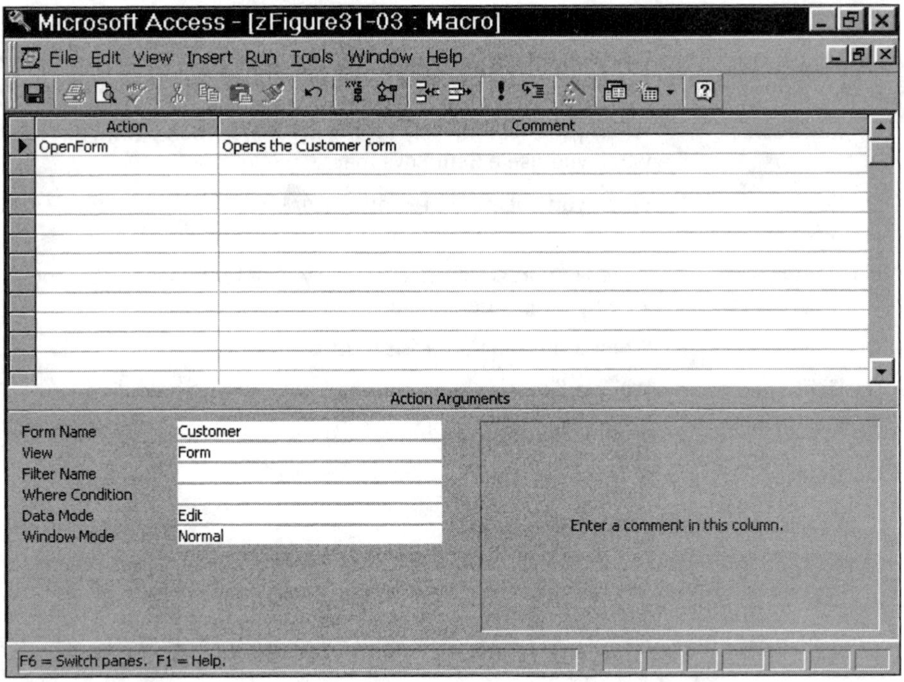

Figure 31-3: A macro to open a form.

The macro in Figure 31-3 has only a single action associated with it, which is the OpenForm action. This action has six possible arguments, although you entered only the form name Customer in the example. You accepted the default values of the other arguments. This action opens the specified form (Customer) for you automatically.

With the OpenCust macro created, you will need to enter design mode for the Pets Display form; attach the macro OpenCust to the form property On Open.

Attaching a macro to a form

With the OpenForm macro saved, you are now ready to *associate,* or *attach,* it with the On Open property of the form Add a Customer and Pets. To attach the OpenCust macro to the form, follow these steps:

1. Click on the Forms tab in the Database window to select the Form list.

2. Select the form named Pets Display Form and bring it into design mode.

3. Display the property sheet by clicking on the Properties button on the toolbar.

   The title of the Property window dialog box should be Form. If it isn't, select the form by clicking on the gray box in the top left corner of the form (where the rulers intersect).

4. Select the Event tab from the tabs at the top of the Property window.

5. Move to the On Open property in the Form property window. Select or type the macro name **OpenCust** in the On Open property cell.

   The property sheet should look similar to the one in Figure 31-4. Notice that the macro name OpenCust is placed in the property area of the On Open property.

6. Save the form and return to the Database window.

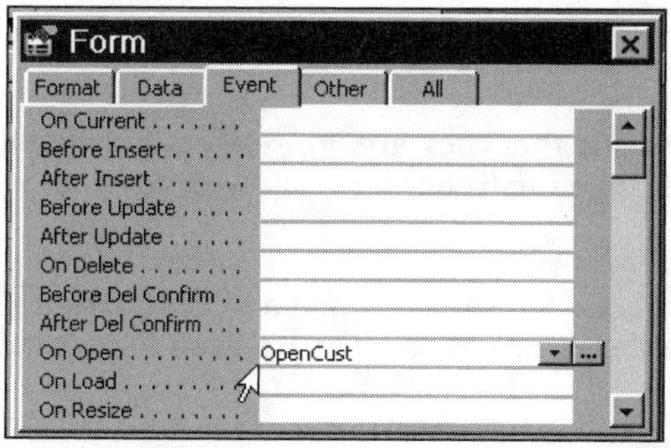

Figure 31-4: Entering a macro in the On Open property of a form.

With the OpenCust macro attached to the form Pets Display, you are ready to try running it. Open the Pets Display form. Notice that Access automatically opens the Customer form for you, placing it behind the Pets Display form. Now you can use either form by clicking on it to look at the individual records. Figure 31-5 shows both forms open.

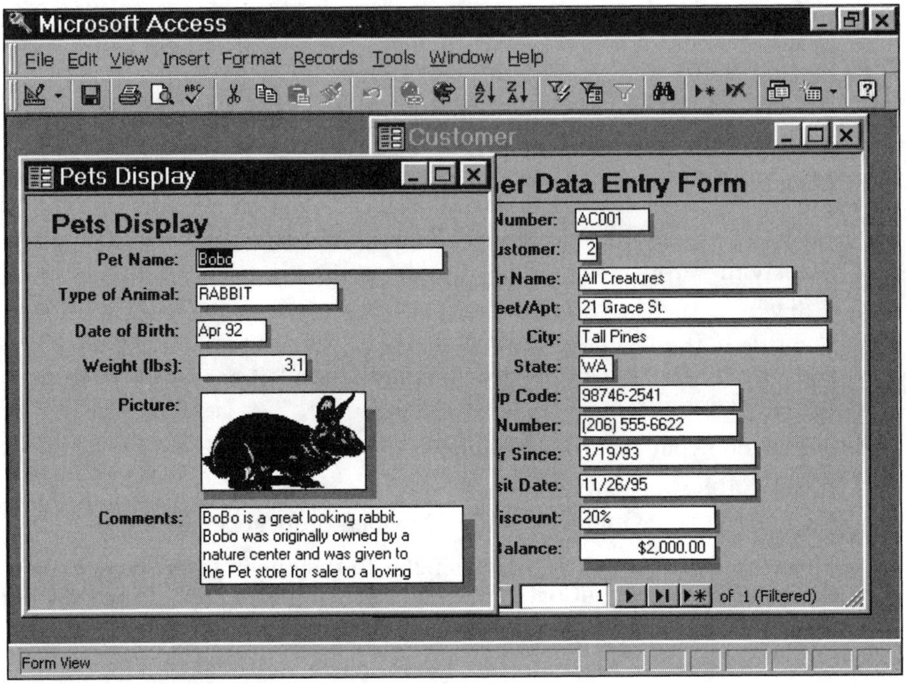

Figure 31-5: Two forms open; one form is opened automatically by a macro attached to the On Open property of the other form.

The only problem with these two forms is that they are not related. Every time you change the pet, it would be nice if the Customer form showed you the correct owner of the pet.

Of all the form-level events, the most common are On Open and On Current. Although the other events are available for use, these two are used for probably 80 percent of all form-level macros.

Synchronizing two forms with On Current

Notice that the forms in Figure 31-5 are independent of each other. Therefore, when you skip through the Pets Display form, the Customer form is not automatically updated to display the related owner information for the pet. To make these two forms work together, you can synchronize them by relating the data between the forms with the On Current property.

You can use the same macro you used before (OpenCust), but now you must specify a Where condition for the OpenForm action. The condition on which to synchronize these two forms occurs when the Customer Number is the same in both forms. To specify the synchronizing condition between these two forms, follow these steps:

1. Open the macro OpenCust in design mode.

2. Click on the Where Condition box of the Action Arguments.

3. Type **[Customer Number] = Forms![Pet Display Form]![Customer Number]**.

4. Resave the OpenCust macro.

Note Notice in Step 3 that you typed **[Customer Number]**, which is the control name for the Customer Number field in the Customer form. You typed this name on the left side of the expression without reference to the form name. The left side of the Where expression in an OpenForm action uses the form specified in the Form Name action argument (three lines above). The right side of the expression requires the keyword *Forms,* the form name, and the control name.

Caution If you specify an unopened form in the Where Condition box, you will get an error message at run time, but not as you create the macro.

Now that you have modified the macro, you need to set the On Current property of the Pets Display form.

To add the OpenCust macro to the form, follow these steps:

1. Remove the macro from the On Open property of the form and add it to the On Current property.

2. Open the Pets Display form in design mode.

3. Move to the On Current property of the Property window.

4. Type **OpenCust** in the On Current parameter box.

5. Save the changes to the form.

Now, when you open the Pets Display form and a pet record is displayed, the Customer form also opens and displays the correct owner for that pet. As you change pets, the Customer form automatically displays the new owner information. These two forms are now synchronized.

Note Even though the two forms are synchronized on the basis of the On Current property, you must still close both forms separately. Closing one form does not automatically close the other. If you want to close both forms at the same time automatically, you need to specify another macro for the On Close property.

To see how these two forms work together, open the Pets Display form and then click on the Datasheet button on the toolbar. The Customer form becomes active and is moved to the front of the Pets Display form. If you click a different pet record in the Pets datasheet, the Customer form is updated automatically to reflect the new owner. Figure 31-6 demonstrates how this process works.

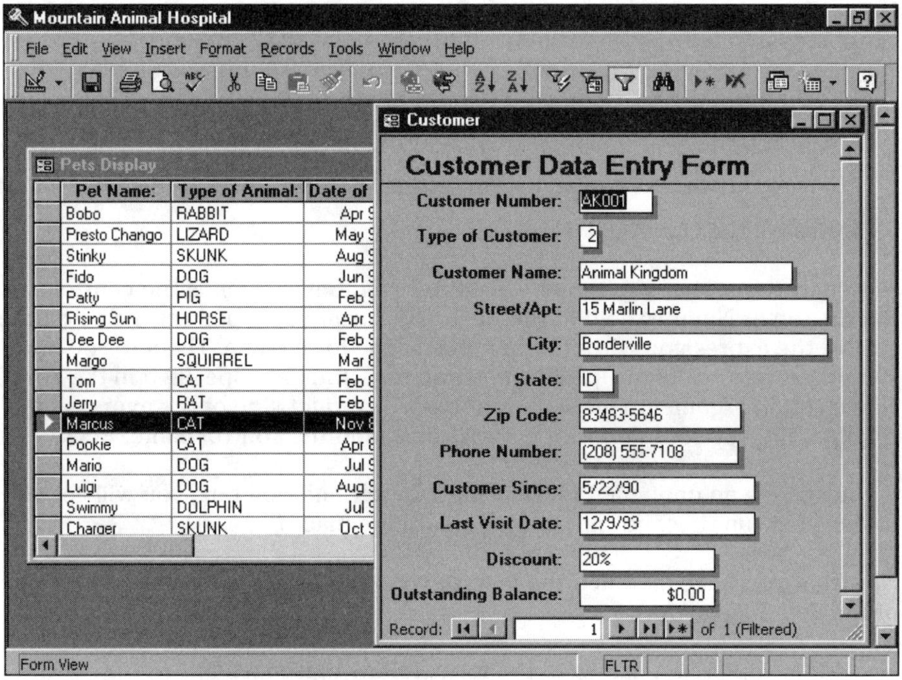

Figure 31-6: Two forms synchronized.

As Figure 31-6 demonstrates, you are not limited to a single-record view when synchronizing forms. The Pets Display form has been set to Datasheet; as you click on different records in the datasheet, the Customer form is updated automatically to reflect the new owner.

The On Current property of the Pets form triggers the OpenCust macro every time the record changes. If you click on the next navigation button, you see that the Customer form shows only one record — the owner record related to the current individual pet record in the Pets form. Notice that in the bottom of the Customer form in Figure 31-6, the record number shows Record 1 of 1 (Filtered). The Where condition in the macro acts as a filter to the Customer form.

If you know this, you can easily understand the use of the On Current property: It activates a macro that performs actions based on the specific record indicated by the form that is using the On Current property. In this case, the current pet record triggers the macro that finds the correct owner in the Customer form. Every time the pet record changes, the On Current property is activated and the next owner is found.

Running a macro when closing a form

At times, you'll want to perform some action when you close or leave a form. For example, you may want Access to keep an automatic log of the names of everyone using the form. Using the two forms from the preceding examples, you may want to close the Customer form automatically every time a user closes the Pets Display form.

To close the Customer form automatically every time the Pets Display form is closed, you need to create a new macro to perform the actions. Then you need to attach the macro to the On Close property of the Pets Display form.

To create a macro that closes a form, follow these steps:

1. Select the OpenCust macro and enter design mode.

2. Activate the Macro Name column by clicking on the Macro Name button on the toolbar. This step lets you create a macro group.

3. Select a blank Macro Name cell below the OpenForm action.

4. In the empty Macro Name cell, type **Close Customer**.

5. Select the empty Action cell alongside the Close Customer macro name.

6. Select the Close action from the pull-down menu.

7. Select the action argument Object Type.

8. Type (or select) **Form**.

9. Select the action argument Object Name.

10. Type (or select) the form name **Customer**. The macro should now look similar to Figure 31-7.

11. Resave the macro with the new changes.

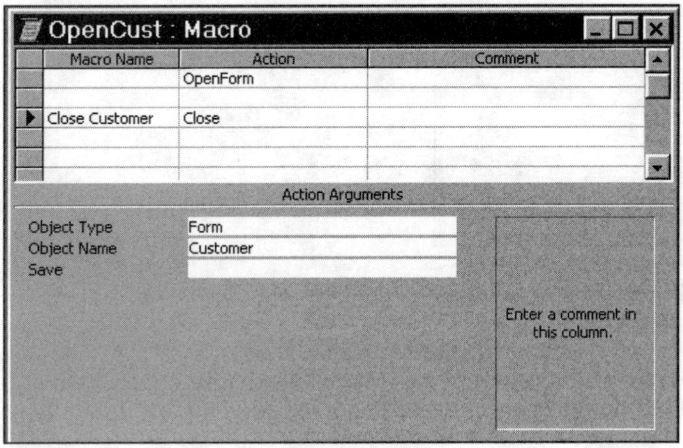

Figure 31-7: Adding a Close action macro to a macro group.

Figure 31-7 shows the new macro Close Customer added to the macro OpenCust. Until now, the OpenCust macro has been a single-purpose macro. Adding another macro has made it into a group macro of two macros. The first macro is the default macro, which opens a form, and the second is a macro named Close Customer.

Cross-Reference Macro groups are covered in Chapter 30.

Notice that the Close Customer macro has only one action: Close. This action has two arguments, both of which you must enter. The first argument is the Object Type, which specifies the type of object you want to close (form or report, for example). The second argument is the Object Name, which specifies by name the object you want to close (in this case, the form named Customer).

Now that you have created the Close Customer macro, you can attach it to the form named Pets Display by following these steps:

1. Select the Pets Display form and click on Design.
2. Activate the property sheet for the form.
3. Select the On Close property in the property sheet.
4. Type **OpenCust.Close Customer** in the On Close property parameter box. The property sheet should look like Figure 31-8.
5. Save the form with the new changes.

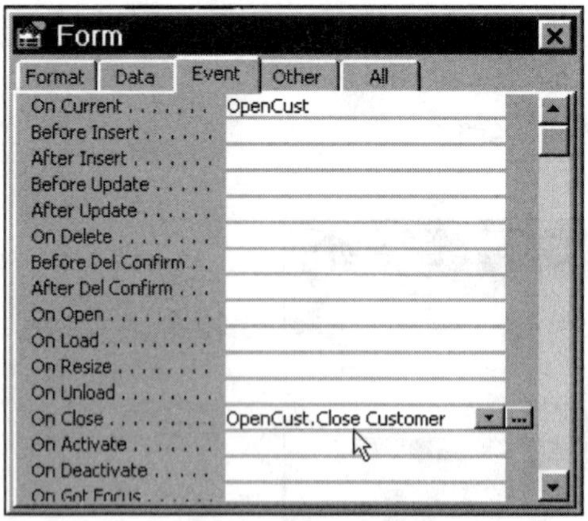

Figure 31-8: The property sheet with the On Close property set.

Note Notice in Figure 31-8 that when you type the macro name in the On Close parameter box, you specify the macro group name. Then you type a period; finally, you type the name of the macro.

Opening the Pets Display form continues to maintain the current owner information in the Customer form because you left the macro with its On Current property set. Now, however, the On Close property is also set. Because you specified On Close with the Pets Display form, the Customer form closes automatically for you when you close the Pets Display form.

The macro attached to the On Close property simply closes the Customer form. If a user accidentally closes the Customer form and then the Pets Display form, Access does not report an error. Therefore, you don't have to specify an On Close for the Customer form to allow closing only via the Pets Display form. Using this principle, you can have one form that specifies the closing of many forms. If the forms are open, Access will close them; otherwise, Access will issue the Close command with no harm done.

Confirming a delete with On Delete

The On Delete property can be used to execute a macro that displays a message and confirms that a user wants to delete a record. For example, to create a macro named ConfirmDelete, follow these steps:

1. Enter the macro design mode, create a new macro, and click on the Condition column.
2. Select the first Condition cell.
3. Type **MsgBox("Do you Want to Delete this Record?", 273, "Delete")<>1**.
4. Select the Action cell next to the Condition box.
5. Select or type the **CancelEvent** action.
6. Select the next Condition cell.
7. Type an ellipsis, which is three periods (...).
8. Select the Action cell next to the Condition box.
9. Select or type the **StopMacro** action.
10. Select the next Action cell.
11. Select or type the **SendKeys** action.
12. Select the Keystrokes action argument.
13. Type **{Enter}**.
14. Save the macro to the name **ConfirmDelete**.

The macro should look like the one in Figure 31-9. Notice that this macro also uses the CancelEvent action. The condition for this macro uses the MsgBox( ) function (for a detailed explanation, see the sidebar "Using the MsgBox( ) function," later in this chapter).

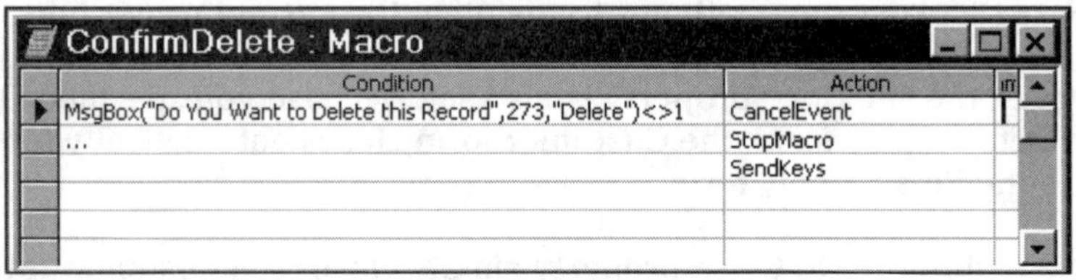

Condition	Action	
▶ MsgBox("Do You Want to Delete this Record",273,"Delete")<>1	CancelEvent	
...	StopMacro	
	SendKeys	

Figure 31-9: A macro to delete a record.

The macro in Figure 31-9 shows the use of another new action: SendKeys. This action lets you send prearranged keystrokes to Access or another active application. The passed keystrokes are processed just as though you pressed them while working in an application. In this case, Access displays a message box like the one in Figure 31-10. Notice that the message box has two buttons: OK and Cancel. Access displays the box and waits for a keystroke. When a user selects the Cancel button, the macro cancels the delete event and stops the macro.

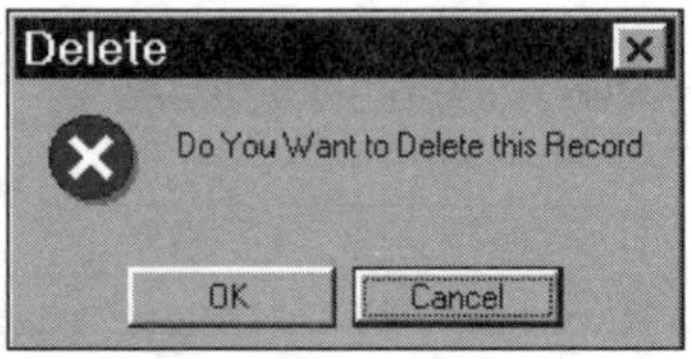

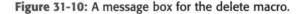

Figure 31-10: A message box for the delete macro.

If a user clicks on the OK button in the message box, the macro performs the SendKeys action. In this case, the macro sends the Enter keystroke. If the user does not take this action, Access displays its Delete message dialog box, forcing the user to verify again that the record should be deleted. Using SendKeys sends the Enter keystroke to the Access Delete message box, telling it to accept the deletion.

Caution This macro does not bypass referential integrity between tables. If you have referential integrity set between the Customer table and the Pets table and have not authorized Cascade Delete through the entire application, the macro fails. To override this, either set up cascade deletes through all the tables or expand the macro to perform a cascade delete by creating an SQL statement and running the SQL statement (use the RunSQL action).

Next, with the delete macro ConfirmDelete completed, you attach it to the Pets Display form by placing the macro name in the entry box of the On Delete property of the form. Figure 31-11 shows the property sheet for the Pets Display form with the On Delete property set.

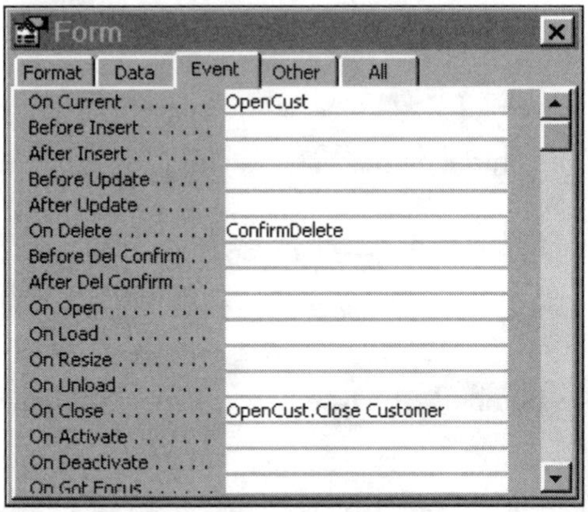

Figure 31-11: Setting an On Delete property.

To see how this macro and the On Delete property work, follow these steps:

1. Display the first record in the Pets Display form.
2. Select Edit⇨Delete Record from the main menu.

   Access responds with the message box you saw in Figure 31-10. In this message box, the Cancel button is the default.
3. Click on the Cancel button to not delete this record.

Control Event Macros

So far, you have worked with event macros at the form level. You can also trigger macros at the control level, using an event as a basis. When you attach a macro at the control level, the macro takes effect against the control. For example, you can immediately verify complex data validation at the field level (rather than when the record is exited) by using the field's Before Update property rather than the property at the form level.

Using the MsgBox( ) function

The MsgBox( ) function is a very powerful function that can be used to display a message in a dialog box, wait for a user response, and then return a value based on the user's choice. The function has three arguments:

MsgBox("*message*" [, *type of msg* [, *box title*]])

The *message* here is the string displayed in the dialog box as a message.

The *type of msg* is the numeric expression controlling the buttons and icons in the dialog box.

The *box title* is the string displayed on the title bar of the dialog box.

Only the message is required. If you don't specify *type of msg* or *box title,* Access displays one button: OK. There is no icon and no title.

Access offers a wide range of type of message numbers. The type of message number specifies three message parts:

Number and type of buttons

Icon style

Default button

The following table describes each:

Number and Button Type	
Value	*Display Button*
0	OK
1	OK, Cancel
2	Abort, Retry, Ignore
3	Yes, No, Cancel
4	Yes, No
5	Retry, Cancel

Icon Style		
Value	*Display*	*Icon*
0	None	
16	x Critical	X in a circle
32	? Warning	Question mark in a balloon
48	! Warning	Exclamation sign in a triangle
64	i	Information in a balloon

Default Button

Value	Button
0	First
256	Second
512	Third

Using the preceding table, you specify the second parameter of the MsgBox( ) function by summing the three option values. For example, you can have a message box show three buttons (Yes, No, and Cancel [3]), use the Question mark (?) [32], and make the Cancel button the default [512]. Just add the three values (512+32+3) to get the second parameter number, which is 548.

If you omit *type of msg* in the function, MsgBox displays a single OK button and makes it the default button with no icon displayed.

Besides displaying the message box with all the options, the MsgBox() function also returns a value that indicates which button the user selects. The number it returns depends on the type of button selected. The following table shows each button and the value that MsgBox() returns:

Button Selected	Value Returned
OK	1
Cancel	2
Abort	3
Retry	4
Ignore	5
Yes	6
No	7

If the dialog box displays a Cancel button, pressing the Esc key is the same as selecting the Cancel button.

Attaching macros to controls

To have a control respond to an event, you write a macro and attach the macro to the property in the control that recognizes the event. Several properties can be polled to trigger macros at the control level. Table 31-2 shows each property, the event it recognizes, and how it works.

As Table 31-2 demonstrates, you can use any of the control-level events to trigger a macro. One of these, On Click, works only with command buttons.

Table 31-2	
The Control-Level Events and Associated Properties	
Event Property	*When the Macro Is Triggered*
Before Update	Before changed data in the control is updated to the table
After Update	After changed data is updated in the control to the data
On Change	When the contents of a text box or combo box's text changes
On Updated	When an OLE object's data has been modified
On Not In List	When a value that isn't in the list is entered into a combo box
On Enter	Before a control receives the focus from another control
On Exit	Just before the control loses focus to another control
On Got Focus	When a nonactive or enabled control receives the focus
On Lost Focus	When a control loses the focus
On Click	When the left mouse button is pressed and released (clicked) on a control
On Dbl Click	When the left mouse button is pressed and released (clicked) twice on a control/label
On Mouse Down	When a mouse button is pressed while the pointer is on a control
On Mouse Move	When the mouse pointer is moved over a control
On Mouse Up	When a pressed mouse button is released while the pointer is on a control
On Key Down	When any key on the keyboard is pressed when a control has the focus or when the SendKeys macro is used
On Key Press	When a key is pressed and released on a control that has the focus or when the SendKeys macro is used
On Key Up	When a pressed key is released or immediately after the SendKeys macro is used

Forms have several different types of objects on them: labels, text boxes, OLE, subforms, command buttons, check boxes, and so on. Each of these has several event properties associated with it. You can attach a macro, an expression, or

Access Basic code to any of them. To see any object's event properties, simply activate the Properties dialog box and select event properties while working with the object.

Working with Macros on Forms

You can group macros for forms in six categories according to their functions:

✦ Validating data

✦ Setting values

✦ Navigating between forms and records

✦ Filtering records

✦ Finding records

✦ Printing records

Each category uses specific macro actions to perform its job.

Validating data

You already worked with macros to validate data at both the form level and control level. When validating data, you worked with several macro actions: MsgBox, CancelEvent, StopMacro, and GoToControl.

The most common event properties that trigger validation macros are the On Delete and Before Update properties, although any property can be used.

Displaying a message

To display a message, you use the MsgBox action. This action has four arguments:

Message	Specifies the user message in a dialog box
Beep	Sounds a computer beep when the dialog box is opened
Type	Specifies the type of icon displayed in the dialog box, such as the stop sign, a question mark, and so on
Title	Specifies a user-entered title for the box

Canceling events

To cancel an event, you use the CancelEvent action. This action has no arguments — it simply cancels the event that triggers the macro to run. For example, if the macro is attached to the Before Update property of a form, the update is canceled.

Stopping a macro

To stop execution of a macro, use the StopMacro action. This action stops execution of the macro immediately and returns the user to the calling form. This action is useful for stopping a macro based on a condition specified in the macro.

Going to a specific control

If you need to return to a specific control (field) in a form, use the GoToControl action. This action has one argument: the control name. If you supply a control name, this action takes you to that control. You normally use this action just before you use the StopMacro action.

Setting values

By setting control, field, and property values with macros, you can make data entry easier and more accurate. Besides having these advantages, you can link several forms, databases, and reports to make them work together more intelligently.

Setting values with a macro can accomplish these tasks:

  ✦ Hide or display a control on the basis of a value in the form (Visible property).

  ✦ Disable or lock a control on the basis of a value in the form (Enable and Locked properties).

  ✦ Update a field in the form on the basis of the value of another control.

  ✦ Set the value of a control in a form on the basis of the control of another form.

The SetValue action is used to set values with a macro. This action has two arguments:

Item   The name of the control or property

Expression   The expression used to set the value

Tip If you use the SetValue action to change the value of a control (field) being validated, do not attach it to the Before Update property. Access cannot change the value of a control while it is being validated; it can change the value only after it has been saved. Therefore, you should use the After Update property instead.

Caution You cannot use the SetValue macro action on bound or calculated controls on reports; the same is true for calculated controls on forms.

Converting a field to uppercase

If you allow entry of a field in either uppercase or lowercase, you may want to store it in uppercase. To accomplish this, create a macro that uses the SetValue action to set the value of the field for you. In the Item argument box, enter the name of the field you want to convert to uppercase. In the Expression argument box, enter the function UCase( ) with the name of the field to be converted. The function UCase( ) must already exist. Figure 31-12 shows the arguments for converting the field Customer Name to uppercase.

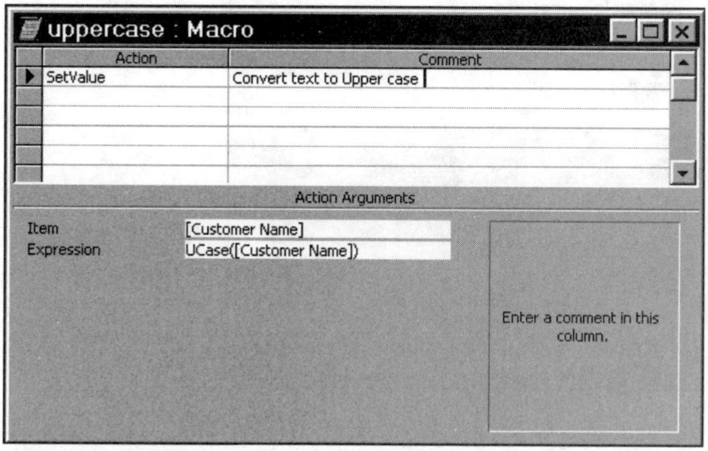

Figure 31-12: Converting a field to uppercase.

After you create the macro, place the macro name in the After Update property sheet.

If the user enters a customer name in lowercase or mixed case, Access automatically runs the macro and converts the field to uppercase when the user completes the update.

Assigning values to new records

When you add new records to a form, it is often convenient to have values automatically filled in for fields using values from another open form. SetValue is also used to do this.

For example, after adding a new customer in the Customer form, you may immediately want to add a pet record in another form and have the Customer Number automatically filled in.

For example, the After Update event on the Customer form can be programmed to add a pet record after the customer record's Pet Name value is changed. A macro opens the Pets Display form in the Add Mode using the OpenForm action. The next macro action, SetValue, automatically sets the value of Customer Number in the Pets Display form to the Customer Number in the Customer form. Figure 31-13 shows the arguments for this macro.

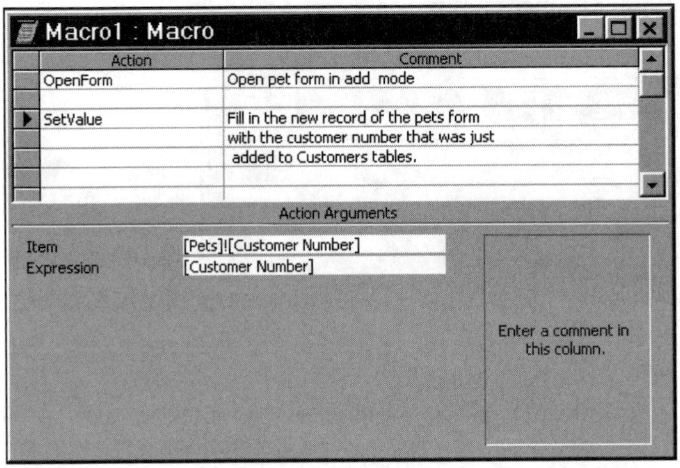

Figure 31-13: Macro arguments to set a field value in another form on the basis of a value in the current form.

> **Tip** The Item argument can also use its full syntax rather than the abbreviation shown in Figure 31-13. The syntax is
>
> ```
> Forms![Pets]![Customer Number]
> ```

The Expression argument references the Customer Number in the open form, which is the Customer form. When working with the SetValue action in this way, you must specify the entire syntax for the name of the field being replaced in the Item box.

Navigating in forms and records

Whenever you need to move to a specific control (field), record, or page in a form, you use the GoToXXXX actions, where XXXX represents the control, record, or page.

Moving to a specific control

To move to a specific control, use the GoToControl action. This action has one argument, which is Control Name. To move to a specific field, simply supply the control name in the argument.

Moving to a specific record

To move to a specific record in a table, query, or form, use the GoToRecord action. This action has four arguments:

Object Type	Type of object (form, table, or query)
Object Name	Name of the object specified in Object Type
Record	Specifies which record to go to (preceding, next, new, first, last, and so on)
Offset	The number of records to offset from (if 10, go back 10 records)

Using this action, you can move to any record in a form, query, or table.

Moving to a specific page

To move to a specific page and place the focus in the first control of the page, use the GoToPage action. This action has three arguments:

Page Number	Specifies the page number you want to move to
Right	The upper left corner of the page (horizontal position)
Down	The upper left corner of the page (vertical position)

This action is useful for working with multiple-page forms.

Filtering records

You can create a macro or series of macros to filter records in a form. For example, you may want to have a Customer form with four buttons to limit the form's records to a single state or to allow all states. (Even though you haven't learned about buttons yet, you can learn how they would interact with a group of macros.) The form will look similar to Figure 31-14. Notice that four buttons are in the box named Filter Records.

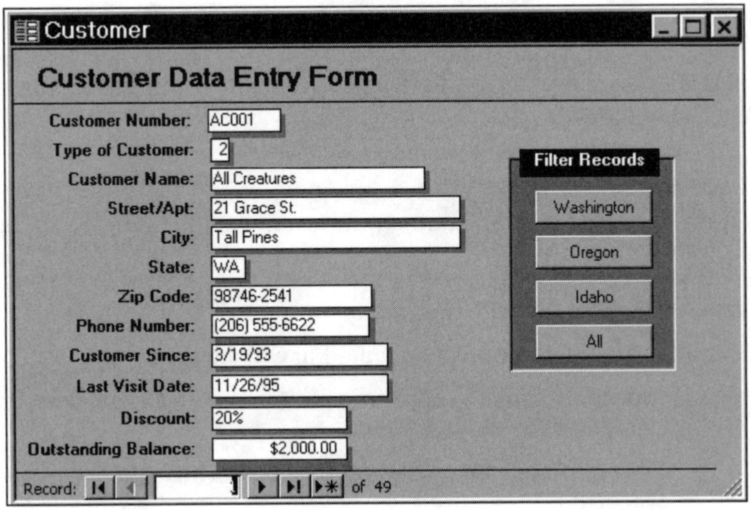

Figure 31-14: A form with buttons used to activate filter macros.

Each button in Figure 31-14 is attached to a different macro. Three of the macros use the ApplyFilter action, and one uses the ShowAllRecords action.

Using the ApplyFilter action

To set a filter condition in a macro, use the ApplyFilter action. This action has two arguments: Filter Name and the Where Condition. You can use either one, but you should use only one unless you predefine a filter and want to filter the filter. For this example, you use the Where Condition argument. To create a macro named StateFilter.WA, follow these steps:

1. Enter the Macro Design window.

2. Enter the macro name **WA** into the group macro StateFilter.

3. Select or type **ApplyFilter** for the action.

4. Type **[State] = "WA"** in the Where Condition argument box.

After you create this macro, you create two more next. One macro is named StateFilter.ID; the other is named StateFilter.OR. These macros set a condition equal to the individual state.

Using the ShowAllRecords action

When you create filter conditions with macros, you should always create another macro that uses the ShowAllRecords action. This action removes an existing filter set by another macro. This action has no arguments. For the next example, create a macro named StateFilter.All with the ShowAllRecords action.

When you complete this process, all four macros should look like the ones in Figure 31-15.

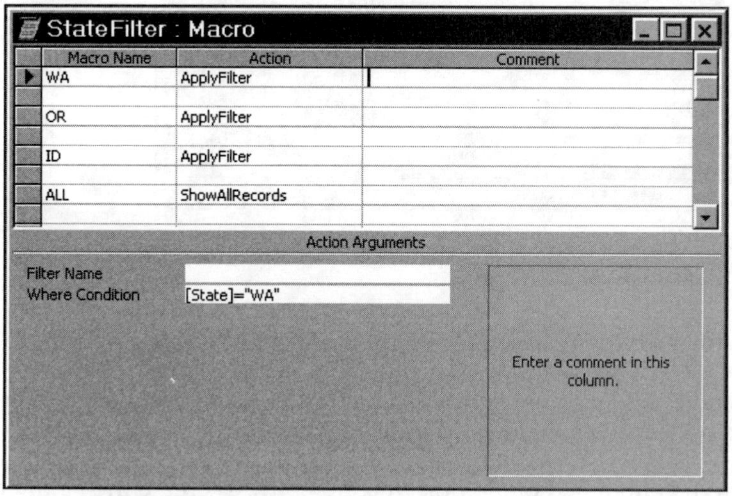

Figure 31-15: A macro group with four filter macros.

Running filter macros

To run a filter macro, simply attach the macro name to the On Click property of the appropriate command button. Then the macro will execute and implement the filter condition every time the button is selected.

Finding records

One of the most powerful ways of using macros is to locate user-specified records. This type of macro uses two macro actions: GoToControl and FindRecord. For example, you can add a search routine to the Customer form, as shown in Figure 31-16. You can create an unbound combo box; as you can see in Figure 31-17, it is named CustomerSelect.

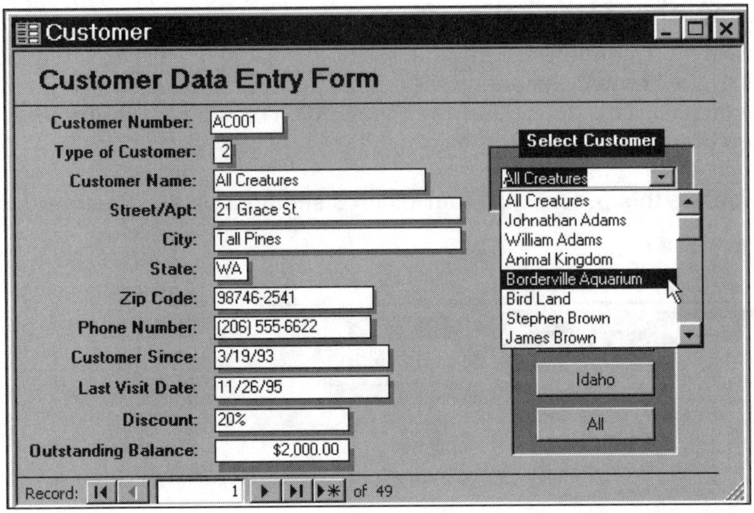

Figure 31-16: The Customer form with a combo box used to find records.

Your property sheet for the combo box should look similar to Figure 31-17.

Beyond completion of these steps, you can beautify the label and combo box area (as a look back at Figure 31-16 shows). These enhancements aren't required.

After you create the unbound combo box, you are ready to create the FindRecord macro to find the customer record by the Customer Name field. To create the macro, follow these steps:

1. Select or type **GoToControl** in the first empty Action cell.

2. Type **[Customer Name]** in the Control Name argument cell.

3. Select or type **FindRecord** in the next empty Action cell.

4. Type **=[CustomerSelect]** in the Find What argument box.

5. Save the macro, naming it **FindRecord**.

That's it! Your macro should now resemble the one in Figure 31-18.

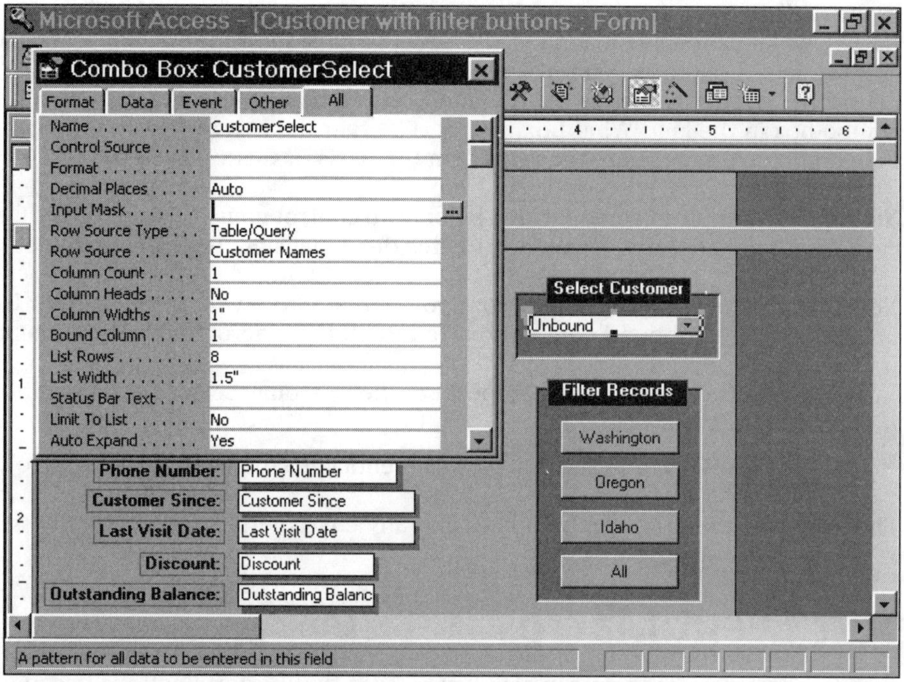

Figure 31-17: The property sheet for the unbound combo box.

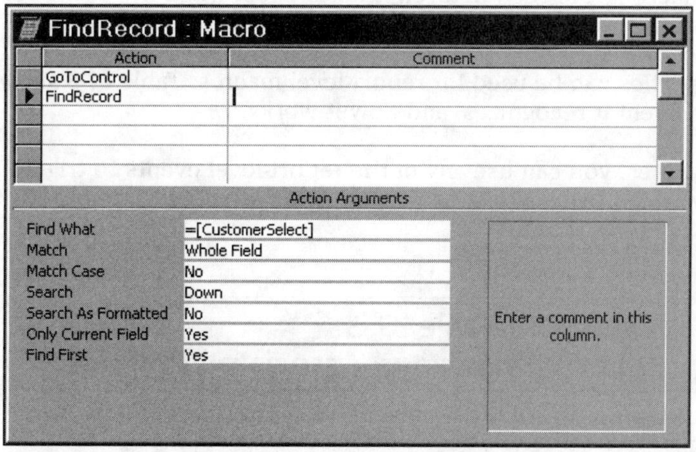

Figure 31-18: A macro to find a record, based on the customer's name.

In the GoToControl argument, you placed the form control name [Customer Name], which is the same as the field name, to limit the scope of the search to the current field (Customer Name). Then, in the FindRecord argument Find What, you placed the control name for the unbound combo box. By placing the unbound combo box in the Find What box, you specify that the macro will find the name via the combo box but update the record on the basis of Customer Name.

Caution   Note that you entered an equal sign before the control name CustomerSelect in the Find What argument box. If you don't enter the equal sign, the macro will not work.

Now that you have created the macro, you're ready to attach it to the After Update property for the unbound combo box. To attach the macro, follow these steps:

1. Move to the After Update property of the CustomerSelect control (unbound combo box).

2. Type **FindRecord** in the Action Arguments cell (the name of the macro).

The form now uses the combo box to find any customer!

Report Event Macros

Just as with forms, reports can also use macros that perform actions based on events you specify. You can work with macros at the report level or the section level. If you attach a macro at the report level, it takes effect when the event occurs against the report as a whole, such as when you open or close the report. If you attach the macro at the section level, it takes effect when the event occurs within a section (such as when you format or print the section).

Several event properties can be used for report-level macros. Table 31-3 shows each property, the event it recognizes, and how it works.

As Table 31-3 illustrates, you can use any of the report-level events to trigger a macro. These events can be used just as you use their counterparts in forms.

Table 31-3
The Report-Level Events and Associated Properties

Event Property	When the Macro Is Triggered
On Open	When a report is opened but before it prints
On Close	When a report is closed and removed from the screen

Event Property	When the Macro Is Triggered
On Activate	When a report receives the focus and becomes the active window
On Deactive	When a different window becomes the active window
On No Data	When the report has no data passed to it from the active table or query
On Page	When the report changes pages
On Error	When a run-time error is produced in Access

Opening a report with a macro

You may want to use the On Open property of a report to run a macro that prompts the user to identify the records to print. The macro can use a filter or use the ApplyFilter action.

For example, you may want to activate a form or dialog box that prompts the user to identify a state or to print the report Customer Mailing Labels. To accomplish this task, you create a filter macro similar to the one in the section on forms and attach it to the On Open property of the report.

Report Section Macros

Besides the report-level properties, Access offers three event properties you can use at the section level for a report macro. Table 31-4 shows each property, the event it recognizes, and how it works.

Table 31-4
The Report Section-Level Events and Associated Properties

Event Property	Event	When the Macro Is Triggered
On Format	Format	When Access knows what data goes in a section (but before laying out the data for printing)
On Print	Print	After Access lays out the data in a section for printing (but before printing the section)
On Retreat	Retreat	After the Format event but before the Print event; occurs when Access has to "back up" past other sections on a page to perform multiple formatting passes

Using On Format

You use the On Format property when a user's response can affect page layout or when the macro contains calculations that use data from sections you don't intend to print. The macro will run before Access lays out the section (following your other property settings for the report, such as Keep Together, Visible, or Can Grow).

You can set the On Format and On Print properties for any section of the report. However, the On Retreat is not available for the page header or page footer sections.

For example, you may want to highlight some data on the form, based on a certain condition the macro determines. If the condition is met, the macro uses the SetValue action to change a control's Visible property to Yes.

Using On Print

You use the On Print property when no user's response affects page layout or when the macro depends on what page it finds the records to be printed. For example, you may want to have a total calculation placed in either the header or footer of each page.

Report Properties

When you work with macros that use the On Print and On Format properties of report sections, you may need to use two special conditional printer properties:

✦ Format Count

✦ Print Count

These two conditional printer properties are used in the Condition Expression column of a macro. Both are read-only properties; Access sets their values. Therefore, you can check these properties, but you cannot change their values. These properties determine when an event occurs twice.

Using Format Count

The Format Count property is used as a macro condition to determine the number of times the On Format property setting is evaluated for the current line on the report.

It is possible for a line to be formatted more than once. For example, when the labels are printed, the last label may not fit on a page; there may be room for only one line of a two-line label. If the label won't fit on the page, Access prints it on the next page. The Format Count for any lines moved from the bottom of the page to the top of the next page is set to 2 because the lines are formatted twice.

If you are accumulating a count of the number of labels being printed, you use the Format Count property in the Condition box of the macro to disregard counting the label a second time.

Using Print Count

Like the Format Count property, the Print Count property is used as a macro condition. This property determines the number of times the On Print setting is evaluated for the current line of the report.

It is possible for part of a record to be printed on one page and the remainder to be printed on the next page. When that occurs, the On Print event occurs twice, so the Print property is incremented to 2. When this occurs, you don't want to have the macro perform its action twice; therefore, you check to see whether the Format Count has changed, and then you stop the macro action.

To understand how this works, suppose that you have a macro that counts the number of records being printed on a page. The record number is placed in the page footer section of each page of the report. If a record is printed across two pages, you want the records counted on only one of the pages.

Working with macros in reports

Like form macros, report macros can be triggered at two levels — report and section. A macro triggered at the report level can prompt a user for a range of records to print before doing anything with the report.

On the other hand, a section-level macro can be used for printing messages on a report when a condition is met. For example, if a customer has not paid on his or her bill in 30 days, the report may print a reminder line that a partial payment is overdue.

Report-level macros can be executed before or after a report is printed or previewed. Section-level macros can be executed before or after a section of the report is printed or previewed. Thus, section-level macros tend to be used for actions that are more refined, such as including conditional lines of text in the report.

Underlining data in a report with a macro

You can use a macro to underline or highlight data dynamically in a report. This is accomplished by hiding or displaying controls and sections.

Suppose that you print the Monthly Invoice Report and you want to underline the Amount Due control if the total amount is more than $500.00. You can do this by adding a control to the group footer named Customer.Customer Number Footer and creating a macro that toggles the Visible property for the control.

Figure 31-19 shows a line added below the Amount Due control. This control is named AmtDueLine.

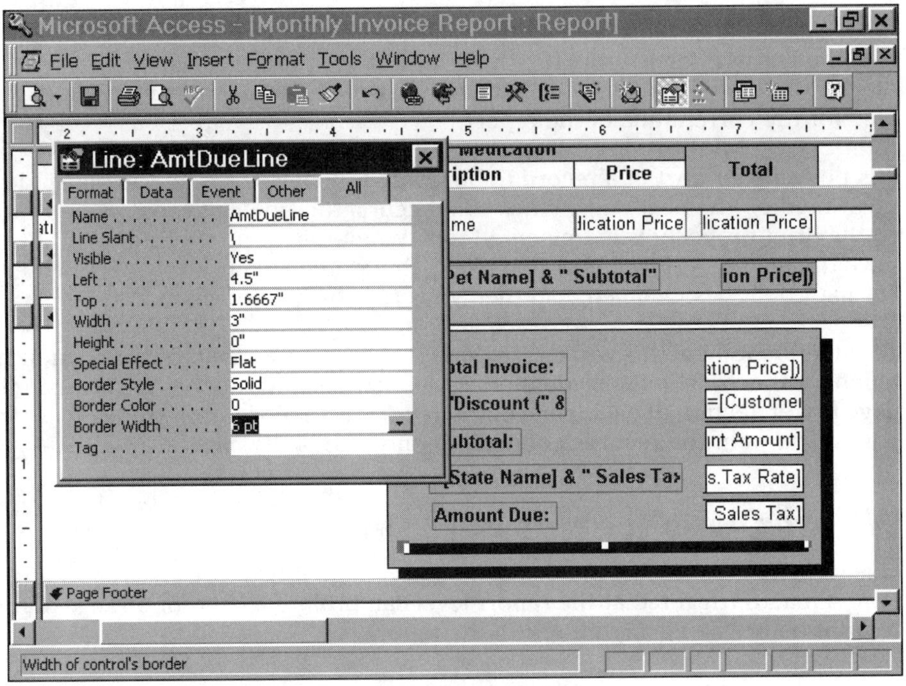

Figure 31-19: A report form with a line added.

In Figure 31-19, notice that the Visible property is set to Yes in the property sheet for the control AmtDueLine.

With the control (line) placed on the report, create a macro that sets the Visible property for this control. This macro requires two conditions — one for [Amount Due]>500 and the other for not being greater than this amount. To create the macro, follow these steps:

1. Create a macro named PrtLine.

2. Select an empty cell in the Condition column.

3. Type **[Amount Due]>500** in the Condition cell.

4. Select the associated Action cell.

5. Select or type **SetValue**.

6. Select the Item argument.

7. Type **[AmtDueLine].Visible**.

8. Select the Expression argument.

9. Type **Yes**.

10. Select another empty Condition cell.

11. Type **Not [Amount Due]>500**.

12. Select the associated Action cell.

13. Select or type **SetValue**.

14. Select the Item argument.

15. Type **[AmtDueLine].Visible**.

16. Select the Expression argument.

17. Type **No**.

18. Save the macro, naming it PrtLine.

The macro should look similar to the one in Figure 31-20. Notice that the macro in this figure has a separate condition to turn the Visible property on (set to Yes) and off.

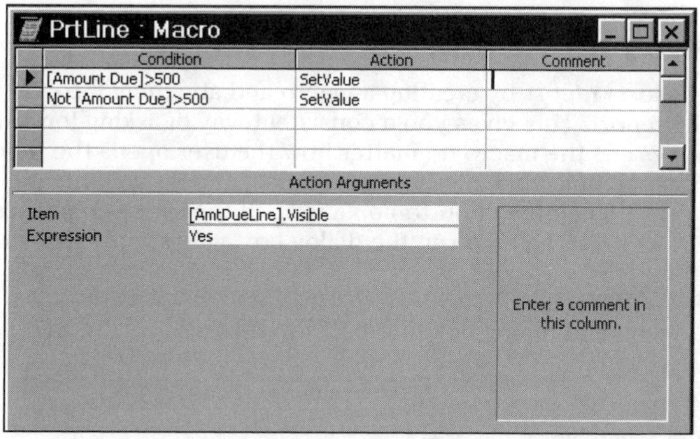

Figure 31-20: A macro to turn the Visible property of a control on or off.

Now that the macro is created, you will need to attach it to the group section named Customer.Customer Number Footer in the Monthly Invoice Report. The macro is attached to the On Format property of the section. Figure 31-21 shows the property sheet with the macro added to the On Format property.

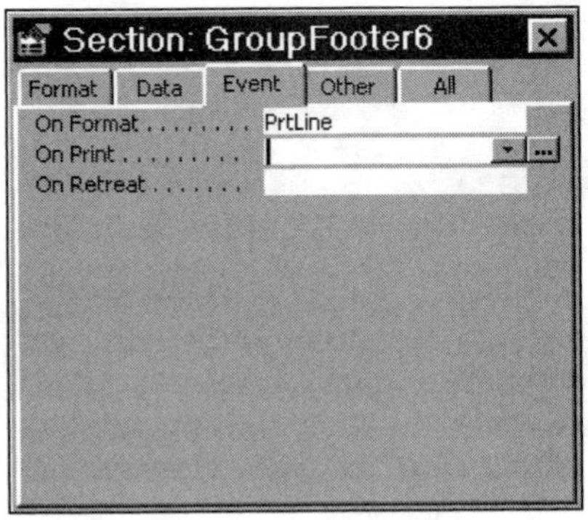

Figure 31-21: A property sheet with a macro name in the On Format property.

Hiding data in a report with a macro

You can hide data in a report with the same method you just used to display or hide a line. You simply set the Visible property to Yes or No in a macro. After you set the property to Yes or No in a macro, attach the macro to the On Format property of the section where the data resides.

Filtering records for a report with a macro

You can filter records for a report by creating a macro and attaching it to the On Open property of the report. This gives you a consistent way of asking for criteria. The On Open property runs the macro no matter how the user opens the report. For example, a user can double-click on the report name, choose a command from a custom menu, or select a command button on a form. If the On Open property is used to trigger the macro, you have to run the dialog box against only this single property.

Cross-Reference Chapter 32 shows a menu and dialog box that perform this type of filtering.

Importing and Exporting Macros

You can easily use data from other formats in Access. You can import, export, and attach tables via commands from the File menu in the Database window. However, if you consistently transfer the same data, you may want to automate the process in a macro.

Using command buttons to import or export

If you create a macro to transfer data, you can activate the macro by using a command button and the On Click property of the button.

When you create the macro, Access provides three actions to help you transfer the data:

+ TransferDatabase
+ TransferSpreadsheet
+ TransferText

By using these actions and their arguments, you can create very powerful (but simple) transfer-data macros.

Creating Accelerator Keys (Hot Keys)

You can assign a macro to a specific key or combination of keys, such as Ctrl+P. After you assign a macro to a key, the key is known as a *hot key*. By assigning hot keys, you can create one macro to perform an action no matter which form, view, or table you're in. For example, the Ctrl+P key combination can be used to print the current record.

You can assign macros to any number of hot keys. All hot-key macros are stored in a single group macro that Access uses. That group macro is known as a key assignment macro. When you open a database, Access looks for a macro name specified in the Options dialog box of the View menu. If the macro exists, it runs automatically, assigning macros to hot keys. Figure 31-22 shows several hot-key assignments in an AutoKeys macro.

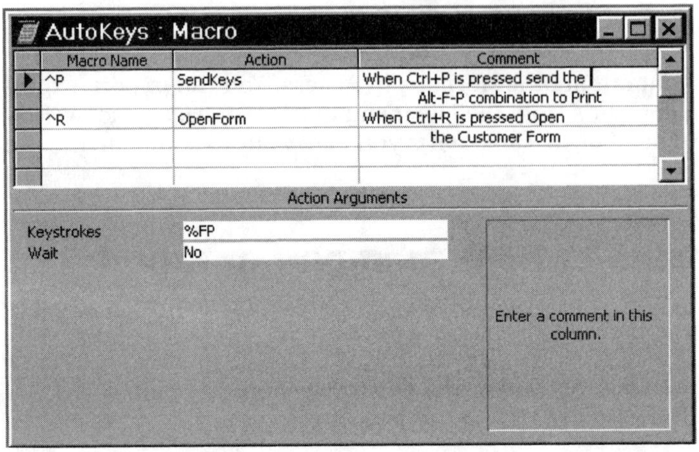

Figure 31-22: A macro to assign hot keys.

Changing the default key assignment macro

You specify the name of the macro for the hot keys in the Options dialog box of the View menu choice in the Database window. The default name for this macro is AutoKeys, but you can give it any name you want. To specify a different hot-key macro name (default key assignment), follow these steps:

1. Select Tools⇨Options from the Database window menu.

2. Click on the Keyboard tab.

3. In the Key Assignment Macro box, replace the default AutoKeys macro name with the name of the macro group that contains the key assignments you want to use.

4. Click on Apply to apply the settings immediately without closing the dialog box; click on OK to apply the settings and close the dialog box. Enter the new name of the hot-key macro in the Key Assignment Macro box of the Items.

You can have several different key assignment macros, each under a different name. To change from one hot-key macro to another, simply enter the new name in the Options box. Then close and reopen the database to make the new key assignment macro active.

Creating a hot-key combination

To create a hot-key combination and assign actions to it requires creating a macro named AutoKeys and using macro names based on the key combination you want to use to specify an action. The macro names can be based on a specific Access syntax called SendKeys syntax; otherwise, they can use the typical macro actions.

Using SendKeys syntax for key assignments

When you enter a key combination in the Macro Name column, you specify the key combination by using a specific syntax known as SendKeys syntax. Table 31-5 shows several key combinations and their corresponding SendKeys syntax. When you assign actions to a key combination, you enter the SendKeys syntax in the Macro Name column.

Using Table 31-5 as a reference, you see that to assign some macro actions to the Tab key, you name a macro {TAB} in the group macro AutoKeys.

Table 31-5
SendKeys Syntax

Key Combo	SendKeys Syntax	Key Combo	SendKeys Syntax
Backspace	{BKSP} or {BS}	F2	{F2}
Caps Lock	{CAPSLOCK}	Ctrl+A	^A
Enter	{ENTER} or ~	Ctrl+F10	^{F10}
Insert	{INSERT}	Ctrl+2	^2
Left arrow	{LEFT}	Shift+F5	+{F5}
Home	{HOME}	Shift+Delete	+{DEL}
PgDn	{PGDN}	Shift+End	+{END}
Escape	{ESC}	Alt+F10	%{F10}
PrintScreen	{PRTSC}	Alt+Up arrow	%{UP}
Scroll Lock	{SCROLLLOCK}	Left arrow ten times	{LEFT 10}
Tab	{TAB}	Shift+BA together	+(BA)

Creating a hot key

To create a hot key, follow these steps:

1. Create a macro named AutoKeys.

2. Type the key combination in the Macro Name column.

3. Type the set of actions you want to associate with the key combination.

4. Repeat Steps 2 and 3 for every hot key to which you want to assign actions.

5. Save the macro.

Access makes the key assignment immediate. When you press the key combination, Access runs the macro actions. In the preceding steps, you can also make several key assignments, creating a macro for each key combination. Just remember to name the macro group AutoKeys (or whatever name you specified in the Options dialog box).

Summary

This chapter provided an in-depth explanation of macro usage. You learned how to use macros in forms and reports and how to create hot keys. The following topics were covered:

✦ An event is some user action. The action may be opening a form, changing data in a record, or clicking on a command button.

✦ Access recognizes user events by using a corresponding property of a form or report. For example, the On Open property is associated with the event of opening a form.

✦ You can attach form macros to the form or to individual controls. Forms can use form-level events and control-level events.

✦ Form-level macros can display messages, open a form, synchronize two forms, and validate data entry.

✦ The two most common form properties for validating data at the form level are On Delete and Before Update.

✦ With the MsgBox( ) function, you can specify conditions in macros. This powerful function displays messages and command buttons to obtain user input.

✦ Control-event macros can be triggered when a user enters or exits a control, clicks on a button, or double-clicks on a control.

✦ You use the SetValue action in macros to hide a control, update a field on the basis of another field value, or disable a control.

✦ Report macros can be triggered at the report level or at the report-section level. Only two event properties are used at the report level; two are used at the report-section level.

✦ By using macros in reports, you can apply a filter to a report, hide or print a line, or hide some other object on a report, basing the macro on a condition.

✦ You can assign macro actions to combinations of keys by using a key assignment macro and macro names based on the SendKeys syntax of Access.

In the next chapter, you work with macros in menus, switchboards, and dialog boxes to further automate your database system.

✦   ✦   ✦

Creating Switchboards, Command Bars, Menus, Toolbars, and Dialog Boxes

Until this chapter, you created individual Access objects: tables, queries, forms, reports, and macros. You worked with each of these objects interactively in Access, selecting the Database window and using the assorted objects.

In this chapter, you tie these objects together into a single database application — without having to write or know how to use a complex database program. Rather, you automate the application through the use of switchboards, dialog boxes, and menus. These objects make your system easier to use; they hide the Access interface from the final user.

What Is a Switchboard?

A switchboard is fundamentally a form. The switchboard form is a customized application menu that contains user-defined command buttons. With these command buttons, you can run macros that automatically select such actions as opening forms or printing reports.

Using a switchboard button, you replace many interactive user steps with a single button selection (or *click*). For example, if you want to open the form Add a Customer and Pets interactively, you must perform three actions: Switch to the Database window, select the Forms tab, and open the form. If you use a switchboard button to perform the same task, you simply click on the button. Figure 32-1 shows the switchboard window with several buttons. Each command button triggers a macro that performs a series of steps, such as opening the Customer form or running the Hospital Report.

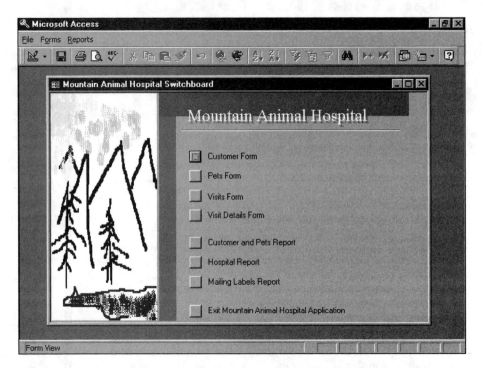

Figure 32-1: A switchboard with several command buttons for forms and reports.

By using a switchboard and other objects covered in this chapter, you can tie your database objects together in a single database application. Rather than the Access interactive interface, the application will have a user interface you create. A primary component of that user-defined interface is the switchboard you create.

Using a switchboard

A switchboard's primary use is as an application interface menu. The switchboard in Figure 32-1 is the application interface menu for the Mountain Animal Hospital database. As you see in the figure, the switchboard contains several command buttons. When the user clicks on any switchboard button, a macro is triggered that performs some action or a series of actions.

Creating the basic form for a switchboard

You create a switchboard by adding command buttons to an existing Access form. The form in Figure 32-1 is a standard Access 97 display form. Forms can have many uses, including data entry, data display, and switchboards.

Because switchboard forms are used as application menus, they tend to use a limited number of form controls. Typically, you find command buttons, labels, object frames (OLE objects, such as pictures), lines, and rectangles. Normally, switchboards lack the other types of form controls, such as text boxes (bound to fields), list and combo boxes, graphs, subforms, and page breaks.

To create a basic switchboard form, you place labels like titles and group headings on the form. In addition to the labels, you may also want to place lines, rectangles, and pictures on the form to make it aesthetically appealing. You create the basic switchboard form by using the techniques you already learned in chapters covering form objects.

Consider, for example, the switchboard in Figure 32-1. Minus the command buttons, this is a typical Access application form. Its major components are a title, some other text controls, various colored rectangles, a line, and a picture (image control).

Working with command buttons

Command buttons are the type of form control you use to run macros or VBA routines. Command buttons are the simplest type of form controls, having the single purpose of executing a macro or VBA procedure that can exist *behind* a form or in a module procedure.

In this example, you will create command buttons that will run macros. As you have learned, macros perform a multitude of tasks in Access, including

✦ Opening and displaying other forms

✦ Opening a pop-up form or dialog box to collect additional information

✦ Opening and printing reports

✦ Activating a search or displaying a filter

✦ Exiting Access

CD-ROM On your CD-ROM in the Mountain Animal Hospital database is a form named Mountain Switchboard-No Buttons. You can use that as a starting point to create your switchboard, as shown in Figure 32-2.

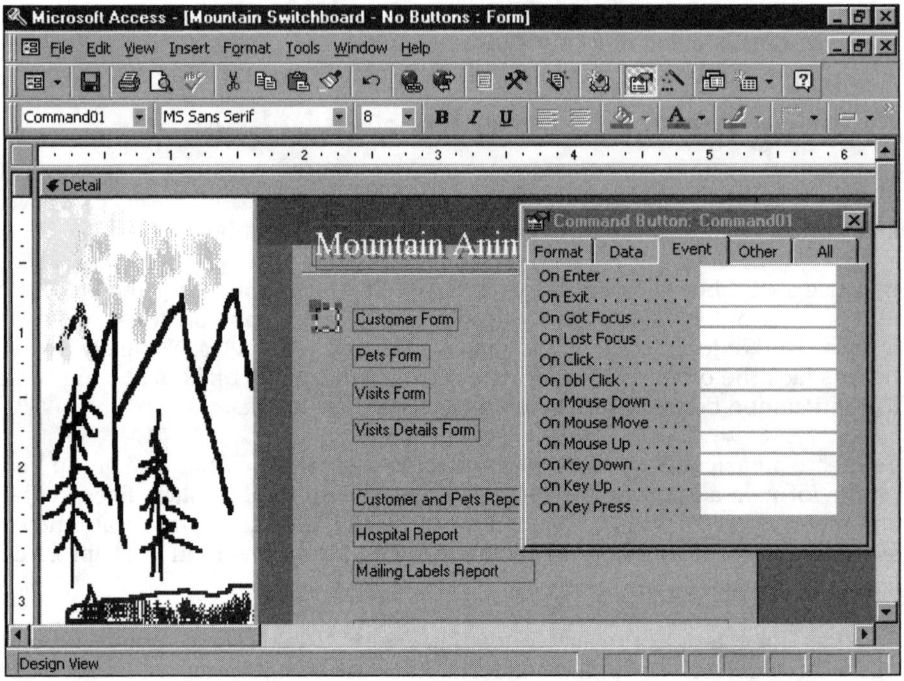

Figure 32-2: A single-button switchboard form with its open property sheet.

Figure 32-2 shows a command button named Command01 and its property sheet. In this property sheet, you see the event properties available for a command button.

Each event property can trigger a macro. For example, to trigger a macro named OpenCust when the user clicks on the button, place the macro name OpenCust in the parameter box for the On Click property. The keyword *On* identifies an event property. The property identifies the user event that must occur to trigger an action.

Caution   On Click and On Dbl Click are mutually compatible. If you activate both the On Click property (giving it a macro name) and the On Dbl Click property, Access follows this order of precedence for the mouse clicking and trapping:

1. On Click (single click)
2. On Dbl Click (double-click)
3. On Click (single click)

In other words, Access processes an On Click first and then an On Dbl Click and, finally, an On Click *again*. Access *always* processes the On Click if it is defined. To prevent the second On Click macro from running, place a CancelEvent action in the On Dbl Click macro.

What is focus?

To understand the terminology associated with command buttons, you need to know the term *focus*. The two command button properties On Enter and On Exit gain or lose focus. In other words, the focus represents the next item of input from the user. For example, if you Tab from one button to another, you lose the focus on the first button as you leave it, and you gain the focus on the second as you enter it. In a form with several command buttons, you can tell which button has focus by the dotted box around the label of the button. Focus does not denote the state of input, as when you press a button; rather, focus is the object that is currently active and awaiting some user action.

The focus for mouse input always coincides with the button down, or pointer, location. Because focus occurs at the moment of clicking on a command button, the property On Enter is not triggered. The reason is that On Enter occurs just before the focus is gained; that state is not realized when you select a command button by using a mouse. The On Enter state never occurs. Rather, the focus and On Click occur simultaneously, bypassing the On Enter state.

In addition, if the macro you call from an On Click opens a dialog box (message box, pop-up form, and so forth), the second click is lost and the On Dbl Click is never reached! If you use On Click and On Dbl Click, the On Click should not open a dialog box if you need to capture the On Dbl Click.

Creating command buttons

A command button's primary purpose is to activate, or run, a macro. Access gives you two ways to create a command button:

✦ Click on the Command Button icon in the Form Toolbox.

✦ Drag a macro name from the database container to the form.

In this chapter, you will see both these methods at least once as you learn how to create the eight command buttons shown in Figure 32-1 (four buttons to display a form, three to display a report, and one to exit the application). In this first example, you see how to create the first form button by using the Command Button Wizard.

When using the Command Button Wizard, you can not only create a command button, but also automatically display text or embed a picture on the button. More importantly, you can create VBA modules to perform tasks, including Record Navigation (Next, Previous, First, Last, Find), Record Operations (Save, Delete, Print, New, Duplicate), Form Operations (Open, Close, Print, Filter), Report Operations (Print, Preview, Mail), Applications (Run Application, Quit, Notepad, Word, Excel), and Miscellaneous (Print Table, Run Query, Run Macro, AutoDialer), even if you don't know a single command in VBA.

**Cross-
Reference**   In Chapter 34, you will learn how to create and edit VBA code with the Command
Button Wizard.

To create the Customer button by using the Command Button Wizard, follow these
steps:

   1. Open the form Mountain Switchboard - No Buttons in design mode.

   2. Make sure that the Control Wizard icon is toggled on.

   3. Click on the Command Button icon in the Toolbox.

   4. Place the cursor on the form in the upper left corner of the Form Display rec-
      tangle and draw a small rectangle.

Note   Command buttons have no control source. If you try to create a button by dragging a field from the Field List, a text box control (not a command button) is created. You must draw the rectangle or drag a macro to create a command button.

The Command Button Wizard displays the dialog box shown in Figure 32-3. You
can select from several categories of tasks. As you choose each category, the list
of actions under the header When button is pressed changes. In addition, the
sample picture changes as you move from action to action. In Figure 32-3, the
specified category is Form Operations, and the desired action is Open Form.

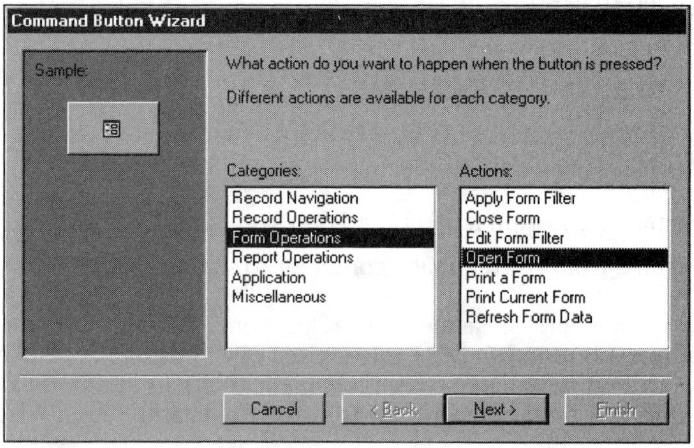

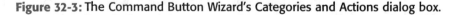

Figure 32-3: The Command Button Wizard's Categories and Actions dialog box.

   5. Choose the Form Operations category and the Open Form action.

   6. Click on the <u>N</u>ext> button to move to the next screen.

      The Wizard displays a list of the Mountain Animal Hospital database's forms.

7. Select the Customer form and Click on the <u>N</u>ext> button to move to the next Wizard screen.

The next screen is a specific dialog box for this button. Because you have chosen the Open Form action, Access uses built-in logic to now ask you what you want to do now with this form. As you can see in Figure 32-4, Access can automatically write a VBA program behind the button to open the form and show all records; if necessary, it can let you specify fields to search for specific values after the form is opened.

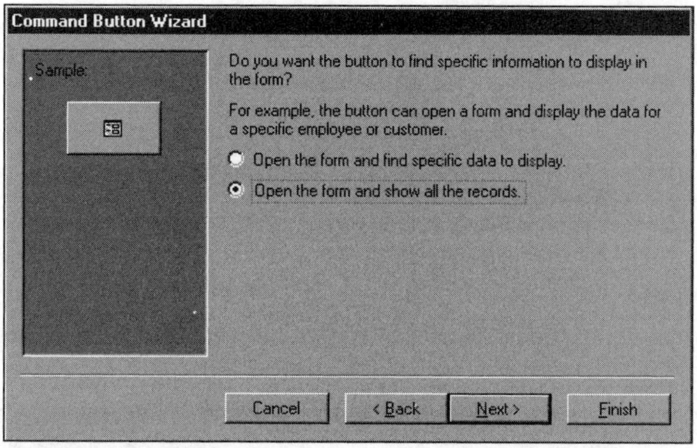

Figure 32-4: The Command Button Wizard open form with a specific data question.

8. Select Open the form and show all the records and Click on <u>N</u>ext> to move on.

The next screen lets you decide what you want to appear on the button. You can display text or a picture on the button. The button can be resized to accommodate any size text. The default is to place a picture on the button. You can choose from the default button for the selected action, or you can click in the Show All Pictures check box to select from over 100 pictures. You also can click on the Browse button to select an icon (.ICO) or bitmap (.BMP) file from your disk. For this example, simply display the text Customer on the button.

9. Click on the Text option button and erase the text Open Form in the text box.

The sample button displays nothing instead of the picture (see Figure 32-5).

10. Click on the <u>N</u>ext> button to move to the final Wizard screen, which lets you enter a name for the button and then display the button on the form.

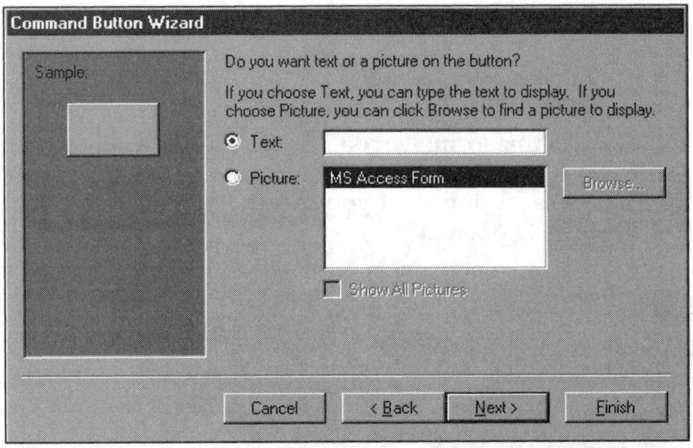

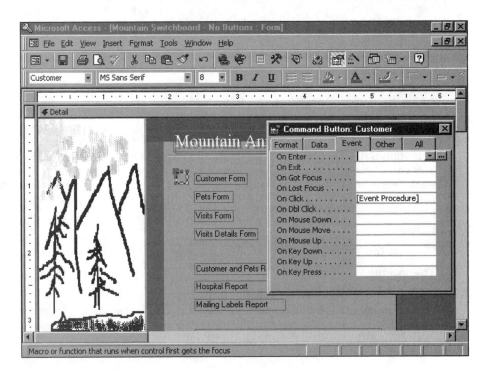

Figure 32-5: Selecting a picture or text for the button.

11. Enter **Customer** as the name of the button. Click on Finish.

The button appears on the Form Design screen, as shown in Figure 32-6.

Figure 32-6: Adding a button to the form design.

Notice the property sheet displayed in Figure 32-6. The On Click property displays Event Procedure, which means that a module is stored *behind* the form. You can see this VBA module library by pressing the Builder button (three dots) next to the [Event Procedure] text. When the Customer button is clicked, the VBA program is run and the Customer form is opened.

A module window appears with the specific VBA program code that's necessary to open the Customer form (see Figure 32-7). There is no need to look at this code unless you plan to change the program. This topic is covered in Chapter 33.

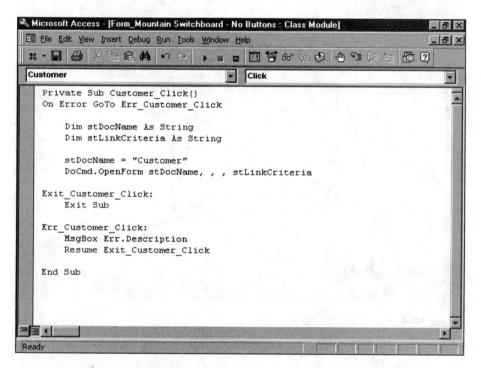

Figure 32-7: The event procedure module for opening the Customer form.

You can create a command button and attach a macro very easily — or attach pictures — without using the Wizard. If you want to dabble in VBA, the Command Button Wizard is a great place to start.

You may want to create buttons for all the forms and reports. You can use the Command Button Wizard, as shown on the previous page (except for the reports you would use the Report Operations options). If you are planning on using a macro or want to create an event procedure yourself, you can also simply click on the first button and choose Edit⇨Duplicate from the menu bar to duplicate the button.

Note This only duplicates the button itself, not the code behind the button.

After you duplicate the Customer button for all the other text entries except the last one, your screen should look like Figure 32-8.

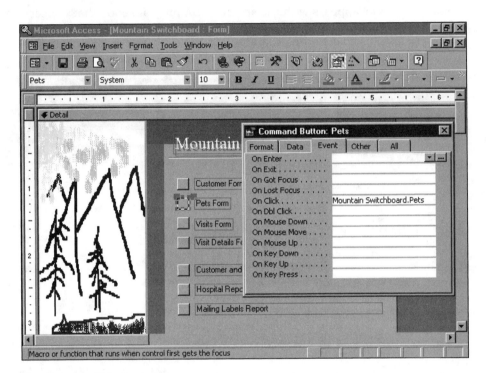

Figure 32-8: All buttons on screen.

Linking a command button to a macro

As soon as you create a command button in the Design window, it is already active. You can click on it, although it doesn't perform any action unless you created it with the Wizard. If you switch to the Form window by clicking on the Form button on the toolbar, you'll see the switchboard. You can use any of the seven buttons you created in design mode.

Every time you click on a button, it graphically pushes down, showing that it has been selected. Except for the Customer button, however, nothing else occurs; only the button movement happens. By switching back to design mode and clicking on the Design button on the toolbar, you can link a macro to the button.

To link a command button to a macro, you enter the macro name into the property cell of one of the command button's event properties. To see the property sheet for a command button, follow these steps:

1. In design mode, click on the Pets command button.

2. Click on the Properties button on the toolbar or select View⇨Properties on.

A property sheet similar to the one in Figure 32-8 should be visible on your screen. Notice the event properties that begin with the word *On* in the property sheet.

The property most commonly used to link a command button to a macro is On Click. This property runs a macro whenever a user clicks on the button. When the button is selected, the On Click property becomes True and the specified macro is run. To associate the macro named Pets in the macro group Mountain Switchboard, follow these steps:

1. Click on the Pets command button.

2. Click on the On Click property cell in the property sheet for the command buttons.

3. Type **Mountain Switchboard. Pets** in the cell and press Enter, as shown in Figure 32-8.

Make sure that you type both the macro group name and then the macro name separated by a period.

Tip   When you enter a macro name, the macro does not have to exist. You can enter the name of a macro that you create later. In this way, you can create the switchboard first and the macros later. If the macro name you enter in the On Click cell does not exist when you open the form and click on the button, Access displays an error message.

Using these methods, you can now complete all seven buttons' properties, assigning a macro for each button on the basis of the On Click property. Table 32-1 shows each button name and the macro it will call.

Table 32-1
The Seven Buttons and Their Macro Names

In Rectangle	Button Name	Macro for On Click
Form	Customer	Event Property (created by Button Wizard)
Form	Pets	Mountain Switchboard.Pets
Form	Visits	Mountain Switchboard.Visits
Form	Visit Details	Mountain Switchboard.Visit Details
Report	Customer and Pets	Mountain Switchboard.Customer and Pets
Report	Hospital Report	Mountain Switchboard.Hospital Report
Report	Customer Labels	Mountain Switchboard.Customer Labels

The macros for the Mountain Switchboard

In this example, each command button opens either a form or a report by using the OpenForm or OpenReport macro actions. The Exit button closes the form with the Quit macro action.

You can create each of the macros and its actions by following these general steps:

1. Enter a macro name in the Macro Name column.
2. Enter a macro action in the Action column (such as OpenForm, OpenReport, or Close) or select the macro action from the drop-down list box.
3. Enter a macro argument (name of form or report) for each action.
4. Optionally, enter a remark (as a reminder) in the Comment Column.

Another way to add a macro action and argument is to drag the form or report from the Database window to the macro's Action column. Access automatically adds the correct action in the Action column, which is OpenForm or OpenReport. Access also adds the correct argument in the Name cell of the arguments.

If you want to create the group macro for this chapter, you can follow Table 32-2. This table shows each macro name, the action for each macro, and the form or report name. (These are shown in Figure 32-9.) The macro Mountain Switchboard should already exist in the Macro Object list of the Database window.

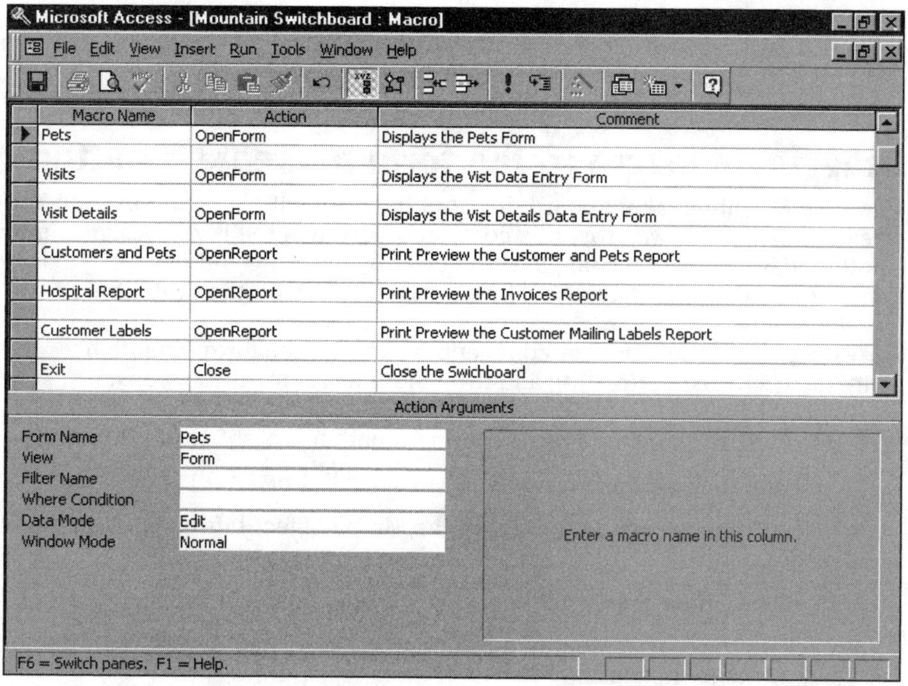

Figure 32-9: The seven macros used for Mountain Switchboard.

Table 32-2
Macros Used in the Group Macro

Macro Name	Action	Argument Name (Form, Report, Object)
Pets	OpenForm	Pets
Visits	OpenForm	Adding General Pet Visit Info
Visit Details	OpenForm	Adding Visit Details
Customer and Pets	OpenReport	Pets & Owners
Hospital Report	OpenReport	Invoices
Customer Label	OpenReport	Customer By State (three snaking columns)
Exit	Close	Mountain Switchboard

Notice that Table 32-2 shows that the action Close will close the form named Mountain Switchboard. These macros work with the actual form named Mountain Switchboard. The Exit command button will be created next.

Dragging a macro to the form to create a button

The form Mountain Switchboard does not have an Exit command button. You already learned one way to add a command button in the Form Design window. Another way to create a command button is by dragging and dropping a macro name from the macro Database window to a position on the switchboard.

For example, to create an Exit command button for the form Mountain Switchboard by using the drag-and-drop method, follow these steps:

1. Enter the design mode for the form Mountain Switchboard - No Buttons.
2. Activate the Database window by pressing F11 or Alt+F1.
3. In the Database window, click on the Macro object button to display all macros.
4. Highlight Mountain Switchboard on the Macro Object list.
5. Click on the macro Mountain Switchboard; drag and drop it onto the form below the rectangles.
6. Click on the button name and change it to **Exit**.
7. Click in the cell of the On Click property of the Exit button.
8. Move to the end of the macro group name and type **.Exit**.

Your screen should now look similar to Figure 32-10. Notice that when you added the macro to the form by the drag-and-drop method, Access automatically created a command button, named it the same as the macro, and placed the macro name (in this case, a group name) in the On Click property of the button.

When you added the macro name to the On Click property, you did not have to add the macro group name. Rather, you moved to the end and placed a period after the group name and then the macro name. Access automatically brought the group name into the On Click property for you.

Tip   If you drag and drop a macro that is not a group macro, Access correctly places the macro name in the On Click property and names the button the same as the macro.

Caution   If you drag a macro group, as you did in this example, and do not add a macro name to the On Click property, Access runs the first macro in the macro group.

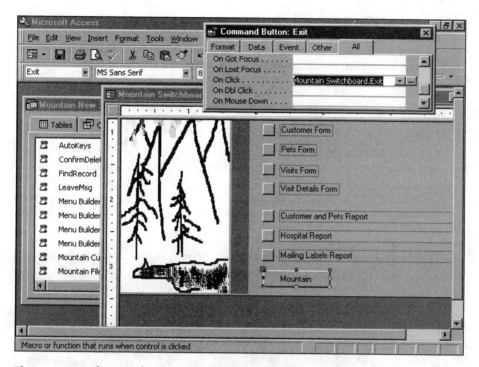

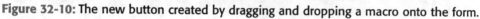

Figure 32-10: The new button created by dragging and dropping a macro onto the form.

Adding a picture to a command button

The first seven command buttons you have created contained nothing in the Caption property of the button. This last button currently contains the text *Mountain* in the Caption property of the command button. However, you can have any button display a picture instead. For example, the CD-ROM in the back of the book contains a file named EXIT.BMP (as well as a sampler of pictures for command buttons), which is a bitmap of an exit sign. You can have the Exit command button show the picture EXIT.BMP rather than the word *Exit*.

To change a command button to a picture button, you can use one of these methods:

✦ Type the name of the bitmap (.BMP) containing the picture into the Picture property of the button.

✦ Use the Picture Builder to select from an icon list that comes with Access.

✦ Specify the name of an icon or bitmap file.

To change the Exit command button to the picture button, EXIT.BMP, follow these steps:

1. In the Mountain Switchboard form, click on the Exit command button.

2. Display the Property window.

3. Select the *Picture* property for the Exit button.

4. Click on the Builder button (three dots on a little button).

   The Picture Builder dialog box appears. No picture appears because the button you are modifying has none. Because you are adding a picture for an Exit button, you may want to see if there is an Exit button in Access. You can scroll down the list of Available Pictures, as shown in Figure 32-11. Access has an Exit picture, but it may not be what you want. You can select any bitmap or icon file on your disk.

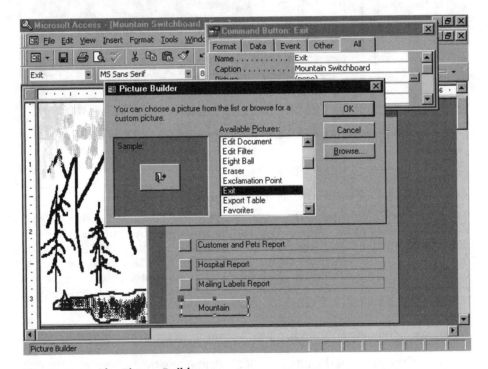

Figure 32-11: The Picture Builder.

5. Click on the Browse button.

The Select Bitmap dialog box shows a standard Windows directory list. Select the directory that contains your file.

6. Select the directory that contains the file **EXIT.BMP,** select the file, and click on Open (see Figure 32-12). The bitmap appears in the sample area. Although it doesn't fit in the sample, it should fit on the button when it is displayed.

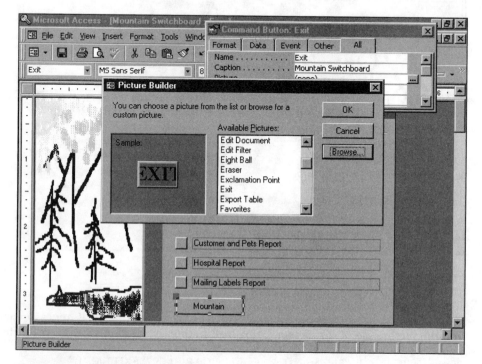

Figure 32-12: The Picture Builder.

7. Click on OK to accept the bitmap.

Access originally places the path of the bitmap in the Picture property. After the picture is saved, Access places the word (bitmap) in the Picture property of the command button.

8. Resize the button so that the picture shows only the word Exit.

Your form should look like Figure 32-13. Notice that Access added the word (bitmap) to the Picture cell for the button Exit.

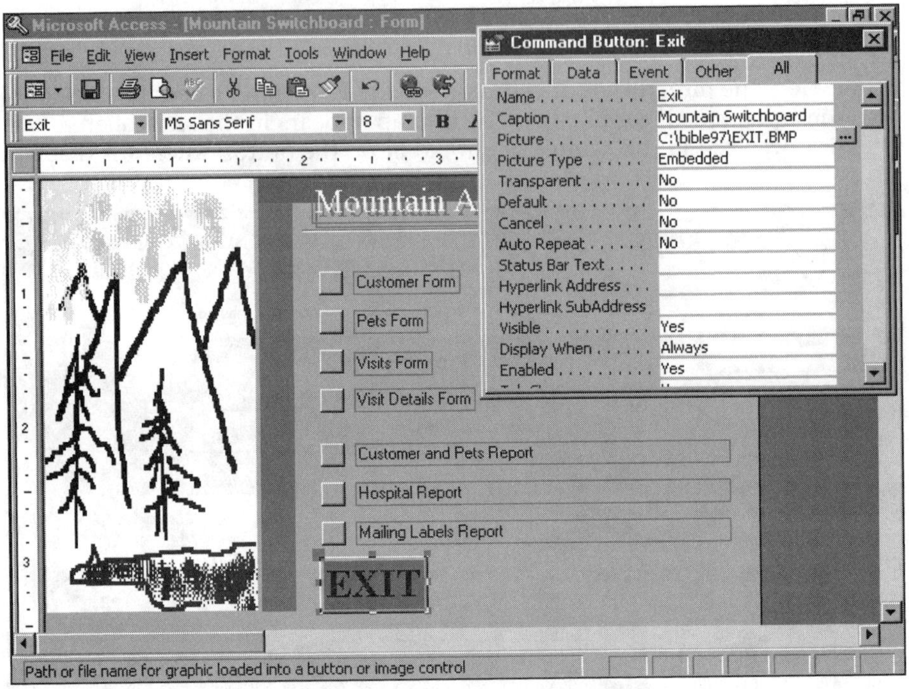

Figure 32-13: The final form with a picture button added.

You also can type the filename directly into the Picture property. If Access cannot find the picture file, it displays a dialog box stating that it couldn't find your file. If you know the drive and directory where the file is located, enter them in the Picture cell with the filename (for example, C:\BIBLE97\EXIT.BMP).

You may want to make all of the buttons into pictures. Click on each button and select the Picture property. Some of the pictures in the Access Picture Builder are 32×32 pixels ($\frac{1}{2}$ inch × $\frac{1}{2}$ inch), and others are 16×16 pixels (.18 inch × .18 inch).

Tip   Cary Prague Books and Software offers a library of over 1,500 button-size pictures like the 100 that come with the Access 97 Picture Builder. If you would like to purchase the Picture Builder Add-On Picture Pack, call Cary Prague Books and Software at 860-644-5891, FAX us at 860-648-0710, or visit our Web site, at www.caryp.com. This product normally costs $99.95. Mention the *Access 97 Bible,* and you can have it for only $59.95!

This action completes the Mountain Switchboard. Save your switchboard. The next task is to customize the menu bar to correspond to the buttons on the switchboard so that the choices can be made from the menu or the buttons.

Creating Customized Menu Bars

Besides creating switchboards with Access, you can create a custom drop-down menu bar that adds functionality to your system. You can add commands to this menu that are appropriate for your application. These commands may be the actions specified in your switchboard command buttons. When you create a custom drop-down menu bar, the new bar will replace the Access menu bar.

Tip   The menu bar is referenced only by a form; you can create a single menu bar and use it for several forms.

Figure 32-14 shows the Mountain Switchboard with a custom drop-down menu bar attached. Notice that each of the three choices on the bar menu (File, Forms, and Reports) has a drop-down menu attached.

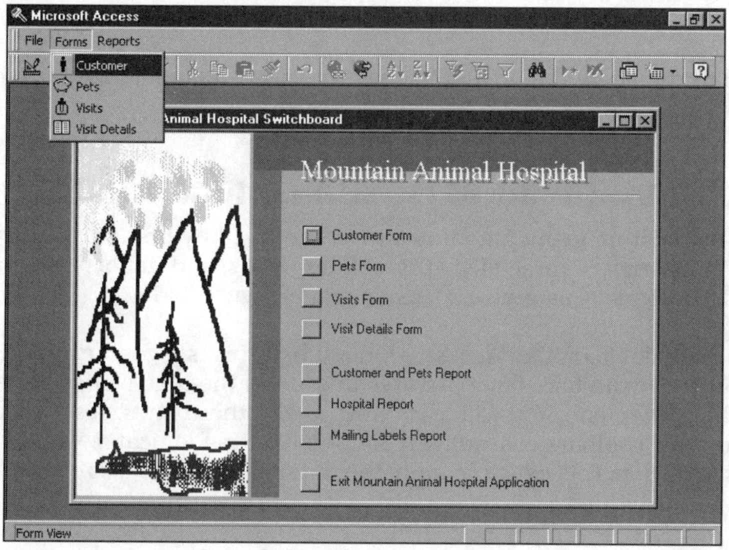

Figure 32-14: The custom drop-down menu bar.

There are two ways to create custom menus in Access 97:

✦ Use the New Access 97 CommandBar Object.

✦ Use macros (this was the only way to create menus in Access 2.0 and Access 95).

Tip If you have menus previously created in Access 2.0 or Access 95, you can convert them to the new menu bar object by selecting the macro to be converted and by then choosing Tools⇨Macro⇨Create Menu from Macro. You can also use the other two options, Create Toolbar from Macro and Create Shortcut Menu from Macro, to create those objects.

Understanding command bars

The new Access 97 Command Bar object allows you to create three types of menus. These are:

Menu Bars	Menus that go along the top of your forms and can have drop down menus too
ToolBars	Groups of icons generally found under the menu bars
Shortcut Menus	Pop-up menus that display when you right-click on an object

This allows you to duplicate the Access 97 user interface, including adding pictures to your menus.

Creating custom menu bars with command bars

You can create the custom menu bar shown in Figure 32-14 by first creating the top-level menu consisting of three elements — File, Forms, and Reports — by first selecting View⇨Toolbars⇨Customize. . ., as shown in Figure 32-15.

If you've never really looked at an Access 97 menu bar, this is a good example because many of the menu bars have pictures in front of the text. Notice the separator lines on the View menu. You will learn how to add these lines. Also notice the check box on the Toolbars cascading menu. This option indicates whether the menu bar is displayed. In this example, only the database menu bar is displayed. The Web menu bar is hidden.

Cross-Reference You will learn about Access 97 and the World Wide Web in the next chapter.

Select Customize. . . and the dialog box appears, as shown in Figure 32-16. Notice that your Office Assistant also is displayed to help you because this is a new feature. Microsoft has decided that you will need help.

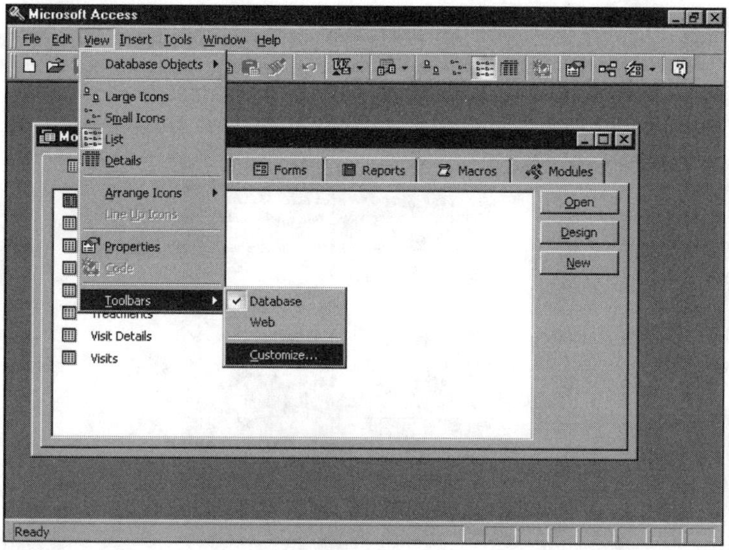

Figure 32-15: Selecting the View⇨Toolbars⇨Customize menu option.

Changing existing menus

From this dialog box, you can also select any of the preexisting menus and customize them by adding, removing, or moving menu items. You can also change pictures and even change the purpose of the menu.

If you decide that you want to change the menu items, you do this by first displaying the toolbar or menu you want to change and then directly changing it by clicking on the menu items you want to manipulate. If you click on a menu item, a submenu item, or a toolbar icon, a little gray button appears over the top of the item. You can then move the icon to a different location by dragging it to the new location. If you want to remove the menu item or icon, you can simply drag it to a place away from the toolbar. If you want to add a new item, you first select the Commands tab in the Customize dialog box, find the category that contains the item you want, and then drag the item to the toolbar or menu.

You can create a whole new item by selecting All Macros or New Menu and dragging it to the menu or toolbar you want it to be on. See the next section of this chapter for adding a new menu.

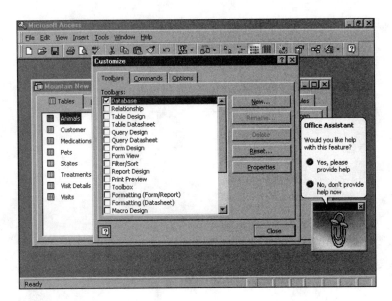

Figure 32-16: The Customize dialog box for toolbars.

Creating a new menu bar

To create a new menu bar, select <u>N</u>ew... from the Customize dialog box, as shown in Figure 32-16. A dialog box appears, asking you to name the custom menu bar. The default is Custom 1. Name this new menu **Mountain Custom Command Bar** and click on the OK button.

A small, gray rectangle appears in the center of the screen, on top of the Customize menu. You will also see the new command bar name appear in the list at the bottom of the Customize menu list, as shown in Figure 32-17.

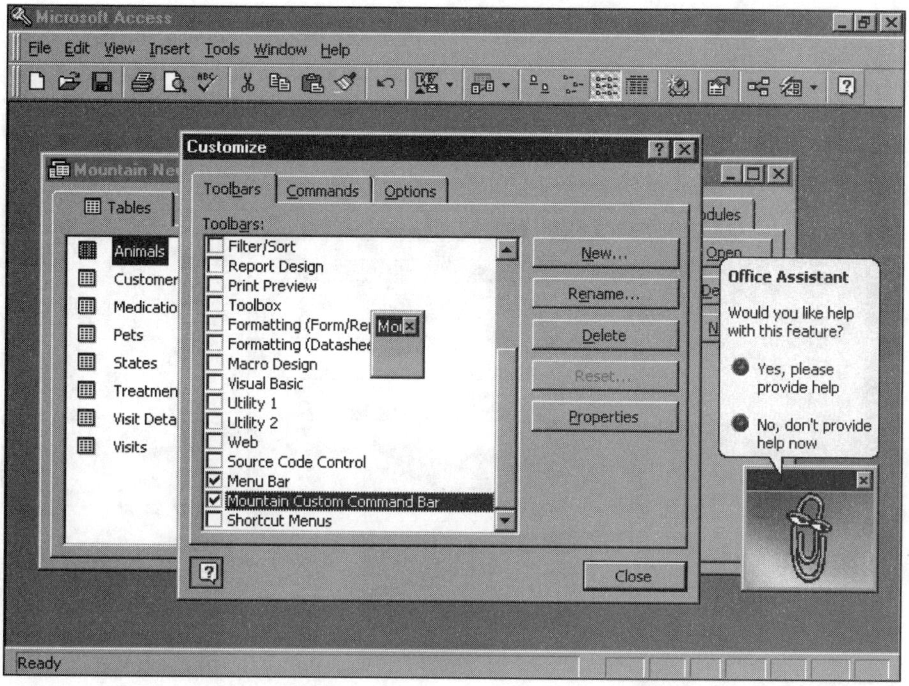

Figure 32-17: A new command bar.

Tip You can move this menu to the top of the screen by dragging it so that it looks like a normal menu bar with no items. You can see this in Figure 32-18. The Mountain bar is at the top, above the standard menu bar.

Before you begin to drag commands or text to the command bar, you must decide what type of command bar it is. You do this by selecting the menu bar (Mountain Custom Command Bar) on the Toolbars tab in the Customize dialog box and then by clicking on the Properties button.

Figure 32-18 shows the Toolbar Properties dialog box. Here you can select each of the command bars in your system. The important portion of this dialog box is the middle portion. The first option is Type.

There are three Type choices:

Menu Bar   Used for drop-down menus of commands containing text only

Toolbar   Used for button bars of pictures

Popup   Used either for drop-down menu lists or shortcut menus; can contain pictures and text

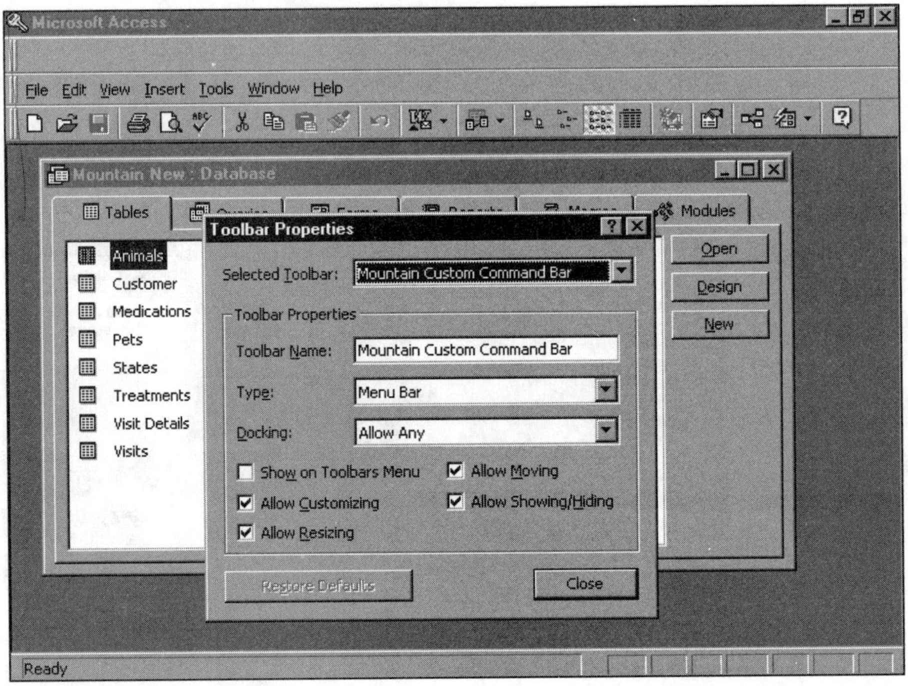

Figure 32-18: The Toolbar Properties dialog box.

For this example, you want to create a menu, so choose the Menu Bar option.

The next option, <u>D</u>ocking, has four options:

Allow Any	Allows docking horizontally or vertically
Can't Change	Cannot change where the command bar is docked
No Vertical	Can dock only horizontally (across the screen)
No Horizontal	Can dock only vertically (up and down the screen)

The rest of the options are five check boxes. These include:

Sho<u>w</u> on Toolbars Menu	Displays the selected toolbar on the <u>V</u>iew⇨<u>T</u>oolbars menu list
Allow <u>C</u>ustomizing	Allows the user to change this through the Customize menu
Allow <u>R</u>esizing	Allows you to resize a floating toolbar or menu bar

Allow <u>M</u>oving   Lets you move the menu or toolbar between floating or docking

Allow Showing/<u>H</u>iding   Lets you show/hide the menu through the View⇨<u>T</u>oolbars menu

For this example, you can select all the choices to give the menu maximum flexibility.

Adding a submenu to a custom menu bar

Most menu commands are placed on submenus. It is rare for a top-level menu item to do anything but display a submenu. The submenu contains the actual menu item that, when clicked on, will run the desired action, such as opening a form or printing a report.

To create a submenu, you essentially repeat the steps you used to create the Mountain Custom Command Bar. To create the submenu menu bar, select New. . . from the Customize dialog box, as originally shown in Figure 32-16, drag it to the Mountain Custom Command Bar, and drop it. The text New Menu appears on the menu bar. Click on it again, and a gray rectangle appears, as shown in Figure 32-19. This is the submenu.

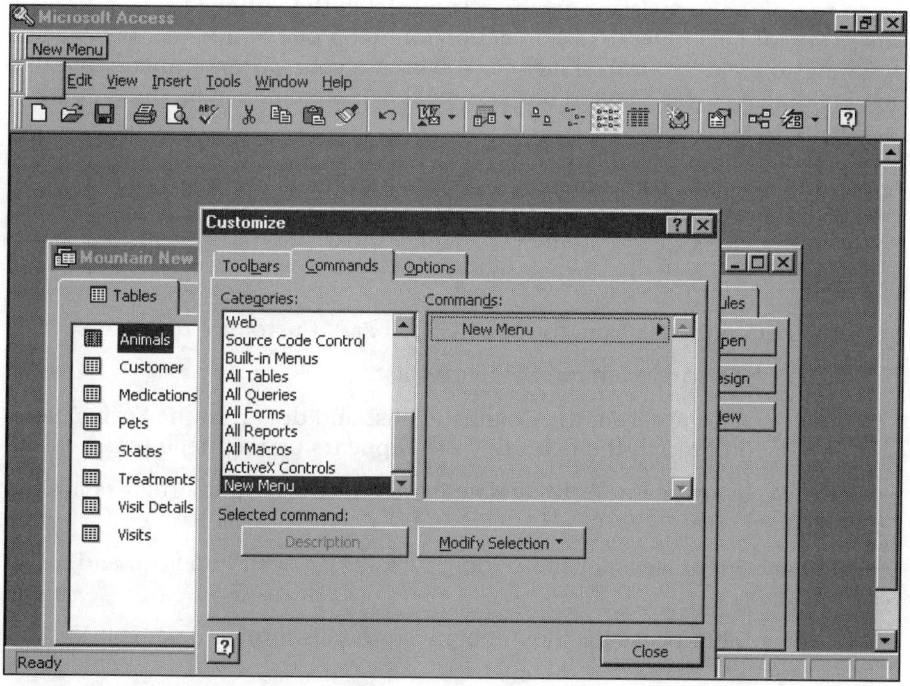

Figure 32-19: Creating a submenu.

You can now edit the name of the submenu by right-clicking on it. Name it File by clicking in the Name area and changing the name from New Menu to File. Repeat these steps for two additional new submenus, and name them Forms and Reports.

After you have your three menus defined, you can begin to add commands to the submenus. Again, you will be able to drag the menu commands directly to the submenu area.

Note Dragging the New Menu item to another menu automatically links the main menu and the submenu and makes the original menu choices nonselectable. The main menu (Mountain Custom Command Bar) is now permanently a menu bar. You can still change the defaults for the submenu items as you create them to display text, pictures, or both.

Caution After you add submenus to a menu bar, you cannot change it to a toolbar or pop-up menu.

Adding commands to a submenu

You can add commands to a custom menu bar by dragging any of the preexisting commands to the menu bar, or you can add any of your tables, queries, forms, reports, or macros to the menu bar.

Using one of the preexisting commands fills in all the options for you. However, unless you are planning to use an action found on one of the Access 97 menus, you want to create your own menus. You create your own new menu option by first creating a new command bar and making it a menu bar, as shown in the previous section of this chapter.

After you have the blank submenus defined on the menu bar, you can drag controls to them. For this example, you might want to add the Forms menu items first. Follow these steps to add an item to display the Customers form when the first item is selected on the Forms menu:

1. Select Commands from the View⇨Toolbars⇨Customize dialog box.

2. Select All Forms from the Categories list.

3. Select Customer from the Commands list and drag it to the Forms menu bar. When you drop it, the text Customer appears on the menu bar.

4. Repeat the process for the Pets command, as shown in progress in Figure 32-20.

5. Repeat the process for the Adding General Pet Visit Info form and name it **Visits**.

6. Repeat the process for the Adding Visit Details form and name it **Visit Details**.

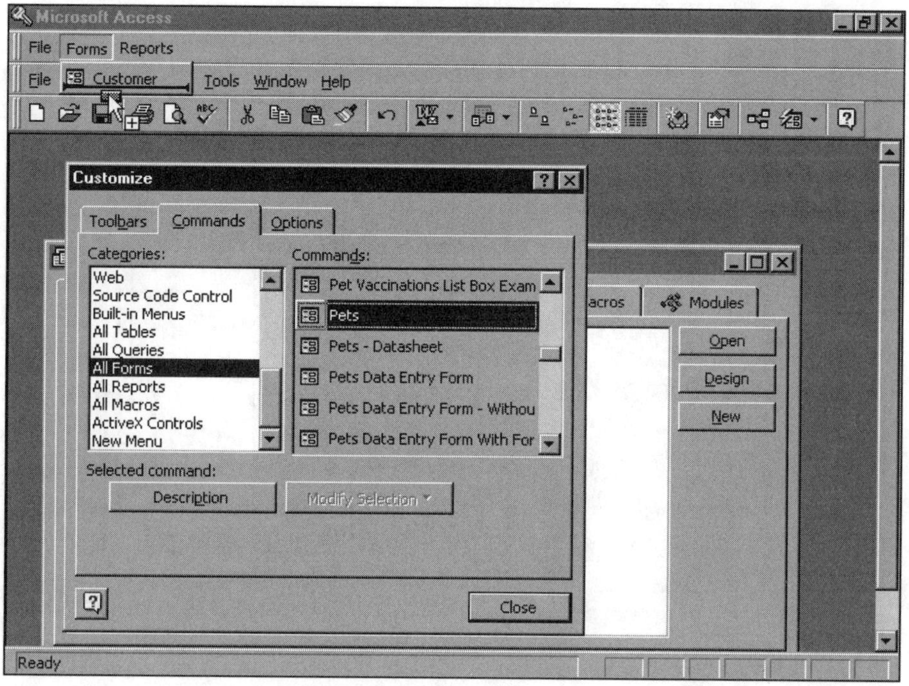

Figure 32-20: Creating a submenu item.

Changing the look of the submenu items

You may notice when you click on the Forms menu that each of the items has a form icon. If you right-click on any of the submenu items with the View⇨Toolbars⇨Customize menu active, you can change the picture or even change whether a picture is displayed at all. Figure 32-21 shows the Change Button Image selection of the View⇨Toolbars⇨Customize menu. Notice that all four of the button images have been changed by simply right-clicking on each menu item, selecting Change Button Image, and then selecting the desired picture.

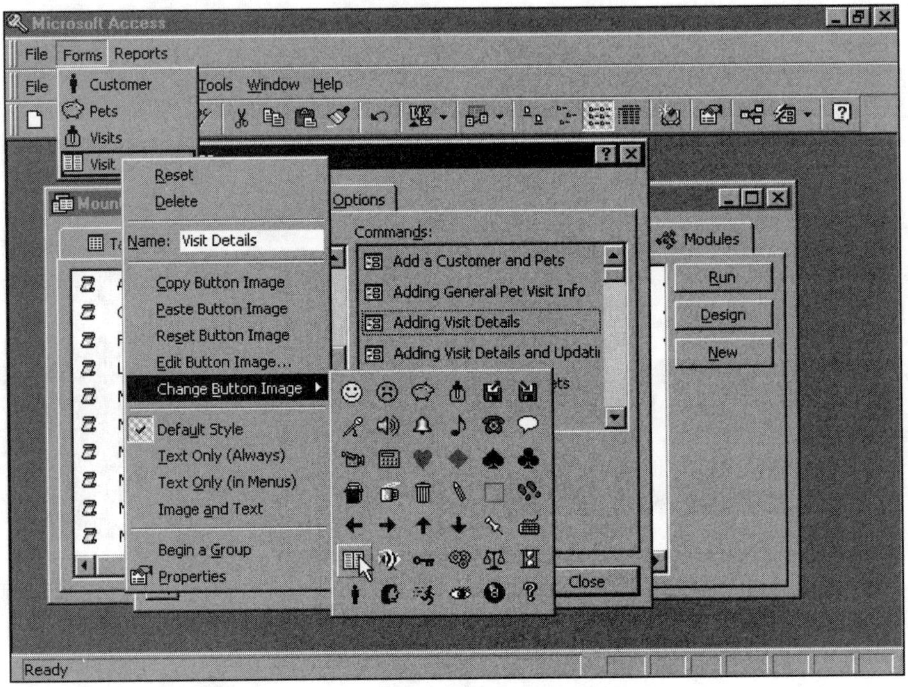

Figure 32-21: Changing the display of a menu bar item.

The shortcut menu contains five options for changing pictures on menus or toolbar icons:

Copy Button Image	Copies the current button face image to the Clipboard
Paste Button Image	Copies the current picture in the Clipboard to the button face
Reset Button Image	Changes the button face image to the default image
Edit Button Image	Uses the internal image editor to change an image
Choose Button Image	Changes the button face image from a list of images stored in Access

There are several ways to change the button image. The easiest is to select from a set of button images that Access stores internally, as shown in Figure 32-21. When you choose a picture and click on OK, the button image changes.

As you can see in Figure 32-21, there are not too many pictures to choose from. You can, however, create your own image and copy it to the Clipboard. After you have an image on the Clipboard, you can use the Paste Button Image option of the shortcut menu to add the image to the button. The image must be sized to fit the button. You can also use the Edit Button Image to change the image after it is on the button face. You can edit the button face by moving the image around and changing individual pixels of color.

As you can also see in Figure 32-21, you can change the caption of the text and the way it is displayed. There are four additional options you can select for how the menu or toolbar option is displayed:

Default Style	Displays image and text for menu bars, pictures for toolbars, and both for pop-ups
Text Only (Always)	Displays text only for menu bars and pop-ups
Text Only (in Menus)	Displays text on menu bars and graphics on toolbars and both on pop-ups
Image and Text	Displays pictures and text on menu bars and pop-ups

Tip

If you want to remove the images and display just text, you can select the Text Only choice for each submenu item.

Tip

If you check the Begin a Group check box, Access will place a horizontal separator line before the menu item.

You can further customize each item for the specific purpose you need. You can display the Properties for any menu by clicking on the Properties button, shown at the bottom of Figure 32-21, as shown in Figure 32-22 for the Customer Item that has been enhanced. Here you set the rest of the actions for the menu item.

Each menu item has a list of properties, as shown in Figure 32-22. After the Control Properties window is displayed, you can change the Selected Control to any of the menu items without returning to the previous menu. You can change the caption, which changes the text on the menu.

Tip

If you want to define a hot key for the menu item, you can add an & in front of the hot-key letter.

Notice that the caption has been changed with the addition of an & in front of the C. This allows you to press the letter *C* after displaying the Forms menu in this example. If you set up an AutoKeys macro list, you can specify the shortcut text, as shown in Figure 32-22. Notice the Ctrl + C next to the Customer menu item as well as in the shortcut text area.

You can also define the tooltip text for the control by entering text in the ToolTip area.

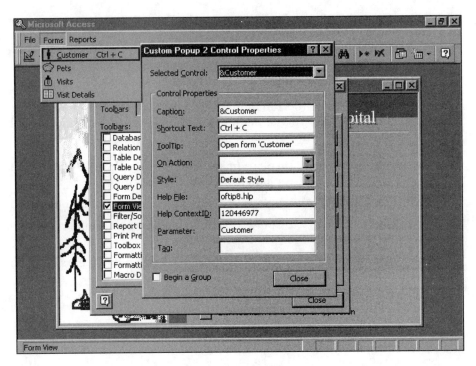

Figure 32-22: Changing the display of a menu bar item.

The most important option is normally the On Action item. This allows you to specify a VBA function or macro that should run when the menu item is selected. Because you dragged each form from the forms list to the menu, the action is already known in the Properties sheet for the item. In fact, the name of the form to open is stored in the Parameter option of the window.

The other options let you choose the Help File name and entry point if you click on Help while selecting the menu. The Parameter entry is used to specify optional parameters when calling a VBA function.

Note You can complete the Reports menu items by dragging the desired reports to the Reports menu item from the All Reports commands. You can add the Exit function to the File menu by dragging the Exit command from the File category.

Attaching the menu bar to a form

After you have completed the submenus and the menu bar named Mountain Custom Command Bar that attach the submenus to, you are ready to attach the menu bar to a form.

To attach a menu bar to a form, open the form in design mode and set the Menu Bar property of the form to the menu bar macro name. To attach the menu bar named Mountain Custom Command Bar to the switchboard form Mountain Switchboard, follow these steps:

1. Open the form Mountain Switchboard in design mode.

2. Display the property sheet by clicking on the Properties button on the toolbar.

3. Click on the small blank box to the left of the ruler (immediately below the toolbar).

   Access displays the title Form for the property sheet.

4. Click on the Menu Bar property of the Property window.

5. Select the Mountain Custom Command Bar from the pull-down menu (or type the menu bar name).

By following these steps, you have just attached the menu bar named Mountain Custom Command Bar with its drop-down menus to the form. You should have a design screen similar to the one in Figure 32-23.

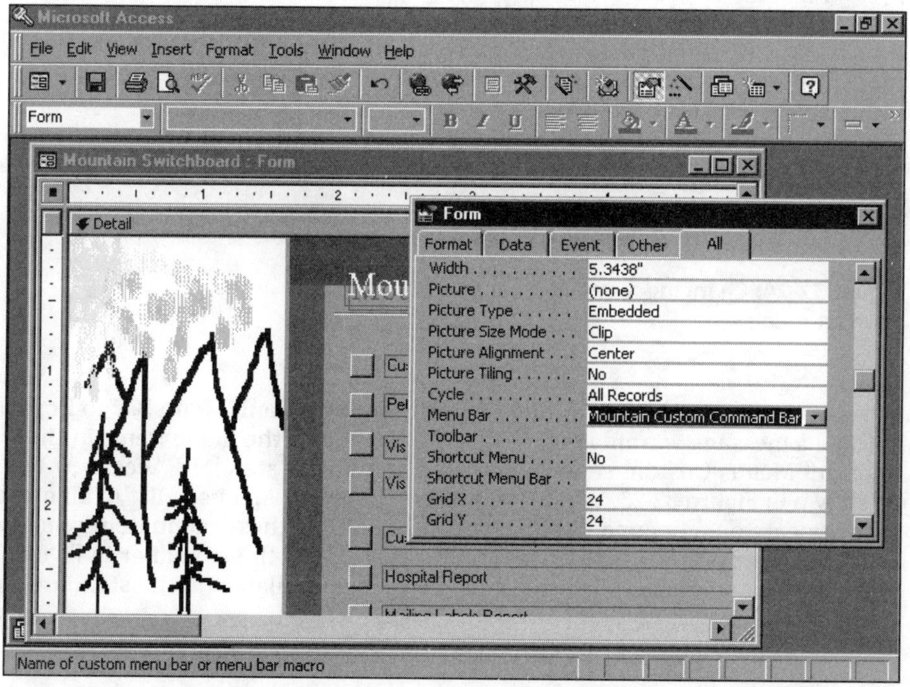

Figure 32-23: Attaching a menu bar to the form using the On Menu property.

Creating shortcut menus

Access 97 allows you to create *custom shortcut menus* that open when the right mouse button is clicked. These menus can replace the standard shortcut menus in Access 97. You can define shortcut menus for the form itself or for any control on the form. Each control can have a different shortcut menu.

A shortcut menu is simply another type of command bar. You can begin a shortcut menu by selecting View➪Toolbars➪Customize and then choosing the New... button from the Toolbars tab of the Customize dialog box. In this example, you can name the new menu **Pets Shortcut**.

After you create the new menu bar, you can select it and click on the Properties button. The Toolbar Properties dialog box is displayed. Change the Type to Popup, as shown in Figure 32-24.

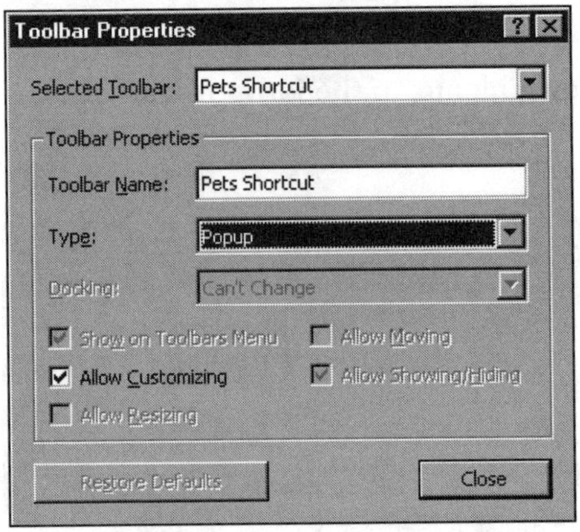

Figure 32-24: Changing a new toolbar to a pop-up shortcut menu.

When you change the type of the toolbar from the default Menu Bar to Popup, you will see a message warning you that you have to edit the menu items in the Shortcut Menus Custom section. Shortcut Menus is a standard Access 97 toolbar, as shown in Figure 32-25. When you click on Shortcut Menus, a list of all menu bars appears on a command bar. If you select any of these menu items, such as Database, Filter, or Form, as shown on the left side of the menu bar in Figure 32-25, you will see a submenu of all the shortcut menus available on the standard Access design screens.

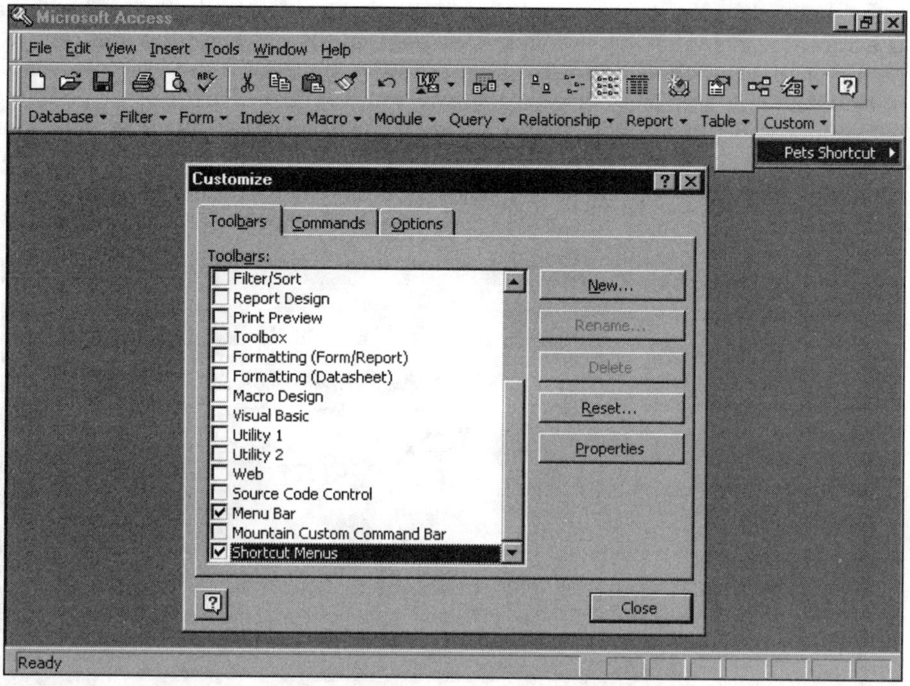

Figure 32-25: Displaying the list of custom shortcut menus.

The last item on the command bar is Custom. When you click on this item, you will see a list of all shortcut (pop-up) menus you have defined yourself. The only shortcut menu defined so far is the Pets Shortcut. Notice the blank menu bar in Figure 32-25, to the left of the Pets Shortcut menu. This is where you will drag your selections.

You add menu items to a shortcut menu in exactly the same way you add any menu item. While the empty Pets Shortcut menu rectangle is displayed as shown in Figure 32-25, click on the Commands tab in the Customize dialog box and then select All Forms in the Categories list. You can then drag any command to the shortcut menu. For this example, you want to add four forms (Pets, Customers, Visits, and Visit Details) by dragging the four forms (Pets, Customers, Adding General Pet Visit Info, and Adding Visit Details) to the menu. Then you want to add three items for the reports — Customer and Pets, Hospital Reports, and Customer Labels — by first selecting All Reports in the Categories list.

As you add each of the forms and reports, you will see them appear on the shortcut menu. Notice that the forms and reports display a different icon next to the menu text. You can display the menu to change the details of each of these menu items by clicking on the item and then right-clicking. Notice in Figure 32-26 that the shortcut menu has been defined and each of the original form and report names have been changed to the more standard names for the example. Also notice the separator line between the forms and reports. This line was created by selecting the Begin a Group option while on the first report, as shown in Figure 32-26. If you wanted to, you could change the pictures for each of the icons next to the menu item by using the button image options.

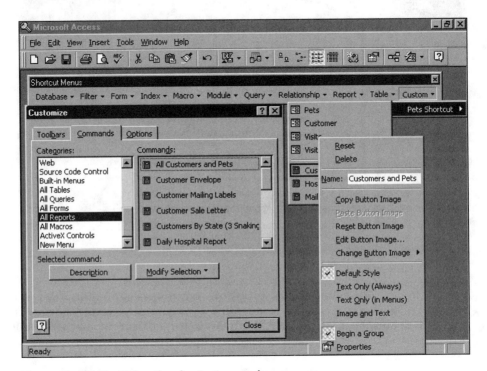

Figure 32-26: Modifying the shortcut menu bar.

Tip   If you click on Properties for any of the menu items, you can set the shortcut keys, ToolTips, actions, and Help file.

After you create the menu definition and save the shortcut menu, you can attach the shortcut menu to either the form or any control on the form. If you attach the shortcut menu to a form, it will override the standard shortcut menu for the form. If you attach a shortcut menu to a control, it will be displayed only when you right-click while on that control. Figure 32-27 shows the Pets shortcut menu being attached to the Shortcut Menu Bar property of the Mountain Switchboard.

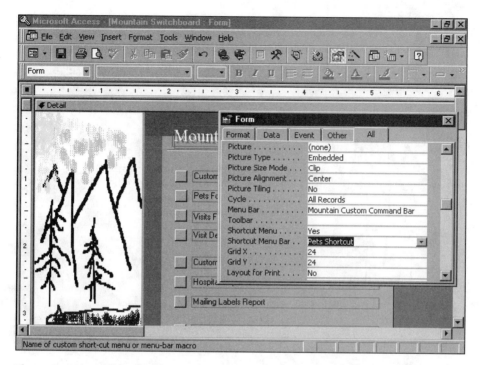

Figure 32-27: Adding the shortcut menu to the form.

You may also notice that the Shortcut Menu property is set to Yes. This is for either the default shortcut menus or shortcut menus you create. If it is set to No, you will not see any shortcut menus when you right-click.

Figure 32-28 shows the shortcut menu on the Mountain Switchboard form. The menu will be displayed to the right of wherever the mouse was clicked, even if it extends beyond the window. Now when you select the desired menu item the actions listed in the menu macro will be run.

Tip If you want to delete a shortcut menu, you must first select the shortcut menu by displaying the list of toolbars in the View➪Toolbars➪Customize dialog box and then click on the Properties button. The Shortcut menus are visible only by then opening the Selected Toolbar combo box. You must change the type from Popup to Menu Bar. After you do this, you can return to the Toolbars tab, where you will now be able to see the shortcut menu and press the Delete button. Remember that when you change a command bar to a pop-up menu, it is visible only on the short-cut menu's Custom tab or in the Selected Toolbar list in the Toolbar Properties dialog box.

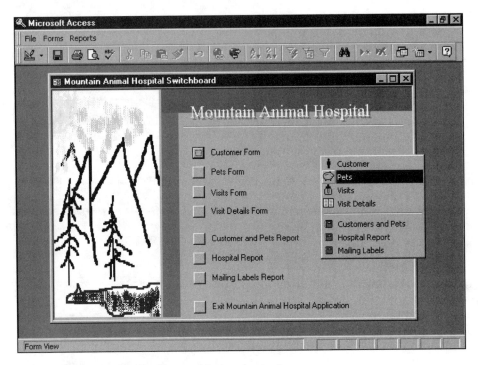

Figure 32-28: Viewing the form with the shortcut menu.

Creating and using custom toolbars

Access has always let you define new toolbars for your application and customize existing toolbars. However, Access 97 also adds features such as customizing the pictures on the buttons (known as button faces). For example, suppose that when you display the Mountain Switchboard, you want to create a new toolbar that lets you open the various forms with one button push. You can create a new toolbar or even add some icons to the standard form toolbar. For this example, you will create a new toolbar.

A toolbar is just another type of command bar.

To create a custom toolbar, follow these steps:

1. Select View➪Toolbars➪Customize.

2. Click on the New button from the Toolbars window.

3. Enter **Mountain Toolbar** in the New Toolbar dialog box and click on OK.

4. Select Properties.

You can see that the new command bar is created as a toolbar. You can close the properties window and drag the four forms to the toolbar. You use the same technique to do this as you saw when creating menu bars and shortcut menus. While the empty Mountain Toolbar rectangle is displayed, click on the Commands tab in the Customize dialog box and then select All Forms in the Categories list. You can then drag any command to the shortcut menu. For this example, you want to add four forms (Pets, Customers, Visits, and Visit Details) by dragging the four forms (Pets, Customers, Adding General Pet Visit Info, and Adding Visit Details) to the menu. You also want to change the button face for each button. When you are done, you can see the toolbar completed, as shown in Figure 32-29. This figure also shows how to change a button image on the last item by first selecting the item and then right-clicking on the item.

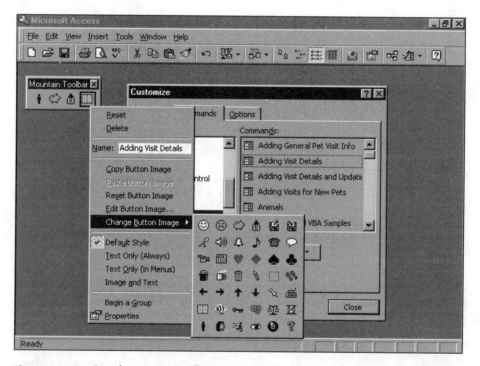

Figure 32-29: Creating a new toolbar.

Tip You can add a space and a separator line between icons by selecting Begin a Group on the icon you want the line to the left of.

The next step is to add the toolbar to a custom form. If you are adding your toolbar to a form, you should do it when the form opens. The general procedure is to use the macro action to display the custom toolbar ShowToolbar. You also will want to turn off the standard Access form toolbar. Figure 32-30 shows the macro changes that make this happen. A new macro action in the Mountain Switchboard named Display Mountain Toolbar has been created.

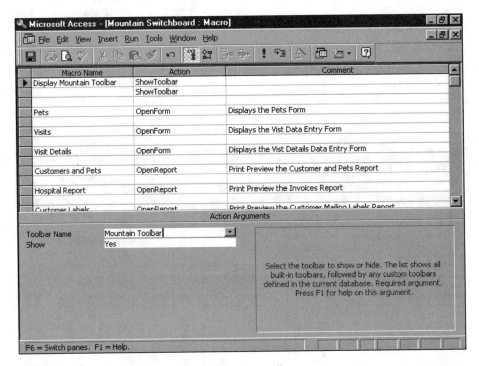

Figure 32-30: Creating a macro to show the toolbar.

The new macro Display Mountain Toolbar contains two actions. The first (pictured at the bottom of Figure 32-30) opens the Mountain toolbar. The Show option has three choices:

Yes	Displays Mountain toolbar on all objects
No	Turns off the display of the toolbar (if it is currently displayed)
Where Appropriate	Displays the toolbar when it makes sense to do so (usually just in forms)

In this example, the Mountain toolbar is displayed where appropriate. The second ShowToolbar action in the Display Mountain Toolbar macro is used to turn off the Form View toolbar.

Tip You should also add the opposite macros to the Exit macro. The first turns off the Mountain toolbar; the other turns back on the Form View toolbar.

After you have made these changes, you can display the Mountain Switchboard, as shown in Figure 32-31. Note the Mountain toolbar on the screen and the tooltip (showing for one of the forms).

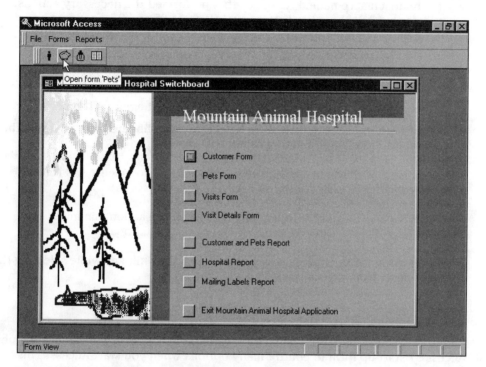

Figure 32-31: Displaying a custom toolbar in a form.

Adding control tips to any form control

Although tooltips must be added using the toolbar customization windows, you can add a tooltip known as a *control tip* to any control. When you place your cursor on a control, textual help resembling a tooltip is displayed with a yellow background. You can create a control tip by entering text into the ControlTip Text property of any control. Whatever you enter into this property is displayed when you place the cursor on a control and leave it there for about a second.

Running a macro automatically when you start Access

After you create the switchboard, a menu bar, and the associated submenus and toolbars, you may want Access to open the form automatically every time you open the database. You can do this in one of two ways. In Access 2.0 the only way was to create a macro named AutoExec that performed the necessary actions. You can still do this, but there is a better way in Access 95 and 97. To create an AutoExec macro to open the switchboard automatically, follow these steps:

1. Create a new macro (you'll name it AutoExec later).
2. Type **Minimize** (or select the action) in the next empty Action cell.
3. Type **OpenForm** (or select the action) in the next empty Action cell.
4. Type **Mountain Switchboard** (or select the switchboard form name) in the Form Name cell in the Action Arguments pane.

Save the macro with the name AutoExec. After you do so, Access will run the macro automatically every time you open the database.

The AutoExec macro shows two actions. The Minimize action minimizes the Database window; the OpenForm action opens the switchboard.

Tip

To bypass an AutoExec macro, simply hold down the Shift key while selecting the database name from the Access <u>F</u>ile menu.

Controlling options when starting Access

Rather than run a macro to open a form when Access starts, you can use the new Access 97 start-up form to control many options when you start Access. This includes setting the following options:

✦ Changing the text on the title bar

✦ Specifying an icon to use when Access is minimized

✦ Global custom menu bar

✦ Global custom shortcut menu bar

✦ Global custom toolbar

✦ Display a form on startup (for example, AutoExec macros)

✦ Control the display of default menus, toolbars, the Database window, and the status bar

Figure 32-32 shows the Access 97 Startup dialog box. You can display this by selecting Tools⇨Startup or by right-clicking on the border of the Database window and selecting Startup.

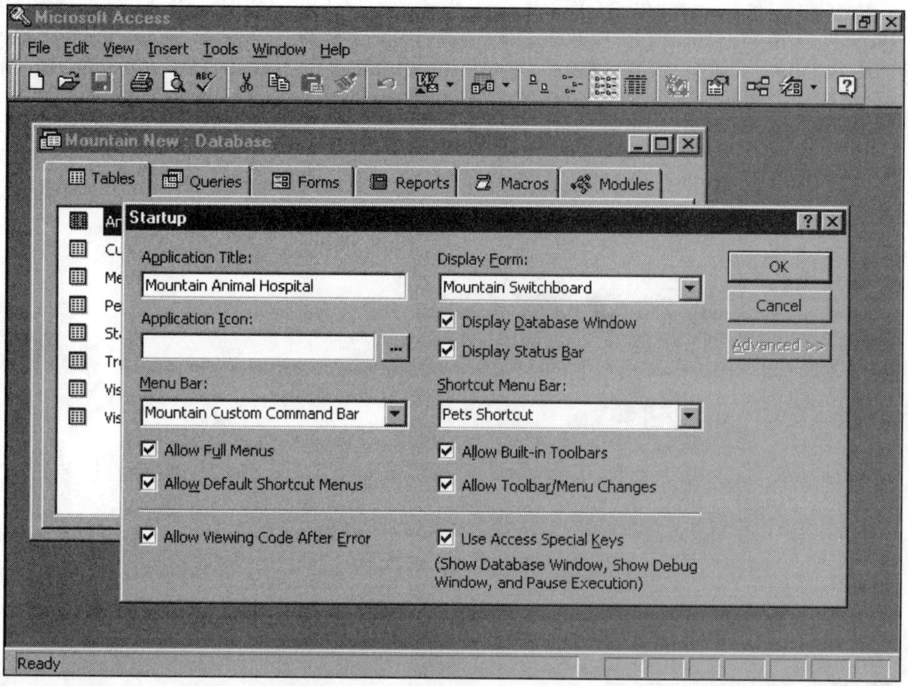

Figure 32-32: The Startup options window.

When you click on the Advanced> button, you can set additional options. These include the following:

✦ Whether to display a code screen after untrapped VBA errors

✦ Whether the special Access keys are enabled to view the Database or Code windows

✦ Whether the special Access keys are enabled to pause execution of a VBA program

Tip   This button replaces both the AutoExec macros and items formerly used in the Access 2.0 INI file.

Creating a Print Report Dialog Box Form and Macros

A dialog box is also a form, but it is unlike a switchboard; the dialog box usually displays information, captures a user entry, or lets the user interact with the system. In this section, you create a complex dialog box that prints reports and labels.

By using a form and some macros, you can create a dialog box that controls printing of your reports. This dialog box can even display a list of pets and their owners (see Figure 32-33), so you can print only a single page of the Pets Directory without having to change the query.

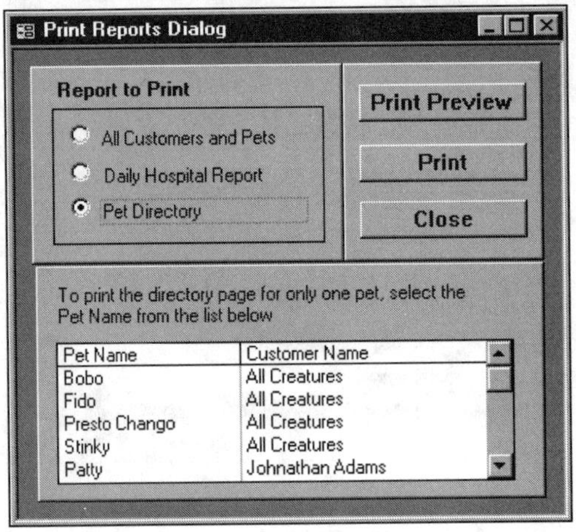

Figure 32-33: A Print Reports dialog box.

Although this dialog box is more complex than a switchboard, it uses the same types of Access objects, which include the following:

✦ Forms

✦ Form controls and properties

✦ Macros

Creating a form for a macro

The form you use in this example displays the various controls. There are three basic sections to the form.

The upper-left corner of the form contains three option buttons, which are placed within an option group. The option buttons let you select one of the three listed reports. Each of the reports is already created and can be seen in the Database window. If you select All Customers and Pets or the Daily Hospital Report, you can print or preview that report. If you select Pet Directory, as shown in Figure 32-33, you see a list box of pets and their owners. You can then choose a pet name for a printout from the Pet Directory report for only that one pet. If you don't choose a pet name, records for all pets are printed from the Pet Directory report.

The upper-right corner of the form contains three buttons. Each button runs a different macro in the Print Report macro library. The first option button, Print Preview, runs a macro that opens the selected report in a Print Preview window. The second option button, Print, runs a macro that will print the selected report to the default printer. The last button, Close, simply closes the form without printing any reports.

To create a form for your macro, first create a blank form and size it properly. Follow these steps:

1. Create a new blank form unbound to any table or query.

2. Resize the form to $3\frac{1}{2}$ inches × 3 inches.

3. Change the Back color to dark gray.

Three rectangles are placed on the form to give it a distinctive look. You can create the three rectangles (as shown in Figure 32-33) by following these steps:

1. Click on the Rectangle button in the Toolbox.

2. Using Figure 32-33 as a guide, create three separate rectangles.

   Each rectangle in this example is shown with the Raised special effect. To create this effect, follow these steps:

3. Select a rectangle.

4. Change the Back color to light gray.

5. Click on the Raised special-effect button in the Special Effect window.

6. Click on the Transparent button in the Border Color window.

7. Repeat Steps 3 through 6 for the second and third rectangles.

   Finally, to enhance the Raised special effect, drag each rectangle away from the adjacent rectangles so that the darker background of the form shows between the rectangle borders. You may need to resize one of the rectangles to line up the edges.

Creating the option group

After you create the form and the special effects, you can then create the necessary controls.

The first set of controls is the option group. In Chapter 19, you learned how to use the Option Group Wizard to create option buttons. To create the option group and option buttons, follow the steps given here and use Figure 32-34 as a guide. In this example, the option group buttons are not bound to a field; they are used to select the dialog box, not to enter data:

1. Click on the Option Group button in the Toolbox, making sure that the Control Wizard icon is on.

2. Draw an option-group rectangle within the upper left rectangle, as shown in Figure 32-34.

3. Enter **All Customers and Pets**, **Daily Hospital Report**, and **Pet Directory** as three separate labels in the first Option Group Wizard.

4. Click on the Finish button to go to the last Wizard screen.

   Your option buttons and the option group appear in the first rectangle. You may need to move or resize the option group's box to fit properly.

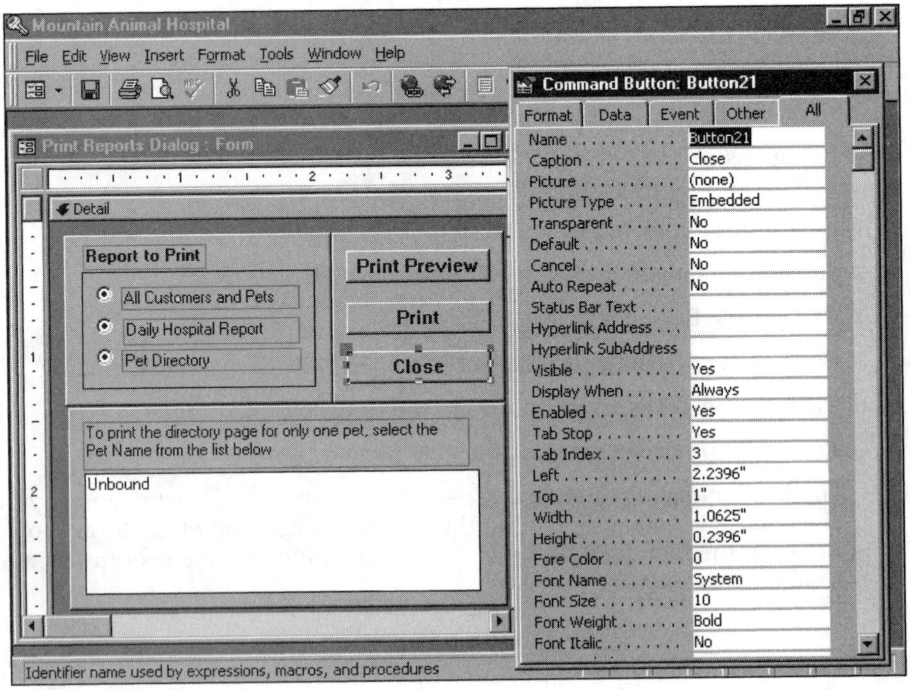

Figure 32-34: The Print dialog box in Design view.

Creating command buttons

After you complete the option group and the option buttons, you can create the command buttons. These pushbuttons trigger the actions for your dialog box. As you can see in Figure 32-34, there are three buttons:

Print Preview   Displays the selected report in the Print Preview window

Print   Prints the selected report to the default print device

Close   Closes the dialog box

To create each command button, follow the next set of steps. Because each button will be the same size, you will duplicate the second and third buttons from the first:

1. Turn the Wizard off; then Click on the command button in the Toolbox.

2. Create the first command button, as shown in Figure 32-34.

3. Select Edit⇨Duplicate to duplicate the first command button.

4. Move the button, as shown in Figure 32-34.

5. Select Edit⇨Duplicate to duplicate the second command button.

6. You may need to move the button into position as shown in Figure 32-34.

   You now need to change the command button captions. The remaining steps show how to make these changes.

7. Select the first command button and change the Caption property to **Print Preview.**

8. Select the second command button and change the Caption property to **Print**.

9. Select the third command button and change the Caption property to **Close**.

Creating a list box on the print report form

The last control you need in the dialog box is the list box that displays the pet name and customer name when the Pet Directory option button is clicked on. To create the list box, follow these steps, using Figure 32-35 as a guide. In this example, you'll create the list box without using the Wizard:

1. Click on the list box button in the Toolbox. Make sure that the Control Wizard icon is off.

2. Using Figure 32-35 as a guide, create the list box rectangle.

3. Move the label control to a position above the list box.

4. Resize the label control so that the bottom right corner is just above the list box, as shown in Figure 32-35.

5. Using the formatting windows, change the Back color of the label to light gray to match the background of the bottom rectangle.

6. Change the Caption property for the list box by clicking on the label of the field (the caption in the label itself) and typing **To print the directory page for only one pet, select the Pet Name from the list below**. The text in the label will wrap automatically as you type.

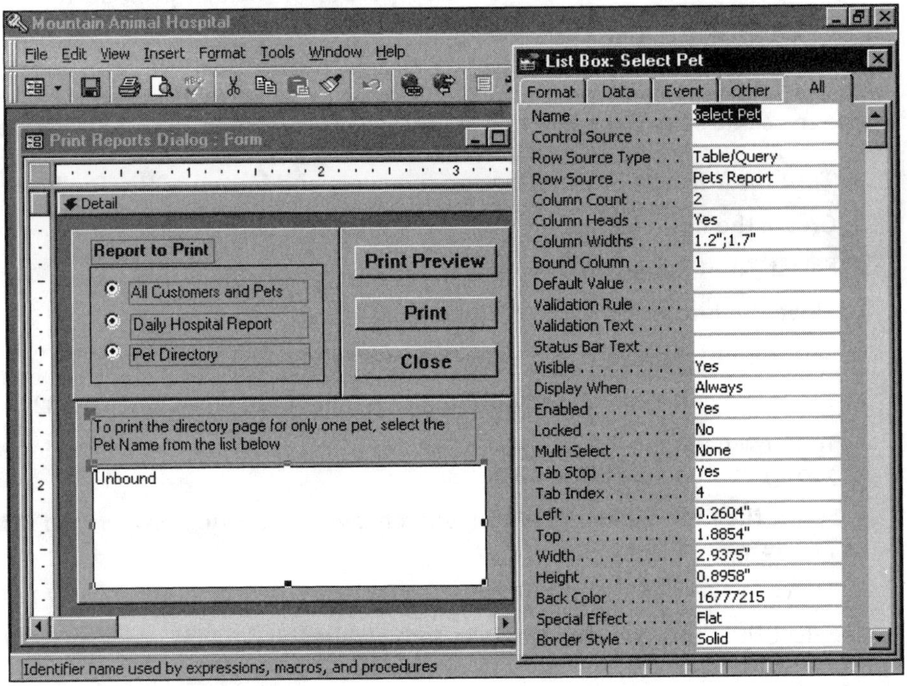

Figure 32-35: The list box definition on the form.

After the list box and label are created, you must define the columns of the list box. To define the columns and data source for the list box, follow these steps, using Figure 32-35 as a guide:

1. Change the Name property to **Select Pet**.

2. Make sure that the Row Source Type indicates **Table/Query.**

3. Change the Row Source to **Pets Report.**

4. Change the Column Count to **2.**

Note The Pets Report must be created before you try to run this form. The Pets Report is a simple query that requires an interesting technique to create (see the following sidebar, "The Pets Report query for the Print Reports form list box," for more information).

5. Change Column Heads to **Yes.**

6. Change the Column Widths to **1.2**, **1.7**.

7. Make sure that the Bound Column property indicates **1**.

Before continuing, you should save the form. Save the file but leave the form on-screen by selecting the menu option File⇨Save. Name the form **Print Reports Dialog Box**.

When the form is completed, you are halfway done. The next task is to create each of the macros you need and create the macro library. When you complete that task, you can add the macros to the correct event properties in the form.

Creating the print macros

As you've learned, macros are attached to the events of controls or objects. These events include entering, exiting, updating, or selecting a control. In this example, macros are attached to several controls and objects. Table 32-3 shows the macros you create for this example and how they will run.

Table 32-3
Macros for the Print Reports Form

Macro Name	Attached to Control/Object	Attached to Property	Description
Show List	Form	On Open	Displays list box if the third option button is on
Show List	Option group	After Update	Displays list box if the third button is selected
Print Preview	Print preview	On Click	Displays selected report in print-preview mode when Print Preview button is selected
Print	Print button	On Click	Prints selected report if Print button is selected
Close	Close button	On Click	Closes form if Close button is selected

The Pets Report query for the Print Reports form list box

The Pets Report is a simple query that has the Customer and Pets tables related by the Customer Number field. The query has two fields displayed: Pet Name from the Pets table and Customer Name from the Customer table. The data is sorted first by Customer Number and second by Pet Name. Figure 32-36 shows the partial datasheet for this list box.

You can see in Figure 32-36 that the Pet Name field is in the first column and the Customer Name field is in the second column. The data is sorted first by the customer number and second by the pet name. As you learned previously, to sort data by two fields, you must place the fields in the Query Design window in the order in which you want the two fields sorted. To sort by the customer number first and then by the pet name, you must place the Customer Number field first in the query but not select it. You then place the Customer Name field third in the query and select it. The query would place Customer Name first in the datasheet. The query design after it is saved and reopened is shown in Figure 32-37. Remember, Access will rearrange fields when a field is not selected to be viewed by unchecking the Show check box.

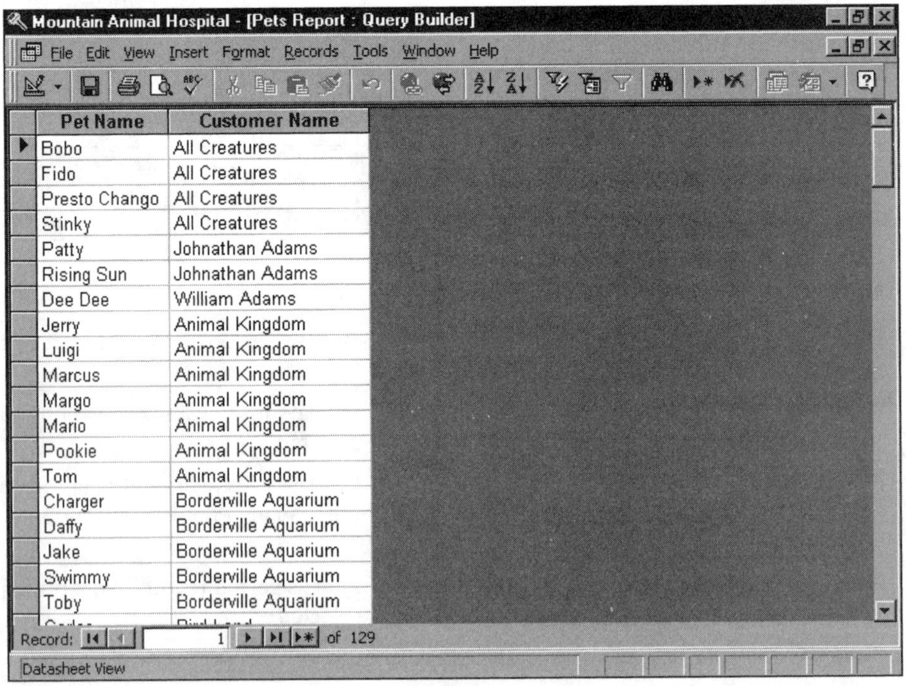

Figure 32-36: The partial datasheet for the Pets Report query.

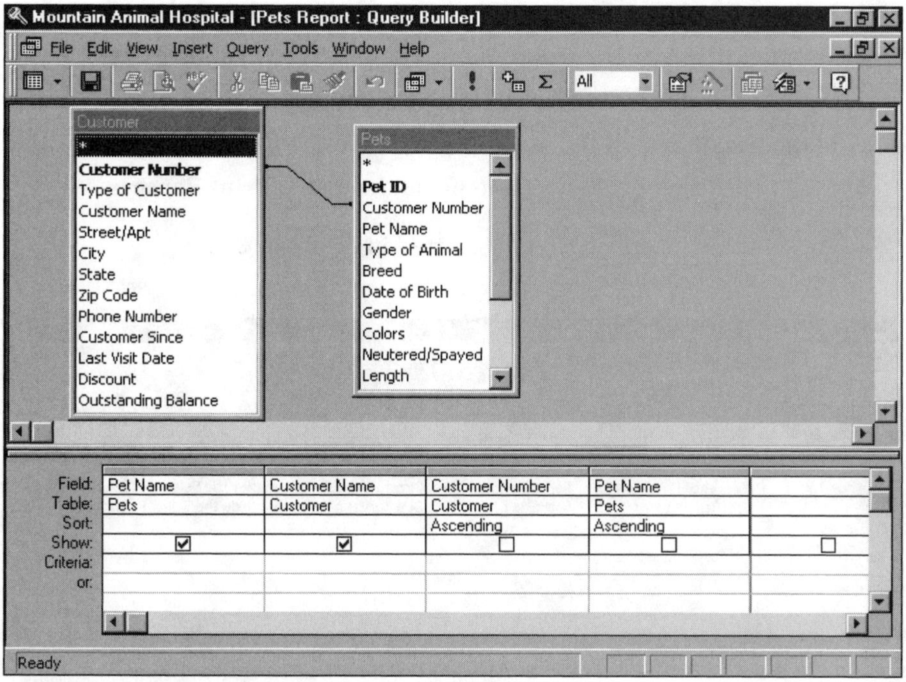

Figure 32-37: The query design for the Pets Report list box.

Creating the Print macro library

In the preceding two chapters, you learned that creating a macro library is the same as creating any macro. You can create this macro library by following these steps:

1. From the Form window toolbar, click on the New Object icon and select New Macro to create a new macro.

2. Select View➪Macro Names or click on the Macro Names button on the toolbar to display the Macro Names column.

3. Select View➪Conditions or click on the Conditions button on the toolbar to display the Condition column.

As you may recall, the Macro Names and Conditions menu options add two columns to the basic Macro window. You will use these columns to enter more parameters into the macro. The Macro Name column is used for creating the individual macro entry points in a macro library. The Condition column determines whether the action in the Action column should be run (on the basis of the conditions). To create the macro, follow these steps:

1. In the third row of the Macro Name column, type **Show List**.

2. In the sixth row of the Macro Name column, type **Print Preview**.

3. In the ninth row of the Macro Name column, type **Print**.

4. In the twelfth row of the Macro Name column, type **Close**.

5. Select File⇨Save As/Export and name the macro **Print Reports**.

You can see these macros correctly created in Figure 32-38.

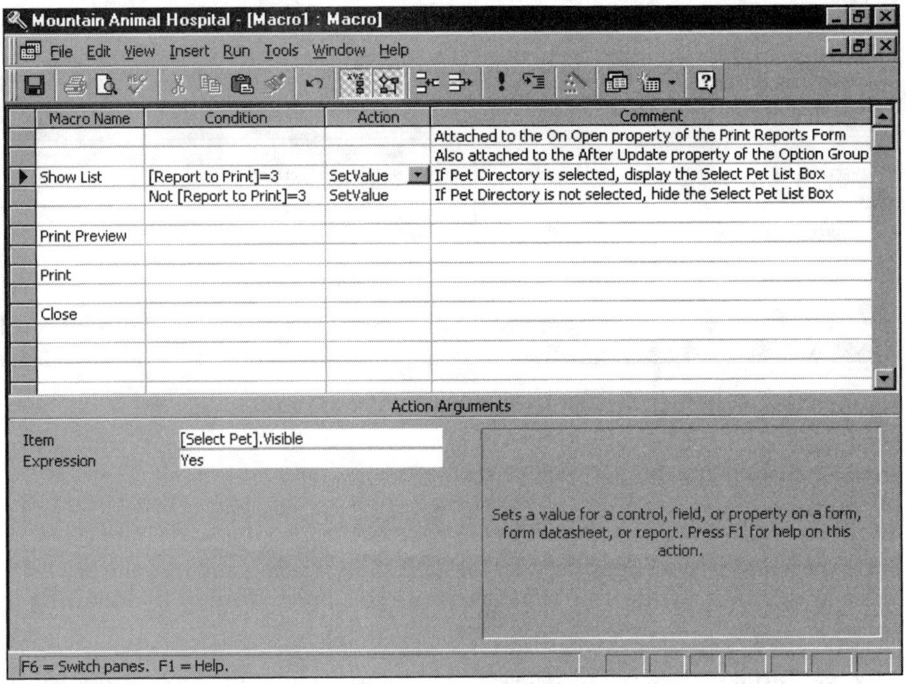

Figure 32-38: Creating the Show List macro and the Print Reports macro group.

Creating the Show List macro

The Show List macro either displays or hides the list box that lists the pet names and customer names. This macro uses the SetValue macro command to run from either the form object or the option group control. The SetValue macro command lets you set a property of a control in the form. In this example, the list box is named Select Pet. The Visible action argument is set to Yes to display the list box or No to hide the list box.

There will need to be two conditions for the Show List macro. The first condition holds if the third option button has been clicked on; the second condition holds if the button has not been clicked on. The Macro Name column has already been set to Show List.

In the first line of the Show List macro, you will set the Condition column to [Report to Print]=3 to reflect the third option button being clicked on in the option group. This line will display the list box, so the action of the macro is set to SetValue, the Item action argument is set to [Select Pet].Visible, and the Expression action argument is set to Yes. Figure 32-38 displays these settings.

You can also see the second line of the Show List macro and comments in Figure 32-38. Notice in the second line that the Condition column indicates that the third option button in the option group has not been clicked on and is therefore set to Not [Report to Print]=3. This line will hide the list box, so the action of the macro is SetValue, the Item property is set to [Select Pet].Visible, and the Expression property is set to No. To create the macro, follow these steps:

1. Type the first two lines in the Comment column, as shown at the top of Figure 32-38.

2. Move the cursor to the first line of the Show List macro row.

3. Place the cursor in the Condition column and type **[Report to Print]=3**.

4. Place the cursor in the Action column and either select or type **SetValue**.

5. Press F6 to move to the Item property in the Action Arguments pane and type **[Select Pet].Visible**.

6. Move to the Expression property and type **Yes**.

7. Press F6 to return to the Action column and then move to the Comments column.

8. Enter the comments in the Comment column, as shown in Figure 32-38.

9. Move your cursor to the second line of the Show List macro row.

10. In the Condition column, type **Not [Report to Print]=3**.

11. In the Action column, type (or select) **SetValue**.

12. Press F6 to move to the Item box in the Action Arguments pane and type **[Select Pet].Visible**.

13. Move to the Expression property and type **No**.

14. Press F6 to return to the Action column and then move to the Comment column.

15. Enter the comments in the Comment column, as shown in Figure 32-38.

When you complete the Show List macro, you can enter the calls to the macro in the form events properties. After this task is completed, you can test the macro. Before continuing, select File⇨Save to save the Print Reports macro library and leave it open on screen.

Entering the Show List macro calls

You are now ready to enter the macro calls for the Show List macro. This macro is called from two places:

✦ The On Open property of the form object

✦ The After Update property of the option group control

As you've learned, these properties are found in the property sheet of the form. To enter the two macro calls, follow these steps:

1. From the Print Reports Macro window, select Window⇨2 Print Reports Dialog: Form.

2. Make sure that the Property window is displayed. If not, click on the Properties button on the toolbar.

3. Display the form's Property window by clicking on the gray square next to the intersection of both form rulers.

4. Enter **Print Reports.Show List** in the On Open property of the Form property sheet.

5. Click on the Option Group control.

6. Enter **Print Reports.Show List** in the After Update property of the Option Group property sheet, as shown in Figure 32-39.

You can test this macro by clicking on the Form View button on the toolbar. As you click on the first and second option buttons, the list box should become invisible. When you select the third option button, the list box should appear. Return to the Design window before continuing.

Creating the Print Preview macro

The Print Preview macro is the next macro you need to create. You can switch to the Macro window by selecting Window⇨3 Print Reports:Macro. This macro is fairly complicated, although it uses only three different macro commands. As you enter the macro commands, you may need to add more lines to the Macro window. Select Insert⇨Row whenever you need to add a new row to the Macro window.

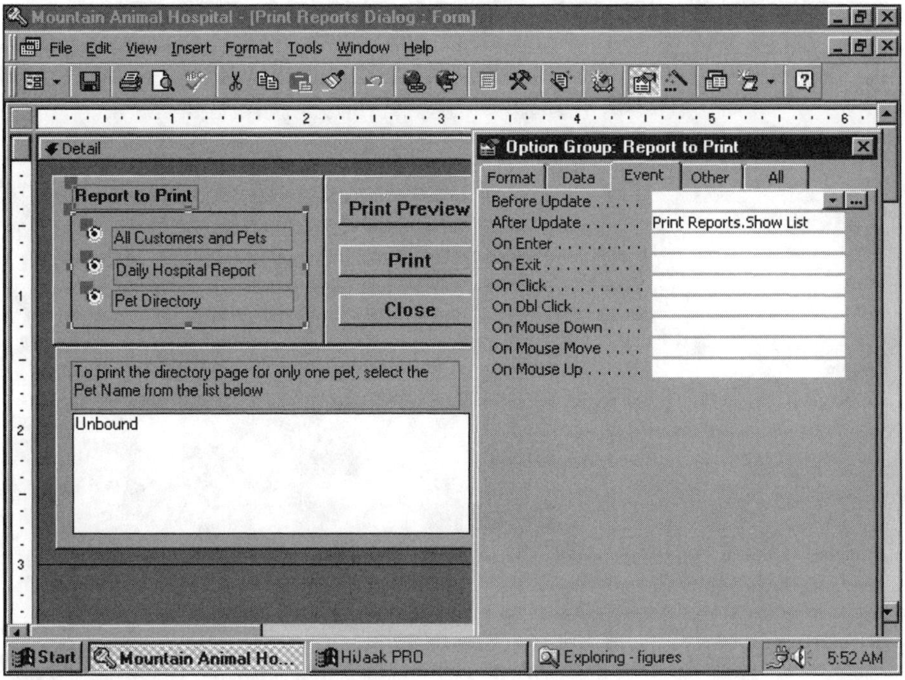

Figure 32-39: Entering the macro call.

Note

You must first select a row to add a new row.

Figure 32-40 shows the completed Print Preview, Print, and Close macros in the Macro window. You can enter all the comments and create the first macro row by following these steps:

1. Type all the lines in the Comment column, as shown in Figure 32-40.

2. Move the cursor to the first line of the Print Preview macro row.

3. In the Action column, type (or select) **SetValue**.

4. Press F6 to move to the Item property of the Action Arguments pane and type **Visible**.

5. Move to the Expression box in the Action Arguments pane and type **No**.

Because no control is specified, it defaults to the form itself. This will hide the entire Form window when the Print Reports macro is started.

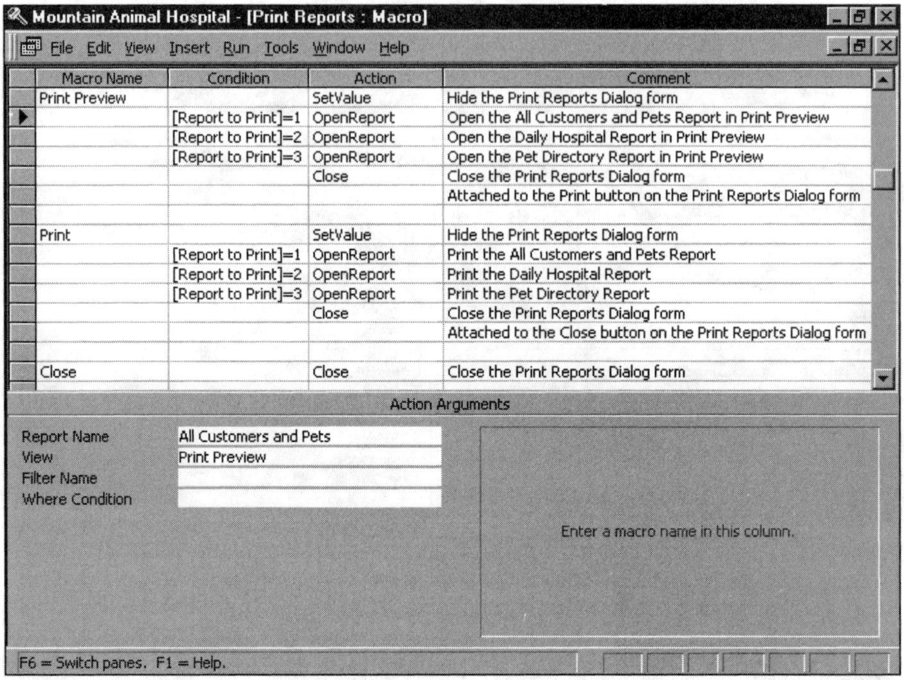

Figure 32-40: Creating the Print Preview macro.

The next three lines of the macro determine the actions to be taken when the Print Preview button is selected for each of the possible option button choices. The first two choices simply display the selected report in a print preview mode. The third choice displays a report by selecting the pet name chosen from the list box. To create the next row, follow these steps:

1. Move your cursor to the second row of the Print Preview macro.

2. In the Condition column, type **[Report to Print]=1**.

3. In the Action column, type (or select) **OpenReport**.

   The OpenReport macro command opens the report specified in the Action Arguments pane of the Macro window.

4. Press F6 to move to the Report Name box in the Action Arguments pane of the Print Preview macro and type **All Customers and Pets**.

5. Move to the View box in the Action Arguments pane and type **Print Preview**.

6. Press F6 to return to the Action column.

These action arguments specify to open the report named All Customers and Pets in a Print Preview window. The second Print row of the Print Preview macro is very similar to the first, except that you must reference the second option button being selected. To create the next row, follow these steps:

1. Move the cursor to the third row of the Print Preview macro.
2. In the Condition column, type **[Report to Print]=2**.
3. In the Action column, type (or select) **OpenReport**.
4. Press F6 to move to the Report Name box in the Action Arguments pane and type **Daily Hospital Report**.
5. Move to the View box in the Action Arguments pane and type **Print Preview**.
6. Press F6 to return to the Action column.

The third OpenReport row contains an extra action argument that the first two rows do not use. The Pet Directory report must use the results of the list box selection to determine whether to print the entire Pets Directory report or print only the report for the specific pet selected. To create the next row, follow these steps:

1. Move the cursor to the fourth row of the Print Preview macro and insert a row.
2. In the Condition column, type **[Report to Print]=3**.
3. In the Action column, type (or select) **OpenReport**.
4. Press F6 to move to the Report Name box in the Action Arguments pane and type **Pet Directory**.
5. Move to the View box in the Action Arguments pane and type **Print Preview**.
6. Move to the Where Condition box and type the following:

   =IIF(Forms![Print Reports Dialog]![Select Pet]Is Null,"","[Pet Name] = Forms![Print Reports Dialog]![Select Pet]")

The Where Condition specifies the condition when the pet name is selected. The condition has two parts. The first part of the IIF function handles the condition when no pet name is selected, and it forms the object hierarchy. The hierarchy is as follows:

Object	Forms
Form name	Print Reports Dialog box
Control name	Select Pet (the list box)
Selection	Is Null

Note

Each of the hierarchy objects is separated by an exclamation mark (!).

If there is no selection, all the pet records are used. The second half of the IIF function is used when a pet name is selected. The second half of the function sets the value of Pet Name to the value chosen in the list box control.

Creating the Print macro

You can create all the macro code for the Print macro by copying each line from the Print Preview macro. Then substitute **Print** for Print Preview in the View box of the Action Arguments pane for each OpenReport action.

Creating the Close macro

The Close macro simply uses Close for the action. Enter **Form** for the Object Type and **Print Reports Dialog** for the Action Arguments object name.

Entering the Print Preview, Print, and Close macro calls

You use the command buttons to trigger an action. Each uses the On Click property. To enter the three macro calls, follow these steps:

1. From the Print Reports Macro window, select Window⇨2 Form: Print Reports Dialog.

2. Make sure that the property sheet is displayed. If not, click on the Properties button on the toolbar.

3. Display the Print Preview command button property by clicking on the Print Preview button.

4. Enter **Print Reports.Print Preview** in the On Click property of the button's property sheet, as shown in Figure 32-41.

5. Display the Print command button property sheet by clicking on the Print button.

6. Enter **Print Reports.Print** in the On Click property of the button's property sheet.

7. Display the Close command button property sheet by clicking on the Close button.

8. Enter **Print Reports.Close** into the On Click property of the button's property sheet.

Sizing the dialog box and changing form properties

The last step in creating a dialog box is to change the Form window properties and size and place the window. You need to set several form properties. Properties and their explanations are listed in Table 32-4.

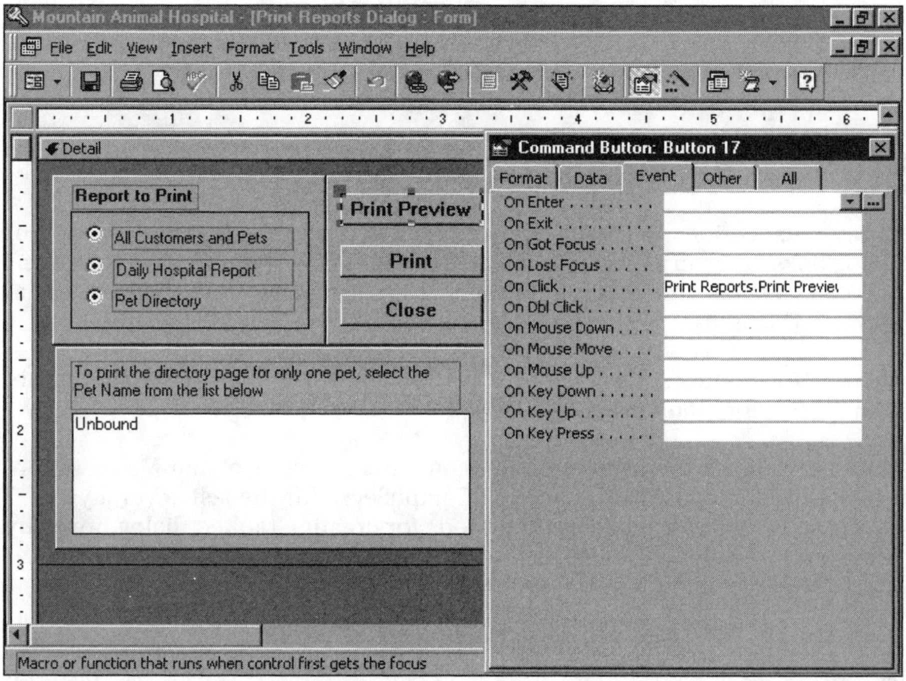

Figure 32-41: Entering the Print Preview macro call into the command button's property sheet.

Table 32-4
Properties for a Form Dialog Box

Property	Value	Description
Default View	Single Form	Displays the form as a single form; necessary for forms that take up less than half a page
Views Allowed	Form	User cannot switch into datasheet mode
Scroll Bars	Neither	(Scroll bars should be omitted in a dialog box)
Navigation Buttons	No	Record navigation buttons are not displayed
Record Selectors	No	Does not display standard record selectors at the bottom left of the form
Auto Resize	Yes	Automatically resizes the form when opened
Auto Center	Yes	Automatically centers the form when opened
Border Style	Dialog	Makes border nonsizable
Pop Up	Yes	Allows the form to be displayed on top of other windows as a pop-up dialog box
Modal	Yes	User must make a choice before leaving the dialog box

You should set the Pop Up property to No if the dialog box will call any other windows. If this property is set to Yes, the dialog box is always displayed on top; you can't get to other windows without first closing the dialog box.

Using the Access 97 Tab Control

Today, most serious Windows applications contain tabbed dialog boxes. Tabbed dialog boxes are very professional looking. They allow you to have many screens of data in a small area by grouping similar types of data and using tabs to navigate between the areas.

Access 97 introduces a native (built-in) Tab control similar to one that has been in Visual Basic for many years.

Note Access 2.0 and 95 themselves do not contain a Tab control, but Microsoft provided a free .OCX Tab control, available on CompuServe for the last several years. There have also been several different methods for creating tabbed dialog boxes by just using lines, rectangles, and either command buttons or even label controls.

Creating a new form with the Access 97 Tab control

The Access 97 Tab control has been added to the standard Form Design toolbar. This control is called a Tab control because it looks like the tabs on a file folder when you use it. Figure 32-42 shows the Access 97 Form Design window with the toolbar showing the Tab control icon and a Tab control already under construction on the design screen.

In this example, you will create another Print Reports Dialog form that will contain a tabbed dialog box that will show a larger view of the Pet Directory so you can see more data.

You create a new Tab control the way you create any Access control. You select the Tab control as shown in the figure above and then draw a rectangle to indicate the size of the control. When the Tab control is initially shown it is displayed with two tab pages.

The Tab control contains pages. Each tab you define creates a separate page. As you choose each tab in Design view, you see a different page. You can place other controls on each page of the Tab control. The control can have many pages. In fact, you can have multiple rows of tabs each having their own page. You can place new controls onto a page or copy and paste them from other forms or other pages. You cannot drag and drop between pages of a Tab control. To change the active page for the Tab control, click on the page you want; it will become active (even in design mode).

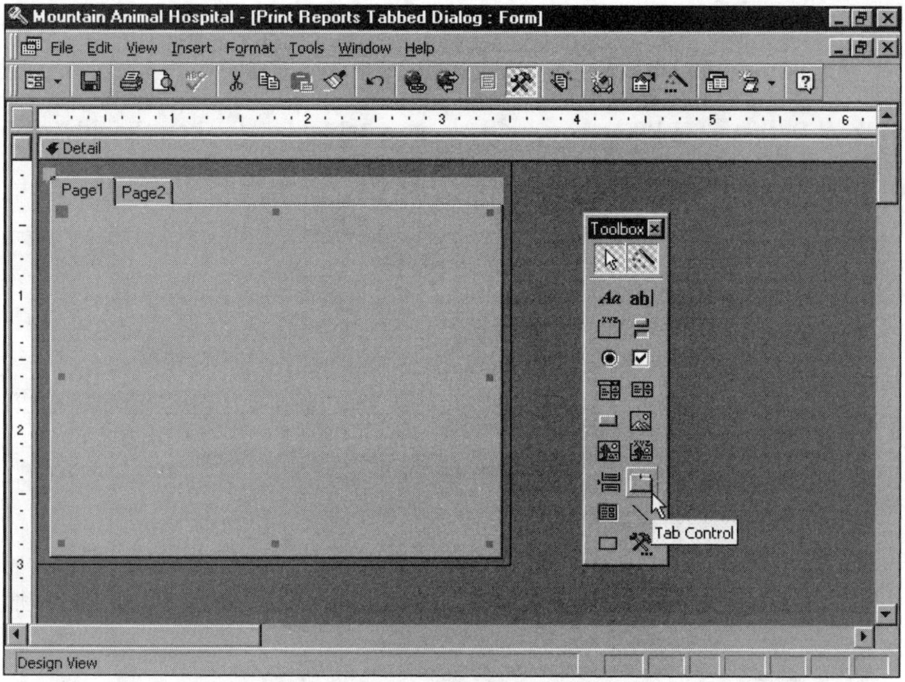

Figure 32-42: Creating an Access 97 Tab control.

You insert new pages by selecting the Insert⇨Tab Control Page option or by right-clicking on a tab and choosing the Insert command. The new page is inserted before the selected page. You delete pages by selecting a tab and pressing the Delete key or by choosing the Edit⇨Delete menu option or by right-clicking on a tab and selecting the Delete command.

Caution
This deletes the active page and all the controls on it.

You can size the Tab control but not individual pages. Individual pages don't have visual appearance properties — they get these from the Tab control itself. You can click on the border of the Tab control to select it. You can click directly on a page to select that page. As with an Access detail section, you cannot size the Tab control smaller than the control in the rightmost part of the page.

Tip
You must move controls before resizing.

Tip For this example, you can copy all the controls from the original Print Report Dialog except the List Box and its caption and paste them on Page1 of the Tab control. Copy and paste the List Box control and its caption to Page2 of the Tab control. Remember, you move between tab pages by simply clicking on the tab — even in Form Design view. When you are done, your tabbed dialog box should look like Figure 32-43.

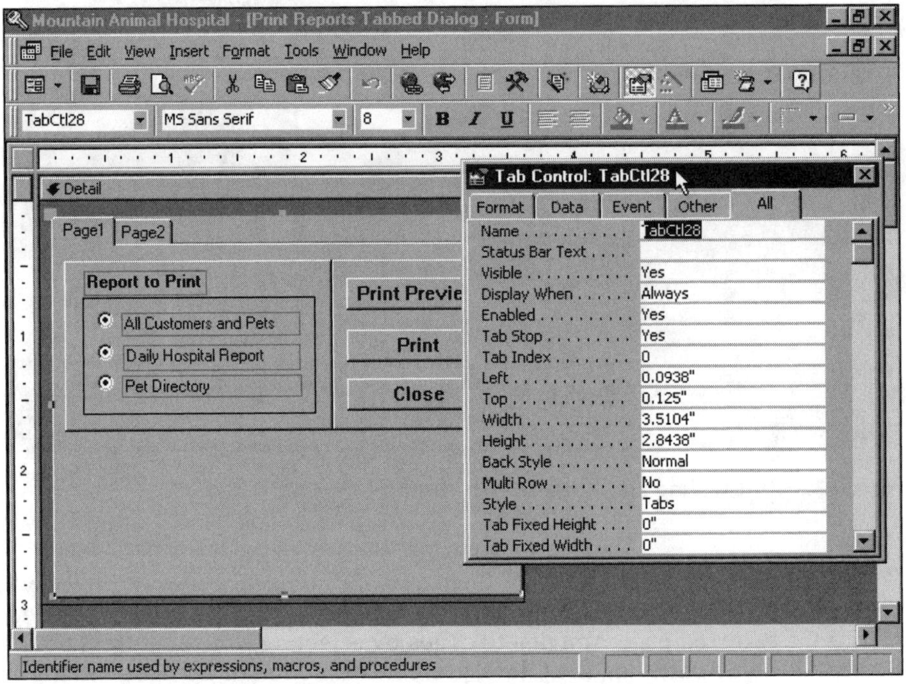

Figure 32-43: Tab control properties.

Access 97 Tab control properties

Like any control, the Tab control has a variety of properties. The Tab control has a separate set of properties for the Tab control itself as well as for each page of the Tab control. Figure 32-43 shows the Property window for the Tab control itself. Notice that there is no Control Source property. The Tab control is only a container for other controls. The form itself can be bound to a table or query, and each control you place on a tab page can be bound to a table field, but the Tab control and its pages cannot be bound by themselves to a data source.

The Tab control itself has many properties found in most controls, such as a Name, Status Bar Text, Visible, Enabled, Tab Stop, and the position and size properties. The Tab control also has several unique properties. Notice the last four properties in the Property window. These the properties are found only in Tab control.

Working with a number of rows

The first unique property is Multi Row. This is either Yes or No. The default is No. When you change the value to Yes and you have more tabs then will fit in the width of the Tab control, the tabs will jump to a new row (see Figure 32-44). If you make the Tab control wider, the tab may return to a single row. You can create as many rows as you have vertical space. The Tab control itself can be as wide as the form width allows. Figure 32-44 shows one-, two-, and three-row Tab controls. Notice that the middle Tab control has an uneven number of tabs on each row. This is perfectly acceptable; the tabs will grow to fill the available space. The Tab control at the bottom was sized too small to fit the number of tabs and the Multi Row property was set to No. Navigation buttons appear to fill the space.

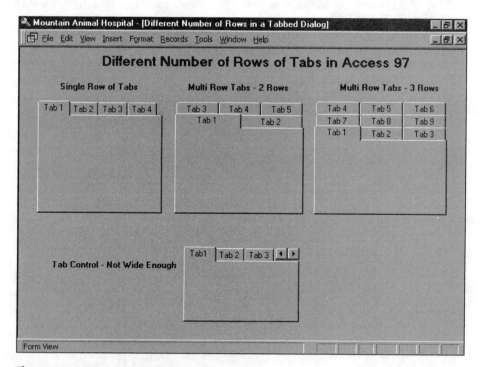

Figure 32-44: Using the Multi Row property.

Setting the height and width of the tabs

Two properties affect the size of the tabs in the Tab control. These are the Tab Fixed Height and Tab Fixed Width properties. The default for both these controls is 0. When the properties are set to 0, each tab is wide enough and tall enough to accommodate its contents. If needed, the width of each tab is increased to span the entire width of the Tab control. If the properties are greater than 0, the tab will be the exact size specified. There is an additional setting. If the Tab Fixed Height or Tab Fixed Width properties are set to –1, then each tab is just wide enough to accommodate its contents, and the tabs will not resize to span the width or height of the control.

The style of a Tab control

The next unique property is the Style property. This has three settings: Tabs, Buttons, and None, as you can see in Figure 32-45. The Tabs setting is the default and creates the standard square tabs. The Buttons setting makes the tabs into buttons, surrounded by a button. The effect shown in Figure 32-45 looks more like the Access 95 Tab Strip control than an actual Tab control and leaves only the buttons and the Tab control set to the first page. You cannot see the rectangle, as with the Tabs setting. The third setting, None, removes the tabs from the Tab control and leaves an empty gray area. When using this setting, the Tab control can act like a multipage form that can be more easily controlled than a standard multipage form because you don't have to worry about navigation from one page to the next.

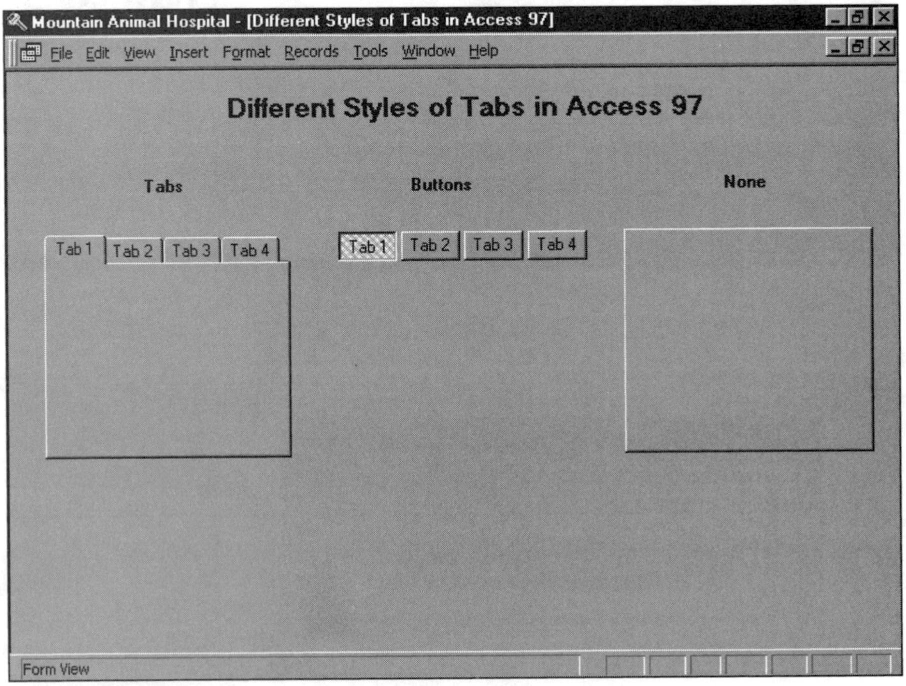

Figure 32-45: Using the Style property.

Changing the page order

Another feature of the Tab control is the ability to change the order of the pages (tabs) in the same way that the tab order of the controls on the form can be changed. Figure 32-46 shows the Page Order dialog box. It lists the text on each tab and lets you use the Move Up and Move Down buttons to rearrange the pages on the Tab control.

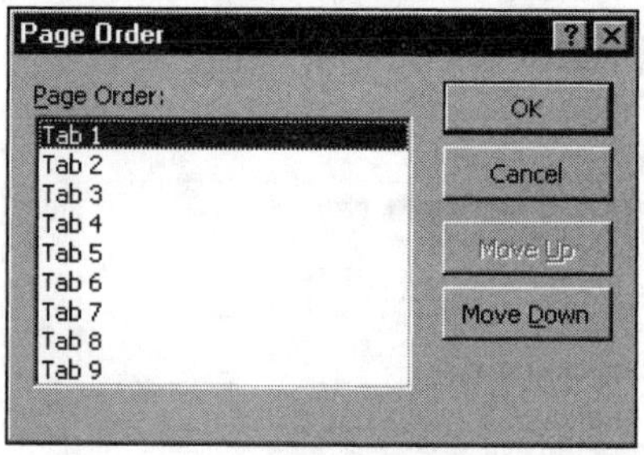

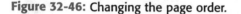

Figure 32-46: Changing the page order.

Using the tab order on a form and the Tab control itself

When you choose View⇨Tab Order, if you have a Tab control on a form, it shows up as a single control in the Tab Order dialog box. The controls inside the Tab control do not show in this dialog box.

To set the tab order for controls within a particular page of a Tab control, choose the Tab Order command from the Tab control's right-click menu or go to the property sheet for the Tab control and click on the builder for the tab index property. You must set the tab order for each page individually.

Tabbing out of the last control inside a Tab control page brings you to the next control in the tab order for the form itself. You cannot jump between pages.

Adding pictures to the Tab control

The page properties of the Tab control have no unique properties, but one of the common properties lets you add a picture to the tab just before the tab text. You use the Picture property just as you would on a command button, toggle button, image control, or unbound OLE object.

You can type the full path and name of the bitmap or icon file or use the Access 97 Picture Builder to select a picture. Figure 32-47 shows the Tab control on the Print Reports Tabbed Dialog with one picture already completed and another being selected. Notice in the figure that the picture of a printer is already beside Page 1. When this picture is selected in the Picture Builder, the document picture will appear next to Page 2.

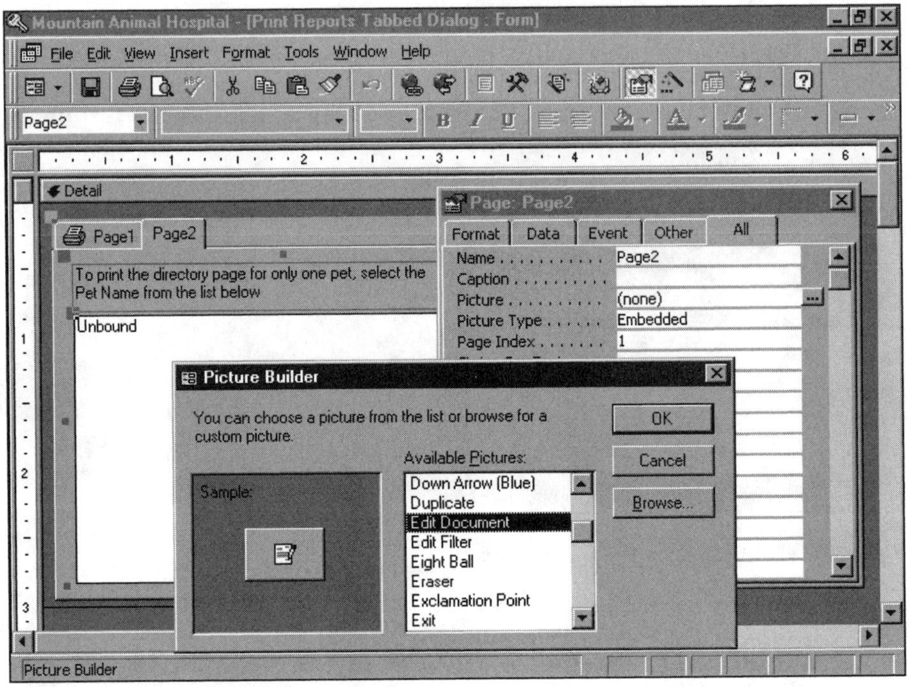

Figure 32-47: Adding a picture to a tab.

Summary

In this chapter, you learned how to create switchboards and dialog boxes by using an Access form. You also learned how to create your own custom menu. The following points were discussed:

✦ Switchboards are forms that usually contain command buttons.

✦ Switchboards are used as menus to help you navigate within your system.

✦ You can create command buttons by using the Toolbox, by dragging a macro onto a form, or by using the Command Button Wizard.

✦ Command buttons trigger macros through several properties.

✦ The best way to create multiple command buttons that are all the same size is by duplicating the first button you created.

✦ You link a command button to a macro by entering the macro name in the proper event (On) property.

✦ You can create macro actions by entering them into the Macro window, selecting them from the Action pull-down menu, or dragging a form or report into a macro's Action cell.

✦ You can have a command button display a picture instead of a text caption by entering the bitmap name into the command button's Picture property or by using the Picture Builder.

✦ Access lets you create custom bar menus through the use of macros.

✦ Each submenu item must be a separate macro. You can specify bar separators and hot keys in a menu.

✦ You can activate a custom bar menu by entering a macro name in the On Menu property of a form or report.

✦ The Access View➪Toobars➪Customize dialog box helps you create a menu.

✦ You can create shortcut menus by using the command bars.

✦ You can create and customize toolbars and use them with Access forms.

✦ You can create a macro that runs automatically when you open a database by naming the macro AutoExec or by using the Startup Properties window.

✦ You can bypass a macro that runs automatically by holding down the Shift key when you open the Database window.

✦ You can create control tips that work like tooltips but can be used with any controls.

✦ A dialog box is nothing more than a form that is used as a pop-up window; usually it contains various controls, such as option buttons, list boxes, and command buttons.

✦ Access 97 contains a Tab control that can be used for multipage forms.

✦ You can set the Access 97 Tab control's style, size, and number of rows.

✦ You can add pictures to a Tab control tab.

✦ A dialog box's pop-up property should be set to No if you are going to open any other windows from the dialog box.

As you have seen in the last chapter, menus, toolbars, and dialog boxes provide powerful uses to navigate your application. In the next chapter, you learn about Access 97 and the Internet.

✦   ✦   ✦

Using the Internet Features of Access 97

The Internet, and particularly the World Wide Web, has become an important part of all businesses today. Whether you simply use the Internet to search for information or are part of a vast corporate intranet, there is a need to be able to use Microsoft Acccess to store and disseminate the data that is moved across the network wire.

Note An *intranet* is a local network that uses HTML technology, such as HTTP or FTP protocols. You can use an intranet much as you use the World Wide Web to store information on home pages and Web sites using the HTML language. Using this technology, you can quickly move between objects, documents, pages, and other destinations by using URL addresses (such as http://www.caryp.com) known as hyperlinks rather than traditional DOS filenames.

Access 97 contains many new features that allow you to store data found on the Internet right within your database container in standard Access tables. You can also create a table, form, or report in Access 97 and save it as an HTML-based table that can be used in any Web site. Using the new Hyperlink data type, you can create Weblike switchboards and specify an Access form or Web site URL to go to when a user presses the right button.

What is HTML?

If you're unfamiliar with HTML, you should make this topic your next learning experience. *HTML,* which stands for HyperText Markup Language, is the language of the Internet. HTML is the universal translator that allows all the different browsers (the two most popular are Microsoft Internet Explorer and Netscape Navigator) to view pages on the World Wide Web. These pages are created using many different tools but ultimately are translated in HTML code. HTML code is simply a prefix known as a tag and some text or numbers. Using Access 97 Internet tools, you can translate Access 97 objects and data into HTML-compatible format.

Using the Web Toolbar with Access 97

Figure 33-1 shows the Access 97 database container with the Web toolbar, which can be turned on by right-clicking on the toolbar and selecting Web or by selecting View➪Toolbars➪Web from any menu. After you have the Web toolbar displayed, you can use it to access Web sites on the Internet or your local intranet. When you use the Web toolbar, you launch the default Web browser on your system.

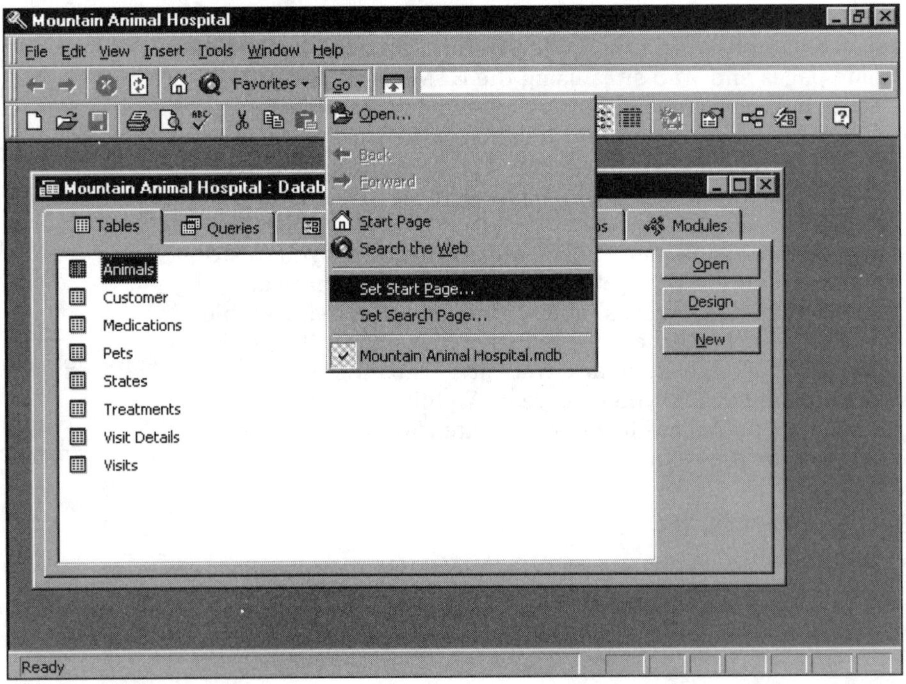

Figure 33-1: The Web toolbar on the Access database container screen.

Note   To take advantage of the Internet features in Access 97, you need a Web browser (such as Microsoft Internet Explorer or Netscape Navigator), a modem, and an intranet connection or other network connection to access the Internet. For access to the World Wide Web, you must purchase services from an Internet provider. You should be able to purchase these services on an unlimited basis for between $9.95 and $19.95 per month.

You can set the default home page by using the Set Start Page... option from the Go menu on the Web toolbar. In Figure 33-1, you can see that the initial URL is `http://www.caryp.com`, the Cary Prague Books and Software home page.

Note   Because this book is about Access 97 and not specifically about the Internet, it is assumed that you own a browser and have some experience visiting Web sites on the World Wide Web.

Easy Publishing to the Web

Many people feel that the process of publishing data to the Web is something to be left to a Webmaster. Access 97 definitely turns this idea into a myth. The Publish to the Web Wizard walks you through the steps of creating the HTML for selected database objects and of placing the generated HTML out on your Web site. You can export data from tables or query dynasets, forms, or reports into HTML.

Suppose that the Mountain Animal Hospital wants to establish a Web site to link its two offices and to allow its more technologically savvy customers to check on their animal's visit history so that they will know the next date for their shots. The hospital could also e-mail notices to its customers.

Using this Wizard, you can create either static or dynamic publications, publish them to the Web, create a home page, and even use templates to obtain a standard look and feel for all your HTML publications!

To start the Publish to the Web Wizard, you go to the Database window and select Save As HTML from the File menu. The Wizard starts as shown in Figure 33-2.

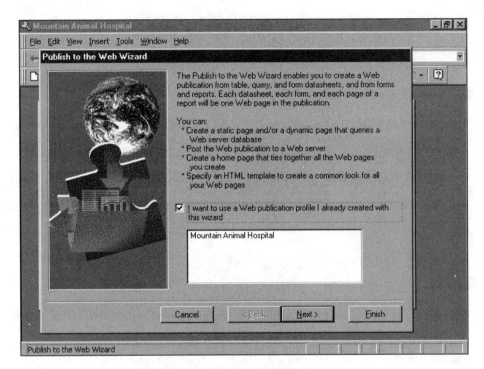

Figure 33-2: The Publish to the Web Wizard introduction screen.

This first screen simply gives you an introduction to the Wizard and allows you to use a previously saved profile, which you have the opportunity to name and save each time you run the Wizard. The Web publication profile is a set of all the selections you made when you used the Wizard. As you can see in the introduction, you can create static pages of data (data at a point in time), or, if you have a Web server, you can create a page that each time it is accessed queries the server for the latest data available. You can also create static or dynamic Web pages of report information as well as create a dynamic form.

Note To create a dynamic query or form page, you must have the Internet Information Server or the new ActiveX server installed at your site.

You also have the opportunity to use the Wizard to create a home page that acts as a switchboard or menu to the other Web pages you create. Finally, you can create an HTML template that specifies a common look for all the Web pages, including backgrounds and common graphics and symbols on each page.

When you are ready, press the Next> button to move to the next Wizard screen.

The second Publish to the Web Wizard screen allows you to select the various objects you want to publish on the Web. As you can see in Figure 33-3, you have the option of selecting any or all of your tables, queries, forms, and reports.

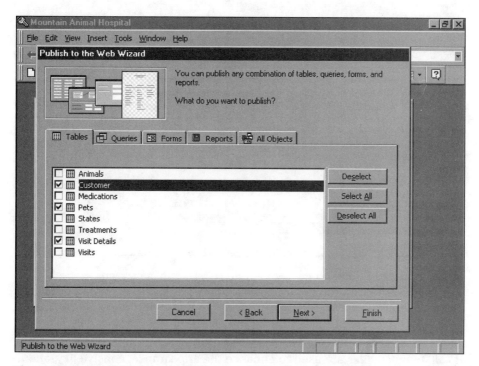

Figure 33-3: The Publish to the Web Wizard object selection screen.

On this screen, you can select as many objects as you want. Later, you can determine the purpose of each object when it is converted to an HTML equivalent. After you have selected the objects to be converted to HTML, you can display the next screen, shown in Figure 33-4.

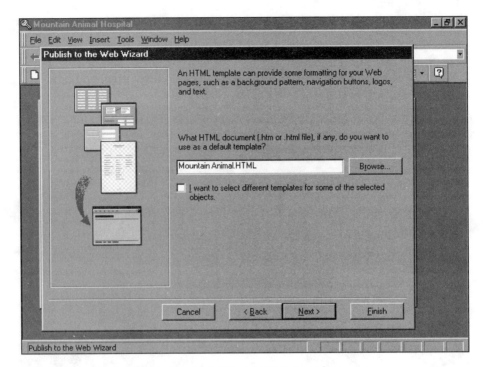

Figure 33-4: The Publish to the Web Wizard HTML template screen.

Using HTML template files

HTML template files are used to enhance the appearance, consistency, and navigation of your World Wide Web application. For example, you may want to include a company logo in the header section, a company-approved background image in the body section, and standard navigation buttons in the footer section of your Web pages.

Tip   If you check the box below the HTML document name, you can then specify a different template for each option you select.

The HTML template can be any text file that includes HTML tags and tokens unique to Access to indicate where to insert data.

When you output a datasheet, form, or report or use the Publish to the Web Wizard and you specify an HTML template file, Access 97 merges the HTML template file with the output files by replacing the tokens with the following:

HTML Template Token	Replacement
<!–AccessTemplate_Title–>	The object name (placed on the title bar of the Web browser)
<!–AcessTemplate_Body–>	The object output
<!–AccessTemplate_FirstPage–>	An anchor tag to the first page
<!–AccessTemplate_PreviousPage–>	An anchor tag to the previous page
<!–AccessTemplate_NextPage–>	An anchor tag to the next page
<!–AccessTemplate_LastPage–>	An anchor tag to the last document page
<!–AccessTemplate_PageNumber–>	The current page number

HTML tags that specify files assume that the files reside in the same folder as the output files created by Access 97. You can specify the folder destination in the Publish to the Web Wizard. If you specify an HTML template file when you output an object to dynamic HTML format, it is merged with the .htx or .asp file during the output operation.

The next screen, shown in Figure 33-5, is very important to what you are actually creating. If you are creating HTML pages from data, you can create either static views of the data (at the point you complete the Wizard) or dynamic views, which change each time the page is accessed as the server is queried.

Understanding dynamic and static views of data

The HTML file format you want to use is based on your application needs. You should use the static HTML format when your data does not change frequently and your World Wide Web application does not require a form. Use dynamic format when your data changes frequently and your Web application needs to store and retrieve live data from your Access 97 database using a form.

How your Web application uses static HTML format

You can create static HTML pages from table, query, and form datasheets and from reports. The resulting HTML files are a snapshot of the data at the time you published your files. If your data changes, you must publish your files again to view the new data in your Web application.

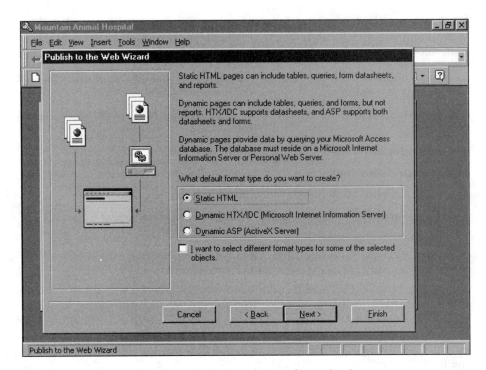

Figure 33-5: The Publish to the Web Wizard page determination screen.

How your Web application uses dynamic IDC/HTX files

When you output an object to IDC/HTX file format rather than an .html file, Access 97 creates an HTML extension file (.htx) and an Internet Database Connector file (.idc). Internet Database Connector (httpodbc.dll) is a component of Microsoft Internet Information Server.

Note   Microsoft Internet Information Server (IDC/HTX files) is the current technology as of December 1996. Starting in early 1997, the Microsoft ActiveX server will become the newer technology. It uses .ASP files.

The .idc file contains a query in the form of an SQL statement and information that Microsoft Internet Information Server uses to connect to an ODBC data source — in this case, an Access 97 database. The connection information includes the data source name and, if user-level security is required to open the database, the user-name and password.

The .htx file is an HTML file that contains formatting tags and instructions and, instead of data, placeholders indicating where to insert the values returned from the query in the .idc file.

After you publish your database and install your Web application, Microsoft Internet Information Server, upon request from a Web browser, opens the Microsoft Access database (using the Microsoft Access Desktop Driver and the .idc file connection information), runs the query in the .idc file to access the data, merges the results and .htx file into one .html file, and then sends the .html file back to the Web browser for display as a Web page.

How your Web application uses dynamic ASP files

When you output an object to dynamic ASP file format, Access 97 creates an ActiveX Server Page (.asp) file instead of an .html file. ActiveX Server is a component of Microsoft Internet Information Server 3.0 or later.

The .asp file contains HTML tags interspersed with one or more queries in the form of SQL statements, template directives, and VBScript code containing references to ActiveX Server Controls. The .asp file also contains ODBC connection information to connect to an ODBC data source — in this case, an Access 97 database. The connection information includes the data source name and, if user-level security is required to open the database, the username and password.

After you publish your database and install your Web application, Microsoft Internet Information Server, upon request from a Web browser, runs the VBScript code, calls the ActiveX Server Controls, opens the Microsoft Access database (using the Microsoft Access Desktop Driver and the .asp file connection information), runs the queries in the .asp file to access the data, merges the results and HTML tags in the .asp file into one .html file, and then sends the .html file back to the Web browser for display as a Web page.

When you use dynamic HTML format files (either IDC/HTX files or ASP files), you need to do the following on a supported Microsoft World Wide Web server to run your Web application:

1. Define either a system or file data source.

2. Either copy the Microsoft Access database to the Web server or define its network location in the ODBC data source definition.

3. Install the Microsoft Access Desktop Driver on the Web server.

4. Ensure that the users of your Web application can log on to the ODBC data source for your Access 97 database.

5. Ensure that the folder containing the .idc or .asp files has the necessary sharing properties, including Execute for Microsoft Internet Information Server and Execute Scripts for Personal Web Server.

Tip
You can use the Publish to the Web Wizard to copy the Access 97 database for you.

The following table summarizes the supported products, platforms, and output files you can use to run your Web application created by Access 97:

Product or Platform	Supported Files
Microsoft Internet Information Server Version 1.x and 2.0 using Internet Database Connector on Windows NT Server Version 3.51	.htm, .html, .idc, .htx
Microsoft Internet Information Server Version 2.0 or later using Internet Database Connector or ActiveX Server on Windows NT Server Version 4.0 or later	.htm, .html, .idc, .htx, .asp
Microsoft Personal Web Server on Windows 95 or later, or on Windows NT Workstation Version 4.0 or later	.htm, .html, .idc, .htx, .asp

Note   After you select either static HTML (for tables and queries) or Dynamic HTX/IDC or Dynamic ASP format, you can press the Next> button to move to a screen (shown in Figure 33-6) that allows you to select the path for the Web objects and whether you want to publish Web objects locally or on an Internet server.

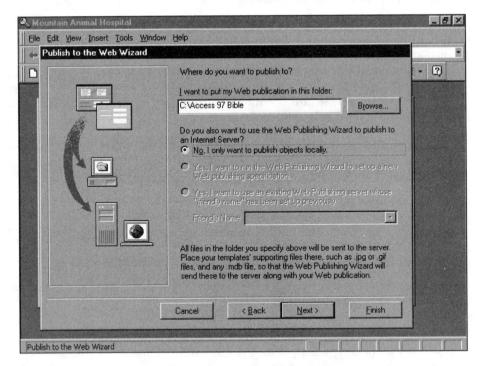

Figure 33-6: The Publish to the Web Wizard publish type screen.

To publish to a Web server, you must have the server installed and recognized by your system.

Note   If your template needs any support files such as compressed icons or graphics (.GIF or .JPG), you must install them in the same directory specified at the top of the screen.

Creating a home page

The next screen (shown in Figure 33-7) lets you create an automatic home page that can link all the published objects together. You simply give it a name, and it is created for you. Of course, you can edit the HTML later and add to it whatever you want.

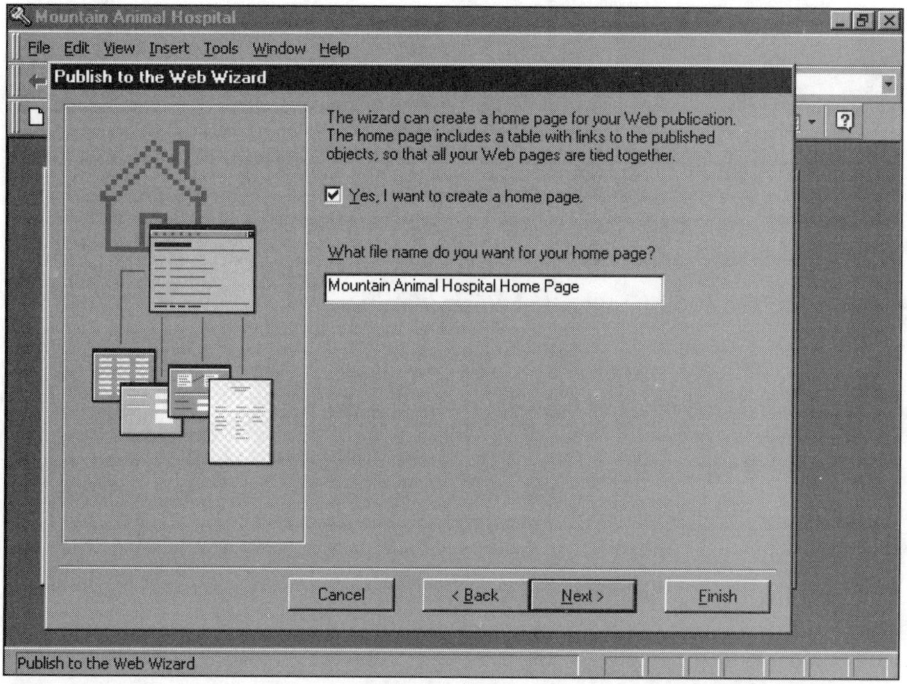

Figure 33-7: The Publish to the Web Wizard screen for creating a home page.

The last screen lets you save all the choices to a new profile, as you saw on the first page of this Wizard (see Figure 33-2). When you check the box, you can enter a new profile. If you use an existing name, the profile is updated, as shown in Figure 33-8.

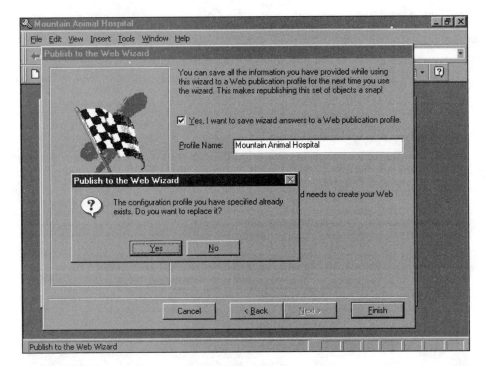

Figure 33-8: The Publish to the Web Wizard final screen.

When you are through, you can display your home page or display any of your other pages you published using the Microsoft Internet Explorer or the browser you use. Figure 33-9 shows the Customer form in Internet Explorer.

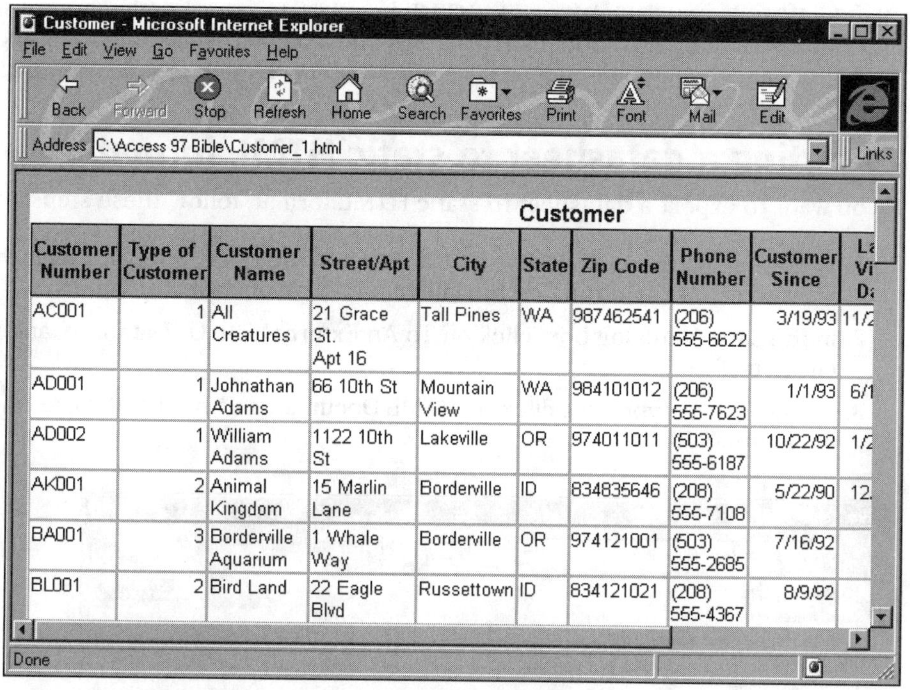

Customer

Customer Number	Type of Customer	Customer Name	Street/Apt	City	State	Zip Code	Phone Number	Customer Since	La Vi Da
AC001	1	All Creatures	21 Grace St. Apt 16	Tall Pines	WA	987462541	(206) 555-6622	3/19/93	11/2
AD001	1	Johnathan Adams	66 10th St	Mountain View	WA	984101012	(206) 555-7623	1/1/93	6/1
AD002	1	William Adams	1122 10th St	Lakeville	OR	974011011	(503) 555-6187	10/22/92	1/2
AK001	2	Animal Kingdom	15 Marlin Lane	Borderville	ID	834835646	(208) 555-7108	5/22/90	12.
BA001	3	Borderville Aquarium	1 Whale Way	Borderville	OR	974121001	(503) 555-2685	7/16/92	
BL001	2	Bird Land	22 Eagle Blvd	Russettown	ID	834121021	(208) 555-4367	8/9/92	

Figure 33-9: The Customer table in Internet Explorer.

Exporting Queries, Forms, and Reports to HTML Format

You have already learned to use the Publish to the Web Wizard by selecting Save As HTML from the File menu. This Wizard outputs one or more datasheets, forms, or reports to static or dynamic HTML format using one or more HTML template files; creates a home page; stores all files to a specified folder as a Web publication; copies the files to the Web server using the Web Publishing Wizard; and saves a Web publication profile to use later. However, you may want to output a single file and not use the Wizard.

You can export individual reports to static HTML format, and you can export datasheets and forms to static or dynamic HTML format. Access 97 creates one Web page for each report page, datasheet, and form you export. Exporting objects to HTML format is useful for creating a simple Web application, verifying the format and appearance of an object's output, or adding files to existing Web applications.

Like the Wizard, you can also use an HTML template file along with your output files. An HTML template contains HTML tags and special tokens unique to Access 97 that enhance the appearance, consistency, and navigation of your Web pages.

Exporting a datasheet to static HTML format

If you want to export a datasheet to static HTML format, follow these steps:

1. In the Database window, click on the name of the table, query, or form you want to export, and then on the File menu, click on Save As/Export.

2. In the Save As dialog box, click on To An External File Or Database, and then click on OK.

3. In the Save as type box, click on HTML Documents (*.html;*.htm), as shown in Figure 33-10.

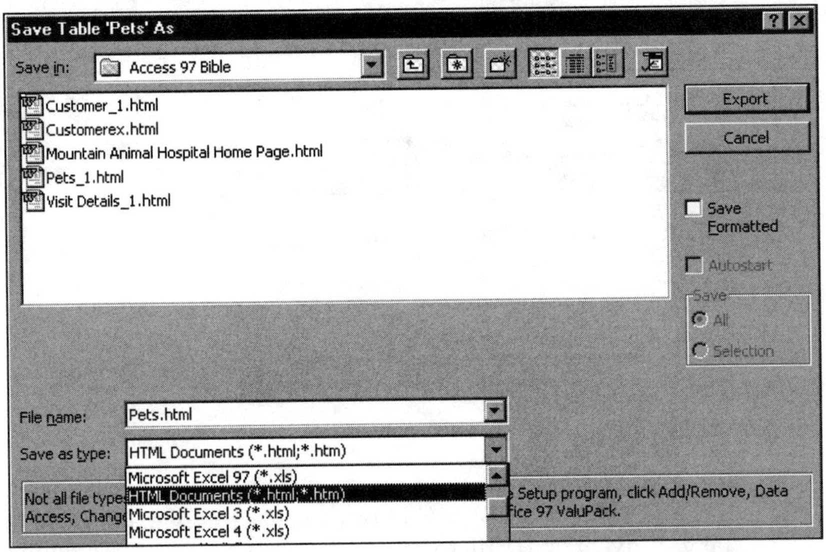

Figure 33-10: Selecting the HTML format in the Save As dialog box.

4. Click on the arrow to the right of the Save in box and select the drive or folder to export to.

5. In the File name box, enter the filename.

6. Select Save Formatted if you want to save the datasheet in a format similar to its appearance in Datasheet view, enable the AutoStart check box, and dis-

play the HTML Output Options dialog box after you click on Export in Step 7. Select AutoStart if you want to display the results in your default World Wide Web browser.

7. Click on Export.

If you selected Save Formatted in Step 6, the HTML Output Options dialog box is displayed. You can specify an HTML template to use. You can also define a default value for the HTML Template option. On the Tools menu, click on Options, and then click on the Hyperlinks/HTML tab, as shown in Figure 33-11.

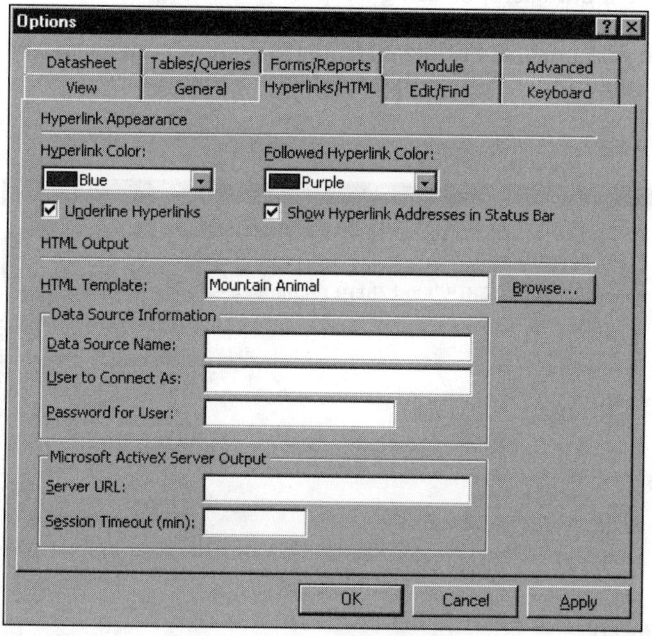

Figure 33-11: The Tools⇨Options⇨Hyperlinks/HTML tab.

The HTML file is based on the recordset behind the datasheet, including any current OrderBy or Filter property settings. If the datasheet contains a parameter query, Access 97 first prompts you for the parameter values and then exports the results. If you selected Save Formatted in Step 6, the HTML table simulates as closely as possible the appearance of the datasheet by creating the appropriate HTML tags to retain attributes such as color, font, and alignment. Values from most fields (except OLE objects and hyperlink fields) are output as strings and are formatted similarly to how they appear in the datasheet, including defined Format or Input Mask properties. Fields with a Hyperlink data type (see the section

"Hyperlinks Connect Your Application to the Internet," later in this chapter) are output as HTML links using <A HREF> tags. All unformatted data types, except Text and Memo, are saved with right alignment as the default. Text and Memo fields are saved with left alignment by default.

The layout of the HTML page simulates the page orientation and margins that are set for the datasheet. To change these settings, display the datasheet, and then use the Page Setup command on the File menu before you export it. A large datasheet may take a long time to output and to display through a Web browser. Consider reducing the size of the datasheet, dividing the datasheet into smaller datasheets by using criteria such as a date field, or using a report or form to view the data.

Figure 33-12 shows the first portion of the HTML that's generated when exporting the data from the Customer table. Notice that the figure shows the first two records in the file.

```
Customerex.html - Notepad                                    _ 8 X
File   Edit   Search   Help
<HTML>
<HEAD>
<META HTTP-EQUIV="Content-Type" CONTENT="text/html; charset=windows-1252">
<TITLE>Customer</TITLE>
</HEAD>
<BODY>
<TABLE BORDER>
<CAPTION>Customer</CAPTION>
<TR>
<TD>AC001</TD>
<TD ALIGN=RIGHT>1</TD>
<TD>All Creatures</TD>
<TD>21 Grace St.
<BR>Apt 16</TD>
<TD>Tall Pines</TD>
<TD>WA</TD>
<TD>987462541</TD>
<TD>2065556622</TD>
<TD ALIGN=RIGHT>3/19/93</TD>
<TD ALIGN=RIGHT>11/26/93</TD>
<TD ALIGN=RIGHT>0.20</TD>
<TD ALIGN=RIGHT>2000.00</TD>
</TR>
<TR>
<TD>AD001</TD>
<TD ALIGN=RIGHT>1</TD>
<TD>Johnathan Adams</TD>
<TD>66 10th St</TD>
```

Figure 33-12: Viewing an HTML representation of the Customer table.

Exporting a datasheet to dynamic HTML format

The process of exporting a dynamic HTML format is essentially the same as exporting a static format except that you choose the Microsoft IIS 1-2 (*.htx;*.idc) or Microsoft ActiveX Server (*.asp) server choice instead of the HTML Documents choice.

To export a datasheet to dynamic HTML format, follow these steps:

1. In the Database window, click on the name of the table, query, or form you want to export, and then on the File menu, click on Save As/Export.

2. In the Save As dialog box, click on To An External File Or Database, and then click on OK.

3. In the Save as type box, click on Microsoft IIS 1-2 (*.htx;*.idc) or Microsoft ActiveX Server (*.asp), depending on which dynamic HTML format you want.

4. Click on the arrow to the right of the Save in box and select the drive or folder to export to.

5. In the File name box, enter the filename.

6. Click on Export.

7. In the HTML Output Options dialog box, you can specify an HTML template to use.

You must specify the machine or file data source name that you will use on the World Wide Web server, and, if required, a username and password to open the database. If you are exporting to ASP file format, you must enter the server URL of the location where the ASP file will be stored on the Web server. For example, if you are storing the ASP files in the \SalesApp folder on the \\Pubweb server, type **http://pubweb//salesapp/**.

When you export to ASP file format, if a form is in Datasheet view or its Default View property is set to Datasheet, then Access 97 outputs the form as a datasheet. If the form is in Form or Design view or its Default View property is set to Single Form or Continuous Forms, then Access 97 outputs the form as a form. The layout of the HTML page simulates the page orientation and margins that are set for the datasheet. To change these settings, display the datasheet and then use the Page Setup command on the File menu before you export it.

Exporting a report to static HTML format

Reports are always output in a static file format type. To export a report, follow these steps:

1. In the Database window, click on the name of the report you want to export, and then on the File menu, click on Save As/Export.

2. In the Save As dialog box, click on To An External File Or Database, and then click on OK.

3. In the Save as type box, click on HTML Documents (*.html;*.htm).

4. Click on the arrow to the right of the Save in box and select the drive or folder to export to.

5. In the File name box, enter the filename.

6. Select AutoStart to display the results in your default World Wide Web browser.

7. Click on Export.

    In the HTML Output Options dialog box, you can specify an HTML template to use. If you do not specify an HTML template file containing navigation tokens, Microsoft Access 97 does not provide a default navigation scheme, and if you selected AutoStart in Step 6, only the first page is displayed.

The HTML file is based on the recordset behind the report, including any current OrderBy or Filter property settings. If the datasheet contains a parameter query, Access 97 first prompts you for the parameter values and then exports the results. Most controls and features of a report, including subreports, are supported except for the following: lines, rectangles, OLE objects, and subforms. However, you can use an HTML template file to include report header and footer images in your output files.

The output files simulate as closely as possible the appearance of the report by creating the appropriate HTML tags to retain attributes such as color, font, and alignment. Fields with a Hyperlink data type are output as HTML links using <A HREF> tags. Access 97 outputs a report, unlike a datasheet, as multiple HTML files, one file per printed page, using the object name and an appendix to create each filename; for example, Products.htm, ProductsPage1.htm, ProductsPage2.htm, and so on. The layout of the HTML pages simulates the page orientation and margins set for the report. To change these settings, display the report in Print or Layout Preview, and then use the Page Setup command on the File menu before you export it.

You cannot output a report to dynamic HTML format.

Exporting a form to dynamic HTML format

You can design an Access 97 form for use in a World Wide Web application and then save it to dynamic HTML format (ASP files only). You can output several types of forms: View forms (to display records), switchboard forms (to act as the home page or to navigate to related pages, such as all reports), and data-entry forms (to add, update, and delete records).

To export a form in dynamic HTML format, follow these steps:

1. In the Database window, click on the name of the form you want to export, and then on the File menu, click on Save As/Export.

2. In the Save As dialog box, click on To An External File Or Database, and then click on OK.

3. In the Save as type box, click on Microsoft ActiveX Server (*.asp).

4. Click on the arrow to the right of the Save in box and select the drive or folder to export to.

5. In the File name box, enter the filename.

6. Click on Export.

You must specify the machine or file data source name that you will use on the Web server, and, if required, a username and password to open the database. If you are exporting to ASP file format, you must enter the server URL of the location where the ASP file will be stored on the Web server. For example, if you are storing the ASP files in the \SalesApp folder on the \\Pubweb server, type **http://pubweb//salesapp/**.

Access 97 outputs a continuous form as a single form. Access 97 outputs most controls as ActiveX controls but ignores any Visual Basic code behind them. The output files simulate as closely as possible the appearance of the form by creating the appropriate HTML tags to retain attributes such as color, font, and alignment. However, all data types are output unformatted, and all Format and InputMask properties are ignored.

When you export to ASP file format, if a form is in Datasheet view or its Default View property is set to Datasheet, then Access 97 outputs the form as a datasheet. If the form is in Form or Design view or its Default View property is set to Single Form or Continuous Forms, then Access 97 outputs the form as a form.

Import or Link (Read-Only) HTML Tables and Lists

Besides exporting an HTML table, you can import or link to a table as well. This process uses the standard Import or Linked Table Wizard shown in Chapter 23. To do this, follow these steps:

1. Open a database, or switch to the Database window for the open database.

2. Do one of the following:

- To import HTML tables or lists, from the File menu, point to Get External Data and then click on Import. To link (formerly known as attaching) HTML tables or lists, from the File menu, point to Get External Data, and then click on Link Tables.

- In the Import or Link dialog box, in the Files Of Type box, click on HTML Documents (*.html;*.htm).

- Click on the arrow to the right of the Look In box, select the drive and folder where the HTML file you want to import or link is located, and then double-click on the filename.

- Follow the instructions for the Import HTML Wizard or the Link HTML Wizard. Click on the Advanced button if you want to edit an import/export specification or specify different file and field formats.

- If your HTML file contains more than one table or list, repeat Steps 1 through 5 for each table or list you want to import or link.

Note A table embedded within a table cell in an HTML file is treated as a separate table when you import or link. A list embedded in a table cell is treated as the contents of a cell, and each item in the list is delimited with the carriage return/line feed characters.

If the data being imported contains a URL link or file hyperlink, then Access converts HTML links to a Hyperlink data type column, but only if all values in a table column or list contain hyperlink addresses defined by an <A HREF> tag. You can change the data type when using the Import HTML Wizard or the Link HTML Wizard. Access 97 ignores GIF and JPEG images embedded in the HTML tables or lists. For data that spans rows or columns, Access 97 duplicates the data in each cell. On the other hand, Microsoft Excel 97 stores the data in the first or upper left cell and then leaves other cells blank.

Hyperlinks Connect Your Application to the Internet

Microsoft Access 97 includes hyperlinks to help you easily connect your application to the Internet or an intranet. A hyperlink can jump to a location on the Internet or on an intranet, to an object in your database or in another database, or to a document on your computer or on another computer connected by a network. Normally, you embed a hyperlink in a form. However, by storing hyperlinks in a table, you can programmatically move to Internet URLs or Office objects such as a Word document using a bookmark, an Excel spreadsheet using a sheet or range, a PowerPoint presentation using a slide, or an Access object such as a table, form, or report.

Using the new Hyperlink data type

Microsoft Access 97 provides a new Hyperlink data type that can contain a hyper-link address. You can define a table field with this data type in order to store hyperlinks as data in a table. Imagine for a moment the future where all patients have e-mail addresses or even their own Web sites. You would want to include a patient's e-mail address or Web site in a linkable file much as automatic phone dialer code is commonly added to a customer's phone number today.

Figure 33-13 shows the Hyperlink data type being defined.

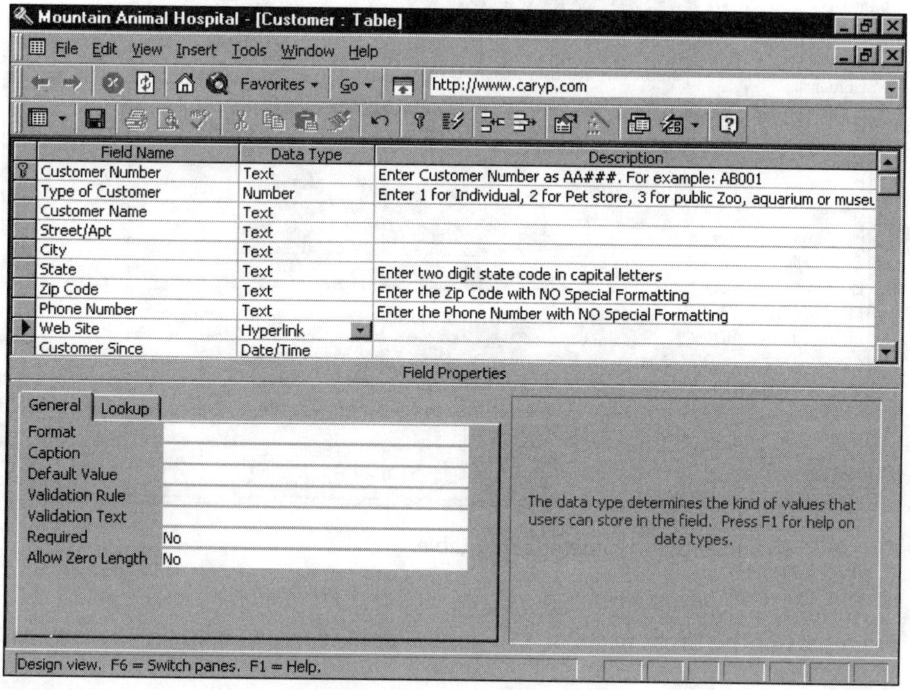

Figure 33-13: Creating a hyperlink in a table design.

When using the Hyperlink data type, you can input text or combinations of text and numbers stored as text and used as a hyperlink address. A hyperlink address can have as many as three parts:

Displaytext	The text that appears in a field or control
Address	The path to a file (UNC path) or Web page (URL)
subaddress	A location within the file or page

The easiest way to insert a hyperlink address in a field or control is to click on Hyperlink on the Insert menu. The Insert Hyperlink dialog box appears as shown in Figure 33-14. As you can see, the Invoice page of the Web site has been input as a URL for Pets R Us.

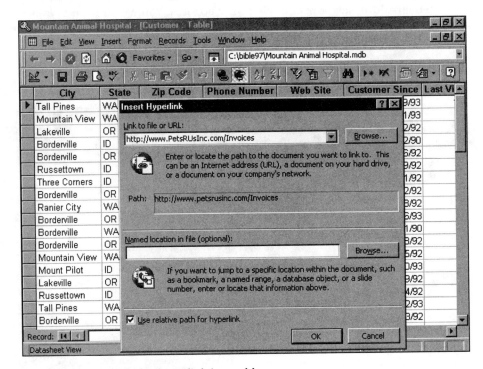

Figure 33-14: Inserting a hyperlink in a table.

Each part of the three parts of a Hyperlink data type can contain as many as 2,048 characters.

When you click on a hyperlink field, Access 97 jumps to an object, document, Web page, or other destination.

Add a hyperlink to a form, report, or datasheet

You can use hyperlinks in forms and datasheets to jump to objects in the same or another Access 97 database; to documents created with Microsoft Word, Microsoft Excel, and Microsoft PowerPoint; and to documents on the global Internet or on a local intranet. You can also add hyperlinks to reports. Although hyperlinks in a report won't work when viewed in Access 97, the hyperlinks will work when you output the report to Word or Microsoft Excel or to HTML.

You can store hyperlinks in fields in tables, just as you store phone numbers and fax numbers. For example, the Suppliers table in the Northwind sample database stores hyperlinks to home pages for some of the suppliers.

You can also create a label or picture on a form or report or a command button on a form that you can click on to follow a hyperlink path. For example, the labels in the Mountain Animal Hospital switchboard can be modified to use the hyperlink address and subaddress properties.

Figure 33-15 shows how to modify the Customer Form label into a hyperlink. When connecting an object in the current database, you leave the Hyperlink Address field blank and fill in the Hyperlink SubAddress with the object type and the object name.

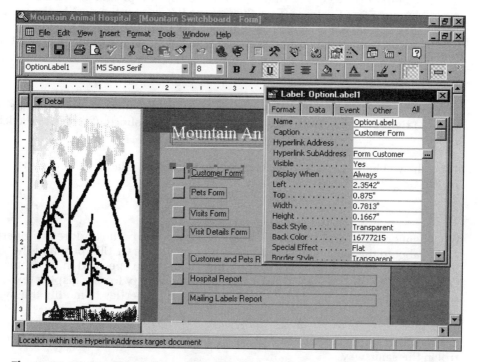

Figure 33-15: Specifying a hyperlink address and subaddress in a form.

Creating a label using the Insert Hyperlink button

If you want to automatically create a label using the Insert Hyperlink button on a form, follow these steps:

1. Open a form or a report in Design view.

2. Click on Insert Hyperlink on the toolbar.

3. In the Insert Hyperlink dialog box, specify a UNC path or a URL in the Link To File Or URL box, or click on the Browse button to navigate to a file on your hard drive, on a local area network, or on an FTP server that you've registered.

4. Leave the Named Location In File box blank or do one of the following:

   To jump to a location in a file, enter a location. For example, type a bookmark name for a Microsoft Word document or a slide number for a PowerPoint presentation.

   To jump to an Access 97 object, enter the object type and object name (for example, Form Customer), or click on the Browse button next to the Named Location In File box. The Browse button opens the Database window for the current or specified database, where you can select the object you want to open.

5. Click on the OK button in the Insert Hyperlink dialog box.

Access 97 adds a label to the form or report. To test the link, click on the label with the right mouse button, point to Hyperlink on the shortcut menu, and click on Open.

Note   If the link will jump to an Access 97 object in the current database, leave the Link To File Or URL box blank.

Note   When you create a label this way, Access 97 sets the Hyperlink Address property of the label to the value you specified in the Link To File Or URL box, and the Hyperlink SubAddress property to the value (if any) you specified in the Named Location In File box. Access 97 uses the Caption property for the display text you see in the label itself. You can change any of these properties to modify the hyperlink.

You can also add hyperlinks to a picture (Image Control) or command button control in the same way.

Figure 33-16 shows the now common cursor hand pointing to a link on a Web site which shows that the label is now a hyperlink. In this example, it will link to the Customer form in the Mountain Animal Hospital database.

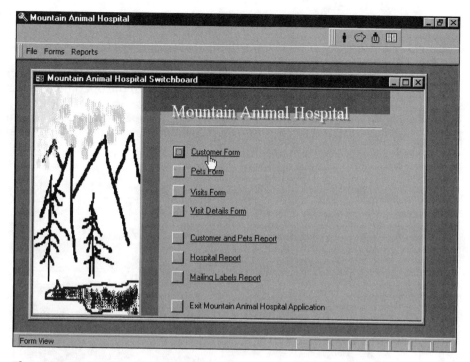

Figure 33-16: Moving to a hyperlink address and subaddress in a form.

Browsing Web Pages with the Web Browser Control

The Microsoft Web Browser control allows you to browse the World Wide Web; view Web pages; access other documents on your computer, the network, or the Internet; and download data from the Internet, all through your application's form.

The Microsoft Web Browser control is an ActiveX control that enables you to view Web pages and other documents on the Internet or an intranet from an Access 97 form. The Web Browser control is provided by Microsoft Internet Explorer 3.0, which is included with Microsoft Office 97. You can also download Microsoft Internet Explorer from the Microsoft corporate Web site (http://www.microsoft.com/) free of charge. You can obtain further documentation about the Web Browser control from the URL http://www.microsoft.com/intdev/sdk/docs/iexplore/.

If you purchased Microsoft Office 97 on CD-ROM, you can view a Help file that contains this information by copying it from the Office 97 ValuPack. For information about obtaining the Web Browser control Help file from the ValuPack, see About the Office 97 ValuPack.

The Web Browser control is automatically registered with the operating system when you install Internet Explorer, so you can use it from Access 97 without first registering it. To add the Web Browser control to a form, click on ActiveX Control on the Insert menu, and then click on Microsoft Web Browser Control in the list of ActiveX controls, as shown in Figure 33-17.

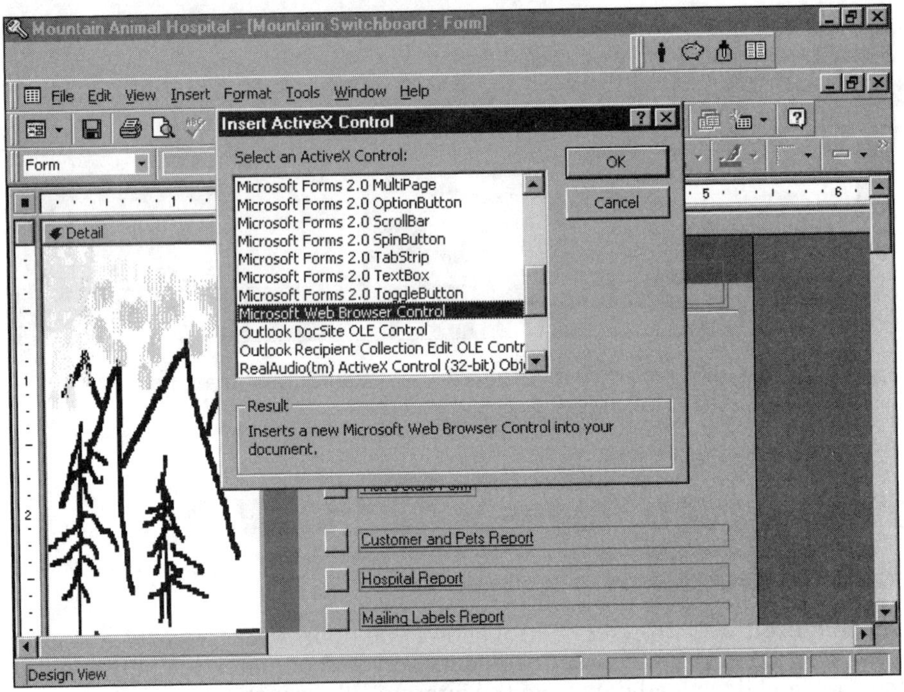

Figure 33-17: Inserting the Web Browser control in Access 97.

After you've added the Web Browser control to a form, you can use the control's Navigate method to open a Web page within the Web Browser window. For example, if you've added a Web Browser control named ActiveXCtl0 to a form, you could create the following Load event procedure for the form:

```
Private Sub Form_Load
        Me!ActiveXCtl0.Navigate "http://www.caryp.com/"
End Sub
```

This procedure would display the Cary Prague Books and Software home page within the control. Figure 33-18 shows the blank area in the Design view of a form and the property sheet for the Web Browser control. When the form is opened, the home page would appear in the blank area. The area can be sized to any size you want.

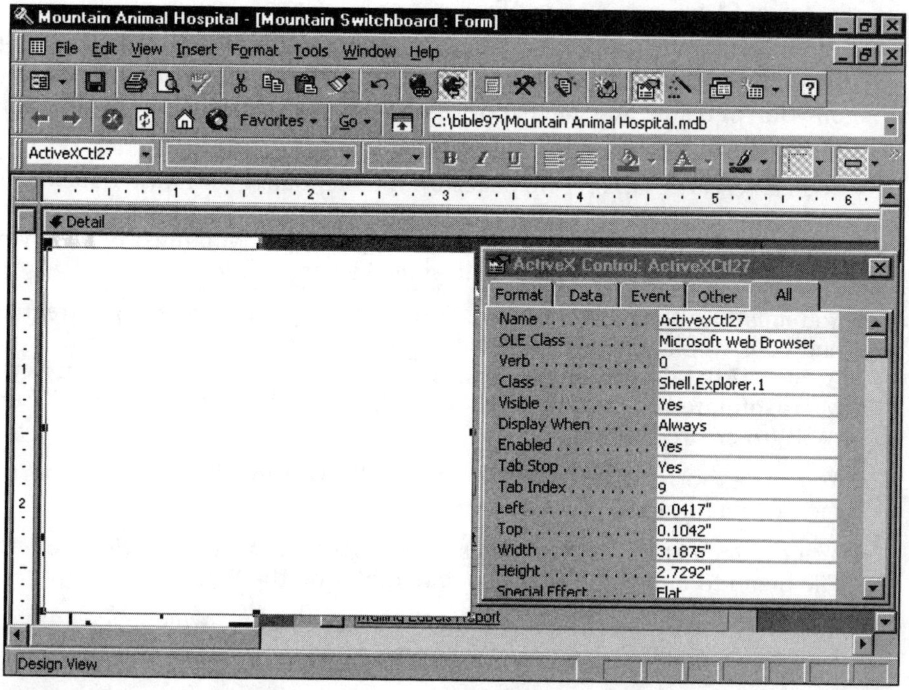

Figure 33-18: The Web Browser control properties.

The Internet is mature yet in its infancy. The ability to access it and program your Microsoft Access 97 environment to take advantage of Internet technology has become very important today.

Summary

In this chapter, you learned how to use the new Internet technology to publish your Access data and how to link to both World Wide Web sites as well as internal corporate intranets. The following points were discussed:

✦ The Internet, and particularly the World Wide Web, has become an important part of all businesses today.

✦ The Web toolbar can be turned on by selecting <u>V</u>iew➪<u>T</u>oolbars➪Web from any menu. After you have the Web toolbar displayed, you can use it to access Web sites on the Internet or your local intranet. When you use the Web toolbar, you launch the default Web browser on your system.

✦ To take advantage of Internet technology, you must have a Web browser installed (Microsoft Internet Explorer or Netscape Navigator).

✦ The Publish to the Web Wizard walks you through the steps of creating the HTML for selected database objects and of placing the generated HTML out on your Web site. You can export data from tables or query dynasets, forms, or reports into HTML.

✦ You can create static HTML pages from table, query, and form datasheets and from reports. The resulting HTML files are a snapshot of the data at the time you published your files. If your data changes, you must publish your files again to view the new data in your Web application.

✦ You must use the dynamic HTML format when your data changes frequently and your Web application needs to store and retrieve live data from your Access 97 database using a form. You must have a Web server such as the Microsoft Internet Information Server (IIS) (IDX/HDC) or the ActiveX Server (ASP) to create Web forms.

✦ You can export individual objects to HTML by using the Save As/Export menu item from the <u>F</u>ile menu.

✦ You can import HTML data by using the Get External Data option from the <u>F</u>ile menu to import or attach to data tables on the Web.

✦ You can create a new data type known as a hyperlink, which can store a Web URL or Microsoft Office object address.

✦ The Hyperlink Address and Subaddress properties in a form label, command button, or image control let you automatically link to a URL or database object and automatically jump to those objects.

✦ The Web Browser control is an ActiveX control that lets you view a Web page within your Access 97 application.

As you have seen in the last chapter of this book, the Internet is an important part of applications in 1997. On the CD-ROM in the back of this book are several bonus chapters on using Visual Basic for Applications (VBA) that will teach you the basics of programming and moving beyond macros with Access 97.

CD-ROM

✦   ✦   ✦

Appendixes

Microsoft Access 97 Specifications

This appendix shows the limits of Microsoft Access databases, tables, queries, forms, reports, and macros.

Databases	
Attribute	*Maximum*
MDB file size	1GB for Access 97, Access for Windows 95, 2.0, and 1.1; 128MB for Access 1.0 (Because your database can include attached tables in multiple files, its total size is limited only by available storage capacity.)
Number of objects in a database	32,768
Number of characters in object names	64
Number of characters in a password	14
Number of characters in a user name or group name	20
Number of concurrent users	255

Tables

Attribute	Maximum
Number of characters in a table name	64
Number of characters in a field name	64
Number of fields in a record or table	255
Table size	1GB
Number of characters in a Text field	255
Number of characters in a Memo field	65,535
Size of OLE object field	1GB
Number of indexes in a record or table	32
Number of fields in an index	10
Number of characters in a validation message	255
Number of characters in a table description	255
Number of characters in a field description	255

Queries

Attribute	Maximum
Number of tables in a query	32
Number of fields in a dynaset	255
Dynaset size	1GB
Number of sorted fields in a query	10
Number of levels of nested queries	50

Forms and Reports

Attribute	Maximum
Number of characters in a label	2,048
Number of characters in a text box	65,535
Form or report width	22 inches (55.87 cm)
Section height	22 inches (55.87 cm)
Height of all sections plus section headers (Design view)	200 inches (508 cm)
Number of levels of nested forms or reports	3 (form-subform-subform)
Number of fields/expressions you can sort or group on (reports only)	10
Number of headers and footers in a report	1 report header/footer; 1 page header/ footer; 10 group headers/footers
Number of printed pages in a report	65,536

Macros

Attribute	Maximum
Number of actions in a macro	999
Number of characters in a comment	255
Number of characters in an action argument	255

Mountain Animal Hospital Tables

The Mountain Animal Hospital Database file is made up of eight tables. There are four main tables and four lookup tables. The main tables are Customer, Pets, Visits, and Visit Details. The four lookup tables are States, Animals, Treatments, and Medications. This appendix displays a database diagram of all eight tables and the relations between them. Screen figures of each of the eight tables are shown in the Table Design window.

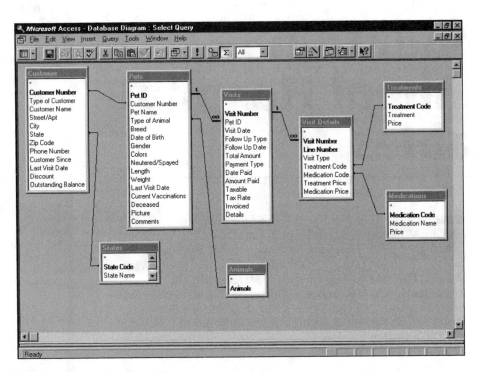

Figure B-1: The database diagram.

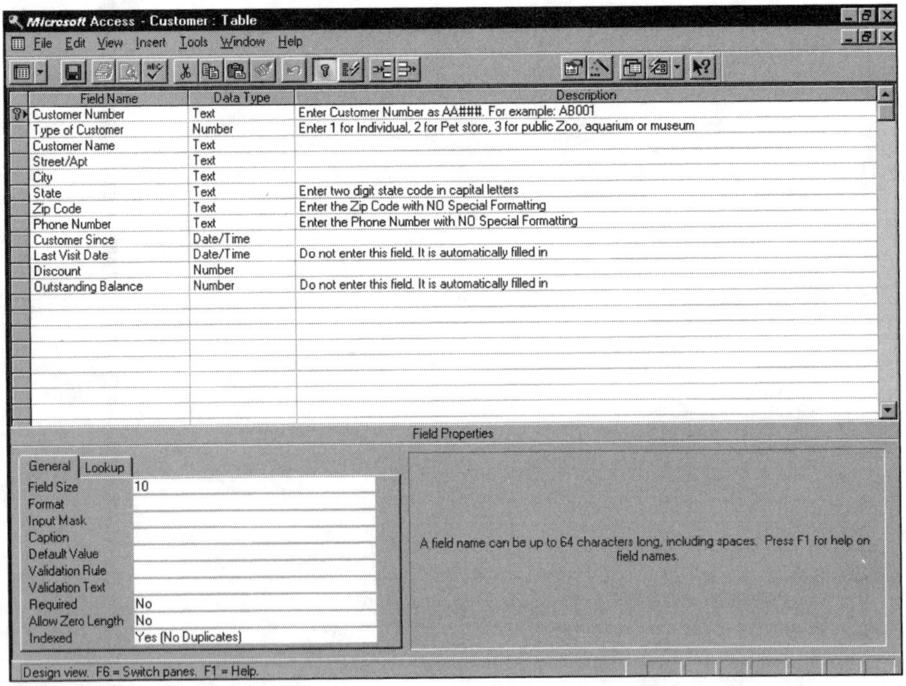

Figure B-2: The Customer table.

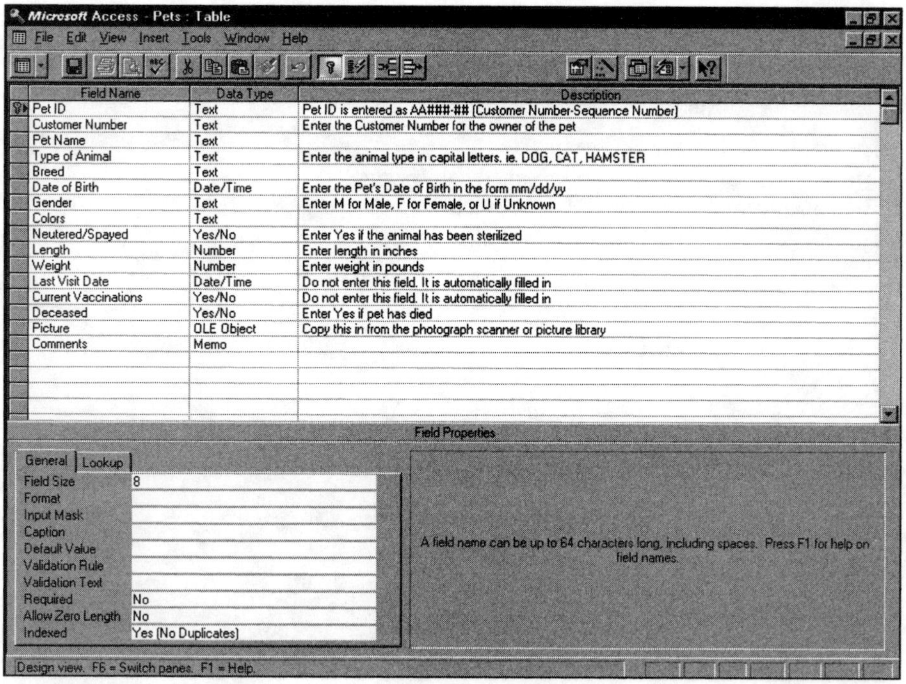

Field Name	Data Type	Description
Pet ID	Text	Pet ID is entered as AA###-## (Customer Number-Sequence Number)
Customer Number	Text	Enter the Customer Number for the owner of the pet
Pet Name	Text	
Type of Animal	Text	Enter the animal type in capital letters. ie. DOG, CAT, HAMSTER
Breed	Text	
Date of Birth	Date/Time	Enter the Pet's Date of Birth in the form mm/dd/yy
Gender	Text	Enter M for Male, F for Female, or U if Unknown
Colors	Text	
Neutered/Spayed	Yes/No	Enter Yes if the animal has been sterilized
Length	Number	Enter length in inches
Weight	Number	Enter weight in pounds
Last Visit Date	Date/Time	Do not enter this field. It is automatically filled in
Current Vaccinations	Yes/No	Do not enter this field. It is automatically filled in
Deceased	Yes/No	Enter Yes if pet has died
Picture	OLE Object	Copy this in from the photograph scanner or picture library
Comments	Memo	

Figure B-3: The Pets table.

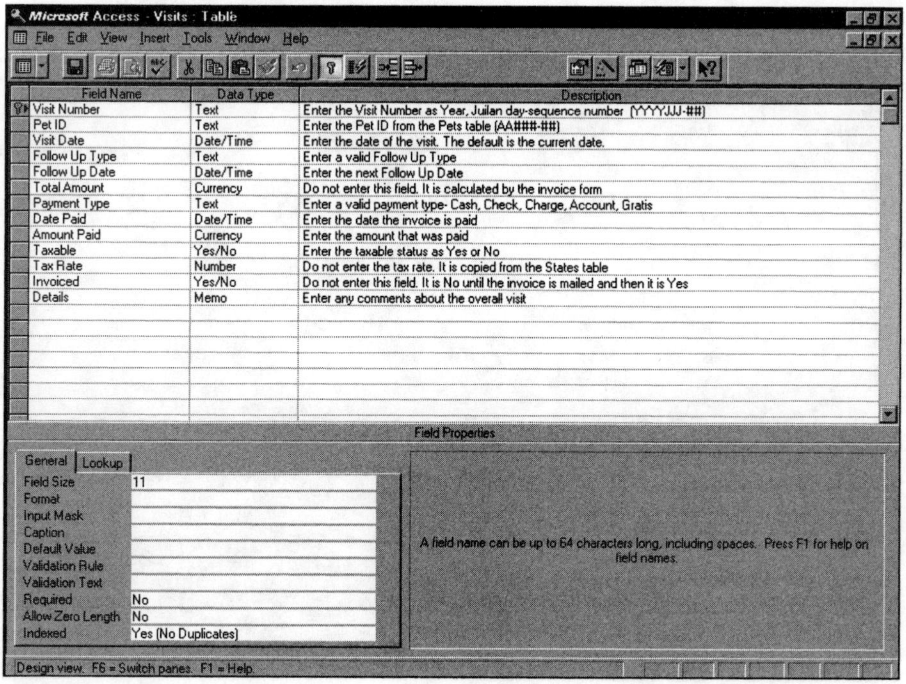

Field Name	Data Type	Description
Visit Number	Text	Enter the Visit Number as Year, Juilan day-sequence number (YYYYJJJ-##)
Pet ID	Text	Enter the Pet ID from the Pets table (AA###-##)
Visit Date	Date/Time	Enter the date of the visit. The default is the current date.
Follow Up Type	Text	Enter a valid Follow Up Type
Follow Up Date	Date/Time	Enter the next Follow Up Date
Total Amount	Currency	Do not enter this field. It is calculated by the invoice form
Payment Type	Text	Enter a valid payment type- Cash, Check, Charge, Account, Gratis
Date Paid	Date/Time	Enter the date the invoice is paid
Amount Paid	Currency	Enter the amount that was paid
Taxable	Yes/No	Enter the taxable status as Yes or No
Tax Rate	Number	Do not enter the tax rate. It is copied from the States table
Invoiced	Yes/No	Do not enter this field. It is No until the invoice is mailed and then it is Yes
Details	Memo	Enter any comments about the overall visit

Figure B-4: The Visits table.

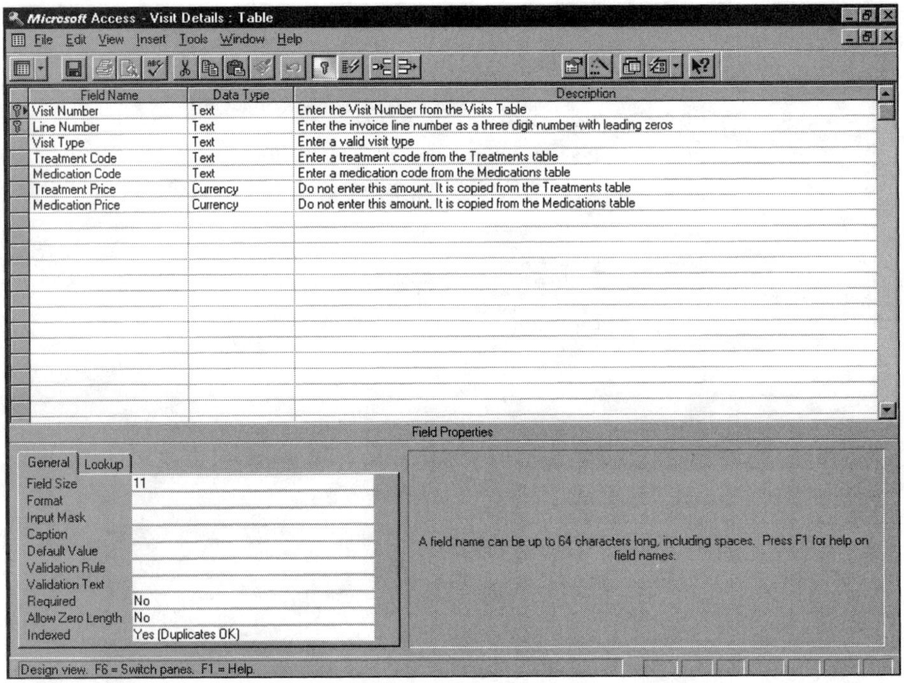

Figure B-5: The Visit Details table.

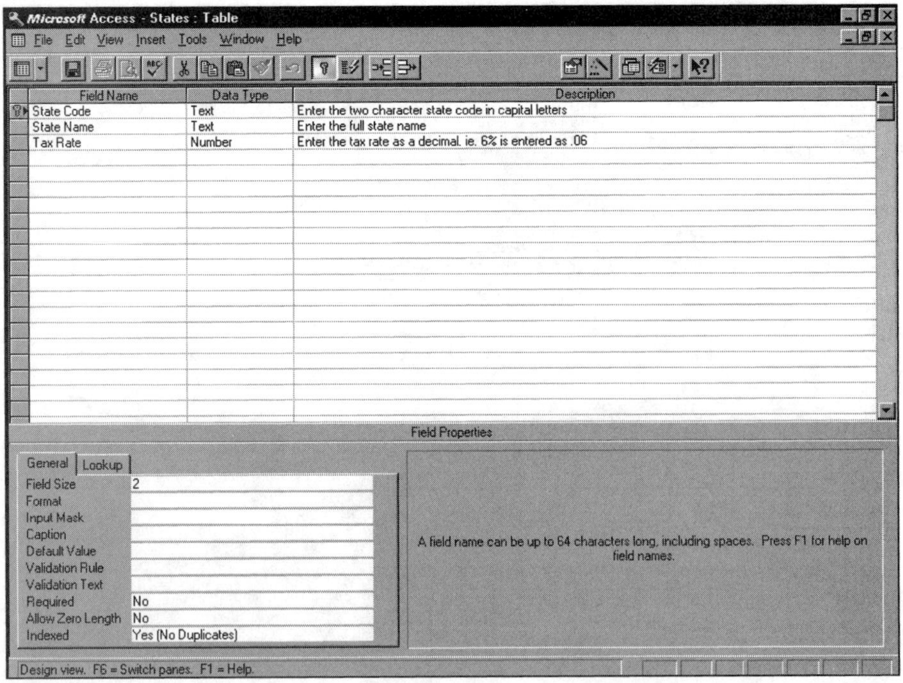

Figure B-6: The States table.

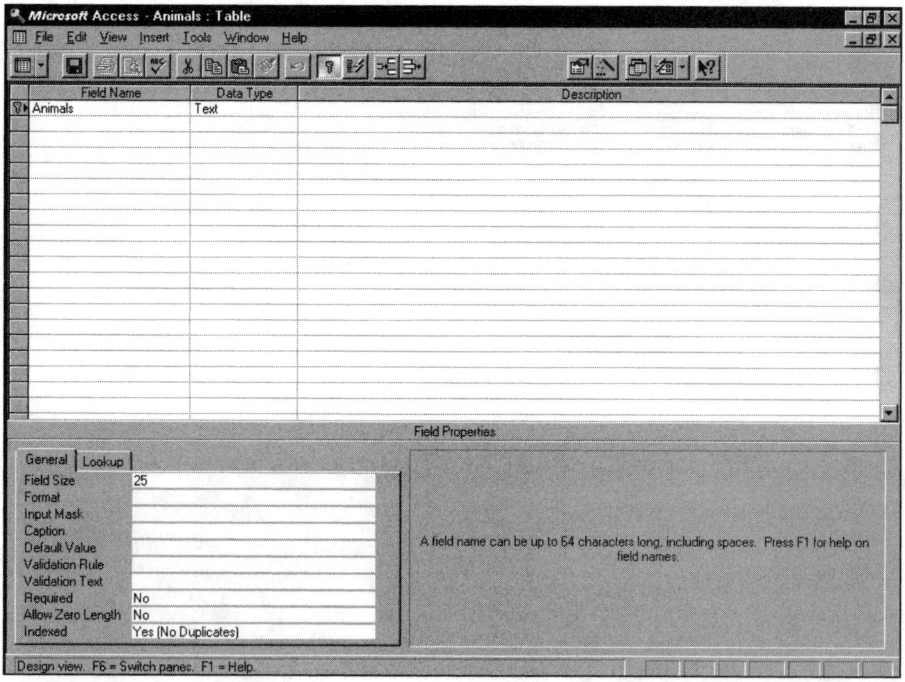

Figure B-7: The Animals table.

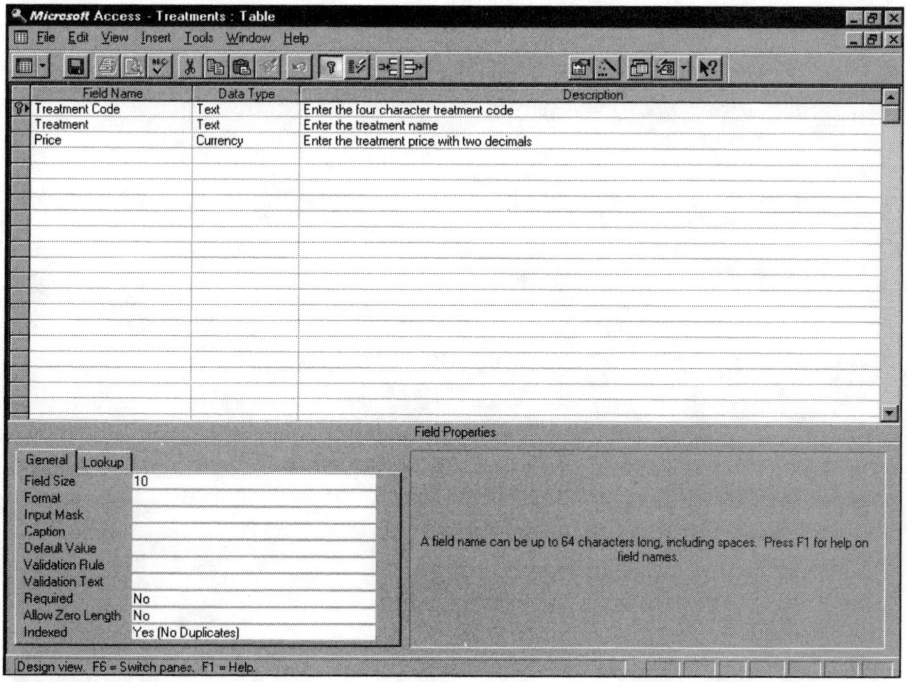

Figure B-8: The Treatments table.

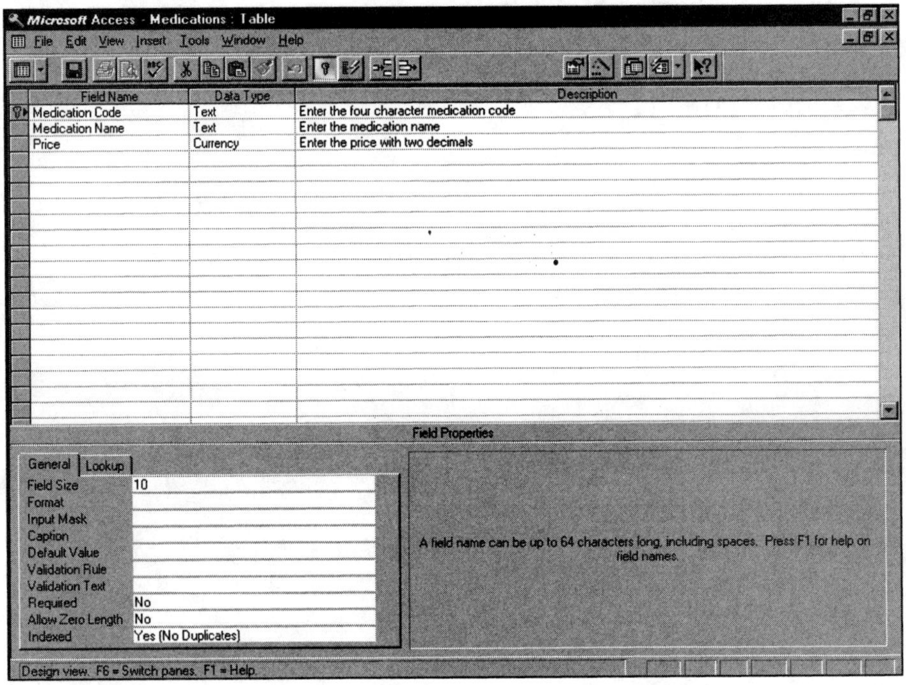

Figure B-9: The Medications table.

What's on the Access 97 CD-ROM

Your CD-ROM contains all of the example files created or referenced in this book.

There are also two bonus chapters on the CD-ROM to teach you the basics of VBA programming in Access 97 and a sample chapter from our new advanced book *Access 97 Secrets*.

Additionally, there are several directories of fully working applications and some demonstration applications, and on-line brochures for Access 97 add-on products as well.

If you would like additional demos of Access 97 add-on products, check out our Web site at www.caryp.com or call our hotline to receive a catalog of over 50 add-on products for Access 97. You can reach us at (860) 644-5891 or by fax at (860) 648-0710.

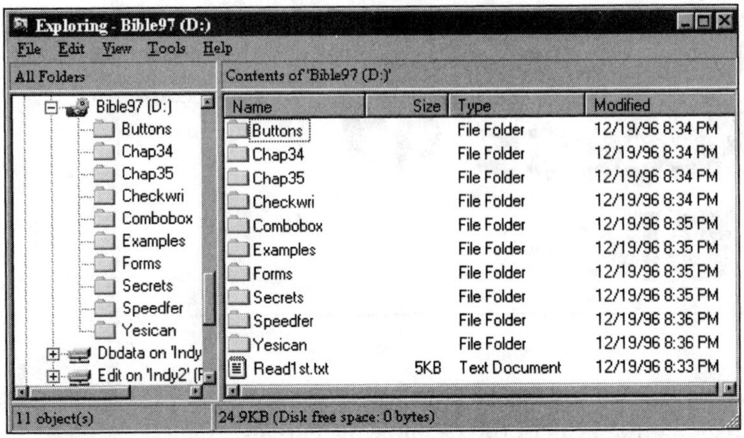

Figure C-1: The directories on the Access 97 Bible CD ROM.

Copying the files to your computer

The files are stored in your CD-ROM in an uncompressed format. You can simply copy them to your hard drive as you want to use them using the Windows 95 or Windows NT 4 Explorer or Windows NT 3.51 File Manager. The sample chapters are stored in Word 6.0/95 format and can be viewed or printed directly from the CD-ROM as long as you don't try to make any changes to the Word files.

Note   All of the .MDB files are Microsoft Access 97 files. They only work in Microsoft Access 97 and do not work in Microsoft Access 95, 2.0, 1.1, or 1.0.

Using the Access 97 Example Files

In the directory **Access 97 Bible Example Files** are three Access 97 .MDB database files:

   ✦ **Mountain Animal Start.MDB** contains the tables only (to get you started).

   ✦ **Mountain Animal Hospital.MDB** contains all of the tables, queries, forms, reports, macros, and modules.

   ✦ **ACTIMPEX.MDB** contains links to various external file formats including dBASE, FoxPro, and Paradox (used in Chapter 24).

There are also several .BMP files used throughout the book to teach you how to properly use graphical objects such as OLE bitmaps and pictures on command buttons and toggle buttons. A variety of files in dBASE and FoxPro (.DBF, .DBT, .NDX), Paradox (.DB) Excel (.XLS) and text files (.TXT) are also included and are used in Chapter 24.

Many of our readers over the years have asked us how we created a specific screen picture or have asked us to provide an example file at each of the steps as we create a form or report. In the *Access 97 Bible*, we have done this for you. If you look at the Forms tab in the Mountain Animal Hospital database you will see many forms named *zFigurexx-yy*. For example, `zFigure16-02` would be the form in the exact state that was used to take Figure 16-2.

Reading the bonus chapters

We have included several chapters as a bonus that we considered beyond the scope and purpose of the *Access 97 Bible*. As products have evolved over the years, it has become increasingly difficult to cover all of the material adequately and yet still produce a book that doesn't require a luggage cart to bring home from the bookstore. More importantly, many of you have asked us to put the book in electronic form on the CD-ROM. In the coming years, you will see more of this. We have started a new trend and added several additional chapters to our CD-ROM. These chapters are more advanced than the rest and even include one chapter from our more advanced book *Access 97 SECRETS*. You will find these chapters in three directories on the CD-ROM:

Chap34 An introduction to the more powerful Access 97 programming language now called Visual Basic for Applications which has replaced Access Basic and is common across all Microsoft Office 97 products including Word and Excel.

Chap35 More on using VBA and programming in it. Contains examples of the most common programming techniques used in Access 97.

Secrets This is a chapter from our other book, *Access 97 SECRETS*.

This chapter explains how to make Access 97 faster and how to take advantage of little-known secrets to make Access 97 really fly. This chapter was written by James Foxall (one of the authors of the *Access 97 SECRETS* book) along with Bill Amo and Cary Prague. If you want the advanced sequel to the *Access 97 Bible*, you can order it directly from the author and take 15 percent off the selling price by calling (800) 277-3117 (U.S. and Canada) or from anywhere at (860) 644-5891 or by fax at (860) 648-0710. You can see the covers of the book and the entire outline by viewing our Web site at `www.caryp.com`.

The chapters stored within these directories contain all of the text and screen pictures from the chapters and can be viewed or printed right from the CD-ROM. You can also copy them to your hard disk if you like. All of the code examples are on the Mountain Animal Hospital database or found additionally in the chapter itself.

Using the additional example files

Besides the sample files used with this book (which include the Mountain Animal Hospital examples) several files are available from Cary Prague Books and Software, the world's largest Microsoft Access add-on vendor.

These are fully working applications that you can use and customize. Each is in its own directory and includes both the Access 97 program and full documentation in Word 6.0/95 format. (You can use Word 97 to view or print the documentation as well.) The programs are as follows:

Check97.mdb: Fully functional Check Writer including Check Register and Check Reconciliation modules. Pay your bills, print checks, and balance your checkbook all with an incredible Access 97 application. This application won the Microsoft Network Access Product of the Year award last year. These files are found in the **Checkwri** directory on the CD-ROM.

BusFrm97.mdb: The Access Business Forms Library Sampler is a sample of our Business Forms Library, a collection of 35 forms and reports. These contain some really innovative techniques that have never been seen anywhere else. The entire library contains tables, forms, reports, and macros for each of the forms and reports. You can integrate them into your own applications, thereby saving you hundreds of hours of work. Microsoft liked these forms so much they distributed this sampler in the Microsoft Access Welcome Kit with Microsoft Access 2.0. These are found along with a user guide in the **Forms** directory on the CD-ROM.

25Combo7.mdb: This is a demonstration database of 25 of the coolest combo and list box techniques. Full documentation is included in the CD-ROM directory named **Combobox.**

All are given to you free of charge for your own use. These are all standard Access database files. To use them, simply copy them to your hard drive and open the database file.

Command Button Images: There is also a set of Microsoft Office-compatible button faces in the **Buttons** directory on your CD-ROM for use in any Windows 95 or NT application. They can be used on Access 97 toolbars as described in Chapter 32. To use these button faces, simply copy the files onto your hard disk or use the bitmaps as they are.

Note   The files named ACTxx.BMP are 32x32 pixel .BMPs perfect for Access command buttons, while the files named ACTxx.B24 are 24x23 pixel .BMPs perfect for Access 97 toolbars and any Office-compatible application.

Online product brochures

If you like our products, we also have a complete set of stand-alone financial applications including General Ledger and Inventory starting at $189.95. Our fully integrated business accounting product which is named **Yes! I Can Run My Business** includes invoices, quotations, purchase orders, general ledger, payroll, inventory, accounts receivable and payable and much more starts at $399.95. A complete brochure is available in the **Yesican** directory on the CD-ROM. You can download demos in any Microsoft Access format from our Web site or BBS as listed below.

The directory **Speedfer** contains a Microsoft Windows help file you can double-click on to display the file. This help file contains information about the newest release of Speed Ferret, a search-and-replace product for Access 97 to let you change the name of a field in a table and have the queries, forms, reports, macros, and modules all changed to match the new field name.

Call for our free catalog including our developer tools, books, and videos.

All of the products are available from:

Cary Prague Books and Software

60 Krawski Dr.

S. Windsor, CT 06074

(860) 644-5891 (International)

(860) 648-0710 (24-hr Fax)

(860) 648-2107 BBS

CompuServe: 71700,2126

Web: www.caryp.com

e-mail: caryp@caryp.com

Index

Symbols and Numbers

A

C

(continued)

(continued)

(continued)

(continued)

H

                              (continued)

M

O

Q

(continued)

(continued)

(continued)

END-USER LICENSE AGREEMENT

<u>Read This</u>. You should carefully read these terms and conditions before opening the software packet(s) included with this book ("Book"). This is a license agreement ("Agreement") between you and IDG Books Worldwide, Inc. ("IDGB"). By opening the accompanying software packet(s), you acknowledge that you have read and accept the following terms and conditions. If you do not agree and do not want to be bound by such terms and conditions, promptly return the Book and the unopened software packet(s) to the place you obtained them for a full refund.

1. <u>License Grant</u>. IDGB grants to you (either an individual or entity) a nonexclusive license to use one copy of the enclosed software program(s) (collectively, the "Software") solely for your own personal or business purposes on a single computer (whether a standard computer or a workstation component of a multiuser network). The Software is in use on a computer when it is loaded into temporary memory (i.e., RAM) or installed into permanent memory (e.g., hard disk, CD-ROM, or other storage device). IDGB reserves all rights not expressly granted herein.

2. <u>Ownership</u>. IDGB is the owner of all right, title, and interest, including copyright, in and to the compilation of the Software recorded on the CD-ROM. Copyright to the individual programs on the CD-ROM is owned by the author or other authorized copyright owner of each program. Ownership of the Software and all proprietary rights relating thereto remain with IDGB and its licensors.

3. <u>Restrictions on Use and Transfer</u>.

   (a) You may only (i) make one copy of the Software for backup or archival purposes, or (ii) transfer the Software to a single hard disk, provided that you keep the original for backup or archival purposes. You may not (i) rent or lease the Software, (ii) copy or reproduce the Software through a LAN or other network system or through any computer subscriber system or bulletin-board system, or (iii) modify, adapt, or create derivative works based on the Software.

   (b) You may not reverse engineer, decompile, or disassemble the Software. You may transfer the Software and user documentation on a permanent basis, provided that the transferee agrees to accept the terms and conditions of this Agreement and you retain no copies. If the Software is an update or has been updated, any transfer must include the most recent update and all prior versions.

4. <u>Restrictions on Use of Individual Programs</u>. You must follow the individual requirements and restrictions detailed for each individual program. These limitations are contained in the individual license agreements recorded on the CD-ROM. These restrictions may include a requirement that after using the program for the period of time specified in its text, the user must pay a registration fee or discontinue use. By opening the Software packet(s), you will be agreeing to abide by the licenses and restrictions for these individual programs. None of the material on this disk(s) or listed in this Book may ever be distributed, in original or modified form, for commercial purposes.

5. <u>Limited Warranty</u>.

   (a) IDGB warrants that the Software and CD-ROM are free from defects in materials and workmanship under normal use for a period of sixty (60) days from the date of purchase of this Book. If IDGB receives notification within the warranty period of defects in materials or workmanship, IDGB will replace the defective CD-ROM.

(b) **IDGB AND THE AUTHORS OF THE BOOK DISCLAIM ALL OTHER WAR-RANTIES, EXPRESS OR IMPLIED, INCLUDING WITHOUT LIMITATION IMPLIED WARRANTIES OF MERCHANTABILITY AND FITNESS FOR A PAR-TICULAR PURPOSE, WITH RESPECT TO THE SOFTWARE, THE PROGRAMS, THE SOURCE CODE CONTAINED THEREIN, AND/OR THE TECHNIQUES DESCRIBED IN THIS BOOK. IDGB DOES NOT WARRANT THAT THE FUNC-TIONS CONTAINED IN THE SOFTWARE WILL MEET YOUR REQUIREMENTS OR THAT THE OPERATION OF THE SOFTWARE WILL BE ERROR FREE.**

(c) This limited warranty gives you specific legal rights, and you may have other rights which vary from jurisdiction to jurisdiction.

6. Remedies.

(a) IDGB's entire liability and your exclusive remedy for defects in materials and workmanship shall be limited to replacement of the Software, which may be returned to IDGB with a copy of your receipt at the following address: Disk Fulfillment Department, Attn: Access 97 Bible, IDG Books Worldwide, Inc., 7260 Shadeland Station, Ste. 100, Indianapolis, IN 46256, or call 1-800-762-2974. Please allow 3–4 weeks for delivery. This Limited Warranty is void if failure of the Software has resulted from accident, abuse, or misapplication. Any replacement Software will be warranted for the remainder of the original war-ranty period or thirty (30) days, whichever is longer.

(b) In no event shall IDGB or the author be liable for any damages whatsoever (including without limitation damages for loss of business profits, business interruption, loss of business information, or any other pecuniary loss) arising from the use of or inability to use the Book or the Software, even if IDGB has been advised of the possibility of such damages.

(c) Because some jurisdictions do not allow the exclusion or limitation of liability for consequential or incidental damages, the above limitation or exclusion may not apply to you.

7. U.S. Government Restricted Rights. Use, duplication, or disclosure of the Software by the U.S. Government is subject to restrictions stated in paragraph (c) (1) (ii) of the Rights in Technical Data and Computer Software clause of DFARS 252.227-7013, and in subparagraphs (a) through (d) of the Commercial Computer—Restricted Rights clause at FAR 52.227-19, and in similar clauses in the NASA FAR supplement, when applicable.

8. General. This Agreement constitutes the entire understanding of the parties and revokes and supersedes all prior agreements, oral or written, between them and may not be modified or amended except in a writing signed by both parties here-to which specifically refers to this Agreement. This Agreement shall take prece-dence over any other documents that may be in conflict herewith. If any one or more provisions contained in this Agreement are held by any court or tribunal to be invalid, illegal, or otherwise unenforceable, each and every other provision shall remain in full force and effect.

Access 97 Bible CD-ROM Installation

The Access 97 Bible CD-ROM contains all of the example files created or referenced in this book.

There are also two bonus chapters on the CD-ROM to teach you the basics of VBA programming in Access 97 and a sample chapter from our new advanced book Access 97 SECRETS.

There are also several directories of fully working applications, demonstration applications, and online brochures for Access 97 add-on products.

The files are stored on the CD-ROM in an uncompressed format. Simply copy the files to your hard drive by using the Windows 95 or Windows NT 4. Explorer (or the Windows NT 3.51 File Manager.)

The sample chapters are stored in Word 6.0/95 format and can be viewed in these versions of Microsoft Word or Microsoft's free Word Viewer program.